Inside AutoCAD LT for Windows, Second Edition

Rusty Gesner
Dennis Hill
Peter Tobey
Tom Boersma
Randall A. Maxey
Bill Valaski

NRP
NEW RIDERS
PUBLISHING

New Riders Publishing, Indianapolis, Indiana

Inside AutoCAD LT for Windows, Second Edition

By Rusty Gesner, Dennis Hill, Peter Tobey, Tom Boersma, Randall A. Maxey, Bill Valaski

Published by:
New Riders Publishing
201 West 103rd Street
Indianapolis, IN 46290 USA

Printed in the United States of America 1 2 3 4 5 6 7 8 9 0

```
***CIP data available upon request***
```

Warning and Disclaimer

Publisher	*Don Fowley*
Associate Publisher	*Tim Huddleston*
Product Development Manager	*Rob Tidrow*
Marketing Manager	*Ray Robinson*
Acquisitions Manager	*Jim LeValley*
Managing Editor	*Tad Ringo*

About the Authors

Rusty Gesner, one of the original members of NRP and formerly New Riders' CAD Publishing Director, is a freelance author and AutoCAD expert. Rusty was born and raised in Indianapolis, and educated at Antioch College and the College of Design, Art, and Architecture at the University of Cincinnati before migrating to Oregon. He is a registered architect, formerly practicing in Oregon and Washington before buying a copy of the original PC release of AutoCAD in early 1983. Prior to joining New Riders in 1986, he was founder and president of CAD Northwest, Inc., one of the first AutoCAD dealerships. Rusty is coauthor and/or developer of various editions of many New Riders books, including *Maximizing AutoCAD, Maximizing AutoLISP*, and *Inside AutoCAD*. He now resides in Boring, Oregon with his wife, Kathy, and their two children, and seven pets (cats, dogs, and horses). In his meager spare time, Rusty skis, bicycles, shoots arrows at unsuspecting bales of excelsior, and rides his tractor in circles.

Dennis Hill is a computer consultant who provides services in AutoCAD and general computer systems to clients of his company, Bandit E.D.S. He has been using AutoCAD since 1985 and studied engineering at San Jose State University. He is one of the authors of *Inside AutoCAD Release 12 for Windows* and *Killer AutoCAD Utilities*. He is also a special contributor to *Maximizing AutoCAD Release 12* and *Maximizing AutoLISP*.

Peter Tobey has pursued a lifelong interest in drafting and design, including the creation of kinetic sculptures, toys, medical equipment prototypes, and the design of large-scale industrial waste-treatment facilities. His continuing self-education in the use of AutoCAD began with version 1.4 in 1984. He works as a freelance AutoCAD consultant outside Portland, Oregon. He is one of the authors of *Inside AutoCAD Release 12 for Windows* and *Killer AutoCAD Utilities*. He is a special contributor to *Maximizing AutoCAD Release 12* and *Maximizing AutoLISP*.

Tom Boersma is a Certified Manufacturing Engineer, an ATC trainer, and a CAD/ CAM training specialist at Grand Rapids Community College in Michigan. He is coauthor of *Inside AutoCAD for Windows, Inside AutoCAD Release 12 for Windows, Inside AutoCAD Release 12*, and *Learn CAD with AutoSketch*.

Randall A. Maxey is the founding owner of R.A. Maxey and Associates, a consulting firm located in Westerville, Ohio. Born and raised in central Ohio, Maxey shares his household with his wife, Sheryl, and their four sons, Andrew, Jason, Joshua, and Jared. Maxey graduated from high school in 1978 and has attended The Ohio State University, Franklin University, and Marion Technical College. His consulting firm, started in 1989, provides technical knowledge and expertise to firms seeking to improve the proficiency of the engineering and design efforts. He has contributed to the books *Hands-On AutoCAD Release 12* and *New Riders' Reference Guide to AutoCAD 13*.

Bill Valaski graduated from the University of Cincinnati with a degree in architectural engineering. He works for CDS Associates, Inc., an A/E firm in Cincinnati, Ohio, where he manages computer operations and is training to become a registered architect. Bill also is a partner in Computer Projects Unlimited (CPU), a computer consulting firm, with Bob Knight, another AutoCAD author. Together they have authored several books, including *AutoCAD: The Professional Reference*; *Using AutoCAD, Second Edition*; *The AutoCAD Quick Reference*; and *New Riders' Reference Guide to AutoCAD Release 12.*

Trademark Acknowledgments

All terms mentioned in this book that are known to be trademarks or service marks have been appropriately capitalized. New Riders Publishing cannot attest to the accuracy of this information. Use of a term in this book should not be regarded as affecting the validity of any trademark or service mark. AutoCAD is a registered trademark of Autodesk.

Acquisitions Editor
STACEY BEHELER

Software Specialist
STEVE WEISS

Production Editor
AMY BEZEK

Copy Editor
LAURA FREY

Technical Editor
WILLIAM BLACKMON

Assistant Marketing Manager
TAMARA APPLE

Acquisitions Coordinator
TRACEY TURGESON

Publisher's Assistant
KAREN OPAL

Cover Designer
KAREN RUGGLES

Cover Illustrator
GREG PHILLIPS

Book Designer
SANDRA SCHROEDER

Production Team Supervisor
LAURIE CASEY

Graphics Coordinator
DENNIS CLAY HAGER

Graphic Image Specialists
CLINT LAHNEN
DENNIS SHEEHAN

Production Analysts
ANGELA BANNAN
BOBBI SATTERFIELD
MARY BETH WAKEFIELD

Production Team
ANGELA CALVERT, DANIEL CAPARO
NATHAN CLEMENT, KIMBERLY COFER
JENNIFER EBERHARDT, KEVIN FOLTZ
DAVID GARRATT, ALEATA HOWARD
SHAWN MACDONALD, JOE MILLAY
ERIKA MILLEN, BETH RAGO
GINA REXRODE, ERICH J. RICHTER
CHRISTINE TYNER, KAREN WALSH
ROBERT WOLF

Indexer
CHRIS CLEVELAND

Contents at a Glance

Introduction,   1

Part One: Tools and Concepts,   23

1   *Getting Off the Ground: CAD Concepts 1A,   25*

2   *Specifying Locations in CAD Space,   65*

3   *Keeping Track of Your Work: Drawings as Files,   107*

4   *Building a Drawing: Using Basic Drawing Tools,   137*

5   *Navigating Views in the CAD Workspace,   171*

6   *Making Changes: Using Basic Editing Tools,   219*

7   *Making Changes: Using Grip Editing,   253*

Part Two: Structure and Control,   295

8   *Preparing Your Workspace: CAD Concepts 1B,   297*

9   *Tailoring Your Work Environment,   339*

10   *Getting Organized: Drawing on Layers,   359*

11   *Achieving Accuracy: The Geometric Power of CAD,   397*

12   *Accessing Your Drawing's Data,   447*

13   *Using Object Properties and Text Styles,   473*

Part Three: Power and Technique,   509

14   *Making More Changes: Editing Constructively,   511*

15   *Modifying Objects and Text,   551*

16   *Increasing Your Drawing Power with Polylines and Double Lines,   585*

17   *Dressing Up Drawings with Hatching,   645*

18   *Leveraging Repetitive Design and Drafting,   673*

19   *Managing and Modifying Blocks and Xrefs,   737*

20   *Applying Dimensions in CAD,   765*

21   *Styling and Editing Dimensions,   797*

22   *Structuring Your Drawing,   831*

23   *Producing Hard Copy,   869*

24   *Moving Beyond the Basics,   905*

Part Four: Appendices, 957

A   *AutoCAD LT Installation and Setup,*   *959*

B   *Troubleshooting Common Problems,*   *969*

C   *Enhancing Performance,*   *981*

D   *System Variables,*   *989*

E   *Dimension Variables,*   *1019*

F   *Command Reference,*   *1027*

G   *The IALT Disk,*   *1049*

     Index,   *1061*

Table of Contents

Introduction   1

  Getting into CAD 2

    Introducing AutoCAD LT for Windows 3

    Who Should Read This Book 4

  Finding Your Way Through This Book 5

    Part One: Tools and Concepts 5

    Part Two: Structure and Control 6

    Part Three: Power and Technique 7

    Part Four: Appendices 9

  Getting the Most from This Book 10

    Notational Conventions 10

    How AutoCAD LT Release 2 Features Are Shown 10

    How Exercises Are Shown 10

    Exercises and Your Graphics Display 14

    Notes, Tips, Warnings, and Command Sidebars 14

    Hardware and Software Requirements 15

  Getting More Help 16

    Taking the Quick Tour 16

    Using Windows Help 17

    Other AutoCAD Books from New Riders 17

    Other Windows Titles from New Riders 18

    Ordering Information 19

    Handling Problems 19

    Contacting New Riders Publishing 20

  Making a Start 21

Part One: Tools and Concepts

  1 Getting Off the Ground: CAD Concepts 1A   25

    Exploring Some Basic Principles of CAD 26

      CAD Methods versus Manual Methods 26

      The Power of CAD 27

      The Responsible CAD Designer 28

Understanding the User Interface 29
Issuing Commands and Options 34
   Using the Pointing Device 36
   Using the Keyboard 43
   Choosing between Mouse and Keyboard 45
Working with Dialog Boxes 46
Recovering from Errors 50
   Using the U Command 50
   Selecting and Erasing Objects 51
Adjusting Your View of the Drawing 54
Accessing the HELP Command 57
   Exploring the Help Windows 57
   Getting Context-Sensitive Help in Commands 61
   Finding Information in the Online Documents 61

2   Specifying Locations in CAD Space   65

Understanding Coordinates and Points 66
   Working with the Coordinate Display 68
   Understanding the Coordinate Display Modes 71
Using AutoCAD LT's Drawing Aids 72
   Locating Points with a Reference Grid 72
   Controlling Points with Snap 73
   Setting Up a Coordinated Grid and Snap 76
   Setting Snap and Grid with Quick Step 81
   Controlling Angles with Ortho Mode 83
Specifying Coordinates from the Keyboard 85
   Understanding Absolute X,Y and Polar Coordinates ... 86
   Understanding Relative X,Y and Polar Coordinates ... 87
   Using Typed X,Y and Polar Coordinates 88
Changing the Origin and Axes with UCSs 90
   Showing the Origin and Axes with the UCS Icon 90
   Controlling the UCS 93
Drawing Isometric Representations 99

3   Keeping Track of Your Work: Drawings as Files   107
      Using Directories to Organize Your Drawing Files 109
      Working with File Commands 111
          Starting a New Drawing 111
          Saving Your Drawing 119
          Working with an Existing Drawing 124
          Leaving AutoCAD LT 128
      Setting Up AutoCAD LT's File Environment 128
          Using the Preferences Dialog Box 129
          Using the File Pull-Down Menu 134

4   Building a Drawing: Using Basic Drawing Tools   137
      Creating Lines, Arcs, Circles, Points, and Text 138
      Working with Lines 139
          The LINE Undo and Close Options...142
          LINE Command Options 144
      Using the ARC Command 146
          ARC Command Options 149
          The Continue Option 151
      Using the CIRCLE Command 152
          CIRCLE Command Options 155
          The Tangent-Tangent-Radius Option 156
      Drawing Points 158
      Working with Text 162
          Using Basic Text Options 165
          Text Justification Options 167

5   Navigating Views in the CAD Workspace   171
      Working with Aerial View 175
          Using the Original AutoCAD LT Release 1 Aerial View 175
          Combining Aerial View Options 184
          Using the Redesigned Aerial View..184
          Adjusting the Aerial View with Its Toolbar Buttons and Menus 190
      Controlling the Display 194
          Working with ZOOM Options 197
          Using the PAN Command...199
          Using the VIEW Command 201

Understanding the Display 206
   Recognizing Sources for Screen Regenerations 206
   Understanding Transparent Commands 207
Setting up Multiple Viewports 212

6 Making Changes: Using Basic Editing Tools   219

Understanding AutoCAD LT's Editing Process 220
Working with Object Selection 221
   Selecting Objects to Edit 221
   Using Selection Options 224
   Changing Selection Behavior 232
   Changing Entity Sorting 237
Using the Basic Editing Commands 237
   Working with the ERASE and OOPS Commands 237
   Constructive Editing with the MOVE and COPY Commands 240
   Specifying Displacements for MOVE and COPY 244
Retracing Your Steps with UNDO and REDO 248
   Understanding UNDO Options 251

7 Making Changes: Using Grip Editing   253

Understanding AutoCAD LT's
  Grip Editing Process 254
Introducing Grip Editing 254
Changing Grip Settings 259
Exploring Grip Editing Modes
  and Methods 260
   Stretch Mode 261
   Grip Editing Options 265
   Snapping to Grips 266
   Stretching and Copying Circles and Arcs 266
   Editing Multiple Objects with Multiple Hot Grips 271
   Move Mode 275
   Snapping Copies to Grids, Distances, and Angles 278
   Specifying a Base Point 279
   Rotate Mode 279
   Scale Mode 286
   Mirror Mode 292

Part Two: Structure and Control

8   Preparing Your Workspace: CAD Concepts 1B   297

    Applying Scale Concepts to CAD Drawings **298**

        Working with the LIMITS Command 299

        Calculating Limits to Fit a Drawing to a Sheet 303

        Applying Scale Settings to Annotation and
         Graphic Elements 308

        Scaling Linetypes, Dimensions, and Other
         Graphic Elements 313

        Working with Drawing Units and Precision Settings 313

        Understanding System Variables 322

        Applying Standards with Prototype Drawings 325

    Using Automatic Setup in AutoCAD LT Release 2 .... **326**

    Planning Your Drawings **332**

        Aiming for Consistency 333

        Applying Standards 333

        Working with Naming Conventions 335

9   Tailoring Your Work Environment   339

    Setting Preferences **340**

        Setting Measurement Defaults 343

        Controlling the Interface Colors 345

        Controlling the Interface Text Fonts 348

    Customizing the Toolbox and Toolbar **350**

        Customizing the Toolbox 350

        Customizing the Toolbar Buttons 356

10   Getting Organized: Drawing on Layers   359

    Understanding Layers **360**

    Setting the Current Layer from the Toolbar **362**

    Working with the Layer Control Dialog Box **363**

        Creating New Layers 363

        Controlling Layer Properties 368

        Renaming Layers 374

Setting Layer Status: Visibility and Selectability **376**

Turning Layers On and Off 376

Reading Layer States 378

Freezing and Thawing Layers for Speed 378

Locking and Unlocking Layers for Selection Control 379

Selecting and Checking Sets of Layers with Filters 382

Using the LAYER Command **387**

Using the Make Option 387

Deleting Named Items **389**

Layer-Naming Considerations **391**

Working with Layer-Naming Conventions 391

Grouping Layers with Wild Cards 392

11 Achieving Accuracy: The Geometric Power of CAD   397

Understanding Object Snap **398**

Constructing Accurate Geometry with Object Snaps 403

Setting and Applying Running Object Snap Modes 420

Tapping into Existing Data in Your Drawing **426**

Setting Temporary Reference Points with the ID Command 426

Assembling Coordinate Points with Point Filters 430

Using Tracking to Specify Coordinates **434**

Placing Points on Objects with MEASURE and DIVIDE **440**

12 Accessing Your Drawing's Data   447

Querying Your Drawing **448**

Making Measurements **448**

Finding Distances and Lengths with the DIST Command 448

Measuring Areas with the AREA Command 452

Using the AREA Command with Objects 456

Examining Objects with the LIST Command **462**

Examining and Modifying Objects with DDMODIFY **468**

13 Using Object Properties and Text Styles   473

Understanding Object Properties **475**

Object Properties and Layer Settings 475

Setting Object Properties **476**

Setting the Current New Object Color 477

Setting the Current New Object Linetype 480

Setting the Current Layer for New Objects 487

Setting the Current Text Style 488

Setting the Elevation for New Objects 488

Setting the Thickness for New Objects 489

Modifying the Properties of Existing Objects **489**

Using the Change Properties Dialog Box 490

Changing an Existing Object's Color Property 492

Changing an Existing Object's Layer Property 493

Changing an Existing Object's Linetype Property 493

Changing an Existing Object's Thickness Property 494

Using the Modify *<Object_type>* Dialog Box to
 Change Properties 494

Using Text Styles and Fonts **497**

Creating and Using Text Styles 497

Creating Text Styles with the Select Text Font Dialog Box 502

Using Style Options 503

Working with Different Font Types 505

Changing the Style of Existing Text with DDMODIFY 505

Part Three: Power and Technique

14   Making More Changes: Editing Constructively   511

Replicating Objects **513**

Laying Out a Design with the OFFSET Command 513

Making Multiple Copies with ARRAY 519

Creating Reflected Copies with MIRROR 524

Editing to Clean Up and Add Detail **528**

Refining a Layout Using the BREAK Command 528

Making Ends Meet with FILLET and CHAMFER 535

Cleaning Up with TRIM and EXTEND 543

15 Modifying Objects and Text   **551**

  Modifying Objects **552**

    Making Changes with the CHANGE Command 553

    Moving Endpoints Using STRETCH 559

    Setting Angles with the ROTATE Command 569

    Adjusting Proportions Using SCALE 575

  Working with Text **578**

    Editing Text 579

    Importing Text from a File 581

16 Increasing Your Drawing Power with Polylines and Double Lines   **585**

  Understanding Polylines **586**

    Using the PLINE Command Options 587

    Modifying Polylines with the PEDIT Command 605

    Exploding Polylines into Lines and Arcs 619

  Drawing Complex Geometry Simply **621**

    Using the POLYGON Command 621

    Creating Donuts and Ellipses 623

    Using the RECTANG Command 628

    Creating Complex Polyline Boundaries with BOUNDARY 630

  Drawing Double Lines with the DLINE Command **637**

17 Dressing Up Drawings with Hatching   **645**

  Understanding Hatch Patterns and Boundaries **646**

    Choosing and Scaling a Hatch Pattern 647

    Choosing Boundaries for Hatch Patterns 648

  Using the HATCH Command and Select Hatch Pattern Dialog Box **649**

    Using the HATCH Command Options 652

  Understanding More About Hatch Patterns **654**

  Using the BHATCH Command and Boundary Hatch Dialog Box **655**

    The Boundary Hatch Dialog Box Options 659

    Controlling Hatch Boundaries 662

    Editing Associative Hatches 666

18   Leveraging Repetitive Design and Drafting   673

Automating Repetitive Elements with Blocks and Xrefs **674**
The Benefits of Using Blocks and Xrefs 675
Inserting Existing Drawings as Blocks **676**
Introducing the INSERT Command 676
Inserting the Component Objects of Blocks 679
Comparing the INSERT Command and the Insert Dialog Box 681
Creating Blocks **683**
Using the Block Definition Dialog Box 683
Defining Blocks with the BLOCK Command 686
Comparing Blocks and Xrefs as Parts, Symbols, and Templates 686
Controlling Block Insertions **690**
Scaling Block Insertions 691
Scaling, Rotating, and Mirroring Unit Blocks 693
Presetting Scale and Rotation 696
Inserting Arrays of Blocks with MINSERT 698
Inserting Blocks Along Objects with DIVIDE and MEASURE **702**
Automating Text with Attributes **707**
Defining Attributes 708
Editing Attribute Definitions 712
Inserting Attribute Definitions 713
Editing Inserted Attributes 716
Referencing External Drawings **719**
Attaching and Detaching Xrefs 720
Updating Xrefs: Editing the Source and Reloading 725
Understanding the Named Items within Xrefs 728
Converting an Xref to a Block 730
Importing Part of an Xref with XBIND 732

19   Managing and Modifying Blocks and Xrefs   737

Editing Whole Blocks **738**
Exploding Blocks to Edit Their Component Objects **739**
Redefining Blocks **742**
Redefining Blocks with INSERT **744**

Understanding Layers, Linetypes, and Colors within Blocks **745**
 Objects with Explicit Properties 745
 Objects with BYLAYER Properties or On Layer 0 745
 Objects with BYBLOCK Properties 747
Creating Block and Xref Libraries **750**
 Managing Layers, Colors, and Linetypes in Blocks 750
 Managing Layers, Colors, and Linetypes in Xrefs 752
 Exporting Blocks and Drawing Data with WBLOCK 753
 Setting the Insertion Base Point 756
Editing, Grips, and Blocks **759**
Nesting Blocks in Blocks and Xrefs **761**
Purging Unused Blocks **763**

20 Applying Dimensions in CAD   765
Understanding Dimensioning Concepts **767**
 Identifying the Components of a Dimension 767
 Harnessing the Associative Power of Dimensions 768
 Controlling Dimension Features with Dimension Variables 768
Dimensioning Your Drawing **769**
 Issuing the Dimensioning Commands 770
 Responding to the Dimension Prompts 772
 Using Linear Dimensioning Commands 774
 Placing Ordinate Dimensions 786
 Inserting Leaders and Text 788
 Dimensioning Circles and Arcs 790
 Applying Angular Dimensioning 794

21 Styling and Editing Dimensions   797
Controlling Dimension Appearance **798**
 The Dimension Styles and Settings Dialog Box 800
 Creating and Using Dimension Styles 814
Editing Associative Dimensions **821**
 Exploding Dimensions 822
 Editing Associative Dimensions 822

22 Structuring Your Drawing — 831

Applying Model Space Views and Viewports 833
Using Views in Your Drawing 833
Setting Up Model Space Tiled Viewports 835
Entering Paper Space 837
Understanding TILEMODE 838
Setting Up a Single Floating Mview Viewport in Paper Space 841
Using Custom Setup to Insert a Title Block and Viewport 847
Composing a Multiview Drawing 851
Defining Multiple Mview Viewports 852
Controlling the Display of Mview Viewports 854
Sizing Text, Symbols, and Dimensions 857
Controlling Viewport Layer Visibility 860
Exploring Additional Paper Space Capabilities 861
Setting Up Mview Viewports Using a 3D Model 862
Controlling Hidden Line Visibility and Linetype Scale 865

23 Producing Hard Copy — 869

Printing and Plotting from AutoCAD LT 870
Making a Quick Check Plot 870
Choosing a Device for Plotting 873
Making Settings with the Plot Configuration Dialog Box 879
Defining What Gets Plotted 884
Specifying Pen Weights and Line Styles 886
Choosing the Proper Paper Size and Rotation 887
Seeing a Preview 889
Understanding Scale Issues 892
Plotting from Model Space 893
Plotting from Paper Space 896
Plotting to a File 897
Managing Plot Settings, Plotters, and Supplies 898
Managing Standard Sets of Plot Settings 898
Dealing with Equipment 900
Managing Media and Supplies 901
Exploring Alternative Output 903

24 Moving Beyond the Basics   **905**

  Developing Standards **906**
    Using Standard Layer-Naming Schemes 907
    Creating Custom Linetypes 910
    Using Hatch Patterns 912
    Using Text Styles 913
    Working with Standard Template Drawings 914
    Using Libraries of Parts and Details 916
    Enforcing and Maintaining Standards 919
  Working in Three Dimensions **921**
    Using the VPOINT Command to View 3D Drawings 921
    Using the VPORTS Command 923
    Using the DVIEW Command 927
    Modifying the Current Coordinate System 930
    Creating and Editing Objects in 3D Space 935
  Sharing Data **940**
  Exchanging File Information with Other Programs **940**
    Using the Drawing Interchange Format (DXF) 941
    Using the Windows Metafile Format (WMF) 943
    Creating PostScript Output 945
  Transferring Information through the Windows Clipboard **948**
    Using the Copy Image Option 948
    Using the Copy Vectors Option 950
    Using the Copy Embed Option 952
    Using the Copy Link Option 952
    Pasting Images into AutoCAD LT 953
    Importing Text with the Paste Command 954
  Looking to Your Future with CAD **956**

Part Four: Appendices

A AutoCAD LT Installation and Setup   **959**

  Preparing for Installation **960**
    Backing Up Your Original Software Disks 960
    Preparing Your Hard Drive before Installation 961

Installing AutoCAD LT **961**

Making Settings **967**

Network Configuration 968

B   Troubleshooting Common Problems   969

Problems with Startup Files **970**

Tailoring Your CONFIG.SYS File 970

Tailoring Your AUTOEXEC.BAT File 972

Common Problems with CONFIG.SYS 973

Common Problems with AUTOEXEC.BAT 974

Memory Problems **976**

Finding Support Files **976**

Tracing and Curing Errors **977**

Clearing Up File Problems After a System Crash **977**

Removing Extraneous Files After a Crash 978

Unlocking Locked Files 978

Other Error Messages **978**

Bugs **979**

AutoCAD LT and Other AutoCAD Releases **979**

C   Enhancing Performance   981

Disk Defragmenting **982**

Setting a Large Permanent Swap File and 32-Bit File Access **982**

Upgrading Your Processor **984**

Installing Additional Memory **985**

Maximizing Available Memory **985**

Running Fewer Applications **986**

Using Faster Video **986**

Keeping Up-to-Date **986**

Using a Disk Cache **986**

Other Tips **987**

D   System Variables   989

E   Dimension Variables   1019

F   Command Reference   1027

G   The IALT Disk   1049

  Installing the IALT Disk **1050**
      Starting AutoCAD LT and Checking the Prototype Drawing 1051
  Installing the IALT Disk's Text Fonts **1054**
  Installing LTHook **1055**
  Installing the AutoCAD LT Release 1 c1a Patch **1056**
  Updating AutoCAD LT Release 1's Plotter Driver **1058**
      Installing the Updated Plotter Driver 1059
  Installing LT_BASIC **1059**

  Index   1061

Introduction

Inside AutoCAD LT for Windows, Second Edition teaches you the mechanics of using AutoCAD LT Release 1 and AutoCAD LT Release 2 for Windows. It also introduces you to some concepts that enable you to use CAD more productively. You see how to use AutoCAD LT for Windows both as a design tool and as a communications tool, thereby capitalizing on the power of CAD.

The arts of drafting and design have roots reaching as far back in history as the roots of language. In fact, illustration was used before written language was created. Drafting was first used as a design communication tool before the pyramids were created.

Today, the preferred method for design drafting is to use a computer. The first acronym given to this new electronic tool was CADD, for Computer-Aided Design and Drafting. As the science of computers and software has progressed, the computer has become more and more of a design tool. The computer's capability to process information for creating and communicating a design goes far beyond the lines and text that appear in a drawing. Today, CAD is simply Computer-Aided Design.

Because CAD evolved from manual drafting, much of the terminology that was used in manual drafting also is used in CAD. For instance, the terms "tool" from drafting and "command" from CAD often are used interchangeably. Such traditional terms as "orthographic," "isometric," "rendering," and many more have carried over into CAD. This book defines terms that are specific to the use of CAD and AutoCAD LT for Windows wherever needed.

The most logical place to begin the process of learning AutoCAD LT for Windows is with a discussion of the benefits of using CAD.

Getting into CAD

Why use CAD? For centuries, paper drawings (and other media) have sufficed for the communication of illustrative ideas. These traditional tools are inexpensive and easy to use. To understand the value of CAD over traditional drafting methods, you need to recognize fundamental differences between these two methods.

When you create a design with CAD, you are actually creating a collection of electronic information called a database. The database includes all the three-dimensional vector geometry required to produce the lines, circles, arcs, solids, and text in the drawing. The database also includes all the background information used to organize the drawing, such as linetypes, fonts, plotter settings, and many more. In addition, you can create and store information that keeps track of inventory items, costs, scheduling dates, and nearly anything else you can imagine. The entire database is contained in a drawing file. The information in this database can simultaneously replace paper drawings, inventory lists, and scheduling documents, just to name a few possibilities.

You can organize information in your drawing in a number of ways and use that organization to extract information with greater efficiency and speed than is possible in a paper drawing. You can group drawing elements together on a common *layer* (like an overlay), or link them together in a named *block* of elements. You can search, or query, the drawing database and export and share its data between computer applications and design disciplines. You can avoid communication errors and any unnecessary duplications of effort.

CAD drawings are not isolated from one another as paper drawings are. The information in a master drawing can be used as a base point for starting other drawings. Background information can be attached as an external reference that is automatically updated whenever the referenced drawing is changed.

The accuracy of CAD's 3D geometry can be used as a sophisticated computer check of your design. The CAD program functions as a calculation engine in which numeric values are recorded as 16-place, floating-point numbers. You can more readily identify areas for potential conflicts. The design is drawn in actual size, and dimensioning becomes a design verification tool.

The CAD drawing is unquestionably superior to manual drafting when it comes to editing. Using editing commands, you can move, rotate, scale, mirror, copy, or stretch drawings with push-button ease and without having to erase any of your work. As you design, you never need to draw anything twice: you can reorganize and reuse as you go. You can freely pursue "what if?" design scenarios, which can be incorporated or abandoned with equal ease. You can respond to changes more quickly and with far less frustration.

All these advantages contribute to your design productivity, enabling you to get more done with the same effort. You can spend more time on perfecting a design when you are not saddled by the mechanics of drawing it by hand. AutoCAD LT for Windows is an easy, accessible entry point for you to begin taking advantage of these benefits in your designs.

Introducing AutoCAD LT for Windows

When AutoCAD was first introduced in 1982, it was a simple tool for creating drawings on a personal computer. The early versions had limited commands for generating basic 2D geometry. The first manual was a loose-leaf binder containing fewer than 150 pages. The program required DOS and could be run on IBM XT systems with 540 KB of RAM and dual (360 KB) floppy drives. It was incredibly slow; you could take a coffee break while performing a regeneration of the screen image. The product succeeded because the only other CAD systems available at the time were mainframe-based programs priced in the six-digit range that cost thousands of dollars per month to operate. What AutoCAD introduced for the first time was true CAD for the masses.

AutoCAD Release 12 has over 175 commands and subcommands, plus dialog boxes. The reference manual is a hardbound book of nearly 700 pages by itself, and it has eight supplemental softcover reference books, all totaling thousands of pages. AutoCAD Release 13 has even more commands, dialog boxes, and documentation.

AutoCAD LT for Windows has much of AutoCAD Release 12's functionality and power, but with a greatly simplified interface. It shares complete file format compatibility with AutoCAD Release 12 and Release 12 for Windows. You can use AutoCAD LT to work on a drawing originally created with Release 12, without experiencing any loss of data when you return to Release 12. AutoCAD LT Release 1's drawing and editing features are described in a 300-page softcover manual accompanied by a short tutorial manual.

AutoCAD LT Release 2 adds several ease-of-use features and a few new commands. These include automated drawing setup, associative boundary hatching, direct distance entry and tracking (inherited from Generic CADD), network support,

Windows-standard menu arrangement, and ToolTips to identify tool and botton icons. AutoCAD LT Release 2 also doubles AutoCAD LT Release 1's printed documentation, expands online Help, and adds online Orientation, What's New, and Tutorial documents.

AutoCAD LT for Windows is priced to be affordable for the small office, the individual user, or the student. In a large firm, AutoCAD LT can be used for training or needs not related to design such as plotting, engineering review, demonstrations, or project management.

Who Should Read This Book

The purpose of *Inside AutoCAD LT for Windows, Second Edition* is to introduce you to a powerful tool for communication involving your computer and AutoCAD LT for Windows. This book is of benefit to any beginner or experienced computer user who is using AutoCAD LT for Windows for the first time. The material covers both the mechanics of using AutoCAD LT for Windows and the concepts of using AutoCAD LT for Windows as a design tool.

◆ If you are experienced in the use of AutoCAD LT Release 1, most material will be a review of existing knowledge; however, you will likely learn even more, and the new information about AutoCAD LT for Windows will certainly benefit you.

◆ If you are experienced in the use of computer-aided design, some of the material will be a review or an adaptation of existing knowledge; the information on the mechanics of using AutoCAD LT for Windows will benefit you the most.

◆ If you are experienced in designing without the use of CAD, or if you are a self-taught CAD user, you will benefit from the discussions of the significance of the tools and how they are used most efficiently in design.

◆ If you are a beginner, you will learn not only the mechanics of using AutoCAD LT for Windows, but also the value gained from using it in the most effective manner.

This book is written to accommodate the beginner. It therefore assumes that you are new to CAD. This book is not written as a tutorial of the DOS or Windows environments, but it does contain information on establishing the AutoCAD LT environment within Windows.

The AutoCAD skills presented in this book will enable you to apply the power of the computer to design problems in engineering or science. Whatever your motivations are, this book helps you to quickly become proficient with AutoCAD LT for Windows. It doesn't matter if you are taking up CAD by choice or because you have a job that

requires it. This book gives you the knowledge and understanding you need to productively harness the power of CAD. If you are trying to learn how to use AutoCAD LT for Windows and you don't know where to start, this book is for you.

The next section outlines the structure of this book. If you are an experienced user seeking information on specific subjects, this section tells you where to find the material that is of particular interest to you.

Finding Your Way Through This Book

Inside AutoCAD LT for Windows, Second Edition is structured to progressively build your knowledge and understanding. To accomplish this, the book is divided into three parts. Part One of the book introduces the fundamental commands and concepts. In Part Two, you learn to use the commands you need to control and structure your drawing and working environment. Finally, in Part Three, you explore advanced tools and techniques for efficiently applying the power of CAD in your design work. The book also has appendixes and an index to enable you to continue to use this book as a reference guide.

Part One: Tools and Concepts

The seven chapters of Part One introduce you to AutoCAD LT for Windows: the basic elements of the program, how you communicate with it, and how it communicates with you and your computer. You learn to create and edit drawing objects while exploring the fundamental concepts of CAD.

Chapter 1 explains AutoCAD LT's interface for you. You learn how the display screen is organized and how you issue commands with either the keyboard or your Windows pointing device. Some basic principles of CAD are outlined early for your consideration as you progress through the mechanics of using AutoCAD LT for Windows. You take AutoCAD LT for Windows for a quick test drive and learn how to create and control drawing objects. The tools for controlling the display of your drawing are introduced, and you learn to access the AutoCAD LT for Windows help facility and AutoCAD LT Release 2's online documentation.

Chapter 2 explains the CAD concept of coordinate space. You learn to use AutoCAD LT's tools for locating objects and keeping track of where you are in a drawing. A few of the AutoCAD LT drawing aids are explained and demonstrated, along with the concept of the AutoCAD custom User Coordinate System or UCS. The new automated setup and direct distance entry features of AutoCAD LT Release 2 are introduced.

Chapter 3 explains the concept and use of drawing files and file commands. These tools provide the access to the computer that you need to create, use, and save drawing files. You learn how to use the **F**ile menu to access these functions. You also learn how to create and utilize a prototype drawing, rename a drawing, set AutoCAD LT to perform automatic file saves for you, recover from a system crash, and exit AutoCAD LT.

Chapter 4 thoroughly explores the basic drawing commands and options for generating lines, arcs, circles, and points. It also discusses how to place text in a drawing and the basic options for controlling the format of your text.

Chapter 5 explores the tools that control what you see. You learn to navigate in a drawing by using the Aerial View (sometimes referred to as a bird's-eye view), as well as the conventional display commands. See how to divide your screen into multiple views, which can each be set to display a different portion of your drawing. The Aerial View features in AutoCAD LT Release 1 and 2 are completely different, so Chapter 5 covers both.

Chapter 6 introduces you to the power of CAD by showing you how to use the basic editing commands. First, the various methods for object selection are explained and demonstrated. Next, you learn how to delete objects and recover from mistakes. Then you learn to move and copy selections of objects.

Chapter 7 continues the coverage of editing with methods of autoediting using grips. Grips are geometric nodes on objects, with which you interactively stretch, move, copy, rotate, scale, and create mirror images of objects.

After you complete Part One, you will be familiar with all the basics of AutoCAD LT for Windows. You will be ready to learn how to best organize your approach to using CAD.

Part Two: Structure and Control

Part Two takes you through the AutoCAD LT tools that help you perform efficiently in CAD. The six chapters help you to set up your working environment, organize the data in your drawings, increase your accuracy, automate your control of point selection, and understand the importance of controlling the properties of drawing objects.

Chapter 8 covers setting up the drawing environment. It reveals some important practices and avoidable pitfalls involved in planning and setting up your work space or drawing environment. You establish how your AutoCAD LT displays coordinate and distance information (units) and at what accuracy level (precision). You discover how the concept of scale is used in a CAD drawing, and how it affects text and linetypes. You learn to set the limits, or the real-world size, of the drawing. You also

see how to use AutoCAD LT Release 2's Quick and Custom drawing setup features to make these settings.

Chapter 9 covers setting up the working environment—AutoCAD LT's user interface. It also covers standards, conventions, and preserving your working and drawing environments through the use of Preferences, system variables and prototype drawings.

Chapter 10 explains the concept of drawing layers and the techniques of using layers to organize the contents of your CAD drawings. You learn about all the commands available for creating, editing, and controlling the layers in a drawing.

Chapter 11 covers drawing accurately. It first explores commands that can be used as support or environment settings for increasing the accuracy of your work. For example, you can create lines that are tangent to arcs or circles. You use object snaps to snap new points and objects to geometric points on existing objects. You also learn how to place new objects at regular intervals along existing lines and curves, how to gain the maximum use from forcing point selections to be parallel to the X or Y axis (Ortho mode), and how to use point filters to control your input. Chapter 11 also covers the use of AutoCAD LT Release 2's new point tracking input mode, and the new DIVIDE and MEASURE commands.

Chapter 12 covers inquiry into the data that makes up a drawing. You learn how to query the data that is part of an object's geometry. You learn how to find distances, perimeters, angles, and areas. Chapter 12 also covers the use of AutoCAD LT Release 2's Modify *<Entity>* dialog box for viewing and changing the geometry of existing objects.

Chapter 13 defines the various properties an object can possess and how they are controlled within AutoCAD LT. You also learn how to define or change the style (font) that text is created with. Chapter 13 also covers the use of AutoCAD LT Release 2's Modify *<Entity>* dialog box for viewing and changing the properties of existing objects.

After completing Part Two, you will have achieved the level of an intermediate user of CAD. Part Three of the book introduces you to some topics that will greatly increase your proficiency.

Part Three: Power and Technique

Part Three explores some of the more advanced and powerful tools and options. You learn to extend the power of the basic tools by using techniques for maximizing the benefits of using CAD. Some advanced drawing and editing tools are introduced, along with techniques for creating and using blocks and external reference files. You also explore the tools for dimensioning a drawing, using paper space to create a drawing with multiple views of your design, and producing a hard copy of your drawing with a printer or plotter. As a final note, you are introduced to some of the topics involved in becoming an advanced CAD user and provided with some guidance as to where you can go next to advance your knowledge and skill as a CAD designer.

Chapter 14 addresses the issue of constructive editing. Several methods for replicating objects are explored, such as offsetting lines and curves, creating arrays of objects, dressing corners with fillets and chamfers, and creating mirror images. You also learn how to break up (explode) objects that are linked together.

Chapter 15 explores more editing commands, including those used for changing points on objects, and stretching, rotating, and scaling objects. You also learn to edit and import text.

Chapter 16 discusses the use of the more advanced drawing and editing tools for creating complex geometry. Learn how to create a line that can have turns and curves in it, yet is treated and edited as a single object called a polyline. You are introduced to AutoCAD LT's ability to draw with two parallel lines at once (double lines). Chapter 16 also covers AutoCAD LT Release 2's new BOUNDARY command, which enables you to create a closed polyline that traces the boundary of a closed area by simply picking a single point in the area.

Chapter 17 covers only one important feature: hatching. You learn how to fill in a designated area with patterns of lines by using a single command (HATCH). These patterns are used to designate materials and can be quite complex, even to the point of appearing random, such as the concrete pattern. The specification of a hatch boundary can be laborious in AutoCAD LT Release 1. Chapter 17 covers AutoCAD LT Release 2's new boundary hatch feature, which enables you to specify an area to hatch by a single point pick. It also enables you to edit hatch patterns, as their boundaries are associative in AutoCAD LT Release 2.

Chapter 18 introduces you to one of the most dramatic advantages of CAD: how to multiply the effect of your creative effort. You learn how to form groups of objects into single-object blocks, and then replicate (insert) them wherever they are needed with a single command. You discover that an entire drawing can be treated as a single block and inserted into any drawing you choose. Finally, you learn how to save storage space and avoid time-consuming updates by using externally referenced drawing files (xref) for drawing background information. Chapter 18 also shows how to insert multiple blocks at regular spacing along linear and curved entities, using AutoCAD LT Release 2's new DIVIDE and MEASURE commands.

Chapter 19 continues the coverage of blocks and xrefs, explaining their structure, management, properties, relationships to layers and colors, and how to edit, redefine, purge, explode, and nest them. The chapter also discusses the creation of libraries of blocks that can be inserted into any drawing you choose.

Chapter 20 explores the concept of dimensioning drawings in AutoCAD LT. You are exposed to a mechanism of semiautomatic dimensioning and how it can be used as a self-check in your drawings. Chapter 20 covers all dimension placement commands in AutoCAD LT, showing how to dimension all types of objects.

Chapter 21 continues coverage of dimensioning with the control and management of dimensions and their appearance. You learn how to control the appearance of your dimensions by setting dimension system variables, and how to save those settings for use later as a named dimension style. You learn to make AutoCAD LT's dimensions meet your standards. A complete architectural dimension style is used as an example.

Chapter 22 introduces advanced topics for structuring and controlling your drawing and its display: working with views and viewports incorporating model space and paper space. You learn how a single design drawing can be used to create all the production drawings you need to manufacture your design. You learn how to control scale and appearance while using paper space, and the layer options related to viewports. Chapter 22 also covers the use of AutoCAD LT Release 2's Custom Setup to set up paper space and insert a title block, date stamp block, and viewport.

Chapter 23 details the procedures for printing and plotting your drawings and how to save custom settings that can be recalled later. Other forms of output available in AutoCAD LT are also discussed.

Chapter 24 points out that this book should be a starting point for you and gives you an idea of future directions. The value of developing styles and standards for your work is discussed, along with the ability to work in three dimensions with AutoCAD LT. The concept of sharing data between other CAD users and even non-CAD programs is discussed. As a final note, you take a look into the future of CAD.

Part Four: Appendices

Appendix A provides guidelines for installing and setting up AutoCAD LT for Windows.

Appendix B is a troubleshooting appendix. Refer to if you have problems.

Appendix C covers optimizing Windows settings and performance for AutoCAD LT.

Appendix D is a complete list of all the system variables used in AutoCAD LT for Windows.

Appendix E is a complete list of all the dimension variables used in AutoCAD LT for Windows.

Appendix F is a quick command reference.

Appendix G consists of instructions on installing the IALT Disk that accompanies the book. In addition to providing starting drawings and support files for many of the book's exercises, the IALT Disk includes a number of extra utility programs.

Getting the Most from This Book

No matter how proficient you are with AutoCAD, Windows, or your computer, and no matter how thoroughly you read this book, you will revisit it again and again as a reference manual. AutoCAD LT offers so many ways for you to accomplish the task of CAD design that you will simply not have the time to explore them all until some need arises. You will then find *Inside AutoCAD LT for Windows, Second Edition* indispensable as you use it to find explanations and examples of specific commands and techniques. To ensure that you are getting the most from this book, read the following sections which explain the notational conventions used throughout the book.

Notational Conventions

The conventions used for showing various types of text throughout this book are, insofar as possible, the same as those used in the *Microsoft Windows User's Guide* and the *AutoCAD LT for Windows User's Guide.* These conventions are shown in this section. Some conventions, such as the use of italics to introduce a new term, are simple. Others, such as those used in the exercises, are worth a closer look.

How AutoCAD LT Release 2 Features Are Shown

ALT2

Features of AutoCAD LT Release 2 not available in AutoCAD LT Release 1 are identified by the icon that appears next to this paragraph. Exercise steps that apply to only AutoCAD LT Release 1 or AutoCAD LT Release 2 are identified.

How Exercises Are Shown

A sample exercise follows. You do not need to work through it or understand the content, but you should look over the format so that you will know how the book's exercises are presented. Most exercises are accompanied by one or more illustrations, most of which were captured from the screen during an actual exercise. Exercises are arranged in two columns, with direct instructions on the left and explanatory notes on the right. Lengthy instructions or explanations sometimes extend across both columns.

Looking at a Sample Exercise

Continue in the SAMPLE drawing from the preceding exercise.

Command: *Turn on the Snap button*	Sets Snap mode on
Command: *Choose* **D**raw, **C**ircle, *then* Center, **R**adius	Issues the CIRCLE command from the Circle child menu of the Draw pull-down
_circle 3P/2P/TTR/<Center point>: *Pick point at* ① *(see fig. I.1)*	Specifies the circle's center point
Radius: **3** Enter	Draws a 6" circle
Command: *Choose* **D**raw, **L**ine	Issues the LINE command
From point: *Click on the Center tool*	Specifies the CENter object snap
_CEN of *Pick the circle at* ②	Starts the line at the circle's center
To point: *Pick* ③	Draws the line
To point: **3,5** Enter	Specifies the coordinates you typed
To point: Enter	Ends the LINE command

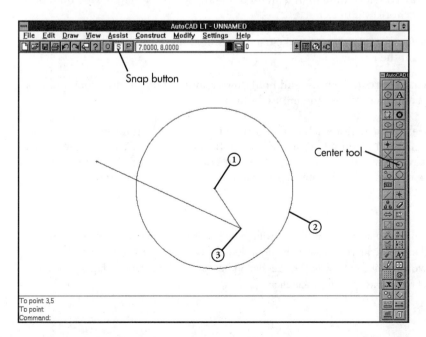

Snap button

Center tool

Figure I.1

A sample exercise illustration.

Because AutoCAD LT for Windows is a Windows application, its interface uses many of the elements used by other Windows applications. The toolbar incorporates buttons for a few commonly used commands. The toolbar also contains the current layer name and the coordinates display. The menu bar always appears above the toolbar. The toolbox contains icons (called tools) for commonly used commands and all of the object snap modes.

You will be using your Windows pointing device (referred to throughout this book as a mouse) for much of your input in AutoCAD LT. You should become familiar with the following terms, which are used to describe mouse actions:

◆ **Click.** To press and release the pick button.

◆ **Click on, click in.** To position the cursor on the appropriate user interface object (icon, input box, menu item, and so on) and click the pick button.

◆ **Double-click.** To press and release the pick button twice, in rapid succession.

◆ **Pick.** To position the cursor on the appropriate object or point and click the pick button.

◆ **Select.** To highlight an object in the AutoCAD LT drawing area by picking it or by using other object selection methods. Also, to highlight an item, word, or character in a drop-down or dialog box list or text input field by clicking on it.

◆ **Choose.** To select an item in a menu or dialog box by either clicking on it or typing its hot-key letter.

◆ **Drag.** To move the mouse and cursor, causing lines or objects on the screen to move with the cursor.

◆ **Press and drag.** To press and hold down a mouse button, drag something on screen, and then release the mouse button.

When you see an instruction such as *Choose* **I**tem in an exercise, it means to move the pointer to **I**tem on the menu bar and click the left mouse button. You also can use a hot key—a key combination consisting of the Alt key and the letter underlined in the menu bar item—to display the menu; for example, to access the **F**ile menu, you would press Alt+F.

Note Some menu items are displayed with three periods following the item name, and others have a right arrow at the right side of the menu. AutoCAD LT uses this notation to indicate items that call dialog boxes and child menus. This book does not reflect this special punctuation.

> Do not be concerned about the leading underscore character included in command prompts to accommodate international versions of AutoCAD LT. You will see the underscore on the screen, but it is not actually part of the command name.

If it is relevant to the context of the exercise, the instructions will include the location from which you are to initiate a command. Exercise steps that use the toolbox instruct you to "*Click on the *** tool.*" Exercise steps that use the toolbar instruct you to "*Click on the *** button.*" Exercise steps that use the pull-down menus instruct you to "choose" the menu identified by its name. If a pull-down menu or dialog box is currently displayed, "choose" refers to an item on it. If no specific direction is given for the source of the command, feel free to use whatever serves you best. (As you progress through the book, you will learn a variety of ways to issue a command. See Chapter 1 for more information on using the command line, the pull-down menus, the dialog boxes, the toolbar, and the toolbox.)

In some cases, you will see the instruction Press Enter. Your computer may have a key labeled Enter, or one labeled Return, or one with an arrow symbol. In any case, *Press Enter* means to press the key that enters a return. You will also see the symbol (Enter) in the exercises. This symbol means the same thing as *Press Enter*.

You often enter commands from the keyboard. Similarly, point coordinates, distances, and option keywords must be typed. The exercise text generally indicates when typed input is required by showing it in bold text following a prompt, such as:

Command: **UNITS** (Enter)

or

To point: **3,5** (Enter)

You should type the input as it appears, and then press Enter.

Early in the book, you will notice that exercises contain numerous prompts and explanations of what is (or should be) happening as you enter commands. Later exercises often omit explanations of familiar effects and prompts that have become routine.

Some exercises end with an instruction to end or save the drawing. You might not want to end a drawing, because some chapters can be completed in one or two sittings. You should save your drawings when instructed, however, to help you build a habit of saving drawings at regular intervals. If you want to proceed at a leisurely pace, you can end your drawing whenever you see the save instruction and reload it later. If you want to take a break and a save or end instruction is not shown, just close and save or end your drawing and reload it later.

Exercises and Your Graphics Display

The authors created this book's illustrations by capturing screen displays during the process of performing the exercises. All screen displays were captured from systems using Super VGA display controllers set for the 800×600-pixel resolution under Windows. If your system has a standard VGA or EGA card or a high-resolution display controller, your screen displays may not agree exactly with the illustrations. Menus and screen elements may appear larger or smaller than they do in the illustrations, and you may want to zoom in or out further than the instructions indicate. You should understand from the outset, in fact, that you must adjust to the task at hand and the resources available. You may find that if you use colors that are different from those designated in the exercises, the objects are easier to see, especially if you are working with a white background rather than a black background.

Setting the Screen Colors in AutoCAD LT

The drawing image will probably be clearer if you set AutoCAD LT to use a black drawing background. To change the colors AutoCAD LT displays, choose **F**ile, then **P**references, then **C**olors. Click on **W**indow Element, and select which part of the screen you want to change, or click in that area of the sample screens on the left. Then simply click on the color you want it to be. Your selection is displayed when you return to the graphics screen. Click on **S**ystem Colors to return to the default settings.

Notes, Tips, Warnings, and Command Sidebars

Inside AutoCAD LT for Windows, Second Edition features many special "sidebars," that are set apart from the normal text by icons. The book includes four distinct types of sidebars: "Notes," "Tips," "Warnings," and "Command Sidebars." These passages have been given special treatment so that you can instantly recognize their significance and easily find them for future reference.

Note A note includes "extra" information you should find useful, but which complements the discussion at hand instead of being a direct part of it. A note might describe special situations that can arise when you use AutoCAD LT for Windows under certain circumstances, and might tell you what steps to take when such situations arise. Notes also might tell you how to avoid problems with your software and hardware.

Tip A tip provides you with quick instructions for getting the most from your AutoCAD system as you follow the steps outlined in the general discussion. A tip might show you how to conserve memory in some setups, how to speed up a procedure, or how to perform one of many time-saving and system-enhancing techniques.

New Riders Publishing
INSIDE
SERIES

Stop A warning tells you when a procedure might be dangerous—that is, when you run the risk of losing data, locking your system, or even damaging your hardware. Warnings generally tell you how to avoid such losses, or they describe the steps you can take to remedy these situations.

For each command, a definition of the command is shown in a special sidebar when the command is first explained. The command sidebars look like the following:

> **CIRCLE.** The CIRCLE command can draw circles by using nearly any geometric method. The most common method (the default) is to specify the center point and radius. You can drag and pick the size of the circle on screen, or you can specify the radius with a keyboard entry.

Hardware and Software Requirements

To use *Inside AutoCAD LT for Windows,* you need the following software and hardware, at the least. This book assumes the following:

◆ You have a computer with both AutoCAD LT for Windows and Windows 3.1 or later installed and configured. Appendixes A and C provide more specific information and recommendations on system requirements and settings, and on installing AutoCAD LT for Windows.

◆ You have at least 3 MB of free hard disk space left after you have installed and configured Windows and AutoCAD LT for Windows. More space is required if you want to install all of the extra utilities on the IALT Disk.

◆ You have a graphics display and pointing device configured to work with Windows (if your system works with Windows, it should work with AutoCAD LT for Windows).

◆ You are familiar with PC DOS/MS-DOS and can use the basic DOS commands and utilities.

◆ You are familiar with Windows and can use it to run applications. If not, use the Windows online help, check the Windows documentation, or go through the Windows tutorial.

Note If AutoCAD LT for Windows is not yet installed on your computer, refer to the instructions in Appendix A.

Getting More Help

Although *Inside AutoCAD LT for Windows* is a thorough tutorial, you will find more details on some commands and features in the *AutoCAD LT for Windows User's Guide*. Also, try the context-sensitive online help (F1) and, in AutoCAD LT Release 2, other online documentation and online tutorial. Chapter 1 also provides more information on using help. Be sure to contact the software retailer or dealer from whom you purchased AutoCAD LT for Windows if you need specific help with setting up AutoCAD LT for Windows to run on your computer system. You can get help directly from Autodesk by calling Autodesk technical support, but you must be prepared to describe your system accurately (both hardware and software) because it is usually impossible to help you without this information. Registered users can call Autodesk technical support free of charge for 90 days (extended support contracts are available after the first 90 days). The technical support number is (206) 485-7086. Other support options are available, including a Fax Back service—call (206) 486-1636, and paid support after the first 90 days.

Another outstanding source for help with AutoCAD LT is CompuServe (GO ARETAIL and choose the AutoCAD LT menu option). Simply address your questions to the SYSOP, and you usually receive an answer within a few days. If you keep your messages public, you often find a wealth of replies and suggestions from other users as well.

If you have questions or problems specifically regarding *Inside AutoCAD LT for Windows, Second Edition*, refer to the section "Handling Problems" toward the end of this introduction.

Because AutoCAD LT for Windows is a Windows application, the best place to search for help with items relating to the operating system is in your *Microsoft Windows User's Guide*. Microsoft also has technical support numbers and CompuServe forums (GO MSOFT and MSSYS).

You may also find the information you need is contained within the Quick Tour.

Taking the Quick Tour

For a brief overview of AutoCAD LT for Windows, try the Quick Tour built into it by clicking on the word **H**elp and then on Quick **T**our (or press Alt+H and then type T). The tour gives you some insights into the organization and use of AutoCAD LT for Windows. All the topics included in the Quick Tour are covered in detail in this book.

Using Windows Help

If you are having difficulties using Windows, be sure to access the help services that are available for each of the Windows programs. Each of the Windows help menus includes a selection for "How to Use Help," from which you can choose a number of topics including Help Basics. In addition, the help menu for Program Manager has a Windows Tutorial available, which steps you through the use of the Windows environment including how to use your mouse in Windows.

For specific help with a Windows program such as File Manager, Program Manager, or Print Manager, use the Contents selection while in the task for which you want help. For example, to learn how to load and run AutoCAD LT from Windows, choose the topic Start an Application from the Program Manager **H**elp menu's **C**ontents selection. Choose the topic "What is File Manager" from the File Manager **H**elp menu's **C**ontents selection to learn the meaning of the various icons used to represent the file types. From the Print Manager, you can get help on how to install and configure a printer (AutoCAD LT for Windows uses the printer you specify in Windows). Similarly, you can obtain help for all the features available from the Windows Control Panel Windows environment options. To maximize the help available to you, use the help screens in conjunction with the *Microsoft Windows User's Guide.*

Other AutoCAD Books from New Riders

New Riders Publishing's *Inside AutoCAD* is the premier reference book for AutoCAD and the best-selling AutoCAD book. New Riders also offers the widest selection of books covering all the various aspects of AutoCAD available anywhere. Although these books are written for the full versions of AutoCAD, there are some you can effectively use as references.

AutoCAD LT for Windows is a subset of AutoCAD Release 12 for Windows. System variables, plot file settings, 3D techniques, UCS commands, viewport settings, and more are available to AutoCAD LT for Windows. Much of the depth of these topics is outside the scope of a book such as *Inside AutoCAD LT for Windows, Second Edition.* For an in-depth look into the program from which AutoCAD LT for Windows' features were derived, see *Inside AutoCAD Release 12 for Windows.* All the advanced drawing controls and techniques available to you in AutoCAD LT for Windows (but outside the scope of this book, which is intended for beginners) are discussed in *Inside AutoCAD Release 12 for Windows.*

If you need a beginning tutorial for AutoCAD Release 12, see *AutoCAD Release 12 for Beginners.* This book covers the 80 percent of AutoCAD that most users need in everyday work, packaged in an easy-to-use text.

If you want a desktop dictionary of all the AutoCAD commands along with their prompts and options, pick up *New Riders' Reference Guide to AutoCAD Release 12.*

If you want to learn to program AutoCAD LT's menus, toolbar, and toolbox with menu macros and the DIESEL language, and to create custom support files, look for *Maximizing AutoCAD Release 12* from New Riders Publishing.

Other AutoCAD titles, although beyond the scope of AutoCAD LT, are available from New Riders, including:

◆ *Inside AutoCAD Release 13 for Windows and Windows NT*

◆ *Inside AutoCAD Release 13 for DOS*

◆ *The AutoCAD API Professional's Toolkit*

◆ *Killer AutoCAD Utilities*

◆ *AutoCAD Drafting and 3D Design*

◆ *The AutoCAD R12 On-Screen Advisor*

◆ *AutoCAD: The Professional Reference, 2nd edition*

◆ *AutoCAD 3D Design and Presentation*

◆ *Managing and Networking AutoCAD*

◆ *Maximizing AutoLISP*

Other Windows Titles from New Riders

If you are new to Windows and want to learn more about this powerful operating environment, see *Inside Windows 3.11, Platinum Edition* from New Riders Publishing. This book is filled with practical examples to help you master Windows commands quickly. The book also features in-depth discussions of basic Windows concepts and provides comprehensive instructions that help you benefit from Windows' powerful features, such as Dynamic Data Exchange and Object Linking and Embedding.

Windows users at all levels can use *Windows 3.1 on Command* from New Riders Publishing. This handy reference is task-oriented; you can use it to learn specific operations without knowing the name of the commands you need. The book covers all the basic Windows file-management operations and shows you how to customize the Windows interface and perform other higher-level functions. This step-by-step guide leads you quickly through even the most complicated Windows-specific tasks.

If you are already proficient with Windows and you want to start customizing or optimizing your Windows system, see *Maximizing Windows 3.1*. This book shows you how to use Windows to program Windows applications, modify existing Windows applications, and optimize memory management.

Other Windows titles available from New Riders include:

- *Windows for Non-Nerds*

- *Windows 3.1 End-User Programming*

- *Windows 3.1 Networking*

- *Inside Windows for Workgroups*

- *Ultimate Windows 3.1*

- *Seven Keys to Learning Windows NT*

- *Inside Windows NT*

- *Windows NT in the Fast Lane*

 Note   New Riders also carries a large line of books on a variety of network products, particularly Novell NetWare and LANtastic.

Ordering Information

You can order any New Riders title by calling 1-800-653-6156 for customer service.

Handling Problems

As you work through the exercises in *Inside AutoCAD LT for Windows, Second Edition*, you might experience some problems. These problems can occur for any number of reasons, from input errors to hardware failures or even typos. If you have trouble performing any step described in this book, take the following actions:

- Check the update text file on the IALT Disk.

- Try again. Double-check the steps you performed in the previous exercise(s), as well as earlier steps in the current exercise.

◆ Check the settings of any AutoCAD LT system variables that were modified in any previous exercise sequences. (See the system variables table in Appendix D for a listing of all system variables.)

◆ Check the *AutoCAD LT for Windows User's Guide* or the AutoCAD LT online help.

If none of the previous suggestions help, call New Riders Publishing at (317) 581-3833, *only* if the problem relates to a specific exercise, instruction, or error in the book. If you need help with general questions on AutoCAD LT, contact Autodesk technical support.

Contacting New Riders Publishing

The staff of New Riders Publishing is committed to bringing you the best in computer reference material. Each New Riders book is the result of months of work by authors and staff, who research and refine the information contained within its covers.

As part of this commitment to you, the NRP reader, New Riders invites your input. Please let us know if you enjoy this book, if you have trouble with the information and examples presented, or if you have a suggestion for future editions.

Please note, however, that the New Riders staff cannot serve as a technical resource for AutoCAD LT or any other applications or hardware. Refer to the documentation that accompanies your programs and hardware for help with specific problems.

If you have a question or comment about any New Riders book, please write to NRP at the following address:

New Riders Publishing
Macmillan Computer Publishing USA
Attn: Associate Publisher
201 W. 103rd Street
Indianapolis, IN 46290

We respond to as many readers as we can. Your name, address, or phone number will never become part of a mailing list or be used for any purpose other than to help us continue to bring you the best books possible.

If you prefer, you can FAX New Riders Publishing at the following number:

(317) 581-4690

Thank you for selecting *Inside AutoCAD LT for Windows, Second Edition*!

Making a Start

Perhaps a little imaginative journey will help you to recognize the position you are in now. You have passed through the security check point at the airport, boarded your own Concorde, and fastened your seatbelt. You are going to be the pilot, so you will need some information to help you get the maximum smooth performance from your vehicle. You are going to a new plateau of design involving "CAD consciousness," from which you probably will never want to return.

Enjoy your flight!

Part I

Tools and Concepts

1   *Getting Off the Ground: CAD Concepts 1A* 25

2   *Specifying Locations in CAD Space* 65

3   *Keeping Track of Your Work:*
    Drawings as Files 107

4   *Building a Drawing: Using Basic*
    Drawing Tools 137

5   *Navigating Views in the CAD Workspace* 171

6   *Making Changes: Using Basic Editing Tools* 219

7   *Making Changes: Using Grip Editing* 253

C H A P T E R

1

Getting Off the Ground: CAD Concepts 1A

This chapter assumes that you are new to CAD and to the AutoCAD LT *user interface*—your means of communicating with the program. Even experienced CAD users can benefit from reading portions of the chapter. In its discussion of CAD concepts, this chapter includes the following topics:

◆ Introducing some basic principles of CAD

◆ Understanding the user interface

◆ Drawing your first CAD objects

◆ Recovering from errors

◆ Adjusting your view of the CAD workspace

◆ Accessing AutoCAD LT's help system

◆ Finding information with AutoCAD LT's online documentation

Don't be concerned if the material seems overwhelming at first; things will become more clear as you explore these topics in depth throughout the rest of the book. On the other hand, if it seems too simple, read on: more complexity awaits you. The rest of the chapters in Part One of this book explain the use of the basic commands and controls, step by step.

Long before his first solo, the would-be pilot studies the mechanics of flight, then moves on to learn the basics of aircraft control, and finally familiarizes himself with the gauges and instruments of his craft. Without this basic knowledge, he or she never leaves the ground.

In much the same way, you need to know the basic mechanics of using CAD so you can start exploring it more thoroughly. To begin working through the exercises in the rest of this book, you need to understand how AutoCAD LT works.

Exploring Some Basic Principles of CAD

If this is your first experience with CAD after spending some time performing manual drafting, then you have come from flying a biplane to strapping yourself into a modern jet aircraft. You will find many new prospects that have not been available to you before.

The first section of this chapter presents some ideas about how using CAD can affect the way you think about and perform your work. If you enjoy exploring concepts, or you are just not quite ready to climb into the cockpit, read along. If you are anxious to get going, however, feel free to skip ahead to the section called "Understanding the User Interface." You can return at your leisure to explore some of the implications of your new pursuit.

CAD Methods versus Manual Methods

Creating a design with CAD essentially is a process of precisely describing the design to the computer. In a typical manual drawing process, you draw a scale image—a depiction—of a design. With CAD, you create the design full size and then plot it at a scale that suits the paper size. Compare this method to manual drafting, in which the fixed paper size requires you to plan how you are going to fit your work to the space. In this sense, CAD is liberating. If you are wondering where to start drawing, the answer is, "Start anywhere!" You have an almost infinite sheet of paper. With experience and practice, you can even develop your AutoCAD LT designs in three dimensions.

The greatest benefit of using CAD as a design tool is that the drawing elements you create remain flexible. Has a design change ever required you to move a portion of a

drawing? To "move" something in a paper drawing, you have to erase your work and draw it all again in the new location. With AutoCAD LT's editing features, you can move something by selecting the objects it comprises and repositioning them. The entire process takes less time than it would take you just to erase your work from the paper drawing.

If you want to pursue a potentially beneficial "what if" scenario, you can make a copy of a drawing file, or just a portion of it, and experiment freely. If you succeed in improving the design, you can bring the changes back into the original drawing; your work is not lost simply because you "sketched it on the side."

CAD can save you from repetitive effort. Have you ever created scale cutouts of equipment or furniture and then moved them around on an outline drawing? After you finish, you are ready to create the arrangement drawing. If you use CAD and move the images electronically, the arrangement drawing is complete the moment you arrive at a satisfactory layout.

The Power of CAD

The flexible nature of CAD drawings makes many new ways of working possible. The following examples illustrate some of these possibilities:

◆ **You have all the information you need to create a part except its final location.** The CAD process frees you from this kind of scheduling problem. By using CAD, you can go ahead and create the part in detail because you can easily position it once its location is set.

◆ **You start a new project similar to one you have done before, and you realize that many of the components are the same.** Using CAD, you can copy elements from the previous job into the new design without having to redraw them. In this way, your work has value beyond the design you are working on at the moment. You can develop libraries of standard drawing components or details to use in future designs.

◆ **You need to work out some complex geometric construct.** Instead of using a 9H or non-photo-blue pencil to sparingly create essential guidelines, AutoCAD LT enables you to place as many guidelines and other reference objects as you need on a scratch layer (similar to a transparent overlay; see Chapter 10, "Getting Organized: Drawing on Layers") and then make them invisible when you plot the finished drawing on paper.

◆ **You need to draw an arc passing through three points.** AutoCAD LT's Arc tool defaults to drawing an arc based on three points (try that with a compass). AutoCAD LT can just as easily find the center of that arc whenever you need it. Design configurations that you might have avoided because they were difficult to calculate or draw are greatly simplified when you use CAD.

◆ **You need to establish a precise location for two holes based on the distance between their edges.** With AutoCAD LT, you might create a new circle at a specific distance from a point on the circumference of a circle you have already drawn. The CAD process enables you to use information derived from one object to create or locate others. Thus CAD serves as a perfect complement to the evolutionary nature of the design process itself.

◆ **You want to draw a line tangent to an arc or a circle.** AutoCAD LT has a tool that can find this point for you. You rediscover the beauty of geometry when you learn to design with CAD. A line segment in geometry is defined by its endpoints; in CAD, you draw a line segment by locating its endpoints. A curve and a line that meet at a point of tangency form a smooth, imperceptible transition. With the kinds of tools available to you in AutoCAD LT, even your "quick and dirty" work can be extremely precise.

The Responsible CAD Designer

To use the design power built into AutoCAD LT most effectively, you need to be aware of and take responsibility for some aspects of the process that may be new to you.

Because of the precision with which CAD drawing elements are defined, your work might communicate more than you intend. One corollary to the preceding example of how precise a "quick and dirty" sketch can be is that when others work with such a drawing, they may not be aware of its inaccuracy.

 Stop People take the precise appearance of a CAD drawing as an indication that its content was created precisely. Be sure that your rough CAD sketches have a note that clearly warns of how imprecisely or inaccurately they were drawn.

Like paper drawings, CAD drawing files contain information about the design they are intended to communicate; in computer terms, the database. CAD drawing files also contain a record of the drawing settings for the CAD program itself, which affect the working environment in which the design is constructed. Any work you do in a CAD drawing affects either this working environment or the drawing database. You need to fully understand the implications of any changes you make to an existing drawing, especially if you are working in a group or exchanging drawing files with others. AutoCAD LT's editing features are like powerful hand tools; you must learn to use them correctly because they have as much potential to do damage as to be constructive.

The following two examples illustrate this point:

♦ **Organizing your drawing through layers.** Just as some manual drawings are assembled from pin-registered transparent overlays, AutoCAD LT drawings can be organized using layers. The commands you use to create and maintain this structure also make it possible to move all the objects in a drawing onto a single layer with a single command. This action effectively (and irreversibly) destroys the organizational information provided by the layers.

♦ **Locating objects on a grid.** Many drawings are constructed based on a reference grid, analogous to graph paper. One of AutoCAD LT's settings enables you to restrict your point selections to an invisible grid. Changing the unit value of the grid, or turning off the setting that restricts points to the grid, can result in improperly located elements. In fact, it is possible (as in the layer example) to move every object in a drawing off an established reference grid with a single command.

CAD drawings have the potential to describe a design in great detail. Individual objects can have significant line-weight and linetype information, like their pencil-on-paper counterparts. In addition, individual objects can be placed on named layers, or they can be members of composite drawing objects (known in AutoCAD LT as *blocks*), to which you can also give names. Poor planning or inattention to the intelligent use of named objects can result in inefficiency, miscommunication, and even loss of valuable data. Truly effective CAD drawings result from knowledgeable use of these named structures, along with care in the construction and placement of drawing objects. The responsibility for producing readily usable CAD drawings rests with the well-informed designer.

As you read through this book and learn to use AutoCAD LT, you will find many more examples of both the power it affords you and some potential pitfalls. Keep the ideas presented here in mind as you start to develop "CAD thinking."

Understanding the User Interface

Designing on a computer involves communicating with the tool itself. Learning to use AutoCAD LT is similar to learning a new language. The stronger your vocabulary becomes, the easier it will be for you to communicate your design clearly and efficiently. This communication is a new challenge to those coming from traditional manual methods.

You must know how to instruct the computer to generate an accurate description of your design. Using AutoCAD LT, you issue these instructions as *commands* that specify point locations, create objects, establish spatial relationships, and much more. The communication is two-way: you communicate your design to AutoCAD LT, and the computer model can feed back information to you. The user interface is designed to simplify your communication with the system.

There are some differences in where tools and buttons are located in the AutoCAD LT Release 1 and AutoCAD LT Release 2 interfaces, and AutoCAD LT Release 2 includes a few items not available in AutoCAD LT Release 1. The AutoCAD LT Release 1 and 2 graphics windows (also called drawing windows) are shown in figures 1.1 and 1.2.

Figure 1.1

The default AutoCAD LT Release 1 graphics window in 800×600 resolution.

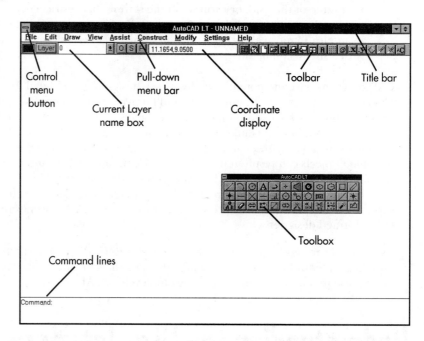

Note   The illustrations in this book generally show the AutoCAD LT Release 2 interface, but differences are noted, where applicable, to assist users of AutoCAD LT Release 1 in following the book's exercises and explanations.

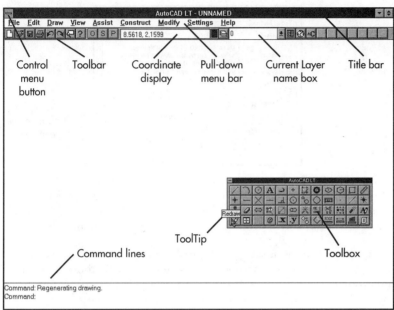

Figure 1.2

The default AutoCAD LT Release 2 graphics window in 800×600 resolution.

The following exercise simply starts AutoCAD LT. The exercise assumes that you have the program installed and are in the Windows Program Manager. If you have not yet installed AutoCAD LT, follow the exercise in Appendix A, "AutoCAD LT Installation and Setup," to do so. If you are not in Windows, type **WIN** at the DOS command prompt, or follow your usual routine for starting Windows.

Starting AutoCAD LT

Open the Windows Program Manager. If the AutoCAD LT program group is minimized, double-click on it to open it.

Double-click on the AutoCAD LT icon in the AutoCAD LT program group to launch the program.

The AutoCAD LT logo appears briefly, and then, in AutoCAD LT Release 1 your screen will appear similar to figure 1.1, or in AutoCAD LT Release 2, the Create New Drawing dialog box appears (see fig. 1.3).

If using AutoCAD LT Release 2, make sure aclt.dwg appears in the Prototype drawing name edit box; if it doesn't, double-click in the edit box and type **aclt.dwg** to ensure that the default prototype is set. If the Use Prototype check box is not checked, click in it.

If using AutoCAD LT Release 2, with your left mouse button click on **N***one, then on* OK	Bypasses the setup methods and starts a new drawing with default settings; your screen should look similar to figure 1.2.

Figure 1.3

The Create New Drawing dialog box.

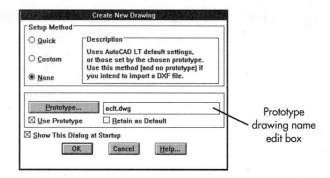

Prototype drawing name edit box

The setup and prototype drawing features of the Create New Drawing dialog box will be covered in Chapters 2, "Specifying Locations in CAD Space," 3, "Keeping Track of Your Work: Drawings as Files," and 9, "Tailoring Your Work Environment."

The AutoCAD LT graphics window is shown in figure 1.1 or 1.2. This window displays the current drawing view and provides access to all of AutoCAD LT's tools. A major step in becoming proficient in the use of AutoCAD LT is learning where to find the tool you need. As you work through this book, you learn where to access each tool and how the function of some tools varies depending on how you initiate them.

Note Refer to the front of this book for a detailed illustration of all the elements of the AutoCAD LT Release 1 and 2 graphics windows.

Like any Windows application, the AutoCAD LT window is resizable and can be moved anywhere on the screen. Most of the interface elements you see in the AutoCAD LT window are Windows objects. If you want to know more about the way Windows objects function, read the Windows documentation, consult the Windows help screens, or go through the Windows Basic Tutorial. This section, however, describes the functions used to access AutoCAD LT's tools in sufficient detail that you should not need to refer to Windows help.

The areas in and around the graphics window contain all the elements available for communicating with AutoCAD LT, accessing CAD files, issuing commands, altering environment settings, and controlling the view of your work. The major elements of the user interface are as follows:

◆ **Title bar.** The AutoCAD LT title bar, at the top of the window, displays the name of the current drawing file. The title bar also contains the control menu button and the window sizing buttons.

◆ **Toolbar.** The toolbar provides direct mouse access to key drawing settings, file commands, viewing options, the PLOT command, point input filters, and layer controls. The toolbar also displays information about the drawing environment. This book refers to the icons on the toolbar as *buttons*.

New Riders Publishing
INSIDE
SERIES

Note   AutoCAD LT ships with a predefined set of toolbar icons and additional empty boxes you can define yourself. The number of icons visible on the toolbar is determined by the size of your AutoCAD LT window, the screen resolution of your system, the size of the toolbar buttons, and the font size. See the *AutoCAD LT Users Guide* (or page 6 of the AutoCAD LT 1.0 README.DOC located in the \ACLTWIN directory) for details about customizing tools and buttons and setting up your display to access all the toolbar buttons.

◆ **Toolbox.** The toolbox is the most direct way to select commands with the mouse. The default toolbox is a *floating* window that can be moved. The toolbox also can be located in a fixed position along either the left or right side of the drawing area, or it can be turned off. The icons in the toolbox issue commands. This book refers to these icons as *tools*.

◆ **ToolTips.** When you place the pointer on a button or tool, an identifying tag pops up at the pointer. This is called a ToolTip, and tells you the name of the button or tool.

Tip   If you press the Enter button (the right mouse button) with the cursor positioned over either the toolbar or toolbox, you open a customization dialog box, which enables you to customize these features. (The *AutoCAD LT Users Guide* describes customizing the toolbox and toolbar.) If you ever open a customization dialog box by mistake, simply press Esc or click on Cancel to close the dialog box.

◆ **Pull-down menu bar.** The pull-down menu bar provides mouse and keyboard access to the pull-down menus, from which you can issue commands and open dialog boxes (described later in this chapter).

◆ **Command line.** The command line is the central point of command and control in AutoCAD LT. It takes all the input from the keyboard, lists command options, and displays *prompts* (requests for required input).

Note   To make the illustrations for this book clearer, we changed the arrangement of the toolbox and moved it. If you want to match your screen to the illustrations, do the following:

Move your cursor to the toolbox, and click with the right mouse button. The Toolbox Customization dialog box opens. Double-click in the box next to the word **F**loating, and type **2**. Click on the OK button. Move the cursor to the title bar of the toolbox, click and hold down the left mouse button while you drag the outline of the toolbox up and to the right (to the edge of the window), and then release the mouse button. Reopen the Toolbox Customization dialog box and click on the OK button to save the location.

In addition to these visible elements, AutoCAD LT maintains a text window to which it writes everything that appears on the command line. Use the F2 key to switch to and from the text window. The display of text is scrollable and stores the last 200 lines of commands, prompts, and messages. Figure 1.4 shows the AutoCAD LT text window as it appears after several commands have been issued. You can use the text window when you want to review commands you have just issued or read the information returned by a query command such as LIST (see Chapter 12, "Accessing Your Drawing's Data").

Figure 1.4

The AutoCAD LT text window.

```
                          AutoCAD LT Text - UNNAMED
Command: U
GROUP
Command:
U  GROUP
Command:
U  GROUP
Command:
U  ARC
Command: '_REDRAW
Command: _ERASE
Select objects: 1 found

Select objects: 1 found

Select objects:

Command: U
ERASE
Command: _ERASE
Select objects: Other corner: 3 found

Select objects:

Command: '_REDRAW
Command: _DSVIEWER
Command: _DSVIEWER
Command: _DSVIEWER
Command: _DSVIEWER
Command:


Command:
Command:
Command: _limits
Reset Model space limits:
ON/OFF/<Lower left corner> <0.0000,0.0000>:

Upper right corner <12.0000,9.0000>:

Command:
```

To use AutoCAD LT, you must know how to access each element of the user interface. The next section discusses the most fundamental aspect of communicating with AutoCAD LT—how to issue commands.

Issuing Commands and Options

Your interaction with AutoCAD LT hinges on one fundamental operation—issuing commands. Even if you only want to query the drawing for some bit of information, you have to tell AutoCAD LT to tell you what you want to know. The following simple exercise demonstrates the basic process of issuing commands.

Issuing Commands

Continue from the previous exercise in the AutoCAD LT graphics window.

Command: *From the toolbox, click on the*
Line tool
           Starts the LINE command

_LINE From point: *Use your mouse to pick*
(click on) location ① *in figure 1.5*
           Locates the start point and displays a
           rubber-band line as you move the cursor

To point: **7,4.5** (Enter)
           Completes a line segment and displays a
           rubber-band line

To point: (Enter)
           Ends the LINE command

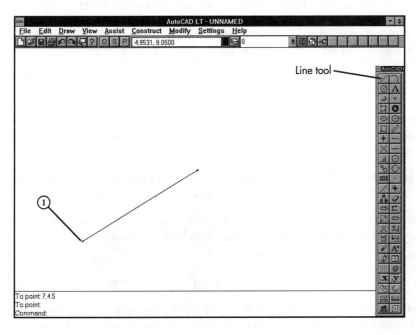

Figure 1.5

Issuing a command and drawing a line.

Most commands follow this pattern in their operation: you issue the command, and AutoCAD LT prompts you for any required input and then draws or modifies something. Some commands, such as ARC and CIRCLE, end when the object is drawn. Other commands, such as LINE, continue until you explicitly end them. As you saw in the preceding exercise, you can end the LINE command by pressing Enter at the To point: prompt. With experience, these patterns become familiar to you.

Most of the AutoCAD LT commands can be placed in one of three categories:

◆ Commands that create new objects (drawing commands)

◆ Commands that modify, manipulate, or replicate objects (editing commands)

◆ Commands that alter environment settings

You use two hardware devices to issue commands to AutoCAD LT: the pointing device and the keyboard.

Using the Pointing Device

The *pointing device* (the Windows mouse device) is used by AutoCAD LT to control the location of the cursor. The cursor usually appears as *crosshairs* in the graphics area and as the Windows pointer whenever the cursor is positioned over a menu selection or an icon. This book assumes the use of a mouse because it is the typical Windows pointing device, although digitizers and trackballs can be used with appropriate Windows drivers.

If you have a two-button mouse, the buttons are defined as follows:

◆ **Pick button.** The pick button (generally the left mouse button) is the button you normally use to select drawn objects, click on Windows objects, and select menu items.

◆ **Enter button.** The Enter button is the other mouse button (generally the right mouse button). This button issues a return just as the Enter key does.

◆ **Pop-up button.** The pop-up button is the Shift+Enter-button (hold down the Shift key while you click the Enter button). This button pops up a menu at the cursor.

If you have a three-button mouse, the buttons are defined as follows:

◆ **Pick button.** The pick button (generally the left mouse button) is the button you normally use to select objects, click on Windows objects, and select menu items.

◆ **Enter button.** The Enter button is the mouse button opposite the pick button (generally the right mouse button). This button issues a return just as the Enter key does.

◆ **Pop-up button.** The pop-up button is the middle button (you also can use the Shift+Enter-button). This button pops up a menu at the cursor.

You have already used the mouse's pick button in the preceding exercise. In the following exercise, try using the pick button along with your other mouse button or buttons.

Using the Mouse Buttons

Continue from the preceding exercise.

Command: *From the toolbox, click on the Circle tool*	Starts the CIRCLE command; notice the Circle ToolTip
_CIRCLE 3P/TTR/<Center point>: *Move the cursor to ① in figure 1.6, and click the pick button on your mouse*	Locates the center and displays a rubber-band line
Radius: *Click the pick button again at ②*	Draws a circle and ends the command
Command: *Press Enter on the keyboard*	Repeats the CIRCLE command
CIRCLE 3P/TTR/<Center point>: *Pick point ③*	Locates the center of a second circle
Radius <2.9849>: *Pick ④*	Completes second circle
Command: *Press the Enter button on your mouse*	Repeats the CIRCLE command again
CIRCLE 3P/TTR/<Center point>: *Press the Shift key and click the Enter button (or just click the third mouse button, if you have one), and choose* **I***ntersection*	Pops up the cursor menu and turns on INTersection object snap
_int of *Pick ⑤*	Locates the center at an intersection of the first two circles
Radius <4.1152>: *Pick ⑥*	Completes the third circle

Figure 1.6

Using the mouse buttons to pick points and issue commands.

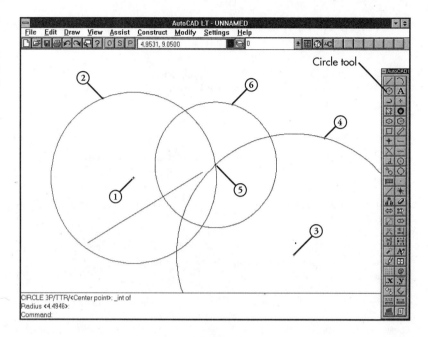

You can repeat the most recent command by pressing the space bar or the Enter key on the keyboard or the Enter button on the mouse. Notice also how the pop-up cursor menu appears near the current location of your cursor when you click the pop-up button. This menu contains *object snap overrides*—commands that assist with the creation of accurate geometry; in this case, locating the intersection of two objects (see Chapter 11, "Achieving Accuracy: The Geometric Power of CAD," for a discussion of these commands).

 Note
Unless an exercise instruction specifies the pop-up button or the Enter button, you should assume that "click" or "pick" refers to the pick button.

This book uses specific terms for all the possible pointing device actions (for example, pick, click on, select). Refer to the section called "Notational Conventions" in the Introduction for a complete list of these terms and how they are applied to both AutoCAD LT and Windows functions.

 Tip
Using a mouse for the first time is not as intuitive as it appears. If you are new to the mouse and experiencing difficulty, go through the mouse lessons in the Windows Tutorial. To do so, choose **H**elp, then **W**indows Tutorial in the Windows Program Manager. Then consider spending some time doing something simple that develops this skill; for instance, you might try playing Windows Solitaire or "doodling" in AutoCAD LT.

As you have seen, you can use the mouse to point to locations in your drawing and to pick tools from the toolbox. The next two sections describe in more detail the elements of the user interface with which you can issue commands by using the mouse: first the toolbar and toolbox, and then the pull-down menus.

Using Toolbar Buttons and Toolbox Tools

The AutoCAD LT toolbar and toolbox offer the most accessible means of issuing commands with the mouse. You have used commands from the toolbox in previous exercises. In the following exercise, you issue two commands from the toolbar as well.

Using the Toolbar and Toolbox to Issue Commands

Continue from the preceding exercise.

Command: *From the toolbox, click on the Circle tool*	Starts the CIRCLE command
_CIRCLE 3P/TTR/<Center point>: *Pick a point*	Locates the center
Radius: *On the toolbar, click on the Cancel (^C) button*	Cancels the CIRCLE command

Notice the small crosses AutoCAD LT leaves on the screen at points you pick. These crosses are temporary markers called *blips* that you can remove at any time with the REDRAW command.

Command: *From the toolbar in AutoCAD LT Release 1, or the toolbox in AutoCAD LT Release 2, click on the Redraw (R) button or tool*	Issues the REDRAW command
'_REDRAW	Removes the blips

The preceding exercise demonstrates an important AutoCAD LT function—*Cancel.* You can cancel any command in progress by pressing Ctrl+C or by clicking on the ^C Cancel button. Cancel stops the current command immediately and returns to the command prompt. Many of the tools, buttons, and menu items issue Cancel before issuing their commands. The cancellation guarantees that the chosen command is issued at the command prompt and is not mistaken for an option to a command already in progress.

Tip   If you find blips annoying, you can turn the blip feature off. To do so, type **BLIPMODE** and press Enter, then type **OFF** and press Enter. Most figures in this book do not show blips.

Likewise, if you find the ToolTips distracting after you learn all of the button and tool icons, you can turn them off by setting the TOOLTIPS system variable to 0 (off). The default is 1 (on). See Chapter 8, "Preparing Your Workspace: CAD Concepts 1B," for more on system variables

The REDRAW command you used in the preceding exercise is a handy way to clean up the display of your drawing. In addition to the blip marks left from picking points, AutoCAD LT drawing and editing commands can leave artifacts that may make the drawing appear to be incorrect. For instance, if two objects overlap and you erase one, the portion of the remaining object that coincided with the erased one disappears. In this case, you can restore the apparently missing portion with REDRAW.

Items in the toolbox and on the toolbar can only be chosen by using the mouse. The other screen element you can use to issue commands—the pull-down menu bar—is equally accessible by using either the mouse or the keyboard.

Note   In the rest of the book, most exercises simply refer to toolbar buttons and toolbox tools in the following way: "Click on the Cancel button" and "Click on the Line tool" instead of first saying "On the toolbar..." or "In the toolbox...".

Using Pull-Down Menus to Issue Commands

The pull-down menus contain the most comprehensive set of commands, and they are accessible to both the mouse and the keyboard. Each menu contains the type of functions indicated by the name that appears on the menu bar. You choose a menu command or option from a pull-down menu to issue it. Any menu item with an arrow to the right of it opens a submenu or *child menu*. Any menu item with three periods after its name opens a dialog box. Any menu item with a check mark in front of it indicates a drawing or system variable that is currently in effect.

In the following exercise, try issuing commands using the pull-down menus.

Using the Pull-Down Menus

Continue from the preceding exercise.

Command: *Click on the **D**raw menu title*   Pulls down the **D**raw menu

*Click on **L**ine*   Starts the LINE command

```
_line From point: Pick ① in figure 1.7     Locates the start point

To point: Pick ②                           Draws a line segment

To point: Pick ③                           Draws another line segment

To point: (Enter)                          Ends the LINE command
```

Now try using the press-and-drag method. Move the cursor to the **D**raw menu title, then press the pick button and hold it down while you move the mouse, as described in the following instruction (see fig. 1.8):

Command: *Press and hold the pick button down* | Pulls down the **D**raw menu, pops up the
on the **D**raw *menu title and drag to move the* | **C**ircle child menu, and issues the CIRCLE
highlight bar down to **C**ircle, *then move to the* | command with the **3** Point option
right into the child menu to **3** Point *and release*
the button

```
_circle 3P/TTR/<Center point>:_          Cancels the CIRCLE command
3p First point: Click on the Cancel
button on the toolbar

First point: *Cancel*

Command: *Cancel*
```

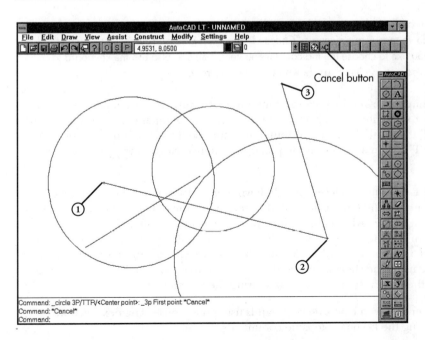

Figure 1.7

Issuing commands from the pull-down menus.

Figure 1.8

The Draw menu and the Circle child menu.

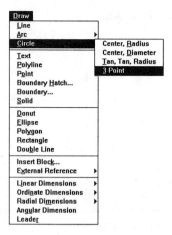

To access pull-down menu items with the mouse, either click on a title in the menu bar and then click on the menu item you want, or press and drag on the menu title and release the mouse button when the menu item you want is highlighted. Dragging the cursor in this way over a menu item with a child menu opens the child menu. You can use the press-and-drag method to select an item from a child menu by continuing to drag the cursor to the right and into the child menu. The command or control option issued is the one highlighted when you release the pick button.

Note Throughout the rest of this book, the directions for issuing commands from the pull-down menus are given as *"Choose **D**raw, then **L**ine..."* You can use any method you like to choose the indicated menu item. You can also use the keyboard to choose menu items, as shown in the next exercise.

Issuing commands from the pull-down menus is easy; just choose a menu, choose a command or menu item, and keep choosing until the command or option you want appears. All the possibilities are presented by name, so if you are unfamiliar with AutoCAD LT's commands, using the pull-down menus is a good way to learn what is available.

AutoCAD LT provides two levels of pull-down menus. By default, the first item on the **S**ettings menu is **F**ull Menu. Choosing this item swaps the default short pull-down menus for the full-length versions, which display a more complete, and more advanced, set of commands and options. When you choose **F**ull Menu, the first item on the **S**ettings menu becomes **S**hort Menu. The first few chapters of this book assume that you are using the short menus and instruct you to choose **F**ull Menu if necessary. In general the book assumes that you are using the full menus.

You have seen how you can issue commands using the mouse. The next section describes using the keyboard to issue commands.

Using the Keyboard

The keyboard is the computer's most basic input device. With the keyboard, you can issue commands and command options to AutoCAD LT by using the pull-down menus or by directly typing the command or option word and pressing Enter or the spacebar.

Note Most AutoCAD LT commands recognize pressing the spacebar or clicking the Enter button as equivalent to pressing Enter. Exceptions to this, such as when you are entering text, are noted in the sections of this book that cover the specific commands.

In the following exercise, you use the keyboard to issue commands both directly and from the pull-down menus.

Using the Keyboard to Issue Commands

Continue from the preceding exercise.

Command: *Press Ctrl+C*	Cancels any active selection or command
Command: **Cancel**	
Command: *Type* **ARC** (Enter)	Starts the ARC command
Center/<Start point>: *Pick ① in in figure 1.9*	Locates start of arc
Center/End/<Second point>: *Pick ②*	Locates second point and displays rubber-band arc
End point: *Pick ③*	Draws the arc
Command: *Press the F10 key*	Highlights the **F**ile menu title
Use the right arrow (cursor) key to move to the **D**raw *menu, and press Enter*	Pulls down the **D**raw menu
Use the arrow keys to move down to the **A**rc *menu, then right into the child menu, then down again to* **3** Point (Enter)	Starts the ARC command with the 3 Point option
_arc Center/<Start point>: *Press Ctrl+C*	Cancels the ARC command

continues

continued

```
*Cancel*

Command: Press Alt+D                          Pulls down the Draw menu

Type A, then 3, (Enter)                       Opens the Arc child menu and starts the
                                              ARC command using the 3 Point method

_arc Center/<Start point>: Press Ctrl+C       Cancels the command
```

Figure 1.9

Using the keyboard to issue commands.

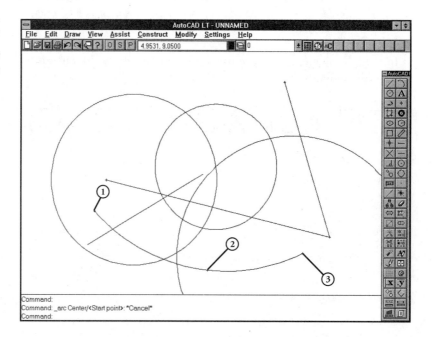

As you saw in the preceding exercise, you can use the keyboard to issue the ARC command in three different ways. You can enter the name of the command itself and press Enter, or you can use two methods with the pull-down menus. To access the pull-down menus with the keyboard, press Alt or F10 and the *hot key* character (the key shown underlined) for the menu you want. Then either type the hot-key character of the item you want to choose, or use the arrow keys to move the highlight bar and press Enter when the item you want is highlighted. In the preceding exercise, each method has the same result—AutoCAD LT begins to draw a three-point arc.

Some commands have *aliases* (abbreviated or alternative forms of their true names). Entering a command alias issues the command just as if you had entered its full name. Command aliases can issue only the command itself, without preselecting an option the way a menu item can. The Appendix F, "Command Reference," lists the

command aliases (also called command shortcuts), which are defined in the ACLT.PGP file. The Command Quick Reference appendix in the AutoCAD LT for Windows *User's Guide* describes how you can add your own command aliases.

TABLE 1.1
Sample AutoCAD LT Command Aliases

Alias	Command	Alias	Command	Alias	Command
A	ARC	C	CIRCLE	L	LINE
M	MOVE	E	ERASE	R	REDRAW
ET	EXIT	Z	ZOOM	P	PAN

AutoCAD LT also includes another file of aliases for users familiar with Generic CADD. See the "Keyboard Shortcuts for Generic CADD Users" appendix in the *AutoCAD LT for Windows User's Guide* for details.

In addition to entering commands and command aliases, AutoCAD LT recognizes a number of special keys and key combinations. The following list describes their functions:

◆ F1 accesses AutoCAD LT Help.

◆ F2 switches between the text and graphics windows.

◆ F5 or Ctrl+E cycles through the Isoplane modes.

◆ F6 or Ctrl+D cycles through the Coordinate Display modes.

◆ F7 or Ctrl+G turns Grid Display on and off.

◆ F8 or Ctrl+O turns Ortho mode on and off.

◆ F9 or Ctrl+B turns Snap mode on and off.

◆ F10 or Alt highlights the pull-down menu bar.

Choosing between Mouse and Keyboard

AutoCAD LT requires the use of both the keyboard and the mouse; each has its place, and neither can provide all the functions required to operate the program. As you work through the exercises in this book and learn to use AutoCAD LT, you will develop a sense of which device is most appropriate to the task at hand. The following list highlights the essential strengths of each device:

◆ **Mouse.** The mouse is efficient for picking points, selecting drawing objects, and selecting user interface items. The mouse is the only way to access items on the toolbar, tools in the toolbox, and the pop-up cursor menu.

◆ **Keyboard.** The keyboard is essential for entering text, including the names of new files. The keyboard is the only accurate way to specify a point location without using AutoCAD LT's snap or object snap functions. The keyboard also is the only way to choose options for commands issued from the toolbox.

For most of the other functions in AutoCAD LT, the choice of which device to use is based more on personal preference. If you are a good typist, for example, you might be most comfortable entering commands with the keyboard. Keep in mind, however, that if you misspell a command, AutoCAD LT will not respond as you expect it to. You might get the error message Unknown Command, or worse, a command might be issued that you did not intend.

AutoCAD LT is simpler than its parent program, AutoCAD Release 12 for Windows, but it retains most of the same commands (many of which have additional options). How can you remember them all, and what if you consistently use one particular option with a command? The toolbox, toolbar, and pull-down menus all provide a ready reference of available commands, and issue them with the click of a mouse button. Commands issued this way are always spelled correctly, and many of the menu items include specific options.

When you are starting out, simply keep the various options in mind as you issue commands and become familiar with the interface. Eventually, you will find a way to access each command that feels right for you and is most appropriate to the task.

Now that you have looked at the most visible interface elements for issuing commands, and understand how to use the mouse and keyboard, you are ready to see how AutoCAD LT deals with its more complex and interactive commands and control options.

Working with Dialog Boxes

The toolbar, toolbox, and pull-down menus are all visible in the default AutoCAD LT window, and the commands they issue tend to have only a few options. For many of its more complex functions, AutoCAD LT uses another interface element that does not appear until certain commands are issued or menu items chosen—dialog boxes.

In the following exercise, you open a dialog box, examine the objects in it, and use it to make a change to your working environment.

Working with Dialog Boxes

Continue from the preceding exercise.

Command: *Choose* **S**ettings, *then* **D**rawing Aids	Opens the Drawing Aids dialog box

Examine the elements of the dialog box and refer to figure 1.10.

Under Modes, *click in the* **O**rtho *check box to place an X*	Places a check mark in the box and sets Ortho mode on
Under **S**nap, *click in the* **X** Spacing *text box, just to the left of the 1, and type* **2**	Changes the snap X-spacing value to 21
Double-click in the same text box, and type **1**	Deletes 21 and changes the value back to 1
Under **I**sometric Snap/Grid, *click in the* On *check box to check it*	Sets grid and snap to display in Isometric mode
Click again in the **I**sometric Snap/Grid On *check box*	Clears the box and sets grid and snap back to display in standard mode
Click on the **T**op *radio button*	Changes Isoplane to top
Click on the OK *button*	Closes the dialog box and applies the change
'_ddrmodes	Echoes the dialog box's command name

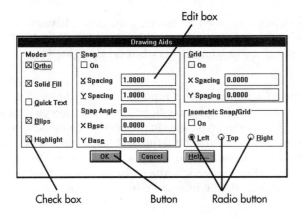

Edit box

Check box   Button   Radio button

Figure 1.10

A sample dialog box with its elements labeled.

Clicking on some elements of the dialog box affects the appearance or condition of other elements. When you check the **I**sometric Snap/Grid On box, for instance, the values in the X Spacing edit boxes for both Snap and Grid turn gray. This gray indicates that you can no longer adjust these values; they are dependent on the

Y-spacing values in Isometric mode. Notice also that the settings you make in the dialog box do not take effect immediately; they are applied when you close the dialog box. In fact, even the DDRMODES command appears on the command line only after you close the dialog box.

AutoCAD LT uses dialog boxes to provide a convenient way to view and change settings, enter and edit text strings, and enter file names. Usually, you open a dialog box in one of two ways: by choosing one of the menu items that are followed by three dots (such as **D**rawing Aids...) or by clicking on certain buttons or tools on the toolbar or in the toolbox (including the Layer, Plot, Grid, and File buttons) or the Object Snap tool in the toolbox. You also can open any dialog box by entering its command name on the command line; for example, DDRMODES for Drawing Aids.

Dialog boxes can present any number of options, making it possible to change several system settings at once, and enabling you to see the interactions between them. Dialog boxes simplify the task of setting up your AutoCAD LT working environment by eliminating the need to remember system variable names and on/off values. Like other windows, you can move a dialog box after you have opened it. Unlike most Windows objects, however, you cannot size a dialog box. Some dialog box selections open child dialog boxes.

Dialog boxes contain one or more of the following elements (see figs. 1.10 and 1.11):

◆ **Button.** Unlike other elements in dialog boxes, buttons initiate immediate actions. All dialog boxes contain at least two buttons, labeled OK and Cancel. These buttons are used to accept or abandon any changes made in the dialog box. Buttons whose labels are followed by three dots open child dialog boxes.

◆ **Check box.** Check boxes are used to change settings that have two conditions, typically on or off. Clicking on a check box either places an X in the box or clears it. Pressing the spacebar when a check box is highlighted has the same effect.

◆ **Edit box.** Edit boxes (sometimes called input boxes or text boxes) are used to enter text or numbers. Clicking in an edit box positions an edit cursor at a point in the entry. You can then type any characters in the edit box, or you can use the arrow keys to move the cursor and the backspace and Del keys to edit the entry. You also can click and drag on any portion of the text to highlight that portion, or double-click to highlight the entire contents. In either case, pressing the Del key deletes the highlighted portion, or typing a new value replaces it.

◆ **List box.** List boxes contain lists of items from which you can select. When a list box is highlighted, you can click on an item to select it, scroll through the list using the scroll bar (if present), or use the keyboard arrow keys. Some list boxes display only one item, with a down arrow on the right. These boxes are normally closed, but when you click on the arrow, a list drops down.

◆ **Radio button.** Radio buttons (sometimes called option buttons) are used to select one among several mutually exclusive options. They take their name from the function of buttons on a car radio, where pressing one button releases any other. When a radio button is highlighted, you can use the arrow keys to move to and select any other button.

◆ **Slider bar.** Slider bars are used to adjust values that vary within a range. You can click on the arrows at the end of a slider bar, click and drag on the slider, or use the arrow keys to adjust a slider bar.

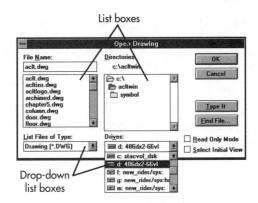

Figure 1.11

More dialog box elements.

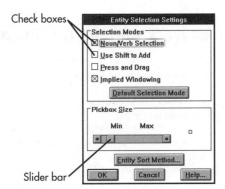

You can use the keyboard to select an item in a dialog box by typing the hot key associated with the object you want to change. Pressing Tab cycles through the selections in a dialog box in order, and pressing Shift+Tab cycles through them in the reverse order.

Your introduction to AutoCAD LT's user interface is now complete. The rest of this chapter discusses several essential functions you must understand to begin working through the book. The next section shows you how to cope with mistakes.

Recovering from Errors

AutoCAD LT always does what you instruct it to do. Unfortunately, this may not always be what you intend. However, AutoCAD LT provides a number of commands you can use to recover from such errors. The next sections show you two simple but essential error-recovery techniques: the U command and the ERASE command.

Using the U Command

In its default configuration, AutoCAD LT keeps track of every command you issue in a given drawing session and can step back through them one by one. To do so, simply enter **U**, for undo, when no command is active. You can press Ctrl+C before entering **U** to ensure that no command is in progress. Try using the U command in the following exercise.

Note AutoCAD LT also has a command called the UNDO command, which has a number of options for undoing more than one step at a time. The U command undoes only one step at a time. (The **U**ndo item on the **E**dit pull-down menu is the same as the U command.) The UNDO command is covered in Chapter 6, "Making Changes: Using Basic Editing Tools."

Stepping Back through Your Work with the U Command

Continue from the preceding exercise. If you have not been following along with the exercises, simply draw a few line segments or circles so you have something to undo.

Command: **U** (Enter)	Issues the U command, which undoes the last command
Command: (Enter)	Undoes the next-to-last command or action
Command: *Press Enter several more times*	Continues to undo previous commands

If you are working from the previous exercises, stop when you undo the arc you drew in the section on "Using the Keyboard." You will still have several objects in your drawing to use in the following section.

U is a command, so pressing Enter or the spacebar repeats it. By repeating the command, you can effectively walk back through every step you have taken to the point at which you opened or started the drawing. U displays the command it is undoing on the command line. The U command undoes settings like Ortho as well as commands.

Tip You can also use the Undo button on the toolbar. If you undo one step too far, click on the Redo button to reverse the last undo.

AutoCAD LT only keeps track of the sequence of settings and commands during a single working session in a drawing. You cannot use the U command to back up to a previous drawing session, nor can you undo the SAVE command or other file operations.

Tip If you discover an error in a drawing session, and you have already saved your work, use the U command repeatedly to back up to a point before the mistake and issue the SAVE command again. This procedure overwrites the mistaken copy of the drawing.

The second simple error-recovery technique you need to know is the use of the ERASE command.

Selecting and Erasing Objects

The U command is indiscriminate; it simply undoes the last action. When you are drawing, it is helpful to be able to remove selected objects without affecting any settings you might have made. The ERASE command enables you to do just that.

You use ERASE in the following exercise to remove some of the circles you drew in earlier exercises. In using the ERASE command, you also practice a fundamental CAD operation—selecting objects.

Selecting Objects and Using ERASE

Continue from the preceding exercise. If you are not continuing from the previous exercises, simply draw a few line segments or circles so you have something to erase.

Command: *Click on the Erase tool (see fig. 1.12)*   Issues the ERASE command

_ERASE

Select objects: *Pick ① and ② in*   Selects two of the circles and highlights
figure 1.12   them

If you drew your own objects for this exercise, simply pick points on two of them. The objects you select should appear *highlighted* (displayed dashed or dotted), as in figure 1.12.

continues

continued

Figure 1.12

Erasing selected objects.

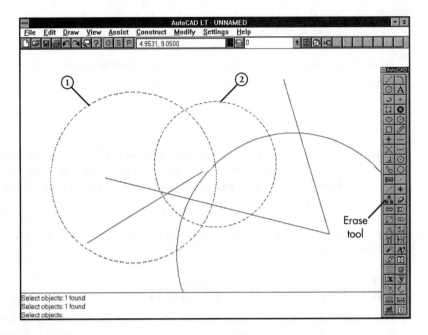

Select objects: **Enter**   Erases the circles

Command: **U Enter**   Undoes the ERASE command

ERASE

Command: *Click on the Erase tool*

_ERASE   Locates the first corner of a selection box
Select objects: *Pick* ① *in figure 1.13,*
not on an object

Move the cursor around. You should see a selection box, which is drawn with solid lines when you move to the right and with dashed lines when you move to the left of this pick point.

Select objects: Other corner: *Pick*   Selects and highlights the circles
②, *with the selection box crossing the circles*

3 found: Erases the circles
Select objects: **Enter**

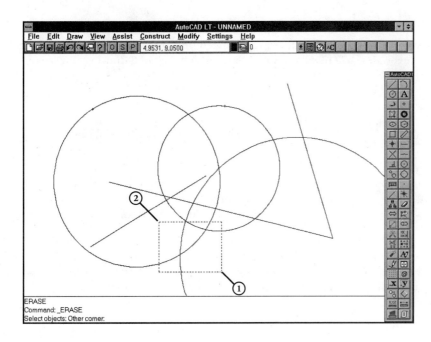

Figure 1.13

Using a selection box.

When you start the ERASE command, the cursor changes to a small square, known as the *pick box*. This pick box is a visual indicator that AutoCAD LT is in selection mode. Clicking with the pick box positioned on an object selects it directly. Clicking in an open area of the drawing locates the corner of a selection box, with which you can select more than one object.

Note The word *object* is used to refer to the lines, circles, arcs, text, and other objects you draw in AutoCAD LT. Unlike paint programs in which the drawn imagery exists only as individual pixels or dots of color, objects drawn in AutoCAD LT exist as whole lines, circles, arcs, text, and other objects that you can select, move, copy, and otherwise manipulate.

In AutoCAD LT Release 1, these objects were also commonly called *entities*. In AutoCAD LT Release 2 and in this book, they are almost always called objects, but are still referred to as entities by a few prompts, options, menu items, and dialog boxes.

Chapter 6, "Making Changes: Using Basic Editing Tools," discusses the object selection process and its options. Many editing commands follow this pattern: you start the command, select objects, and press Enter to have AutoCAD LT apply the command to the selected objects.

For now, you know enough to be able to recover from accidentally drawing a line or circle where you did not mean to draw one. You need only one more tool to be ready to start on the exercises; you need a way to control which part of a drawing you see on screen.

Adjusting Your View of the Drawing

A key to success in the use of CAD is the ability to control the view of your design. This skill enables you to work in any size drawing while confined to a small screen. AutoCAD LT offers several methods for controlling the view. The following exercise demonstrates one of the most accessible options, the Aerial View window.

The Aerial Viewer differs significantly between early versions of AutoCAD LT Releases 1 and later versions of AutoCAD LT Release 1 or AutoCAD LT Release 2. Use which-ever one of the following two exercises matches your version of AutoCAD LT. In these exercises, you *zoom* in on (enlarge) a portion of the drawing, then zoom back out to the original view.

In AutoCAD LT Release 1, the Aerial View button is the second one to the right of the coordinate display box on the toolbar.

Using the Aerial View Window in Early AutoCAD LT Release 1

Continue from the preceding exercise.

Command: *Click on the Aerial View button (see fig. 1.14)*	Opens the Aerial View window in Zoom mode
Pick ① *in figure 1.14, then* ②	Specifies the corners of a zoom window and enlarges the view in the graphics window
Pick two points in the Aerial View window again, this time as near the lower left and upper right corners as possible	Zooms to a view similar to the previous view

When you move the cursor into the Release 1 Aerial View window, it changes to the Windows pointer. Picking a start point in the default Zoom mode locates one corner of a zoom window box, which you drag to include the portion of the drawing you want to zoom in on. Picking the other corner causes the graphics window's view to change to display the selected area of your drawing. The Aerial View window is updated with an outline indicating the area displayed in the graphics window.

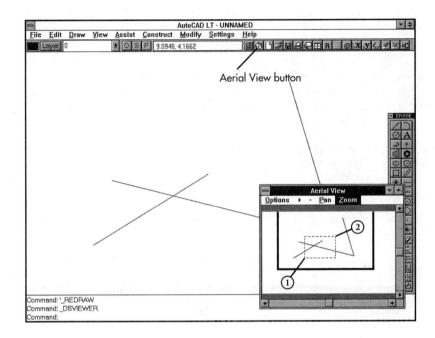

Figure 1.14

*Using the Aerial
View window in
early AutoCAD
LT Release 1.*

In AutoCAD LT Release 2, the Aerial View button is the second one to the right of the layer name box on the toolbar.

ALT2

Using the Aerial View Window in Later AutoCAD LT Release 1 and AutoCAD LT Release 2

Continue from the preceding exercise.

Command: *Click on the Aerial View button (see fig. 1.15)*
Opens the Aerial View

With the pointer in the Aerial View, press the Enter (right mouse) button and move the pointer slightly to the left
Enters Zoom mode, displays a zoom box, and zooms the drawing window image

Press the Enter button and move the pointer to place the X in the center of the box on ① (see fig. 1.15)
Enters Pan mode and pans the drawing window image

Press the Enter button and move the pointer to size the box like that shown in figure 1.15
Changes to Zoom mode and zooms the drawing window image

continues

continued

Click the pick button   Completes the zoom operation

When you complete the zoom operation, the drawing window is zoomed to match the current Aerial View zoom box, the Aerial View is zoomed to show the entire drawing extents, and the current view of the drawing window is indicated in the Aerial View by the reverse (black) background area. Control returns to the drawing window.

In the Aerial View, click several times on the   Zooms the Aerial View but not the drawing
Minus button, until the Aerial View shows a   window
bit more than the entire previous view of the
whole drawing

Press the Enter button and use Zoom and Pan   Zooms to the original view
mode to zoom to the original view, then click the
pick button

Figure 1.15

*Using the Aerial
View window in
AutoCAD LT
Release 2.*

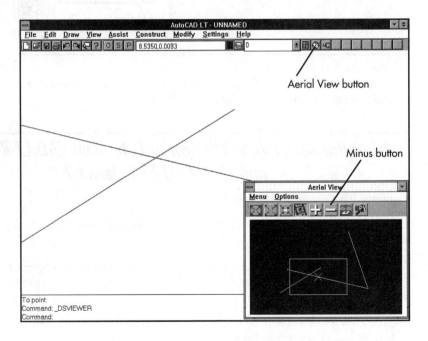

When you move the cursor into the Release 2 Aerial View window, it changes to the Windows pointer. Pressing the Enter mouse button enters Zoom mode, where moving the pointer sizes the zoom box. Pressing the Enter button again switches between Zoom and Pan modes. In Pan mode, moving the pointer moves the zoom box, which you drag to include the portion of the drawing you want to zoom in on. Pressing the mouse pick button accepts the current zoom box, zooms the drawing and updates the Aerial View window, indicating the area displayed in the drawing window.

One of the biggest hurdles in moving from manual drafting to CAD is retraining your sense of scale and location. It can be difficult to know how large an object is or where you are in your drawing. This transition is not always easy, but working in the AutoCAD LT environment builds familiarity.

The Aerial View window is covered in much greater detail in Chapter 5, "Navigating Views in the CAD Workspace." This brief introduction to it should be enough to get you going in the first few chapters. The last section of this chapter introduces you to AutoCAD LT's help system.

Accessing the HELP Command

Help information is always available in AutoCAD LT. To get help when you need it, however, you need to know how to use the AutoCAD LT help feature effectively. Fortunately, the help system even includes help on how to use the help system. The following section briefly gets you started and shows you the main features of the help system.

Exploring the Help Windows

You can get help with AutoCAD LT in several ways. You can issue the HELP command by entering **HELP** or **?**, pressing the F1 key, or choosing **H**elp, then **C**ontents, from the pull-down menu. Any of these choices displays the Contents section in the AutoCAD LT Help window. The Help window differs somewhat between AutoCAD LT Releases 1 and 2. Figure 1.16 shows the Help window for AutoCAD LT Release 1, and figure 1.17 shows the Help window for AutoCAD LT Release 2.

Figure 1.16

The Contents section displayed in the AutoCAD LT Release 1 Help window.

Control menu button

Figure 1.17

The Contents section displayed in the AutoCAD LT Release 2 Help window.

Control menu button

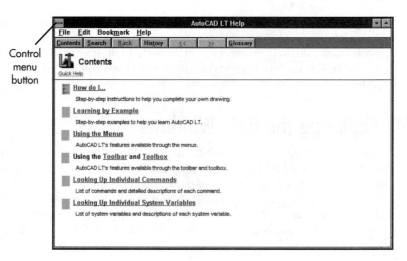

In the following exercise, you open the AutoCAD LT Help window and explore the Contents section.

New Riders Publishing
INSIDE SERIES

Looking at the Contents of AutoCAD LT Help

Command: *Choose **H**elp, **C**ontents*	Opens the Help window (see fig. 1.16 or 1.17)

Move the cursor to an underlined item; it changes to a pointing hand.

Click on <u>Keyboard entry</u> *in AutoCAD LT Release 1 or on* <u>Looking Up Individual Commands</u> *in AutoCAD LT Release 2*	Displays the Command Reference section from A to D
Click on <u>CIRCLE</u>	Displays the CIRCLE help window
*Click on the **B**ack button*	Returns to the Command Reference section
Click on <u>E-P</u>	Displays Command Reference for 'ELEV through PURGE
Double-click on the control menu button (see fig. 1.16 or 1.17)	Closes the Help window

AutoCAD LT Help **C**ontents comprises three main parts, each with one or more underlined subtopics, as shown in figure 1.16 or 1.17. To access any of the subtopics, move the cursor to it and click when the pointing hand's index finger points to the desired item. The main parts are:

♦ **To learn how to use Help, press F1** or click on the F1 symbol.

♦ **Menus** includes items for help with both the short pull-down menus and the full pull-down menus.

♦ **Commands** are accessed from the Keyboard entry menu item, which leads to three submenus listing all the AutoCAD LT commands alphabetically.

The **H**elp pull-down menu provides the following additional three choices:

♦ **Search for Help On...** contains help for each command and system variable in AutoCAD LT.

♦ **Quick Tour** is a brief guide to procedures for various tasks in AutoCAD LT.

♦ **About AutoCAD LT** relates information on your specific copy of AutoCAD LT and the text found in the ACLT.MSG file.

Tip   If any help window contains more information than fits in it, scroll bars are displayed at the right (and sometimes at the bottom) that you can use to see all the information. You can also resize, move, and manipulate the help window, like any other window.

Near the top of the LT Contents window in figures 1.16 and 1.17 are the **C**ontents, **S**earch, **B**ack, His**t**ory, **<<**, **>>**, and **G**lossary buttons.

◆ **Contents** displays the Contents menu.

◆ **Search** opens the Search dialog box, in which you can select or enter key words and phrases to search for help on a specific topic.

◆ **Back** returns to the previously displayed help window.

◆ **History** displays a list of the previously displayed help window from the current help session. You can select one to reopen it.

◆ **<< and >>** page to the previous and next topics in the alphabetical topic list for the current window.

◆ **Glossary** displays a glossary of terms.

In addition to the buttons, the pull-down menu bar at the top of the Help Contents window contains pull-down menus labeled **F**ile, **E**dit, Book**m**ark, and **H**elp. Press F1 in the Help Contents window to learn how to use these menus, which offer features that include marking your place in the help files and copying text from help windows.

Using **S**earch for Help on… is the quickest way to get information on a specific subject. You can access this section of Help directly from AutoCAD LT's Help pull-down menu. Figure 1.18 shows the AutoCAD LT Release 2 Help menu; the AutoCAD LT Release 1 Help menu is similar, but lacks the **O**rientation and **T**utorial items.

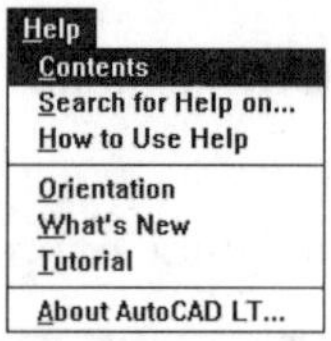

Figure 1.18

The AutoCAD LT Release 2 Help menu.

Practice using the Search for Help on… function by looking up the LINE command in the following exercise.

Searching in AutoCAD LT's Help

Start in the AutoCAD LT graphics window.

Command: *Choose* **H**elp, *then* **S**earch for Help on...	Opens the Search dialog box in the AutoCAD LT Help window

Press and drag on the box in the middle of the slider bar to quickly scroll the list to the LINE entry. This list is long, so you may need to get as close as you can with the slider box and then click on the up and down arrows to find LINE.

Double-click on LINE	Puts LINE in the upper box, LINE Command in the lower box, and changes the **G**o To button from gray to black
Click on the **G**o To *button*	Displays the LINE Command entry in the AutoCAD LT Help window
Double-click on the control menu button	Exits AutoCAD LT help and closes the Help window

---

Getting Context-Sensitive Help in Commands

Another way to use the HELP command is to issue it while using the command about which you want to learn more. This method is called context-sensitive help. To do so, you can enter **HELP** or a question mark prefaced with an apostrophe (**'HELP** or **'?**), or you can press F1. The apostrophe issues the HELP command *transparently* (without canceling the active command).

 Tip
Most dialog boxes contain a Help button, which you can choose to display the specific Help window for their commands.

Finding Information in the Online Documents

In addition to three Help window access items, **C**ontents, **S**earch for Help on..., and **H**ow to Use Help, the AutoCAD LT Help menu offers items which offer more information. The AutoCAD LT Release 2 Help menu offers a **W**hat's New item, and it also offers **O**rientation and **T**utorial items, as shown in figures 1.19, 1.20, and 1.21.

Figure 1.19

The AutoCAD LT Release 2 Tutorial window.

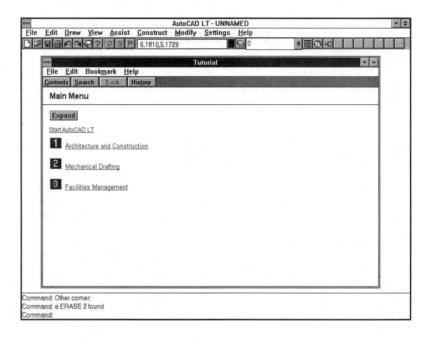

The Tutorial uses the Windows Help system, so it functions much like the previously described help items.

Figure 1.20

The AutoCAD LT Release 2 What's New window.

The **W**hat's New and **O**rientation items open interactive documents that you similarly navigate by clicking on buttons and underlined labels or keywords.

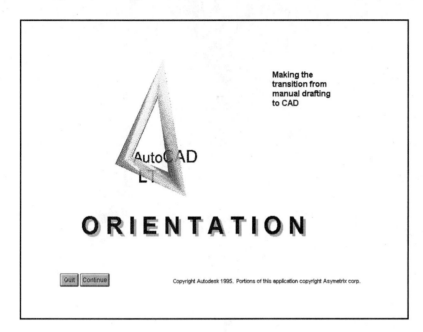

Figure 1.21

The AutoCAD LT Release 2 Orientation window.

In this chapter, you've become familiar with the AutoCAD LT interface, and drawn a few lines and circles. Every object created in CAD is located and sized by its coordinates, which you simply picked in this chapter. The next chapter discusses how to accurately specify and use coordinates in AutoCAD LT.

C H A P T E R

2

Specifying Locations in CAD Space

Most drawings require accuracy in order to convey information clearly. CAD requires you to provide some form of accurate point location information. Fortunately, AutoCAD LT provides several methods and tools to help you place objects easily and accurately and keep track of where you are.

This chapter shows you:

- ◆ What coordinates are and the role they play in CAD

- ◆ How to understand and use the coordinate display

- ◆ How to set up a reference grid

- ◆ How to use drawing aids such as Snap and Ortho to control point input

- ◆ How to specify points using absolute coordinates

- ◆ How to locate points relative to one another

- ◆ What a User Coordinate System (UCS) is, and how to use it

- ◆ How to use an isometric snap grid to draw

The coordinate system, which forms the basic structure of your CAD design space and is important for you to understand, is explained in this chapter.

AutoCAD LT, like most CAD systems, locates the objects in your drawing using the *Cartesian* (or rectangular) coordinate system. The endpoints of lines, the centers of circles—all are recorded as points having X, Y, and Z coordinate values within a three-dimensional grid. The first section of this chapter introduces the coordinate system and shows you how to identify points within it.

In this chapter, you explore coordinates and drawing aids by creating a drawing that resembles figure 2.1. If you take a break during the exercises, click on the Save button and name the drawing SSBRAKET.

Figure 2.1

A shaft support bracket.

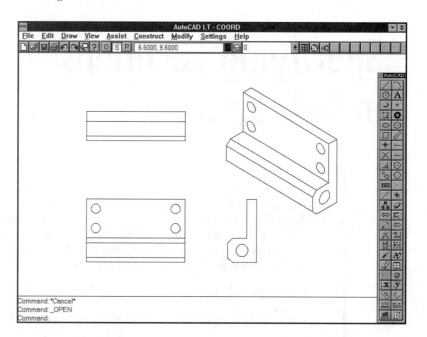

Understanding Coordinates and Points

You create AutoCAD LT drawings within a three-dimensional Cartesian coordinate system. The program locates a point in 3D space by specifying its distance from an *origin*, measured along three perpendicular axes: the X, Y, and Z axes. The origin is the point 0,0,0 (or just 0,0 for 2D). Only the X and Y axes are used for 2D drawings. Figure 2.2 shows the coordinate system you use to create 2D drawings.

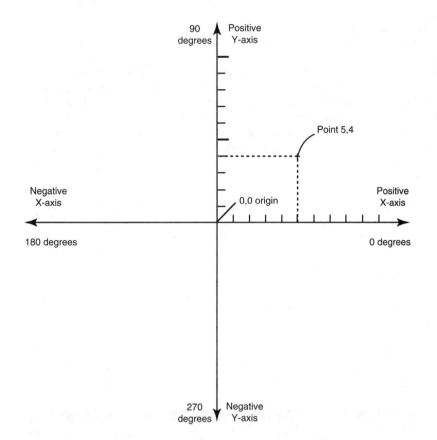

Figure 2.2

The X and Y axes in a 2D Cartesian coordinate system.

In the AutoCAD LT coordinate system, the X axis is normally horizontal, and the Y axis is normally vertical. The Z axis is perpendicular to both the X and Y axes. The axes intersect at the origin, and coordinate values increase as you move away from the origin. As you look at the graphics window, X coordinate values to the right of the origin are normally positive; X coordinates to the left of the origin are normally negative. Y coordinate values above the origin are normally positive, and Y coordinate values below the origin are normally negative.

When you enter a point, whether by picking it or by entering it from the keyboard, AutoCAD LT reads the point as a set of numbers in the form X,Y,Z. Each number represents the distance from the origin in the specified axis. In 2D drawings, you can omit the Z-axis value; AutoCAD LT automatically assigns it a value (the default is 0). For example, the coordinates 5,4 specify a point five units in the positive X axis and four units in the positive Y axis, measured from the 0,0 origin, as illustrated in figure 2.2.

In most drawings, the origin is at the lower left corner of the drawing area, but its location can vary. You can change your view to place the origin anywhere you choose in the drawing window. You can draw equally well in any region of this coordinate space.

You can also reset the origin to any point you choose in the drawing by using the UCS command, as explained later in this chapter.

AutoCAD LT relies on this coordinate system. Every object in a drawing has a precise location in CAD space—it requires coordinate location data as part of its definition. If you had to calculate each point, working in CAD would be hopelessly cumbersome. You can use a variety of methods to supply the location information when you create or manipulate objects. Even with all those methods, you sometimes need to enter coordinate values at the keyboard to accurately specify point locations or relationships.

Specifying coordinate locations is one of the key elements of your communication with AutoCAD LT. As a guideline, any prompt with the word "point" in it requires some form of location or coordinate input. You can specify a coordinate point in AutoCAD LT in two ways. You can point to a location with the mouse, or you can enter a coordinate value using the keyboard. AutoCAD LT provides a handy means of keeping track of the current location of your cursor—the coordinate display.

Working with the Coordinate Display

The coordinate display is located near the center of the toolbar. Figure 2.3 shows the coordinate display with the cursor at the point 3.6099,2.5817. In its default mode, the coordinate display provides a constant readout of the cursor location. You can use it to keep track of the location of your cursor in a drawing.

Figure 2.3

The coordinate display, on AutoCAD LT's toolbar.

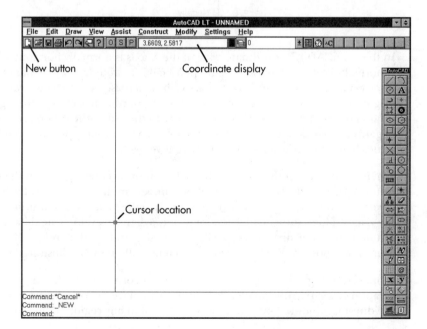

In the following exercise, you use the coordinate display to explore how AutoCAD LT's coordinate system works. You see how the display changes depending on your activity, and you learn to change the format of the coordinate display's readout. You also see how inaccurate uncontrolled point input is.

In a default new drawing, the origin is exactly at the lower left corner of the drawing area. In the following exercise, you use the ZOOM command to display a slightly larger view, so that you can see both positive and negative coordinates. ZOOM is discussed in detail in Chapter 5, "Navigating Views in the CAD Workspace," but you need only follow the instructions given here to use it in this exercise.

In the following exercise, you use the coordinate display to help draw the rectangular outline of the shaft support.

Using the Coordinate Display

In AutoCAD LT Release 1, click on the New
button, and press Enter

Begins a new, blank drawing

In AutoCAD LT Release 2, click on the New
button (see fig. 2.3), choose **N**one *then* OK

Opens the Create New Drawing dialog
box, then begins a new, blank drawing

Use the mouse to move the cursor around to the lower left and upper right corners of the drawing area. Watch the coordinate display change, and note the values displayed at the corners.

Command: **Z** (Enter)

Issues the ZOOM command

All/Center/Extents/Previous/Window/
<Scale(X/XP)>: **.8** (Enter)

Zooms out to display a larger area

Move the cursor to the corners again, and watch the coordinate display. It changes from positive values to negative. See if you can accurately place the cursor at the 0.0000,0.0000 origin. You can't, can you?

Use the coordinate display to *try* to pick points as accurately as possible in the following LINE command.

Command: *In the toolbox, click on the Line tool*

Issues the LINE command

_LINE From point: *Pick*
1.0000,5.2000 at ① *(see fig. 2.4)*

Starts a line and displays a rubber-band line

Move the cursor and watch the X,Y values in the coordinate display change as you move the rubber-band line. Use the crosshairs to help pick the next points approximately.

continues

continued

`To point:` *Pick 5.2000,5.2000 at* ②	Draws the first line
`To point:` *Pick 5.2000,6.4000 at* ③	Draws another line
Click on the coordinate display	Freezes the coordinate display

Move the cursor around the screen; notice that the coordinate display doesn't change.

`To point:` *Use the crosshairs to pick at* ④	Updates the coordinate display to display the point approximately 1.0000,6.4000
Press F6 or click on the coordinate display, and then move the cursor	Restores the continuously updated coordinate display, but it now displays in a *distance<angle* format

`To point:` *Use the distance<angle coordinate display to pick 1.2000<270 at* ①

Press F6 several times again, or click on the coordinate display, or press Ctrl+D, and then move the cursor. The coordinate display cycles through X,Y, frozen, and distance<angle modes. Set the coordinate display to distance<angle mode.

`To point:` (Enter)	Exits the LINE command and returns to X,Y mode

Note how the distance<angle format (called *polar* coordinates) displays the distance and angle from the previous point, shown by the rubber-band cursor, while the X,Y coordinates are relative to the 0,0 origin.

When you started the exercise, the coordinates displayed as a pair of numbers separated by a comma. This format matches the Cartesian coordinate system; the first number is the X coordinate, the second is the Y coordinate. As you move the mouse, the crosshair pointer and the coordinate numbers change, indicating the current position of the crosshair pointer within the coordinate system.

 Note   You can set the coordinate display to various units with various degrees of precision—see the section on units in Chapter 8, "Preparing Your Workspace: CAD Concepts 1B," for details. Although the default is four decimal places of precision, the exercise instructions in this book generally only show as many places as needed to tell you which points to pick.

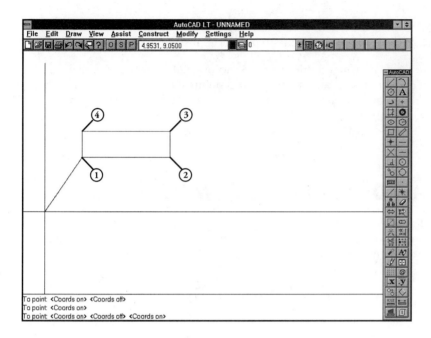

Figure 2.4

The polar coordinate display format.

Understanding the Coordinate Display Modes

When you click on the coordinate display, the display mode changes. Pressing F6 or Ctrl+D has the same effect. The coordinate display appears in one of three modes:

- ◆ **Dynamic Cartesian.** X,Y coordinates, continuously updated

- ◆ **Dynamic Polar.** Polar coordinates during certain commands, but X,Y otherwise, both continuously updated

- ◆ **Static.** X,Y coordinates, updated only when you pick a point

Normally, one of the X,Y modes is displayed. The polar display appears only when a rubber-band line is visible on the screen. The polar format is useful because you often specify points "relative" to the previous point.

Tip   When you draw circles or arcs by picking their centers, you can then use the polar mode to display the radius as you pick it.

When you are working in AutoCAD LT, you use coordinates constantly, even if not consciously. You use coordinates to locate the lines, arcs, and circles you draw. You use them to place objects when you use MOVE, COPY, and other editing commands.

You can specify exact coordinate locations with keyboard input, but it is often more intuitive and efficient to use the mouse to pick locations.

Although the rectangle you just drew may look accurate, it isn't. In the preceding exercise, you could not accurately pick the exact points specified. The reason is that the points you pick are translated from the pixel (screen display dot) you pick to the nearest drawing coordinates. To pick points accurately, you need the assistance of some special tools—AutoCAD LT's drawing aids.

Using AutoCAD LT's Drawing Aids

AutoCAD LT provides a variety of tools you can use to locate points accurately by using the mouse. The primary aids, grid and snap, enable you to pick points accurately at any rectangular increment.

Locating Points with a Reference Grid

The simplest drawing aid is called the grid, and it serves the same purpose as the lines on a sheet of graph paper. The grid provides a visual indicator of the location of coordinates, but it does not impose any accuracy over the points you pick. The grid is displayed as a rectangular array of points. Take a look at the grid in the following exercise.

Using the Reference Grid

Continue from the preceding exercise.

Command: *Press F7*   Turns on the default grid

<Grid on>

The default grid in AutoCAD LT Release 1 is one-unit square; in AutoCAD LT Release 2 it is $^1/_2$-unit square (see fig. 2.5).

Try to place the cursor on the grid dot at 2,2. You can't; the cursor is still inaccurate.

Press Ctrl+G   Turns off the grid dots and redraws the
                                                 drawing area

<Grid off>

Command: *Press F7*   Turns on the grid again

<Grid on>

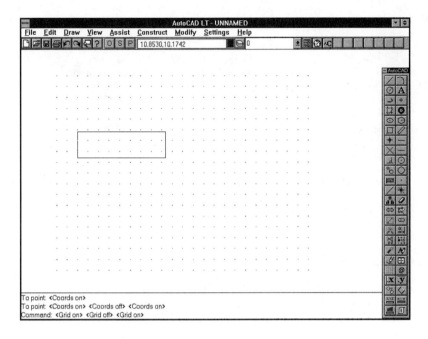

Figure 2.5

Displaying a reference grid.

As you saw in the exercise, when you turn off the grid, AutoCAD LT must redraw the drawing area to remove the grid dots. You can turn the grid on or off with F7 or Ctrl+G, or by using the Drawing Aids dialog box covered later in this chapter.

Notice that the default X and Y grid spacings are equal. The grid, along with the coordinate display, helps you find points, but you need to use snap to pick them accurately.

Controlling Points with Snap

Snap adds real control to picking points by working in concert with the grid and the coordinate display. Snap is an invisible grid that constrains points picked with the mouse.

Try out snap in the following exercise, and start to draw the front view of the shaft support.

Using Snap to Control Point Picking

Continue from the preceding exercise, with the grid on.

Command: *Click on the S (Snap) button*   Turns on snap

continues

continued

```
<Snap on>
```

Move the mouse and notice that the cursor and coordinate display jump in increments. In AutoCAD LT Release 1, they jump in one-unit increments; in AutoCAD LT Release 2, they jump in ½-unit increments.

Move to the point 2,2 (see fig. 2.6). The coordinate display shows exactly 2.0000,2.0000.

`Command:` *Click on the Line tool*	Issues the LINE command
`_LINE From point:` *Pick 1,1 at* ① *(see fig. 2.7)*	Starts a line

Use the polar coordinate display to help pick the next point.

`To point:` *Pick 1<90 at* ②	Draws a 1-unit long line

Try to put the cursor on the point 4.2<0 at ③; you can't because it is not on a snap point.

`To point:` *Press Ctrl+G*	Turns off the grid dots

```
<Grid off>
```

Again, move the cursor and notice that snap acts the same whether grid is on or off.

Press F9 or Ctrl+B	Turns off snap

```
<Snap off>
```

Try again to put the cursor on the point 4.2<0; you still can't because point picking without snap is inaccurate.

`To point:`	Exits the LINE command

You can turn snap on or off with F9 or Ctrl+B, or by using the Drawing Aids dialog box. Snap enables you to accurately set points a snap increment larger than the screen pixel spacing, so that the points you pick are translated and rounded off from the nearest pixel to controlled drawing-coordinate increments.

Grid and snap are actually independent. The grid is just a visual aid, while the snap provides point control regardless of the grid setting or visibility. Although grid and snap are independent, they work best in coordination.

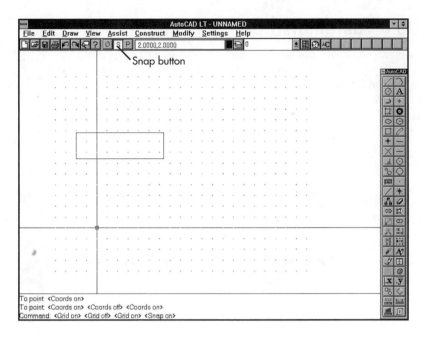

Figure 2.6

Snapping to the point 2,2.

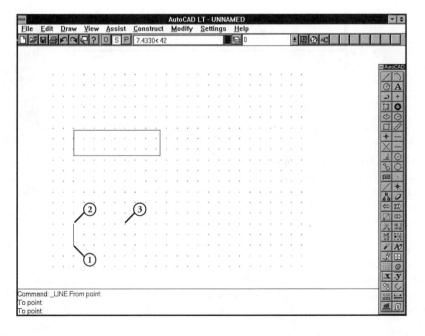

Figure 2.7

Using the snap grid to pick points accurately.

Setting Up a Coordinated Grid and Snap

You can set grid and snap with the GRID and SNAP commands, or by using the Drawing Aids dialog box. To open the Drawing Aids dialog box, you can choose **S**ettings, then **D**rawing Aids, or just click on the Drawing Aids (DDRMODES) button in AutoCAD LT Release 1 or the Drawing Aids tool in AutoCAD LT Release 2. The Drawing Aids dialog box is shown in figure 2.8. In AutoCAD LT Release 2, you also can coordinate snap and grid by using the setup methods in the Create New Drawing dialog box.

Figure 2.8

The Drawing Aids dialog box.

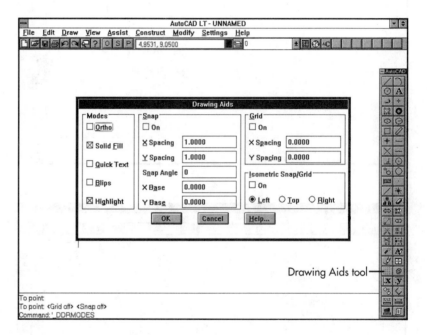

The default setting, with a ¹/₂-unit or one-unit grid and snap, is not very useful. By setting up a proportionally coordinated grid and snap, you can use the grid to estimate locations, and you can count the snap increments between grid dots. A grid of one unit and a snap of 0.25, for example, enables you to easily count four snap increments between grid dots.

All the coordinates in the shaft support drawing are on 0.1-unit increments, so you will set an 0.5-unit grid with an 0.1-unit snap in the following exercise. Then, as you draw the front view of the shaft support, you easily can snap to the specified points. Use the grid to estimate locations and the coordinate display to confirm points. If you make a mistake, you can click on the Undo button to reverse it.

Using a Coordinated Snap and Grid

Continue from the preceding exercise, with grid and snap off.

Command: *Click on the Drawing Aids button or tool (see fig. 2.8)*	Issues DDRMODES command and opens the Drawing Aids dialog box

Notice that the default snap setting is 1.0000 in AutoCAD LT Release 1 and 0.5000 in AutoCAD LT Release 2, but the default grid setting is 0.0000. A zero grid setting makes the grid equal to the snap.

*In the **G**rid section, click in the* On *box*	Puts an X in the box, which indicates grid is on
*If using AutoCAD LT Release 2, in the **G**rid section, double-click in the* X S**p**acing *box and type* **1**	Specifies X grid dot spacing of one-unit
*In the **G**rid section, double-click in the* Y Spa**c**ing *box and type* **.5**	Specifies Y grid dot spacing of one-half unit
Click on OK	Closes the dialog box and turns on the grid

Notice that the grid dot spacing is unequal for the X and Y axes (see fig. 2.9).

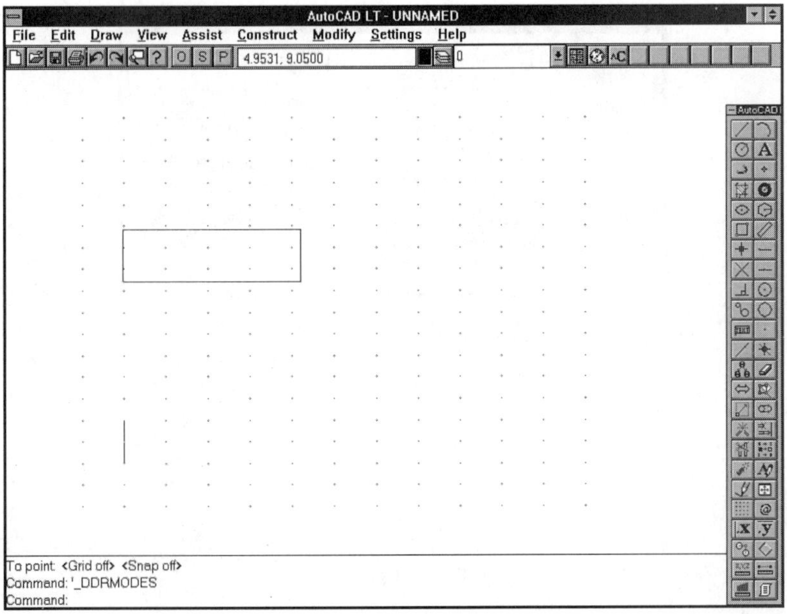

Figure 2.9

Unequal X and Y grid spacing.

continues

continued

You also can control the grid by using the GRID command.

Command: **GRID** (Enter)

Grid spacing(X) or ON/OFF/Snap/   Sets X and Y grid to 0.25
Aspect <A>: **.25** (Enter)

Command: *Choose* **S**ettings, *then* **D**rawing Aids   Issues DDRMODES command and opens
                                            the Drawing Aids dialog box; notice
                                            the X and Y grid spacing is 0.25

In the **G**rid *section, double-click in the* X **Sp**acing   Specifies X grid spacing of 0.5
box and type **.5**

Press Enter   Accepts 0.5 X spacing and sets Y to match it

In the **S**nap *section, double-click in the* **X**   Specifies X snap increment of 0.1
Spacing *box and type* **.1**

In the **S**nap *section, click in the* On *box*   Puts an X in the box and sets Y to match X

The resulting Drawing Aids dialog box settings are shown in figure 2.10.

Figure 2.10

*Coordinated grid
and snap settings
in the Drawing
Aids dialog box.*

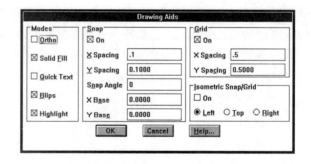

Click on OK   Closes the dialog box, turns on 0.1 snap, and
                                            displays 0.5-unit grid (see fig. 2.11)

Command: *Click on the Line tool*   Issues the LINE command

_LINE From point: *Pick point 1,2*   Sets first point of line
at ① *(see fig. 2.11)*

To point: *Pick 4.2<0 at* ②   Draws line

To point: *Pick 1.0<270 at* ③

To point: *Pick 4.2<180 at* ④

To point: (Enter)   Ends LINE command

Command: (Enter)   Repeats LINE command

LINE From point: *Pick 1.0,1.2 at* ⑤

To point: *Pick 4.2<0 at* ⑥

To point: (Enter)   Ends LINE command

Repeat the LINE command and draw another 4.2-unit line at ⑦.

Repeat the LINE command and draw from ① to ⑧ to ⑨ to ②, using the snap increment and the grid dots shown in figure 2.11 to locate the points.

Command: *Click on the Save button,*   Saves and names the drawing
type **SSBRAKET**, *and choose* OK

_saveas Current drawing name set C:\ACLTWIN\SSBRAKET.

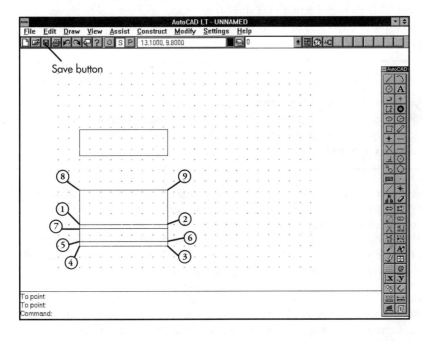

Figure 2.11

Front view drawn with grid and snap.

Notice how easy it is to find a point and select it with the help of snap and grid. Your snap is now set to 0.1 and your grid is spaced at 0.5 units. You will benefit most from a grid-to-snap ratio of about 4 to 1 or 5 to 1. Such a ratio affords you a good visual reference of your location without a lot of excess clutter from superfluous grid dots.

Notice that the grid spacing is balanced between X and Y. When you change the X value in the Drawing Aids dialog box without specifying a Y value, the Y value defaults to the X value. This setting is useful because you normally want the X and Y grid spacing to match.

Note   You might notice that the spacing of a line or a row or column of grid dots looks just a little off on the display. Do not be alarmed—it just looks that way because the grid and drawn lines must be rounded off to the nearest pixel on the display. They are still accurate, and the lines will plot as accurately as your printer or plotter can reproduce them.

When you are turning the grid on or off, the F7 and Ctrl+G keys are more efficient than opening the Drawing Aids dialog box. You also can use the dialog box to change the grid spacing, however. For quick changes in the snap or grid increments, you might prefer to use the SNAP and GRID commands instead of the dialog boxes.

GRID. The GRID command controls the visibility and spacing of a visual reference grid of dots. The grid can also be set by using the Drawing Aids dialog box, without issuing the GRID command.

SNAP. The SNAP command turns the snap grid on and off, and sets its spacing. It also provides options for setting Aspect (different X and Y values) and switching to an isometric snap grid. The snap grid settings can also be made by using the Drawing Aids dialog box, without issuing the SNAP command.

Snap and grid are useful even in drawings in which most elements do not fall on snap and grid spacings. You can use snap and grid to create construction lines. During the layout stage of a facilities project, for example, set the grid to 20' and the snap to 5'. Use the grid as a column spacing reference, and then use other means of controlling accuracy for elements that do not fall on snap increments. You can also use snap and grid to place dimensions and annotations in an orderly manner.

Tip   Instead of turning snap off (as you will be tempted to do from time to time), set the snap increment to a smaller increment, use typed coordinates, or use one of the other methods of accuracy control, which are discussed in Chapter 11, "Achieving Accuracy: The Geometric Power of CAD."

Notice that the grid does not cover the entire drawing area. Remember that you zoomed the display to show a larger area, including negative coordinate areas, in an earlier exercise. The display still shows this larger area, but the grid only covers the 12-unit by 9-unit area set as the default drawing limits. Drawing limits (the defined area to which you normally confine your drawing) are discussed further in Chapter 8, "Preparing Your Workspace: CAD Concepts 1B."

You also can set snap and grid when you begin a new drawing in AutoCAD LT Release 2 by using the setup methods offered by the Create New Drawing dialog box, discussed in the following section. If you are using AutoCAD LT Release 1, skip this section.

Setting Snap and Grid with Quick Step

The Create New Drawing dialog box in AutoCAD LT Release 2 offers two setup methods: **Q**uick and **C**ustom. The Quick method enables you to set snap, and turn on both snap and grid, but sets grid to 0 (equal to snap). The Custom method provides a button to access the full Drawing Aids dialog box for settings. Both methods also provide other settings and are covered in more detail in Chapter 3, "Keeping Track of Your Work: Drawings as Files," and Chapter 8, "Preparing Your Workspace: CAD Concepts 1B." Try setting snap and grid using the Quick method in the following exercise.

Setting Snap and Grid with Quick Setup

If you are using AutoCAD LT Release 1, skip this exercise. If you are using AutoCAD LT Release 2, continue.

Command: *Choose the New button*	Opens the Create New Drawing dialog box (see fig. 2.12)
Choose **Q**uick, *then* OK Drawing Setup	Specifies Quick setup and opens the Quick dialog box (see fig. 2.13)
Put checks in the Turn on **G**rid *and* Turn on **S**nap *boxes*	Turns on snap with the default 0.5 spacing and sets grid equal to snap
Double-click in the **X** Spacing *box and type* **0.1**	Specifies X snap of 0.1
Choose OK	Sets Y snap equal to X snap, closes dialog box, and redraws screen with a 0.1 grid
Command: **G** (Enter)	Specifies alias for GRID command

continues

continued

```
GRID
```

```
Grid spacing(X) or ON/OFF/Snap/          Sets X and Y grid to 0.5
Aspect <0.0000>: .5 (Enter)
```

Move the cursor; it snaps to 0.1 increments between the 0.5 grid dots.

Choose **F**ile	Opens the File menu and lists previously opened drawings at the bottom of the menu
Choose **1** C:\ACLTWIN\SSBRAKET	Specifies drawing to reopen and displays dialog box stating "The current drawing has been changed. Do you want to save the changes?"
Choose **N**o	Discards current drawing and reloads SSBRAKET

Figure 2.12

The Create New Drawing dialog box.

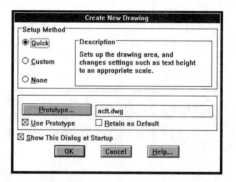

Figure 2.13

Setting snap and grid in the Quick Drawing Setup dialog box.

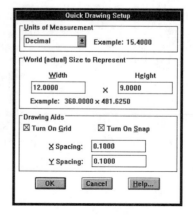

Grid can guide your eye to pick points, and snap can help you pick them with precision, but you still need a steady hand to pick points. The next drawing aid will increase both your accuracy and speed in picking points at 90-degree incremental angles.

Controlling Angles with Ortho Mode

Ortho mode is a tool to help you draw "orthogonally," meaning in horizontal or vertical directions. This mode keeps the objects you create square with each other and aligned to the coordinate system. Ortho snaps points to 90-degree angular increments. You can set Ortho mode by clicking on the O (Ortho) button on the toolbar, pressing F8 or Ctrl+O, or by clicking in the **O**rtho box in the Modes section of the Drawing Aids dialog box. The O (Ortho) button on the toolbar indicates the current setting; if the button is greyed and raised, Ortho is off. If the button is white (highlighted) and depressed, Ortho is on.

Experience the effect of this tool in the following exercise as you draw the right side view. To help locate points, you can also use the coordinates display and align the crosshairs with corresponding lines in the front view.

Using Ortho to Draw at 90-Degree Increments

Continue from either of the two preceding exercises, with grid and snap on.

Command: *Click on the Line tool*   Issues the LINE command

_LINE From point: *Pick the point 8,1*   Sets first point of line
at ① *(see fig. 2.14)*

Move the cursor and observe that the rubber-band line moves freely to any angle.

Turn on Ortho by clicking on the O *(Ortho) button*   Turns on Ortho mode and highlights button

Move the cursor and observe that the rubber-band line jumps to angles of 0, 90, 180, and 270 degrees. You need to carefully position the cursor in either the X axis or the Y axis, not both.

To point: *Move the cursor to* ② *(see fig. 2.14)*   Rubber-bands and draws line to ⑦
and pick at 2.6<90

To point: *Continue drawing, picking*   Draws three more orthogonal lines
④, ⑤, *and* ⑥ *(see fig. 2.15)*

Try to put the rubber-band line on ⑦; you can't unless you turn Ortho off.

To point: *Press Ctrl+O and pick* ⑦   Turns off Ortho and draws diagonal line to ⑦

Finish drawing the right side view, turning Ortho off and on as needed. Leave it turned off.

Figure 2.14

Using Ortho to draw.

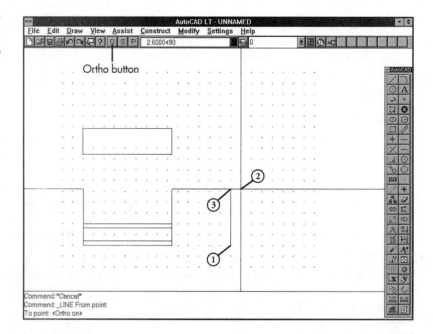

Figure 2.15

Drawing with Ortho on and off.

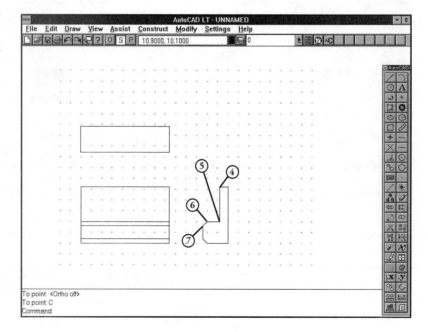

Creating geometry that is parallel to the axes with Ortho is extremely simple, fast, and accurate if you also use snap.

If you need to, you can also rotate the axes to draw orthogonally at other angles, as explained later in the UCS section of this chapter.

Note In subsequent exercises, the instructions will simply say to turn Ortho on or off, rather than instructing you to click on the O button or press F8 or Ctrl+O. This arrangement should avoid the confusion that would result if your current setting does not match the setting used in the exercise.

When Snap and Ortho do not enable you to accurately pick the point you need, you must use another method. You can use one of the accuracy methods in Chapter 11, "Achieving Accuracy: The Geometric Power of CAD," or you can type coordinate values.

Specifying Coordinates from the Keyboard

Often, the simplest and most efficient way to specify points is to enter coordinates at the keyboard, particularly points that do not fall on a reasonable snap increment or on existing geometry. These typed coordinates are much like the values you have seen displayed in the coordinate display. You can even use typed coordinates to specify a known location that is off the screen.

You can specify typed coordinates in two ways: as absolute coordinates and as relative coordinates. You can use either way to specify either X,Y or polar coordinates. The example typed coordinate values shown in the following sections are illustrated in figure 2.16.

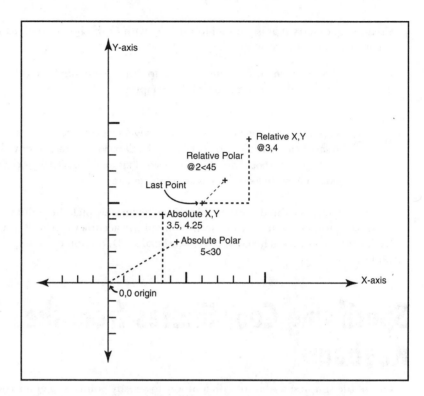

Understanding Absolute X,Y and Polar Coordinates

When the coordinate display shows X,Y point locations, it is displaying absolute X,Y coordinates, which means that the point is offset from the 0,0 origin by the X and Y values. You can specify any point by using absolute X,Y coordinates, if you know its X and Y values. The AutoCAD LT drawing file database stores all object locations using absolute X,Y coordinates.

Absolute X,Y coordinates are most useful when some key feature of design is at the origin and the other features are all located from it. An example might be locating data points from a benchmark when creating maps from survey information.

When AutoCAD LT prompts you for a point, you can enter absolute X,Y coordinates by typing them on the command line. Type the X value of the coordinate, a comma, the Y value of the coordinate, and then press Enter. For example, the following enters an absolute coordinate 3.5 units to the right of the origin (in the X direction) and 4.25 units above it (in the Y direction):

3.5,4.25 *Press Enter*

Although absolute X,Y coordinate points are specified with parentheses (3.5,4.25) in most mathematical conventions, you should not include parentheses when you type coordinates at the keyboard in AutoCAD LT. Also, do not insert any spaces.

You can also type absolute polar coordinates. The polar coordinate values you have seen in the coordinate display (such as 4.2000<90.0000) were relative polar coordinates. In other words, the coordinate display showed the distance and angle offset of the cursor relative to the last previous point. Absolute polar coordinates are similar, but they are offset from the 0,0 origin instead of from the last point. To specify an absolute polar coordinate, type the distance, followed by a left angle bracket (<) and the angle, and then press Enter. For example, to specify a point 5 units at 30 degrees from the 0,0 origin, you would type the following absolute polar coordinate.

5<30 *Press Enter*

Absolute polar coordinates are not often used, but relative polar coordinates are frequently used.

Understanding Relative X,Y and Polar Coordinates

The use of relative coordinates depends on keeping track of the last point. Each time you type or pick a point, the new point becomes the AutoCAD LT *last point*. AutoCAD LT remembers the last point, so you can easily enter new points relative to its location. Relative coordinates are based not on the 0,0 origin, but on the last point. To enter a relative point from the keyboard, you precede the coordinate value with an **@** (at sign).

The following relative X,Y example specifies a point three units to the right (in the X axis) and four units above (in the Y axis) the current last point.

@3,4 *Press Enter*

Use relative X,Y coordinates when you know the X and Y distances from your last point to the next one, for example, when you want to create a horizontal or vertical line exactly 4.2 units long. Relative X,Y coordinates are often easier to specify than absolute coordinates. For example, if your last point is 3.625,2.9375 and you want to draw exactly 3.5 units straight up along the Y axis, it is much simpler to enter the relative coordinates @0,3.5 than to calculate and enter the absolute coordinates 3.625,6.4375.

Tip   If you enter the @ symbol by itself in response to any command asking for a point, AutoCAD LT will use the last point. Entering @ alone is the same as entering @0,0.

When a point is at a non-orthogonal angle from the last point, it is often easiest to specify it with a relative polar coordinate. To enter a relative polar coordinate, type the **@** symbol, the distance, followed by a left angle bracket (**<**), then the angle, and then press Enter. For example, to specify a relative polar point 2 units from the last point at an angle of 45 degrees, enter the following:

    @2<45 *Press Enter*

Using Typed X,Y and Polar Coordinates

Experiment with keyboard coordinate input in the following exercise to redraw and finish the inaccurate top view you started earlier. Be careful to include @ signs, decimal points, and < signs as shown. Use Undo if you make an error.

Using the Keyboard to Input Coordinates

Continue from the preceding exercise, with Ortho off.

`Command:` *Click on the Erase tool (see fig. 2.17)*	Issues the ERASE command
`_ERASE` `Select objects:` *Pick each line of the rectangle in the top view, then press Enter*	Erases the four top view lines
`Command:` *Click on the R (Redraw) button in AutoCAD LT Release 1 or Redraw tool in AutoCAD LT Release 2*	Redraws the grid
`Command: L` (Enter)	Specifies the alias for the LINE command
`LINE From point: 1,5.2` (Enter)	Specifies the starting point at ①, in absolute coordinates relative to the origin (see fig. 2.17)
`To point: 1,6.4` (Enter)	Specifies absolute point relative to the origin and draws the line to ②
`To point: @4.2,0` (Enter)	Specifies the third point in coordinates relative to the last point and draws the line to ③
`To point: @1.2<270` (Enter)	Specifies the fourth point in polar coordinates relative to the third point and draws the line to ④

To point: **C** (Enter)	Closes the series of lines to the starting point and ends the command
Command: (Enter)	Repeats LINE command
LINE From point: **@0,.2** (Enter)	Starts line at ⑤ relative to the last point (which is ④, not the closing point)
To point: **@-4.2,0** (Enter)	Specifies the point relative to ⑤ and draws the line
To point: (Enter)	Ends the LINE command
Command: (Enter)	Repeats LINE command
LINE From point: **1,6** (Enter)	Specifies the point at ⑥ in absolute coordinates
To point: **@4.2<0** (Enter)	Specifies the point in polar coordinates relative to ⑥ and draws the line to 5.2,6
To point: (Enter)	Ends the LINE command

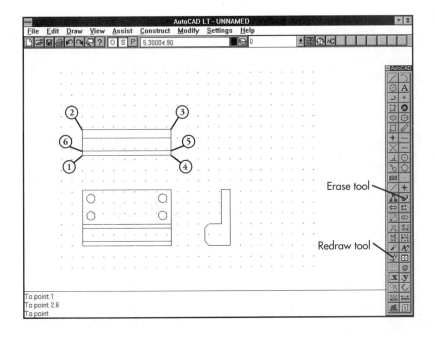

Figure 2.17

Top view redrawn with typed coordinates.

Tip   You can abbreviate distances, points, and other numbers by omitting insignificant leading zeros, trailing zeros following the decimal point, and trailing decimal points. Enter **0.25,75.0000** as **.25,75**, for example, to save typing.

Relative coordinates are also used to specify *offsets* in many editing commands. This usage will become more significant to you in the editing chapters.

Relative coordinates are efficient for entering a sequential series of known points, but they don't help much when you want to enter several points relative to a single known point. The way to handle this is to use the UCS command to reset the location of the 0,0 origin and then to use absolute coordinates, which are relative to the new origin.

Changing the Origin and Axes with UCSs

The UCS command enables you to establish your own coordinate system. You can change the origin point by changing the position of the coordinate system, and you can rotate the axes by changing the angle of the coordinate system. The default coordinate system is called the *WCS* (*World Coordinate System*), and a user-defined coordinate system is called a *UCS* (*User Coordinate System*). Although the drawing has only one "real" origin (0,0,0 of the WCS), the UCS options permit you to locate alternate origin points and rotate the X,Y,Z reference plane in 3D space to accommodate your design needs. By default, all 2D points you specify are placed in the plane of the X,Y axes.

Although the UCS command was developed to address 3D drawing, it is quite useful in 2D drafting. You can show the current location and orientation of the origin and axes by turning on the UCS icon.

Showing the Origin and Axes with the UCS Icon

If you look at the UCS icon in figure 2.18, you see that the X arrow points along the positive X axis, and the Y arrow points along the positive Y axis. The "W" on the Y arrow means that the current UCS is the default World Coordinate System (WCS). The "+" on the UCS icon indicates that the icon is displayed at the origin of the current UCS (0,0).

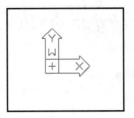

Figure 2.18

*The UCS icon at
the WCS origin.*

The UCS icon reflects any rotation of the X,Y axes. If the icon is set to display at the
origin, it also can indicate the location of the origin of the current UCS. The UCS
icon shown in figure 2.19 has been rotated to a 45-degree angle and set to display at
the origin. The grid, axes, and crosshairs are also offset and rotated with any changes
to the UCS.

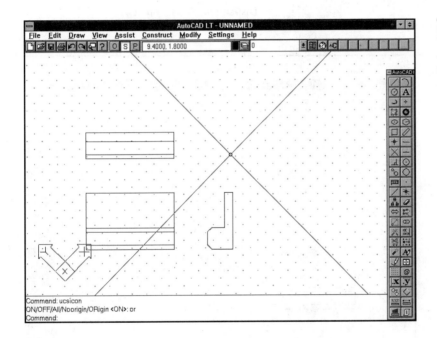

Figure 2.19

*Rotated UCS
icon, grid, and
crosshairs.*

If you are using AutoCAD LT Release 1, to use the menu for the UCS and UCSICON
commands, you must first turn on the **F**ull Menu option in the **S**ettings menu. You
can then access the UCS items on the **A**ssist menu. You do so in the following exercise, and then turn on the UCS icon and set it to display at the origin. If you are using
AutoCAD LT Release 2, the full menu is the only menu.

Turning on the UCS Icon

Continue from the preceding exercise.

Command: If using AutoCAD LT Release 1, *choose* **S**ettings, *then* **F**ull Menu	Sets pull-down menu display to full menus
Command: *Choose* **A**ssist, U**C**S icon	Issues the UCSICON command
ON/OFF/All/Noorigin/ORigin <OFF>: ON (Enter)	Displays the UCS icon at the lower left corner of the drawing area
Command: (Enter)	Repeats the UCSICON command
UCSICON ON/OFF/All/Noorigin/ORigin <ON>: OR (Enter)	Displays the UCS icon at the origin (see fig. 2.20)

Figure 2.20

Displaying the UCS icon at the WCS origin.

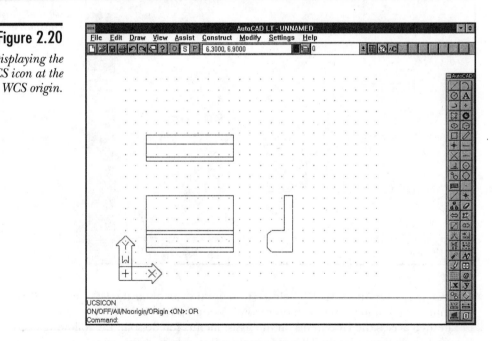

When the ORigin option is off, or the origin is too close to the edge of the drawing area, the UCS icon displays at the lower left corner of the drawing area.

> **UCSICON.** The UCSICON command controls the visibility and placement of the UCS Icon.

The UCSICON command has the following options:

◆ **ON.** The ON option displays the icon.

◆ **OFF.** The OFF option turns off the display of the icon.

◆ **All.** The All option applies the current settings to multiple viewports (see Chapter 5, "Navigating Views in the CAD Workspace).

◆ **Noorigin.** The Noorigin option displays the icon at the lower left corner.

◆ **ORigin.** The ORigin option displays the icon at the UCS origin, if possible.

The UCS icon also displays information about your location in 3D space. The box formed by the intersection of the arrows, for example, indicates a positive Z-axis direction. This book does not explore the topic of 3D: you can refer to some of the books referenced in the introduction for more information.

Controlling the UCS

The UCS is quite useful in 2D design. With it, you can set the origin to any relevant point or rotate the axes to any relevant angle. For example, you can set the origin to a datum feature of a machined part, use any survey point in a map as a reference, or set the origin at the intersection of walls or a foundation corner. Rotating the UCS coordinate system also rotates the Grid, Snap, and Ortho functions. This makes it easy to work on objects aligned orthogonally with each other, but rotated relative to the orientation of the default WCS.

Try setting the UCS in the next exercise, and use an offset origin to place the holes in the front and side views of the shaft support.

Changing and Drawing in UCSs

Continue from the preceding exercise, with the UCS icon on and full menus enabled.

Command: *Choose* **A**ssist, Set **U**CS   Displays the UCS child menu (see fig. 2.21)

Choose **Z** Axis Rotate   Issues UCS command with the Z option

continues

continued

```
_ucs
Origin/ZAxis/3point/Entity/View/X/Y/Z/
Prev/Restore/Save/Del/?/<World>: _z
```

`Rotation angle about Z` `axis <0>:` **45** (Enter)	Rotates UCS and axes 45 degrees, as shown earlier in figure 2.19

Notice that the Grid, Snap, and Ortho drawing aids are aligned to the new UCS orientation, and that the grid covers the entire drawing area.

Command: *Click on the Undo button*	Undoes the UCS rotation

```
_U GROUP
```

Figure 2.21

The UCS child menu.

Command: *Choose* **A**ssist, Set **U**CS, **O**rigin	Issues UCS command with the ORigin option

```
_ucs
Origin/ZAxis/3point/Entity/View/X/Y/Z/
Prev/Restore/Save/Del/?/<World>: _origin
```

`Origin point <0,0,0>:` **1.4,2.4** (Enter)	Moves the UCS origin and icon (see fig. 2.22)

Move the cursor around and watch the coordinate display to see where positive and negative coordinates are now located.

Command: *Click on the Circle tool*	Issues CIRCLE command
`_CIRCLE 3P/TTR/<Center` `point>:` **0,0** (Enter)	Sets center at new UCS origin

```
Radius: .2 (Enter)
```
Draws circle (see fig. 2.22)

```
Command: (Enter)
```
Repeats CIRCLE command

```
CIRCLE 3P/TTR/<Center
point>: 0,.8 (Enter)
```
Sets center 0.8 above new
UCS origin

```
Radius <0.2000>: (Enter)
```
Draws circle

Repeat the CIRCLE command to draw the other two circles shown in figure 2.22, at 3.4,0 and
3.4,0.8.

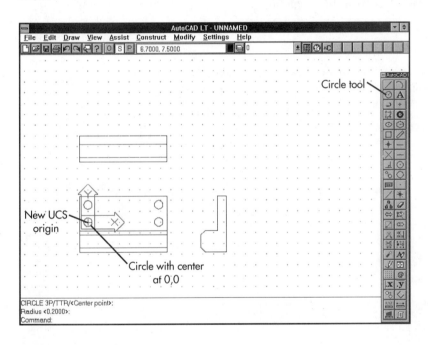

Figure 2.22

*Circle drawn with
offset UCS origin.*

```
Command: Choose Assist, Set UCS,
Entity
```
Issues the UCS command with
the Object option

```
_ucs
Origin/ZAxis/3point/Entity/View/X/Y/Z/
Prev/Restore/Save/Del/?/<World>: _entity
```

```
Select object to align UCS: Pick the
line at ① (see fig. 2.23)
```
Moves the UCS origin and
aligns the X axis to the line

Notice that the positive X axis is now vertical and the positive Y axis points to the left.

continues

continued

Use the CIRCLE command to draw the 0.25-radius circle shown at 0.5,0.6 in figure 2.23.

Next, set the UCS to the lower left corner of the side view, using the 3 Point option.

Command: *Choose* **A**ssist, Set **U**CS, **3** Point	Issues the UCS command with the 3 Point option

```
_ucs
Origin/ZAxis/3point/Entity/View/X/Y/Z/
Prev/Restore/Save/Del/?/<World>: _3point
```

Origin point <0,0,0>: *Pick point* ① *(see fig. 2.24)*	Sets the new origin point
Point on positive portion of the X-axis <-2.0000,0.0000,0.0000>: *Pick point* ②	Sets the direction of the positive X axis
Point on positive-Y portion of the UCS XY plane <-3.0000,1.0000,0.0000>: *Pick any point above the line* *(see fig. 2.24)*	Sets the direction of the positive Y axis and displays the UCS icon at the new origin

Figure 2.23

Drawing with the UCS aligned to an object.

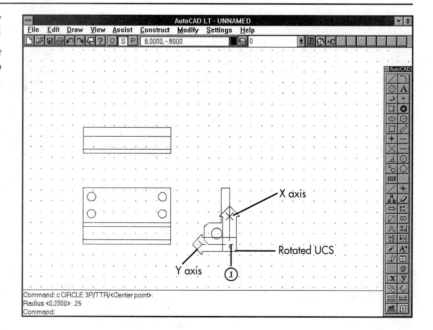

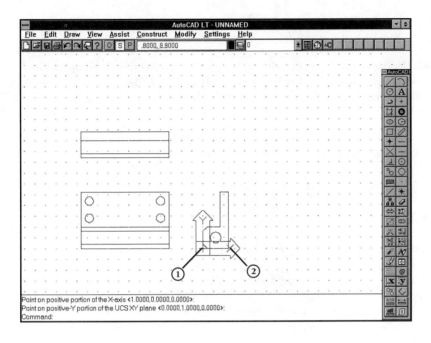

Figure 2.24

The side view UCS set with the 3 Point option.

Because this book does not explore the subject of 3D, it concentrates on those features of the UCS command most relevant to 2D.

> **UCS.** The UCS command is used to set up and manage User Coordinate Systems. It provides a range of options, including setting the origin, specifying rotation about any axis, aligning with objects, saving, listing, and restoring.

The UCS command prompt shows all of the command's options. The full UCS child menu available from the **A**ssist pull-down menu was shown earlier in figure 2.21. The options useful for 2D work, and their functions, are as follows:

- ◆ **World.** The World option sets the UCS to the WCS.

- ◆ **Origin.** The Origin option shifts the UCS origin without affecting the orientation of the reference axis.

- ◆ **3 Point.** The 3 Point option sets the UCS origin to a supplied point, the positive X axis in the direction of a second point, and the positive Y axis in the direction of a third point.

◆ **Entity.** The Entity option aligns the UCS to a selected object with respect to the point at which the object was selected.

◆ **View.** The View option orients the UCS with the current view. This option is most useful when using the VIEW command (Chapter 4, "Building a Drawing: Using Basic Drawing Tools," and Chapter 17, "Dressing Up Drawings with Hatching").

◆ **Z.** The Z option rotates the orientation of the X,Y axes and plane of the UCS around the Z axis and origin by the angle you specify.

◆ **Prev.** The Prev option restores the previous UCS.

◆ **Save.** The Save option saves the current UCS to the name you specify.

◆ **Restore.** The Restore option restores the named UCS you specify.

◆ **Del.** The Del option deletes the named UCS you specify

◆ **?.** The ? option enables you to list all named UCS, or one or more UCSs that you specify. You can use wild cards, such as ? or *, to specify a set of names.

Note that you use the Z option, *not* the ZAxis option, to rotate the X,Y axes. The ZAxis option is for reorienting the direction of the Z axis in 3D.

You often use a few UCSs repeatedly in a drawing. To do so easily, you can assign names to the UCSs and then set them current by name. You can use the Prev, Restore, Save, Del, and ? options of the UCS command, but it is easier to use the UCS Control dialog box (see fig. 2.25).

Figure 2.25

The UCS Control dialog box.

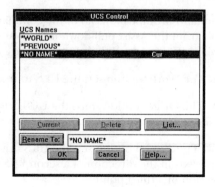

You will save the current UCS, naming it RSIDE, and then restore the WCS in the following exercise.

Saving and Setting Named UCSs

Continue from the preceding exercise, with the UCS set to the right side view.

Command: *Choose* **A**ssist, **N**amed UCS	Issues the DDUCS command and opens the UCS Control dialog box (see fig. 2.26)
Click on *NO NAME*	Selects the current unnamed UCS (notice the "Cur" indication) and enters *NO NAME* in the box next to the **R**ename To button
Click in the box next to the **R**ename To *button, delete the contents, type* **RSIDE**, *and choose the* **R**ename To *button*	Renames *NO NAME* to RSIDE
Click on *WORLD* *and choose* **C**urrent	Sets the WCS current
Choose OK	Accepts changes and resets the UCS back to the original WCS

Figure 2.26

The UCS Control dialog box, after changes.

You should also know about one final drawing aid that is available from the Drawing Aids dialog box: **I**sometric Snap/Grid.

Drawing Isometric Representations

AutoCAD LT's isometric features enable you to quickly and easily draw isometric representations of 3D objects. Although the resulting drawing is actually in 2D, just like an isometric drawing you draw on a drafting board, it has a 3D appearance due to the angles used.

AutoCAD LT's isometric features enable you to set the Grid, Snap, and Ortho drawing aids to three preset sets of isometric angles, called isometric planes (*isoplanes*). These isoplanes are called Top, Left, and Right because they align to the top, left, and right faces of an isometric cube (see fig. 2.27). The left isoplane is shown in figure 2.28. The coordinate system, however, does not change, rendering most coordinate values irrelevant to what you are drawing.

 Tip   Isometric mode is most useful when you can use relative polar coordinates at angles of 30, 90, 150, 210, 270, and 330 degrees. At these angles, relative distances are valid. You can either type relative polar coordinates or pick them using snap and the coordinate display. Using Ortho makes drawing at these angles easier.

Figure 2.27

The isoplanes on an isometric cube.

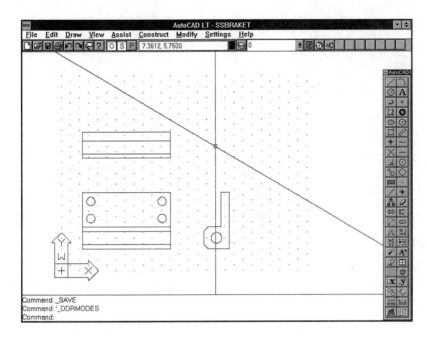

Figure 2.28

The grid and cursor in the left isoplane.

You can set Isometric mode with the SNAP command or the Drawing Aids dialog box. You can switch between isoplanes with the Drawing Aids dialog box or with the F5 or Ctrl+E keys.

You use Isometric mode to draw the shaft support in the following exercise. Use the relative polar coordinates display when picking points.

Using the Isometric Snap/Grid

Continue from any previous exercise in this chapter, with the WCS current and snap on (check the S button on the toolbar).

Command: *Turn on the O (Ortho) button*	Turns on Ortho mode
Command: *Click on the Drawing Aids button or tool*	Opens the Drawing Aids dialog box
In the **I***sometric Snap/Grid section, click in the* On *box*	Puts an X in the box and sets Isometric mode on
Choose OK	Closes the dialog box and turns on Isometric mode (see fig. 2.28)

continues

continued

The crosshairs and grid are now both skewed at exactly 30 degrees. This is the left isoplane, so draw the left face first.

Command: *Click on the Line tool*	Issues the LINE command
_LINE From point: *Pick the grid dot at ① (see fig. 2.29)*	Sets first point of line
To point: *Pick point 1.6<90 at ④*	Draws line
To point: **@4.2<330** (Enter)	Draws line to ③
To point: *Pick point 1.6<270 at ②*	Draws line
To point: **C** (Enter)	Draws closing line to ①
Command: *Press F5*	Switches to the top isoplane (see fig. 2.29)
<Isoplane Top>	
Command: (Enter)	Repeats the LINE command
LINE From point: *Pick ②*	Sets first point of line
To point: *Pick point 0.4<30 at ⑤*	Draws line
To point: *Pick point 4.2<330 at ⑥*	Draws line
To point: *Pick point 0.4<210 at ③*	Draws line
To point: (Enter)	Ends LINE command

The left and top faces should now look like figure 2.29.

Press Ctrl+E	Switches to the right isoplane
<Isoplane Right>	
Command: (Enter)	Repeats the LINE command
LINE From point: *Pick ⑥ (see fig. 2.30)*	Sets first point of line
To point: *Pick point 2.6<270 at ⑦*	Draws line
To point: *Pick point 1<210 at ⑧*	Draws line
To point: *Turn off Ortho and pick point 0.2<150 at ⑨*	Draws line

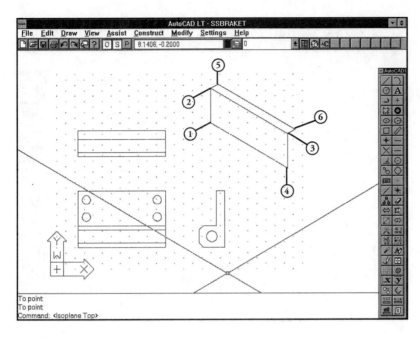

Figure 2.29

*Left and top faces
of the shaft
support.*

The 0.2 distance from ⑧ to ⑨ is misleading, but the point is 0.2 up and 0.2 to the left.

To point: *Pick point 0.6<90 at* ⑩   Draws line

To point: *Pick 0.3464<60 at* ⑪   Draws line

Again, the distance is misleading; the point is 0.2 up and 0.2 to the right.

To point: *Pick point 0.6<30 at* ⑫   Draws line

To point: **(Enter)**   Ends LINE command

Change to the left isoplane, draw a 4.2-unit line from ⑨ to ⑬, and continue drawing lines to match figure 2.30.

You also need to add bolt and shaft holes to the shaft support. To do this, AutoCAD LT provides an Isometric mode to its ELLIPSE command. In Isometric mode, the ELLIPSE command works much like the CIRCLE command, but draws ellipses aligned to the current isoplane. The ELLIPSE command is covered in Chapter 16, "Increasing Your Drawing Power with Polylines and Double Lines," but for drawing isometric holes in the following exercise, you can just follow the instructions here.

Figure 2.30

The isometric shaft support.

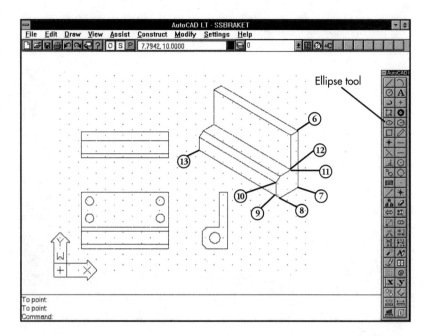

Drawing Isometric Circles

Continue from the preceding exercise, with the left isoplane set.

Command: *Choose* **D**raw, **E**llipse	Issues the ELLIPSE command
_ellipse	
<Axis endpoint 1>/Center/ Isocircle: **I** (Enter)	Sets Isometric mode
Center of circle: *Pick* ① (*see fig. 2.31*)	Sets center
<Circle radius>/Diameter: **.2** (Enter)	Draws ellipse in the left isoplane

Repeat the ELLIPSE command to draw the other three bolt holes in the left face.

Set the isoplane to the right face and repeat the ELLIPSE command with a 0.25-unit radius to draw the shaft hole in the right face, shown in figure 2.31.

Command: *Click on the Drawing Aids button or tool*	Opens the Drawing Aids dialog box

New Riders Publishing
INSIDE
SERIES

In the **I**sometric Snap/Grid *section, click in the* On *box*	Removes the X from the box
Click on OK	Closes the dialog box and turns off Isometric mode

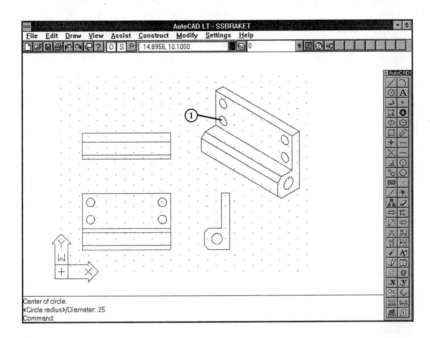

Figure 2.31

The shaft support with isometric holes.

Notice that when you switch from normal to isoplane mode, the Snap and Grid X Spacing options become unavailable. Only equal valued spacings are allowed in Isometric mode, so only the Y value, which applies to all isometric axes, can be set.

 Note Because this chapter deals with the grid, the grid is shown in this chapter's illustrations. In the rest of the book, the illustrations usually don't show the grid for clarity. You should, however, use the grid while you are working.

You have now been checked out on all the basic tools for controlling your drawing environment. You are ready to begin drawing with AutoCAD LT. The next chapter revisits the basic commands you glanced at in Chapter 1, "Getting Off the Ground: CAD Concepts 1A," and explores them thoroughly. You will also learn an essential communication skill: how to annotate a drawing with text.

The brakes are off and you are headed down the runway!

Keeping Track of Your Work: Drawings as Files

In CAD, drawings are stored on disk as data files. To use CAD effectively, you must be able to create, access, revise, and save these files. This chapter presents the tools and techniques for managing drawing files with AutoCAD LT. The following topics are included:

- How to use directories to organize your drawing files

- How to start a drawing with the NEW command

- What prototype drawings are and how to use them

- How to use the SAVE and SAVEAS commands to save your work

- What drawing files are and how your system stores them

- How to name drawing files

- How to open an existing drawing

- When to use the END or the EXIT command to leave AutoCAD LT

◆ How file locking works

◆ How AutoCAD LT searches for support files

When you keep your drawing files organized, they are easier for both you and your computer to find. The time you save more than compensates you for the effort required. This chapter gives you some guidelines for organizing your files.

No matter how much skill a pilot has, he can fly only one plane at a time. When you were working at a drafting table, you could work on only one drawing at a time. AutoCAD LT has a similar limitation: you can have only one drawing open at a time. Even so, you can change to a different AutoCAD LT drawing in less time than it takes to peel the tape off a paper drawing. Moreover, you have access to every drawing you need without leaving your desk.

Instead of using sheets of paper, AutoCAD LT uses the electronic media of computer disks to store your drawings. Each drawing is stored on a disk drive as a file of data that describes the drawing to AutoCAD LT. To work on a specific drawing, you must first load it from disk into AutoCAD LT's drawing editor. Then after you have worked on the drawing, you must save it back to disk.

Tip   If you are new to using Windows, you should read this entire chapter. If you are familiar with Windows, you might want to skip most of the text and just quickly step through the exercises. As you will see, AutoCAD LT's file operations are similar to most Windows applications. You should, however, read the sections on prototype, temporary and support files, as well as the file locking and file environment sections, for procedures unique to AutoCAD LT.

Appendix G, "The IALT Disk," explains how to set up a directory for the files that accompany the book, as well as how to create a separate icon to launch AutoCAD LT when you are working on the book's exercises. Appendix G shows you how to set up a "working directory" for AutoCAD LT in the Windows Program Manager. You can also use the same technique to create multiple unique configurations of the program.

Stop   The exercises throughout the rest of the book (including those in this chapter) assume that you have read Appendix G, "The IALT Disk," and have your system configured so that the files from the IALT disk are readily accessible. If you have not done so yet, do it now.

To organize your files, DOS provides a directory structure that you can access in Windows file dialog boxes. The next section shows you how to use this structure.

Using Directories to Organize Your Drawing Files

DOS and Windows use a file organization structure consisting of drives, directories, and subdirectories. In the first exercise, you use the AutoCAD LT OPEN command to examine this structure.

Looking at Files and Directories

Start AutoCAD LT using the IALT icon created by the Appendix G installation.

If using AutoCAD LT Release 2 choose Cancel in the Create New Drawing dialog box.

Click on the Open button (see fig. 3.1)	Issues the OPEN command and displays the Open Drawing dialog box

The DGWS\IALT directory should be current, as set up by the Appendix G installation.

Click in the Dri**v**es *list box*	Opens the Dri**v**es drop-down list
Use the slider bar to view the available drives, and click on the drive where you installed AutoCAD LT	Scrolls the list of available drives, selects the drive, and closes the list box
Click in the **D**irectories *list box*	Activates the **D**irectories list box
Double-click on the root directory, for example, on c:\	Displays all the directories under the root directory
Use the slider bar, if necessary, to find the ACLTWIN *directory, and double-click on* ACLTWIN	Sets the ACLTWIN directory current and lists its contents and subdirectories (see fig. 3.1)
Use the slider bar to view the available drawing files in the File **N**ame *list box*	Displays drawing files, including the SSBRAKET drawing from Chapter 2, "Specifying Locations in CAD Space"
Click on Cancel	Closes the Open Drawing dialog box without opening a drawing

3

Figure 3.1

The C:\ACLTWIN directory shown in the Open Drawing dialog box.

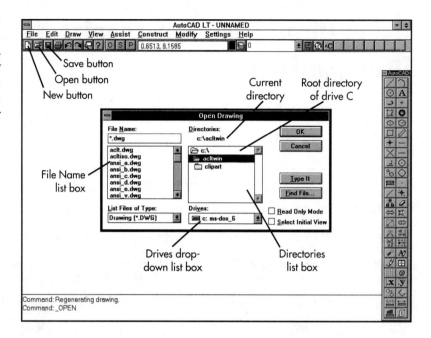

Notice that the file-folder symbols in the file list represent directories and sub-directories. These symbols are analogous to file folders in a cabinet. You often hear the DOS file structure referred to as a tree on which the directories and sub-directories branch off a common root directory. Each disk drive has its own root directory, and there is only one root directory per disk drive. People have one common problem with this directory tree analogy: most file management programs display the tree with the root directory at the top of the screen, so you have to imagine that the tree is hanging upside down.

The *path* to a file (or more simply, a file's path) is made up of the combined names of each directory or subdirectory under which a file might be stored. The file's path works in much the same way that your home address makes a path to your home. The state in your address indicates in which of the country's directories you live. The city indicates in which of the state's subdirectories you live. The street indicates which subdirectory of the city you are in, and your house number is the file name of your home in the street subdirectory. Notice that the same file name can occur in different locations and still be a unique address, just as someone on a different street, or in a different city or state, can have the same address number as you.

The directory structure is the way DOS organizes files. Directories, subdirectories, and files all have the same name constraints in DOS: the name cannot be more than eight characters in length, but it can have an optional extension name of up to three characters. A name can be any combination of letters, numbers, or the following

characters: exclamation point (!), number sign (#), dollar sign ($), apostrophe ('), parentheses ( ), hyphen (-), at sign (@), percent sign (%), caret symbol (^), amper-sand (&), underscore (_), back quote (`), braces ({ }), and tilde (~). The combination of the file's drive name, directory path, and the name of the file itself forms the file's full address.

You should use directory names to help keep track of what is kept in the directory. Make the directory names descriptive, and use the directory and subdirectory branch structure to make meaningful path names when they are combined into the full path. As you develop large collections of drawing files, you will need to keep them orga-nized. The easiest way to accomplish this organization is to start now. Use short descriptive names like DWGS for the directory off the root, and then use a specific contract name or number for each job's subdirectory. Creating deeper subdirectories can add even more organization; for example, C:\DWGS\IALT\CHAP03. If you have a large project, it might be wise to give the project its own directory off the root.

Working with File Commands

Having acquired an understanding of the structure in which AutoCAD LT's file commands operate, you can now turn your attention to the first of those commands and start a new drawing.

Starting a New Drawing

In AutoCAD LT, you use the NEW command, which opens the Create New Drawing dialog box, to start a new drawing. You can create a new drawing without a name; in fact, in AutoCAD LT Release 1 the Create New Drawing dialog box does not require you to supply a name, and in AutoCAD LT Release 2 the Create New Drawing dialog box does not even accept a name. If you do not name the drawing, AutoCAD LT assigns it UNNAMED as a temporary name.

You must, however, assign a name to your drawing to save it to disk. If you issue the SAVE command from an unnamed drawing, AutoCAD LT opens the Save Drawing As dialog box, and you must supply a name before it saves your work. If you issue the SAVE command from a named drawing, AutoCAD LT simply saves it. Any drawing is an investment of your time, and saving your drawing frequently protects against accidental loss.

You can start your drawing based on a *prototype drawing*. The prototype can contain a variety of predefined elements and settings tailored to your specific work. This method is like starting a new drawing from a copy of another.

ALT2

The Create New Drawing dialog box differs from AutoCAD LT Release 1 to AutoCAD LT Release 2. In AutoCAD LT Release 2, the Create New Drawing dialog box lacks features for specifying a new drawing name, but includes setup methods lacking in AutoCAD LT Release 1.

The next sections show you how to use the NEW command to start a drawing with the Create New Drawing dialog box and how to use prototype drawings.

Using the Create New Drawing Dialog Box

In the following exercise, you open the Create New Drawing dialog box (see fig. 3.2) using the NEW command. You also practice starting a new drawing under different circumstances.

Figure 3.2

The AutoCAD LT Release 1 Create New Drawing dialog box.

Figure 3.3

The AutoCAD LT Release 2 Create New Drawing dialog box.

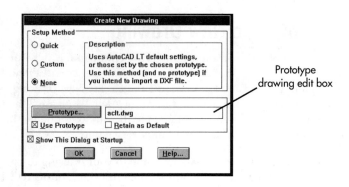

Using the Create New Drawing Dialog Box

Continue from the preceding exercise.

Command: *Click on the New button*

Issues the NEW command and opens the Create New Drawing dialog box (see fig. 3.2 or 3.3)

If using AutoCAD LT Release 1, type **NEWDWG** *in the* New **D**rawing Name *edit box and and press Enter*	Closes the Create New Drawing dialog box and starts a new drawing named NEWDWG
If using AutoCAD LT Release 2, choose **N**one *in the* Setup Method *section, then choose* OK	Bypasses the setup method feature, closes the Create New Drawing dialog box, and starts a new UNNAMED drawing
Command: *Click on the Line tool, and draw a line anywhere on the screen*	
Command: *Choose* **F**ile, **N**ew	Opens an AutoCAD LT alert box (see fig. 3.4)

AutoCAD LT always alerts you before closing the current drawing if any changes were made to it.

```
The current drawing has been changed.
Do you want to save the changes?
```

Click on **N**o, *or press* **N**	Abandons the changes and opens the Create New Drawing dialog box
If using AutoCAD LT Release 1, Click on the New **D**rawing Name *button*	Opens the Create Drawing File dialog box, which is similar to the AutoCAD LT Release 2 dialog box shown in figure 3.5
If using AutoCAD LT Release 2, choose OK	Closes Create New Drawing dialog box and starts an UNNAMED drawing
If using AutoCAD LT Release 2, click on the Save button	Issues the SAVE command and opens the Save Drawing As dialog box (see fig. 3.5)
Double-click on the DWGS *directory (see fig. 3.5)*	Makes the DWGS directory current
Double-click in the File **N**ame *edit box, and enter* **NEWDWG**	Returns to the Create New Drawing dialog box and places the drawing name and path in the New **D**rawing Name edit box
Press Enter, or click on OK	Creates a new drawing named NEWDWG in the DWGS directory

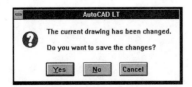

Figure 3.4

An AutoCAD LT alert box: you must save the file or lose your changes.

Figure 3.5

The Save Drawing As dialog box.

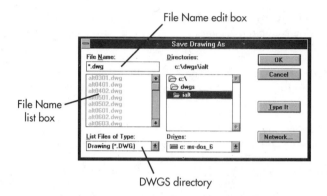

Notice that the Create New Drawing dialog box opens with the cursor in the New **D**rawing Name edit box. You only need to enter a file name to complete the command. Similarly, the Save Drawing As or Create Drawing File dialog box opens with the cursor in the File **N**ame edit box. The SAVE command is completely covered later in this chapter.

In AutoCAD LT Release 1, when you click on the New **D**rawing Name button in the Create New Drawing dialog box, the Create Drawing File dialog box opens. When you save an UNNAMED drawing, the nearly identical Save Drawing As dialog box opens. The default file list shows the files with a DWG extension in the working directory. The file names appear grayed out, but you can choose a name from the list. When you are creating a series of drawings with similar names, because you can click on and edit an existing name. The name you enter is then passed back to the Create New Drawing dialog box or used to save the file, with a complete path.

NEW. The NEW command is used to create a new drawing in AutoCAD LT. A drawing name can be assigned, and a prototype drawing can be designated.

 Stop   The NEW command opens the Create New Drawing dialog box as long as the FILEDIA system variable is set to 1 (on). This system variable controls AutoCAD LT's automatic display of dialog boxes. You can change this setting only at the command line, by entering **FILEDIA**. If no dialog boxes appear when you use the NEW command, check the status of your FILEDIA variable.

Using the Create New Drawing dialog box is simple: you type a file name, then press Enter or click on OK. Or, in AutoCAD LT Release 1, you can click on the New **D**rawing Name button to open the Create Drawing File dialog box, which offers the same file and directory features as the Save Drawing As dialog box (see fig. 3.3):

◆ **File Name.** The File **N**ame edit box is the default focus where you enter a file name. If the dialog box focus is elsewhere, a single click positions the cursor for text editing, and a double-click highlights for text replacement.

◆ **File Name list box.** The File Name list box displays existing files of the specified file type.

◆ **Dri**v**es.** The Dri**v**es drop-down list box enables you to select a different disk drive. A single click selects a drive and changes the list in the **D**irectories box to the drive's current path setting.

◆ **Directories.** The **D**irectories box lists the current drive and directory along with any subdirectories. A double-click selects a directory and lists the files that match the type specified in the **L**ist Files of Type box.

◆ **List Files of Type.** The **L**ist Files of Type drop-down list sets the file extension for the files that are listed in the File **N**ame edit box. The default is Drawing(*.DWG). The list scrolls to enable you to choose a file extension from a selection of 20 with a single click.

To help you match names or avoid using the same name, you can use the File Name list box to see what file names already exist (and the **D**irectories box to see where they are). The file names in the File Name list box are grayed out to remind you that using the same name overwrites the original. You can create a series of names, such as CAMSHFT1, CAMSHFT2, and so on, simply by selecting an existing name and changing the desired character to create a unique name. The new file is created in the selected drive and directory (when saved).

The Create New Drawing dialog box in both Release 1 and 2 provides a powerful option called a *prototype*. The next section explores the use of prototype drawings.

Using Prototype Drawings

The Create New Drawing dialog box has a section for specifying a prototype drawing name (if any) to be used as the starting point for a new drawing. The following exercise explores the use of a prototype specification.

Using a Prototype Drawing

Continue from the preceding exercise, or start AutoCAD LT using the IALT icon.

Command: *Click on the New button (unless the* Create New Drawing *dialog box is already open)*

Issues the NEW command and opens the Create New Drawing dialog box

Click on the **P***rototype button (see fig. 3.6)*

Opens the Prototype Drawing File dialog box

Click on the Dri**v***es list box, and select a different drive*

Changes the drive and directory to your choice

Click on the **D***efault button*

Resets the drive and directory to the default (where AutoCAD LT is installed)

Use the Dri**v***es and* **D***irectories list boxes as required to access the directory where your* Inside AutoCAD LT *files are located*

Selects the C:\DWGS\IALT directory (if the book files were installed in the default directory)

In the file name list box, click on the ALT0301.DWG *file (scroll the list as required to reach this file)*

Selects the ALT0301 drawing as the prototype drawing file

Click on OK

Closes the Prototype Drawing File dialog box and displays C:\DWGS\IALT\ALT0301 in the Create New Drawing dialog box

If using AutoCAD LT Release 2, choose OK, then click on the Save button

Closes the Create New Drawing dialog box, opens an UNNAMED drawing with an ANSI B-size drawing border, and opens the Save Drawing As dialog box

In the New **D***rawing Name edit box (in AutoCAD LT Release 1) or* File **N***ame edit box (in AutoCAD LT Release 2), enter* **ANSI-B** *(type it and press Enter)*

Closes the Create New Drawing or Save Drawing As dialog box and creates a new drawing named ANSI-B with an ANSI B-size drawing border (see fig. 3.7), which it inherited from the ALT0301 prototype

---

Figure 3.6

The Prototype Drawing File dialog box.

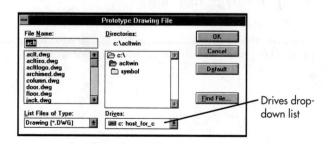

Drives drop-down list

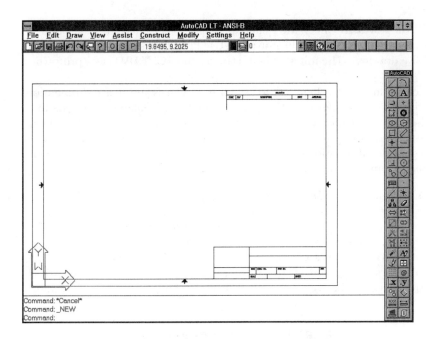

Figure 3.7

*Starting a
drawing from
a prototype.*

The Prototype Drawing File dialog box is similar to the Create Drawing File dialog box described in the preceding section. The Prototype Drawing File dialog box has the same features for selecting drives, directories, file types, and file names. The files are not grayed out because the overwrite hazard is not present. The Default button restores all selections to the current prototype file and its location.

What is the concept of a prototype all about? A *prototype* drawing serves as a pattern or template when creating a new drawing. The new drawing takes on all the settings, configuration, objects, and named references or definitions—everything contained in the prototype. In other words, the new drawing begins as a clone of the prototype. AutoCAD LT ships with two sample prototype drawings: ACLT.DWG (set up for American/English sheet size and units) and ACLTISO.DWG (set up for ISO/metric). The differences between these sample prototype drawings are minor.

The Create New Drawing dialog box has two additional check-box options relating to the prototype drawing:

♦ **No Prototype.** In AutoCAD LT Release 1, check the **N**o Prototype box to start a new drawing with the AutoCAD LT defaults. This is equivalent to using the default ACLT.DWG prototype.

♦ **Use Prototype.** In AutoCAD LT Release 2, clear **U**se Prototype box to start a new drawing with the AutoCAD LT defaults. This is equivalent to using the default ACLT.DWG prototype.

◆ **Retain as Default.** Check the **R**etain as Default box to make the specified prototype drawing or the **N**o Prototype or **U**se Prototype setting the default for successive drawings. The initial default is to use the ACLT.DWG as a prototype.

Default prototypes are an excellent way to establish standards and to avoid repetitious setup procedures, such as snap and grid settings. You can use default prototypes to get a "running start" on typical drawings; you then simply make the specific modifications and issue the drawing. You also can use portions of an existing drawing, such as background graphic information or notes. To create prototype drawings, remove job-specific elements and save them as a general-purpose detail.

In AutoCAD LT Release 1, you can specify a prototype without using the Prototype Drawing File dialog box. To use this method, open the Create New Drawing dialog box and enter a new drawing name in the New **D**rawing Name edit box, with the format NEW=OLD, where NEW is the new drawing name and OLD is an existing drawing name (see fig 3.8). Keep in mind, however, that this method is open to typographical errors. Also, if you are specifying existing files in different directories, it may be faster to use the Prototype Drawing File dialog box than to type their path names.

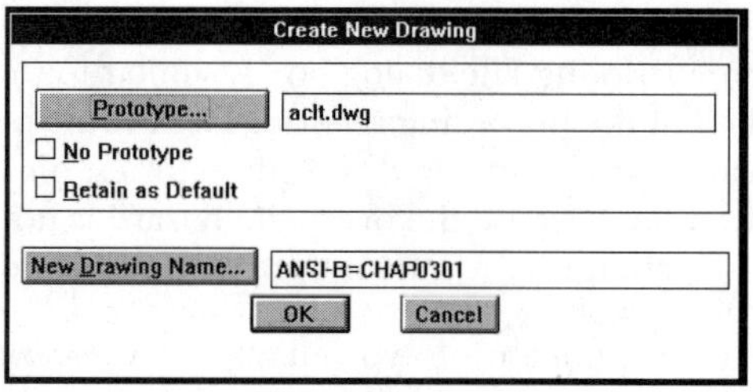

Figure 3.8

Creating the ANSI-B drawing using the NEW=OLD format in AutoCAD LT Release 1.

Create New Drawing
Prototype...   aclt.dwg
☐ No Prototype
☐ Retain as Default
New Drawing Name...   ANSI-B=CHAP0301
OK   Cancel

Note   This book uses the prototype mechanism to start exercise drawings in which you work with files provided on the IALT disk. You start the exercise drawing by using the drawing from the disk as a prototype. This technique leaves the original drawing unaltered if you have a power failure or if you simply want to perform the exercise again.

So far in this chapter, you have only started new drawings. AutoCAD LT doesn't actually write a file to disk (other than an autosave file, which is discussed later in this chapter) until you use another file command—the SAVE command, which you have used several times if you are using AutoCAD LT Release 2. The next section fully explores saving drawings.

Saving Your Drawing

AutoCAD LT makes it easy to save your work. You can save a drawing in several ways: by clicking on the Save button on the toolbar (shown earlier in figure 3.1), by choosing **F**ile and then **S**ave from the pull-down menu (see fig. 3.9), or by entering SAVE on the command line.

The following exercise demonstrates these methods for saving a drawing.

Saving a Named Drawing

Continue from the previous exercise, with the ANSI-B drawing open.

Command: *Click on the Save button*	Issues the SAVE command and saves the drawing
Command: *Choose* **F**ile, **S**ave	Issues the QSAVE command and saves the drawing again
Command: **SAVE** (Enter)	Saves the drawing again
Command: **SA** (Enter)	Uses the command alias to issue the SAVE command and save the drawing

SAVE

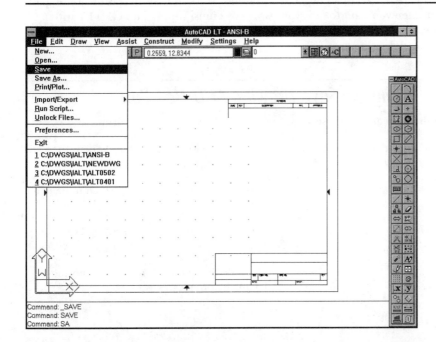

3

Figure 3.9

The Save and Save As menu items on the File menu.

> **SAVE.** The SAVE command saves your drawing to a file on disk. The current drawing's path and file name are used if a name has been assigned. If the file already exists, the SAVE command first renames it with a BAK extension.

Note The pull-down menu issues the QSAVE command, which works the same as the SAVE command in AutoCAD LT. (The name originates from a "Quicksave" command in earlier versions of the AutoCAD program.)

As you can see, using the SAVE command with a named drawing file is easy; you simply issue the command, and AutoCAD LT writes the file to disk and then returns control to you. The SAVE command works differently with an unnamed drawing, as you will see in the next section.

Using the Save Drawing As Dialog Box

When you save an unnamed drawing, the SAVE command opens the Save Drawing As dialog box. You can also use the Save Drawing As dialog box to save a named drawing, giving it a different name.

When you first start AutoCAD LT, or begin a new drawing in AutoCAD LT Release 2, or when you use the NEW command in AutoCAD LT Release 1 and don't specify a file name, you are placed in an unnamed drawing. You can draw in this file as long as you like, but when you want to save your work, you must supply AutoCAD LT with a name for the file. In the following exercise, watch what happens when you attempt to save an unnamed drawing.

Using the Save Drawing As Dialog Box

Continue from the preceding exercise, or start AutoCAD LT using the IALT icon.

Command: *Click on the New button (unless the* Create New Drawing *dialog box is already open)*
Issues the NEW command and opens the Create New Drawing dialog box

Choose OK, *or press Enter*
Closes the dialog box and starts an unnamed drawing

Click on the Save button
Opens the Save Drawing As dialog box (see fig. 3.10) *with* *.dwg *in the* File **N**ame *edit box*

Click on OK
Rejects the command; requires a drawing name before it can save

Scroll to the bottom of the File Name list and double-click on the ANSI-B.DWG *file*	Specifies an existing name and displays an alert box (see fig. 3.10)
Click on **N**o *or press N*	Aborts and returns to the Save Drawing As dialog box
Enter **MYDWG** *in the* File **N**ame *edit box (type it and press Enter or choose* OK)	Specifies MYDWG as the name, closes the Save Drawing As dialog box, and saves the drawing with the new name

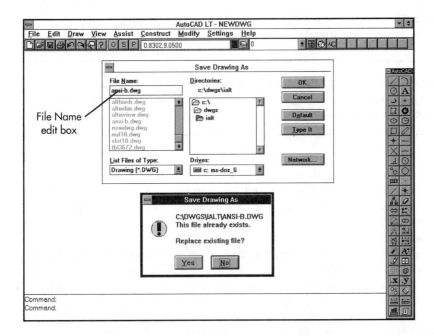

File Name edit box

Figure 3.10

The Save Drawing As dialog box and its alert box.

3

AutoCAD LT will not save an unnamed drawing. When you choose a file name, AutoCAD LT is careful not to allow you to overwrite an existing file with SAVE or SAVEAS (similar to the NEW command). If you choose not to overwrite an existing file, AutoCAD LT returns to the Save Drawing As dialog box.

The Save Drawing As dialog box is almost identical to the Create Drawing File dialog box discussed earlier. The difference between these two dialog boxes is in the results achieved: the Create Drawing File dialog box simply assigns a name to the current drawing in AutoCAD LT's memory, whereas the Save Drawing As dialog box follows through and stores the drawing as a file on disk. This difference is important to recognize, because if you exit AutoCAD LT without saving your work, you will lose it. All the information stored in the computer's memory (RAM) is abandoned when you exit AutoCAD LT. If your system fails for some reason, the information is also lost.

Tip Save your work frequently to avoid losing it in the event of a power or computer failure. Also, see the Automatic Save section, later in this chapter.

The Save Drawing As dialog box has two buttons not found in the other dialog boxes you have looked at so far:

◆ **Default.** Click on the D̲efault button to set the file type to *.DWG and the drive and directory to the AutoCAD LT working directory.

◆ **Type It.** Click on the T̲ype It button to close the Save Drawing As dialog box and enter a file name directly on the command line.

SAVEAS. The SAVEAS command opens the Save Drawing As dialog box and enables you to save your drawing to a file on disk after renaming it. You can assign a new path as well as a new file name.

Stop If the file name you supply to the SAVEAS command already exists, the existing file is overwritten and cannot be recovered; however, you are warned by the alert box that this will happen. The SAVEAS command does not create a backup file (a file with a BAK extension).

When entered at the command line, the SAVEAS command opens the Save Drawing As dialog box directly. The SAVEAS command tells AutoCAD LT to change the name of the current drawing and save to a file under the new name. The SAVEAS command can be used to create a new design based on an existing one, like a prototype drawing, without overwriting the existing one. Just open the desired existing drawing, then use SAVEAS to save it with a new name. The SAVEAS command gives you a good way to pursue "what-if" scenarios. With SAVEAS, you can save a series of variations or options based on a similar design.

The SAVE and SAVEAS commands raise a major issue—how to name your drawings. The next section discusses this issue of file names.

Working with File Names

A key element in good CAD management is the careful specification of file names. This aspect of CAD is too often overlooked. Files that have been assigned cryptic names tend to get lost and end up as mysteries that clutter disk directories. Inattention to this seemingly minor detail can reduce the efficiency of your CAD system; therefore, it is well worth your time to consider this issue.

New Riders Publishing
INSIDE SERIES

First, what is a *file*? AutoCAD LT stores drawings as data files on disk. AutoCAD LT drawing data files are binary (machine-readable) files stored under a proprietary format established by Autodesk. These files are fully compatible with AutoCAD Release 11 and 12 on all computer platforms supported by AutoCAD.

AutoCAD LT, being a Windows application, uses files that have DOS file characteristics. As discussed earlier, these characteristics include an eight-character name with a DWG file extension. Like directory names, file names should be chosen to help you keep your work organized. A typical job can have many drawing files. Plan your file names so that they can cover the entire job in an easy-to-follow format.

Your computer can assist with sorting and searching if you set up your files correctly. With only eight characters, file names usually represent some kind of code. When establishing such a code, you should keep several key points in mind:

◆ Do not include a date in the file name unless it has some special significance, because DOS always stores files with a date/time stamp.

◆ Structure your file names with the most general information at the beginning of the name and the most specific at the end (for example, *JOB,DISCIPLINE,SHEET*# might be ABCMECH1 or ABC-M001).

◆ Use a template when creating names for similar files. In other words, decide on a key *character string* (a series of numbers or characters) for the start of the name, and then use the last characters to make each name unique. This system keeps similar files grouped together in the directory and keeps them sorted in sequence when listed alphanumerically.

◆ Use leading zeros, when applicable, for numeric strings. Your computer then sorts the file names in the correct order. For example, use ABC-M001, ABC-M002...ABC-M099...ABC-M100, not ABC-M1, ABC-M2...ABC-M99... ABC-M100.

When files are listed alphanumerically in ascending order, numbers precede letters and are sorted from 0 to 9. Letters are treated as capitalized and sorted from A to Z. The sort sequence for all the valid characters in ascending order is as follows:

! # $ % & ' ( ) - <numbers **0** to **9**> @ <letters **A** to **Z**> ^ _ ` { } ~

This order is established by the ASCII code value of the characters. Your Windows manual has a list of the Extended ASCII Character Set codes.

Almost any system for naming your drawings is better than no system at all. An easy approach is to choose the eight most significant characters you use when you are filing a print of the drawing. The issue of drawing names becomes especially critical when you exchange files with clients or contractors (see the discussion of this issue in Chapter 24, "Moving Beyond the Basics"). Documenting a standard for naming drawings helps operators to conform and actually saves time by removing indecision when selecting a new file name. People can cooperate more readily when the reasons for a naming convention are made clear.

The focus of this chapter has been on new files. You also need to know how to recall an existing drawing when you want to work on it.

Working with an Existing Drawing

Most of the work you do in AutoCAD LT involves existing drawings. For this reason, AutoCAD LT provides easy access to these files with the Open Drawing dialog box. You already have used this dialog box to explore directory structures in the first exercise of this chapter. In the following exercise, you use the OPEN command to open and look at one of the drawings from the *Inside AutoCAD LT for Windows, Second Edition* disk.

Using the Open Drawing Dialog Box

Continue from the preceding exercise or start AutoCAD LT using the IALT icon.

If using AutoCAD LT Release 2, choose Cancel in the Create New Drawing dialog box.

Command: *Click on the Open tool (refer to figure 3.1 or the inside cover illustraion, if needed)*	Issues the OPEN command and displays the Open Drawing dialog box (see fig. 3.11)
Scroll, if needed, to locate the ALT0502.DWG *file name, then double-click on it*	Opens the drawing named ALT0502
Command: *Press Enter or choose* **F**ile, **O**pen	Issues the OPEN command and redisplays the Open Drawing dialog box
Find and double-click on ANSI-B.DWG	Repens the ANSI-B.DWG drawing
Command: **OPEN** (Enter)	Displays the Open Drawing dialog box
Double-click on MYDWG	Reopens the MYDWG drawing

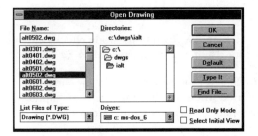

Figure 3.11

*The Open
Drawing
dialog box.*

> **OPEN.** The OPEN command closes the current drawing (prompting you to save any changes) and retrieves a specified drawing file from disk. You can specify the path as well as the file name.

The OPEN command displays the Open Drawing dialog box. Most of the elements in this dialog box are familiar if you have worked through this chapter's exercises. The Open Drawing dialog box has the following standard file features:

◆ **Drives.** The Drives drop-down list enables you to select a different disk drive.

◆ **Directories.** The Directories list enables you to select a different directory.

◆ **List Files of Type.** The List Files of Type drop-down list setting determines the type of file that is displayed.

◆ **File Name.** The File Name edit box and list enable you to select a file name by choosing it from the list or by entering it directly. If you double-click or press Enter, the designated file opens and the Open Drawing dialog box closes.

◆ **OK.** The OK button accepts the designated file name and closes the Open Drawing dialog box.

◆ **Cancel.** The Cancel button cancels the command and closes the Open Drawing dialog box.

◆ **Type It.** The Type It button closes the Open Drawing dialog box and takes you to the command line with the prompt Enter name of drawing followed by the current default drawing name, which you can accept by pressing Enter.

In addition, the Open Drawing dialog box offers three new options:

◆ **Read Only Mode.** Click on the **R**ead Only Mode check box to open a drawing for viewing or for using as a prototype only.

◆ **Select Initial View.** Click on the **S**elect Initial View check box to specify a named view to be displayed when the drawing opens. (Chapter 5, "Navigating Views in the CAD Workspace," discusses named views.)

◆ **Find File.** Click on the **F**ind File button to open the Find File dialog box discussed in the next section.

> **Tip**
>
> AutoCAD LT will open any valid AutoCAD drawing file regardless of the file's extension, but it will only save to a file with a DWG extension. You can use this feature to protect your prototype drawings from being accidentally overwritten. To do so, use the DOS COPY, RENAME, or MOVE commands or the Windows File Manager to rename prototype files to an extension other than DWG.

Although the commands described in the preceding sections are essential tools for putting together a set of drawings and developing your designs, the OPEN command is central to managing your drawings. AutoCAD LT's OPEN command provides access to any existing drawing. You also can use the OPEN command to view any drawing files in your system. Whether you are a designer or an engineer, a CAD operator or a project manager, the OPEN command is your means of monitoring drawings.

Using the Find File Dialog Box

The Open Drawing dialog box provides one way of tracking down drawing files with the **F**ind File button. When you click on the **F**ind File button, the Find File dialog box opens. In the following exercise, you use this dialog box to search your system for drawing files.

Using the Find File Dialog Box

Continue from the preceding exercise, or open the MYDWG file you created earlier.

Command: *Click on the Open tool*	Issues the OPEN command and displays the Open Drawing dialog box (refer to fig. 3.11)
Click on the **F**ind File *button*	Opens the Find File dialog box (see fig. 3.12)
Click on the **E**dit Path *button*	Opens the Edit Path dialog box (see fig. 3.12)

*Click on the path name listed in the **S**earch Path list box, then click on the **D**elete button*	Removes the current directory from the Search Path list box
*Double-click on the DWGS directory in the **D**irectories list box*	Places the DWGS directory in in the **P**ath edit box
*Click on the **A**dd button*	Places the DWGS directory in the **S**earch Path list box
*Double-click on the IALT directory in the **D**irectories list box, then click on the **A**dd button*	Adds the IALT directory to the **S**earch Path list box, as shown in figure 3.12
*Click on the **C**lose button*	Returns to the Find File dialog box

In the Search Location box, make sure that Path Only appears in the Dri**v**es drop-down list box. If not, open the list box and select it.

*Click on the **S**tart Search button*	Lists the number of drawing files found, and lists their names in the F**i**les Found list box
Click on the Cancel button	Closes the Find File dialog box
Click on the Cancel button	Closes the Open Drawing dialog box

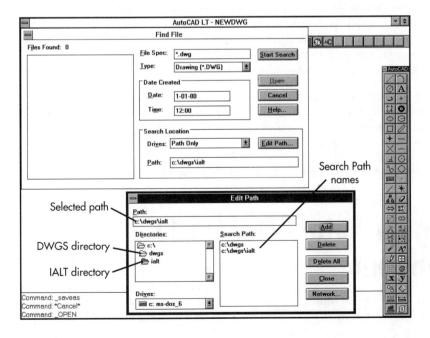

Figure 3.12

The Find File and Edit Path dialog boxes.

3

The preceding exercise uses the **E**dit Path option in the Find File dialog box to search the DWGS and IALT directories for drawing files. When you close the Edit Path dialog box, it returns the search path(s) you chose to the Find File dialog box. When you click on the **S**tart Search button, Find File then performs a search of the Search Location path.

Notice that the Edit Path dialog box has options for creating not only a multiple-directory search path but also a search path across multiple drives, if necessary. In addition, the Find File dialog box has options for selecting files based on a file type other than *.DWG or the file date.

Although you have only skimmed the surface of this powerful tool, remember that if you don't know the name of a file, or don't know where a file is located, Find File can help you. As your skills and knowledge of the AutoCAD LT environment increase, you will find the other Find File options easy to understand.

So far, this chapter has discussed the NEW, SAVE, SAVEAS, and OPEN commands. The final file command in this chapter applies only at the end of an AutoCAD LT design session—the EXIT or QUIT command.

Leaving AutoCAD LT

When the time comes to leave AutoCAD LT, you can type **EXIT** or **QUIT** and press Enter, or you can choose **F**ile and then E**x**it. Before closing, if you have made any changes since the last time you saved the drawing, AutoCAD LT asks if you want to save the changes. As with the NEW and OPEN commands, the Save Drawing As dialog box opens if you say you want to save and the current drawing is unnamed. If you want to exit and save your drawing without being asked, enter **END**.

AutoCAD LT is a Windows application, so the standard methods for terminating a Windows application also apply. You can double-click on the control menu button or press Alt+F4. As with the EXIT command, an alert box opens with an option to save if there are any unsaved changes.

When you exit AutoCAD LT, control returns to the Program Manager.

Setting Up AutoCAD LT's File Environment

AutoCAD LT offers several settings that affect the way it works with files. With these settings, you can prevent two people from working on a drawing simultaneously, save

your work automatically at regular intervals, and control where AutoCAD LT looks for its support files and stores its temporary files. The file control settings are accessed from the Preferences dialog box.

Using the Preferences Dialog Box

To customize AutoCAD LT, you can make many changes. You can effect most of these changes from the Preferences dialog box. The AutoCAD LT Release 2 Preferences dialog box is shown in figure 3.13. The AutoCAD LT Release 1 version is similar, but differs slightly in its layout and lacks the Menu File and User Name items. This chapter covers file-related aspects of the Preferences dialog box; other features are covered in Chapter 9, "Tailoring Your Work Environment." The file settings tell AutoCAD LT where to look for and where to place various files.

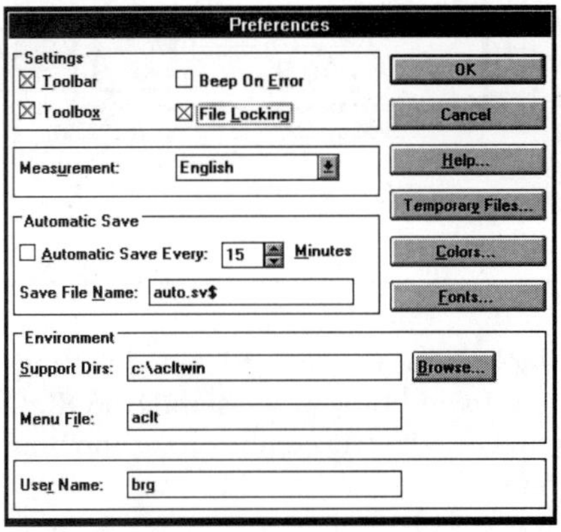

Figure 3.13

The Preferences dialog box.

In the following exercise, you open the Preferences dialog box but make no changes. The purpose of the exercise is to familiarize you with the controls that are available.

Using the Preferences Dialog Box

Continue from the preceding exercise, or reopen the MYDWG file you created earlier.

Choose **F**ile, Pre**f**erences   Opens the Preferences dialog box (see fig. 3.13)

Examine the dialog box

Click on the Temporar**y** Files *button*   Opens the Temporary Files dialog box

continues

continued

Notice that with the **U**se Drawing Directory box checked (the default), the **D**irectory and **B**rowse features are disabled (see fig. 3.14).

Click on the Cancel *button*	Closes the Temporary Files dialog box
Click on the Cancel *button*	Closes the Preferences dialog box

---

Figure 3.14

The Temporary Files dialog box.

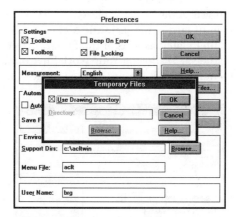

Notice that the Preferences dialog box has four areas labeled Settings, Measurement, Automatic Save, and Environment. In addition to the standard OK, Cancel, and **H**elp buttons, the Preferences dialog box also has three buttons at the bottom labeled Temporar**y** Files, **C**olors, and **F**onts.

The following list briefly describes the file-related Preferences dialog box settings:

◆ **File Locking.** The File **L**ocking check box enables or disables the file-locking function (described later in this section).

◆ **Automatic Save Every:.** The **A**utomatic Save Every: check box enables or disables the automatic save feature (described later in this section).

◆ **Minutes.** The **Mi**nutes edit box specifies the time interval for the automatic save feature.

◆ **Save File Name.** The Save File **N**ame edit box specifies the file name that is used by the automatic save feature.

◆ **Support Dirs.** The **S**upport Dirs edit box specifies AutoCAD LT's file search path (described later in this section).

◆ **Temporary Files.** The Temporary Files button opens the Temporary Files dialog box, which is used to specify where AutoCAD LT places its temporary files (described later in this section).

The purpose of this section of the chapter is to examine those settings related to files; specifically, file locking, automatic save, support directories, and temporary files. For more information on the other Preferences dialog box settings, see Chapter 9, "Tailoring Your Work Environment."

Understanding File Locking

File locking is a feature that supports the use of AutoCAD LT in a networked environment. In such an environment, it is possible for one person to open a drawing file that someone else is working on without either party being aware of the other's efforts. Under such circumstances, the network drawing file will only reflect the work of the last person to save her work because the work the previous person saved is overwritten. To avoid such an incident, AutoCAD LT offers a file-locking mechanism, and AutoCAD LT Release 2 offers control over the user name. The file lock feature creates a file with the same name as the drawing file and a DWK extension. As long as this DWK file exists, AutoCAD LT does not allow anyone to open the DWG file.

Checking the File **L**ocking box in the Preferences dialog box enables the file-locking function. When you try to open a file that is already in use, you get an alert message that states Unable to lock file.... The message also specifies whether the file was opened by an AutoCAD LT user and when the file was opened. This alert message indicates that the file is already open and that AutoCAD LT prevents a second user from also opening it.

In AutoCAD LT Release 2, the Use**r** Name edit box in the Preferences dialog box enables you to specify a unique user name, which is used by AutoCAD LT Release 2 to identify what user is working on a file or has locked a file.

ALT2

If you turn off your system or experience a system failure while working in a locked file, you might need to unlock the file before you can resume working on it. The final section of this chapter discusses how to unlock files.

Note File locking serves no purpose unless you are working on a network where others might access your files. If so, make sure the File **L**ocking check box is checked. However, if you are not working on a network, clear the File **L**ocking check box to avoid the nuisance of having to unlock files after a system or power failure.

Controlling the Automatic Save Feature

A good habit to develop is to save your work frequently. This habit can spare you the frustration of having to re-create your work after a power failure or a system crash. Remembering to periodically save your drawing file can be difficult, however, especially when you are concentrating on what you are trying to do. To relieve you of this need to remember, AutoCAD LT has an automatic save feature. In the following exercise, you enable this feature.

Enabling the Automatic Save Feature

Continue from the preceding exercise.

Choose **F***ile,* Pre**f**erences	Opens the Preferences dialog box
Put a check in the **A**utomatic Save Every *check box*	Activates the automatic save feature

If you want to change the time interval, double-click in the The Every: [nn] **M**inutes box and enter a new value, or click on the up or down arrow buttons to change the time interval.

Click on the OK *button*	Closes the Preferences dialog box

With the automatic save feature enabled, AutoCAD LT saves your work to the specified file name at the specified interval. The automatic save feature actually requires some command to be issued before it checks the clock, so it will not continue to save a file that is dormant while you are at lunch. If required, the automatic save feature saves upon completion of the next command.

The default file name that is used for the save file is AUTO.SV$. If you decide to change this file name, be sure to choose a name or an extension you will never use for an actual drawing to avoid accidentally overwriting your work. The time interval can be any number of minutes from 1 to 600 (10 hours). Set the time interval to be frequent enough not to lose much work, but not so frequent as to become a nuisance.

If the power fails or your system crashes, use the OPEN command and specify the AUTO.SV$ file in the **F**ile Name edit box. If the file represents the latest version of your drawing, use the SAVEAS command to rename it as your working drawing and then continue.

Setting Up AutoCAD LT's Search Path

AutoCAD LT uses several types of files, collectively referred to as support files. These support files include the following:

◆ The ACLT.MNU and ACLT.MNX menu files (these define the short menu in AutoCAD LT Release 1, or the standard and only menu in AutoCAD LT Release 2)

◆ The full menu files (ACLT2.MNU and ACLT2.MNX) in AutoCAD LT Release 1

◆ Various text font style files (*.SHX)

◆ Various PostScript font files (*.PFB)

◆ English and metric linetype files (ACLT.LIN and ACLTISO.LIN)

◆ The English and metric hatch pattern files (ACLT.PAT and ACLTISO.PAT)

AutoCAD LT accesses these support files in a variety of ways. Each time you open a drawing, for example, AutoCAD LT looks for a menu file. Similarly, any drawing file can be inserted into another with the INSERT command (described in Chapter 18, "Leveraging Repetitive Design and Drafting"). AutoCAD LT needs to know where support files are located before it can use them.

In AutoCAD LT Release 2, the Menu File edit box enables you to specify a default menu name independently of the search path.

ALT2 **3**

AutoCAD LT can only find support files located in the current working directory or in a directory specified in a support directory's search path. To create a search path, enter the full drive and path name in the **S**upport Dirs edit box of the Preferences dialog box. The default path is the AutoCAD LT directory (the directory in which you installed AutoCAD LT). You can add other paths by separating them with a semicolon, or you can click on the **B**rowse button to open the Edit Path dialog box (which functions like the Find File dialog box, described earlier in this chapter).

Locating Temporary Files

AutoCAD LT opens several temporary files while you work. These temporary files have extensions such as AC$ and serve to manage your screen image, divide large drawings into manageable pieces, keep a record of your work in case you want to undo, and perform many more background functions. The temporary files are closed and removed when you exit AutoCAD LT properly. By default, these temporary files are opened in the same directory as your drawing.

The Temporary Files button in the Preferences dialog box opens the Temporary Files dialog box. You can use this dialog box to specify a different path for your temporary files. You must first clear the **U**se Drawing Directory box and then enter the desired directory name. The **B**rowse button opens the Edit Directory dialog box, which enables you to select a directory in a manner similar to the Edit Path dialog box.

Using the File Pull-Down Menu

You already have seen or used most of the commands found on the **F**ile pull-down menu. This section briefly describes the remaining selections.

The full **F**ile pull-down menu includes all the file commands described earlier in this chapter, as well as the following selections:

◆ **Print/Plot.** The **P**rint/Plot selection opens the Plot Configuration dialog box (as does the Plot button on the toolbar). Chapter 23, "Producing Hard Copy," covers plotting.

◆ **Import/Export.** The **I**mport/Export selection leads to a child menu with options for working with several file formats other than AutoCAD LT's own drawing files. Supported formats include AutoCAD slides (*.SLD), Drawing Interchange (*.DXF), Windows Metafile (*.WMF), and PostScript files (see fig. 3.14).

AutoCAD LT comes with a symbol library installed under the AutoCAD LT directory if the default installation is used. The symbol library is divided into four subdirectories named ARCHITEC, BUSINESS, ELECTRON, and ENGINEER. These subdirectories are further divided by topic. A total of 376 Windows Metafiles are located in the topic subdirectories. You can import these files directly into your drawings by using the **I**mport menu's **W**MF In feature.

◆ **Run Script.** The **R**un Script selection opens the Select Script File dialog box. Script files enable you to run automated or "canned" sequences of AutoCAD LT commands stored in an ASCII text file.

Script files are AutoCAD LT's way of automating your drawings. A script file is an ASCII text file containing sequences of commands, options, location and angle data, text, and any other information you could otherwise enter at the command line. AutoCAD LT reads a script file just as it would read your input from the command line.

◆ **Unlock Files.** The **U**nlock Files selection opens the File(s) to Unlock dialog box, which enables you to remove invalid *.DWK drawing lock files without having to leave AutoCAD LT (see the discussion of file locking earlier in this chapter).

If you suffer a power failure or your system crashes while you are in AutoCAD LT, you will probably need to use the **U**nlock File feature before accessing the drawing and menu you were in prior to your system's failure. To unlock a file, simply select the locked file's name from the File **N**ame list and answer **Y**es to the alert box prompt. If you are on a network, be sure to check with the network supervisor first.

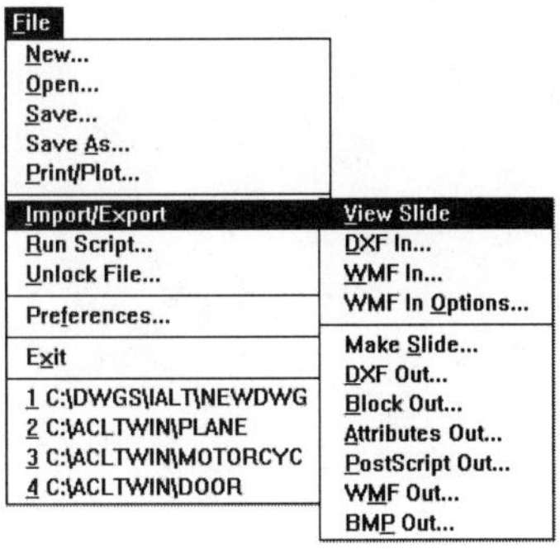

File	
New...	
Open...	
Save...	
Save As...	
Print/Plot...	
Import/Export	View Slide
Run Script...	DXF In...
Unlock File...	WMF In...
	WMF In Options...
Preferences...	
	Make Slide...
Exit	DXF Out...
1 C:\DWGS\ALT\NEWDWG	Block Out...
2 C:\ACLTWIN\PLANE	Attributes Out...
3 C:\ACLTWIN\MOTORCYC	PostScript Out...
4 C:\ACLTWIN\DOOR	WMF Out...
	BMP Out...

Figure 3.15

The File pull-down menu with the Import/Export child menu open.

Tip

The AutoCAD LT **F**ile pull-down menu includes a shortcut for reopening a drawing file in which you recently worked. The last items (up to four) on the **F**ile pull-down menu list the most recently open drawings. To open one of these drawings, simply click on its name in the list (you will be prompted if there are any unsaved changes to the current drawing).

Now that you have seen how space is defined in AutoCAD LT (see the discussion on coordinates in Chapter 2, "Specifying Locations in CAD Space") and how the information you create (the drawing file) is stored and retrieved, it's time to start learning how to fly AutoCAD LT.

3

C H A P T E R

4

Building a Drawing: Using Basic Drawing Tools

The first step toward preparing intelligent CAD documents is to learn to use the basic drawing tools appropriately. This chapter shows you how to use the AutoCAD LT tools that create four common geometric objects found in drawings: lines, arcs, circles, and points. Then you learn to create and place text objects and to annotate your drawings. Along the way, you learn to use all the options available for each of these drawing commands, and you gain some insight into their most appropriate uses.

In this chapter, you will learn:

◆ How to draw lines, arcs, and circles

◆ How to place point objects

◆ How to create and place text

◆ How to use these objects to create the geometry and annotation you need for a particular drawing

The majority of drawings are made up mostly of the elements you learn to create in this chapter, and the methods you use to create them are typical of the way most of the other drawing commands in AutoCAD LT work.

The most effective uses of CAD rely on an intelligent construction of the drawing database. With paper drawings, it is the job of those who create and use a drawing to interpret the symbols correctly, based on their own knowledge and experience. With a well-constructed CAD drawing, you can query the drawing database to learn more about a particular object.

In paper drawings, objects are just pictorial representations—pencil marks on a page. In a CAD drawing, you create objects with exact definitions. With CAD, you can integrate into a drawing a wealth of information that the manual drafting process cannot include.

Creating Lines, Arcs, Circles, Points, and Text

Lines, arcs, and circles are the three most common objects in most drawings. It follows that the commands you use the most often are the ones that create these objects. You use the LINE command to draw a straight line, CIRCLE to draw holes, and ARC or PLINE (polyline, a series of lines and/or arcs) to draw curves. The POINT command creates a point object. Although the point object is not as useful as lines, arcs, and circles, it comes in handy sometimes. Nearly every drawing requires the use of the TEXT command for annotation.

You have already used three of the basic drawing commands. In the exercise in Chapter 1, "Getting Off the Ground: CAD Concepts 1A," you drew a simple figure. Then, in Chapter 2, "Specifying Locations in CAD Space," you learned about coordinates, and about some of the tools for positioning objects precisely. In this chapter, these tools are combined with the basic drawing commands to show you how to create objects with more accuracy. The exercises focus on creating the elements found in the fixture base shown in figure 4.1.

The exercises in this chapter use the ALT0401.DWG file as a prototype drawing. Because metric units are appropriate for this mechanical drafting, this file was created using the ACLTISO.DWG instead of the ACLT.DWG as a prototype. Distances and coordinates represent millimeters.

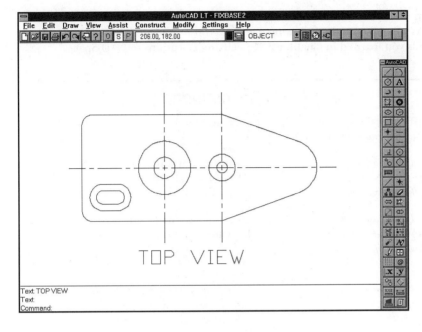

Figure 4.1

*The fixture base
with view title
text.*

Although ALT0401.DWG appears to be an empty drawing file, it includes several important settings. Snap is set to 2, grid is set to 10, Ortho is off, and the drawing is zoomed to the area in which you will initially draw. This drawing is set up for center and hidden linetypes as well as continuous lines. Linetypes (and drawing colors) in this drawing are controlled by *layers*. Drawing on layers is somewhat like manual drafting on transparent overlays. The initial layer is CENTER, for drawing centerlines. Layers and linetypes are covered comprehensively in Chapter 8, "Preparing Your Workspace: CAD Concepts 1B," and Chapter 10, "Getting Organized: Drawing on Layers."

Working with Lines

The most common object in a drawing is the line. Lines are versatile. Construction lines are frequently used for laying out geometry. Centerlines are used to locate other geometry. Border lines indicate a drawing's constraints. Hidden lines show features obscured by other features. The majority of edit commands work with lines. Creating lines is one of the most basic drafting tasks in AutoCAD LT.

The first step in the fixture base drawing is laying out centerlines with the LINE command. As you do so in the following exercise, you'll practice some of the point entry methods you learned in Chapter 2, "Specifying Locations in CAD Space."

Using the LINE Command

Start AutoCAD LT using the IALT icon. Unless the Create New Drawing dialog box is already open, click on the New button to open it.

If using AutoCAD LT Release 1, type **FIXBASE=ALT0401** *in the* New Drawing Name *input box, then choose* OK	Creates new drawing file named FIXBASE in the DWGS\IALT directory, using ALT0401 as a prototype
If using AutoCAD LT Release 2, make sure Setup Method **N**one *is selected, then type* **ALT0401** *in the Prototype input box and choose* OK	Creates new unnamed drawing file using ALT0401 as a prototype
If using AutoCAD LT Release 2, choose the Save button, *type* **FIXBASE** *in the* File **N**ame *input box, then choose* OK	Opens the Save Drawing As dialog box, and names and saves the drawing file as FIXBASE in the DWGS\IALT directory
`Command: Choose `**D**`raw, `**L**`ine`	Issues the LINE command
`_line From point: `**38,88** (Enter)	Starts the line at ① (see fig. 4.2)
`To point: `**@208,0** (Enter)	Specifies a relative X,Y coordinate and draws a line to ②

The resulting line has a center linetype because it was drawn on the CENTER layer.

`To point: `*Click on the Line tool*	Cancels the current line and issues the LINE command again
`Command: *Cancel*`	
`Command: _LINE From point:` **112,32** (Enter)	Starts the line
`To point: `*Turn on the Ortho toolbar button (click on it)*	Turns on Ortho mode

If the coordinate display doesn't show distance<angle coordinates, click in it once or twice until it does.

`<Ortho on> `*Pick point 112.00<90.00, using the coordinates display*	Picks a relative polar point to draw a 112 mm line at 90 degrees

`To point:` *Press Enter or click the Enter mouse button*	Ends the LINE command
`Command:` `L` (Enter)	Issues the LINE command using the command alias
`LINE From point:` *Pick point 156,144*	Starts the line
`To point:` **@112<270** (Enter)	Specifies a relative polar point
`To point:` *Press Ctrl+C* `*Cancel*`	Cancels the LINE command

The resulting centerlines are shown in figure 4.2.

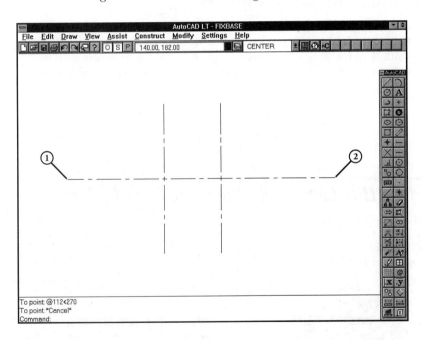

Figure 4.2

Centerlines created with the LINE command.

AutoCAD LT indicates what it is drawing by showing you a rubber-band line from the previous point to the cursor position. The rubber-band line enables you to visualize how the line will appear if you pick a point at the current location of the crosshair pointer.

LINE. The LINE command draws one or more straight 2D or 3D line segments. Press Enter at the From point: prompt to continue from the endpoint of the last line drawn or tangent to the last arc drawn. Enter **C** at the To point: prompt to close two or more line segments, creating a line from the last endpoint to the original start point. Press Enter or cancel at the To point: prompt to end the LINE command.

Tip You can activate the Drawing Aids dialog box to control the snap and grid spacing, as needed, while you are in the LINE command.

The LINE Undo and Close Options

In the preceding exercise, you created all the centerlines you need for this portion of the drawing. They were drawn with the predefined linetype set for the CENTER layer. To create the outline of the fixture base, using a continuous linetype, you need to make OBJECT the current layer. Notice that the toolbar displays the current layer name.

In the following exercise, you first change the current layer from CENTER to OBJECT. Then you draw the first object lines, using the Undo and Close options of the LINE command. You will draw a closed rectangle, and then erase one of the lines.

Using the LINE Command's Undo and Close Options

Continue from the preceding exercise.

Command: *On the toolbar, click on* Pulls down a list of the layers
CENTER *in the layer name box* defined in the drawing (see fig 4.3)

Click on OBJECT *in the layer name list* Sets the OBJECT layer current

---

Figure 4.3

The layer name lists in AutoCAD LT Releases 1 and 2.

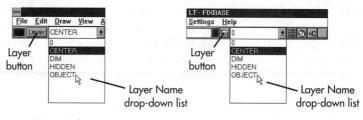

AutoCAD LT Release 1   AutoCAD LT Release 2

Command: *Click on the Line tool*   Issues the LINE command

_LINE From point: *Pick point 156.00,*   Starts at the upper right corner, on the
128.00 at ① *(see fig. 4.4)*   centerline

To point: *Pick point 108.00<180.00 at* ②   Draws a 108 mm line at 180 degrees

To point: *Pick point 80.00<270.00 at* ③   Draws an 80 mm line at 270 degrees

To point: *On the toolbar, click in the*   Switches the display to X,Y coordinates
coordinate display

Next, you deliberately pick the wrong point instead of 156,48, so you can see how to recover
from such errors.

<Coords on> *Pick point 150,48*   Draws a line just short of the centerline

Next, you use the LINE command's Undo option to recover from selecting this point.

To point: *Enter* **U** *or click on the Undo*   Undoes the last line segment
button (see fig. 4.4)

_U

To point: *Pick point 156,48 at* ④   Draws a 108 mm line to the centerline

Next, you use the Close option to close the rectangle.

To point: *Enter* **C** *or click on the Close*   Draws a line closing the rectangle (see
button or tool   fig. 4.4) and ends the LINE command

The fixture base is angled at the right end, so the right side of the rectangle is not actually
needed. See if Undo will remove it.

Command: *Click on the Undo button*   Undoes the entire previous LINE command

_U LINE   Removes the entire rectangle

When you undo a completed LINE command, all line segments created during the command
are removed. Use REDO to recover from the undo.

Command: *Click on the Redo button*   Restores the four lines

_REDO

Command: *Pick the line at* ⑤   Highlights the line and displays its grips

Type **E** *and press Enter*   Issues the ERASE command and erases
     the line

continues

continued

Figure 4.4

The closed rectangle.

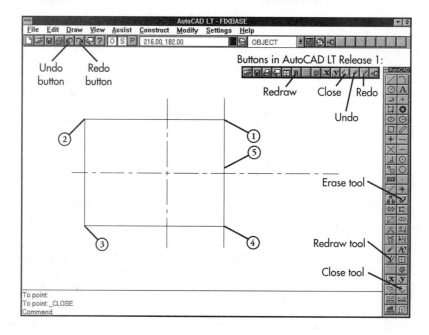

```
_ERASE 1 found
```

Now the needed three sides are displayed, but a portion of a centerline appears to be missing.

| Command: *Click on the Redraw button or tool* | Issues the REDRAW command |
| `'_REDRAW` | Restores the image of the centerline (see fig. 4.5) |

 Note   When you erase or move an object in CAD, objects underneath the object you erased or moved are not affected. They may temporarily disappear until the image is redrawn, however.

LINE Command Options

The LINE command gives you some versatility with the following five options.

◆ **From point.** At the `From point:` prompt, your input specifies the first point of the first line.

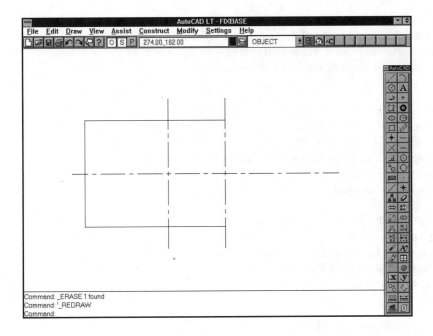

Figure 4.5

Three sides of the fixture base.

◆ **Continue.** Press Enter at the From point: prompt to start the line from the endpoint of the most recently drawn line or arc.

◆ **To point.** At the To point: prompt, your input specifies the point to which a line is drawn from the previous point.

◆ **Undo.** At the To point: prompt, you enter **U** (Undo) or click on the Undo button on the toolbar to undo the last line segment, stepping back to the previous point.

◆ **Close.** At the To point: prompt, you enter **C** (Close) or click on the Close button or tool to close a series of two or more line segments. AutoCAD LT creates a line from the last endpoint to the first point of the series.

Note that pressing Enter or clicking the Enter mouse button at the From point: prompt will set the start point of the line at the endpoint of the most recently drawn line or arc. When starting from an arc, the line is started tangent to the arc. Pressing Enter or the Enter button at the To point: prompt ends the LINE command. You can also end the LINE command by clicking on the Cancel (^C) button on the toolbar or by pressing Ctrl+C.

4

The Undo option is handy when only the last line segment in a series is wrong. If you enter **U** repeatedly to undo several line segments, you will step back through the sequence of points you picked. Undo makes it easy to remove incorrect segments without having to exit and restart the LINE command.

Tip When you are creating a long chain of line segments, press Enter (or click the Enter button) three times when you are satisfied with your progress. By pressing three times, you will close one LINE command, start another, and resume from the last endpoint. Then, if you use the U (Undo) command at the command prompt, it will undo only the last LINE command's series of segments instead of all the segments. You cannot, however, use the Close option to close the entire chain.

If you try to use the LINE command's Close option with only one line segment drawn, you will get a `Cannot close until two or more segments drawn` error message. If you create two segments in line with each other and use the Close option, a third segment will be created over the top of the other two. You will then have three objects drawn when only one is needed.

Tip Ortho mode is especially helpful for creating lines that are perpendicular to the X,Y axes. The Ortho button on the toolbar and the function key F8 make it easy for you to switch Ortho on and off, even during a command.

Using the ARC Command

The ARC command is used to create circular arcs. It can be used in the same way you would draw with a traditional compass, but its options make it much easier to draw an arc. Like the LINE command, ARC can be controlled with drawing aids.

In the following exercise, you will draw an arc by specifying three points on its circumference, then undo it and draw two other small arcs to round the corners of the fixture base. Use the coordinates display and snap to aid in picking points.

Using the ARC Command

Continue in the drawing from the preceding exercise.

Command: **ARC** (Enter)   Begins the ARC command

Center/<Start point>: *Pick point 156,48*   Sets the start point of the arc
at ① *(see fig. 4.6)*

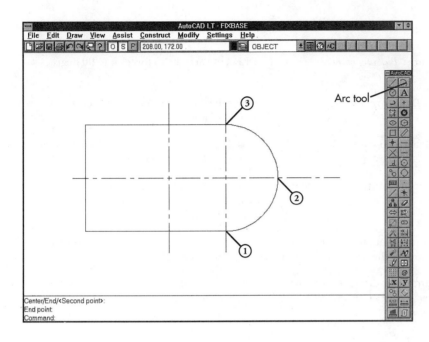

Figure 4.6

Drawing a three-point arc.

`Center/End/<Second point>:` *Pick point 196,88 at* ②

Sets second point of the arc

Drag the cursor and watch the rubber-band arc stretch.

`End point:` *Pick point 156,128 at* ③

Sets the endpoint and draws the arc

`Command:` *Click on the Undo button*

Removes the arc

`_U ARC`

`Command:` *Choose* **D**raw, **A**rc, *then* Start, Center, **E**nd

Issues the ARC command with Start, Center, End option

`_arc Center/<Start point>:` *Pick point 56,128 at* ④ *(see fig. 4.7)*

Sets the start point of the arc, then the menu issues the Center option for the next point

`Center/End/<Second point>: _c Center:`
56,120 (Enter)

Specifies the center of the arc at ⑤

Move the cursor around and watch the rubber-band arc snap to 90-degree increments because Ortho is on.

continues

continued

Angle/<End point>: *Pick any point near 40,120*	Draws the arc; ortho forces it to 90 degrees
Command: *Choose* **D**raw, **A**rc, *then* Start, Center, **A**ngle	Issues the ARC command with Center and Angle options
_arc Center/<Start point>: *Pick point 48,56 at* ⑥	Sets the start point of the arc, then the menu issues the Center option
Center/End/<Second point>: _c Center: **@8,0** (Enter)	Specifies the center of the arc at ⑦ with relative coordinates, then the menu issues the Angle option

Turn off the Ortho button, move the cursor and watch the arc drag. The angle controlled by the cursor is relative to the arc's center, with zero degrees to the right.

Angle/<End point>: _a Included angle: *Turn on Ortho and pick any point directly above the arc's center*	Specifies a 90-degree angle and draws the arc (see fig. 4.7)
Command: *Click on the Save button*	Saves your drawing to disk

Figure 4.7

Creating rounded corners with the ARC command.

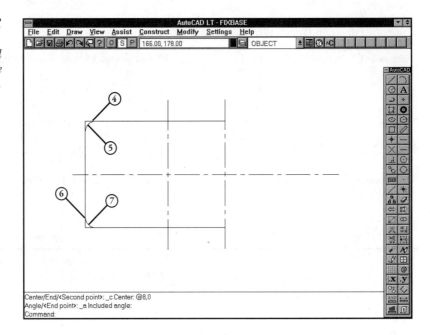

Unlike the LINE command, the ARC command ends when the arc is completed. In addition to the menu items that issue ARC with specific options, you can issue the default 3 point ARC command with the **3** Point Arc menu item or the Arc tool.

> **ARC.** The ARC command creates a circular arc. You can choose the arc's dimensions and location by specifying three pieces of information. This information may be any combination of the start point, a point on the circumference, endpoint, center, and included angle that defines an arc. The default is a three-point arc that uses a starting point, a point on the arc, and an endpoint.

Notice the effect that Ortho mode has on the ARC command. With Ortho on, arcs with their center point specified are created with included angles that are multiples of 90 degrees. Right-angle curves are easy to create by this method.

 Note   An arc is not drawn until all three pieces of information have been supplied. If you cancel the command before you supply the third piece of information, nothing is created.

Although the ARC command has a number of options, the command itself is simple to use. When AutoCAD LT prompts you to do so, provide the point or angle requested. When you give AutoCAD LT enough information, it draws the arc and completes the command.

When AutoCAD LT has enough information to do so, it drags a rubber-band arc as you move the cursor to indicate how it will draw the arc.

ARC Command Options

You can control the information you provide and the order in which you provide it with the ARC command's options.

♦ **Start point.** At the Start point: prompt, your input specifies the first point of the arc. This option is the default.

♦ **Second point.** At the Second point: prompt, your input specifies a second point of a three-point arc, anywhere on the curve of the arc.

♦ **Center.** You can enter **C** to prompt for a center point. At the Center: prompt, your input specifies the center of the arc.

♦ **End.** You can enter **E** to prompt for an endpoint. At the End point: prompt, your input specifies the endpoint of the arc.

◆ **Angle.** You can enter **A** to prompt for the included angle. At the `Included angle:` prompt, your input specifies the included angle of the arc. By default, the base angle is from the center point to the start point and the angle is measured counterclockwise.

◆ **Continue.** Press Enter at the `Start point:` prompt to begin an arc tangent to the last line or arc object created.

To define an arc in AutoCAD LT, you must supply three pieces of information chosen from the list of start point, second point, endpoint, center point, and/or included angle. The valid combinations of these values yield the seven sets of options. When you use the Continue option, the starting point and angle are taken from the preceding line or arc, and only the endpoint is required to complete the arc. You often need to think ahead a little to know how and where to start an arc and which options to use to have AutoCAD LT create the arc you want. The **H**elp menu provides help on all seven combinations.

Note   If you use the cursor to indicate the angle, the input angle is counterclockwise relative to the arc's center point and with zero degrees being to the right, but the resultant angle is applied to the arc's base angle from the center point to the start point.

You do not need to remember all the combinations if you use the **D**raw pull-down menu. The short menu has the three most common options listed, and the full menu lists all seven possible combinations (see fig. 4.8). You can also follow the command prompts and enter the indicated option letters according to the information most available to you for creating the arc.

Figure 4.8

The full Arc pull-down child menu.

Draw	
Line	
Arc	Start, Center, End
Circle	Start, Center, Angle
	Start, End, Angle
Text	Center, Start, End
Polyline	Center, Start, Angle
Point	3 Point
Hatch...	
Solid	Continue Line/Arc
Donut	
Ellipse	
Polygon	
Rectangle	
Double Line	
Insert Block...	
External Reference ▶	
Linear Dimensions ▶	
Ordinate Dimensions ▶	
Radial Dimensions ▶	
Angular Dimension	
Leader	

Tip   AutoCAD LT draws arcs counterclockwise by default. To draw an arc clockwise, use a negative value for the included angle.

The Continue Option

The ARC and LINE commands can be used in conjunction with one another by using their Continue options. The following exercise demonstrates this feature, creating the slotted hole in the fixture base.

Using the Arc and Line Continue Option

Continue in the drawing from the preceding exercise and make sure the Ortho button is on.

Command: *Click on the Line tool*	Issues the LINE command
_LINE From point: *Pick point 64,56 at* ① *(see fig. 4.9)*	Starts the lower line of the slot
To point: **@12,0** (Enter)	Draws line to ②
To point: *In the toolbox, click on the Arc tool*	Cancels the LINE command and starts the ARC command
_ARC Center/<Start point>: (Enter)	Specifies the Continue option and starts the arc tangent to the line
End point: *Pick point 76,76 at* ③	Draws the arc
Command: *Click on the Line tool*	Issues the LINE command
_LINE From point: (Enter)	Specifies the Continue option and starts the line tangent to the arc
Length of line: **12** (Enter)	Specifies the length and draws the line to ④
To point: *Click on the Arc tool*	Cancels the LINE command and starts the ARC command
_ARC Center/<Start point>: (Enter)	Specifies the Continue option and starts the arc tangent to the line
End point: *Pick the endpoint of the lower slot line at* ①	Completes the arc and finishes the slot (see fig. 4.9)

4

Figure 4.9

The fixture base with a slot.

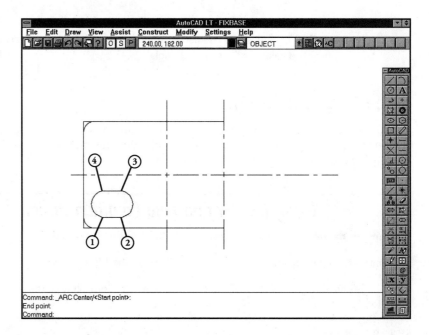

The finished example drawing of the fixture base shows the part with rounded corners on the left side. You have the tools now to create the outline of the part using the LINE and ARC commands with the Continue option.

Note   Chapter 14, "Making More Changes: Editing Constructively," explains the FILLET command, which is an easy alternative way to create arcs tangent to adjacent lines.

Using the CIRCLE Command

The third basic geometric element you will find in most designs is the circle. Circles are used to represent holes, wheels, shafts, columns, trees, instrument symbols, and so on. As with manual drafting methods, you use tools in CAD for constructing circular geometry, but the tools present in AutoCAD LT provide precision and instant construction that is unimaginable with a compass.

Use the CIRCLE command to draw the holes and sleeves in the fixture base.

Using the CIRCLE Command

Continue in the drawing from the preceding exercise.

Command: *Click on the Circle tool*	Issues the CIRCLE command
`_CIRCLE 3P/TTR/<Center point>:` *Pick point 156,88 at* ① *(see fig. 4.10)*	Sets the center of the circle

Move the cursor and watch the radius and rubber-band circle drag. The coordinate display shows changing X,Y coordinates as you drag (if not, click on it until it does).

If you are using AutoCAD LT Release 1, the prompt will be `Radius:` instead of the following:

`Diameter/<Radius>:` *Click twice in* *the coordinate display on the toolbar*	Changes the display to polar coordinates— watch them change as you drag
`<Coords off> <Coords on>` *Pick point* *4.00<0.00 at* ②	Sets the circle radius to 4 mm and draws the circle
Command: `Enter`	Repeats the CIRCLE command
`_CIRCLE 3P/TTR/<Center point>:` `@Enter`	Re-enters the last point and sets the center of the circle

The following prompt is for AutoCAD LT Release 1 users:

`Radius <4.00>:` *If using AutoCAD LT* *Release 1, enter* **10**	Specifies a radius and draws the circle

The following two prompts are for AutoCAD LT Release 2 users, who have a diameter option available:

`Diameter/<Radius> <4.00>:` *If using* *AutoCAD LT Release 2, enter* **D**	Prompts for the diameter
`Diameter <8.00>:` **20** `Enter`	Specifies a diameter and draws the circle
Command: *Choose* **D**raw, **C**ircle, **3** point	Starts a circle with the three-point option
`_circle 3P/TTR/<Center point>: _3p` `First point:` *Pick point 104,88 at* ③	Sets the first point on the circle 8 mm to the left of the left centerlines
`Second point:` *Pick point 112,96 at* ④	Sets the second point on the circle 8 mm above the centerlines

Move the cursor and watch the rubber-band circle drag. Notice that X,Y coordinates are being displayed, which reminds what you to input next.

continues

4

continued

Figure 4.10

Using the CIRCLE command.

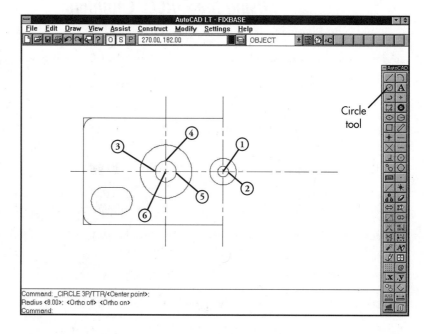

Circle tool

Third point: *Pick point 120,88 at* ⑤	Sets the second point on the circle 8 mm above the centerlines
Command: *Click the Enter button*	Repeats the CIRCLE command in its default center-radius mode
CIRCLE 3P/TTR/<Center point>: *Pick point 112,88 at* ⑥	Sets the center point

Next, experiment with the effects of Ortho mode.

Radius <8.00>: *Turn off the Ortho button*	Turns off Ortho mode

Move the cursor around while watching the polar coordinate display. Notice the odd radius values that are generated.

<Ortho off> *Turn on the Ortho button*	Turns on Ortho mode

Move the cursor while you watch the polar coordinate display. Notice that the values are all increments of the snap setting.

<Ortho on> *Pick a radius of 20*	Draws the circle (see fig. 4.10)
Command: *Click on the Save button*	Saves your drawing to disk

> **CIRCLE.** The CIRCLE command can draw circles by using nearly any geometric method. The most common method (the default) is to specify the center point and radius. You can drag and pick the size of the circle on screen, or specify the radius with a keyboard entry.

CIRCLE Command Options

The CIRCLE command provides you with several options for controlling the sequence in which you create the circle. In addition to the default center point and radius shown in the command definition, you can create a circle by specifying three points on the circumference, or by selecting two objects (lines, circles, or arcs) to which the circle is to be tangent, and then specifying a radius.

◆ **Center point.** You type or pick the center point, and the CIRCLE command then prompts you for a radius.

If you are using AutoCAD LT Release 2, the prompt, `Diameter/<Radius>` `<default>:` also offers a diameter option.

◆ **Radius.** The radius option is the default. When AutoCAD LT prompts you for the radius, you enter a distance or pick two points to show a distance for the radius.

◆ **Diameter.** If you are using AutoCAD LT Release 2 and want to specify the circle by its diameter, enter a **D** at the `Diameter/<Radius>` prompt, then specify a distance for the diameter.

◆ **3P.** (3 point) You enter **3P** to prompt for three points. The points you enter specify a circle by three points on the circumference.

◆ **TTR.** (Tangent-Tangent-Radius) You enter **T** to prompt for two tangential objects and a radius. Then, select two line, circle, or arc objects that form tangents to the circle, and specify a radius.

All of the previous methods are available in the **C**ircle submenu on the **D**raw pull-down menu. The menu items issue the CIRCLE command along with the indicated options.

You can use the Ortho and Snap modes together when picking the radius of center-radius circles to force the radius value to an increment of the snap setting. Ortho mode has no effect when creating circles with the 3P option. Although you can use the 3 point option to create an extremely large circle from points close together, AutoCAD LT prevents you from specifying colinear points, which would make a circle of infinite radius.

The Tangent-Tangent-Radius Option

The last circle creation option, TTR, introduces two new concepts, the tangent spec and the object snap box. Experiment with the TTR option in the following exercise.

Creating Circles Tangent to Other Objects

Continue in the drawing from the preceding exercise.

Command: *Choose **D**raw, **C**ircle, then **T**an,* Tan, Radius	Issues CIRCLE command with the Tangent, Tangent, Radius option
`_circle 3P/TTR/` `<Center point>:_ttr`	Displays an object snap box at the crosshairs
Enter Tangent spec: *Pick anywhere on* *top line near* ① *(see fig. 4.11)*	Specifies that the circle is to be tangent to the line
Enter second Tangent spec: *Pick the* *left side line near* ②	Specifies that the circle is also to be tangent to this line
`Radius <20.00>:` **16** (Enter)	Specifies a radius of 16 mm and draws the circle
Command: *Click on the Circle tool*	Issues the CIRCLE command in its default center-radius mode
`CIRCLE 3P/TTR/<Center point>:` **TTR** (Enter)	Specifies the Tangent, Tangent, Radius option
Enter Tangent spec: *Pick the circle you* *just created*	Selects the first object for tangency
Enter second Tangent spec: *Pick the* *large circle at* ③	Selects the second object for tangency
`Radius <16.00>:` **8** (Enter)	Specifies the radius
`Circle does not exist.`	Indicates that the specified parameters do not create a circle

Try the same tangency elements with a larger radius.

Command: *Choose **D**raw, **C**ircle, then **T**an,* Tan, Radius	Starts a circle with the TTR option

`Enter Tangent spec:` *Again pick the circle you just created*	Selects the first object for tangency
`Enter second Tangent spec:` *Pick the large circle at* ③	Selects the second object for tangency
`Radius <16.00>:` *Pick point 84,100 at* ④	Sets the first point of a distance to specify radius
`Second point` *Turn off Ortho and switch the coordinate display to X,Y mode*	
`<Ortho off> <Coords on>` *Pick point 88,112 at* ⑤	Creates the circle using the distance between the two points as the radius (see fig. 4.11)
`Command:` *Click on the Undo button three times, then click on the Redraw tool or button*	Removes the tangent circles, also resetting Ortho and coordinate modes, and then redraws

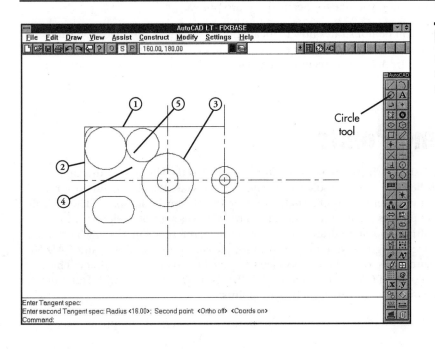

Figure 4.11

Creating circles tangent to other objects.

4

Drawing a circle with the Tangent-Tangent-Radius option has two unique aspects. The first is the `Tangent spec:` prompt. AutoCAD LT is simply asking you to select an object to which you want the desired circle to be tangent. The command attempts to draw a circle with the radius you specify by finding points of tangency between the objects you select (not an easy task with only a compass and straightedge). This type of intelligence is found in many CAD operations and becomes familiar to you as you use AutoCAD LT more.

The object snap box mentioned in the exercise defines the area in which AutoCAD LT searches for objects to consider for the tangent spec. In this exercise, there was only one object in the box. The object snap box is used for geometric *object snap* modes, which are explained in more detail in Chapter 11, "Achieving Accuracy: The Geometric Power of CAD."

The second unique feature is the radius specification. Because the circle's center is not yet known, the program cannot display the usual rubber-band line radius. You can enter a radius value or specify two points to "show" AutoCAD LT a radius. You can use any method you like to specify these two points.

The next section demonstrates how to locate points at a given distance. You can combine points with object snap modes to provide precise construction references (see Chapter 11, "Achieving Accuracy: The Geometric Power of CAD," for further details).

Drawing Points

The most basic drawing command is POINT. POINT is the simplest of drawing commands because it is used solely to create its namesake. Points are dimensionless and abstract representations of a single location in 3D coordinate space. The default point object plots as a dot, and as such, has little value as a graphic element. In manual drafting, you often draw temporary points as reference marks to which you later measure or align, or you use points to stipple surfaces or sections. AutoCAD LT provides better ways to do these tasks (see Chapter 11, "Achieving Accuracy: The Geometric Power of CAD," and Chapter 17, "Dressing Up Drawings with Hatching"), but you will occasionally resort to drawing points.

In the following exercise, you create a few points and change their appearance.

Using the POINT Command

Continue from either the "Using the CIRCLE Command" or the "Creating Circles Tangent to Other Objects" exercises.

Command: *Click on the Point tool* (*see fig. 4.12*)	Starts the POINT command
`_POINT Point:` *Pick* ① (*see fig. 4.12*)	Draws a dot

You can't see the point very well because it is obscured by a blip, unless you have turned BLIPMODE off.

Command: *Click on the Redraw tool or button*	Redraws and displays the dot

The point is a single-pixel dot, which is still a bit hard to see. You can change the way it appears.

Command: *If using AutoCAD LT Release 1, choose* **S**ettings, **F**ull Menu	Switches to the full menu (AutoCAD LT Release 2 has only a full menu)
Command: *Choose* **S**ettings, **Po**int style	Opens the Point Style dialog box (see fig. 4.13)
`'_ddptype` *Click on a point style other than the first and second*	Changes the current point style setting
Click on OK	Closes the dialog box
Command: *Choose* **D**raw, **Po**int	Issues the POINT command and repeats it until canceled
`_point Point:` *Pick three more point locations*	Displays points (see fig. 4.12)
Command: `_point Point:` *Press Ctrl+C*	Cancels the POINT command
`*Cancel*`	

The new points display in the new style, but the original point will not until regenerated.

Command: *Choose* **V**iew, **Reg**en	Issues REGEN command
`_regen Regenerating drawing.`	Regenerates and displays original point in new style

Click on the Undo button repeatedly until all points are undone.

Command: *If using AutoCAD LT Release 1, choose* **S**ettings, **S**hort Menu	Switches back to short menu

Figure 4.12

*Points displayed
with style 34.*

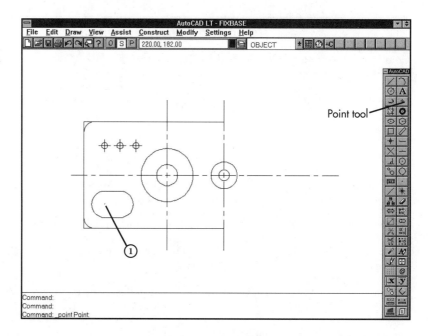

Figure 4.12

*Points displayed
with style 34.*

Figure 4.13

*The Point Style
dialog box.*

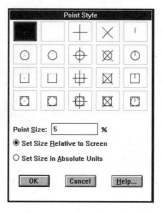

Points are the easiest object to create in AutoCAD LT. When you use the POINT
command, AutoCAD LT asks you to locate the point you want. You can pick a location with the cursor or enter the coordinates from the keyboard. AutoCAD LT uses
the coordinates you specify to create a *point object* (an object called a point) in the
drawing database. You can use the AutoCAD LT editing commands to move and copy
points.

> **POINT.** The POINT command draws a point object with X,Y,Z coordinates anywhere in space. Points are sometimes used for reference marks and as nodes to snap to with the NODe object snap mode.

The P<u>o</u>int item on the **D**raw pull-down menu issues a repeating form of the POINT command, useful when locating a number of reference points at one time.

The appearance of points can be selected from 20 different "styles" (see fig. 4.14). In addition to using the Point Style dialog box, you can set the point style by its number by entering the PDMODE system variable at the command prompt.

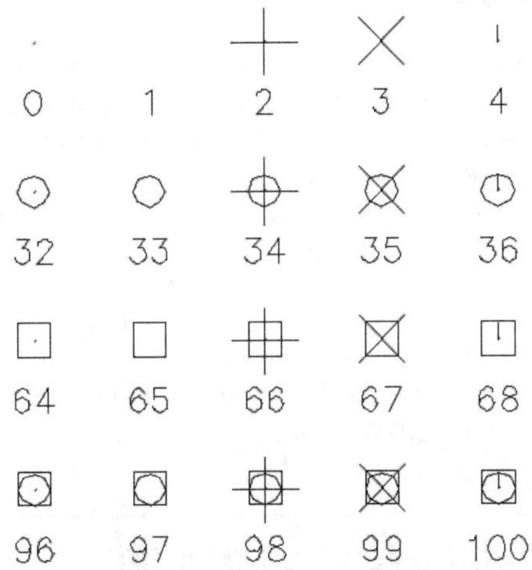

Figure 4.14

The 20 available point styles and their numbers.

.		+	×	ı
0	1	2	3	4
⊙	○	⊕	⊗	◔
32	33	34	35	36
⊡	□	⊞	⊠	▯
64	65	66	67	68
◎	▢	⊕	⊠	◫
96	97	98	99	100

Point size controls the display size of a point symbol. Two options are available for setting this size. Setting the point size to a negative value causes the point symbols to be sized relative to the screen display. Points appear the same size on the display regardless of the zoom magnification. Setting a positive point size value displays points at a fixed size like other objects. You can set point size in the Point Style dialog box or by entering the PDSIZE system variable at the command prompt.

Tip Avoid the temptation to use points as dots to represent concrete or gravel. This procedure creates many individual objects which are difficult to find, erase, and work with, and their appearance is affected by Point Styles settings. Use a hatch pattern instead (see Chapter 17, "Dressing Up Drawings with Hatching").

Points are useful for identifying reference locations. Survey information is typically a collection of point data that can be input directly with the POINT command. Points are frequently returned from finite element analysis and similar engineering software. They are also used by some Geographical Information Systems (GIS) software to associate text data with other graphic elements. Object snap (see Chapter 11, "Achieving Accuracy: The Geometric Power of CAD") can locate a point, hidden among other objects, by its unique object type.

Although points have their uses, they are in fact rarely found in the typical finished drawing. In contrast, drawings nearly always include text, the last basic drawing object discussed in this chapter.

Working with Text

The graphic elements of a drawing are powerful communicators, but normally the graphics do not provide enough information on their own. Text is usually required to clarify the purpose of the drawing. Text labels and notes are a commonplace practice for including information that goes beyond the scope of the graphics in a drawing. (Dimensioning text is placed with powerful automatic dimensioning commands, discussed in Chapter 20, "Applying Dimensions in CAD.")

The principal command for creating text in an AutoCAD LT drawing is the DTEXT command (for Dynamic TEXT). Discover for yourself in the next exercise how easily DTEXT allows you to place text in your drawing. You replace your FIXBASE drawing with a new one based on the ALT0402.DWG file.

Using the DTEXT Command

Continue from the previous exercise or start AutoCAD LT using the IALT icon. Unless the Create New Drawing dialog box is already open, click on the New button.

If continuing from the previous exercise choose **N**o *at the* Do you want to save the changes? *message*	Discards the FIXBASE drawing and opens the Create New Drawing dialog box
If using AutoCAD LT Release 1, type **FIXBASE=ALT0402** *in the* New Drawing Name *input box, then choose* OK	Creates new drawing file named FIXBASE in the DWGS\IALT directory, using ALT0402 as a prototype
If using AutoCAD LT Release 2, make sure Setup Method **N**one *is selected, then type* **ALT0402** *in the Prototype input box and choose* OK	Creates new unnamed drawing file using ALT0402 as a prototype

If using AutoCAD LT Release 2, choose the Save *button,* type **FIXBASE** *in the* File **N**ame *input box, then choose* OK	Opens the Save Drawing As dialog box, and names and saves the drawing file as FIXBASE in the DWGS\ALT directory
In the alert box, which warns FIXBASE already exists, choose **Y**es	Replaces old FIXBASE drawing
`Command:` *Click on the Text tool*	Starts the DTEXT command
`_DTEXT Justify/Style/<Start point>:` *Pick point 140,170 at* ① *(see fig. 4.15)*	Sets the start point for the text
`Height <3.50>:` **8** (Enter)	Sets 8 mm text height
`Rotation angle <0.00>:` (Enter)	Accepts the default text rotation (not rotated)
`Text:` **THIS IS LEFT** (Enter)	Draws text and spaces down one line to continue the DTEXT command

Notice that the text appears on the screen as you type it.

`Text:` **JUSTIFIED** (Enter)	Draws text below first line
`Text:` (Enter)	Ends the DTEXT command

You must press Enter because the DTEXT command does not accept the Enter button or the spacebar as a return at the `Text:` prompt.

`Command:` (Enter)	Repeats the DTEXT command
`DTEXT Justify/Style/<Start point>:` (Enter)	Sets the start point below the previous line of text
`Text:` **TEXT** (Enter)	Adds the line of text
`Text:` *Pick point 140,22 at* ②	Moves the start point for the next line of text

You can set a new location for a new line of text at any time during text input.

AND MORE (Enter)	Draws the text
`Text:` **TEXT**	Draws the text below the previous line
`Text:` *Press Backspace*	Deletes T at end of TEXT
`Text:` TEX *Continue pressing Backspace until MORE is deleted*	Deletes text, stepping back to previous line

continues

continued

`Text:` *Press Ctrl+C*   Cancels the DTEXT command and discards
the rest of the current text

`*Cancel*`

A DTEXT command must be completed properly by pressing Enter, or all input is discarded.

Figure 4.15

Using the DTEXT command.

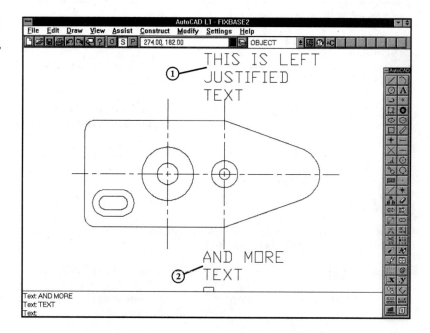

Placing text in your drawings is an essential part of communicating your design. The flexibility provided by the Text tool allows placing several pieces of text at different locations with a single command. With planning, you could conceivably annotate an entire drawing, while issuing the DTEXT command only once, but remember that a single Undo would remove all the text. The DTEXT command must be completed properly before any text is actually placed in the drawing.

> **DTEXT.** The DTEXT command places text objects in a drawing. It prompts for insertion point, text style, justification, height, and rotation, and places one or more lines of text, either directly below the first, or at other locations selected. Preview text appears on-screen as it is entered.

DTEXT allows for placement of multiple lines of text at various locations, without ending and restarting the command. When you press Enter after typing text, DTEXT starts a new line of text below the preceding line, with the same justification, text height, and other settings. When you press Enter in response to the Start point: prompt, DTEXT finds the last text object created in the current drawing session and starts the new text below the existing, matching its properties.

 Tip   You can use an INSert object snap at the Start point: prompt to select any previous text string, then press the spacebar, then Enter at the Text: prompt to place a new text string below any existing text string. See Chapter 11, "Achieving Accuracy: The Geometric Power of CAD," for information on object snap.

Another text command, called simply TEXT, is also available in AutoCAD LT, but it lacks the flexibility and dynamic qualities of DTEXT. The principal differences between TEXT and DTEXT are that DTEXT displays the text in the drawing as you type it while TEXT does not, and that TEXT creates only a single line of text at a time. Both commands are available in AutoCAD LT, but only DTEXT appears in its menus and tools.

Using Basic Text Options

The DTEXT command works differently from most other drawing commands. When you start DTEXT, the first prompt presents you with three options; a fourth option is also available but is not shown in the prompt. The initial four DTEXT command options are described in the following list:

♦ **Justify.** If you enter **J**, DTEXT prompts you to select from five alternative text justifications (see the following section, "Text Justification Options"). When you make a justification selection, DTEXT prompts for the insertion point or points it needs, according to your selection, and then proceeds to the next prompt (see the discussion following this list).

♦ **Style.** If you enter **S**, DTEXT prompts you for a text style to use. (Text styles are discussed in Chapter 13, "Using Object Properties and Text Styles.") You can press Enter at this point to leave the current text style unchanged, or you can enter the name of a previously defined style, which becomes the current one. DTEXT then repeats the initial prompt.

♦ **Start point.** If you simply pick or enter a point location, DTEXT uses it as the insertion point of the new text, with the default *left* justification, which is the bottom left corner of the first character. Once it has an insertion point, DTEXT proceeds to the next prompt (see the discussion following this list).

◆ **Press Enter.** If you press Enter instead of selecting one of the first three options, and you have previously created text in the current drawing session, AutoCAD LT highlights the most recently drawn text and applies the justification, style, height, and rotation values used for it to the text you are about to enter. DTEXT then skips its other normal prompts, and proceeds to prompt for a new text string. Unless you pick a new location at this point, DTEXT aligns the new text directly below the highlighted text. If DTEXT finds no previous text to use as a model, it issues the error message `Point or option keyword required`, and repeats the initial prompt.

Tip   If you want to use a justification other than left (the default), you can bypass the Justify option prompt by simply entering the justification keyword character at DTEXT's initial prompt. See the following "Text Justification Options" section.

You can change the style selection as many times as you care to; DTEXT simply repeats the same prompt. However, once you supply DTEXT with an insertion point (unless you choose the option of pressing Enter), DTEXT prompts for the rest of the information it needs, as follows:

◆ `Height<0.2000>:` You enter the height of the text. This prompt does not appear if you select *aligned* justification, as this option defines the text height, or if the selected text style is defined with a non-zero height (see Chapter 13, "Using Object Properties and Text Styles"). The default is the value of the *TEXTSIZE* system variable, which is updated to the height most recently specified.

◆ `Rotation angle<0>:` You specify the angle at which you want the text drawn. This prompt does not appear if you select *aligned* or *fit* justification, as these options define this angle (see the justification options list following). The rotation angle defaults to 0 (horizontal, left to right) initially, and to the most recently specified angle during a drawing session.

Eventually, all options lead to the final prompt that fulfills the purpose of the DTEXT command:

◆ `Text:` You type a text string and press Enter to create a line of text. Enter additional text to have DTEXT format it like a paragraph, with each line aligned with the previous one, at a (usually) readable distance below it. You can pick a new insertion point at any time to have the next text you enter located at the new point. Press Enter twice at the end of a line to complete the command and draw all the text entered.

Text Justification Options

AutoCAD LT provides several justification options to allow you to place text properly in relation to other objects in the drawing.

◆ **Left.** Left justification is the default. You specify a point at the Start point: prompt for the left end of the text string baseline.

◆ **Align.** You enter **A** and specify the beginning and ending points of the text baseline. The text height is scaled as needed to fit the text between these points without distortion, hence the height may not match other text in the drawing.

◆ **Fit.** You enter **F** and specify the beginning and ending points of the text baseline. The text width is adjusted to fit the text between these points without changing the height. This option will distort the appearance of your text.

◆ **Center.** You enter **C** and specify a point for the center of the text string baseline.

◆ **Middle.** You enter **M** and specify a point for the horizontal and vertical midpoint of the text string.

◆ **Right.** You enter **R** and specify a point for the right end of the text string baseline.

The preview text that DTEXT displays appears left-justified, regardless of the justification you select.

 Tip If you know the justification you want, you can enter it at the Start point: prompt without first entering the Justify option.

In the following exercise, try the Aligned and Center options.

Using Text Justification Options

Continue from the preceding exercise.

Command: *Click on the Text tool*	Starts the DTEXT command
`_DTEXT Justify/Style/` `<Start point>:` **J** (Enter)	Specifies the Justify option
`Align/Fit/Center/Middle/Right:` **A** (Enter)	Specifies Aligned text

continues

continued

`First text line point:` *Pick 210,112 at* ① *(see fig. 4.16)*	Sets the start point for the DTEXT
`Second text line point:` *Pick point 82.02<45 at* ②	Sets the alignment angle (45 degrees) and endpoint
`Text:` **ALIGNED** `(Enter)`	Enters the text
`Text:` `(Enter)`	Redraws the text, aligned (see fig. 4.16)

The text is scaled to fit between the alignment picks, so the prompts for aligned text do not ask for text height or rotation angle.

Figure 4.16

Aligned text.

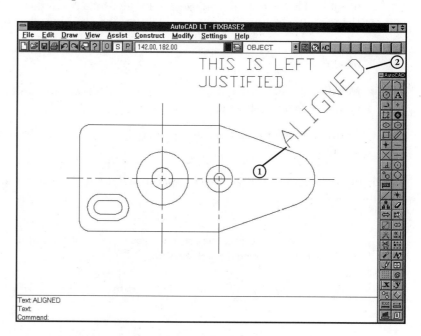

`Command:` *Click on the Undo button three times*	Removes the text
`Command:` *Choose **D**raw, **T**ext*	Starts the DTEXT command
`_dtext Justify/Style/<Start point>:` `C` `(Enter)`	Specifies centered text
`Center point:` *Pick point 132,16 at* ① *(see fig. 4.17)*	Sets the center point for the text
`Height <3.50>:` `10` `(Enter)`	Sets height to 10

`Rotation angle <0.00>:` (Enter)	Accepts the default
`Text:` **TOP VIEW** (Enter)	Enters the text

The text does not appear correctly centered until the DTEXT command is ended.

`Text:` (Enter)	Draws the centered text and exits DTEXT (see fig. 4.17)
`Command:` *Click on the Save button*	Saves your drawing

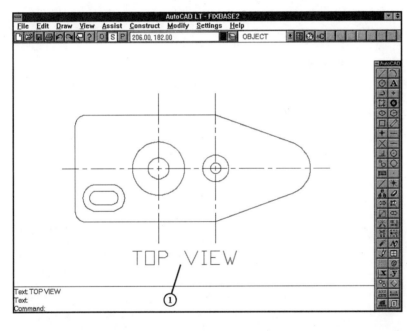

Figure 4.17

Centered text created with DTEXT.

Text in AutoCAD LT involves more than the basics of the DTEXT command. For instance, the default appearance is not always appropriate, so Chapter 13, "Using Object Properties and Text Styles," explains how to use the STYLE command to place text in different fonts. Chapter 10 shows you how to easily edit text in AutoCAD LT, and how to import text from an ASCII text file. Chapter 20, "Applying Dimensions in CAD," shows you how to place dimensioning text.

The next chapter expands your knowledge of AutoCAD LT to include the other major activity involved in creating and working with CAD drawings—modifying and replicating existing objects, the commands used for editing.

You are off the ground now, on your first solo. It's time to learn to make the adjustments required for a smooth, successful flight.

CHAPTER

5

Navigating Views in the CAD Workspace

This chapter introduces tools for controlling your view in CAD. The chapter includes the following topics in its discussion of navigating views:

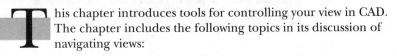

◆ Working with the Aerial View window and its menu options

◆ Using the ZOOM, PAN, and VIEW commands

◆ Understanding drawing regenerations

◆ Using commands transparently

◆ Setting up multiple viewports with the VIEWPORTS command

The efficient use of the display control commands is central to working productively in a CAD environment.

Every pilot is required to spend time reading and interpreting navigational charts. Determining where you are and knowing how to get to where you are going are critical skills in aviation. These skills also are important in CAD. Because you are working with a drawing area that can be nearly any size, you need to know where you are at all times.

To acquire these skills, you must first develop a sense that you are looking at the drawing through a fixed window. You control what you see by moving the drawing around under the window. You can only control a drawing in this way if you know your location relative to the whole drawing, even while you are focused in on a particular feature.

To be able to work on your design, you need to get close to what you are doing. A standard D-size drawing can be a small image even on an expensive high-resolution 21-inch monitor. In CAD, there is no fixed relationship between the size of your view and the drawing size. You can shrink the earth to fit on your screen as if you were looking at it from deep in space. You also can enlarge the head of a pin to fill the same area as if you were looking at it through a microscope. The sense of where you are controls your understanding of the graphic information on your screen.

As an example of the control you have over how a drawing is viewed, look at the map of Oregon shown in figure 5.1. Figure 5.2 shows the same map with the city of Portland enlarged to fill the screen.

Figure 5.1

The full extents of the Oregon map.

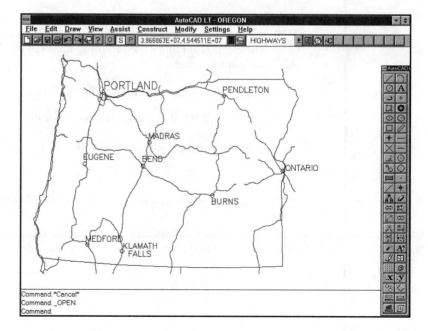

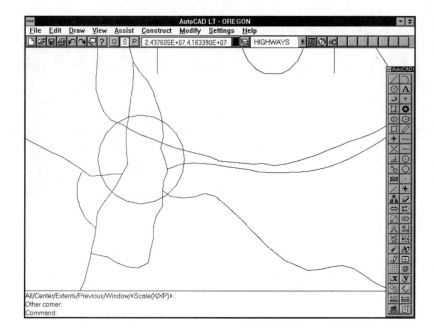

Figure 5.2

*Zooming in
on the city of
Portland.*

AutoCAD LT's display tools help you to set up your drawing so you can easily work in specific areas. You can zoom in (enlarge) or zoom out (shrink) to view an area in greater detail or greater scope. You can even have more than one view on the screen at a time. With viewports, you can divide your screen to show from 1 to 64 separate views, and you can move from view to view during a drawing command such as LINE, ARC, or CIRCLE.

Viewports are used in figures 5.3 and 5.4 to further illustrate the infinite variety of ways in which you can view a drawing. In figure 5.3, all four views have a different magnification or scale displayed even though the views themselves are the same size. In figure 5.4, the views are all the same size and magnification, but their position relative to one another is meaningless. Normally, the view on your screen has no meaning in a measurable sense. Your view of the drawing is only a tool for seeing what you need to see while working on various portions of your design—an extremely important tool.

Figure 5.3

Four differently scaled views of the Oregon map.

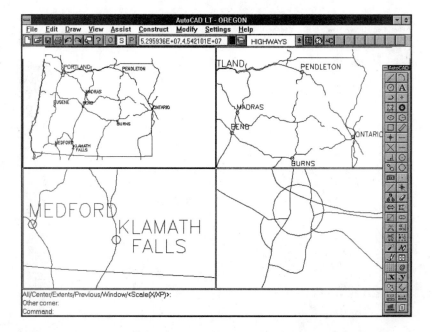

Figure 5.4

Four views at one scale of different locations on the map.

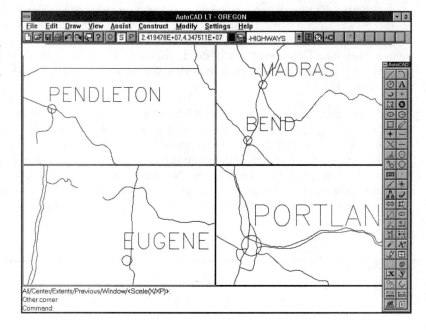

Working with Aerial View

AutoCAD LT provides a powerful yet easy-to-use tool for both navigating in your drawing and controlling your view of it: the Aerial View window. You can use Aerial View to adjust the amount of drawing area you see in the display.

The Aerial View window was redesigned in later versions of AutoCAD LT Release 1 and in AutoCAD LT Release 2. Use the following section to explore the Aerial View in early versions of AutoCAD LT Release 1 (your Aerial View window looks like that in figure 5.6). If you are using a recent version of AutoCAD LT Release 1 (your Aerial View window looks like that in figure 5.12), or are using AutoCAD LT Release 2, skip to the later section on the redesigned Aerial View.

Using the Original AutoCAD LT Release 1 Aerial View

In the following exercise, you use the original Aerial View window to examine an existing drawing.

Exploring a Drawing with the Original Aerial View Window

Start AutoCAD LT using the IALT icon.

Command: *Click on the New button*	Issues the NEW command and opens the Create New Drawing dialog box
*Click on the **P**rototype button, and then double-click on the file name* ALT0501.DWG *located in the \DWS\IALT directory*	Uses the ALT0501.DWG file that came with *Inside AutoCAD LT for Windows, Second Edition* as the new drawing prototype
Click in the New **D**rawing Name *field, and enter the name* **ZOOM-PAN**	Starts a new drawing named ZOOM-PAN based on the drawing ALT0501 (see fig. 5.5)
Command: *Click on the Aerial View button (see fig. 5.5)*	Issues the DSVIEWER command
_DSVIEWER	Opens the Aerial View window (see fig. 5.6) in Zoom mode
Pick points ① *and* ② *(see fig. 5.6)*	Specifies a zoom window and zooms in on the bathroom (see fig. 5.7)

The heavy black box in the Aerial View indicates the area of the current drawing display.

Pick a window from ③ *to* ④ *(see fig. 5.7)*	Zooms in on the bathtub (see fig. 5.8)

continues

continued

Figure 5.5

The initial drawing view.

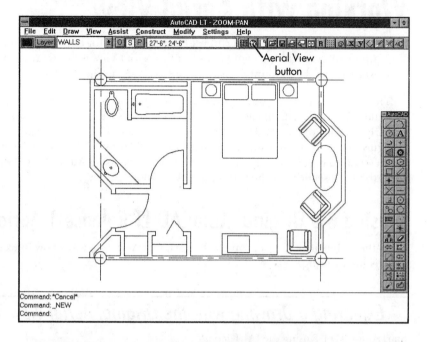

Figure 5.6

Picking a zoom window around the bathroom in the Aerial View.

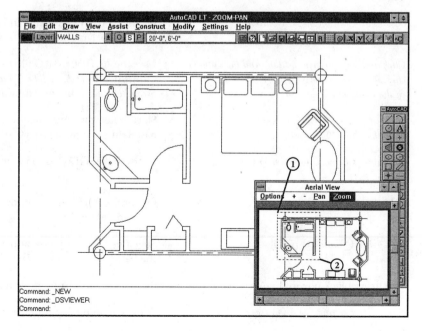

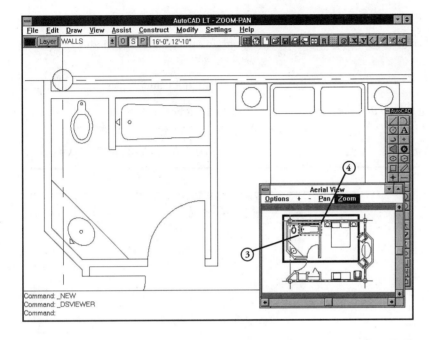

Figure 5.7

Zooming in on the bathtub.

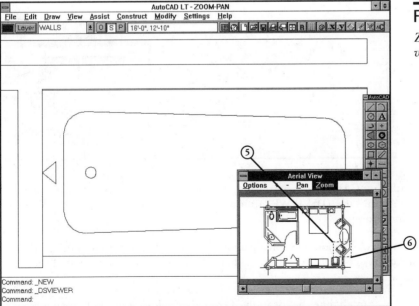

Figure 5.8

Zooming to a view of a chair.

continues

continued

Pick a window from ⑤ to ⑥ (see fig. 5.8)	Zooms in on a chair by the window (see fig. 5.9)
*Click on **P**an*	Enters Pan mode and displays a pan window
Move the cursor to position the window as shown in figure 5.9, then pick	Pans to the other chair by the window
*Double-click on **Z**oom*	Zooms to the full area of the Aerial View

Figure 5.9

Panning to a view of the other chair.

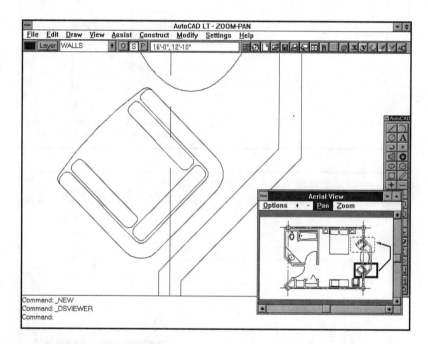

In the default AutoCAD LT configuration, Aerial View is not open until you either click on the Aerial View (DSVIEWER) button on the toolbar or enter DSVIEWER at the command prompt.

Zoom is analogous to a zoom lens on a camera. Zoom does not actually change the size or scale of objects—just your view of them. Zoom is the default mode of the Aerial View window.

Aerial View also can change the location of your view. This method of moving your viewpoint around a design is called a *pan*, taken from the term for moving a camera up, down, and/or sideways in cinematography. When you use the PAN command, the magnification remains unchanged.

Notice that when you move the cursor into the Aerial View window, the crosshairs become highlighted. Clicking within the Aerial View picks one corner of a zoom window (sometimes called a zoom box). You then drag the other corner and pick to specify the zoom area and perform the zoom.

The currently displayed area of the drawing is outlined in the Aerial View window by a heavy black box. This box provides a constant reference to the location of your current view relative to the overall drawing.

Notice also that the resultant view does not necessarily match the zoom window you picked. AutoCAD LT zooms to include everything you enclosed in the zoom window, but the view may also include a bit more because the shape of the graphics window does not change.

Did you notice that a Ctrl+C combination does not cancel a window selection the way it does in the graphics window? The Aerial View is a separate window. The commands and keys of the AutoCAD LT graphics window do not work in the Aerial View window.

 Tip   To cancel a zoom in the Aerial View window after picking the first point, click on Zoom, or press the F10 or Alt key (menu bar toggle) twice.

Using **P**an changes the cursor in the Aerial View window to a highlighted pan box. When you position this box and pick a point, the view in the graphics window is moved, without changing its scale, to the location indicated by the box within the Aerial View.

Zoom or **P**an affects the graphics window only. The area shown in the Aerial View is left unchanged. When you double-click on **Z**oom, the view in the graphics window zooms to match the view in the Aerial View window.

Finally, notice that the zooms and pans conducted in the Aerial View window are not echoed at the command line. This has a side effect when it comes to using the U and UNDO commands. The undo commands act to undo the last command line function along with any intervening Aerial View operations affecting the graphics window. In the case of the preceding exercise, a single undo would reverse all the screen functions performed in the Aerial View window although no command line functions were used.

 Stop   The U and UNDO commands return the graphics window to the view present before the Aerial View window was used. In most cases, however, AutoCAD will also undo previous commands.

The Aerial View window has a menu with several options. The next section examines these options.

Understanding the Original Aerial View Options

The default settings of the original Aerial View window will work for most of your basic needs. You also can tailor the Aerial View window to suit the job at hand by using the following options available from the window's menu bar:

◆ **+ (plus).** The + option magnifies the image in the Aerial View window 2× to display less of the drawing (does not affect the graphics window).

◆ **– (minus).** The – option shrinks the image in the Aerial View window .5× to display more of the drawing (does not affect the graphics window).

◆ **Pan.** The Pan option pans the drawing in the graphics window to the view you specify in the Aerial View window (does not change the zoom magnification). To aid your view selection, the Aerial View window displays a dashed box sized to match the current view.

◆ **Zoom.** The Zoom option zooms the drawing in the graphics window to the area defined by the two corner points you pick in the Aerial View window. If you double-click on Zoom, the drawing in the graphics window zooms to the entire area currently visible in the Aerial View window.

The Aerial View Options menu items (see fig. 5.10) are as follows:

◆ **Global View.** The Global View option displays the current extents or the virtual screen (whichever is less) in the Aerial View window (does not affect the graphics window). The virtual screen and extents are described later in this chapter.

◆ **Locate.** The Locate option displays, in the Aerial View window, a bird's-eye view of the cursor location as you move it around in the graphics window. You can right-click to open the Magnification dialog box, which enables you to adjust the view magnification by clicking in the value box and entering a new value, or by using a slider bar, or by choosing + or – (the default is 8×). When you pick a point in the graphics window, the graphics window zooms to the view displayed in the Aerial View window, and the Aerial View reverts to its previous view.

◆ **Statistics.** The Statistics option displays memory and entity count statistics for the current viewport.

◆ **Auto Viewport.** When the Auto Viewport option is checked, AutoCAD LT constantly updates the Aerial View window to the current viewport. The only change you generally see is in the heavy boundary line in the Aerial View window indicating the view area of the drawing. When this option is cleared, AutoCAD LT does not update the Aerial View window when you switch viewports until you reactivate the Aerial View window. The Auto Viewport option is discussed further at the end of this chapter.

◆ **Window on Top.** When the Window on **T**op option is checked, the Aerial View window remains on top of the graphics window. If this setting is not checked, the Aerial View window goes behind the graphics window immediately after you use it.

◆ **Dynamic Update.** When the Dynamic **U**pdate option is checked, the Aerial View window updates as you edit the drawing in the graphics window. When this option is cleared, the Aerial View window updates only when you reactivate it. You can clear this option when you edit complex drawings to increase AutoCAD LT's speed.

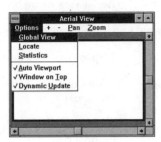

Figure 5.10

The Aerial View Options menu.

In addition to these menu commands and options, you also can use the Aerial View's scroll bars to pan the view in the Aerial View. The scroll bars are at the right side and the bottom of the Aerial View. You can click on the arrow buttons at the top or bottom or the left or right of the scroll bars, or you can drag the slider box (the box in the center of the scroll bar) up or down or left or right to pan the view in the Aerial View. The scroll bars do not affect the graphics window.

In the following exercise, you use several of the Aerial View options, including the + and –, the scroll bars, and the Locate option.

Using the Original Aerial View Options and Controls

Continue using the Aerial View in the ZOOM-PAN drawing.

Click on – (minus) *twice*	Shrinks the drawing in the Aerial View
Choose **O**ptions, **G**lobal View	Resets the Aerial View
Click on + (plus) *twice*	Zooms in on the drawing in the Aerial View

Use the Aerial View scroll bars to center the bathtub, by clicking repeatedly on the up arrow in the vertical scroll bar until the right end of the tub is visible, then clicking several times on the left arrow in the horizontal scroll bar.

continues

5

continued

Click on **Z**oom	Sets Zoom mode
Pick a window around the tub fixture and drain (see fig. 5.11)	Zooms the drawing
Reset the image by choosing **O**ptions, *then* **G**lobal View, *and double-click on* **Z**oom	Resets the Aerial View and restores the original view
Choose **O**ptions, **L**ocate	Changes the cursor to a plus and grays the Aerial View menu bar

Move the cursor in the graphics window, and watch the image displayed in the Aerial View.

Move the cursor to the tub fixture and drain	Displays that area in the Aerial View
Pick a point at the same bathtub fixtures as before	Zooms the drawing to the image seen in the Aerial View
Reset the image as you did before	Resets the Aerial View and restores the original view in the graphics window
Choose **O**ptions, *then* **L**ocate, *and then right-click (click the Enter button)*	Opens the Magnification dialog box

Click repeatedly on the minus button, to the left of the number 8, to reset the zoom factor used by the **L**ocate option to 2.

Move the cursor in the graphics window, and watch the image displayed in the Aerial View.

Click on the Aerial View title bar to cancel	
Choose **O**ptions, *and click on* Window on **T**op	Turns off the Window on **T**op option
Zoom in on the bathtub fixtures and drain again	

The Aerial View disappears as soon as the zoom selection is made.

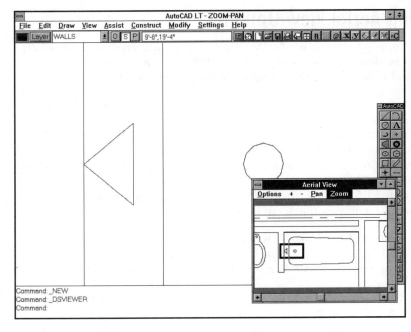

Figure 5.11

Zooming in on the bathtub fixtures.

Notice that when you click on + or –, AutoCAD LT's reaction is immediate. When you close the Aerial View and then reopen it, it reverts to Zoom mode. If you leave the Aerial View open or use the Aerial View toolbar button to redisplay it, its current mode will be the one that was last used.

The **L**ocate option temporarily reverses the relationship of the Aerial View and the graphics window. The Aerial View becomes a magnifying-glass view of the area under the cursor. The **L**ocate option also provides a preview of what your zoomed image will look like.

The extent of the drawing area displayed in the Aerial View window can be altered but not saved. Each time a drawing is loaded into AutoCAD LT, the Aerial View defaults to a display of the drawing's extents or virtual screen, whichever is less.

Remember that you can always return to a full view of the drawing by choosing the Aerial View's **G**lobal View option and then double-clicking on **Z**oom.

Tip   When you are working with the Aerial View "always on top," take into account the area of the screen occupied by the window itself. Size and center the graphics window view in the area free of the Aerial View.

Combining Aerial View Options

By combining options, you can use Aerial View to display your drawing in many ways. In a very large or densely cluttered drawing, for example, you can use the + option to make the Aerial View display a smaller subset of the graphics window.

The Aerial View, although it is dependent on AutoCAD LT, is a separate window within the Windows environment. Like any window, you can move and size it to suit your needs. The Aerial View has its own control menu bar, and a double-click on the control menu button closes the window. Whether the Aerial View is open, minimized, on top, or behind the graphics window, you can access it by pressing Alt+Tab one or more times, even from another program. The Minimize button causes the Aerial View to minimize to an icon, which is usually hidden by the graphics window. The toolbar Aerial View button redisplays the Aerial View regardless of its status.

The size and location of the Aerial View are retained between sessions and are stored in the AVIEW.INI file. You can maximize the Aerial View to a full-screen display, but this configuration is not retained when you close and reopen the window.

The navigational qualities of the Aerial View are most useful in a large drawing in which it is easy to lose track of where you are. The Aerial View can display the entire drawing in its separate window, which can be kept visible or immediately accessible. You can then use the Aerial View to pan or zoom quickly to any area within the graphics window that you want.

This completes coverage of the original Aerial View window.

If you are using a recent version of AutoCAD LT Release 1 (your Aerial View window looks like that in figure 5.12) or are using AutoCAD LT Release 2, use the following section to explore the redesigned Aerial View. If you are using an early version of AutoCAD LT Release 1, skip the following section and refer to the previous section, which covers the original Aerial View.

Using the Redesigned Aerial View

In the following exercise, you use the redesigned Aerial View window to examine an existing drawing.

Exploring a Drawing with the Redesigned Aerial View Window

Start AutoCAD LT using the IALT icon. Unless the Create New Drawing dialog box is already open, click on the New button to open it.

If using AutoCAD LT Release 2, make sure Setup Method **N**one is selected.

Type **ALT0501** *in the Prototype input box and choose* OK

Creates new unnamed drawing (see fig. 5.12), using the ALT0501 file that came with *Inside AutoCAD LT for Windows, Second Edition* as a prototype

Choose the Save button, type **ZOOM-PAN** *in the File* **N***ame input box, then choose* OK

Opens the Save Drawing As dialog box, and names and saves the drawing file as ZOOM-PAN in the DWGS\IALT directory

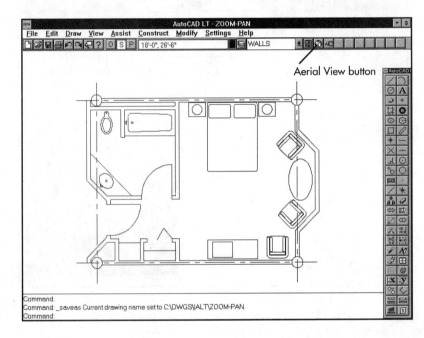

Figure 5.12

The initial drawing view.

Command: *Click on the Aerial View button (see fig. 5.12)*

Issues the DSVIEWER command

_DSVIEWER

Opens the Aerial View window (see fig. 5.13); the reverse background indicates the area of the current graphics area view

Move the pointer to the center of the bathroom in the Aerial View window and click the Enter mouse button

Enters zoom mode and displays a view box with an X at the center

Move the mouse left and right

Resizes the view box and changes the view in the graphics area

continues

continued

Move the mouse so the view box matches (approximately) that in figure 5.13, then click the pick button	Specifies a zoom window and zooms in on the bathroom, displaying the view shown in figure 5.13

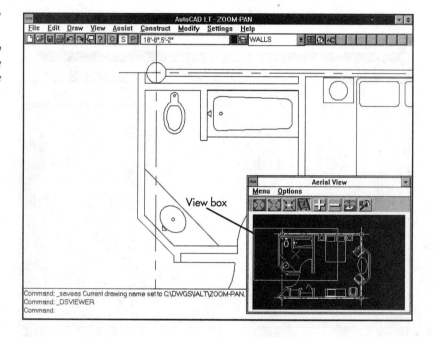

Figure 5.13

Making a view box around the bathroom in the Aerial View.

The reverse background (see fig. 5.14) in the Aerial View now indicates the zoomed-in area of the current drawing display. Cursor control returns to the graphics area.

Place the pointer in the middle of the bathtub in the Aerial View and click the Enter button, then move the mouse to the left until the view box encloses just the bathtub, then click the pick button	Zooms in on the bathtub (see fig. 5.14); the reverse background (see fig. 5.15) now indicates the new zoomed-in area and the cursor returns to the graphics area
Place the pointer in the reverse background area in the Aerial View, click the pick button, then move the mouse	Enters pan mode, displaying a view box with crosshairs in the Aerial View; as the mouse moves, the view box and graphics area view pan
Move the mouse to position the view box as shown in figure 5.15, then click the pick button	Pans the view box and graphics area view to the chair by the window

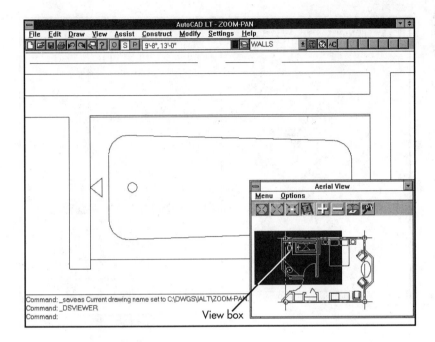

Figure 5.14

*Zooming in on
the bathtub.*

Place the pointer on the other chair by the
window, outside the reverse background area,
then click the pick button

Command: **U** (Enter)

Instantly pans the view box and graphics
area view to the other chair, as shown in
figure 5.16

Undoes all Aerial View operations, restoring
the full drawing view just as it was when you
opened the Aerial View

Click on the Spyglass button (see fig. 5.16),
move the view box around in the graphics
window, and move to center it on the chair
from the previous view

Displays a view box and crosshairs in the
graphics window; the box pans the view
in the Aerial View as you move it in the
graphics window

Press the Enter button and move the
mouse around, then move to size the
view box to encompass just the chair,
then click the pick button

Changes the view box to zoom mode and
zooms the view in the Aerial View as you
move it in the graphics window; it zooms
the graphics window and restores the
previous Aerial View view (see fig. 5.16)
when you click the pick button

Figure 5.15

Panning to a view of a chair.

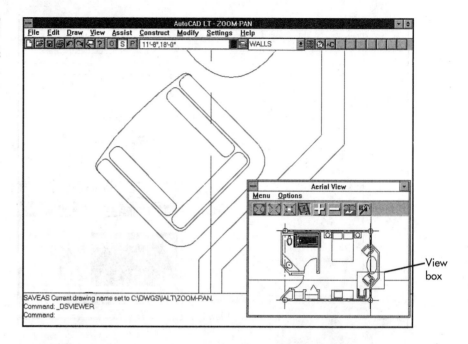

Figure 5.15

Panning to a view of a chair.

Figure 5.16

Panning to a view of the other chair.

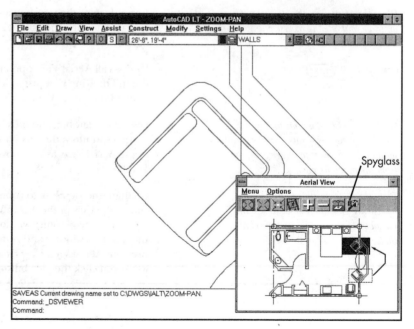

In the default AutoCAD LT configuration, the Aerial View is not open until you either click on the Aerial View (DSVIEWER) button on the toolbar or enter DSVIEWER at the command prompt.

Zoom is analogous to a zoom lens on a camera. Zoom does not actually change the size or scale of objects—just your view of them. Zoom is the default mode of the Aerial View window.

Aerial View also can change the location of your view. This method of moving your viewpoint around a design is called a *pan*, taken from the term for moving a camera up, down, or sideways in cinematography. When you use the PAN command, the magnification remains unchanged.

The currently displayed area of the drawing is outlined in the Aerial View window by a reverse background area, generally black. This background area provides a constant reference to the location of your current view, relative to the overall drawing.

When you move the cursor into the Aerial View window, the pointer appears. If you click the Enter mouse button, it enters zoom mode and a view box without crosshairs appears. If you click the pick button within the reverse background area, it enters pan mode and a view box with crosshairs appears. When already in either the Aerial View or Spyglass zoom or pan mode, clicking the Enter button switches to the other (zoom or pan) mode. Moving the mouse drags the size (in zoom mode) or position (in pan mode) of the view box. This is called dynamic zooming or panning. Then, clicking the pick button completes the operation.

When not already in zoom or pan mode, clicking the pick button in the Aerial View but outside the reverse background area instantly pans the view box to the point picked. This is called nondynamic panning.

Pressing Ctrl+C does not cancel Aerial View operations. The Aerial View is a separate window. The commands and keys of the AutoCAD LT graphics window do not work in the Aerial View window.

 Tip   To close the Aerial View window, choose **M**enu, then E**x**it in the Aerial View window, or double-click on the Aerial View window's control menu button. Any pending operation will be discarded. To exit the Aerial View window without closing it or completing a pending operation, just move the pointer back to the graphics window. This is easy to do in pan mode, but escaping the Aerial View in zoom mode often requires a quick movement, because a slow-moving pointer often remains trapped in the Aerial View.

Zooming and panning in the Aerial View affects the graphics window only. The area shown in the Aerial View is left unchanged.

Finally, notice that the zooms and pans conducted in the Aerial View window are not echoed at the command line. This has a side effect when it comes to using the U and UNDO commands. The undo commands act to undo the last command line function, along with any intervening Aerial View operations affecting the graphics window. In the case of the preceding exercise, a single undo reversed all the screen functions performed in the Aerial View window even though no command line functions were used.

 Stop The U and UNDO commands return the graphics window to the view present before the Aerial View window was used. In most cases, however, AutoCAD will also undo previous commands.

The Aerial View window has two menus and several toolbar buttons, identified in figure 5.17. The next section examines these.

Figure 5.17

The Aerial View Window.

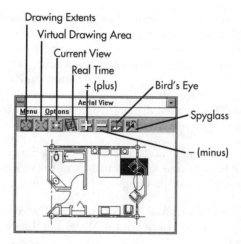

Adjusting the Aerial View with Its Toolbar Buttons and Menus

The default view in the Aerial View window will work for most of your basic needs. You also can adjust the area shown in the Aerial View window to suit the job at hand by using buttons on the window's toolbar. Additional buttons control the method of panning and zooming, and how the graphics window view updates. The Aerial View buttons are the following:

◆ **Drawing Extents.** The Drawing Extents button zooms the Aerial View to show the entire drawing extents (the smallest area showing all drawing objects). The graphics window is unaffected.

◆ **Virtual Drawing Area.** The Virtual Drawing Area button zooms the Aerial View to show the largest drawing area possible without causing a regeneration (regeneration is explained later in this chapter). This is generally several times the area of the drawing extents. The graphics window is unaffected.

◆ **Current View.** The Current View button zooms the Aerial View to show the area of the current graphics window view (the reverse background area). The graphics window is unaffected.

◆ **Real Time.** The Real Time button controls how the view in the graphics window updates. The default is on for real time updating, so the view in the graphics window pans and zooms as you adjust the view box in the Aerial View window. If you turn it off, the view in the graphics window does not pan or zoom until you complete the Aerial View operation. Clicking on the Real Time button turns real time updating on or off.

◆ **+ (plus).** The + button magnifies the image in the Aerial View window by a small increment each time you click on it. This displays less of the drawing. The graphics window is unaffected.

◆ **− (minus).** The − button shrinks the image in the Aerial View window by a small increment each time you click on it. This displays more of the drawing. The graphics window is unaffected.

The Aerial View offers two methods of panning and zooming the graphics window: the Bird's Eye (the default) and the Spyglass.

◆ **Bird's Eye.** The Bird's Eye button displays a view box in the Aerial View. This is used for zooming or panning the area of the graphics window. As you adjust the view box, its current area is shown in the graphics window (unless Real Time is off). You move the mouse to adjust the view box size or position. You switch between zoom and pan modes by clicking the Enter mouse button, and complete the operation by clicking the pick button. Picking causes the graphics window view to pan or zoom to show the area specified by the view box, and the Aerial View indicates this area with a reverse background.

◆ **Spyglass.** The Spyglass button displays a view box in the graphics window instead of in the Aerial View. This is useful for zooming in on a precise area. As you adjust the view box, its current area is shown in the Aerial View window. You move the mouse to adjust the view box size or position. You switch between zoom and pan modes by clicking the Enter mouse button and complete the operation by clicking the pick button. Picking causes the graphics window view to zoom to show the area specified by the view box, and the Aerial View returns to its previous area, indicating the graphics window area with a reverse background. The Aerial View returns to the default bird's eye method after you complete a spyglass operation.

5

Note Changes to the area shown in the Aerial View window are unaffected by undo and redo operations.

The Aerial View also has two menus, **M**enu and **O**ptions. The **M**enu menu offers the following two items:

◆ **Set to Current VP.** In AutoCAD LT, you can use multiple viewports in the graphics window to display more than one view of the drawing. This is described later in this chapter. The Aerial View, however, only shows the view of one viewport. If you switch viewports in the graphics window and enter the Aerial View, you will see a VP icon with the international symbol for "No" to warn you. Choosing any of the Aerial View buttons updates the Aerial View to the current viewport, but might not produce the results you expect. For predictable results, choose **S**et to Current VP to reset it to show the current viewport before performing Aerial View operations.

◆ **Exit.** The **E**xit item closes the Aerial View.

The **O**ptions menu offers the following three items:

◆ **Big Icons.** If the **B**ig Icons item is checked, the Aerial View displays the toolbar icons shown in the preceding figures. If you clear the **B**ig Icons item, it displays smaller icons.

◆ **Tool Bar.** When the **T**ool Bar item is checked, the Aerial View window displays the toolbar. If you clear the **T**ool Bar item, the toolbar is not displayed. You still can use the Aerial View, but only its default Bird's Eye method.

◆ **Auto-Update.** When the **A**uto-Update item is checked, the Aerial View window updates as you edit the drawing in the graphics window. When this option is cleared, the Aerial View window updates only when you reactivate it. You can clear this option when you edit complex drawings to increase AutoCAD LT's speed.

In addition to these menu commands and options, you also can drag the Aerial View's titlebar or border to move or resize it, and use its control menu to move, resize, minimize, and restore it like any other window. You cannot maximize it. The size and location of the Aerial View, and the state of its menu item options, are retained between sessions. The graphics window Aerial View button toolbar redisplays the Aerial View regardless of its status.

In the following exercise, you use several of the Aerial View menu items and toolbar buttons.

Using the Redesigned Aerial View Controls

Continue using the Aerial View in the ZOOM-PAN drawing.

Click on the – (minus) button twice	Shrinks the image in the Aerial View
Click on the + (plus) button twice	Enlarges the image in the Aerial View
Click on the Current View button	Fills the Aerial View with the current drawing view
Click on the Virtual Drawing Area button	Zooms the image in the Aerial View way out
Click on the Drawing Extents button	Zooms the image to fill the Aerial View with the whole drawing
Pick in the center of the chair in the reverse background area, then move the mouse around	Enters bird's eye zoom mode and pans the graphics window view as you move the mouse
Click on the Real Time button, and move the mouse around again, then pick in the middle of the lavatory sink	Turns off real time updating so it no longer updates the graphics window view as you move the mouse, but it updates the graphics view when you pick the sink
Draw a circle in the graphics window	Updates the Aerial View to show the circle
Choose Options, Auto-Update	Turns off automatic updating
Draw a line in the graphics window	It doesn't show up in the Aerial View
Click on the Aerial View titlebar	Updates the Aerial View to show the line
Choose Options, Auto-Update	Turns on automatic updating

Notice that when you click on + or –, AutoCAD LT's reaction is immediate. When you close the Aerial View and then reopen it, it reverts to Bird's Eye mode. If you leave the Aerial View open, its current mode will be the one that was last used.

The Spyglass temporarily reverses the relationship of the Aerial View and the graphics window. The Aerial View becomes a magnifying-glass view of the area under the cursor. The Spyglass also provides a preview of what your zoomed image will look like.

The extent of the drawing area displayed in the Aerial View window can be altered but not saved. Each time a drawing is loaded into AutoCAD LT, the Aerial View defaults to a display of the drawing's extents or virtual screen, whichever is less.

5

By combining options, you can use Aerial View to display your drawing in many ways. In a very large or densely cluttered drawing, for example, you can use the + option to make the Aerial View display a smaller subset of the graphics window.

The navigational qualities of the Aerial View are most useful in a large drawing in which it is easy to lose track of where you are. The Aerial View can display the entire drawing in its separate window, which can be kept visible or immediately accessible. You can then use the Aerial View to pan or zoom quickly to any area within the graphics window that you want.

The Aerial View provides access to the basic display controls, but AutoCAD LT has several other display commands. In some cases, these display commands might be easier to use or might provide controls beyond those of the Aerial View.

Controlling the Display

AutoCAD LT provides two specific commands, ZOOM and PAN, for performing some of the functions you have used in the Aerial View. These commands work directly within the graphics window. The ZOOM command, like Aerial View's Zoom mode, permits you to adjust your view of the drawing by altering the magnification factor, the focal area, or both. The following exercise introduces several of the options provided by the ZOOM command.

Using the ZOOM Command

Reopen or continue to work in the ZOOM-PAN drawing. Start with a view of the entire room (see fig. 5.18; reset with Aerial View if needed), and then double-click on the Aerial View control menu button if needed to close the Aerial View.

Command: *Click on the Zoom button*	Issues the ZOOM command
`'_ZOOM`	
`All/Center/Extents/Previous/Window/` `<Scale(X/XP)>:` *Pick ① (see fig. 5.18)*	Specifies first corner of a window
`Other corner:` *Pick ②*	Defines zoom window and zooms in (see fig. 5.19)
`Command:` *Enter*	Reissues the ZOOM command
`'ZOOM`	

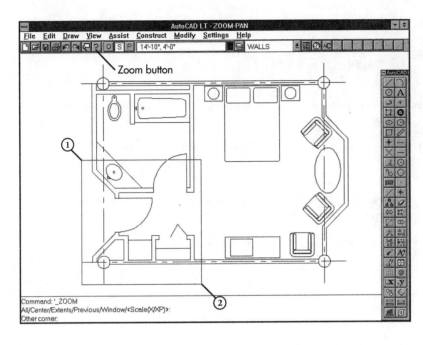

Figure 5.18

*Zooming in
on the hotel
room entry.*

`All/Center/Extents/Previous/Window/` `<Scale(X/XP)>:` **P** Enter	Specifies the Previous option, which restores the previous view
`Command:` Enter	Reissues the ZOOM command
`'ZOOM`	
`All/Center/Extents/Previous/Window/` `<Scale(X/XP)>:` **C** Enter	Specifies the Center option
`Center point:` *Pick a point at the center of the table between the chairs*	Sets the center of the view
`Magnification or Height <21'-5 3/8">:` **10'** Enter	Sets the height of the view at 10' and performs the zoom
`Command:` *Choose* **V**iew, **Z**oom, **E**xtents	Issues the ZOOM command with the Extents option

`'_zoom`
`All/Center/Extents/Previous/Window/`
`<Scale(X/XP)>:` `_extents`
`Regenerating drawing.`
	Zooms to a view encompassing all of the drawing's objects

continues

continued

`Command: Z` (Enter)	Issues the ZOOM command
`ZOOM`	
`All/Center/Extents/Previous/Window/` `<Scale(X/XP)>:` **2X** (Enter)	Specifies a zoom magnification factor relative to the current view
`Command:` (Enter)	Reissues the ZOOM command
`ZOOM`	
`All/Center/Extents/Previous/Window/` `<Scale(X/XP)>:` **.5** (Enter)	Specifies a zoom magnification factor relative to the entire drawing
`Command:` *Click on the Zoom button*	Issues the ZOOM command
`'_ZOOM`	
`All/Center/Extents/Previous/Window/` `<Scale(X/XP)>:` **A** (Enter)	Specifies the All option and zooms to display the entire drawing
`Regenerating drawing.`	

Figure 5.19

The zoomed-in entry.

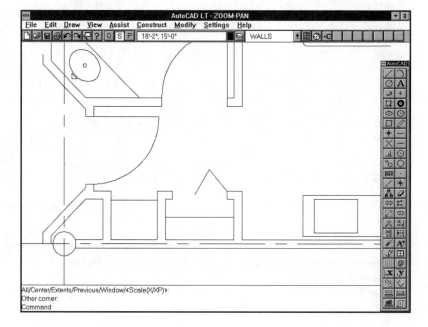

The ZOOM command affects the view of the graphics window directly. The default option is a window selection that uses a rubber-band box. Using the pull-down menu enables you to select the type of zoom from a list of options.

> **ZOOM.** The ZOOM command controls the display in the current viewport, zooming in (magnifying the image) or zooming out (shrinking the image). Zoom in to view a small part of the drawing in greater detail, or zoom out to view a larger part in less detail.

Working with ZOOM Options

The ZOOM command has the following options:

◆ **All.** You enter an **A** to zoom to display the entire drawing. In 2D (plan view), the All option displays a rectangular area that includes all objects in the drawing (the *extents)* and the defined drawing *limits.* For now, just think of limits as the area covered by the grid; see Chapter 8, "Preparing Your Workspace: CAD Concepts 1B," for a full explanation of limits. In a 3D view, the All option displays the extents (just like the Extents option).

◆ **Center.** You enter a **C** and the Center option prompts for the center point and the height (in drawing units) or the magnification (for example, 5×), and then zooms to center a view of that height or magnification.

◆ **Extents.** You enter an **E** to display all drawing objects as large as possible in the current viewport.

◆ **Previous.** You enter a **P** to restore the previous view for the current viewport. The Previous option restores the previous view whether it was generated by the Aerial View or by the ZOOM, PAN, or VIEW commands. Up to ten previous views are stored for each viewport, and you can step back through them by repeatedly using ZOOM Previous.

◆ **Window.** The Window option zooms to the rectangular area you specify by picking two diagonally opposite corner points. Unless the X,Y proportions of the window you specify exactly match the proportions of the screen or viewport, extra width or height is added to the image. The Window option is the default for point input; you need not enter a W to use the Window option.

◆ **Scale(X/XP).** You enter a magnification factor by which to zoom. The Scale(X/XP) option is the default for numerical input (other than points). A number by itself designates a scale factor relative to the drawing limits. A number with an **X** suffix designates a scale factor relative to the current view.

A number with an XP suffix designates a scale factor relative to a view in paper space (see Chapter 22, "Structuring Your Drawing"). Use a fractional magnification to zoom out.

You can use the Center option to emulate the PAN command or to change the scope of the current view. If you pick a new center and press Enter at the `Magnification or Height` prompt, your view *pans* (moves the display without changing the zoom magnification) to the new center point. If you press Enter at the new center-point prompt instead of specifying a new point, the center point remains unchanged as the display height or magnification changes according to the value you supply at the `Magnification or Height` prompt.

When you first open a drawing in AutoCAD LT, the view of the drawing is the one with which it was last saved.

 Tip Use ZOOM All or ZOOM Extents before you save and close or exit a drawing, so that, when you reopen the drawing, the entire drawing is displayed. You can cut the zoom short with a Ctrl+C or the Cancel button—it still gets stored as if the zoom were completed. When you reopen the drawing, you can also cut its initial generation short, then zoom to any portion you desire.

The ZOOM command in the graphics window has advantages and disadvantages compared to the zoom mode of the Aerial View window. The advantages of the ZOOM command in the graphics window are:

◆ It doesn't take up space in the graphics window, and it has a short command alias (Z).

◆ The graphics window is normally larger than the Aerial View, so you can specify a zoom window with greater precision with the ZOOM command than you can with the Aerial View.

◆ You can use a combination of ZOOM Window and ZOOM Previous to go back and forth between an overall view and several detailed work views at different points.

◆ The ZOOM command does not require additional graphics memory overhead.

 Tip The fastest way to perform a ZOOM Previous command is to use the command alias Z with the P option. In other words, you enter **Z**, then **P**, and your previous view is displayed.

The disadvantages of the ZOOM command compared to the Zoom feature of the Aerial View window are as follows:

◆ You cannot see the entire drawing without a ZOOM All or ZOOM Extents, each of which performs a regeneration of the screen, which is slower than Aerial View. (See the discussion of regeneration in the section "Understanding the Display," later in this chapter).

◆ You cannot define a zoom window that extends beyond the current view except by entering the coordinates from the keyboard.

◆ The Aerial View provides a more natural and interactive interface.

The PAN command is the other way you can directly control the drawing view. The next section discusses the PAN command.

Using the PAN Command

PAN is the simplest of the display control commands. This command's effect is that of moving the drawing around at a fixed distance behind the graphics window.

Try using the PAN command in the following exercise.

Using the PAN Command

Reopen or continue to work in the ZOOM-PAN drawing. Start with a view of the entire room (like that shown in fig. 5.18; ZOOM All if needed).

Command: *Click on the Pan button or tool*	Issues the PAN command
`'_PAN Displacement:` *Pick a point in the bathroom sink*	Sets the start point of the pan
`Second point:` *Pick a point in the middle of the screen*	Defines the offset and performs the pan (see fig. 5.20)
Command: *Enter* **Z***, then* **P**	Zooms to the previous view

Use the ZOOM command with the default window option to zoom in on the entry as in the preceding exercise (see fig. 5.18 and 5.19).

`Command:` **P** (Enter)	
`Displacement:` `12'<225` (Enter)	Specifies the distance and angle for the offset

continues

continued

Figure 5.20

*A view of
the room after
using PAN.*

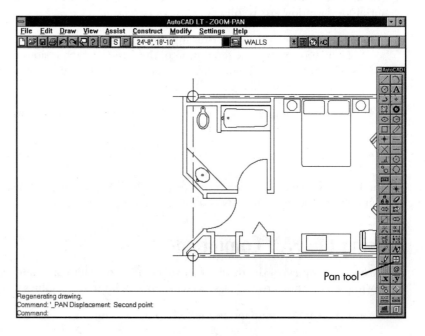

Pan tool

Second point: **(Enter)**	Accepts displacement and performs the pan
Command: *Click on the Aerial View* *button*	Shows the overall drawing and the location of the present view (see fig. 5.21)

_DSVIEWER

Figure 5.21 shows the panned view in the original Aerial View; the redesigned Aerial View shows the panned view with a reversed background.

> **PAN.** The PAN command moves the view up, down, and sideways in the drawing without changing the current zoom magnification. You can pick points or enter a displacement (offset). PAN has no command options.

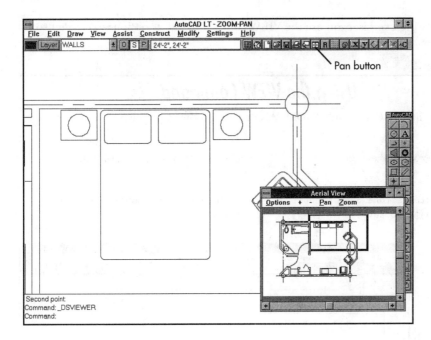

Figure 5.21

The panned view, shown in the graphics and original Aerial View windows.

The PAN command works like its counterpart in the Aerial View. The center of the view shifts while the zoom factor remains constant. The action is like moving the drawing beneath a window; the first point you pick in the drawing moves to the screen location of the second point you pick.

In AutoCAD LT, you can specify a PAN displacement by picking or entering two points from the keyboard or by entering a coordinate at the `Displacement:` prompt and pressing Enter at the `Second point:` prompt. When you press Enter at the `Second point:` prompt, AutoCAD LT interprets the first coordinate as a displacement from 0,0. You can enter either an X,Y or distance<angle displacement using this method. You must enter a value at the `Displacement:` prompt.

The next display control command, VIEW, enables you to save your view under a name that you specify. You can then use this name to redisplay the view whenever you want.

Using the VIEW Command

With ZOOM Previous, you can step back through previous views, but you cannot switch directly from one view to another or return to the view from which you previously zoomed. With the VIEW command, however, you can create, save, and then redisplay views in any sequence you like.

In the following exercise, you use the VIEW command and its options to create two named views.

Using the VIEW Command

Reopen or continue to work in the ZOOM-PAN drawing. Zoom in on the bathroom as shown in figure 5.22.

Command: *Choose* **V**iew, **V**iew, **S**ave	Issues the VIEW command with the Save option
`'_view ?/Delete/Restore/Save/Window:` `_save  View name to save:` **BATH** (Enter)	Saves the current view under the name of BATH

Figure 5.22

A view of the bathroom to be saved as BATH.

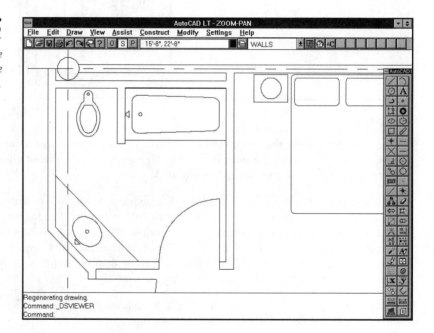

Zoom in on the table and chairs as shown in figure 5.23.

Choose **V**iew, **V**iew, **S**ave	Issues the VIEW command with the Save option
`'_view ?/Delete/Restore/Save/Window:` `_save  View name to save:` **WINDOW** (Enter)	Saves the view under the name WINDOW

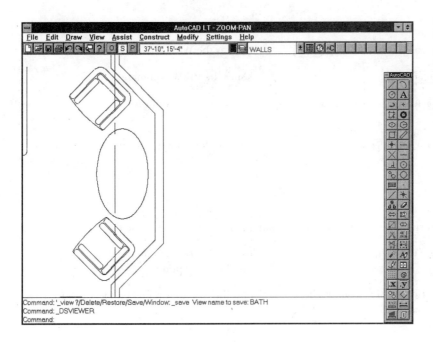

Figure 5.23

*Another view,
to be saved as
WINDOW.*

Command: (Enter)	Repeats the VIEW command
'VIEW ?/Delete/Restore/Save/Window: ? (Enter)	Specifies the list option
View(s) to list <*>: (Enter)	Displays the text window and lists all the named views in the drawing

```
Saved views:
View name                    Space
BATH                         M
WINDOW                       M
```

Press F2	Returns to the graphics window
Command: **VIEW** (Enter)	Issues the VIEW command
?/Delete/Restore/Save/Window: **R** (Enter)	Specifies the Restore option
View name to restore: **BATH** (Enter)	Restores the view named BATH
Command: (Enter)	Repeats the VIEW command
VIEW ?/Delete/Restore/Save/Window: **D** (Enter)	Specifies the Delete option

continues

5

continued

View name(s) to delete: **WINDOW** (Enter)	Deletes the WINDOW view
Command: **V** (Enter)	Issues the VIEW command
VIEW ?/Delete/Restore/Save/Window: **?** (Enter)	Specifies the list option
View(s) to list <*>: (Enter)	Lists all the named views in the drawing

```
Saved views:
View name                         Space
BATH                              M
```

Press F2 to return to the graphics window. Zoom in on an area around the closet.

Command: *Choose* **V**iew, **V**iew, **W**indow	Issues the VIEW command with the Window option
'_view ?/Delete/Restore/Save/Window: _window View name to save: **CLOSET** (Enter)	Specifies the view name that will be saved
First corner: *Pick point* ① *(see fig. 5.24)*	Starts a window
Other corner: *Pick point* ②	Completes the window and saves the CLOSET view
Command: (Enter)	Repeats the VIEW command
'VIEW ?/Delete/Restore/Save/Window: **R** (Enter)	Specifies the Restore option
View name to restore: **CLOSET** (Enter)	Displays the Closet view

The VIEW command enables you to return to any saved view at any time in the future. AutoCAD LT makes this possible by saving the view names within the drawing database. The VIEW Window option creates a view defined by the specified window, but it does not change the current view. The VIEW command can also list the views you have created. Other VIEW options depend on other display commands to set up views.

> **VIEW.** The VIEW command saves the current viewport's view or a user-specified window as a named view with a name (up to 31 characters). Saved views are then restored with the VIEW Restore option.

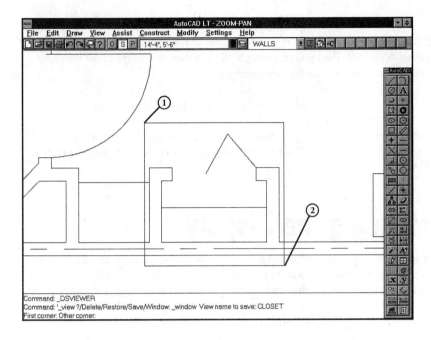

Figure 5.24

Creating a view named CLOSET using the Window option.

The VIEW command has the following options:

◆ **?.** You can enter a **?** to display a list of all saved viewport configurations, or use wild cards to list a specific set of views. (Chapter 10, "Getting Organized: Drawing on Layers," contains a full explanation of wild cards.) The list shows an M or a P to designate whether the view is defined in model space (M) or paper space (P). (See Chapter 22, "Structuring Your Drawing," for a discussion of model space and paper space.)

◆ **Delete.** You enter a **D**, and then enter the name of a view you want to delete. You can use wild cards to specify a group of views to delete.

◆ **Restore.** You enter an **R**, and then enter the name of a saved view to display it in the current viewport.

◆ **Save.** You enter an **S**, and then enter a name (up to 31 characters) to save the current viewport's view.

◆ **Window.** You enter a **W**, then a name, and then specify two corner points to define a window to save as a view by specifying its corners.

You can use the VIEW command to set up working areas in large drawings. VIEW enables you to move easily from one part of the drawing to another. You also can use VIEW to prepare on-screen presentations and to define the plot area (see Chapter 23, "Producing Hard Copy").

Tip ZOOM All requires a screen regeneration. Perform a ZOOM All, and save a view named A (for All). Then you can enter **V**, **R**, and then **A** anytime to get the same view as Zoom All, without the regeneration.

You now understand the basic display control commands, which are central to productivity in a CAD environment. The display control commands play such a crucial role that AutoCAD LT has provisions for using each of them *transparently* (in the middle of other commands). The next section explains this important aspect of using AutoCAD LT.

Understanding the Display

How does AutoCAD LT produce the image you see on the screen? It uses the geometry you create to determine which screen pixels (dots) are to be lit (turned on) and which are not. When you open a drawing, AutoCAD LT creates this pixel image in a memory area called the *virtual screen*. Then when you tell AutoCAD LT to look at a portion of the drawing (a view), it simply recalls that portion of the virtual screen. This action also takes place in a redraw. Redrawing or recalling a portion of the virtual screen takes very little time, even in a complex drawing.

As you work in the drawing, AutoCAD LT updates the virtual screen memory area; however, a few commands cause AutoCAD LT to recreate the entire virtual screen from scratch, reading back through the whole drawing database. This operation is called a *screen regeneration*, and it takes much more time than simply recalling or redrawing a portion of the virtual screen, particularly in a complex drawing.

Recognizing Sources for Screen Regenerations

As you might have guessed, screen regenerations (or simply *regens*) should be avoided if at all possible. Fortunately, the size of the virtual screen can be quite large, depending on how much memory is available to AutoCAD LT. A real need to regenerate the virtual screen occurs infrequently. The following commands and procedures automatically force a regeneration:

- ◆ REGEN
- ◆ ZOOM All
- ◆ ZOOM Extents
- ◆ VPORTS

- Defining a new linetype (Chapter 13, "Using Object Properties and Text Styles")

- Defining a new text style (Chapter 13, "Using Object Properties and Text Styles")

- Redefining a block definition (Chapter 19, "Managing and Modifying Blocks and Xrefs")

- Resizing the graphics window

The purpose of the REGEN command is to force a regeneration of the virtual screen. As an example, you might want to use the REGEN command in the following situation: you are zoomed in to a small area and find that the vectors used to define curved surfaces are too few to provide clarity. Be aware that when you attempt to zoom back out, AutoCAD LT will need to do another screen regeneration.

The ZOOM All command must calculate whether it should display the limits of the drawing or the extents. The drawing *extents* are defined as the window that would be required to enclose all the objects within the drawing. If objects exist outside the limits, then a ZOOM Extents is performed.

To determine whether the current virtual screen includes the drawing extents, AutoCAD LT would have to examine each object in the database and then compare the extracted data with the limits defined in the virtual screen. AutoCAD LT takes a faster approach to this problem and simply recalculates the virtual screen. Because ZOOM All and ZOOM Extents both involve this problem, both cause regenerations.

The VPORTS command creates multiple views of the drawing, each of which is handled in a separate viewport. Whenever the number of displayed viewports is changed, a new virtual screen must be created; therefore, the VPORTS command forces a regeneration.

With the speed of the modern PC and the amount of memory available for the virtual screen, screen regenerations are not the nightmare they once were. A regeneration in a large, dense drawing can still be rather lengthy, but now you know how to avoid regenerations.

At the opposite end of the spectrum from those commands that require a regeneration are the commands that can be performed transparently. The next section discusses transparent commands.

Understanding Transparent Commands

The display commands described in the first section of this chapter are typical of AutoCAD LT commands that you might need to use while you are in the middle of another command. You already have used some transparent commands in a previous exercise. In the following exercise, pay close attention to the behavior of these commands.

Using Commands Transparently

Reopen or continue to work in the ZOOM-PAN drawing. If needed, zoom in on the closet as previously shown in figure 5.24.

Open the Aerial View and click on its minimize button or use its control menu to minimize it for later access.

Command: *Click on the Line tool*	Issues the LINE command
_LINE From point: *Pick a point in the middle of the closet*	Starts a line
To point: *Choose* **V**iew, **V**iew, **R**estore	Issues the VIEW command with the Restore option
'_view >>?/Delete/Restore/Save/Window: _restore >> View name to restore: **BATH** (Enter)	Restores the BATH view
Resuming LINE command.	
To point: *Pick a point in the center of the room at* ① *(see fig. 5.25)*	Locates the second endpoint in the bathroom
To point: *Click on the Pan button or tool*	Issues the PAN command
'_PAN >>Displacement: *Pick point* ②	
>> Second point: *Pick point* ③	Pans into the lower right corner of the hotel room
Resuming LINE command.	
To point: *Pick a point in the middle of the round column*	Locates the third endpoint in the center of the column
To point: *Click on the Zoom button*	Issues the ZOOM command
'_ZOOM >>Center/Previous/Window/ <Scale(X/XP)>: **C** (Enter)	Specifies the Center option

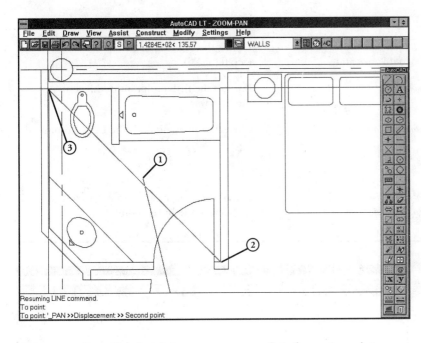

Figure 5.25

Locating an endpoint in the BATH view and designating a PAN.

>>Center point: *Pick the point 18',12'* | Sets the center point

>>Magnification or Height <9'-0">: **22' (Enter)** | Specifies the height and zooms to show the room

Resuming LINE command.

To point: *Pick a point in the middle of the bed at 19'-6",18'-0"* | Locates the fourth endpoint in the center of the bed

To point: *Click on the Aerial View button* | Issues the DSVIEWER command

_DSVIEWER
Point or option keyword required. | Indicates an invalid command

AutoCAD LT does not allow you to open the Aerial View transparently. Use Windows methods to redisplay the Aerial View. In AutoCAD LT Release 1, you can use Alt+Tab or double-click on its minimized icon (which might be hidden by the graphics window). In AutoCAD LT Release 2, you must click on its minimized icon (which is always visible on top of the graphics window).

Double-click on the minimized Aerial View icon or press Alt+Tab one or more times until the Aerial View appears | Opens the Aerial View

continues

continued

Specify a window around the entry then minimize the Aerial View again	Zooms the drawing to a view of the entry (see fig. 5.26)
`To point:` *Pick point* ④	Locates the fifth endpoint in the center of the doorway
`To point:` *Click on the Close button or tool*	Closes the line and ends the LINE command
`_CLOSE`	
`Command:` *Click on the Aerial View button and zoom to the view shown in figure 5.27*	Opens the Aerial View and zooms to the full view of the hotel room

Figure 5.26

Locating an endpoint after using the Aerial View.

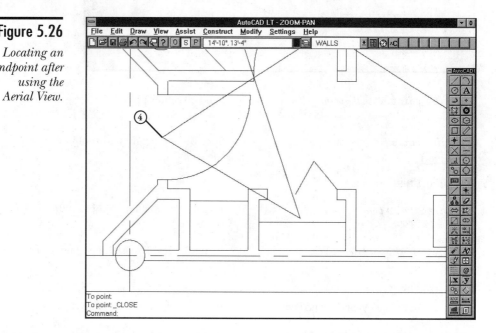

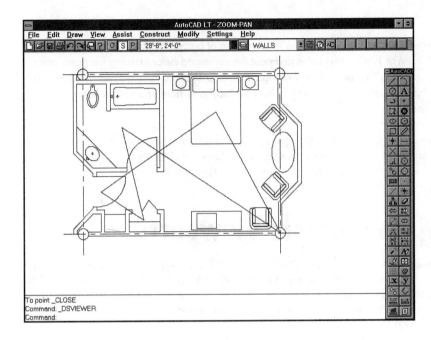

Figure 5.27

*A line generated
with intermediate
transparent
commands.*

The buttons, tools, and menu items issued VIEW, PAN, and ZOOM commands with
leading apostrophes. This symbol issues the command transparently, which means
that instead of canceling a running command like LINE, the transparent command
runs underneath the running command. The prompt shows the ">>" symbol to
indicate a transparent command.

The ZOOM command has fewer options when it is run transparently. The All and
Extents options are not present because they require regenerations, and AutoCAD LT
cannot be regenerated during a command.

You can issue many commands transparently. To enter a command transparently
from the keyboard, precede the standard command name with an apostrophe. When
you complete or cancel the transparent command, you return to the command you
interrupted. Other transparent commands include 'COLOR, 'GRID, 'HELP, 'LAYER,
'LIMITS, 'ORTHO, 'OSNAP, 'REDRAW, 'SNAP, 'STYLE, plus many of the dialog box
commands and most system variables.

Transparent display control commands are invaluable when you need to do the
following:

◆ Copy or move objects from one small, crowded area of a drawing to another

◆ Use a command repeatedly at multiple locations in a large drawing

◆ Draw or place large features in proper relation to small details

Tip

When alternating between the repeated use of a command and a transparent ZOOM or PAN, press Enter to repeat the command *before* issuing the transparent command. You then take advantage of AutoCAD LT's command repeat feature while you move transparently to the next location where you need to use the command.

You have now seen ways of adjusting your view of a drawing within the graphics window. AutoCAD LT also provides a way to display several views of a drawing at one time (called *viewports*). This subject is discussed in the last section of this chapter.

Setting Up Multiple Viewports

You can use the Aerial View or the ZOOM and PAN commands to focus your view of the drawing anywhere you choose and in any size. You can use the VIEW command to save and restore as many specific views as you need, but so far you see only one view at a time. Viewports offer a solution when you need to perform close work simultaneously in several locations.

The following exercise emulates placing conduit runs in an electrical plan. This application illustrates a typical use for viewports, but you can probably imagine other uses in your own work. In the following exercise, you work with some of the VPORTS command options.

Using Multiple Viewports

Create a new drawing named VIEWPORT, using the ALT0502.DWG as a prototype.

Command: *If using AutoCAD LT Release 1 and full menus are not currently displayed, choose* **S**ettings, **F**ull Menu

Selects the full menu

Command: *Choose* **V**iew, Viewp**o**rts, **3** Viewports

Issues the VPORTS command with the 3 (viewports) option

```
_vports
Save/Restore/Delete/Join/SIngle/?/2/
<3>/4: _3
```

`Horizontal/Vertical/Above/Below/Left/` `<Right>:` (Enter)	Accepts the default Right side configuration
`Regenerating drawing.`	Creates viewports like those shown in figure 5.28, and regenerates the drawing
`Command:` *Click in the upper left viewport*	Makes the upper left viewport active
`Command:` *Click on the Aerial View button*	Opens the Aerial View
`_DSVIEWER` *Zoom in on the bathroom to match figure 5.28, then close the Aerial View*	
`Command:` *Click in the lower left viewport*	Makes the lower left viewport active
`Command:` *Click on the Zoom button*	Issues the ZOOM command
`'_ZOOM All/Center/Extents/Previous/` `Window/<Scale(X/XP)>:` *Pick point* ① *(see fig. 5.28)*	Sets first window point to zoom in on the chase
`Other corner:` *Pick point* ②	Zooms the lower left viewport to match figure 5.29
`Command:` *Click on the Arc tool*	Issues the ARC command
`_ARC Center/<Start point>:` *Pick point* ③ *(see fig. 5.29)*	Sets the start point of the arc
`Center/End/<Second point>:` *Pick point* ④	Sets a point on the curve of the arc
Click in the upper left viewport	Makes the upper left viewport active
`End point:` *Pick point* ⑤	Sets the endpoint of the arc in the bathroom

5

Figure 5.28

*Zooming in on
the electrical
chase.*

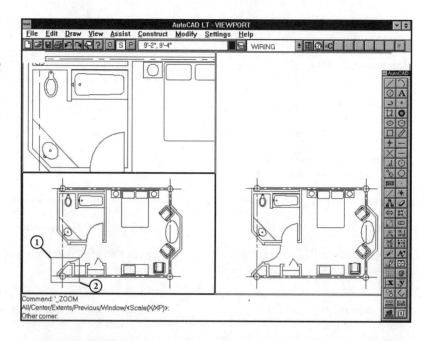

Figure 5.29

*Running a wire
from the chase to
the bathroom.*

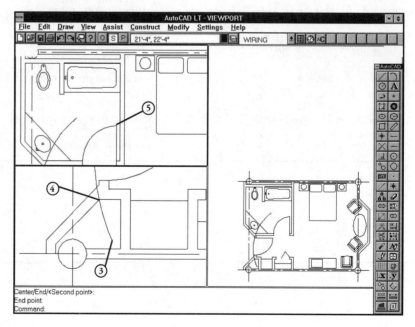

The same drawing appears in three viewports. The viewport outlined by a dark line is *active*. The cursor changes as you move across the three viewports: it appears as crosshairs in the active viewport and as an arrow pointer in the inactive viewports. The PAN and ZOOM commands apply only to the active viewport. The Aerial View displays a black outline or reverse background indicating the area displayed in the active viewport. In AutoCAD LT Release 2, you might need to choose Menu, then **Set** to Current VP in the Aerial View or click in the Aerial View with the *not-VP cursor* (the circled and slashed VP symbol) to update it to the current viewport.

The actual command name is VPORTS (or VIEWPORTS). This command is not available from the short menu.

> **VPORTS or VIEWPORTS.** With the TILEMODE system variable set to 1 (1 = on, which is the default), the VPORTS command divides your screen into tiled viewports. The current view (viewpoint or perspective), and the SNAP, GRID, ISOMETRIC, and UCSICON settings can differ in each viewport. Each viewport can be zoomed independently.

The VPORTS command has Save and Restore options, like the VIEW command. VPORTS also has options to help you create viewport configurations to suit your specific application. The VPORTS command has the following options:

◆ **Save.** You enter an **S** and a name (up to 31 characters) to save the current viewport configuration.

◆ **Restore.** The Restore option restores any saved viewport configuration. You enter an **R**, and then enter a specific name to restore or a **?** to list saved viewport configurations. After you list the viewports, you will be reprompted for the name to restore. See the description of the **?** option for more on listing viewports.

◆ **Delete.** You enter a **D** and a name to delete a saved viewport configuration.

◆ **Join.** You enter a **J** and specify two viewports to combine or join. You can press Enter to accept the current viewport as the first (dominant) viewport, or click in another viewport to select it as dominant. Then you click in the viewport you want to join to the dominant viewport. The two viewports must be adjacent and form a rectangle. The resulting viewport inherits the view and settings of the dominant viewport.

◆ **SIngle.** You enter **SI** to change the screen to a single viewport, which displays the view of the current viewport.

5

◆ **?.** You enter a **?** to list the name and location of each viewport. Then you enter an asterisk to list all the defined viewport configurations, or use wild cards to list a specific set of viewports. The list is displayed in the text window; press F2 to return to the graphics window.

◆ **2.** You enter a **2** to divide the current viewport into a horizontal or vertical pair of viewports.

◆ **3.** You enter a **3** or press Enter at the initial prompt to divide the current viewport into three viewports. You then specify the configuration you want from six available options: all Horizontal, all Vertical, one Above, one Below, one on the Left, and one on the Right (the default).

◆ **4.** You enter a **4** to divide the current viewport into four equal viewports.

In the viewport listing, a viewport is located by its lower left and upper right corners. The screen is considered to be one unit wide and one unit high in display coordinates (not drawing coordinates). The corners are then located using X and Y coordinates between 0.00 and 1.00.

In the following exercise, you save, list, join, and restore viewports, then return to a single viewport.

Using the VPORTS Command Options

Continue to work in the VIEWPORT drawing from the preceding exercise.

Command: **VPORTS** (Enter)   Issues the VPORTS command

Save/Restore/Delete/Join/SIngle/?/2/   Specifies the Save option
<3>/4: **S** (Enter)

?/Name for new viewport configuration: Saves the current viewport configuration
WIRING (Enter)   under the name WIRING

Command: (Enter)   Repeats the VPORTS command

VPORTS

Save/Restore/Delete/Join/SIngle/?/2/   Specifies the List option
<3>/4: **?** (Enter)

Viewport configuration(s) to list <*>:   Lists all the defined viewports and
(Enter)   their screen coordinates, as follows:

```
Current configuration:
id# 3
  corners: 0.0000,0.5000 0.5000,1.0000
id# 4
  corners: 0.0000,0.0000 0.5000,0.5000
id# 2
  corners: 0.5000,0.0000 1.0000,1.0000

Configuration WIRING:
    0.0000,0.5000 0.5000,1.0000
    0.0000,0.0000 0.5000,0.5000
    0.5000,0.0000 1.0000,1.0000
```

Locates viewports:
Locates the upper left viewport

Locates the lower left viewport

Locates the right side viewport

Shows that the WIRING configuration
has three viewports located at these
display coordinates

Press F2

Returns to the graphics window

Command: (Enter)

Repeats the VPORTS command

VPORTS

Save/Restore/Delete/Join/SIngle/?/2/
<3>/4: **J** (Enter)

Specifies the Join option

Select dominant viewport <current>:
(Enter)

Selects the current upper left viewport

Select viewport to join: *Click in the*
lower left viewport

Joins the two viewports on the left

Regenerating drawing.

Changing the number of viewports always causes a regeneration.

Command: *Click on the Aerial View*

Opens the Aerial View

Use pan mode to center the view and exit the
Aerial View

Pans, and closes the Aerial View

Command: *Choose* **V**iew, Viewp**o**rts, **R**estore

Issues the VPORTS command with the
Restore option

_vports
Save/Restore/Delete/Join/SIngle/?/2/
<3>/4: _restore

?/Name of viewport configuration to
restore: **WIRING** (Enter)

Restores the WIRING viewport configuration

Regenerating drawing.

Restores a single viewport

continues

continued

Click in the right viewport	Makes it current
Command: **(Enter)**	Repeats the VPORTS command
VPORTS	
Save/Restore/Delete/Join/SIngle/?/2/ <3>/4: **SI** **(Enter)**	Specifies the SIngle option
Regenerating drawing.	Restores a single viewport

The list of the saved viewports specifies the location of each viewport defined in it. The Join option uses the current viewport as the default for the dominant viewport. The view in the dominant viewport becomes the view in the joined viewport. You cannot join two viewports that would not form a rectangle, such as the one on the lower left with the one on the right. The single viewport has the same view and settings as the viewport from which it was created.

Viewports are handy when your work involves doing similar or related work in different parts of a large drawing. Often two viewports are enough, although a third can serve as an overview if you don't use the Aerial View. If three or four viewports are not enough, try subdividing one of the viewports into two or more viewports, and then dividing one of those, and so on. AutoCAD LT stops you when the viewports get too small for the screen or if the division would create more than 16 viewports.

In paper space (see Chapter 22, "Structuring Your Drawing"), AutoCAD LT provides another type of viewport, which is useful for composing and plotting a drawing, as well as for working in and viewing multiple views.

Now you know how to move around in your drawings and adjust your view so that you can see what you are working on. The next chapter introduces you to one of the fundamental processes you use to create drawings using AutoCAD LT: using editing commands to replicate and modify existing objects.

C H A P T E R

6

Making Changes: Using Basic Editing Tools

This chapter introduces you to the real power of CAD—how easily you can make changes. You learn to delete, move, and copy objects and to recover quickly from mistakes. You also learn to make changes by using an interactive editing feature called *grip editing*. This chapter includes the following topics in its discussion of the AutoCAD LT editing process:

◆ Selecting objects for editing

◆ Controlling selections with selection options

◆ Setting AutoCAD LT's selection and editing modes

◆ Correcting errors with the ERASE and OOPS commands

◆ Working with the MOVE and COPY commands

◆ Backstepping with the UNDO command

The first section of the chapter focuses on object selection, which is central to the process of editing. The second section continues the discussion of the selection options and covers the three basic editing commands, ERASE, MOVE, and COPY, as well as ERASE's counterpart, OOPS. The U (Undo) command is used throughout this chapter. For more complete control over errors and changes, the final section of this chapter explores the U, UNDO, and REDO commands. Chapter 7, "Making Changes: Using Grip Editing," explores editing with grips, which enables you to grab and directly manipulate objects by geometric points such as endpoints, midpoints, and center points.

The skilled pilot, like any master, makes a smooth flight look easy. Flying is an active endeavor, requiring the pilot's constant attention to small details of the aircraft's performance and the outside environment while he makes control, navigation, and communication decisions. Similarly, the best CAD drawings are the result of skillful attention to detail, and you achieve this attention to detail with editing as much as with careful drawing.

Editing in CAD is an important skill. Your editing ability will probably be the key factor in determining your efficiency in CAD. To develop good editing skills, it is important for you to understand AutoCAD LT's editing process, as well as the mechanics of making object selections, editing objects, and recovering from errors.

Understanding AutoCAD LT's Editing Process

Editing in AutoCAD LT can actually involve two distinct and different processes:

1. You can replicate and modify objects in AutoCAD LT through the use of editing commands. In the traditional command-oriented method (sometimes called *verb-noun editing*), the user issues a command to initiate the editing process, and then selects the objects to edit. AutoCAD LT offers an alternative for most editing commands (sometimes called *noun-verb editing*), in which you select the objects and then issue the command that acts upon them. This chapter covers both verb-noun and noun-verb editing with editing commands.

2. AutoCAD LT also provides an alternative grip editing process for replicating and modifying objects. *Grips* are small boxes that appear at the points (such as endpoints, midpoints, and centers) of selected objects. In this alternative grip editing process, you first select the objects to edit, then manipulate their grip points to modify or copy them. Grip editing is always a noun-verb process. By careful object selection and the use of grip points and options, you can do a wide variety of editing in a fluid, interactive manner. Chapter 7, "Making Changes: Using Grip Editing," covers editing with grips.

Grips are enabled or disabled by the GRIPS AutoCAD LT system variable. (See Chapter 8, "Preparing Your Workspace: CAD Concepts 1B," for more on system variables.) By default, grips are initially enabled. To clarify the distinction between traditional object selection and the grip editing process, the following quick exercise disables grips. You can then work with selection options and editing commands before you learn how grip editing works in the next chapter.

Disabling Grips

Start AutoCAD LT with a new unnamed drawing.

Command: **GRIPS** (Enter)	Prompts for a new GRIPS system variable setting
New value for GRIPS <1>: **0** (Enter)	Disables grips

 Note The GRIPS setting is stored in AutoCAD LT itself rather than in the drawing that happens to be current at the time. Grips will remain disabled until you change the GRIPS setting in the next chapter. Keep this in mind if you should decide to skip ahead to a chapter that uses grips.

You start your examination of the editing process with a look at the selection options.

Working with Object Selection

To manual drafters, changes and edits are the bane of their existence. To move a pencil line, the drafter has to erase the line and redraw it in a new location. The drafter *selects* a line to erase by positioning an eraser. This procedure often requires skill with an erasing shield and is long, tedious, and demoralizing work. Changing inked drawings is even more difficult.

CAD changes all that. CAD editing is much easier than manual drafting, although design work in CAD drawing is often more editing than drawing. Much of the power of CAD lies in the ease with which you can modify and replicate drawing objects.

Selecting Objects to Edit

CAD drawing elements are objects that are defined within the drawing database, and displayed on screen or plotted. The process of selecting these objects is a fundamental part of editing.

In the following exercise, you observe how object selection works.

Selecting Objects

Create a new drawing named FIXBASE (replacing the old FIXBASE drawing), using the ALT0601.DWG drawing file as a prototype. GRIPS should be turned off from the preceding exercise.

`Command:` *Click on the Erase tool*	Issues the ERASE command
`_ERASE`	
`Select objects:` *Pick the line at* ① *(see fig. 6.1)*	Selects and highlights the line
`1 found`	
`Select objects:` *Pick the line at* ②	Selects and highlights the line
`1 found`	
`Select objects:` *Pick point* ③ *and move the cursor to* ④	Starts a window
`Other corner:` *Pick point* ④	Selects the objects contained in the window
`2 found`	
`Select objects:` *Pick point* ⑤ *and move the cursor to* ⑥	Starts a crossing window
`Other corner:` *Pick point* ⑥	Selects all the objects within or crossing the window
`4 found`	

Five lines, two circles, and an arc should now be highlighted and selected.

`Select objects:` **Q** (Enter)	Enters an invalid option; AutoCAD LT prompts with valid options

`*Invalid selection*`
`Expects a point or Window/Last/Crossing/ BOX/ALL/Fence/WPolygon/CPolygon/Add/`
`Remove/Multiple/Previous/Undo/AUto/SIngle`	

`Select objects:` (Enter)	Erases the selections
`Command:` *Click on the U (undo) button*	Issues the U command

`_U ERASE`	Restores the objects

Next, reselect the same objects before issuing the ERASE command.

Command: *Pick the line at* ①	Selects the line
Command: *Pick the line at* ②	Selects the line
Command: *Pick point* ③	Starts a window
Other corner: *Pick point* ④	Selects the contained objects
Command: *Pick point* ⑤	Starts a window
Other corner: *Pick point* ⑥	Selects crossing objects
Command: **E** (Enter)	Issues the ERASE command and erases the selections

`_ERASE 8 found`

Command: *Click on the U (Undo) button*	Issues the U command

`_U ERASE`   Restores the objects

Command: *Click on the Save button*	Saves the FIXBASE drawing

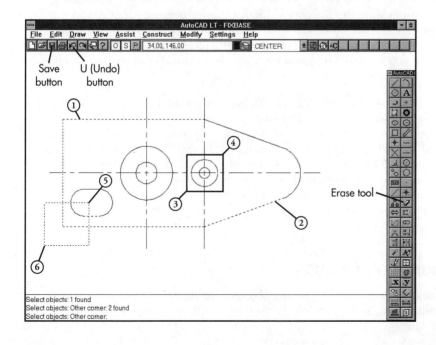

Figure 6.1

Selecting objects in AutoCAD LT.

6

The preceding exercise demonstrates two basic approaches to selection and editing: you can start the command and then select the objects, or you can make the object selection first, then issue the command.

If you view CAD as a language, the editing command is a verb, and the objects being edited are the nouns. In command-selection editing, you issue the command (verb) first, then select the objects (nouns). This is called verb-noun editing. In selection-command editing you select the objects (nouns) first, then issue the command (verb). This is called noun-verb editing.

In the first method (verb-noun), when AutoCAD LT prompts for a selection to be made (with the `Select objects:` prompt), the cursor changes to a small square, called the *pick box*. Objects are *highlighted* when they are selected. You can select them by picking, windowing, or several other methods. When you select more objects, they are added to a *selection set*. The object selection process has many options (even though they are not listed at each prompt). Pressing Enter completes object selection, and the command then acts upon the selection set. Pressing Ctrl+C or choosing the Cancel button instead of pressing Enter cancels object selection and deselects any objects in the selection set.

 Note The highlighting of very small circles and arcs may not be visible.

In the second method (noun-verb), when objects are selected before issuing the command, the appearance of the cursor doesn't change because AutoCAD LT doesn't know what you are doing yet. As in the first method, the objects are highlighted as you select them. Issuing a command completes object selection, and the command then acts upon the selection set. Canceling instead of entering a command deselects all the objects.

Either method works with most editing commands. A few commands (ones that only accept picking, not windowing) require issuing the command first. Whether you choose objects before or after commands, the selection process is a distinct and required step. If you have not made an object selection prior to invoking an editing command, AutoCAD LT prompts you to select objects before any editing actually begins. The selection process ends when you press Enter and the actual editing begins. On the other hand, if you make your object selections prior to invoking an editing command, the selection process begins when you select something and ends when you issue a command.

Using Selection Options

Although the default methods of picking objects individually and using windows or crossing windows usually accomplish what you need, the other object selection options can save you a great deal of time under the right circumstances. Familiarity with these options will enable you to use the most efficient object selection methods possible.

The object selection options are not listed on any menu or within any dialog box, but they are available whenever AutoCAD LT prompts you to select objects. In the first exercise, you used an invalid selection option character to force AutoCAD LT to display its object selection options. The following object selection prompt was displayed:

```
*Invalid selection*
Expects a point or Window/Last/Crossing/BOX/ALL/Fence/WPolygon/
CPolygon/Add/Remove/Multiple/Previous/Undo/AUto/SIngle
```

The default method (if implied windowing—the PICKAUTO system variable—is on) is a combination of the first three methods shown in the following list: pick, Window, and Crossing. If no object is found by a pick, object selection enters Window/Crossing mode. Then AutoCAD LT determines whether to make a window or crossing selection by whether the second pick is to the right or left of the first. (You can explicitly specify this combination method by using the AUto option.)

AutoCAD LT provides the following object selection methods:

- **Object pick.** The default pick method enables you to pick individual objects. When you pick objects, AutoCAD LT searches for and selects the most recently created object that falls within or crosses the pick box. Some editing commands, such as TRIM, can act on only one object at a time and require picking by a point or a fence.

- **Window.** The window method selects objects contained within a window you specify. You can pick two points left to right, or enter **W** and pick any two points. AutoCAD LT selects only those objects that are enclosed entirely within the window. Lines that are overlapped by the window edge are considered to be enclosed.

- **Crossing.** The crossing method works the same as window, except that crossing also includes any object that is partially within (or crossing) the window. You can pick two points right-to-left, or enter **C** and pick any two points.

- **Fence.** The Fence option enables you to pick a series of points defining an open polyline fence. When you press Enter, all objects touched by the polyline fence are selected. Some editing commands, such as TRIM, can act on only one object at a time and require picking by a point or a fence. If you use a fence to select objects, each is treated as if picked at the point where the fence line first crosses the object.

6

◆ **WPolygon.** The WPolygon option is similar to the Window selection, but it enables you to pick a series of points defining an irregular polygon. When you press Enter, all objects completely within the polygon are selected.

◆ **CPolygon.** The CPolygon option is similar to the Crossing selection, but it enables you to pick a series of points defining an irregular polygon. When you press Enter, all objects inside or crossed by the polygon are selected.

◆ **Multiple.** The Multiple option enables you to pick multiple objects in close proximity. This option speeds up selection by making multiple selections possible without highlighting or prompting. An extra Enter is required to complete the multiple selection and return to normal object selection. Multiple also prevents AutoCAD LT from otherwise finding the same object repeatedly instead of finding multiple objects near the same point.

◆ **ALL.** The ALL option selects all objects in the drawing that are not on a locked or frozen layer.

◆ **Last.** The Last option selects the most recently created object.

◆ **Previous.** The Previous option reselects the entire preceding selection set (from a previous command or object selection session) as the current selection set. Erasing the previous objects or undoing the previous editing command clears the previous selection set.

◆ **Remove.** The Remove option switches to Remove mode. Subsequently selected objects are removed from the selection set (not from the drawing). You also can use Shift to remove selected objects from the set.

◆ **Add.** The Add option switches from the Remove mode back to normal object selection so that you can again add to the selection set. If the Use Shift to Add setting is on (the PICKADD system variable is off), you also can use Shift to add selected objects to the set.

◆ **Undo.** The Undo option undoes or reverses the last selection operation. Each Undo undoes one selection operation.

The final three options are intended for use in menu items that preset the selection options. The manual use of these three options is no more efficient than the previous options and methods.

◆ **AUto.** The AUto option combines the default methods of pick, Window, and Crossing, in a combined method called implied windowing. AUto mode is always available if the Implied Windowing selection setting is on (the PICKAUTO system variable is set to 1).

◆ **BOX.** The BOX option combines the Window and Crossing options. Pick two points from left to right for a window selection or from right to left for a crossing selection.

◆ **SIngle.** The SIngle option works in conjunction with the other selection options. If you precede a selection with SIngle, object selection automatically ends after the first successful selection without having to press Enter, as normally required to exit object selection.

Tip You can force AutoCAD LT to make a window or crossing selection by entering the Window or Crossing option if the first pick would otherwise find and select an object.

The objects selected are referred to as a *selection set*. Creating selection sets is a fundamental part of the CAD process. To find quick ways to create the selection set you need, practice using the various selection options. Note that it is often easier to select more than you need and then remove some of the objects.

Objects must be at least partially visible to be selected with any method except the ALL option, which selects all objects in the database regardless of visibility. Window selections ignore off-screen portions of objects, so if you window the entire visible portion of an object that extends beyond the current view, the object will be selected.

Note If snap and object snap (see Chapter 11, "Achieving Accuracy: The Geometric Power of CAD") are used together, AutoCAD LT snaps first and then performs the object snaps from that snapped point.

Turn snap off for object selections if you need to pick an object that is off the snap grid. Be sure to turn snap back on before picking drawing or edit points.

In the preceding exercise, you used the default object pick, window, and crossing window methods of object selection. If you picked a point on an object, it was selected. If you picked in an open area, you entered Window/Crossing mode, where you selected a window left to right or a crossing window right to left. By contrast, the following exercise uses explicit Window, Crossing, and several other options for selecting objects.

Using Selection Options

Continue in the FIXBASE drawing from the preceding exercise.

Command: *Click on the Erase tool*   Issues the ERASE command

continues

6

continued

```
_ERASE
```

`Select objects: W (Enter)`	Specifies the Window option
`First corner:` *Pick the line at* ① *(see fig. 6.2)*	Starts a window

Notice that the line was not selected even though you picked it. Move the cursor around; it defines a window (not crossing window) no matter what direction you move it.

`Other corner:` *Pick point* ②	Defines the window and selects the arc
`1 found`	
`Select objects: C (Enter)`	Specifies the Crossing option
`First corner:` *Pick* ① *again*	Starts a crossing window

Move the cursor around again; it defines a crossing window no matter where you move it.

`Other corner:` *Pick point* ②	Defines the crossing window and selects both angled lines, the center line, and the arc
`4 found (1 duplicate)`	Indicates that the arc was already selected
`Select objects:` *Press Ctrl+C*	Cancels the ERASE command and deselects all the objects

Figure 6.2

Defining a window selection.

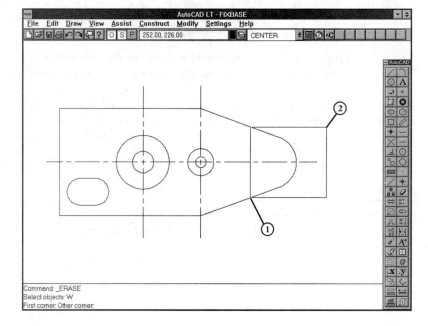

Command: **(Enter)**	Repeats the ERASE command
ERASE	
Select objects: **CP** **(Enter)**	Specifies the CPolygon (crossing polygon) option
First polygon point: *Pick* ③ *(see fig. 6.3)*	Starts a closed polygon
Undo/<Endpoint of line>: *Turn off ortho and pick the points* ④ *through* ⑨, *then turn ortho back on*	Defines a polygon outlining the end of the fixture base
Undo/<Endpoint of line>: **(Enter)**	Completes the selection
7 found	

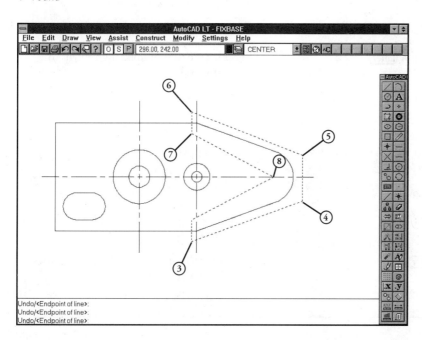

Figure 6.3

Using the crossing polygon option.

Select objects: **R** **(Enter)**	Specifies the Remove option, which switches to removing objects from the selection set
Remove objects: *Pick the line at* ⑩ *(see fig. 6.4)*	Deselects and dehighlights the line

continues

continued

```
1 found, 1 removed
```

Remove objects: *Pick the intersection of the*   Deselects one of the lines
center lines ⑪

```
1 found, 1 removed
```

Remove objects: *Pick again at* ⑪   Finds the same line again, so it does nothing

```
1 found
```

Remove objects: **M** (Enter)   Specifies the Multiple option

Remove objects: *Pick twice again at* ⑪,   Finds both center lines, ends Multiple mode,
and press Enter   and deselects the second line

```
2 selected, 2 found, 1 removed
```

Remove objects: **A** (Enter)   Specifies the Add option, and returns to
          selection mode

Select objects: *Pick the circle at* ⑫   Adds the circle to the selection set

```
1 found
```

Select objects: *Hold down Shift while*   Deselects the line
picking the bottom line at ⑬

```
1 found, 1 removed
```

Select objects: (Enter)   Completes object selection and erases the
          selected objects

Command: **U** (Enter)   Enters U (Undo) command, which undoes
          the ERASE command.

ERASE

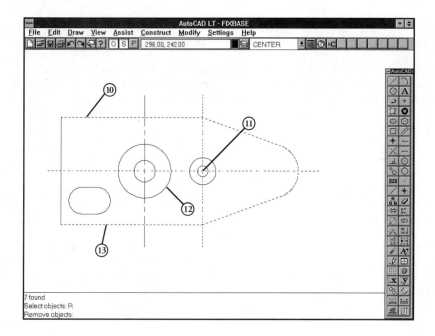

Figure 6.4

Objects deselected with the Remove option and Shift+pick.

The default mode for any object selection is to add objects with default object pick, Window, and Crossing window methods. AutoCAD LT also accepts selection options at any `Select objects:` or `Remove objects:` prompt so that you can switch to another selection option without interrupting the selection process. To enter a selection option, you need only enter the letters shown in uppercase in the object selection options prompt.

Each time a selection is made, AutoCAD LT normally reports how many objects were found (and any duplicates) and removed (if any). This feedback is useful, but it can get in the way when you attempt to select multiple objects at the same point. In Multiple mode, this feedback is suspended, so you can pick any number of objects without AutoCAD LT repeatedly finding the same object when you pick several times at one point. Multiple suspends feedback and highlighting until you press Enter, and then it reports the number selected and the number found. You cannot use other selection options during Multiple mode.

You can use any selection option in either Add or Remove mode. When you are in the default Add mode, a selection made with Shift held down removes objects from the selection set. The opposite is not true, however; when you are in Remove mode, a shifted selection does not add objects.

6

When you want to start a window at a point occupied by an object, use the Window or the Crossing option to prevent the first pick from selecting the object.

Specifying the Undo option at the Select objects: prompt undoes the last selection. The CPolygon, WPolygon, and Fence options have an additional Undo option of their own that releases the last point selected, so that you can adjust a window, polygon, or fence without having to start over. Specifying U with a window creates an error that drops the first point and lets you pick again.

The Window, Crossing, CPolygon, WPolygon, and Fence selections must be completed once they are started. If you use Ctrl+C (Cancel) to end a selection, the current command (such as ERASE) will also be canceled. If you start one of these options in error, you should complete the operation and then use U (Undo) to reverse the selection.

The preceding exercise used only a few of the many options available when AutoCAD LT prompts to select objects. Other selection options are used in exercises later in this chapter. In these exercises, you learn to use selection options within specific editing commands.

In this chapter so far, you have used the default selection settings. AutoCAD LT makes it possible to alter these settings to change AutoCAD LT's selection behavior. The next section discusses how to change selection settings.

Changing Selection Behavior

By default, AutoCAD LT gives you the option of selecting objects before or after issuing a command. Also, you can start either a Window or a Crossing window with a pick in empty space. AutoCAD LT provides control over these and other settings affecting the selection process with the Entity Selection Settings dialog box.

In the following exercise, you open the Entity Selection Settings dialog box and make some changes to the default settings. You can open this dialog box by entering the DDSELECT command or choosing Selection Style from the full **S**ettings menu.

In the exercise, you start by confirming how the defaults work, and then you test the effect of changes to AutoCAD LT's selection settings. You will turn off **N**oun/Verb Selection, which disables selecting before issuing a command. You will also turn on **P**ress and Drag, which enables you to indicate windows by pressing the pick button, dragging, and releasing the button instead of using two distinct picks to indicate a window. You will also turn on **U**se Shift to Add. Previously, objects were added to the selection set as they were selected, and a Shift-pick removed objects from the set. Instead, **U**se Shift to Add causes a Shift-pick to add to the set and an unshifted pick to replace the previous set. You also adjust the size of the pick box, which determines how far AutoCAD LT searches for objects.

Changing Selection Settings

Continue in the FIXBASE drawing from any preceding exercise.

Command: *Pick point* ① *(see fig. 6.5)*	Starts a window
Other corner: *Pick point* ②	Selects a crossing window
Command: *Pick the circle at* ③	Adds the circle to the selection set
Command: **E** (Enter)	Issues ERASE and performs the erase
ERASE 5 found	
Command: *Click on the Undo button*	Reverses the erase

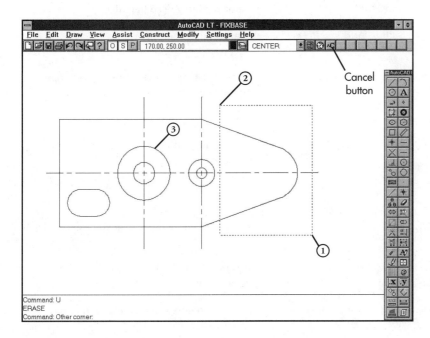

Figure 6.5

Selecting objects.

If using AutoCAD LT Release 1 and the **S**ettings menu does not show a Sele**c**tion Style item, choose **S**ettings, then **F**ull menu.

Command: *Choose* **S**ettings, Sele**c**tion Style	Issues the DDSELECT command and opens the Entity Selection Settings dialog box (see fig. 6.6)

continues

6

continued

```
'_ddselect
```

Remove the X *from the* **N**oun/Verb Selection *check box (click on it), and click on* OK	Turns off Noun/Verb Selection and closes dialog box

Try to repeat the previous crossing selection; nothing happens with **N**oun/Verb Selection off.

Next, you turn on **P**ress and Drag and **U**se Shift to Add, and adjust the size of the pick box.

Command: (Enter)	Reopens the Entity Selection Settings dialog box

```
'_DDSELECT.
```

Choose **D**efault Selection Mode	Restores **N**oun/Verb default
Put checks in the **U**se Shift to Add *and* **P**ress and Drag *check boxes*	Turns on these settings
Click and drag the box in the Pickbox **S**ize *slider bar*	Adjusts the pick box size (watch it change the indicator box at the right)
Click on OK	Makes settings and closes dialog box
Command: *Pick at* ① *(refer back to fig. 6.5)*	Makes a single point crossing window and finds nothing

```
Other corner:
```

Command: *Press pick button at* ①*, hold it down and drag to* ②*, then release*	Starts, drags, and completes a crossing window selection and selects the lines and arc
Command: *Touch the circle at* ③ *with the corner of the pick box and pick*	Searches for and selects the circle, replacing the previous selections
Command: *Hold down Shift while repeating the press-and-drag pick from* ① *to* ②*, then release*	Makes a crossing window selection and adds it to the selection set
Command: *Hold down Shift and pick the circle at* ③ *again*	Removes the circle from the selection set
Command: *Click on the Cancel button*	Clears the selection set

```
Command: *Cancel*
```

`Command:` ⟨**Enter**⟩	Reopens the Entity Selection Settings dialog box
`Command:` `'_DDSELECT`	
Click on the **E***ntity Sort Method button, and look at the available options*	Opens the Entity Sort Method dialog box (see fig. 6.6)

The Entity Sort Method options are discussed in the following section.

Click on Cancel	Closes the Entity Sort Method dialog box
Click on the **D***efault Selection Mode button*	Restores default **N**oun/Verb and **I**mplied Windowing
Click and drag the Pickbox **S**ize *slider to its previous size*	Resets pick box size
Click on OK *in the* Entity Selection Settings *dialog box*	Makes settings and closes dialog box

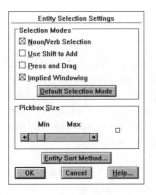 

Figure 6.6

The Entity Selection Settings and Entity Sort Method dialog boxes.

The setting options in the Entity Selection Settings dialog box enable you to change the way the editing process works. These settings are a matter of personal preference and are as follows:

- ◆ **Noun/Verb Selection.** When **N**oun/Verb Selection is enabled, you can create a selection set at the command line before issuing an editing command. When **N**oun/Verb Selection is disabled, you cannot select before issuing a command. When it is on and you select before issuing a command, you can use only the default pick or window/crossing methods. The other selection options are only available during editing commands. If you issue a command when a

6

noun/verb selection set is active (objects are highlighted), the command immediately acts on that selection set. When the **N**oun/Verb Selection setting is turned on, the crosshairs display the pick box when the Command: prompt is active.

◆ **Use Shift to Add.** After you enable the **U**se Shift to Add setting, you must hold down the Shift key to add to a selection set; otherwise, each selection results in a new selection set. This is the standard behavior of many other Windows-based programs; however, the default setting in AutoCAD LT is off. Whether **U**se Shift to Add is on or off, shift-selections of previously selected objects removes them from the selection set.

◆ **Press and Drag.** When you enable the **P**ress and Drag setting, you change the way in which you specify selection windows. In the press-and-drag method, you press the pick button to locate the first corner of the window, and hold down the pick button while you drag the cursor to the second corner, then release. Releasing the button sets the second corner, as opposed to making two distinct picks. This is the standard behavior of many other Windows-based programs and non-Windows programs that use a graphical user interface (GUI); however, the default setting in AutoCAD LT is off.

◆ **Implied Windowing.** *Implied windowing* means that if a pick does not find an object, AutoCAD LT assumes that you wanted to make a window or crossing selection. When **I**mplied Windowing is on (the default setting), the default object pick, window, and crossing window methods are always available during object selection. Even if you disable **I**mplied Windowing, only the first pick in an object selection session is affected, and only in editing commands. If that first pick fails to find an object, nothing happens. Subsequent picks, however, start a window unless they find an object. Implied windowing is always in effect during noun/verb selection, regardless of the setting.

These settings are stored with the AutoCAD LT configuration, not in the drawing. The rest of this book uses the default settings, but we encourage you to experiment, practice, and determine which methods you prefer.

You can freely adjust the pick-box size to suit your selection needs. The size is the number of pixels that AutoCAD LT searches up, down, left, and right from the crosshairs. A smaller pick box can make it harder to pick objects (and thereby easier to accidentally initiate a selection window); however, a smaller pick box also enables you to identify specific objects more easily when you are selecting in crowded areas.

Tip   The smallest pick box size you can set in the Entity Selection Settings dialog box is 1, but you can even set it to 0 for pinpoint selections by using the PICKBOX system variable.

Changing Entity Sorting

The Entity Sort Method dialog box (refer back to fig. 6.6) controls the order in which entities (objects) are selected, displayed, and output. Make changes to this setting only if you have a specific reason to do so. The default setting searches for, displays, or outputs objects in the fastest way for all operations except plotting and PostScript output, for which the object creation order is used. To cause object creation order to be used for other operations, put checks in the boxes. For example, if you want object selection searches to give preference to the most recently created object, check the **O**bject Selection box.

Having seen the selection methods and practiced some of the selection options, you are now ready to use the selection options with the editing commands. This section has not explored all the possible selection options, but you will use additional selection options as you work through the following sections.

Using the Basic Editing Commands

The most basic editing functions in AutoCAD LT are the ERASE, OOPS, MOVE, and COPY commands. You use the ERASE command to remove errors or unneeded construction objects, and the OOPS command to reverse the effects of an ERASE command. You use the MOVE command to relocate objects as dictated by your design needs, and the COPY command as a simple means of replicating repetitive work.

This section explores each of these basic editing commands and several of the selection options not yet tried. You start with the commands most closely tied to the human condition ("nobody's perfect").

Working with the ERASE and OOPS Commands

You have already used ERASE in many previous exercises in this book. In the following exercise, you use the ERASE command with Last, a very common selection option, and then you use ERASE's counterpart, the OOPS command.

Using ERASE, the Last Option, OOPS, and U

Continue in the FIXBASE drawing from any preceding exercise.

Command: **E** (Enter)   Issues the ERASE command, using its alias

continues

6

continued

ERASE

Select objects: **L** (Enter)	Specifies the Last option and selects the last drawn object, the arc at ① (see fig. 6.7)
1 found	
Select objects: (Enter)	Erases the arc
Command: *Choose* **M**odify, **E**rase	Issues the ERASE command
_erase	
Select objects: **L** (Enter)	Specifies the Last option and selects the line at ②
1 found	
Select objects: **L** (Enter)	Reselects the same line
1 found (1 duplicate)	
Select objects: (Enter)	Erases the line
Command: *Choose* **M**odify, **O**ops	Issues the OOPS command and restores the erased line
_oops	
Command: (Enter)	Repeats OOPS command
OOPS *Invalid*	Does nothing; OOPS only restores the most recent erasure
Command: *Click four times on the Undo button*	Issues the U command four times
_U OOPS	Undoes the invalid OOPS
_U OOPS	Undoes the first OOPS, re-erasing the line
_U ERASE	Undoes the second ERASE, restoring the line
_U ERASE	Undoes the first ERASE, restoring the arc

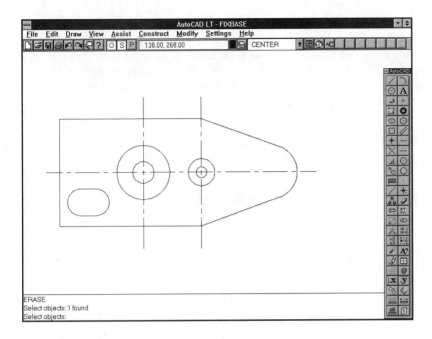

Figure 6.7

Selecting items for ERASE, OOPS, and U.

The ERASE command is straightforward and unambiguous, with no options.

The OOPS command is the complement to ERASE. OOPS reverses the effect of ERASE, but only for the most recent erasure. Although OOPS reverses ERASE, it will do so even if other commands have been used in the meantime. The U (Undo) command, however, can step back through an entire drawing session, undoing ERASE, OOPS, and any other commands, in order.

ERASE. The ERASE command deletes a selection set from the drawing database.

OOPS. The OOPS command restores the objects that were erased with the last ERASE command. (The BLOCK command, covered in Chapter 18, "Leveraging Repetitive Design and Drafting," also performs an erase operation, and OOPS will restore those objects as well.) OOPS restores the erased objects, even if other commands have been used after the ERASE command. OOPS only restores objects erased in the last erase operation; objects erased in earlier erase operations cannot be restored.

6

The Last selection option is often used with the ERASE command. This selection option identifies the most recently created object that is visible on screen. The Last option works only once within a selection because it selects only the one object. If the entire drawing is visible and you repeatedly used the ERASE command with the Last selection option, it would step back through the drawing, erasing in the opposite order from which it was created.

Having explored the commands that address our tendency to make mistakes, you now examine two editing commands that address both our need for change and the benefits of duplication—the MOVE and COPY commands.

Constructive Editing with the MOVE and COPY Commands

The time has come to actually use the selection process for constructive editing. The following exercise uses the MOVE and COPY commands, along with the Fence and Previous selection options.

Using MOVE, COPY, and the Fence and Previous options

Create a new drawing using the ALT0602.DWG drawing file as a prototype.

Command: *Choose* **F**ile, *then* Save **A**s, *and save the drawing as* FIXBASE, *replacing the previous FIXBASE drawing*

Command: *Click on the Move tool*   Issues the MOVE command and prompts for a selection set

_MOVE

Select objects: **F** (Enter)   Specifies the Fence selection option

First fence point: *Pick point* ①   Starts a fence line
(see fig. 6.8)

Undo/<Endpoint of line>: *Turn off*   Defines a fence line segment
the Ortho button and pick point ②

Undo/<Endpoint of line>: (Enter)   Ends Fence mode and completes the selection

4 found   Selects the circles and center lines

```
Select objects: Hold down Shift while        Removes the horizontal center line from
picking the line at ③                        the selection set

1 found, 1 removed

Select objects: (Enter)                       Completes the selection set

Base point or displacement: Pick the          Sets the reference point for the move and
point at ④                                    drags image of the objects
```

Move the cursor around, and notice that the coordinates displayed are all relative to the base point.

```
Second point of displacement: Use the         Moves the objects 60 mm to the right
coordinate display to pick point 60<0
```

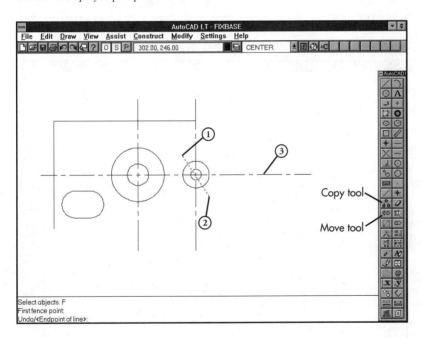

Figure 6.8

Using the Fence selection option.

```
Command: UN (Enter)                           Issues the UNDO command

UNDO Auto/Back/Control/End/Group/             Sets a mark for a later exercise on UNDO,
Mark/<number>: M (Enter)                      at the end of this chapter

Command: Click on the Copy tool               Issues the COPY command and prompts for a
                                              selection set
```

continues

continued

```
_COPY

Select objects: P (Enter)                    Reselects previous set

3 found

Select objects: (Enter)                      Completes the selection set

<Base point or displacement>/               Sets the reference point for the copy
Multiple: Pick any point in
the right half of drawing

Second point of displacement:               Copies the objects 60 mm to the left,
Pick point at coordinates 60<180            their original position (see fig. 6.9)
```

Figure 6.9

Moved and copied objects.

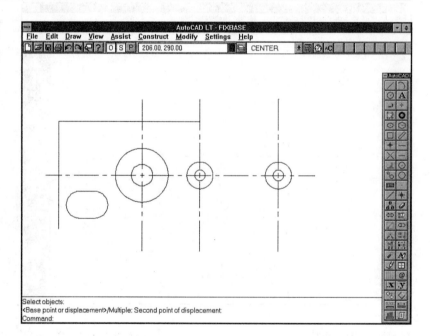

Stop Do not use the Copy Image, Copy Vectors, Copy Embed, Copy Link, or Paste items Edit menu for routine drawing editing. These are special command items intended for copying and linking graphic data between AutoCAD LT and other Windows applications. For more information on these items, see Chapter 24, "Moving Beyond the Basics," or the use AutoCAD LT HELP command (Enter HELP, and choose Full Menus, then Edit).

Notice that the Fence selection option works like the edge of a crossing window; everything the fence line touches is selected when you press Enter. The Previous selection option shows how AutoCAD LT retains each selection set until a new one is defined (or the old one is erased or undone).

The Previous selection option is a big time-saver. This option makes it possible to perform several editing operations on the same group of objects. To take full advantage of this capability, however, you need to plan ahead when you create the selection set so that you can use the Previous option to reselect for various successive commands. Note that when you use the Previous selection option after a COPY command, AutoCAD LT selects the original set, not the copies.

Stop   AutoCAD LT's selections consider only visible objects; therefore, the Fence selection option selects only objects that it visibly touches. If a selection fence passes through a gap created in a line by the linetype (such as in a center line), the line is not selected.

The MOVE command is simple and has no options. You supply MOVE with a selection set and with a displacement, which is the distance and angle by which the moved or copied objects will be offset. The MOVE displacement in the preceding exercise was specified by the distance and angle between the two points you picked. As you will see in the next exercise, these points can be indicated in several ways, or you can specify a single displacement value.

The COPY command is very similar to the MOVE command, except that it duplicates instead of relocates, and it has one option, Multiple. The COPY displacement works just like MOVE. The COPY example in the preceding exercise showed that it is the displacement between the points that matters, not the particular points you pick. The base point need not be on one of the objects, although it is often logical to pick it on an object. When you use the Multiple selection option, as you will see in the next exercise, each copy is displaced from the same base point.

MOVE. The MOVE command relocates selected objects by the 2D or 3D displacement you specify. You can indicate the displacement by two points, from which a relative distance and angle for the move is derived. Or you can specify a coordinate value at the first displacement prompt and press Enter at the second displacement prompt, in which case the coordinate value is interpreted as the relative distance and angle, or displacement, for the move.

6

COPY. The COPY command copies selected objects by the displacement you specify. The selected objects are not modified. You can indicate the displacement by two points, from which a relative distance and angle for the copy is derived. Or you can specify a coordinate value at the first displacement prompt and press Enter at the second displacement prompt, in which case the coordinate value is interpreted as the relative distance and angle, or displacement, for the copy. You can use the Multiple option to make multiple copies, specifying a single base point with multiple displacements (multiple second points).

In a typical CAD drawing session, you will use the COPY and MOVE commands frequently. You may often find it easier to copy and modify an object than to create a similar object from scratch.

 Tip For a quick way to explore a design idea while leaving the original untouched, you can use COPY to reproduce the design off to the side of the drawing area and then explore the design idea by modifying the copy. If you like the effects of your idea, you can erase the original design and use MOVE to replace the original with the new version.

Specifying Displacements for MOVE and COPY

The displacement is central to the MOVE and COPY commands. Several methods are available for specifying this information. How you specify the displacement is unimportant. In different situations, however, different methods may be easier to pick, enter, conceive, or calculate. When using the Multiple COPY option and known displacements, for example, it is often easiest to pick a base point on the object and enter relative displacements. Try using different methods in the following exercise.

Specifying Displacements with MOVE and COPY

Continue in the new FIXBASE drawing from the preceding exercise.

Command: *Choose* **C**onstruct, **C**opy   Issues the COPY command

_copy

Select objects: **P** (Enter)   Selects the objects that were previously
                                      selected—not the copies that were created

3 found

`Select objects: R` `Enter`	Specifies the Remove option
`Remove objects:` *Pick the line at* ① *(see fig. 6.10)*	Removes the line from the selection set
`1 found, 1 removed`	
`Remove objects:` `Enter`	Completes the selection set
`<Base point or displacement>/` `Multiple: M` `Enter`	Specifies the Multiple option and reprompts for a base point
`Base point:` *Pick intersection at* ②	Sets base point of displacement at center of circles

Placing the base point at the center enables you to easily pick a known point as the center of a new copy or to enter a known relative offset as a displacement.

`Second point of displacement:` *Pick point* ③	Copies circles to new center point
`Second point of displacement:` `@146<180` `Enter`	Copies circles by relative polar displacement to ④
`Second point of displacement:` `@0,-28` `Enter`	Copies circles by relative X,Y displacement to ⑤
`Second point of displacement:` `Enter`	Completes the command

To specify relative displacements in COPY Multiple mode, you must enter a base point and then relative coordinates. For moves and single copies, you can simply specify a relative displacement without the @ sign, as follows.

`Command:` *Pick the circle at* ⑥ *(see fig. 6.10)*	Selects the circle
`Command: M` `Enter`	Issues the MOVE command, with the circle selected
`MOVE 1 found`	
`Base point or displacement: 44,0` `Enter`	Specifies coordinate value for displacement
`Second point of displacement:` `Enter`	Accepts coordinate value as relative displacement and moves the circle to center it at ⑦

continues

6

continued

Note that no @ sign was required for the relative displacement coordinate value; you entered 44,0, not @44,0.

Command: **U** (Enter)	Undoes the MOVE command
MOVE	
Command: *Click on the Move tool*	Issues the MOVE command
_MOVE	
Select objects: **P** (Enter)	Specifies the Previous selection option
No previous selection set.	Undo cleared the previous selection set
Select objects: *Pick the circle at* ⑥	Selects the circle
1 found	
Select objects: (Enter)	Completes the selection set
Base point or displacement: **44<0** (Enter)	Specifies polar coordinate value for displacement
Second point of displacement: (Enter)	Accepts coordinate value as relative polar displacement and moves the circle to ⑦
Command: **CP** (Enter)	Issues the COPY command
COPY	
Select objects: **P** (Enter)	Reselects the circle
1 found	
Select objects: (Enter)	Completes the selection set
Base point or displacement: *Pick the center of the circle at* ⑦	Enters a coordinate value
Second point of displacement: (Enter)	Uses the coordinate value as a relative displacement

Was the circle copied? To see it, open the Aerial View window.

Command: *Click on the Aerial View button*

_DSVIEWER

Press Alt+minus or click on the minus menu label (AutoCAD LT Release 1), or click several times on the minus icon (AutoCAD LT Release 2) until the circle appears (see fig. 6.10)	Expands Aerial View, displaying copied circle in upper right of the Aerial View

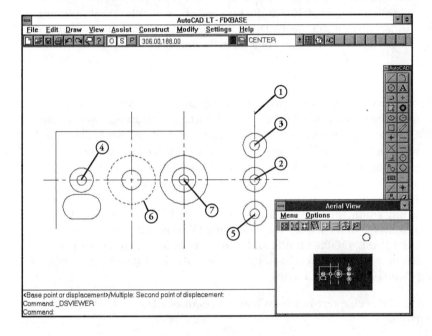

Figure 6.10

Specifying offsets, with results shown in the revised Aerial View.

The original Aerial View appears similar to the revised Aerial View shown in figure 6.10.

The preceding exercise illustrates various methods of specifying the displacement by which selected objects are copied or moved. You can use absolute or relative coordinates for either the base point or the second point, but if you know the relative coordinates, it is usually easiest to just specify a displacement at the Base point or displacement: prompt.

When you specify coordinates at the Base point or displacement: prompt, and press Enter for the second point, AutoCAD LT interprets the coordinates as a relative displacement. Both the MOVE and COPY commands work this way. The last example in the exercise illustrates a common mistake. In this case, "accidentally" pressing Enter at the Second point of displacement: prompt caused the coordinates of the center point you picked to be interpreted as a displacement. The center point coordinates were 156,200, so the copied circle was displaced 156 mm to the right and 200 mm up, beyond the current view.

A similar mistake is to accidentally use an @ sign when entering an intended displacement at the Base point or displacement: prompt. If you do so and then press Enter at the Second point of displacement: prompt, the value you enter is interpreted as specifying a coordinate relative to the last point, and the resulting coordinate is then interpreted as the displacement. For example, if the last point you specified was 32,20 and you entered @10,5 instead of 10,5 at the Base point or displacement: prompt, the resulting displacement would be 42,25 (32,20 plus 10,5) instead of the intended 10,5. Either of these mistakes can cause objects to disappear or to appear in strange places.

Stop   If any command appears to have no effect or displaces objects to unexpected locations, try to determine what happened. If the objects disappear, you can use ZOOM Extents to see if they were transported to a distant coordinate. The safest approach is to issue an Undo and try again. The worst thing you can do is to try again without first using an Undo—this step simply compounds a problem if the command is having an unwanted effect of which you are unaware.

Many more editing commands are available (see Chapter 14, "Making More Changes: Editing Constructively," and Chapter 15, "Modifying Objects and Text"), but these four commands, ERASE, OOPS, MOVE, and COPY, are good examples of the way editing commands work. The next chapter covers an entirely different way of editing your drawings: using AutoCAD LT grips.

The last section of this chapter shows you how to use AutoCAD LT's UNDO and REDO commands.

Retracing Your Steps with UNDO and REDO

You are already familiar with U, the single-step Undo command, and the REDO command. The U and REDO commands are accessible from toolbar buttons, and they are issued by the first two items on the **E**dit pull-down menu, **U**ndo and **R**edo. AutoCAD LT also has a more inclusive UNDO command for controlling access to the history of the current drawing session. The UNDO command is available only by entering it at the command line.

If you type **UNDO** at the command line and press Enter, AutoCAD LT issues the following option prompt:

```
Auto/Back/Control/End/Group/Mark/<number>:
```

You take a look at a couple of these options and the REDO command in the following exercise, then explore them in more depth.

The REDO command reverses the effect of the last U command or the Back or number option of the UNDO command. REDO must be issued immediately after the U or UNDO command. REDO reverses only one use of U or UNDO at a time; if you issue multiple U commands, REDO will recover only from the last one, after which it will prompt:

```
Previous command did not undo things
```

You may see slight differences in the following exercise if you deviated from the preceding exercises.

Exploring UNDO and REDO

Continue from the previous two exercises, with the UNDO Mark option set in the first MOVE, COPY exercise.

Command: **UNDO** (Enter)	
Auto/Back/Control/End/Group/Mark/ <number>: **3** (Enter)	Undoes three steps, to before the mirror edit if you made no errors during mirroring
_DSVIEWER COPY MOVE	Lists the commands undone
Command: **REDO** (Enter)	Reverses the effects of the previous UNDO command
Command: **UN** (Enter)	Issues the UNDO command
UNDO Auto/Back/Control/End/Group/Mark/ <number>: **B** (Enter)	Undoes to the mark you set before the first COPY command, if you made no errors
_DSVIEWER COPY MOVE GROUP COPY Mark encountered	Lists all intervening commands and undoes back to the beginning of the first COPY
Command: (Enter)	Repeats the UNDO command

continues

6

continued

UNDO Auto/Back/Control/End/Group/Mark/ <number>: **B** (Enter)	Undoes to before the mark, back to the beginning
This will undo everything. OK? <Y> **Y** (Enter) MOVE GROUP Everything has been undone.	
Command: *Choose* **F**ile, E**x**it, **N**o	Quits AutoCAD LT, discarding changes

This quick exploration illustrates several details of how UNDO, U, and REDO work. UNDO, U, and REDO ignore Ctrl+Cs themselves, but treat canceled commands as steps. Intervening settings such as ortho and snap are undone and redone when the prior command is undone or redone, but are not counted as an undo step. UNDO reversed the view change in the Aerial View, but did not close it. REDRAW and REGEN are treated as steps by UNDO, U, and REDO, but the screen is not redrawn or regenerated unless the redraw or regeneration was caused by a pan or zoom. File commands such as SAVE or SAVE AS are treated as steps by UNDO, U, and REDO, but undoing or redoing a file operation has no effect. Most commands issued by pull-down menu items are treated and identified as GROUPs by UNDO and REDO, as the SAVEAS and COPY commands were when you used the pull-down menu to access them. In the next chapter, you will see that each grip editing operation is counted as a single command called GRIP_EDIT by UNDO, U, and REDO.

> **UNDO.** The UNDO command reverses the effect(s) of one or more previous commands, and can step back through the drawing to its state at the beginning of the drawing session. The UNDO command includes options for controlling how many previous drawing steps are stored, controlling how far back to undo previous steps, grouping operations as if single steps, and for turning off the undo feature.

> **REDO.** The REDO command restores everything undone by a U or UNDO command, if REDO is used immediately after the U or UNDO command. REDO reverses only a single previous U or UNDO command.

Understanding UNDO Options

The function of each of the UNDO command's options is as follows:

- **Auto.** The Auto option turns Auto mode on and off. When Auto is on, UNDO and U treat any series of commands issued from a menu item like a single command and undo or redo the series as a single step.

- **Back.** The Back option undoes everything to the last UNDO mark (see the Mark option) or to the beginning of a drawing session if no mark has been set. If no mark has been set, AutoCAD LT prompts to warn you that it is about to undo everything.

- **Control.** The Control option controls how much drawing history AutoCAD LT stores for possible undoing. The Control option presents a prompt with additional options, which are described separately after this list.

- **End.** The End option signals the end of a group (see the Group option).

- **Group.** The Group option instructs AutoCAD LT to treat the commands that follow it (until the End option is issued) as a single step for the purpose of UNDO and U.

- **Mark.** The Mark option places a marker in the stream of your commands. The UNDO's Back option will stop at the mark.

- **<number>.** The number option is the default. Enter the number of steps you want to undo, or press Enter to undo one step (the equivalent of the U command).

You can use the Group option if you want to try out some alternative way of solving a geometric problem. Begin a group with UNDO and the Group option, work through the drawing problem, and then if you want to discard the results, use the U command to undo the entire sequence. If you won't be sure until later whether or not you want to save the sequence, use UNDO with the End option to encapsulate it as a single step. Then, if you later do undo it, a single undo step will undo the entire sequence.

In a similar way, you can use UNDO's Mark option to leave a bookmark in your work. If you want to experiment with your design, but you may want to return it to its current condition, use UNDO and place a mark with the Mark option. Later, issue UNDO and use the Back option to restore the drawing in one step to the condition it was in before the mark was placed. For quick trips into the think tank, an UNDO mark is faster than establishing a temporary drawing.

6

Note An UNDO group or mark is not stored in the drawing's database. When you exit a drawing, any UNDO groups or marks are lost.

The UNDO command's Control option has the following additional options:

◆ **All.** The All option is the default for the Control option. This option causes AutoCAD LT to keep a history of all the commands you perform, which enables you to step back through an entire drawing session if you want.

◆ **None.** The None Control option turns the undo history off and clears it. When this option is set, no undo history is kept; therefore, there is nothing to step back through when you try to undo anything. To turn undo back on, use All or One.

◆ **One.** The One Control option clears the undo history and limits the UNDO function to a one-step history. You can use the UNDO or U commands only for one prior operation at a time with the One Control option set.

The Control options are provided to limit the number of disk-space requests AutoCAD LT makes on your system. Normally, the undo history is kept in a temporary file. If you work for an extended period of time in one drawing on a system with limited free disk space, you may run out of space, causing AutoCAD LT to shut down. You can avoid this problem by using the None or One options to limit the size of the undo history file. But don't forget to also save your drawing periodically.

In the next chapter, you continue your exploration of editing methods by using AutoCAD LT's interactive grip editing tools.

C H A P T E R

7

Making Changes: Using Grip Editing

This chapter introduces you to grips, which provide an easy, yet powerful way to move, copy, rotate, scale, stretch, and make mirror images of objects with an interactive editing feature called *grip editing*. This chapter includes the following topics in its discussion of the AutoCAD LT grip editing process:

◆ Selecting objects for grip editing

◆ Setting AutoCAD LT's grip editing settings

◆ Stretching, moving, copying, rotating, scaling, and mirroring objects with grip editing

◆ Using hot, cold, and multiple grips to manipulate objects

◆ Working with AutoCAD LT's grip edit modes and options

The first section of the chapter provides a quick tour of grip editing. The second section introduces and explains the Grips dialog box settings. The third and major section of the chapter thoroughly covers all grip editing modes, methods, and options.

Understanding AutoCAD LT's Grip Editing Process

AutoCAD LT's grip editing feature is an interactive process for replicating and modifying objects. *Grips* are small boxes that appear at the points (such as endpoints, midpoints, and centers) of selected objects. In grip editing, you first select the objects to edit, then manipulate their grip points to modify or copy them. By careful object selection and the use of grip points and options, you can do a wide variety of editing in a fluid, interactive manner.

Grips are enabled or disabled by the GRIPS system variable, which can be controlled by the Grips dialog box. By default, grips are initially enabled; however, you turned them off in Chapter 6 to clarify the distinction between traditional object selection and the grip editing process.

You use the Grips dialog box to turn grips back on in the following quick exercise. In AutoCAD LT Release 1, the Grips dialog box is accessible only from the **F**ull menu, so you must change to the **F**ull menu if you are currently using the **S**hort menu.

Enabling Grips

Start AutoCAD LT with a new unnamed drawing.

If using AutoCAD LT Release 1, choose **S**ettings, then **F**ull Menu if **G**rips Style is not already available in the menu.

Command: *Choose* **S**ettings, **G**rips Style	Opens the Grips dialog box
Put a check in the **E**nable Grips *check box, then choose* OK	Turns grip editing on

---

The GRIPS setting is stored in AutoCAD LT itself rather than in the drawing that happens to be current at the time. Grips should remain on for the rest of the book.

Introducing Grip Editing

Using commands to edit drawings is more structured than the AutoCAD LT alternative—grips. Editing with grips is a free-form interactive approach to editing, using only the mouse, the Shift key, and a few option keys. Despite this simple interface, you can do most editing with grips. Grips are small boxes that appear at geometric

points (such as center, mid-, and endpoints) on selected objects. By picking and dragging grips, you can modify and copy objects. In fact, grip editing is so flexible that you will, in this chapter, create the entire drawing shown in figure 7.1 simply by copying and manipulating the five objects in the upper left corner.

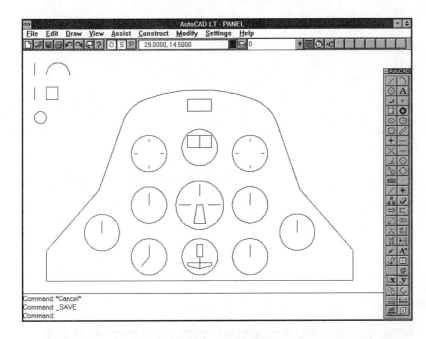

Figure 7.1

An instrument panel created by grip editing.

First, take a quick introductory tour of grip editing with the following exercise.

Manipulating Grips

Continue from the previous exercise. Draw a line, arc, and circle, in the middle of the drawing area, as shown in figure 7.2 (they won't yet appear highlighted or display the grips shown in the figure).

Command: *Select all three objects*
Selects the objects and displays their grips (see fig. 7.2)

Command: *Pick an endpoint of the line object*
Highlights the grip point and enters Stretch mode

```
** STRETCH **
<Stretch to point>/Base point/Copy/
Undo/eXit: Move the cursor around,
then click the Enter mouse button
```
Stretches the line's endpoint, then switches to Move mode

continues

continued

** MOVE ** <Move to point>/Base point/Copy/ Undo/eXit: *Move the cursor around,* *then click the Enter button*	Drags all three objects, then switches to Rotate mode
** ROTATE ** <Rotation angle>/Base point/Copy/ Undo/Reference/eXit: *Move the cursor* *around, then click the Enter button*	Rotates all three objects, then switches to Scale mode
** SCALE ** <Scale factor>/Base point/Copy/Undo/ Reference/eXit: *Move the cursor* *around, then click the Enter button*	Scales all three objects, then switches to Mirror mode
** MIRROR ** <Second point>/Base point/Copy/Undo/ eXit: *Move the cursor around, then* *click the Enter button*	Mirrors (drags and rotates a mirror image of all three), then returns to Stretch mode
** STRETCH ** <Stretch to point>/Base point/Copy/ Undo/eXit: *Pick a new point*	Stretches and relocates the selected endpoint, then exits grip editing mode

The objects remain selected, with their grips displayed.

Figure 7.2

*Grip points on a
line, an arc, and
a circle.*

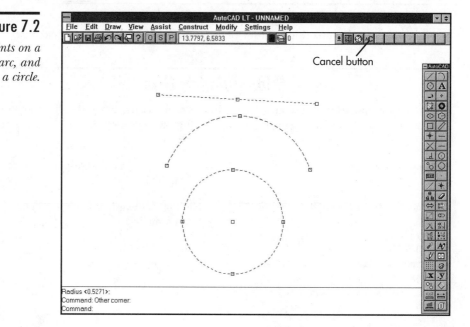

Command: *Pick an endpoint grip of the arc*

Highlights the grip point and enters
Stretch mode

** STRETCH **
`<Stretch to point>/Base point/Copy/`
`Undo/eXit:` *Drag the grip and pick a new point*

Stretches the arc to the new endpoint,
then exits grip editing mode

Command: *Pick a quadrant grip on the circle*

Highlights the grip point and enters
Stretch mode

** STRETCH **
`<Stretch to point>/Base point/Copy/`
`Undo/eXit:` *Drag the grip and pick a new point*

Changes the diameter of the circle and
redraws it through the point picked,
then exits grip editing mode

Command: *Pick the midpoint grip of the line*

Highlights the grip point and enters
Stretch mode

** STRETCH **
`<Stretch to point>/Base point/Copy/`
`Undo/eXit:` *Drag the grip and pick a new point*

Moves the line to the new midpoint, then
exits grip editing mode

Command: *Pick the grip at the center of the circle*

Highlights the grip point and enters
Stretch mode

** STRETCH **
`<Stretch to point>/Base point/Copy/`
`Undo/eXit:` *Drag the grip and pick a new point*

Moves the circle to the new center
location, then exits grip editing mode

Command: *Hold down Shift, and pick a
non-grip point on the circle*

Deselects and dehighlights the circle, but
its grips remain

Command: *Pick the grip at the center
of the circle*

Enters Move mode, using the center of the
circle as the reference point

** MOVE **
`<Move to point>/Base point/Copy/`
`Undo/eXit:` *Drag the cursor and pick
a new point*

Moves the selected objects (line and
arc), but not the circle

Command: *Press Ctrl+C*

Deselects the objects, but the grips remain

`*Cancel*`

Command: *Press Ctrl+C again*

Removes the grips

`*Cancel*`

continues

continued

Command: *Reselect the objects*	Highlights the objects and displays their grip points
Command: *Click on the Cancel button*	Issues two Ctrl+Cs, deselecting the objects and removing their grips

When either noun-verb selection, grips, or both are enabled, the crosshair cursor displays a small square box at its center. This box indicates that you can make selections at the Command: prompt. (If you try to select objects from the Command: prompt without either noun-verb selection or grips mode active, nothing happens because AutoCAD LT does not know what you are trying to do.) When you make a selection with grips enabled, objects are highlighted and small boxes (grips) appear at key geometric points on each object. Pressing Ctrl+C once deselects the selected objects but doesn't remove the displayed grips. Pressing a second Ctrl+C clears the grips. Clicking on the toolbar Cancel button issues two Ctrl+Cs, so it both deselects the objects and clears the grips.

If you are in a grip editing mode, such as Stretch, the first Ctrl+C exits grip editing mode, the second Ctrl+C deselects the objects, and the third Ctrl+C clears the grips. Issuing a non-editing command, such as LINE, will also deselect objects and clear grips, if you are not in a grip editing mode. If noun-verb selection is enabled, most editing commands accept the selection set and clear the grips.

 Note The toolbar's Cancel button issues two Ctrl+Cs, thus both deselecting objects and hiding their displayed grip points. Most commands issued by the toolbox or menus also issue two Ctrl+Cs. Keep this in mind as you work through the rest of this chapter.

When grips are visible, picking a grip makes it *active* (sometimes referred to as *hot*). When you make a grip active, AutoCAD LT enters Stretch mode (in most cases), and a grip editing prompt line of options appears. Pressing Enter, the spacebar, or clicking the Enter button cycles through the following grip edit modes: Stretch, Move, Rotate, Scale, and Mirror. Each mode can have a slightly different effect, depending on the type of object(s) selected and the location of the selected grip(s) on the object(s).

Each of the grip edit modes is discussed in detail later. First, you examine the available grip settings that you can use to control the way grips look and work in AutoCAD LT.

Changing Grip Settings

AutoCAD LT enables you to change several settings that affect the way your grips appear and perform. Earlier, you used the Grips dialog box to turn grips on. In the following exercise, you open the Grips dialog box and examine the rest of its settings.

Using the Grips Dialog Box

Continue from the preceding exercise, with grips on.

Command: *Choose* **S**ettings, **G**rips Style	Issues the DDGRIPS command and opens the Grips dialog box (see fig. 7.3)
`'_ddgrips`	
Click on the **U**nselected *button in the* Grip Colors *section*	Opens the Select Color dialog box

If you want to change the color of unselected (inactive) grips, select another color and click on OK. Otherwise, click on Cancel to exit the Select Color dialog box and keep the default color.

Click on the **S**elected *button in the* Grip Colors *section*	Also opens the Select Color dialog box

If you want to change the color of selected (active or hot) grips, select another color and click on OK. Otherwise, click on Cancel to exit the Select Color dialog box.

If you feel that the grip boxes are too small or too large, you can drag the box in the **G**rip Size slider to change the grip size (watch the sample grip box in the display change).

Click on OK (*or* Cancel *if you made no changes*)	Closes the Grips dialog box

From the Grips dialog box, you can make five changes that affect grips in AutoCAD LT:

- ◆ **Enable Grips.** With the **E**nable Grips check box, you can enable or disable grips. The GRIPS system variable also controls this setting (0 = disabled, 1 = enabled).

- ◆ **Enable Grips Within Blocks.** When you select a block object (see Chapters 18 and 19 about blocks) with the Enable Grips Within **B**locks box cleared (disabled), a single grip is displayed at the block's insertion point. When you enable (put a check in) this box, all the usual grip points are displayed on all the objects in the block. Normally, this option produces unnecessary clutter, so enable it only if needed.

Figure 7.3

The Grips dialog box.

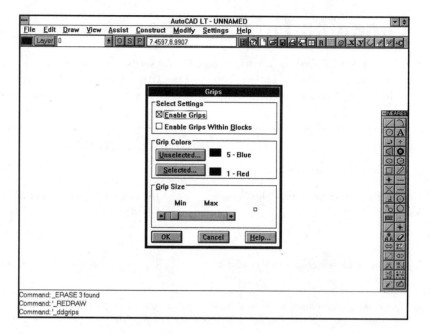

◆ **Grip Colors.** With the **U**nselected and **S**elected buttons, you can change the color of inactive and active (hot) grips.

◆ **Grip Size.** With the **G**rip Size slider bar, you can adjust the size of the grip box to suit your vision, your display, and the density of your drawing(s). Unlike the pick box discussed earlier, the size of the grip box has no effect on AutoCAD LT's behavior, but large grip boxes can be difficult to distinguish from one another in congested areas.

Make sure that the **E**nable Grips box is checked. You are now ready to experiment further with the grip editing modes and options.

Exploring Grip Editing Modes and Methods

For several years, Autodesk has held an annual Top Gun Competition. In these competitions, AutoCAD professionals test their skills against one another. One year's contest required that contestants recreate a target drawing starting with a prototype consisting of only a line, a circle, and a piece of text. The stipulation was that only editing commands could be used.

7

Although creating objects with only editing commands is not the most efficient way to draw, the point is that it's possible. In the next series of exercises, you create a drawing using a similar approach. You see the power within the grip edit modes to stretch, move, rotate, scale, and mirror objects, with options for copying in each mode. You do this entire drawing without using any drawing commands. Although this is by no means the most efficient way to create a drawing, it will thoroughly expose you to grip editing. In this section, you are introduced to the grip editing modes in the order in which they appear when you enter grip editing mode.

Grip editing looks simple, and basically it is, but with many possible ways to combine the available options, you sometimes need to pay close attention to get the result you want. With practice, editing with grips can be extremely efficient. Fasten your flight harness, and follow along. Remember that if you make a mistake, you can use Undo and Ctrl+C at any time.

Stretch Mode

Autodesk chose Stretch as the default mode for grips because Stretch is clearly the most versatile option. With Stretch, depending on the object and grips, you can stretch, move, and copy. With grips, however, flexibility often connotes complexity, and the Stretch mode is no exception to this rule of thumb. Keep this caution in mind if you get frustrated as you try these first exercises. If you can get through the Stretch mode, you will have a good grasp of the use of grips.

The drawing you are about to use has been prepared with five objects on three layers. The grid is set to 1, and snap is set to 0.25. In the first exercise, you use the Grip Stretch mode first to replicate and then to modify some lines.

 Note As you work through this exercise and subsequent exercises, change the coordinate display mode between X,Y and polar as needed to easily pick the points indicated.

Using Stretch Mode to Copy and Stretch Lines

Create a new drawing named PANEL, using the ALT0701.DWG drawing file as a prototype.

Command: *Pick the red line object at* ① *(see fig. 7.4)*   Highlights the line and displays its grips

Command: *Pick the midpoint grip at* ①   Activates the grip and enters Stretch mode

```
** STRETCH **
<Stretch to point>/Base point/Copy/
Undo/eXit: Press and hold down Shift
while picking the point 2.0,1.5
```
Enters Stretch (multiple) or Copy
mode and copies the line to the new
midpoint

continues

continued

```
** STRETCH (multiple) **                          Exits grip editing mode and
<Stretch to point>/Base point/Copy/              deactivates the grip
Undo/eXit: Click the Enter button
```

Figure 7.4

*Copying an
existing line
using grips.*

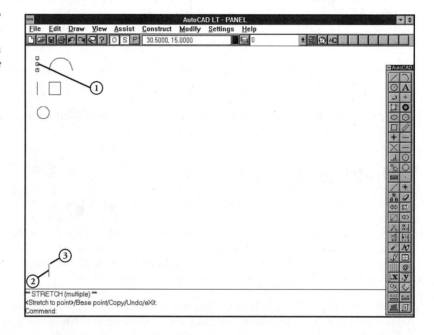

The original line is still selected, with inactive grips displayed.

Command: *Click on the Cancel button*   Clears the selection and grips

Command: *Pick the line object at* ②   Highlights the line and displays its grips

Command: *Pick the upper endpoint grip at* ③   Enters Stretch mode

```
** STRETCH **                                     Stretches the endpoint to ④ (see fig. 7.5)
<Stretch to point>/Base point/Copy/              and completes the grip operation
Undo/eXit: Pick the point 2.00,3.50
```

Command: *Pick the endpoint grip at* ④   Activates the grip and enters Stretch mode

```
** STRETCH **                                     Specifies Copy option which enters
<Stretch to point>/Base point/Copy/              Stretch (multiple) mode
Undo/eXit: C (Enter)
```

```
** STRETCH (multiple) **
<Stretch to point>/Base point/Copy/
Undo/eXit: Pick point 28,1
```
Stretches and copies the line to the
new endpoint at ⑤

```
** STRETCH (multiple) **
<Stretch to point>/Base point/Copy/
Undo/eXit: Click the Enter button
```
Completes the grip operation

```
Command: Pick the lower endpoint grip at ⑥
```
Enters Stretch mode

```
** STRETCH **
<Stretch to point>/Base point/Copy/
Undo/eXit: Shift-pick point 5.5,8.5
```
Stretches and copies the line to ⑦
and enters Stretch (multiple) mode

```
** STRETCH (multiple) **
<Stretch to point>/Base point/Copy/
Undo/eXit: Click the Enter button
```
Completes the grip operation

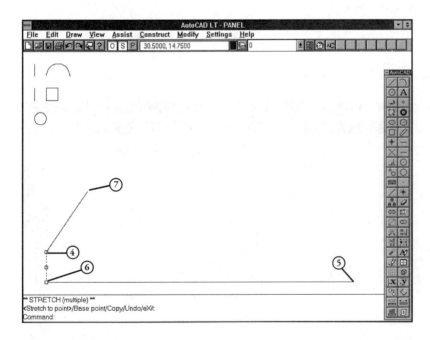

Figure 7.5

*Creating new
lines from existing
ones with grips.*

The line (at ⑨ in fig. 7.6) is still selected.

```
Command: Pick the new line at ⑧ (see fig. 7.6)
```
Adds line to selection set, and displays its grips

```
Command: Shift-pick the line at ⑨ (not on a grip)
```
Deselects the original line

continues

continued

Command: *Pick the endpoint grip at* ⑩	Activates grip and enters Stretch mode
** STRETCH ** <Stretch to point>/Base point/Copy/ Undo/eXit: *Shift-pick point 8.5,14*	Stretches and copies only the highlighted line to ⑪
** STRETCH (multiple) ** <Stretch to point>/Base point/Copy/ Undo/eXit: *Click the Enter button*	Completes the grip operation
Command: *Pick the new line at* ⑪	Adds new line to selection set and displays its grips
Command: *Pick the common endpoint grip at* ⑫	Activates grip and enters Stretch mode
** STRETCH ** <Stretch to point>/Base point/Copy/ Undo/eXit: *Pick the point 6.50,8.50*	Stretches the endpoints of both selected lines to match figure 7.7
Command: *Click on the Cancel button*	Clears selection and grips
Command: *Click on the Save button*	Saves the PANEL drawing

Figure 7.6

Building on existing geometry with grips.

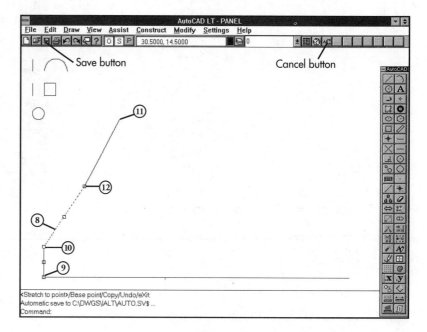

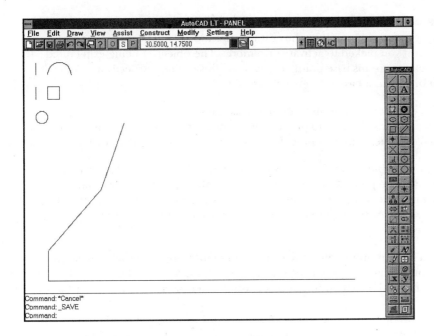

Figure 7.7

The PANEL drawing at the end of the exercise.

7

Notice that you can't stretch a midpoint of a line to another location; therefore, when Stretch mode is applied to a midpoint of a line, it acts like a move. Using the Shift key with any mode enters Multiple mode (the same as the Copy option), so stretching a line's midpoint grip with Shift held down copies the line. When Stretch is applied to an endpoint grip, it works as its name implies; it leaves the inactive endpoint in place and stretches the line's active endpoint to the new location. Holding down Shift leaves the original line intact and creates a new one (multiple).

Selecting a highlighted object with Shift held down deselects the object, but the grips remain. Selecting the object a second time with Shift held down removes the object's grips.

Grip edits affect only highlighted (selected) objects. A grip common to two selected objects will affect both.

Grip Editing Options

The Stretch mode offers several options in its prompt. Most of these options apply to the other grip edit modes. The following list examines each of the Stretch mode options:

◆ **Stretch to point.** The Stretch to point option is the default. You specify a point to which the active grip(s) are stretched or moved.

◆ **Base point.** The Base point option enables you to specify a point to use for the base reference point for the editing operation. The default base point is the grip point you picked to activate grip mode. The object(s) being grip-edited drag relative to this base point. You can use this option to specify any other point or grip as a base reference point.

◆ **Copy.** The Copy (multiple) option works the same as holding down Shift when picking the first "Stretch to point." The Copy option enters Multiple mode, which continues until you press Enter, enter **X** (see the eXit option), or Cancel.

◆ **Undo.** The Undo option reverses the last grip edit or option. For example, you can undo Base point, Copy option, or a multiple copy or stretch. You cannot back out of the Stretch mode itself, however; you must use Cancel. Using the Undo button or the U command after exiting grip edit mode undoes the entire grip session.

◆ **eXit.** The eXit option ends the grip editing mode and deactivates all active grips, but it leaves objects selected and grips displayed. In Multiple mode, you can exit with the eXit option or by pressing Enter or clicking the Enter button.

Many of these options are common to all grip modes, although the default prompt changes to reflect the particular mode in use. A few modes have an additional prompt, which is described in their respective sections.

Snapping to Grips

When snap is on, as you have seen, the cursor snaps to points on the snap grid. Similarly, during a grip operation, the cursor snaps to grip points, whether or not they are active, and whether or not they are on selected objects. When you move the cursor into the area of a grip box, it snaps to the grip's center. This mechanism is true in any grip mode and provides a geometric snap function similar to the object snap modes (described in Chapter 11, "Achieving Accuracy: The Geometric Power of CAD"). Because grips appear at geometric points such as center points, endpoints, and midpoints, snapping to grips enables you to precisely stretch, move, copy, and so on to existing geometric points.

You can use this simple but powerful feature as another means of achieving accuracy in locating objects. You will use it in the next exercise to stretch and copy an arc.

Stretching and Copying Circles and Arcs

The way the Stretch mode works varies with different kinds of objects. Stretch is a little trickier to use with arcs than with lines. In the following exercise, you create two

new arcs and add them to the figure. You will use an inactive grip as a point to which you will snap one of the arcs. You also will use Stretch mode to move and scale a circle.

Using Stretch Mode on Arcs and Circles

Continue from the preceding exercise. To better see the effect of snapping to grips, turn off the S (snap) toolbar button.

Command: *Pick the line at* ① *(see fig. 7.8), then Shift-pick the same line at a non-grip point*	Highlights the line and displays its grips, then deselects the line, leaving the grips displayed
Command: *Pick the arc at* ② *(see fig. 7.8)*	Highlights the arc and displays its grips
Command: *Pick the arc's right endpoint grip at* ②	Activates grip and enters Stretch mode
** STRETCH ** `<Stretch to point>/Base point/Copy/` `Undo/eXit:` *Move the cursor slowly in and out of a few grip boxes*	Drags the arc, snapping it to the grips' centers
Shift-pick the grip at ①	Creates the large arc in figure 7.8
** STRETCH (multiple) ** `<Stretch to point>/Base point/Copy/` `Undo/eXit:` *Click the Enter button*	Completes the grip operation
Command: *Shift-pick the original arc (not at a grip point)*	Deselects the arc
Command: *Pick the new arc*	Selects it and displays grips
Command: *Pick the left endpoint grip at* ③	Enters Stretch mode
** STRETCH ** `<Stretch to point>/Base point/Copy/` `Undo/eXit:` *Turn on the Snap button and pick point 10.5,16*	Stretches only the new arc's endpoint to ④; see the large arc in figure 7.9
Command: *Pick the new arc's midpoint grip at* ⑤ *(see fig 7.9)*	Enters Stretch mode
** STRETCH ** `<Stretch to point>/Base point/Copy/` `Undo/eXit:` *Pick the point 9.25,15.25*	Stretches the midpoint to ⑥ and completes the grip operation

continues

continued

Figure 7.8

Copying an arc using grips.

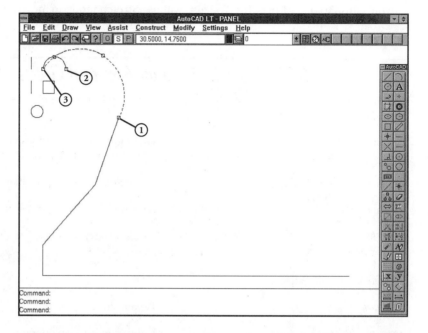

Figure 7.9

Changing an arc's endpoints and curvature (midpoint) using grips.

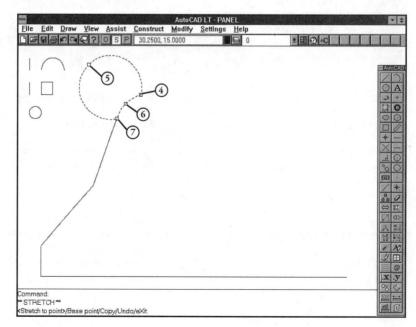

Create the arc shown between ⑧ and ⑨ in figure 7.10. First copy the last arc you created by stretching its endpoint from ⑧ to 19.5,16 at ⑨, Shift-picking to copy it. Then deselect the original arc and stretch the other endpoint of the copy from ⑩ to ⑧. Finally, adjust the midpoint of the copy, stretching it to point 15,16.75.

Command: *Click on the Cancel button*   Clears the selection and grips

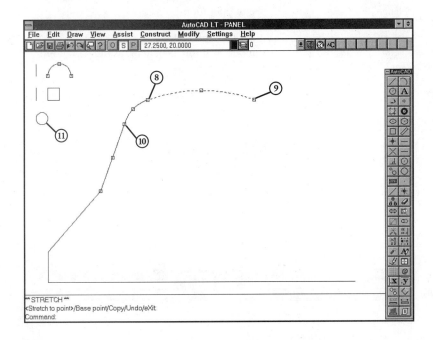

Figure 7.10

Copying and modifying an arc using grips.

Command: *Pick the circle object at* ⑪   Highlights the circle and displays its grips
(see fig. 7.10)   *(see fig. 7.11)*

Command: *Pick the center-point grip at* ⑫   Enters Stretch mode
(see fig. 7.11)

```
** STRETCH **
<Stretch to point>/Base point/Copy/
Undo/eXit: Shift-pick point 15,7.25
```
Copies the circle to the new center point at ⑬

```
** STRETCH (multiple) **
<Stretch to point>/Base point/Copy/
Undo/eXit: Click the Enter button
```
Completes the grip operation

Command: *Pick the new circle*   Selects it and displays grips

continues

continued

Command: *Pick the right quadrant grip near* ⑭   Enters Stretch mode and activates
                                                            quadrant grip

```
** STRETCH **
<Stretch to point>/Base point/Copy/
Undo/eXit: @1.5,0 (Enter)
```
Changes diameter, stretching grip to point
17.00,7.25 at ⑭, and completes the grip
edit operation

Command: *Shift-pick the grip at* ⑭, *Shift-pick*   Activates two grips and enters Stretch
another quadrant grip , then pick the   mode, with the grip at ⑭ as the base point
grip at ⑭ *again (without Shift)*

```
** STRETCH **
<Stretch to point>/Base point/Copy/
Undo/eXit: Move the cursor
```
Moves the circle instead of stretching it

Command: *Click twice on the Cancel button*   Exits Stretch mode, and clears the
                                                            selection and grips

Command: *Click on the Redraw button or tool*   Cleans up the display

Command: *Click on the Save button*   Saves the PANEL.DWG drawing

Figure 7.11

*Creating and
enlarging a circle
using grips.*

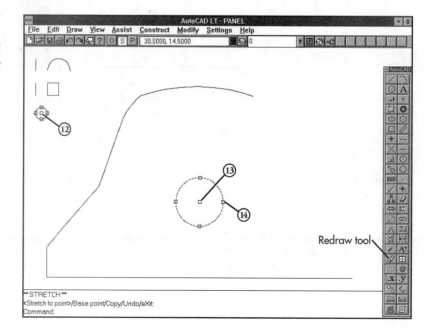

When you stretch a grip, it affects other grip points on the object. Grip editing affords great control and flexibility, but you must exercise care when selecting which grip to use. For example, when you apply Stretch to a circle, it moves or copies if you activate the center grip or more than one grip, whereas it changes the radius if you activate a single quadrant grip.

In this exercise, you typed the relative coordinate **@1.5,0** to demonstrate that you can enter coordinates as well as pick points during grip editing.

 Tip   Relative coordinates entered during grip editing are relative to the grip base point, not the last point picked or entered.

Editing Multiple Objects with Multiple Hot Grips

You can have more than one grip active (or hot) at the same time. As you saw with the circle in the preceding exercise, multiple active grips on a single object can change how the edit affects the object. You can also have multiple active grips on multiple objects. In the following exercise, you use multiple active grips to affect more than one object at once. The square in the drawing is a single polyline object (see Chapter 16, "Increasing Your Drawing Power with Polylines and Double Lines"), so grip editing treats it as a single object. You also get the opportunity to use the Copy option again.

Using Multiple Active Grips

Continue from the preceding exercise.

`Command:` *Pick the square at* ① *(see fig. 7.12)*   Highlights the square and displays its grips

`Command:` *Hold down Shift, and select the grip at each of the square's corners*   Activates all four grips so that Stretch mode will move the square

`Base point:` *Pick the lower left corner grip at* ②   Enters Stretch mode with that grip as the base point

`** STRETCH **`
`<Stretch to point>/Base point/Copy/`
`Undo/eXit:` `C` `(Enter)`   Specifies the Copy option and enters Multiple mode

`** STRETCH (multiple) **`
`<Stretch to point>/Base point/Copy/`
`Undo/eXit:` *Pick the point 14.00,15.00*   Copies the square to ③

continues

continued

```
** STRETCH (multiple) **
<Stretch to point>/Base point/Copy/
Undo/eXit: Pick points 14,12 and 14.5,5.75
```
Copies the square twice,
to ④ and ⑤

```
** STRETCH (multiple) **
<Stretch to point>/Base point/Copy/
Undo/eXit: Click the Enter button
```
Completes the grip operation

Figure 7.12

Creating multiple copies of a square using grips.

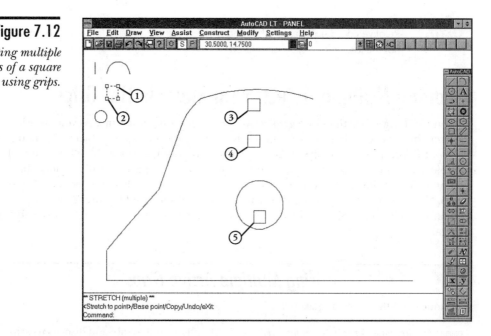

```
Command: Pick two new squares at
③ and ④ (see fig. 7.12)
```
Highlights the squares and displays
their grips

```
Command: Shift-pick the grips at ⑥, ⑦, ⑧,
and ⑨ (see fig. 7.13)
```
Activates the four grips on the right side
of the squares

```
Command: Pick any activated grip
```
Enters Stretch mode and makes that grip
the base point

```
** STRETCH **
<Stretch to point>/Base point/Copy/
Undo/eXit: Move the cursor around
```
Drags the four grips, distorting the
squares into parallelograms

*Pick a point one unit to the
right of the base point grip*
Changes both squares into
2×1 rectangles (see fig. 7.14)

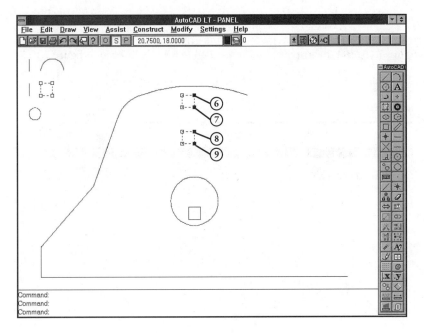

Figure 7.13

*Picking multiple
grips to stretch
a box.*

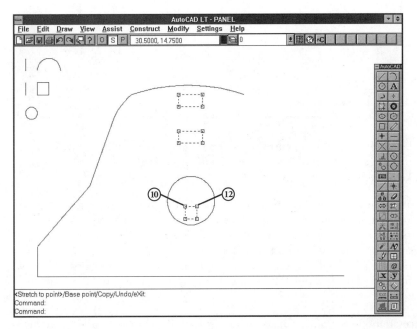

Figure 7.14

*Two boxes
modified
simultaneously
with grips.*

continues

continued

Stretch the lower square to match figure 7.15. Stretch the grip at ⑩ in figure 7.14 to ⑪ (14.75,7.25) in figure 7.15, and the grip at ⑫ in figure 7.14 to ⑬ (15.25,7.25) in figure 7.15.

Command: *Click on the Cancel button*   Clears selections and grips

Command: *Click on the Save button*   Saves the PANEL.DWG drawing

---

Figure 7.15

Two corners distorted by grip editing.

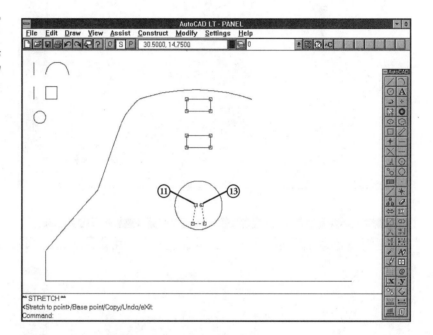

Note that selected objects with no currently activated grips were unaffected. When you make multiple grips on an object active, the edit affects them all in the same way. This can make Stretch move or copy, or distort a box into a parallelogram.

The square object in the preceding exercise is a polyline (covered in Chapter 16, "Increasing Your Drawing Power with Polylines and Double Lines"). A *polyline* is a special kind of line in which any number of joined line and arc segments can be treated as a single object. Notice that the midpoints of the sides of the polyline segment do not get grips; only the endpoints of polyline segments get grips. You can pick any number of grips on a polyline, in which case they will be simultaneously stretched.

The Grip Stretch mode is a powerful and complex tool. Experiment with it by trying to stretch an arc with two active grips (hard to control), or by trying to stretch one of

the squares with three corners picked. The Stretch mode is similar to an editing command, STRETCH, which is described in Chapter 15, "Modifying Objects and Text."

Tip   The STRETCH command is often easier to use when stretching multiple objects because you can use a window selection method to indicate which parts of multiple objects to stretch, instead of individually picking numerous grips.

Now that you have seen how the Stretch mode works, you can take a look at the other modes. The Stretch mode is unique among grip editing modes because it affects only objects with active grips, and only those objects' active grip points. The other modes, such as the Move mode discussed in the next section, affect all selected objects.

Move Mode

The Grip Move mode works like the MOVE command described in the previous chapter. You have already used the Stretch mode to perform a move function. In the following exercise, try using the Move mode.

Using the Grip Move Mode

Continue from the preceding exercise, or create a new drawing again named PANEL.DWG, using the ALT0702.DWG drawing file as a prototype.

Command: *Pick the blue line at ① (see fig. 7.16)*   Highlights the line and displays its grips

Command: *Pick the endpoint grip at ①*   Enters Stretch mode

```
** STRETCH **
<Stretch to point>/Base point/Copy/
Undo/eXit: Click the Enter button
```
Advances to Move mode

```
** MOVE **
<Move to point>/Base point/Copy/Undo/
eXit: Shift-pick point 10.75,3
```
Enters Move Multiple mode and copies the line to ②

```
** MOVE (multiple) **
<Move to point>/Base point/Copy/Undo/
eXit: Pick the point 15,8
```
Places another line at ③ and prompts for the next

```
** MOVE (multiple) **
<Move to point>/Base point/Copy/Undo/
eXit: Click the Enter button
```
Completes the grip operation

continues

continued

New Riders Publishing
INSIDE SERIES

Figure 7.16

*Making multiple
copies of lines
with Move mode.*

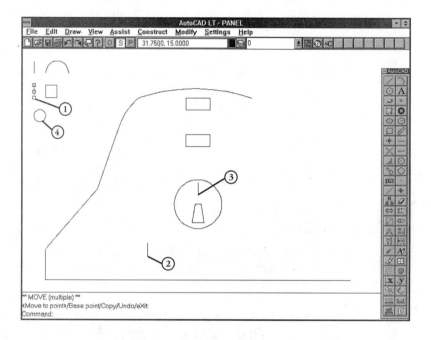

Command: *Click on the Cancel button*   Clears selection and grips

Use Stretch Multiple mode to copy the circle at ④, dragging its center grip from ⑤ (see fig. 7.17) to the end of the line at ⑥ (with a circle's center grip hot, Stretch acts just like Move, so you need not cycle to Mode). Then use Stretch again to increase the new circle's radius by 1".

Command: *Click on the Cancel button*

Command: *Select the new circle at ⑧ and the*   Selects objects, activates grip, and enters
line at ⑨, then pick the center grip at ⑩   Stretch mode
(see fig. 7.18)

```
** STRETCH **                                Moves the circle but stretches the line
<Stretch to point>/Base point/Copy/          (it may be hard to see the line stretching)
Undo/eXit: Move the cursor
```

Press Enter   Cycles to Move mode

```
** MOVE **                                   Moves both the circle and line
<Move to point>/Base point/Copy/Undo/
eXit: Move the cursor
```

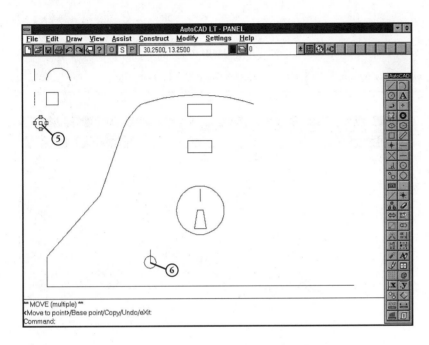

Figure 7.17

Circle copied with Stretch mode.

Shift-pick point 15,3

Copies the circle and line to ⑪ and enters Move Multiple mode

```
** MOVE (multiple) **
<Move to point>/Base point/Copy/Undo/
eXit: Release Shift and move the cursor
```

Drags the circle and line freely

Press Shift while moving the cursor

Snaps the dragged circle and line to an invisible grid, with an increment equal to the distance of the first copy

Shift-pick ⑫ and ⑬

Places two more copies of the circle and line on the invisible grid

```
** MOVE (multiple) **
<Move to point>/Base point/Copy/Undo/
eXit: Release Shift, and pick points
15,12 and 6.75,5
```

Places copies at ⑭ and ⑮, unconstrained by the invisible grid

```
** MOVE (multiple) **
<Move to point>/Base point/Copy/Undo/
eXit: Click twice on the Cancel button
```

Ends grip edit mode and clears the selections and grips

continues

continued

`Command:` *Click on the Redraw button or tool*   Cleans up the display

`Command:` *Click on the Save button*   Saves the PANEL.DWG file

Figure 7.18

Creating copies on an invisible grid with grips.

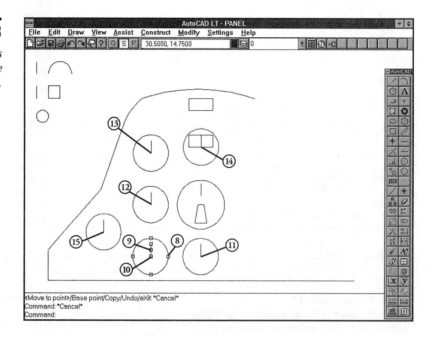

The Grip Move mode works like the MOVE command. Using the Copy option or Multiple mode creates a new object. The Move mode affects all selected objects, regardless of which grip is picked. You must be careful with Move and the other modes. Objects whose grips are not active may still be selected and could be affected by the operation you perform (this is not the case with the Stretch mode).

Snapping Copies to Grids, Distances, and Angles

The preceding exercise demonstrated an important special effect of Shift with the Copy option or Multiple mode. After you pick a point in Multiple mode, holding down Shift causes the cursor to snap to invisible points. In this way, you can place copies on a regular spacing. In Stretch or Move modes, Shift snaps subsequent "Move to" points to an invisible grid. The X,Y spacing and angle of the grid are equal to the distance and angle from the base point to the first point picked. In Rotate mode, Shift snaps subsequent points to increments of the angle from the base point to the first point picked. In Scale mode, Shift snaps subsequent points to increments of the distance from the base point to the first point picked. You can reset the spacing, distance, and angle used by picking a copy point without Shift.

This feature does not affect Mirror mode. The ARRAY command (described in Chapter 14, "Making More Changes: Editing Constructively") can create similar effects.

You will snap rotation angles about a base point in the next exercise.

Specifying a Base Point

You have used the default base point for grip editing operations thus far. The default base point is typically the grip point picked to enter grip editing mode. This base point is the point relative to which the selected objects are moved, scaled, rotated, and so on.

You can also use the Base point option in the grip mode prompts to respecify the base point. By doing this, you can modify an object in relation to other objects or points in the drawing. You try this in the next exercise, as you move on and take the Rotate mode for a spin.

Rotate Mode

You use the Grip Rotate mode to (guess what) rotate selected objects. In the following exercise, you add some details to your drawing by using the Grip Rotate mode. As you think about rotation angles, recall that the base 0-degree angle is oriented to the right. In one rotation, you will snap multiple copies to an angular increment, and use the Base point option to set a base point on a non-grip point.

Using the Grip Rotate Mode

Continue from the preceding exercise.

Command: *Pick the line at* ① *(see fig. 7.19),* | Highlights the line, displays its
then pick the endpoint grip at ① | grips, and enters Stretch mode

** STRETCH ** | Cycles to Move mode, then Rotate mode
<Stretch to point>/Base point/Copy/
Undo/eXit: *Click the Enter button twice*

** ROTATE ** | Rotates the line smoothly with Ortho
<Rotation angle>/Base point/Copy/ | off, but rotates it to 90-degree
Undo/Reference/eXit: *Move the cursor* | increments with Ortho on
around, turn on the O (Ortho) button,
then move the cursor again

continues

continued

Figure 7.19

Grip points on the line, before rotation.

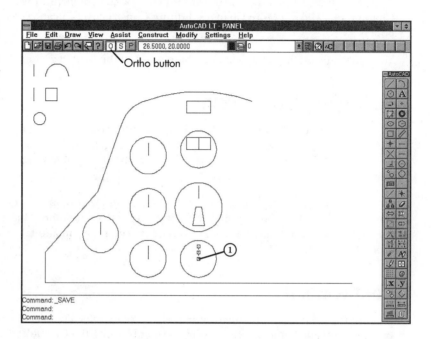

<Ortho on> *Pick a point to the left of* ① — Rotates the line 180 degrees as shown in figure 7.20

Command: *Click on the Cancel button* — Clears the selection and grips

Command: *Turn off Ortho*

<Ortho off>

Pick the line at ② *(see fig. 7.20), then pick the endpoint grip at* ③ — Highlights the line, displays its grips, and enters Stretch mode

** STRETCH **
<Stretch to point>/Base point/Copy/
Undo/eXit: *Click the Enter button twice* — Cycles to Move mode, then Rotate mode

** ROTATE **
<Rotation angle>/Base point/Copy/Undo/
Reference/eXit: *Click one or more times on the coordinate display, until it displays polar mode, and move the cursor* — Displays distance and rotation angle

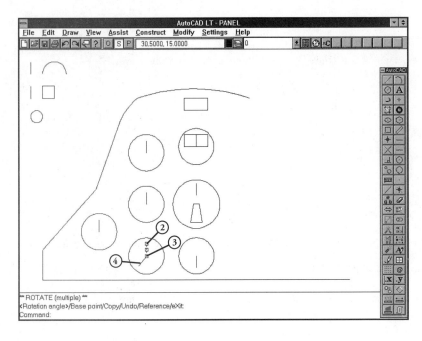

Figure 7.20

First line rotated, and grips on second line to copy-rotate.

Shift-pick any point at a 135-degree angle	Creates a rotated copy of the line at ④, 135 degrees from the original

`** ROTATE (multiple) **`
`<Rotation angle>/Base point/Copy/`
`Undo/Reference/eXit:` *Click twice on the Cancel button*
	Exits Rotate mode and clears the selection and grips

`Command:` *Pick the line at* ⑤ *(see fig 7.21), then pick any of its grips, then click the Enter button twice*	Highlights the line, displays its grips, and cycles to Rotate mode

Move the cursor around; the line rotates relative to the grip picked, which is the default base point.

`** ROTATE **`
`<Rotation angle>/Base point/Copy/`
`Undo/Reference/eXit:` **B** (Enter)
	Specifies the Base point option

`Base point:` *Pick the point 15,7.25 and move the cursor around*	Resets rotation base point; the line now rotates around center of circle at ⑥

continues

continued

```
** ROTATE **
<Rotation angle>/Base point/Copy/
Undo/Reference/eXit: Shift-pick
any point at a 90-degree angle
```
Creates a rotated copy on the left, 90 degrees from the original

```
** ROTATE (multiple) **
<Rotation angle>/Base point/Copy/
Undo/Reference/eXit: Move the cursor
around without Shift, then hold down
Shift while moving it
```
Line rotates freely without Shift, but snaps to 90-degree angles with Shift held down

Shift-pick any point below ⑥

Creates a rotated copy on the right, snapped to 0 degrees

```
** ROTATE (multiple) **
<Rotation angle>/Base point/Copy/Undo/
Reference/eXit: Click twice on the Cancel button
```
Exits and clears the selection and grips

`Command:` *Click on the* Redraw *button or tool*

Issues the REDRAW command and clears up the screen

`Command:` *Click on the Save button*

Saves the PANEL.DWG file

Figure 7.21

Snapping rotated copies of a line to 90-degree angular increments.

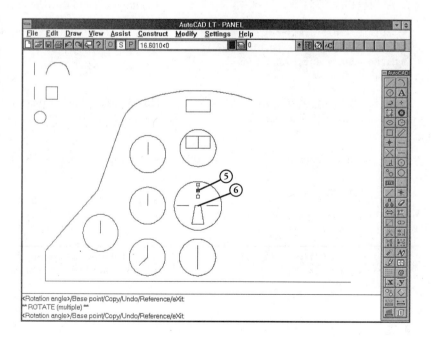

Notice that holding down Shift while you pick "Rotate to" points locks the points into an angle increment of the first angle picked.

You can pick multiple active grips, but this has no effect on the operation of the Grip Rotate mode. Rotate rotates all objects currently selected, whether or not they have an active grip, and only the grip picked to enter grip editing mode affects the rotation. This grip becomes the default base point, the center of rotation, used by the Rotate mode. As you did in the exercise, you can use the Base option to reset this base point. If you reset the base point, the selected objects rotate about the new base point, and no active grips have any effect on the rotation.

Stop If your initial rotation angle was picked at zero degrees, Shift-picking subsequent rotation angle points in Multiple mode is meaningless. It snaps to increments of zero degrees, which locks the cursor at whatever angle it is at when you press Shift.

The rotation angle is relative to a base angle of zero degrees, normally to the right. In addition to being able to reset the base point, you can reset the base angle of the Rotate mode by using the Reference option.

Tip In Rotate mode, you can simply type the rotation angle and press Enter. This is often easier than picking points, and picking points cannot always be used to precisely indicate angles other than increments of 45 degrees because they will not usually coincide with the snap grid.

Most of the Rotate mode options are similar to the Stretch mode options, as listed in the earlier section on the Stretch mode. The Rotate mode has an additional option:

◆ **Reference.** The Reference option enables you to specify a starting angle other than the default of 0 by entering **R** and specifying an angle. You can enter an angle or pick two points to indicate an angle. You also can enter the @ sign to specify the base point as one of these points.

Note When you use two points to specify an angle, the first point is interpreted as the origin, and the angle is measured to the second point according to your Units Style settings. The default is counterclockwise from the X axis, with zero degrees to the right.

In the following exercise, you use Rotate's Reference option to further develop your PANEL drawing.

Using Rotate's Reference Option

Continue from the preceding exercise.

Command: *Click on the Aerial View button*	Issues the DSVIEWER command and opens the Aerial View window

_DSVIEWER *Zoom in on the upper left circle (see fig. 7.22)*

Command: *Pick the line at ① and use Stretch mode to stretch the grip at ① to point 10.75,12.75*	Shortens the line and swings the endpoint around to ② in figure 7.23
Command: *With the line at ② selected, pick the grip at ③ and click the Enter button twice*	Activates the grip and enters Rotate mode

** ROTATE ** <Rotation angle>/Base point/Copy/ Undo/Reference/eXit: **B** (Enter)	Specifies the Base point option

Base point: *Pick the circle's center point 10.75,11.5*	Locates the rotation base point at ④

Move the cursor and observe that the 0-degree base angle is to the right. It is often easier to work if you use the Reference option to align it to the object being rotated, as follows.

** ROTATE ** <Rotation angle>/Base point/Copy/ Undo/Reference/eXit: **R** (Enter)	Specifies the Reference option

Reference angle <0>: **90** (Enter)	Resets the base angle

Again, move the cursor; the base angle aligns with the line.

** ROTATE ** <New angle>/Base point/Copy/Undo/ Reference/eXit: *Shift-pick point* ⑤	Copies the line to the 9 o'clock position and enters Multiple mode

** ROTATE (multiple) ** <New angle>/Base point/Copy/Undo/ Reference/eXit: *Shift-pick points* ⑥ *and* ⑦	Creates lines at the 3 o'clock and 6 o'clock positions, snapping their angles to increments of the first copy's angle

** ROTATE (multiple) ** <New angle>/Base point/Copy/Undo/ Reference/eXit: *Click twice on the Cancel button*	Exits and clears the selection and grips

Use the Aerial View to restore the full view of the panel, then save the drawing.

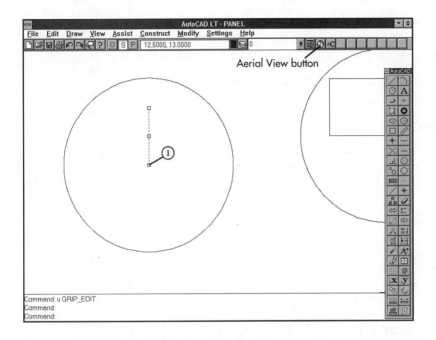

Figure 7.22

Modifying a line object using grips.

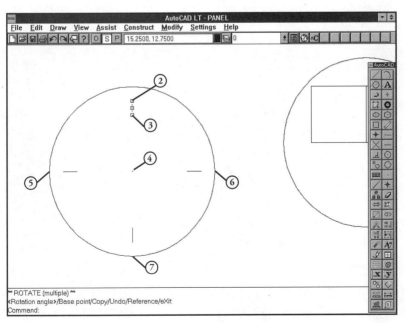

Like the Stretch and Move modes, the Rotate mode has an editing command counterpart, the ROTATE command, which is described in detail in Chapter 15, "Modifying Objects and Text."

In the next section, you do some fitting work with the Scale mode.

Scale Mode

You use the Grip Scale mode to change the size of objects, adjusting their X and Y scale factors equally. In the following exercise, you copy a rectangle, make a rotated copy of it, and then scale the rectangle and its rotated copy for use in a new location.

Using the Grip Scale Mode

Continue from the preceding exercise.

Use Move Multiple mode to copy the rectangle from ① in figure 7.24 to the point 17,2 at ②, then clear the selection and grips.

Figure 7.24

Using grips to create a new rectangle.

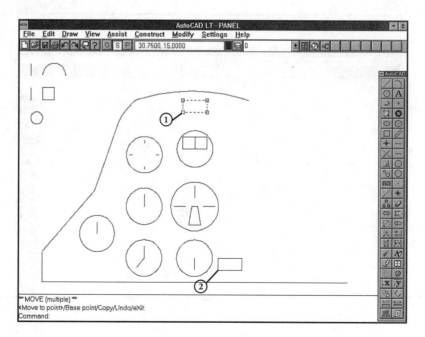

Use the Aerial View or ZOOM to zoom to the view of the bottom right circle and new rectangle shown in figure 7.25.

Use Rotate Multiple mode to copy the new rectangle, shown selected in figure 7.25, to create another new rectangle at ③.

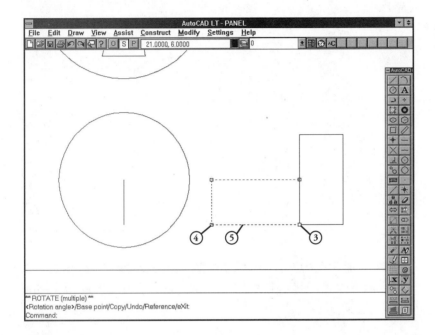

Figure 7.25

Using grips to create a rotated copy.

Command: *Pick both rectangles, then pick the grip at* ④ *(see fig. 7.25), and click the Enter button three times*	Makes the grip active, as the base point, with both rectangles selected, and cycles to Scale mode

`** SCALE **`
`<Scale factor>/Base point/Copy/Undo/`
`Reference/eXit:` *Pick the point 17.5,2 at* ⑤
	Specifies a point one-half unit from the base point, so it reduces the rectangles to half-size (see fig. 7.26)

Use Move mode to move the rectangles to the positions shown in figure 7.27. Then, use Stretch mode to distort the lower rectangle to match figure 7.28.

Command: **Z** (Enter)	Issues the ZOOM command

`ZOOM`
`All/Center/Extents/Previous/Window`
`/<Scale(X/XP)>:` **P** (Enter)
	Specifies the Previous option and restores the full view of the panel

Command: *Click on the Save button*	Saves the PANEL.DWG file

Figure 7.26

Objects scaled to half-size using grips.

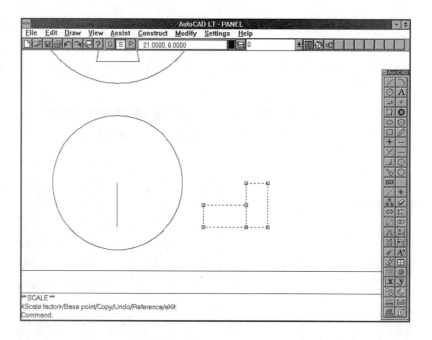

Figure 7.27

Scaled rectangles, relocated with Move mode.

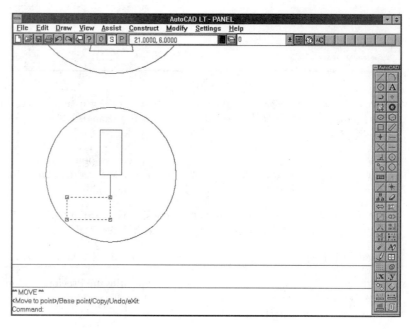

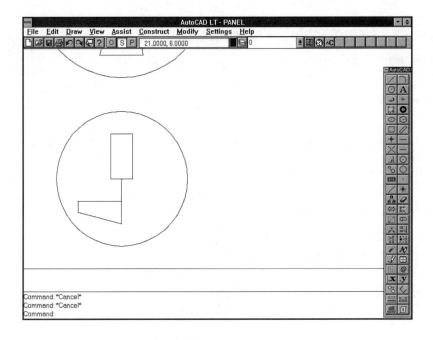

Figure 7.28

*Lower rectangle
after distortion
with Stretch mode.*

The Scale mode enables you to enlarge or reduce all the selected objects by the scale factor provided, relative to a base point. The default operation uses the picked grip as the base point and the actual distance from the base point to a second picked point as the scale factor. You can use the Base option to reset the base point. You also can enter a specific value for the scale factor. For example, you could have entered 0.5 instead of picking the point 17.5,2 in this exercise. This alternative works well if you are in a very large-scale drawing, in which one unit is an extremely small distance on the screen.

Note In Multiple mode, holding down Shift causes the cursor to snap to invisible points. In Scale Multiple mode, using Shift snaps subsequent points to increments of the distance from the base point to the first point picked, not to the snap grid points.

The Scale mode, like the Rotate mode, offers a Reference option. The Reference option can be quite useful, especially when you need to match one dimension to another. The following exercise illustrates this feature.

Using Scale's Reference Option

Continue from the preceding exercise.

Command: *Pick a crossing window (right to left) that selects all the objects in the PANEL drawing*	Highlights everything and displays their grips
Command: *Pick the midpoint grip at* ① *(see fig. 7.29), then click the Enter button three times*	Sets the base point and cycles to Scale mode

`** SCALE **`
`<Scale factor>/Base point/Copy/Undo/`
`Reference/eXit:` **R** `Enter`
	Specifies the Reference option

`Reference length <1.0000>:` **@** `Enter`	Specifies the base point ① as the first point of the reference distance
`Second point:` *Pick the grip at* ②	Specifies the ① to ② distance as the reference distance to be scaled

`** SCALE **`
`<New length>/Base point/Copy/Undo/`
`Reference/eXit:` *Pick the grip at* ③
	Scales reference distance to the distance between the base point and ③, scaling the selected objects (see fig. 7.30)

Command: *Click on the Cancel button*	Clears the selection and grips
Command: *Click on the Undo button*	Restores the original scale
`_U GRIP_EDIT`	
Command: *Click on the Redraw button or tool*	Cleans up the display

Scale mode has its counterpart in the SCALE editing command described in Chapter 15, "Modifying Objects and Text."

The next section covers the last of the grip modes, the Mirror mode.

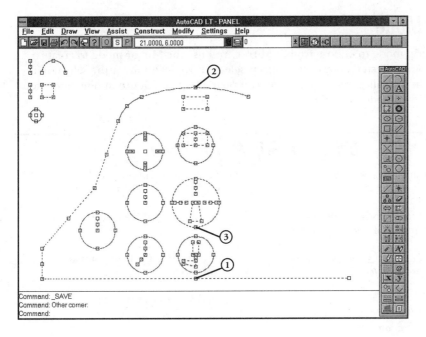

Figure 7.29

Using Scale mode with the Reference option.

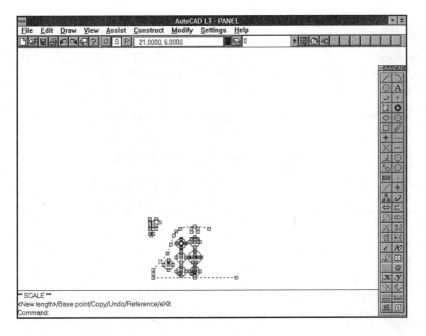

Figure 7.30

The PANEL drawing after scaling all the objects.

Mirror Mode

The final grip mode to choose from is Mirror. You use the Mirror mode to create a reflection or a reflected copy of the objects selected. You can mirror the selection at any angle. In the following exercise, you complete the panel figure in one quick step by using Mirror mode.

Using the Grip Mirror Mode

Continue from any preceding exercise, and use the available objects in the PANEL.DWG drawing.

Select all objects shown with grips in figure 7.31 (note that the angled line at ① is NOT selected; use Shift-pick if needed to deselect it).

Command: *Pick the grip at* ② *(see fig. 7.31) and click the Enter button four times*   Activates the grip, as a base point and cycles to Mirror mode

** MIRROR **
<Second point>/Base point/Copy/Undo/   Drags and rotates a mirror image
eXit: *Move the cursor around*   of the selected objects

Turn on the Ortho button and Shift-pick ③,   Creates a mirror-image copy of the objects
straight up from the ② *base point*   selected (see fig. 7.32)

** MIRROR (multiple) **
<Second point>/Base point/Copy/Undo/   Drags and rotates a mirror image, but the
eXit: *Move the cursor around*   base point has changed

Click twice on the Cancel button   Exits Mirror mode, and clears the grips and selections

Command: *Click on the Redraw button or tool*   Redraws the screen

Command: *Click on the Save button*   Saves the completed PANEL.DWG (see fig. 7.32)

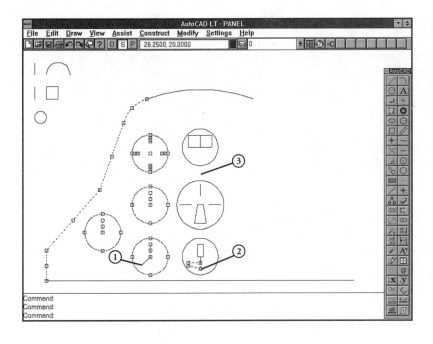

Figure 7.31

*Selecting objects
and the base point
to mirror using
grips.*

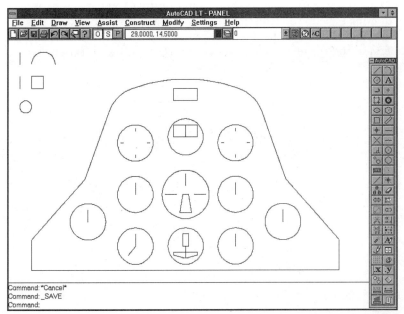

Figure 7.32

*The finished
PANEL drawing.*

The Grip Mirror mode works a little differently from the other grip modes. Instead of a "to" point, Mirror prompts for a second point. This second point sets the other endpoint of the imaginary line about which the selected objects are mirrored. The first point defaults to the base point, initially the active grip. In Mirror Multiple mode, when you are creating multiple copies, the base point gets reset to the second point of each previous copy. You can use the Base point option to specify an alternate base point.

If you do not use Shift-pick or the Copy option to use the Multiple mode, the Mirror mode simply flips the selected objects to the other side of the mirror line. You will more often draw half of something and want to mirror-copy that half to complete it, as you did in the preceding exercise.

If you made it through this series of exercises, congratulations! You may be a candidate for the Top Gun Awards someday. This sketch is rather crude, but you can easily refine it by continuing to practice the grip edit modes you have learned.

This concludes Part One, "Tools and Concepts," of *Inside AutoCAD LT for Windows, Second Edition.* You have now advanced through the basics of using AutoCAD LT as a design tool, and you are ready to see how to structure and control your design environment to best suit your specialized needs.

Begin your exploration into Part Two, "Structure and Control." You see how to apply the concept of drawing scale to your full-size designs. You are introduced to the AutoCAD LT variables and settings that control the way your design environment appears and operates, and the techniques you need to use to ensure consistency in your work.

Part II

Structure and Control

8 *Preparing Your Workspace: CAD Concepts 1B* 297

9 *Tailoring Your Work Environment* 339

10 *Getting Organized: Drawing on Layers* 359

11 *Achieving Accuracy: The Geometric*
Power of CAD 397

12 *Accessing Your Drawing's Data* 447

13 *Using Object Properties and Text Styles* 473

New Riders Publishing

INSIDE SERIES

Preparing Your Workspace:
CAD Concepts 1B

In manual drafting, you cannot simply pull a sheet of paper from a drawer, tape it down, and start drawing. At a minimum, you have to plan where on the paper to start drawing and what scale to use. Starting a CAD drawing requires a similar kind of planning and preparation. AutoCAD LT provides several tools to prepare your CAD workspace, make settings appropriate to a specific project, and control the final appearance of your drawings. This chapter examines the following CAD concepts:

◆ Working with scale in CAD

◆ Defining your working area with the LIMITS command

◆ Applying scale factors to drawing objects

◆ Specifying drawing units and precision settings

◆ Using system variables to adjust your working environment

◆ Setting up drawings with the AutoCAD LT Release 2 Create New Drawing dialog box setup methods

◆ Planning your drawing

◆ Developing drawing and naming standards

◆ Renaming blocks, dimension styles, layers, linetypes, text styles, UCSs, views, and viewports

◆ Saving setups in prototype drawings

The time you spend learning to set up drawings and control these factors could save you hours of work over the life of a single drawing.

Historically, the concept of flight has served as a metaphor for freedom. Consider the expression "free as a bird." Once aloft, you are ostensibly free to go where you want. If every pilot exercised such freedom, however, it would soon lead to serious problems. Pilots are generally required to file a flight plan every time they leave the ground.

CAD affords the designer a similar freedom. Almost everything you can create can be changed at any time, unlike the ink on linen of old. Even with CAD, however, changes take time. As the number and the complexity of your drawings increase, the time and effort required to revise them can become significant. Without some advance planning, both the efficiency and the clarity of your design communication suffer.

This chapter explores several aspects of planning your work in AutoCAD LT. These aspects have parallels in traditional drafting practice, such as calculating the scale at which your design is represented, and selecting the appropriate drawing units.

Start by looking at how CAD differs from traditional drafting methods in dealing with the concept of scale. Then you learn to define and control your working area in AutoCAD LT space.

Applying Scale Concepts to CAD Drawings

Regardless of which drawing process you choose (manual or CAD), some designs can be represented in their actual size, while others must be scaled before they can be represented on standard-sized drawing sheets. When you create a scale drawing, you apply a multiplier or a divisor to the actual measured distances in the drawing to determine how they are represented in the final design.

In a paper drawing done to scale, all the elements have a scale factor applied to them when they're drawn. You begin by determining what scale to use so that the design fits on the sheet size selected for the job. Conversely, all CAD designs are created full size. A CAD drawing, however, is typically plotted at some scale to fit a particular sheet size; therefore, you still need to consider the final scale in planning your drawing.

To achieve the desired appearance when you apply a plotting scale to your drawing, you must first understand how AutoCAD LT structures your workspace. The LIMITS command provides a way of keeping track of your planned drawing area.

Working with the LIMITS Command

A drawing that extends beyond the edge of a sheet of paper is considered bad form. When you work with pencil and paper, it's easy to see when this happens. When you work with AutoCAD LT, however, you have an almost unlimited sheet of paper. Without some kind of structure to represent the ultimate size of the paper you intend to plot on, it's not easy to know where the edges of the paper are. The LIMITS command provides the structure you need to define and control the area in which you work.

In the following exercise, you use the LIMITS command to see the effect of setting drawing limits and to understand what constitutes legitimate drawing limits. You also enable AutoCAD LT's limits-checking function. The drawing in this exercise starts out identical to the default ACLT.DWG prototype drawing, except that snap and grid are turned on and set to 0.25.

Using the LIMITS Command to Define Your Working Area

Create a new drawing named LIMITS, using the ALT0801.DWG file as a prototype.

`Command:` *Click on the Zoom button*	Issues the ZOOM command

`'_ZOOM`
`All/Center/Extents/Previous/Windows/`
`<Scale(X/XP)>:` **.75** `Enter`
	Zooms to display from approximately -2,-1.5 to 17,10.5, but the grid covers only the default 12×9 limits

`Command:` *Choose* <u>S</u>ettings, Dra<u>w</u>ing, <u>L</u>imits	Issues the LIMITS command
`_limits`	

`Reset Model space limits:`
`ON/OFF/<Lower left corner>`
`0.0000,0.0000>:` `Enter`
	Retains the default 0,0 lower left limit

continues

continued

`Upper right corner <12.0000,9.0000>:` *Pick point 6.25,5.0*	Sets the upper right limit and completes the command

Notice that the screen redraws to redisplay the grid within the new limits (see fig. 8.1).

`Command:` (Enter)	Repeats the LIMITS command

`LIMITS`

`Reset Model˙ space limits:`
`ON/OFF/<Lower left corner>`
`6.0000,5.0000>:` *Pick point -1.0,-1.0*
	Sets a lower left limit with a negative value

`Upper right corner <0.0000,0.0000>:` *Pick point 9.0,7.0*	Sets the upper right limit; the grid redraws

Draw a line from -2,-1 to 5,4. Nothing stops you from drawing outside the limits.

`Command:` **`LIMITS`** (Enter)	Executes the LIMITS command

`Reset Model space limits:`
`ON/OFF/<Lower left corner>`
`<-1.0000,-1.0000>:` **`ON`** (Enter)
	Turns on limits checking

Try to draw another line starting at -2,-1. Limits checking rejects the point outside the limits and issues a warning:

`**Outside limits`

`From point:` *Click on the Cancel button*

`Command:` **`LM`** (Enter)	Issues the LIMITS command

`LIMITS`

`Reset Model space limits:`
`ON/OFF/<Lower left corner>`
`<-1.0000,-1.0000>:` **`OFF`** (Enter)
	Turns off limits checking so you can draw
	anywhere you like

`Command:` *Choose* <u>S</u>*ettings, Dra*<u>w</u>*ing,* <u>L</u>*imits*	Issues the LIMITS command

```
_limits
```

Reset Model space limits: ON/OFF/<Lower left corner> <-1.0000,-1.0000>: **0,0** (Enter)	Sets the lower left limit at 0,0
Upper right corner <9.0000,7.0000>: **36,24** (Enter)	Sets the upper right limit at 36,24
Command: *Click on the Zoom button*	Issues the ZOOM command
' _ZOOM	
All/Center/Extents/Previous/Window/ Scale(X/XP)>: **A** (Enter)	Specifies the All option and regenerates the drawing
Regenerating drawing.	Displays the grid covering the new drawing limits (see fig. 8.2)

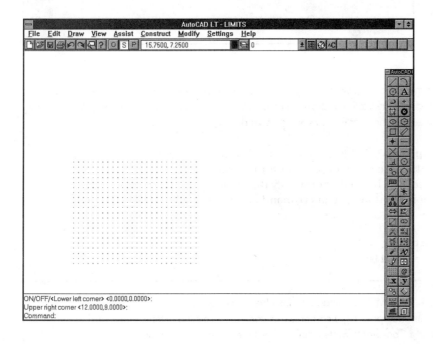

Figure 8.1

Limits set from
0,0 to 6.25,5.0.

8

Figure 8.2

*Limits set from
0,0 to 36,24.*

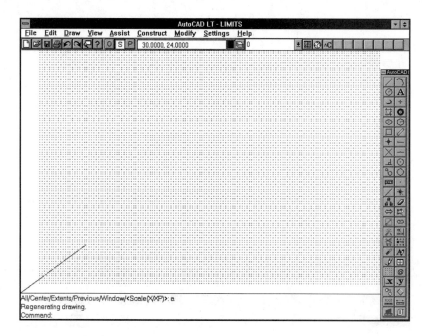

ote   In the sample drawings for this chapter, the displayed grid is set deliberately dense to clearly indicate the drawing limits. Use a more practical grid setting, such as four times the snap setting, in your own work.

Notice that in the WCS, the grid appears only within the confines of the drawing limits. The LIMITS command prompts for the lower left corner and then for the upper right corner. If you do not specify the second point up from and to the right of the first point, you will get an error and be reprompted to specify the limits, as follows:

```
Invalid limits.
Reset Model space limits:
```

> **LIMITS.** The LIMITS command defines the drawing area by the coordinates of its lower left and upper right corners. This command sets the extents of the grid in the World Coordinate System and defines the minimum area for the ZOOM All command.

The LIMITS command has the following options:

♦ **ON.** The ON option turns on limits checking to prevent points from being picked outside the limits.

♦ **OFF.** The OFF option turns off limits checking (the default) to enable you to pick points outside the limits.

♦ **Lower left corner.** The Lower left corner sets the coordinates for the lower left corner of the limits (the default is 0,0).

♦ **Upper right corner.** The Upper right corner sets the coordinates for the upper right corner of the limits (the default is 12,9).

Think of the drawing limits as defining the edges of your CAD "sheet." AutoCAD LT uses the current settings of the LIMITS command to determine the minimum area to display when you issue the ZOOM All command. (However, ZOOM All can display a larger area. The last zoom in the exercise displayed a larger area than the limits, in order to include the line drawn beyond the limits.) Conveniently, one of the plotting options is to plot to the limits of the drawing.

With LIMITS turned off, there is no limits checking and you can draw anywhere. With limits checking turned on, you cannot draw outside the drawing limits. There are exceptions to this rule, however. If you define a circle or an arc by specifying points within the drawing limits, it will be created even if it extends outside the limits. Similarly, you can move and copy objects to a location outside the limits as long as the base point and the second point are both within the drawing limits. Ultimately, keeping the geometry within the drawing limits is your job.

While you are still creating your drawing, you need to consider the scale at which you will eventually plot it. The LIMITS command provides an easy way to define a visual drawing area suitable to your plotting scale and sheet size.

Calculating Limits to Fit a Drawing to a Sheet

Ordinarily, you set drawing limits to represent the edge of the sheet on which you intend to plot. As you create your design in full size, think of the limits *sheet* as being an area large enough to encapsulate your design plus room for a border. Depending on what you are drawing, this area could require a very large or a very small sheet.

Imagine your house with a huge drawing sheet laid out around it. This sheet would have to be scaled up to fit around the house. Scale is achieved in CAD in a similar manner. You draw full size, in real-world units, and scale up the sheet (limits) and border by a factor that corresponds to a standard drawing scale. To accomplish this, you use an inverse of the plot scale. As an example, if you intend to plot a drawing at the scale $^1/_4$"=1'-0", which is equivalent to 1:48, you would need to scale up your sheet by a factor of 48. A standard architectural D-size sheet (24" by 36") at this 1:48 scale is 96' by 144' in your drawing—big enough to fit a good-sized house.

Two of AutoCAD LT's prototype drawings, ACLT.DWG and ACLTISO.DWG, have limits set to 12 by 9 and 420 mm by 297 mm, respectively. The limits-checking function is set to OFF by default.

The following exercise illustrates how to calculate and set new limits for an architectural plan. The drawing in this exercise uses architectural units. Units settings are covered in detail later in this chapter. When you initially open the drawing, you will see an 11 by 8 $^1/_2$-inch rectangle, which represents an A-size sheet, as shown in figure 8.3. You will zoom out to see how this relates to the full-size plan, then set limits and scale the rectangle appropriately for a $^1/_4$" = 1'-0" (1:48) plot.

Calculating Limits for an Architectural Drawing

Create a new drawing, again named LIMITS, using the ALT0802.DWG file as a prototype.

Move the cursor to ① and ② (see fig. 8.3) and observe the coordinate display to verify the size of the 11 by 8 $^1/_2$-inch rectangle, which represents an A-size sheet. The $^1/_2$-inch grid shows the current limits.

Figure 8.3

A Rectangle representing an A-size sheet.

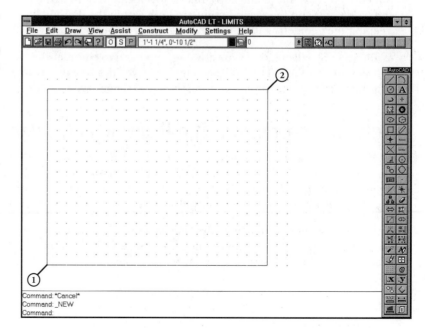

Command: *Click on the Zoom button*	Issues the ZOOM command

`'_ZOOM`
`All/Center/Extents/Previous/Window`
`<Scale<X/XP)>: A` (Enter)
	Zooms to display the full-size architectural plan (notice the 11 by 8 ½-inch rectangle in the lower left corner)

Move the cursor to ③ and ④ (see fig. 8.4) and observe the coordinate display to see the size of the drawing—about 27' by 22'.

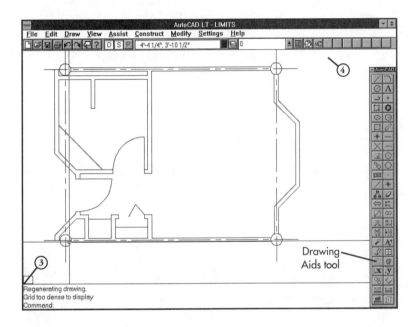

Figure 8.4

A Full-size plan with A-size rectangle in corner.

The drawing would fit on an 11 by 8 ½-inch (A-size) detail sheet if plotted at a ¼"=1'-0" (1:48) scale. To see this, set the limits to the size of a scaled-up A-size sheet of paper, as follows:

Command: *Choose **S**ettings, Dra**w**ing, **L**imits*	Issues the LIMITS command
`_limits`	

`Reset Model space limits:`
`ON/OFF/<Lower left corner>`
`<0'-0",0'-0">:` (Enter)
	Accepts the 0,0 setting for the lower left corner

`Upper right corner <1'-0",0'-9">:` **`44',34'`** (Enter)	Sets the upper right corner to match an A-size sheet at a scale of 1"=4'
Command: *Click on the Drawing Aids tool or button*	Opens the Drawing Aids dialog box

continues

continued

`_DDRMODES`

Change the Snap settings to 1", the Grid settings to 6", and click on OK	Changes the grid and snap, and redraws the grid

Repeat the ZOOM command with the All option to zoom the drawing to the new limits (see fig. 8.5).

Move the cursor to ⑤ (see fig. 8.5) to verify the 44'×34' limits.

`Command:` *Pick the rectangle twice at 0,0* ③ *(see fig. 8.4), and press Enter three times*	Selects rectangle, activates grips and enters Scale mode

`**SCALE**`
`<Scale factor>/Base point/Copy/Undo/`
`Reference/eXit:` **48** (Enter)
	Scales up rectangle 48 times, as shown in figure 8.5

Figure 8.5

Drawing limits and sheet size for 1:48 plot scale.

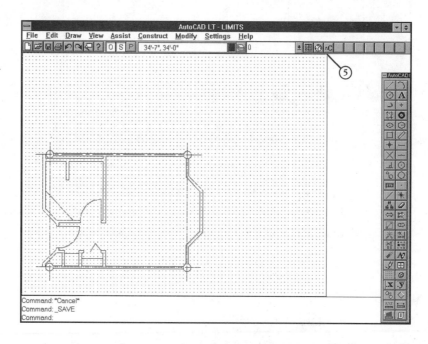

The preceding exercise is a simple example of determining a scale and using the LIMITS command to reflect the resultant sheet size. After you know the actual size of the design and the sheet size for the plot, you can apply a typical scale factor and see if the design fits.

In the preceding exercise, the room plan is a little over 24 feet wide. The plot will be made on 11 by 8 ¹/₂-inch paper. The exercise uses a common architectural scale of ¹/₄"= 1'-0", which is the same as 1"=4'. You can figure it in this way: every inch of paper can hold four feet of design. This formula equates to 1 paper inch equaling 48 design inches (4'=48") or 1:48; therefore, your 11 by 8 ¹/₂-inch sheet needs to be scaled up by 48 and becomes 44' by 34'—large enough to fit around the room plan. Any border or title block you might use should be scaled by this same factor, unless you use paper space (see Chapter 22, "Structuring Your Drawing"). When you plot the drawing, you scale it down by 48 to fit on the 11 by 8 ¹/₂-inch paper.

Three factors go into the scale calculation:

◆ **Size of the figure.** What is the overall size of what you are drawing? Usually, this size is a given. The design is the size it needs to be to function, but you might need to rough out the design before you know the exact size. When deciding on the overall size, you should allow for white space around the design and leave room for possible changes, dimensions, annotations, a border, and a title block.

◆ **Size of the sheet.** What is the size of the sheet on which you intend to plot? This size often is set by a company or a client standard. Sheet size also may be dictated by the limitations of your plotting device. A wide range of standard sizes is available for both English and metric work.

◆ **Plot scale.** To produce a scalable plot of your drawing, you need to know what standard scales are preferred by the people who will be using the drawing. Each discipline has its favorites. Architectural drawings often use fractional inches to represent feet, whereas mechanical drawings might use a unitless ratio. Electrical drawings are usually at a scale of 1:1 or enlarged, whereas civil drawings seldom get larger than 1"=10' and can even be 1"=200' or smaller.

Typically, the plot scale will be the variable you adjust when the other two factors are known. On occasion, however, a certain scale may be required. When this situation occurs, you need to adjust the sheet size or break up the figure into multiple sheets. The time to experiment with different limits settings and plot scales is early in the design layout process. If a design grows, you can easily change the drawing limits, but changing the plot scale becomes more difficult after you apply dimensions and annotations (see the next section).

 Note   Because a CAD file can represent a design far more precisely than even the best-quality plot, some designs are supplied in electronic form (on disk). In such instances, detailed information often is read directly from the drawing file; the plot is supplied only for reference and can therefore be scaled to any convenient size.

A scale multiplier is the key to creating drawings with consistent appearance. After you determine a plot scale factor, you calculate the drawing limits by multiplying the actual sheet dimensions by the inverse of the apparent (plotted) scale factor. These calculations are as follows:

1 ÷ (Plot Scale Factor) = Scale Multiplier

Actual Sheet Width × Scale Multiplier = Horizontal Limit

Actual Sheet Height × Scale Multiplier = Vertical Limit

The inverse of the plot scale is your scale multiplier. You use the scale multiplier to determine the sizes of many other elements in your drawing, such as text size, linetype scale, and dimension scale. In the preceding exercise, the plot scale was $1/4$"=1'-0", which was found to be the same as 1:48 or $1/48$ scale. The inverse of this plot scale is $48/1$ or simply 48; therefore, the scale multiplier for a drawing to be plotted at $1/4$"=1'-0" is 48.

In the next section, you see how the scale multiplier is applied to other elements of your drawing to create a consistent, legible plot.

Applying Scale Settings to Annotation and Graphic Elements

When you work with scale, the real issue is how to reconcile the following two types of drawing elements:

◆ **Elements of the design itself.** This drawing element type consists of the lines, arcs, circles, and so on, that actually represent your design. These elements are drawn dimensionally correct, but they can appear to be different sizes when represented at different scales.

◆ **Annotation, symbols, and graphics.** This consists of all the other drawing elements. These elements appear the same regardless of the scale of your drawing. They include notes, dimensions, borders, title blocks and other notational symbols, and other graphical elements (such as the spacing of crosshatch lines and the size and spacing of dots and dashes in noncontinuous linetypes).

You can easily change your limits settings at any time. Concentrate on the design until you are satisfied with its overall size, and then reset the limits appropriately.

 Stop Make any adjustments that affect the scale multiplier *before* adding text, symbols, dimensions, and other annotations to the drawing.

The changes you make to the drawing limits and the scale multiplier have no effect on the design elements (other than the apparent size in the plotted drawing). The changes you make to the scale multiplier do, however, affect elements like dimensions, notes, title blocks, and linetypes. After you determine a scale factor, you use the resultant scale multiplier to calculate the size of these features. For this reason, try to establish a scale factor before developing any annotation, dimensioning, or sheet-layout elements.

Scaling Text

Sizing text is a good example of applying scale to non-design drawing elements. In the following exercise, you use the DTEXT command and the scale value you determined in the preceding exercise to create appropriately sized notes.

Recall that the intended plot scale is $1/4"=1'$ or 1:48, so the scale multiplier is 48. To produce text that is $1/8$ inch high on the plotted drawing, you need to scale it up by factor of 48 ($48 \times 0.125" = 6"$).

Applying a Scale Factor to Text

Continue in the LIMITS drawing from the preceding exercise.

Command: *Click on the Text tool*	Issues the DTEXT command
_DTEXT Justify/Style/<Start point>: **8'10,4'6** (Enter)	Specifies a point in the closet
Height <0'-0 3/16">: **6** (Enter) inch ($48 \times .125 = 6$)	Sets the text height for a plotted size of $1/8$
Rotation angle <0.00>: (Enter)	Accepts the default angle
Text: **CLOSET** (Enter)	Specifies and displays the text string
Text: (Enter)	Completes the DTEXT command
Command: (Enter)	Repeats the DTEXT command
DTEXT Justify/Style/<Start point>: **5',1'** (Enter)	Specifies a point in the lower left corner of the drawing
Height <0'-6">: **12** (Enter)	Sets the text height for a plotted size of $1/4$ inch ($48 \times .25 = 12$)

continues

continued

Rotation angle <0.00>: Enter	Accepts the default rotation angle value
Text: **TYPICAL ROOM PLAN** Enter	Specifies the text string
Text: Enter	Completes the DTEXT command (see fig. 8.6)
Command: *Click on the Save button*	Saves the LIMITS drawing

Figure 8.6

Adding text that is sized with a scale multiplier.

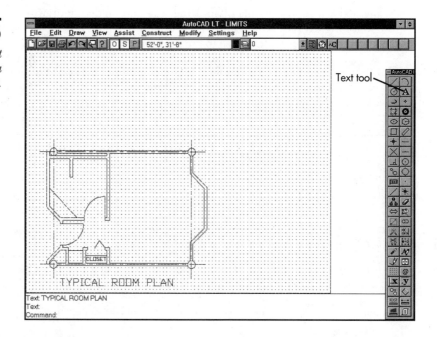

Tip   If you find it difficult to judge the text size without plotting, use the grid. For example, in the preceding exercise the grid is set to 6 inches; therefore, each grid dot would be 6 divided by 48 or $^1/_8$ inch apart at the plot scale of $^1/_4$"=1'-0". The text height of the text string (CLOSET) fits between two rows of grid dots, and the drawing title (TYPICAL ROOM PLAN) is twice this height.

The initial text size in the default ACLT.DWG prototype is 0.20, which shows as rounded off to $^3/_{16}$" in the preceding exercise. This would plot very small in an architectural plan drawing. Table 8.1 shows the drawing text size required to achieve a desired plotted text size when plotting at some common scales. Table 8.2 shows some standard sheet sizes.

TABLE 8.1
Common Text Sizes at Various Scales

Scale	Scale Multiplier ×	Plotted Text Size =	Drawing Text Size
$^1/_8$"=1'-0"	96	$^1/_8$"	12"
1"=8'-0"		$^3/_{16}$"	18"
1:96		$^1/_4$"	24"
$^3/_{16}$"=1'-0"	64	$^1/_8$"	8"
1"=5'-4"		$^3/_{16}$"	12"
1:64		$^1/_4$"	16"
$^1/_4$"=1'-0"	48	$^1/_8$"	6"
1"=4'-0"		$^3/_{16}$"	8"
1:48		$^1/_4$"	12"
$^3/_8$"=1'-0"	32	$^1/_8$"	4"
1"=2'-8"		$^3/_{16}$"	6"
1:32		$^1/_4$"	8"
$^1/_2$"=1'-0"	24	$^1/_8$"	3"
1"=2'-0"		$^3/_{16}$"	4.5"
1:24		$^1/_4$"	6"
$^3/_4$"=1'-0"	16	$^1/_8$"	2"
1"=1'-4"		$^3/_{16}$"	3"
1:16		$^1/_4$"	4"
1"=1'-0"	12	$^1/_8$"	1.5"
1"=12"		$^3/_{16}$"	2.25"
1:12		$^1/_4$"	3"
1 $^1/_2$"=1'-0"	8	$^1/_8$"	1"
1"=8"		$^3/_{16}$"	1.5"
1:8		$^1/_4$"	2"

continues

TABLE 8.1, CONTINUED
Common Text Sizes at Various Scales

Scale	Scale Multiplier	×	Plotted Text Size	=	Drawing Text Size
1:2	2		0.125"		0.25"
			0.1875"		0.375"
			0.25"		0.5"
1:10	10		0.125"		12.5"
			0.1875"		18.75"
			0.25"		25"
2:1	0.5		0.125"		0.0625"
1:0.5			0.1875"		0.09375"
			0.25"		0.125"

TABLE 8.2
Standard Sheet Sizes

U.S. Engineering · *International*

Sheet	Width (in.)	Length (in.)	Sheet	Width (mm)	Width (in.)	Length (mm)	Length (in.)
A	8.5	11	A0	841	33.11	1189	46.81
B	11	17	A1	594	23.39	841	33.11
C	17	22	A2	420	16.54	594	23.39
D	22	34	A3	297	11.69	420	16.54
E	34	44	A4	210	8.27	297	11.69

The DTEXT command accepts a height value directly and applies it to the text you place. The height of text also can be controlled by the text style, but this method limits your flexibility in placing text (Chapter 13, "Using Object Properties and Text Styles," discusses text style).

Scaling Linetypes, Dimensions, and Other Graphic Elements

The sizes of other non-design drawing elements are controlled by AutoCAD LT's system variables (system variables are discussed more thoroughly later in this chapter). As an example, you use system variables to set scale factors for dimensions and linetypes. You apply the same basic principle demonstrated with text.

Noncontinuous linetypes (center lines, hidden lines, and so on) are scaled according to the LTSCALE system variable. AutoCAD LT's linetypes do not precisely meet either ANSI or ISO standards, but you can approximate these or your own office standards by setting the LTSCALE value to $^1/_4$ to $^1/_2$ of the scale multiplier (see the system variables section in this chapter to set it). Similarly, hatch patterns should be scaled by the scale multiplier. You may find that a factor of $^1/_2$ to $^2/_3$ of the scale multiplier creates hatching that is close to standards.

As another example, various elements of dimension objects are all scaled by setting the DIMSCALE variable. This value should be set equal to the scale multiplier.

Borders, title blocks, and symbols are commonly placed in a drawing as blocks using the INSERT command (described in Chapter 18, "Leveraging Repetitive Design and Drafting"). You use the scale multiplier as the insertion scale factor to size these elements correctly.

In AutoCAD LT, you work in real-world units and apply a scale factor when you plot. The next section discusses how to select and set the design units and the precision level with which they are used.

Working with Drawing Units and Precision Settings

A paper drawing uses a scale factor to represent any size of design on a standard sheet. In AutoCAD LT, you develop your designs in full size in units that are appropriate to the type of project on which you are working. A technical researcher uses decimal or scientific notation; a mechanical designer draws machine parts in metric units or inches; an architect or facilities manager works in feet and inches; and a surveyor chooses decimal feet or even miles as units. The units style selected affects both the coordinate display and the type of input AutoCAD LT accepts. AutoCAD LT also has settings for angle units, which affect how angles are displayed and measured and how angle input is interpreted.

In addition to setting the type of units, you can specify the precision AutoCAD LT displays for the distances, angles, and relationships between objects in your drawing. When you work with paper drawings, precision is determined by how well you can read a scale or a protractor and draw lines. In AutoCAD LT, your drawing is stored with 16 decimal places of accuracy. You probably will never have a need for such accuracy unless you intend to draw objects on a galactic or molecular level at 1:1 scale. You still need to control the precision of your input to avoid problems with lines not meeting or incorrect dimensions being calculated.

The Units Control dialog box (see fig. 8.7) is used to set both units and precision. So far in this chapter, you have been working in AutoCAD's Architectural units. In the following exercises, you explore changing and using various units and precision settings.

Figure 8.7

The Units Control dialog box, with Decimal units and angles.

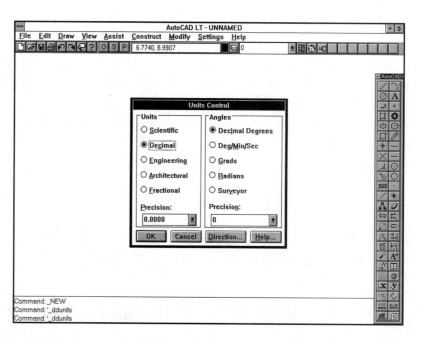

Changing the Drawing Units and Precision Settings

Continue in the LIMITS drawing from the preceding exercise.

Command: *Choose* **S**ettings, **U**nits Style   Opens the Units Control dialog box
                                                        (see fig. 8.7)

`'_ddunits`

Note that the **A**rchitectural radio button is set in the Units area.

Click on each of the other Units *radio buttons,*   Changes units and precision to the equivalent
noting the changes in the **P**recision *box*   setting for each units style selected

Click on the **E**ngineering *radio button*	Sets the units to **E**ngineering
Click on the **P**recision *drop-down list box or arrow*	Opens the **P**recision drop-down list
Click on 0'-0.000 (use the scroll bar if this value is not visible)	Changes the precision value to three decimal places

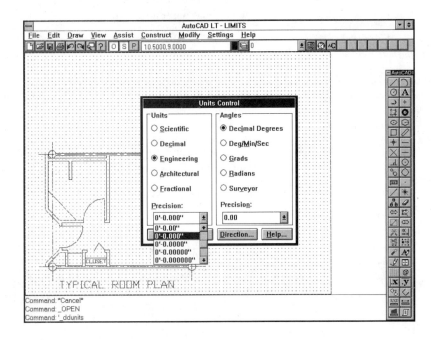

Figure 8.8

The Units Control dialog box, with Engineering units and three decimal places of precision.

8

Note that the Dec**i**mal Degrees radio button is set on the Angles side.

Click on each of the other Angles *radio buttons, noting the* Precisio**n** *values displayed*	Changes the precision to the equivalent setting for each Angles type selected
Click on the Dec**i**mal Degrees *radio button*	Sets the Angles control back to Dec**i**mal Degrees
Click on the Precisio**n** *drop-down list box or arrow*	Opens the Precisio**n** drop-down list
Click on 0 (use the scroll bar if this value is not visible)	Changes the precision value to zero decimal places
Click on the **D**irection *button at the bottom of the Units Control dialog box*	Opens the Direction Control dialog box (see fig. 8.9)

continues

continued

Note the default settings of **E**ast and **C**ounter-Clockwise, as well as the other settings that are available.

Click on the Cancel *button*	Closes the Direction Control dialog box
Click on the OK *button*	Closes the Units Control dialog box and saves the Engineering setting

Command: *Click on the Line tool and turn off the Snap and Ortho buttons*

_LINE From point: <Snap off><Ortho off> *Pick point* ① *and move the cursor to* ②, *observing the coordinate displayed (click on the coordinate display if needed to show polar distance and angle mode)*	Displays the coordinates in feet and decimal inches in three decimal places, with decimal angles in one decimal place of precision (see fig. 8.10)
To point: *Choose the Cancel button*	Cancels the LINE command

Move the cursor to the lower left and upper right limits (grid extents) and observe the coordinate display.

Figure 8.9

The Direction Control dialog box.

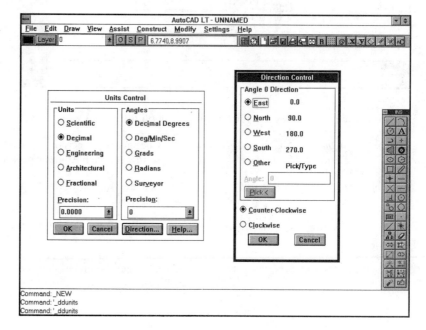

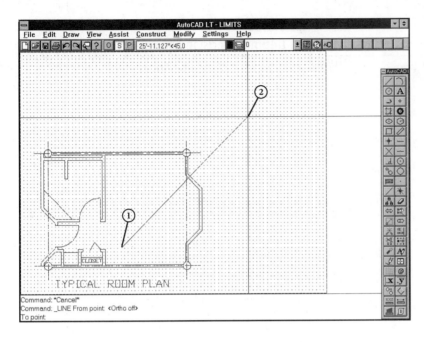

Figure 8.10

Dragging a line in Engineering units.

8

You can also use the UNITS command to set linear and angular units and precision; however, the Units Control dialog box is quicker and easier to use. The UNITS command simply steps you through settings on the command line for each of the items in the dialog box.

In a way, the default precision setting is inherited from the previous units setting in the Units Control dialog box. In the preceding exercise, with the initial Architectural units, precision was $1/16$. This same precision was applied to Fractional units. When you set Decimal units or Engineering, the precision became four decimal places (0.0000), which is considerably more precise than $1/16$. AutoCAD LT keeps track of fractional precision in powers of 2 and decimal units in decimal places. For example, $1/16$ precision, which is 1 divided by two to the fourth power, becomes 0.0000 precision, which is four decimal places. See table 8.3.

TABLE 8.3
Fractional and Decimal Precision Equivalents

Power of Two	Fraction	Decimal Places
0	$1/1 = 1$	0
1	$1/2$	0.0
2	$1/4$	0.00

continues

TABLE 8.3, CONTINUED
Fractional and Decimal Precision Equivalents

Power of Two	Fraction	Decimal Places
3	$^1/_8$	0.000
4	$^1/_{16}$	0.0000
5	$^1/_{32}$	0.00000
6	$^1/_{64}$	0.000000
7	$^1/_{128}$	0.0000000
8	$^1/_{256}$	0.00000000

The precision setting affects only the displayed values of the coordinates. The precision setting is *not* a form of snap! Only snap can guarantee the incremental value of the points you pick.

The type of units you choose affects not only the display of coordinates but also what constitutes valid input. You see this effect in the following exercise. You return to the Units Control dialog box and explore the impact that various units have on units display and on your keyboard input. After setting each style of units in the following exercise, move the cursor around and observe the coordinate display format. Notice the differences between the display and input formats.

Display and Input in Various Units

Continue in the LIMITS drawing from the preceding exercise, with units set to Engineering, and the Snap and Ortho buttons off.

Command: **L** (Enter)   Issues the LINE command

Engineering units work in feet and in decimal inches, so you can specify feet and inches in fractional, decimal, or scientific notation formats in your input, as follows.

LINE From point: **15-1/2',6'2"** (Enter)   Specifies the starting point using fractional
                                                           feet and feet and inches

Click one or more times in the coordinate display to display continuous X,Y coordinates, and move the cursor to the limits while observing the coordinate display. Check the limits each time you reset units in the following.

To point: **2.097917E+01',16.192708'** (Enter)   Accepts scientific notation and decimal feet
                                                           for the second point

`To point:` *Choose* **S**ettings, **U**nits Style	Issues the DDUNITS command and opens the Units Control dialog box transparently
`'_ddunits`	
Click on the De**c**imal *radio button*	Sets the drawing units to Decimal (with 0.000 precision)
Click on the OK *button*	Closes the Units Control dialog box, saves setting, and resumes LINE command
`To point:` **15'6,6'** `(Enter)`	Attempts to draw a line
`Point or option keyword required.` `To point:`	

AutoCAD rejected this input because it did not conform to the input requirements for the present units style. Only Architectural and Engineering units accept explicit feet or inches.

`To point:` **186,72** `(Enter)`	Accepts the same starting point expressed in decimal units (which you can interpret as inches)

As long as you do not include feet or inches in your input, you can use fractional input in any units style, as follows.

`To point:` **231.75,194-5/16** `(Enter)`	Specifies the second point in a mixture of decimal and fractional input formats
`To point:` **'DDUNITS** `(Enter)`	Opens the Units Control dialog box transparently (be sure to include the apostrophe—the **U**nits Style menu item also issues '_DDUNITS transparently)
Click on the **F**ractional *radio button*	Sets the drawing units to Fractional
Click on the OK *button*	Closes the Units Control dialog box and resumes the LINE command
`To point:` **15.5',8'6** `(Enter)`	
`Point or option keyword required.` `To point:`	Rejects feet in the input
`To point:` **186,102** `(Enter)`	Accepts implied inches
`To point:` **201-3/4,164.3125** `(Enter)`	Accepts a mixed-format input

continues

continued

To point: (Enter)	Completes the LINE command
Command: **U** (Enter)	Undoes the line and units settings

For the following steps, do not move the cursor or mouse.

Command: **DU** (Enter)	Issues the DDUNITS command and opens the Units Control dialog box
Press Alt+A	Turns on the **A**rchitectural radio button and units, with ¹/₈ precision
(Enter)	Closes the Units Control dialog box and saves settings

Without moving the cursor, observe the coordinate display.

Command: (Enter)	Reopens the Units Control dialog box
Press Alt+P and then press the Down arrow key three times	Activates the **P**recision box and sets precision to 0'-0 ¹/₆₄"
(Enter)	Closes the Units Control dialog box and saves settings

Without moving the cursor, observe the coordinate display, then press F9 to turn on snap and observe again.

Move the cursor, observing the coordinate display, then turn off the Snap button. Move the cursor and observe again.

Each change of the units style displays the limits differently, even though the limits setting is actually unchanged. The limits are actually from 0,0 to 528,408 units. Only in Architectural and Engineering units are units formatted in feet and inches, showing the upper limits as 44'-0",34'-0". All the other units settings indicate the limits as some decimal form of 0,0 to 528,408 units because 44 feet converted to inches (44 by 12) is 528 inches and 34 feet is 408 inches.

AutoCAD LT's basic drawing unit can represent any unit you like. In the English measurement system, you generally assume it to represent inches. In metric drawings, you assume the same basic unit to represent millimeters. Architectural and Engineering units assume the basic unit represents inches, and displays anything over 12 inches as feet. Architectural and Engineering units display foot (') and inch (") marks, and AutoCAD LT's dimensioning automatically reflects this. You can use

AutoCAD LT's dimension style text suffix feature to automatically add alternative units indicators to dimensioning; see Chapter 21, "Styling and Editing Dimensions," for details.

Tip To represent Surveyor's units (decimal feet), use decimal units and add the foot mark (') with AutoCAD's dimension style text suffix feature. To represent millimeters, use decimal units and add mm as a suffix with AutoCAD's dimension style text suffix feature.

You probably noticed a difference in AutoCAD LT's units display and input formats. For example, 201'-7 3/4" is the format AutoCAD LT uses for display of Architectural units, but you input the same value as **201'7-3/4"** because spaces are not allowed in input. AutoCAD LT interprets a space in input as being the same as pressing Enter.

Tip Although you must use an apostrophe (') to separate feet from inches in input, AutoCAD LT does not require you to include the inch (") mark in your input. Inches are the basic drawing unit in Architectural and Engineering units, so if you do not designate a unit type, inches are assumed. For example, either **201'7-3/4"** or **201'7-3/4** and either **7"** or **7** are equivalent input.

In Architectural units at the end of the previous exercise, you observed $1/8$ and $1/64$ precision. With snap off and $1/8$ precision, the coordinate display showed values similar to 32'-9 5/8", 23'-7 1/4". With $1/64$ precision, the same coordinate would display as 32'-9 5/8", 23'-7 15/64". With snap on (set to 1"), the same coordinate would display as 32'-10", 23'-7". With snap off, your coordinate display may have showed scientific notation, like 2.875309E+2. When the coordinate display cannot fit a value in the current units format, it displays scientific notation. You can use snap, or move the cursor slightly, to cure this.

Stop Too large a precision setting can cause deceptive results. If you set the precision to $1/8$ inch, everything is rounded to $1/8$ inch when displayed, even if the displayed coordinate may not be accurate. A value which is actually 3'-7 $15/64$" would inaccurately display as 23'-7 $1/4$" at a large precision setting such as $1/8$.

Tip Even though you may not need finer fractions than $1/8$ inch in a particular drawing, you can ensure precision by setting a smaller value, such as $1/64$, and by always using snap, typed input, or another method of accuracy control (see Chapter 11, "Achieving Accuracy: The Geometric Power of CAD"). To make drawing errors show up, you set the precision to a smaller value, such as $1/64$; then, if a value displays as $61/64$ inch when it should be 1 inch, you know that it is not correct.

The style of units you use to specify locations in your design should be dictated by convenience and accuracy. As the preceding exercise demonstrates, AutoCAD LT does not pose many restrictions on what input formats you can or cannot use, as summarized in the following:

◆ Any style of units can accept input in decimal, fractional, or scientific notation formats. This input can represent any form of units you like, such as millimeters, feet, inches, or miles.

◆ Only Engineering or Architectural units styles can accept input with feet (') or inch (") marks (however, any units style can *represent* inches).

Tip You can use the SCALE command (covered in Chapter 15, "Modifying Objects and Text") to convert a drawing in which AutoCAD's basic units represent one type of measurement to another type of measurement. For example, to convert a drawing from feet and inches to millimeters, set units to decimal and scale the entire drawing by a factor of 25.4. To convert a drawing from millimeters to feet and inches, set units to Architectural and scale the entire drawing by a factor of 1/25.4 (0.0393700787402). Similarly, to convert a survey plan, in which decimal units represent feet, to feet and inches, scale it by 12 and set units to Architectural.

All of the settings discussed in this chapter are stored as AutoCAD LT system variables. In addition to using specific commands and dialog boxes to make these settings, you can also tailor the way AutoCAD LT works by directly adjusting system variables. The next section briefly explains system variables and how to use them.

Understanding System Variables

AutoCAD LT uses what are called *system variables* to control many aspects of creating, editing, and displaying objects in a drawing and also to control the overall characteristics of the drawing itself (such as the current display window). System variables are analogous to the switches and knobs on an aircraft's control panels. Setting system variables enables you to change and store such information as text style and height, last point picked, lower left and upper right corners of the drawing limits, and many more.

AutoCAD provides two ways to directly set system variables: at the command line, and with the SETVAR command. As an example of setting a system variable, try setting the LTSCALE system variable, which controls the scale of noncontinuous linetypes (center lines, hidden lines, and so on). The LTSCALE value is typically ¼ to ½ of the scale multiplier discussed earlier in this chapter. For a 1:1 plot scale, you might use a scale of 0.5, as shown in the following exercise. With the default LTSCALE of 1, the hidden and center linetypes appear as shown in figure 8.11. The two outer rectangles

in the figure represent an 11 by 8 $\frac{1}{2}$ sheet with a $\frac{1}{2}$-inch border. The small dashes in these linetypes will plot about $\frac{1}{4}$-inch long—about twice as long as most standards recommend. Try changing their linetype scale using the LTSCALE system variable.

Setting the LTSCALE System Variable

Begin a new drawing named LTSCALE, using the ALT0803.DWG file as a prototype (see fig. 8.11).

Command: **SETVAR** (Enter)	Prompts for a variable name
Variable name or ?: **LTSCALE** (Enter)	Prompts for a new value
New value for LTSCALE <1.0000>: **.5** (Enter)	Sets the value, but the drawing is unaffected until regenerated
Command: **REGEN** (Enter)	Regenerates the drawing, updating the linetypes to half their previous scale
Command: **LTSCALE** (Enter)	Issues the LTSCALE system variable prompt
New scale factor <0.5000>: **1** (Enter)	Changes the value and regenerates the drawing

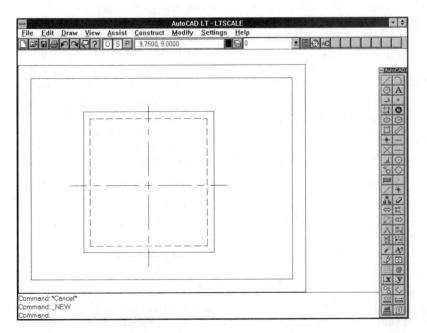

Figure 8.11

Linetypes with the default LTSCALE of 1.

8

AutoCAD LT has over 150 system variables. The values of some system variables are stored in each individual drawing file and take effect when the drawing is loaded. The values of other system variables are recorded in one of AutoCAD LT's program or configuration data files and affect every drawing.

Many system variables are set by various commands and are the result of your actions. These variables change as you work; for example, picking a point in a command sets the LASTPOINT variable, and creating a circle sets the CIRCLERAD (default radius) variable. Many system variables are set by the choices you specify in the dialog boxes you access from the **S**ettings pull-down menu.

You do not often need to deal with system variables directly. In fact, some system variables simply hold information (such as the current time and date or the name of your drawing) and can be read but not changed (read only). Many of the system variables' default values are appropriate for the way most people work, and you may never need to change these values.

You can enter new values for most system variables simply by entering the variable name like a command, followed by the new value. Typing **LTSCALE** (the system variable used to set the scale of linetypes) and entering a new value at the command line is an example of controlling a system variable directly. (Although most system variables can be entered like commands, they are not considered AutoCAD LT commands.)

Some system variables require using the SETVAR command to change their values. The SETVAR command displays and changes system variables. Some system variables, ones that are read-only, can be displayed by SETVAR, but can only be changed indirectly by commands that use them. Some system variables, those used for dimensioning and whose names begin with DIM, are called Dimension Variables and can be set by SETVAR, by the Dimension Style and Settings dialog boxes, or directly by name at either the Command: or Dim: prompts. See Chapter 21, "Styling and Editing Dimensions," for details. Some system variables are not even displayed by the SETVAR command. Most of these are not used by AutoCAD LT, but are included in its drawing file data for compatibility with the full AutoCAD Release 12. Appendixes D, "System Variables," and E, "Dimension Variables," list all system variables.

> **SETVAR.** The SETVAR command lists and changes the values of system variables. You can enter a specific variable to change, or enter a question mark (?) to list one or more variables.

The SETVAR command has the following options:

◆ **?.** The ? option prompts for system variable names to list. You can respond with a specific name or use wild cards (wild cards are discussed later in this chapter).

♦ **Variable name.** Entering a variable name prompts for a new value for the specified variable, unless it is read-only. The prompt offers the current value as a default. If the variable is read-only, the prompt displays its current value and indicates that it is read-only.

Stop System variable settings can affect the basic structure of a drawing. For this reason, do not change any system variable in a drawing that has been set up previously without being certain of what you are doing and what the change's full consequences will be.

All system variables have default values. These can be preset by using prototype drawings, so that each new drawing you start has the defaults you set in the prototype.

Applying Standards with Prototype Drawings

AutoCAD LT's prototype drawing mechanism provides an easy method for applying many of the preparatory steps discussed in this chapter to all your new drawings. A prototype drawing is nothing more than a drawing that contains all the settings and graphic elements you desire to have preset and preexisting in other new drawings. To create a prototype drawing, you include system variable settings, layer names and settings, text styles, borders, title blocks, other symbol blocks, and scale-related settings such as limits and text height in an ordinary drawing. If much of your work is similar, identify any additional elements that might be included, such as standard details. It takes little effort to remove or edit objects from a drawing, so you come out ahead by including the objects even if they are needed in only two or three drawings.

To quickly start new drawings, you can maintain a library of standard prototype drawings for a variety of special purposes. If a series of four drawings contains a common special element, you might create a temporary prototype that includes that element. Your single effort is duplicated three times—such is the advantage of using CAD.

In many of the exercises in this and previous chapters, you already have seen how to start a new drawing using prototypes. In AutoCAD LT Release 2, the prototype drawing settings can also be modified when you start a new drawing by using the setup methods in the Create New Drawing dialog box.

If you are using AutoCAD LT Release 2, you can use the two setup methods in its Create New Drawing dialog box to set most of the settings covered in the preceding sections of this chapter. These setup methods are covered in the next section. If you are using AutoCAD LT Release 1, skip the next section.

Using Automatic Setup in AutoCAD LT Release 2

ALT2

The Create New Drawing dialog box in AutoCAD LT Release 2 (see fig. 8.12) provides two setup methods: **Q**uick and **C**ustom. So far in this book, you have used the **N**one option to bypass automatic setup. **N**one ensures that the prototype drawing and its settings are used unaltered. (If the **U**se Prototype check box is not checked, the settings will be the same as the original default ACLT.DWG prototype.) If you select either **Q**uick or **C**ustom setup, the prototype drawing (if selected) is modified by setup.

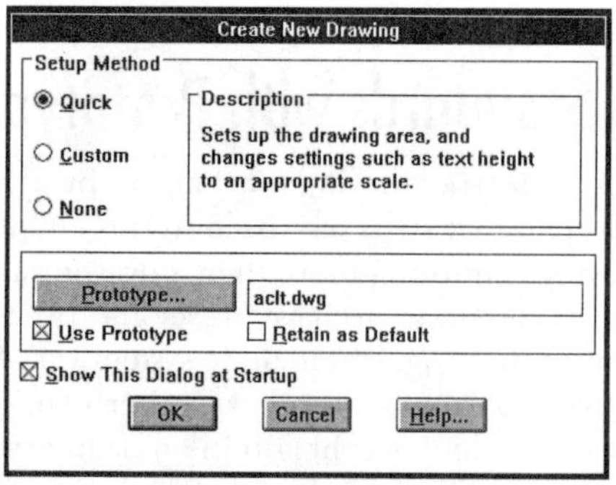

Figure 8.12

The AutoCAD LT Release 2 Create New Drawing dialog box.

> **Create New Drawing**
>
> ┌─ Setup Method ──────────────────────────────┐
> │ ◉ **Q**uick   ┌─ Description ─────────────┐ │
> │   │ Sets up the drawing area, and │ │
> │ ○ **C**ustom   │ changes settings such as text height │ │
> │   │ to an appropriate scale. │ │
> │ ○ **N**one   └──────────────────────────┘ │
> └───┘
>
> ┌───┐
> │   [**P**rototype...]   aclt.dwg   │
> └───┘
> ☒ **U**se Prototype   ☐ **R**etain as Default
>
> ☒ **S**how This Dialog at Startup
>
>   [OK]   [Cancel]   [Help...]

Quick setup (see fig. 8.13) defaults to the prototype drawing's settings, but enables you to alter some of these settings. You can alter the type of units, limits (called World (actual) Size to Represent in the dialog box), snap, and grid in the Quick Drawing Setup dialog box. **Q**uick setup does not provide control of units precision or angle units, and always sets the grid spacing equal to the snap spacing.

In addition to the features of **Q**uick setup, **C**ustom setup (see fig. 8.14) provides complete control over all aspects of units, and all drawing aids settings, including independent grid and snap settings. **C**ustom setup optionally inserts a predefined title block and date stamp block in the new drawing. **C**ustom setup also sets up the new drawing in a floating paper space viewport (see Chapter 22, "Structuring Your Drawing").

In the following exercise, try using quick setup on a new drawing created from a prototype drawing. The prototype's settings match those of your LIMITS drawing just after you changed it to Engineering units.

New Riders Publishing
INSIDE SERIES

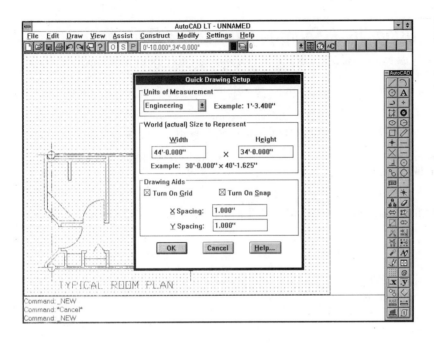

Figure 8.13

The Quick Drawing Setup dialog box.

8

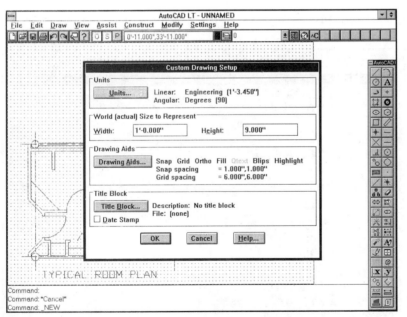

Figure 8.14

The Custom Drawing Setup dialog box.

Using Quick Setup to Start a New Drawing

Command: *Click on the New button, choose* **N**o *to discard changes, then enter* ALT0804 *in the Prototype edit box, then choose* **Q**uick, *then* OK	Opens the Quick Drawing Setup dialog box using the ALT0804 prototype drawing with the defaults as shown in figure 8.13

Notice the current grid in the drawing in the background behind the dialog box and the limits that the grid indicates. Notice also the rectangle that exists in the drawing, outlining the limits.

Click on Engineering *in the* **U**nits of Measurement *drop-down list and select* Architectural	Changes units to Architectural and redisplays all defaults in Architectural units
Click in the **W**idth *box and type* **36**', *then in the* **H**e**i**ght *box and type* **24**', *then press Tab*	Changes the limits and resets the snap spacing to ³/₄"

Quick setup recalculates and sets snap, but doesn't always come up with a useful value.

Press Tab two more times to highlight **X** Spacing, *then type* **3** *and press Tab*	Sets both X and Y spacing to 3"
Choose OK	Closes the dialog box, makes the settings, and zooms to the new limits
Command: *Choose* **V**iew, **Z**oom, **A**ll	Zooms to show rectangle marking old limits (see fig. 8.15)

Figure 8.15

The new drawing after Quick setup.

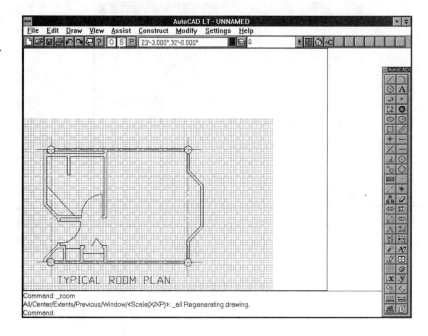

Both **Q**uick and **C**ustom setup inherit their default settings from the prototype drawing and make the changes you specify to the settings presented in their dialog boxes.

Quick and **C**ustom setup also make changes to certain settings whether or not you accept the defaults or make specific selections. The affected settings are listed in Table 8.4.

TABLE 8.4
Settings Affected by Quick and Custom Setup

Variable Name	Controls	ACLT.DWG Default 9 × 12 limits	After Setup with 18 × 24 limits
CHAMFERA	1st chamfer bevel	0.5000	1.0000
CHAMFERB	2nd chamfer bevel	0.5000	1.0000
DIMASZ	dim arrow size	0.1800	0.3600
DIMCEN	dim center mark	0.0900	0.1800
DIMDLI	dim line increment	0.3800	0.7600
DIMEXE	dim extension length	0.1800	0.3600
DIMEXO	dim extension offset	0.0625	0.1250
DIMGAP	dim text/line gap	0.0900	0.1800
DIMTXT	dim text size	0.1800	0.3600
DONUTID	donut inside diameter	0.5000	1.0000
DONUTOD	donut outside diameter	1.0000	2.0000
FILLETRAD	fillet radius	0.5000	1.0000
GRIDUNIT	grid (0 = same as snap)	0.0000,0.0000	0.0000,0.0000
HPSCALE	hatch pattern scale	0.5000	1.0000
HPSPACE	hatch line spacing	0.2500	0.5000
LIMMAX	limits	12.0000,9.0000	24.0000,18.0000
LTSCALE	linetype scale	1.0000	2.0000
SNAPUNIT	snap	0.5000,0.5000	1.0000,1.0000
TEXTSIZE	text height	0.2000	0.4000

Setup uses the limits and units you specify and attempts to factor the above settings by logical values. Sometimes, as in the case of snap in the previous exercise, the results are not what you want. Setup also sets other, non-scalar variables such as LASTPOINT, VIEWCTR, and VIEWSIZE.

Stop   Setup changes settings whether or not you make specific choices. Quick setup always sets grid to 0, which makes it equal to snap, even if you already had a proportional snap and grid set in the prototype drawing. Setup scales dimension variables unless the prototype has DIMSCALE set to 0—this can have serious implications to dimensioning. See Chapter 21, "Styling and Editing Dimensions," for more information.

In the following exercise, try using custom setup on the same prototype drawing as in the previous quick setup exercise.

Using Custom Setup to Start a New Drawing

Command : *Click on the New button, choose* **N**o   Opens the Custom Drawing Setup dialog box
to discard changes, then enter ALT0804 *in the*   using the ALT0804 prototype drawing
Prototype edit box, then choose **C**ustom, *then* OK   with the defaults as shown in figure 8.14

Notice the current grid and the rectangle that exists in the drawing, outlining the limits, in the background behind the dialog box.

Choose **U**nits   Opens the Units Control dialog box

Choose **A**rchitectural, *then set* **P**recision   Changes units to Architectural, closes
to 0'-0 1/64" *and choose* OK   Units Control dialog box and redisplays
    all defaults in Architectural units

Click in the **W**idth *box and type* **36'**, *then in*   Changes the limits and resets the snap
the **H**eight *box and type* **24'**, *then press Tab*   spacing to $^{45}/_{64}$" and grid to 4"

Custom setup recalculates and sets snap and grid, maintaining their default proportions, but doesn't always come up with useful values.

Choose **D**rawing Aids *and set* **S**nap *to*   Opens Drawing Aids dialog box, resets snap
3 *and* **G**rid *to* 1' *then choose* OK   and grid, and returns to the Custom Drawing
    Setup dialog box

Choose Title **B**lock, *then select*   Opens the Title Block dialog box (see
Arch/Eng (in) *and choose* OK   fig. 8.16), selects a title block, and returns to
    Custom Drawing Setup

Put a check in the **D**ate Stamp *check box*   Tells AutoCAD LT to insert a date stamp
    block

Choose OK	Closes the dialog box, makes the settings and displays the drawing, zoomed to the new limits, in a floating paper space viewport within the title block (see fig. 8.17)
Command: *Choose* **V**iew, **T**ile Mode	Exits paper space and shows drawing in the normal model space you are familiar with, zoomed to the extents, showing the rectangle marking old limits (see fig. 8.15)

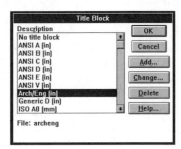

Figure 8.16

The Title Block dialog box.

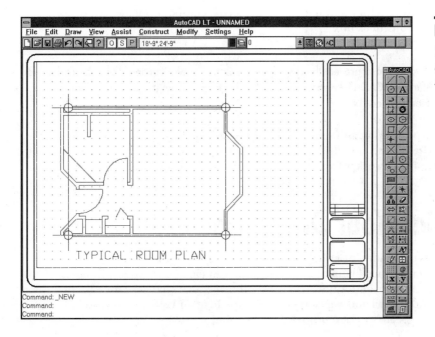

Figure 8.17

The new drawing after Custom setup.

The Custom Drawing Setup dialog box sets up the drawing in a single floating viewport in paper space, even if you select none for the Title **B**lock. If you want to use multiple viewports, see Chapter 22, "Structuring Your Drawing," which covers the use of floating viewports in paper space. If you want to set up tiled model space but use the full units, snap, and grid control that the Custom Drawing Setup dialog box provides, use the technique shown in the last step of the preceding exercise. (Tiled model space is what you have been working in and will continue to work in through-out the book, until Chapter 22.)

 Tip   To use the Custom Drawing Setup dialog box for full units, snap, and grid control in the normal tiled model space, go ahead and make the desired settings, choose none for the Title **B**lock and, after setup is complete, choose **V**iew, **T**ile Mode from the pull-down menu. This exits paper space and zooms the drawing to its previous limits in a single, full viewport in tiled model space. If you need to change the limits, you have to do so after setup.

The Create New Drawing dialog box offers two other controls over prototype draw-ings. First, to start new drawings with no prototype (so the default settings are the same as the standard original default ACLT.DWG prototype) clear the **U**se Prototype check box. Second, if you want to always use no prototype (set the check box) or a specific prototype (enter its name in the **P**rototype edit box) put a check in the **R**etain as Default check box.

 Tip   If you want to prevent the display of the Create New Drawing dialog box when you start AutoCAD LT Release 2, clear the check mark from its **S**how This Dialog at Startup check box.

The prototype drawing and setup methods are an important part of planning a drawing. The next section discusses how you can improve both your productivity and the quality of your work with a little additional advance planning.

Planning Your Drawings

The process of creating drawings with AutoCAD LT, like any complex endeavor, benefits from advance planning. Certainly, you can change almost anything in a CAD drawing at any time, and AutoCAD LT's tools make such changes far easier than they ever were with pencil and paper. The most expedient and efficient method of working is to create a design properly the first time.

This section focuses on two phases of planning your AutoCAD LT drawings: first, strategies for developing a consistent approach to creating drawings; and second, the use of prototype drawings to simplify the process of applying drawing standards.

Some facets of the following discussion apply to subjects not yet covered in this book. The discussion is intended principally as a brief introduction to those aspects of producing CAD drawings that can benefit most from advance planning. If you do not understand parts of the discussion now, you may want to reread this section after you are more familiar with AutoCAD LT.

Aiming for Consistency

Faced with the wide variety of commands, options, settings, system variables, styles, and so forth, you can easily get lost in the complexity of AutoCAD LT. Aim for consistency in your drawings to avoid some of this confusion.

A consistent approach to drawing creation has three benefits:

♦ You need to make a decision only once regarding each issue of a drawing setting. You can then focus your attention on your design rather than on the drawing process.

♦ When drawings are created similarly each time, they become easier to edit later. Furthermore, you can rely on your ability to reuse some elements from your previous work with little or no rework involved.

♦ When the appearance of your drawings is consistent, clients and others in your office will find it easier to read and use them. This promotes more business and enhances your ability to handle it.

The best place to begin to establish consistency is the process of defining and applying drawing standards. The next section discusses these procedures.

Applying Standards

Drawing standards follow a simple rule: almost any standard is better than none. At the very least, you have something defined, and you can argue about it and compromise with it. Standards work only when they are clearly understood and agreed to by everyone involved. Standards are relatively easy to develop if you are working alone, but be sure to get input from your clients. They will appreciate your concern and your efforts to involve them in the design process. Developing standards is more intricate if you are working in a group. You need to consider how the work is distributed, sequenced, and accomplished and to get input from everyone involved.

In defining and applying drawing standards, the following are some basic concerns:

◆ Decide on a standard sheet size, or a range of sizes, for each type of drawing. This size might be set by your printer or plotter or by client requirements.

◆ Create or acquire a border and title block. Use these elements to project a consistent appearance and to promote a professional presentation. To simplify the output, coordinate the border and title block with the sheet size and your printer or plotter. (See Chapter 18, "Leveraging Repetitive Design and Drafting," Chapter 19, "Managing and Modifying Blocks and Xrefs," and Chapter 22, "Structuring Your Drawing," for the use of reference files and paper space with borders and title blocks.)

◆ Designate standard drawing scales and text heights, and specify when to use them.

◆ Designate standard text styles (see Chapter 13, "Using Object Properties and Text Styles").

◆ Assign drawing colors to plotted line weights (see Chapter 23, "Producing Hard Copy").

◆ Define dimension styles and standards (see Chapter 21, "Styling and Editing Dimensions").

The nature of your work dictates other standards, such as the following:

◆ Assign standard snap and grid settings when you create electrical or process schematics.

◆ Develop discipline-specific symbol libraries (see Chapter 18, "Leveraging Repetitive Design and Drafting"), and use them exclusively.

◆ Develop a layering standard (see Chapter 10, "Getting Organized: Drawing on Layers"), and place predefined sets of appropriate layers in each prototype drawing.

After you decide on a set of standards, document them in concise language with appropriate illustrations. Prepare a CAD drafting manual that lists the standards for reference. You should provide explanations of the reasoning behind the standards, because people will more readily cooperate with standards when they understand why they are required.

The real benefit of standardization is freedom from repetitive decision making. Each designer can concentrate more on the project at hand than on the mechanics of its creation.

Another aspect of CAD drawings that benefits from planning is the assignment of names to drawings and to various objects and structures in the drawings. The next section examines this often-underrated task.

Working with Naming Conventions

Unlike the pencil marks that make up paper drawings, many elements of CAD drawings require that the designer assign names to them. This name then becomes part of the element's definition. The names are the means by which both you and AutoCAD LT can keep track of elements such as the following:

◆ Layers (see Chapter 10, "Getting Organized: Drawing on Layers")

◆ Blocks (see Chapter 19, "Managing and Modifying Blocks and Xrefs")

◆ Text styles (see Chapter 13, "Using Object Properties and Text Styles")

◆ Linetypes (also see Chapter 13)

◆ Views (see Chapter 5, "Navigating Views in the CAD Workspace")

Chapter 3, "Keeping Track of Your Work: Drawing as Files," discussed guidelines for naming your drawing files. Although some similar considerations apply to any named object, other considerations apply specifically to AutoCAD LT's named objects. These considerations include the following:

◆ Make names descriptive.

◆ Use simple, short codes for common features.

◆ Apply a structure or template to names to enable the use of wild cards (discussed later in this section).

When you develop standard names for layers and blocks, you can create and identify them more easily. This practice speeds the process of creating drawings while eliminating the confusion, replication of effort, and waste of time that occur when you have to reinvent names.

Renaming Names

Various objects and structures in AutoCAD drawings have names that you may at times need to change. These include blocks, dimension styles, layers, linetypes, text styles, UCSs, views, and viewports, all of which are covered in other chapters of this book. What all of these named things have in common is that you can use the Rename dialog box or the RENAME command to change their names. You used named views in Chapter 5, "Navigating Views in the CAD Workspace." Try naming and renaming a view in the following exercise.

Renaming Views

Create an unnamed new drawing, using no setup method and the default ACLT prototype.

First, you create a view and name it.

Command: **VIEW** (Enter)

?/Delete/Restore/Save/Window: **S** (Enter)   Saves the current view

View name to save: **ORIGINAL** (Enter)   Names the current view ORIGINAL

Now, rename the view with the Rename dialog box.

Command: *Choose* **M**odify, **R**ename   Issues DDRENAME command and opens
                                  Rename dialog box (see fig. 8.18)

_ddrename

Click on View *in the* **N**amed Objects *list*   Displays current view names in the **I**tems list

Click on ORIGINAL *in the* **I**tems *list*   Inserts ORIGINAL in **O**ld Name box

Click in the **R**ename To *edit box*   Specifies new name
(see fig. 8.18) and type **REVISED**

Click on the **R**ename To *button*   Changes name to REVISED in the **I**tems list

Click on OK   Closes Rename dialog box and renames the
                                  view

Now, rename the view again with the RENAME command.

Command: **RENAME** (Enter)

Block/Dimstyle/LAyer/LType/Style/   Prompts for a view name to change
Ucs/VIew/VPort: **VI** (Enter)

Old view name: **REVISED** (Enter)

New view name: **RENAMED** (Enter)   Changes the view's name

Exit AutoCAD LT

The previous name in the **R**ename To edit box of the Rename dialog box is not
automatically cleared. To clear it, double-click in the **R**ename To edit box before
entering the new name.

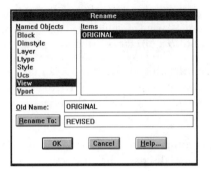

RENAME. The RENAME command changes the names of blocks, dimension styles, layers, linetypes, text styles, UCSs, views, and viewports. All eight of its options work the same, prompting for the old name and then for the new name.

Tip You can copy an old name to the new name box and edit it in the Rename dialog box. To copy the old name, double-click in the **O**ld Name box and press Ctrl+Ins, then click or double-click in the **R**ename To edit box and press Shift+Ins. You can then edit the name.

Using Wild Cards for Groups of Names

By using structured names, you can take advantage of one specific AutoCAD LT feature. AutoCAD LT accepts two *wild-card* characters in many operations involving lists of named objects. These AutoCAD LT wild-card characters are similar to the standard DOS wild-card characters. A question mark (?) represents any single character in a particular location, and an asterisk (*) represents any number of characters from its location to the end of a string.

External blocks (see Chapter 18, "Leveraging Repetitive Design and Drafting") grouped together into symbol libraries are prime candidates for a naming convention. The first letter of the block name can indicate the specific engineering discipline for which it is used; for example, E for electrical, M for mechanical, C for civil. Successive characters can then be used to indicate the general class of object the block represents; for example, LT for lighting equipment, VL for valve, or SP for survey point. The remaining five characters of the name can specify the unique characteristics of the individual block.

The main idea of a naming convention is that you can use a template to assemble names with specific types of information encoded in specific locations in the name string. In this way, you could list electrical block names by simply specifying E*;

similarly, you could list all mechanical valve symbols with the specification MVL*. As Chapter 3, "Keeping Track of Your Work: Drawings as Files," suggested, a naming convention also lends organization to a directory listed in alphabetical order.

By planning the names of all your drawing elements, you can take advantage of wild cards to specify groups of named objects for AutoCAD LT to apply a command to or to list. The layer name filter mechanism (covered in Chapter 10, "Getting Organized: Drawing on Layers") also uses wild cards to isolate groups of layers.

You must apply the results of planning and developing standards before they can be of any benefit. Many of the standards discussed in this section can be incorporated into every drawing you produce simply by creating and using prototype drawings.

Planning your prototypes and standards, setting scale factors, drawing limits and units settings, and using AutoCAD LT Release 2's setup methods all affect the design space in which you work. AutoCAD LT also provides several ways to modify the user interface (the screen elements that make up the tools of your work environment). The next chapter explores some of the methods used to control the user interface.

Tailoring Your Work Environment

I n Chapter 8, "Preparing Your Workspace: CAD Concepts 1B," you learned to modify and control AutoCAD LT's drawing settings and environment. AutoCAD LT also provides several ways to modify the *user interface* (the screen elements that make up the tools of your work environment). This chapter explores some of the methods used to control the user interface.

This chapter examines the following interface features:

◆ Using the interface features of the Preferences dialog box

◆ Controlling toolbar and toolbox visibility

◆ Setting the default measurement system through standard prototype drawings

◆ Controlling interface colors

◆ Choosing interface fonts

◆ Adjusting the toolbox position and shape

◆ Customizing and adding tools to the toolbox and toolbar

AutoCAD LT presents a workable user interface right out of the box. All the tools you need are accessible, and the program uses reasonable colors, text styles, and sizes. You can modify many of these elements and tailor your work environment in any way you choose. Some elements are controlled from within AutoCAD LT with the Preferences dialog box, whereas other elements are controlled by commands or by setting system variables. AutoCAD LT provides a large number of system variables that affect command settings and behavior. Most of these are stored in your drawings; the values and settings of these system variables affect many aspects of working with the program.

This section is organized into two parts. In the first part, you learn to use the Preferences dialog box to change the appearance of the screen elements that make up AutoCAD LT's user interface. In the second part, you learn to customize tools and buttons.

Setting Preferences

The easiest way to change the elements of the user interface is with the Preferences dialog box, which is shown in figures 9.1 and 9.2. In Chapter 3, "Keeping Track of Your Work: Drawings as Files," you explored the file-related functions of this dialog box. In this chapter, you learn to use the Preferences dialog box to control user interface elements, such as whether the toolbar and the toolbox appear on-screen, what colors AutoCAD LT uses to display its graphics and text windows, and what fonts it uses for the text in these windows.

Figure 9.1

The AutoCAD LT Release 1 Preferences dialog box.

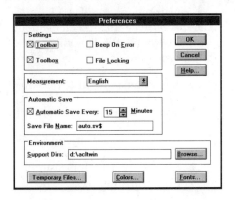

Figure 9.2

The AutoCAD LT Release 2 Preferences dialog box.

In the next exercise, you visit the Preferences dialog box and use it to make some very visible changes to your AutoCAD LT system.

Note The U and UNDO commands have no effect on changes made to AutoCAD LT preferences settings, even though you might use commands to make some of the changes. For this reason, whenever you make changes to AutoCAD LT preferences settings, keep track of what you do so that you can set the system back to the way it was.

Making Changes to the User Interface with the Preferences Dialog Box

Create a new unnamed drawing, using the ACLT default prototype drawing. If using AutoCAD LT Release 2, make sure None is selected as the Setup Method.

`Command:` *Choose* **F**ile, Pre**f**erences	Issues the PREFERENCES command and opens the Preferences dialog box (see figs. 9.1 and 9.2)
`_preferences`	
Remove the checks from the **T**oolbar *and* Toolbo**x** *boxes (click on them)*	Turns off display of the toolbar and toolbox
Click on the OK *button*	Closes the Preferences dialog box and regenerates without the toolbar and toolbox

continues

continued

```
Regenerating drawing.
```

Command: **PF** (Enter)	Issues the PREFERENCES command and opens the Preferences dialog box
Put checks in the **T**oolbar *and* Toolbo**x** *check boxes*	Restores their display

Leave the Preferences dialog box open for the next exercise.

The Preferences dialog box gives you control over the display of the toolbar and toolbox, AutoCAD LT's default measurement settings, automatic save, support directory and temporary file locations, the screen colors, and the screen fonts. The following list describes the Preferences dialog box setting options:

◆ **Toolbar.** When you check the **T**oolbar box, the toolbar is displayed (the default is on).

◆ **Toolbox.** When you check the Toolbo**x** box, the toolbox is displayed (the default is on).

◆ **Beep on Error.** When you check the Beep on **E**rror box, an audible warning is issued in the event of an error condition (the default is off). Such errors include attempting to draw outside the limits if limits checking is on.

◆ **File Locking.** The File **L**ocking check box enables or disables the file-locking function (see Chapter 3).

◆ **Measurement.** The Meas**u**rement drop-down list box enables you to choose between the English or metric versions of AutoCAD LT's prototype drawings, which affects the defaults of many unit-related settings as well as the default linetype and hatch-pattern files.

◆ **Automatic Save Every.** The Automatic Save Every check box enables or disables the automatic save feature (see Chapter 3).

◆ **Save File Name.** The Save File **N**ame edit box specifies the file name that is used by the automatic save feature.

◆ **Support Dirs.** The **S**upport Dirs edit box specifies AutoCAD LT's file search path (see Chapter 3).

◆ **Menu File.** The <u>M</u>enu File edit box (AutoCAD LT Release 2 only) specifies the default menu, which defines the pull-down menus, toolbar, and toolbox.

◆ **User Name.** The Use<u>r</u> Name edit box (AutoCAD LT Release 2 only) specifies your user name, which is used for networking and file locking.

◆ **Temporary Files.** The Temporar<u>y</u> Files button opens the Temporary Files dialog box, which is used to specify where AutoCAD LT places its temporary files (see Chapter 3).

◆ **Colors.** When you click on the <u>C</u>olors button, the AutoCAD LT Window Colors dialog box opens. In this dialog box, described later in this section, you can assign the colors of your choice to various screen elements of AutoCAD LT's graphics and text windows.

◆ **Fonts.** When you click on the <u>F</u>onts button, the Fonts dialog box opens. In this dialog box, described later in this section, you can specify any available Windows font for the text elements of AutoCAD LT's graphics and text windows.

ote The settings you make in the Preferences dialog box are saved in AutoCAD LT's ACLT.INI file rather than in the drawing file. Consequently, the setting choices you make will be used for all the drawings you view, create, or edit, until you change these setting choices.

Setting Measurement Defaults

The Meas<u>u</u>rement drop-down list box enables you to indirectly control many settings related to units and dimensioning. It controls whether AutoCAD LT uses the ACLT.DWG or ACLTISO.DWG file as a prototype for new drawings. The new drawings you have started so far in this book have either used prototype drawings from the IALT Disk or have used the default ACLT.DWG.

The ACLT.DWG is set up for English measurements, with default limits of 12 by 9 and decimal units which are assumed to represent inches. The ACLTISO.DWG file is set up according to ISO standards for metric units, with default limits of 420 by 297 and decimal units which are assumed to represent millimeters. Both files have reasonable settings for all units-related settings, including dimensioning settings, based upon these limits and units.

The Meas<u>u</u>rement setting also controls whether English or metric versions of AutoCAD LT's linetype and hatch-pattern files are the defaults. Take a look at the default environments provided by this setting in the following exercises.

Setting AutoCAD LT's Measurement System

Continue from the previous exercise, with the Preferences dialog box open.

Click in the Measurement *drop-down list box*	Opens the list and displays options for English and Metric
Choose Metric	Selects Metric
Click on the OK *button*	Opens the message dialog box shown in fig. 9.3
Click on the OK *button*	Closes both dialog boxes and regenerates the drawing

```
Regenerating drawing.
```

Press F7 and F9 to turn on the grid and snap so you can see the default 12 by 9 limits. Check the limits with the cursor and coordinate display. These are the original limits from the ACLT.DWG prototype—you must start a new drawing to use the new settings from the ACLTISO.DWG prototype.

Command: **DIMTXT** (Enter)	Displays the DIMTXT dimension variable prompt
New value for DIMTXT <0.1800>: (Enter)	Accepts current value of 0.18, representing inches

---

Figure 9.3

An AutoCAD LT message regarding measurement changes.

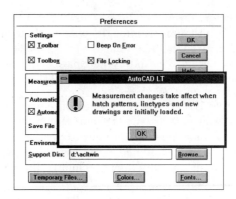

The Measurement setting has had no effect on the current drawing. You must begin a new drawing for the changes to take effect.

Examining the ACLTISO Measurement Settings

Continue from the previous exercise.

Command: *Click on the New button*   Opens the Create New Drawing dialog box

Notice that the default **P**rototype drawing has changed to ACLTISO.DWG.

Choose OK   Begins a new unnamed drawing

Press F7 and F9 to turn on the grid and snap so you can see the default 420 by 297 limits. Check the limits with the cursor and coordinate display (the snap setting of 10 prevents it from reaching 297).

Command: **DIMTXT** (Enter)   Displays the DIMTXT prompt

New value for DIMTXT <2.5000>:   Accepts current value of 2.5, representing
(Enter)   millimeters

Use the Preferences dialog box to reset the system of measurement to English.

Begin a new unnamed drawing, noticing that the default prototype drawing name is again ACLT.DWG.

The Meas**u**rement setting does not affect existing drawings you open—only new ones created with the default prototype that it sets.

 Stop   If you work with both English and metric drawings, be sure to remember to check the Meas**u**rement setting before starting a new drawing, and reset it if needed.

Controlling the Interface Colors

You can also change the colors used by the AutoCAD LT interface. The **C**olors button opens a Colors dialog box, which enables you to set colors for various elements of the Graphics and Text windows. The following exercise assumes that you have a color monitor.

Setting a Screen Color

Continue from the previous exercise or create an unnamed new drawing.

Command: *Choose **F**ile, Pre**f**erences*   Opens the Preferences dialog box

continues

continued

*Choose **C**olors*	Opens the AutoCAD LT Window Colors dialog box (see fig. 9.4)

The default **W**indow Element to which a selected color will be applied is Graphics window background.

Click on the blue box (fifth in the top row) in the Basic Colors *section*	Changes the background in the sample Graphics Window to blue

Figure 9.4

Exploring the AutoCAD LT Window Colors dialog box.

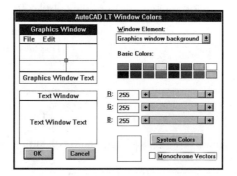

The sample windows in the AutoCAD LT Window Colors dialog box preview the changes you make. These changes are not displayed in the real windows until you choose OK in both the AutoCAD LT Window Colors dialog box and the Preferences dialog box, as you will do in the next exercise.

You can choose from the standard 16 basic colors by clicking on their color buttons. The top row colors are gray, red, green, yellow, blue, magenta, cyan, and white. The bottom row colors are dark versions of each of these (with dark gray being black). The large box in the bottom center of the dialog box shows the currently selected color.

You can specify custom colors by entering RGB (Red, Green, Blue) color values in the **R**, **G**, and **B** boxes or by adjusting the RGB sliders. The RGB controls give you more than 16 million colors to choose from, but if your Windows video driver supports fewer colors, the custom colors you specify may be created by dithering (mixing alternating pixels of available pure colors), which generally does not look good. It's best to use only the pure colors that your Windows video driver supports.

The following two items in the AutoCAD LT Window Colors dialog box deserve special note:

- ◆ **System Colors.** When you click on the **S**ystem Colors button, the Windows system colors (specified in the Colors dialog box of the Windows Control Panel)

are applied to AutoCAD LT's windows and dialog boxes. Using this setting makes the appearance of AutoCAD LT consistent with your other Windows applications. You can use this button to reset the standard colors after experimenting.

♦ **Monochrome Vectors.** When you check the **M**onochrome Vectors box, the AutoCAD LT drawing area displays only black-and-white. This setting option improves visibility on monochrome displays (such as some laptop computers) and simplifies creating black-and-white screen illustrations (such as the ones used in this book).

You can specify the window element to change by clicking on it in the sample windows. You may find it impossible to click on the sample crosshair, but you can also specify the window element to change by selecting it from the Window Element drop-down list. Try both methods in the next exercise.

Setting More Screen Colors

Continue from the previous exercise.

Click on the words Text Window Text *in the sample* Text Window	Changes the **W**indow Element list setting to Text window text color
Click on the cyan box in the Basic Colors *menu*	Changes the words Text Window Text in the sample Text Window to bright cyan
Click in the sample Text Window, *but not on the words* Text Window Text	Changes the **W**indow Element control setting to Text window background
Click on the dark blue color in the Basic Colors *menu*	Changes the background in the sample Text Window to dark blue
Click on the down arrow in the **W**indow Element *drop-down list box*	Opens the drop-down list box
Click on Crosshair color (XOR) *(use the scroll bar if it is not visible)*	Activates the Crosshair color control
Click on the white color in the Basic Colors *menu*	Changes the crosshair colors in the sample Graphics Window to white
Choose OK	Closes the AutoCAD LT Window Colors dialog box
Choose OK	Closes the Preferences dialog box and applies the changes to the real windows

continues

continued

Press F2 to see the text window changes, then press F2 again to return to the graphics window.

Command: *Choose* **F**ile, Pre**f**erences, **C**olors   Opens the Preferences dialog box, then
                                                            the AutoCAD LT Window Colors dialog box

Click on the **S**ystem Colors *button*   Resets your Windows defaults

Choose OK, *then choose* OK *again*   Closes the AutoCAD LT Window Colors and
                                            Preferences dialog boxes and restores colors

 Tip   Some studies have shown that a blue background is easier on the eyes, and even may reduce dyslexia in affected individuals.

Controlling the Interface Text Fonts

You can set fonts by using the Preferences Fonts dialog box (see fig. 9.5). The current font, font style (italic, bold, and so on), and size are shown in the sample box in the lower right of the Fonts dialog box. The graphics window font you choose affects the text displayed on the toolbar and on the command lines. The text in the AutoCAD LT title bar, toolbox title bar, pull-down menus, and dialog boxes is controlled by the Windows display driver and not affected by AutoCAD LT's font settings. Furthermore, these font settings do not affect text you create in a drawing (see the STYLE command, covered in Chapter 13, "Using Object Properties and Text Styles," for a discussion of assigning fonts to drawing text).

Figure 9.5

*The Fonts
dialog box.*

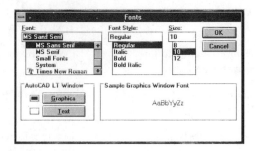

 Tip   If you experiment with the screen font, be sure to note the current settings first so that you can restore them. The AutoCAD LT default graphics window font is MS Sans Serif, Regular style, 10-point size. The AutoCAD LT default text window font is Courier, Regular style, 10-point size.

Try setting fonts in the following exercise.

Setting Interface Text Fonts

Continue from the previous exercise, or create an unnamed new drawing.

`Command:` *Choose* **F**ile, Pre**f**erences	Opens the Preferences dialog box
Choose **F**onts	Opens the Fonts dialog box (see fig. 9.5)

The Graphics button is active, so any changes you make affect the graphics window, not the text window. Note the current settings, which are highlighted and shown in the sample box.

Scroll the **F**ont *selection box, and click on* MS Serif	The sample window displays the MS Serif font
Click on Bold Italic *in the* Font St**y**le *box and* 12 *in the* **S**ize *box*	Makes the font larger and italicizes it (see the sample box)
Choose **T**ext *in the* AutoCAD LT Window *section*	Changes to the text window font controls

Note the current text window font settings (probably 10-point Courier), which are highlighted and shown in the sample box.

Click on Bold *in the* Font St**y**le *box*	Makes the font bold (see the sample box)
Choose OK	Closes the Fonts dialog box
Choose OK	Closes the Preferences dialog box and applies font changes

Press F2 to see the text window changes, then press F2 again to return to the graphics window.

`Command:` *Choose* **F**ile, Pre**f**erences, **F**onts	Opens the Preferences dialog box, then the Fonts dialog box

Reset your previous settings.

Choose OK, *then choose* OK *again*	Closes the dialog boxes and restores your fonts

---

 Note   Changing the graphics window font, style, or size can affect the number of buttons that appear on the toolbar and the apparent location of the floating toolbox. See the discussion of this topic in Appendix A, "AutoCAD LT Installation and Setup."

One important user interface element has its own controls—the toolbox.

Customizing the Toolbox and Toolbar

In AutoCAD LT, you can modify and add to the toolbox tools and toolbar buttons with no programming knowledge. All you need to know are the command names you want to create tools or buttons for, and that \3 means Ctrl+C (cancel). First, explore the toolbox in the following section.

Customizing the Toolbox

The toolbox is one of the most accessible ways to issue commands. AutoCAD LT provides several adjustments you can make to the toolbox. You can size and position it, choose to have it present or not, and customize the number and selection of tools available from it.

Without delving into toolbox customization, you can simply change the location and the width (and therefore the shape) of the toolbox in either its floating or locked state. The following exercise shows you how. The exercise assumes that your toolbox is currently floating, similar to the one illustrated in figure 9.6. If not, simply repeat the TOOLBOX command to cycle the toolbox through its various positions.

Setting the Toolbox Position

Continue from the preceding exercise, or create an unnamed new drawing.

Command: *Click on the Toolbox button*	Issues the TOOLBOX command
_TOOLBOX	Moves the toolbox to a fixed location in the upper left corner of the graphics screen
Command: (Enter)	Repeats the TOOLBOX command
TOOLBOX	Turns off the toolbox
Command: **TOOLBOX** (Enter)	Places the toolbox in a fixed location in the upper right corner of the graphics screen
Command: **TL** (Enter)	Issues the TOOLBOX command
TOOLBOX	Restores the floating toolbox

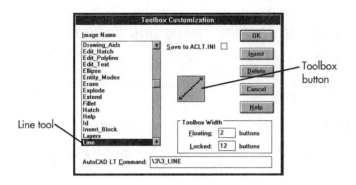

Figure 9.6

The Toolbox Customization dialog box.

Note The AutoCAD LT Release 1 Toolbox Customization dialog box is the same as the AutoCAD LT Release 2 Toolbox Customization dialog box shown in figure 9.6, except for the tool image names. In AutoCAD LT Release 1, the image names are simply the names of the associated commands. In AutoCAD LT Release 2, the image names are used as the ToolTip text for the tools, so they have been revised to make them more readable and informative. The drawback to the revised names is that you must supply the correct command name when customizing the toolbox by adding tools.

The simplest adjustment you can make to the toolbox is to have it appear or not appear (see the previous section of this chapter on using the Preferences dialog box). By clicking on the Toolbox button on the toolbar, you also can select from the following four possible display states: floating (the default), locked in either the upper left or the upper right corner of the graphics window, or not present on the screen. Using the TOOLBOX command or button to suppress the toolbox display does not affect the Preferences dialog box setting, only the current AutoCAD LT session. The next time you start AutoCAD LT, the Preferences dialog box setting will control whether or not the toolbox is displayed.

In its floating state, the toolbox is a standard window and can be positioned anywhere on the screen. As with any Windows element, you can press and drag on the title bar to position the toolbox's outline wherever you want; you place the toolbox by releasing the mouse button. You can also change the shape of the toolbox and add or reassign tools, as shown in the following exercise.

Adjusting the Toolbox Shape and Position

Continue from the preceding exercise.

Command: *Right-click on the Line tool*	Opens the Toolbox Customization dialog box (see fig. 9.6)
Clear the **S**ave to ACLT.INI *box (click on it)*	Makes changes temporary
In the Toolbox Width *section, double-click in the* **L**ocked *edit box and enter* **12**	Changes the width setting for the toolbox when it is displayed in a fixed location
Click on the OK *button*	Places the changes in effect and closes the Toolbox Customization dialog box
Command: *Click four times on the Toolbox button, observing each state*	Displays 12×4 toolboxes in the fixed (corner) locations, but doesn't affect the floating state
Command: *Press and drag the toolbox title bar*	Places the floating toolbox where you release the mouse button

---

In the Toolbox Width section of the Toolbox Customization dialog box, you can set the width of the toolbox in each display state, floating or locked. This setting effectively changes the toolbox's displayed shape. Depending on how you work, you may want to keep the toolbox in one place most of the time. You can easily move it out of the way when necessary.

Tip   When you make temporary changes to the toolbox settings, make sure that the **S**ave to ACLT.INI check box is *not checked*. This cautionary step prevents any changes from being written to the ACLT.INI file and ensures that your original toolbox settings are restored the next time you start AutoCAD LT.

When you click the Enter mouse button with the cursor over one of the icons in the toolbox, you open the Toolbox Customization dialog box (see fig. 9.6). The Toolbox Customization dialog box enables you to assign any command (or sequence of commands) to any toolbox icon. You also can delete or add tools (up to a total of 40 tools in AutoCAD LT Release 1 or 60 in AutoCAD LT Release 2). In figure 9.6, the **I**mage Name list shows the available predefined tools. The large box in the center shows the currently selected (Line) icon, magnified. The AutoCAD LT **C**ommand box shows the command defined for the selected tool.

The following two exercises demonstrate how easily you can add tools to the toolbox in AutoCAD LT Release 1 or AutoCAD LT Release 2. Follow the exercise that matches your version of AutoCAD LT, and skip the other exercise.

Adding a Tool to the Toolbox in AutoCAD LT Release 1

Continue from the preceding exercise.

Command: *Right-click on the Line tool*	Opens the Toolbox Customization dialog box with the Line tool selected

Notice that the AutoCAD LT Command edit box shows \3\3_LINE. This makes the tool issue two Cancels (Ctrl+Cs, because \3 is the code for Ctrl+C), then the LINE command. The underscore character prefacing the LINE command is for international compatibility in menu design.

Scroll up in the **I**mage Name list *and click on* DDINSERT	Displays the DDINSERT icon in the icon box and DDINSERT in the AutoCAD LT **C**ommand box
Click in the AutoCAD LT **C**ommand *box, then press Home*	Positions text cursor before the word DDINSERT

WARNING: Do **not** click on OK or you will replace the selected Line tool.

Type \3\3 *and choose* **In**sert	Adds two Ctrl+C codes to the command text (see fig. 9.7), closes the Toolbox Customization dialog box, and inserts the new tool before the Line tool (similar to fig. 9.8)
Command: *Click on the new DDINSERT tool*	Issues DDINSERT command and opens Insert dialog box (see Chapter 18, "Leveraging Repetitive Design and Drafting," for details)
Click on Cancel	Closes Insert dialog box
Command: *Right-click on the DDINSERT tool*	Opens the Toolbox Customization dialog box with the DDINSERT tool selected
Choose **D**elete	Closes the Toolbox Customization dialog box and deletes the DDINSERT tool

Figure 9.7

Adding a new DDINSERT tool in AutoCAD LT Release 1.

The process of adding a tool to AutoCAD LT Release 2 is the same as in AutoCAD LT Release 1, except the Image Name list and the default text inserts in the AutoCAD LT **C**ommand box differ, as shown in the following exercise.

Figure 9.8

A new Insert Block tool in AutoCAD LT Release 2.

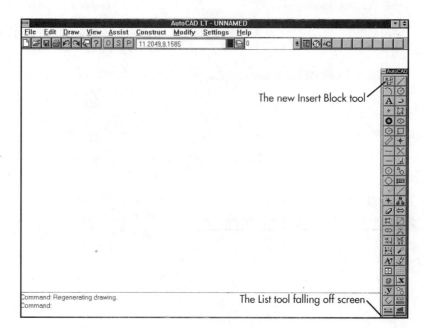

Adding a Tool to the Toolbox in AutoCAD LT Release 2

Continue from the preceding Adjusting the Toolbox... exercise.

Command: *Right-click on the Line tool*

Opens the Toolbox Customization dialog box with the Line tool selected

Notice that the AutoCAD LT Command edit box shows `\3\3_LINE`. This makes the tool issue two Cancels (Ctrl+Cs, because `\3` is the code for Ctrl+C), then the LINE command. The underscore character prefacing the line command is for international compatibility in menu design.

Click on Ellipse *in the* **I**mage Name *list*

Displays the Ellipse icon in the icon box and `\3\3_ELLIPSE` in the AutoCAD LT **C**ommand box

The Ellipse tool is an existing tool, so it has a predefined icon and command string, including the Ctrl+C codes.

Click on Insert_Block *in the* **I**mage Name *list*

Displays the Insert_Block icon in the icon box and Insert_Block in the AutoCAD LT **C**ommand box

The Insert Block tool, unlike the Ellipse tool, is not in the default toolbox, so it has a predefined icon but no predefined command string. Selecting the Insert_Block image name simply inserts the Insert_Block image name in the AutoCAD LT **C**ommand box. Next you change it to a proper command string.

Double-click in the AutoCAD LT **C**ommand *box, then press Del*

Clears the AutoCAD LT **C**ommand box

WARNING: Do **not** click on OK or you will replace the selected Line tool.

Type `\3\3_DDINSERT` *and choose* **In**sert

Defines the command text string (similar to fig. 9.7), closes the Toolbox Customization dialog box, and inserts the new tool before the Line tool (see fig. 9.8)

Notice that the List tool might be pushed off the bottom of the screen. You can reposition the toolbox to access it.

Command: *Click on the new Insert Block tool*

Issues DDINSERT command and opens Insert dialog box (see Chapter 18, "Leveraging Repetitive Design and Drafting," for details)

Click on Cancel

Closes Insert dialog box

continues

continued

Command: *Right-click on the Insert Block tool*	Opens the Toolbox Customization dialog box with the Insert Block tool selected
Choose **D**elete	Closes the Toolbox Customization dialog box and deletes the Insert Block tool

Tip   To make a tool (or button) for a transparent command, omit the \3 codes and preface the command string with an apostrophe ('). To make a tool (or button) for an editing command that accepts noun-verb selection sets, omit the \3 codes.

Note   In AutoCAD LT Release 1, the editing tools which can accept a noun-verb selection have no \3 (cancel) codes. This enables you to make a noun-verb selection and then click on the tool. When you click on the tool, it accepts the selection and immediately acts on it.

ALT2   In AutoCAD LT Release 2, these editing tools have \3 codes, which prevents you from making a noun-verb selection and then clicking on the tool to accept the selection and immediately act on it. This unnecessarily eliminates a very convenient feature. You can restore this feature by editing the Copy, Erase, Move, Rotate, Scale, Change, and Explode tools and deleting their \3 codes.

You also can modify the toolbar.

Customizing the Toolbar Buttons

The process of customizing the toolbar, using the Toolbar Button *nn* Customization dialog box (see fig 9.9), is nearly the same as the process of customizing the toolbox in the preceding exercises. The differences and features are as follows:

◆ You cannot modify the toolbar position.

◆ You cannot modify the Ortho, Snap, or Paper Space buttons, the Coordinate Display, the Current Color button (Entity Creation Modes dialog box), or the Current Layer drop-down list.

◆ Customizable buttons are identified by number.

◆ You can replace existing buttons with new definitions, or delete existing buttons to make them blank, but you cannot directly insert new ones between existing ones.

◆ Right-clicking on existing buttons opens the dialog box with a S<u>e</u>lect Image list; Right-clicking on blank buttons opens the dialog box with a S<u>e</u>lect Character list, as shown in figure 9.9.

◆ Selecting from the S<u>e</u>lect Image list places the selected icon image on the button; selecting from the S<u>e</u>lect Character list places the selected character on the button. You can switch between the S<u>e</u>lect Image list and Select Character list by choosing the Ima<u>g</u>e and <u>C</u>haracter buttons.

◆ You can cycle though the buttons by choosing the <u>N</u>ext and <u>P</u>revious buttons.

Note If you do not provide a command string in the AutoCAD LT **C**ommand box, nothing happens when you choose OK.

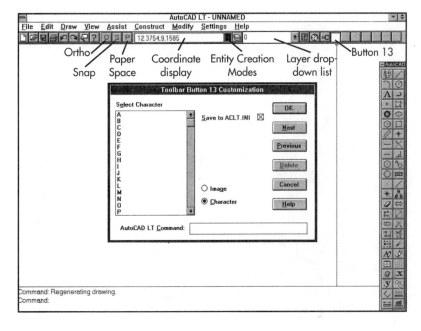

Figure 9.9

The Toolbar Button 13 Customization dialog box.

9

The *AutoCAD LT for Windows User's Guide* (shipped with the product) and the book *Inside AutoCAD Release 12* (New Riders Publishing) covers the customization of the toolbox and toolbar tools and buttons in more detail. *Inside AutoCAD Release 12* also describes how to create your own icon images.

The next chapter covers the topic of layers. Layers are one of the drawing elements for which you need to develop standards. Layers are the most important tool you have for keeping data organized within your drawings. More time has probably been spent debating layer standards than any other topic in CAD. Before deciding on a layer standard for your work, study the next chapter carefully.

Getting Organized: Drawing on Layers

One of the keys to becoming an effective CAD software user is the organization of the component parts of your drawing. This chapter shows you how to organize your drawing through the use of layers. In its discussion of layers, this chapter includes the following topics:

◆ Introducing the concept of layers

◆ Creating, naming, and assigning colors and linetypes to layers

◆ Changing the color and linetype properties of layers

◆ Setting the current layer

◆ Using layers effectively for organizing, displaying, and grouping various objects in your drawing

◆ Controlling the visibility and selectability of objects by layer

◆ Controlling layer lists with filters and wild cards

The effective use of layers in your drawing is one of the most important ways to work smarter. Layers enable you to organize your drawing in such a way that the benefits of CAD over manual drafting are readily apparent. As your drawings become more involved and complex, layers can be a great time-saver and a way to avoid unnecessary confusion.

You learned in Chapter 1 that the effective use of CAD relies on the intelligent construction of the drawing database. One of the most important aspects of organizing the drawing data is controlling the layers upon which entities reside. Every object in an AutoCAD LT drawing is associated with a particular layer.

Using layers is an efficient way to organize your drawing, and one of the most powerful. Giving some forethought to your layer-naming conventions and the properties you assign to layers can greatly increase your efficiency in using AutoCAD LT. This chapter explains how to create, modify, control, and draw on layers.

Understanding Layers

Layers in CAD can be thought of as overlays, similar to pinning together several mylar drawings in manual drafting to form a composite drawing. In an architectural drawing, for example, one layer might contain the dimensions for the drawing, another layer might contain the architectural background, yet another layer might contain a reflected ceiling plan for the building, and so on.

This same concept is used in AutoCAD LT. Figure 10.1 illustrates the example just described. On the left side of the figure is a plan view as you might normally see it on screen or plotted in an architectural drawing. On the right side of the figure, you see a depiction of the layers used in the drawing: layer DIMS is used for the dimensions; layer FLOOR is the layer for the walls, doors, and windows; and layer CEILING is the reflected ceiling plan to show the layout of the ceiling tiles.

Figure 10.1

Using layers in AutoCAD LT.

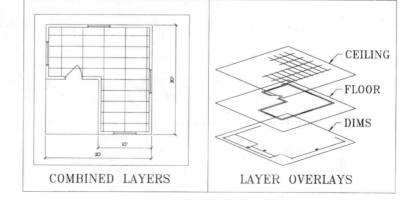

COMBINED LAYERS   LAYER OVERLAYS

An architectural drawing is used as an example here, but all drafting disciplines benefit greatly from the judicious use of layers. In machine design, structural design, civil engineering, and all other drafting specialties, you can increase your flexibility, control, and productivity by using layers.

AutoCAD LT provides several ways of working with layers:

◆ Opening the Layer Control dialog box by clicking on the Layers (DDLMODES) button (see fig. 10.2) on the toolbar

◆ Opening the Layer Control dialog box by choosing **S**ettings, then **L**ayer Control from the pull-down menu

◆ Opening the Layer Control dialog box by entering the **DDLMODES** command

◆ Entering the **LAYER** command, then entering options and layer names on the command lines

◆ Setting the current layer by clicking on the Current Layer name box on the toolbar and then choosing a layer name from the Current Layer name drop-down list

The first four methods in the above list provide complete layer control. The first three methods open the Layer Control dialog box, which is the method you will use most. This dialog box, shown in figure 10.3, presents an intuitive graphical interface for the myriads of layer settings and options.

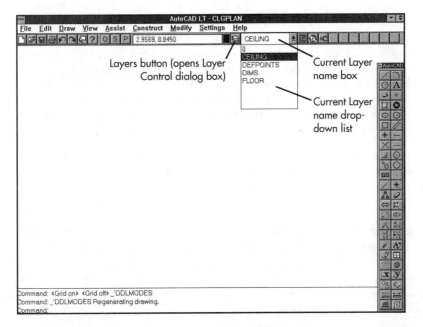

Figure 10.2

The toolbar's layer control features.

10

In AutoCAD LT Release 1, the Layers button is labeled "Layer" instead of with an icon and the Layers ToolTip.

Figure 10.3

The Layer Control dialog box.

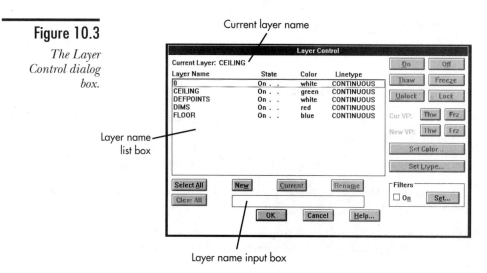

Current layer name

Layer name list box

Layer name input box

Setting the Current Layer from the Toolbar

The easiest way to set a layer current is with the Current Layer name box on the toolbar (see fig. 10.2). You have already done this in previous chapters. You did so by clicking on the Current Layer name box, which dropped down a list of layers to select from. If your drawing contains more than eight layers, a vertical scroll bar appears to the right of the list. To make a layer current, you click on its name in the Current Layer name drop-down list. The layer name you select is then displayed in the Current Layer name box. In various exercises in this chapter, you use the Current Layer name box to set the current layer.

If a layer is frozen, its name does not appear in the Layer Name drop-down list, because a frozen layer cannot be current. If a layer is off, however, its name does appear in the drop-down list and can be set current.

Stop If you select a layer that is off from the Current Layer name drop-down list, it will be made current without warning. Anything you subsequently draw will be created on that layer, but will not appear on-screen until you turn on the layer.

The easiest way to create layers and to change their colors, linetypes, and visibility is by using the Layer Control dialog box.

New Riders Publishing
INSIDE SERIES

Working with the Layer Control Dialog Box

The Layer Control dialog box consists of a list box, numerous buttons, and an input box. The Layer Name list box provides a list of the layers defined in the drawing. The list shows their status (to be discussed later), their colors, and which linetypes are associated with the layers. The buttons enable you to control and establish the properties of layers and which layers are displayed in the list box. A detailed list of the buttons and their functions follows the exercise. The input box at the bottom of the Layer Control dialog box (just above the OK and Cancel buttons) is for user entry of layer names.

Creating New Layers

You begin working with layers in the following exercise. To do so, you must first create layers. You will create a new drawing and use the Layer Control dialog box to create a new layer named OBJECT in the following exercise.

Creating New Layers

Create a new drawing named LAYERS, using the default ACLT prototype drawing. If using AutoCAD LT Release 2, make sure Setup Method None is selected. Set snap to 0.1 and grid to 0.5, and turn on both.

Click on the Layers button	Issues the DDLMODES command
' _DDLMODES	Displays the Layer Control dialog box (see fig. 10.4)
Type **OBJECT** *in the input box, and choose* Ne**w**	Creates a new layer named OBJECT and adds it to the Layer Name list box
Click on OBJECT *in the* Layer Name *list box*	Selects a layer for a subsequent action
Choose **C**urrent	Makes OBJECT the current layer
Click on OK	Closes the Layer Control dialog box and saves the changes

The Current Layer name box on the toolbar now shows OBJECT.

Use the LINE command to draw a rectangle 8 units wide by 3 units high with the lower left corner at coordinates 2,2, as shown in figure 10.5.

10

Figure 10.4

*Creating the
OBJECT layer in
the Layer Control
dialog box.*

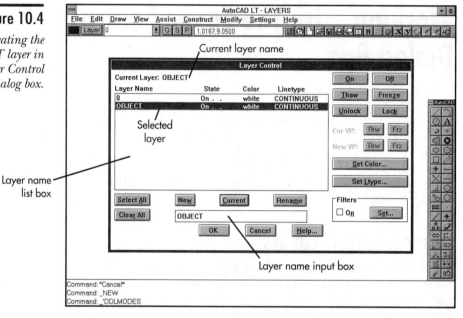

Figure 10.5

*A rectangle
drawn on the
OBJECT layer.*

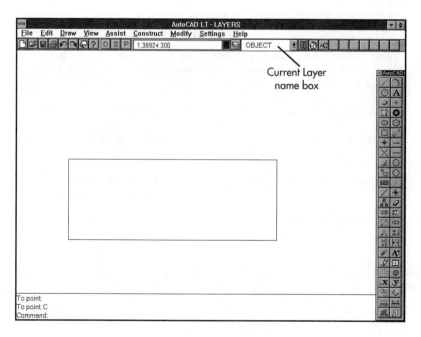

You just created a new layer named OBJECT and made it the current layer. Making a
layer current means that the entities you draw will be placed on that layer until you

make another layer current. The rectangle appears on the OBJECT layer, but it doesn't look any different than if it were drawn on layer 0. All new layers are created with the same default color and linetype (white and continuous) as layer 0. You learn to change these layer properties later in this chapter.

When you make a layer current, the layer name appears in the Current Layer name box on the toolbar. By glancing at the toolbar while you are drawing, you can always tell on what layer your entities will be placed (see fig. 10.5).

 Note   You can also use the keyboard to select layers in the Layer Name list box. To do so, press Alt+Y, use the Up and Down arrow keys to move the dotted box that appears to the desired layer, and then press the spacebar to select or deselect it.

The Layer Control dialog box contains numerous options, as shown in figure 10.4:

◆ **Current Layer name.** Shows what layer is current in the drawing.

◆ **Layer Name list box.** Lists layers defined in the drawing. The layer names listed can be controlled through the use of filters, as discussed later in this chapter. You can select or deselect layers by clicking on their names. Selected layers are highlighted. You can use the numerous buttons in the dialog box to control the status or properties of selected layers. When only one layer is selected, its name appears in the input box.

◆ **Select All button.** Selects and highlights all the layers currently displayed in the Layer Name list box.

◆ **Clear All button.** Deselects and dehighlights all layers in the list box.

◆ **New button.** Creates new layers with the name currently in the input box.

◆ **Current button.** Sets a selected layer current. (This button is grayed out if more than one layer is selected.)

◆ **Rename button.** Renames the selected layer to match the name in the input box. (This button is grayed out if more than one layer is selected.)

◆ **Input box.** Enables you to specify names for layers that you want to create and to rename layers.

◆ **On/Off buttons.** Control the On/Off status of selected layers. Layers that are off are not displayed, but they are still invisibly regenerated.

◆ **Thaw/Freeze buttons.** Control whether the selected layers are frozen or thawed. Layers that are frozen are neither displayed nor regenerated.

10

◆ **Unlock/Lock buttons.** Control the Unlock/Lock status of selected layers. Layers that are locked are displayed and are recognized by object snaps (see Chapter 11, "Achieving Accuracy: The Geometric Power of CAD"), but their objects cannot be selected to prevent accidental editing.

◆ **Cur VP Thw/Frz buttons.** Control the current layer Thaw/Freeze status of layers within individual model space viewports in paper space (see Chapter 22, "Structuring Your Drawing").

◆ **New VP Thw/Frz buttons.** Control the default layer Thaw/Freeze status in subsequently created viewports (see Chapter 22).

◆ **Set Color button.** Opens the Select Color dialog box, which assigns a color to the selected layer(s).

◆ **Set Ltype button.** Opens the Select Linetype dialog box, which assigns a linetype to the selected layer(s).

◆ **Filters On check box.** Filters the names displayed in the Layer Name list box. When checked (on), only layer names matching the currently defined filters are listed.

◆ **Filters Set button.** Opens the Set Layer Filters dialog box, which enables you to limit the display of layer names according to their status, properties, or names.

◆ **OK button.** Closes the Layer Control dialog box and saves the current settings.

◆ **Cancel button.** Closes the Layer Control dialog box and discards any changes made.

◆ **Help button.** Activates Windows Help for the Layer Control dialog box.

The Layer Control dialog box always shows a layer named "0" (zero). Every new AutoCAD LT drawing has to have some place to store entities, so it always has layer 0. You cannot delete or rename layer 0. Think of it as a clean sheet of paper. You would not begin a painting without a canvas; likewise, AutoCAD LT cannot begin a drawing without a layer for the entities you draw.

You do not have to use layer 0 as long as you have other layers in your drawing. As a matter of fact, many AutoCAD LT users may never use layer 0 in their drafting because they have already created the layers they need for their drawing.

 Note   It is good practice to avoid using layer 0 for normal drawing because it has special characteristics concerning the creation and insertion of blocks (see Chapter 18, "Leveraging Repetitive Design and Drafting").

Layer Naming

The layer names you assign must not contain any spaces. You can use underscores, dollar signs, or hyphens in addition to the standard alphanumeric characters. For example, EXTERIOR WALLS is not a valid layer name, but EXTERIOR_WALLS or EXTERIOR-WALLS is valid. AutoCAD LT converts all layer names to uppercase.

You can assign meaningful names to your layers. You are allowed 31 characters in length for layer names, so feel free to be descriptive in your layer names, especially if you use many layers. The last section of this chapter addresses layer-naming conventions that help provide consistency and flexibility and control over layers.

Multiple Layer Creation

There is no limit to the number of layers that are in a drawing. In fact, in larger drawings, it is not unheard of to use dozens—perhaps hundreds—of layers. Later in this chapter, you learn to give some thought to the layer names you assign so that they can be grouped together using wild cards.

You can easily create multiple layers at one time with the Layer Control dialog box. You simply enter several layer names separated by commas—no spaces—in the input box and then choose Ne<u>w</u>. In the following exercise, you create two additional layers for your drawing and then place objects on each layer.

Creating Multiple Layers and Setting the Current Layer

Continue from the preceding exercise.

`Command:` *Choose* <u>S</u>ettings, <u>L</u>ayer Control	Issues the DDLMODES command
`'_DDLMODES`	Opens the Layer Control dialog box
Type **CENTER,TEXT** *in the input box, and choose* <u>N</u>ew	Creates two new layers named CENTER and TEXT and lists them in the La<u>y</u>er Name list box
Click on the CENTER *layer name in the* La<u>y</u>er Name *list box*	Selects and highlights the CENTER layer
Choose <u>C</u>urrent	Makes the selected CENTER layer current and displays its name as the current layer
Click on OK	Closes the Layer Control dialog box and displays CENTER in the Current Layer name box

continues

10

continued

Draw a line from point 1.5,3.5 to point 10.5,3.5 through the center of the rectangle.

Command: *Click on the Current Layer name box (see fig. 10.6)*	Displays the Current Layer name drop-down list
Click on TEXT	Sets layer TEXT current and displays its name in the Current Layer name box

Click on the Text tool and use DTEXT with a height of 0.2 to place the text "BASEPLATE BLANK" above the rectangle (see fig. 10.6). If you need help with text, refer to Chapter 4, "Building a Drawing: Using Basic Drawing Tools."

Figure 10.6

Creating objects on various layers.

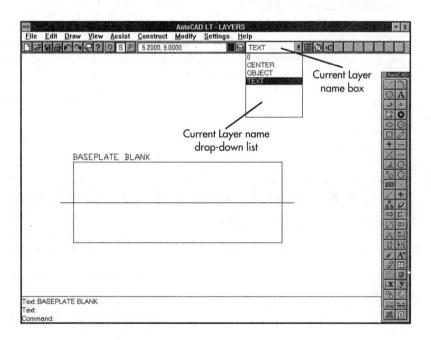

You created three new layers in your drawing and drew an object on each. The problem is that all the layers have the same default *properties*. Specifically, all the layers are white with the CONTINUOUS linetype, which means that everything looks the same in your drawing.

Controlling Layer Properties

To take full advantage of AutoCAD LT's layers, you need to use different linetypes and colors to differentiate objects on different layers in your drawing. For instance,

any layer can have any of AutoCAD LT's 255 available colors and any of 24 predefined linetypes (sometimes called line styles) assigned to it.

Uses for Color and Linetype

In addition to making it easy to differentiate objects on-screen, colors and linetypes are essential to the information that the drawing conveys. Various objects and types of lines in the drawing require different plotted line weights (widths) to clearly communicate a design. Colors are used in AutoCAD LT as the primary method of controlling line weight. You assign colors to layers (or objects—see Chapter 13, "Using Object Properties and Text Styles) in your drawing, and then you assign those colors to specific plotter pens. To control the plotted line width or color, the pens can be different widths or different colors. Even laser, inkjet, and electrostatic plotters and printers can use this method to assign colors to logical pens that simulate real pens.

Drafting practices and standards dictate that various linetypes have different meanings in a drawing. For example, a center linetype is used to denote the center of objects such as holes (circles) or other objects such as the baseplate in your drawing. A hidden linetype is used to denote objects in your drawing that would normally be hidden from view.

Note Although many plotters provide *logical* (plotter-defined) linetypes that can be assigned at plot time to AutoCAD LT colors, you generally obtain better results by using AutoCAD LT's linetype definitions. AutoCAD LT's linetypes also have the advantage of being visible on the screen.

You have placed a center line on the CENTER layer in your baseplate drawing; however, it is displayed as continuous instead of being displayed with a CENTER linetype. The center line also is displayed with the default color of white. These default characteristics appear because you have not yet assigned properties to the layers in your drawing.

In the next few exercises, you assign color and linetype properties to the layers in your baseplate drawing. Before assigning linetypes to a layer, however, you must first load the desired linetypes into your drawing, as shown in the following exercise.

Linetype Storage and Loading

AutoCAD LT stores its standard linetype definitions, which specify how a linetype appears, in a file named ACLT.LIN. This file determines the length and pattern of dashes and dots that make up each linetype. There is also an ACLTISO.LIN file which defines ISO-standard linetypes. Before you can assign linetypes to layers with the Layer Control dialog box, you must first load them with the LINETYPE command. In the following exercise, you load all linetypes by using an asterisk as a wild card.

Loading Linetypes

Continue from the preceding exercise, and make sure that the full pull-down menus are set to display if you are using AutoCAD LT Release 1.

Choose **S**ettings, Li**n**etype Style, **L**oad	Issues the LINETYPE command with the Load option
`Command: '_linetype` `?/Create/Load/Set: _load`	
`Linetype(s) to load: * `**Enter**	Specifies loading all linetypes and opens the Select Linetype File dialog box
Press Enter	Accepts the default file name ACLT.LIN

`Linetype BORDER loaded.`
`Linetype BORDER2 loaded.`
`Linetype BORDERX2 loaded.`
`...`
`Linetype PHANTOM loaded.`
`Linetype PHANTOM2 loaded.`
`Linetype PHANTOMX2 loaded.`
	Lists all 24 linetypes as they load
	(not all are shown here)

`?/Create/Load/Set: `**Enter**	

The asterisk is a wild card that matches any name, so it specifies that you want all the linetypes loaded.

> **LINETYPE.** The LINETYPE command enables you to load new linetypes into a drawing, list the currently loaded linetypes, and set the current new object linetype. This command is also used to create user-defined linetypes on the fly.

Because you will probably not use all linetypes, AutoCAD LT enables you to selectively load needed linetypes by specifying specific names. You can use any of AutoCAD LT's wild cards, and you can specify multiple names separated by commas at the `Linetype(s) to load:` prompt.

Tip You can delete unused linetypes by using the PURGE command. The PURGE command is covered later in this chapter.

Color and Linetype Layer Assignments

Now that you have the linetypes loaded into your drawing, you can assign them to layers in the following exercise. You will also assign different colors to each layer.

Assigning Layer Properties

Continue from the preceding exercise.

Command: *Click on the Layers button*   Opens the Layer Control dialog box

Click on CENTER *in the* La**y**er Name *list box*   Selects and highlights the layer to modify

Choose **S**et Color   Opens the Select Color dialog box (see fig. 10.7)

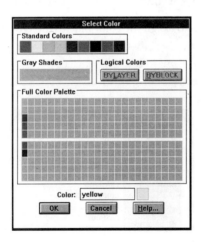

Figure 10.7

Selecting yellow in the Select Color dialog box.

10

Click on the yellow box in Standard Colors   Specifies the color for the layer; "yellow"
at the top of the dialog box   appears in the Color input box

continues

continued

Click on OK	Closes the Select Color dialog box

The color name "yellow" appears in CENTER's Color column in the Layer Name list box.

Choose Set **L**type	Opens the Select Linetype dialog box (see fig. 10.8)
Click on the dashed line next to CENTER	Specifies and highlights the CENTER linetype; "CENTER" appears in the **L**inetype input box
Click on OK	Closes the Select Linetype dialog box

The linetype name "CENTER" appears in CENTER's Linetype column in the Layer Name list box.

Click on OK	Closes the Layer Control dialog box and saves the settings

The drawing regenerates and displays the center line with the CENTER linetype and yellow color (see fig. 10.9). It may be hard to see if you have a white drawing background.

Use the Layer Control dialog box again to assign the color blue to the OBJECT layer and green to the TEXT layer.

Command: *Click on the Save button*	Saves the drawing

Figure 10.8

Selecting CENTER in the Select Linetype dialog box.

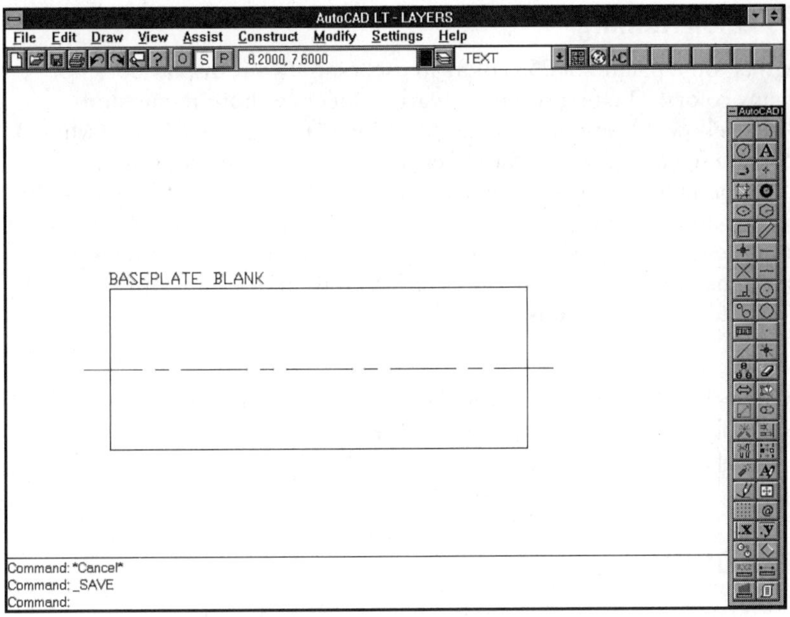

Figure 10.9

The center line displayed with the CENTER linetype on the CENTER layer.

The Layer Control dialog box makes it easy to assign various colors and linetypes to layers. After you have assigned colors and linetypes, anything you draw on these layers inherits the color and linetype properties you have defined. You can experiment with your drawing by changing layers (making another layer current) and placing objects on the current layer. If you experiment, erase or undo the added objects and reset layer TEXT current before continuing.

 Note The appearance of linetypes is controlled by the linetype scale (LTSCALE system variable) setting. An inappropriate LTSCALE for your drawing can make all linetypes appear continuous on the screen. The LTSCALE value is typically $1/4$ to $1/2$ of the scale multiplier (the inverse of plot scale). Chapter 8, "Preparing Your Workspace: CAD Concepts 1B," provides details on figuring scale and an example of setting the LTSCALE system variable.

 Tip When you are selecting layers in the La**y**er Name list box in the Layer Control dialog box, you can select more than one layer by clicking on the layers of interest. To select all of the layers, click on Select **A**ll in the Layer Control dialog box. To deselect all of the previously selected layers, click on Clea**r** All.

AutoCAD LT's Color Naming

AutoCAD LT gives you a palette of 255 colors to use, even if your display does not support that many colors. The first seven standard colors have both names and numbers: red (1), yellow (2), green (3), cyan (4), blue (5), magenta (6), and white (7). You can pick these colors, or you can enter their names or numbers in the Color input box. Other colors have only numbers. If your display supports fewer colors, the unsupported colors appear gray in the Select Color dialog box. You can still select other colors, but they appear gray in the drawing. These colors are sometimes used to assign plotter pens or to designate textures or materials in drawing data exported from AutoCAD LT to other programs.

Note   On a white background, color 7 (white) appears black. You may find light colors such as yellow easier to see if you use the **C**olors button in the Preferences dialog box to set the graphics window background to black.

Renaming Layers

You can rename a layer if desired. Perhaps you have received a drawing from an associate in which the layer names do not conform to your desired naming scheme. Perhaps you find that a layer name is not descriptive enough, or you may have originally misspelled the layer name.

You can rename a layer in several ways. One method is by using the Rena**me** button in the Layer Control dialog box. In the following exercise, you use the LAYERS drawing from the previous exercises and rename the TEXT layer to PART_LABEL, the CENTER layer to CENTERLINE, and the OBJECT layer to ROUGH_CUT.

Renaming Layers Using the Layer Control Dialog Box

Continue from the preceding exercise.

Command: *Click on the Layers button*	Opens the Layer Control dialog box
Click on TEXT *in the* La**y**er Name *list box*	Selects the layer to rename and displays "TEXT" in the input box
Double-click on TEXT *in the input box, and type* **PART_LABEL**	Deletes "TEXT" and specifies the new name for the layer
Choose Rena**me**	Renames the layer in the La**y**er Name list
Click on CENTER *in the* La**y**er Name *list box*	Selects CENTER, but grays out the Rena**me** button because two layers are selected

Click on PART_LABEL *in the* Layer Name *list box*	Deselects PART_LABEL and displays CENTER in the input box
Click in the input box to the right of the word CENTER, *and type* **LINE**	Changes CENTER to CENTERLINE in the input box (see fig. 10.10)
Choose Rename	Renames the layer in the Layer Name list

Repeat these steps to rename the OBJECT layer to ROUGH_CUT.

Choose OK	Closes the Layer Control dialog box and saves the names

The Current Layer name box on the toolbar displays "PART_LABEL."

Command: *Click on the Current Layer name box*	Opens the Current Layer name drop-down list, displaying the new names
Click on the down-arrow button to the right of the Current Layer Name box	Closes the list without changing the curren layer; the box still displays the PART_LABEL name

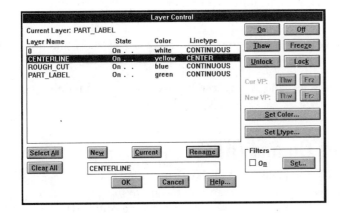

Figure 10.10

Renaming a layer using the Rename button.

10

Note The Current Layer name box on the toolbar displays as many characters of the layer name as it can fit. Use the Layer Control dialog box to see the entire name of long layer names; the entire selected name is always shown in the Layer name input box.

AutoCAD LT provides other ways to rename layers. The Rename item on the **M**odify pull-down menu issues the DDRENAME command, which opens the Rename dialog box. The RENAME command can also be used to change named items at the command line. You can use the RENAME command and the Rename dialog box to rename blocks, layers, linetypes, text styles, and other named items. See Chapter 8 for examples of using RENAME and the Rename dialog box.

Setting Layer Status: Visibility and Selectability

Having many layers is a very effective way of organizing your drawing. Having them all displayed at once, however, can be confusing or make it difficult to edit a particular part, especially if your drawing is very complex. AutoCAD LT provides several ways to control the display and selectability of layers. The three layer status controls discussed in this chapter are On/Off, Freeze/Thaw, and Lock/Unlock. The following list describes the effects of these layer status controls:

◆ **On, thawed, and unlocked.** Visible, selectable, recognized by object snaps (see Chapter 11, "Achieving Accuracy: The Geometric Power of CAD"), and require regeneration time.

◆ **Off.** Invisible, unselectable, unrecognized by object snaps, but still require regeneration time.

◆ **Freeze.** Invisible, unselectable, unrecognized by object snaps, and don't take regeneration time.

◆ **Lock.** Visible, unselectable, recognized by object snaps, and require regeneration time.

Turning Layers On and Off

Turning a layer on or off controls whether or not the objects on that layer are displayed. You might turn off layers that aren't relevant to the work you are currently doing in your drawing. By turning off layers, you are telling AutoCAD LT not to display them. The objects on those layers are out of your way while you work on other layers, but they still require processing time during regenerations.

You might also turn off layers for plotting purposes. Perhaps you want the layer that contains dimensions to be plotted on one sheet, but not on another. Layers are used in this way to create many drawing sheets from one drawing file.

You control whether a layer is on or off by using the Layer Control dialog box. In the following exercise, you use the baseplate drawing from the previous exercises.

Turning Off a Layer

Continue in the LAYERS drawing from the preceding exercise.

Command: *Click on the Layers button*   Opens the Layer Control dialog box

Notice the On in the State column of the Layer Name list.

Click on CENTERLINE *in the* Layer   Selects the layer to modify
Name *list box*

Choose O**ff**   Sets the layer's state to off

Notice that the On in the State column is replaced by a dot, which means off (see fig. 10.11).

Click on OK   Closes the Layer Control dialog box

The drawing window redraws, turning off the line on the CENTERLINE layer.

Use the Layer Control dialog box to turn the CENTERLINE layer back on, repeating the preceding steps but choosing **O**n instead of O**ff**. The On reappears in the State column.

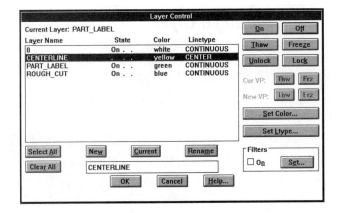

Figure 10.11

Turning off the
CENTERLINE
layer.

10

You can select multiple layers and turn them on or off at once. Use Select **A**ll and **O**n if you need to be sure that all layers are on.

Stop   A layer that is off can also be the current layer, but this is not recommended. Any objects you draw or place in your drawing will be placed on that layer, but because the layer is off, your new objects will not be displayed. You should make sure that your current layer is always on.

Reading Layer States

The current states of the layer status controls are displayed in the State column of the Layer Name list box in the Layer Control dialog box. In tilemode, there are three subcolumns in the State column: On, Freeze, and Lock. In paper space, there are two additional subcolumns for the Cur VP and New VP settings (see Chapter 22, "Structuring Your Drawing"). The On subcolumn displays On for on or a dot for off; the Freeze subcolumn displays an F for frozen or a dot for thawed; and the Lock subcolumn displays an L for locked or a dot for unlocked.

Freezing and Thawing Layers for Speed

Freezing a layer also turns off the display of the objects on that layer, but it has one important difference from turning off a layer. When a layer is frozen, AutoCAD LT ignores the objects on that layer when it regenerates the drawing. In other words, if you perform a ZOOM or PAN command that requires AutoCAD LT to regenerate the display, it ignores the objects on frozen layers in the interest of time.

In the following exercise, you freeze and then thaw the PART_LABEL layer.

Freezing a Layer

Continue in the LAYERS drawing from the preceding exercise.

Command: *Click on the Layers button*	Opens the Layer Control dialog box
Make sure all layers are on, then click on PART_LABEL *in the* Layer Name *list box*	Selects the layer to modify
Choose Free<u>z</u>e	Displays `Cannot freeze the current layer` at the bottom of the Layer Control dialog box
Choose Clea<u>r</u> All, *click on* ROUGH_CUT, *then choose* <u>C</u>urrent	Sets layer ROUGH_CUT current
Choose Clea<u>r</u> All, *click on* PART_LABEL, *then choose* Free<u>z</u>e	Sets the state to frozen, displaying an F in the State column
Click on OK	Closes the Layer Control dialog box and regenerates, except for the PART_LABEL layer

Thaw the PART_LABEL layer, repeating the preceding steps but choosing <u>T</u>haw instead of Free<u>z</u>e. A dot replaces the F in the State column, and the drawing regenerates when you choose OK.

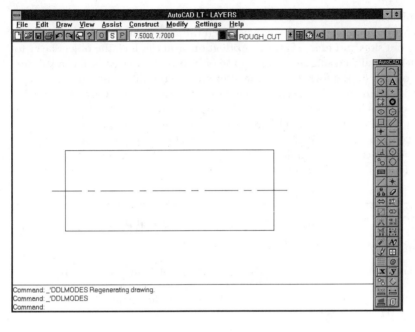

Figure 10.12

Freezing the PART_LABEL layer.

When the drawing regenerates, all objects on frozen layers are totally ignored. In this case, the text disappears from your screen. Rest assured that it is still a part of your drawing. You have just told AutoCAD LT to ignore it until you thaw the layer.

Unlike a layer that is off, the current layer cannot be frozen. If you try to freeze the current layer, AutoCAD LT reports an error message stating that it cannot freeze the current layer.

Note Layer visibility can be controlled in individual viewports in your drawing. Chapter 22, "Structuring Your Drawing," discusses viewports in more detail. In paper space, you can have several viewports in your drawing, each one with different layers frozen and thawed. This is a powerful feature for creating many views from one drawing.

Another state you can assign to a layer is whether it is locked or unlocked.

Locking and Unlocking Layers for Selection Control

Locking a layer prevents you from accidentally modifying the objects on that layer. This feature is useful when you need to have a layer on both for visibility and as a layout guide, but you don't want to change the objects on that layer. A locked layer can be current, you can still draw on it, and you can use object snap to snap points to objects on any locked layer.

As an example, suppose your engineering department has finalized the outside dimensions for the baseplate blank you have been working on in this chapter. Now it is time to lay out slots and holes on it for production. You can lock the object layer to keep from accidentally erasing or changing the objects on that layer. You can still see and use the objects on the locked layer for reference. In the following exercise you use the ID command and INTersection object snap to draw a circle relative to the intersection of lines on a locked layer. The ID command reports the coordinates of a specified point and resets the LASTPOINT system variable to that point so you can use relative coordinates from that point. The INTersection object snap snaps a picked point to the intersection of two objects. These are fully explained in the next chapter; for now just follow the prompts.

Selection and Object Snapping with a Locked Layer

Continue in the LAYERS drawing from the preceding exercise.

Command: *Click on the Layers button*	Opens the Layer Control dialog box
Make sure all layers are on and thawed, then click on ROUGH_CUT *in the* La**y**er Name *list box*	Selects the layer to modify
Choose Loc**k**	Locks the layer, displaying an L in the La**y**er Name list and a warning at the bottom of the dialog box (see fig. 10.13)
Choose OK	Closes the dialog box; all layers are displayed

Next, you see how the lock affects selection.

Command: *Select all objects, then type* **E** *and press Enter*	Issues the ERASE command with all objects selected
ERASE 6 found 4 were on a locked layer.	Erases the center line and text and notifies you about the lines on the locked layer
Command: **OOPS** (Enter)	Restores the erased line and text

Now, to begin adding holes, you use the ID command to snap the last point to the lines on the locked layer, and then you draw a circle relative to it.

Command: **ID** (Enter)

`Point:` *Click on the Intersection tool*	Issues the INTersection object snap
`_INT of` *Pick* ① *(see fig. 10.14)*	Snaps and sets the last point to the intersection on the locked layer
`X = 2.0000, Y = 2.0000, Z = 0.0000`	
`Command:` *Click on the Circle tool*	Issues the CIRCLE command
`_CIRCLE 3P/TTR/<Center point>:` `@.5,.5` (Enter)	Sets center relative to intersection at last point
`Radius:` `.2` (Enter)	Draws a circle on the locked layer
`Command:` *Pick the new circle, then type* **CP** *and press Enter*	Issues the COPY command with the circle selected
`_COPY 1 found` `1 was on a locked layer.`	Rejects the circle because its layer is locked
`Select objects:` *Click on the Cancel button*	Cancels the COPY command; you must unlock the layer to copy its objects

Unlock the ROUGH_CUT layer, repeating the preceding steps in the Layer Control dialog box, but choosing **U**nlock instead of Loc**k**. A dot replaces the L in the State column.

Use the COPY command to copy the circle to the other three corners (see fig. 10.14).

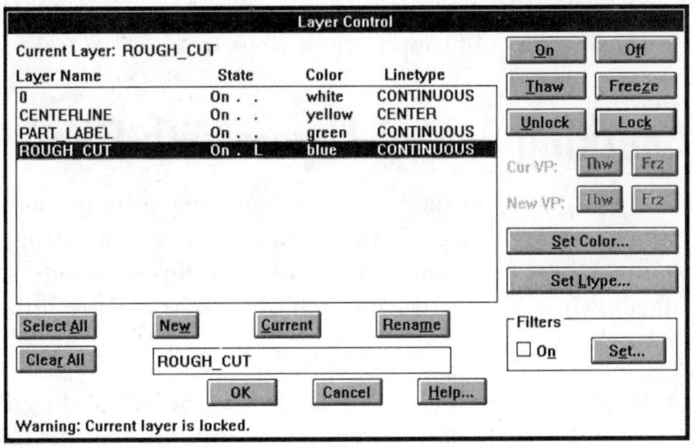

Figure 10.13

Locking the ROUGH_CUT layer.

10

Figure 10.14

*Editing with a
locked layer.*

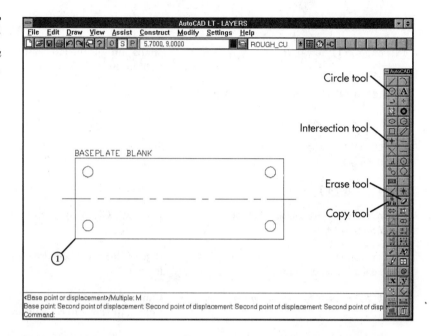

The Layer Control dialog box shows that the layer is locked by placing an "L" under State. You can lock the current layer, but AutoCAD LT warns you when you do so.

If you try to select an object on a locked layer, AutoCAD LT reports: 1 was on a locked layer. If your drawing becomes crowded with many objects, it may sometimes be helpful to lock the layers with which you are not immediately concerned. You can still set them current, draw on them, and snap to their objects.

Selecting and Checking Sets of Layers with Filters

By using filters to selectively display layer names in drawings that contain many layers, you narrow the list of names to search through if you want to review or change their properties or visibility status. Filters help you to deal with complex drawings, such as the architectural drawing shown in figure 10.15, which often have a large number of layers.

The drawing file you use in the next exercise contains only a portion of this 900K drawing file, but it contains all 58 layers. If all layers are on and thawed, the drawing is an unintelligible mess, as shown in figure 10.16.

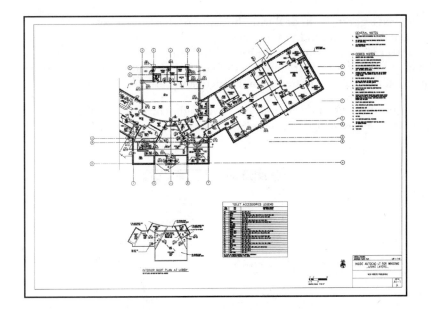

Figure 10.15

A complex, multilayer drawing.

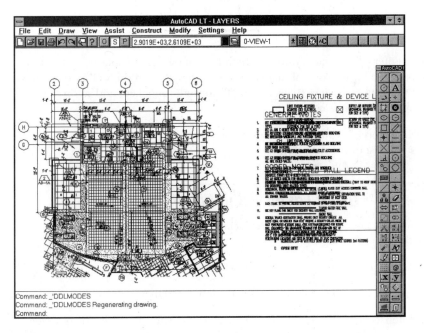

Figure 10.16

A portion of a complex drawing with all 58 layers displayed.

10

Obviously, you need a good way to deal with the status of these many layers. When a drawing has more layers than can fit in the Layer Name list box, the list box provides a scroll bar that you can use to find any desired layer. Despite the scroll bar, however, it still can be hard to work with a large number of layers. Fortunately, you can filter the layer names, states, and properties to limit which layers are listed in the list box.

You may have noticed the Filters section in the lower right corner of the Layer Control dialog box. Choosing Set opens the Set Layer Filters dialog box (see fig. 10.17).

Figure 10.17

The Set Layer Filters dialog box.

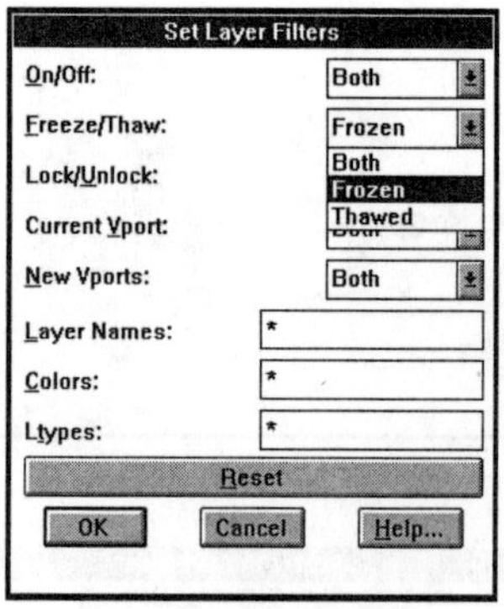

Set Layer Filters	
On/Off:	Both
Freeze/Thaw:	Frozen
Lock/Unlock:	Both / Frozen / Thawed
Current Vport:	
New Vports:	Both
Layer Names:	*
Colors:	*
Ltypes:	*
Reset	
OK Cancel Help...	

The Set Layer Filters dialog box controls which layer names are displayed in the Layer Name list box of the Layer Control dialog box. The default is to show all layer names regardless of their state (frozen, thawed, on, off, locked, unlocked, and so on) or their properties (color or linetype).

In the following exercise, you use layer filters to selectively display layer names in a drawing. First you list only frozen layers.

Using Layer Visibility Filters

Create a new drawing again named LAYERS (replacing the previous file), using the ALT1001.DWG file as a prototype.

Command: *Click on the Layers button*   Opens the Layer Control dialog box

Use the scroll bar in the Layer Name list box to see the layers and their states and properties.

Choose Set in the Filters *section*   Opens the Set Layer Filters dialog box (see fig. 10.17)

Notice that all of the visibility settings read "Both."

Press Alt+F, or click on Both *next to* **F**reeze/Thaw	Opens the **F**reeze/Thaw drop-down list
Click on Frozen	Specifies that frozen layer names will be displayed
Choose OK	Closes the Set Layer Filters dialog box and checks the O**n** box in the Filters section

Use the scroll bar in the La**y**er Name list box to see that only frozen layer names are now listed (see fig. 10.18).

Choose OK	Closes the Layer Control dialog box

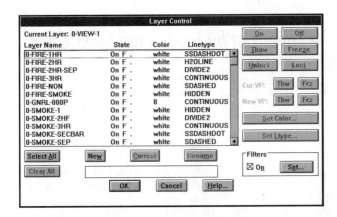

Figure 10.18

Filtered layer list displaying only frozen layer data.

The current filter settings affect the layer list only when the O**n** box in the Filters section is checked. You can turn this on or off by choosing O**n**. When off, all of the layer names display.

Using the visibility state filters is a good way to quickly determine which layers are on, off, frozen, thawed, and so on. As an example, when you choose **O**n/Off in the Set Layer Filters dialog box and select Off from the drop-down list, the La**y**er Name list box displays only the layers that are off. If none are found, AutoCAD LT displays an empty layer list and the message No layers match filter criteria in the Layer Control dialog box.

Similarly, you can use the color and linetype filters to determine which layers are set to specific colors and linetypes. The asterisks shown in the input boxes beside **L**ayer Names, **C**olors, and L**t**ypes in the Set Layer Filters dialog box specify that all the layers will be listed, regardless of the name, color, or linetype. The asterisk is a wild card that matches any or all characters.

10

The layer names filter is also useful for freezing, thawing, or turning on or off a set of layers by using wild cards. The drawing in these exercises is a part of an architectural drawing that is used to generate three separate sheets: a dimensioned floor plan, a reflected ceiling plan, and a callout plan. Because this drawing is used to generate several plots, a layer-naming convention was established to facilitate grouping them with wild cards (such as * and ?) for display and plotting purposes; for example, all architectural floor plan layers begin with an A.

You can use the input boxes in the Set Layer Filters dialog box to filter the list of the layers by names and properties. In the following exercise, for example, you use an asterisk wild card to list only the architectural layers of your drawing, which are those layer names beginning with an A, and then you use the color filter to list only those architectural layers that are yellow.

Filtering the Layer List by Layer Name and Color

Continue from the preceding exercise.

Command: *Click on the Layers button*	Opens the Layer Control dialog box; the Filter **On** check box is cleared (off) again
Click on the **Se**t *button*	Opens the Set Layer Filters dialog box; the **F**reeze/Thaw filter has reset to Both
Click in the **L**ayer Names *input box, press Home, and type* **A**	Sets the names filter to A*, which means all layer names beginning with A
Double-click in the **C**olors *input box, and type* **YELLOW**	Replaces * with YELLOW, setting the layer color to display
Choose OK	Closes the Set Layer Filters dialog box; lists only layers beginning with A and only if they are also yellow (see fig. 10.19)

Figure 10.19

Using name and color filters to selectively list layer names.

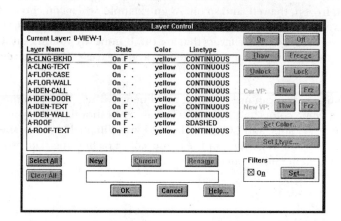

Notice that the filters were cleared when you reopened the Layer Control dialog box after closing it in the preceding exercise. You also can clear the filters with the **R**eset button in the Set Layer Filters dialog box.

Wild cards are important tools for filtering layers and are further discussed in the last section of this chapter.

Using the LAYER Command

In addition to the Layer Control dialog box and the Current Layer name box and Current Layer name drop-down list on the toolbar, AutoCAD LT provides a LAYER command for creating, modifying, and setting current layers. You can enter **LAYER** or the **LA** abbreviation at the Command: prompt.

The following prompt shows the various options for the LAYER command:

```
?/Make/Set/New/ON/OFF/Color/Ltype/Freeze/Thaw/LOck/Unlock:
```

Except for Make, all of these options are the same as those in the Layer Control dialog box. (The Set option has the same effect as the **C**urrent dialog box button or the Current Layer name box on the toolbar.)

Although the Layer Control dialog box accomplishes everything the LAYER command does, it is sometimes quicker to tap a few keys on the keyboard to manipulate layer settings than to access and use the dialog box.

Using the Make Option

The Make option of the LAYER command is similar to the New option, except that it enables you to select only one layer name and, at the completion of the command, makes that layer current. You just enter **LA**, then **M**, then the layer name, and the layer is created and made current. This procedure would otherwise take several steps using the Layer Control dialog box.

Perhaps you need to add a layer to the drawing from the preceding exercise for use in preparing a pre-bid take-off. In the following exercise, you create a new layer named A-ESTIM and make it current by using the LAYER command's Make option.

10

Using the LAYER Make Option

Create a new drawing, or continue in the LAYERS drawing from the preceding exercise.

Command: **LA** (Enter)	Issues the LAYER command
LAYER ?/Make/Set/New/ON/OFF/Color /Ltype/Freeze/Thaw/LOck/Unlock: **M** (Enter)	Specifies the Make option
New current layer <0-VIEW-1>: **A-ESTIM** (Enter)	Names the new layer to create and make current
?/Make/Set/New/ON/OFF/Color/Ltype /Freeze/Thaw/LOck/Unlock: (Enter)	Ends the LAYER command and sets the new layer current

---

The layer name shown in the toolbar changes to display the name for your newly created current layer (see fig. 10.20).

Figure 10.20

A new layer created and set current with the Make option.

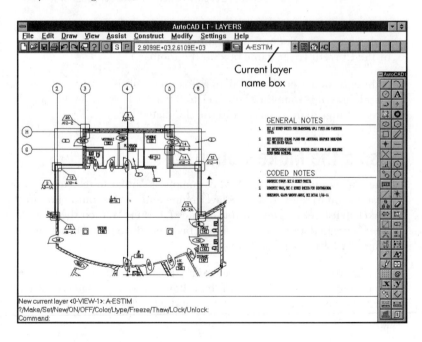

The Make option of the LAYER command creates a layer and sets it current. You still need to assign properties and visibility states to the new layer, unless you want it to have the defaults.

> **LAYER.** The LAYER command offers the same control over layers as does the Layer Control dialog box (except for freezing of layers in specific mview viewports in paper space). LAYER's options—? (lists layers), Make (creates and sets current layer), Set (current), New, ON, OFF, Color, Ltype, Freeze, Thaw, LOck, and Unlock—provide the same functions as the features of the Layer Control dialog box. For an explanation of these features, see the previous option list for the Layer Control dialog box.

The command to freeze layers in specific mview viewports in paper space is VPLAYER (see Chapter 22, "Structuring Your Drawing").

Tip   If the layer name you enter already exists, Make just makes it current, without causing an error.

Deleting Named Items

The quickest way to load several linetypes is to load the entire linetype file, as you did earlier in this chapter. This step saves typing or even having to know the names of the specific linetypes you need. The disadvantage to this step is that storing unneeded linetype definitions in the drawing file uses up disk space. You also may find drawings cluttered with unneeded layer definitions, particularly drawings created from standard prototypes that define every layer you might conceivably use. Fortunately, you can use the PURGE command to remove unused blocks, dimension and text styles, layers, linetypes, and shapes from a drawing. You cannot purge after drawing or editing commands are used, unless you first save the drawing. In some cases, such as to purge new layers or to purge existing layers after erasing all of their objects, you must save and reopen the drawing before you can purge.

Try purging unused layers from the architectural plan of the preceding exercise. First, before you can purge, you need to save and reopen the drawing.

Purging Unneeded Layers

Continue from the preceding exercise.

Command: *Click on the Open button, and enter* **Y**

Saves the current drawing and displays the Open Drawing dialog box, with the current drawing name as the default

continues

continued

Choose OK	Reopens the newly saved current drawing
Command: **PURGE** (Enter)	Prompts for the type of item to purge
Purge unused Blocks/Dimstyles/LAyers/ LTypes/SHapes/STyles/All: **LA** (Enter)	Specifies purging layers
Purge layer 0-VIEW-1? <N> (Enter)	Skips the 0-VIEW-1 layer
Purge layer TITLE? <N> (Enter)	Skips the TITLE layer
Purge layer A-OVHD-CASE? <N> (Enter)	Skips the A-OVHD-CASE layer
Purge layer 0-VIEW-1TXT? <N> (Enter)	Skips the 0-VIEW-1TXT layer
Purge layer 0-GNRL-000P? <N> (Enter)	Skips the 0-GNRL-000P layer
Purge layer A-ESTIM? <N> **Y** (Enter)	Deletes the A-ESTIM layer and completes the purging

The current layer name box now shows layer 0, the default, because the current A-ESTIM layer was purged.

You cannot purge an item that is referenced in any object or by any other named item. If the 0-VIEW-1TXT layer, for example, contained a text object using the SIMPLEX text style, then neither the layer nor the style could be purged.

> **PURGE.** The PURGE command removes definitions of unused blocks, dimension and text styles, layers, linetypes, and shapes from a drawing. The PURGE command must be used on a newly opened drawing, before any drawing or editing commands are used. When you enter any option (type of named item), PURGE prompts for confirmation for purging each unreferenced definition of that type.

If you want to delete several types of named items, repeat the PURGE command for each.

Note Because of the way blocks are defined and stored, totally purging all unused named items might require two or more cycles of saving, reopening, and purging. See Chapter 19, "Managing and Modifying Blocks and Xrefs," for more information.

Layer-Naming Considerations

Layer names give you quite a bit of flexibility: you can use up to 31 letters, digits, dollar signs ($), hyphens (-), and underscore (_) characters. You need to control this flexibility to avoid confusion and to facilitate easy layer manipulation in complex drawings (such as the architectural plan in the previous exercises). You can achieve this control by establishing conventions and using wild cards.

Working with Layer-Naming Conventions

Because layers are so vital to the organization and layout of your drawing, the layer names you assign have been a topic of debate ever since CAD came into being. Personal preferences often dictate the layer names used in a drawing. Office standards often override personal preferences. National standards often take precedence over office standards. Standardizing layer names becomes more important as more and more offices and agencies exchange CAD drawing files.

A good naming convention facilitates manipulating groups of layers with wild cards. For example, if you were designing a new wing for one of the local university's educational buildings, you might use the system shown in table 10.1.

10

TABLE 10.1
Sample Layer-Naming Conventions

Layer Name	Objects on the Layer
AEWALL-FULL	Existing interior full-height partition lines
AEWALL-EXTERIOR	Existing exterior wall lines
AEDOOR-FULL	Existing interior doors
AEDOOR-EXTERIOR	Existing exterior doors
A-WALL-FULL	Proposed interior full-height partition lines
A-WALL-EXTERIOR	Proposed exterior wall lines
A-DOOR-FULL	Proposed interior doors
A-DOOR-EXTERIOR	Proposed exterior doors

You can see a logical grouping by the way the layer name is designed. The first letter, A, signifies an architectural layer as opposed to a mechanical or electrical layer. The second character determines whether the conditions are existing (E) or proposed (-). The next four characters determine the grouping of objects—DOOR, WALL, WNDW (window), and so on. The last characters of the layer names further detail the objects.

By using this general-to-specific layer-naming scheme, you can organize the objects in your drawing into logical groupings. All of the A* layers are architectural, all of the *DOOR* layers contain doors, and so on. Even the placement of the characters can facilitate the grouping of layers. You can specify or filter groups of layers named in this manner by using wild cards.

Many other layer-naming standards are in use, including CSI and AIA standard formats. Contact your industry's standards body to see if established standards exist for your type of work.

Grouping Layers with Wild Cards

Wild cards are special characters that AutoCAD LT uses to enable it to group names together. The two most common wild cards are the question mark (?) and the asterisk (*). You had your first experience with wild cards in the exercise on layer filters. Remember the asterisk?

The asterisk replaces any number of characters in a name. The question mark replaces a single character. For example, suppose you have the layer names VIEW1, VIEW2, and VIEW3 in your drawing. By using the question mark when AutoCAD LT asks for layer names, instead of typing **VIEW1,VIEW2,VIEW3**, you could type **VIEW?**. This specifies all layer names that begin with "VIEW," regardless of what the fifth character is.

The architectural drawing in the following exercise contains many layers, as you previously saw in figures 10.18 and 10.19. Layer A-WALL-FURR shows wall lines representing furring. Layer A-WALL-FULL shows proposed wall lines. To group the two layer names together, you would enter **A?WALL-????** or **A?WALL-*** when specifying layer names.

In the following exercises, you freeze all the layers by using the * wild card, and you thaw layers A-WALL-FURR and A-WALL-FULL by using the ? wild card.

Using the ? Wild Card

Continue in the previous architectural drawing, or Create a new drawing again named LAYERS, using the ALT1001.DWG file as a prototype.

Command: *Click on the Layers button*   Opens the Layer Control dialog box

Choose Select **A**ll   Highlights all the layers

Choose Free**z**e   Freezes all but the current layer

Choose S**e**t *in the* Filters *section*   Opens the Set Layer Filters dialog box

Double-click in the **L**ayer Names *input box,*   Specifies all layer names beginning with any
and type **?-WALL-????** *(see fig. 10.21)*   character, followed by "-WALL-" and then by
                                                         any four characters

Click on OK   Closes the Set Layer Filters dialog box and
                                                         lists only A-WALL-FURR and A-WALL-FULL

Choose **T**haw   Thaws the selected layers

Click on OK   Closes the Layer Control dialog box

The drawing regenerates with only the current and ?-WALL-???? layers. When you click on the Current Layer name box, you see the names shown in figure 10.22.

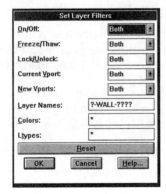

Figure 10.21

Filtering layer names with the ? wild card.

10

Figure 10.22

*Current and ?-WALL-????
layers thawed
with ? wild-card
filters.*

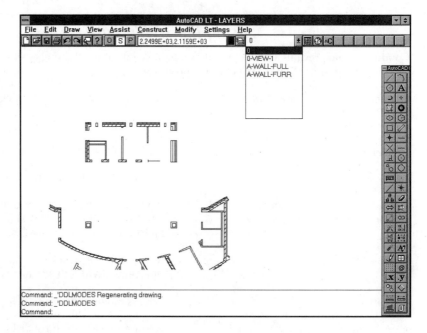

The asterisk (*) is perhaps a more powerful wild card than the question mark. When used to specify layer names, it replaces more than one character. For example, if you have many layers in your drawing beginning with the letter A, you could group them together by typing **A***. The asterisk in this case means, "I want all the layer names beginning with A, and I don't care what characters follow."

Similarly, if several layer names end with the characters "WALL", you could group them together by typing ***WALL**. This is the same as saying, "I want all the layer names ending with WALL, and I don't care what or how many characters precede it."

The asterisk wild card also can be used in the middle to sort out layer names. "A-*-WALL" would group all the layer names beginning with "A-" and ending with "-WALL".

In the following exercise, you thaw all the layers with names beginning with "A-FLOR" to show the items on the floor layers.

*Using the * Wild Card*

Continue from the preceding exercise.

Command: *Click on the Layers button*	Opens the Layer Control dialog box
Choose Se*t in the* Filters *section*	Opens the Set Layer Filters dialog box
Double-click in the **L**ayer Names *input box, and type* **A-FLOR***	Specifies layer names beginning with A-FLOR
Click on OK	Closes the Set Layer Filters dialog box, listing five layer names beginning with A-FLOR
Choose Select **A**ll	Highlights all listed layers
Choose **T**haw	Thaws the selected layers
Click on OK	Closes the Layer Control dialog box

The drawing regenerates with the previously thawed layers and the newly thawed A-FLOR* layers. When you click on the Current Layer name box, you see the names shown in figure 10.23.

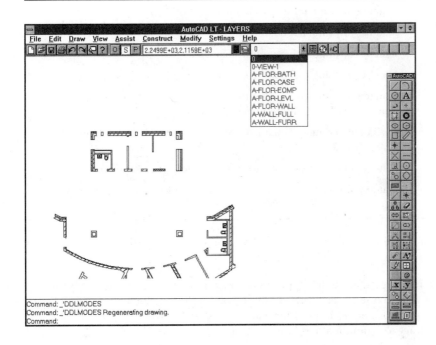

Figure 10.23

A-FLOR layers thawed using the * wild card.*

10

Note When you specify file names in DOS, the asterisk wild card replaces all characters to the end of the file name or extension. As examples, * and *ABC are equivalent, and PART*ABC, PART*XYZ, and PART* are equivalent, because DOS replaces all characters to the end of the name with the wild card, ignoring the ABC and the XYZ. In AutoCAD LT, however, the asterisk wild card replaces all characters only until the next character encountered. As examples, PART* is equivalent to PART*ABC and PART*XYZ, and PART*ABC is equivalent to PART*C, but PART*ABC and PART*XYZ are not equivalent.

Table 10.2 lists the wild cards that are available in AutoCAD LT:

TABLE 10.2
Available Wild Cards

Wild Card	Meaning
?	Matches any single character
*	Matches any character or characters, including an empty (null) character string
@	Matches any alphanumeric character
#	Matches any numeric character
.	Matches any nonalphanumeric character
~	Matches any single character except the one that follows the tilde
[ ]	Matches any single character that matches one of the characters in the brackets, such as [abc] to match a, b, or c
-	Designates a range of characters in brackets, such as [1-6] to match 1, 2, 3, 4, 5, or 6
[~]	Matches anything except any of the characters enclosed after the tilde
`	Matches the special character that follows; for example, `? matches a ? instead of interpreting the ? as a wild card

You can even combine these wild cards, but the question mark and asterisk are all you usually need.

The last several chapters have developed your CAD setup and organizational skills. You are probably anxious to take off and draw again. In the next chapter, you'll learn just how easily you can achieve the superb accuracy that AutoCAD LT offers in its drawing accuracy tools and features.

Achieving Accuracy: The Geometric Power of CAD

AutoCAD LT provides tools for drawing objects accurately and for obtaining accurate information from your drawing (querying). You have already learned about the Snap and Ortho modes, which relate to the drawing's environment. In this chapter, you explore drawing tools that relate to objects and to alternative methods of specifying accurate locations. From this chapter's discussion of these AutoCAD LT tools, you learn the following operations:

◆ Using object snap modes to snap points to existing geometry

◆ Identifying and using point locations with the ID command and the LASTPOINT system variable

◆ Working with point filters as an alternative to construction lines

◆ Using tracking to locate coordinates in AutoCAD LT Release 2

◆ Placing points on objects with the DIVIDE and MEASURE commands in AutoCAD LT Release 2

The tools in this chapter demonstrate the way in which AutoCAD LT supports the evolution of a design that builds on itself. The geometric power of CAD depends on the accuracy that these tools enable you to achieve.

To make a smooth landing in aviation, a pilot must approach his destination accurately. The path of the plane should intersect the runway in a perfect tangent, preferably exactly on the runway's center line. Achieving this kind of accuracy in flight requires careful attention to minute details and skillful use of the available controls. These same accuracy requirements apply when you are preparing a design in AutoCAD LT.

You can use AutoCAD LT to make sketches or simply to try out ideas without any particular regard for accuracy, but one of the powerful features of CAD is its range of tools for easily creating extremely accurate drawings. As you begin to master AutoCAD LT, you will discover that drawing accurately is often no more difficult than simply sketching. In fact, because of the way CAD stores all its information at the same level of accuracy, the objects in a rough sketch are as intricately defined as those in a finished drawing. The accuracy of the information in a drawing is therefore entirely dependent on the care with which the drawing was created.

This chapter begins with a discussion of the most powerful tools available in AutoCAD LT for accurately defining relationships between objects in your drawing—the object snap modes.

Understanding Object Snap

Most design work requires some degree of accuracy for the placement of objects in space. You have already learned to set and use a snap grid that aligns itself with the current coordinate system definition (UCS). Frequently, however, you need to align one object with another regardless of the coordinate system. Whether you are designing intricate machine parts or multiple-acre shopping malls, the relationship between the elements in a design is important.

Designers have traditionally applied graphical methods to the problems of drafting analytical geometry. A geometric construction is often the only way to solve design problems. Drafting textbooks have sections describing such geometric construction methods; for example, bisecting an angle using only a compass and a straightedge (see fig. 11.1) or drawing an arc tangent to two other arcs.

The need to apply graphical methods to geometric construction problems has not changed, but CAD provides many new tools to assist the process. These tools yield three clear benefits: (1) construction is simpler and therefore easier to perform; (2) the geometry is more accurate, as are the points derived from the geometry; and (3) the results can be consistently maintained with far more precision than was possible with manual drafting methods.

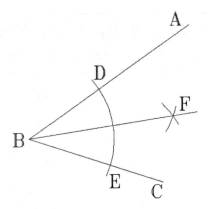

Figure 11.1

A classic graphical solution to a geometric problem—bisecting an angle.

The *object snap modes* are a set of tools in AutoCAD LT for creating accurate geometric constructions. These object snap tools are used to directly identify key points within objects. Each of the object snap modes uses the geometric definitions of an object and full floating-point precision to derive mathematically correct endpoints, midpoints, centers, perpendiculars, tangents, and so on. The object snap modes are accessible as tools in the toolbox and as items on the cursor pop-up menu (see fig. 11.2). You also can access the object snap modes from the keyboard by entering their first three letters (as shown on the left side of fig. 11.2).

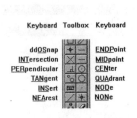

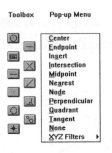

Figure 11.2

Accessing the object snap modes from the toolbox, the pop-up menu, and the keyboard.

You can open the pop-up menu in two ways. If you have a three-button mouse, it opens at the cursor location when you click the middle (pop-up) mouse button. You can also press Shift while clicking the Enter button instead of clicking the pop-up button. If you have a two-button mouse, you will have to Shift-click the Enter button when instructed to click the pop-up button or use the pop-up menu.

In the following exercise, you use some of AutoCAD LT's object snap functions to solve the classic geometric construction problem illustrated in figure 11.1. You observe how AutoCAD LT simplifies this procedure.

Bisecting an Angle Using Object Snap Modes

Create a new drawing named OSNAP, using the ACLT.DWG prototype and no setup method. Use the LINE command to draw two lines, from ① to ② to ③ (see fig. 11.3).

Command: *Choose* **D**raw, **A**rc, *then* Center, **S**tart, End option	Issues ARC command with the Center
_Arc Center/<Start point>:	
_c Center: *Click on the Endpoint tool*	Activates the ENDPoint object snap
_ENDP of *Pick the upper line at* ④ *(see fig. 11.3)*	Snaps to the closest endpoint of the line at ② as the center for the arc
Start point: *Click on the Nearest tool*	Activates the NEArest object snap
_NEAREST to *Pick the lower line at* ⑤	Snaps to the point on the line that is closest to the pick location
Angle/<End point>: **ENDP** (Enter)	Activates the ENDPoint object snap
of *Pick the upper line at* ⑥	Snaps to the closest endpoint of the line and draws the arc shown in figure 11.4

Figure 11.3

Creating an arc using object snap object modes.

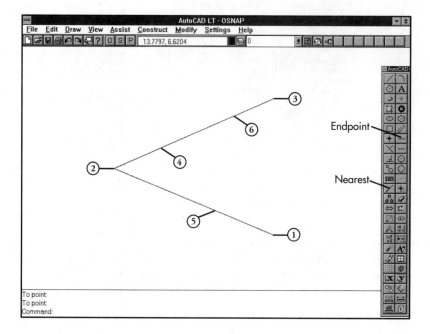

```
Command: Click on the Line tool
```

```
_LINE From point: Click                    Opens the pop-up menu
the middle (pop-up) mouse button
or Shift-click the Enter button
```

```
Choose Endpoint                            Activates the ENDPoint object snap and
                                           closes the pop-up menu
```

```
_endp of Pick the lower line at            Snaps to the endpoint closest
⑦ (see fig. 11.4)                          to the pick point
```

```
To point: Click on the  Midpoint           Activates the MIDpoint object snap
tool
```

```
_MID of Pick any point on the arc          Snaps to the midpoint of the arc and draws
                                           the line shown in figure 11.4
```

```
To point: (Enter)
```

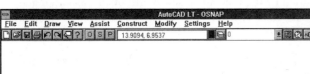

Figure 11.4

Bisecting an angle using the midpoint of an included arc.

You often need to start a line precisely at the end of another line. In the preceding exercise, the two lines you initially drew have a common endpoint because of the way the LINE command works. When you draw a series of lines, the LINE command makes the starting point of each segment coincident with the endpoint of each segment if you draw them consecutively. On the other hand, the ENDPoint object snap enables you to access the endpoint of any existing line whenever you need to.

The object snap works like a magnet. You specify an object snap when AutoCAD LT is asking for a point. Then, when you pick a point, the resulting coordinate is attracted to the nearest point that meets the specified object snap requirements.

During object snap mode, the cursor changes to a larger box at the intersection of the crosshairs, called the target box or *aperture*. You can change the size of the aperture box, as you will see later in this section.

When you are seeking an object's endpoint, for example, you do not need to have the endpoint physically within the aperture box; you need only have a portion of the object within the aperture box. You simply pick near the endpoint you want, and AutoCAD LT snaps to the object's endpoint that is closest to the point you pick. Most of the object snap modes operate in a similar manner (the exception is the INTersection object snap—the desired intersection must be within the aperture box).

The point returned is determined by the object you select and by the specified active object snap mode(s). When more than one object snap mode is active, the calculated point closest to the picked point is the one that is returned.

AutoCAD LT has 11 object snap modes and an optional modifier. The following list gives a simple description of each object snap mode:

- ◆ **CENter.** The CENter mode finds the center of a circle or an arc.

- ◆ **ENDPoint.** The ENDPoint mode finds the endpoint of a line or an arc.

- ◆ **INSert.** The INSert mode returns the insertion point of text objects and block references.

- ◆ **INTersection.** The INTersection mode locates the intersection of two lines, arcs, or circles or the intersection of any combination of these objects.

- ◆ **MIDpoint.** The MIDpoint mode finds the midpoint of a line or an arc.

- ◆ **NEArest.** The NEArest mode returns a point (on an object) that is nearest to the point you pick.

- ◆ **NODe.** The NODe mode returns the location of a point object.

- ◆ **NONe.** The NONe mode instructs AutoCAD LT not to use any object snap mode.

- ◆ **PERpendicular.** The PERpendicular mode returns a point at the intersection of the object selected and a line perpendicular to that object from either the last or the next point picked.

- ◆ **QUAdrant.** The QUAdrant mode finds the closest 0-, 90-, 180-, or 270-degree point (relative to the current UCS) on a circle or an arc.

- ◆ **TANgent.** The TANgent mode locates a point that is tangent to the selected circle or arc from either the last or the next point picked.

As illustrated in figure 11.2, the object snap modes are available as tools in the toolbox (left side of fig. 11.2) and as items on the cursor pop-up menu (right side of fig. 11.2). Each mode can also be specified by entering the three letters capitalized in the preceding list.

Stop Although you can activate the ENDPoint object snap mode by entering **END**, you should instead enter four letters (**ENDP**) to avoid it being interpreted as an END command and accidentally ending your AutoCAD LT session.

AutoCAD LT's object snap modes include a QUIck modifier; in addition, you can activate multiple modes. The section of this chapter called "Setting and Applying Running Object Snap Modes" discusses these topics and provides an explanation of why a NONe object snap mode is needed.

You can use object snaps in two ways. The next section describes using object snaps as overrides that apply only to the next pick. The other method of using object snaps is to set running object snap modes that apply to every point picked until you change the mode setting or specify an override. The latter method is described in the section called "Setting and Applying Running Object Snap Modes."

Constructing Accurate Geometry with Object Snaps

By default, AutoCAD LT has no object snap modes enabled. Thus your point picks are constrained only by a snap grid (if Snap is on) and an orthogonal direction (if Ortho is on). *Object snap overrides* generate coordinates calculated or extracted from an object or from its relationship to other locations or objects. Such object snap modes are called overrides because they override Snap, Ortho, and any running mode currently set, including NONe. These overrides must be applied each time you need them and only while AutoCAD LT is prompting for a point location. Object snaps work the same whether you use them as overrides or as running modes, but overrides are the easiest way to explore the unique effects of each of the individual object snaps.

11

The following series of exercises use object snaps and point filters to create most of the drawing shown in figure 11.5.

Figure 11.5

The finished shaft arm bracket.

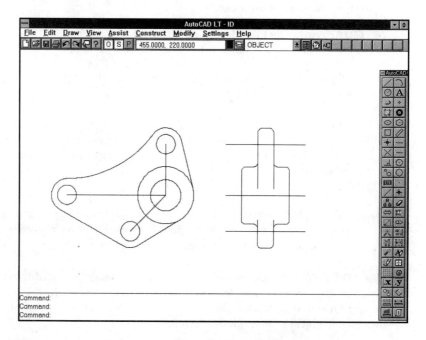

Snapping to Endpoints, Centers, Midpoints, and Quadrants

In the following exercise, you use the four object snap modes (ENDPoint, MIDpoint, CENter, and QUAdrant) that locate specific geometric features of single objects. The example drawing also has text and other objects you use in later exercises, but simply ignore them now.

Using Geometric Object Snap Modes on Geometric Features

Create a new drawing, again named OSNAP, using the ALT1101.DWG drawing as a prototype and no setup method. Draw a circle at 150,100 with a radius of 20.

Command: *Click on the Line tool*

_LINE From point: *Click on the Center tool*   Specifies the CENter object snap

_CEN of *Pick any point on the circle*   Starts a line at the center of the circle

To point: @125<0 (Enter)

To point: *Click on the Circle tool*	Cancels, then issues the CIRCLE command
Command: _CIRCLE 3P/TTR/ <Center point>: *Click on the Endpoint tool*	Specifies the ENDPoint object snap
_ENDP of *Pick the line at* ① *(see fig. 11.6)*	Snaps the center of the circle to the endpoint of the line
Radius <20.0000>: **35** (Enter)	
Command: (Enter)	Repeats the CIRCLE command
CIRCLE 3P/TTR/<Center point>: *Click the pop-up button and choose* **C**enter *from the pop-up menu*	Specifies the CENter object snap
_center of *Pick the circle at* ②	Snaps to the center of existing circle, to draw a concentric circle
Radius <35.0000>: *Click on the Midpoint tool*	Specifies the MIDpoint object snap
_MID of *Pick anywhere on the line*	Snaps the radius to the line's midpoint
Command: *Pick the circle at* ③, *then type* **CP** *and press Enter*	Issues the COPY command with the circle selected
<Base point or displacement>/ Multiple: **CEN** (Enter)	Specifies the CENter object snap
of *Pick the circle at* ③	Snaps the reference point of the copy to the center
Second point of displacement: *Click* *on the Quadrant tool*	Specifies the QUAdrant object snap
_QUAD of *Pick the circle at* ④	Snaps copy of small circle to the 90-degree quadrant point of the large circle
Erase the large circle at ④.	
Command: *Click on the Arc tool*	
_ARC Center/<Start point>: *Choose* **M**idpoint *from the pop-up menu*	Specifies the MIDpoint object snap
_mid of *Pick anywhere on the line*	Starts the arc at the midpoint of the line
Center/End/<Second point>: **C** (Enter)	Prompts for center point of arc

continues

continued

Figure 11.6

Drawing with object snaps.

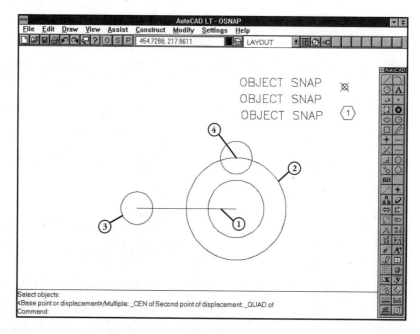

`Center: ` **`ENDP`** (Enter)	Specifies the ENDPoint object snap
`of ` *Pick the line at* ①	Snaps the center of the arc to the endpoint of the line
`Angle/<End point>: ` *Choose* **Q**uadrant *from the pop-up menu*	Specifies the QUAdrant object snap
`_QUAD of ` *Pick the circle at* ⑤ *(see fig. 11.7)*	Snaps the endpoint to the quadrant of the circle, extending the arc to align with that point
`Command: ` *Pick the circle at* ⑥, *then click on the Copy tool*	Issues the COPY command with circle selected
`<Base point or displacement>/ Multiple: ` *Choose* **C**enter *from the pop-up menu*	Specifies the CENter object snap
`_cen of ` *Pick the circle at* ⑥ *again*	Snaps the reference point of the copy to the center
`Second point of displacement: ` *Choose* **M**idpoint *from the pop-up menu*	Specifies the MIDpoint object snap

_mid of *Pick anywhere on the arc*   Snaps the copy of the circle to the midpoint
                                            of the arc at ⑦

Erase the arc, click on the Redraw tool or button, and save the OSNAP drawing. At this point,
it should look like figure 11.7, except the arc at ⑦ is gone.

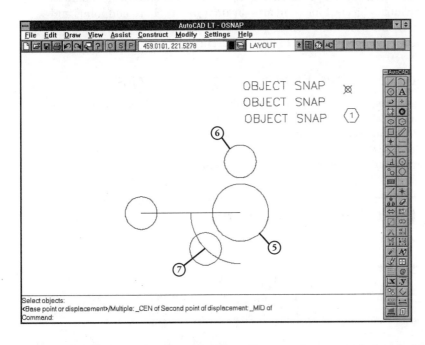

Figure 11.7

*Snapping a circle
to the midpoint of
an arc.*

When you are using the object snap modes, you do not need to pick at the actual
point you want. You should make sure, however, that you select the correct type of
object. AutoCAD LT issues an error message if you pick the wrong type of object for a
specific object snap mode. If multiple points are possible, pick nearer to the desired
point than to other points that also qualify for the object snap mode. To pick the
center of an arc or a circle, you must pick on the object itself rather than pick near its
center.

Tip   If you accidentally specify the wrong object snap mode, just enter any type of
             invalid input or pick a point in a clear area. AutoCAD LT issues an error message
             and reissues the prompt for a point. You can then specify the correct mode.

Frequently, the geometric features of several objects coincide, so you might have
several possible ways to specify the same point using object snaps. For example, in the
preceding exercise, you could have snapped the center of the arc to the center of the
circle instead of the end of the line.

As your design becomes more involved and detailed, keep in mind that each of the modes you just used can snap to points at some distance from the actual point you pick. If the location you want to pick is crowded, this feature of object snaps is helpful.

Each object snap mode in the preceding exercise located geometrically defined points on individual objects. Lines and arcs, by their nature, have endpoints and midpoints. Arcs and circles have center points. In addition, circles have four quadrant points, and arcs can have from zero to four quadrant points.

Snapping to Intersections, Perpendiculars, and Tangents

In the following exercise, you look at three object snap modes that enable you to snap to points defined by geometric relationships—either between two objects or between an object and a point you pick. The three object snap modes are INTersection, PERpendicular, and TANgent. First you draw some construction lines on the LAY-OUT layer, and then you use them with object snaps to draw a tangent arc.

Using Object Snaps Involving Geometric Constructions

Continue working with the OSNAP drawing from the preceding exercise.

Command: *Click on the Line tool*

`_LINE From point:` *Click on the Center tool*	Activates the CENter object snap
`_CEN of` *Pick the upper circle at* ① *(see fig. 11.8)*	Snaps to the center
`To point:` *Click on the Center tool*	Activates the CENter object snap
`_CEN of` *Pick the left circle at* ②	Snaps to the center point and draws a line segment
`To point:` `@190<90` (Enter)	Draws line to ③
`To point:` *Press Enter twice*	Ends, then repeats, the LINE command
`LINE From point:` `15,270` (Enter)	Begins line in upper left corner
`To point:` *Click on the Perpendicular tool*	Activates the PERpendicular object snap
`_PER to` *Pick angled line* ④	Snaps the line to ⑤, perpendicular to the slope of the angled line
`To point:` (Enter)	

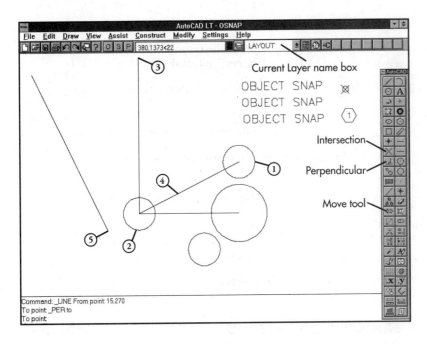

Figure 11.8

*Creating
construction lines
using object
snaps.*

Next, you will move the last line to bisect the angled line between the circles.

`Command:` *Pick the new line at* ⑤, *then type* **M** *and press Enter*	Issues the MOVE command for the line selected
`Base point or displacement:` *Click on the Endpoint tool*	Activates the ENDPoint object snap
`_ENDP of` *Pick the line at* ⑤	Snaps the reference point for the move to the endpoint of the line
`Second point of displacement:` *Click on the Midpoint tool*	Activates the MIDpoint object snap
`_MID of` *Pick the line at* ④	Snaps the moved line to the midpoint of the angled line

Click on the current layer list and change to the OBJECT layer.

Click on the Arc tool

`_ARC Center/<Start point>:` **C** (Enter)	Prompts for the center point
`Center:` *Click on the Intersection tool*	Activates the INTersection object snap

continues

continued

`_INT of` *Pick the intersection at* ⑥ *(see fig.11.9)*	Snaps the center of the arc to the intersection of the lines
`Start point:` *Click on the Intersection tool*	Activates the INTersection object snap
`_INT of` *Pick point* ⑦	Snaps the start point and drags the arc to the intersection of the line and the left circle

Because the center and start points are on a line perpendicular to the left circle, the arc is tangent to the left circle.

`Angle/<End point>:` *Click on the Center tool*	Activates the CENter object snap
`_CEN of` *Pick the circle at* ⑧	Snaps the end of the arc to align with the angle from the arc's center to the circle's center

Because the arc's center is on the perpendicular line bisecting the line between the circles, the end of the arc is tangent to the circle.

Figure 11.9

Creating an arc using construc-tion lines and object snaps.

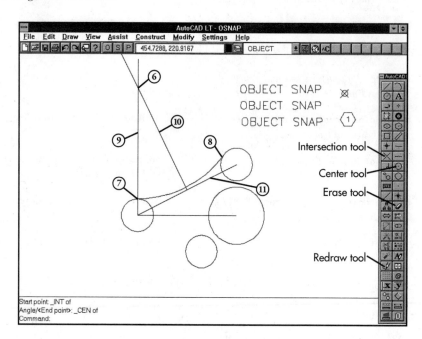

Erase the construction lines at ⑨, ⑩, and ⑪, and then click on the Redraw tool or button.

Next, you will set an UNDO mark, so you can easily undo the following experiments with the effects of the TANgent and PERpendicular object snaps.

Command: **UNDO** (Enter)	Starts the UNDO command
Auto/Back/Control/End/Group/Mark/ number>: **M** (Enter)	Sets a Mark
Command: **L** (Enter)	Issues the LINE command
LINE From point: *Click on the* *Perpendicular tool*	Activates the PERpendicular object snap
_PER to *Pick the line at* ⑫ *(see fig. 11.10)*	Selects the existing line, but doesn't display a rubber-band line yet
To point: *Click on the Tangent tool*	Activates the TANgent object snap
_TAN to *Pick the circle at* ⑬	Calculates and draws a line tangent to the side picked on the upper circle and perpendicular to the existing line
To point: *Press Enter twice*	Ends and reissues the LINE command
LINE From point: **PER** (Enter)	Activates the PERpendicular object snap
to *Pick the circle at* ⑭	Selects the circle but doesn't display a rubber- band line yet
To point: **TAN** (Enter)	Activates the TANgent object snap
of *Pick the arc at* ⑮	Calculates and draws a line perpendicular to the circle and tangent to the arc
To point: *Choose* **P***erpendicular from* *the pop-up menu*	Activates the PERpendicular object snap
_per to *Pick the line at* ⑯	Snaps a perpendicular line from the last point to the horizontal line
To point: *Press Enter twice*	Ends and reissues the LINE command
LINE From point: *Click on the* *Perpendicular tool*	Activates the PERpendicular object snap
_PER to *Pick the arc at* ⑮	Selects the arc but doesn't display a rubber- band line yet
To point: *Click on the Perpendicular tool*	Activates the PERpendicular object snap
_PER to *Pick the circle at* ⑰	Calculates and draws a line perpendicular to the arc and through the large circle perpen- dicular to the side picked

continues

continued

`To point:` *Press Enter twice*	Ends and reissues the LINE command
`LINE From point:` *Pick point* ⑱	
`To point:` *Click on the Perpendicular tool*	Activates the PERpendicular object snap
`_PER to` *Pick the arc at* ⑮	Displays an error message; a perpendicular line from ⑱ cannot be drawn

`No Perpendicular found for`
`specified point.`
`Point or option keyword required.`	

`To point:` *Click on the Cancel button*	Cancels the LINE command

Figure 11.10

Experimenting with the PERpendicular and TANgent object snap modes.

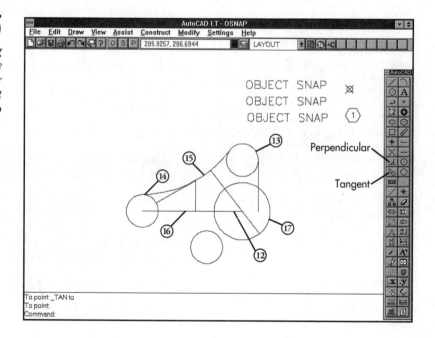

`Command:` **UNDO** (Enter)	Starts the UNDO command
`Auto/Back/Control/End/Group/Mark/` `number>:` **B** (Enter)	Specifies the Back option and undoes the lines
`GROUP GROUP GROUP LINE` `Mark encountered`	

Command: *Click on the Redraw tool or button*

Next you will use the TANgent object snap to add the lines shown in figure 11.11.

Command: *Click on the Line tool*

`_LINE From point:` *Click on the Tangent tool*	Activates the TANgent object snap
`_TAN to` *Pick the circle at* ⑲ *(see fig. 11.11)*	Selects the circle but doesn't display a rubber-band line yet
`To point:` *Click on the Tangent tool*	Activates the TANgent object snap
`_TAN to` *Pick point* ⑳	Calculates and draws a line tangent to the sides picked on the left and lower circles

`To point:` *Press Enter*

Repeat the LINE command with TANgent object snaps to draw the lines from ⑳ to ㉑ and ㉑ to ㉒, and then save the OSNAP drawing.

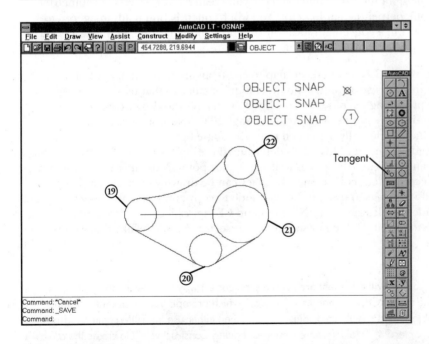

Figure 11.11

Creating lines simultaneously tangent to two circles.

With the INTersection object snap mode, both intersecting objects must be within the aperture. The INTersection object snap mode is one of the most commonly used modes. With this object snap mode, you can easily place columns on a grid.

Tip   You can use the INTersection object snap to locate a point at any distance along a line at any angle by snapping a circle center to the starting point on the line and entering the desired distance as the radius. The resulting circle will intersect the line at the desired point, to which you can snap with the INTersection mode.

Circles (in most cases) and arcs (in many cases) have more than one possible point for a PERpendicular or TANgent object snap. In these cases, the point on the side closest to the pick point is used. Both the PERpendicular and TANgent object snap modes can snap either the first end, the second end, or both ends of a line. When you use these object snaps with the first point (the From point) of a line, no rubber-band line appears until you pick the next point (the To point).

The PERpendicular object snap mode can snap to a projected point that is not on a selected line, but perpendiculars to arcs must be on the arc. The PERpendicular object snap applied to a circle or an arc constructs a *normal* to the curve—a line whose slope passes through the center of the curvature.

In the beginning of the preceding exercise, you created another classic geometric construct—the perpendicular bisector. You will frequently find it advantageous to create an object in a convenient location (the perpendicular line, in this case) and then move it precisely into place using object snaps.

You cannot use the TANgent object snap to create an arc that is tangent to two circles. You need to use a construction technique similar to that used in the beginning of the preceding exercise. To specify an arc tangent to two circles, you need to know either the arc's radius or its included angle. The exercise used the included angle, which coincidentally happened to be the angle between the vertical line and the bisecting line (see fig. 11.9). This determined the center point (shown at bubble number 6) and radius of the arc, as well as the start point. Most arcs won't benefit from such a convenient coincidence, but they can be drawn with a similar construction. The easiest way is to use grip Rotate mode to copy and rotate the bisector by half of the included angle, then use ENDPoint and CENter object snaps to move the rotated line to the circle's center so that it intersects the bisector like the example in the exercise.

Tip   If you know the tangent arc's radius, the easiest way to draw the tangent arc is to use the CIRCLE command's TTR option, which prompts you to pick the two tangent objects and specify the radius. You can then either use the TRIM command (see Chapter 14, "Making More Changes: Editing Constructively") to create the arc by deleting part of the circle, or use object snaps to draw an arc over the circle and then erase the circle and use REDRAW to redisplay the arc.

New Riders Publishing
INSIDE SERIES

Although many of the design construction techniques in CAD are similar to those used with a compass and a straightedge, CAD affords some pleasant freedoms. In CAD, for example, you can draw a circle more easily than you can draw an arc. In fact, drawing and erasing circles in CAD is far easier than it ever was on paper. You are therefore free to use complete circles (liberally), whereas a designer on paper would only use an arc (sparingly).

Snapping to Nearest Points, Point Objects, Text Objects, and Blocks

Three other object snap modes find points associated with an object's location. In the following exercise, you use the NEArest, NODe, and INSert object snap modes. NEArest snaps to the closest point on any object. NODe snaps to point objects (point objects are used in dimensions). Text objects and blocks (see Chapter 4, "Building a Drawing: Using Basic Drawing Tools," and Chapter 18, "Leveraging Repetitive Design and Drafting") are located by their insertion points. You use the INSert object snap to locate insertion points of text and block objects.

Using the NEArest, NODe, and INSert Object Snap Modes

Continue working with the OSNAP drawing from the preceding exercise and change to the NOTES layer.

Command: *Click on the Line tool*

_LINE From point: *Click on the Nearest tool*   Activates the NEArest object snap

_NEAREST to *Pick the arc at* ① *(see fig. 11.12)*   Snaps the line's start point to the point
                                                          on the arc nearest to the point picked

To point: *Click on the Center tool*   Activates the CENter object snap

_CEN of *Pick any point on the arc*   Draws the line to the center of the arc

To point: *Press Enter*   Completes the line

Use the LINE command to draw another
new line from 50,10 to @325<0

Command: *Pick the point object at*   Issues the MOVE command with the point
②, *then type* **M** *and press Enter*   object selected

Base point or displacement: *Click*   Activates the NODe object snap
on the Node tool

_NODE of *Pick the point object again*   Snaps the reference point for the move to the
                                                          point object

continues

continued

Figure 11.12

Creating a radial line of an arc.

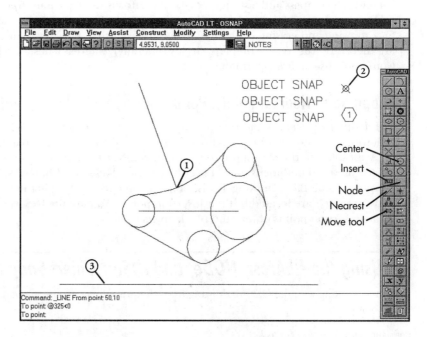

Second point of displacement: **NEA** (Enter)	Activates the NEArest object snap
to *Pick near the left end of the line at* ③	Moves the point object to the location on the line nearest the pick point
Command: *Pick the point object, then press Enter*	Repeats MOVE command with the point object selected
Base point or displacement: **5<90** (Enter)	Specifies a displacement
Second point of displacement: (Enter)	Uses 5<90 displacement to move point object up 5 units
Command: *Click on the Line tool*	
_LINE From point: *Click on the Insert tool*	Activates the INSert object snap
_INS of *Pick the top text object at* ④ *(see fig. 11.13)*	Snaps to the insertion point, at the right end of the text
To point: *Choose* In**s**ert *from the pop-up menu*	Activates the INSert object snap
_ins of *Pick the second text object at* ⑤	Snaps the line to the insertion point at the center of the text

To point: *Click on the Insert tool and pick the text at ⑥*	Snaps the line to the insert at the left end of the text
To point: **INS** ⏎Enter	Activates the INSert object snap
of *Pick the text "1" (not the hexagon) at ⑦*	Snaps the line to the insertion point at the middle of the text
To point: *Click on the Cancel button, then the Undo button*	Cancels and undoes the lines

The insertion point of text depends on what justification was used to create it. The text used here was right, center, left, and middle justified.

Command: *Pick the text at ⑥, then type* **M** *and press Enter*	Issues the MOVE command with the bottom line of text selected
Base point or displacement: *Click on the Insert tool*	Activates the INSert object snap
_INS of *Pick the same line of text* ⑥	Snaps the base point to the insertion point of the text
Second point of displacement: *Click on the Node tool*	Activates the NODe object snap
_NODE of *Pick the point object at* ⑧	Moves the text to the point's location
Command: *Pick the hexagonal object* ⑨ *and press Enter*	Repeats the MOVE command with the hexagonal object and the text "1" both selected because they are a single block object (see Chapter 18, "Leveraging Repetitive Design and Drafting")
Base point or displacement: *Click on the Insert tool*	Activates the INSert object snap
_INS of *Carefully pick the hexagon at* ⑨ *(don't pick the text)*	Snaps to the insertion point of the block object (a point left of the hexagon)
Second point of displacement: *Click on the Nearest tool*	Activates the NEArest object snap
_NEAREST to *Pick the line at* ⑩	Moves the hexagon and the text to the point on the line that is nearest to the pick point

Erase the two text objects at ④ and ⑤ and the point object at ⑧. Click on the Redraw tool or button, and then save the OSNAP drawing (see fig. 11.14).

Figure 11.13

Working with the INSert and NODe object snaps.

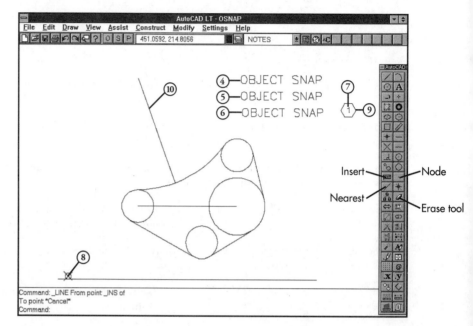

Figure 11.14

The OSNAP drawing after the exercise is complete.

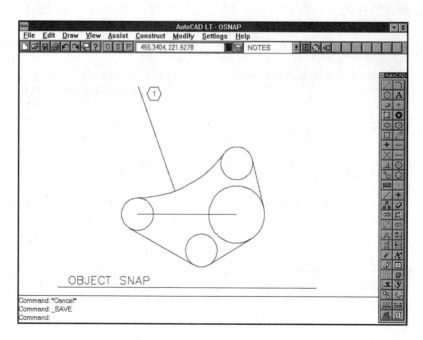

The NEArest object snap mode simply finds a point on an object closest to the point you specify. In the preceding exercise, the line drawn from a nearest point on the arc to its center was its radius by definition. The NEArest object snap mode is often used in measurement; the section of the next chapter called "Finding Distances and Lengths with the DIST Command" gives examples of this usage. Whenever you need to reference a location on an object but do not need (or cannot easily snap to) a specific point like a midpoint or an endpoint, you can use the NEArest object snap mode.

The NODe mode is uniquely single-minded among the object snap modes. The NODe object snap finds the location of point objects exclusively; *point entities* are those objects created with the POINT command. In a dense drawing, you can use point objects to place reference points, then use NODe object snap to snap to them later. You can snap to point objects when many other types of objects are crowded together because the NODe object snap mode ignores everything except point objects.

Although the point object in the preceding exercise had an easily visible point style (see Chapter 4, "Building a Drawing: Using Basic Drawing Tools"), you can place points with a less obtrusive style so that they display as a small dot.

 Tip   When you create blocks (see Chapter 18, "Leveraging Repetitive Design and Drafting"), you can put point objects in them to provide snap points for NODe object snaps.

Associative dimensions (see Chapter 20, "Applying Dimensions in CAD") use point objects as their reference points. You can use NODe to snap to these points.

You can apply the INSert object snap mode to a variety of objects, such as text, blocks, and block attributes (blocks are discussed in Chapter 18, "Leveraging Repetitive Design and Drafting"). As illustrated in the preceding exercise, you can also use the INSert object snap mode to determine the justification used when a text object was created.

Text and block objects (unlike lines, arcs, and circles) do not have intrinsic geometric definition points; you specify their insertion points in the process of creating them. You can achieve good control over text placement using the INSert object snap during a move, rotate, or copy by specifying the appropriate justification when you create the text. To place a label in the center of a circular or hexagonal feature, for example, you would use middle-justified text.

You have seen how each mode works as an override. The next section examines the other method of working with object snaps—setting running object snap modes.

Setting and Applying Running Object Snap Modes

The object snap overrides must be specified for each point you pick. If you need to snap to many similar points, or if you want more than one object snap active at the same time, you should use a running object snap. Running object snaps remain in effect and apply to every point picked, unless they are overridden.

The running object snap modes perform the same as the object snap overrides. You set these running object snap modes by using the Running Object Snap dialog box (see fig. 11.15). You can access this dialog box by clicking on the Object Snap tool (DDOSNAP command) in the toolbox, or choosing the **O**bject Snap item on the **A**ssist pull-down menu, or by entering **DDOSNAP** (**OS** for short) at the command line.

Figure 11.15

The Running Object Snap dialog box.

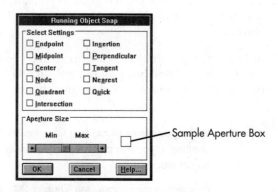

Sample Aperture Box

In the following exercise, you set a combined running object snap mode and use it with the CIRCLE and ARC commands to modify the figure you have created in previous exercises.

Setting and Applying Running Object Snap Modes

Continue working with the OSNAP drawing from the preceding exercise, and change to the LAYOUT layer.

Command: *Click on the Object Snap tool*	Issues DDOSNAP command and opens the Running Object Snap dialog box (see fig. 11.15)
'_DDOSNAP	
Put check marks in the **E**ndpoint *and* **C**enter *boxes (click in them)*	Sets ENDPoint and CENter as running object snaps

Use the Aperture Size slider bar to make the sample aperture box a little smaller.

Click on OK	Closes the dialog box and saves the settings

Command: *Click on the Line tool*

_LINE From point: *Pick the lower circle at* ① *(see fig. 11.16)*	Snaps the start point of a line to the center of the circle
To point: *Pick the large circle at* ②	Snaps and draws the line from center to center
To point: *Pick the upper circle at* ③	Snaps another line to the center of the upper circle

To point: (Enter)

Change to the OBJECT *layer*

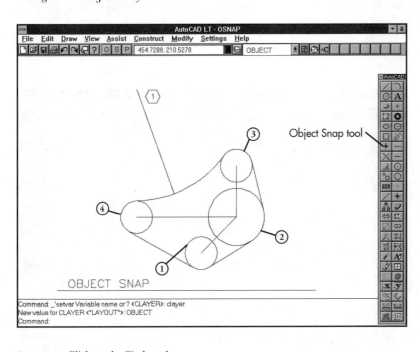

Figure 11.16

Drawing lines using a running CENter object snap.

Command: *Click on the Circle tool*

_CIRCLE 3P/TTR/<Center point>: *Pick the left circle at* ④	Snaps to the center, to start a concentric circle
Radius: **12** (Enter)	Specifies the radius and draws the circle

continues

continued

Command: *Pick the new circle, then then type* **CP** *and press Enter*	Issues the COPY command with the circle selected
`<Base point or displacement>/` `Multiple:` **M** (Enter)	Specifies Multiple copy option
`Base point:` *Pick the left circle at* ⑤ (see fig. 11.17)	Snaps the base point to the center of the circle
`Second point of displacement:` *Pick the lower circle at* ⑥ *and the upper circle at* ⑧	Snaps new concentric circles existing circles
`Second point of displacement:` (Enter)	Ends the multiple copies
Command: *Click on the Circle tool*	
`_CIRCLE 3P/TTR/<Center point>:` *Pick the large circle at* ⑦	Snaps to the center to a concentric circle
`Radius <12.0000>:` **19** (Enter) (*see fig. 11.17*)	Draws the circle

Figure 11.17

Creating concentric circles with a running CENter object snap.

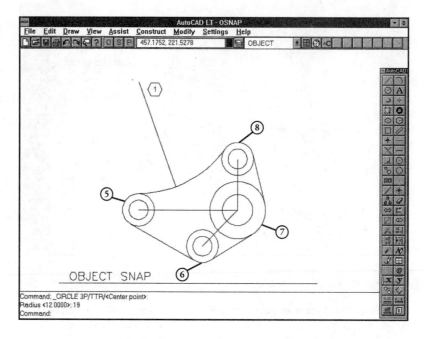

Erase the four construction circles at ⑤, ⑥, ⑦, and ⑧, and then click on the Redraw tool or button (see fig. 11.18).

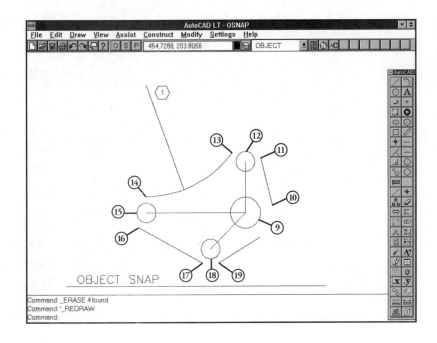

Figure 11.18

Replacing construction circles using the CENter and ENDPoint object snaps.

```
Command: Click on the Circle tool
```

`_CIRCLE 3P/TTR/<Center point>:` *Pick the large circle at* (9) *(see fig. 11.18)*	Snaps to the center to start a concentric circle
`Radius <19.0000>:` *Pick the endpoint at* (10)	Snaps the radius to the endpoint to re-create the large circle on the OBJECT layer
`Command:` *Choose* **D**raw, **A**rc, *then* Start, Center, **E**nd *option*	Issues the ARC command, with the Center option following the start point
`_arc Center/<Start point>:` *Pick the endpoint at* (11)	Snaps the start of the arc to the end of the line
`Center/End/<Second point>: _c Center:` *Pick the circle at* (12)	Snaps the center of the arc to the center of the circle
`Angle/<End point>:` *Pick the endpoint at* (13)	Snaps to the end of the line and draws the arc

Repeat the ARC command twice, creating an arc at (14), (15), and (16) and another arc at (17), (18), and (19).

Click on the Redraw tool or button, then click on the Save button (see fig. 11.19)

Figure 11.19

The OSNAP drawing with tangential arcs.

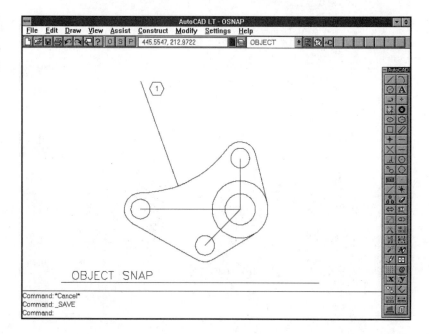

The preceding exercise showed that snapping to objects with a running mode is as easy as picking an object. When you picked a circle, AutoCAD LT snapped to its center, but when you picked a line or the end of an arc, AutoCAD LT snapped to its endpoint. AutoCAD LT bases the mode to apply on the type(s) of objects found in the aperture box and their proximity. For example, with the mode combination ENDPoint, INTersection, and CENter, if there is more than one object in the aperture box and they intersect, the INTersection mode prevails. If not, one of the following applies to the object nearest the pick point. If it is an arc and the pick is less than the arc's radius from an endpoint, then the ENDPoint mode applies; otherwise, the CENter mode prevails. If it is a circle, the CENter mode is used. If it is a line, the ENDPoint mode is applied.

Tip   CEnter, INTersection, ENDPoint is probably the most useful combination. It will find most of the points you want, and can be overridden in the few cases when you need another mode or no object snapping.

Other mode combinations are tricky. When you use the ENDPoint mode with the MIDpoint mode, you must pick nearer the end than the middle to indicate which mode you intend. When you combine the PERpendicular and the TANgent modes, proximity distance determines which mode you want applied to an arc or a circle.

Some mode combinations just don't work. The NEArest mode does not combine well with anything because it overpowers everything. Similarly, if you combine the CENter and QUAdrant modes and the radius of a circle or arc is much larger than the aperture, it is impossible to snap to the center. For such large circles and arcs, the distance from the pick point to the center is always greater than the distance to a quadrant point. However, you can still snap to the center of small circles and arcs by placing the crosshairs as close as possible to the center point while picking the circle or arc with the aperture. When in doubt, just override the running mode combination with a mode that you know will work.

 Note When you pick a location with an object snap override, it snaps to an object if a suitable one is found and returns an error if no suitable object is found. However, when you pick a location with a running object snap, it returns the pick point, not an error, if no suitable object to snap to can be found.

Many users like to have a common set of running object snaps, such as INTersection and ENDPoint, routinely set, and override them when they need other modes or no object snap.

 Tip If you have running object snaps active and you need to make a selection without any object snap, you can click on the Snap None tool in the toolbox to have the NONe object snap override disable the running object snaps during the selection. The NONe object snap can also be accessed from the cursor pop-up menu or from the keyboard by entering **NONe** or **NON**.

AutoCAD LT normally examines all objects within the aperture and finds the closest point matching one of the criteria in the search. You can combine the QUIck mode modifier with any mode. Using the QUIck mode modifier quickens the process in large or cluttered drawings, because it examines the most recently created objects within the aperture and finds the first (not necessarily the closest) point matching the search criteria.

 Tip A smaller object snap aperture enables you to more accurately pick the desired object or objects in crowded drawings, but it requires a steadier hand.

Object snaps are a fundamental tool in AutoCAD LT for achieving accuracy and will be used throughout the rest of this chapter and throughout the *Inside AutoCAD LT for Windows, Second Edition* book. The remaining sections of this chapter discuss a variety of other aids and techniques for creating precise and accurate drawings, but many of the exercises continue to demonstrate the use of the object snap modes in combination with these other tools. In the next section, for example, you explore two techniques for locating new points relative to existing geometry, a task almost impossible to do accurately without using object snaps.

Tapping into Existing Data in Your Drawing

AutoCAD LT provides several ways to precisely place new points relative to existing geometry. This section describes two methods. In the first method, the ID command saves the location of an existing point so you can specify a new point relative to it using relative coordinates. This method is similar to using a scale and adjustable triangle or a drafting machine in manual drafting. In the second method, the point filter mechanism aligns new points with the X and/or Y coordinates of existing geometry. This method is similar to using construction lines in manual drafting.

Setting Temporary Reference Points with the ID Command

In a typical CAD application, you are not usually concerned with the coordinate locations of points in a drawing; however, there are times when you need this information. In such situations, you can use the ID command to return the coordinate location of the point specified. If you use an object snap to pick the location, you can use the ID command to return specific geometric points. As examples, you could find the precise coordinates of the center of a circle or the midpoint of a line.

The ID command has a second important function: it resets the AutoCAD LT system variable LASTPOINT. This function enables you to set a temporary reference point anywhere you need for use with a relative coordinate input.

In the following exercise, you use the ID command to verify coordinates of points. The part in the exercise is similar to the one you drew in the first section of this chapter. Then you begin to set up to draw a side view of the part, using combinations of ID and relative coordinates.

Using the ID Command to Set Temporary Reference Points

Create a new drawing named ID, using the ALT1102.DWG file as a prototype and no setup method. A running object snap of ENDPoint and CENter is set in the prototype drawing, so pick points will snap to end or center points if found within the aperture. The aperture size, stored in your configuration, is the same as you left it.

Command: *Choose* **A**ssist, **I**D Point	Issues the ID command
_ID Point: *Pick the left circle at* ① (*see fig. 11.20*)	Snaps to the center point of the circle and displays its coordinates

To help you see the points picked, the figures for this exercise show the blips that appear when you pick points.

```
X = 60.0000   Y = 120.0000   Z = 0.0000
```

Command: **(Enter)**	Repeats the ID command
ID Point: *Pick the line at* ③	Snaps to the endpoint at ④ and displays its coordinates

```
X = 50.4032   Y = 102.4529   Z = 0.0000
```

Command: **ID (Enter)**	Starts the ID command
Point: *Pick the large circle at* ⑤	Snaps to the circle's center point at ⑥ and displays its coordinates

```
X = 185.0000   Y = 120.0000   Z = 0.0000
```

Command: **LASTPOINT (Enter)**	Issues prompt for the LASTPOINT system variable and displays its current value, the last ID point
New value for LASTPOINT <185.0000,120.0000,0.0000>: **(Enter)**	Leaves the last point unchanged

The LASTPOINT system variable stores the last ID point, so you can draw a new line relative to that point using relative coordinates.

Command: *Click on the Line tool*	
_LINE From point: **@75<0 (Enter)**	Starts line 75 units to the right of the ID point; this start point becomes the new last point
To point: **@100<0 (Enter)**	Draws line to point 100 units to the right of the last point (the start point)
To point: **(Enter)**	
Command: **LASTPOINT (Enter)**	Displays the LASTPOINT value, now the end of the new line

continues

continued

Figure 11.20

Creating a line relative to the LASTPOINT location.

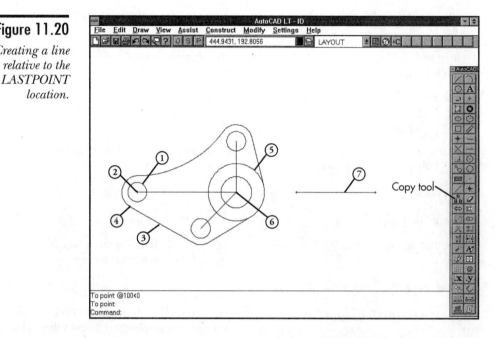

```
New value for LASTPOINT          Leaves the default value unchanged
<360.0000,120.0000,0.0000>: Enter

Command: ID Enter                Starts the ID command

Point: Pick the large circle at ⑤   Snaps the last point to the center
                                    of the circle

X = 185.0000   Y = 120.0000   Z = 0.0000

Pick the line at ⑦, (see fig.    Issues the COPY command with
11.21), then type CP and press Enter   the line selected


<Base point or displacement>     Uses the LASTPOINT value at the center
/Multiple: @ Enter               of the large circle

Second point of displacement: Pick   Creates the line at ⑨, using a
the circle at ⑧                      displacement from the center of the large
                                     circle to the center of the upper circle

Click on the Save button         Saves the ID drawing (see fig. 11.21)
```

 New Riders Publishing
INSIDE SERIES

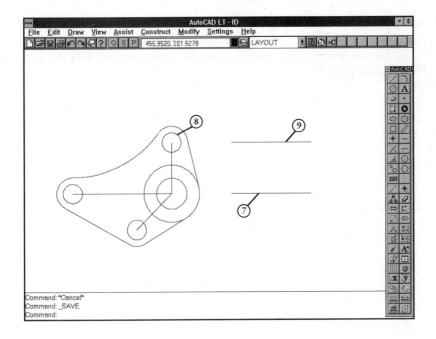

In the preceding exercise, you saw that the ID command reports only the X, Y, and Z coordinate values. You can use object snaps to snap to the exact geometric point you want identified. Multiple running object snaps can make it unclear which point is actually snapped to, but you can use blip marks to see the point AutoCAD LT snapped to.

> **ID.** The ID command prompts for a point and returns the X, Y, and Z coordinates of the point specified. The system variable LASTPOINT is set to the coordinates returned. Normally, the current elevation setting is used for the Z value. You can pick the point, and you can use snap, object snap, point filters, and absolute or relative coordinates.

To use the coordinate stored in the LASTPOINT variable, you must use a relative coordinate (type an input starting with, or consisting of, the @ symbol) in response to the next location prompt, without first picking other points. The @ symbol alone returns the last point.

Stop A few object-selection operations change the LASTPOINT system variable. AUto and implied window or implied crossing window selections always set LASTPOINT to the last corner picked. Picking an object sets LASTPOINT to the pick point

continues

(modified by object snap modes) only during a command selection mode, but not if you use noun-verb selection and pick the object before issuing the command. Other explicit selection modes, such as Window, Crossing, WPolygon, and BOX, do not affect LASTPOINT.

Drawing a new object in a precise relationship to a point on the existing geometry is the easiest and most common use of the ID/LASTPOINT technique. The first line created in the preceding exercise is an example of this usage. Be careful to apply the relative coordinate input to the first point of the object specified—the start of the line, the center of the circle, and so on. Each point specified during a drawing or editing command resets the LASTPOINT variable.

The ID command provides the quickest way to determine the exact coordinates of a specific point. You can use ID to determine if objects are truly placed on the snap grid. In some drawings, such as those used for civil engineering and machine-component design, the origin (0,0,0) is a datum reference. In such situations, you can use the ID command to read locations directly from the drawing.

In summary, you can use object snaps to locate points on objects, and you can use the ID command and relative coordinates to locate points at a distance (if you know the relative offset distance and the angle). Both of these techniques, however, are limited to specifying a single coordinate. To locate multiple new points based on existing geometry, you can use point filters.

Assembling Coordinate Points with Point Filters

If you need to locate a point to align with the X, Y, or Z coordinate of another point, you use point filters. You can assemble a coordinate location from the X, Y, or Z values of any set of points you can specify. To add accuracy to your point specification, you can use snap, object snap, and the LASTPOINT value.

In the following exercise, you continue to construct the side view of the part developed in the previous exercises. You use point filters to accurately align points in the side view with the Y coordinates of the existing figure's endpoints. The X and Y point filters are accessible from the toolbar by clicking on the .X and .Y tools or buttons. In addition, you can choose the <u>X</u>YZ Filters item from the pop-up menu for access to all six possible filter combinations.

Locating Points Using Point Filters

Continue working with the ID drawing from the preceding exercise.

Command: *Click on the Object Snap tool* Opens the Running Object Snap dialog box

`'_DDOSNAP` *Click as required to remove the checks* Turns off any running object snap modes
*from the **E**ndpoint and **C**enter check boxes,*
then click on OK

Command: *Pick the line at* ① *(see fig. 11.22),* Issues the COPY command with the
then type **CP** *and press Enter* line selected

`<Base point or displacement>/Multiple:` Activates the MIDpoint object snap
Click on the Midpoint tool

`_MID of` *Pick anywhere on the same line* Snaps the base point to the midpoint
of the line

`Second point of displacement:` *Click* Activates the X filter
on the .X tool or button

`.X of` *Click on the @ tool or button* Sets the X coordinate to that of the line's
midpoint (using the LASTPOINT variable)

`@ (need YZ):` *Click on the Center tool* Activates the CENter object snap

`_CEN of` *Pick the lower circle at* ② Snaps to the center of the lower circle,
extracts the Y coordinate of that point,
combines it with the previous X
coordinate, and offsets the copy of the
line to the resulting point

Change the current layer to OBJECT

Command: *Click on the Line tool*

`_LINE From point:` *Click on the* Activates the Y filter
.Y tool or button

`.Y of` *Click on the Quadrant tool* Activates the QUAdrant object snap

`_QUAD of` *Pick the upper arc at* ③ Snaps to the arc's top quadrant point and
extracts its Y coordinate

continues

11

continued

`(need XZ): 300,0` (Enter)	Specifies the X and Z coordinates that AutoCAD combines with the previous Y coordinate, and draws the line to the resulting point
`To point:` *Click on the .Y tool or button*	Activates the Y filter
`.Y of` *Click on the Endpoint tool*	Activates the ENDPoint object snap
`_ENDP of` *Pick near the line endpoint at* ④	Snaps the endpoint and extracts its Y coordinate
`(need XZ): @` (Enter)	Extracts the X and Z values of the LASTPOINT variable (300,0), combines them with the previous Y coordinate, and draws the line
`To point:` *Click the Enter button twice*	Ends and repeats the LINE command
`LINE From point:` *Click on the .X tool or button*	Activates the X filter
`.X of` *Click on the @ tool or button*	Extracts the X coordinate of the LASTPOINT variable (300)
`@ (need YZ):` *Click on the Endpoint tool*	Activates the ENDPoint object snap
`_ENDP of` *Pick the line at* ⑤	Extracts the Y and Z coordinates of the line's upper endpoint, combines them with the previous X coordinate, and starts the line
`To point:` *From the pop-up menu, choose* **X**YZ Filters, .YZ	Activates the YZ filter
`.YZ of` *Click on the Quadrant tool*	Activates the QUAdrant object snap
`_QUAD of` *Pick the bottom of the lower radius arc at* ⑥	Extracts the Y and Z coordinates of the arc's bottom quadrant point
`(need X):` *Click on the @ tool or button*	Extracts the X of the LASTPOINT, which is the line's start point, not the YZ pick point
`To point:` *Click the Enter button twice*	Ends and repeats the LINE command
`LINE From point:` *Turn on the Snap button, and click on the .X tool or button*	Turns on snap and activates the X filter
`<Snap on> .X of` *Pick the point 280,150*	Extracts the X coordinate (280) from the snapped point, and prompts for Y and Z

(need YZ): \<Snap off\> *Turn off the Snap button, and click on the Intersection tool*	Turns off snap and activates the INTersection object snap
_INT of *Pick the intersection of the vertical line and the large circle at* ⑦	Extracts the Y and Z of the specified intersection and starts the line
To point: **.XZ** (Enter)	Activates the XZ filter
of *Click on the @ tool or button*	Extracts the X and Z (280 and 0) of the LASTPOINT (the start point)
@ (need Y): *Click on the Quadrant tool*	Activates the QUAdrant object snap
_QUAD of *Pick near the bottom of the large circle at* ⑧	Extracts the Y of the circle's bottom and draws the line
Click on the Cancel button, then the Save button	Ends the line and saves the ID drawing

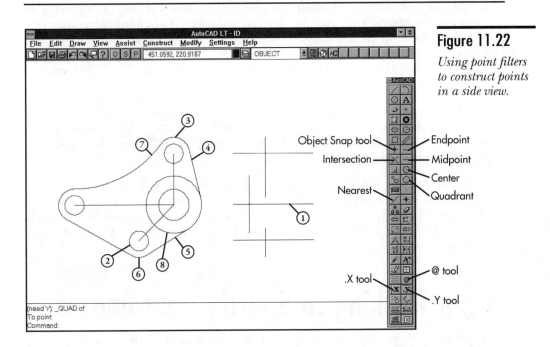

Figure 11.22

Using point filters to construct points in a side view.

Recall that points in AutoCAD LT are defined by X, Y, and Z coordinates and that in a 2D environment you need only X and Y (Z defaults to 0). Whenever you are prompted for a point, you can respond with one or two point-filter designators. The cursor pop-up menu's **X**YZ Filters child menu lists the six possibilities for a point-filter specification. If you supply a single coordinate value by using a point filter, such as X, AutoCAD LT prompts for the other two values (need YZ). Specifying a second point supplies these two values. AutoCAD LT then assembles the inputs into a single

3D-point coordinate. When you are prompted for two values (for example, XZ), you must input two numbers. When you enter absolute coordinates from the keyboard, these two numbers are input on the same line separated by a comma.

You can supply individual coordinate values by picking points, specifying locations with snap or object snap, entering absolute coordinates from the keyboard, or using the LASTPOINT value by way of a relative input (@ symbol). As you saw in the exercise, points picked to supply partial coordinates (such as at the .X of prompt) do not affect the LASTPOINT. When the point filter operation is complete, LASTPOINT is set to the resulting point.

Using point filters accomplishes what you would use construction lines to do in manual drafting. It is somewhat like applying Ortho mode to partial coordinate values. All points with the same Y value lie along a horizontal line while points with the same X value form a vertical line. Specifying a new point with an X value taken from one existing point and a Y value from another existing point finds the intersection of imaginary orthogonal construction lines drawn from each of the two points. In the preceding exercise, you used this method of transferring position values from one object to another to start drawing the side view of an object. Figure 11.05 showed the completed side view, created from those lines using editing tools discussed in Chapter 14, "Making More Changes: Editing Constructively," and Chapter 15, "Modifying Objects and Text."

Points resulting from using point filters are treated the same as any point you might pick. As an example, you can rotate the User Coordinate System (UCS) to project points at any angle. In addition, object snaps and Snap or Ortho mode affect the points from which point filters extract coordinates.

If you are using AutoCAD LT Release 2, you have two more methods of accurately specifying points. These are placing relative points with the tracking feature, and placing point objects at regular intervals along lines and curves with the DIVIDE and MEASURE commands. If you are using AutoCAD LT Release 1, skip the rest of this chapter.

Using Tracking to Specify Coordinates

AutoCAD LT Release 2's tracking feature combines elements of the ID command, the @ (relative) modifier, ortho, and point filters. It enables you to specify points relative to any point or object in an interactive manner. Tracking is commonly combined with object snap and direct distance entry.

ALT2

In AutoCAD LT, there is usually more than one way to draw anything. In the following exercise, you will use tracking to reproduce the results of the previous ID and point filters exercises.

Using Tracking to Place Relative Points

Create a new drawing again named ID, using the ALT1102.DWG file as a prototype and no setup method. A running object snap of ENDPoint and CENter is set in the prototype drawing.

Command: **L** (Enter)

Issues the LINE command

LINE From point: *Click on the Tracking tool*

Enters tracking mode

TRACKING First tracking point: *Pick the large circle at* ① *(see fig. 11.23)*

Snaps to the center of the circle (CENter is on) and sets the current tracking point

Next point (Press RETURN to end tracking): *Move the cursor around, passing over the current tracking point to switch between up/down and left/right rubber-banding*

Rubber-bands in the same manner as if ortho were on (it isn't), switching between up/down and left/right rubber-banding only when you pass the cursor over the current tracking point (the center of the circle)

Move the cursor to the right (so that the rubber-band line snaps to 0 degrees, like ortho does), and then enter **75**

Uses direct distance entry to track to a point 75 units to the right of the center of the circle, making it the new current tracking point

Next point (Press RETURN to end tracking): (Enter)

Ends tracking and accepts the current tracking point as the input point, starting a line at ②

To point: *Turn on ortho, move the cursor to the right, then enter* **100**

Uses ortho and direct distance entry to draw the line to ③

<Ortho on>

To point: **TK** (Enter)

Enters tracking mode

First tracking point: *Move the cursor up/down and left/right (switching by passing the cursor over the current tracking point) and pick a series of tracking points (pick some on objects using object snap), ending up near* ④

Tracks orthogonally from one point to the next, each time displaying a single orthogonal rubber-band line from the current tracking point

continues

11

continued

Next point (Press RETURN to end tracking): (Enter)	Ends tracking and draws a line from ③ to the last tracking point at ④
To point: U (Enter)	Undoes the last line segment
To point: (Enter)	Ends the LINE command, leaving only the line from ② to ③

Notice the similarity of using tracking with direct distance entry to enter the first point and using ortho with direct distance entry to enter the second point in the exercise. Whether or not ortho is on, tracking points are always placed orthogonally to the previous tracking point. Even if ortho is on, however, the results of tracking are not constrained by ortho, as the line drawn from ③ to ④ demonstrated in the exercise.

Figure 11.23

Using tracking to start a line relative to a circle's center.

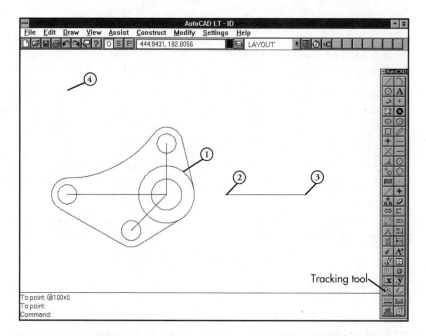

You can enter tracking mode by entering TK or TRAcking (only the first three characters are required), by clicking on the Tracking tool, or by selecting Tracking from the pop-up menu.

Tip If snap is on, it might be impossible to get tracking to switch between up/down and left/right tracking because you cannot get the cursor to pass close enough to the current tracking point. If this happens, turn snap off.

In the preceding exercise, you used tracking to set a point relative to a single existing point. Like point filters, tracking is also useful for aligning a point with the X coordinate of one point and the Y coordinate of another. In the following exercise, you use tracking to copy the line drawn in the previous exercise. You copy it relative to the centers of the small upper and lower circles, and aligned with the existing line's endpoint, instead of using point filters or the @ (relative) modifier. Next you use tracking to draw a new line offset 20 units from the end of an existing line and aligned with the top and bottom quadrants of an existing circle.

Tracking Points Relative to Two Objects

Continue from the previous exercise, with ortho on and the ENDPoint and CENter running object snaps set.

Command: *Pick the line at* ① *(see fig. 11.24) and enter* **CP**

Issues the COPY command with the line selected

COPY 1 found

<Base point or displacement>/Multiple: **M** (Enter)

Specifies multiple copy mode

Base point: *Pick* ①

Snaps to the endpoint

Second point of displacement: **TRA** (Enter)

Enters tracking mode

First tracking point: *Pick the circle at* ②

Tracks to the circle's center

Next point (Press RETURN to end tracking): *Pick the line at* ①

Tracks to a point orthogonal to both the center of the circle and end of the line

Next point (Press RETURN to end tracking): (Enter)

Accepts the point and copies the line to ③

Second point of displacement: *Click the popup button (hold Shift and click the Enter button), then select* **T**racking

Enters tracking mode using the pop-up menu

_tk First tracking point: *Pick the line at* ①

Tracks to the endpoint

continues

continued

Next point (Press RETURN to end tracking): *Pick the circle at* ④	Tracks to a point orthogonal to both the center of the circle and end of the line
Next point (Press RETURN to end tracking): `Enter`	Accepts the point and copies the line to ⑤
Second point of displacement: `Enter`	Ends the COPY command
Command: **L** `Enter`	Issues the LINE command
LINE From point: **TK** `Enter`	Enters tracking mode
First tracking point: *Pick the line at* ①	Starts tracking at end of line
Next point (Press RETURN to end tracking): *Move cursor to track to the right and enter* **20**	Doesn't work—it was supposed to use direct distance entry to track 20 units to the right, but the running ENDPoint object snap made it snap back to ①
Next point (Press RETURN to end tracking): **NON** `Enter`	Overrides ENDPoint object snap with NONe
Move cursor to track to the right and enter **20**	Uses direct distance entry to track 20 units to the right
Next point (Press RETURN to end tracking): **QUA** `Enter`	Overrides running object snaps with QUAdrant
of *Pick circle at* ⑥	Snaps to quadrant at ⑥ and tracks to point at ⑦
Next point (Press RETURN to end tracking): `Enter`	Accepts the point and starts a line at ⑦
To point: **TK** `Enter`	Enters tracking mode
First tracking point: **@** `Enter`	Starts tracking at ⑦
Next point (Press RETURN to end tracking): **QUA** `Enter`	Overrides running object snaps with QUAdrant
of *Pick circle at* ⑧	Snaps to quadrant at ⑧ and tracks to point at ⑨

Next point (Press RETURN to end tracking): (Enter)	Accepts the point and draws a line to ⑦
To point: (Enter)	Ends the LINE command

Notice, for the second copy, that using the pop-up menu and having running object snap modes set enabled you to make the copy without ever taking your hand off the mouse.

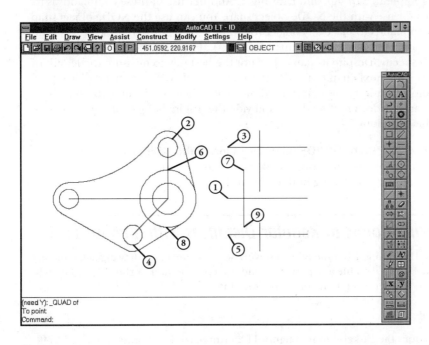

Figure 11.24

Copying and drawing lines relative to an existing line and circles.

Tip To find the center of a rectangle, use tracking and MIDpoint object snaps to specify a point relative to the midpoints of two adjacent sides.

In Chapter 14, "Making More Changes: Editing Constructively," you will use tracking to break (remove portions) off existing objects. If you want, you can continue to use tracking to draw the other lines shown in figure 11.24.

Another new feature in AutoCAD LT Release 2 is the ability to place point objects at regular intervals along lines and curves with the MEASURE and DIVIDE commands. If you are using AutoCAD LT Release 1, skip the following section.

Placing Points on Objects with MEASURE and DIVIDE

ALT2

In AutoCAD LT Release 2, the MEASURE and DIVIDE commands are useful tools for placing points or other objects at regular intervals along existing objects. By default, they place point objects, but you can also use them to place blocks (see Chapter 18, "Leveraging Repetitive Design and Drafting"). Another use of these commands is to create points for use with the NODe object snap. You can use the NODe object snap and other commands to place any object you want at or relative to these points. The MEASURE command places the points (or blocks) at intervals determined by a distance you specify. Despite its name, it is not the best way to measure the length of an object—see the next chapter for a better way. The DIVIDE command places the points (or blocks) at intervals determined by the number of segments you specify. Despite its name, it does not break or subdivide the original object, it only places points (or blocks) along it.

One use for MEASURE or DIVIDE might be to locate the positions for holes at a minimum interval of 25 units along a gasket, such as the circular flanged pipe gasket shown in figure 11.25. Try using both commands to do this in the following exercises.

Placing Points at Regular Distances with MEASURE

Continue in the ID drawing from the previous exercise or create a new drawing again named ID, using the ALT1102.DWG file as a prototype and no setup method. A running object snap of ENDPoint and CENter is set in the prototype drawing.

Erase everything.

Use CIRCLE to draw the gasket shown in figure 11.25 (three circles at center points 160,140 with radii of 100, 110, and 120).

Use LINE to draw two 100-unit-long lines at points 320,20 and 360,20 as shown in figure 11.25.

Turn off snap and ortho, and the ENDPoint and CENter running object snaps.

Command: *Choose* **S**ettings, P**o**int Style	Opens the Point Style dialog box (see Chapter 4, "Building a Drawing: Using Basic Drawing Tools")
`'_ddptype`	
Select the middle point style icon in the second row, then click on OK	Sets an easily visible point style and closes the dialog box

New Riders Publishing
INSIDE
SERIES

Command: Choose **C**onstruct, Mea**s**ure	Issues the MEASURE command
_measure	
Select object to measure: *Pick the line at* ① *(see fig. 11.25)*	Specifies the object to measure
<Segment length>/Block: **25** (Enter)	Specifies the distance between points and completes the command, placing points along the line (see fig. 11.26)
Command: (Enter)	Repeats the MEASURE command
MEASURE	
Select object to measure: *Pick the middle circle at* ② *(see fig. 11.26)*	Specifies the object to measure
<Segment length>/Block: **25** (Enter)	Specifies the distance between points and completes the command, placing points along the circle (see fig. 11.26)

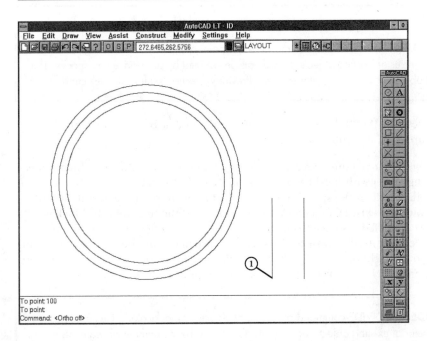

Figure 11.25

A circular gasket and two lines.

Figure 11.26

Points placed along a circle with MEASURE.

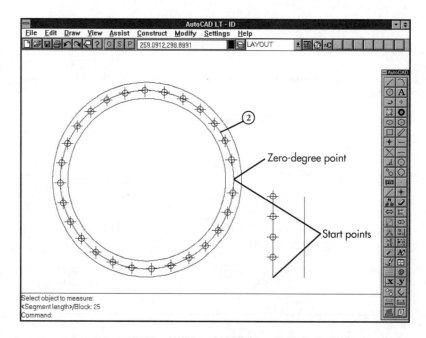

MEASURE. The MEASURE command places point objects or blocks along the length or perimeter of existing objects, at intervals determined by a distance you specify. The point objects or blocks are placed in the Previous selection set for later selection.

You can access MEASURE by typing the command name or by choosing **C**onstruct, then Mea**s**ure from the pull-down menu.

On open objects, such a lines, arcs, and open polylines (see Chapter 16, "Increasing Your Drawing Power with Polylines and Double Lines"), the first point or block is placed by MEASURE at the specified distance from the endpoint nearest the point you use to pick the existing object. On closed polylines, the first point or block is placed at the specified distance from the first vertex. On circles, the first point or block is placed counterclockwise at the specified distance from the zero-degree point (default is to the right of center). MEASURE places a point (or block) at the ending point of open and closed objects if the segment length is appropriate.

DIVIDE. The DIVIDE command places point objects or blocks along the length or perimeter of existing objects, at intervals determined by the number of segments you specify. The point objects or blocks are placed in the Previous selection set for later selection.

You can access DIVIDE by typing the command name, or choosing **C**onstruct, then Divid**e** from the pull-down menu.

On open objects, such a lines, arcs, and open polylines (see Chapter 16, "Increasing Your Drawing Power with Polylines and Double Lines"), the first point or block is placed by DIVIDE at the specified distance from the endpoint nearest the point you use to pick the existing object. On closed polylines or circles, the first point or block is placed at the first vertex or zero-degree point (default is to the right of center). DIVIDE does not place a point (or block) at the ending point of open or closed objects.

In the previous exercise, MEASURE left an undesirable gap at the start point, and a distance of 25 units came out uneven. DIVIDE is a better way if you need even spacing, but how many segments should you specify? Since MEASURE left a gap at the start point, one more segment than the number of points MEASURE placed would guarantee no less than 25 units between segments. You could count the points, then erase them and use DIVIDE, but it's easier to let AutoCAD LT's object selection count them for you, as shown in the following exercise.

Selecting and Counting Points Placed by MEASURE

Continue in the ID drawing from the previous exercise.

Command: **E** (Enter)	Issues the ERASE command
ERASE Select objects: **P** (Enter)	Selects the Previous selection set, the points that MEASURE created along the circle
27 found	Displays count of points inserted by MEASURE
Select objects: (Enter)	Erases the 27 points
Command: *Click on the Redraw tool or button*	Cleans up the image

---

You can use Previous to select the set of point objects or blocks placed in the Previous selection set by DIVIDE or MEASURE. You can use Previous to select the set of points anytime in the current drawing session until you use the U or UNDO command or an editing command that uses object selection. This enables you to use the points and NODe object snap points to place other geometry, and then later erase the point objects or blocks.

Tip   To simply count the points (or blocks) inserted by DIVIDE or MEASURE, use the SELECT command and Previous option.

Now that you know you need 28 points with DIVIDE, try using it on the gasket, and on the other line, in the following exercise.

Defining a Number of Segments with DIVIDE

Continue in the ID drawing from the previous exercise.

Command: *Choose* **C**onstruct, Divi**de**	Issues the DIVIDE command
_divide	
Select object to divide: *Pick the middle circle at* ① *(see fig. 11.27)*	Specifies the object to measure
<Number of segments>/Block: **28** (Enter)	Specifies the number of "segments" and completes the command, placing points along the circle between each "segment" (see fig. 11.27)
Command: (Enter)	Repeats the DIVIDE command
DIVIDE	
Select object to divide: *Pick the line at* ②	
<Number of segments>/Block: **5** (Enter)	Specifies the number of "segments" and completes the command, placing points along the line between each "segment"

DIVIDE placed points evenly around the circle, and because the number of segments was divisible by four, they also align nicely with the circle's quadrant points.

You continue to use object snap modes and tracking in many of the exercises throughout the exercises in the rest of this book. To produce drawings that accurately describe and depict your designs, the object snap modes (and the other tools presented in this chapter) are essential. If you use them as a matter of habit in all your work, you will find that the task of editing and refining your designs will be greatly facilitated.

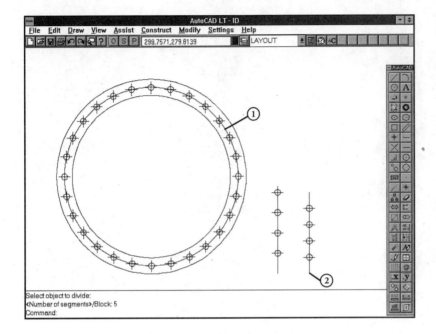

Figure 11.27

Points placed along a circle and a line with DIVIDE.

Now you have the necessary tools for creating accurate geometry and applying editing tools with precision. In the next chapter, you learn some techniques for deriving information from your drawings, including measuring and querying the objects you create.

C H A P T E R

12

Accessing Your Drawing's Data

AutoCAD LT provides tools for drawing objects accurately, but the graphic appearance of your drawing is only part of the value of a CAD drawing. Because you draw accurately in CAD, you can extract accurate information about the objects in your drawing. In this chapter, you examine some tools that enable you to obtain information about your design and about the objects that make up the design. From this chapter's discussion of these AutoCAD LT tools, you learn the following operations:

- ◆ Taking measurements with the DIST and AREA commands

- ◆ Measuring the area of objects with the AREA command

- ◆ Using the LIST command to query object data

- ◆ Using the DDMODIFY command to examine an object's data

- ◆ Using the DDMODIFY command to modify an object's geometric data

For a safe and smooth flight, a pilot depends on the accuracy of his data. The usability of CAD drawings for construction and manufacturing, and even the safety of the resulting structures and products, likewise depends on the accuracy of data. In the following sections you will see how to examine and modify that data.

Querying Your Drawing

Distances, angles, and other values critical to the design are often derived from the graphic development of the design itself. The paper-bound designer always had to be proficient at using scales and a protractor. AutoCAD LT replaces these interpretive tools with powerful functions for directly measuring and querying the elements of a drawing.

The next section discusses the DIST and AREA commands, which enable you to take measurements of objects and relationships in a drawing. Later, you explore the LIST command, which displays the information that makes up an object's definition.

Making Measurements

A major part of the design process involves trial-and-error refinements. You start with some given information and some restraints to work within, and you then develop design solutions. You spend time in a loop that consists of evaluating a design, determining any errors, modifying and refining the design to correct those errors and incorporate changes, and then evaluating the design again. At its most fundamental level, design evaluation is invariably a dimensional or spatial issue. You must be able to make measurements.

AutoCAD LT has two basic tools for measuring—the DIST and AREA commands. These commands measure distances, circumferences, lengths of lines, arcs and polylines, designated areas, and the areas contained within objects.

Finding Distances and Lengths with the DIST Command

The DIST command is straightforward—it measures distances. The design process presents numerous applications for the DIST command. You can use DIST to measure a line from endpoint to endpoint to find its length. You can use DIST to find the radius of an arc or a circle by measuring from the center to a point on the

circumference. You can use DIST with object snap modes to find the distance be-tween any two points critical to your design. The DIST command is more than a glorified tape measure, however, because it also returns two angle measurements (the angle in the XY plane and the angle from the XY plane toward the Z axis) as well as the X, Y, and Z offset components of the distance between the specified points.

In the following exercise, you use the DIST command to make measurements in a drawing like the one you created in the first section of this chapter. You change the current units style to see the effect of different units on the information that DIST displays. The ENDPoint and CENter running object snaps are turned on.

Measuring Distances and Lengths with the DIST Command

Create a new drawing named MEASURE, using the ALT1201.DWG file as a prototype and using no setup method.

Command: *Choose* **A***ssist,* **D***istance*	Issues the DIST command
`'_dist First point:` *Pick the left circle at* ① *(see fig. 12.1)*	Snaps to the center of the circle and displays a rubber-band reference line
`Second point:` *Pick the upper circle at* ②	Snaps to the center and displays the distance, angle, and offset information between the two center points

`Distance = 139.7542, Angle in XY Plane = 27, Angle from XY Plane = 0`
`Delta X = 125.0000, Delta Y = 62.5000, Delta Z = 0.0000`

Command: *Choose* **S***ettings,* **U***nits Style*	Opens the Units Control dialog box
In the Units *area, change the* **P***recision setting to* 0	Sets units to display integers with no decimals
In the Angles *area, change the* Precisio**n** *setting to* 0.00	Sets angles to display two decimals
Choose OK	Closes the Units Control dialog box and saves the settings
Command: `DIST` (Enter)	Issues the DIST command
`First point:` *Pick the left circle again at* ①	Snaps a rubber-band line to the center
`Second point:` *Pick the upper circle again at* ②	Snaps to the center and displays the information between the two center points

continues

12

continued

```
Distance = 140, Angle in XY Plane = 26.57, Angle from XY Plane = 0.00
Delta X = 125, Delta Y = 63, Delta Z = 0
```

Command: **DISTANCE** (Enter)	Issues the DISTANCE system variable prompt
DISTANCE = 140 (read only)	Reports the last measured distance
Command: *Click four times on the Undo button*	Undoes the measurements and restores the units precision to 0.0000
Command: **DISTANCE** (Enter)	Issues the DISTANCE system variable prompt
DISTANCE = 139.7542 (read only)	Still reports the last measured distance, but with the restored precision

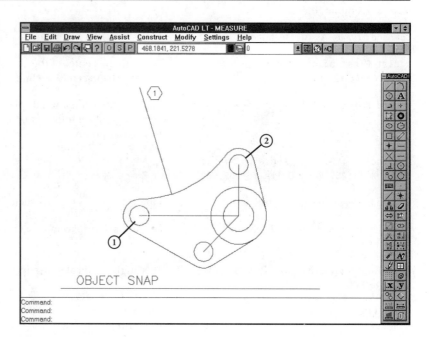

Figure 12.1

Obtaining design information with the DIST command.

Notice the differences between the information reported by the two measurements. In the first, distances show four decimal places of precision and angles are rounded off to integers. In the second, distances are rounded off to integers and the angles have two places of precision. The actual distances and angles haven't changed, only the measurement's displayed accuracy. The actual accuracy stored by AutoCAD LT is constant, unaffected by units and angle precision.

The DISTANCE system variable stores and reports the last measured distance in the current units. Notice that the DISTANCE value was not altered by undoing the settings or measurements.

The DIST command, like many of the other drawing and editing commands, displays a rubber-band cursor. The points used by DIST are affected by Snap, Ortho, and the object snap modes. The DIST command does not create anything (the points picked do not even affect the LASTPOINT variable); DIST simply returns the distance, angle, and offset information between the two points selected. The format of the DIST command's output depends on the current units and the precision settings.

> **DIST.** The DIST command calculates and displays the distance, angle, and X,Y,Z offsets between any two points that you specify.

The DIST command returns the following pieces of information:

◆ **Distance.** Distance denotes the distance between the two points displayed in the current units.

◆ **Angle in XY Plane.** Angle in XY Plane denotes the angle in the XY plane, specified according to the current 0-angle rotation direction and displayed according to the current units angle setting.

◆ **Angle from XY Plane.** Angle from XY Plane denotes the angle from the XY plane toward the Z axis, specified as a spherical coordinate would be and displayed according to the current units angle setting (0 in 2D drawings).

◆ **Delta X.** Delta X is the offset distance in the X axis between the two specified points displayed in the current units.

◆ **Delta Y.** Delta Y is the offset distance in the Y axis between the two specified points displayed in the current units.

◆ **Delta Z.** Delta Z is the offset distance in the Z axis between the two specified points displayed in the current units.

Object snap modes, particularly multiple modes, can sometimes trick you by snapping to the wrong point. You can use the rubber-band cursor to see where the first point is, but you need to be sure that the second point is what you intend. You can double-check the measurement by measuring again in the opposite direction. If you have blips on, they provide a visual reference of the point selected.

Heed Chapter 8's warning on the value of the units precision setting. Be sure that the precision display value is set to a level beyond what your design requires so that you can detect errors. This warning also applies to the precision display of angles.

12

Remember that angle precision defaults to integers; if you need to know the angle's value more precisely, you must change the precision setting in the Units Control dialog box.

The Delta X and Delta Y values are often helpful. In the preceding exercise, the actual distance between the left hole and the upper hole is less significant than are their distances from the large pivot hole. Because the centers of the holes form a right angle, with a single operation, the DIST command provides this information as the Delta X and Delta Y offset distances.

The DIST command is limited to measuring linear distances, offsets, and the angles between two points. DIST doesn't directly measure objects, although you can use it with object snaps to pick points on objects. The AREA command, on the other hand, doesn't measure linear distances, but it does measure areas, objects, and much more.

Measuring Areas with the AREA Command

As the name implies, you use the AREA command primarily to measure areas. AREA offers several options and two basic methods. The first method (the default) works in much the same way as the DIST command works. You specify points to define a perimeter and then press Enter, and AREA calculates and returns the area and perimeter in the current units. The second method works with circles and polyline objects (see Chapter 16, "Increasing Your Drawing Power with Polylines and Double Lines"). You can use this method to find the areas and perimeters of complex shapes with a single pick.

First, you examine the AREA command in the default point specification method. In the following exercise, you use a sample architectural drawing to practice making area measurements. A running INTersection object snap has been set in the proto-type drawing.

Measuring Areas with the AREA Command

Create a new drawing named AREA, using the ALT1202.DWG file as a prototype and using no setup method.

Command: *Choose **A**ssist, **A**rea*   Issues the AREA command

_area

<First point>/Entity/Add/Subtract: Snaps to the intersection in the bottom
Pick point ① *(see fig. 12.2)*   left column and starts the area definition

Note that the AREA command provides no rubber-band references, lines, or highlighting. Also, the points defining the perimeter must be selected in sequence, either clockwise or counterclockwise.

Next point: *Pick point* ②	Establishes a counterclockwise direction for the remaining points
Next point: *Pick point* ③	
Next point: *Pick point* ④	Defines the final point desired
Next point: *Click the Enter button*	Closes the area and displays the calculated results

```
Area = 45360.00 square in.
(315.0000 square ft.),
Perimeter = 71'-6"
```

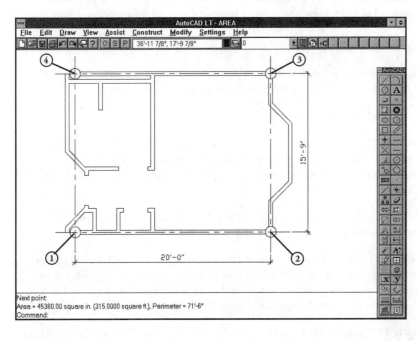

Figure 12.2

Using the AREA command to calculate the gross area of the hotel room.

In the default point specification method, AutoCAD LT calculates the area of the region within the boundary based on straight lines between the points specified. When you press Enter, the AREA command closes the first and last perimeter points. This method is best for simple areas that can be defined with a few straight lines or for situations in which the accuracy lost in approximating curves is unimportant.

In the preceding exercise, you saw that the AREA command defaults to prompting for points. In this mode, AREA simply continues to repeat the Next point: prompt with no indication given of the points picked and no rubber-band cursor such as the one produced with the WPolygon or CPolygon selection options. Consequently, you need to pay attention while you are picking points and pick the points in a sequential order that forms an enclosing outline. Blips help you to visualize the process (or at least to see where you have been). You press Enter to complete the point input. AREA then returns the calculated area and the total length of the perimeter you defined. AREA's report format is affected by the units and angles precision settings. The calculated area is given in two forms when in engineering or architectural units—square inches and square feet. Other units settings report the calculated area only in a single appropriate format.

> **AREA.** The AREA command calculates and displays the total of one or more areas and perimeter distances defined by a series of three or more points that you pick (the default method) or defined by one or more selected circles or polylines (the Entity option).

The area and perimeter are displayed in current units. If Architectural or Engineering units are current, both square inches and square feet are displayed.

The AREA command has the following options:

◆ **First point.** The First point option starts the point definition method. You select points outlining the perimeter in a clockwise or a counterclockwise sequence, and then you press Enter to complete the point input. This option is the default.

◆ **Entity.** The Entity option (covered in the following section) prompts for a circle or a polyline and reports the area and perimeter of the object selected.

◆ **Add.** The Add option changes the AREA command to its ADD mode, which continues to reissue the initial AREA prompt (without the Add option) after each region is defined or object is selected until you press Enter twice. Each individual area is reported and added to a running total.

◆ **Subtract.** The Subtract option changes the AREA command to its SUBTRACT mode. This mode functions like the ADD mode, but successive areas are subtracted from the total area.

In the following exercise, you use the AREA command to find the combined net floor area of the bedroom and hallway.

Adding Areas

Continue from the preceding exercise.

Command: **AREA** (Enter)	Starts the AREA command
<First point>/Entity/Add/Subtract: **A** (Enter)	Enters ADD mode and prompts for the first point
<First point>/Entity/Subtract: *Pick point* ⑤ *(see fig. 12.3)*	Starts defining the bedroom area
(ADD mode) Next point: *Pick points* ⑥, ⑦, ⑧, ⑨, ⑩, ⑪, ⑫, ⑬, *and* ⑭	Completes the bedroom perimeter (treating the round columns as chamfered corners)
(ADD mode) Next point: (Enter)	Closes, calculates, and displays the bedroom area

```
Area = 27910.21 square in.
(193.8209 square ft.),
Perimeter = 55'-3 3/8"
Total area = 27910.21 square in.
(193.8209 square ft.)
```

<First point>/Entity/Subtract: *Pick point* ⑮	Starts defining the hallway area
(ADD mode) Next point: *Pick points* ⑯, ⑰, ⑱, *and* ⑲	Completes the hallway perimeter (ignoring the wing wall)
(ADD mode) Next point: (Enter)	Closes and calculates the area of the hallway, adds it to the area of the bedroom, and displays the total area

```
Area = 9882.02 square in.
(68.6251 square ft.),
Perimeter = 32'-6"
Total area = 37792.23 square in.
(262.4460 square ft.)
```

<First point>/Entity/Subtract: *Click the Enter button*	Completes the AREA command

12

Figure 12.3

Finding a combined area using the Add option of the AREA command.

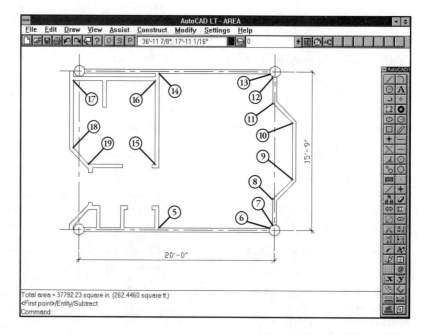

You can use the Add and Subtract options to sum up as many areas as you need. The Subtract option is used in the next section.

If you need to measure an area with a complex or curved outline accurately, or if you need to know the length of a curved or complex path, you should use the AREA command's Entity option.

 Note When adding or subtracting areas, you must specify the Add or Subtract option before picking points; otherwise, the AREA command will end after the first area is defined.

Using the AREA Command with Objects

If the AREA command only calculated the area of one or more regions bounded by points you pick, it would be a useful tool. When you add the capability to calculate the areas of objects (polylines in particular), the AREA command becomes an extremely powerful tool for design.

Polylines are single objects composed of one or more lines and arcs. Chapter 16, "Increasing Your Drawing Power with Polylines and Double Lines," covers polylines in detail. You do not need a deep understanding of polylines, however, to calculate their area. Because a polyline is a single object (even though you might view it as a collection of lines and arcs), you can select a polyline, and the AREA command does the work of calculating its area and perimeter.

The following exercise uses a copy of the drawing you created earlier in this chapter. The figure has been replicated at the right (see fig. 12.4). The original figure at the left consists entirely of individual line, arc, and circle objects, except for the line at bubble number 3 and the arc at bubble number 4, which are single-segment polyline objects. The perimeter of the figure at the right is a multi-segment polyline. The objects within this polyline are circles, which you subtract from the polyline in the following exercise.

Applying the AREA Command to Objects

Create a new drawing named AREA, using the ALT1203.DWG file as a prototype and using no setup method.

Command: **AA** (Enter)   Issues the AREA command

AREA

<First point>/Entity/Add/Subtract: Specifies the Entity option
E (Enter)

Select circle or polyline: *Pick the*   Displays the circle's area and circumference
circle at ① *(see fig. 12.4)*

Area = 3848.4510,
Circumference = 219.9115

Command: (Enter)   Repeats the AREA command

AREA

<First point>/Entity/Add/Subtract: Specifies the Entity option
E (Enter)

continues

12

continued

`Select circle or polyline:` *Pick the line at* ②	Displays an error message
`Entity selected is neither a circle nor a 2D/3D polyline`	

The AREA command accepts only circles or polylines, although a polyline may contain only a single line or an arc segment, as follows:

`Select circle or polyline:` *Pick the polyline at* ③	Displays the length (a single segment has no area)
`Area = 0.0000, Length = 136.2500`	
`Command:` (Enter)	Repeats the AREA command
`AREA`	
`<First point>/Entity/Add/Subtract:` **E** (Enter)	Specifies the Entity option
`Select circle or polyline:` *Pick the arc at* ④	Displays the length and area
`Area = 1181.5582, Length = 126.3440`	
`Command:` **PERIMETER** (Enter)	Issues the PERIMETER system variable prompt
`PERIMETER = 126.3440 (read only)`	Reports the last perimeter, length, or circumference
`Command:` **SETVAR** (Enter)	Issues the system variable prompt
`Variable name or ? <PERIMETER>:` **AREA** (Enter)	Issues the AREA system variable prompt
`AREA = 1181.5582 (read only)`	Reports the last area

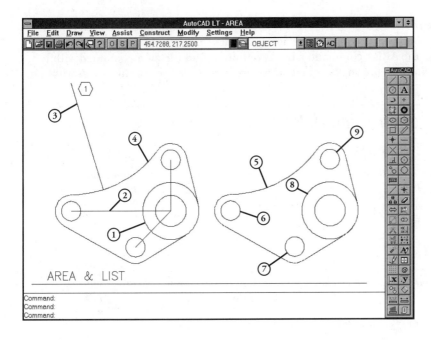

Figure 12.4

*Finding the area
of objects with the
AREA command.*

In the preceding exercise, you saw that using the AREA command with the Entity option is a one-shot process. The area value is returned immediately, and the command is ended. In addition, the AREA command's Entity option is selective about the objects it measures—only circles and 2D and 3D polylines are accepted. If you select other objects, you get the error message `Entity selected is neither a circle nor a 2D/3D polyline`. When the Entity option is applied to an open-ended polyline, it returns the total length of the open polyline and the area that would be contained if it were closed by a straight line between the open endpoints. In the case of a polyline arc, this area is calculated as if the arc were closed with a chord.

 Tip   AREA recognizes if a selected polyline object is not a closed region and reports a length instead of a perimeter. You can use this distinction as a mental flag to note when the AREA command has calculated the area based on the polyline being closed by an imaginary line between its endpoints.

 Tip   You can use the PERIMETER and AREA system variables at any time to redisplay the last perimeter (or length or circumference) or area. PERIMETER can be entered at the `Command:` prompt, but you must use the SETVAR command to access AREA because the system variable name conflicts with the AREA command name. You can access these transparently, from within other commands, by prefacing them with a single quotation mark (for example, **'PERIMETER** or **'SETVAR**).

12

The outline of the figure on the right is made up of one continuous, closed polyline, as you can demonstrate by picking it at the Command: prompt. In the following exercise, you use the AREA command's Entity option to find the area contained within this object, and you use the Subtract option to deduct the area of the circles within it.

Subtracting Holes from a Polyline's Area

Continue from the preceding exercise.

Command: *Pick the arc on the right at* ⑤ *(refer to figure 12.4)*

Highlights the entire outline, showing that it is a single polyline

Command: **AA** (Enter)

Deselects the polyline and issues the AREA command

AREA

<First point>/Entity/Add/Subtract:
A (Enter)

Enters ADD mode (note the following prompts)

<First point>/Entity/Subtract:
E (Enter)

Specifies the Entity option

(ADD mode) Select circle or
polyline: *Pick the polyline at* ⑤

Displays the polyline's area and perimeter, along with the current total area

Area = 14971.9163,
Perimeter = 503.0538
Total area = 14971.9163

(ADD mode) Select circle or
polyline: (Enter)

Exits ADD mode and returns to the previous option prompt

<First point>/Entity/Subtract:
S (Enter)

Enters SUBTRACT mode

<First point>/Entity/Add: **E** (Enter)

Specifies the Entity option

(SUBTRACT mode) Select circle or
polyline: *Pick the circle at* ⑥

Displays its area and circumference, and subtracts the area from the total

Area = 452.3893,
Circumference = 75.3982
Total area = 14519.5270

(SUBTRACT mode) Select circle or polyline: *Pick the circle at* ⑦	Displays its area and circumference, and subtracts the area from the total
Area = 452.3893, Circumference = 75.3982 Total area = 14067.1377	Reports data for the circle at ⑦
Continue with the circles at ⑧ *and* ⑨	
Area = 3848.4510, Circumference = 219.9115 Total area = 10218.6867	Reports data for the circle at ⑧
Area = 452.3893, Circumference = 75.3982 Total area = 9766.2973	Reports data for the circle at ⑨
(SUBTRACT mode) Select circle or polyline: (Enter)	Exits SUBTRACT mode
<First point>/Entity/Add: (Enter)	Completes the AREA command

Press F2 to review the results in the text window.

Using AREA's Entity option on a polyline is the only way to measure along a length other than a straight line. If you need to calculate the area of a complex shape with accuracy, you should consider creating a polyline outline of the complex shape. This technique is useful in facilities management, civil engineering, geographical work, or any task involving combinations of close tolerances, expensive materials, and complex shapes.

 Note   If you want to add or subtract object areas, you must specify the Add or Subtract option; otherwise, the AREA command will end after displaying the objects' area.

When you are in the AREA command's ADD or SUBTRACT mode, you can alternate between defining areas with points (the default method) and defining areas by picking objects (the Entity method). You can also alternate between the ADD and SUBTRACT modes. If you have a large, complicated area to calculate, take a moment to decide whether it might be faster to define the area in pieces (add), to start from an overall area and cut pieces out (subtract), or to add and subtract areas.

> **Tip**
>
> The BOUNDARY command, a new feature in AutoCAD LT Release 2, is particularly useful for finding irregular areas. The BOUNDARY command generates a closed polyline boundary within a closed area, requiring you to only pick a single point within the area. If the area has islands within it, BOUNDARY generates additional polyline boundaries for them. The objects enclosing the area might overlap and need not meet precisely. Recall the two areas in figure 12.2; they required carefully picking 14 points. Instead, you could draw two lines closing the doorways, use BOUNDARY to create two polylines, and then use AREA's Entity mode to find the areas. You can even use BOUNDARY to indirectly obtain areas of objects that the AREA command doesn't accept. See Chapter 16, "Increasing Your Drawing Power with Polylines and Double Lines," for the use of BOUNDARY.

As the previous exercises have demonstrated, you cannot always distinguish between polylines and individual line or arc objects. The last section of this chapter introduces a tool you can use to identify and examine all types of objects in your drawing—the LIST command.

Examining Objects with the LIST Command

The structure of an AutoCAD LT drawing file includes an object database in which each object is represented as a record of the data required to define it. The LIST command displays this data record in the text window. In the following exercise, you use the LIST command to examine several different types of objects.

Examining Objects with the LIST Command

Create a new drawing named AREA, again using the ALT1203.DWG file as a prototype and using no setup method; or continue working in the AREA drawing from the preceding exercise and press F2 to return to the drawing window.

Command: *Choose **A**ssist, **L**ist*   Issues the LIST command

`_list`

`Select objects:` *Pick the line at* ①
(see fig. 12.5)

`1 found`

```
Select objects: (Enter)          Ends selection, and lists the line's object data
                                 in the text window

      LINE      Layer: LAYOUT
                Space: Model space
  from point, X=  60.0000  Y= 100.0000  Z=   0.0000
    to point, X= 185.0000  Y= 100.0000  Z=   0.0000
Length = 125.0000,  Angle in XY Plane =     0
Delta X = 125.0000, Delta Y =   0.0000, Delta Z =   0.0000

Command: LIST (Enter)            Starts the LIST command and returns to the
                                 drawing window

Select objects: Pick the arc at (2)

1 found

Select objects: (Enter)          Lists the arc's data

      ARC       Layer: OBJECT
                Space: Model space
center point, X=  60.0000  Y= 100.0000  Z=   0.0000
radius   20.0000
 start angle      90
   end angle     241

Command: LS (Enter)              Issues the LIST command

LIST

Select objects: Pick the circle at (3)

1 found

Select objects: (Enter)          Lists the circle's data

        CIRCLE    Layer: OBJECT
                  Space: Model space
     center point, X= 185.0000  Y= 100.0000  Z=   0.0000
     radius   35.0000
circumference  219.9115
         area 3848.4510

Command: Pick the text at (4), and press Enter    Repeats the LIST command with the text
                                                  selected
```

continues

12

continued

```
        TEXT        Layer: NOTES
                    Space: Model space
    Style = NOTES    Font file = ROMANS.SHX
    start point, X=  29.5714  Y=  15.6944  Z=   0.0000
    height   10.0000
      text AREA & LIST
 rotation angle      0
    width scale factor    1.0000
obliquing angle      0
generation normal
```

Figure 12.5

A drawing containing a variety of types of objects to examine.

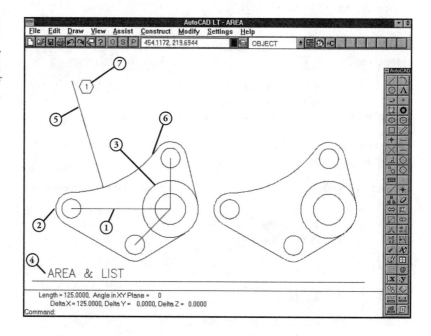

The LIST command supports all the object selection options. As with most editing commands, selected objects are highlighted. Pressing Enter completes the selection set and changes to the text window in which the data record is displayed. If you use noun/verb selection, LIST displays the data in the text window as soon as you issue the command. The data displayed vary with the type of object selected.

If you select more than one object, or if you select a complex object such as a multi-segment polyline, the listing pauses with a `Press RETURN to continue:` prompt; otherwise, all the data might not fit in the text window. If you want to see previously displayed data, or if your text window is sized too small to view all the data, you can resize the window or use the scroll bars to view more data.

> **LIST.** The LIST command prompts for a selection set, changes to the text window, and lists the object data for each selected object.

The LIST command reveals a wealth of information, including the following:

◆ Type of object, such as: line or polyline? block or xref?

◆ The layer on which the object resides

◆ The object's color and linetype definition (if any)

◆ Most of the information included in the DIST and AREA commands

◆ The coordinates of any defining points and the radius of arcs and circles

You can use the LIST command when you are uncertain of an object's type. As an example, a polyline line and an arc appear the same as a normal line and an arc. Likewise, an object usually looks the same whether it is included in a block object or not.

In the preceding exercise, you listed a line, an arc, and a text object. In the following exercise, you list two types of complex objects: polylines and block references. Complex objects contain subentities, whose data are similar to the simple objects in the preceding exercise.

Listing Complex Objects

Continue from the preceding exercise.

Command: *Pick the polyline at* ⑤   Repeats the LIST command with the polyline
(see fig. 12.5), then press Enter   selected

LIST first lists the polyline's global properties and then the data for each vertex (endpoint) subentities. (Polylines are covered in Chapter 16, "Increasing Your Drawing Power with Polylines and Double Lines.")

```
            POLYLINE  Layer: NOTES
                      Space: Model space
          Open
starting width    0.0000
  ending width    0.0000

            VERTEX    Layer: NOTES
```

continues

12

continued

```
                     Space: Model space
        at point, X= 100.7324  Y= 126.2310  Z=   0.0000
starting width    0.0000
  ending width    0.0000

          VERTEX    Layer: NOTES
                     Space: Model space
        at point, X=  60.0000  Y= 256.2500  Z=   0.0000
starting width    0.0000
  ending width    0.0000

       END SEQUENCE  Layer: NOTES
                     Space: Model space
     area    0.0000
   length  136.2500

Press RETURN to continue: (Enter)
```

Command: *Pick the polyline arc at* ⑥, *then press Enter*

Repeats the LIST command with the polyline arc selected (compare it to the previous arc)

```
        POLYLINE  Layer: OBJECT
                     Space: Model space
        Open
starting width    0.0000
  ending width    0.0000

          VERTEX    Layer: OBJECT
                     Space: Model space
        at point, X=  60.0000  Y= 120.0000  Z=   0.0000
starting width    0.0000
  ending width    0.0000
        bulge    0.2361
       center X=  60.0000  Y= 256.2500  Z=   0.0000
       radius  136.2500
   start angle    270
     end angle    323

          VERTEX    Layer: OBJECT
                     Space: Model space
        at point, X= 169.0000  Y= 174.5000  Z=   0.0000
starting width    0.0000
  ending width    0.0000

Press RETURN to continue: (Enter)

        bulge    0.2361
```

```
        END SEQUENCE  Layer: OBJECT
                    Space: Model space
        area 1181.5582
     length   126.3440
```

Command: *Pick the hexagon at* ⑦, *then click the Enter button*	Repeats the LIST command with the hexagon selected

The hexagon is a block reference (insert) object. Blocks are covered in Chapter 19, "Managing and Modifying Blocks and Xrefs."

```
        BLOCK REFERENCE  Layer: NOTES
                    Space: Model space
        KEYNOTE
        at point, X=  64.6031  Y= 241.5569  Z=   0.0000
        X scale factor    50.0000
        Y scale factor    50.0000
  rotation angle       0
        Z scale factor    50.0000

        ATTRIBUTE  Layer: 0
                    Space: Model space
    Style = NOTES    Font file = ROMANS.SHX
      mid point, X=  78.6656  Y= 249.6759  Z=   0.0000
   height     6.2500
   value 1
      tag ITEMNO
  rotation angle       0
   width scale factor    1.0000
 obliquing angle       0
   flags normal
generation normal

Press RETURN to continue: (Enter)

        END SEQUENCE  Layer: NOTES
                    Space: Model space
```

The text inside the hexagon is an attribute. *Attributes* are block subentities that store text information as a value for the attribute *tag* (name). Note the value and tag information in the attribute data list.

When you apply the LIST command to a polyline, the location of each vertex is listed. As with the DIST command, this information includes the X, Y, and Z offsets of the line's endpoints. This information is sometimes helpful, such as when you are working with the rise and run of stairs or with the pitch of a roof.

12

LIST is the only means available in AutoCAD LT Release 1 to examine some object information. For example, LIST gives the start and end angles of an arc, LIST reveals the style with which text was created, and LIST shows the names of blocks and attribute tags. Many other examples could be cited, but you only need to remember to use the LIST command when nothing else you have tried has told you what you want to know.

In AutoCAD LT Release 2, you have another means of examining and modifying the drawing data of objects: DDMODIFY. If you are using AutoCAD LT Release 1, skip the rest of this chapter.

Examining and Modifying Objects with DDMODIFY

ALT2

In AutoCAD LT Release 2, the DDMODIFY command opens a Modify *object_type* dialog box tailored to the selected object type. Figure 12.6 shows a Modify Line dialog box. The Modify *object_type* dialog boxes display the same data as the LIST command. In addition, Modify *object_type* dialog boxes enable you to change the selected object's geometric data and properties. This section shows the use of the Modify *object_type* dialog box for displaying object data, and for modifying geometric data. The next chapter covers the use of the Modify *object_type* dialog box for changing object properties.

Figure 12.6

A Modify Line dialog box.

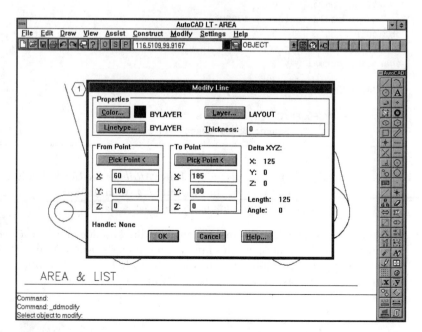

In the following exercises, you use the same objects as in the previous LIST exercises, but you examine and alter them with Modify *object_type* dialog boxes.

Examining a Line with a Modify Line Dialog Box

Continue working in the AREA drawing from the preceding exercise, or create a new drawing using the ALT1203.DWG file as a prototype and using no setup method.

Command: *Choose **M**odify, Modi**f**y Entity*   Issues the DDMODIFY command and prompts for selection

Select object to modify: *Pick the line*   Selects the line and opens the Modify Line
at ① (see fig. 12.7)   dialog box (see fig. 12.6)

Leave the dialog box open for the next exercise.

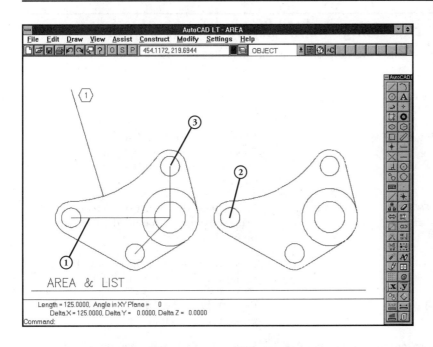

Figure 12.7

A variety of object types to examine and modify.

DDMODIFY. The DDMODIFY command prompts for selection and opens a Modify *object_type* dialog box, such as a Modify Circle dialog box if a circle is selected. Selection must be by picking a single object. The contents of the dialog box vary with the selected object type. Modify *object_type* dialog boxes enable you to view and change the selected object's geometric data and properties.

12

You can access the Modify *object_type* dialog box by entering DDMODIFY or by choosing **M**odify, then Modi**f**y Object from the pull-down menu.

The top part of a Modify *object_type* dialog box displays the object's properties (see the next chapter). The lower part displays the object's geometric data and provides buttons and edit boxes that you use to modify the data. The Modify Line dialog box in figure 12.6, for example, displays the lines defining geometric data (the X, Y, and Z coordinates) in its From Point and To Point boxes. You can edit the coordinates in the **X**, **Y**, and **Z** edit boxes, or use the **P**ick Point and Pic**k** Point buttons to temporarily close the dialog box and pick new points. Derived data, such as the X, Y, and Z length components (Delta XYZ) and the overall Length and Angle are displayed at the right, but cannot be directly modified.

Use the Modify *object_type* dialog box to examine and modify additional objects in the following exercise.

Examining and Modifying Various Objects

Continue working in the AREA drawing from the preceding exercise, with the Modify Line dialog box open.

Double-click in the To Point **X** *box and* *enter* **260**	Changes 185 to 260
Choose **P**ick Point *in the* From Point *area*	Closes the dialog box, displays a rubberband line and prompts for a point; notice the other end has moved to 260,100 (②in figures 12.7 and 12.8)
From pt: *Use ENDPoint object snap to* *pick the line at* ③	Moves the endpoint to ③ and reopens the dialog box; notice that the derived data has updated
Choose OK	Closes the dialog box and accepts the changes, as shown in figure 12.8
Command: **Enter**	Repeats the DDMODIFY command and prompts for selection
_DDMODIFY Select object to modify: *Pick* *the circle at* ④ *(see fig. 12.8)*	Selects the circle and opens the Modify Circle dialog box (see fig. 12.9)
Double-click in the **R**adius *box, type* **25**, *and* *choose* OK	Closes the dialog box and accepts the change, enlarging the circle

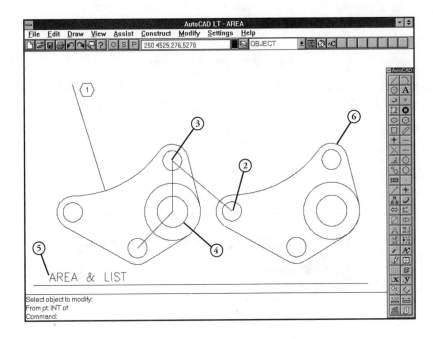

Figure 12.8

The modified line.

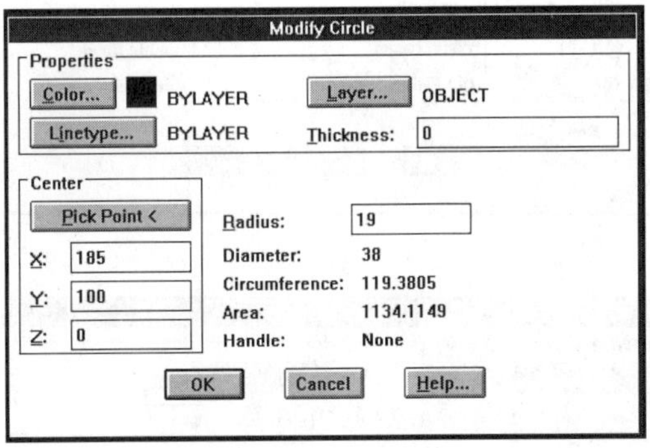

Figure 12.9

The Modify Circle dialog box.

Command: *Choose* **M**odify, Modif**y** Entity	Issues the DDMODIFY command and prompts for selection
Select object to modify: *Pick the text at* ⑤	Selects the text and opens the Modify Text dialog box (see fig. 12.10) with the text in the T**e**xt edit box highlighted
Type **DDMODIFY** *then double-click on* 10 *in the* **H**eig**h**t *edit box and type* **12**	Replaces text, highlights and replaces existing height
Choose OK	Closes the dialog box and accepts the changes

continues

12

continued

Command: **(Enter)**	Repeats the DDMODIFY command and prompts for selection
_DDMODIFY Select object to modify: *Pick the polyline at* ⑥ *(refer to figure 12.8)*	Selects the polyline and opens the Modify Polyline dialog box (see fig. 12.11)
Click several times on the **N**ext *button*	Changes to list the data for each successive vertex (see Chapter 16, "Increasing Your Drawing Power with Polylines and Double Lines")
Choose Cancel	Closes dialog box without making changes

Figure 12.10

The Modify Text dialog box, after changes.

Figure 12.11

The Modify Polyline dialog box.

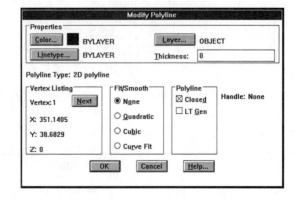

You can view and modify any kind of data for any kind of object. In the next chapter, you examine the tools for controlling, viewing, and modifying the properties and appearance of objects.

Using Object Properties and Text Styles

Manual drafting offers a variety of ways to depict different types of information and to identify different elements in your drawing. One method of differentiating information is with line weights. You usually implement this method by using drafting pens of varying widths or pencils with lead of varying degrees of hardness. Additionally, different types of lines, such as dashed lines, typically represent different types of information. The lines showing a building's structural grid, for example, are entirely different from those showing the foundation footings. You also can use different fonts for the text that appears in your drawing; general notes might appear in one font and titles in another.

In an AutoCAD LT drawing, by contrast, you depict different types of information and identify different drawing elements by using object properties, also called entity properties. When the drawing is plotted, the object properties are drawn to appear exactly like their manual-drafting counterparts.

In this chapter, you learn how to perform the following operations:

◆ Presetting object properties with the DDEMODES command

◆ Changing the properties of existing objects with the DDCHPROP command

◆ Setting the proper linetype generation for polyline objects

◆ Making different linetypes available to your drawings by using the LINETYPE command

◆ Viewing and changing an object's properties with the Modify *<Object_type>* dialog box (DDMODIFY command)

◆ Making different fonts and text styles available to your drawings by using the STYLE command and the Select Text Font dialog box

◆ Viewing and changing a text object's style with the Modify Text dialog box (DDMODIFY command)

Object properties affect the way an object appears in AutoCAD LT and on the plotted output (see fig. 13.1). By learning how to control object properties, you can make your drawings more informative and clear to the viewer.

When you construct your first drawings in AutoCAD LT, you use default settings to create the objects. Initially, all objects are placed on layer 0, with a color of white (the color white displays white when the drawing editor background is black, and black when the background is white) and a linetype of CONTINUOUS. The color, linetype, and layer characteristics of an object are called *object or entity properties*. All objects in AutoCAD LT have color, linetype, and layer properties.

Figure 13.1

The floor plan with new titles, linetypes, and colors.

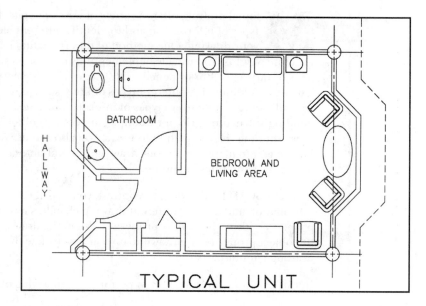

In Chapter 10, you learned to create new layers, make layers current, and change the layer properties that affect the appearance of objects. This chapter shows you how to control the appearance of objects by setting and changing object properties. This chapter also shows you how to use and change text styles.

Understanding Object Properties

Object properties control how objects in your drawing are displayed in the drawing area and plotted on paper. Each object in a drawing has up to four different properties—color, linetype, layer, and thickness. The thickness property controls the extrusion distance of an object for creating 3D drawings and is discussed in Chapter 24, "Moving Beyond the Basics."

Before AutoCAD LT displays or plots an object, it reads the object's properties (along with other object data) to determine what the appearance of the object should be. The appearance of an object is controlled by its linetype and color properties. By default, an object's linetype and color properties reference (are derived from) the color and linetype settings of its layer. However, an object's linetype and color properties can also be set *explicitly*, which means that they are independent of the layer settings.

When an object references its layer for linetype or color information, AutoCAD LT looks at the object's layer property to get the object's layer name. Then AutoCAD LT looks at the settings of the object's layer to determine how to draw the object.

When an object is created, AutoCAD LT stores the current layer name, the current object linetype, and the current object color as the object's properties. Although you may not have been aware of it, you learned to set the current layer object property for new objects in Chapter 10, "Getting Organized: Drawing on Layers." You can set the current linetype and color properties for new objects as well. You can even change an object's properties after it has been created.

Object Properties and Layer Settings

In general, you should manage the linetype and color of objects by using layer settings rather than by using explicit linetype and color object properties. It is easier to make changes to the linetype and color of objects by using layer settings. If you use layers to organize objects, you can quickly modify the appearance of those objects by using the Layer Control dialog box. With little effort, you can change the color or linetype of any layer you select—and all objects on that layer with properties defined by layer—all at once.

In contrast, if you explicitly set the properties of objects and you decide that the linetype or color of the objects needs to be modified, you must select the objects to change. This can be difficult if there are many objects to be modified mixed with many objects on the same layer that do not need to be modified. However, if it is useful to have a few objects with explicit object properties sharing the same layer as objects with different object properties, explicit object properties are an option.

Setting Object Properties

You use the Entity Creation Modes dialog box to set the current new object properties. To access the Entity Creation Modes dialog box, you choose **S**ettings, then **E**ntity Modes, or you can click on the Current Color button. You also can access the Entity Creation Modes dialog box by entering the DDEMODES command. Figure 13.2 shows the Current Color button and Entity Creation Modes dialog box in AutoCAD LT Release 2. In AutoCAD LT Release 1, the Current Color button is at the far left side of the toolbar.

Figure 13.2

The Entity Creation Modes dialog box.

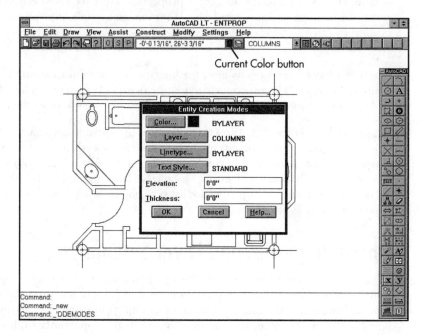

> **DDEMODES.** The DDEMODES command displays the Entity Creation Modes dialog box, which is used to control the properties of new objects. These properties include color, layer, linetype, and thickness. The property settings in the Entity Creation Modes dialog box affect the creation of all new objects. The Entity Creation Modes dialog box also enables you to set the elevation and the current text style.

13

Setting the Current New Object Color

Object color in AutoCAD LT serves two purposes. The primary purpose for the use of color in AutoCAD LT is to control the line weight of plotted objects. When the drawing is plotted, line weight is assigned according to the colors used for the objects. Chapter 23, "Producing Hard Copy," provides information about plotting your drawings. The second purpose for color is to provide a visual cue to distinguish groups of objects. Colors can be used to indicate line weight, layer, plotter linetype, or any other category of object.

In this chapter's first exercise, you start to draw column center lines. You create the column center lines on the COLUMNS layer because they relate to column information. However, the column center lines need to be a different line weight and linetype than the columns themselves.

The exercise shows you how to set the current new object color. In the exercise, you set the current new object color using the Select Color dialog box (see fig. 13.3), accessed from the Entity Creation Modes dialog box.

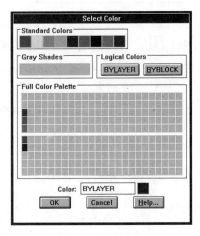

Figure 13.3

The Select Color dialog box.

Center marks for the columns have already been added for you in the exercise's prototype drawing. (You learn how to add center marks in Chapter 20, "Applying Dimensions in CAD.") Figure 13.4 shows what your drawing should look like after you have added two of the four center lines. The first line is drawn in the color of the current layer, and the second line is drawn in the color you set using the Entity Creation Modes dialog box.

Figure 13.4

The ENTPROP drawing with two horizontal column center lines added.

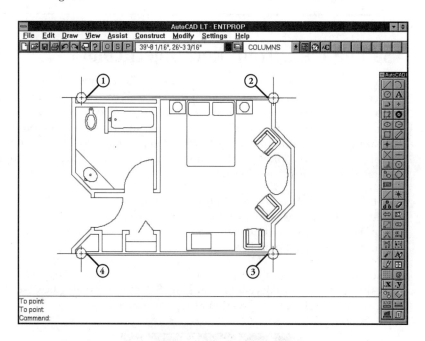

Setting the New Object Color Explicitly

Create a new drawing named ENTPROP, using ALT1301.DWG as a prototype and with no setup method, and zoom to the view shown in figure 13.4.

Command: *Click on the Object Snap tool and set an* **E**ndpoint *running object snap*	Sets object snap to ENDPoint
Command: *Click on the Line tool*	Issues the LINE command
_LINE From point: *Pick point* ① *(see fig. 13.4)*	Specifies the starting point for the first column center line
To point: *Pick point* ②	Specifies the endpoint for the column center line
To point: (**Enter**)	Ends the LINE command

Command: *Click on the Current Color button on the toolbar*	Opens the Entity Creation Modes dialog box
Click on the **C**olor *button in the Entity Creation Modes dialog box*	Opens the Select Color dialog box
Choose the sixth color, magenta, from the Standard Colors *box, then click on* OK *twice*	Selects the color to use and closes the Select Color dialog box
Command: *Click on the Line tool*	Starts the LINE command
LINE From point: *Pick point* ③	Specifies the starting point for the second column center line
To point: *Pick point* ④	Specifies the endpoint for the second column center line
To point: (Enter)	Ends the LINE command
Command: *Choose the Save button*	Saves the current drawing to disk

The current new object color determines the value of the color object property for all new objects. When you click on the **C**olor button in the Entity Creation Modes dialog box, the Select Color dialog box opens (refer back to fig. 13.3). This dialog box has color chips for all 255 colors that AutoCAD LT supports. When you choose one of the color chips, either the color name or the color number appears in the Color edit box.

AutoCAD LT provides names for the first seven standard colors; these colors are displayed in the Standard Colors group and have the names red, yellow, green, cyan, blue, magenta, and white. Colors 8 and 9, which also appear in the Standard Colors group, have no associated names. All other colors are referenced by number. The Gray Shades group shows colors 250 to 255, and the Full Color Palette box displays colors 10 to 249. The colors in the upper portion of the Full Color Palette group are all even numbers, and the colors in the lower portion of the box are all odd numbers.

The BY**L**AYER and **B**YBLOCK buttons in the Logical Colors group in the Select Color dialog box enable you to specify two additional new object color property settings—BYLAYER and BYBLOCK. The BYLAYER object color property setting causes an object to display using the color of the object's layer. BYLAYER is the default color for new objects. The BYBLOCK object color property setting affects the color of objects inserted as a block. BYBLOCK causes an object inserted as a block to display in the color of the object into which the block is inserted. Chapter 18, "Leveraging Repetitive Design and Drafting," provides more information on creating and using blocks.

In the preceding exercise, the first line was drawn with the default BYLAYER object creation settings. The second line was drawn with the new object color set to MAGENTA and the default BYLAYER linetype. In later exercises, you change the properties of these objects so that they are the same color and have a center linetype.

Setting the Current New Object Linetype

The various linetypes in manual drafting (Hidden, Center, Phantom, and so on) are also used in AutoCAD LT. Different types of lines provide visual cues that enable the viewer to quickly identify the meaning of the line. In Chapter 10, "Getting Organized: Drawing on Layers," you learned how to set the layer linetype that controlled the appearance of all objects on that layer. However, like object color, an object's linetype can be controlled independently of the object's layer.

When you click on the Linetype button in the Entity Creation Modes dialog box, the Select Linetype dialog box opens (see fig. 13.5). This dialog box controls the current linetype of new objects. Loaded linetype names appear alphabetically in the Select Linetype dialog box. To choose a linetype, you can select it from the list by clicking on its pattern, or you can enter its name in the Linetype edit box. If many linetypes are available in the current drawing, you might need to scroll the list or use the Next and Previous buttons to view more of the linetype list.

Figure 13.5

The Select Linetype dialog box.

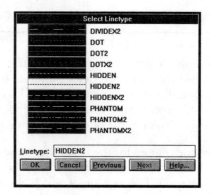

In the following exercise, you use hidden and center linetypes to add vertical center lines to the columns (later, you change the hidden linetype to a center linetype). The hidden line initially appears continuous or with a very fine pattern until you set the linetype scale appropriately for the drawing.

Setting the New Object Linetype Explicitly

Continue working in the ENTPROP drawing from the preceding exercise.

Command: *Choose* Settings,
Linetype Style, Load

Issues the LINETYPE command
with the Load option

Linetype(s) to load: * (Enter)

Specifies all available linetypes

Choose the ACLT.LIN *file from the Select Linetype File dialog box*	Closes the dialog box and loads all linetypes defined in the file
`?/Create/Load/Set:` **S** (Enter)	Specifies the Set option to set a current linetype
`New entity linetype (or ?)` `<CONTINUOUS>:` **HIDDEN2** (Enter)	Specifies the HIDDEN2 linetype for subsequently created objects
`?/Create/Load/Set:` (Enter)	Ends the LINETYPE command
`Command:` *Click on the Line tool*	Starts the LINE command for the horizontal column lines
`From point:` *Pick point* ① *(see fig. 13.6)*	Specifies the starting point for the third column center line
`To point:` *Pick point* ②	Specifies the endpoint for the third column center line
`To point:` (Enter)	Ends the LINE command

The line appears continuous or very fine. You need to set the linetype scale.

`Command:` *Choose* **S**ettings, Li**n**etype Style, Lin**e**type Scale	Issues the LTSCALE command
`'_ltscale` `New scale factor <1.0000>:` **24** (Enter)	Sets the linetype scale to 24 (half of the drawing scale factor of 48)
`Regenerating drawing.`	Regenerates and displays the hidden line as shown in figure 13.6
`Command:` *Click on the Current Color button*	Opens the Entity Creation Modes dialog box, which shows HIDDEN2 as the current linetype
Click on the Li*netype button in the Entity Creation Modes dialog box*	Opens the Select Linetype dialog box

The linetypes that were loaded by the LINETYPE command are displayed in the Select Linetype dialog box, as shown in figure 13.5.

Choose the CENTER2 *linetype from the list, then click on* OK	Selects the linetype for new objects and closes the Select Linetype dialog box
Click on OK *in the Entity Creation Modes dialog box*	Closes the Entity Creation Modes dialog box

continues

continued

Command: *Click on the Line tool*	Issues the LINE command for the final horizontal column center line
LINE From point: *Pick point* ③	Specifies the starting point for the fourth column center line
To point: *Pick point* ④	Specifies the endpoint for the fourth column center line
To point: (Enter)	Ends the LINE command
Command: *Choose the Save button*	Saves the current drawing to disk

Figure 13.6 shows the resulting drawing with all the column lines.

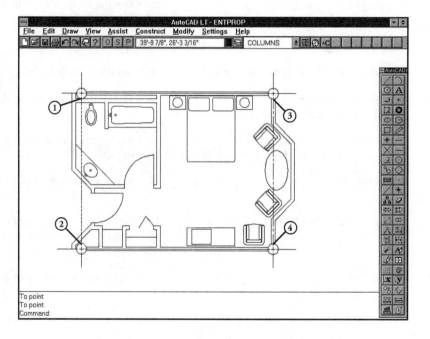

Figure 13.6

The ENTPROP drawing with all the floor plan column lines.

You set the linetype scale for the final plotted appearance of the drawing, not the on-screen appearance. For architectural work using the *NAME*2 linetypes such as HIDDEN2 and CENTER2, a linetype scale from half of to the full drawing scale factor works well. With the *NAME* linetypes such as HIDDEN and CENTER, a linetype scale of from one-fourth to half of the drawing scale factor works well. The ENTPROP drawing is meant to be plotted at 1/4"=1'-0" (1/48 scale) on an 8 1/2"×11" sheet, so its

drawing scale factor is 48. See Chapter 8, "Preparing Your Workspace: CAD Concepts 1B," for more on linetypes, scale, and drawing setup.

Initially, three linetypes are available for use by new objects. These linetypes are CONTINUOUS, BYLAYER, and BYBLOCK. BYLAYER is the default linetype setting for new objects. As with the color property, the BYLAYER setting determines whether new objects follow the object property settings defined by the layer on which the object is placed. The BYBLOCK setting causes objects within a block to reflect the settings of the object into which the block is inserted.

Loading New Linetypes

When you begin a new drawing, only one style of line is available—a continuous, solid line. To add more linetype definitions to your drawing, you use the Load option of the LINETYPE command. Linetype definitions are loaded from an external file. AutoCAD LT has two default linetype definition files. ACLT.LIN provides the AutoCAD standard default line patterns, and ACLT.ISO provides line patterns of the International Standards Organization and scales for metric work. You learned how to load linetypes in Chapter 10, "Getting Organized: Drawing on Layers."

If you use the LAYER and CHANGE commands to modify layer settings or object properties, the linetypes are automatically loaded when they are entered in response to each command's prompts.

Occasionally, you might have more linetypes loaded than you use in the drawing. The more linetypes you use in a drawing, the longer it takes the Select Linetype dialog box to open, the longer it takes to locate a linetype in the dialog box, and the drawing file size becomes slightly larger. To eliminate unused linetypes, use the PURGE command (discussed in Chapter 10, "Getting Organized: Drawing on Layers"). The PURGE command eliminates unused layers, linetypes, blocks, dimension styles, text styles, and shapes from the drawing.

Controlling the Linetypes of Polylines

As you learn in Chapter 16, "Increasing Your Drawing Power with Polylines and Double Lines," a polyline is a single complex object, which is made from multiple straight and curved segments. Because of these multiple and different segments, the patterns of dashes, dots, and spaces of some linetypes make it difficult to apply linetypes to a polyline object properly. By default, linetype patterns are shown as if each segment of a polyline were a separate object. If a linetype pattern sequence is longer than a polyline segment, the segment appears solid. When you apply a linetype to a polyline that is made up of short and long segments as well as curves, the end product is sometimes strange (see fig. 13.7). The effect is most visible on spline-fit polylines. In AutoCAD LT, linetype patterns can be drawn continuously over the length of a polyline, thus eliminating the restarting of the linetype pattern at each segment.

Linetype generation for new polyline objects is controlled by the PLINEGEN system variable. Linetype generation for existing polylines is controlled by the PEDIT command (discussed in detail in Chapter 16, "Increasing Your Drawing Power with Polylines and Double Lines"). When polyline generation is turned off, the linetype pattern is restarted at each polyline segment. If polyline generation is turned on, the linetype pattern is generated continuously from one end of the polyline to the other. The multi-segmented polyline is drawn correctly at the first example at the top of figure 13.7, with polyline generation off, and incorrectly in the second example, with polyline generation turned on (notice the corners of the polyline). However, the spline-fit polyline in the third example is rendered incorrectly with polyline generation off because the spline is represented by small arc segments that are shorter than the linetype pattern length. The polyline is rendered correctly in the fourth example with polyline generation turned on.

Figure 13.7

The effects of linetype generation on several polylines.

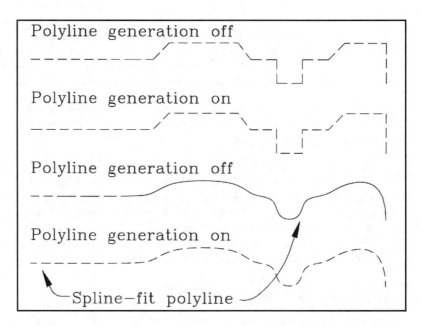

In the following exercise, you add a polyline that represents the edge of a roof to the architectural floor plan. First you draw the polyline with polyline generation on (see fig. 13.8), and then you turn off polyline generation to see its effect on the polyline.

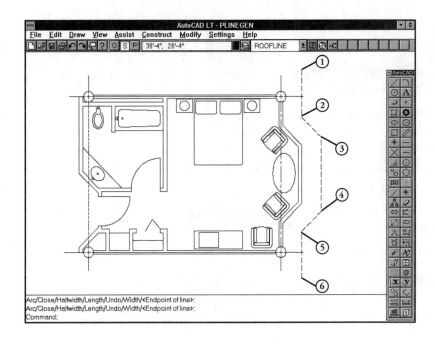

Figure 13.8

*The roof line
with polyline
generation
turned on.*

13

Controlling Polyline Linetype Generation

Continue working with the ENTPROP drawing from the preceding exercise, or create a new
drawing named PLINEGEN using ALT1302.DWG as a prototype and using no setup method.

Command: *Click on the* Layers button, *then set
the ROOFLINE layer current and set the
ROOFLINE linetype to DASHED*

Command: *Turn off the ENDPoint running
object snap*

Command: *Click on the Current Color
button and set the color and linetype
object creation modes to* BYLAYER

Command: **PLINEGEN** (Enter)   Issues the PLINEGEN system variable prompt

New value for PLINEGEN <0>: **1** (Enter)   Turns on polyline generation (0=off, 1=on)

Command: *Click on the Polyline tool*   Issues the PLINE command

_PLINE

continues

continued

`From point:` *Pick point* ① *(see fig. 13.8)*	Specifies the starting point of the roof line
`Arc/Close/Halfwidth/Length/Undo/Width/` `<Endpoint of line>:` *Pick point* ②	Specifies the next point of the roof line
`Arc/Close/Halfwidth/Length/Undo/Width/` `<Endpoint of line>:` *Pick points* ③, ④, ⑤, *and* ⑥	
`Arc/Close/Halfwidth/Length/Undo/Width/` `<Endpoint of line>:` (Enter)	Ends the PLINE command

The roofline is rendered incorrectly with polyline generation turned on (see fig 13.8)—there are unwanted gaps at the corner segments of the polyline.

Next, you turn off polyline generation of the existing polyline to render the roofline correctly.

`Command:` *Choose* **M**odify, Edit Pol**y**line	Issues the PEDIT command
`Select polyline:` *Click on the polyline*	Selects the polyline that was created
`Close/Join/Width/Edit vertex/Fit/` `Spline/Decurve/Ltype gen/Undo/` `eXit <X>:` **L** (Enter)	Modifies the polyline's linetype generation setting
`Full PLINE linetype ON/OFF <On>:` **OFF** (Enter)	Turns off polyline generation setting and restarts the pattern at each vertex
`Close/Join/Width/Edit vertex/Fit/` `Spline/Decurve/Ltype gen/Undo/` `eXit <X>:` (Enter)	Exits the PEDIT command
`Command:` **PLINEGEN** (Enter)	Issues the PLINEGEN system variable prompt
`New value for PLINEGEN <1>:` **0** (Enter)	Turns off polyline generation
`Command:` **SAVE** (Enter)	Saves the drawing

Figure 13.9 shows the correct dashed roof line for the architectural plan.

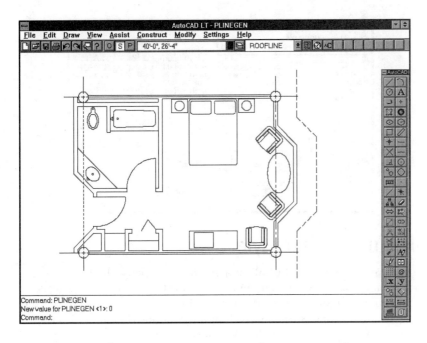

Figure 13.9

*The roof line
with polyline
generation
turned off.*

13

Setting the Current Layer for New Objects

Because Chapter 10, "Getting Organized: Drawing on Layers," covers layers thoroughly, this chapter does not go into detail about how to use them. The current layer for new objects is set by using the DDLMODES command with the Layer Control dialog box or by using the LAYER command. The Layer Control dialog box can be accessed by choosing the **L**ayer button in the Entity Creation Modes dialog box, as well as by the methods described in Chapter 10.

When you click on the **L**ayer button in the Entity Creation Modes dialog box, the Layer Control dialog box opens (see fig. 13.10). This dialog box is the same as that accessed by the DDLMODES command discussed in Chapter 10, "Getting Organized: Drawing on Layers." With the Layer Control dialog box, you can select the layer on which you want new objects placed by highlighting the layer name (in the La**y**er Name list box) and choosing the **C**urrent button. You also can make modifications in this dialog box, such as setting the layer color or linetype for objects that have their color and linetype properties set to BYLAYER.

Figure 13.10

The Layer Control dialog box.

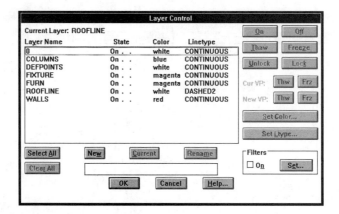

Setting the Current Text Style

Although the current text style is technically not an object property, the Entity Creation Modes dialog box enables you to set the current style for new text objects. When you click on the Text **S**tyle button in the Entity Creation Modes dialog box, the Select Text Style dialog box opens (see fig. 13.17 in the section "Creating a Text Style"). This dialog box displays a list of all style names defined in the drawing and illustrates a few of the characters of the current text style. The Select Text Style dialog box also displays information regarding the font file name and style parameters. This dialog box and text styles are discussed in detail later in this chapter.

Setting the Elevation for New Objects

Elevation is not an object property. However, there was a time in AutoCAD's history when elevation was an object property. In AutoCAD LT, elevation in effect presets the Z coordinate of points specified with only X and Y coordinates for drawing objects in AutoCAD's 3D Space. For example, if the elevation for new objects was set to 5 and you specified the start point of a line at 3,4, the start point of the line would be 3,4,5. Although you can use the elevation setting to control the Z coordinate of objects, it is better to use the UCS command discussed in Chapter 2 to control the Z-axis position of new objects in 3D space.

You use the **E**levation edit box in the Entity Creation Modes dialog box to set the default Z coordinate for specified points. By default, the elevation is set to 0. You also can use the ELEV command or the ELEVATION system variable to control the Z coordinate of specified points. Some drawings, such as three-dimensional models, require different elevations for different elements.

Usually, when you are drawing in AutoCAD LT, you look *down* at the drawing in the XY plan view. When you are viewing a drawing in plan view, it is difficult, if not

impossible, to decipher the Z coordinate of an object. You can use the LIST or DDMODIFY commands (described in Chapter 12, "Accessing Your Drawing's Data") to query an object's data from the drawing database to determine an object's position in 3D space. You also can use the 3D viewing commands (DVIEW and VPOINT, discussed in Chapter 24, "Moving Beyond the Basics") to view your drawing from a location in 3D space and thereby observe an object's position in the Z direction. Elevation is discussed in Chapter 24 in more detail because it is used to create 3D objects.

Setting the Thickness for New Objects

The thickness of new objects is the last item that is set with the Entity Creation Modes dialog box. Thickness is an object property like layer, linetype, and color. The thickness property adds 3D height to basic objects by extruding them the distance of the thickness setting in the Z direction. You use the **T**hickness edit box in the Entity Creation Modes dialog box to control this setting. You can also use the ELEV command and the THICKNESS system variable to set the thickness for new objects. This property is used in AutoCAD LT to create three-dimensional models.

As with elevation, it is difficult to see an object's thickness in the plan view. You can use the LIST command or the 3D viewing commands to see an object's thickness in 3D space. Because object thickness is used for drawing 3D objects, it is discussed in detail in Chapter 24, "Moving Beyond the Basics."

Modifying the Properties of Existing Objects

No drawing is perfect the first time you create it. The beauty of CAD is that the objects in a drawing can be modified more easily than their manual drafting ink-on-film counterparts can. AutoCAD LT provides two commands to modify the properties of objects already in a drawing—the CHPROP and DDCHPROP commands. DDCHPROP is the Change Properties dialog box version of the CHPROP command. Both CHPROP and DDCHPROP enable you to change the color, layer, linetype, and thickness of selected objects.

In addition, AutoCAD LT Release 2 provides the DDMODIFY command (Modify *<Object_type>* dialog box), with which you can view and change both the properties and geometry of an object. While DDMODIFY provides more functionality than DDCHPROP, it can modify only one object at a time.

ALT2

When you issue the CHPROP or the DDCHPROP command, you are first prompted to select an object or a group of objects to modify. After you have selected the objects to modify with DDCHPROP, the Change Properties dialog box opens (see fig. 13.11). This dialog box enables you to modify all object properties. The properties of the selected object or objects are displayed in the Change Properties dialog box beside the property buttons (**C**olor, **L**ayer, and L**i**netype). If you select a group of objects that have different values of object properties (such as a line with a color of red and a circle with a color of green), the text next to the property button will read VARIES.

Figure 13.11

*The Change
Properties
dialog box.*

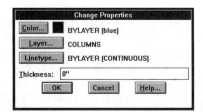

Using the Change Properties Dialog Box

When you need to modify the properties of objects that are in a drawing, you use the Change Properties dialog box. You can open this dialog box either by entering **DDCHPROP** at the Command: prompt or by clicking on the Change Properties tool in the toolbox. From the Change Properties dialog box, you can set most of the same properties you set from the Entity Creation Modes dialog box. Typically, however, you use the Change Properties dialog box after objects are placed in the drawing and the Entity Creation Modes dialog box before objects are created.

In the following exercise, you change and correct the object properties of the column center lines using the Change Properties dialog box.

Changing the Properties of Drawing Objects

Continue working with the ENTPROP drawing from the preceding exercise, or create a new drawing using ALT1303.DWG as a prototype and using no setup method.

Command: *Choose* **M**odify, Chan**g**e Properties   Issues the DDCHPROP command and
                                                           prompts for selection

Select objects: *Pick the line at* ①   Selects the top column center line
(see fig. 13.12)

Select objects: (Enter)   Ends all object selection and opens the
                                                           Change Properties dialog box

The Change Properties dialog box displays the current settings of the object's properties. Next, you change the object to the correct color and linetype.

Click on the **C**olor *button*	Opens the Select Color dialog box
Click on the Green color in the Standard Colors *group, then click on* OK	Sets the color object property of the line to Green and closes the dialog box
Click on the **L**inetype *button*	Opens the Select Linetype dialog box
Select CENTER2 *from the list, then click on* OK	Changes the linetype of the selected object to CENTER2 and closes the Select Linetype dialog box
Click on OK *in the Change Properties dialog box*	Closes the dialog box and regenerates the line with the new object property values
`Command:` *Click on the Change Properties tool*	Issues the DDCHPROP command and prompts for selection
`Select objects:` *Pick the lines at* ②, ③, *and* ④ *(see fig. 13.12)*	Selects the remaining three column center lines
`Select objects:` Enter	Ends all object selection and opens the Change Properties dialog box

This time the Change Properties dialog box displays VARIES next to the **L**inetype button because the selected objects do not share the same linetype. MAGENTA, however, is displayed next to the **C**olor button because all the objects share that color.

Click on the **C**olor *button*	Opens the Select Color dialog box
Click on the Green color in the Standard Colors *group, then click on* OK	Sets the color object property of the lines to Green and closes the dialog box
Click on the **L**inetype *button*	Opens the Select Linetype dialog box
Select CENTER2 *from the list, then click on* OK	Changes the linetype of the selected objects to CENTER2 and closes the Select Linetype dialog box
Click on OK *in the Change Properties dialog box*	Closes the dialog box and regenerates the lines with the new object property values
Save the drawing	

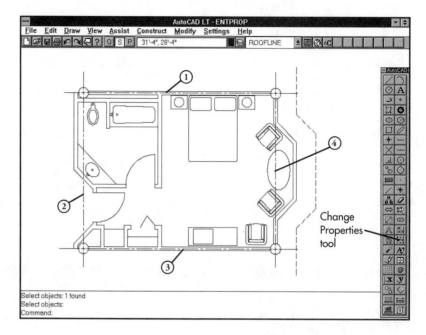

Figure 13.12

The changed column center lines.

The preceding exercise changed the object properties of the column center lines so that the center lines would plot at the same line weight as the center marks and have the proper linetype. Another way to organize the column center line objects would be to create a new layer for the center lines and use the DDCHPROP command to change the layer property of the lines to the new layer and change color property of the lines to BYLAYER. By using this technique, you could control the visibility and line weight of the column center lines independently of the columns themselves, thus providing more flexibility in your drawing organization.

> **DDCHPROP.** The DDCHPROP command is used to change the object properties of existing objects in the drawing. These properties include color, layer, linetype, and thickness. After the DDCHPROP command is issued, the Change Properties dialog box is displayed. The current values of the selected objects' properties are displayed in the dialog box.

Changing an Existing Object's Color Property

The **C**olor button in the Change Properties dialog box activates the Select Color dialog box. This dialog box is the same as the one that appears when you click on the

<u>C</u>olor button in the Entity Creation Modes dialog box; however, it affects the selected object's color instead of the default color for subsequently created objects. As explained previously, the Select Color dialog box has color chips for all 255 colors and buttons for the two logical colors (BYLAYER and BYBLOCK) that AutoCAD LT supports. After you select a color and click on OK, the selected object or objects are set to that value. If the color of the selected objects varies, all objects will be set to the chosen value.

Changing an Existing Object's Layer Property

The <u>L</u>ayer button in the Change Properties dialog box activates the Select Layer dialog box (see fig. 13.13). This dialog box enables you to change the layer of the selected objects. If the objects you choose are all from the same layer, that layer name is highlighted in the Select Layer dialog box; if the selected objects come from several different layers, no names in the Layer Name list are highlighted.

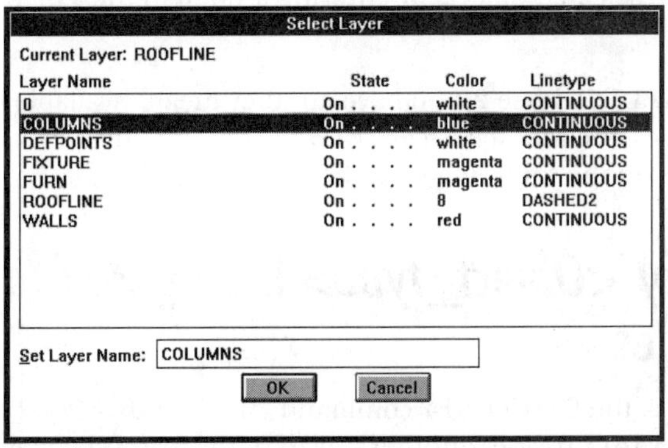

```
                          Select Layer
Current Layer: ROOFLINE

Layer Name                    State      Color    Linetype
0                             On . . . . white    CONTINUOUS
COLUMNS                       On . . . . blue     CONTINUOUS
DEFPOINTS                     On . . . . white    CONTINUOUS
FIXTURE                       On . . . . magenta  CONTINUOUS
FURN                          On . . . . magenta  CONTINUOUS
ROOFLINE                      On . . . . 8        DASHED2
WALLS                         On . . . . red      CONTINUOUS




Set Layer Name:  COLUMNS
                     OK        Cancel
```

Figure 13.13

The Select Layer dialog box.

Changing an Existing Object's Linetype Property

The <u>L</u>inetype button in the Change Properties dialog box activates the Select Linetype dialog box (see fig. 13.14). The Select Linetype dialog box displays all of the linetypes currently loaded in the drawing. The linetype names appear in a narrow list, and the linetype representation appears above the list. If you select a linetype from the list, the pattern of the linetype is displayed in the box above the list. As in the Select Layer dialog box, the linetype name is highlighted if all the selected objects share the same linetype. You set the linetype property for the selected objects by choosing a linetype name and clicking on OK.

Figure 13.14

The Select Linetype dialog box.

Changing an Existing Object's Thickness Property

The **T**hickness option in the Change Properties dialog box enables you to set the extrusion distance of the selected objects. If the selected objects have different values for their thickness, the word VARIES appears in the **T**hickness edit box. You set the thickness property for the selected objects by entering a value in the **T**hickness edit box.

If you are using AutoCAD LT Release 2, you have another means available for changing object properties, the Modify *<Object_type>* Dialog Box. If you are using AutoCAD LT Release 1, skip the following section.

Using the Modify *<Object_type>* Dialog Box to Change Properties

ALT2

In AutoCAD LT Release 2, the DDMODIFY command (the Modify *<Object_type>* dialog box—see figure 13.15) provides another way to both view and change the properties of an existing object. You might prefer it to the DDCHPROP command (Change Properties dialog box) because it also enables you to display and modify the geometric data of the selected object. For text objects, it even enables you to change the style and justification, as you will see later in this chapter. The disadvantage to the Modify *<Object_type>* dialog box is that it can only be used to modify a single object.

Try using the DDMODIFY command to change the layer and linetype of several lines, using Modify Line dialog boxes. You'll also change the endpoints of one line.

New Riders Publishing
INSIDE
SERIES

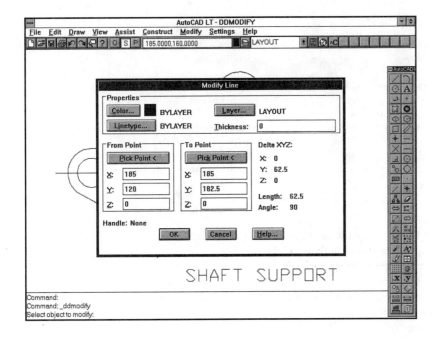

Figure 13.15

A Modify Line dialog box.

13

Changing Object Properties and Geometry with DDMODIFY

Create a new drawing named DDMODIFY using ALT1304.DWG as a prototype and using no setup method.

Command: *Choose* **M**odify, Modi**f**y Entity	Issues the DDMODIFY command and prompts for selection
_ddmodify Select object to modify: *Pick the line at* ① *(see fig. 13.16)*	Selects the line and opens the Modify Line dialog box, showing the line's current properties and geometric data as shown in figure 13.15
Choose **L**ayer	Opens the Select Layer dialog box
Select LAYOUT, *then choose* OK	Sets the line's layer to LAYOUT and returns to the Modify Line dialog box
Choose **Li**netype	Opens the Select Linetype dialog box
Select CENTER2, *then choose* OK	Sets the line's linetype to CENTER2 and returns to the Modify Line dialog box

continues

continued

In the From Point area, choose **P**ick Point	Returns to the drawing for end point specification
From pt: *Turn on ortho and pick* ②	Changes the line's lower endpoint and returns to the Modify Line dialog box
In the To Point area, choose Pic**k** Point	Returns to the drawing for the point
To point: *Pick* ③	Changes the line's upper endpoint and returns to the Modify Line dialog box
Choose OK	Accepts the changes and closes the Modify Line dialog box

Repeat DDMODIFY to change the layer and linetype of the other two lines at ④ and ⑤. The drawing should appear as shown in figure 13.16

The center lines are not evenly balanced on the circles; you'll learn how to correct this with dimensioning center marks in Chapters 20, "Applying Dimensions in CAD," and 21, "Styling and Editing Dimensions."

Figure 13.16

Modified center lines.

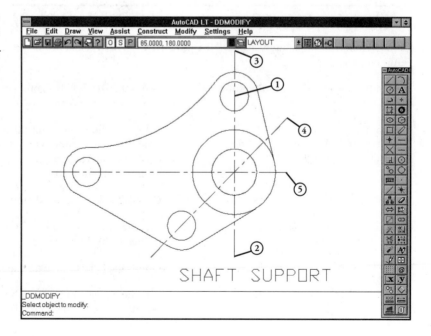

You also can use DDMODIFY for changing text style and justification, but first look at how to use other commands to define and modify text styles.

Using Text Styles and Fonts

AutoCAD enables you to change the appearance of text in many ways. You can control the font, its height, width, and obliquing angle. Text can also be drawn backwards, upside-down, or vertical. With all these parameters controlling text, it could become quite a headache to manage several different kinds of text. AutoCAD LT groups all of these text parameters together into a *text style*. In AutoCAD LT, you can create, name, and recall different text styles for different types of text. For example, you can have a large bold text style for section labels, an easy-to-read sans-serif style for notes and dimensions, and a fancy text style for logos or brand names.

Creating and Using Text Styles

Up to this point, you have added text to a drawing using AutoCAD LT's default text style, STANDARD. To create new text styles, you use the STYLE command. AutoCAD LT enables you to have an almost unlimited number of text styles in a drawing. After you create a new text style, it automatically becomes the current style for new text objects.

The current text style for new objects can be set by clicking on the Text **S**tyle button in the Entity Creation Modes dialog box and selecting a defined text style from the list in the Select Text Style dialog box (see fig. 13.17). Also, you can use the STYLE command to set the current text style for new text objects.

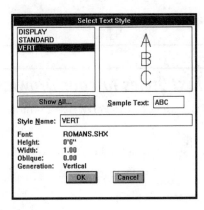

Figure 13.17

The Select Text Style dialog box.

Because the size of text in the AutoCAD drawing is determined by multiplying the intended plot text height by the drawing scale factor, text styles are usually created when you set up a drawing or at least before you draw any text. You can automate the setting up of text styles by using prototype drawings. If you create text styles in a prototype drawing, they will be available for every new drawing that uses the prototype.

In the following exercise, you create two new text styles, add some text to your drawing, and change the STANDARD style to use a better-looking font. The DISPLAY style is for large text labels such as drawing titles, detail labels, and section labels. The VERT style is set for vertical text and has a fixed text height. Figure 13.18 shows the text that you add in the following exercise.

Figure 13.18

Text with various styles added to the drawing.

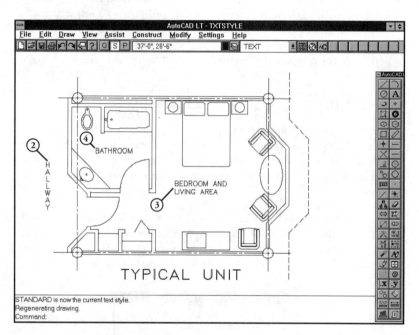

Adding New Text Styles to Your Drawing

Create a new drawing named TXTSTYLE using ALT1305.DWG as a prototype and using no setup method.

Command: **STYLE** (Enter)   Issues the STYLE command

Text style name (or ?)   Creates a new text style named DISPLAY
<STANDARD>: **DISPLAY** (Enter)

New style.

Double-click on the ROMAND.SHX *font file in the* File **N**ame *list box*	Specifies the ROMAND font for the text style and opens the Select Font File dialog box
`Height <0'-0">:` (Enter)	Accepts the default variable text height
`Width factor <1.0000>:` **1.25** (Enter)	Specifies a text width that is wider than normal
`Obliquing angle <0.00>:` (Enter)	Accepts the default obliquing angle
`Backwards? <N>` (Enter)	Accepts the default forward-reading text
`Upside-down? <N>` (Enter)	Accepts the default right-side-up text
`Vertical? <N>` (Enter)	Accepts the default horizontal text
`DISPLAY is now the current text style.`	
`Command:` **STYLE** (Enter)	
`Text style name (or ?)` `<DISPLAY>:` **VERT** (Enter)	Creates a new text style named VERT and opens the Select Font File dialog box
`New style.`	
Double-click on the ROMANS.SHX *font file in the* File **N**ame *list box*	Specifies the ROMANS font for the text style
`Height <0'-0">:` **6"** (Enter)	Specifies a fixed text height of 6 inches
`Width factor <1.0000>:` (Enter)	
`Obliquing angle <0.00>:` (Enter)	
`Backwards? <N>` (Enter)	
`Upside-down? <N>` (Enter)	
`Vertical? <N>` **Y** (Enter)	Causes text that uses the VERT text style to be drawn vertically
`VERT is now the current text style.`	
`Command:` *Click on the Current Color button*	Opens the Entity Creation Modes dialog box
Click on the Text **S**tyle *button*	Opens the Select Text Style dialog box
Choose the DISPLAY *text style from the list of fonts, then click on* OK	Sets the current text style and closes the Select Text Style dialog box

continues

continued

Click on OK	Closes the Entity Creation Modes dialog box
Command: *Click on the Text tool*	Issues the DTEXT command
_DTEXT Justify/Style/<Start point>: *Pick point* ① *(see fig. 13.18)*	Accepts the current style, DISPLAY, and default justification, left
Height <2'-0">: **1'** ⟨Enter⟩	
Rotation angle <0.00>: ⟨Enter⟩	
Text: **TYPICAL UNIT** ⟨Enter⟩	
Text: ⟨Enter⟩	

> **STYLE.** The STYLE command enables you to create, name, and recall sets of text style parameters including font, text height, text width, and obliquing angle, as well as backwards, upside-down, and vertical orientation. The STYLE command sets a newly defined text style or a changed text style as the current style for the drawing.

In the following exercise, you select and use the VERT style, and then use the DTEXT command instead of the Entity Creation Modes dialog box to set the current style to STANDARD. Because the STANDARD style is so simple that it looks rather crude, you then use the STYLE command to redefine, changing its font from TXT to ROMANS.

Selecting, Using, and Redefining Text Styles

Continue from the previous exercise.

Command: *Click on the Current Color button*	Opens the Entity Creation Modes dialog box
Click on the Text **S**tyle *button*	Opens the Select Text Style dialog box
Choose the VERT *text style from the list of fonts, then click on* OK	Sets the current text style and closes the Select Text Style dialog box
Click on OK	Closes the Entity Creation Modes dialog box
Command: *Click on the Text tool*	Issues the DTEXT command
_DTEXT Justify/Style/<Start point>: *Pick point* ② *(see fig. 13.18)*	

Rotation angle <270.00>: `Enter`

Text: **HALLWAY** `Enter`

Text: `Enter`

The DTEXT command did not prompt you for text height because the VERT style is defined using a fixed text height. You can also set the style in the DTEXT command, as follows.

Command: **T** `Enter`	Issues the DTEXT command
DTEXT Justify/Style/<Start point>: **S** `Enter`	Prompts for text style
Style name (or ?) <VERT>: **STANDARD** `Enter`	Specifies the STANDARD style
Justify/Style/<Start point>: *Pick point* ③	
Height <0'-0 3/16">: **6"**	
Rotation angle <0.00>: `Enter`	
Text: **BEDROOM AND** `Enter`	
Text: **LIVING AREA** `Enter`	
Pick point ④	
Text: **BATHROOM** `Enter`	
Text: `Enter`	

The default STANDARD style is a bit crude. Use the STYLE command to redefine it.

Command: **STYLE** `Enter`	Issues the STYLE command
Text style name (or ?) <STANDARD>: `Enter`	Defaults to modify the existing STANDARD text style,
Existing style.	Opens Select Font File dialog box
Type **ROMANS** *in the* File **N**ame *edit box, then click on* OK	Changes the font file definition to ROMANS.SHX (you might need to type ROMANS.SHX, the full file name)
Height <0'-0">: `Enter`	Accepts the default variable text height
Width factor <1.0000>: `Enter`	Accepts the default width factor

continues

continued

`Obliquing angle <0.00>:` (Enter)	Accepts default obliquing angle
`Backwards? <N>` (Enter)	Accepts default forward-reading text
`Upside-down? <N>` (Enter)	Accepts default right-side-up text
`Vertical? <N>` (Enter)	Accepts default horizontal text

`STANDARD is now the current text style.`

`Regenerating drawing.`

The text using the old STANDARD style is updated when the drawing is regenerated after the style command.

Save the drawing

Tip
The advantage to the simple TXT font is that it regenerates and plots quickly. In drawings that have a lot of text, you can use it for a text style as you work and for making check plots, then redefine the style before making final plots.

Creating Text Styles with the Select Text Font Dialog Box

You also can create new text styles by using the Select Text Font dialog box from the Settings menu. If you choose **S**ettings, then Text **S**tyle, AutoCAD displays the Select Text Font dialog box (actually, an *icon menu*—see fig. 13.19). This dialog box enables you to choose a font for the text style visually. The Select Text Font dialog box displays the names of the fonts that come with AutoCAD LT. This dialog box also displays a small icon image for each font file, showing the font name and some sample letters. Because all the fonts do not fit on a single screen, the **N**ext button enables you to see the next page of fonts. To view a second screen of font images, you simply click on the **N**ext button. When you select either the name of the font from the font list or its graphic image, a style with the name of the font is created, and the selected font is automatically set as the style's font.

Using the menu to define text styles is not as flexible as the STYLE command. The menu system does not allow you to specify a name for the style; it uses the name of the font file as the style name. The font file name is too cryptic to be useful and does not convey any other information about the style such as text height, width, or other

style settings. You can use the DDRENAME command (covered in Chapter 8, "Preparing Your Workspace: CAD Concepts 1B") to change the name of any named item in AutoCAD. This command displays the names of items such as text styles, layer names, and block names. When you rename a text style with the DDRENAME command, you can also respecify the various style parameters and options.

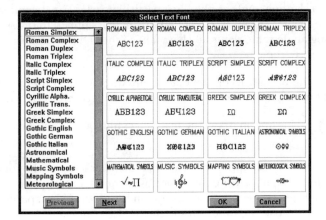

Figure 13.19

The Select Text Font dialog box.

Using Style Options

When you added new fonts to the drawing in the previous exercise, you were asked several questions regarding which options to use for the style.

- ◆ `Text style name or ? <STANDARD>`: The first question you are asked is the name for a new style or the name of an existing style. If you specify the same name as an existing style, the settings you designate for the style options redefine all existing text that uses that style name. This operation could cause unexpected results in your drawing; therefore, you should approach this action cautiously.

- ◆ `File:` The second text style option is a request for the font file name. All text has an associated font file that defines how the characters are drawn. Most AutoCAD LT fonts are shape files and have a file extension of SHX. In addition, AutoCAD LT supports PostScript Type 1 fonts; these font files have an extension of PFB. Which font file you use depends entirely on the types of text you want to place in your drawing.

- ◆ `Height <0,00>`: The third text style option defines character height (also called text height). The default value for this option is 0, which means that character height is not set until you issue the DTEXT or TEXT command. If you do set a value for this option, all text using that style name is set to that height. In some cases, this condition might be desirable. If you want to use a style in a variety of different heights, you should keep this value at 0.

◆ `Width factor <1.0>:` The fourth text style option defines the font width factor. This value, which defaults to 1, determines how many times wider than normal width the text is drawn. You can stretch a font by specifying a number larger than 1 or squeeze a font by specifying a number between 0 and 1.

◆ `Obliquing angle <0>:` The fifth text style option defines an obliquing angle. An *obliquing angle* is a slanting angle applied to a particular style. The default is a value of 0 degrees, which means in effect that no angle is applied to the style. A positive obliquing angle value slants all characters to the right; a negative value slants all characters to the left.

◆ `Backwards? <N>:` The Backwards option determines whether the font is drawn backwards (right to left) rather than in the normal manner (left to right).

◆ `Upside-down? <N>:` This option draws the text object mirrored about the baseline of a font.

◆ `Vertical? <N>:` The Vertical option determines if the characters of the font are drawn from left to right or from top to bottom. Not all fonts support this option. You cannot determine whether this option is supported by a particular font until you actually load the font by using the STYLE command or the Select Text Font dialog box.

Figure 13.20 shows some of the different text style options applied to the ROMANS font style. The effects shown here are typical of those you will see across the range of fonts supplied with AutoCAD LT.

Figure 13.20

The ROMANS font with various style options applied.

Text style parameters		
Width factor 0.75 ⟶	ABC 123	R
Width factor 1.00 ⟶	ABC 123	O
Width factor 1.25 ⟶	ABC 123	M
Oblique angle 0 ⟶	ABC 123	A
Oblique angle 10 ⟶	ABC 123	N
Oblique angle 20 ⟶	ABC 123	S
Oblique angle 45 ⟶	ABC 123	V
Upside down ⟶	∀BC 123	E R T I C A L
Backwards ⟶	ABC 123	

Working with Different Font Types

When you choose a style from the Select Text Font dialog box, you are using the font definition from a particular font file. AutoCAD LT supports two different types of font files—shape fonts and PostScript fonts. You can plot shape fonts and PostScript outline fonts to any plotter that AutoCAD LT supports. This capability makes AutoCAD LT fonts fairly universal.

Not all the PostScript Type 1 fonts that come with AutoCAD LT are strictly outline fonts. A majority of those fonts are designed to be filled, but this filling can occur only when the drawing is plotted to a PostScript printer. To plot these types of fonts in their true manner, you must use the PSOUT command to create a proper PostScript plot file. The PSOUT command encodes the proper information that tells the PostScript printer how to fill the font, thereby giving you the type of output you desire. Chapter 23, "Producing Hard Copy," discusses plotting in detail.

In addition to redefining styles, you can modify existing text objects by assigning a new style to them. In AutoCAD LT Release 1, you must do this by using the CHANGE command, which is covered in the Chapter 15, "Modifying Objects and Text." If you are using AutoCAD LT Release 1, skip the rest of this chapter. In AutoCAD LT Release 2, you can also use the Modify Text dialog box (DDMODIFY command) to change any aspect of an existing text object, as shown in the following section.

Changing the Style of Existing Text with DDMODIFY

In AutoCAD LT Release 2, the DDMODIFY command opens the Modify Text dialog box (see fig. 13.21) when a text object is selected. It can be used to view or modify the object properties, text properties, style, or geometric placement of an existing text object.

ALT2

Try using DDMODIFY in the following exercise to change the existing text in the DDMODIFY drawing from the earlier DDMODIFY exercise.

Changing Existing Text with the Modify Text dialog box

Reopen your DDMODIFY drawing or create a new drawing named DDMODIFY using ALT1304.DWG as a prototype and using no setup method.

Command: *Choose **M**odify, Modi**f**y Entity*	Issues the DDMODIFY command and prompts for selection
`_ddmodify` `Select object to modify:` *Pick the text at* ① *(see fig. 13.21)*	Selects the text and opens the Modify Text dialog box, showing the text's current properties, style, and geometric data as shown in figure 13.21

continues

continued

Figure 13.21

An existing text object and its Modify Text dialog box.

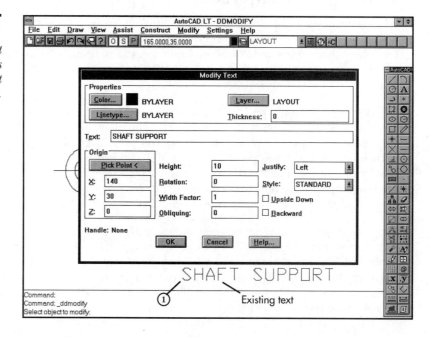

Choose **L**ayer, *then select* NOTES, *then* choose OK	Opens the Select Layer dialog box, specifies a new layer for the text, and returns to the Modify Text dialog box
Click in the **J**ustify *drop-down list box and* choose Center	Opens the drop-down list and changes the justification from Left to Center
Click in the **S**tyle *drop-down list box and* choose NOTES	Opens the drop-down list and changes the style from STANDARD to NOTES
Click in the T**e**xt *edit box to the right of the text, press the Spacebar, and type* **BRACKET**	Changes text to SHAFT SUPPORT BRACKET
Choose OK	Accepts the changes and closes the Modify Text dialog box (see fig. 13.22)

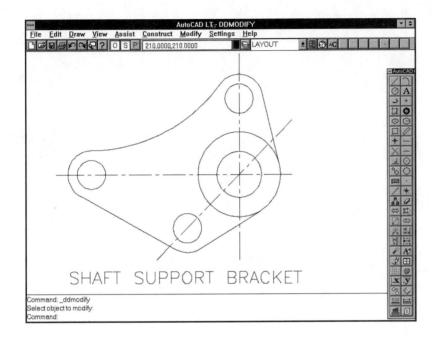

Figure 13.22

Text after modifications.

Now that you have learned how to create objects and modify their properties, it's time to learn how to edit them in more advanced ways. In Chapter 14, "Making More Changes: Editing Constructively," you learn how to create more objects from existing objects and how to change existing objects. You will discover that in AutoCAD LT, it is often more efficient to recycle objects rather than to create new ones.

Part III

Power and Technique

14 Making More Changes: Editing
    Constructively 511

15 Modifying Objects and Text 551

16 Increasing Your Drawing Power with
    Polylines and Double Lines 585

17 Dressing Up Drawings with Hatching................ 645

18 Leveraging Repetitive Design and Drafting......... 673

19 Managing and Modifying Blocks and Xrefs 737

20 Applying Dimensions in CAD........................... 765

21 Styling and Editing Dimensions 797

22 Structuring Your Drawing................................ 831

23 Producing Hard Copy 869

24 Moving Beyond the Basics 905

C H A P T E R

14

Making More Changes: Editing Constructively

In this chapter, you learn how to apply many of AutoCAD LT's editing commands to the process of creating a drawing. The chapter divides the editing commands discussed into two groups roughly based on function. In practice, you use all these commands in a variety of ways. The real power of AutoCAD LT comes from the skilled use of combinations of editing tools to accomplish your task.

In this chapter, you learn how to:

◆ Replicate objects using the OFFSET, ARRAY, and MIRROR commands

◆ Use editing tools to convert construction lines into permanent parts of the drawing

◆ Clean up your drawings and add detail with the BREAK, FILLET, TRIM, and EXTEND commands

The tools in this chapter demonstrate the way AutoCAD LT supports a design as it evolves from a sketchy layout to a final drawing. These same tools can also be effectively applied to incorporate revisions and updates to completed designs.

The ideal flight would never require a course correction, a change in radio or navigation frequencies, a weather update, a change in cabin temperature, a calculation of fuel load vs. consumption, a headwind update, or any of the hundreds of other details that remain in flux throughout the flight. The aircraft that made the ideal flight would not require any controls for making corrections or changes, and its pilot would be unneeded between takeoff and landing.

The ideal flight does not exist in reality. Nothing works perfectly, and a tool that does not address the issue of change is soon obsolete. You have seen some of AutoCAD LT's tools for making changes to your designs; now, this chapter will introduce you to more of the editing tools.

The process of creating CAD drawings often consists more of using editing commands to replicate and modify previously drawn objects than using the drawing commands themselves. Editing in this sense is a constructive process. Commands can be distinguished according to these two functions, but in practice, CAD blurs the line between the "drawing" and "editing" activity.

Through the course of this chapter's exercises, you create a conceptual design of a residential entrance, as shown in figure 14.1. Within this context, the chapter introduces each command and gives simple examples of its use. The chapter also attempts to illustrate methods of working in AutoCAD LT.

Figure 14.1

The completed entrance drawing.

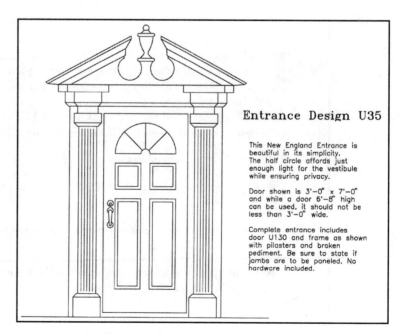

Entrance Design U35

This New England Entrance is beautiful in its simplicity. The half circle affords just enough light for the vestibule while ensuring privacy.

Door shown is 3'-0" x 7'-0" and while a door 6'-8" high can be used, it should not be less than 3'-0" wide.

Complete entrance includes door U130 and frame as shown with pilasters and broken pediment. Be sure to state if jambs are to be paneled. No hardware included.

You begin editing constructively with three commands that create new objects from existing ones: OFFSET, ARRAY, and MIRROR.

Replicating Objects

You have already looked at the most common editing command for replicating existing objects, the COPY command. AutoCAD LT has three other commands that create new objects based on existing ones: OFFSET, ARRAY, and MIRROR. Each command is useful for both layout and detail work.

These three commands are introduced first in this chapter to help quickly build the framework for the design. They also have many applications in detail work. OFFSET, ARRAY, and MIRROR are all found on the **C**onstruct pull-down menu. They are not included in the default toolbox.

To start the discussion of replicating objects, look at one of the most useful commands for accurate layout work—the OFFSET command.

Laying Out a Design with the OFFSET Command

As its name implies, you use the OFFSET command to create new drawing objects that are offset from existing ones. The result depends on the type of object selected. Apply OFFSET to a line, and you get a new parallel line of the same length. Use it with ARC or CIRCLE, and you get a smaller or larger arc or circle. Use it with a polyline (including rectangles, ellipses, complex curves, and polygons), and it creates a new object parallel to the original (see Chapter 16, "Increasing Your Drawing Power with Polylines and Double Lines").

In the first exercise, you draw some reference lines and then offset them to create a rough layout of the entrance. You also draw and offset an arc and a rectangle. The RECTANG command is covered in Chapter 16, "Increasing Your Drawing Power with Polylines and Double Lines," but you can simply follow the instructions in the exercise to create what you need.

The prototype drawing contains several layers and is set up as an architectural C-size drawing intended for plotting at 1" = 1' scale. It has a grid set to 6", and snap is set to 1".

Using OFFSET to Lay Out a Design

Create a new drawing named ENTRANCE using ALT1401.DWG as a prototype and using no setup method. Ortho is on and the current layer is CENTER.

Draw a center line from 6'0",0'6" to @11'<90. The CENTER linetype should be clearly visible on-screen, but you might have to look closely in figure 14.2 to see it. Remember, linetype scale is set for plotted appearance, not screen appearance.

Set the LAYOUT layer current and draw a horizontal line from 1'6",1'0" to @9'<0.

Next, you use the Distance mode of the OFFSET command.

Command: *Choose* **C**onstruct, **O**ffset	Issues the OFFSET command
_offset	
Offset distance or Through <Through>: **2'1** (Enter)	Sets the distance to offset
Select object to offset: *Pick the center line*	Identifies the center line as the object to be offset
Side to offset? *Pick any point to the right of the line*	Creates the copy of the line at ① (see fig. 14.2)
Select object to offset: *Pick the center line again*	
Side to offset? *Pick any point to the left of the line*	Creates another copy of the line to the left at ②
Select object to offset: (Enter)	Completes the OFFSET command

Repeat the preceding offset sequence using an offset distance of 1'-6" to create the two new lines at ③ and ④.

Choose the Change Properties tool or Cha**n**ge Properties from the **M**odify menu, and change the two newest lines to the LAYOUT layer. The drawing should now match figure 14.2.

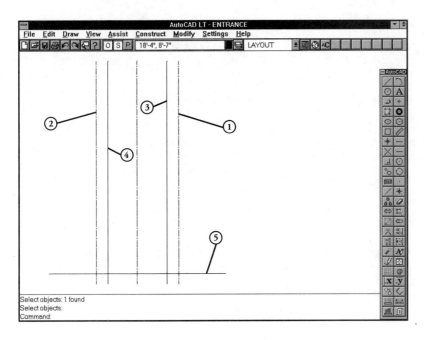

Figure 14.2

Using the OFFSET command.

Next, you use the Through option of OFFSET to offset a line through a point.

Command: *Pick the baseline at* (5)	Highlights the baseline and displays its grips
Command: **OFFSET** (Enter)	Begins the OFFSET command but ignores the baseline because you cannot preselect objects to offset
Offset distance or Through <1'-6">: **T** (Enter)	Specifies the Through mode
Select object to offset: *Pick the baseline at* (5) *again*	Identifies the baseline as the object to be offset
Through point: *Pick any point with a Y coordinate value of 1'2"*	Offsets the baseline by the Y distance to the point
Select object to offset: (Enter)	Completes the OFFSET command

continues

continued

Command: **OF** (Enter)	Issues the OFFSET command
OFFSET	
Offset distance or Through <Through>: **7'** (Enter)	Switches OFFSET to Distance mode by specifying a distance
Select object to offset: **L** (Enter)	Attempts to use the Last selection option
Invalid point.	Indicates that the Last option is not accepted by OFFSET
Select object to offset: *Pick the new line at* ⑥ *(see fig. 14.3)*	Selects the line as the object to be offset
Side to offset? *Pick any point above the line*	Creates the line at ⑦ exactly 7' above the original
Select object to offset: (Enter)	

Use OFFSET with a distance of 1' to copy the line at ⑦ up to ⑧.

Set the DETAIL layer current. Draw a line from 6'2",6'9" ⑨ to 11"<0 ⑩.

Use the Ce**n**ter, Start, Angle option to draw the arc at ⑪ with its center at 6'0",6'9". Use the ENDPoint object snap to place its start point at the right end of the line at ⑩ and then specify 180 degrees.

Command: *Choose* **D**raw, Rectangle	Issues the RECTANG command
First corner: *Pick the point 4'11",2'0" at* ⑫	
Other corner: **@11,11** (Enter)	Draws the rectangle and completes the command

The square is a polyline (see Chapter 16), so OFFSET will treat it as a single object. First, however, you offset the arc.

Command: **OF** (Enter)	Issues the OFFSET command
Offset distance or Through <1'-0">: **T** (Enter)	Specifies the Through mode
Select object to offset: *Pick the arc at* ⑪	
Through point: **ENDP** (Enter)	Activates the ENDPoint object snap

`_endp of` *Pick the line at* ⑨	Creates a small arc at ⑨
`Select object to offset:` (Enter)	Completes the command

In order to change offset modes, you must end the command and reissue it.

`Command:` (Enter)	Repeats the OFFSET command
`Offset distance or Through` `<Through>:` **1** (Enter)	Switches OFFSET to Distance mode by specifying a distance
`Select object to offset:` *Pick the* *rectangle at* ⑫	
`Side to offset?` *Pick any point inside* *the rectangle*	Creates a second rectangle 1" inside the first
`Select object to offset:` (Enter)	

Save the drawing. It should now match figure 14.3.

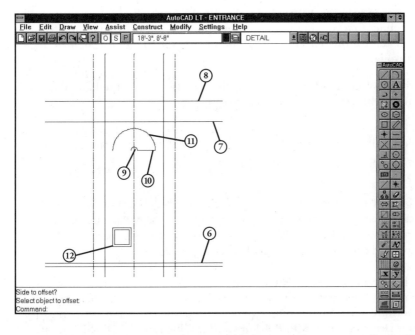

Figure 14.3

Using the OFFSET command on non-line objects.

OFFSET initially prompts for a *Through* distance. You can specify the distance by selecting two points, or entering a value. OFFSET then prompts for the object to offset. Pick the object, and OFFSET prompts for the direction in which to offset the object. This method creates a new copy of the selected object, parallel to the original at the specified distance from it. OFFSET acts on only one object at a time. It does not recognize noun/verb selection or the normal selection options such as Last. Instead, it requires that you pick an object to offset.

> **OFFSET.** The OFFSET command creates a parallel copy of a selected line, circle, arc, or 2D polyline. The copy is created offset by a specified distance or drawn through a specified point (the initial default).

OFFSET operates in two modes. The initial mode is *Through.* If you press Enter at the <Through> prompt, you are prompted to select the object to be offset and a point through which the copy is to pass. Selecting two points or entering a specific value at the <Through> prompt establishes the distance by which the copy is offset. You are prompted to select the object to be offset and to specify the direction for the offset.

In the *Distance* mode, OFFSET prompts first for the distance of the offset. The previous distance is offered as the default. You can choose any two points or enter a value. You are then prompted for the direction for the offset.

If you enter **T** to change to the Through mode from the initial distance prompt, AutoCAD LT assumes that you do not want to specify a new offset distance and prompts immediately for the object to offset. It then asks for a point for the new object to pass through.

During a drawing session, AutoCAD LT retains the last offset mode used and the last distance specified (when Distance mode is used).

With lines, OFFSET works somewhat like COPY with relative coordinates, and a direction perpendicular to the line. More generally, OFFSET does its best to create a object *parallel* to the one you pick, at the specified distance.

Note OFFSET creates only lines that are parallel to the original. Therefore, when you are selecting a point for an offset line to pass through, only the distance perpendicular to the original object is used. Although the new line might not actually pass through the specified point, it would if it were long enough to do so.

When used with arcs and circles, OFFSET creates a concentric arc or circle with the radius determined by the original radius and the offset distance. The rectangle object you drew is a polyline; it is a single complex object (described in detail in Chapter 16, "Increasing Your Drawing Power with Polylines and Double Lines"). OFFSET creates a new polyline whose elements are offset according to the same rules applied to normal lines, arcs, and circles. In this case, the effect is to create a square within the square.

Note OFFSET has no effect on nonlinear objects such as block, solid, dimension, text, or point objects.

Careful use of the OFFSET command can avoid a lot of calculations. Offsetting a line drawn at an angle replicates the original angle. The distance is always interpreted as perpendicular; you do not even need to know the angle. For example, when drawing a section through a pipe with insulation, you can simply offset the pipe's outside diameter by the thickness of the insulation. This guarantees that the thickness is correct and the overall diameter is concentric with the pipe—you do not need to calculate the new circle's diameter value. As pointed out in Chapter 12, "Accessing Your Drawing's Data," you can use the LIST command to reveal the new circle's diameter if you need to know what it is.

Tip Use OFFSET to create construction lines to which you can snap with object snap modes. You can later erase these lines, or use other editing commands such as BREAK, TRIM, EXTEND, or FILLET to convert them into part of the final drawing, as you will do later in this chapter.

OFFSET is especially useful with polylines. Use polyline for instance, to create a complex foundation or building wall outline; then use OFFSET to create a perimeter footing or double-line plan.

Offsetting polylines may yield unexpected results (as shown in fig. 14.4), but if you analyze them, you can see why OFFSET creates what it does. The bottom half of the figure shows two original polylines, and the top shows copies of the polylines with offset polylines inside and outside them. Offset must maintain a parallel distance, so the inside offset line on the left ignores the pockets in the original polyline. Likewise, the offset polylines of the figure eight can't stay parallel if they cross like the original, so they only offset from one lobe.

The second editing tool that creates replicas of an original object is the ARRAY command.

Making Multiple Copies with ARRAY

ARRAY is a powerful tool for creating many identical copies of a group of objects in a regular pattern. The ARRAY command is as aptly named as OFFSET. Use it to create multiple copies of selected objects in a *rectangular* or *polar* (circular) array. Unlike OFFSET, ARRAY works with any number or type of objects, and all the selection options are available.

Figure 14.4

Unexpected results with the OFFSET command and polylines.

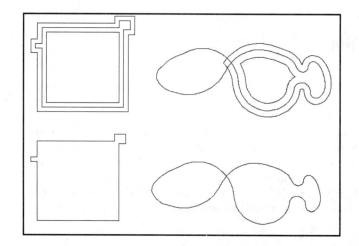

Note Most "benchmark programs" used to rate the performance of AutoCAD or other CAD software on a particular computer include an operation that creates a large array of complicated objects. Very few commands can create drawing data as rapidly as the ARRAY command can, so it is very adept for this purpose.

In the following exercise, you use ARRAY to replicate the door panels and complete the semicircular light (the window in the door).

Making Multiple Copies with ARRAY

Continue from the preceding exercise.

Command: *Choose* **C**onstruct, **A**rray	Issues the ARRAY command
_array	
Select objects: *Select both squares near* ① *(see fig. 14.5)*	Specifies the objects to be arrayed
2 found	
Select objects: (Enter)	Completes the selection set
Rectangular or Polar array (R/P) <R>: (Enter)	Accepts the default Rectangular array option

`Number of rows (---) <1>:` **`2`** `Enter`	Specifies the number of rows for the array
`Number of columns (¦¦¦) <1>:` **`2`** `Enter`	Specifies the number of columns
`Unit cell or distance between rows (---):` *Pick the lower left corner of the square at* ① *(see fig. 14.5)*	Specifies the base point for the array
`Other corner:` *Pick the point 6'2",3'3" at* ②	Specifies the row and column offsets for the array and copies the squares
`Command:` *Pick the line object at* ③ *and enter* **AR**	Issues the ARRAY command with the line selected
`ARRAY 1 found`	
`Select objects:`	
`Rectangular or Polar array (R/P) <R>:` **`P`** `Enter`	Specifies the Polar array option
`Center point of array:` *Click on the Center tool*	Activates the CENter object snap
`_CEN of` *Pick the arc at* ④	Snaps to the center of the arc
`Number of items:` **`5`** `Enter`	Specifies that four new arcs are to be created (the existing arc counts as one)
`Angle to fill (+=ccw, -=cw) <360>:` *Pick a point left of the arc's center*	Uses Ortho mode to specify a 180-degree angle
`Rotate objects as they are copied? <Y>` `Enter`	Accepts the default and creates the new lines rotated around the arc's center

ARRAY originally defaults to rectangular arrays. The rectangular array is aligned orthogonally to the current UCS. You can use the UCS command to rotate the alignment. As with OFFSET, ARRAY retains the Rectangular/Polar option specified in the previous usage as the default selection.

ARRAY. The ARRAY command makes multiple copies of objects, creating a rectangular array (copies arranged parallel to the X,Y axis) or a polar array (copies arranged in a circular pattern). Objects in polar arrays can be rotated about the array's center point or copied with their original orientation.

Figure 14.5

Using the ARRAY command.

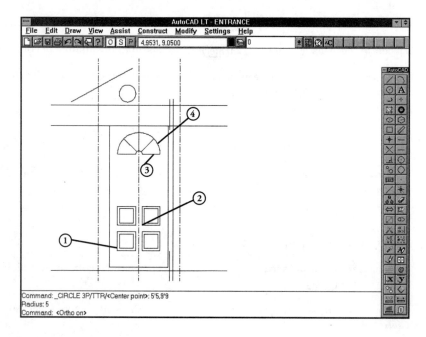

The ARRAY command has the following options:

◆ **Rectangular.** The Rectangular option displays the following prompts:

```
Number of rows (---) <1>:
Number of columns (¦¦¦) <1>:
Unit cell or distance between rows (---):
Distance between columns (¦¦¦): or Other corner:
```

If you choose rectangular, ARRAY prompts for the number of horizontal rows for the array, and then the number of vertical columns. Accept the default number (one) for either horizontal rows or vertical columns, and AutoCAD LT does not prompt for the corresponding distance. To create an array, you must specify at least two rows or two columns; accept all the defaults and AutoCAD LT does nothing (One-element array, nothing to do).

AutoCAD LT then asks you to specify the unit cell distances. These may be entered as individual values, or by specifying two opposite corners of a *unit cell* (the corners of a box whose sides represent the horizontal and vertical offsets of the array). You can "show" AutoCAD LT the unit cell, as you did at the start of the exercise, or enter either absolute or relative coordinates for the corners of the box. The first corner selected becomes the base point for the direction of the array created.

If you specify the distances, you can either enter them or "show them" to AutoCAD LT with two points. The prompts include simple symbols to remind you of the direction being specified. By using the pointing device to specify the unit cell or distances between rows and columns, you can base the array on other features within your drawing such as the snap grid or object snaps.

◆ **Polar.** The Polar option displays the following prompts:

```
Center point of array:
Number of items:
Angle to fill (+=ccw, -=cw) <360>:
Angle between items:
Rotate objects as they are copied? <Y>
```

The Polar option of the ARRAY command is used to create circular arrays. The center point specifies the base point around which the objects are created. As with the rectangular array, the number of items is the total, including the existing items being arrayed. Unless you are filling 360 degrees, you usually want to specify one more copy than the angle to fill, divided by the angle between copies. For example, in the preceding exercise, 180 degrees divided by 45 degrees between copies equals four, so you specified five items. The angle to fill is the included angle from the center to each existing item, to the end of the array. The default angle is 360. If you specify a 360-degree angle, AutoCAD LT spaces the number of copies equally around a circular array. With the default angle direction settings (see Chapter 8, "Preparing Your Workspace: CAD Concepts 1B"), a positive angle causes AutoCAD LT to construct the array in a counterclockwise direction (like arcs); a negative angle constructs the array clockwise. ARRAY accepts angle values between 1 and 360, (and –1 and –360); larger values are treated as if all possible whole multiples of 360 had been subtracted first.

The final prompt when using the Polar option enables you to choose whether AutoCAD LT rotates each group of objects as it is copied. The default is yes, which creates an array like that in the exercise. This situation is more common. Choosing no causes ARRAY to place each copy at a new angular location but with the original rotation. Because each object is located based on its original relationship to the array's center, this option can have unexpected results.

Tip You can use ARRAY to create multiple copies, and then use ERASE to remove some of the objects if the required array is not completely regular or consistent.

Use a rotated UCS to create rectangular arrays at angles other than 0 and 90.

Both OFFSET and ARRAY create copies identical to the objects you select (or at most rotated). To create copies within a symmetric design, you will need to use the MIRROR command.

Creating Reflected Copies with MIRROR

Many designs have elements that are mirror images of each other. AutoCAD LT's MIRROR command enables you to easily draw such elements once and replicate them mirrored about a central axis.

In the following exercise, you use MIRROR to quickly develop some symmetric portions of the entrance. The new prototype drawing reflects the state of the ENTRANCE drawing at the end of the preceding exercise except that the door has been drawn using the RECTANG command, and the door's bottom and vertical layout lines have been erased. You create sketched lines on the current LAYOUT layer to suggest outlines of the parts of the columns and the pediment, and a circle to locate the figured cutout (see fig. 14.6).

Using MIRROR to Lay Out a Symmetric Design

Use the ALT1402.DWG file as a prototype, using no setup method, to create a new drawing named ENTRANCE.

With Ortho on, draw a line from 7'9",0'6" ① (see fig. 14.6) to 9'0"<90 for left side of right column. Then draw two 1'6" lines at 90 degrees from 7'7",0'6" ② , and 7'7",8'0" ③.

Turn Ortho off and draw a line from 5'8",11'0" ④ to 2'6",9'4" ⑤.

Finally, draw a 5" radius circle with its center at 5'5",9'9" ⑥, and turn Ortho back on. The drawing should now match figure 14.6.

Command: *Choose* **C**onstruct, **M**irror	Issues the MIRROR command
_mirror	
Select objects: *Select the three lines you just drew at the right of the door, press Enter*	Uses standard object selection methods
First point of mirror line: *Click on the Midpoint tool*	Activates the MIDpoint object snap
_MID of *Pick the column center line at* ⑦	Uses the center line as the mirror axis

`Second point:` *Pick above or below the first point (with Ortho on)*	Specifies a vertical axis
`Delete old objects? <N>` (**Enter**)	Completes the MIRROR command and copies the lines to the left of the door

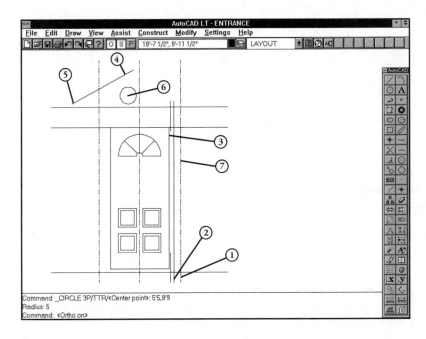

Figure 14.6

Creating elements that are symmetrical to the door's center line.

The MIDpoint object snap only ensured that you had a point on the center line. It was not necessary to use the exact center of the line; the NEAr or INTersection object snaps would have worked equally well.

Next, you use the OFFSET command to create the rightmost line of the entrance.

`Command:` **OF** (**Enter**)	Issues the OFFSET command
`Offset distance or Through <Through>:` **4** (**Enter**)	Specifies a 4" offset distance
`Select object to offset:` *Pick the new line at* ⑧ *(see fig. 14.7)*	Specifies the objects to be offset
`Side to offset?` *Pick a point to the right to create the line at* ⑨	Creates the right edge of the complete entrance
`Select object to offset:` (**Enter**)	Completes the OFFSET command

continues

continued

`Command:` *Select all seven lines to the right of the door plus the circle and the angled line above it, then enter* `MI`	Issues the MIRROR command with the objects selected
`MIRROR 9 found`	
`First point of mirror line:` *Click on the Midpoint tool*	Activates the MIDpoint object snap
`_MID of` *Pick the center line of the door at* ⑩	Specifies the base point for the mirror operation
`Second point:` *Turn Ortho off and move the cursor around*	Rubber-band images reflect that any angle for the mirror axis is now possible
`<Ortho off>` *Turn Ortho back on*	
`<Ortho on>` *Pick directly above or below the first point*	Specifies a vertical axis
`Delete old objects? <N>` ⟨Enter⟩	Mirrors all objects to the opposite side of the door center line (see fig. 14.7)

Figure 14.7

Using the MIRROR command to copy the symmetric door elements.

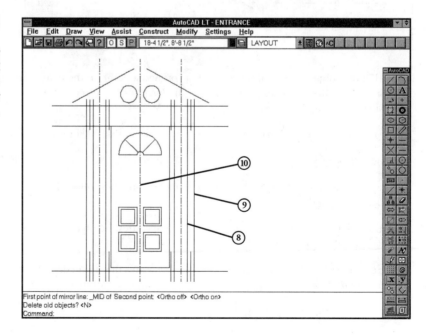

MIRROR is simple; select the objects to be mirrored and show AutoCAD LT the mirror axis. The only option is whether or not to delete old objects. The axis line can be at any angle; MIRROR accurately transposes objects across the axis.

MIRROR. The MIRROR command creates a mirror image of selected objects. The selected objects can be retained (the default) or deleted.

The MIRROR command has the following prompts:

◆ `First point of mirror line:` At this prompt, you must specify the first point of an axis about which the selection set is to be mirrored.

◆ `Second point:` At this prompt, you must specify the second point of an axis about which the selection set is to be mirrored.

◆ `Delete old objects? <N>:` At this prompt, you must answer **N** to keep the original in place and make a mirror copy, or **Y** to mirror the object and delete the original.

MIRROR works with all types of drawing objects, including text. AutoCAD LT provides a system variable, **MIRRTEXT**, which enables you to use MIRROR to place text at its mirrored location without reversing the text itself. Use the default MIRRTEXT setting of 1 to cause text to be mirrored literally (as it appears in a mirror), or change the setting to 0 to have text read correctly even though it is mirrored.

The preceding exercise used **MIRROR** to create symmetric elements of the entrance figure. MIRROR is equally useful for simply creating an opposite hand image of a single figure; just respond yes to the `Delete old objects?` prompt. Also, you picked points on the center lines for the axis reference. MIRROR does not require that you use lines; you may specify any two points as the axis.

The MIRROR and ARRAY commands have a "broad brush" quality. They work well in quickly laying out designs—developing relationships and proportions. Both commands can do double duty; objects to be mirrored or arrayed often start out as simple outlines or references. As the design develops, detail added to individual elements can be replicated as well. It is important to plan ahead—include as many elements as you can in the portion of the design to be mirrored or arrayed. You may find it easier to erase the copies and repeat the ARRAY or MIRROR command rather than to perform multiple edits as details change or evolve.

Stop It is a very bad practice to create half-length lines perpendicular to a mirror axis, and then mirror them along with other features. This practice creates two separate line segments that appear as one. Such lines may not meet perfectly or may plot with a blip of ink where they meet because pen plotters aren't perfect.

AutoCAD LT makes this sort of back-and-forth design process quick and easy. Examples are included in the remainder of the exercises in this chapter. In the next section, you look at the commands for refining details of your design. In many cases, once you have developed the "big picture," you clean up your design and reapply the "broad brush" commands to apply the finish refinements.

Editing to Clean Up and Add Detail

The previous section described commands used to create new objects from existing objects. This section shows you the commands you can use to refine your design elements: BREAK, FILLET, CHAMFER, TRIM, and EXTEND. Each of these commands is used to modify existing objects. They are commonly used to refine a design that has been laid out quickly with drawing commands and editing commands such as those previously described in this chapter.

For example, in the previous section, you used the OFFSET and MIRROR commands to work out the proportions of the columns and the pediment of a residential entrance design. In practice, once you had the proportions you wanted, you might erase all but one set of layout lines, change them to your detail layer, develop one-half of the column outline in detail, and then repeat the mirroring process to complete the design. The following exercises continue to work on this design, using this strategy.

Refining a Layout Using the BREAK Command

With the BREAK command, you can break one object into two, or remove a section of a circle to make an arc. The BREAK command works only with lines, arcs, circles, and polylines, and it requires selection by picking points. It does not use the noun/verb selection set mechanism, nor do the normal selection options apply.

In the following exercise, you use the BREAK command to divide layout lines and to break a circle. If you are using AutoCAD LT Release 2, you can also try BREAK in conjunction with tracking and direct distance entry.

In the exercise, you specify break points that leave lines overlapping the ends of other lines, so the overlapping lines can be used in later exercises to demonstrate other editing commands. These lines will become parts of separate features. In the prototype drawing, most of the other layout lines created in the previous exercises have been erased, and a single vertical line and several horizontal lines have been added to the detail layer. These lines are used to construct the base and capital of the right column (see fig. 14.8). The snap increment has been set to ½", to suit the greater level of detail. Notice that the current layer, NOTES, is irrelevant because editing commands such as BREAK do not change the layer of the objects they affect.

Developing a Design with the BREAK Command

Create a new drawing named ENTRANCE, using the ALT1403.DWG as a prototype and using no setup method.

Command: *Click on the Break tool*	Issues the BREAK command
_BREAK Select object: *Pick the outside line at* ① *(see fig. 14.8)*	Selects the line and sets the first break point
Enter second point (or F for first point): *Pick the same line at* ②	Erases the line between the two points
The original line is now two lines.	
Command: **Enter**	Repeats the BREAK command
BREAK Select object: *Pick the same line at* ③	Selects the line and sets the first break point
Enter second point (or F for first point): @ **Enter**	Specifies the same point and breaks the line at that point
Command: *Select the same line above* ③	Highlights the segment to confirm that it is now two lines
Command: *Choose* **M**odify, **B**reak	Issues the BREAK command
_break Select object: *Pick the circle at* ④ *(see fig. 14.9)*	Selects the circle and sets the first break point

continues

continued

Figure 14.8

Using the BREAK command.

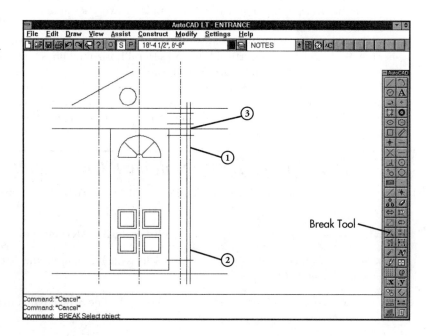

```
Enter second point (or F for first       Specifies the second break point and
point): Pick the circle again at ⑤       breaks the circle

Command: BR (Enter)                       Issues the BREAK command

BREAK Select object: Pick the line
at ⑥

Enter second point (or F for first       Erases the portion of the line to the
point): Pick a point beyond the left     left of the selected point
end of the line ⑦                        (see fig. 14.10)
```

Save the drawing

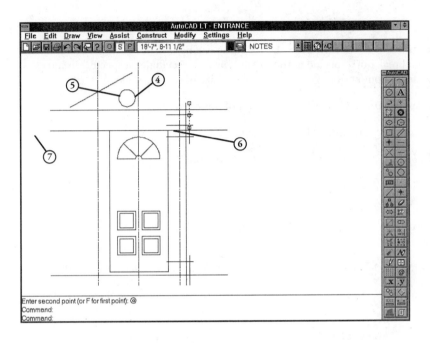

Figure 14.9

Breaking a circle into an arc and breaking off the end of a line.

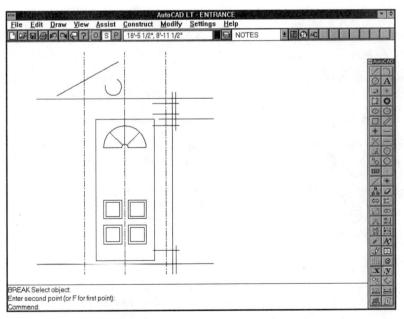

Figure 14.10

The results of using the BREAK command.

continues

ALT2

continued

If you are using AutoCAD LT Release 2, try the following example of using tracking and direct distance entry. You break out a specific portion of an object, a rectangle, at specific distances from corner points, without knowing the coordinates or size of the rectangle.

If you are using AutoCAD LT Release 1, skip the rest of this exercise.

Zoom to the view shown in figure 14.11 and turn off Snap.

Command: BR **(Enter)**	Issues the BREAK command
BREAK Select object: *Pick the rectangle at* ⑧ *(see fig. 14.11)*	
Enter second point (or F for first point): **F (Enter)**	Enables you to respecify the first point
Enter first point: **TK (Enter)**	Enters tracking mode (see Chapter 11)
First tracking point: *Use an INTersection object snap to pick* ⑨	Sets first tracking point and displays a rubberband tracking line from it
Next point (Press RETURN to end tracking): *Turn off Snap and move the cursor left and right over* ⑨ *then move to* ⑩ *to ensure that it is tracking to the right, type* **2** *and press Enter*	Sets tracking direction horizontally to the right, then uses direct distance entry to track to a point 2" to the right of ⑨
Next point (Press RETURN to end tracking): **(Enter)**	Accepts the current tracking point as the first break point
Enter second point: **TK (Enter)**	Enters tracking mode for second break point
First tracking point: *Use an INTersection object snap to pick* ⑪	Sets first tracking point and displays a rubberband tracking line from it
Next point (Press RETURN to end tracking): *Move the cursor up and down over* ⑪ *then move to* ⑫ *to ensure that it is tracking down, type* **2** *and press Enter*	Sets tracking direction vertically down, then uses direct distance entry (see Chapter 2) to track to a point 2" below ⑪
Next point (Press RETURN to end tracking): **(Enter)**	Accepts the current tracking point as the second break point and breaks the rectangle to match figure 14.12
Command: **U (Enter)**	Undoes the break

BREAK

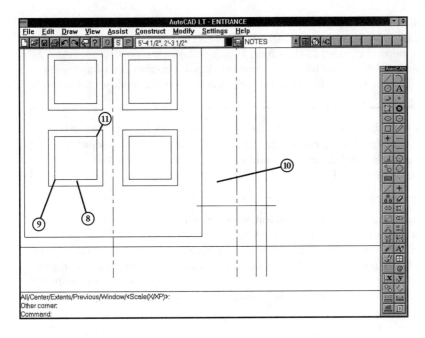

Figure 14.11

Using tracking and direct distance entry with BREAK.

14

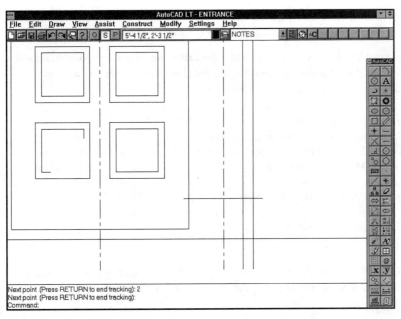

Figure 14.12

Rectangle after breaking.

BREAK uses the point you pick as the default for the first break point. The second pick need not be "on" the object—AutoCAD LT projects to the nearest point on the object. Picking beyond the end of the object removes the entire portion from the first point. Using the @ symbol for the second break point creates two objects with coincident endpoints. BREAK is applied to circles in a counterclockwise direction.

> **BREAK.** The BREAK command erases portions of objects between two specified points. You can break lines, circles, arcs, and 2D polylines. The point you pick to select an object to break becomes the default first break point, but you can use the F option to respecify this first point.

The BREAK command has only one option, which was demonstrated in the tracking and direct distance entry example at the end of the previous exercise. After picking an object to break, enter **F** to specify a different first point for the break. This is very useful when a break point you want to specify is too near another object to select in a single pick. It also enables you to select anywhere on the object you want to break, and then use object snaps to identify the actual break points, for example, where it intersects another object.

Stop Circles break counterclockwise from the first selected point to the second. If you reverse the points, you end up with the opposite section of the circle.

You cannot break closed polylines across the first vertex. If you try, you end up with the portion of the polyline between the break points that includes the first vertex (probably the opposite of what you intended).

One very common use of break is for "erasing" portions of objects "hidden" by others, for instance, if one pipe crosses over another. You draw each pipe as continuous lines, and then use the BREAK command to remove a portion of the more distant pipe. You can also use the TRIM command (described later in this section), but BREAK has a flexibility that enables you to specify new endpoints anywhere, not just at boundaries. Also, although AutoCAD LT does not accept blocks as trim boundaries, you can use object snap modes (such as INTersection) with the BREAK command to "trim" objects at features contained within blocks.

Tip To get rid of an unwanted portion of a long line that extends beyond the display, use the BREAK command at two visible points on the line, then erase the unwanted portion.

BREAK is very useful for rough cleanup and detailing. To do precise work with BREAK, however, you need to use it with object snaps. Two other commands that

you can use for cleanup, FILLET and CHAMFER, incorporate greater precision into their function.

Making Ends Meet with FILLET and CHAMFER

FILLET and CHAMFER are closely related commands used to create filleted, beveled, or precise intersections between lines or at the intersections between adjacent straight segments of polylines. FILLET also works with arcs. The command names are derived from woodworking and machining operations that impart rounded or faceted features to sharp edges.

In the following exercise, you use the FILLET command to first make lines meet precisely, then to form filleted intersections between lines and arcs, and then to apply radii to all the vertices of a polyline. Start with using FILLET on the lower right corner of the entrance as shown in figure 14.13.

Making Ends Meet with FILLET

Continue from the preceding exercise. Zoom in on the lower right half of the door and column base (see fig. 14.13).

Command: *Choose* **C***onstruct,* **F***illet*	Issues the FILLET command
_fillet Polyline/Radius/<Select first object>: *Pick the line at* ①	Specifies the first segment for the fillet
Select second object: *Pick the line at* ②	Specifies the second segment and creates a clean corner (the current radius is 0)
Command: (Enter)	Repeats the FILLET command
FILLET Polyline/Radius/<Select first object>: **R** (Enter)	Specifies the Radius option
Enter fillet radius <0'-0">: **3** (Enter)	Sets a 3-inch fillet radius

Next, you use the FILLET command on the same two lines.

Command: (Enter)	Repeats the FILLET command
FILLET Polyline/Radius/<Select first object>: *Pick the line at* ①	Specifies the first line for the fillet

continues

continued

`Select second object:` *Pick the line at* ②	Specifies the second line and creates a 3-inch radius corner
`Command:` **F** `Enter`	Issues the FILLET command

Figure 14.13

Working with the FILLET command.

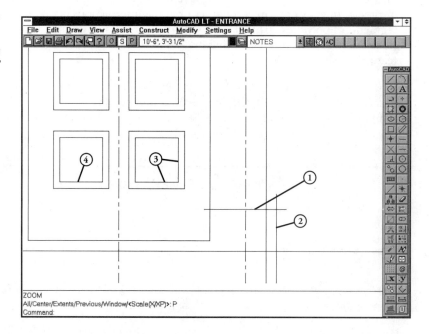

Unless you use one of AutoCAD LT Release 2's setup methods, the default FILLET radius value is 0, which makes the elements meet at a coincident point (their physical or projected intersection). You can specify a different radius to fillet corners with arcs. The radius, once entered, is retained as the default.

> **FILLET.** The FILLET command creates an arc between any combination of two lines, circles, or arcs. You also can use FILLET to create an arc between two adjacent segments of a 2D polyline, or at all vertices of a single 2D polyline. If the selected objects do not intersect, or if they extend past their intersection, FILLET extends or trims them as needed. You also can use FILLET to set a default fillet radius (initially 0, unless you use Quick or Custom Setup) that is used by subsequent FILLET commands.

FILLET has the following options:

◆ **Polyline.** Use the P option to apply fillets to all vertices of a polyline where two straight segments (with lengths greater than the specified radius) meet.

◆ **Radius.** Use the R option to change the default fillet radius.

In the following exercise, you will see how the FILLET command affects polylines (see Chapter 16, "Increasing Your Drawing Power with Polylines and Double Lines," for more on polylines).

Filleting Polylines

Continue from the preceding exercise to discover the effect the FILLET command has on polylines.

`FILLET Polyline/Radius/<Select first object>:` *Pick one side of the polyline square at* ③ *(see fig. 14.13)*	Specifies the first segment for the fillet
`Select second object:` *Pick the adjacent side of the square at* ③	Specifies the second segment and creates a 3-inch radius corner
`Command:` (Enter)	Repeats the FILLET command
`FILLET Polyline/Radius/<Select first object>:` **P** (Enter)	Specifies the Polyline option
`Select 2D polyline:` *Pick any side of the polyline square at* ④	Selects the polyline and fillets all of its corners with a 3-inch radius
`4 lines were filleted`	Reports the number of sides filleted (see fig. 14.14)

Next, you reset the radius back to 0" and repeat the last three FILLET commands.

`Command:` (Enter)	Repeats the FILLET command
`FILLET Polyline/Radius/<Select first object>:` **R** (Enter)	Specifies the Radius option
`Enter fillet radius <0'-3">:` **0** (Enter)	Sets a 0" fillet radius

continues

continued

Figure 14.14

Rounding off corners with the FILLET command.

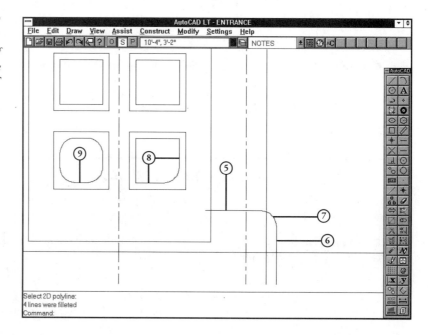

Command: **Enter**	Repeats the FILLET command
FILLET Polyline/Radius/<Select first object>: *Pick the line at* ⑤ *(see fig. 14.14)*	Specifies the first line for the fillet
Select second object: *Pick the line at* ⑥	Specifies the second line, creates a square corner, but leaves the previous fillet arc

Erase the arc at ⑦ before refilleting the polyline square at ⑧.

Command: **F Enter**	Issues the FILLET command
FILLET Polyline/Radius/<Select first object>: *Pick one side of the polyline square at* ⑧	Specifies the first segment for the fillet
Select second object: *Pick the adjacent side of the square at* ⑧	Specifies the second segment and changes the corner to square, removing the arc segment
Command: **Enter**	
FILLET Polyline/Radius/<Select first object>: **P Enter**	Specifies the Polyline option

`Select 2D polyline:` *Pick any side of the polyline square at* ⑨	Selects the polyline and squares all its corners, removing the arcs
`4 lines were filleted`	Reports the number of sides filleted

When you used the P option, AutoCAD LT applied FILLET to every intersection of straight segments on the polyline.

Stop Applying FILLET to a polyline with existing arc segments bounded by straight segments changes all the arcs to the radius specified by the FILLET command. If this is not the desired result, use FILLET without the P option to fillet the desired individual vertices (see the discussion of polylines in Chapter 16, "Increasing Your Drawing Power with Polylines and Double Lines").

FILLET creates a separate tangent arc when applied to lines (or arcs). Changing the radius of a fillet arc requires undoing or erasing the arc and trying again. In contrast, polyline fillet arcs are created as part of the polyline; changing the radius of a single polyline fillet is simply a matter of applying the command again.

The FILLET and CHAMFER commands work essentially the same way. The initial prompt offers options for radius (FILLET) or distances (CHAMFER). Unless you use Quick or Custom Setup, the default value is 0, which makes the elements meet at a coincident point (their physical or projected intersection). The radius or distances, once entered, are retained as the default for the next occurrence of the command. Both commands can be used to modify polylines (the squares) in the same way individual line objects are modified, or you can use the P option and have AutoCAD LT apply FILLET or CHAMFER to every intersection of straight segments that occurs on the polyline.

Note Each new fillet arc or chamfer segment is created with the layer, color, and linetype properties of the objects selected—if both objects have the same properties. If the objects do not have the same layer, color, and linetype properties, the fillet arc or chamfer segment is created with the current object layer, color, and linetype property settings.

The most common use for the FILLET command involves setting the radius to 0 and using it to force lines (perhaps quickly sketched) to meet at precise intersections. This procedure gives you a quick and easy way to clean up a quickly produced layout.

Tip If you frequently need to use FILLET with a non-zero radius, use CHAMFER with distances set to 0 for cleanup. In this way, you can avoid having to reset the FILLET default (or the other way around if you use CHAMFER more often).

In the following exercise, you continue in the entrance design using the CHAMFER command to develop the details of the column base and capital.

Beveling Corners with CHAMFER

Continue from the preceding exercise.

Command: *Choose* **C**onstruct, C**h**amfer	Issues the CHAMFER command
_chamfer Polyline/Distances/ Select first line>: **D** (Enter)	Specifies the Distance option
Enter first chamfer distance <0'-0">: **1-1/2** (Enter)	Sets the length of the chamfer's first side
Enter second chamfer distance <0'-1 1/2">: (Enter)	Accepts the default length, which matches the first side
Command: (Enter)	Repeats the CHAMFER command
CHAMFER Polyline/Distances/<Select first line>: *Pick the line at* ⑤ *(see fig. 14.14)*	Specifies the first line for the chamfer
Select second line: *Pick the line at* ⑥	Specifies the second line and creates the chamfer

Use the Aerial View to pan to the upper right corner of the entrance, as shown in figure 14.15.

Command: **CF** (Enter)	Issues the CHAMFER command
CHAMFER Polyline/Distances/<Select first line>: *Pick the line at* ⑩	Specifies the first line for the chamfer
Select second line: *Pick the line at* ⑪	Specifies the second line and creates the chamfer

Repeat the CHAMFER command and select the lines at ⑫ and ⑬ (see fig. 14.16).

CHAMFER creates straight segments. Therefore, unlike FILLET, which can remove or modify existing arc radii when applied to polylines, CHAMFER does not remove or modify previously created chamfer segments. Using CHAMFER a second time on a polyline, with a distance setting that is less than the previous one, will create all new chamfers at some or all of the previously created chamfer vertices.

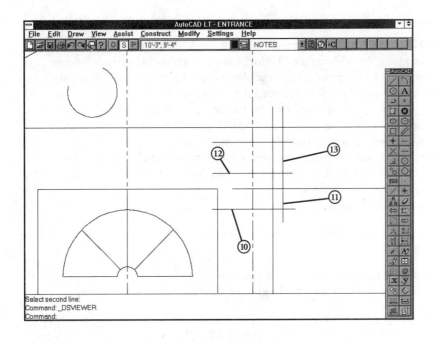

Figure 14.15

Using the CHAMFER command.

14

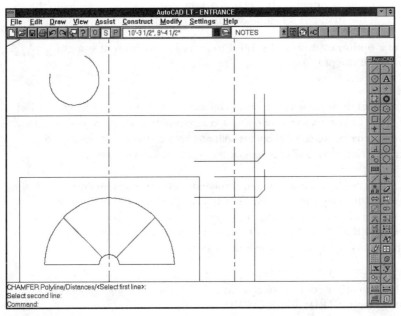

Figure 14.16

Intersections changed into chamfers.

CHAMFER. The CHAMFER command creates an angled line connecting two intersecting lines. You also can use CHAMFER to create an angled segment between two adjacent straight segments of a 2D polyline, or at all vertices of straight segments throughout a single 2D polyline. You can set the distance (default 0, unless you use Quick or Custom Setup) measured from the real or projected intersection of the lines to the start of the chamfer on each line. CHAMFER extends or trims the lines to those distances from their intersection and then joins the endpoints with a new line or segment. The first line you select is modified by the first chamfer distance, and the second line is modified by the second distance. The default value for the second distance is always equal to the first.

CHAMFER has the following options. The first is essentially the same as the FILLET Polyline option:

◆ **Polyline.** Use the P option to apply chamfers to all vertices of a polyline where two straight segments (with lengths greater than the specified distance) meet.

◆ **Distances.** Use the D option to specify the distances back from the intersection to the ends of the CHAMFER segment. CHAMFER requires two distances (one for each line segment). The second distance you specify defaults to the same value as the first, but it can be different from the first if you so specify.

You can use the P option to apply CHAMFER to every intersection of straight segments that occurs on the polyline.

Note Unlike FILLET, in which the P option can be used with a zero radius to remove fillet arcs, using CHAMFER with distances set to zero has no effect on a polyline. If the previous command created chamfers with non-zero distances, changing to a distance setting of zero will not remove the segments that were created.

The exercises illustrate the potential for multiplying your efforts. The entrance design shown has panels with sharp square corners. You can quickly see the effect of filleted or chamfered corners by erasing all but one (inner or outer) square, applying FILLET or CHAMFER with the P option to it, and then using the OFFSET and ARRAY commands as you did in the previous section.

While you use FILLET and CHAMFER primarily to clean up the ends of objects, AutoCAD LT has two other commands that you can also use to make objects meet others at a distinct point: TRIM and EXTEND.

Cleaning Up with TRIM and EXTEND

During design development, objects you draw may often overlap, extend beyond where they should, or stop short of some feature they need to intersect. AutoCAD LT has two related commands you can use to redefine the endpoints of one object in terms of its intersection with another object: TRIM and EXTEND.

These two commands do exactly what their names imply. You use TRIM to remove a portion of one object when it projects beyond another. You use EXTEND to project an object until it intersects with another. In each case, only the trimmed or extended objects' endpoints change. Arcs retain their radii, lines retain their angles, and both retain their original opposite endpoints.

In the first exercise in this section, you use the TRIM command to clean up the outlines of the column's capital (see fig. 14.17). Next, with these parts defined, you use COPY and MIRROR to develop the elements of the complete capital. Finally, you use EXTEND to finish the horizontal details and clean up the circular detail in the pediment.

14

Cleaning Up with TRIM

Create a new drawing named ENTRANCE based on the ALT1404.DWG prototype, using no setup method.

Zoom in on the upper half of the door and column capital (see fig. 14.17).

Command: *Click on the Trim tool*	Issues the TRIM command
Command: _TRIM Select cutting edge(s)...	
Select objects: *Pick the lines at* ①, ②, ③, *then press Enter* *(see fig. 14.17)*	Selects the lines and completes the selection of edge objects
<Select object to trim>/Undo: *Pick the line at* ④	Trims the line at the ③ line intersection (see fig. 14.18)
<Select object to trim>/Undo: *Pick the line at* ⑤	Trims the line at the ② line intersection
<Select object to trim>/Undo: *Pick the line at* ⑥	Removes the portion of the line between the ① line and the ② line

continues

continued

```
<Select object to trim>/Undo:
Choose Modify, Trim
```
Cancels the current trim operation
and reissues the TRIM command

```
*Cancel*
```

Figure 14.17

Using the TRIM command.

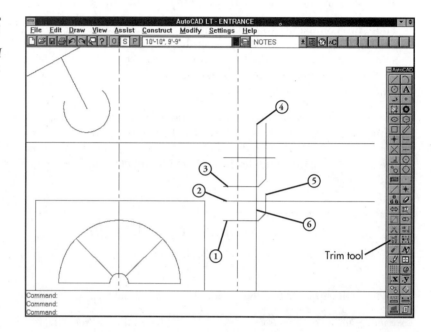

The previously trimmed objects should look like figure 14.18.

```
Command: _trim
Select cutting edge(s)...
```

```
Select objects: Pick the lines
at ⑦, ⑧, ⑨, then press Enter
(see fig. 14.18)
```
Selects the lines and completes the
selection of edge objects

```
<Select object to trim>/Undo:
Pick the line at ⑩
```
Trims the line at the ⑨ line

```
<Select object to trim>/Undo:
Pick the line at ⑪
```
Trims the line at the ⑦ line

```
<Select object to trim>/Undo:
Pick the line at ⑫
```
Trims the line off at the ⑧ line

`<Select object to trim>/Undo:` **Enter**	Completes the TRIM command (see the results in fig. 14.19)

Save the drawing

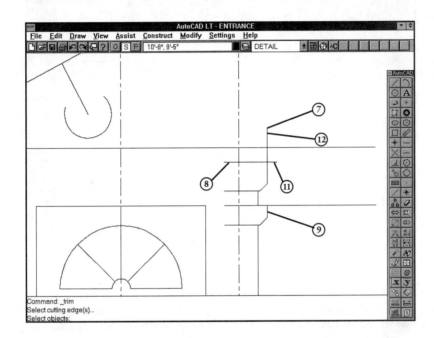

Figure 14.18

Trimming objects that are also selected as trim edges.

Unlike the BREAK, FILLET, and CHAMFER commands, the TRIM command uses a normal selection process for cutting edges. However, objects to be trimmed must be picked individually or by the Fence selection method. The portion of an object that is to be removed is controlled by the location of the pick point. The same object can be trimmed by several others within the same command by selecting several trim points. Each object is trimmed at the nearest edge it crosses; successive picks trim the object at successive edges. Objects selected as trim boundaries can also *be trimmed* by other objects selected as trim boundaries at the same time. The command alias for the TRIM command is TR.

> **TRIM.** The TRIM command removes portions of lines, arcs, circles, and 2D polylines that cross a selected cutting edge. You can select lines, circles, arcs, and polylines as cutting edges. An object can act as a cutting edge *and* be an object that is trimmed within the same command.

Figure 14.19

Results of the TRIM command exercise.

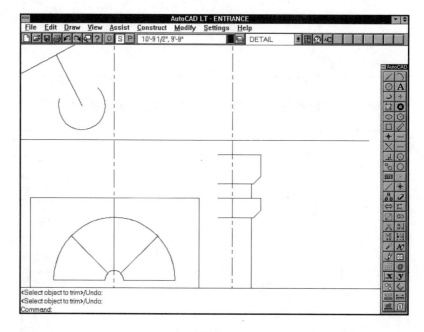

The TRIM command is very useful (like BREAK) for removing portions of objects that are depicted as being "behind" others. Simply select the foreground objects and trim away anything they should obscure. TRIM is also good for creating detail drawings from copied portions of larger figures. Simply create a boundary outline and then trim everything that extends beyond it. Use a polyline for boundary and you can select it with a single pick.

TRIM is a simple command. Its only option is Undo, which reverses the effect of the most recent pick. To trim objects, create a cutting edge selection set, then pick the objects to be trimmed on the side of the cutting edge where you want the excess removed. EXTEND is similar, and almost as simple as TRIM; you use EXTEND in the next exercise to complete the capital.

Before working with the EXTEND command, you need to create the lines for the right edge of the entrance's cornice by copying the three upper elements of the column edge. Next, you mirror the vertical elements of the right side of the column to the left (see fig. 14.20). You will then be ready to finish the capital by extending the horizontal lines into place. During the exercise, you will also experiment with the effect of extending an arc.

Filling in the Details with EXTEND

Continue from the preceding exercise.

Copy the three uppermost vertical/angled elements of the capital three inches to the right to create the cornice edge.

Use the MIRROR command to replicate all six vertical/angled elements of the right side of the capital (and column) to the left, about the center line (use the MIDpoint object snap to select the center line for the first point of the mirror line selection).

The results are shown in figure 14.20.

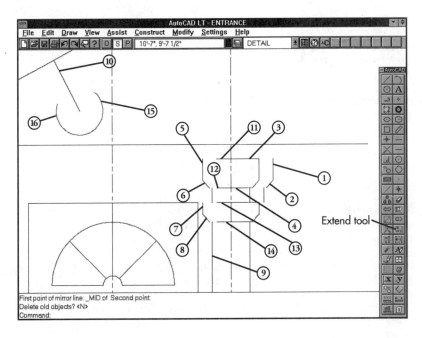

Figure 14.20

Components of the EXTEND exercise.

14

Command: *Click on the Extend tool*	Issues the EXTEND command

```
_EXTEND
Select boundary edge(s)...
```

Select objects: *Pick the vertical line at ① (see fig. 14.20) and the angled line at ②, then press Enter*	Selects the lines as boundary edges and completes the edge selections

continues

continued

`<Select object to extend>/Undo:` *Pick the top of the column at* ③	Extends the line to the cornice edge
`<Select object to extend>/Undo:` *Pick the horizontal line at* ④	Extends the line to the angled cornice edge
`<Select object to extend>/Undo:` **Enter**	Completes the EXTEND command
`Command:` *Choose* **M**odify, E**x**tend	Issues the EXTEND command
`_extend` `Select boundary edge(s)...`	
`Select objects:` *Pick the vertical line at* ⑤, *the left column lines at* ⑥, ⑦, ⑧, *and* ⑨, *and the angle line near the arc at* ⑩, *and then press Enter*	Selects the lines as boundary edges and completes the edge selections
`<Select object to extend>/Undo:` *Pick the top of the column at* ③	Fails because there is no boundary edge on that side
`No edge in that direction.`	
`<Select object to extend>/Undo:` *Pick the top of the column at* ⑪	Extends the line to the left face of the column
`<Select object to extend>/Undo:` *Continue to pick the horizontal lines at* ⑫, ⑬, *and* ⑭	Extends each line to the nearest boundary face, but the line at ⑭ needs further extension
`<Select object to extend>/Undo:` *Pick the line at* ⑭ *again*	Extends the line again—to the next boundary line
`<Select object to extend>/Undo:` *Pick the arc at* ⑮	Extends the arc clockwise to the line
`<Select object to extend>/Undo:` **U** **Enter**	Retracts the extension
`<Select object to extend>/Undo:` *Pick the arc at* ⑯	Extends the arc counter clockwise to the line
`<Select object to extend>/Undo:` **Enter**	Completes the EXTEND command

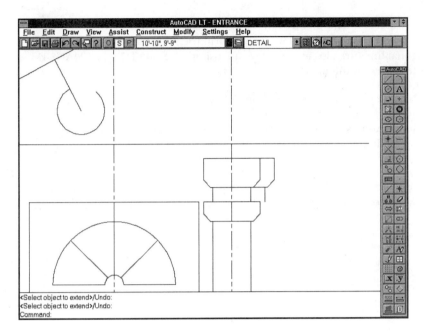

Figure 14.21

The nearly completed capital after using the EXTEND command.

14

Tip   The Fence object selection method is a quick and efficient way to trim or extend several objects at once. Each object is selected and extended as if picked at the point where it intersects the Fence selection line. In the previous exercise, you could have extended the lines at ⑪, ⑫, ⑬, and ⑭ with a Fence selection intersecting all four lines.

Like TRIM, EXTEND uses the standard object selection to define its boundary edges. You must then pick objects to extend individually or by the Fence selection method. AutoCAD LT attempts to extend each selected object in the direction of the endpoint nearest the point you pick. Each object is extended to the first boundary edge it reaches; successive picks extend the object to any successive boundaries.

EXTEND. The EXTEND command projects selected lines, arcs, and open polylines to meet selected boundary edges. You can use lines, arcs, circles, and polylines as boundary edges. You can select an object as both a boundary edge and as an object to extend.

The EXTEND command works in much the same sequence as the TRIM command. You first select object(s) to define the boundary lines, and then pick the individual objects to be extended. The objects to be extended must project to intersect the boundary objects; AutoCAD LT does not project the boundary objects.

EXTEND is very useful in completing mirrored details (as you were shown in the exercise), and it is the most practical way to perform the same task with lines at any angle. Orthogonal lines are also easy to elongate using the STRETCH or CHANGE commands (described in the next chapter).

Most of the entrance design can now be completed by simply repeating the steps depicted in the exercises presented so far. By working back and forth between refining the details and using COPY or MIRROR to replicate the results, you can quickly develop, evaluate, or revise almost any design you might need.

In this chapter, you have used editing commands to replicate existing features and to clean up the points at which they intersect. The next chapter describes four more editing commands you can use to modify objects and further enhance your drawing power.

Modifying Objects and Text

I n this chapter, you learn how to apply several AutoCAD LT edit commands that change the geometry of existing objects to the process of developing a drawing and modifying text. The first section of the chapter discusses commands that change the size and shape of objects. The second section of this chapter deals with editing and importing text.

In this chapter, you learn how to:

◆ Modify objects using the CHANGE command to change their endpoints

◆ Modify objects using the STRETCH command to stretch some points while others remain in place

◆ Modify objects using the ROTATE command, aligning them with other objects with the Reference option

◆ Modify the SCALE command to resize them

◆ Edit text using the Edit Text dialog box (DDEDIT)

◆ Import predefined text using the AutoCAD LT/Windows text-file import features

The tools in this chapter continue the demonstration begun in the previous chapter, showing how editing tools aid in the evolution of a design from a sketchy layout to a final drawing. Even after a drawing is supposedly final, these same tools aid in making revisions and updates.

You have seen and used most of AutoCAD LT's tools for making changes to your designs; now, this chapter introduces you to the rest of the editing tools. Through the course of this chapter's exercises, you continue the creation of a conceptual design of a residential entrance, as shown in figure 15.1. Within this context, the chapter introduces each command and gives simple examples of its use and illustrates methods of working in AutoCAD LT. The exercises also include further examples of using the commands covered in the previous chapter.

Figure 15.1

The completed entrance drawing.

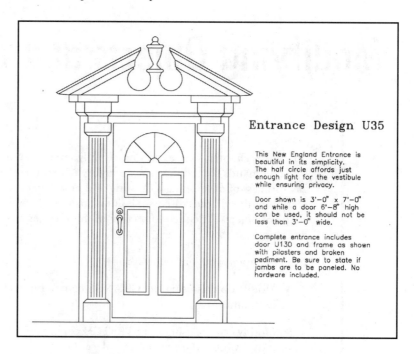

You begin with commands that modify existing objects independently of their relationship to others.

Modifying Objects

In this section, you learn to use four new commands to modify existing objects: CHANGE, STRETCH, ROTATE, and SCALE.

These tools set CAD far apart from traditional methods of design. Used in combination with grip editing or COPY and the other commands that replicate objects, these are the tools that provide the "draw it once, use it often" functionality. If the circle you drew is too small or too large—change it. If the building plan is too short or too long—stretch it. You do not need to redraw something to change its angular orientation or relative size.

Each of these commands has an important role in AutoCAD LT. The trick is learning to apply each one appropriately. Begin now with the CHANGE command. Although this command promises much, it requires good judgment if it is to be used to its best effect.

Making Changes with the CHANGE Command

The CHANGE command is a relic of the earliest versions of AutoCAD. It was originally used to move and change the radii of circles, move the endpoints of lines, move and rotate block insertions, make a variety of changes to text objects, and alter the properties of all types of objects. Other commands have been added that fulfill many of these needs better or more easily, but CHANGE still has some unique capabilities.

The prototype drawing used in the first exercise of this section contains the work you did in the preceding exercise, mirrored to both sides of the door and developed further. It includes a finial above the door, five short lines that will be elongated to represent the grooves on the columns, and several text objects. In the exercise, you use CHANGE to adjust the radius of the ball at the top of the finial (see fig. 15.2), and use TRIM to clean up the intersecting lines.

Using CHANGE to Modify a Circle

Create a new drawing named ENTRANCE using the ALT1501.DWG as a prototype and using no setup method. Zoom in on the finial at the top center of figure (see fig. 15.2).

Command: **CH** (Enter)	Issues the CHANGE command
CHANGE	
Select objects: *Pick the circle at* ① *(see fig. 15.2), and press Enter*	Selects the circle and ends object selection
Properties/<Change point>: *Pick the point at 6'2",11'6"*	Changes the radius of the circle to pass through the point picked

continues

continued

Figure 15.2

Changing the finial.

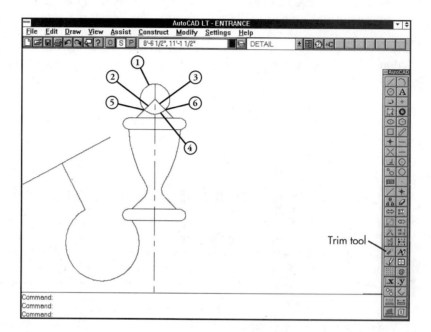

Trim tool

Command: **(Enter)**   Repeats the CHANGE command

CHANGE

Select objects: **P (Enter)**   Reselects the previous selection set

1 found

Select objects: **(Enter)**   Completes the selection

Properties/<Change point>: **(Enter)**   Prompts for a radius

Enter circle radius: **1-1/2 (Enter)**   Changes the radius of the circle to 1¹/₂"

Next, you clean up this detail using the **TRIM** command to remove portions of lines within the circle, and the circle between lines, then add a line at the base of the new arc.

Command: **TR (Enter)**   Issues the TRIM command

TRIM
Select cutting edge(s)...

Select objects: *Pick the circle at* ① *, the*   Specifies the cutting edge selection
line at ② *, and the line at* ③ *, then press Enter*

`<Select object to trim>/Undo:` *Pick the line at ②, the line at ③, and the circle at ④*	Specifies the objects to be trimmed and performs the trims
`<Select object to trim>/Undo:` *Click on the Line tool*	Cancels the TRIM command and issues the LINE command; the completed trims remain in effect
`_LINE From point:` *Use ENDPoint object snap to pick ⑤*	
`To point:` *Use ENDPoint to pick ⑥*	Draws a line across the base of the arc
`To point:` *(Enter)*	Completes the LINE command (see fig. 15.3)

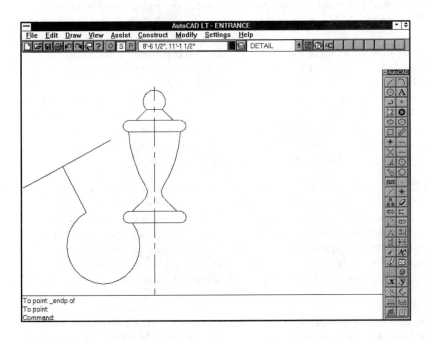

Figure 15.3

The changed finial.

15

The CHANGE prompts differ depending on the type of object selected. With a circle, CHANGE will change only the radius. With lines, CHANGE can change the endpoint location of one or more lines. Ortho mode has an effect similar to applying XY filtering to "change point." CHANGE can modify the location, text style, height, rotation, and even the text string of text objects or attribute definitions (see Chapter 13, "Using Object Properties and Text Styles").

Note The CHANGE command was once the only method available in AutoCAD for changing a line of text. An entire line of text had to be re-entered to correct a single character. AutoCAD LT has other text editing tools, which you will discover later in this chapter.

> **CHANGE.** The CHANGE command modifies the geometry and properties of existing objects. Its default is Change point, which specifies a new primary point for most objects. The effect varies with the object type.

Note The CHPROP command and the Change Properties dialog box provide a more efficient and easier way to change properties.

CHANGE has no options as such, except for Properties. It presents a series of prompts, which differ with each type of object. With a line or circle, CHANGE prompts for the "change point." Pick a point, and CHANGE relocates the nearest endpoint of the line to a new point, or adjusts the radius of a circle to pass through a point. Grip editing (see Chapter 7, "Making Changes: Using Grip Editing") works just as well for these functions. Press Enter at the <Change point> prompt for a circle, and CHANGE prompts for a new radius value. This is the only practical way to enter a new radius for a circle; you can't do that efficiently with grips.

The CHANGE command is a handy and powerful way to make a variety of changes to text. It is the easiest way to alter text style and height (CHANGE does not prompt for height if the style specified is defined with non-zero height—see Chapter 13, "Using Object Properties and Text Styles"). The location and angular orientation are easier to adjust with the MOVE and ROTATE commands. An existing text string can be replaced using CHANGE, but not edited. It is far easier and more flexible to use the DDEDIT command. (The ROTATE and DDEDIT commands are discussed later in this chapter.)

CHANGE can also be used to move or rotate block insertions, but using grips, or the specific commands for these operations, is more convenient. CHANGE does not work with arc or polyline objects.

Using Ortho with CHANGE applied to multiple lines at once is a powerful tool. Lines can be of varying lengths and at varying angles to start (reflecting a hasty layout perhaps). The CHANGE command arranges them in parallel with their changed endpoints in orthogonal alignment.

In the following exercise, you use CHANGE to elongate the lines of the column fluting, and alter the appearance, position, and content of the text. You also use MIRROR to copy the column fluting lines.

Using CHANGE to Stretch Lines

Continue from the previous exercise.

Use the ZOOM command with the Previous option to return to the full view, then make sure Ortho is turned off.

Command: *Select the five short lines at the top of the right column*	Highlights the lines and displays their grips
Command: **CH** (Enter)	Issues the CHANGE command with the lines selected
CHANGE 5 found	
Properties/<Change point>: *Pick just above the base of the right column*	Extends the five lines to converge at the point picked
Command: (Enter)	Repeats the CHANGE command
CHANGE	
Select objects: **P** (Enter)	Reselects the Previous selection
5 found	
Select objects: *Turn on Ortho and press Enter*	Sets Ortho to make lines parallel and completes selection
<Ortho on> Properties/<Change point>: *Pick any point at the bottom of the right column with a Y value of 1'-9"*	Extends all five lines parallel, with Y endpoint coordinates of 1'9", and completes the CHANGE command

Next, you mirror the five new lines into the left column.

Command: **MI** (Enter)	Issues the MIRROR command
Select objects: **P** (Enter)	Uses Previous selections

continues

continued

```
5 found

Select objects: (Enter)
```

```
First point of mirror line: Choose          Creates the mirrored objects
the midpoint of the center line
```

```
Second point: Pick any point directly       Creates the mirrored objects
above or below first point
```

```
Delete old objects? <N> (Enter)
```

```
Command: Turn Ortho off
```

```
<Ortho off> CH (Enter)                       Issues the CHANGE command
```

```
CHANGE
```

```
Select objects: Pick the word "Design"       Selects the text
and press Enter
```

```
Properties/<Change point>: Pick at           Moves the text
point 10'-6",4'-0"
```

```
Text style: NOTES                            Prompts with current style; changes the
New style or RETURN for no change:           text style to FANCY
FANCY (Enter)
```

```
New height <0'-3">: 4-1/2 (Enter)            Enlarges the text from 3" to 4-1/2"
```

```
New rotation angle <0>: Turn Ortho on
```

```
<Ortho on> Pick a point above the D in       Rotates the text 90 degrees
the text
```

```
New text <Design>: Entrance Design           Changes the text string
U35 (Enter)
```

```
Command: Click on the Redraw button or tool  Cleans up the image (see fig. 15.4)
```

Save the drawing

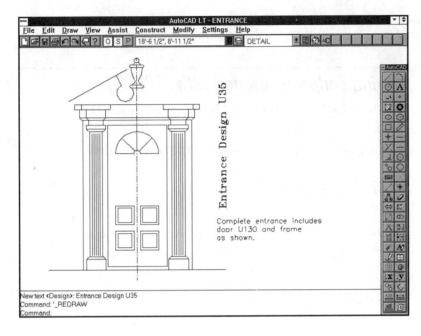

Figure 15.4

*The entrance after
a few changes.*

AutoCAD LT provides a more specific but related command for changing the locations of individual endpoints of objects: the STRETCH command.

Moving Endpoints Using STRETCH

You can use CHANGE to relocate the endpoints of lines, but AutoCAD LT provides a more powerful tool for moving endpoints and redefining the points of a variety of objects. STRETCH can move and shrink or extend groups of objects while maintaining connections to adjacent objects. If you need to lengthen or shorten a figure you have already drawn, or relocate a feature that is connected to others, you will appreciate the power of STRETCH.

The way STRETCH operates is unique and somewhat complicated. It uses the standard selection mechanism, but requires that defining points (points to be relocated) be specified with a window or polygon. AutoCAD LT bases the scope of the stretch on the last window used to select objects and ignores previous selections. Selected objects within the window or polygon are moved by STRETCH, while certain types of selected objects that cross the crossing window or crossing polygon are stretched.

In the following exercise, you use STRETCH to adjust the proportions of the panels in the door, and make a small change to the height of the column bases.

Moving Endpoints around with STRETCH

Continue in the ENTRANCE drawing from the preceding exercise. Make sure Ortho is turned on.

Command: *Click on the Stretch tool*   Issues the STRETCH command

```
_STRETCH
Select objects to stretch by window or
polygon...
```

Select objects: *Pick a window*   Defines a window but does not select
from ① *to* ② *(see fig. 15.5)*   anything

```
0 found
```

Select objects: *Pick the top of the*   Selects the square to stretch
outer square at ③

```
1 found
```

Select objects: **Enter**   Completes the selection

Base point or displacement: *Pick*   Establishes the base point for the stretch
any point   and displays a rubber-band reference

Second point of displacement: *Pick a*   Performs the stretch (see fig. 15.5)
point 2'-3" above the base point

These steps stretched only the selected box, moving the segment that was in the window and stretching the segments that crossed the window.

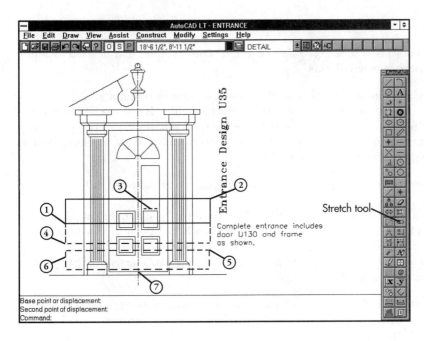

Figure 15.5

Stretching a door panel.

STRETCH prompts for a window or polygon selection, then for a displacement. In the first stretch of the preceding exercise, the window established a relationship to the defining points of the objects, but no objects were selected until you picked the square at ③.

STRETCH. The STRETCH command stretches objects that cross a crossing window. You can stretch lines, arcs, solids, traces, polylines (including all polyline and polyface meshes), and 3D faces. For stretchable objects, endpoints that lie inside the crossing window are moved while endpoints outside the window remain fixed. All objects entirely in the window move. Text, blocks, shapes, and circles move only if their insert or center points are in the window.

The effect of STRETCH depends on three things:

◆ Which objects were selected. Any object selection method may be used to add or remove selected objects.

◆ A specified window or polygon. At least one window or polygon must be specified, although it does not have to select anything. It is the relationship of the defining points of each object to the last specified window or polygon that determines what is stretched, moved, or ignored. Only the last specified window or polygon affects this relationship.

◆ The selected object types. Different types of objects are affected differently.

You specify the displacement for the STRETCH command just like the displacement for the MOVE or COPY commands. You can enter an X,Y or polar displacement or use any combination of pointing device or keyboard input, relative or absolute coordinates to indicate it with a base point and second point. The use of Ortho greatly increases your control.

In the following exercise, you use a crossing window and a crossing polygon to both select the objects and define the relationship of the defining points of each object to the window or polygon.

Stretching with Crossing Windows and Polygons

Continue from the preceding exercise.

Command: **S** (Enter)	Issues the STRETCH command
STRETCH Select objects to stretch by window or polygon...	
Select objects: *Pick a crossing window from* ② *to* ④	Defines a crossing window and selects objects to stretch
26 found	
Select objects: (Enter)	Completes the selection
Base point or displacement: (Enter)	Specifies a polar displacement
Second point of displacement: @2'3"<90 (Enter)	Accepts the displacement

This affected only the selected objects, moving segments that were within the window and stretching segments that crossed the window.

`Command:` (Enter)	Repeats the STRETCH command

`STRETCH`
`Select objects to stretch by window or`
`polygon...`	

`Select objects:` *Pick a crossing* *window from* ⑤ *to* ⑥	Selects objects and specifies a window that encloses the column base caps
`30 found`	
`Select objects:` (Enter)	Completes the selection
`Base point or displacement:` *Pick* ⑦	Starts the rubber-band reference line
`Second point of displacement:` *Turn* *Ortho off and drag the cursor around*	Allows the objects to stretch in all directions
`<Ortho off>` *Turn Ortho on again*	Constrains displacement to vertical or horizontal
`<Ortho on>` *Pick 6" above* ⑦	Performs the stretch
`Command:` *Click on the Stretch tool*	Issues the STRETCH command

`_STRETCH`
`Select objects to stretch by window or`
`polygon...`	

`Select objects:` **P** (Enter)	Reselects the previous objects
`30 found`	
`Select objects:` (Enter)	Attempts to complete the selection set
`You must select a window or polygon` `to stretch.`	Refuses to accept the selection without a window

Although the objects were selected, no window was specified to tell STRETCH how to treat the
objects.

`Command:` (Enter)	Repeats the STRETCH command

`STRETCH`
`Select objects to stretch by window or`
`polygon...`	

continues

continued

`Select objects:` **`CP`** `(Enter)`	Specifies the crossing polygon selection option
`First polygon point:` *Pick* ⑥	Starts the polygon
`Undo/<Endpoint of line>:` *Continue to pick points defining a polygon that selects the column bases as before, but avoids the panels in the door, then press Enter after the polygon is defined*	Selects objects and defines a polygon
`30 found`	
`Select objects:` `(Enter)`	Completes the selection
`Base point or displacement:` **`4<90`** `(Enter)`	
`Second point of displacement:` `(Enter)`	Moves all selected segments within the polygon and stretches selected segments that cross it (see fig. 15.6)

Save the drawing

Figure 15.6

The entrance modified by the STRETCH command.

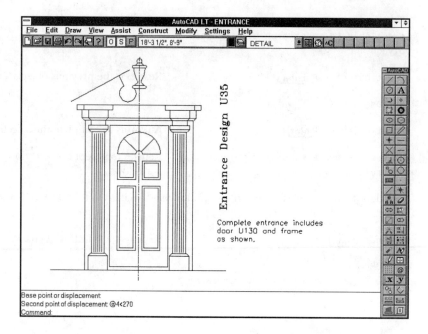

Although you used a crossing polygon to make the last selection and specify the object to polygon relationship, you could have used a crossing window and then used the Remove selection mode to deselect the door panels.

Note   There is a problem affecting the use of polygon selection with STRETCH in some releases of AutoCAD LT Release 1. See the end of the LT_BUG.TXT file from the IALT DISK for a description of this problem.

Although the specific effect of STRETCH depends on the types of objects (some object types can only be moved, not stretched), the general effects are as follows:

◆ Selected objects whose defining points are entirely within the extents of the window or polygon are moved without stretching.

◆ Selected objects whose defining points are entirely outside the extents of the window or polygon are ignored.

◆ Selected objects with some defining points inside and some outside the extents of the window or polygon are stretched. For example, selected lines with only one endpoint in the specified window act like taffy—they are literally pulled to anywhere you specify.

It is important to know how the STRETCH command affects different objects, and what it considers the defining point of each object you select. Some objects are modified by STRETCH: it relocates the endpoints of lines and arcs, vertices of polylines, and definition points of associative dimensions (see Chapter 21, "Styling and Editing Dimensions"). For other objects, STRETCH simply acts like the MOVE command. If the window includes point objects, the centers of circles, or the insertion points of text objects or blocks (including hatches), they are simply moved by the offset distance specified in the STRETCH operation.

Note   The insertion points of blocks, particularly hatches, may not be near the visible objects (see Chapters 17, "Dressing Up Drawings with Hatching," and 18, "Leveraging Repetitive Design and Drafting," for more on blocks and hatches). This insertion point must, however, be within the stretch window or polygon for STRETCH to affect the block or hatch.

As you saw in the exercise, you can use STRETCH to interactively adjust proportions to change the size and shape of objects. The STRETCH command can save you hours of work when you need more room in a tight area of a schematic, or the dimensions of a building plan change slightly. If you include the definition points of associative dimensions in the stretch window, the dimension value will automatically be updated to reflect the new dimension.

15

The polygon selection options are very helpful. You will often need these options to get the results you want.

Tip

Use any type of selection you like to specify the objects to stretch and move with STRETCH, then use a window or polygon (not the crossing variety) to establish which of the selected objects to move and which to stretch, based on the relationship of the defining points of the objects to the window or polygon. Using a non-crossing window or polygon helps avoid messing up the previous selections, and the window or polygon need not select anything. If it does select something you don't want affected, use the Remove selection option and pick the objects to remove (do not use window or polygon to remove them).

You need to be careful when defining the points for the STRETCH operation and selecting the objects to be stretched. The fact that the last window or polygon is the one that counts limits your selection flexibility. One option for selecting objects is to use the SELECT command to help build the selection set.

Building a Complex Selection Set with SELECT

SELECT seems to be a little-known command. It is most useful in conjunction with custom menu items, and with the STRETCH command because of the way STRETCH uses a window or polyline definition during the selection process. By itself, the SELECT command is not an editing command. It is used as a support utility in conjunction with the other editing commands for the purpose of building a selection set (see Chapter 6, "Making Changes: Using Basic Editing Tools") that is used in the subsequent editing operation. Whatever you select with the SELECT command becomes the previous selection set, available to any command that accepts the Previous option.

In the following exercise, you use the SELECT command to select objects to be excluded from a subsequent stretch operation (see fig. 15.7). You use SELECT and STRETCH together to adjust the height of the column capitals, much like the adjustment you made to the bases in the preceding exercise.

Using SELECT to Simplify STRETCH Selection

Continue in the ENTRANCE drawing from the preceding exercise. Verify that Ortho is on.

Command: *Choose* **A**ssist, **S**elect, **A**dd   Issues the SELECT command with the
                                                         Add option

```
_select
Select objects: _add
```

New Riders Publishing
INSIDE
SERIES

`Select objects:` *Pick a window from* ① *(see fig. 15.7) to* ②	Specifies a window that selects all the elements of the light
`7 found`	
`Select objects:` (Enter)	Completes the selection and ends the SELECT command

The selected objects are now in the previous selection set.

`Command:` **SE** (Enter)	Issues the SELECT command
`SELECT`	
`Select objects:` **P** (Enter)	Specifies the Previous selection option and highlights the light
`7 found`	
`Select objects:` (Enter)	Repeats the selection and ends the SELECT command
`Command:` **S** (Enter)	Issues the STRETCH command
`STRETCH` `Select objects to stretch by window or polygon...`	
`Select objects:` *Pick a crossing window from* ③ *to* ④	Selects the lower half of the column caps, the columns, and a portion of the light
`34 found`	
`Select objects:` **R** (Enter)	Specifies the Remove selection option
`Remove objects:` **P** (Enter)	Specifies the Previous selection option and removes the light elements included
`7 found, 4 removed`	
`Remove objects:` (Enter)	Completes the selection
`Base point or displacement:` *Pick any point*	Establishes the base point
`Second point of displacement:` *Pick a point 1 1/2" below the base point*	Stretches the column capitals (see fig. 15.8)

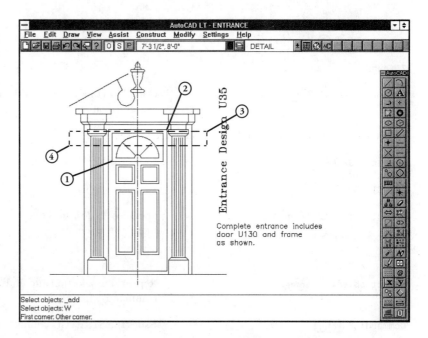

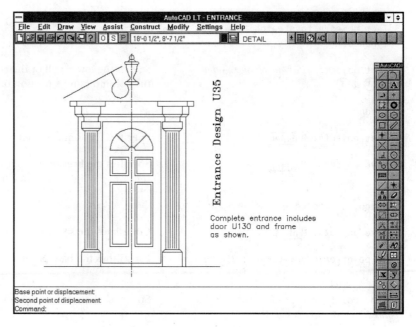

The SELECT command doesn't do anything; it simply creates a selection set of objects you can access from a subsequent command by way of the Previous selection option. The effect of this exercise is similar to the adjustment you made to the proportions of the column bases in the STRETCH command exercise by using the CPolygon selection option. Usually, the polygon selection is more intuitive and easier, but SELECT can simplify this kind of operation, especially when working in a crowded area of the drawing.

> **SELECT.** The SELECT command creates a selection set that you can later recall by using the Previous object selection option. Select can use all the selection options.

SELECT works equally well with any command that allows the Previous selection option. STRETCH benefits most because the extra meaning it places on window and polyline definitions during the selection process often necessitates that objects be selected for addition or deletion in advance.

Tip You can use the SELECT command in conjunction with the LAYER command to select objects on a specific layer for use in subsequent editing commands. Make the desired layer current, and turn off or freeze all the others. Use the SELECT command to build a selection set of objects to be affected on that layer. Use the LAYER command again to turn all layers back on. Then use your editing command with the Previous option to select and act on the objects you had just isolated according to layer.

As described earlier in this chapter, the all-powerful CHANGE command can be used to change the angular orientation of certain types of objects. Just as the STRETCH command provides a better solution for relocating endpoints, the ROTATE command is a more versatile tool for rotating objects than CHANGE.

Setting Angles with the ROTATE Command

The angular orientation, or rotation, of objects is one of the aspects you need to be able to change and control as you draw. AutoCAD LT provides a specific tool for manipulating this angular orientation, appropriately named the ROTATE command.

Like the other commands in this section, ROTATE uses the standard selection options so you can build a set of objects to rotate all at one time (thereby ensuring that all the rotations use the same angle). The basic operation prompts for the objects to be rotated, then for the base point around which the objects will be rotated, and finally, for the rotation angle.

In the following exercise, you use the ROTATE command to put the title text into the proper orientation.

Changing Angular Alignments with ROTATE

Create a new drawing named ENTRANCE, using the ALT1502.DWG as a prototype and using no setup method. Make sure Ortho is on.

Command: *Click on the Rotate tool*   Issues the ROTATE command

_ROTATE

Select objects: *Select the vertical
text at* ① *(see fig. 15.9), and press Enter*

Base point: *Pick at the point 10'-6",*   Sets the base point
5'-0" (near ①*)*

<Rotation angle>/Reference: *Pick*   Rotates the text 270 degrees (restores it
below ① *(angle <270>)*   to horizontal)

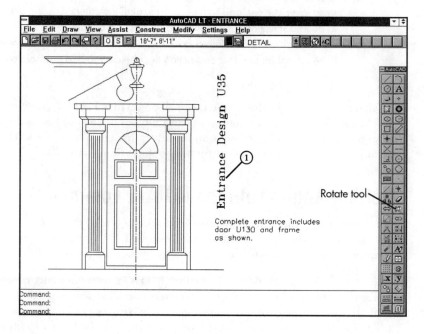

Figure 15.9

Rotating text.

The ROTATE command acts predictably to rotate the selected object about a base point that you specify.

> **ROTATE.** The ROTATE command rotates objects in the X,Y plane around a specified base point using a relative rotation angle that you enter or a reference angle that you indicate by picking points.

The ROTATE command's only real option is the Reference angle. It permits a variety of input for defining the initial and final angles. For the reference angle, you can enter a specific angle (which is always in reference to the current UCS), or utilize selection tools such as Ortho, Snap, point filters, and object snap modes to specify two points that define the angle from the current UCS zero direction. You may want to use a constant rotation base for defining one particular direction, or you might create a named UCS. You define the new angle similarly. You can enter a specific angle for the new angle (which is always defined in respect to the reference angle and the current direction of angle measurement rotation), or point to it. AutoCAD LT drags a rubber-band cursor from the rotation base point to the new angle. The distance from the base to the cursor is irrelevant because AutoCAD LT looks only at the angle.

ROTATE is easy to use. It is particularly handy when, as in the preceding exercise, a feature is created in some other orientation, or objects are replicated at several points in the drawing, but at different angles. For orthogonal rotation and cases where you know the exact angle, pointing or entering the new angle directly is the quickest and easiest method to use. The Reference option is a powerful assistant; it eliminates the need to measure or calculate angles in order to align objects precisely (bye-bye protractor).

Try using ROTATE with the Reference option to align the pediment molding with the layout line created in the first section of this chapter. The molding has already been detailed in the new prototype drawing using the MIRROR and EXTEND commands in ways similar to the strategies previously described. Details such as molding are often easier to construct while aligned orthogonally. You then simply rotate and move them into place, as demonstrated in this exercise

---

Rotating Objects into Alignment with the Reference Option

Continue from the previous exercise.

Zoom in on the upper left of the entrance (see fig. 15.10).

Command: **RO** (Enter)   Issues the ROTATE command

ROTATE

continues

continued

`Select objects:` *Select the nine lines that make up the molding in the upper left near ② and press Enter*

`Base point:` *Use INT object snap to pick the upper right endpoint of the molding at ② (see fig. 15.10)*   Sets the base point

`<Rotation angle>/Reference:` **R** `Enter`   Specifies the Reference option

`Reference angle <0>:` **@** `Enter`   Respecifies the base point

`Second point:` *Pick a point below the base point (angle 270)*   Specifies vertical reference angle

`New angle:` *Turn Ortho off and move the cursor around*   Rotates the rubber-band line image around the base point

`<Ortho off>` *Click on the Perpendicular tool*   Activates the PERpendicular object snap mode

`PER to` *Pick the angled layout line at ③ (see fig. 15.10)*   Rotates the molding parallel to the layout line

Figure 15.10

Placing the molding above the entrance.

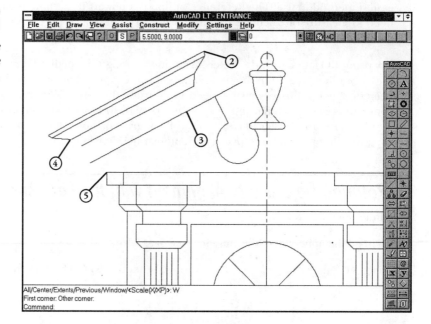

Erase the angled layout line at ③

`Command:` *Select all nine molding objects, then type* **M** *and press Enter*	Starts the MOVE command with the molding selected
`MOVE 9 found`	
`Base point or displacement:` *Use ENDPoint object snap to pick point* ④	Sets the base point
`Second point of displacement:` *Use ENDPoint to pick point* ⑤	Moves the molding
`Command:` *Click on the Trim tool*	Issues the TRIM command
`TRIM` `Select cutting edge(s)...`	
`Select objects:` *Pick the lines at* ⑥ *and* ⑦ *(see fig. 15.11), then press Enter*	
`<Select object to trim>/Undo:` *Pick the line at* ⑦	Trims the molding
`<Select object to trim>/Undo:` *Pick the line at* ⑧	Trims layout line and leaves a connecting line
`<Select object to trim>/Undo:` (Enter)	Completes the TRIM command
`Command:` *Pick all the pediment parts except the finial and turn Ortho on*	
`Command: <Ortho on>` **MI** (Enter)	Issues the MIRROR command with all the objects selected
`MIRROR 11 found`	
`First point of mirror line:` *Use MIDpoint object snap to pick the center line*	
`Second point:` *Pick the center line again above the first point*	
`Delete old objects? <N>` (Enter)	Completes the MIRROR command

Use the ZOOM command with the Previous option (see fig. 15.12). Save the drawing.

15

Figure 15.11

Using the TRIM command to clean up the pediment.

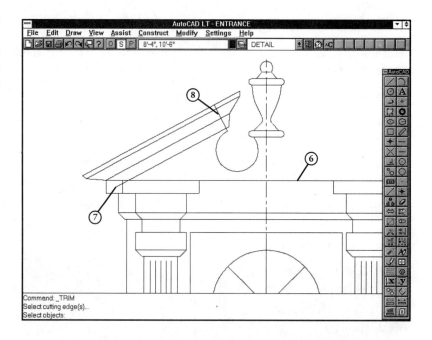

Figure 15.12

The ENTRANCE drawing with the text rotated and the full pediment.

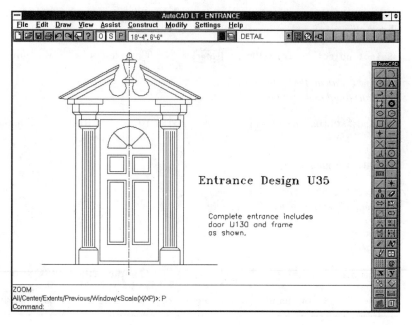

The Reference option enables you to set the starting angle to any relevant angle. It is often useful to set up a relationship between the start and ending angles based on an orthogonal direction or the direction to an object snap point.

ROTATE may have power over relative angles, but you need a different tool to control an object's relative size. To change the relative size of an object or group of objects, you need the SCALE command.

Adjusting Proportions Using SCALE

The SCALE command is used to increase or decrease the size of selected objects proportionately, based on a specified reference point. The SCALE command may not seem too useful, because in AutoCAD LT, you usually draw objects at their actual size. However, in developing a design, you may not know exact dimensions in the beginning. In such cases, you can draw objects close to final size, maintaining any required relationships between elements. Once the controlling dimension is determined, use the SCALE command to adjust the group of objects as a whole. Other designs may involve multiple instances of a feature repeated at different sizes. In this case, you can draw one of the objects, use COPY to replicate it as required, and then use the SCALE command to adjust the size of each one as required.

In the following exercise, you use the SCALE command to adjust the size of the finial (acquired from a generic library of parts) to suit the geometry of this specific entrance. You also change the height of all the descriptive text while maintaining the proportions between text height, and character and line spacing. Figure 15.13 shows the pick points.

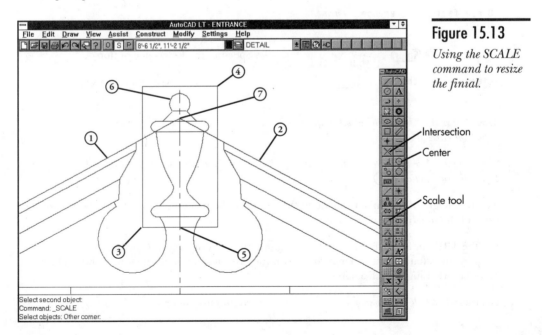

Figure 15.13

Using the SCALE command to resize the finial.

Using SCALE to Adjust Size Proportionately

Continue in the ENTRANCE drawing from the preceding exercise. Zoom to the view shown in figure 15.13.

Command: **F** (Enter)	Issues the FILLET command
FILLET Polyline/Radius/<Select first object>: *Pick the line at* ① *(see fig. 15.13)*	
Select second object: *Pick the line at* ②	Creates the intersection of the molding lines at ⑦
Command: *Click on the Scale tool*	Issues the SCALE command
_SCALE	
Select objects: *Select a window from* ③ *to* ④*, then press Enter*	Completes the window and selects the finial objects
18 found	
Base point: *Use INTersection object snap to pick* ⑤	Sets the base point at the base of the finial
<Scale factor>/Reference: *Turn off Ortho*	
<Ortho off> **R** (Enter)	Specifies the Reference option
Reference length <1>: **@** (Enter)	Respecifies the base point by using the last point
Second point: *Use CENter object snap to pick the circle at* ⑥	
New length: *Use INTersection object snap to pick the intersection at* ⑦	Completes the SCALE command

Now the height of the finial is such that the center of the ball is at the exact intersection of the slope of the molding on either side.

Use the TRIM or FILLET commands to clean up the molding lines, removing the portion you temporarily extended to ⑦. Then zoom with the Previous option to the view shown in figure 15.14 before using SCALE again.

Command: *Select all four lines of text*	Highlights the text

Command: **SC** (Enter)	Issues the SCALE command with the text selected
SCALE 4 found	
Base point: *Use INSert object snap to pick the title text at* (8) *(see fig. 15.14)*	Activates the Insert object
<Scale factor>/Reference: **.75** (Enter)	Specifies the scale factor and scales the text
Command: *Click on the Redraw button or tool*	Clears the screen (see fig. 15.14)

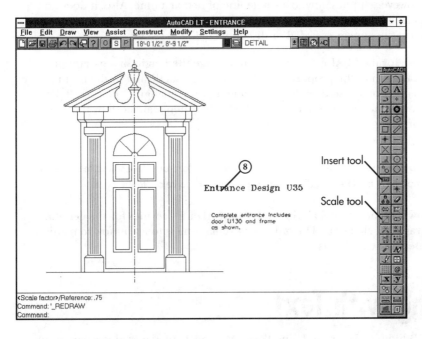

Figure 15.14

The ENTRANCE drawing after the scale command exercise.

15

As with the ROTATE command, the SCALE command works predictably to change the size and position of selected objects in proportion to each other, relative to a specified point. The Reference option enables you to set up a relationship between a specific existing distance and its scaled counterpart.

> **SCALE.** The SCALE command changes the size of existing objects relative to a specified base point, by a specified scale factor, by referencing one specified distance to another, or by a combination of these two methods.

The SCALE command and its options are very similar to the ROTATE command. You first select the objects to be scaled, then specify a base point, and determine the scale factor last. The Reference option also works similarly. You can enter a referenced distance or use a base point and a second point to indicate a reference distance, and then use any method to specify the new distance. The reference distance is scaled to fill the new distance. AutoCAD LT drags a rubber-band cursor from the base point to show the proposed new distance. Unlike the ROTATE command, the direction of the cursor from the base point is irrelevant—with the SCALE command, AutoCAD LT looks only at the distance.

Earlier, you used the CHANGE command to adjust text height. The CHANGE command, however, applies only to a single line of text at a time. Also, it does not affect the spacing between lines of text, so multiple lines of text that have been changed in size can appear crowded or disconnected.

A common use for the SCALE command is to change the height of a paragraph of text, while maintaining the proportion of line spacing established by the font requirements. This is especially useful with leadered text, when changing the overall plot scale of a drawing. You select the text and the leader, then scale both by the inverse of scale factor change.

Tip You may need to use the STRETCH command before or after scaling leadered text created by the LEADER dimensioning command, to relocate the note.

You have now seen how to use all the tools AutoCAD LT provides for the general editing of graphical elements. The only thing remaining is to learn how to manipulate the content of text objects.

Working with Text

Chapter 4, "Building a Drawing: Using Basic Drawing Tools," introduced you to the DTEXT command as the basic drawing tool for creating text. Most drawings eventually contain at least some descriptive text. As with any other drawing element, you need to be able to modify text objects. Earlier in this chapter, you saw how to use the CHANGE command to make both graphic changes to text objects, and to replace their contents. AutoCAD LT provides a more flexible method for directly editing the character string within a text object. For unusually long strings and paragraphs of text, you may want to use a word processing program or an ASCII text editor to create the text outside the drawing. AutoCAD LT provides a simple means of importing text from a file on disk.

Start by looking at DDEDIT, the primary editing command for text within an AutoCAD LT drawing, which uses the Edit Text dialog box.

Editing Text

Unless you type and spell perfectly, and your designs spring to life full-blown, complete, and error-free, you need to be able to make changes to the string content of text objects in your drawings. You have seen how to do this with the sledgehammer approach provided by the antique CHANGE command. AutoCAD LT provides a more convenient dialog box interface for text editing, which is accessed by the DDEDIT command.

In the next exercise, you use DDEDIT to make a simple change to a line of text.

Using DDEDIT to Edit Text

Create a new drawing named ENTRANCE using the ALT1503.DWG as a prototype and using no setup method.

Command: *Click on the Edit Text tool*	Issues the DDEDIT command
`_DDEDIT`	
`<Select a TEXT or ATTDEF object>/` `Undo:` *Pick text at* ① *(see fig. 15.15)*	Selects the text and opens the Edit Text dialog box
Click in edit box, to right of the period *following* `"...as shown."`	Positions the text input cursor after the period
Press space bar once or twice, then type **`Hardware not included.`**	Adds a new sentence to the line
Press Enter or click on the OK *button*	Replaces the text and prompts for more
`<Select a TEXT or ATTDEF object>/` `Undo:` (Enter)	Completes the DDEDIT command

Save the drawing

15

Figure 15.15

The ENTRANCE drawing with edited text.

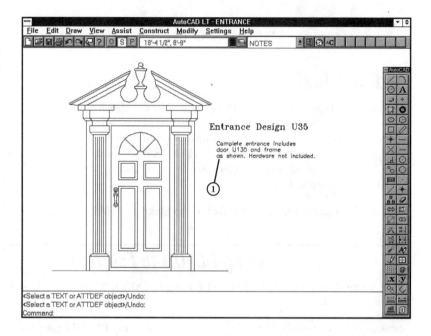

DDEDIT works like any other editing dialog box. When it opens, the entire text string is highlighted for replacement. Clicking in the box positions the cursor. Any new text is inserted at the cursor's location and replaces all highlighted text. Clicking on OK closes the dialog box and applies the changes (OK is also the default meaning for pressing the return key). The command continues to prompt for another text string to edit until you press Enter at the text selection prompt or cancel the command.

> **DDEDIT.** The DDEDIT command (Dynamic Dialogue EDIT) prompts for a text or attribute string and opens the Edit Text dialog box with the selected string highlighted. DDEDIT can also be used to edit the tag, prompt, and default values of attribute definitions. Use DDATTE to edit attributes after they have been inserted as a block. DDEDIT repeats for additional text selections until you press Ctrl+C or Enter at its selection prompt.

DDEDIT enables you to make minor edits to text without having to retype an entire string. It also enables you to edit multiple text strings without reissuing the command each time.

Tip You can use the Windows cut-and-paste feature to move text from one text string to another. To do so, highlight the string in the Edit Text dialog box and press Ctrl+Ins to store it or Shift+Del to store and delete it. Then close the dialog box and select the second text string to add the stored text to. Position the cursor in the second text string in the Edit Text dialog box, and press Shift+Ins to insert it. You can also use this cut-and-paste feature to import or export text between AutoCAD LT and another program by using the Clipboard. See your Windows documentation for details.

Tip If you want to edit text and change its properties or position, you can use the CHANGE command in AutoCAD LT Release 1 or the DDMODIFY command in AutoCAD LT Release 2.

Although DDEDIT is convenient, you can still only edit one line of text at a time. If you have multiple occurrences of the same error, you are likely to be better off changing one and using it to replace the others. AutoCAD LT stores text objects as separate objects within the drawing database. A paragraph of text consists of several individual text objects; each with its own insertion point that keeps it separate from the others. You therefore cannot edit a paragraph as a single object, and DDEDIT doesn't do groups. A more practical way to deal with multiple lines of text is to use a text editor outside of AutoCAD LT and import the results back into AutoCAD LT.

Importing Text from a File

Although not a text editing tool (strictly speaking), AutoCAD LT does provide a mechanism for importing text from standard ASCII text files directly into drawings. The final exercise in this chapter demonstrates this function. In this exercise, you use the Windows File Manager application to retrieve a paragraph of descriptive text from a file provided on the IALT disk. The exercise assumes that you have a standard Windows installation which includes File Manager. If you need help using File Manager, press F1 after opening File Manager.

Importing ASCII Text into a Drawing

Continue in the ENTRANCE drawing from the preceding exercise and erase the three lines of smaller text.

Press Alt+Tab one or more times, until the Windows Program Manager appears.

Open or switch to the File Manager (its icon is usually located in the Main program group).

continues

continued

Adjust the size of the File Manager window if necessary, so part of the AutoCAD LT window is visible behind it.

Display the drive and contents of the directory where the IALT files are located (probably C:\DWGS\IALT).

Find the file named ALT15.TXT.

Click in the AutoCAD LT window to return to the drawing.

Command: *Click on the Text tool*	Issues the DTEXT command
DTEXT Justify/Style/<Start point>: *Pick ① at 9'-9", 7'-0" (see fig. 15.17)*	Sets the insertion point
Height <0'-3">: **2** (Enter)	Specifies the text height
Rotation angle <0>: (Enter)	Accepts the default value
Text: *Press Alt+Tab to switch to File Manager*	

Position the cursor on the ALT15.TXT file, and press and drag it (hold the pick button down) over the AutoCAD LT window (see fig. 15.16), then release the button.

This New England Entrance is	The text in the file is imported
Text: beautiful in its simplicity.	directly into the drawing
Text: The half circle affords just	
Text: enough light for the vestibule	
Text: while ensuring privacy.	
Text:	
Text: Door shown is 3'-0" x 7'-0"	
Text: and while a door 6'-8" high	
Text: can be used, it should not be	
Text: less than 3'-0" wide.	
Text:	
Text: Complete entrance includes	
Text: door U130 and frame as shown	
Text: with pilasters and broken	
Text: pediment. Be sure to state if	
Text: jambs are to be paneled. No	
Text: hardware included.	
Text: (Enter)	Completes the DTEXT command (see fig. 15.17)

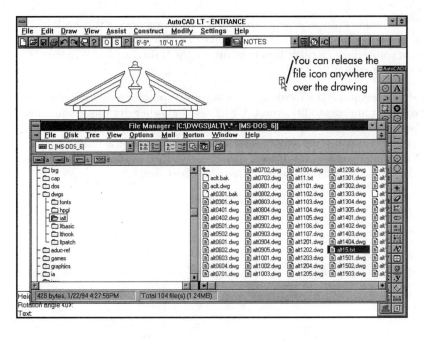

Figure 15.16

Using the Windows drag-and-drop feature.

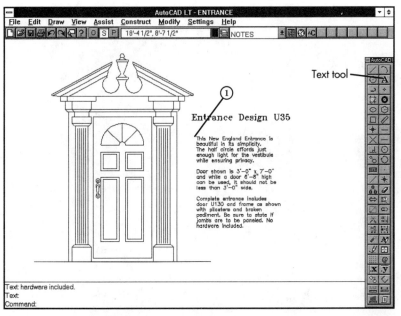

Figure 15.17

Importing text from an ASCII file.

15

This AutoCAD LT import function depends on the outside services of various Windows utilities. You may use the editor of your choice to create and edit the text files, but be sure that your editor can save files in standard ASCII format. The Windows Notepad is a suitable editor.

You now have all the AutoCAD LT editing tools at your disposal. These tools provide a great deal of power and capability. AutoCAD LT also has other drawing commands that will further enhance your drawing power. In the next chapter, you finally meet the polyline commands you've heard so much about, as well as several other AutoCAD LT drawing features with unforgettable names, such as DONUT. The flight attendant will even bring you some coffee with the donuts!

Increasing Your Drawing Power with Polylines and Double Lines

What you have learned to this point will enable you to produce quality drawings with AutoCAD LT. Placing text, creating lines, circles, and other objects, and modifying these objects are the basics for using CAD effectively. In this chapter, you learn some additional commands that will increase your productivity and enhance your creativity. These commands enable you to create something more than straight line segments and simple circles and arcs. Specifically, this chapter provides a detailed discussion of the following topics:

◆ Drawing and editing polylines (a *polyline* is a single object made of connected line or arc segments)

◆ Exploding polylines into lines and arcs

◆ Creating donuts, polygons, rectangles, and ellipses

◆ Creating polyline boundaries automatically

◆ Using the DLINE (Double LINE) command to draw parallel lines

Effective use of these elements can make the difference between an average drawing and an excellent one. The use of polylines—particularly those created by the ELLIPSE, RECTANG, POLYGON, DONUT, and BOUNDARY commands—and of double lines also can save drawing time.

As you gain more experience with AutoCAD LT, you will discover that there is usually more than one way to accomplish the same task. The key is to determine which way is most effective and quickest for the task at hand. The commands introduced in this chapter are useful tools for constructing your drawings more intelligently. These commands enable you to use polylines, double lines, donuts, ellipses, and other complex geometry in your design process.

Polylines have many potential uses. You could use polylines to outline the shape of a room in an architectural floor plan. You also could use polylines to create the outline of a machined part or cross section. By using polylines in this manner, you need to edit only one object if changes are necessary. Additionally, polylines provide all kinds of useful data to aid in the design process. To construct and edit polylines, AutoCAD LT provides the PLINE, PEDIT, 3DPOLY, and POLYGON commands.

Double lines are used in constructing walls on architectural floor plans. They might also be used in designing a new gasket for a pump. Anywhere an interior and exterior edge line follow the same center line, you can use double lines to avoid having to draw the two parallel lines separately. To draw double lines, AutoCAD LT provides the DLINE command.

Ellipses are in reality polylines that can be used to show isometric representations of holes. Donuts are a special kind of polyline and have all sorts of creative uses, from designating junction points on an electrical schematic to representing O-rings in a mechanical assembly drawing. To create ellipses and donuts, AutoCAD LT provides the ELLIPSE and DONUT commands.

Understanding Polylines

A *polyline* is a single AutoCAD LT object that can consist of one or more line segments or arcs or both. These line segments and arcs are joined together at their endpoints. Figure 16.1 illustrates several types of polylines.

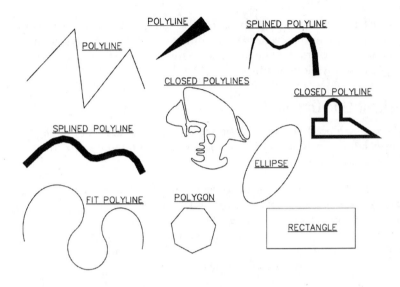

Figure 16.1

Polyline examples.

As you can see in figure 16.1, polylines afford limitless possibilities for creativity. They are useful for creating logos for clients, free-form layouts for landscaping beds, various shapes for design and artwork layout—the potential uses are endless.

Using the PLINE Command Options

To create polylines in AutoCAD LT, you use the PLINE command and its options. You issue the PLINE command by selecting the **P**olyline item from the **D**raw pull-down menu, choosing the Polyline tool in the toolbox, or entering **PLINE** or the PL alias at the Command: prompt. When constructing polylines, you can specify line segments (the Line option), arc segments (the Arc option), or both. As you will see in the following exercises, you are presented with two different sets of options depending on whether you specify line segments or arc segments.

> **PLINE.** The PLINE command enables you to construct a single polyline object consisting of line and arc segments joined at their endpoints. A polyline can be opened or closed. A polyline contains width information for each vertex.

If you make a mistake while creating any segment of the polyline, you can use the PLINE Undo option. Each time you use the PLINE command's Undo option without drawing a new segment, you undo the preceding polyline segment. If you are drawing a complex polyline and make a mistake, don't panic. You can correct your error by using the Undo option to reverse what you have done.

16

In addition to specifying line or arc segments, you also can specify starting width and ending width for each segment. Polylines are the only AutoCAD LT objects to which you can assign explicit widths to the line or arc segments. Refer to figure 16.1 for examples of polylines with various widths.

Using the Default Line Option

The process of creating a polyline can be as simple as drawing a series of line segments. You already know how to draw lines by specifying two endpoints. To create polylines, you use the same procedure.

In the following exercise, you edit a drawing of an architectural detail. The drawing represents a cross section of a shelf attached to a wall. You create a polyline consisting of several straight line segments representing a break symbol at the top and bottom of the wall portion. After you create the polyline, you use the LIST command to see what data AutoCAD LT maintains on polylines. To facilitate the picking of points, the drawing has been set up with grid and snap turned on.

Creating and Examining a Simple Polyline

Create a new drawing named SHELF, using the ALT1601.DWG file as a prototype and using no setup method. Zoom to the view shown in figure 16.2.

Command: *Choose* **D**raw, **P**olyline	Issues the PLINE command
`_pline`	
From point: *Pick point* ① *(see fig. 16.2)*	Defines the start point of the polyline
Current line-width is 0'-0"	Provides information regarding the current line width
Arc/Close/Halfwidth/Length/Undo/ Width/<Endpoint of line>: *Pick point* ②	Specifies the vertex for the polyline
Arc/Close/Halfwidth/Length/Undo/ Width/<Endpoint of line>: *Turn Ortho off and pick point* ③	
Arc/Close/Halfwidth/Length/Undo/ Width/<Endpoint of line>: *Turn Ortho on and pick point* ④	
Arc/Close/Halfwidth/Length/Undo/ Width/<Endpoint of line>: *Turn Ortho off and pick point* ⑤	

New Riders Publishing
INSIDE
SERIES

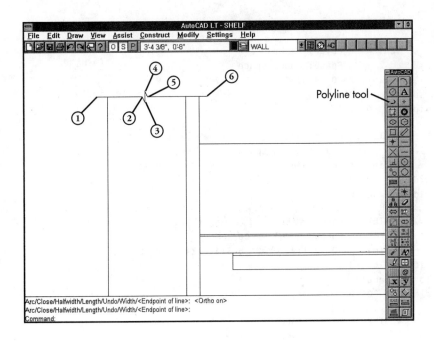

Figure 16.2

Creating a break symbol.

Arc/Close/Halfwidth/Length/Undo/
Width/<Endpoint of line>:
Turn Ortho on and pick point ⑥

Arc/Close/Halfwidth/Length/Undo/   Exits the PLINE command
Width/<Endpoint of line>: (Enter)

Next, you use LIST to examine the polyline.

If you are using AutoCAD LT Release 2, you can instead use the DDMODIFY command and click on the Next button in the Modify Polyline dialog box to examine each vertex.

ALT2

Command: **LIST** (Enter)   Issues the LIST command

Select objects: *Pick the polyline you just*   Specifies the object to list—notice that it is
drew   selected as a single object

1 found

Select objects: (Enter)   Ends selection and lists the data, as follows:

```
            POLYLINE  Layer: WALL
                      Space: Model space
          Open                      Notice the "Open" indication
   starting width      0'-0"
     ending width      0'-0"
```

continues

continued

```
                    VERTEX    Layer: WALL
                              Space: Model space
               at point, X=-0'-4 3/4"  Y=    0'-7"  Z=    0'-0"
      starting width    0'-0"
        ending width    0'-0"


                    VERTEX    Layer: WALL
                              Space: Model space
               at point, X=-0'-2 5/8"  Y=    0'-7"  Z=    0'-0"
      starting width    0'-0"
        ending width    0'-0"


                    VERTEX    Layer: WALL
                              Space: Model space
               at point, X=-0'-2 1/2"  Y=0'-6 3/4"  Z=    0'-0"
      starting width      0'-0"
Press RETURN to continue:
        ending width    0'-0"


                    VERTEX    Layer: WALL
                              Space: Model space
               at point, X=-0'-2 1/2"  Y=0'-7 1/4"  Z=    0'-0"
      starting width    0'-0"
        ending width    0'-0"


                    VERTEX    Layer: WALL
                              Space: Model space
               at point, X=-0'-2 3/8"  Y=    0'-7"  Z=    0'-0"
      starting width    0'-0"
        ending width    0'-0"


                    VERTEX    Layer: WALL
                              Space: Model space
               at point, X=0'-0 3/8"  Y=    0'-7"  Z=    0'-0"
      starting width    0'-0"
        ending width    0'-0"


               END SEQUENCE  Layer: WALL
                              Space: Model space
               area    0.00 sq in (0.0000 sq ft)

Press RETURN to continue: [Enter]

               length 0'-5 15/16"
```

Notice that the length, but no area or perimeter, is listed because the polyline is open, not closed.

Use ZOOM Previous to zoom to the original view, and then copy this break symbol from ⑦ (see fig. 16.3) to the bottom of the wall section at ⑧. When you select it, notice that it is a single object.

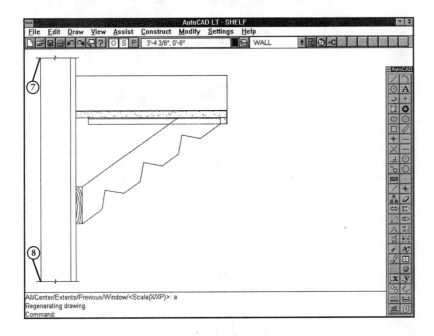

Figure 16.3

Copying a polyline as a single object.

AutoCAD LT maintains more data on polylines than on standard line objects. When you use the LIST command on a polyline, AutoCAD LT lists the layer name for the main polyline entity as well as for each vertex. (A *vertex* is the location at which two segments of the polyline meet at their endpoints.) The LIST command designates whether the object is in paper space or in model space. In addition, the location (X,Y,Z) of each vertex is listed, as well as the starting width and ending width of each line or arc segment. The LIST command calculates the area enclosed by the polyline as if the endpoint of the polyline and the start point were connected. When you create a polyline, you have the option of creating a *closed* polyline—a polyline in which the start point and endpoint are coincident (the same). Closed polylines are useful for determining areas enclosed by the polyline. Finally, the LIST command calculates the total length of the polyline. This length represents the sum of the linear length of all the segments of the polyline.

In the following exercise, you continue to use the SHELF drawing you created in the preceding exercise. You create a closed polyline representing a cross section of a

$1 \frac{1}{2} \times 1 \frac{1}{2} \times \frac{1}{8}$-inch steel angle support for the shelf unit. Later, you use the FILLET command to radius the corners properly.

Creating a Closed Polyline

Zoom in to the area of the drawing where the shelf attaches to the wall (see fig. 16.4). Set the STEEL layer current.

Command: *Click on the Polyline tool*	Issues the PLINE command
_PLINE	
From point: *Pick point* ① *(see fig. 16.4)*	Defines the start point of the polyline
Current line-width is 0.0000	Provides information regarding the current line width
Arc/Close/Halfwidth/Length/Undo/ Width/<Endpoint of line>: *Pick point* ②	Specifies the next vertex
Arc/Close/Halfwidth/Length/Undo/ Width/<Endpoint of line>: *Pick point* ③	
Arc/Close/Halfwidth/Length/Undo/ Width/<Endpoint of line>: *Pick point* ④	
Arc/Close/Halfwidth/Length/Undo/ Width/<Endpoint of line>: *Pick point* ⑤	
Arc/Close/Halfwidth/Length/Undo/ Width/<Endpoint of line>: *Pick point* ⑥	
Arc/Close/Halfwidth/Length/Undo/ Width/<Endpoint of line>: **C** (Enter)	Closes the polyline
Command: **LIST** (Enter)	Issues the LIST command
Select objects: **L** (Enter)	Selects the polyline you just drew
1 found	
Select objects: (Enter)	

```
               POLYLINE  Layer: STEEL
                         Space: Model space
              Closed
      starting width     0'-0"
        ending width     0'-0"
```

Notice the "Closed" indication

```
                VERTEX    Layer: STEEL
                          Space: Model space
              at point, X=    0'-0"  Y=    0'-0"  Z=    0'-0"
    starting width    0'-0"
      ending width    0'-0"
```

The rest of the vertexes are listed...then the last vertex, as follows:

```
                VERTEX    Layer: STEEL
                          Space: Model space
              at point, X=    0'-0"  Y=-0'-1 5/8"  Z=    0'-0"
    starting width    0'-0"
      ending width    0'-0"

              END SEQUENCE  Layer: STEEL
                            Space: Model space
          area    0.38 sq in (0.0026 sq ft)
```

Press RETURN to continue: (Enter)

```
          perimeter 0'-6 1/4"
```

Notice that the area and perimeter are listed because the polyline is closed.

Save the drawing for a later exercise

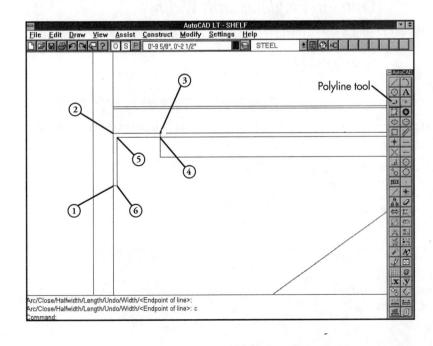

Figure 16.4

Creating a closed polyline.

16

As mentioned previously, polylines can have explicit widths assigned to them. The width can vary from vertex to vertex. This width should not be confused with pen widths or line weights of lines plotted on paper. Pen widths are assigned according to entity color. (Chapter 23, "Producing Hard Copy," provides a detailed discussion on plotting your drawing.) Polyline line widths, on the other hand, are specified as the physical width of the segments at each vertex.

AutoCAD LT provides two methods of assigning line widths to polylines. One method is to specify the halfwidth of the polyline; the other is to specify the width. Although these methods may seem redundant, assigning halfwidths has specialty applications in printed circuit board design and other fields. The most common method for assigning a width to a polyline, however, is to specify the width. The width method is used in this chapter.

When you assign widths to polylines, you can specify width values for each segment of the polyline or for each vertex. Each vertex can even have a width value different from the previous or subsequent vertex. Think of each endpoint of each segment of the polyline as being assigned a width. This affords great creativity in creating polylines. A width of zero is the default.

In the following exercise, you create a polyline arrow as a single object (a line with an arrowhead), using varying width values.

Creating Polylines with Width

Make sure the SHELF drawing is saved, then create a new drawing named ARROW, using the ALT1602.DWG file as the prototype and using no setup method.

Command: **PLINE** (Enter)	Issues the PLINE command
From point: **2,2** (Enter)	Specifies the start point for the polyline
Current line-width is 0.0000	Provides information about the current line-width setting
Arc/Close/Halfwidth/Length/Undo/ Width/<Endpoint of line>: **W** (Enter)	Specifies the Width option
Starting width <0.0000>: (Enter)	Specifies the starting width for the next polyline segment
Ending width <0.0000>: **1/8** (Enter)	Specifies the ending width for the next segment
Arc/Close/Halfwidth/Length/Undo/ Width/<Endpoint of line>: **2-3/8,2** (Enter)	Defines the location of the endpoint

Arc/Close/Halfwidth/Length/Undo/
Width/<Endpoint of line>: **W** (Enter)

Starting width <0.0625>: **.03** (Enter)

Ending width <0.0300>: (Enter)

Arc/Close/Halfwidth/Length/Undo/
Width/<Endpoint of line>: **3,2** (Enter)

Arc/Close/Halfwidth/Length/Undo/
Width/<Endpoint of line>: (Enter)

Specifies the Width option again

Exits the PLINE command

Your polyline leader should resemble figure 16.5.

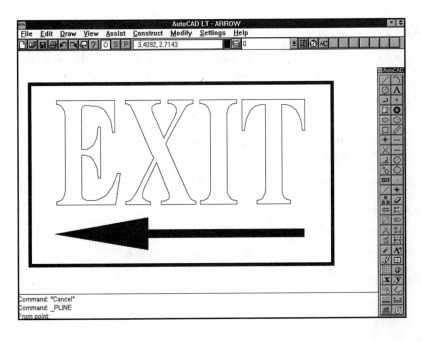

Figure 16.5

A polyline leader.

The Length option of the PLINE command creates a new polyline segment a specified length in the same direction as the last segment. If the Length option is specified
for the first segment of the polyline, a direction of 0 (zero) is assumed.

Using the Arc Option

As mentioned in this chapter's introduction, a polyline can contain arc segments as
well as line segments. You can draw an arc segment by specifying the endpoint of
the arc, the included angle of the arc, the center point, the arc direction from the

previous polyline segment, or the radius; for a three-point arc, you specify two additional points.

In the following exercise, you use the Arc option of the PLINE command to create the knockouts or cutouts in the metal studding used for routing electrical and plumbing in the SHELF drawing.

Creating a Polyline with Arcs

Open the SHELF drawing you saved earlier in the chapter. Turn on Ortho.

Command: *Click on the Polyline tool*	Issues the PLINE command
_PLINE	
From point: *Pick point* ① *(see fig. 16.6)*	Specifies the start point of the polyline
Current line-width is 0'-0"	Provides information regarding the current line width
Arc/Close/Halfwidth/Length/Undo/ Width/<Endpoint of line>: *Pick point* ②	Specifies the endpoint of the first line segment
Arc/Close/Halfwidth/Length/Undo/ Width/<Endpoint of line>: **A** (Enter)	Specifies the Arc option
Angle/CEnter/CLose/Direction/ Halfwidth/Line/Radius/Second pt/ Undo/Width/<Endpoint of arc>: *Pick point* ③	Specifies the endpoint of the arc segment
Angle/CEnter/CLose/Direction/ Halfwidth/Line/Radius/Second pt/ Undo/Width/<Endpoint of arc>: **L** (Enter)	Specifies the Line option
Arc/Close/Halfwidth/Length/Undo/ Width/<Endpoint of line>: *Pick point* ④	
Arc/Close/Halfwidth/Length/Undo/ Width/<Endpoint of line>: **A** (Enter)	Specifies the Arc option
Angle/CEnter/CLose/Direction/ Halfwidth/Line/Radius/Second pt/ Undo/Width/<Endpoint of arc>: **CL** (Enter)	Closes the polyline with an arc

New Riders Publishing
INSIDE
SERIES

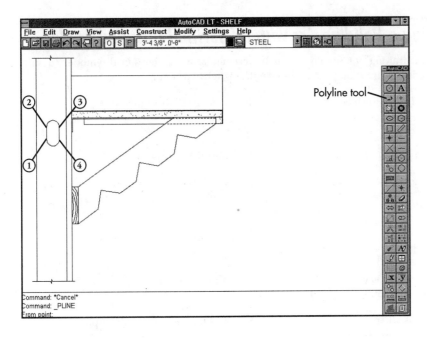

Figure 16.6

Creating a polyline with arc segments.

In the next exercise, you add a wood bullnose detail to the edge of the shelf. To do so, you create a polyline arc segment by specifying the included angle of the arc. An *included angle* is the angle created by two imaginary lines passing through the endpoints and center of the arc (see fig. 16.7).

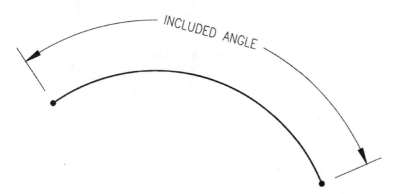

Figure 16.7

Included angle of an arc.

16

Creating a Polyline Arc with a Specified Included Angle

Using the SHELF drawing, set Snap to $^1/_{16}$-inch increments, and turn on Ortho mode. Zoom in to the outer edge of the shelf unit, and make the WOOD layer current.

Command: *Choose* **D**raw, **P**olyline	Issues the PLINE command
`_pline`	
From point: *Pick point* ① *(see fig. 16.8)*	Specifies the start point
`Current line-width is 0'-0"`	Provides information regarding the current line width
`Arc/Close/Halfwidth/Length/Undo/` `Width/<Endpoint of line>:` *Pick point* ②	
`Arc/Close/Halfwidth/Length/Undo/` `Width/<Endpoint of line>:` **A** (Enter)	Specifies the Arc option

`Angle/CEnter/CLose/Direction/`
`Halfwidth/Line/Radius/Second pt/`
`Undo/Width/<Endpoint of arc>:`
A (Enter)
	Specifies the included Angle option

`Included angle:` **90** (Enter)	Specifies the included angle of the arc
`Center/Radius/<Endpoint>:` *Pick point* ③	Defines the endpoint of the arc

`Angle/CEnter/CLose/Direction/`
`Halfwidth/Line/Radius/Second pt/`
`Undo/Width/<Endpoint of arc>:`
L (Enter)
	Specifies the Line option

`Arc/Close/Halfwidth/Length/Undo/` `Width/<Endpoint of line>:` *Pick point* ④	
`Arc/Close/Halfwidth/Length/Undo/` `Width/<Endpoint of line>:` **C** (Enter)	Closes the polyline back to ①
Command: *Choose* **V**iew, **Z**oom, **P**revious	

Save the drawing for a later exercise

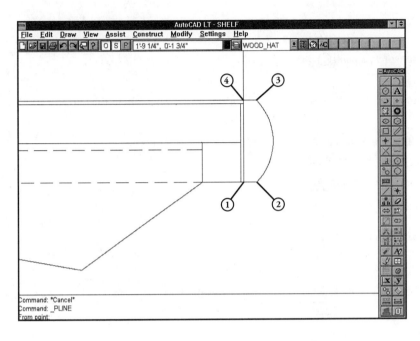

Figure 16.8

Adding a bullnose detail using a polyline.

Notice that after you specify the Angle option, you are presented with an additional prompt:

`Center/Radius/<Endpoint>:`

In the preceding exercise, you specified an endpoint for the arc. You might also have specified a center point or a radius to draw the arc segment. Refer to Chapter 4's discussion of arc options for creating arcs. You can use the same options for polyline arc segments.

In the following exercise, you add a door symbol to a drawing using a multiwidth polyline. You use a 1 ¹/₂-inch width for the door line segment and a width of zero for the arc segment representing the swing of the door. You use the Center option to create the arc segment.

Creating an Arc with the Center Option

Make sure the SHELF drawing is saved, then create a new drawing named DOORSYM, using the ALT1603.DWG file as a prototype and using no setup method.

Command: *Click on the Polyline tool*   Issues the PLINE command

`_PLINE`

continues

continued

From point: _ENDP of *Pick point* ① *(see fig. 16.9)*

Current line-width is 0'-0"	Provides information about the current line width

Arc/Close/Halfwidth/Length/Undo/ Width/<Endpoint of line>: **W** (Enter)	Specifies the Width option

Starting width <0'-0">: **1.5** (Enter)

Ending width <0'-1 1/2">: (Enter)

Arc/Close/Halfwidth/Length/Undo/ Width/<Endpoint of line>: **@36<90** (Enter)	Draws wide polyline to ②

Arc/Close/Halfwidth/Length/Undo/ Width/<Endpoint of line>: **W** (Enter)	Specifies the Width option

Starting width <0'-1 1/2">: **0** (Enter)

Ending width <0'-0">: (Enter)

Arc/Close/Halfwidth/Length/Undo/ Width/<Endpoint of line>: **A** (Enter)	Specifies the Arc option

Angle/CEnter/CLose/Direction/ Halfwidth/Line/Radius/Second pt/ Undo/Width/<Endpoint of arc>: **CE** (Enter)	Specifies the CEnter option

Center point: *Click on the Endpoint tool*

_ENDP of *Pick point* ①	Specifies the center point

Angle/Length/<End point>: *Make sure Ortho is on, then pick near* ③	Specifies the second endpoint of the arc

Angle/CEnter/CLose/Direction/ Halfwidth/Line/Radius/Second pt/ Undo/Width/<Endpoint of arc>: (Enter)	Ends the PLINE command

Save the drawing for a later exercise

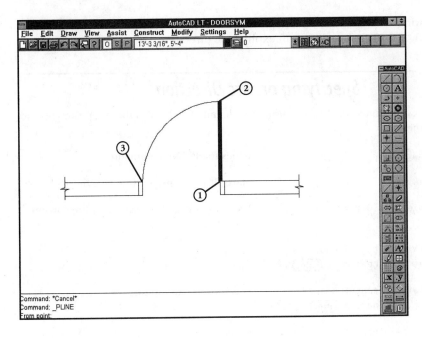

Figure 16.9

A door symbol using a polyline arc.

When you create a polyline arc segment using the Direction option, you can draw arcs that are not tangent to the previous polyline segment. The Direction option determines the starting direction for the arc. If the arc is the first segment of the polyline, a starting direction of zero degrees is assumed.

Figure 16.10 illustrates the concept. If you visualize an imaginary circle completing the arc, it is easier to determine whether an arc segment is tangent to the polyline segment. In effect, by specifying an arc direction, you are determining the starting direction or the direction in which the arc will be drawn.

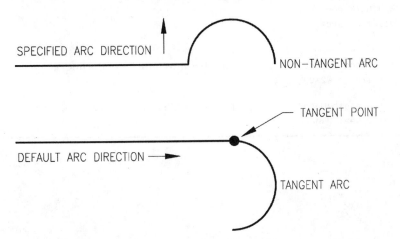

Figure 16.10

Tangent/non-tangent polyline arc segments.

In the following exercise, you create a polyline arc segment (similar to the top polyline in fig. 16.10) by specifying an explicit arc direction.

Specifying an Arc Direction

Create a new drawing named PLINEARC, using the default ACLT.DWG file as a prototype and using no setup method.

Command: **PLINE** (Enter)	Issues the PLINE command
From point: *Pick a point*	Starts drawing the polyline (see fig. 16.11)
Current line-width is 0.0000	Provides information regarding the current line width
Arc/Close/Halfwidth/Length/Undo/ Width/<Endpoint of line>: **@2<0** (Enter)	
Arc/Close/Halfwidth/Length/Undo/ Width/<Endpoint of line>: **A** (Enter)	Specifies the Arc option
Angle/CEnter/CLose/Direction/ Halfwidth/Line/Radius/Second pt/ Undo/Width/<Endpoint of arc>: **D** (Enter)	Specifies the Direction option
Direction from start point: **@2<90** (Enter)	Specifies the new direction
End point: **@2<0** (Enter)	Specifies the endpoint of the arc
Angle/CEnter/CLose/Direction/ Halfwidth/Line/Radius/Second pt/ Undo/Width/<Endpoint of arc>: **L** (Enter)	Specifies the Line option
Arc/Close/Halfwidth/Length/Undo/ Width/<Endpoint of line>: **@2<0** (Enter)	Specifies the endpoint of the line segment
Arc/Close/Halfwidth/Length/Undo/ Width/<Endpoint of line>: (Enter)	Exits the PLINE command

---

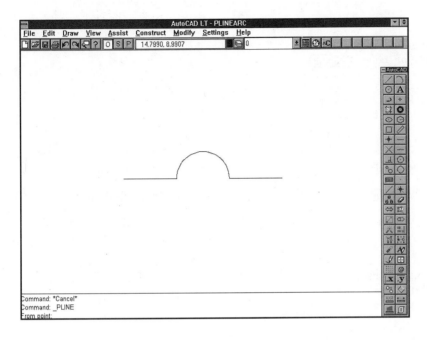

Figure 16.11

Specifying an arc direction.

An arc segment also can be drawn by specifying a radius for the arc. This method is useful in situations in which the radius is predetermined and must be maintained at that value.

In the following exercise, you create a polyline shape that represents a corner guard, which might be used on a wall or a piece of equipment to protect the corner. The radius of the arc is 2 units (see fig. 16.12).

Specifying an Arc Radius

Continue using the PLINEARC drawing from the preceding exercise.

Command: **PL** (Enter)   Issues the PLINE command

PLINE

From point: *Pick a point*   Defines the start point of the polyline

Current line-width is 0.0000   Provides information about the current line
                                                          width

Arc/Close/Halfwidth/Length/Undo/
Width/<Endpoint of line>: **@2<0** (Enter)

continues

continued

`Arc/Close/Halfwidth/Length/Undo/` `Width/<Endpoint of line>:` **A** (Enter)	Specifies the Arc option

`Angle/CEnter/CLose/Direction/`
`Halfwidth/Line/Radius/Second pt/`
`Undo/Width/<Endpoint of arc>:` **R** (Enter)
	Specifies the Radius option

`Radius:` **2** (Enter)	Defines the arc radius
`Angle/<End point>:` **A** (Enter)	Specifies the included Angle option
`Included angle:` **180** (Enter)	Defines the included angle of the arc
`Direction of chord <0>:` **@2<45** (Enter)	Determines the direction of the imaginary line connecting the endpoints of the arc segment

`Angle/CEnter/CLose/Direction/`
`Halfwidth/Line/Radius/Second pt/`
`Undo/Width/<Endpoint of arc>:` **L** (Enter)
	Specifies the Line option

`Arc/Close/Halfwidth/Length/Undo/` `Width/<Endpoint of line>:` **@2<90** (Enter)	
`Arc/Close/Halfwidth/Length/Undo/` `Width/<Endpoint of line>:` (Enter)	Ends the PLINE command

Figure 16.12

Specifying an arc radius.

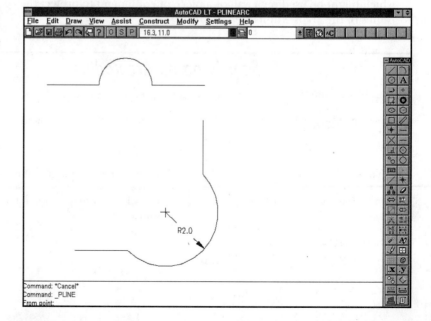

Another option for drawing a polyline arc segment involves specifying three points for the arc: a start point (assumed as the last point specified on the polyline), a second point, and an endpoint. This Second point option is used to specify a three-point arc segment when you know the start point, endpoint, and a point that the arc must pass through. The disadvantage to three-point arc segments is that they will not necessarily align tangentially to adjacent segments. Experiment on your own with creating polyline arc segments using the Second point option. Figure 16.13 shows an example of a polyline created with this option. The pick points have been added for clarification.

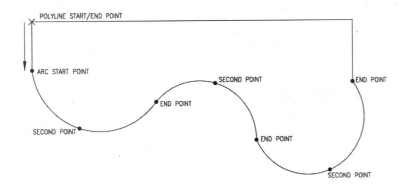

Figure 16.13

Using three-point specification for polyline arc segments.

 Note Three-dimensional polylines can be created in AutoCAD LT using the 3DPOLY command. 3D polylines can contain only straight line segments; no arc segments are allowed. The 3DPOLY command is similar to the PLINE command, except that a Z ordinate can be specified in addition to the required X and Y coordinates.

16

> **3DPOLY.** The 3DPOLY command enables you to construct polylines in three-dimensions (X,Y,Z). A three-dimensional polyline can contain only line segments.

Modifying Polylines with the PEDIT Command

Because polylines are a collection of arc and line segments considered to be one object by AutoCAD LT, they are unique in the way that they must be changed or edited. The PEDIT command is used exclusively for editing polylines and their unique features. You know by now that each endpoint of each segment of a polyline is a vertex. With the PEDIT command, you can move and insert vertices, straighten polyline segments, create a break in the polyline, and so on.

Using the PEDIT command, you also can create a spline curve based on a quadratic or cubic B-spline equation. You can control the appearance of how a linetype is generated with the PEDIT command. In addition, you can use the PEDIT command to assign a uniform width to all the polyline segments and to change the individual width of each vertex.

PEDIT. The PEDIT command enables you to alter a polyline. With PEDIT, you can add or move vertices, change overall and vertex width values, and break and straighten polylines. You also can apply three types of curves to a polyline.

The PEDIT command provides many powerful options for controlling the appearance of polylines.

Using the PEDIT Command Options

You can issue the PEDIT command by selecting the Edit Polyline item in the **M**odify pull-down menu, or entering **PEDIT** or its alias, **PE**, at the Command: prompt. When you issue the PEDIT command, you are prompted to select a polyline. The most reliable method for doing so is by picking the polyline. After you select a polyline, you are presented with the following prompt:

```
Close/Join/Width/Edit vertex/Fit/Spline/Decurve/Ltype gen/Undo/eXit <X>:
```

The next section discusses each of these options.

The Close option of the PEDIT command simply draws a line segment from the last vertex to the first segment of the polyline. Figure 16.14 illustrates a polyline before and after using the Close option.

The Join option of the PEDIT command is used to add to the polyline separate line and arc objects that share an endpoint with the polyline. This option works only for open polylines. If you want to create a polyline from several arcs and lines that meet at their endpoints, you can do so with the PEDIT Join option. If you select a line or arc that is not already a polyline, the PEDIT command prompts you by asking if you want to convert that object into a polyline. If you respond "Yes," you can then use the Join option or any other PEDIT option on that new polyline.

In the SHELF drawing, the bottom edge of the angled wood shelf support has been constructed of separate line segments. In other words, you have an existing shape created from separate line objects. In the following exercise, you create a single polyline from these objects by using the PEDIT Join option.

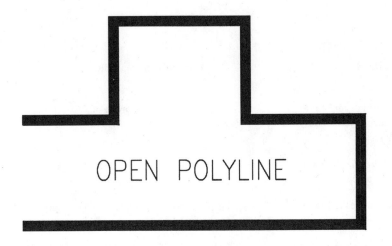

Figure 16.14

*Using the Close
option of the
PEDIT command.*

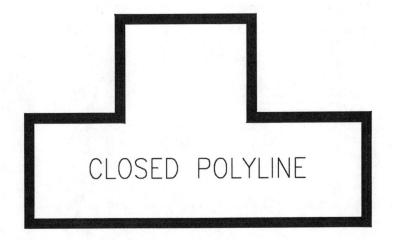

16

Using the PEDIT Join Option

Open the SHELF drawing that you saved earlier, and use ZOOM All.

`Command:` *Choose **M**odify, Edit Pol**y**line*	Issues the PEDIT command
`_pedit Select polyline:` *Pick a line at* ① *(see fig. 16.15)*	Selects the polyline to edit

continues

continued

`Entity selected is not a polyline`	
`Do you want to turn it into one?` `<Y>` (Enter)	Converts entity into a polyline

`Close/Join/Width/Edit vertex/Fit/`
`Spline/Decurve/Ltype gen/Undo/`
`eXit <X>: J` (Enter)
	Specifies the Join option

`Select objects:` *Select the ten lines* *representing the bottom of the brace*	Determines the objects to add to the previously selected polyline
`9 segments added to polyline`	Displays how many segments were joined to the polyline

`Open/Join/Width/Edit vertex/Fit/`
`Spline/Decurve/Ltype gen/Undo/`
`eXit <X>:` (Enter)
	Exits the PEDIT command

Figure 16.15

Adding segments to a polyline.

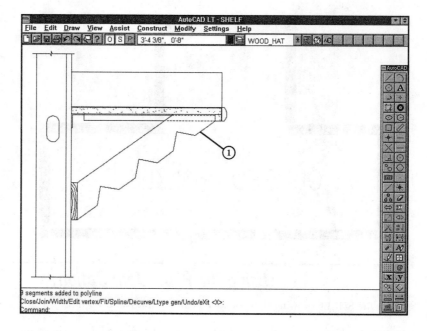

The Width option of the PEDIT command enables you to specify a width for all segments or vertices of a polyline. This option creates the same width for all vertices of the polyline. When you select the Width option, you are asked for the new width for all the polyline segments. You can enter a width, or you can specify a width by picking two points on the screen.

In the following exercise, you use the PEDIT Width option to modify the polyline representing the bullnose trim. You assign this polyline a width of 0.03 inches.

Assigning a Width to a Polyline

Continue working with the SHELF drawing from the preceding exercise. Zoom in to the area of the bullnose, as shown in figure 16.16.

Command: *Choose* **M**odify, Edit Pol**y**line   Issues the PEDIT command

_pedit Select polyline: Selects the polyline to edit
Pick the polyline at ① *(see fig. 16.16)*

Open/Join/Width/Edit vertex/Fit/   Specifies the Width option
Spline/Decurve/Ltype gen/Undo/
eXit <X>: W (Enter)

Enter new width for all segments: Defines the new width
.03 (Enter)

Open/Join/Width/Edit vertex/Fit/   Exits the PEDIT command
Spline/Decurve/Ltype gen/Undo/
eXit <X>: (Enter)

Command: *Choose* **V**iew, **Z**oom, **A**ll

Save the drawing for a later exercise

16

Figure 16.16

Assigning a width to a polyline.

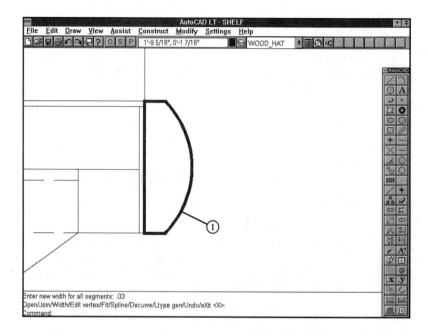

The Edit vertex option of the PEDIT command is discussed in the next section.

The Fit option of the PEDIT command calculates a smooth curve fitting all the vertices of the polyline. The curve is made up of two arcs for every pair of vertices in the polyline. To produce a smooth curve, AutoCAD LT adds extra vertices to the polyline. If the final appearance is not what you want, you can use PEDIT's Decurve option to restore the polyline to its original state. You also can use the Edit vertex option or grips to reposition a vertex for the desired appearance.

The Spline option of the PEDIT command generates a cubic or quadratic B-spline using the vertices of the polyline as control points. In other words, instead of forcing a curve through every vertex as in a fit curve, the vertices serve more as control points for the curve. A spline curve is "anchored" at the start point and endpoints of the polyline. The spline curve does not necessarily pass through each vertex. Each vertex between the start point and endpoint of the polyline "pulls" the curve toward it. The more vertices you have in your polyline, the more force each vertex exerts on the curve.

Figure 16.17 illustrates four types of polyline curves—a normal, fit, cubic B-spline, and quadratic B-spline polyline curve. The *frame* or original polyline is shown so that you can see how each type of curve is affected by the original polyline vertices.

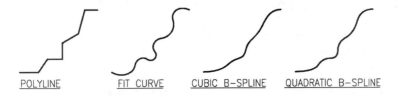

Figure 16.17

Types of polyline curves.

POLYLINE   FIT CURVE   CUBIC B-SPLINE   QUADRATIC B-SPLINE

AutoCAD LT has a few system variables that control the appearance of the curve and the type of curve that the PEDIT command generates (refer to Appendix D, "System Variables").

The system variable SLPINETYPE should be set to a value of 5 to generate a quadratic B-spline. SPLINETYPE=6 generates a cubic B-spline.

SPLFRAME is a system variable that controls whether the original polyline frame is displayed when you generate a curve. A value of 1 displays the frame, and a value of 0 (the default) does not display the frame.

SPLINESEGS is a system variable that designates how many control points are inserted for the curve approximation. The default value is 8. A higher number adds more control points to the curve, thereby increasing its accuracy and approaching the ideal mathematical curve. If you increase the value of SPLINESEGS, however, you substantially increase the amount of time it takes to generate the polyline because more segments must be calculated.

For most situations, unless you are plotting mathematical functions, the default values for these system variables are suitable.

When you use the LIST command on a curved polyline (fit or spline), AutoCAD LT lists the vertices that were added for the curve data. A splined polyline list could therefore be lengthy because of the number of additional vertices required for the curve data.

In the following exercise, you modify the wooden shelf brace in the SHELF drawing by changing the bottom edge to a spline curve.

Creating a Spline Curve from a Polyline

Continue working with the SHELF drawing from the preceding exercise.

Command: *Choose* **M**odify, Edit Pol**y**line	Issues the PEDIT command
_pedit Select polyline: *Pick the polyline at* ① *(see fig. 16.18)*	Selects the polyline to edit

continues

continued

`Close/Join/Width/Edit vertex/Fit/`
`Spline/Decurve/Ltype gen/Undo/`
`eXit <X>: S` **(Enter)**
	Specifies the Spline option

`Close/Join/Width/Edit vertex/Fit/`
`Spline/Decurve/Ltype gen/Undo/`
`eXit <X>:` **(Enter)**
	Exits the PEDIT command

`Command:` *Choose* **V**iew, **Z**oom, **A**ll

Figure 16.18

Creating a spline curve.

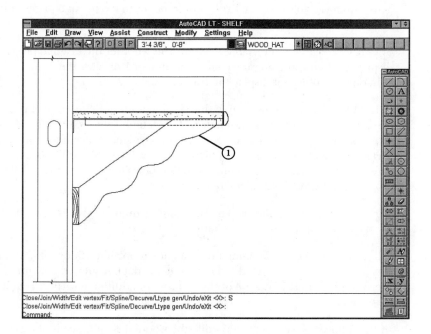

The Decurve option of the PEDIT command removes the curve information from a polyline and restores the polyline to its original state.

The Ltype gen option of the PEDIT command controls how a linetype is generated in a polyline. Normally, AutoCAD LT treats each polyline segment between vertices as a separate item when calculating the spacing and placement of dashes and dots representing a linetype. With linetype generation on, AutoCAD LT essentially ignores the vertices of the polyline between the start point and endpoint. Figure 16.19 illustrates the difference between having linetype generation on and off in a polyline. The system variable PLINEGEN is an on/off toggle that controls whether new polylines are created with linetype generation.

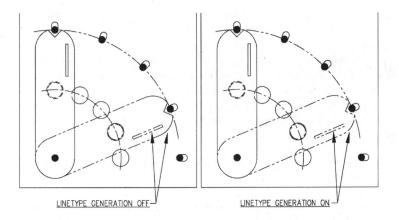

Figure 16.19

Linetype generation in a polyline.

Editing Polyline Vertices

The Edit vertex option of the PEDIT command presents a whole new set of options with the following prompt:

```
Next/Previous/Break/Insert/Move/Regen/Straighten/Tangent/Width/eXit <N>:
```

These options enable you to change the appearance of a polyline by modifying vertices. When you choose the Edit vertex option of the PEDIT command, an X appears at the start point of the polyline. This X marks the vertex that is currently being edited. You use the Next and Previous options to navigate around the polyline to each vertex.

The Break option enables you to separate the polyline into two separate polylines. This option is an alternative (and more complicated) method to using the BREAK command in AutoCAD LT. Nevertheless, the Break option is presented here as one method for breaking polylines.

The break can occur at the same vertex or between two vertices. When you choose the Break option, the current vertex is used as the first break point. You are then presented with the following prompt:

```
Next/Previous/Go/eXit <N>:
```

You can choose the second break point with the Next or Previous options, or you can use the same vertex as the first break point. When you are ready to break the polyline, you choose the Go option.

The Insert option is a powerful editing feature that enables you to add a vertex to an existing polyline. To add a vertex, you position the X marker at the vertex before the location of the new vertex. AutoCAD LT then prompts:

```
Enter location of new vertex:
```

After you specify a new point for the new vertex, the polyline is modified to include this new vertex.

The Move option of the Edit vertex option of the PEDIT command enables you to modify the position of an existing vertex. This function is accomplished by placing the X marker on a vertex and specifying a new location for that vertex. You can achieve the same results more easily by using grip editing, which is discussed later in this chapter. You might also want to refer to the discussion in Chapter 7, "Making Changes: Using Grip Editing."

The Regen option is used primarily for regenerating the polyline to see the effects of assigning a new width value to a vertex.

The Straighten option is convenient for removing vertices from between two other vertices on the polyline and replacing them with a straight segment. This option is similar to the Break option in that you place the X marker on the two vertices that will become the endpoints of the straight segment and then choose the Go option. If the start point and endpoint markers are at the same vertex, AutoCAD LT straightens the segment following that vertex if it is an arc.

The Tangent option enables you to assign a tangent direction (similar to the earlier fig. 16.10) to the current vertex. This information is used by the curve-fitting options discussed later. When specifying this tangent angle, you can enter an explicit angle or pick a point on the screen to show AutoCAD LT the direction from the current vertex.

The Width option is interesting because it enables you to assign a separate width value to each vertex of the polyline, if desired. This option prompts for a starting width and ending width for the segment immediately following the current vertex. An important distinction to note is that the Width option at the Edit vertex option prompt is different from the Width option at the main PEDIT prompt. The PEDIT Width option specifies a new width for all vertices in the polyline, whereas the Edit vertex Width option assigns width values to a specific vertex.

By far the simplest method of moving vertices in a polyline is by using their grips. Chapter 7, "Making Changes: Using Grip Editing," discusses grips in detail. When you use the Stretch mode of grip editing on polylines, you can move any vertex to a new location, thereby changing the shape of the polyline. Other grip editing modes (such as Rotate, Scale, and Move) also work on polylines, but they treat the polyline as one object. In other words, you cannot rotate, scale, or move just one segment of a multisegment polyline.

In the following exercise, you change the shape of the bullnose detail in the SHELF drawing by modifying the arc radius using grips.

Using Grips to Modify Polylines

Continue from the preceding exercise, using the SHELF drawing. Turn on Ortho mode, set Snap to $^1/_{16}$-inch increments, and zoom in to the area of the bullnose.

Command: *Pick the polyline at* ①   Selects the object to edit
(see fig. 16.20)

Command: *Pick the grip at* ①

** STRETCH **

<Stretch to point>/Base point/Copy/   Uses the Stretch mode of grip editing to
Undo/eXit: *Move the highlighted (hot)*   stretch the polyline
grip $^1/_8$ *inch to the left*

Command: *Choose* **V**iew, **Z**oom, **A**ll

Save the drawing for a later exercise

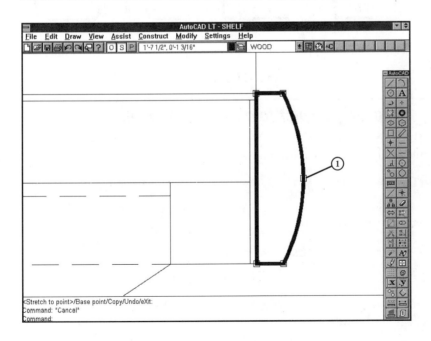

Figure 16.20

Using grips to edit polylines.

16

Applying Fillets and Chamfers to Polylines

The FILLET and CHAMFER commands work as well on polylines as they do on separate AutoCAD LT objects. AutoCAD LT can treat each segment of adjoining polylines separately when applying a fillet or chamfer.

Whole polylines are treated a little differently, however, in that you can fillet or chamfer every vertex, if desired. The FILLET and CHAMFER commands operate on every corner of a polyline with one pick point. Figure 16.21 illustrates a polyline before and after filleting.

Figure 16.21

Applying the FILLET command to a polyline.

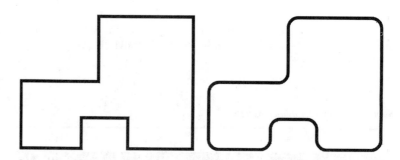

In the following exercise, you apply a fillet to an entire polyline representing the base of a widget.

Applying a Fillet to an Entire Polyline

Make sure the SHELF drawing is saved, then create a new drawing named WIDGET, using the ALT1604.DWG file as the prototype and using no setup method.

Command: *Choose* **C**onstruct, **F**illet	Issues the FILLET command
_fillet Polyline/Radius/ <Select first object>: **R** (Enter)	Specifies the Radius option
Enter fillet radius <0'-0">: **.3** (Enter)	Specifies the new radius for the fillet
Command: (Enter)	Repeats the FILLET command
FILLET Polyline/Radius/ <Select first object>: **P** (Enter)	Specifies the Polyline option
Select 2D polyline: *Pick the polyline at* ① *(see fig. 16.22)*	Selects the polyline to fillet and draws four fillet arcs
4 lines were filleted	Displays how many segments were filleted

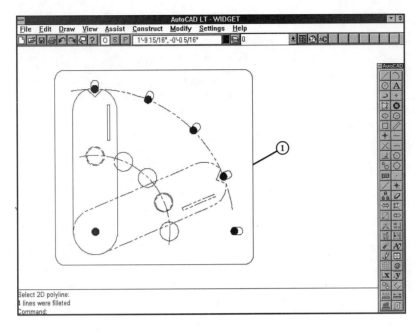

Figure 16.22

Filleting a polyline.

In the preceding exercise, you applied a fillet to every vertex of a polyline. However, you also can fillet two adjoining segments of a polyline. In the following exercise, you apply a fillet to a cross section of a steel angle to show the filleted edges.

Applying a Fillet to Polyline Segments

Open the SHELF drawing that you saved earlier. Zoom in to the view of the steel angle support, as shown in figure 16.23. Turn off Snap.

Command: *Choose* **C**onstruct, **F**illet	Issues the FILLET command
_fillet Polyline/Radius/ <Select first object>: **R** (Enter)	Specifies the Radius option
Enter fillet radius <0'-0">: **.12** (Enter)	Defines the new radius
Command: (Enter)	Repeats the FILLET command
FILLET Polyline/Radius/ <Select first object>: *Pick the polyline segment at* ① *(see fig. 16.23)*	Selects the first segment to fillet

continues

16

continued

Select second object: *Pick the segment at* ②

Selects the second segment to fillet and draws the fillet arc

Command: (Enter)

Repeats the FILLET command

FILLET Polyline/Radius/ <Select first object>: *Pick the segment at* ③

Select second object: *Pick the segment at* ④

Command: (Enter)

FILLET Polyline/Radius/ <Select first object>: *Pick the segment at* ⑤

Select second object: *Pick the segment at* ⑥

Command: **R** (Enter)

Issues the REDRAW command

REDRAW

Save your drawing

Figure 16.23

Applying fillets to polyline segments.

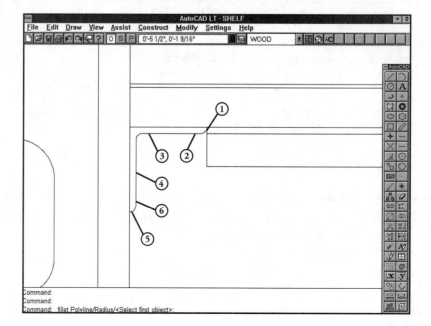

Sometimes, to edit polylines, you need to convert them into individual line and arc objects.

Exploding Polylines into Lines and Arcs

AutoCAD LT includes the EXPLODE command for you to use when you need to break complex entities, also called compound objects, into their constituent objects. Polylines explode into simple lines and arcs. To issue this command, you can select the Explode item from the **M**odify pull-down menu, choose the Explode tool in the toolbox, or enter **EXPLODE** or the **EP** alias at the Command: prompt. EXPLODE uses normal object selection, so you can select any numbers of objects to explode.

Try using EXPLODE to convert the five-segment break line and the door symbol to individual lines and arcs in the following exercise.

Using EXPLODE to Convert Polylines to Lines and Arcs

Open the DOORSYM drawing you saved in the earlier "Creating an Arc with the Center Option" exercise.

Command: *Pick the break line at* ①   Selects and highlights the five-segment
(see fig. 16.24)   break line as a single object

Command: *Pick the door at* ②   Selects and highlights the wide line and zero-
     width arc as a single object

Command: **EP** (Enter)   Issues the EXPLODE command with the two
     objects selected, and explodes them; press F2
     to see the full following message

```
2 found.
Exploding this polyline has lost width information.
The UNDO command will restore it.
```

Command: *Pick the line at* ①   Selects only one line segment, a line entity,
     and highlights its grips (see fig. 16.25)

Command: *Pick the arc at* ②   Selects only the arc segment, an arc entity,
     and highlights its grips

16

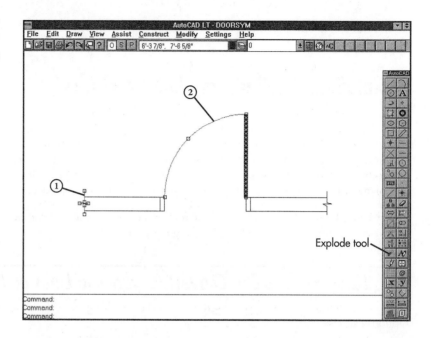

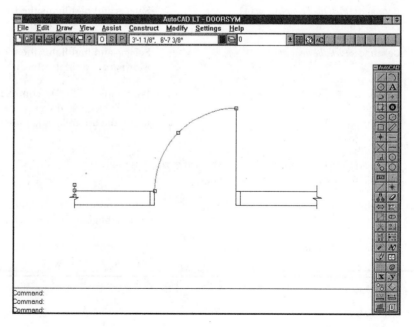

When you explode a polyline with non-zero width or curve-fitting, EXPLODE warns you. When you explode simpler objects, it converts them without any feedback, and you probably won't see any difference until you select one of the resulting objects.

> **EXPLODE.** The EXPLODE command replaces complex or compound objects such as polylines, block insertions, associative dimensions, and associative hatch patterns with their constituent objects.

Curve fit polylines explode into their line and arc segments, but spline fit polylines explode into many tiny line segments that approximate the spline curve. Other compound objects such as block insertions, associative dimensions, and associative hatch patterns have their own quirks and limitations when exploded—see the following chapters where these commands are covered for details.

Drawing Complex Geometry Simply

The power of CAD lies in its capability to eliminate or minimize some of the tedious tasks involved in producing drawing documents. Because CAD software takes advantage of the immense speed and power of the computer system, you can do in seconds what might normally take you minutes or hours when drawing by hand or even when using the CAD software and not taking advantage of its automated features.

One example of this timesaving quality is AutoCAD LT's capability to produce polygons and ellipses quickly with a few points. AutoCAD LT takes over the task of computing the geometry calculations and construction aids you would normally have to struggle with. For creating complex geometry, the compass and protractor are tools of the past. AutoCAD LT is the new tool of your trade.

When AutoCAD LT constructs polygons and ellipses, it is actually calculating the vertices of a polyline and then creating the polyline. In effect, AutoCAD LT is plotting a mathematical function, much as you did in your geometry class. With AutoCAD LT, therefore, you don't have to remember all the rules for creating these objects.

Using the POLYGON Command

The POLYGON command is used to create regular polygons with sides of equal length. You can draw a polygon that is made up of from 3 to 1,024 sides. A *polygon* is really a polyline of zero width that contains no tangent direction information.

> **POLYGON.** The POLYGON command creates multisided polygons consisting of from 3 to 1,024 sides. The POLYGON command creates a polyline with no width value.

To create polygons, you can use two different methods:

◆ Circumscribed about a circle: With this method, the midpoint of each side of the polygon lies on an imaginary circle.

◆ Specifying one edge of the polygon: With this method, you are asked to specify the two endpoints of one edge of the polygon, and AutoCAD LT draws the rest of the sides accordingly.

Figure 16.26 illustrates these two methods.

Figure 16.26

Two methods for creating polygons.

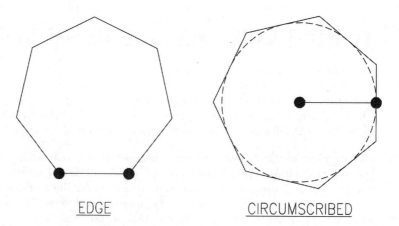

EDGE   CIRCUMSCRIBED

In the following exercise, you create a polygon by specifying the radius of the circle about which you want the polygon circumscribed or drawn around. Suppose that you are a mechanical designer who has been asked to finish the detail drawing of a specialty fastener. You are to draw a six-sided polygon representing the head of a bolt. The polygon must measure $^3/_8$" from flat to flat, or across the polygon.

Creating a Polygon

Create a new drawing named BOLT, using the ALT1605.DWG file as a prototype and using no setup method.

Command: *Click on the Polygon tool*   Issues the POLYGON command

```
_POLYGON
Number of sides <4>: 6 (Enter)
```
Specifies the number of sides

```
Edge/<Center of polygon>: Click on
the Center tool
```

```
_CEN of Pick the circle at ① (see fig. 16.27)
```
Specifies the center of the polygon

```
Radius of circle: @3/16<0 (Enter)
```
Specifies the radius of the circle passing through the midpoints of the sides of the polygon (see fig. 16.27) and draws the polygon

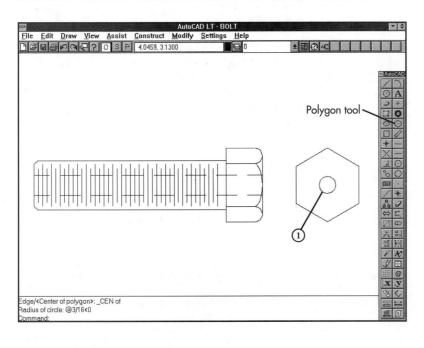

Figure 16.27

Creating a polygon.

Creating Donuts and Ellipses

AutoCAD LT offers a fanciful treat called *donuts*, which are really polylines consisting of arc segments with a width. The DONUT command enables you to draw donuts. To issue this command, you can select the **D**onut item from the **D**raw pull-down menu, choose the Donut tool in the toolbox, or enter **DONUT** or the **DO** alias at the Command: prompt. Donuts are created by specifying an inside diameter and an outside diameter, and then picking center point(s). AutoCAD LT then keeps prompting you to place the donuts until you press Enter. Figure 16.28 illustrates various forms of donuts.

Figure 16.28

Donuts in drawings.

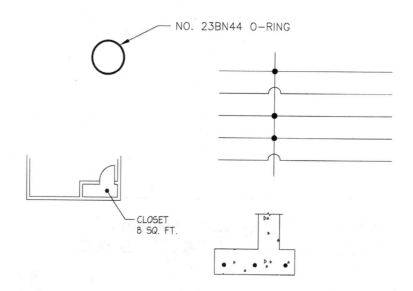

Try using DONUT to fill the circle in the center of the bolt head in the BOLT drawing with a solid dot.

Using DONUT to Make a Solid Filled Dot

Continue in the BOLT drawing from the previous exercise.

`Command:` *Click on the DONUT tool*	Issues the DONUT command
`_DONUT`	
`Inside diameter <0.5000>:` **0** `Enter`	Sets the inside diameter to make a solid dot
`Outside diameter <1.0000>:` *Use the QUAdrant object snap to pick the circle at ① (see fig. 16.29)*	Sets first point of distance indicating outside diameter
`Second point:` *Use the QUAdrant object snap to pick ②*	Sets second point of distance and sets diameter to match circle
`Center of doughnut:` *Use the CENter object snap to pick the circle*	Draws the donut, as shown in figure 16.29
`Center of doughnut:` `Enter`	Exits the DONUT command

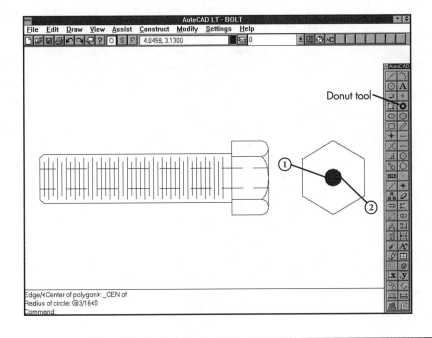

Figure 16.29

Solid filled dot created with DONUT.

DONUT. The DONUT command is used to create polyline *circles* that can vary in width. A donut is created by specifying an inside diameter and an outside diameter.

A trick often used by experienced AutoCAD LT users when they need a dot on their drawing is to create a donut with a zero inside diameter and an outside diameter greater than zero. This trick has the effect of a filled circle that can have many uses. Electrical designers use such donuts for junction points on ladder or schematic diagrams. Structural engineers use them for showing the cross section of a reinforcing bar (rebar). Architects might use them at the ends of leaders to label the square footage of a small room on a floor plan. The possibilities are endless.

An *ellipse* is constructed as a polyline with short line segments approximating a true elliptical curve. To draw an ellipse, you use the ELLIPSE command. To issue this command, you can select the **E**llipse item from the **D**raw pull-down menu, choose the Ellipse tool in the toolbox, or enter **ELLIPSE** or the **EL** alias at the Command: prompt. Ellipses are used to represent circles that are not parallel with the viewer's viewing plane. Isometric views and mechanical drawings commonly use ellipses.

16

If you have a basic understanding of the geometry of an ellipse, you can easily construct one. An ellipse has a major and a minor axis (see fig. 16.30). Geometrically speaking, an ellipse actually has two center points. For the sake of simplicity, however, AutoCAD LT considers the intersection of the major and minor axes as the center of an ellipse.

Figure 16.30

The geometry of an ellipse.

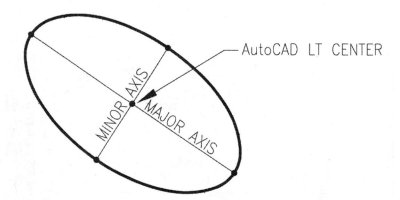

AutoCAD LT CENTER

MINOR AXIS

MAJOR AXIS

ELLIPSE. The ELLIPSE command is used to create zero-width polylines simulating an elliptical shape. In AutoCAD LT, you can create an ellipse by specifying the major- and minor-axis endpoints, the endpoints of one axis, and a rotation angle (as if rotating a circle on a diameter axis) or by specifying the center point and the axis endpoints.

AutoCAD LT enables you to construct an ellipse by specifying the endpoints of the axes or by specifying the center point and one endpoint of each of the axes. Additionally, if the Snap style is set to Isometric, AutoCAD LT can construct an ellipse (isocircle) in the current isometric plane by using a specified radius or diameter.

In the following exercise, you construct ellipses to represent holes that are projected at an angle on a machine part. The top view and side view of the part require ellipses to truly represent the angled hole (see fig. 16.31). To assist you in drawing the ellipses, construction lines have been drawn to show the projections of the angled hole. Draw the ellipses for the side view (left side of your drawing) that represents the angled hole. The hidden portion of the hole has been completed for you.

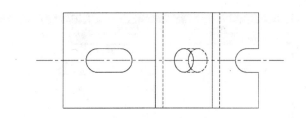

Figure 16.31

Holes represented by ellipses.

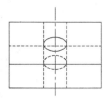
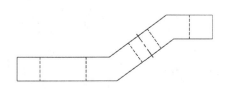

Constructing Ellipses

Create a new drawing named TOOLJIG, using the ALT1606.DWG file as a prototype and using no setup method. Make certain that the OBJECT layer is current.

Command: *Click on the Ellipse tool*   Issues the ELLIPSE command

_ELLIPSE

<Axis endpoint 1>/Center: *Click on the Intersection tool*

_INT of *Pick point* ① *(see fig. 16.32)*   Defines one end of one axis

Axis endpoint 2: *Click on the Intersection tool*

_INT of *Pick point* ②   Defines the other end of the axis

<Other axis distance>/Rotation: *Click on the Perpendicular tool*

_PER to *Pick point* ③   Defines the first endpoint of the second axis (the other endpoint is assumed)

Construct the ellipse for the top view similarly.

Freeze the CONSTRUCTION_LINES layer.

16

Figure 16.32

*Constructing
ellipses to
represent circles
viewed at an
angle.*

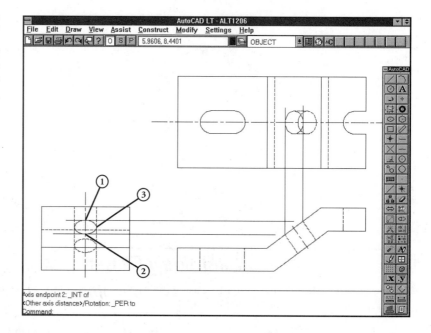

One of the options of the ELLIPSE command, Rotation, enables you to construct an ellipse that represents a circle that has been tilted away from the viewer. In other words, AutoCAD LT simulates a circle rotated about its diameter (the major axis of the ellipse) away from the viewing plane. The specified rotation angle projects a circle into an ellipse as though the viewer is rotating the circle about its diameter away from himself. The Rotation option is useful in situations in which you want to simulate a three-dimensional look in a two-dimensional drawing. If you know the approximate viewing angle, you can project a circle by using the ELLIPSE Rotation option.

Using the RECTANG Command

One of the most useful commands in AutoCAD LT is the RECTANG command for constructing rectangles. When you specify two points—one corner and the opposite corner—AutoCAD LT quickly constructs the appropriate rectangle. To issue the RECTANG command, you can select the Rectangle item from the **D**raw pull-down menu, choose the Rectangle tool in the toolbox, or enter **RECTANG** or the **RC** alias at the Command: prompt.

RECTANG. The RECTANG command creates a rectangular polyline using the current polyline width. The rectangle is created by specifying its two opposite corners.

The rectangle is one of the most common shapes used in drawing creation. A *rectangle* is a closed polyline consisting of four line segments. When a rectangle is drawn, it assumes the current width setting of the system variable PLINEWID (the polyline width used last). Once you realize the ease of constructing rectangles with the RECTANG command, you will use it all the time. Using the RECTANG command is certainly much quicker than figuring the placement of four separate line segments and trimming them to create a rectangle.

In the following exercise, you modify the SHELF drawing by creating a backsplash for the shelf using the RECTANG command. You also use the RECTANG command to create the plastic laminate covering for the backsplash.

Using the RECTANG Command

Open the SHELF drawing, and set the WOOD layer current. Zoom to the view in figure 16.33.

Command: *Click on the Rectangle tool*   Issues the RECTANG command

_RECTANG

First corner: *Use an INTersection object*   Specifies one corner of the rectangle
snap to pick a point ① *(see fig. 16.33)*

Other corner: @.75,4 (Enter)   Specifies the opposite corner and draws the
          rectangle to ②

Set the PLAM layer current for adding the plastic laminate covering for the backsplash. Set snap to ¹/₁₆ and create the rectangles shown from ③ to ④ and ② to ⑤ in figure 16.30 for the plastic laminate. The laminate should be ¹/₁₆" thick. Set snap back to ¹/₈.

Save the drawing for a later exercise

Figure 16.33

Creating a backsplash using the RECTANG command.

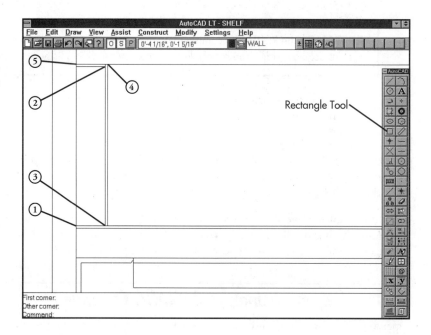

If you are using AutoCAD LT Release 2, you have one more tool for creating complex polylines automatically: the BOUNDARY command. If you are using AutoCAD LT Release 1, skip to the last section of this chapter, "Drawing Double Lines with the DLINE Command."

Creating Complex Polyline Boundaries with BOUNDARY

ALT2

In AutoCAD LT Release 2, the BOUNDARY command creates one or more closed polylines by tracing the inside perimeter(s) of specified area(s). It is a subset of the BHATCH command (see the next chapter). To issue the BOUNDARY command, you can select the Boundary item from the **D**raw pull-down menu, or enter **BOUNDARY** at the Command: prompt. BOUNDARY opens the Boundary Creation dialog box (see fig 16.34), which provides control over the objects considered, point picking, and methods of finding the bounding objects. The bounding objects can overlap and need not meet endpoint-to-endpoint, but they must form an enclosed area. If they don't, you can simply add temporary objects to complete the enclosure.

The BOUNDARY command is quite useful for finding the inside area or perimeter length of a complex area. Use it to create a bounding polyline, then use the Entity option of the AREA command (see Chapter 12, "Accessing your Drawing's Data") to extract the polyline's area or perimeter length. Try doing this to find three simple interior areas in the following exercise. The initial drawing is shown in figure 16.35. The boundary polylines will be drawn on layer AREA (color blue), which has been set

current. Several lines have been drawn on layer AREA across the doorways, so BOUNDARY properly closes the doorways.

Figure 16.34

The Boundary Creation dialog box.

Making a Polyline Boundary

Create a new drawing named BOUNDARY, using the ALT1607.DWG drawing as a prototype, and using no setup method.

Command: *Choose* **D**raw, Boundary	Issues the BOUNDARY command and displays the Boundary Creation dialog box—make sure your settings match those shown in figure 16.34
Choose **P**ick Points	Temporarily closes the dialog box and prompts for points
_boundary Select internal point: *Pick* ① *(see fig. 16.35)*	Specifies point in area within which BOUNDARY will search to generate a boundary
Selecting everything... Selecting everything visible... Analyzing the selected data...	Tells you the progress
Non-uniformly scaled Block encountered. Non-uniformly scaled Block encountered. Non-uniformly scaled Block encountered. Non-uniformly scaled Block encountered. Non-uniformly scaled Block encountered. Non-uniformly scaled Block encountered. Non-uniformly scaled Block encountered.	Informs you of encounter; such blocks are ignored
Analyzing internal islands...	Completes analysis and highlights proposed boundaries, then prompts for another point

continues

continued

```
Select internal point: Pick ②

Analyzing internal islands...          Completes analysis and highlights proposed
                                       boundaries, then prompts for another point

Select internal point: Pick ③

Analyzing internal islands...

Select internal point: (Enter)        Completes boundary specification

BOUNDARY created 13 polylines         Completes the command and draws the
                                      polylines, but they are probably obscured


Command: Click on the Layer button and    Displays resulting boundary polylines; see
turn off all layers except AREA           ①, ②, and ③ in figure 16.35

Command: Choose Assist, Area

_area

<First point>/Entity/Add/Subtract:
E (Enter)

Select circle or polyline: Pick the       Displays area and perimeter of large room
polyline at ① (see fig. 16.36)

Area = 60796.00 square in. (422.1944
square ft.), Perimeter = 107'-2"

Command: Press Enter                      Repeats AREA command

AREA
<First point>/Entity/Add/Subtract: E (Enter)

Select circle or polyline: Pick ②         Displays area and perimeter of small room

Area = 6068.00 square in. (42.1389
square ft.), Perimeter = 26'-10"

Command: UNDO (Enter)

Auto/Back/Control/End/Group/Mark/<number>: 4 (Enter)

AREA
AREA
'DDLMODES
GROUP
Everything has been undone
```

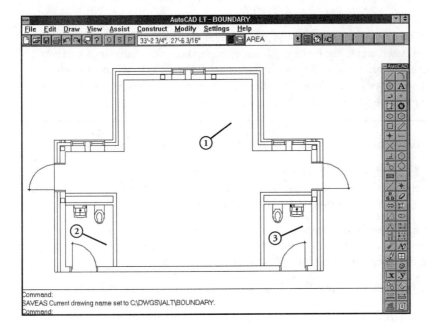

Figure 16.35

Specifying points for boundaries.

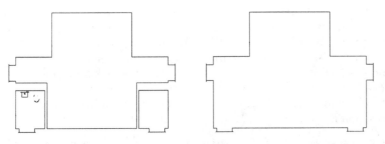

Figure 16.36

Composite illustration of the resulting boundaries.

16

The columns, doors, lavatories, and water closets are blocks (see the next chapter). Those that are mirrored, or flipped from their defined orientation, are reported as Non-uniformly scaled... and are ignored. The rest of the blocks within the specified boundary areas are analyzed, generating the island boundaries of the lavatory and water closet shown near ② in figure 16.36. These are the extra ten of the thirteen polylines created. Having Island **D**etection on can generate superfluous boundaries such as these, in addition to the boundary you want. Turning Island **D**etection off, however, can cause BOUNDARY to reject pick points, displaying a Boundary Definition Error dialog box, claiming Point is outside of boundary.

> **BOUNDARY.** The BOUNDARY command creates polyline boundaries within specified closed areas. The Boundary Creation dialog box provides settings to control the process, including controlling the boundary set (which objects are considered). The existing objects must fully enclose the area, but can overlap each other. The resulting polyline traces the boundary of the enclosure.

The Boundary Creation dialog box provides the following settings and controls:

◆ **From E̲verything on Screen.** This radio button causes the boundary calculation to consider all visible objects. This can be time-consuming in a large drawing. See the following Make N̲ew Boundary Set item.

◆ **From E̲xisting Boundary Set.** This radio button causes the boundary calculation to consider only those visible objects that are in a specified boundary set. See the following Make N̲ew Boundary Set item.

◆ **Make N̲ew Boundary Set.** This button temporarily closes the Boundary Creation dialog box and prompts for selection of objects to be considered by the boundary calculation.

◆ **R̲ay Casting:.** This drop-down list enables you to specify where the boundary tracing process starts, relative to your pick point (see the following P̲ick Points item). The default, Nearest, causes BOUNDARY to find the nearest object and trace the boundary counterclockwise from that nearest point. The optional +X, -X, +Y, and -Y selections cause BOUNDARY to start at the pick point and find the first object encountered in the specified direction: positive X, negative X, positive Y, or negative Y, and then trace the boundary counterclockwise from that nearest point.

◆ **Island D̲etection.** Causes BOUNDARY to create boundary polylines for islands (independent closed sets of objects) found within the primary boundary.

◆ **Pick P̲oints.** This button temporarily closes the Boundary Creation dialog box and prompts for points within the desired boundaries. As you specify each point, BOUNDARY reports the results of its consideration and highlights the resulting boundary lines. After you specify all desired points and press Enter at the Select internal point: prompt, BOUNDARY creates the polyline boundaries on the current layer and ends the command.

The pick point and the ray casting method combine to determine what is considered inside and outside the boundary. If you use Nearest or +X and an object within the desired enclosed area is nearest to or to the right (+X) of the pick point, it will be found and BOUNDARY will report "Point is outside of boundary." you generally can avoid changing the ray casting method by picking an appropriate point near the

desired boundary. You can change the ray casting method only when Island **D**etection is on, but you can then turn Island **D**etection off and use the newly selected method.

It is often necessary, particularly in complex drawings, to use Make **N**ew Boundary Set to limit the objects considered, so BOUNDARY doesn't waste time with irrelevent objects. Turning off or freezing layers is another good way to limit what is considered.

You can also use Make **N**ew Boundary Set to exclude objects that interfere with the desired boundary. For example, to find the entire inside area of the building in figure 16.35, you need to exclude the toilet rooms. Try doing so in the following exercise.

Finding Complex Areas with BOUNDARY

Continue from the previous exercise or create a new drawing named BOUNDARY, using the ALT1607.DWG drawing as a prototype, and using no setup method.

Command: *Choose* **D**raw, Boundary	Issues the BOUNDARY command and displays the Boundary Creation dialog box
Choose Make **N**ew Boundary Set	Temporarily closes the dialog box and prompts for object selection
_boundary Select objects: **ALL** (Enter)	Selects everything
201 found	
Select objects: **R**	Enters Remove mode
Remove objects: *Select all toilet room walls and the fixtures and doors within the rooms*	Removes the toilet rooms from the set of objects to consider
20 found	
Remove objects: *Press Enter*	Completes selection
Analyzing the selected data... Non-uniformly scaled Block encountered. Non-uniformly scaled Block encountered. Non-uniformly scaled Block encountered. Non-uniformly scaled Block encountered.	Analyzes selection set and reopens the Boundary Creation dialog box
Choose **P**ick Points	Temporarily closes dialog box and prompts for points
Select internal point: *Pick* ① (*see fig. 16.35*)	Specifies point in area within which BOUNDARY will search

continues

continued

`Analyzing internal islands...`	Completes analysis and highlights proposed boundaries, then prompts for another point
`Select internal point:` *Press Enter*	Completes boundary specification
`BOUNDARY created 1 polyline`	Completes the command and draws the polyline, but it is probably obscured

Turn off all layers but AREA and use the AREA command's Entity option to select the new boundary polyline (see ④ in figure 16.36). The area (shown at ④ in figure 16.36) should be 529.6111 square ft., and the perimeter should be 109'-10". Then use UNDO to undo everything.

This was not a very complex drawing, but the same techniques can be used to create polylines and find areas within any closed set of objects. It is a little trickier to generate a polyline boundary of an area within the outside of a closed set of objects. You might think you could draw a closed polyline that fully encloses but does not touch the object(s) you want the area of, then use the BOUNDARY command with Island **D**etection checked (on) and pick a point between the enclosing polyline and the desired object(s). Theoretically, that should create one polyline boundary for the enclosing polyline and one for each enclosed object, but this actually works only for simple sets of objects. For more complex areas, even for the outside area of the building in figure 16.35, a trickier solution is required, as the following tip explains.

 Tip   To find the outside area of a building plan or any other object composed of multiple objects use the following trick:

1. Set a temporary layer, such as AREA, current.

2. Draw a closed polyline (such as a large rectangle) that fully encloses but does not touch the object(s) you want the area of.

3. Draw a line that touches both the enclosed objects and the enclosing polyline.

4. Use the BOUNDARY command with Island **D**etection cleared (off). Use Make **N**ew Boundary Set to exclude other unwanted objects that touch or protrude from the object you want the area of, and other extraneous objects, to avoid conflicts and simplify the calculations.

5. Use Pick **P**oint and pick a point between the enclosing polyline and the desired object(s). It will create one polyline boundary that traces the enclosing polyline, the line connecting the enclosing polyline to the enclosed objects, and the enclosed objects themselves (see fig. 16.37).

6. Use editing commands such as BREAK, TRIM, PEDIT, and ERASE to get rid of the enclosing polyline, the line connecting the enclosing polyline to the enclosed objects, and the portions of the polyline boundary that traces them. This leaves just the portions of the polyline boundary that trace the enclosed objects themselves. Use PEDIT to close it.

7. Use the Entity option of the AREA command to pick the resulting polyline. Use UNDO to return the drawing to its previous state.

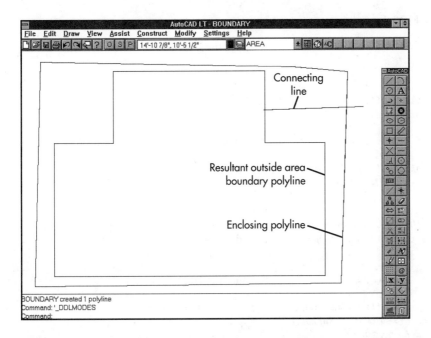

Figure 16.37

Creating an outside area boundary.

Drawing Double Lines with the DLINE Command

Double lines are useful when you need to have continuous line and arc segments parallel to one another, such as for wall lines. To create double lines, AutoCAD LT provides the DLINE command. You can issue this command by selecting the Dou**b**le Line item from the **D**raw pull-down menu, choosing the Double Line tool in the toolbox, or entering **DLINE** or the **DL** alias at the Command: prompt. Architects use the DLINE command for laying out walls because it can automatically trim corners and intersections, and create endcaps for a finished look. Of course, other applications also benefit from use of the DLINE command.

Try the DLINE command with its default settings (except Width) to add two walls the building plan from the previous exercise.

Drawing Walls with DLINE

Continue from the previous exercise or create a new drawing named BOUNDARY using the ALT1607.DWG drawing as a prototype, and using no setup method.

Set the A-WALL-FULL layer current.

Command: *Click on the Double Line tool*	Issues the DLINE command
`_DLINE`	
`Break/Caps/Dragline/Offset/Snap/Undo/` `Width/<start point>:` **W**	
`New DLINE width <1/16">:` **6**	
`Break/Caps/Dragline/Offset/Snap/Undo/` `Width/<start point>:` *Use MIDpoint object* *snap to pick* ① *(see fig. 16.38)*	Starts the double line
`Arc/Break/CAps/CLose/Dragline/Snap/` `Undo/Width/<next point>:` *Use MIDpoint* *object snap to pick* ②	Completes the double line, drawing it and breaking the two intersecting wall lines at the endpoints
Command: **DL**	Issues the DLINE command
`Break/Caps/Dragline/Offset/Snap/Undo/` `Width/<start point>:` *Use MIDpoint object* *snap to pick* ③ *(see fig. 16.39)*	Starts the double line
`Arc/Break/CAps/CLose/Dragline/Snap/` `Undo/Width/<next point>:` **@48,0**	Draws a double line segment, breaking the intersecting wall line at the start point
`Arc/Break/CAps/CLose/Dragline/Snap/` `Undo/Width/<next point>:` *Press Enter*	Ends the DLINE command and draws an end cap on the new double line
`REDRAW`	

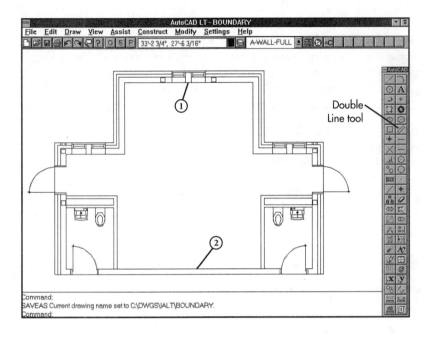

Figure 16.38

Drawing a double line between walls.

Double Line tool

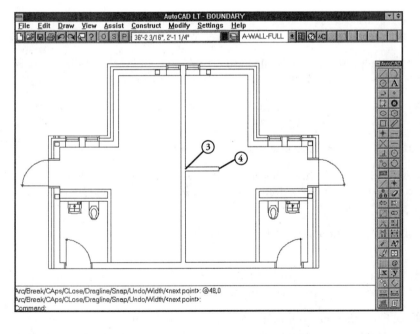

Figure 16.39

Adding a capped double line.

16

> **DLINE.** The DLINE command is used to construct parallel line and arc segments at a specified offset width. Its options provide control over offset from the line of the pick points, offset from the start point, breaks at intersecting lines, capping ends, width, drawing arc or straight segments, and snapping to existing objects.

The prompt that appears after the DLINE command is first issued enables you to preset many of the double line parameters. The DLINE command creates separate line and arc segments—not polylines. The initial prompt is

```
Break/Caps/Dragline/Offset/Snap/Undo/Width/<start point>:
```

After you pick the first point, the prompt for drawing straight line segments with the DLINE command is as follows:

```
Arc/Break/CAps/CLose/Dragline/Snap/Undo/Width/<next point>:
```

The DLINE command's options provide the following features:

◆ **Arc.** When you choose the Arc option of the DLINE command, you are presented with another prompt:

```
Break/CAps/CEnter/CLose/Dragline/Endpoint/Line/Snap/
Undo/Width/<second point>:
```

The Arc option presents additional CEnter, Endpoint, and second point prompts. These options function similarly to the PLINE arc options.

◆ **Break.** When you choose the Break option of the DLINE command, you are presented with the following prompt:

```
Break Dline's at start and end points?  OFf/<ON>:
```

The Break option determines whether AutoCAD LT creates a gap where a line intersects the start or end of a double line. Figure 16.31 illustrates a double line with the Break option on.

◆ **CAps.** The CAps option of the DLINE command determines whether endcaps are drawn when you finish drawing your double lines.

◆ **CLose.** The CLose option of the DLINE command closes the double lines by drawing double lines to the start point and cleaning up the final corner.

◆ **Dragline.** The Dragline option of the DLINE command is a powerful option and requires additional explanation. When you choose the Dragline option, the following prompt appears:

```
Set dragline position to Left/Center/Right/
<Offset from center = 0">:
```

After you specify the first point for the DLINE command, AutoCAD LT's rubber-band line appears. The Dragline option enables you to determine what offset relationship the double lines have to this dragline. The DLINE command defaults to the dragline being the center line of the double lines. You can change it to be the left or right line or specify a distance as an offset from the center. By setting the Dragline option, you have more control over the placement of the double lines.

◆ **Snap.** The Snap option of the DLINE command presents the following prompt:

```
Set snap size or snap On/Off. Size/OFF/<ON>:
```

The Snap option terminates the double line by snapping to an object. This option might be useful in situations in which you want a double line to meet an existing line on your drawing. If the Break option is on, the object snapped to will be broken by a gap the width of the double line. The Snap option also enables you to set the aperture size in pixels at the crosshair location.

◆ **Undo.** The Undo option of the DLINE command operates in the same manner as the Undo option of the LINE or the PLINE command. It undoes the last segment of the double line.

◆ **Width.** The Width option of the DLINE command is also similar to the Width option of the PLINE command. It determines the spacing of the double lines.

In the following exercise, you use the DLINE command with its Arc, and the Arc CEnter and Angle options to add a routed detail to the backsplash in your SHELF drawing.

Creating a Double Line

Open the SHELF drawing that you saved in an earlier exercise. Zoom in to the backsplash area, as shown in figure 16.40. Set Snap to $^1/_4$-inch increments. All of your pick points will be on grid dots.

Command: *Choose* **D**raw, Dou**b**le Line	Issues the DLINE command
`_dline`	
`Break/Caps/Dragline/Offset/Snap/` `Undo/Width/<start point>:` **W**	Specifies the Width option

continues

16

continued

`New DLINE width <1/16">: ` **`1/4`**	Sets the new width for the double lines
`Break/Caps/Dragline/Offset/Snap/` `Undo/Width/<start point>: ` *Pick* *point* ① *(see fig. 16.40)*	Specifies the start point

`Arc/Break/CAps/CLose/Dragline/`
`Snap/Undo/Width/<next point>: `
Pick point ②
	Specifies the endpoint of the segment

`Arc/Break/CAps/CLose/Dragline/` `Snap/Undo/Width/<next point>: ` **`A`**	Specifies the Arc option

`Break/CAps/CEnter/CLose/Dragline/`
`Endpoint/Line/Snap/Undo/Width/`
`<second point>: ` **`CE`**
	Specifies the CEnter option

`Center point: ` *Pick point* ③	Specifies the center point of the arc segment
`Angle/<Endpoint>: ` **`A`**	Specifies the Angle option
`Included angle: ` **`-90`**	Sets the included angle of the arc

`Break/CAps/CEnter/CLose/Dragline/`
`Endpoint/Line/Snap/Undo/Width/`
`<second point>: ` **`L`**
	Specifies the Line option

`Arc/Break/CAps/CLose/Dragline/`
`Snap/Undo/Width/<next point>: `
Pick point ④	

`Arc/Break/CAps/CLose/Dragline/` `Snap/Undo/Width/<next point>: ` **`A`**	Specifies the Arc option

`Break/CAps/CEnter/CLose/Dragline/`
`Endpoint/Line/Snap/Undo/Width/`
`<second point>: ` **`CE`**
	Specifies the CEnter option

`Center point: ` *Pick point* ⑤	Specifies the center point of the arc segment
`Angle/<Endpoint>: ` **`A`**	Specifies the Angle option
`Included angle: ` **`-90`**	Sets the included angle of the arc

`Break/CAps/CEnter/CLose/Dragline/`
`Endpoint/Line/Snap/Undo/Width/`
`<second point>: `**`L`**
	Specifies the Line option

`Arc/Break/CAps/CLose/Dragline/`
`Snap/Undo/Width/<next point>:`
Pick point ⑥	

`Arc/Break/CAps/CLose/Dragline/` `Snap/Undo/Width/<next point>: `**`A`**	Specifies the Arc option

`Break/CAps/CEnter/CLose/Dragline/`
`Endpoint/Line/Snap/Undo/Width/`
`<second point>: `**`CE`**
	Specifies the CEnter option

`Center point: `*Pick point* ⑦	Specifies the center point of the arc segment
`Angle/<Endpoint>: `**`A`**	Specifies the Angle option
`Included angle: `**`-90`**	Sets the included angle of the arc

`Break/CAps/CEnter/CLose/Dragline/`
`Endpoint/Line/Snap/Undo/Width/`
`<second point>: `**`L`**
	Specifies the Line option

`Arc/Break/CAps/CLose/Dragline/`
`Snap/Undo/Width/<next point>:`
Pick point ⑧	

`Arc/Break/CAps/CLose/Dragline/` `Snap/Undo/Width/<next point>: `**`A`**	Specifies the Arc option

`Break/CAps/CEnter/CLose/Dragline/`
`Endpoint/Line/Snap/Undo/Width/`
`<second point>: `**`CE`**
	Specifies the CEnter option

`Center point: `*Pick point* ⑨	Specifies the center point of the arc segment
`Angle/<Endpoint>: `**`A`**	Specifies the Angle option
`Included angle: `**`-90`**	Sets the included angle of the arc

The DLINE command automatically terminates and closes the lines when it reaches its start point.

16

Figure 16.40

Creating a routed detail in the backsplash.

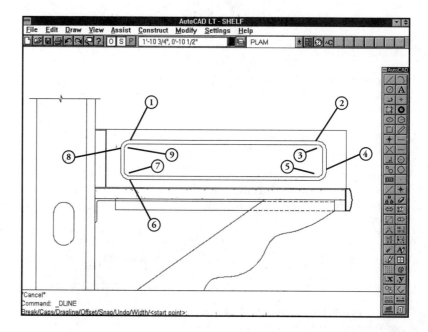

By now you have learned to create a variety of different objects in AutoCAD LT. In the next chapter, you learn to dress up your drawings by using hatch patterns.

C H A P T E R

17

Dressing Up Drawings with Hatching

By now you can draw almost anything effectively, including drawing and editing lines, arcs, circles, text, polylines, and other objects. In this chapter, you learn to dress up your drawings with hatch patterns—patterns that you apply to fill closed areas. Specifically, this chapter provides a detailed discussion of the following topics:

- ◆ Selecting, scaling, and defining hatch patterns

- ◆ Using the HATCH command to apply non-associative (non-editable) hatch patterns in AutoCAD LT Release 1

- ◆ Using the BHATCH command to apply associative (editable and updatable) hatch patterns in AutoCAD LT Release 2

- ◆ Editing and updating associative hatch patterns

Effective use of hatches can make the difference between an average or incomplete drawing and an excellent and attractive one.

Understanding Hatch Patterns and Boundaries

A *hatch pattern* (architects call it *poché*) is used in drafting practices to specify or differentiate types of materials or to attain a decorative effect. Figures 17.1, 17.2, and 17.3 show the various hatch patterns available in AutoCAD LT.

Figure 17.1

AutoCAD LT standard hatch patterns.

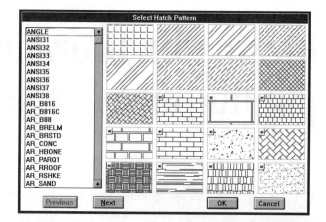

Figure 17.2

Additional AutoCAD LT standard hatch patterns.

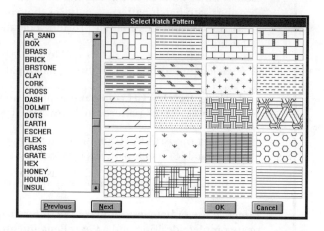

In AutoCAD LT Release 1, the **H**atch item from the **D**raw pull-down menu displays the Select Hatch Pattern dialog box (the icon menu shown in figs. 17.1, 17.2, and 17.3). You can use this dialog box to choose patterns, or use the HATCH command and type the desired pattern name.

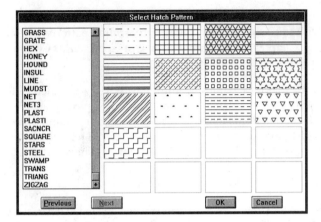

Figure 17.3

Additional AutoCAD LT standard hatch patterns.

In AutoCAD LT Release 1, you must use the HATCH command to apply hatch patterns to areas. In AutoCAD LT Release 2, you can still use the HATCH command and type the desired pattern name, but there is a better alternative—the **H**atch item in the **D**raw pull-down menu and the Select Hatch Pattern dialog box have been replaced by the Boundary **H**atch item and Boundary Hatch dialog box (the BHATCH command). The BHATCH command offers three major advantages over the HATCH command: ease of use, acceptance of overlapping objects in the hatch boundary selection set, and associativity. Associativity enables you to edit the hatch pattern or change the hatch boundary and have the changes reflected in the pattern.

Choosing and Scaling a Hatch Pattern

You can choose a hatch pattern in AutoCAD LT Release 1 in two ways. One way is through the Select Hatch Pattern dialog box (see figs. 17.1, 17.2, and 17.3). You open this dialog box by choosing the **H**atch item from the **D**raw pull-down menu. You select the pattern by name or visually by its pattern, then the dialog box issues the HATCH command with the selected pattern.

Another way to specify a hatch pattern is with the HATCH command. You can issue the HATCH command by choosing the HATCH tool in the toolbox (AutoCAD LT Release 1 only) or by entering **HATCH** or the **H** alias at the Command: prompt. AutoCAD LT presents a prompt showing the last-used pattern name and giving you the option to change the pattern.

In AutoCAD LT Release 2, you use the Boundary Hatch dialog box (BHATCH command), instead of the Select Hatch Pattern dialog box or HATCH command.

Most of the predefined patterns are designed for use at a 1:1 scale in a drawing to be plotted at full size. Like linetypes, you scale them for their plotted appearance, not their screen appearance. If you are zoomed in to an area that will plot approximately

17

the same size as the dimensions of your screen, they should look similar to how they will plot. For drawings plotted at other than full size, try scaling patterns by your drawing scale factor (see Chapter 8, "Preparing Your Workspace: CAD Concepts in 1B"), then adjust that pattern scale if needed.

The architectural patterns that have names beginning with AR_ are scaled differently. They are generally designed to be scaled 1:1 in a drawing to be plotted at $\frac{1}{2}$"=1'0" scale, and they should be scaled accordingly. You should use, for example, a scale of two for AR_CONC in a drawing to be plotted at $\frac{1}{4}$"=1'0" scale. Those that represent scalar materials, however, such as AR_BRSTD (standard brick) should always be scaled 1:1.

Tip
Some patterns can represent different materials when applied at different scales. The AR_SAND pattern, for example, works well as sand in a detail section at 1:1 scale and also can be used to represent concrete in a plan at 1:20 scale.

In addition to predefined patterns, AutoCAD LT gives you the option of creating a user-defined hatch pattern consisting of lines. These lines can be at any angle and at any spacing, and can be single-hatched (only one set of lines) or double-hatched (two sets of lines crossing at 90 degrees to one another).

Choosing Boundaries for Hatch Patterns

When creating a hatch pattern in AutoCAD LT, you must choose the objects that will serve as the boundary for the pattern. Creating hatch patterns in AutoCAD LT can be somewhat tricky with the HATCH command. For the HATCH command to calculate where to place the hatch pattern, an acceptable boundary is required. An acceptable boundary selection set is one in which all the objects in the boundary meet precisely at their adjoining endpoints to form an unambiguous closed boundary. Boundary objects cannot overlap each other. Lines, arcs, circles (alone), and polylines are valid boundary objects, even those within blocks. You can select and hatch multiple boundaries, and one boundary can be within another, forming an island within the hatch pattern. AutoCAD LT is even smart enough to hatch around text objects, treating them as islands, but text cannot form part of a boundary.

If boundary objects overlap or fail to form a closed area, the resulting hatch pattern spills out, as shown in the left side of figure 17.4.

ALT2

The BHATCH command in AutoCAD LT Release 2 solves the problem of overlapping objects, but it ignores nonuniformly scaled blocks (mirrored or unequal X, Y, or Z scales—see the next chapter).

Tip

A trick of most seasoned AutoCAD LT users is to create a temporary closed polyline boundary around the area they want to hatch, as shown in the middle of figure 17.4. AutoCAD LT then has a nice, clean boundary to hatch, and you don't have to worry about whether the existing boundary set will yield the desired results. Figure 17.4 illustrates the difference between a good boundary selection set and a bad one.

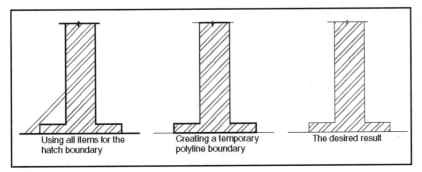

Using all items for the hatch boundary

Creating a temporary polyline boundary

The desired result

Figure 17.4

The importance of a good boundary selection set for hatching.

The BHATCH command is covered later in the chapter; the HATCH command is covered in the following section.

Using the HATCH Command and Select Hatch Pattern Dialog Box

In the next two exercises, you add hatch patterns to the building plan shown in figure 17.5. The hatch patterns shown in figure 17.5 don't yet exist in the drawing—you will apply them. (The next two figures show the AutoCAD LT Release 1 interface because the exercises are mainly for AutoCAD LT Release 1 users.)

In the first exercise, you apply the predefined AR_CONC hatch pattern to the concrete walls. You have to create a polyline boundary to get some of the walls hatched correctly. Then, in the second exercise, you apply a user-defined pattern to hatch the brick facing. The first exercise uses the Select Hatch Pattern dialog box; if you are using AutoCAD LT Release 2, you do not need to perform the exercises, but read them over to better understand hatching.

17

Figure 17.5

Applying hatch patterns.

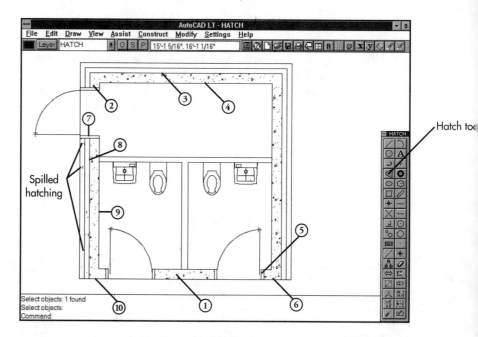

Hatch tod

Spilled hatching

Applying a Predefined Hatch Pattern

Create a new drawing named HATCH, using the ALT1701.DWG file from the IALT Disk as a prototype, and using no setup method. A layer named HATCH has been created and set current.

Command: *Choose* **D**raw, **H**atch box	Opens the Select Hatch Pattern dialog and displays the first page of patterns (see fig.17.1)
Click twice on **N**ext	Changes to the second, then the third page of patterns (see figs 17.2 and 17.3)
Click on the last pattern (the stair-stepped lines)	Scrolls the pattern name list and highlights both the pattern and its name, ZIGZAG
Scroll back to the top of the list and click on the name AR_CONC	Displays the first page of patterns and highlights both the pattern and its name
Choose OK	Closes the dialog box, issues the HATCH command with the AR_CONC pattern selected, and prompts for scale

```
_hatch
Pattern (? or name/U,style): ar_conc
```

New Riders Publishing
INSIDE
SERIES

`Scale for pattern <1.0000>:` **2** (Enter)	Defines the scale factor for the hatch pattern
`Angle for pattern <0>:` **45** (Enter)	Determines the angle at which to draw the hatch pattern
`Select objects:` *Use a Window to select the lines bounding the area shown hatched at* ① *in figure 17.5*	Selects the lines forming the hatch boundary
`4 found`	
`Select objects:` (Enter)	Ends object selection and creates the hatch pattern, as shown in figure 17.5
`Command:` (Enter)	Repeats the HATCH command, skipping the pattern selection, scale, and angle prompts, using the previous settings, and prompting for boundary selection
`Select objects:` *Pick the lines and polylines at* ②, ③, ④, ⑤, *and* ⑥	Specifies boundary objects (notice that the lines at ② and ⑥ overlap the ends of polyline at ③)—will the hatch spill out?
`Select objects:` (Enter)	Ends selection and draws the hatch correctly— sometimes you get lucky; if you had used a zero angle, the pattern would have spilled out

Repeat the HATCH command again and pick the lines at ⑦, ⑧, ⑨, and ⑩. The lines at the ends also overlap—will the hatch spill out? Complete the command and you find that they indeed do spill, as shown near ⑦ and ⑩ in figure 17.5.

`Command:` **U** (Enter)	Undoes the hatch.

Use INTersection object snap and PLINE to draw a polyline enclosing the desired hatch area. Then repeat the HATCH command and select the polyline (use the Last selection option)—it hatches correctly, as shown in figure 17.7 (see the next exercise).

Use ERASE with the Previous selection option to erase the polyline, then use REDRAW to clean up the image.

Tip   All hatches are placed and aligned relative to the current snap origin and rotation angle in the current UCS (default 0,0 and zero degrees—see Chapter 2, "Specifying Locations in CAD Space"). Patterns such as AR_CONC can fill certain areas better, such as small areas in detail drawings, if rotated 45 degrees. It also can help to adjust the hatch origin by offsetting the 0,0 base of the current UCS. Fine dots in patterns such as AR_CONC might require setting plotter pen size to .005 or larger to prevent them from dropping out of plots.

17

The Select Hatch Pattern dialog box is just a convenient way to select a pattern and issue the HATCH command, which actually applies the hatching.

> **HATCH.** The HATCH command is used to apply a predefined or user-defined pattern (or poché) to an area. A boundary selection set must be specified in addition to the pattern name, scale, and rotation angle of the pattern. User-specified patterns consisting of only evenly spaced lines also can be used.

Using the HATCH Command Options

When you issue the HATCH command to apply a hatch pattern, you are presented with the following prompt:

```
Pattern (? or name/U,style) <U>:
```

The HATCH command options are as follows:

◆ **?.** The ? option lists, by name or wildcard, the hatch patterns stored in the ACLT.PAT file. To list all patterns, enter an asterisk after entering the ? option.

◆ **name.** The name you specify determines the pattern used, and then HATCH prompts you for scale and angle. You can enter *name* alone to use the default hatching style, or enter *name,style* to specify both—see the following style option. You can enter the name of any valid hatch pattern defined in the ACLT.PAT file.

◆ **U.** The U option indicates a user-defined pattern, and then HATCH prompts you for angle, spacing, and whether to double-hatch the area. You can enter the U alone to use the default hatching style, or enter U,*style* to specify both—see the following style option. You can enter the name of any valid hatch pattern defined in the ACLT.PAT file.

◆ **style.** The style you specify determines how HATCH treats islands, or smaller boundaries within the outermost boundary or boundaries. You enter any valid hatch pattern name, or U (user-defined pattern), followed by a comma and either an N, O, or I, to determine how AutoCAD LT hatches the selection set. The three styles of hatching are Normal, Outermost, and Ignore. For example, AR_CONC,N specifies the AR_CONC pattern with the normal style and U,I specifies a user-defined pattern with the Ignore style. Figure 17.6 illustrates the differences between these styles. The flaw in the Outermost example in this figure also illustrates that sometimes, no matter how hard you try, AutoCAD LT does not produce the proper hatching. To achieve the desired result, you must sometimes manipulate your selection set differently or create new, temporary borders.

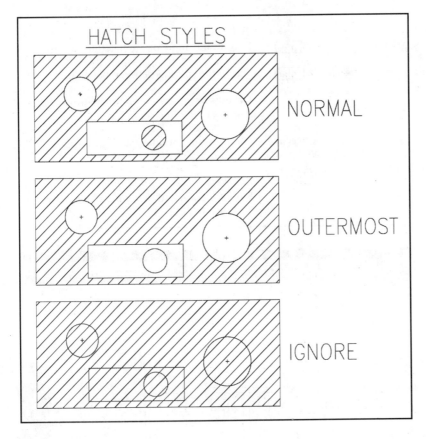

Figure 17.6

Hatch styles.

In the following exercise, you hatch the brick walls with a user-defined hatch pattern. Short lines capping the ends of the brick walls have already been drawn on layer HATCH. If you are using AutoCAD LT Release 2, you do not need to perform the exercise, but read it over to better understand hatching.

Applying a User-Defined Hatch Pattern

Continue working with the HATCH drawing from the preceding exercise.

Command: *Click on the Hatch tool*	Issues the HATCH command

`_HATCH`

Pattern (? or name/U,style) `<ar-sand>: U` Enter	Specifies the User-defined option

continues

continued

`Angle for crosshatch lines <0>:45` (Enter)	Defines the angle of the hatch lines
`Spacing between lines <1.0000>: 2` (Enter)	Sets 2" the spacing between hatch lines
`Double hatch area? <N>` (Enter)	Defaults to *not* draw additional lines at 90 degrees to the first set of hatch lines
`Select objects:` *Pick the lines and polylines at* ① *(see fig. 17.7),* ②, ③, *and* ④ *(use small Window selections to pick the wall end lines at* ① *and* ④*)*	Specifies the boundary set
`Select objects:` (Enter)	Ends selection and draws the hatch pattern, as shown in figure 17.7

Figure 17.7

Hatching the brick wall with a user-defined pattern.

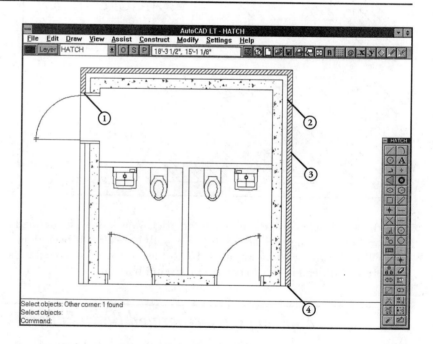

Understanding More About Hatch Patterns

Hatch patterns are stored in a file named ACLT.PAT, which can be customized with your own hatch patterns—see your *AutoCAD LT User's Guide* or *Maximizing AutoCAD*

Release 12 from New Riders Publishing. If you decide to customize AutoCAD LT in this manner, however, be sure to save a backup copy of the original ACLT.PAT file.

The hatch pattern is considered a block object in AutoCAD LT, which means that all the lines and dots making up a hatch pattern are one object. An advantage of the hatch pattern being one object is that you save drawing space by not having all of these separate objects cluttering up the drawing. Another advantage is that if you need to modify the hatch pattern or to erase the old one and create a new one, you don't have hundreds of objects to erase.

Hatches behave normally with most editing commands, such as MOVE. STRETCH, however, is a special case. Although hatches are placed and aligned relative to the current snap origin and rotation angle in the current UCS (default 0,0 and zero degrees), the hatch pattern block has an insertion point of 0,0,0 in the WCS, which is not necessarily the same as the current UCS. If you want to stretch objects that include a hatched area, the hatch insertion point must be included in the STRETCH command's selection window. The pattern can be moved, but the lines within it cannot be stretched unless the pattern is exploded. See the next chapter for more information on blocks, and Chapter 15, "Modifying Objects and Text," for the STRETCH command.

Stop Exploding a hatch pattern is inadvisable. This warning is especially applicable for patterns containing many dots and short line segments. The chances are that you would never be able to erase all the resulting little bits of lines after exploding a hatch pattern. You should therefore explode with extreme caution.

The rest of this chapter covers the AutoCAD LT Release 2 BHATCH command, which solves many of the quirks of HATCH. If you are using AutoCAD LT Release 1, skip the rest of the chapter. If you are using AutoCAD LT Release 2, be sure you've read the general information on hatch pattern selection and scaling in the preceding sections titled "Understanding Hatch Patterns and Boundaries" and "Understanding More About Hatch Patterns."

Using the BHATCH Command and Boundary Hatch Dialog Box

Instead of laboriously requiring you to pick objects or create boundaries, the BHATCH command prompts for points within the areas to be hatched, finds their boundaries, and hatches them.

ALT2

In AutoCAD LT Release 2, the Boundary **H**atch item in the **D**raw pull-down menu and the Boundary Hatch tool both issue the BHATCH command, which is a much better alternative to the HATCH command. The BHATCH command is easier to use, ignores the overlapping portions of boundary objects, and provides editing associativity. You can edit the resulting hatched area or change the hatch boundary and have the changes reflected in the pattern. The BHATCH command, whether issued by menu, toolbox, or entering its name by typing, displays the Boundary Hatch dialog box, as shown in figure 17.8.

Figure 17.8

The Boundary Hatch dialog box.

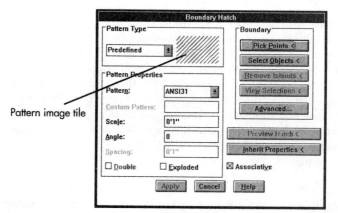

The boundary specification aspects of BHATCH are the same as for the BOUNDARY command, which was covered in Chapter 16, "Increasing Your Drawing Power with Polylines and Double Lines." Therefore, the details of boundary specification are not covered in this chapter, so refer to Chapter 16 for more information.

By using the BHATCH command in the following exercise, you can quickly create the hatching that took careful selection of boundary objects, and even required you to draw new boundary objects, in the previous two exercises. You use the AR_CONC predefined pattern and a user-defined pattern for brick.

Applying Hatch Patterns with BHATCH

Create a new drawing named HATCH, using the ALT1701.DWG file from the IALT Disk as a prototype, and using no setup method. A layer named HATCH has been created and set current.

Command: *Click on the Boundary Hatch tool*   Issues the BHATCH command and displays the Boundary Hatch dialog box

_BHATCH

New Riders Publishing
INSIDE
SERIES

Click several times on the pattern image tile (see fig. 17.8)	Cycles through the predefined patterns, displaying each in the pattern image tile and its name in the Patter**n** drop-down list box
In the Pattern Properties area, click in the Patter**n** *drop-down list box, scroll down to* AR_CONC, *and select it*	Opens the list box, selects the pattern, and displays it in the pattern image tile and its name in the drop-down list box
Double-click in the Sca**l**e *box and type* **2**	Sets the scale
Double-click in the **A**ngle *box and type* **45**	Sets the angle
In the Boundary area, choose Pick **P**oints	Temporarily closes the dialog box and prompts for point specification
`Select internal point:` *Pick* ① *(see fig. 17.9—the hatch patterns shown are not yet visible)*	Specifies the first area to hatch and highlights its boundary

Notice that the overlapping portions of the lines that interfered and caused the pattern to spill in the earlier HATCH exercise are not highlighted.

`Selecting everything...`
`Selecting everything visible...`
`Analyzing the selected data...`
	Tells you the progress

`Non-uniformly scaled Block encountered.`
`Non-uniformly scaled Block encountered.`
`Non-uniformly scaled Block encountered.`
`Non-uniformly scaled Block encountered.`
`Analyzing internal islands...`
	Informs you of the blocks encountered —such blocks are ignored

`Select internal point:` *Pick* ②	Specifies another area and highlights its boundary
`Analyzing internal islands...`	
`Select internal point:` *Pick* ③	Specifies a third area and highlights its boundary
`Analyzing internal islands...`	
`Select internal point:` **(Enter)**	Accepts the points and reopens the Boundary Hatch dialog box
Choose Apply	Closes the dialog box and draws the three concrete wall hatches (see fig. 17.9)

continues

17

continued

Command: (Enter)	Repeats the BHATCH command and opens the Boundary Hatch dialog box
Click on Predefined *in the* Pattern T**y**pe *drop-down list*	Opens the list, offering choices of Pre-Defined User-defined, and Custom
Select User-defined	Specifies the user-defined option

The user-defined option clears the pattern image tile, grays the Patter**n** drop-down list and Sc**a**le boxes, and ungrays the **S**pacing and **D**ouble (double-hatch) boxes. The **A**ngle is still 45 from before.

Double-click in the Spacing *box and type* **2**	Sets the spacing to 2" to indicate brick
In the Boundary area, choose Pick **P**oints	Temporarily closes the dialog box and prompts for point specification
Select internal point: *Pick* ④	Specifies the area to hatch and highlights its boundary

The status messages appear, like before, but they aren't shown here.

Select internal point: *Pick* ⑤	Specifies another area to hatch and highlights its boundary
Select internal point: (Enter)	Accepts the points and reopens the Boundary Hatch dialog box
Choose Apply	Closes the dialog box and draws the two brick hatches (see fig. 17.9)

 Note In early versions of AutoCAD LT Release 2, if Architectural or Engineering units are current, the Sc**a**le box displays a distance in the current units instead of a scale factor. This causes a scale such as 32 to display as 2'8".

BHATCH. The BHATCH command (Boundary Hatch dialog box) is used to apply a predefined pattern (or poché) to one or more closed areas, automatically detecting islands within the area(s). A name, scale, and rotation angle must be specified for the pattern, or a user-specified pattern consisting of only evenly spaced lines can be specified. A boundary selection set must be specified, either by selecting objects, by picking one or more points in the area(s) to hatch, or both. BHATCH finds the boundary of the specified area, and does not require the defining objects to meet precisely, unlike the HATCH command. Unlike hatch patterns created with the HATCH command, those created by BHATCH are associative and can be edited, automatically adjusting as their boundaries are modified.

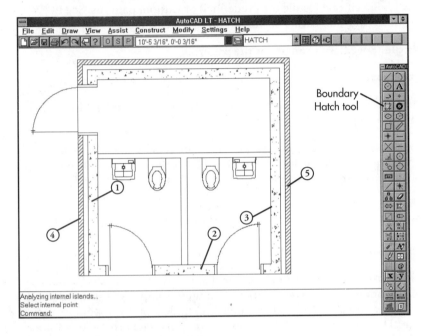

Figure 17.9

Hatches applied by boundary hatching.

As you saw in the previous exercise, the Boundary Hatch dialog box offers several controls over the pattern and the boundary.

The Boundary Hatch Dialog Box Options

The options and controls of the Boundary Hatch dialog box are as follows:

◆ **Pattern Type.** The Pattern Type drop-down list enables you to specify a Predefined pattern (from the ACLT.PAT file), a User-defined pattern (a single or double set of spaced lines), or a Custom pattern. A Custom pattern is a user-defined pattern that can consist of multiple broken lines, like the patterns in ACLT.PAT. A Custom pattern is defined in a PAT file where the file name is the pattern name.

◆ **Pattern Properties.** The Pattern Properties area defines the patterns treatment. Those options not relevant to the specified pattern type are grayed and inactive. The options are as follows:

17

◆ **Pattern.** The name of a predefined pattern from the ACLT.PAT file.

◆ **Custom Pattern.** The name of a custom pattern file—a file with a PAT extension that contains a single custom pattern definition. Use the name 2x2TILE, for example, to specify the pattern in the 2X2TILE.PAT file.

◆ **Scale.** Specifies the scale for Predefined or Custom patterns. See the previous Note and earlier section in this chapter on hatch scale.

◆ **Angle.** Specifies the angle for the pattern.

◆ **Spacing.** Specifies the spacing between lines of a User-defined pattern.

◆ **Double.** If checked, causes a User-defined pattern to be double-hatched, with two sets of lines 90 degrees apart.

◆ **Exploded.** Although not recommended for general use, the Exploded option, if checked, causes the pattern to be drawn as many individual line objects instead of as a single associative hatch pattern.

◆ **Boundary.** The options in the Boundary area control what is considered in the boundary and how it is considered. See the BOUNDARY command in Chapter 16, "Increasing Your Drawing Power with Polylines and Double Lines," for more information. The options are as follows:

◆ **Pick Points.** Temporarily closes the dialog box and prompts for point specification. At the Select internal point: prompts, you pick a point in each area you want hatched, or enter **U** to undo a previous point specification. The areas must be fully enclosed by objects. The proposed boundaries are highlighted as they are found. When you finish picking points, you press Enter to return to the dialog box. See also A**dv**anced.

◆ **Select Objects.** This enables you to select boundary objects in the same manner as with the old HATCH command. The objects must meet the same restrictive, nonoverlapping requirements, so this is not very useful. This is *not* the same as the BOUNDARY command's Make **N**ew Boundary Set option—for BHATCH, that option is within the A**dv**anced sub-dialog box.

◆ **Remove Islands.** When Island **D**etection is on (the default is on—see A**dv**anced), picking points can generate island boundaries within the primary outer boundary that is found. If so, the hatch pattern stops at the island (unless the style is set to Ignore). You can use **R**emove Islands to remove these islands from consideration, so the hatch pattern does not stop at their boundaries.

◆ **View Selections.** Displays the current boundary set. If none has been specified, this is grayed and inactive.

◆ **Advanced.** Opens the Advanced Options dialog box (see fig. 17.10). Its controls are listed separately, following this list.

◆ **Preview Hatch.** Displays, in the drawing, a temporary preview of the hatches that the current settings and selections would generate.

◆ **Inherit Properties.** Temporarily closes the dialog box and prompts for selection of an existing associative hatch. When you pick an associative hatch at the `Select hatch object:` prompt, the dialog box reopens, with the pattern type and properties of the selected pattern. Inherit Properties does not recognize nonassociative hatches, such as those created by AutoCAD Release 12 or AutoCAD LT Release 1.

◆ **Associative.** This check box turns associativity on and off. Hatch patterns created by BHATCH are associative by default if HANDLES is on. If the HANDLES and Associative settings are both on, editing the boundary of a boundary hatch updates the hatch. HANDLES is both a command name and a system variable, and can only be turned on and off by the HANDLES command. Handles are unique identifiers, assigned to each object in a drawing, that are used by applications and commands such as BHATCH to keep track of those objects. HANDLES is on by default in new drawings created by AutoCAD LT Release 2, unless they use a prototype in which HANDLES is off. HANDLES is off by default in AutoCAD LT Release 1, so be careful to turn it on if adding hatches to drawings created in AutoCAD LT Release 1.

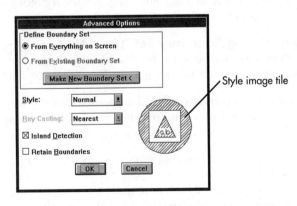

Figure 17.10

The Advanced Options dialog box.

17

Stop If you turn off HANDLES, hatch associativity is destroyed. Regardless of the HANDLES and Associative settings, if the boundary of a boundary hatch is edited in AutoCAD LT Release 1 or AutoCAD Release 12, the hatch is not updated. The

continues

hatch does not, however, lose associativity in AutoCAD LT Release 2. You can later update the hatch by selecting it in the HATCHEDIT command and choosing Apply in the Hatchedit dialog box.

AutoCAD LT Release 2 associative hatches are not compatible with AutoCAD Release 13 associative hatches. You can edit a Release 13 hatch only in Release 13, and an LT hatch only in LT.

Controlling Hatch Boundaries

The pick point you use might not always find the desired boundary, particularly if islands and intersecting objects interfere. Also, in complex drawings, BHATCH examines all objects visible in the current viewport, which can be time-consuming. The Advanced Options dialog box, displayed by the A**d**vanced button, aids both of these problems. The options in the Define Existing Boundary Set area, and the **R**ay Casting and Island **D**etection options are identical to options in the BOUNDARY command's Boundary Creation dialog box (see Chapter 16, "Increasing Your Drawing Power with Polylines and Double Lines," for examples and discussion of their use and effects). The advanced options are as follows:

◆ **Define Existing Boundary Set.** The options in the Define Existing Boundary Set area control which objects are considered in the boundary calculation. These options are as follows:

   ◆ **From E**v**erything on Screen.** This radio button causes the boundary calculation to consider all objects visible in the current viewport. This can be time-consuming in a large drawing. See the following Make **N**ew Boundary Set item.

   ◆ **From E**x**isting Boundary Set.** This radio button causes the boundary calculation to consider only those visible objects that are in a specified boundary set. See the following Make **N**ew Boundary Set item.

   ◆ **Make N**ew **Boundary Set.** This button temporarily closes the Boundary Creation dialog box and prompts for selection of objects to be considered by the boundary calculation.

◆ **S**tyle. This drop-down list enables you to specify the style of hatching: Normal, Outer, or Ignore. These styles are the same as those in the earlier HATCH command discussion—refer back to it for details on their effects. When you select a style, its effect is illustrated by the Style image tile. Clicking on the style image tile cycles through the three styles and displays the selected style in the **S**tyle drop-down list.

- ◆ **Ray Casting.** This drop-down list enables you to specify where the boundary tracing process starts, relative to your pick point (see the following **P**ick Points item). The default, Nearest, causes BHATCH to find the nearest object and trace the boundary counterclockwise from that nearest point. The optional +X, -X, +Y, and -Y selections cause BHATCH to start at the pick point and find the first object encountered in the specified direction: positive X, negative X, positive Y, or negative Y, and then trace the boundary counterclockwise from that nearest point.

- ◆ **Island Detection.** When on, Island **D**etection causes BHATCH to find boundaries of islands (independent closed sets of objects) found within the primary boundary. The effect of turning off Island **D**etection is often the same as using the Ignore style.

- ◆ **Retain Boundaries.** This check box, when on (it's off by default) causes BHATCH to create and retain polyline boundary objects for each hatch pattern it creates. If off, polyline boundary objects for each hatch pattern are temporary and are discarded when the BHATCH command completes. These polyline boundary objects are identical to those that would be created by the BOUND-ARY command. This does not affect associativity, which depends on HANDLES not on the polyline boundaries.

In the following exercise, you use a number of these BHATCH options to create a reflected ceiling plan of the building that you hatched in the previous exercises. You use the Patter**n**, **A**ngle, **S**pacing, **D**ouble, Pick **P**oints, Preview Ha**t**ch, **R**emove Islands, and A**dv**anced options, and then use the Advanced Options dialog box's Make **N**ew Boundary Set, **S**tyle, and Retain **B**oundaries options.

Using the Boundary Hatch Dialog Box Options and Features

Continue from the previous exercise or create a new drawing named HATCH, using the ALT1701.DWG file from the IALT Disk as a prototype, and using no setup method.

Make a new layer named CEILING, set it current, and turn off layer HATCH.

Use INTersection object snap to draw three lines across the inside of the doorways, and save the drawing. Your drawing should match figure 17.11, except the hatch patterns shown are not yet visible. Be sure to turn off INTersection before continuing.

Command: *Click on the Boundary Hatch tool*	Issues the BHATCH command and displays the Boundary Hatch dialog box
Set Patter**n** *to* User-defined, **A**ngle *to* 0, **S**pacing *to* 24 (2'0"), *and put a check in the* **D**ouble *check box*	Sets options for a 24" square ceiling grid

continues

17

continued

Choose Pick **P**oints	Temporarily closes the dialog box and prompts for point specification
`Select internal point:` *Pick* ①, ②, *and* ③ *then press Enter (see fig. 17.11)*	Specifies three areas to hatch, highlights their boundaries, and returns to the Boundary Hatch dialog box
Choose Preview Ha**t**ch	Displays a preview of the hatches (see fig. 17.11)

The hatch at ① is OK, but the lavatory interferes with that at ② and the door interferes with that at ③.

Figure 17.11

Creating a reflected ceiling plan with BHATCH options.

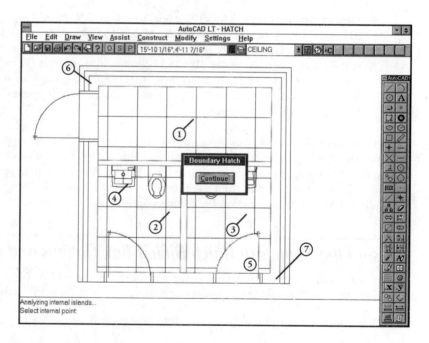

Choose **C**ontinue	Returns to the Boundary Hatch dialog box
Choose **R**emove Islands	Redisplays the preview and prompts for island selection
`Select island to remove:` *Pick the highlighted line in the lavatory at* ④	Removes the lavatory island from consideration
`<Select island to remove>/Undo:` *Pick the highlighted door at* ⑤	

`Removal of outer boundary not allowed.`	Tells you that you can't remove an object that is part of the enclosed area's boundary
`<Select island to remove>/Undo:` (Enter)	Returns to the Boundary Hatch dialog box
Choose Preview Ha<u>t</u>ch, *look at it, then choose* <u>C</u>ontinue	Previews the change and returns to the Boundary Hatch dialog box

The lavatory problem is fixed, but the door at ⑤ still interferes. (If your results don't match the preceding, try again with a new HATCH drawing. In the Boundary Hatch dialog box, choose A<u>d</u>vanced and make sure the settings match those shown in figure 17.10.)

Choose Cancel, *then Press Enter*	Cancels BHATCH and closes and reopens the Boundary Hatch dialog box for another try
Set Patter<u>n</u> *to* User-defined, <u>A</u>ngle *to* 0, <u>S</u>pacing *to* 24 (2'0"), *and put a check in the* <u>D</u>ouble *check box*	Sets options for a 24" square ceiling grid
Choose A<u>d</u>vanced	Opens the Advanced Options dialog box (see fig. 17.10)

From E<u>v</u>erything on Screen is selected and Island <u>D</u>etection is on.

Choose Make <u>N</u>ew Boundary Set	Temporarily closes the dialog box and prompts for object selection
`Select objects:` Select a Window from ⑥ to ⑦	Selects the desired objects
`21 found.`	
`Select objects:` *If it is selected, shift-pick the door at* ⑤, *then press Enter*	Removes the door from the boundary selection set
Set <u>S</u>tyle *to* Ignore *and put a check in the* Retain <u>B</u>oundaries *check box, then choose* OK	Causes BHATCH to ignore the lavatory islands and to retain polyline boundary objects for each hatch pattern it creates, and returns to the Hatch dialog box
Choose Pick <u>P</u>oints *and pick* ①, ②, *and* ③, *then press Enter*	
Choose Preview Ha<u>t</u>ch, *look at it, then choose* <u>C</u>ontinue	Previews the hatches—they look OK—and returns to the Boundary Hatch dialog box
Choose Apply	Closes the dialog box and draws the three hatches

continues

continued

Command: *Turn off all layers except* CEILING

Shows only the three hatches and their polyline boundaries (see fig. 17.12)

Save the drawing

Figure 17.12

Reflected ceiling plan created with Advanced Options dialog box settings.

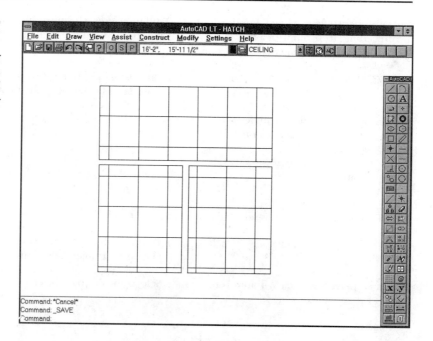

The correct areas are hatched, but the hatches are not centered on the rooms. Because the hatching is associative, you can edit them to fix this.

Note Some of the settings in the Advanced Options dialog box are retained between uses of the BHATCH command, so be sure to check its settings if you have difficulty getting the hatch boundary you want.

Editing Associative Hatches

You have two primary means of editing associative hatches: the HATCHEDIT command's Hatchedit dialog box, and the normal AutoCAD LT editing commands and grip editing methods. As you can see in figure 17.13, the Hatchedit dialog box is identical to the Boundary Hatch dialog box; however, all controls over boundary specification except Advanced are grayed and inactive. Within HATCHEDIT's Advanced Options dialog box, only the **S**tyle option is available.

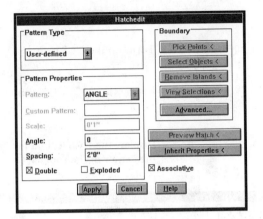

Figure 17.13

The Hatchedit dialog box.

First, try using the UCS command with point filters to reset the origin, and then use the HATCHEDIT command to update the ceiling plan to center it. Then, in a later exercise, you use editing commands to alter a hatch boundary.

Updating an Associative Hatch with HATCHEDIT

Continue from the previous exercise, with only the CEILING layer turned on.

Command: *Choose* **A**ssist, Set **U**CS, **O**rigin	Issues the UCS command with the Origin option

`_ucs`
`Origin/ZAxis/3point/Entity/View/X/Y/Z/`
`Prev/Restore/Save/Del/?/<World>: _origin`	

`Origin point <0,0,0>:` **.X** `Enter`	Specifies an X point filter and prompts for a point
of *Use a MIDpoint object snap to pick* ① *(see fig. 17.14)*	Sets the X origin to the center of the room and prompts for the X (and Z) point
of (need YZ): *Use a MIDpoint object snap to pick* ②	Sets the Y origin to the center of the room (don't pick the left side of the polyline boundary, because the doorway caused the creation of multiple segments on that side)
Command: *Choose* **A**ssist, UCS I**c**on	Issues the UCSICON command
`_ucsicon`	

continues

continued

```
ON/OFF/All/Noorigin/ORigin <OFF>:        Turns on the UCS icon
ON (Enter)

Command: (Enter)                          Repeats the UCSICON command

UCSICON

ON/OFF/All/Noorigin/ORigin <ON>:         Displays the UCS icon at the origin,
OR (Enter)                                the center of the room at ③
```

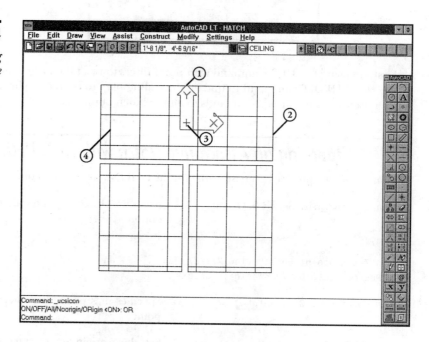

Figure 17.14

Off-center ceiling plan before HATCHEDIT.

```
Command: Choose Modify, Edit Hatch        Issues the HATCHEDIT command and
                                          prompts for selection

Select hatch object: Pick the hatch       Selects the hatch and opens the Hatchedit
                                          at ④ dialog box

Choose Apply                              Closes the Hatchedit dialog box and updates
                                          the hatch, centering it

Analyzing hatch object
Select hatch object:

Command: Choose the Redraw tool or button  Cleans up the screen (see fig. 17.15)
```

Command: *Choose **A**ssist, Set **U**CS, **W**orld*   Sets the UCS origin back to the WCS

Save the drawing

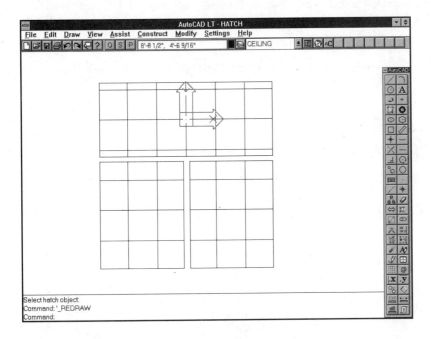

Figure 17.15

Centered ceiling plan after HATCHEDIT.

In addition to simply updating the hatch pattern, you also can use the Hatchedit dialog box to specify a different pattern, respecify the angle and spacing, and remove associativity.

Stop   In early versions of AutoCAD LT Release 2, associativity might be lost if you choose Cancel to exit the Hatchedit dialog box. If this happens, use the U command to undo the HATCHEDIT command.

Two problems remain in the ceiling plan. First, the hatch at ④ should be adjusted to eliminate the small border tiles. You can do so by setting the UCS origin to 12 inches below the center of the room and reapplying HATCHEDIT. Second, when you centered the hatch at ④, it also changed the hatches in the toilet rooms. All three rooms are part of a single associative hatch object because they were applied by a single use of the BHATCH command. If you need to edit hatch patterns independently, apply each with a separate use of BHATCH.

17

Stop In early versions of AutoCAD LT Release 2, HATCHEDIT does not correctly handle multiple hatched areas created by multiple pick points in a single use of the BHATACH command. It might fail to update all but the area of the first pick point, or it might fail to update any areas and remove associativity. If you might need to later edit multiple hatched areas, you should separately hatch each area with repeated BHATCH commands .

You can also use an editing command, such as STRETCH, to modify hatch boundaries, and the associativity automatically updates the hatches. Try it in the following exercise.

Updating an Associative Hatch with STRETCH

Continue from the previous exercise and turn on all layers (see fig. 17.16). Make sure all running object snaps are off.

Command: *Click on the Stretch tool*   Issues the STRETCH command

```
_STRETCH
Select objects to stretch by window
or polygon...
```

Select objects: *Select a Crossing window from* ① *to* ② *(see fig. 17.16)*

```
28 found
```

Select objects: (Enter)   Ends selection

Base point or displacement: **24,0** (Enter)   Specifies a 2' stretch

Second point of displacement: (Enter)   Accepts displacement and stretches all selected objects

```
Analyzing associative hatch...
```
     Updates affected hatches

Command: *Click on the Redraw tool*   Cleans up the image (see fig. 17.17)

By now you have learned to create and edit a variety of different objects in AutoCAD LT. In the next chapter, you learn new ways to combine and repeat objects in groups with AutoCAD LT's many methods for automating repetitive elements, called blocks and xrefs.

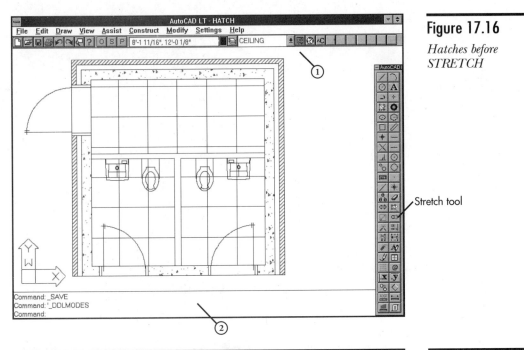

Figure 17.16

Hatches before STRETCH

Stretch tool

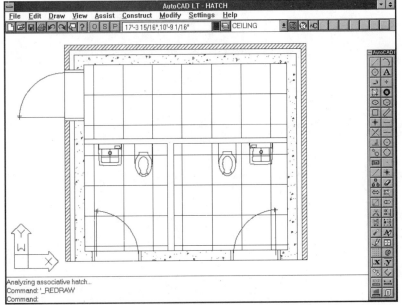

Figure 17.17

Hatches after STRETCH.

17

Leveraging Repetitive Design and Drafting

W hen an aerospace company builds an airliner, it does not sequentially create and assemble each basic component. Rather, subcontractors and subdivisions of the aerospace company build component assemblies that are then assembled. Many of these component assemblies are duplicated many times in one airliner—for example, the seats—and all are duplicated at least once in each aircraft.

A complex CAD drawing involves similar duplication and is created in somewhat the same way, although you might create your own drawing subcomponents rather than obtaining them from a consultant. These drawing subcomponents are the repetitive elements of your drawing: fixtures, doors, nuts and bolts, standard details, material lists, title blocks, and symbols. Redrawing these standard items from scratch each time you need one would be slow and boring. Once you have created a drawing subcomponent in AutoCAD LT, blocks and xrefs enable you to quickly insert or attach it any number of times in any drawing.

This chapter explores the use of blocks and xrefs, including the following:

◆ Using blocks and xrefs as parts, symbols, and templates

◆ Creating and inserting blocks at various scales and rotations

◆ Inserting arrays of blocks as a single object

◆ Inserting multiple copies of a block along linear and curved objects

◆ Using block attributes to automate and control text

◆ Using xrefs to include externally stored drawing data in the current drawing

An understanding of these topics will enable you to take advantage of blocks and xrefs in your drawings to reduce repetitive drawing tasks.

In CAD, blocks and xrefs are the tools for automating repetition. The two primary types of repetitive elements are objects that occur repeatedly in a single drawing and those that occur once in each of multiple drawings. Any repetitive element can be stored as a block definition or as a drawing to insert or attach as a block or xref. Each insertion or attachment is a perfect duplicate of the original.

The need for repetition in design and drawing is the primary reason CAD exists. Although many drawing and editing tools are quite efficient, CAD would have little advantage over manual drafting if everything you drew were totally unique, with no repetition to automate. Even in manual drafting, repetitive elements are automated with tools such as tracing templates, preprinted stick-on standard details, material schedule templates, preprinted title block sheets, and base plans on pin-registered polyester overlays.

Automating Repetitive Elements with Blocks and Xrefs

A *block* is an AutoCAD term loosely applied to both the definition (in a drawing) of a named group of objects, and to the insertion in the same drawing of a reference to that definition. A *block definition* assigns a name to a group of any number of objects. These objects exist only in the block definition. A *block insertion* does not create copies of the original objects, but is instead a single object, which displays as an image of the original objects.

An *xref* is an external reference in a drawing to the contents of another drawing, including all of the referenced drawing's objects as well as named items such as layers, linetypes, and blocks. Like a block, an *xref* does not create copies of the original objects, but is a single object which displays as an image of the original objects. The main difference between an xref and a block is that the block is defined in the current drawing, while the xref is defined in another, external drawing.

In addition to alleviating the boredom of repetitive drafting, blocks and xrefs offer advantages in quality, speed, efficiency, versatility, standardization, reduced disk storage space, and control over updating drawing data.

The Benefits of Using Blocks and Xrefs

Quality, speed, efficiency, and standardization result from eliminating repetition by inserting or attaching perfect copies instead of redrafting from scratch. Standardization also results from using attributes to control the insertion parameters of text.

Blocks and xrefs are versatile because you can insert or attach them at any scale or rotation angle, and edit them or extract their component elements.

Blocks reduce disk space because their component objects are defined only once in each drawing in which they are inserted. Each insertion saves space by referring to the single definition instead of duplicating the data for each component object. In comparison, if you draw repetitive elements and use the COPY command to duplicate them, each duplicate uses as much space as the original. Xrefs further reduce disk space because the drawing data exists only once, in one drawing file that is external to the drawings to which it is attached, instead of existing once in *each* file in which it is referenced.

Blocks offer control over updating drawing data by enabling you to explicitly update all insertions of a block in a single drawing by redefining the block definition in that drawing. Xrefs offer control over updating drawing data by automatically updating the data in all drawings that reference them the next time the drawing is loaded. Because the xref drawing data exists in a drawing file that is external to the drawings to which it is attached, edits to that external drawing file are automatically reflected in subsequently loaded drawings that reference it.

You can use a block for anything you can use an xref for, and the opposite, except that you can't automate text with xrefs. The deciding factor for which to use is the way they are stored and updated: internally or externally, and explicitly or automatically. Because blocks are a little simpler to use, they are explored before xrefs in this chapter.

18

Inserting Existing Drawings as Blocks

Any drawing file can be inserted into another drawing as a block. To insert a drawing as a block, you use the INSERT command.

Introducing the INSERT Command

The INSERT command inserts a reference to a block definition and defines the block in the current drawing. In the following exercise, try inserting a nut into the mechanical part drawing from earlier chapters. The 10 mm nut is in the NUT10.DWG file and the mechanical part is in the ALTMVIEW.DWG file, which is set up with metric units.

Inserting a Nut in a Drawing

Create a new drawing named INSMECH using the ALTMVIEW.DWG file as a prototype drawing and no setup method.

Turn off layer DIM, set layer OBJECT current, and turn on snap and set it to 2. The drawing should look like figure 18.1 except for the nut at ①.

`Command:` *Choose* **D**raw, Insert Bloc**k**	Issues DDINSERT command and opens the Insert dialog box (see fig. 18.2)
`_ddinsert`	
Click in the file name input box next to the **F**ile *button, type* **NUT10**, *and press Enter*	Enters **NUT10.dwg** in the file name input box and **NUT10** in the block name input box (see fig. 18.2)
Choose OK *and move the cursor*	Closes dialog box, drags an image of the nut on the screen and prompts as follows
`Insertion point:` *Pick the center of the slot at* ① *(see fig. 18.1)*	Sets the center of the nut at ①
`X scale factor <1> / Corner / XYZ:` (Enter)	Defaults X scale to 1
`Y scale factor (default=X):` (Enter)	Defaults to same as X scale

```
Rotation angle <0>: (Enter)        Defaults to zero rotation and inserts image of
                                   NUT10 block

Command: IN (Enter)                Issues the INSERT command

INSERT Block name (or ?)           Prompts for block name listing
<NUT10>: ? (Enter)

Block(s) to list <*>: (Enter)      Lists all block definitions

Defined blocks.  NUT10

User    Unnamed
Blocks  Blocks
   1       2
```

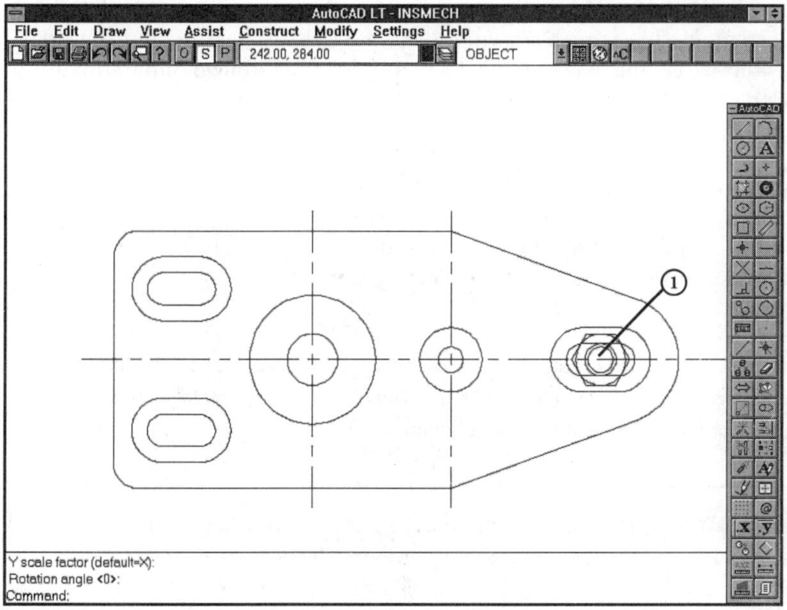

Figure 18.1

Nut inserted into mechanical part drawing.

18

Figure 18.2

*The Insert
dialog box.*

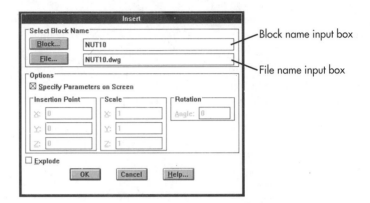

When you insert a drawing file as a block, AutoCAD LT creates a block definition in the current drawing. This block definition is not visible, but it contains the data from the inserted file. The INSMECH drawing database now contains an invisible definition of the NUT10 block. Inserting a drawing file as a block also creates an inserted block reference—a visible image of the block. The INSMECH drawing now contains a visible image of the NUT10 block. Once inserted, a block will not be updated unless you do so explicitly.

The insertion point locates the block relative to an insertion base point defined in the block. For an inserted drawing file, this defaults to the 0,0 point (actually, the 3D 0,0,0 point, but this chapter ignores the Z coordinate) of the current UCS. You can reset this point by using the BASE command; see the next chapter.

Note Inserting a drawing file creates a block definition even if you cancel the INSERT or DDINSERT command at or after the `Insertion point:` prompt. In such cases, you can use U or UNDO to remove the definition.

INSERT and DDINSERT. The INSERT and DDINSERT (Insert dialog box) commands insert an image of and reference to a previously defined block, or they insert a drawing file to create a block definition as well as an image of and reference to that new definition. The inserted block reference is a single object, regardless of the number of objects in the drawing file or previously defined block. If, however, the block name is prefaced with an asterisk (like ***NUT10**) with the INSERT command or the **E**xplode box in the Insert dialog box is checked, AutoCAD LT simply copies the objects in the block definition or drawing file and does not create a block reference or definition. The INSERT command and Insert dialog box have options for listing defined blocks, and for specifying the block's insertion point, scale, and rotation.

The INSERT command and Insert dialog box options are listed later in this chapter. In the next section, you insert blocks as their individual constituent objects.

Inserting the Component Objects of Blocks

In the following exercise, you insert NUT10 again, but this time as individual objects, not as a block reference. You can then turn the nut into a bolt head by erasing the inner (bolt shaft) circles. You also erase the inner slot polylines and replace them by inserting the SLOT10 drawing as individual objects. SLOT10 is a 10mm slot drawn using hidden lines for the portions that will be "under" the head or the nut.

Inserting the NUT10 Block's Objects

Continue from the preceding exercise, and press F2 to redisplay the drawing window.

Command: *Pick the previous nut block insertion*	Selects the entire block reference, a single object
Command: **INSERT** (Enter)	
Block name (or ?) <NUT10>: ***NUT10** (Enter)	Prefaces name with asterisk, to insert component objects

Notice that the image of the block does *not* drag with the cursor.

Insertion point: *Pick the center of the slot at* ① *(see fig. 18.3)*	Sets the base point of the insertion
Scale factor <1>: (Enter)	Defaults X scale to 1
Rotation angle <0>: (Enter)	Defaults to zero and inserts objects of NUT10 block
Command: *Select the two inner (bolt) circles of the new nut, and the three polyline slots at* ②,③, *and* ④, *then type* **E** *and press Enter*	Selects and erases the two newly inserted circle objects, as well as the polyline slots
Command: **I** (Enter)	Issues the DDINSERT command and opens the Insert dialog box

Notice that the **E**xplode box is now checked, because you used an asterisk with the previous INSERT command.

Enter **SLOT10** *in the file name input box and choose* OK	Enters **SLOT10.dwg** in file name box and **SLOT10** in the block name box and closes dialog box

continues

18

continued

`Insertion point:` *Pick* ①	Sets the insertion point at the nut's center
`X scale factor <1> / Corner` `/ XYZ:` `Enter`	Defaults X scale
`Y scale factor (default=X):` `Enter`	Defaults to same as X scale
`Rotation angle <0>:` `Enter`	Defaults rotation and inserts individual objects of SLOT10 block

At the other two slot locations, use **INSERT** to insert *SLOT10 or the Insert dialog box to insert SLOT10 with the **E**xplode box checked.

The drawing should match figure 18.3. Now, list the blocks you've inserted:

`Command:` *Choose* **D**raw, Insert Bloc**k**, **B**lock	Opens Insert dialog box, then the Blocks Defined in this Drawing dialog box (see fig. 18.4)

Only the NUT10 block is listed. Inserting *SLOT10 or SLOT10 with **E**xplode checked did *not* create a block definition.

Choose Cancel *twice*	Closes both dialog boxes

`Command:` *Click on the* Save *button*

Figure 18.3

Inserting exploded NUT10 and SLOT10 blocks.

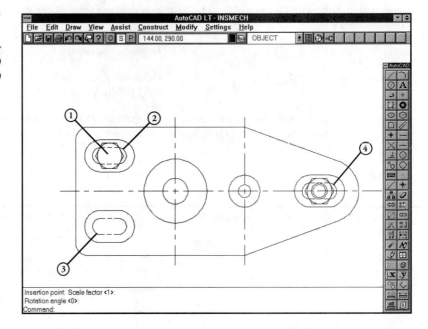

Figure 18.4

The Blocks Defined in this Drawing dialog box.

Inserting a file's data exploded (with an asterisk prefacing the name or with the **E**xplode box checked) does *not* create a block definition—it only copies the file's component objects.

Tip You can explode a block after insertion if its X, Y, and Z scales are equal. To do so, use the EXPLODE command (see Chapter 16, "Increasing Your Drawing Power with Polylines and Double Lines") and select the block insertion. It will be replaced by its component objects. The block definition remains in the drawing.

Blocks cannot be inserted exploded unless their X, Y, and Z scales are equal, so only one scale factor was requested in the exercise. The resulting objects are ordinary objects, and can be edited like any other objects.

Stop Any previous Insert dialog box uses and INSERT commands both affect the **E**xplode box default. Specifying a block name with or without an asterisk in the INSERT command affects the **E**xplode setting. Check the **E**xplode setting each time you use the Insert dialog box, or you may inadvertently insert individual objects when you wanted a block, or the opposite.

Comparing the INSERT Command and the Insert Dialog Box

Practically speaking, there is not much difference between using the Insert dialog box and the INSERT command. The Insert dialog box is a little cleaner for listing blocks and easier if you want to select the block or drawing file name from a list instead of typing the name. The **F**ile button opens the Select Drawing File dialog box. The **B**lock button opens the Blocks Defined in this Drawing dialog box shown in figure 18.4. You can click on a name to select it or type a name in the **S**election box. If you have a lot of blocks defined, you can use wild cards in the **P**attern box to filter the list.

18

When you specify a block name in the INSERT command, it checks to see if the block is defined in the current drawing. If so, it uses that definition; if not, it searches the AutoCAD LT support path on disk for it.

In the Insert dialog box, if the file name input box is filled in, the block is inserted from disk. If only the block name is specified and the file name input box is blank, AutoCAD LT searches for an existing definition in the current drawing. If it can't find the specified file or block name, it reports an invalid name error.

Tip

You can insert a drawing using a block name that is different than the file name. In the INSERT command, you do this by entering names with an equal sign, like **BLOCKNAME=FILENAME**. In the Insert dialog box, you do this by entering the file name first, then a different block name. You must make sure that the cursor is *not* in the file name input box when you choose OK, or the block name will be changed to match the file name. If the block doesn't already exist, it is created with the file contents. If it already exists, it is redefined (see block redefinition in the next chapter).

If the block and file names are both filled in, but do not match you will either redefine an existing block or create a new one.

Stop

In the Insert dialog box, make sure that the block and file names match or that only one is filled in unless you want to insert or redefine a drawing file and use a different block name. For example, if the block name is NUTTY and the file name is NUT10.dwg, a new block definition will be created named NUTTY, containing the data from the NUT10 file. If you do want the names to differ, do *not* press Enter or choose OK when the cursor is in the file name input box. Doing so changes the block name to match the file name.

After you specify the block or file name, unless the **S**pecify Parameters on Screen box is checked, the Insert dialog box behaves exactly like the INSERT command. If the **S**pecify Parameters on Screen box is not checked, you must specify the Insertion Point, Scale, and Rotation options in the Insert dialog box. This is generally impractical because it requires specifying the insertion point by typing X, Y, and Z coordinates. The Insert dialog box and INSERT command options are discussed and used further in the Controlling Block Insertions section later in this chapter.

Creating Blocks

Unless you insert it exploded, inserting a drawing file creates a block definition. Another way to define blocks is by using the Block Definition dialog box or the BLOCK command.

Using the Block Definition Dialog Box

Defining a block is quite simple. You specify its name, its insertion (base) point, select its objects, and the block is defined.

In the following exercise, you make a block named HEAD from the objects inserted in the preceding exercise as the *NUT10 block.

Making and Inserting a New HEAD Block

Continue from the preceding exercise, with *NUT10 inserted and its two inner circles erased.

`Command:` *Choose* **C**onstruct, Make **B**lock	Issues the BMAKE command and opens the Block Definition dialog box (see fig. 18.5)
`_bmake`	

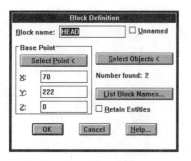

Figure 18.5

The Block Definition dialog box.

Type **HEAD** *and choose* Select **P**oint	Enters HEAD in the block name input box, and returns to drawing for point specification
`Insertion base point:` *Pick center of head at* ① *(see fig. 18.6)*	Reopens dialog box, with 70 and 222 in **X** and **Y** fields
Choose **S**elect Objects	Returns to drawing for object selection
`Select objects:` *Select both the circle and polygon at* ② *and press Enter*	Reopens dialog box, displaying `Number found: 2`

continues

continued

Clear the **R**etain Entities *check box*	Causes selected objects to be erased during block definition
Choose OK	Closes dialog box, erases selected objects, and defines the HEAD block
Press Enter and choose **L**ist Block Names	Repeats BMAKE command, reopens dialog box, then lists all defined blocks in the Block Names in This Drawing dialog box
Choose OK, *then* Cancel	Closes both dialog boxes

Use the Insert dialog box (with the **E**xplode box and the file name input box cleared) or the INSERT command to insert two HEAD blocks at the two left-side slots (see fig. 18.7).

Command: *Click on the Save button*

Figure 18.6

Specifying an insertion point and selecting objects to define a block.

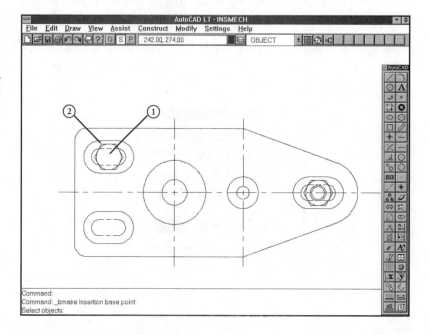

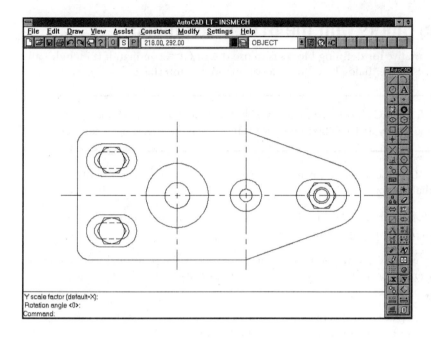

Figure 18.7

The INSMECH drawing with two HEAD blocks inserted.

The drawing now contains a block definition named HEAD, as listed in the Block Names in This Drawing dialog box. The original objects were deleted, but if you had left the **R**etain Entities box checked, they would not have been erased.

The Block Names in This Drawing dialog box is similar to the earlier Blocks Defined in this Drawing dialog box (see fig. 18.4). The only differences are the lack of the **S**election input box and the inclusion of unnamed or anonymous blocks in the list. For example, in the exercise, the dialog box listed the new HEAD block, the previously defined NUT10, and two others: *D1 and *D2. Block names that are listed with a leading asterisk, like *D1, are anonymous blocks, such as those created by dimension and hatch objects. (Do not confuse this with using an asterisk in the INSERT command to insert the constituent objects of a block.)

Note Although you can create an unnamed block by putting a check in the **U**nnamed check box, there is no practical reason to do so. You cannot control the name of unnamed or anonymous blocks, and you cannot insert them by name.

18

Defining Blocks with the BLOCK Command

Another alternative for defining blocks is to use the BLOCK command. It includes all of the features of the dialog box, but in a command line interface.

BLOCK. The BLOCK command defines a block with the name and insertion (base) point you specify and the objects you select. The objects are erased upon completion.

Most of the BLOCK command prompts are similar to those issued by the Block Definition dialog box:

◆ `Block name (or ?):`. At this prompt, you specify a name, or enter a question mark to list currently defined blocks.

◆ `Insertion base point:`. At this prompt, you specify the point that will be used as the insertion point by the INSERT command or Insert dialog box to locate the block.

◆ `Select objects:`. At this prompt, you select all objects to include in the block. This prompt is the normal object selection prompt.

You use the BLOCK command in the next exercise, which is in the next section.

 Tip   The BLOCK command does not have a Retain Objects option, so the selected objects are always erased. You can, however, restore them with the OOPS command.

The names you assign to your blocks are important for avoiding confusion and enabling good drawing management. See the naming conventions section of Chapter 24, "Moving Beyond the Basics."

Comparing Blocks and Xrefs as Parts, Symbols, and Templates

Although you use blocks and xrefs for many repetitive elements, the primary uses of blocks and xrefs fall into four categories, as shown in figure 18.8 and listed in the following:

◆ **Parts.** Parts are representations of real objects such as propellers, desks, doors, door jambs, fixtures, nuts and bolts, structural steel sections, IC chips, and bearing assemblies. Because real objects have real dimensions, parts are usually drawn full scale and inserted or attached at 1:1 scale, like the nut and bolt in the preceding exercises.

◆ **Unit parts.** Unit parts are representations of real objects in which several sizes of a part differ only in size. One of these parts can be conveniently represented by scaling a single block or xref definition at the time it is inserted or attached. Good candidates for unit parts include cross-sections of lumber, doors and their swing arcs in plan view, a universal size nut or bolt head, and some types of fixtures and fasteners. Unit parts are drawn at one unit large, and inserted at whatever scale is required. For example, the 10 mm nut and head in the preceding exercises could have been drawn and defined at one unit (1 mm diameter) and then inserted at a scale of 10 (resulting in a diameter of 10 mm).

◆ **Symbols.** Symbols may be non-scalar representations of real objects, such as electrical receptacles, drains, utility poles, or schematic IC components, or they may be labels and callouts such as numbered door or window symbols, room labels, or bubbles like those in this book's illustrations. Symbols are usually drawn at their plotted size and inserted at the inverse of this plot scale. For example, you would define a $^3/_{16}$ " bubble and insert it at a scale of 48 in a drawing to be plotted at $^1/_4$"=1'-0". See Chapter 8, "Preparing Your Workspace: CAD Concepts 1B," for more on scaling.

◆ **Templates.** Templates include title blocks, materials lists, schedules, standard details, and other items that you modify or add to after insertion. Templates such as title blocks and schedules are scaled like symbols. Standard details are scaled like parts.

You have already defined and inserted parts. In the following sections, you work with unit parts, symbols, and templates.

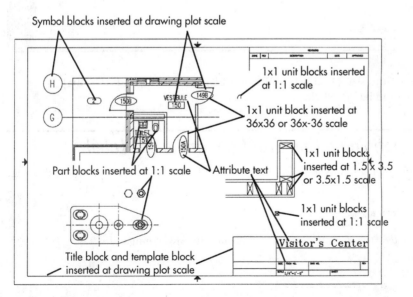

Symbol blocks inserted at drawing plot scale

1x1 unit blocks inserted at 1:1 scale

1x1 unit block inserted at 36x36 or 36x-36 scale

1x1 unit blocks inserted at 1.5 x 3.5 or 3.5x1.5 scale

1x1 unit blocks inserted at 1:1 scale

Part blocks inserted at 1:1 scale Attribute text

Title block and template block inserted at drawing plot scale

Figure 18.8

Parts, unit parts, symbols, and templates.

18

Creating Unit-Scale Part Blocks and Symbol Blocks

Defining unit parts and symbol blocks is just like part block definition; the only difference is the scale. Unit parts are generally defined as one unit in diameter, height, and/or width. Symbols are generally defined at the size they should appear when plotted.

In the following exercise, you use the room plan from Chapter 12, "Accessing Your Drawing's Data," (see fig. 18.9). A running INTersection object snap is currently set.

Figure 18.9

A room plan.

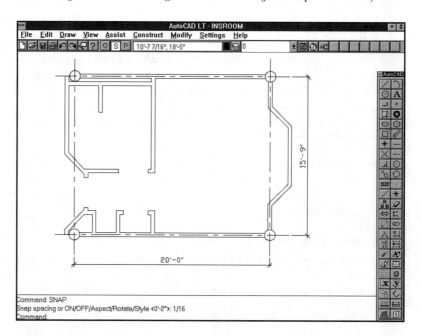

You will create unit-size (1"×1") DOOR and LUMBER blocks, and a ¼" high RMLABEL (room label) block.

Defining a Unit-Size Door and a ¼" Label

Create a new drawing named INSROOM, using the ALT1202.DWG file as a prototype drawing, and no prototype method.

Turn on snap and set it to ¹/₁₆.

Command: *Click on the Arc tool*   Issues the ARC command

`_ARC Center/<Start point>:` *Pick any point in a clear area of the drawing*	Sets start point
`Center/End/<Second point>: C` (Enter)	Prompts for center point
`Center: @0,-1` (Enter)	Sets center point 1 unit below start point
`Angle/<End point>: @-1,0` (Enter)	Sets endpoint 1 unit left of center, and draws a tiny arc

Zoom in on the tiny arc until it is large enough to work with (see fig. 18.10—your arc may appear coarsely segmented unless you perform a regeneration).

Use the LINE command to draw a line from ① to ② (see fig. 18.10).

`Command:` *Click on the Rectangle tool*	Issues the RECTANG command
`_RECTANG`	
`First corner:` *Pick point at* ③	Starts the rectangle
`Other corner: @.5,.25` (Enter)	Draws $1/2 \times 1/4$ box at ③

Repeat the RECTANG command to draw a 1" square at ④ and use the LINE command to put an X in it.

`Command: B` (Enter)	Issues the BLOCK command
`BLOCK Block name (or ?): DOOR` (Enter)	Names the block
`Insertion base point:` *Pick* ⑤	Sets the base point
`Select objects:` *Select the line and arc, then press Enter*	Creates the block, erasing the included objects

Repeat the BLOCK command and define a block named RMLABEL. Pick the insertion base point at the center of the rectangle and select the rectangle.

Repeat the BLOCK command and define a block named LUMBER. Pick the insertion base point at ④ and select the square and X lines in it.

Zoom back to the previous full plan view (the view in fig. 18.9), set snap back to 2", and save the drawing.

18

Figure 18.10

Defining DOOR and LUMBER unit-size blocks, and RMLABEL symbol block.

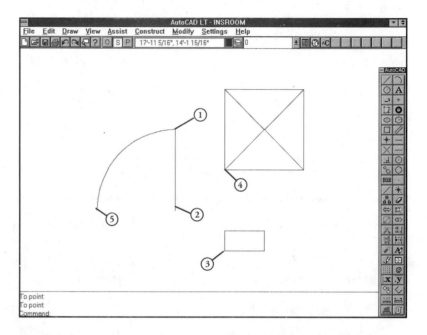

You now have the RMLABEL, LUMBER, and DOOR blocks defined in the current drawing. To insert RMLABEL, you need to control the block scale, and to insert DOOR and LUMBER, you need to control scale and rotation.

Controlling Block Insertions

You control block insertions with the Insert dialog box or the INSERT command options. The INSERT command has the following prompts and options. The Insert dialog box shares all but the first of these prompts and options:

◆ `Block name (or ?) <default>:`. At this prompt, you enter a block name to insert, press Enter to accept the previous name as a default, or enter a question mark to list the currently defined blocks.

◆ `Insertion point:`. At this prompt, you specify the point at which the insertion base point defined in the block will be placed, or enter a preset scale or rotation option (S, X, Y, Z, R, PS, PX, PY, PZ, or PR—see the Preset Scale and Rotation section of this chapter). If you preset scale or rotation, you will be reprompted for the insertion point. The block insertion is scaled and rotated relative to this point.

- Scale factor <1>:. This prompt appears only if you specify the block name with an asterisk in the INSERT command, or put a check in the **E**xplode box in the Insert dialog box. Exploded blocks must have equal X, Y, and Z scales.

- X scale factor <1> / Corner / XYZ:. At this prompt, you press Enter to set scale to 1:1, or enter a scale factor for the X scale, or pick a corner point to indicate the X and Y scale factors. When you pick a corner point, AutoCAD LT sets the X scale factor to the distance from the insertion point to the X coordinate of that point and sets the Y scale factor to the distance from the insertion point to the Y coordinate of that point. (The Corner option is redundant because you can specify the scale by corner point without first entering the option.) The Z scale factor defaults to the same as X unless you enter XYZ (or just X) to request prompting for X, then Y, and then Z scale.

- Y scale factor (default=X):. At this prompt, you enter the Y scale factor or press Enter to accept the X scale as the default.

- Rotation angle <0>:. At this prompt, you press Enter to accept zero rotation, or enter an angle relative to the insertion point, or pick a point to indicate the angle.

Although you can set the scale and rotation in the Insert dialog box, to do so you must also enter the X, Y, and Z coordinates of the insertion point, which is generally impractical. Therefore, you usually use these options whether you use the INSERT command or Insert dialog box.

Scaling Block Insertions

The simplest means of scaling is to enter a scale factor, as you will do with the RMLABEL block in the following exercise. You will also enter some text, to see how the symbol scale and text scale are coordinated.

Inserting and Scaling a Room Label Block

Continue from the preceding exercise, with the RMLABEL, LUMBER, and DOOR blocks defined and snap set to 2. Your drawing should look like figure 18.9.

Command: **I** (Enter)	Opens the Insert dialog box
Choose **B**lock, *then select* RMLABEL	Opens the Blocks Defined in this Drawing dialog box, and specifies the block to insert
Choose OK, *then* OK *again*	Closes both dialog boxes
Insertion point: *Pick* ① *(see fig. 18.11)*	

continues

18

continued

Notice the scale drag by the corner as you move the cursor; however, dragging and picking is not an effective way to specify the scale of non-unit-size blocks.

`X scale factor <1> / Corner / XYZ:` `48` **(Enter)**	Sets X scale factor to 48
`Y scale factor (default=X):` **(Enter)**	Defaults to same as X scale
`Rotation angle <0.00>:` **(Enter)**	Defaults rotation to zero
`Command:` *Click on the Text tool*	Issues DTEXT command
`_DTEXT` `Justify/Style/<Start point>:` `M` **(Enter)**	Specifies Middle justification
`Middle point:` `@` **(Enter)**	Places it at the last point, the block's insertion point
`Height <0'-0 3/16">:` `6` **(Enter)**	
`Rotation angle <0.00>:` **(Enter)**	Defaults rotation
`Text:` `1302` **(Enter)**	Enters text
`Text:` **(Enter)**	Completes DTEXT command and redraws text (see fig. 18.11)

Figure 18.11

Inserting and scaling the RMLABEL symbol block and text.

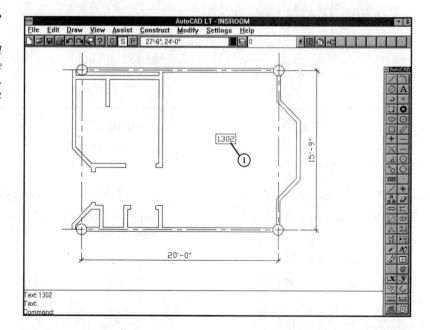

The text is 6" high, intended to be plotted at a scale of 1:48, which yields ¹/₈" plotted text. Using the same ratio, the label is 12" high inserted at a scale of 48, and will plot ¹/₄" high, the same as the size at which it was drawn and defined.

As you saw, dragging the scale by the corner didn't relate to the geometry of the block. Dragging and picking the corner point to specify scale works better in unit-size blocks.

Scaling, Rotating, and Mirroring Unit Blocks

Unit blocks, such as the DOOR and LUMBER blocks you created earlier, are drawn 1×1. When you set their scale, the scale factor becomes the size. For example, if you scale the door by a factor of 36, it becomes 36". In the following exercise, try inserting and scaling the DOOR and LUMBER blocks. Dragging the corner of a unit block like LUMBER is like using the RECTANG command. You will also rotate these blocks and use a negative scale factor to insert a mirror image of the DOOR block.

Inserting and Rotating Unit-Size Blocks

Continue from either of the two previous exercises, with the LUMBER and DOOR blocks defined, snap set to 2, and a running INTersection object snap.

Command: **IN** (Enter)	Issues the INSERT command
INSERT Block name (or ?) <RMLABEL>: **DOOR** (Enter)	Specifies block name
Insertion point: *Pick* ① *(see fig. 18.12)*	Sets insertion point

You can drag the corner with the cursor, but typing the scale factor avoids accidentally distorting the X,Y scale at this snap setting.

X scale factor <1> / Corner / XYZ: **36** (Enter)	Scales door to 36 inches
Y scale factor (default=X): (Enter)	Defaults to same as X
Rotation angle <0.00>: *Pick point* ②	
Command: (Enter)	Repeats INSERT command
INSERT Block name (or ?) <DOOR>: (Enter)	Accepts default name
Insertion point: *Pick* ③	

continues

18

continued

X scale factor <1> / Corner / XYZ: **36** `Enter`	Sets X size to 36
Y scale factor (default=X): **-36** `Enter`	Sets Y size to minus 36, mirroring the block
Rotation angle <0.00>: *Pick* ④	Rotates block 90 degrees

Figure 18.12

Inserting and rotating unit-size DOOR blocks.

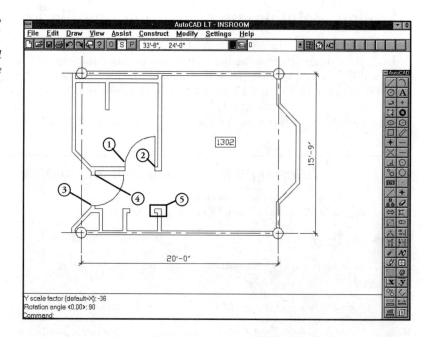

To set up for inserting the LUMBER block, zoom in on the door jamb at ⑤ of figure 18.12, to match the view shown in figure 18.13.

Set snap to ¹/₄ and grid to 1, and turn them on, and use the OFFSET command with a distance of ¹/₂ to offset the wall lines inward. Then, use TRIM, or the FILLET command with radius 0, to clean up the corners, to match figure 18.13.

Next, you insert the LUMBER block scaled to nominal 2×4 size (1 ¹/₂"×3 ¹/₂"), using the grid to judge the 1 ¹/₂ dimension.

Command: **IN** `Enter`	Issues the INSERT command

INSERT Block name (or ?) <DOOR>:
LUMBER `Enter`

Insertion point: *Pick* ⑥ *(see fig. 18.14)* Sets one corner

X scale factor <1> / Corner / XYZ: Sets the other corner
Drag and pick ⑦

Rotation angle <0.00>: *Pick* ⑧ Sets the rotation and places the block

Repeat INSERT with the LUMBER block to insert and rotate the other 2×4s shown in figure 18.14.

Zoom back to the full drawing plan, and set snap back to 2 and grid to 1' (12").

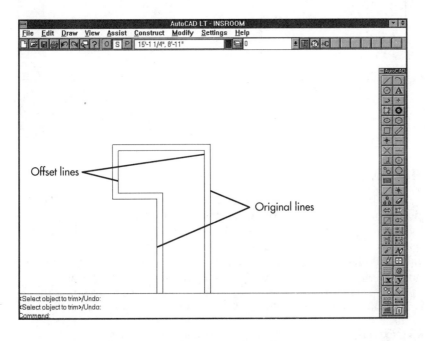

Figure 18.13

Setting up wall lines for LUMBER block insertion.

When you scale the insertion of a unit-size block by its corner point, AutoCAD LT stretches the block to the corner point you pick. This feature provides a versatile and interactive way to insert appropriate types of blocks.

 Note You cannot enter units (such as 2'6") to scale a block. You must use a scale factor such as 30, not a distance.

As you dragged the blocks prior to setting their insertion points in the previous exercises, they displayed at their original sizes. The DOOR block, for example, was tiny. It would be more convenient and make placement easier if you could set the scale and rotation before dragging the block into place and picking the insertion point.

18

Figure 18.14

*Inserting unit-size
LUMBER block
by picking its
corners.*

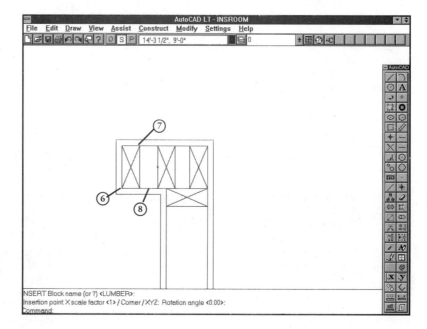

Presetting Scale and Rotation

The INSERT command and the Insert dialog box enable you to preset any or all of the scale and rotation settings before you specify the insertion point. This presetting makes block placement easier because you can see exactly how a block fits as you drag it. In the Insert dialog box, with the **S**pecify Parameters on Screen box cleared, you can preset scale and rotation, but only if you also preset the insertion point. This defeats the purpose of presetting. However, if you use the Insert dialog box with a check in the **S**pecify Parameters on Screen box, you can use the same presets as the INSERT command after you close the Insert dialog box.

In the following exercise, try presetting scale and rotation on a door.

Dragging a Block with Preset Scale and Rotation

Continue from any of the three previous exercises, with the DOOR block defined.

If you are continuing from the Unit-Size Blocks exercise, zoom to the full plan, and set snap to 2 and grid to 12 (or click repeatedly on the U button, until the full plan returns).

Erase the door at ① (see fig. 18.15), if it exists, so you can reinsert it with presets.

Command: **I** (Enter)   Opens the Insert dialog box (make sure the **E**xplode box is cleared)

Enter **DOOR** *in the block name input box, then*   Closes dialog box and prompts for input
choose OK

From this point on, the Insert dialog box and INSERT command prompts are identical.

`Insertion point: S` (Enter)   Defers the insertion point until after prompt
ing for XYZ scale

`Scale factor: 36` (Enter)   Scales X, Y, and Z equally

The DOOR block now drags at a 36" size, but it still needs to be flipped (mirrored).

`Insertion point: Y` (Enter)   Defers the insertion point until after Y scale

`Y scale factor: -36` (Enter)   Flips the block

`Insertion point: R` (Enter)   Defers the insertion point until after rotation

`Rotation angle: 90` (Enter)   Rotates the block

Now the door drags with the desired scale and orientation.

`Insertion point:` *Pick* ①   Inserts the DOOR (using the running
INTersection object snap)

Because you preset XYZ scale and rotation, the prompts ended with the `Insertion point` prompt. If you had preset only some of the values, the normal prompts for the others would have followed.

Several other options for presetting values are available, but they are not shown as prompts during the INSERT command. The complete preset options are listed in the following:

♦ **Scale and PScale.** These options prompt for a single preset scale factor which is applied equally to X, Y, and Z scale.

♦ **Xscale and PXscale.** These options preset only the X-scale factor.

♦ **Yscale and PYscale.** These options preset only the Y-scale factor.

♦ **Zscale and PZscale.** These options preset only the Z-scale factor.

♦ **Rotate and PRotate.** These options preset the rotation angle. Enter this value from the keyboard or by picking two points.

You need only enter the first one or two (capitalized) characters of these preset options to indicate what you want preset.

18

Figure 18.15

*Inserting a door
with preset scale
and rotation.*

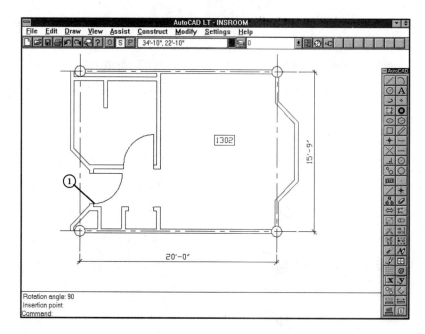

Notice that two sets of options are shown. Those that begin with a P (for preliminary, not preset) set only a preliminary scale and/or rotation. This provides a visual aid to block insertion, but after insertion you can reset the scale and rotation at the normal insert prompts and defaults. Those that begin with S, X, Y, Z, and R are fixed presets and do not prompt further after insertion.

Note   You cannot mix fixed presets (such as Scale or Xscale) with preliminary presets (such as PRotate or PYscale). If you try to mix them, the preliminary presets become fixed, and AutoCAD LT does not prompt you again for their values.

Fortunately presets are forgiving of errors, so you don't have to start over if what you enter doesn't have the desired effect.

Tip   You can repeat presets. For example, if you enter **S** for scale and make an error in setting the scale you want, you can enter **S** again and respecify the scale.

Inserting Arrays of Blocks with MINSERT

You used the ARRAY command in Chapter 14, "Making More Changes: Editing Constructively," to duplicate objects in a rectangular pattern. ARRAY works for any

number or type of objects. You can use the ARRAY command for arraying a block. If you do so, it copies the selected block, creating a number of identical block references. For example, using ARRAY to array a block in three rows and four columns would create a total of 12 block insertions, each a separate object. You can create the same effect with blocks by using the MINSERT command, which creates an array of images of a block's objects, but as a single object.

In the following exercise, you insert a 5×2 array of table blocks in a room. Then, you move the entire array as a single object. The prototype drawing is one you used earlier in Chapter 10, "Getting Organized: Drawing on Layers."

Arraying Blocks with MINSERT

Create a new drawing named MINSERT, using the ALT1001.DWG file as a prototype drawing, and using no setup method.

Turn off layers *IDEN* and S-GRID* (by using wild-card filters), and zoom to the view shown in figure 18.16.

Command: **MN** (Enter)   Issues the MINSERT command

The following prompts are just like those of the INSERT command.

MINSERT Block name (or ?): **TBL3672** (Enter)   Specifies block name; AutoCAD LT finds the TBL3672.DWG file

Insertion point: *Pick* ① *(see fig. 18.16)*

X scale factor <1> / Corner / XYZ: (Enter)

Y scale factor (default=X): (Enter)

Rotation angle <0>: (Enter)

The following prompts are just like those of the ARRAY command.

Number of rows (---) <1>: **2** (Enter)

Number of columns (¦¦¦) <1>: **5** (Enter)

Unit cell or distance between
rows (---):**9'** (Enter)

Distance between columns (¦¦¦): 8' (Enter)   Inserts image of ten tables, as shown in figure 18.16

continues

18

continued

Command: *Select any of the tables*	Highlights entire array and displays a grip at the single insertion point
Command: *Pick the grip*	Enters Stretch mode and drags the entire array
** STRETCH ** <Stretch to point>/Base point/Copy/ Undo/eXit: *Pick ②*	Moves the entire array as shown in figure 18.17
Command: *Click on the Save button*	Saves the drawing for a later exercise

Figure 18.16

Inserting an array of tables with MINSERT.

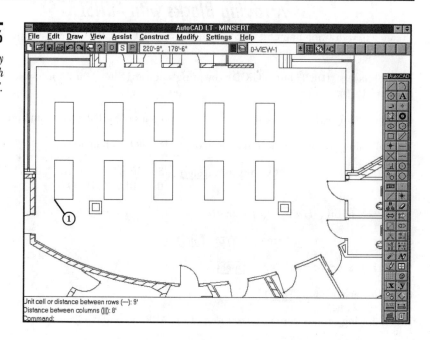

When you array blocks with ARRAY, you create a number of individual block reference objects. When you create a block array with MINSERT, you create a single object containing multiple images of a single block reference. MINSERT is more efficient in terms of the drawing data required to define the block array, and the entire block array can be manipulated as a single object, but the individual block images within it cannot be independently moved, exploded, or edited.

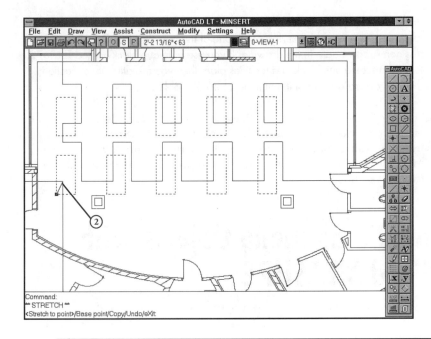

Figure 18.17

The moved array.

MINSERT. MINSERT is similar to a combination of the INSERT and ARRAY commands. MINSERT is limited to rectangular arrays. It inserts multiple images of, and a single reference to, a previously defined block (or a drawing file which it inserts to create a block definition). The inserted block array is a single object, regardless of the number of rows and columns or objects in the drawing file or previously defined block. You cannot preface the block name with an asterisk (like *NUT10) with the MINSERT command, and you cannot explode an array created with MINSERT. The MINSERT command has options for listing defined blocks, for specifying the block's insertion point, scale, and rotation, and for specifying the number and spacing of the rows and columns in the array it creates.

The MINSERT command prompts and options are identical to those of the ARRAY command (in Chapter 14, "Making More Changes: Editing Constructively") and the INSERT command (earlier in this chapter), so they are not repeated here.

Note The table in the preceding exercise could have been a unit-size block. Although you can use unit-size blocks for many things, sometimes it may be advantageous to use full-scale part blocks with unique names instead. For example, a 1×1 square block could be inserted at any size to represent any size of table, any rectangular column,

continues

18

or numerous other rectangular objects. These objects would all inherit the same block name, however. This interferes with one of the benefits of CAD: to be able to access non-graphic data in the drawing. If you use a unique block named TBL3672 instead of a scaled unit block in a facilities plan, then you use attribute extraction methods to extract a count of the number of 36×72 tables.

If you are using AutoCAD LT Release 2, you have two other commands that you can use to insert multiple blocks: DIVIDE and MEASURE. Unlike MINSERT, divide and measure insert an individual block insertion at each insertion point. If you are using AutoCAD LT Release 1, skip the following section and proceed to the "Automating Text with Attributes" section.

Inserting Blocks Along Objects with DIVIDE and MEASURE

ALT2

The AutoCAD LT Release 2 DIVIDE and MEASURE commands were introduced in Chapter 11, "Achieving Accuracy: The Geometric Power of CAD." In that chapter they are used to place point objects along linear and curved objects. DIVIDE and MEA-SURE can also be used to insert blocks instead of points. Doing so is exactly like using them to insert points, except you specify the Block option, block name, and block alignment before specifying the number of segments or segment length.

The specified block is always inserted at 1:1 scale. If you need to scale it, create a new block at the proper scale. You can nest the original block in the new block, as described in the next chapter. It is also inserted at zero degrees rotation, unless you specify to align it with the object along which it is inserted.

When DIVIDE and MEASURE prompt you for block alignment, you can align the blocks with the specified object or use the block's original alignment. If you align them with the object, each insertion is rotated to the angle or tangent angle of the object at the insertion point. You can combine alignment with an insertion base point that is offset from the block to offset the inserted blocks from the objects that they are inserted along.

The MEASURE command places the blocks at intervals determined by a distance you specify. The DIVIDE command places the blocks at intervals determined by the number of segments you specify. You can access MEASURE by typing the command name, or choosing **C**onstruct, then Mea**s**ure from the pull-down menu. You can access DIVIDE by typing the command name, or choosing **C**onstruct, then Divid**e**

from the pull-down menu. Chapter 11 demonstrated the differences between DIVIDE and MEASURE; this chapter uses only the DIVIDE command to demonstrate their behavior with blocks instead of points. The MEASURE command behaves the same way.

One use for DIVIDE is to place bolts around a shaft housing. Try using it to do so in the following exercises.

Placing Points at Regular Distances with MEASURE

Create a new drawing named DIVIDE, using the ALT1803.DWG file as a prototype and no setup method. The drawing is set up the same as the earlier INSMECH (ALTMVIEW) drawing, with metric units. The drawing should look like figure 18.18, except the bolt heads shown in the figure are not yet inserted.

Command: *Choose* **C**onstruct, Divid**e**   Issues the DIVIDE command

`_divide`

`Select object to divide:` *Pick the polyline*   Selects the object, set to start the at
at ① *(see fig. 18.18)*   the nearest endpoint, which is ①

`<Number of segments>/Block:` **B** (Enter)   Specifies the Block option

`Block name to insert:` **HEAD** (Enter)   Specifies the block name to use

`Align block with object? <Y>` **N** (Enter)   Specifies using the block definition's
            orientation

`Number of segments:` **24** (Enter)   Inserts 24 blocks

There are two problems with the results of the exercise. First, the bolt heads are too large. You can fix this by creating a new, smaller bolt head block. Second, the heads are centered on the outside line of the housing, instead of between the lines. You can fix this either by creating a temporary offset polyline centered between the existing lines and selecting it with DIVIDE, or by defining the head block with an offset base point. You'll fix these problems in the next exercise. But first, review how MEASURE and DIVIDE determine their start points.

On open objects, such a lines, arcs, and open polylines (see Chapter 16, "Increasing Your Drawing Power with Polylines and Double Lines"), the insertion point of the first block is placed by MEASURE at the specified distance from the endpoint nearest the point you use to pick the existing object. On closed polylines, the insertion point of the first block is placed at the specified distance from the first vertex. On circles, the insertion point of the first block is placed counterclockwise at the specified

18

distance from the zero-degree point (default is to the right of center). MEASURE places a block at the ending point of open and closed objects if the segment length is appropriate.

Figure 18.18

Bolt head blocks inserted non-aligned along a polyline by DIVIDE.

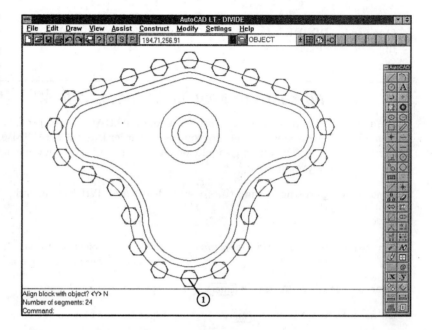

On open objects, such as lines, arcs, and open polylines, the insertion point of the first block is placed by DIVIDE at the specified distance from the endpoint nearest the point you use to pick the existing object. On closed polylines or circles, the insertion point of the first block is placed at the first vertex or zero-degree point (default is to the right of the circle's center). DIVIDE does not place a block at the ending point of open or closed objects.

Tip You can use Previous to select the entire set of inserted blocks, which are placed in the Previous selection set by DIVIDE or MEASURE.

Try creating and inserting a new, smaller block that has an offset origin in the following exercise. Insert it along both the perimeter polyline and the shaft collar circle. The block needs to be half the original size. The distance between the perimeter lines of the housing is 12 mm, so you need to offset the block's origin by 6mm. For this offset to work correctly, the block must be inserted aligned with the polyline and circle.

Placing Points at Regular Distances with MEASURE

Continue from the previous exercise. Use ERASE and the Previous selection option to erase the HEAD blocks previously inserted by DIVIDE.

Use INSERT to insert the HEAD block in a clear area at half-size, exploding it as its component objects by specifying its name as ***HEAD**. Use a scale of .5 and zero rotation.

Zoom in on the inserted components, as shown in figure 18.19, then use BLOCK to define a new block named SMHEAD with an offset origin, using tracking and direct distance entry, as follows:

Command: **B** (Enter)	Issues the BLOCK command
BLOCK Block name (or ?): **SMHEAD** (Enter)	Names the new block
Insertion base point: **TK** (Enter)	Starts tracking mode
First tracking point: *Turn off Snap, then use a CENter object snap to pick the circle at* ①	Snaps to ②
Next point (Press RETURN to end tracking): *Move the cursor down so it tracks to* ③, *then enter* **6**	Tracks down, then uses direct distance entry to specify a point 6 units below ②
Next point (Press RETURN to end tracking): (Enter)	Ends tracking and accepts the point
Select objects: *Pick both the circle and hexagon, then press Enter*	Selects and erases the new block's objects and creates the block definition

Zoom to the previous view. It should appear like figure 18.20, except the small head blocks are not yet inserted.

Command: *Choose* **C**onstruct, Divid**e**	Issues the DIVIDE command
_divide	
Select object to divide: *Pick the polyline at* ④ *(see fig. 18.20)*	Selects the polyline
<Number of segments>/Block: **B** (Enter)	Specifies the Block option
Block name to insert: **SMHEAD** (Enter)	Specifies the block name to use

continues

18

continued

Figure 18.19

*Creating the
SMHEAD block,
using tracking to
offset the base
point.*

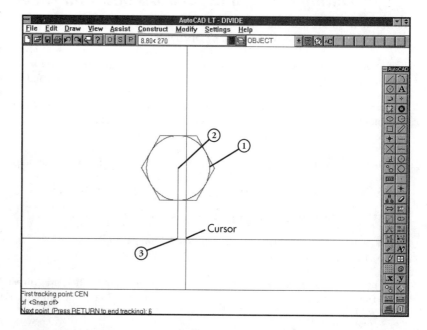

Align block with object? <Y> (Enter)   Defaults to align them

Number of segments: 24 (Enter)   Inserts 24 blocks as shown in figure 18.20

Repeat the DIVIDE command with six segments to insert the blocks on the circle shown at ⑤.

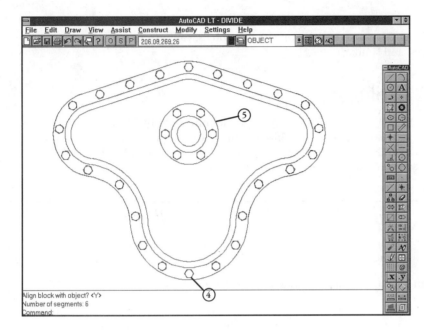

Figure 18.20

Half-size bolt heads inserted and aligned with an offset origin.

Automating Text with Attributes

The primary purpose of attributes is to define and store non-graphic (alphanumeric) data in the drawing, and to extract it for data analysis and reporting. Attributes are text data (sometimes called strings) defined and inserted in blocks. Attributes have *tags* (names or labels), prompts, and default values. They can be visible or invisible, and *constant* (the same value in each insertion) or *variable* (defined at the time of insertion or after insertion), or they can insert default text that you can later change. The attribute text can have any of the visible characteristics available to normal text, such as style, height, or rotation.

Extracting attribute data for analysis and reporting is beyond the scope of this book (see *Inside AutoCAD Release 12* or *Maximizing AutoLISP*). If you have significant data extraction, analysis, and reporting requirements, you should use AutoCAD Release 12 or 13 with their SQL features, which are covered thoroughly in *The AutoCAD Professional's API Toolkit*, from New Riders Publishing.

However, attributes have another use in AutoCAD LT for drafting applications: to automate text. You can define attributes with specific text styles, specify their relative positions, define prompts to the user, and even set default values, and include any number of these attributes in a block. Then, when you insert the block, the attribute

18

text is automated and controlled. This method is useful for inserting and controlling standardized but variable text that appears in bubbles, callouts, title blocks, materials lists, schedules, and similar items.

Defining Attributes

In the following exercise, you add two attribute definitions to the title block drawing from Chapter 3. These attribute definitions control text that needs to change from one drawing to another. The drawing already contains several text labels that do not need to change from one drawing to another. It also contains the needed text styles.

Adding Attribute Text to a Title Block

Create a new drawing named TBLK1117, using the ALT0301.DWG file as a prototype drawing, and using no setup method.

Turn on snap and set it to ¹/₁₆, then zoom to the view shown in figure 18.21.

Command: *Choose* **C**onstruct, **D**efine Attribute	Issues DDATTDEF command and opens Attribute Definition dialog box (see fig. 18.22)
_ddattdef	
In the Attribute area, enter **TITLE** *in the* **T**ag *input box and enter* **Enter project title** *in the* **P**rompt *input box*	Sets the tag (the attribute's name) and its insertion prompt
In the Text Options area, select TITLES *from the* **T**ext Style *drop-down list, and enter* **0.3125** *in the* **H**eight *input box*	Sets the text style and height
In the Insertion Point area, choose Pic**k** point	Closes dialog box and prompts for insertion point
Start point: *Pick* ① *(see fig. 18.21)*	Sets attribute text insertion point and reopens dialog box
Choose OK	Closes dialog box and inserts the attribute tag at ①
Command: **AD** (Enter)	Issues ATTDEF command
ATTDEF Attribute modes — Invisible:N Constant:N Verify:N Preset:N Enter (ICVP) to change, RETURN when done: (Enter)	Accepts default modes

`Attribute tag:` **SCALE** (Enter)	Defines the tag (the attribute's name)
`Attribute prompt:` **Enter sheet scale** (Enter)	Defines the insertion prompt
`Default attribute value:` **Varies** (Enter)	Defines the default text value

From this point on, the prompts are the same as those of the TEXT and DTEXT commands.

`Justify/Style/<Start point>:` **S** (Enter)	Prompts for text style
`Style name (or ?) <TITLES>:` **ROMANC** (Enter)	Sets text style
`Justify/Style/<Start point>:` *Pick* ②	
`Height <0.3125>:` **.09375** (Enter)	
`Rotation angle <0>:` (Enter)	Accepts default and inserts attribute tag at ②
`Command:` *Click on the Save button*	Saves title block for insertion in the next exercise

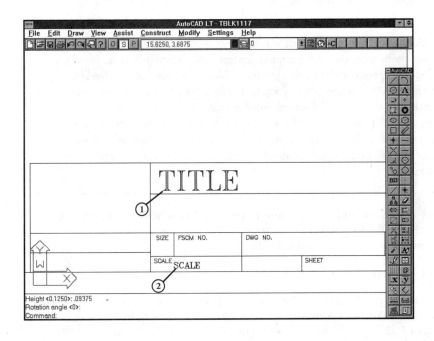

Figure 18.21

Title block drawing with two attributes defined.

Figure 18.22

*Defining the
TITLE attribute
in the Attribute
Definition
dialog box.*

Attribute Definition

Mode
☐ Invisible
☐ Constant
☐ Verify
☐ Preset

Attribute
Tag: TITLE
Prompt: Enter project title
Value:

Insertion Point
Pick Point <
X: 0.0000
Y: 0.0000
Z: 0.0000
☐ Align below previous attribute

Text Options
Justification: Left
Text Style: TITLES
Height < 0.3125
Rotation < 0

OK   Cancel   Help...

Until you insert them as part of a block, the attributes you defined display their tag
names.

You can use either the ATTDEF command or the Attribute Definition dialog box to
define attributes. The abbreviated alias, DAD, issues the DDATTDEF command and
opens the Attribute Definition dialog box.

> **ATTDEF.** The ATTDEF command defines an attribute for inclusion and insertion in a
> block. An attribute consists of a tag name, an optional prompt (otherwise the tag is
> used), and an optional default value (otherwise blank) for insertion with the block.
> When an attribute is defined, its tag appears. When the attribute has been included
> in a block and inserted, its default value or the value you enter at the time of insertion
> appears. The attribute tag and value text can use any of the options available to
> normal text, such as style, height, or rotation. Attributes can be defined to insert as
> visible or invisible and constant or variable. They can be set to automatically insert
> default text.

The ATTDEF command and the Attribute Definition dialog box provide the same
options. See the DTEXT options in Chapter 4 for the insertion point and text
options; the other options are listed following.

The ATTDEF command's prompt involves four possible modes:

◆ Enter (ICVP) to change, RETURN when done:. This option of ATTDEF controls
  the Invisible, Constant, Verify, and Preset modes (see the following four items).
  You enter I, C, V, or P to turn these on or off. The Attribute modes—
  Invisible:N Constant:N Verify:N Preset:N prompt indicates the current
  state of each of these modes with a Y (on) or N (off). The defaults are all off (N):
  visible, variable, non-verified, and not preset.

The Attribution Definition dialog box provides buttons to set these modes. The four modes work as follows:

- ◆ **Invisible.** The Invisible check box or the I ATTDEF option sets the attribute to be invisible when inserted.

- ◆ **Constant.** The Constant check box or the C ATTDEF option sets the attribute to be constant (having the same value in each insertion) when on or variable, or variable (defined at the time of insertion or after insertion) when off. Constant attribute text values cannot be changed after insertion. Variable attribute text values can be changed at any time.

- ◆ **Verify.** The Verify check box or the V ATTDEF option causes the INSERT command or the Insert dialog box to prompt for verification after you enter the text value during block insertion.

- ◆ **Preset.** The Preset check box or the P ATTDEF option causes the INSERT command or the Insert dialog box to insert the default variable text value and bypass prompting for the value. You can edit variable values later.

The ATTDEF command's prompts or the Attribute Definition dialog box also enable you to specify the following features:

- ◆ **Tag.** The Tag defines the attribute's name. This is the tag name by which its data is extracted and identified.

- ◆ **Prompt.** The Prompt defines a prompt that the INSERT command or Insert dialog box uses to request variable attribute input.

- ◆ **Value.** The Value defines the value of constant attributes or the default value of variable attributes.

- ◆ **Insertion point or Start point.** This option sets the insertion point of the attribute text.

- ◆ **Align below previous attribute.** The Align below previous attribute check box causes the new attribute definition to be placed below the previous definition. Pressing Enter at the ATTDEF `Justify/Style/<Start point>:` prompt has the same effect.

The options used in the ATTDEF command and the Attribute Definition dialog box affect each other's defaults.

18

Stop Check and reset the ICVP (Invisible, Constant, Verify, and Preset) modes each time, or you may get unexpected results when you later insert the attribute block. Be careful to provide a default for all preset attributes, or the Preset mode will cause a blank attribute to be inserted.

You can use the default value as a sort of reminder that you need to fill in a value at a later time.

Tip Rather than leaving a default blank, it is safer to provide a value such as !SCALE NEEDED! to avoid inserting a blank value or forgetting to later fill in the value. You can search on such values later by searching on a wild-card string such as !*!.

To see how these attribute definitions automate text, you need to insert them as part of a block. As with any other object, you can select attribute definitions with the BLOCK command to define an attribute-laden block, or you can define them in a drawing such as the TBLK1117 drawing, and then insert the drawing into another drawing to define and insert a block.

Editing Attribute Definitions

You can use the DDEDIT and CHANGE commands to edit attribute definitions. The DDEDIT command enables you to edit the tag, prompt, and default value using the Edit Attribute Definition dialog box (see fig. 18.23), after prompting you to select an ATTDEF (Attribute Definition). The CHANGE command enables you to edit its text characteristics as well as tag, prompt, and default value. The CHANGE command edits attribute definitions in the same way it edits text objects—see Chapter 15, "Modifying Objects and Text."

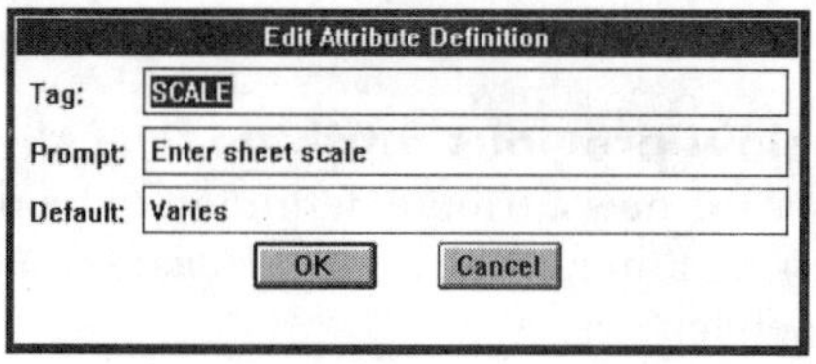

Figure 18.23

The Edit Attribute Definition dialog box.

Edit Attribute Definition	
Tag:	SCALE
Prompt:	Enter sheet scale
Default:	Varies

OK   Cancel

If you insert an exploded block or drawing, copies of the original attribute definitions will be inserted instead of the values. These copies of the original attribute definitions can be edited.

Inserting Attribute Definitions

When attribute definitions are inserted as part of a block, they become attribute subentities of the block. After the normal insertion information is provided, the INSERT command or the Insert dialog box inserts constant or preset attribute text values and prompts for non-preset variable attribute text values.

In the following exercise, you open the MINSERT drawing from the previous section of this chapter and insert the TBLK1117 drawing you just created into it. You insert the title block at a scale of 96, suitable for plotting at a $1/8$"=1'-0" scale on a 17×11 sheet. After you respond to the normal insertion prompts, the INSERT command prompts for the TITLE and SCALE variable attribute values.

Inserting a Title Block with Attribute-Automated Text

Open the MINSERT drawing that you created earlier in this chapter.

Use the Aerial Viewer to zoom to a view about three times as large as the plan (similar to the view in figure 18.24).

Command: **IN** (Enter)   Issues the INSERT command

The following prompts are identical to the normal insertion prompts:

INSERT Block name (or ?): **TBLK1117** (Enter)

Insertion point: **S** (Enter)

Scale factor: **96** (Enter)

Insertion point: *Pick* ① *(see fig. 18.24)*

Rotation angle <0>: (Enter)   Accepts default

Enter attribute values   Prompts for text values with the following
                                                  prompts that you defined in the attribute
                                                  definitions

Enter project title: **Visitor**   Enters TITLE attribute text value
Center (Enter)

Enter sheet scale <Varies>:   Enters SCALE attribute text value and
1/8"=1'-0" (Enter)   completes the block insertion (see fig.
                                                  18.24)

Zoom in to a view similar to that shown in figure 18.25 and view the attributes at ② and ③.

18

Figure 18.24

Inserting an attribute-laden title block.

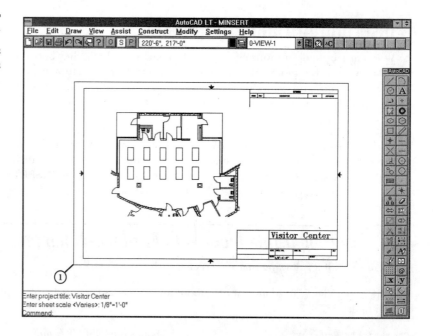

Figure 18.25

Zoomed-in view of the TITLE and SCALE attributes.

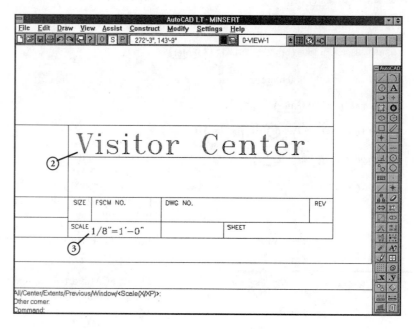

When you insert a block, all attributes are inserted with it. The inserted attributes inherit the text characteristics and locations within the block from their attribute definitions. Text height is, of course, scaled with the block and the attributes are rotated with the block. However, you can later modify the placement, object properties, or text characteristics of variable attributes, as explained in the next section of this chapter.

Tip

If you are using AutoCAD LT Release 2, you can use the Custom Drawing Setup feature to insert title blocks, but it does not support attributes in title blocks. You can, however, insert a separate attribute-laden block after the drawing setup process.

Although you only defined two variable attributes in the title block, you could have defined any number of attributes, with any combination of modes. Constant attributes are inserted without prompting, as are preset variable attributes. Variable attributes defined with Verify mode on reprompt for verification of their values after insertion, unless Preset mode is also on.

Note

Insertion presents attributes in the reverse order of their creation in the inserted drawing or their selection during block creation.

If you prefer to input attributes in a dialog box, you can do so by setting the ATTDIA system variable to 1 (on); just enter **ATTDIA** at the Command: prompt, and then enter **1**. After you respond to the normal insertion prompts, the Enter Attributes dialog box opens (see fig. 18.26). The Enter Attributes dialog box displays prompts for all variable attributes with all defined defaults displayed. You then modify or enter any desired text values and choose OK. Preset mode is meaningless when ATTDIA is on because all defaults are displayed and those that you do not change are entered when you choose OK.

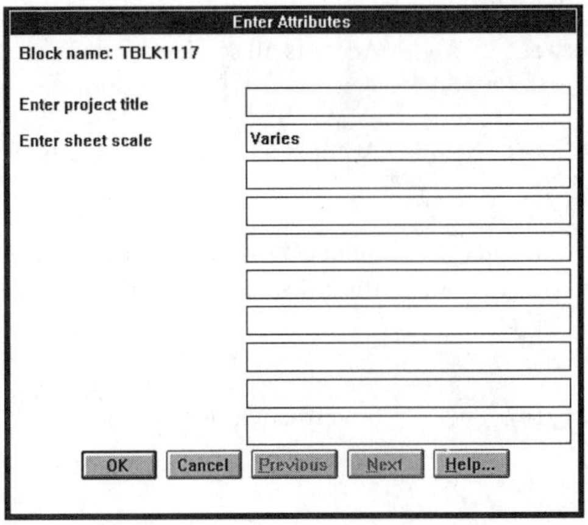

Enter Attributes
Block name: TBLK1117
Enter project title
Enter sheet scale — Varies
OK   Cancel   Previous   Next   Help...

Figure 18.26

Entering attributes with the Enter Attributes dialog box.

18

The Enter Attributes dialog box makes inserting attributes easier and reduces the chance of error. You may want to turn it on in your prototype drawing files. An identical dialog box can be used to edit the values of inserted attributes.

Editing Inserted Attributes

Unlike other objects within blocks, attributes can be edited after insertion. AutoCAD LT provides two commands for editing attribute text. The DDATTE command (Edit **A**ttribute on the **M**odify menu) prompts you to select a block and then displays all of its variable attributes for editing in the Edit Attribute dialog box. Except for its title bar, the Edit Attribute dialog box is identical to the Enter Attributes dialog box shown in figure 18.26. The Enter Attributes dialog box edits only text values; it cannot change placement, object properties, or text characteristics.

If you need to edit placement, visibility, or text characteristics, you use the ATTEDIT command. It prompts for selection using several filters, then presents each attribute for modification. In the following exercise, you use the ATTEDIT command to move and edit the value of the TITLE and SCALE attributes you created and inserted in the previous exercises.

Modifying Inserted Attributes

Continue in the MINSERT drawing from the preceding exercise, with the title block inserted.

Command: **ATTEDIT** (Enter)	Starts the ATTEDIT command
Edit attributes one at a time? <Y> (Enter)	Sets ATTEDIT to prompt for changes for each attribute selected
Block name specification <*>: (Enter)	Accepts all selected blocks
Attribute tag specification <*>: (Enter)	Accepts all selected attribute tags
Attribute value specification <*>: (Enter)	Accepts all selected attribute values
Select Attributes: *Pick the text values at* ① *and* ② *(see fig. 18.27), then press Enter*	Selects both attributes without highlighting, then displays an X on the first one
2 attributes selected.	
Value/Position/Height/Angle/Style/ Layer/Color/Next <N>: **V** (Enter)	Specifies Value option

`Change or Replace? <R>: C` (Enter)	Prompts for string to change
`String to change: Visitor` (Enter)	Specifies search string
`New string: Visitors'` (Enter)	Specifies replacement string and changes the text value
`Value/Position/Height/Angle/Style/` `Layer/Color/Next <N>: P` (Enter)	Specifies Position option
`Enter text insertion point:` *Pick the* *point one snap increment to the left*	Moves the attribute text
`Value/Position/Height/Angle/Style/` `Layer/Color/Next <N>:` (Enter)	Cycles to next selected attribute
`Value/Position/Height/Angle/Style/` `Layer/Color/Next <N>: P` (Enter)	Specifies Position option
`Enter text insertion point:` *Pick the* *point up one snap increment*	Moves the attribute text
`Value/Position/Height/Angle/Style/` `Layer/Color/Next <N>:` (Enter)	Exits ATTEDIT

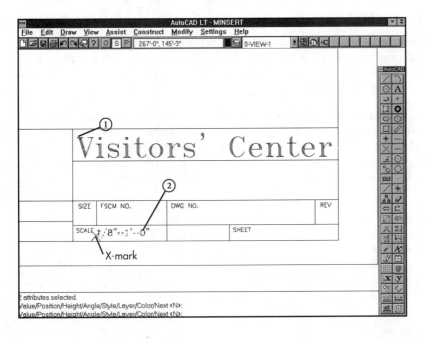

Figure 18.27

Editing attribute text and position with ATTEDIT.

Although you only relocated the attributes slightly and changed one text string, you could just as easily have rotated them, changed the text style or height, and changed their object color or layer properties.

Note ATTEDIT presents selected attributes in the reverse order of their creation in the inserted drawing or their selection during block creation.

Instead of individually picking attributes, you can use a combination of wild-card filters and standard selection set methods. ATTEDIT's prompts and options provide great flexibility, as described in the following list.

◆ `Edit attributes one at a time? <Y>.` At this prompt, you press Enter for individual prompting for changes to each selected attribute, or enter N to apply the changes globally to all selected attributes.

◆ `Block name specification <*>:.` At this prompt, you enter a block name filter to restrict the selection of attributes. Selected attributes in blocks that do not match the name are rejected. You can use wild cards, such as ? and * in ??LABEL*, to accept multiple block names.

◆ `Attribute tag specification <*>:.` At this prompt, you enter a tag name filter to restrict the selection of attributes. Selected attributes whose tags do not match the name are rejected. You can use wild cards, such as ? and *, to accept multiple tag names.

◆ `Attribute value specification <*>:.` At this prompt, you enter a text value filter to restrict the selection of attributes. Selected attributes whose values do not match the text value filter are rejected. You can use wild cards, such as ? and *, to accept multiple values.

◆ `Select Attributes:.` At this prompt, you select one or more attributes by any one, but only one, of the standard object selection methods. Selections are not highlighted. You can pick any number of attributes, but to use options such as Crossing or Fence, you must enter the option without picking. As soon as one option selection is successfully made, attribute selection ends and the first attribute is marked.

◆ `Value/Position/Height/Angle/Style/Layer/Color/Next <N>:.` At this prompt, you enter the first letter of the desired modification option, or press Enter (for the default Next option) to cycle to the next selected attribute. Position relocates the insertion point to the point you specify. Height, Angle, and Style modify the text height, rotation angle, and style specified during attribute

definition. Layer and Color change the object properties of the attribute. The Value option has Replace and Change suboptions that enable you to replace the entire text value or change a portion of it. If you specify the Change option, ATTEDIT searches for all occurrences of the string you specify and replaces them with the new string.

Tip To quickly select large numbers of attributes, plan their tag names so you can use appropriate filters and then select everything with a crossing window. All non-attribute objects are ignored, and well-planned filters can eliminate undesired attributes.

Attributes are a powerful yet flexible way to automate and standardize many kinds of text in drawings due to their editing flexibility, control of text values and characteristics, insertion prompting, and defaults.

Tip You can use the ATTDISP command to display invisible attributes.

In the previous exercises, you inserted the title block as a block. A title block is a good candidate for insertion as an external reference.

Referencing External Drawings

External references, often called xrefs, are references in a current drawing to the contents of another (external) drawing, including all of the objects and named items such as styles, linetypes, and even blocks or other xrefs that the external drawing might contain. Like a block, an *xref* is a single object, which displays as an image of the referenced objects. It does not define a block in the current drawing, nor does it place a copy of any object or data from the external drawing in the current drawing's database. Only an image is placed in the current drawing; the xref data is defined only in the external drawing. The insertion of an xref is called *attachment*. Like a block insertion, the external reference can be scaled and rotated during attachment; however, any attributes it contains are ignored.

Xrefs take up less space in a drawing file than blocks, and cannot be edited from within the drawing to which they are attached. Any drawing file can be attached as an xref. There are differences between the editing and updating of xrefs compared to blocks. To edit the contents of an xref, you must edit the original external drawing file. Each time a drawing containing an xref is opened, the current version of the

18

referenced drawing is loaded and the current drawing is updated. In contrast, a block can be edited in the current drawing by using the EXPLODE command to explode it or by inserting it exploded, editing its component objects, and then redefining the block (see the next chapter). Editing a block affects only the current drawing. Editing an xref's external drawing affects all drawings that reference it.

Xrefs are used for two primary purposes. First, they are an efficient way to import standard elements, such as title blocks, which do not need to be modified in the current drawing. Second, they provide a way for the same drawing data to be used in multiple drawings, and to be automatically updated in all drawings. Several people can work on a project in a coordinated manner, using the same data. For example, a building design team of several people can simultaneously work on the building's structural plan, floor plan, electrical plan, and plumbing plan. All team members can use the same base plan by attaching it as an xref. If any change is made to the base plan, it is automatically updated in the drawings to which it is attached.

Stop   In a team situation, it is the responsibility of the person making the change to notify the others; XREF does not provide automatic notification or identification of changes.

Attaching and Detaching Xrefs

Xrefs are attached, detached, listed, and updated with the XREF command. You attach xrefs with the XREF command. Xref attachment is much like block insertion, with many of the same prompts.

The following exercise begins with an empty drawing named XREFPLAN, using a prototype file that has appropriate units, limits, snap, and grid settings defined. To this drawing, you attach a title block and plan as xrefs. The plan is like that used earlier in the MINSERT exercise.

Attaching Plan and Title Block Xrefs

Open the ALT1802 drawing file and use SAVEAS to save it as BASEPLAN.

Create a new drawing named XREFPLAN, using the ALT1801.DWG file as a prototype drawing, and using no setup method.

Command: *Choose* **D**raw, E**x**ternal Reference, **A**ttach	Issues XREF command with the Attach option (see fig. 18.28)

```
_xref                                    Menu issues the Attach option, and a tilde
?/Bind/Detach/Path/Reload/<Attach>:      (~) to open the Select File to Attach dialog
_attach                                  box (the normal file dialog)
Xref to Attach: ~
```

Attach Xref ALT0301: *Select*
ALT0301.DWG *and choose* OK

```
Attach Xref ALT0301: ALT0301.DWG        Indicates attachment name and path
ALT0301 loaded.
```

The following prompts are identical to the INSERT command and Insert dialog box prompts.

```
Insertion point: 0,0 (Enter)            Specifies insertion point

X scale factor <1> / Corner / XYZ: 96 (Enter)

Y scale factor (default=X): (Enter)

Rotation angle <0>: (Enter)
```

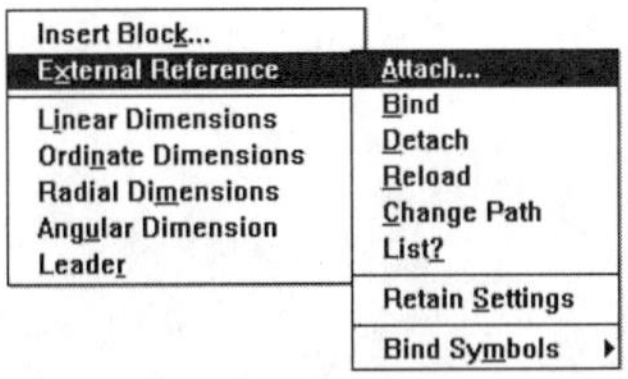

Figure 18.28

*The External
Reference
submenu of the
Draw menu.*

```
Command: XR (Enter)                     Issues the XREF command

XREF

?/Bind/Detach/Path/Reload/<Attach>:     Specifies the Attach option
A (Enter)

Xref to Attach <ALT1801>:               Specifies PLAN xref name and BASEPLAN
PLAN=BASEPLAN (Enter)                    drawing name

Attach Xref PLAN: BASEPLAN
PLAN loaded.

Insertion point: 0,0 (Enter)            Specifies insertion point

X scale factor <1> / Corner / XYZ:      Accepts default 1:1 scale
(Enter)
```

continues

18

continued

```
Y scale factor (default=X):  (Enter)

Rotation angle <0>:  (Enter)                   Attaches the plan (see fig. 18.29)

Command:  Pick a point on the plan            Selects and highlights the entire plan;
                                              you can't edit just a portion

Command:  (Enter)                             Repeats XREF command

XREF

?/Bind/Detach/Path/Reload/                    Specifies inquiry option
<Attach>:  ? (Enter)

Xref(s) to list <*>:  (Enter)                 Lists all xref names and paths (path and file
                                              names)


   Xref Name              Path
. . . . . . . . . . . . . . . . .    . . . . . . . . . . . . . . .


   ALT0301                ALT0301.DWG
   PLAN                   BASEPLAN

Total Xref(s): 2
```

Press F2 to return to the drawing window.

Command: *Click on the Save button*   Saves drawing for the next exercise

---

The drawing now contains a title block and base plan, each attached as an xref. Notice that the BASEPLAN drawing was attached as the PLAN xref, and that the block array of tables created in an earlier exercise by MINSERT is part of the xref image. Each is a single object which can be moved, rotated, and scaled, but the component objects cannot be edited directly. The object created by attaching an xref is actually a special block reference object.

Tip Although you cannot select individual objects in an xref, you can use object snap modes to snap to them.

A drawing file cannot be simultaneously inserted as a block and as an xref.

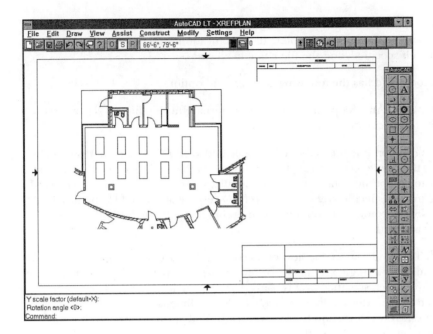

Figure 18.29

Xrefs of a title block and a plan attached to the current drawing.

 Note   You cannot insert as a block a drawing that is already attached as an xref. You must first detach it, or insert it under a different block name (see the next chapter), or rename the block. Likewise, you cannot attach as an xref a drawing whose name matches a current block name unless you attach it with a different name. You can rename xref names by using the Block option of the RENAME command, or by detaching and reattaching with a different name.

XREF. The XREF command attaches references to external drawings, in a manner similar to inserting a block. The primary difference between an xref and a block is that a block is defined in the current drawing, while the xref's data resides entirely in the external drawing's database. Only a reference to the external file is placed in the current drawing's database. The XREF command options enable you to attach, detach, and list xrefs, to reload or respecify the path to an external drawing file to update the xref, and to bind (convert to a normal block) specified xrefs. Once bound, the named items defined in the external drawing, such as blocks, dimension or text styles, layers, linetypes, UCSs, views, and tiled viewports, can be used independently in the current drawing.

The *path* of an xref has a slightly different meaning than the directory path of a file. The path of an xref means the complete file specification used to attach it: the directory path if specified, and the file name in all cases.

The XREF command has the following prompts and options:

◆ **Attach.** The Attach option attaches the external drawing file whose name you specify to the current drawing as an xref.

◆ **?.** The ? option lists the names of the specified xrefs in the current drawing, as well as the referenced drawing file names and paths used to attach them. Press Enter to accept the default asterisk to list all xrefs, or enter a name or wild-card string to list a specific xref or set of xrefs. (Xrefs are also listed by the BLOCK and INSERT commands, but only their xref names are listed, not their file names and paths.)

◆ **Bind.** The Bind option enables you to convert the specified xref(s) to block(s). You can enter a single xref name, or several names separated by commas, or use wild cards. Each specified xref is converted to a block, and the named items defined in the external drawing, such as blocks, dimension or text styles, layers, linetypes, UCSs, views, and tiled viewports, (called *dependent symbols*) become independently available in the current drawing. (See the Understanding the Named Items within Xrefs section of this chapter for the special names assigned to these named items.)

◆ **Detach.** The Detach option removes specified xrefs from the drawing. You can enter a single xref name, or several names separated by commas, or use wild cards.

◆ **Path.** The Path respecifies the external drawing file name and/or directory path associated with an xref. You can enter a single xref name, or several names separated by commas, or use wild cards. XREF then prompts for an old and new path for each specified xref. The Path option updates the specified xrefs.

◆ **Reload.** The Reload option updates specified xrefs to the latest versions of their referenced drawing files, without exiting the current drawing. You can enter a single xref name, or several names separated by commas, or use wild cards. Reload is useful in a networked environment in which other people may edit the drawings that are referenced in your current drawing.

 Stop   If you send a drawing file containing an xref to someone to use or to plot, be sure to include a copy of the referenced external drawing file. Otherwise, opening or plotting the drawing file containing the xref will display a "Can't open file" message box and an xref error message.

How attributes are treated depends on their type. Variable attributes are ignored in attached xrefs, but constant attribute values still appear.

 Note If you bind an xref that contains variable attributes, it will be converted to a block without attributes. Subsequent insertions of that block will not include variable attributes unless you redefine it upon insertion; see the block redefinition section of the next chapter. After redefinition, subsequent insertions of that block prompt for attributes, but the previous insertions are unaffected. If you want to insert attribute-controlled text along with an xref, such as a title block, define the attributes in a separate file and insert it after attaching the xref.

The primary advantage of xrefs is how they automatically update to reflect changes in the referenced drawing.

Updating Xrefs: Editing the Source and Reloading

To update an xref, you modify its external source drawing, and reload the xref. Reloading is automatic when the drawing containing the xref is reopened. If the external source drawing is modified by others, you can force reloading with the XREF Reload option.

In the following exercise, you open and edit the BASEPLAN drawing, the source of the PLAN xref.

Modifying the Source Plan

Continue from the preceding exercise, with the two xrefs attached and the drawing saved.

Open the BASEPLAN drawing (see fig 18.30).

Use STRETCH to select the crossing window shown from ① to ② and stretch the selected objects with a displacement of 0,8' (8 feet). Then use MOVE to select and move each of the leftover wall hatch objects by the same displacement. Use REDRAW to check the results, as shown in figure 18.31.

Save the drawing

18

Figure 18.30

The BASEPLAN drawing during STRETCH and before MOVE.

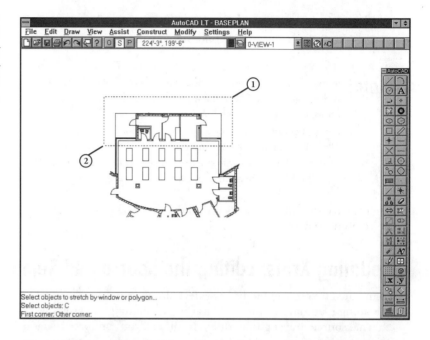

Figure 18.31

The BASEPLAN drawing after STRETCH and MOVE.

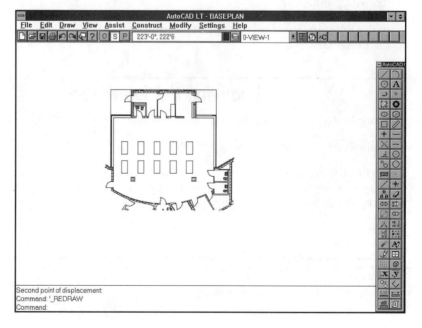

You have edited the xref's source file just as you would edit any drawing file. With the base plan modified, you can reopen the XREFPLAN drawing and observe the updating.

Updating the Xref

Continue from the preceding exercise, with the BASEPLAN drawing modified and saved.

Open the XREFPLAN drawing (see fig. 18.32). The following is displayed as it is loaded:

```
Command: _OPEN
Resolve Xref ALT0301: ALT0301.DWG
ALT0301 loaded.
Resolve Xref PLAN: baseplan
Duplicate DEFPOINTS layer entry ignored.
PLAN loaded.
```

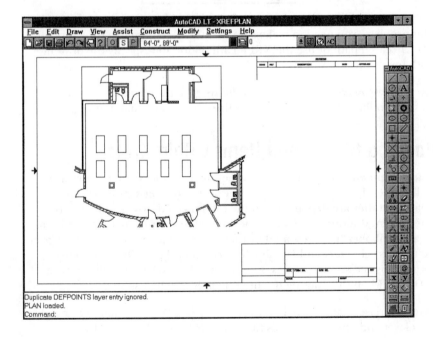

Figure 18.32

The XREFPLAN drawing with the BASEPLAN xref automatically updated.

18

As it loads the drawing, AutoCAD LT locates and loads any external drawings it references. If the external drawing itself contains xrefs, their drawings are also loaded. If all are found and loaded without problems, the xrefs are reported to be *resolved*. If AutoCAD LT has problems loading anything, it displays a message dialog box like that shown in figure 18.33, and command line messages like the following:

```
Resolve Xref PLAN: baseplan
** Error resolving Xref PLAN.
11 unresolved dependent layer(s).
2 unresolved dependent linetype(s).
```

Figure 18.33

The "Can't open file" error message dialog box.

To resolve this problem, you need to make sure that the file(s) are in a directory on the AutoCAD LT search path or use the XREF Path option to respecify the drawing name and path for the unresolved xref.

The unresolved *dependent layer(s)* and *dependent linetype(s)* reported in the command line error messages refer to the named items defined in the external drawing.

Understanding the Named Items within Xrefs

The named items defined in the external drawing, such as blocks, dimension or text styles, layers, linetypes, UCSs, views, and tiled viewports, are called *dependent symbols*. *Dependent* means that they are dependent on the referenced drawing, and are not defined in the current drawing. *Symbol* is the term used to refer to such named items because they are symbolically represented by their names. Except for the special layer names 0 (see the next chapter) and DEFPOINTS (used by dimensioning), these named items are assigned strange names, such as layer PLAN|A-DOOR or linetype ALT0301|HIDDEN, when the drawing defining them is attached as an xref.

In the following exercise, you use the Layer Control dialog box to examine some of the dependent layer and linetype symbols in the PLAN and ALT0301 xrefs.

Examining the Named Dependent Symbols of an Xref

Continue from the preceding exercise, with the XREFPLAN drawing reopened and the PLAN xref updated.

Command: *Click in the Current Layer name drop-down list box on the toolbar*	Opens drop-down list, listing only layers 0 and DEFPOINTS
Command: *Click on the Layers button*	Opens Layer Control dialog box (see fig. 18.34)
Select the PLAN|A-DOOR *layer*	Displays name in the input box, but grays the Current and Rename buttons
Choose the Set **L**type *button*	Opens the Select Linetype dialog box
Click on any of the noncontinuous linetypes	Displays Xref not allowed error message
Choose Cancel, *then* Cancel *again*	Closes both dialog boxes

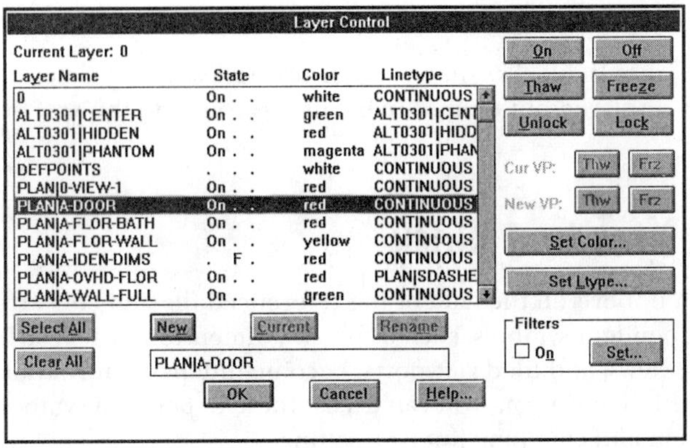

Figure 18.34

Layer Control dialog box, including the dependent layers and linetypes of xrefs.

The Current Layer name drop-down list excludes dependent layers because you can't set them current or draw on them. Similarly, dependent linetypes are displayed, but cannot be set current, and dependent blocks cannot be inserted independently. The Layer Control dialog box, however, does list dependent layers because you can temporarily modify their properties and visibility settings. These names consist of the xref name, a vertical bar character (|), and the original symbol name from the referenced drawing, for example, PLAN|A-DOOR or ALT0301|HIDDEN. This naming scheme prevents duplicate names, which could interfere with settings in the current drawing.

18

When you select an xref layer in the Layer Control dialog box, the **C**urrent and Rena**m**e buttons are disabled and grayed (and Ne**w** is unusable, although not grayed), but the other buttons are still active. You can assign any color to xref-dependent layers, and set them on/off, frozen/thawed, and locked/unlocked. You can assign them any linetype defined in the current drawing, but the xref-dependent linetypes are not assignable, even though they are displayed in the Select Linetype dialog box. Unless you turn on the VISRETAIN system variable, even the assignments and settings that can be made are only temporary and all original dependencies are restored when the drawing or the xref is reloaded. To save these settings within the current drawing, choose **D**raw, then E**x**ternal Reference, then Retain **S**ettings and set the value of VISRETAIN to 1 (on).

 Stop You can reset the linetype of an xref-dependent layer to any linetype defined in the current drawing, but you cannot reset it back to its original linetype without reloading the drawing or xref.

 Tip You can use the Filters feature of the Layer Control dialog box to exclude dependent layers.

The other dependent symbols, blocks, dimension or text styles, UCSs, views, and tiled viewports, are similarly displayed but unmodifiable unless you bind the xref or specific symbols.

Converting an Xref to a Block

The XREF Bind option imports all the data of the referenced file and converts the xref to a block. The dependent symbols, such as blocks, dimension or text styles, layers, linetypes, UCSs, views, and tiled viewports, become independently available in the current drawing. After conversion, you can access these dependent symbols, for example, renaming them and changing linetype settings.

In the following exercise, you bind the title block xref, converting it to a normal block. Its dependent symbols are also converted but are changed to names such as ALT0301$0$CENTER.

Binding the Title Block Xref

Continue from either of the previous two exercises, with the XREFPLAN drawing open.

Command: *Select the title block*   Highlights the xref

Command: **LS** (Enter)	Issues the LIST command with the xref selected and displays its data

LIST 1 found
       BLOCK REFERENCE   Layer: 0
                      Space: Model space
       ALT0301
       External reference
	The External reference denotation identifies it as an xref
	
	(coordinate, scale, and rotation data follow here)

Press F2 to return to the drawing window.

Command: *Choose* **D**raw, **Ex**ternal Reference, **B**ind	Issues XREF command with Bind option
_xref ?/Bind/Detach/Path/Reload/<Attach>: _bind	
Xref(s) to bind: **ALT*** (Enter)	Specifies all names beginning with ALT; only ALT0301 matches
Scanning...	Scans for matching names and binds them
Command: *Select the title block and reissue the LIST command*	Displays identical data, but without the External reference denotation

Press F2 to return to the drawing window.

Command: *Click on the Layers button*	Opens Layer Control dialog box (see fig. 18.35)
Select the ALT0301$0$CENTER *layer*	Displays name in the input box
In the input box, delete ALT0301$0$ *and choose* **Rena**m**e**	Renames layer to CENTER
Choose OK	Accepts change and closes dialog box
Command: *Click on the Current Layer name drop-down list box on the toolbar*	Opens drop-down list

The drop-down list lists only layers 0 and DEFPOINTS, and the converted and renamed ALT0301$0$HIDDEN, ALT0301$0$PHANTOM, and CENTER.

Command: *Choose* **M**odify, Re**n**ame	Opens the Rename dialog box
In the **N**amed Objects *area, select* Ltype, *then in the* **I**tems *area, select* ALT0301$0$CENTER	Enters ALT0301$0$CENTER in the **O**ld Name box

continues

18

continued

Enter **CENTER** *in the* **R**ename To *input box, then choose* **R**ename To, OK	Specifies new name and renames linetype

`1 Ltype(s) renamed.`

Figure 18.35

Layer Control dialog box, with converted layers and linetypes from xrefs.

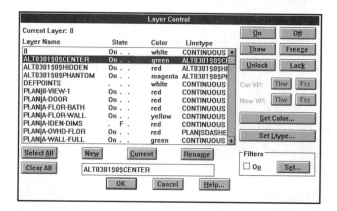

The naming scheme used by XREF Bind eliminates the possibility of duplicate names, but generates strange names that you may want to rename. It takes the vertical bar in names such as ALT0301|CENTER and replaces it with a number nested in a pair of dollar signs (0), creating a name such as ALT0301$0$CENTER. If the name ALT0301$0$CENTER happens to exist already, AutoCAD LT uses the next higher digit between the dollar signs, for example, ALT0301$1$CENTER, ALT0301$2$CENTER, and so on.

If you need to import only a specific item from an xref, you can bind specific dependent symbols instead of the entire xref.

Importing Part of an Xref with XBIND

XBIND binds (imports and converts) specified dependent symbols, such as blocks, dimension or text styles, layers, linetypes, UCSs, views, and tiled viewports, from an external drawing that is attached as an xref. Once bound, these items can be independently used in the current drawing, even after the xref is detached. Because they receive strange names when converted, as discussed in the previous section, you will probably want to rename them after binding them. You can use the Rename dialog box or the RENAME command to do so.

The abbreviated alias for the XBIND command is XB, or you can select it from the Bind Symbols submenu of the External Reference submenu of the **D**raw menu (see fig. 18.36).

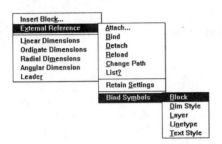

Figure 18.36

The Bind Symbols submenu.

In the following exercise, you list the xrefs and blocks, convert the PLAN|DOORR dependent block to an ordinary block, rename it, and insert it.

Importing a Door Block from an Xref with XBIND

Continue from any of the previous three exercises, with the XREFPLAN drawing open.

Command: **B** (Enter)	Issues BLOCK command
BLOCK Block name (or ?): **?** (Enter)	Specifies List option
Block(s) to list <*>: (Enter)	Lists all blocks (Xdep indicates dependent blocks)

```
Defined blocks.
  ALT0301
  PLAN                  Xref: resolved
  PLAN¦COLCONC          Xdep: PLAN
  PLAN¦DOORR            Xdep: PLAN
  PLAN¦LAVFS            Xdep: PLAN
  PLAN¦TBL3672          Xdep: PLAN
  PLAN¦WCWALL           Xdep: PLAN

User    External    Dependent   Unnamed
Blocks  References  Blocks      Blocks
  1         1          5          17
```

Press F2 to return to the drawing window.

continues

18

continued

Command: *Choose* **D**raw, E**x**ternal Reference, Bind Sy**m**bols, **B**lock	Issues XBIND command with Block option

```
_xbind
Block/Dimstyle/LAyer/LType/Style: _block
```

Dependent Block name(s): **PLAN¦DOORR** (Enter)	Specifies name to bind
Scanning... 1 Block(s) bound.	Searches for and binds the PLAN¦DOORR dependent symbol as the PLAN0DOORR block

Use the Block option of the RENAME command or the Rename dialog box to change the PLAN0DOORR block name to DOORR.

Repeat the BLOCK command with the ? list option. The list is the same as before, except the PLAN¦DOORR dependent symbol has been replaced with the ordinary DOORR block.

Use the INSERT command with a preset scale of 42 and preset rotation of 90 to insert the DOORR block at ① (see fig. 18.37).

Figure 18.37

The converted, renamed, and inserted DOORR block.

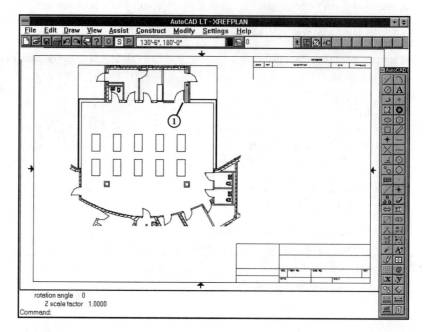

The PLAN xref is still intact, but its dependent DOORR block is now a permanent part of the current drawing. Any dependent symbol can similarly be bound and renamed for independent use in the current drawing. Binding an xref or its dependent symbols has no effect on the external referenced file.

> **XBIND.** The XBIND command enables you to convert specified dependent symbols (blocks, dimension or text styles, layers, linetypes, UCSs, views, and tiled viewports) that are defined in an externally referenced drawing into normal blocks, dimension or text styles, layers, linetypes, UCSs, views, and tiled viewports. You specify what type of symbol to bind at the initial `Block/Dimstyle/LAyer/LType/Style:` prompt, and XBIND prompts for a specific symbol name of that type. You can enter a single name, or several names separated by commas, or use wild cards. Each specified symbol is bound and becomes independently available in the current drawing. If a bound item references another dependent symbol in the xref, that other symbol is also bound. For example, binding a layer causes a linetype assigned to that layer to be bound as well.

 Tip   You can attach a library file containing predefined named items such as dimension styles or blocks, use XBIND to import specific ones, rename them to usable names, and then detach the xref.

This chapter has given you a power boost on productivity, with highly effective and efficient ways to quickly produce the repetitive elements in your drawing. You might compare it to going from a single-engine Piper Cub to a twin-engine Lear Jet. The next chapter continues the coverage of blocks and xrefs with an exploration of their structure, editing methods, and important management issues.

18

Managing and Modifying Blocks and Xrefs

I f you are working on drawings of any significant complexity, you will quickly accumulate numerous blocks and drawing files that are inserted or attached as blocks or external references. To avoid confusion and error, you need to be aware of several issues such as how blocks are structured, redefined, and managed. This chapter includes the following topics to address these issues:

- ◆ Exploding blocks and editing their constituent objects

- ◆ Redefining blocks

- ◆ Understanding layers, linetypes, and colors within blocks

- ◆ Block and xref libraries

- ◆ Exporting drawing data to external drawing files

- ◆ Controlling the insertion base point

- ◆ Rescaling and mirroring blocks

◆ How grips work with blocks

◆ Nesting blocks in blocks and xrefs

◆ Purging blocks

Many aspects of block management and editing are common sense, or just like dealing with other types of objects.

Editing Whole Blocks

Some editing operations with whole blocks are too simple to require demonstration here. The basic rules are as follows:

◆ Like other named items, blocks can be renamed with the RENAME command or the Rename dialog box.

◆ Like any other object, blocks can be copied, moved, mirrored, rotated, scaled, and so on. (How grips work with blocks is covered later in the chapter.)

◆ You can use object snap modes to snap to objects within the block.

◆ Copying a block creates a new block reference object—an image of the block definition just like the block reference that it was copied from.

◆ Rotating or scaling a block changes the rotation or scale data of the block reference, just as if you inserted it with a different scale or rotation angle.

◆ Mirroring a block makes one or more of its scales negative.

◆ Stretch moves a block if the insertion point is in the crossing window or polygon; the visible objects are irrelevant to stretch.

◆ You can't stretch part of a block unless you explode it.

Modifying block components and redefining blocks, however, is a bit more involved and requires demonstration in the following sections. You have already seen how to modify xrefs. To modify blocks, you must redefine them, and if you want to modify their constituent or component objects, you first need to explode them or insert them exploded.

Exploding Blocks to Edit Their Component Objects

You can use the EXPLODE command to explode a single block reference object into its constituent objects, or you can insert the individual constituent objects of a block by using an asterisk (like ***NUT10**) with the INSERT command or the **E**xplode box in the Insert dialog box. In either case, what you get is not a block reference, but its constituent objects, which can be edited like any other objects.

Note   As you explore blocks, bear in mind that, on a white drawing background, the color "white" (7) appears black.

In the previous chapter, you inserted the NUT10 block as its component objects by prefacing its name with an asterisk in the INSERT command. You also inserted the SLOT10 block as its component objects by using the Insert dialog box with a check in the **E**xplode box. In the following exercise, you revisit the mechanical drawing (see fig. 19.1) from the previous chapter and modify its nuts and bolts. You'll copy, explode, and edit the objects of the HEAD and NUT10 blocks to refine their appearance.

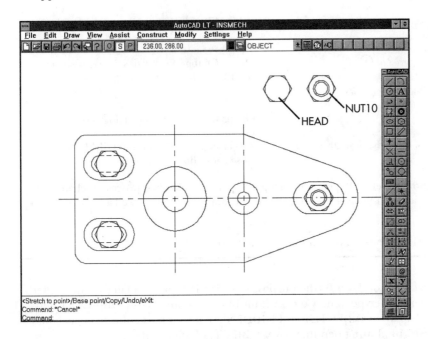

Figure 19.1

Mechanical drawing with nut and bolt head blocks.

Exploding Blocks and Editing Their Component Objects

Create a new drawing named INSMECH (replacing the previous file), using the ALT1901.DWG file as a prototype drawing, and using no setup method (see fig. 19.1).

Zoom in on the nut and bolt head in the upper right of the drawing, to the view shown in the background of figure 19.2. Turn off snap.

Command: *Pick the nut, then the head*	Selects and highlights each as a single object
Command: *Choose **A**ssist, **L**ist*	Issues LIST command and lists data for both blocks

Note that both the HEAD and NUT10 blocks are on layer OBJECT. Press F2 to return to the drawing and note that they are red, the layer's color.

Command: *Pick the nut and the head, then type* **X** *and press Enter*	Issues EXPLODE and explodes both blocks; they change to black or white
Command: *Pick a circle from the nut and from the head*	Selects and highlights each as individual circle objects
Command: *Choose **A**ssist, **L**ist*	Issues LIST command and lists data for both circles

Note that the circles are on layer 0, which is color white (7), then press F2 to return to the drawing window.

Command: *Pick the circles at* ① *and* ② *(see fig. 19.2), then choose **M**odify, Cha**ng**e Properties*	Opens Change Properties dialog box (see fig. 19.2), with the two circles selected
Choose **L**ayer	Opens the Select Layer dialog box
Select OBJECTLT, *then* OK, *then* OK *again*	Sets layer of both circles to OBJECTLT and closes both dialog boxes

The circles are now magenta. Repeat the Change Properties dialog box process to change the circle at ③ (see fig. 19.3) to layer HIDDEN. It also becomes magenta, as well as changing to a hidden linetype.

Zoom to the previous view (the view in fig. 19.1) and save the drawing.

Now the objects are on layer 0 (the purpose of which is explained later in the Understanding Layers, Linetypes, and Colors within Blocks section), layer OBJECTLT and layer HIDDEN. Layers OBJECTLT and HIDDEN are magenta, a color to be assigned to a lighter weight plotting pen than layer OBJECT, which is red.

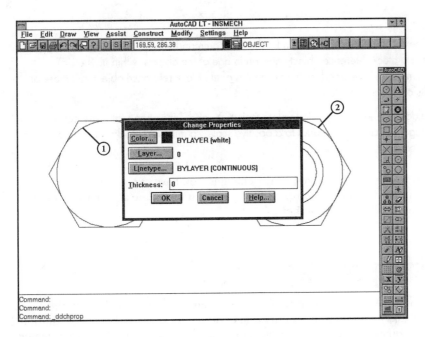

Figure 19.2

The head and nut and the Change Properties dialog box.

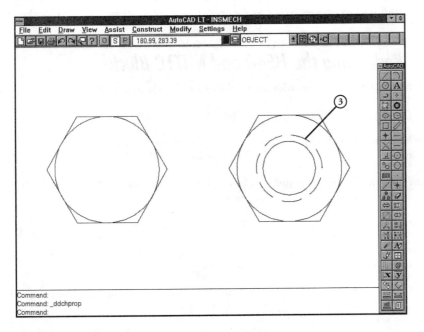

Figure 19.3

Head and nut with circles on changed layers.

Note   The color and linetype shown by the LIST command can be confusing. You cannot see a block reference object—just an image of the objects within it. The LIST command, however, lists the properties of the block reference object, not those of its component objects.

Blocks cannot be exploded unless their X, Y, and Z insertion scales are equal. A negative scale is not equal to a positive scale, so mirrored blocks cannot be exploded.

The inserted blocks are unaffected by the changes. You have exploded two block references and modified their component objects, but to update all occurrences of the blocks, you need to redefine them.

Redefining Blocks

If you attempt to define a block using the name of an existing block definition, AutoCAD LT asks if you want to redefine the existing block. That's block redefinition in a nutshell. You can use either the BLOCK command or the Block Definition dialog box. Try each in the following exercise, as you redefine the HEAD and NUT10 blocks.

Redefining the HEAD and NUT10 Blocks

Continue from the preceding exercise, with the modified head and nut objects.

Command: *Choose* **C**onstruct, Make **B**lock	Opens Block Definition dialog box
Enter **HEAD** *in the block name input box, then choose* **S**elect Objects	Specifies block name and prompts for object selection
Select objects: *Select the circle and hexagon of the modified head, then press Enter*	Selects objects and reopens Block Definition dialog box
Choose Select **P**oint	Prompts for base point
Insertion base point: *Turn on snap and pick the center of the modified head*	Sets point and reopens Block Definition dialog box
Clear the **R**etain Entities *check box and choose* OK	Displays the Warning dialog box shown in figure 19.4
Choose **R**edefine	Closes dialog boxes and redefines the HEAD block

```
Redefining block HEAD
```

```
Command: B (Enter)
```
Issues BLOCK command

```
BLOCK Block name (or ?): NUT10 (Enter)
```
Specifies block to redefine

```
Block NUT10 already exists.
Redefine it? <N> Y (Enter)
```
Confirms redefinition

```
Insertion base point: Pick the center of the
modified nut
```

```
Select objects: Select all objects of the modified
nut, then press Enter
```
Selects objects and redefines
NUT10 block (see fig. 19.5)

```
Block NUT10 redefined
Regenerating drawing.
```

```
Command: Click on the Save button
```
Saves for a later exercise

```
Command: Pick a nut and a head, then choose
Assist, List
```
Issues the LIST command and lists the data
for both blocks

Press F2 to return to the drawing window.

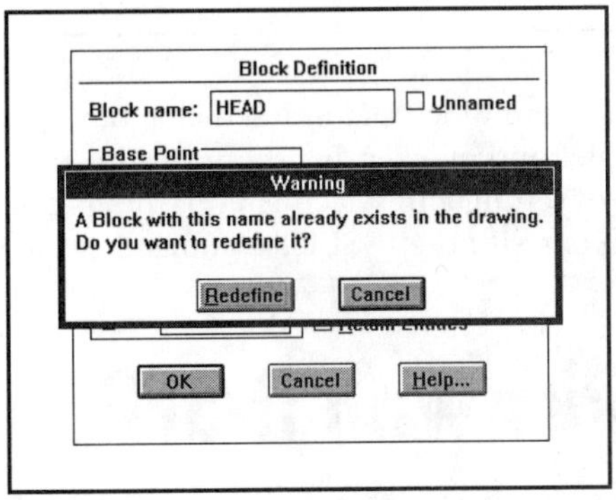

Figure 19.4

*The Warning
dialog box for
block redefinition.*

The redefined block references take on the new block definitions just as if newly
inserted. (Any exploded blocks, however, would be unaffected.)

The modified objects of the redefined blocks in the preceding exercise retain the
settings of the OBJECTLT and HIDDEN layers (magenta, and a hidden linetype) in
spite of the fact that the LIST command reports that the blocks are on layer OBJECT.
Why? And why do the hexagons and circle that were on layer 0 before block redefinition now appear red (look closely), the color of layer OBJECT instead of the color of
layer 0? To understand why, you need to understand how layers, linetypes, and colors

work in blocks. To answer these questions, see the Understanding Layers, Linetypes, and Colors within Blocks section, which follows the next brief section on redefining blocks during insertion.

Figure 19.5

Redefined HEAD and NUT10 blocks in the INSMECH drawing.

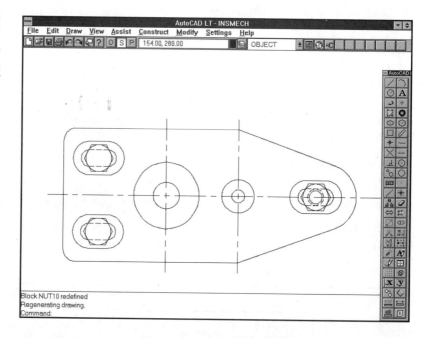

Either the BLOCK command or the Block Definition dialog box redefines blocks, but the BLOCK command is simpler and quicker. In addition, it warns you before you've gone through all the trouble of setting and selecting everything. You can also redefine blocks by inserting a drawing with the INSERT command or the Insert dialog box.

Redefining Blocks with INSERT

If you use the INSERT command to insert a block and enter both a block name and file name using an equal sign to link them, like ***BLKNAME=FILENAME***, then INSERT will search for the specified file name on disk and insert it as the specified block name, defining the block in the process. If the block name already exists, INSERT will prompt `Block BLKNAME redefined`, but will not ask for confirmation. If you continue or cancel without undoing the INSERT command, all occurrences of that block will be redefined in the current drawing. If you don't want it redefined, then you must cancel and undo the INSERT command.

To enter different block and file names in the Insert dialog box, you should enter the block name last or it may put the file name in the block name input box. If you press

Enter or choose OK when the cursor is in the file name box, the Insert dialog box insists on changing the block name to match the file name (you have to look quickly to see it). If the block name already exists, the Insert dialog box will display a Warning dialog box and ask Do you want to redefine it?. If you choose Redefine, the block will be redefined (even if you subsequently cancel at the insertion prompts). Use U (undo) if you accidentally redefine a block. If you choose Cancel, it returns you to the Insert dialog box.

Understanding Layers, Linetypes, and Colors within Blocks

Linetypes and component objects in a block can have their object color and linetype properties set to BYLAYER (the default), to BYBLOCK, or to explicit colors or linetypes. Objects in blocks can be on layer 0 (the default) or on named layers. These settings affect the flexibility and appearance of the block.

Objects with Explicit Properties

Objects with explicit object color and linetype properties are not affected by layer color and linetype settings, whether they are in a block or not. An object that has an object color magenta and object linetype hidden remains magenta and hidden regardless of the layer on which it resides, and regardless of inclusion in a block.

Stop   Use caution: try to avoid assigning explicit properties to objects in blocks. They are inflexible and cannot be changed without redefining the block. Explicit properties in blocks often cause problems in drawings provided to consultants and others, who may need to change the color or linetype of objects in blocks to use the drawing as a base plan or to conform to their CAD standards.

Objects with BYLAYER Properties or On Layer 0

Objects that have BYLAYER object properties always assume the color and linetype of their layer, *unless* they are on layer 0 and in a block inserted on another layer. For example, recall the previous exercises. The circles that were changed to layers OBJECTLT and HIDDEN had BYLAYER properties, so they took on the appearance of their layers both before and after they were defined and inserted with the HEAD and NUT10 blocks. The hexagons and inner nut circle, however, changed from black (or white) to red when they were defined and inserted with the HEAD and NUT10 blocks because they are on layer 0.

Layer 0 is a special layer, with chameleon-like properties. If an object with BYLAYER properties is on layer 0 and in a block, then when you insert the block, the image of the object takes on the layer properties of the layer on which the block is inserted.

To further demonstrate this, the INSMECH drawing contains a layer named DOT-TED, with the color green and linetype DOTX2. (If your drawing window background color makes green dots hard to see, use another color.) In the following exercise, insert a NUT10 block on layer DOTTED and change a HEAD block to layer DOTTED. Make some changes to the layer settings, then explode the NUT10 block and see the dotted parts revert to layer 0's properties.

Observing BYLAYER Properties and the Chameleon-Like Layer 0

Continue from the preceding exercise, with the HEAD and NUT10 blocks redefined.

Set the current layer to DOTTED and zoom in to the area shown in figure 19.6.

Use the INSERT command to insert the NUT10 block in the upper left.

Pick the existing HEAD block reference and use the Change Properties dialog box to change its layer to DOTTED.

The images of the objects on layer 0 in both blocks now have a green and dotted appearance, as shown in figure 19.6.

Use the Layer Control dialog box to set the colors of layer DOTTED to blue and layer OBJECTLT to yellow. The objects defined on layer 0 become blue and those defined on OBJECTLT become yellow.

Command: *Click twice on the Undo button*   Restores layer color settings and returns the HEAD block to layer OBJECT

Command: *Pick the dotted NUT10 block, then type* **X** *and press Enter*   Issues EXPLODE; the dotted green lines become white or black as they revert to layer 0

Set the current layer back to OBJECT, and save the drawing for a later exercise.

This exercise confirms that BYLAYER objects on layer 0 assume the appearance of the layer upon which the block resides, such as OBJECT to DOTTED. If you change the layer of the block reference object or the layer settings after insertion, the layer 0 objects assume the appearance of the new layer or settings. However, BYLAYER objects on named layers such as OBJECTLT assume the current color and linetype settings of the layer that the objects are on, regardless of the layer the block is on.

AutoCAD LT has another object setting that yields even more flexibility: BYBLOCK.

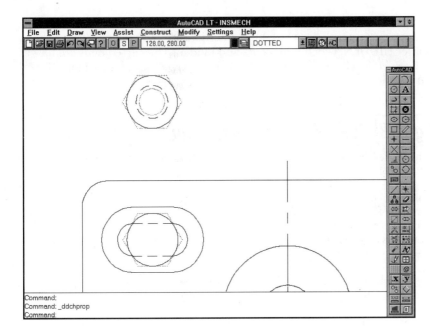

Figure 19.6

Chameleon-like layer 0 objects in block on layer DOTTED.

19

Objects with BYBLOCK Properties

Objects with BYBLOCK color or layer properties work similarly to those with BYLAYER settings on layer 0. Think of BYBLOCK settings as being not yet defined. BYBLOCK objects in blocks take on the current object (entity) color and linetype settings at the time the block is inserted instead of the settings current when the block is defined. BYBLOCK objects are completely flexible, unlike those with BYLAYER settings on layer 0, which are predestined to assume only the default color and linetype of the layer on which the block is inserted.

In blocks, objects with color and linetypes set BYBLOCK adopt the settings current at the time of their insertion, whether the current setting is BYLAYER or explicit, or even BYBLOCK. In blocks, objects drawn on layer 0 with settings BYBLOCK act exactly like primitive objects, both floating to the current layer and adopting the current properties at the time of insertion. These make good general-purpose blocks, such as one-unit squares and circles that are stretched to insert as rectangles and ellipscs.

Tip   You might insert a BYBLOCK block with the current settings BYBLOCK if you intend to nest it (include it as an object) in another block. See the section on nesting blocks later in this chapter.

The following exercise creates a block from the four objects of the inner slot (see fig. 19.7). The objects currently all have BYLAYER linetype and colors settings. The dashed lines are on layer HIDDEN, which is magenta and hidden. The curved ends are on layer OBJECT, which is red and continuous. You will change the color and linetype of the curved ends to BYBLOCK, make a block, and experiment with inserting it.

Observing BYBLOCK Blocks Adopting Insertion-Time Settings

Continue from the preceding exercise, with the layer settings and HEAD block restored, the newly inserted NUT10 block exploded, and snap on.

Copy the four objects of the inner slot from ① to ② (see fig. 19.7).

Use the Change Properties dialog box to change the color and linetype of the curved ends to BYBLOCK. BYBLOCK is an explicit setting, overriding the OBJECT layer settings, so the ends become black (or white) and continuous.

Use BLOCK to define a block named BYB, selecting all four objects at ②. Enter **OOPS** to restore the objects after defining the block.

Click on the Current Color (DDEMODES) button, which opens the Entity Creation Modes dialog box. Confirm that object (entity) color and linetype are BYLAYER, and close the dialog box.

Use INSERT to insert the BYB block at ③. The ends assume the current BYLAYER setting and assume the red and continuous appearance of the current OBJECT layer.

Use the Entity Creation Modes dialog box to change current object color and linetype to blue and HIDDEN2.

Insert the BYB block at ④. The ends assume the current explicit blue and HIDDEN2 settings, overriding the red and continuous appearance of the current OBJECT layer.

Use the Entity Creation Modes dialog box to change current object color and linetype to BYBLOCK.

Insert the BYB block at ⑤. The ends assume the current explicit BYBLOCK settings, appearing black (or white) and continuous and overriding the current OBJECT layer.

Use the Change Properties dialog box to change the four objects at ② and the three blocks at ③, ④, and ⑤ to layer DOTTED. Only the hidden lines at ② and curved ends at ③ assume the layer's properties, green and dotted (see fig. 19.8).

Use the Change Properties dialog box to change the four objects at ② and the three blocks at ③, ④, and ⑤ to color cyan and linetype HIDDEN2. All objects at ② and all curved ends of the blocks become cyan and HIDDEN2.

Use the Change Properties dialog box to change the four objects at ② and the three blocks at ③, ④, and ⑤ to color and linetype BYLAYER. All objects at ② and all curved ends of the blocks assume the layer's properties, green and dotted.

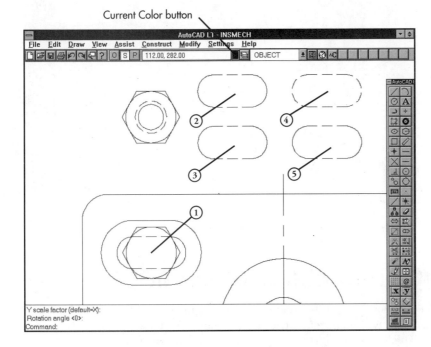

Current Color button

Figure 19.7

BYBLOCK blocks inserted with various settings.

19

When you inserted the blocks, the objects with properties BYBLOCK assumed the current object settings. If the current settings are BYLAYER, the BYBLOCK objects assume the BYLAYER setting and the current layer's color and linetype. If BYBLOCK objects in a block are inserted with BYLAYER current and the block is then changed to a different layer, the objects assume the new layer's properties, as did the curved ends in the exercise when changed to the DOTTED layer. If the current settings are explicit when inserted, the BYBLOCK objects assume the current object color and linetype properties and are not affected by subsequent changes to different layers, unless the blocks are first changed to color and linetype BYLAYER. They are also affected by explicit changes to the object color and linetype settings.

 Tip Use BYBLOCK if you need the colors and linetypes of objects to vary, like a primitive object that varies from one insertion to another.

Figure 19.8

BYBLOCK objects and blocks after changing to layer DOTTED.

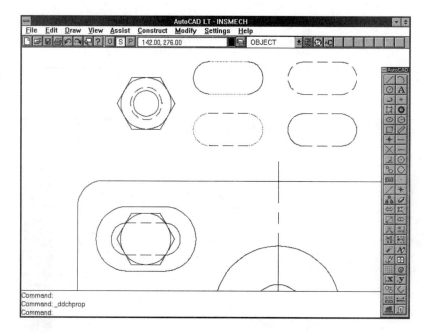

Creating Block and Xref Libraries

The two most important aspects of creating and managing block and xref libraries are layer, color, and linetype management, and block name, file name, and directory management. This section summarizes layer, color, and linetype management for blocks and xrefs, demonstrates how to use the **WBLOCK** command to export blocks and objects to create drawings that can be inserted as blocks or attached as xrefs in other drawings, and discusses block name, file name, and directory management. It also demonstrates the use of the **BASE** command to control the insertion base point of drawings to be inserted as blocks or attached as xrefs in other drawings.

Managing Layers, Colors, and Linetypes in Blocks

The decision to use BYLAYER, BYBLOCK, or explicit colors and linetypes is important to your block construction. When the block is defined, explicit settings are locked in. This means that you cannot easily change the settings unless you redefine the block. However, if you set color and linetype BYLAYER, you can change them by simply changing the layer. By organizing your drawings BYLAYER, you can impose a structure that you can easily control by turning layers on/off and freezing/thawing them. Simple schemes for blocks are usually better than complex ones.

Tip It helps to think of layer 0 as if it were called "layer BYBLOCK." Blocks created on layer 0 float to the layer current at the time of their insertion.

Confusion can result if you mix explicit settings with layer settings. For typical blocks, such as parts and single-purpose symbols, you can use BYLAYER object settings to control your symbols and parts. For multipurpose symbols, use BYLAYER on layer 0, and control your blocks by layer insertion.

You should generally create blocks and drawings to be inserted as blocks or xrefs with all objects on layer 0 and/or with object properties set to BYLAYER or BYBLOCK. Then you can use layer settings to control color and linetype, enabling you and others to change the appearance as needed. Blocks containing objects with inflexible explicit properties have the potential to create problems in every drawing in which they are inserted or attached.

Any layers that are part of an inserted block, but do not exist in the drawing before the insertion, are created when the block is inserted. Use standardized, common layers whenever possible to keep the number of layers in a drawing to a minimum.

For multipurpose symbols and for unit parts, you can create your symbols by using BYLAYER on layer 0 and control the appearance of your blocks by controlling the layer on which you insert them. This technique is useful for symbols that do not require unique layers, but which must assume the characteristics of other objects in the drawing that have color and linetype characteristics associated by layer. This technique is essential if you have clients who require you to utilize their layering standard.

For even finer control, use layer 0 with color and linetype defined BYBLOCK; you still achieve the same effect as described earlier. These settings place your blocks on the current layer with the current color and linetype characteristics. If both your layer and linetype are set BYLAYER when you insert the symbol, the symbol takes on the characteristics of the layer upon which it is inserted. If, however, linetype and color are explicitly set (to red, yellow, DASHED, BYBLOCK, or anything other than BYLAYER), the symbol uses the explicit settings rather than the layer settings.

BYBLOCK offers the most flexibility, because by simply changing color and linetype settings prior to insertion, you can change the appearance of blocks when you insert them. This procedure also enables you to insert multiple instances of the same symbol on the same layer, but have them take on different color and linetype properties. You should use this procedure sparingly, however, because explicit properties become permanent after insertion.

Managing Layers, Colors, and Linetypes in Xrefs

Xrefs behave much differently than blocks when it comes to layers, linetypes, and colors. The difference is caused mainly by the way layers are treated when an xref is attached to a drawing. When a block containing layers that already exist is inserted in the destination drawing, the layers are merged. If the objects in the block are set BYLAYER, the destination drawing's settings override those of the block's. Objects in the block that are on the matching layers take on the characteristics of the destination drawing's layers.

An xref's layers do not behave the same way. When an xref is attached, its layer names, with one exception, are not duplicated in the drawing. Instead, they are prefixed by the name of the xref. For example, if an xref named DOOR28 contains a layer named OBJECT, the layer becomes DOOR28|OBJECT when the xref is attached to the destination drawing. If a layer named OBJECT already exists in the destination drawing, it is unaffected. The xref's objects on layer DOOR28|OBJECT retain their original characteristics, because the layer is unique.

As is most often the case, the exception is layer 0. Any objects that exist on layer 0 in the xref come in on layer 0 in the destination drawing. They then assume the characteristics of the destination drawing's layer 0 just as a block insert would. The following list describes how xref objects created on layer 0 behave when they are attached to a drawing, based on their color and linetype settings:

◆ **BYLAYER.** The objects assume the color and linetype characteristics of the destination drawing's layer 0.

◆ **BYBLOCK.** The objects assume the color and linetype characteristics that are current at the time the xref is attached.

◆ **EXPLICIT.** The objects retain their original explicit color and linetype settings.

Because an xref's layers do not merge with the destination drawing's layers (except layer 0), you can simply create the xref's objects on any layer other than 0 to make layers, colors, and linetypes remain as they are in the original.

If you want the xref to temporarily assume different characteristics in the destination drawing, you can change the settings of the xref's layers in the destination drawing. For example, you can change the color of layer DOOR28|OBJECT. Unless the VISRETAIN system variable is 1 (on), however, these changes do not survive from one drawing session to another. When the drawing is reloaded, the xref layers revert to the original settings of the drawing they reference. To permanently make the xref objects assume the properties of their destination drawing, create the xref's objects on layer 0 with properties BYLAYER or BYBLOCK, or set VISRETAIN to 1.

Exporting Blocks and Drawing Data with WBLOCK

Often you may create blocks in the current drawing that you later want to use in other drawings. You need not redraw them as separate drawing files; you can use the WBLOCK command to export them. The WBLOCK command creates a drawing file from the drawing data you export with it. If the file already exists, WBLOCK offers to replace it. You can export a block defined in the current drawing, or selected objects, or the entire current drawing. The WBLOCK command does *not* create a new block, either in the current drawing or in the drawing file it creates, but the file it creates can be inserted as a block or attached as an xref in any drawing.

In the following exercise, you export an existing block with WBLOCK.

Exporting the NUT10 Block with WBLOCK

Continue from either of the two previous exercises, with the layer settings and HEAD block restored, the NUT10 block exploded, and snap on.

Erase any slots left from the BYBLOCK exercise, and zoom to the view shown in the background of figure 19.9.

Click on the Current Color (DDEMODES) button, which opens the Entity Creation Modes dialog box. Set color to BYLAYER, layer to 0, and linetype to BYLAYER, and close the dialog box.

`Command:` *Choose* **F**ile, **I**mport/Export, **B**lock Out	Issues WBLOCK command and opens Create Drawing File dialog box
`_wblock`	
Enter **HEAD10** *in the* File **N**ame *input box, then choose* OK	Specifies file name to create and prompts for the block name
`Block name:` **HEAD** (Enter)	Creates the HEAD10 drawing file, duplicating the contents of the HEAD block definition

The current drawing directory now contains a new drawing file named HEAD10. This new file contains all of the objects defined in the current drawing's HEAD block. It also contains all named items, such as nested blocks, dimension or text styles, layers, and linetypes, which are referenced by objects in the HEAD block definition. It does not contain definitions of any named items that are irrelevant to the exported data. This new drawing file is now available for importing in other drawings as a block or attaching as an xref.

Figure 19.9

Using WBLOCK to export from the INSMECH drawing.

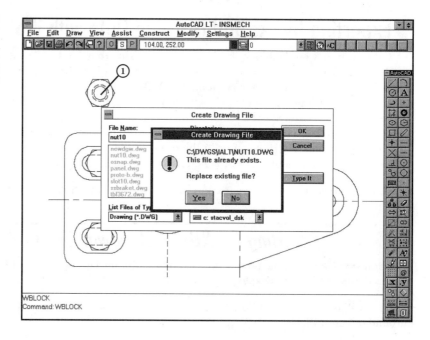

WBLOCK. The WBLOCK command creates a new drawing file or replaces an existing one with the data you select from the current drawing. As data to export, you can specify a block name defined in the current drawing, or press Enter and specify an insertion base point and select objects to export, or enter * to export the entire current drawing. Selected objects are erased upon completion. The WBLOCK command does *not* create a new block, either in the current drawing or in the drawing file it creates. The 0,0 base point of the new file is the insertion base point of the specified block, or the point specified at the Insertion base point: prompt for selected objects, or the 0,0 point of the current UCS if you enter * to export the entire drawing. Settings such as units, limits, snap, and grid are also exported.

Tip If you specify a drawing file name to create, then enter an equal sign at the Block name: prompt, WBLOCK searches the current drawing for a block definition whose name matches the file name specified.

In the following exercise, you export a selected set of objects with WBLOCK, and then export the entire current drawing.

Exporting Selected Objects and an Entire Drawing with WBLOCK

Continue from the preceding exercise.

Command: `Enter`	Repeats WBLOCK and dialog box
Enter **NUT10** *in the* File **N**ame *input box, then choose* OK	Specifies file name to create and displays warning dialog box (refer to fig. 19.9)
Choose **Y**es	Closes warning dialog box and prompts for the block name
`Block name:` `Enter`	Prompts base point for objects instead of using an existing block definition
`Insertion base point:` *Pick* ① *(see fig. 19.9)*	Sets insertion base point
`Select objects:` *Select all exploded nut objects at* ①, *then press Enter*	Replaces the NUT10 drawing, using the selected objects, and deletes the objects
`Command:` **W** `Enter`	Issues WBLOCK command and opens dialog box
Enter **MECHPART** *in the* File **N**ame *input box, then choose* OK	Specifies file name to create and prompts for the block name
`Block name:` ***** `Enter`	Creates the MECHPART drawing, using the entire contents of the current drawing, but does not delete any objects

The current drawing directory now contains an updated NUT10 drawing file and a new drawing files, named MECHPART. This new file contains all of the objects defined in the current drawing including all named items, such as nested blocks, dimension or text styles, layers, and linetypes, which are currently in use. It does not contain definitions of any named items that are not currently in use. This new drawing file is now available for importing in other drawings as a block or attaching as an xref.

 Tip   You can use U (undo) or OOPS to restore the objects deleted by WBLOCK. Undo will not undo the file creation, just the deletion.

You can do the following as a substitute for the PURGE command: use WBLOCK with an asterisk, specifying the same file name as the current drawing, and then reopen the file without saving the current drawing. (See Chapter 10, "Getting Organized: Drawing on Layers," and the last section of this chapter for more on the PURGE command.) The PURGE command is selective, but WBLOCK purges all unused named items from the file it creates. Use WBLOCK with caution, or you might purge items you did not intend to purge.

 Note Use the UCS command or BASE command (see the next section) to reset the base point before using WBLOCK with an asterisk to export an entire drawing.

 Tip You can use WBLOCK to export the definitions of named items, such as blocks, dimension or text styles, layers, and linetypes, to a new drawing file by exporting blocks or objects that use these named items. You can then import those named item definitions into other drawings by using INSERT to insert the new drawing file, canceling the insertion at the `Insertion point:` prompt. You can later purge the block definition this creates, as well as any unneeded named items.

 Note Users often refer to "a wblock." There is no such thing as a wblock. The WBLOCK command does not create a new block, either in the current drawing or in the drawing file it creates. All WBLOCK does is create a new drawing file (or replace an existing one). The confusion probably stems from the fact that the drawing file created can then be inserted as a block.

The process of creating a drawing with WBLOCK exports current settings. However, when you insert the resulting drawing into another, it does not import any setting—just objects and named items referenced by objects. This prevents insertions from changing current drawing settings. You can observe this in the following Base Point exercise.

The 0,0 base point in the MECHPART drawing you created with WBLOCK is the 0,0 point of the current UCS, which may not be the point you desire. If you didn't plan ahead and reset it with UCS or BASE, you can reset it in the new drawing with the UCS or BASE command.

Setting the Insertion Base Point

WBLOCK exports and blocks are imported relative to the base point in the current UCS. The default base point is 0,0,0. You can use the BASE command to reset the base point without affecting the 0,0 of the UCS. See Chapter 2, "Specifying Locations in CAD Space," for the use of UCS, and the following for the use of the BASE command.

In the following exercise, you will change the base point in the MECHPART drawing you just created, then insert it in a new drawing. You can also observe the

import/export behavior of setting and named items. If you did not perform the preceding exercise, you can begin a new drawing named MECHPART using the ALT1902.DWG file as a prototype.

Setting the Insertion Base Point with the BASE Command

Open the MECHPART drawing you created in the preceding exercise. You can discard the current drawing.

Use ZOOM All to zoom to the view shown in figure 19.10.

Examine the layers and settings to see that they were exported by the previous WBLOCK command.

Command: *Choose* **S**ettings, Dra**w**ing, *then* **B**ase	Issues BASE command
Base point <0.00, 0.00, 0.00>: *Pick point* ① *(see fig. 19.10)*	Resets the base point for insertions in other drawings
Command: *Click on the Save button*	Saves the new base point

Begin a new drawing again named INSMECH (replacing the previous INSMECH file), using the ACLTISO metric prototype drawing from the ACLTWIN directory, and using no setup method.

Use INSERT to insert the drawing named MECHPART, dragging it around (see fig. 19.11) to observe the insertion base point before entering point **200,75**, scale **1**, and rotation **0**.

Examine the layers and settings to see that named items but not settings were imported by INSERT.

Command: *Click on the Save button*	Saves for the next exercise

The new base point you set became the drag point for the insertion.

When you reset the UCS, the base point is adjusted so as to remain in the same place relative the drawing.

> **BASE.** The BASE command resets the base point in the current UCS. The base point is used as the insert base point when the drawing is inserted in or attached to other drawings.

Figure 19.10

Resetting the base point.

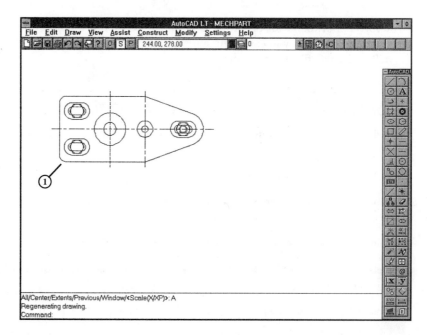

Figure 19.11

Dragging the MECHPART insertion by its new base point.

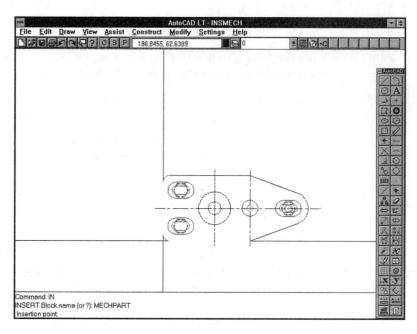

Note The base point affects how the STRETCH command treats blocks, including hatch patterns, which are anonymous blocks. If the base point is not within the crossing window or polygon used to select objects in STRETCH, the block or hatch will be ignored and not moved because visible parts ignored by the crossing window or polygon. This often causes a problem by ignoring hatches when you are stretching the lines bounding them. The base points of hatches are always placed at the WCS origin, regardless of the current UCS. The solution is to move the hatch objects after stretching, as you did in the previous chapter when updating xrefs. You can find the insertion point by picking the block or hatch at the Command: prompt and looking for the grip that appears there.

Editing, Grips, and Blocks

Edit processes involving a whole block are just like editing any other object, except that the block normally has only one grip point to use in grip editing. This is the insertion point grip. The grips of the objects internal to the block are suppressed by default to avoid clutter. Sometimes, however, you want to edit relative to other grip points.

For example, in the following exercise, you will rotate the MECHPART block by the center of a circle within the block. To do so, you must turn on grips in blocks. You can turn on grips in blocks with the Grips Style dialog box (or the GRIPBLOCK system variable).

Rotating a Block about an Internal Grip

Continue from the preceding exercise.

Command: *Pick the block*	Highlights the block and displays a grip at the insertion point
Command: *Choose **S**ettings, **G**rips Style*	Opens Grips dialog box (see fig. 19.12)
Put a check in the Enable Grips Within **B**locks *check box, then choose* OK	Sets internal grips to display in blocks
Command: *Pick the block*	Highlights the block and displays numerous grips
Command: *Pick the center grip at* ① *(see fig. 19.13)*	Makes center grip of circle hot and enters Stretch mode

continues

continued

```
** STRETCH **                          Cycles to Rotate mode
<Stretch to point>/Base point/Copy/
Undo/eXit: Press Enter twice
```

```
** ROTATE **                           Rotates the block 90 degrees and exits grip
<Rotation angle>/Base point/Copy/Undo/   editing
Reference/eXit: Pick the grip at ②
```

Command: *Click on the Cancel button, then on*   Clears selection and grips, cleans up screen,
the Redraw button or tool, then on the Save button   and saves

---

Figure 19.12

Turning on internal grips in blocks in the Grips dialog box.

Figure 19.13

Rotating a block with internal grips.

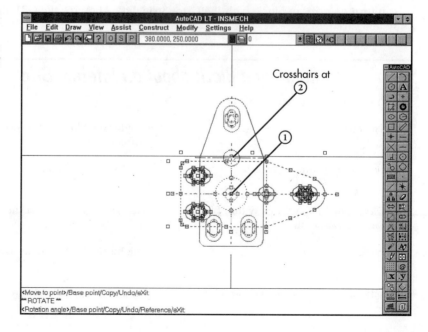

With internal grips on, grip editing blocks is just like grip editing other objects, except that you can only manipulate the block as a whole.

If you think back, you may have noticed that some of the internal objects of the MECHPART block were themselves blocks, nested in the MECHPART block. If you use the ? option of the BLOCK or INSERT commands, you will find that the HEAD and NUT10 blocks are defined in the drawing, as well as the MECHPART block.

Nesting Blocks in Blocks and Xrefs

Blocks and xrefs can contain any type of object, even other blocks and xrefs. And those blocks and xrefs can contain other blocks and xrefs, and so on. This arrangement is called *nesting*, and blocks and xrefs can be nested as deeply as you want. You can even redefine a nested block without exploding the block that contains it. The only restriction of nesting is that you cannot create a *circular block reference*, which means a block that, somewhere in the nesting, references itself.

You created a nested block by inserting a drawing containing blocks. The MECHPART drawing contained line, arc, polyline, and circle objects, and the HEAD and NUT10 blocks. When you inserted it into the current INSMECH drawing, you created the MECHPART block. The MECHPART block contains all of the MECHPART drawing's objects including the HEAD and NUT10 blocks, which are nested in the MECHPART block.

In the following exercise, you will check the current block status, then redefine a block that is nested in the MECHPART block, creating a nested block in a nested block. Then you will explode the outer block of the nest, the MECHPART block.

Examining Nested Blocks

Continue from the preceding exercise, with the MECHPART block inserted and zoom into the view shown in figure 19.14. Turn snap on.

Use the BLOCK or INSERT ? option with an asterisk wild card to list all blocks. It lists HEAD, MECHPART, and NUT10. Press F2 to return to the drawing window.

Command: *Pick one of the HEAD blocks*   Selects and highlights the entire MECHPART block, in which the HEAD block is nested

Create a hexagonal washer bolt head by drawing a 10 mm radius circle at ① (see fig. 19.14) and inserting the HEAD10 drawing as a block at ①.

Command: *Select the new washer circle   Issues the BLOCK command with the
and HEAD10 block, then enter* **B**   objects selected

continues

continued

`Command: B/` `BLOCK Block name (or ?): HEAD `**Enter**	Specifies block name
`Block HEAD already exists.` `Redefine it? <N> Y `**Enter**	Confirms redefinition
`Insertion base point: `*Pick center of circle*	

`2 found`
`Block HEAD redefined`
`Regenerating drawing.`
	Accepts preselected objects and redefines existing head block as a nested block containing the HEAD10 block

The two HEAD blocks nested in the MECHPART block are updated and redrawn. The HEAD10 blocks are now nested in the HEAD blocks, which are nested in the MECHPART block.

`Command: `*Pick the MECHPART block, then type* **X** *and press Enter*	Issues the EXPLODE command and explodes the MECHPART block

The NUT10 and newly redefined HEAD blocks are now unnested and can be selected.

`Command: `*Pick one of the HEAD blocks*	Selects only the newly redefined nested HEAD block
`Command: `*Click on the Save button*	Saves for next exercise

When you explode a nested block, only the outermost block is exploded. To explode a nested block, you must explode the outer block(s), then the nested block. To explode a deeply nested block requires repetitive EXPLODE commands.

Note   Because objects within blocks cannot be edited unless exploded, deeply nested blocks make drawing management difficult and the use of BYLAYER or BYBLOCK properties essential for flexibility.

The INSMECH still contains the MECHPART block definition, but no insertions of it. When you exploded the MECHPART drawing, the image of the block definition's objects were replaced with actual copies of the objects. Now these objects exist twice, in the exploded block and in the block definition. Leaving unused block definitions in a drawing unnecessarily increases the drawing file size and load time. The way to remove them is to use the PURGE command.

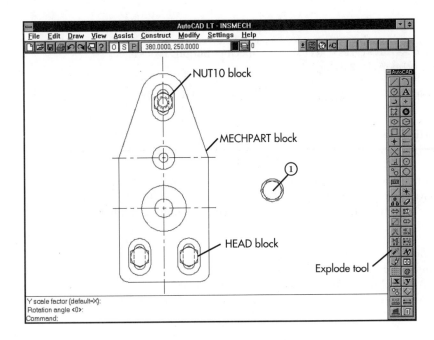

Figure 19.14

Defining a nested block that redefines another nested block.

Purging Unused Blocks

The PURGE command (see Chapter 10, "Getting Organized: Drawing on Layers") is used to remove unused block definitions from a drawing. The INSMECH still contains the now unused MECHPART block definition, which you will purge in the following exercise. First you must reload the drawing because, although PURGE can be used after a SAVE, it won't recognize that the MECHPART block is no longer referenced until after you reload the drawing.

Deleting Unused Blocks with PURGE

Continue from the preceding exercise, with the MECHPART block exploded.

Use the OPEN command to reopen the INSMECH drawing.

Command: **PR** (Enter)   Issues the PURGE command

PURGE

continues

continued

```
Purge unused Blocks/Dimstyles/LAyers/          Specifies purging blocks
LTypes/SHapes/STyles/All: B Enter

Purge block MECHPART? <N> Y Enter          Purges MECHPART block
```

Use the BLOCK or INSERT Command ? option and enter an asterisk to list all defined blocks and verify MECHPART's deletion.

The limitation of the PURGE command is that it cannot purge blocks, dimension or text styles, layers, ltypes, or shapes that are referenced or used by any objects, blocks, dimension or text styles, layers, ltypes, or shapes. For example, if you have the following situation:

An unused block containing
    An unused nested block containing
        A text object with an otherwise unused text style
        And an object on an otherwise unused layer that is set to
            An unused linetype...

You have to repeatedly reopen, save, and purge the drawing to eliminate all of these unused items. The first purge cycle can purge the outer block, the second can purge the nested block, the third can purge the text style and layer, and the fourth can purge the linetype.

With the previous chapter's tools and techniques of creating and using blocks and xrefs, and this chapter's insights into block organization, structure and management, you've moved your AutoCAD LT skills and productivity to supersonic levels, with highly effective and efficient ways to manage and quickly produce the repetitive elements in your drawing. The next chapter presents similarly powerful CAD tools that help you measure your progress in your flight through AutoCAD LT: the automatic dimensioning tools.

Applying Dimensions in CAD

Dimensions are required on most types of mechanical and architectural drawings to completely convey the message of the drawing. In this chapter, you learn to use the AutoCAD LT dimensioning commands to generate accurate dimensions from a drawing. In most cases, the dimensions are automatically generated with little effort on your part. Occasionally, however, you must use special techniques in applying dimensions to meet your technical requirements. This chapter teaches you how to perform the following operations:

◆ Dimensioning linear distances, diameters, radii, and angles by picking points or selecting objects

◆ Dimensioning successive linear distances with baseline or ordinate (datum) dimensions or with continuous strings of dimensions

◆ Drawing center marks and leader lines with text notes

◆ Using associative dimensions to update measurements automatically when associated objects are edited

The first dimensioning exercises might seem surprisingly simple, but they will build your confidence and show you how easy dimensioning can be with CAD. This chapter focuses on dimension placement tools and techniques, and the next chapter shows how to control dimension appearance and edit dimensions to get the exact results you need. The dimension variables and dimension styles in the next chapter might appear rather challenging, especially if you are new to CAD dimensioning. Fortunately, after you learn to dimension your specific types of drawings, you do not need to fully comprehend all the dimensioning features AutoCAD LT makes available to you.

The geometry of a design is only a small part of an AutoCAD LT drawing. After you draw the object, you usually add notes, symbols, and dimensions to the drawing. In Chapters 4, 13, and 15, you learned many of the techniques for adding text to a drawing. In this chapter, you learn to use the AutoCAD LT dimensioning tools to add dimensions like those shown in figure 20.1. This procedure is done in the AutoCAD LT dimensioning mode, which has its own collection of commands.

Figure 20.1

Dimensions on a mechanical drawing.

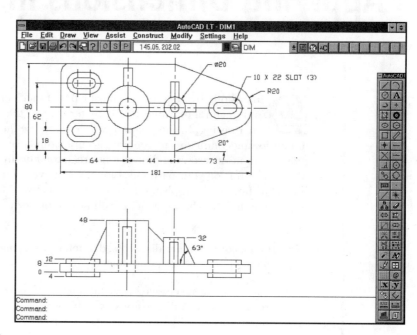

Note This chapter uses a mechanical example for dimensioning. Architectural dimensioning requires adjustment of dimension variables and styles. The particular type of drafting example and your particular dimensioning standards are not important to learning the dimensioning concepts and the dimension placement

commands and techniques. The adjustment of dimension variables and styles is explained in the next chapter, using both mechanical and architectural examples to meet common dimensioning standards.

Understanding Dimensioning Concepts

CAD dimensioning will be successful only if the drawing has been created accurately. Chapter 11, "Achieving Accuracy: The Geometric Power of CAD," emphasized the importance of drawing accurately. Proper use of coordinates and of the object snap tools ensures an accurate drawing. Commands such as DISTANCE and ID are used to query the coordinates of the objects. AutoCAD LT calculates dimensions exactly from the drawing objects; therefore, accurate geometry produces accurate dimensions.

In training industrial CAD users, we have observed that many of them have not had formal training in proper dimensioning techniques. If you cannot properly dimension drawings manually, don't expect that CAD dimensioning will produce professional results. Many different disciplines use a wide variety of dimensioning standards. You should take some time to learn the proper dimensioning standards for your type of work.

Note Publications such as *ANSI Y14.5* provide detailed instructions and examples for mechanical dimensioning standards. Other dimensioning standards for architectural or engineering applications are published in appropriate technical drafting books.

Identifying the Components of a Dimension

AutoCAD LT dimensions are composite objects that consist of lines, arcs, and text. Like blocks, you select dimensions as single objects unless they have been exploded into separate objects.

Dimensions are located by definition points. Although you must specify these points, AutoCAD LT maintains them for future use if the dimension is modified. *Extension lines* extend away from the definition points, and therefore, away from the geometry. Extension lines are sometimes referred to as *witness* lines. A *dimension line* drawn between witness lines indicates the direction in which the dimension measures a distance, an angle, or a location. A dimension line is terminated on both ends with an arrowhead, tick mark, or other symbol. *Dimension text,* positioned near or embedded in the dimension line, indicates the size of the dimension, along with optional prefixes and suffixes. Figure 20.2 identifies these components on a typical dimension.

Figure 20.2

*Components
of a typical
dimension.*

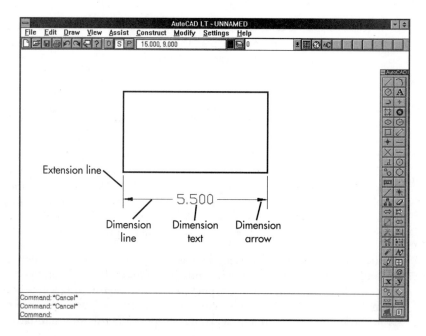

Harnessing the Associative Power of Dimensions

Perhaps you have noticed a special note on CAD drawings specifying "No Manual Changes." With manual drawings, engineering changes were often accomplished simply by changing the value of a dimension rather than redrawing and redimensioning the geometry. The associative features of CAD dimensions allow the value of the dimension to change automatically as the object is moved or resized. In CAD, you should not simply edit the dimension value without changing the objects associated with that dimension. Doing so results in an inaccurate drawing, possibly causing inaccurate dimensions to later be generated. In the next chapter, you learn to change the associative properties of dimensions, and you see the results on your drawing.

Controlling Dimension Features with Dimension Variables

Dimension variables control the appearance of dimensions created with AutoCAD LT. By using dimension variables, you can tailor dimensions to meet any drafting standard or personal preference. Dimension variables are part of the many system variables that control AutoCAD LT.

Note   Appendix E, "Dimension Variables," provides a complete list of the AutoCAD LT dimension variables, including a brief description of the function of each variable. All the system variables beginning with DIM are referred to as dimension variables.

In earlier chapters, you learned to set system variables that controlled features such as units, limits, text appearance, and other common settings. Figure 20.3 illustrates how the same dimensioning command produces different results based on the current dimension variable settings.

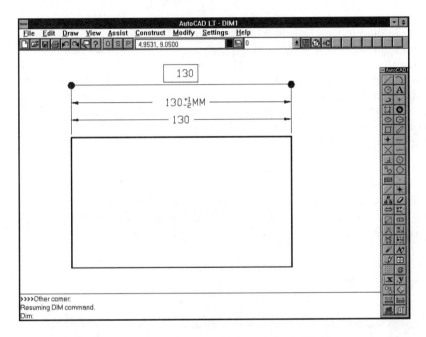

Figure 20.3

The same dimension created with different dimension variables.

20

The first dimensioning exercises in this chapter use the dimension variable settings that have been saved with the ALT2001.DWG drawing file. In the next chapter, you change the dimension variables to obtain the desired results.

Dimensioning Your Drawing

Before you explore the individual dimensioning commands, you should become familiar with the overall structure of the dimensioning commands in AutoCAD LT. Depending on your preferences, you can execute the dimensioning commands by using the **D**raw pull-down menu or by typing the commands.

Figure 20.4 shows the five basic types of dimensions at the bottom of the **D**raw menu. The submenu for L**i**near Dimensions is also shown. Ord**i**nate Dimensions and Radial Di**m**ensions also have submenus.

Figure 20.4

The dimension choices from the Draw pull-down menu.

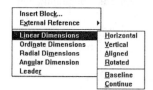

Remember one of the fundamental rules of using AutoCAD LT: Watch the command line to see what information the software is requesting. You can execute a new command when the prompt reads Command:. The dimensioning commands, however, do not function at this prompt; instead, you must first enter dimensioning mode by entering **DIM**. When the Command: prompt changes to the Dim: prompt, you can enter a dimensioning command. You remain in dimensioning mode and the Dim: prompt continues to display on the command line until you exit dimensioning mode. To exit dimensioning mode, enter **EXIT**, or **E**, or press Ctrl+C at the Dim: prompt.

Note   The dimensioning commands on the **D**raw pull-down menu use the DIM1 command to automatically enter dimensioning mode, then issue a dimensioning command. The DIM1 command automatically exits dimensioning mode after one dimensioning command is used.

You can abbreviate dimensioning commands by entering the least number of characters unique to a command.

Tip   Although you can abbreviate some dimensioning commands to one or two characters, they are easier to remember if you use three-character abbreviations, which works for all dimensioning commands.

Issuing the Dimensioning Commands

Many of the dimensioning commands share common prompts and options. After you understand what action AutoCAD LT expects at each prompt, you will be able to use any one of the dimensioning commands as easily as another.

In the following exercise, you use the HORIZONTAL dimensioning command, which is explained in detail after the exercise. Explanations of the HORIZONTAL command prompts also follow the exercise.

Exploring Common Dimension Prompts

Create a new drawing named DIM1, using the ALT2001.DWG file as a prototype, and using no setup method. Zoom to the view shown in figure 20.5.

Command: **DIM** (Enter)	Enters dimensioning mode
Dim: **HOR** (Enter)	Specifies a horizontal dimension
First extension line origin or RETURN to select: *Use an INTersection* *object snap to pick* ① *(see fig. 20.5)*	Locates first point
Second extension line origin: *Use an INTersection object snap to pick* ②	Locates second point
Dimension line location (Text/ Angle): *Pick near* ③	Places the dimension line
Dimension text <181>: (Enter)	Accepts the default text for this dimension
Dim: **EXIT** (Enter)	Exits dimensioning mode and returns to Command: prompt
Command: *Choose* **D**raw, **L**inear Dimensions, **H**orizontal	Issues the DIM1 and HORIZONTAL dimen- sion commands
_dim1 Dim:_horizontal	
First extension line origin or RETURN to select: (Enter)	Enters object-selection mode
Select line, arc, or circle: *Turn* *snap off, then pick line at* ④	
Dimension line location (Text/ Angle): *Turn snap on, then pick point* ⑤	
Dimension text <40>: (Enter)	Accepts the default text for this dimension
Command: **U** (Enter)	Undoes the last dimension
Command: **U** (Enter)	Undoes the first dimension

20

Figure 20.5

Two horizontal dimensions added to the DIM1 drawing.

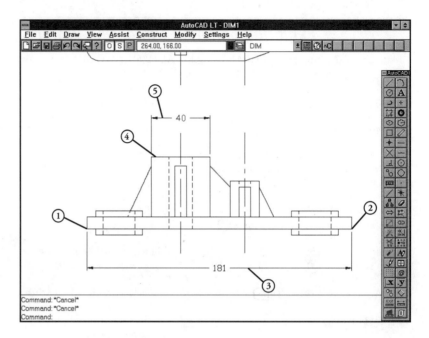

 Tip

Unfortunately, most dimensioning commands require three clicks to select them from the **D**raw menu. Fortunately, Windows provides a more efficient press-and-drag method of selecting menu items, which enables you to select any menu item with a single dragged click. For example, you can select the **H**orizontal dimensioning item by pressing the pick button on **D**raw, holding down the button, and dragging to **L**inear Dimensions, which pops up the submenu, and dragging to **H**orizontal, then releasing the button. With a little practice, you can do this quickly and efficiently.

When you do dimensioning from the **D**raw pull-down menu, dimensioning mode is entered automatically. When the dimension is completed, you are back at the Command: prompt.

 Note

The DIM1 command enters dimensioning mode to execute a dimensioning command but exits back to the Command: prompt when the dimension is complete. The effect is similar to that of issuing dimensioning commands from the **D**raw pull-down menu.

Responding to the Dimension Prompts

The following list explains each of the dimensioning command prompts and describes the possible actions AutoCAD LT expects.

◆ First extension line origin or RETURN to select: You can use one of two methods to dimension: either select points to define the dimension (the default), or press Enter to select an object to dimension. If you pick a point in response to this prompt, AutoCAD LT uses it as the first point for the dimension—the point you are dimensioning *from*.

◆ Second extension line origin: If you pick a point in response to the First extension line origin or RETURN to select: prompt, AutoCAD LT asks for the point to dimension *to*.

 Stop When you pick dimension points, always use object snaps so that you create accurate dimensions.

◆ Select line, arc, or circle: If you press Enter at the First extension line origin or RETURN to select: prompt, AutoCAD LT asks you to select an object, which it then uses to determine the dimension points. You can select polyline segments as well as line, arc, and circle objects. A wide polyline is dimensioned from its center line.

◆ Dimension line location (Text/Angle): At this prompt, you specify a point through which you want the dimension line to pass. Use an appropriate snap value for neat and regular placement and spacing.

◆ Dimension text <default>: AutoCAD LT calculates the exact dimension for the object or points you specify and offers the calculated value as a default. You can enter a different dimension text string, or you can press Enter to use the calculated default value for the dimension. If you want blank dimension text, press the space bar and then press Enter.

You also can precede or follow the calculated default dimension value with a notation or with other text. By entering a pair of less-than (<) and greater-than (>) symbols, you can indicate the location of the calculated text, preceded and/or followed by the text to add. As an example, to get This is 2.50 the added text., you enter:

Dimension text <2.50>: **This is <> the added text.**

In the preceding exercise, you exited the DIM command by entering **EXIT**. You also can use Ctrl+C; there is essentially no difference in the effects of using EXIT or Ctrl+C at the Dim: prompt.

Dim: **EXIT.** The EXIT dimensioning command leaves dimensioning mode and returns you to the Command: prompt.

With this background on dimensioning mode and its prompts, you can begin to dimension your DIM1 drawing.

Using Linear Dimensioning Commands

Linear dimensions are the most common type of dimension found on a drawing. AutoCAD LT provides six options for linear dimensioning. These options are all similar in the manner in which they are executed. Figure 20.6 shows the various applications of these six types of linear dimensions.

Figure 20.6

Six types of linear dimensions.

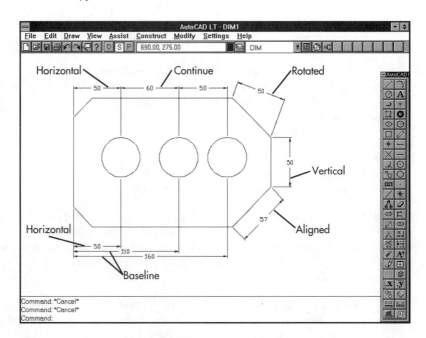

Horizontal and Vertical Dimensions

Horizontal and vertical dimensions are the most frequently used and the most basic types of dimensions; they are the cornerstone of dimensioning. In AutoCAD LT, horizontal and vertical dimensions operate very similarly. Take a closer look at the HORIZONTAL command you used earlier.

> Dim: **HORIZONTAL.** The HORIZONTAL dimensioning command draws a horizontal dimension line. You can pick the first and second extension-line origins, or you can press Enter to select an object to dimension.

If you select a circle, its diameter is dimensioned using the 0- and 180-degree quadrant points as the extension-line endpoints. If you select other objects, the horizontal projection of their endpoints is dimensioned.

In the following exercise, you dimension the mount plate's overall width with a horizontal dimension. You use the DIM1 command this time to execute only a single dimensioning command. You also use object snaps for precision.

Placing Horizontal Dimensions

Continue from the preceding exercise with the mount plate drawing named DIM1.

Command: *Choose* **D**raw, L**i**near Dimensions, **H**orizontal	Issues the dim1 and HORIZONTAL dimension commands
`_dim1` `Dim:_horizontal`	
`First extension line origin or` `RETURN to select:` **ENDP** (Enter)	
of *Pick point* ① *(see fig. 20.7)*	Locates first point
`Second extension line origin:` **QUAD** (Enter)	
of *Pick point* ②	Locates second point
`Dimension line location (Text/` `Angle):` *Pick point* ③	Places the dimension line
`Dimension text <181>:` (Enter)	Accepts the default text for this dimension, draws the dimension, and returns to the `Command:` prompt

Figure 20.7

A horizontal dimension.

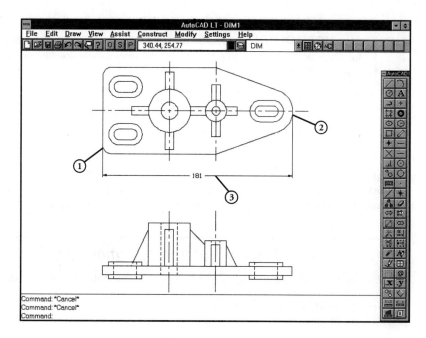

Although this dimension might not appear exactly the way your dimensioning standards dictate, in the next chapter you learn to control its appearance. You can change many characteristics of a dimension's appearance, including text style, spacing between the dimension and the object, the number of decimal places, or the unit type AutoCAD LT uses to measure (decimal, architectural, fractions, and so on).

You place a vertical linear dimension in exactly the same way as you place a horizontal one. The only difference between horizontal and vertical dimensioning is the dimension's orientation.

If you select a circle, its diameter is dimensioned using the 90- and 270-degree quadrant points. If you select other objects, the vertical projection of their endpoints is dimensioned.

In the following exercise, you dimension the mount plate's overall height with a vertical dimension.

Placing a Vertical Dimension

Continue from the preceding exercise, using the DIM1 drawing. Turn Snap off.

Command: *Choose* **D**raw, L**i**near
Dimensions, **V**ertical

```
_dim1
Dim: _vertical

First extension line origin or
RETURN to select: ENDP (Enter)
```

of *Pick point* ① *(see fig. 20.8)*   Locates first point

```
Second extension line origin:
ENDP (Enter)
```

of *Pick point* ②   Locates second point

```
Dimension line location (Text/
Angle): Pick point ③
```
Places the dimension line

```
Dimension text <80>: (Enter)
```
Accepts the default text

Save the drawing

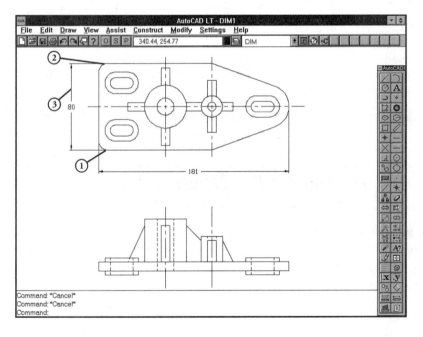

Figure 20.8

*A vertical
dimension.*

In the preceding exercise, you saw that the steps for placing a vertical dimension are
almost identical to the steps for placing horizontal dimensions. The default orientation for dimension text is horizontal, regardless of the dimension's orientation. As
you learn in the next chapter, you also can set the text orientation to align with the
dimension line.

Stop If you inadvertently enter the VERTICAL dimensioning command and then enter the points for a horizontal dimension, AutoCAD LT draws the vertical dimension. The result is a zero-length dimension if the points are aligned vertically. When the resulting dimension surprises you, double-check the dimensioning command you used.

Dim: **VERTICAL.** The VERTICAL dimensioning command draws a vertical dimension line. You can pick the first and second extension-line origins, or you can press Enter to select an object to dimension.

Dimensioning a Series with the BASELINE and CONTINUE Commands

Frequently, you need to dimension a series of features. To avoid repeatedly specifying the original or previous extension-line origin, you can use the BASELINE or the CONTINUE dimensioning command.

The BASELINE command draws baseline dimensions, or dimension stacks. *Baseline dimensions* are multiple dimensions, all beginning at the same start point, the baseline. First you create or select a linear dimension, and then you use BASELINE to add other dimensions that use the same first extension-line origin. Each dimension in the stack is a separate dimension object.

In the following exercise, you place several baseline dimensions along the side of the mount plate.

Creating Baseline Dimensions

Continue from the preceding exercise. Begin by erasing the vertical 80 mm dimension.

Command: *Choose* **D**raw, L**i**near
Dimensions, **V**ertical

First extension line origin or
RETURN to select: **ENDP** (Enter)

of *Pick point* ① *(see fig. 20.9)*   Locates first point

Second extension line origin:
QUAD (Enter)

of *Pick point* ②   Locates second point

Dimension line location (Text/   Places the dimension line
Angle): *Pick point* ③

Dimension text <18>: `Enter`   Accepts the default text

Command: *Choose* **D**raw, **Li**near
Dimensions, **B**aseline

_dim1
Dim: _baseline

Second extension line origin or
RETURN to select: **QUAD** `Enter`

of *Pick point* ④

Dimension text <62>: `Enter`   Accepts the default text

Command: *Choose* **D**raw, **Li**near
Dimensions, **B**aseline

Second extension line origin or
RETURN to select: **ENDP** `Enter`

of *Pick point* ⑤

Dimension text <80>: `Enter`   Accepts the default text

Save the drawing

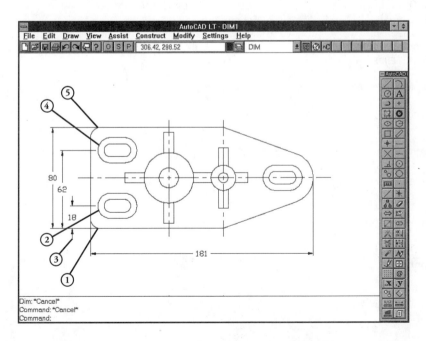

Figure 20.9

*Baseline
dimensions.*

> Dim: **BASELINE.** The BASELINE dimensioning command calculates and draws a dimension in a series from a single first extension-line origin. Create or select any linear dimension, and then use BASELINE to dimension successive distances. You enter only the second extension-line origin point for each successive dimension.
>
> Each dimension is offset from and parallel to the previous or the selected dimension and shares the same first extension-line origin.

The CONTINUE dimensioning command works in much the same way as the BASELINE dimensioning command. CONTINUE draws *chained dimensions*, or dimension strings, rather than baseline dimensions. Each new chained dimension starts at the second extension line of the previous or selected linear dimension. The dimension lines are aligned.

In the following exercise, you dimension some features near the bottom of the mount plate by using consecutive (chained) dimensions.

Placing Chained Dimensions

Continue from the preceding exercise, using the drawing named DIM1.

Command: *Choose* **D**raw, **L**inear Dimensions, **H**orizontal   Issues the Dim: HORIZONTAL command

First extension line origin or RETURN to select: **ENDP** (Enter)

of *Pick point* ① *(see fig. 20.10)*   Locates first point

Second extension line origin: **ENDP** (Enter)

of *Pick point* ②   Locates second point

Dimension line location (Text/ Angle): *Pick point* ③   Places the dimension line

Dimension text <64>: (Enter)   Accepts the default text

Command: *Choose* **D**raw, **L**inear Dimensions, **C**ontinue

_dim1
Dim: _continue

```
Second extension line origin or
RETURN to select: ENDP (Enter)
```

of *Pick point* ④

```
Dimension text <44>: (Enter)
```
Accepts the default text

```
Command: Choose Draw, Linear
Dimensions, Continue
```

```
_dim1
Dim: _continue
```

```
Second extension line origin or
RETURN to select: QUAD (Enter)
```

of *Pick point* ⑤

```
Dimension text <73>: (Enter)
```
Accepts the default text

Save the drawing

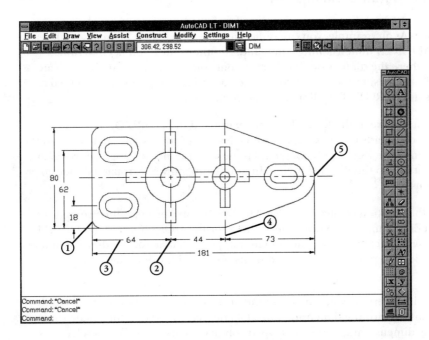

Figure 20.10

Continuous dimensions.

Tip

Because CONTINUE aligns the consecutive dimensions and BASELINE places the dimensions at a uniform spacing, these two commands can produce quite professional-looking dimensions.

`Dim:` **CONTINUE.** The CONTINUE dimensioning command dimensions multiple distances, each measured from the previous or selected second extension-line origin. You create or select any linear dimension, and then you use CONTINUE to dimension successive distances. AutoCAD LT aligns each dimension with the previous or selected linear dimension and uses its second extension line as the new first extension line. You enter only the second extension-line origin point for each successive dimension.

The CONTINUE and BASELINE commands align the dimensions to any angle established by the previous or selected dimension. The next two types of linear dimensions discussed are not restricted to horizontal or vertical dimension lines.

Aligned and Rotated Dimensions

At times, you need to draw a dimension parallel to the line of the points being dimensioned. As an example, you can dimension the true length of an angled line using the ALIGNED dimensioning command. At other times, you need to draw a dimension where the dimension line is set to some other reference angle. You can, for example, dimension the projected distance between two points at a specified angle by using the ROTATED dimensioning command.

The difference between the ROTATED command and the HORIZONTAL and VERTICAL commands is that ROTATED enables you to specify any angle to align the dimension line. The ROTATED command is useful for dimensioning features at an angle not parallel to the dimension line. In most cases, however, rotated dimensions are seldom used.

Except for the addition of the `Dimension line angle <0>:` prompt, the prompts for the ROTATED command are the same as those for the HORIZONTAL and VERTI-CAL dimensioning commands. You can enter a specific angle for the dimension line, or you can pick two points to align the dimension line with other objects in the drawing.

In the following exercise, you dimension the projected distance between the edges of the two bosses, with the dimension line at 45 degrees. To set up for a later Undo exercise, use dimensioning mode and typed commands instead of menu selections.

Placing a Rotated Dimension

Continue from the preceding exercise, using the DIM1 drawing. Pan to the view shown in figure 20.11.

Command: **DIM** (Enter)	Enters dimensioning mode
Dim: **ROT** (Enter)	Specifies a rotated dimension
Dimension line angle <0>: **45** (Enter)	Sets the dimension line's angle
First extension line origin or RETURN to select: **ENDP** (Enter)	
of *Pick point* ① *(see fig. 20.11)*	Locates first point
Second extension line origin: **ENDP** (Enter)	
of *Pick point* ②	Locates second point
Dimension line location (Text/ Angle): *Pick point* ③	
Dimension text <52>: (Enter)	Accepts the default text

Continue to the next exercise without exiting dimensioning mode.

> Dim: **ROTATED.** The ROTATED dimensioning command calculates the dimension and draws the dimension line at any specified angle. You can pick the first and second extension-line origins, or you can press Enter to select a line, a circle, an arc, or a polyline to dimension. ROTATED draws the extension lines perpendicular to the dimension line.

In the preceding exercise, you saw that the ROTATED command calculated the projected distance between the two points, using 45 degrees as a reference. The ALIGNED command, by comparison, dimensions from point to point.

> Dim: **ALIGNED.** The ALIGNED dimensioning command calculates the point-to-point dimension between the two extension-line origin points you specify and aligns the dimension line parallel to an imaginary line between the points. If you press Enter to select a line, a circle, an arc, or a 2D polyline to dimension, the dimension line aligns with the object.

Figure 20.11

Rotated versus aligned dimensioning.

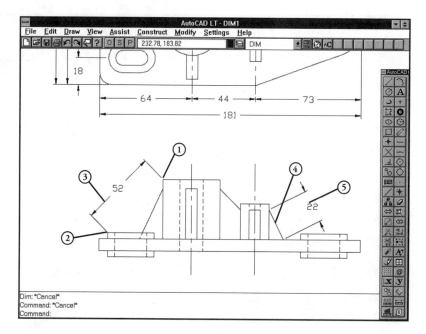

The ALIGNED dimensioning command's prompts are identical to those of the HORIZONTAL and VERTICAL dimensioning commands.

In the following exercise, you dimension the rib length using the ALIGNED command and select the line for calculating the dimension instead of choosing the two endpoints.

Placing an Aligned Dimension

Continue from the preceding exercise.

Dim: **ALI** (Enter)   Specifies an aligned dimension

First extension line origin or
RETURN to select: (Enter)

Select line, arc, or circle:
Pick line at ④ *(see fig. 20.11)*

Dimension line location (Text/
Angle): *Pick point* ⑤

Dimension text <22>: (Enter)   Accepts the default value

Continue to the next exercise without exiting dimensioning mode.

After you use the object-selection option with the ALIGNED command, the resulting alignment depends on the type of object selected. The dimension line aligns to the points derived from the object. ALIGNED uses the endpoints of arcs and lines (or polyline segments). If you select a circle, ALIGNED uses the pick point and the diameter point on the opposite side.

The Undo Option in Dimensioning Mode

You might not always dimension perfectly, but if you make an error, you can fix it. You can undo dimensions in three ways. After you exit dimensioning mode, you can use the ERASE command to erase specific dimensions. You also can use the U or the UNDO command after exiting dimensioning mode. These two commands, however, undo the entire Dimensioning mode session. If you are using dimensioning mode (not DIM1) and you need to undo a specific dimensioning command, you can use the dimensioning mode UNDO command.

Try undoing the previous rotated and aligned dimensions (which were created in dimensioning mode) in the following exercise. First use dimensioning mode UNDO, and then exit and use the regular AutoCAD LT UNDO.

Undoing Dimensions

Continue from the preceding exercise.

Dim: **U** (Enter)   Removes the aligned dimension

Dim: *Press Ctrl+C*   Exits dimensioning mode

Cancel

Command: **U** (Enter)   Removes the rotated dimension

Save the drawing

> Dim: **UNDO.** The UNDO dimensioning command cancels the latest dimensioning command, including any dimension variable settings made since the previous command. You can repeat UNDO to step back to the beginning of the current dimensioning session. After you exit dimensioning mode, however, AutoCAD LT treats the entire dimensioning session as a single step.

Stop Be careful when you undo dimensions. You cannot reverse dimensioning mode UNDO command; dimensioning mode does not have a REDO command. Also be careful with the regular UNDO command after you exit dimensioning mode, because it undoes the entire dimensioning session.

Placing Ordinate Dimensions

Ordinate (datum) dimensions indicate the positions of points or features relative to the current User Coordinate System (UCS) origin. You can use ordinate dimensions to designate the elevations of floors in a building section, to mark increments along the X and Y axes of a graph, or to dimension a large number of holes in a part. Like baseline dimensions, a set of ordinate dimensions typically uses a common base point (*datum point*). Ordinate dimensions use only leader lines and dimension text; they do not include dimension lines or extension lines. When you dimension a large number of features from a common base, ordinate dimensions create a less cluttered drawing. Ordinate dimensions also facilitate numerical control (NC) programming for parts that must be machined.

Tip You can specify several leader endpoints to form a "dog-leg" leader from the feature to the text.

Because the ORDINATE command calculates the dimensions from 0,0, you usually need to change the User Coordinate System (UCS) base point when you use this command. Chapter 2, "Specifying Locations in CAD Space," covered the UCS icon settings and the methods of defining a UCS.

In the following exercise, you dimension the various heights of the mount plate with ordinate dimensions. Before using the ORDINATE command, you set the UCS origin to the base of the plate.

Drawing Ordinate Dimensions

Continue working with the DIM1 drawing. Be sure that Ortho mode is on.

Use the UCSICON command to set the UCS icon to ON and ORIGIN. Use the Origin option of the UCS command to set the UCS origin to the base of the plate, as shown in figure 20.12.

```
Command: Choose Draw, Ordinate
Dimensions, Y-Datum

_dim1
Dim: _ordinate
```

Select Feature: **ENDP** (Enter)

of *Pick point* ① *(see fig. 20.12)*

Leader endpoint (Xdatum/Ydatum): **Y**   Issues the Y option

Leader endpoint: *Pick point* ②   Specifies the leader length

Dimension text <4>: (Enter)   Accepts the default text

Command: *Choose* **D**raw, Ordi**n**ate Dimensions,
Y-Datum

Select Feature: **ENDP** (Enter)

of *Pick point* ③

Leader endpoint: *Pick point* ④

Dimension text <12>: (Enter)   Accepts the default text

Continue using this method to place ordinate dimensions at the 0, 8, 32, and 48 locations.

Set the UCS back to WORLD.

Save the drawing

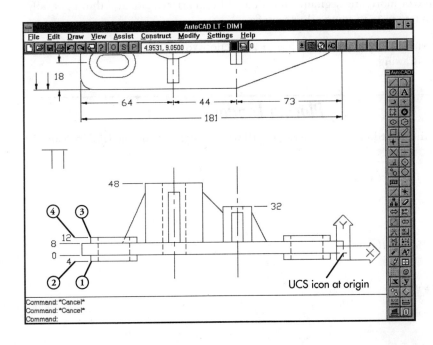

Figure 20.12

A series of ordinate dimensions.

> `Dim:` **ORDINATE.** The ORDINATE dimensioning command draws a leader line and calculates dimension text for ordinate or datum dimensions. The text aligns with the leader line. You pick the *feature* to dimension (the leader's first point) and the leader endpoint. This command calculates the distance along the X or Y axis from 0,0 to the feature point, depending on the first (feature) and second leader points.

The ORDINATE command has the following options:

- **Select Feature.** At the `Select Feature:` prompt, you pick the leader's first point.

- **Leader endpoint.** At the `Leader endpoint:` prompt, you pick the second point.

- **Xdatum/Ydatum.** The Xdatum/Ydatum option enables you to enter an **X** or **Y** to force an X-datum or Y-datum dimension, regardless of leader line points. ORDINATE asks for the second leader endpoint.

Inserting Leaders and Text

In addition to dimensions, drawings usually contain a number of leaders. *Leaders* consist of one or more line segments terminated by an arrowhead, and they generally point from a text note to some other feature.

In the following exercise, you add a leader and a note to call out a typical slot in the mount plate drawing.

Placing Leaders

Continue from the preceding exercise, using the DIM1 drawing. Turn off the UCS icon and Ortho mode.

`Command:` *Choose* **D**raw, Leade**r**

`_dim1`
`DIM: _leader`

`Leader start:` *Pick point* ①
(see fig. 20.13)

`To point:` *Pick point* ②

`To point:` *Pick point* ③

To point: (Enter)   Ends leader placement

Dimension text <48>: **10 X 22**   Replaces the default text
SLOT (3) (Enter)

Save the drawing

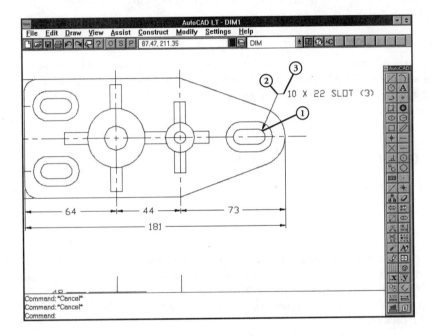

Figure 20.13

A leader and text callout.

20

If you continued from the ordinate dimensioning exercise, the default leader text came from the last ORDINATE command. The default is useful for calling out another type of dimension in which the text does not fit. Just enter a space for the original dimension text, and then use LEADER to place the text elsewhere, pointing to the original dimension line.

Dim: **LEADER.** The LEADER dimensioning command draws an arrowhead, one or more leader lines at any angle, and horizontal text.

The LEADER command has the following prompts:

◆ Leader start: At the Leader start: prompt, you pick the point for the arrowhead.

◆ To point: At the To point: prompt, you pick as many points as you want, a procedure similar to that of the LINE command. The To point: prompt repeats until you press Enter. If the angle of the last two points is not horizontal, LEADER adds a short horizontal line.

◆ Dimension text <default>: At the Dimension text <default>: prompt, you press Enter to accept the default text (the text from the most recently calculated dimension), or you enter your own text.

Tip   To draw a leader with no text, enter only a space as text. To enter additional lines of text, use the DTEXT command, pick the leader text as the start point with the INS object snap mode, and then enter a space and press Enter to step down for the next line of text.

Dimensioning Circles and Arcs

AutoCAD LT makes the dimensioning of objects and geometric relationships easy and automatic. Even though you can dimension circles and arcs with linear dimensions, AutoCAD LT includes three dimensioning commands to use specifically with circles and arcs: DIAMETER, RADIUS, and CENTER.

The RADIUS dimensioning command is almost identical to the DIAMETER dimensioning command. To use the DIAMETER or the RADIUS command, you must select a circle, an arc, or an arc polyline segment by picking a point on the object. The diameter or radius dimension line passes through the center of the arc or circle and aligns with the pick point.

In the following exercise, you use the DIAMETER command to dimension the small boss on the mount plate. You also use the RADIUS command to dimension the radius on the right side of the plate. One dimension variable, DIMTIX, will have to be turned off to keep the text out of the center of the arcs and circles.

Dimensioning with the DIAMETER and RADIUS Commands

Continue from the preceding exercise, using the DIM1 drawing.

Command: **DIMTIX** (Enter)	Accesses the DIMTIX dimension variable
New value for DIMTIX<1>: **0** (Enter)	Turns off DIMTIX
Command: *Choose* **D**raw, Radial Di**m**ensions, **D**iameter	Issues the DIAMETER dimensioning command

New Riders Publishing
INSIDE
SERIES

```
_dim1
Dim: _diameter
```

```
Select arc or circle: Pick circle at ①
(see fig. 20.14)
```

```
Dimension text <20>: Enter
```
Accepts the default text

```
Enter leader length for text:
Pick point ②
```

Command: *Choose* **D**raw, Radial Di**m**ensions, **R**adius
Issues the RADIUS dimensioning command

```
_dim1
Dim: _radius
```

```
Select arc or circle: Pick the arc at ③
```

```
Dimension text <20>: Enter
```

```
Enter leader length for text:
Pick near ④
```

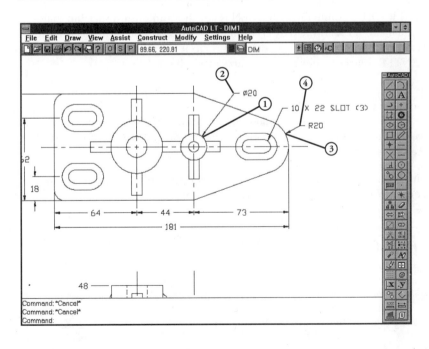

Figure 20.14

Diameter and radius dimensions.

Dim: **DIAMETER.** The DIAMETER dimensioning command dimensions arcs and circles. The dimension line is placed at the point where you pick the arc or circle. Whether the text is placed inside or outside the circle depends on the size of the text compared to the size of the circle. Several dimension variables, explained in the next chapter, also control the text placement.

Dim: **RADIUS.** The RADIUS dimensioning command dimensions the radius of an arc or a circle. The point where you select the radius determines the leader placement for the radius dimension.

DIAMETER draws a leader only if the dimension text is larger than the circle or arc, but RADIUS can draw the leader inside or outside the circle or arc. You can drag the leader to either side of the arc. You also can create an inside radius leader by entering a negative leader length. The DIAMETER command calculates the diameter of a circle and displays it with the ANSI diameter symbol ($\oslash$), whereas the RADIUS command displays the radius with an R in front of the value.

In the preceding exercise, you saw that the DIMTIX dimension variable affected the DIAMETER and RADIUS commands. DIMCEN is another dimension variable that affects both the DIAMETER and RADIUS commands. This variable controls whether center marks are created for dimensioned arcs and circles. A separate dimensioning command, CENTER, places center marks on arcs or circles.

If DIMCEN is set to a positive value, CENTER draws a cross at the circle's center. The larger the value of DIMCEN, the larger the cross. If DIMCEN is set to a negative value, CENTER also draws center lines that extend outside the circle by that value. If DIMCEN is 0, trying to use CENTER produces the message, DIMCEN = 0,0, not drawing center cross. *Invalid*.

In the following exercise, you use a negative DIMCEN setting of −3 to place a center cross and a center line on each of the two arcs in the upper left slot.

Placing Center Marks with the CENTER Command

Continue working with the DIM1 drawing.

Dim: **DIMCEN** (Enter)   Accesses the DIMCEN dimension variable

Current value <0.00> New value: Assigns a new DIMCEN value
-3 (Enter)

```
Command: Choose Draw, Radial Dimensions,     Issues the CENTER command
Center Mark

_dim1
Dim: _center

Select arc or circle: Pick arc at ①
(see fig. 20.15)

Command: Choose Draw, Radial Dimensions,     Issues the CENTER command
Center Mark

Select arc or circle: Pick arc at ②
```

Save the drawing

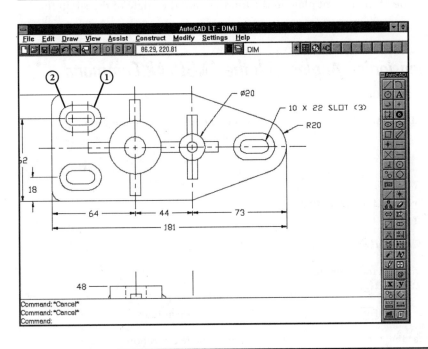

20

Figure 20.15

Center lines and mark drawn with a negative DIMCEN.

Dim: **CENTER.** The CENTER dimensioning command draws a center mark (a cross) or a center mark and center lines in circles and arcs. The DIMCEN dimension variable controls the center-mark size and whether center lines also are drawn.

Tip Use the CENTER command, along with various DIMCEN settings, to begin placing center lines on a view with many circles. Then draw the remaining center lines, as needed, to complete the view. Sometimes the BREAK or the STRETCH command also is needed to get your center lines to look technically correct.

Applying Angular Dimensioning

You can use the ANGULAR dimensioning command to dimension the angle between two lines. ANGULAR also displays the angle subtended by an arc or adds an angular measurement to indicate part of a circle.

In the following exercise, you use the ANGULAR command to dimension the angle on the right side of the mount plate in the top view and the angle of the rib in the front view.

Dimensioning Angles with the ANGULAR Command

Continue working with the DIM1 drawing.

Command: *Choose* **D**raw, Ang**u**lar Dimension	Issues the ANGULAR dimensioning command
`_dim1` `Dim: _angular`	
`Select arc, circle, line, or RETURN:` *Pick line at* ① *(see fig. 20.16)*	
`Second line:` *Pick line at* ②	
`Enter dimension arc line location` `(Text/Angle):` *Pick point* ③	
`Dimension text <20>:` (Enter)	Accepts the default text
`Enter text location (or` `Return):` (Enter)	Centers the text location
Command: *Choose* **D**raw, Ang**u**lar Dimension	
`Select arc, circle, line,` `or RETURN:` *Pick line at* ④	
`Second line:` *Pick line at* ⑤	

`Enter dimension arc line location` `(Text/Angle):` *Pick point* ⑥	Locates the dimension arc inside the angle
`Dimension text <63>:` (Enter)	Accepts the default text
`Enter text location (or Return):` *Pick point* ⑦	Locates text outside the angle

Save the drawing

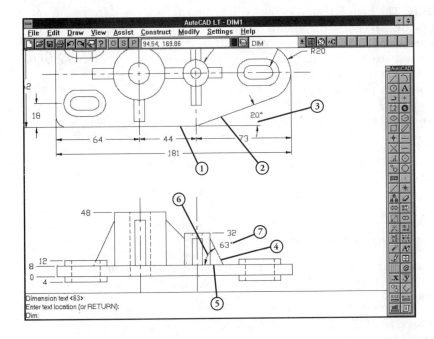

Figure 20.16

Angular dimensions.

20

> `Dim:` **ANGULAR.** The ANGULAR dimensioning command dimensions an angle by picking one of the following object combinations: two non-parallel lines or polyline segments; an arc or polyline arc segment; a circle and another point; or three points. All object-selection methods require selection by picking points.

The ANGULAR command prompts you to select an arc, circle, or line, or to press Return, as follows:

◆ **Arc.** The Arc option enables you to dimension the angle by picking an arc or polyline arc segment and then specifying the dimension arc location and the dimension text location. The extension lines pass from the center point to or through the endpoints.

◆ **Circle.** The Circle option enables you to dimension an angle by picking a circle and then specifying a second angle endpoint, the dimension arc location, and the dimension text location. The extension lines pass from the center point to or through the circle pick point and second angle endpoint.

◆ **Line.** The Line option enables you to dimension the angle between two lines from their intersection by picking two non-parallel lines or polyline segments and then specifying the dimension arc location and the dimension text location.

◆ **RETURN.** The Return option enables you to dimension an angle by specifying three points. To choose the Return option, you press Enter and are prompted for three points to determine the angle: Angle vertex:, First angle endpoint:, and Second angle endpoint:. Then you specify the dimension arc location and the dimension text location. The extension lines pass from the center point to or through the first and second angle endpoints.

After you have chosen the geometry to specify the angle, three more prompts appear:

◆ Enter dimension arc line location (Text/Angle). Except for the two-line option, AutoCAD LT uses the point you specify for the dimension line arc location to determine whether to dimension the angle inside or outside the extension lines. For the two-line option, AutoCAD LT considers the lines to extend through their intersection, creating four possible angles to dimension. AutoCAD LT uses the point you specify for the dimension arc line location to determine which angles to dimension, drawing any needed extension lines.

◆ Dimension text <*default*>. The Dimension text <*default*>: prompt is the standard default text prompt. At this prompt, you press Enter or enter an alternate value.

◆ Enter text location. At the Enter text location (or Return): prompt, you specify the text location or press Enter to center the text in the dimension arc.

Depending on the complexity of the angular dimensioning you must perform, you might want to experiment further with the ANGULAR options.

Now that you know how to apply dimensions with all of the dimensioning commands, you need to learn how to control their appearance in order to meet your dimensioning standards. The next chapter shows you how to use a combination of dimension variables and dimension creation techniques, along with some dimension editing commands, to dimension a drawing to specific standards.

Styling and Editing Dimensions

In Chapter 20, you learned to use the AutoCAD LT dimensioning commands to generate accurate dimensions from a drawing. Dimension standards, however, vary widely from one type of application to another, and even within the same application, from one office or trade to another. AutoCAD LT provides dimension variables and styles to adapt dimensions to meet various standards. This chapter teaches you how control AutoCAD's dimension variables and styles, and how to edit dimensions. It also does the following:

◆ Shows how a couple changes in settings can make a big difference in dimension appearance

◆ Explains every setting in the Dimension Styles and Settings dialog box

◆ Demonstrates settings for center marks, tolerances, limits, zero suppression, and rounding

◆ Explains how to create named dimension styles that establish certain sets of settings

◆ Demonstrates styles and settings suitable for architectural dimensioning

◆ Explains how associative dimensions update measurements automatically when edited

◆ Demonstrates how to edit dimensions and dimension text

The myriad of dimension variables and dimension style dialog boxes might appear rather challenging, especially if you are new to CAD dimensioning. Fortunately, if you set them up for your specific types of drawings, you can create named dimension styles and use them over and over again to easily dimension drawings.

Controlling Dimension Appearance

Many different dimensioning standards exist, and AutoCAD LT has the capability to conform to these different dimensioning standards. When a dimension is created, many of its characteristics are determined by the current variable settings. A dimension reflects the current units as well as the current text style. Already, in the previous chapter, you have changed a few of the dimension variables in the exercises when you used the CENTER and DIAMETER dimensioning commands. The following section on dimension variables should make you aware of most of the dimensioning capabilities of AutoCAD LT.

To view or change a setting quickly, you can enter a dimension variable (like any other system variable) at the Command: prompt. We recommend that you learn to access the variables through the dialog boxes. This method requires much less memorization of variable names. Later, you may find that you prefer to access the variables directly through the Command: prompt.

Before you read further about the functions of the dimension settings, try changing a few settings to see how the changes affect your dimensions. First, draw a horizontal dimension for comparison. Then, change the size of the dimension features—text height, arrow size, and so on—and add a suffix of mm to show that the dimensions are in millimeters. Create a new horizontal dimension and notice the feature changes. Then, change the dimension settings again to create a basic dimension with a box around it, and change the arrows to dots. Create one more dimension to see the new changes. The exercise drawing is the same as that used in Chapter 20, except it has been scaled (enlarged) by a factor of 1.333333 so that the features no longer measure in even millimeters. Running object snaps of INTersection and ENDPoint are set in the prototype, and snap is on, to aid in placing dimensions.

Changing Dimension Appearance with New Dimension Settings

Create a new drawing named DIM2 using the ALT2101.DWG file as a prototype, and using no setup method. Zoom to the view shown in figure 21.1. The dimensions shown do not yet exist.

Command: *Choose* **D**raw, **L**inear Dimensions,
Horizontal

First extension line origin or
RETURN to select: *Pick line at* ①
(see fig. 21.1)

Second extension line origin: *Pick
line at* ②

Dimension line location
(Text/Angle): *Pick* ③

Dimension text <59>: Enter   Draws a dimension

Command: *Choose* **S**ettings, Di**m**ension Style   Opens Dimension Styles and Settings
                                                  dialog box

'_ddim

Choose Scale and **C**olors   Opens Scale and Colors dialog box

Double-click in the **F**eature Scaling box, *type* **.75**   Sets DIMSCALE to .75 and returns to the
and choose OK   Dimension Styles and Settings dialog box

Choose Text F**o**rmat, *and type* **mm** *in the* Te**x**t   Opens the Text Format dialog box and sets
Suffix *box, choose* OK, *then* OK *again*   DIMPOST to mm, then closes both dialog
                                                  boxes

Use the HORIZONTAL dimension command again to draw the dimension at ④. It has text and arrows 75 percent the size of the previous dimensions, and a mm suffix.

Command: *Choose* **S**ettings, Di**m**ension Style   Opens Dimension Styles and Settings
                                                  dialog box

'_ddim

Choose Dimension **L**ine, *and put a check in the*   Opens Dimension Line dialog box and sets
Basic **D**imension *check box, then choose* OK   DIMGAP to –3, to create basic dimensions

Choose **A**rrows, *and click on the* **D**ot *radio button,*   Opens the Arrows dialog box, sets DIMBLK
choose OK, *then* OK *again*   to DOT, then closes both dialog boxes

continues

continued

Use the HORIZONTAL dimension command a third time to draw the dimension at ⑤. It has a basic dimension box with dot dimension line terminators.

Save the drawing

Figure 21.1

Creating dimensions with new dimension settings.

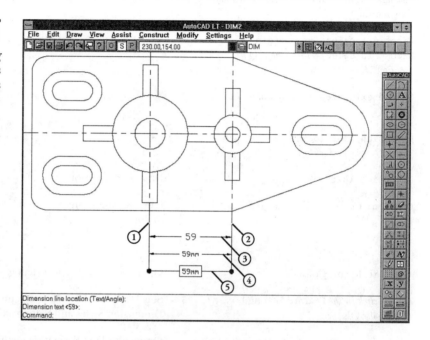

As setting just these few dimension variables demonstrates, a couple of settings can greatly change the appearance of a dimension. There are many more variables you can control with the Dimension Styles and Settings Dialog box.

The Dimension Styles and Settings Dialog Box

AutoCAD LT has over 40 dimension variables, all of which are listed in Appendix E. All the AutoCAD LT system variables that begin with *DIM* are referred to as *dimension variables.* Each one controls some aspect of a dimension or its appearance. You can change many variables or just a few, depending upon the effects you want to achieve. A specific configuration of dimension variables produces a *dimension style.* Creating a new dimension style can be tedious, but AutoCAD LT enables you to save the variable settings under a dimension style name. From then on in that drawing, you can set the dimension style by specifying its name.

By using a series of dialog boxes, you can control all the dimension variables. You can display the top-level dialog box, Dimension Styles and Settings, from the Di**m**ension

Style item of the **S**ettings pull-down menu. The DDIM command also displays this dialog box. From the Dimension Styles and Settings dialog box, you can assign new dimension style names, recall named styles, and display the Dimension Settings dialog boxes. Figure 21.2 shows the Dimension Styles and Settings dialog box.

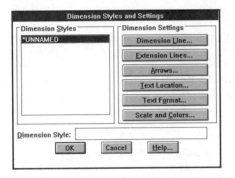

Figure 21.2

The Dimension Styles and Settings dialog box.

Note When you display the Dimension Styles and Settings dialog box for the first time, the Dimension **S**tyles box lists one dimension style, *UNNAMED. This style is defined by the AutoCAD LT default dimension variable settings and is suitable for full-size drawings in a variety of fields and disciplines. If you are using a prototype drawing, you will have the variable settings that were established in that drawing.

To change dimension variables, click on the appropriate Dimension Settings button. You do not need to know the dimension variable names, only the aspect of the dimension you want to change.

Note Throughout the various subdialog boxes displayed by the Dimension Styles and Settings dialog box, there are various height, size, extension, offset, gap, and increment settings. These control the size and relative placement of the parts of dimensions. They should be set to the actual plotted size that your standards dictate, and the plot scale adjustment should be made by setting **F**eature Scaling (DIMSCALE), which affects all these settings equally. See the section on the Scale and Colors dialog box for details and for an important warning to AutoCAD LT Release 2 users.

The Dimension Line Dialog Box

The Dimension Line dialog box shown in figure 21.3 controls the variables that affect how the dimension line is drawn.

◆ **Force Interior Lines.** When you check the Force **I**nterior Lines box, you force AutoCAD LT to draw interior dimension lines even when the dimension text does not fit between the extension lines. This is commonly used for architectural dimensioning.

◆ **Basic Dimension.** When you check the Basic **D**imension box, a basic dimension (such as that used in geometric tolerancing) is designated by the dimension text being placed in a box.

◆ **Text Gap.** The Text **G**ap setting controls how much of the dimension line AutoCAD LT removes to embed dimension text.

◆ **Baseline Increment.** The **B**aseline Increment setting controls the distance between baseline dimensions.

Figure 21.3

The Dimension Line dialog box.

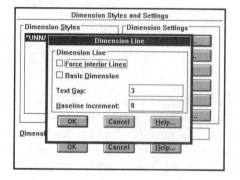

The Extension Lines Dialog Box

The Extension Lines dialog box shown in figure 21.4 controls the variables that affect how AutoCAD LT draws extension lines (witness lines).

◆ **Extension Above Line.** You use the **E**xtension Above Line edit box to set the distance that the extension line continues past the dimension line.

◆ **Feature Offset.** The Feature **O**ffset edit box sets the distance between the definition point and the point where AutoCAD LT begins drawing the extension line. This setting enables you to have a gap between the object and the extension line itself. You might need to increase this setting for dimensions of curved objects.

◆ **Visibility.** The Visibilit**y** drop-down list box enables you to suppress one or both extension lines, which is useful to prevent overlapping extension lines when a dimension line ends on the dimensioned object or if an extension line exists. Although unsuppressed dimensions might look OK on screen, the overlapping lines might plot poorly. If it doesn't affect your plotted appearance, don't bother with it.

◆ **Center Mark Size.** The Center Mark Size edit box defines the size of the cross AutoCAD LT draws at the center of an arc or a circle after you enter the DIAMETER, RADIUS, or CENTER dimensioning command. A zero setting suppresses center marks but is, of course, invalid with the CENTER command. This sets the DIMCEN variable.

◆ **Mark with Center Lines.** The Mark with Center Lines check box determines whether center lines are placed with the DIAMETER, RADIUS, or CENTER dimensioning commands. If the text is placed inside the arc or circle with DIAMETER or RADIUS dimensions, this setting is ignored and no center lines are drawn. This controls the DIMCEN value, setting it positive for no center lines and negative for center lines.

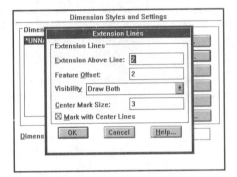

Figure 21.4

The Extension Lines dialog box.

21

 Tip If you draw center lines (using a CENTER linetype and the LINE command), their dashes rarely align properly at the centers of circles and arcs. You should instead turn on the Mark with Center Lines check box (a negative DIMCEN) and use CENTER to place center marks, then use a CENTER linetype, the LINE command, and an ENDPoint object snap to snap to the ends of the center mark lines to complete the center lines.

In the following exercise, try trimming the existing center lines from two circles and replacing them. Use center marks only in one circle and both center marks and lines in the other circle.

Using Center Marks and Lines

Continue in the DIM2 drawing from the previous exercise and zoom to the view shown in figure 21.5.

Command: *Click on the Trim tool*   Issues the TRIM command

continues

continued

```
_TRIM
Select cutting edge(s)...
```

```
Select objects:
```
Pick the circles at ① *and* ② *(see fig. 21.5), then press Enter*

Specifies trim edges, then ends selection

```
<Select object to trim>/Undo:
```
Pick each of the four center lines at ③ *and* ④, *then press Enter*

Trims the center lines from within the circles, then ends the TRIM command

```
Command:
```
Choose **S**ettings, Di**m**ension Style

Opens Dimension Styles and Settings dialog box

In the Dimension Line *dialog box, clear the* Basic **D**imension *check box and choose* OK, *then in the* Arrows *dialog box, choose the* **A**rrow *radio button then choose* OK

Clears the last setting from the previous exercise and returns to the main Dimension Styles and Settings dialog box

In the Extension Lines *dialog box, set* **C**enter Mark Size *to* **3** *and make sure that the* **M**ark with Center Lines *check box is cleared, then choose* OK

Sets to draw 3 mm center marks and returns to the main Dimension Styles and Settings dialog box

Choose OK

Exits the Dimension Styles and Settings dialog box and saves the settings

```
Command:
```
Choose **D**raw, Radial Di**m**ensions, **C**enter Mark *and pick the circle at* ① *(see fig. 21.6)*

Issues the CENTER dimension command and draws a center mark as shown in figure 21.6

```
Command:
```
Choose **S**ettings, Di**m**ension Style, *and in the* Extension Lines *dialog box, put a check in the* **M**ark with Center Lines *check box, then choose* OK *twice*

Sets to draw center marks and lines

```
Command:
```
Choose **D**raw, Radial Di**m**ensions, **C**enter Mark *and pick the circle at* ②

Issues the CENTER dimension command and draws a center mark as shown in figure 21.6

Save the drawing

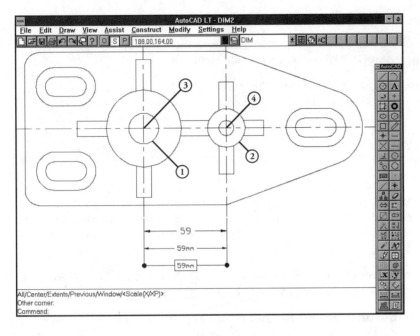

Figure 21.5

*Trimming center
lines from circles.*

21

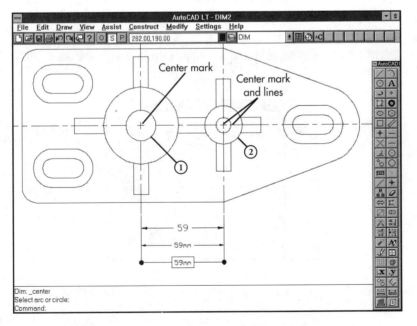

Figure 21.6

*Center marks
and lines added
to circles.*

The Arrows Dialog Box

The Arrows dialog box shown in figure 21.7 controls the dimension variables that determine how AutoCAD LT terminates dimension lines.

◆ **Arrow, Tick, Dot, and User.** The Arrow, Tick, Dot, and User radio buttons enable you to select an arrow (the default), a tick mark (diagonal slash), a dot, or a user-defined symbol as the dimension line terminator. You used a dot in the first exercise of this chapter.

◆ **Arrow Size.** The Arrow Size edit box sets the size of the arrow, tick mark, dot, or user symbol.

◆ **User Arrow.** If you select the User radio button, the User Arrow edit box is ungrayed, and you can enter the name of the block to use as a terminator. The user arrow should be designed as a 1×1 unit sized block, so it is scaled appropriately.

◆ **Separate Arrows.** If checked, you can specify different user arrow blocks in the First Arrow and the Second Arrow boxes.

◆ **First Arrow and Second Arrow.** If you check the Separate Arrows box, the First Arrow and Second Arrow edit boxes are ungrayed, and you can enter the names of individual blocks to use as terminators.

◆ **Tick Extension.** The Tick Extension box is ungrayed after you select Tick, so you can specify how far the dimension line extends through the tick marks and past the extension lines.

Figure 21.7

The Arrows dialog box.

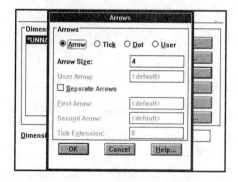

You'll use tick marks and the tick extension setting in an architectural dimension style exercise later in this chapter.

The Text Location Dialog Box

The Text Location dialog box shown in figure 21.8 controls the dimension variables that determine the size of dimension text and where AutoCAD LT locates the dimension text relative to the dimension line.

◆ **Te̱xt Height.** The Te̱xt Height edit box controls the height of dimension text.

◆ **Tolerance Height.** The T̲olerance Height edit box controls the height of dimension tolerances if they are drawn (see the section on the Text Format dialog box).

◆ **Ho̱rizontal and V̲ertical**. The text placement boxes, Ho̱rizontal and V̲ertical, enable you to locate text embedded in the dimension line, above or below the dimension line, centered along the length of the dimension line, and inside or outside the extension lines.

◆ **Relative P̲osition.** The Relative P̲osition edit box provides an additional adjustment that allows a defined text position at a vertical distance from the dimension line.

◆ **Al̲ignment.** The Al̲ignment box enables you to control whether dimension text is always horizontal, aligned with the dimension line, or varied. The effect of this setting depends upon whether the dimension text is inside or outside the extension lines.

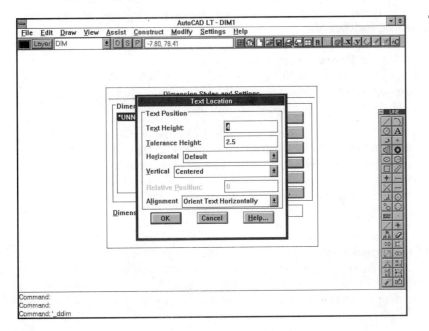

Figure 21.8

The Text Location dialog box.

Stop If you are using a text style with a fixed text height, this height will override your dimension text height setting.

The Text Format Dialog Box

The Text Format dialog box shown in figure 21.9 controls the dimension variables that determine the content of dimension text. The Basic Units section contains the following options:

◆ **Length Scaling.** The Length **S**caling edit box in the Basic Units section enables you to enter a factor that AutoCAD LT applies to the actual measured length to calculate the value shown by the dimension text. Unless you use this with paper space, it is not normally used in CAD drawings because they are normally drawn at real-world size. If you draw a 2× detail, however, you can enter a Length **S**caling factor of .5, and the dimension text reflects the correct dimension.

Note Sometimes you need to dimension a drawing in units other than those in which it was created, for example to dimension a drawing in millimeters when it was drawn in inches. You can do so by setting a Length **S**caling factor, but it is clearer and less confusing to instead create a new, empty drawing in the desired units and to use the INSERT command to insert the original drawing into the new one, exploded and using the appropriate scale factor. Then the resulting drawings units will match the dimension measurements.

◆ **Scale in Paper Space Only.** Turning on the Scale in Paper Space **O**nly check box causes the Length **S**caling edit box value to affects only dimensions applied to objects which are in an mview floating viewport in paper space. Chapter 22, "Structuring Your Drawing," discusses this topic.

◆ **Round Off.** The **R**ound Off edit box enables you to enter an increment for AutoCAD LT to round off dimensions independent of the unit settings. You can work with a coordinate display set to five decimal places, but have all dimensions rounded to only three decimal places. This does not affect the number of significant digits, which is controlled by the units setting, so a rounded dimension can have trailing zeros unless you truncate them with the Zero Suppression settings.

◆ **Text Prefix and Text Suffix.** The Text Pre**f**ix and Te**x**t Suffix edit boxes enable you to enter text strings to add before and after the dimension text. For example, you might want to suffix basic dimensions with the word BASIC rather than draw a box around the text, or you might want to suffix reference

dimensions with REF rather than surround the text with parentheses. The suffix box is commonly used to dimension in units other than those available in the UNITS command and Units Control dialog box, such as mm for millimeters.

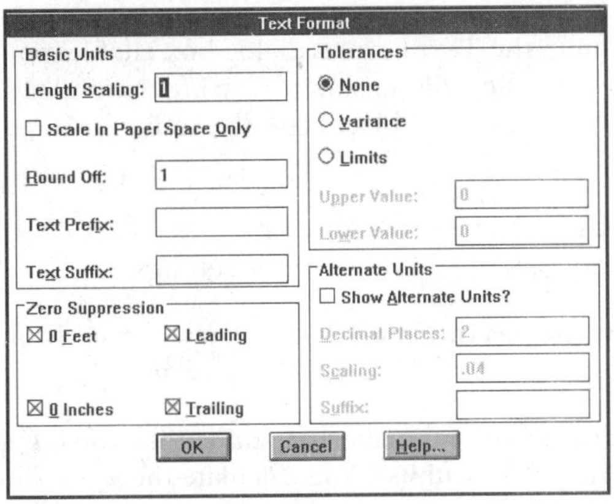

Figure 21.9

The Text Format dialog box.

The Zero Suppression section in the Text Format dialog box contains four check boxes. These check boxes enable you to suppress zeros in dimension text. Several combinations allow many different output formats.

- ◆ **0 Feet.** A check in the 0 Feet check box suppresses zero feet text if the dimension is less than one foot (3 ½ " instead of 0'-3 ½").

- ◆ **0 Inches.** A check in the 0 Inches check box suppresses zero inch text if the dimension is an even number of feet (3' instead of 3'-0").

- ◆ **Leading.** A check in the Leading check box suppresses leading zeros in decimal dimensions (.375 instead of 0.375).

- ◆ **Trailing.** A check in the Trailing check box suppresses trailing zeros in decimal dimensions (3.25 instead of 3.2500).

The Tolerances section in the Text Format dialog box contains three radio buttons that control how dimension text reflects tolerance settings, and two edit boxes that specify the tolerance values.

- ◆ **None.** The None option prints the measured dimension only.

- ◆ **Variance.** The Variance option prints a plus and a minus tolerance value after the measured dimension text.

- ◆ **Limits.** The Limits option replaces the dimension text with two values—the measured dimension plus the upper value, and the measured dimension minus the lower value.

◆ **Upper Value and the Lower Value.** The Upper Value and the Lower Value boxes are ungrayed when the **V**ariance or **L**imits options are selected. The Upper Value and the Lower Value settings specify the tolerance values used in the tolerance text or used to calculate dimension limits.

The Alternate Units section in the Text Format dialog box enables you to control the display of an alternate, or reference, dimension text string that follows the primary dimension text. The number of decimal places and the suffix are independent of the primary dimension text.

◆ **Show Alternate Units?** The Show **A**lternate Units? check box turns on alternate units and ungrays the following three settings.

  ◆ **Decimal Places.** Sets the number of decimal places displayed in the alternate units.

  ◆ **Scaling.** Sets the scale of the alternate units (like the Length **S**caling edit box does for the primary units). You calculate the value shown in alternate units from the primary dimension by applying a scaling factor. The default value of 25.4 enables you to add alternate metric dimensions to the drawings you create in inches.

  ◆ **Suffix.** Sets the suffix text to add to the alternate units.

You already used the Te**x**t Suffix feature to add mm to a dimension in your DIM2 drawing. Try some of the other Text Format dialog box settings in the following exercise. Although you might not have known it, the reason the 59 mm dimensions are an even 59 is that the **R**ound Off is set to 1 and zero suppression is on. Try changing **R**ound Off, turning off zero suppression, and using the Tolerances features in the following exercise. You'll use the DIMUPD (DIMension UPDate command—covered later in this chapter) to see the effects.

Dimensioning with Tolerances, Limits, Rounding, and Zeros

Continue from the previous exercise in the DIM2 drawing. Zoom to the view shown in figure 21.10.

Command: *Choose* **S**ettings, Di**m**ension Style	Opens Dimension Styles and Settings dialog box
In the Text Format *dialog box, clear the* **L**eading *and* **T**railing *check boxes in the* Zero Suppression area	Sets to include zeros
Choose OK *twice*	Exits dialog boxes and saves settings
Command: *Choose* **M**odify, Ed**i**t Dimension, **U**pdate Dimension	Issues the DIM1 and UPDATE commands

```
_dim1
Dim: _update
```

Select objects: *Pick the dimension at* ① *(see fig. 21.10), then press Enter*	Updates dimension, still rounded, but now showing trailing zeros (see fig. 21.11)
Command: *Choose* **S**ettings, Di**m**ension Style, *and in the* Text Format *dialog box, set* **R**ound Off *to 0.01, then choose* OK *twice*	Sets to show two decimal places
Command: *Choose* **M**odify, Ed**i**t Dimension, **U**pdate Dimension, *and update the dimension at* ②	Updates the dimension to 58.67 mm (see fig. 21.11)
Command: *Choose* **S**ettings, Di**m**ension Style, *and in the* Text Format *dialog box, choose the* **V**ariance *radio button, set* U**p**per Value *to* 0.1 *and* Lo**w**er Value *to* 0.06, *then choose* OK *twice*	Sets to draw dimensions with tolerances

Draw the horizontal dimension shown at ③ in figure 21.11.

Command: *Choose* **S**ettings, Di**m**ension Style, *and in the* Text Format *dialog box, choose the* **L**imits *radio button, then choose* OK *twice*	Sets to draw dimensions with limits

Draw the horizontal dimension shown at ④ in figure 21.11.

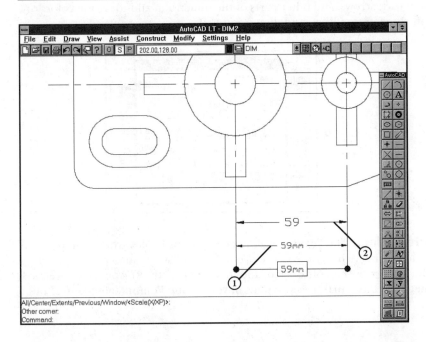

Figure 21.10

Dimensions before settings changes.

Figure 21.11

Dimensions after changes and with tolerances and limits.

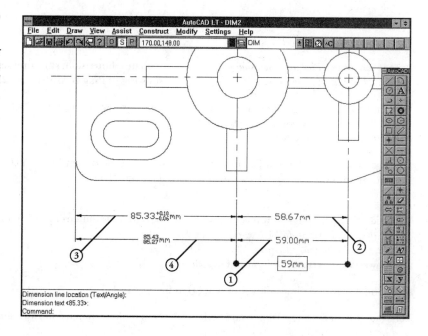

The Scale and Colors Dialog Box

You use the Scale and Colors dialog box shown in figure 21.8 to set the plotted size of the dimension text, arrows, and other parts of the dimension and to set the colors of dimension lines, extension lines, and dimension text.

Figure 21.12

The Scale and Colors dialog box.

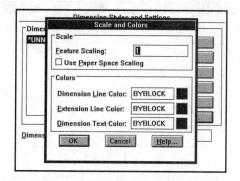

◆ **Feature Scaling.** The Feature Scaling edit box sets DIMSCALE, an important dimension variable that controls the overall scale of size-related parameters (height, size, extension, offset, gap, and increment settings). You set size-related parameters to the actual sizes you want in your plotted output, and control the

plot scale adjustment by setting **F**eature Scaling (DIMSCALE), which affects all of these settings equally. You set the **F**eature Scaling value to the drawing scale factor (the inverse of the plot scale). Consider the following example: To get 0.125-inch dimension text in a 1:12 plot, set the dimension text height to 0.125 and the **F**eature Scaling value to 12. The Te**x**t Height setting (in the Text Location dialog box) is multiplied by the **F**eature Scaling value. A 0.125 Te**x**t Height setting appears as 1.5 inches in the drawing (.125×12), but it appears as 0.125 inches when plotted at 1:12. The default setting for **F**eature Scaling is 1. See the following important warning if you are using AutoCAD LT Release 2.

 Note

The **F**eature Scaling value (DIMSCALE variable) is a factor that affects all other numerical dimension settings, such as text size, arrow size, extension-line offsets, and other similar settings. Try to avoid changing all of these settings individually for different plotting scales.

Whether you use AutoCAD LT Release 1 or AutoCAD LT Release 2, when you change the **F**eature Scaling value of existing dimensions, you might see unexpected changes in dimension appearance. These changes occur because more or less room is needed for text, arrows, and other dimension features. You can adjust the settings which control these features.

The **Q**uick and **C**ustom setup methods of the AutoCAD LT Release 2 Create New Drawing dialog box can have a significant effect on dimension settings, as explained in the following warning.

 Stop

If you use either the **Q**uick or **C**ustom setup methods of AutoCAD LT Release 2, feature scaling might operate completely differently. Although the authors of this book strongly disagree with their reasoning, Autodesk changed the way in which dimensions of *UNNAMED dimension styles are scaled when these setup methods are used, unless DIMSCALE is set to zero. These setup methods, instead of simply scaling the **F**eature Scaling (DIMSCALE) setting, leave DIMSCALE unchanged and individually scale each of the size-related variables, such as DIMASZ and DIMTXT. The values assigned to these size-related variables are based upon the drawing limits (called "World (actual) Size to Represent" in the setup dialog boxes), and they are actually useless and misleading because setup does not take plot scale into account. This means that, although to a new user the dimensions might look OK on screen, they probably require further adjustment in scale to plot according to proper standards. Adjusting them to a proper scale, however, is no longer an easy matter of setting DIMSCALE to your plot scale factor. You have to individually change each size-related variables, or deal with a confusing combination of the size-related variable settings and the DIMSCALE setting.

 ALT2

continues

21

This behavior is completely contrary to the de facto standards used by nearly every experienced AutoCAD user, and presents confusing and often irrelevant defaults in the size-related settings of the Dimension Styles and Settings dialog boxes.

You can, and should, prevent AutoCAD LT Release 2's setup from individually scaling each of the size-related variables by using named dimension styles or setting DIMSCALE to 0 (the same as putting a check in the Use **P**aper Space Scaling check box) in each of the prototype drawings that you use. Then the size-related variables are unaffected by setup, but if you set DIMSCALE to 0, you have to set **F**eature Scaling (DIMSCALE) before dimensioning (unless you want to actually use paper space sizing—see Chapter 22).

◆ **Use **P**aper Space Scaling.** When you check the Use **P**aper Space Scaling box, DIMSCALE is set to 0 and the dimension features are automatically scaled to the scale factor of the paper space viewport. This topic is further explained in Chapter 22.

◆ **Dimension **L**ine Color, **E**xtension Line Color, and **D**imension Text Color.** These three drop-down lists enable you to independently control the color of each of these dimension components. The default setting for each of these components is BYBLOCK, but you can set them to BYLAYER or any explicit color. Clicking on any of the three color swatch boxes opens the Select Color dialog box for color selection.

Tip   Because AutoCAD LT colors can control the pen assignments on a plotter, assigning different colors to objects is one method of controlling the pen width with which the objects are plotted.

Creating and Using Dimension Styles

After you have changed one or more dimension variables, you can create a new style by entering a name in the **D**imension Style edit box of the Dimension Styles and Settings dialog box (see fig. 21.10). The new name appears in the Dimension **S**tyles list box. The first name you enter replaces the *UNNAMED style, and additional names are appended to the list. After you enter a new name, it is highlighted. If you exit the Dimension Styles and Settings dialog box with OK, the highlighted name becomes the current style. You also can select a new style from the Dimension **S**tyles list box by picking the name (it then appears in the **D**imension Style edit box) and clicking on OK.

Tip   In a typical CAD drafting department, it is difficult for several drafters to produce uniform dimensions if they must individually set all the dimension values. Establish several standard dimension styles for everyone to use. Of course, there will always be several settings (such as the size of center marks or extension-line visibility) that must be adjusted during a drawing session.

Architectural dimensioning makes a good example for creating a couple of dimension styles because it requires adjusting many settings. Figure 21.13 shown a plan with two dimension that were created with all dimension variables and dialog box settings set to their defaults (except DIMSCALE). This drawing is intended for plotting at ¼"=1'-0" scale, so DIMSCALE (the Feature Scaling setting) is set to 48.

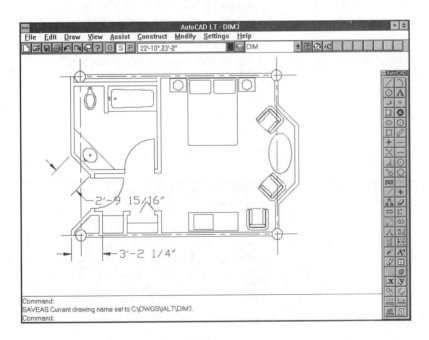

Figure 21.13

An architectural plan with default dimensioning.

Obviously, these dimensions will not do. In the following exercise, you adjust all the settings needed for architectural dimensions that meet common office standards. You also create a text style for dimensioning, using the ARCHS hand-letter font that is included on the IALT Disk.

Creating an Architectural Dimension Style

Create a new drawing named DIM3 using the ALT2102.DWG file as a prototype, and using no setup method (see fig. 21.13). Running object snaps of INTersection and ENDPoint are set in the prototype, and snap is on to aid in placing dimensions.

Command: *Choose* **S**ettings, Di**m**ension Style	Opens Dimension Styles and Settings dialog box
In the Dimension Line *dialog box, turn on* Force **I**nterior Lines *and choose* OK	Causes a dimension line to always be drawn
In the Extension Lines *dialog box, set* **E**xtension Above Line *to* $^1/_{16}$ *and* Feature **O**ffset *to* $^3/_{32}$ *and choose* OK	Sets the extension line extension past the dimension line and the gap between the dimensioned feature and the beginning of the extension line
In the Arrows *dialog box, choose the* Tic**k** *radio button, and set both* Arrow Si**z**e *and* Tick E**x**tension *to* $^3/_{64}$ *and choose* OK	Sets to draw diagonal tick marks, sets the tick size, and sets the dimension line to extend past the extension line
In the Text Location *dialog box, set* Te**x**t Height *to* $^3/_{32}$, Ho**r**izontal *to* Force Text Inside, **V**ertical *to* Above, *and* A**l**ignment *to* Align With Dimension Line *and choose* OK	Sets text height, forces it between extension lines and above the dimension line, and aligns it with the dimension line
In the Text Format *dialog box, clear the* **0** Inches *check box and choose* OK	Always includes 0, like 12'-0 ½" instead of dimensions such as 12'-½"
In the main Dimension Styles and Settings *dialog box, click in the* **D**imension Style *box and type* **ARCH** *then press Enter*	Defines dimension style ARCH with the current settings, displays message "New style ARCH created from *UNNAMED" and replaces *UNNAMED with ARCH in the Dimension **S**tyles list box
Choose OK	Exits dialog box and saves settings
Command: *Choose* **M**odify, Ed**i**t Dimension, **U**pdate Dimension, *and update the two existing dimensions*	Updates the dimensions to the new settings (see fig. 21.14)

The updated dimensions are close to common architectural standards, but still take up too much space and aren't in an "architectural" style font. Both of these problems can be resolved by defining a new text style.

Use the STYLE command to create a text style named ARCHS. Use the ARCHS.SHX font file from the IALT Disk. ARCHS.SHX should be in your \DWGS\FONTS directory; if not, see Appendix G. Create the style with 0 Height, 0.75 Width, and default all other settings. This becomes the current text style.

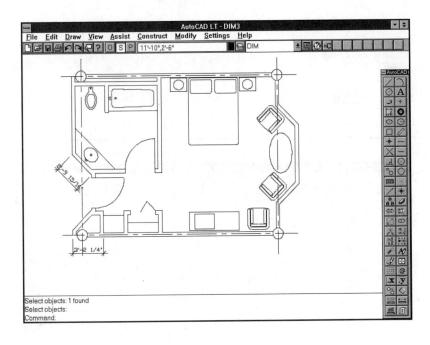

Figure 21.14

An architectural plan updated to new style settings.

Zoom in to the view in figure 21.15.

Command: *Choose* **M**odify, Ed**i**t Dimension, **U**pdate Dimension, *and update the two existing dimensions*	Updates the dimensions to the new style (see fig. 21.15)

Next, you add a couple of continued dimensions, using point filters to set the extension line origin so it is clear of the wall line.

Command: *Choose* **D**raw, L**i**near Dimensions, **C**ontinue	Issues the DIM1 and CONTINUE commands

`_dim1`

`Dim: _continue`

Second extension line origin or RETURN to select: **(Enter)**	Enables you to select a dimension
Select continued dimension: *Pick the dimension at* ① *(see fig. 21.15)*	Selects dimension to continue from
Second extension line origin or RETURN to select: **.X (Enter)**	Specifies .X point filter
of *Pick* ②	Sets X origin to corner of closet

continues

continued

(need YZ): *Use a NEArest object snap*   Sets the origin on the center line
to pick the center line at ③

Dimension text <2'-6">: (Enter)   Accepts the text and draws the dimension

Repeat the CONTINUE command to draw the 3'-6" dimension in figure 21.15.

Figure 21.15

An architectural plan updated to new text style.

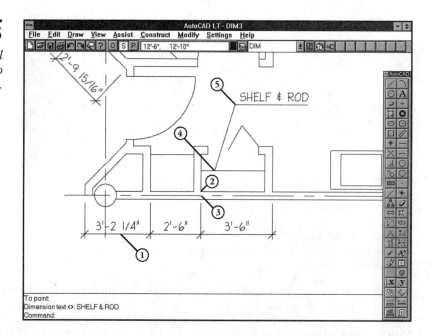

This is about as good an architectural style as you can achieve with AutoCAD LT. You might prefer numerator-over-denominator fractions instead of the numerator/denominator fractions here. If so, you need AutoCAD Release 13.

Don't confuse dimension and text styles. Text styles are created with the STYLE command and dimension styles are created with the DDIM command (Dimension Styles and Settings dialog box). There is also a STYLE command in Dim: mode, but it only sets a new text style current. The current text style and current dimension style are used for all new and updated dimensions.

Tip

The prototype drawing for the previous exercise has units precision (in the Units Control dialog box) set to 1/64". Although you might not need to draw to such small increments, you need this setting in order to set dimension settings to small values.

You might want to use the color settings in the Scale and Colors dialog box of the Dimension Styles and Settings dialog box to assign specific colors to the parts of the dimension. Colors are used to control plotted line weight. Most architects probably also prefer a heavier tick mark, but there is no color setting for it. You can use a user-defined arrow block instead of a tick, and design your "arrow" so it looks like a heavier tick. The process is similar to that shown in the following exercise, which uses a user arrow for leader notes.

In the following exercise, you try drawing a leader with the current style, as shown at ④ and ⑤ in figure 21.15. Then you create a new dimension style for leader notes. The ARROWHD block used is drawn as a unit-sized block. You can insert and examine it if you like. In the exercise, you have to insert it before it is available for dimensioning, but you can cancel the insertion. When you cancel an insertion, the block definition is still imported.

Creating a Dimension Style for Leader Notes

Continue in the DIM3 drawing from the previous exercise.

Command: *Choose* **D**raw, Leade**r**	Issues the DIM1 and LEADER commands
_dim1	
Dim: _leader Leader start: *Use a NEArest object snap to override the running modes and pick* ④ *(see fig. 21.15)*	Sets start point of leader
To point: *Pick* ⑤	Sets next point
To point: (Enter)	Ends leader lines
Dimension text <>: **SHELF & ROD** (Enter)	Draws leader and text (see fig. 21.15)

The leader lacks an arrow head and you might not like having the leader line under your callout text.

Command: *Click on the Undo button*	Undoes the leader and text
_U GROUP	

You need a new NOTES dimension style to fix this, as follows:

Command: **IN**	Issues the INSERT command
INSERT Block name (or ?): **ARROWHD** (Enter)	Specifies the ARROWHD block from the \DWGS\IALT directory

continues

21

continued

`Insertion point:` *Choose the Cancel button*	Cancels the INSERT command, but the block is already imported and remains available for the following NOTES style
`*Cancel*`	
`Command:` *Choose* **S**ettings, Di**m**ension Style	Opens Dimension Styles and Settings dialog box
Double-click in the **D**imension Style *box and type* **NOTES** *then press Enter*	Defines dimension style NOTES with the current settings, displays message "New style NOTES created from ARCH" and adds NOTES to the Dimension **S**tyles list box
In the Arrows *dialog box, choose the* **U**ser *radio button*	Ungrays the User Arrow box
Double-click in the User Arro**w** *edit box, enter* **ARROWHD**, *then choose* OK	Sets to use the ARROWHD block you imported
In the Text Location *dialog box, set* **V**ertical *to* Centered, *then choose* OK	Sets text along side instead of above the leader line
Choose OK	Exits Dimension Styles and Settings dialog box and saves NOTES settings
`Command:` *Choose* **D**raw, Leade**r** *and redraw the previous leader and text*	Creates the leader and text shown in figure 21.16

 Stop   Be sure you have the correct dimension style set current before you create, update, or edit dimensions. The DIMSTYLE dimension variable, the STATUS and VARIABLES dimensioning commands, and the highlighted name in the Dimension Styles and Settings dialog box should indicate the current dimension style.

 **ALT2**

In early versions of AutoCAD LT Release 2, however, the uppermost style name might be highlighted in the Dimension Styles and Settings dialog box, and the DIMSTYLE dimension variable, the STATUS and VARIABLES dimensioning commands might erroneously list *UNNAMED regardless of the actual style current. Early versions of AutoCAD LT Release 2 might also experience loss of settings in styles, reverting to the settings of the uppermost style name in the Dimension Styles and Settings dialog box.

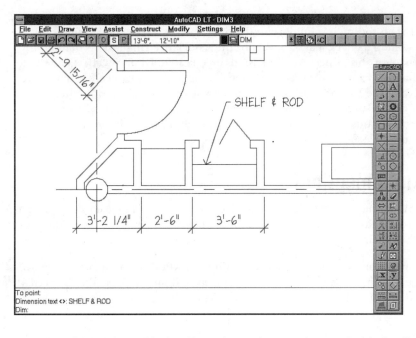

Figure 21.16

An architectural plan with the new NOTES style and leader.

In AutoCAD Release 13, the dimension style name is stored with the dimensions created with that style and protected from accidental changes due to updating or editing. In AutoCAD LT, the dimension style current when the dimension is created, updated, or edited determines the dimension's appearance.

 Tip   You can create a set of named dimension styles and import them into any drawing. To do so, create the styles in an empty drawing, then use the INSERT command to insert that drawing into any other drawing. You can cancel the INSERT command at the `Insertion point:` prompt. Even though canceled, the dimension styles will be imported and available.

Editing Associative Dimensions

An *associative dimension* is a single dimension object. In AutoCAD LT, a single dimension object consists of arrowheads, dimension lines, dimension text, and extension lines. If you stretch one or more objects, any associative dimension related to the feature also changes automatically; you do not have to redimension it. You will discover many advantages to using associative dimensions.

You make dimensions associative by setting the DIMASO dimension variable to ON (the default). This setting is so important that it is listed as a separate **S**ettings pull-down menu item. If a check mark appears by the Associati**v**e Dimensions item, the setting is turned on and associative dimensions are created. DIMASO affects linear, angular, ordinate, diameter, and radius dimensioning. Leaders and center marks are not associative. If the DIMASO setting is on when you create a dimension, the dimension is created as a single associative dimension object. All of the dimensions you have created in this and the previous chapter have been associative (unless you accidentally turned associativity off).

Exploding Dimensions

If the DIMASO setting is off when you create a dimension, the dimension is created as individual arrowheads (blocks), dimension lines, dimension text, and extension lines, each component being a separate AutoCAD LT object.

When you explode an associative dimension with the EXPLODE command, you have the same objects as if you had created a non-associative dimension. All the individual items of the dimension, such as text, arrows, and extension lines, can be edited individually.

Stop   In many production CAD applications, it is not recommended that you use exploded or non-associative dimensions unless there is a special reason to do so.

Editing Associative Dimensions

When you use associative dimensions, you create definition points on a layer named DEFPOINTS. Definition points associate the dimension to the object being dimensioned. You can snap to definition points with the NODe object snap mode. Definition points exist at each extension-line origin and at the intersection of the dimension line with the second extension line.

You can use the STRETCH command to stretch associative dimensions or to move associative dimension text. If you catch a definition point in the STRETCH command's crossing window, the dimension is stretched. Although the dimension text does not have an actual definition point at the center, it behaves as if there were. You can use STRETCH to move dimension text by selecting it with a small crossing window centered on the text.

AutoCAD LT provides six dimensioning commands for editing the appearance of associative dimensions. Three of these commands are presented here, and the others are covered later in the chapter. Figure 21.17 shows these commands in the **M**odify pull-down menu under the Ed**i**t Dimension item.

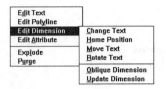

Figure 21.17

The editing commands for associative dimensions.

The remaining exercises in this chapter use an architectural drawing. Because this is an architectural drawing, it would be proper to place the text above the dimension line and use ticks instead of arrows. After you change these two settings, you use the UPDATE command to update the existing four dimensions.

In the following exercise, you use the STRETCH command to widen the closet by 12 inches—the dimension is automatically updated to 4'-6"—and use grip editing to move (stretch) dimension text. You also use the NEWTEXT command to change the text of an 8 ¼" dimension to 8". Figure 21.18 shows the drawing before you edit the dimensions.

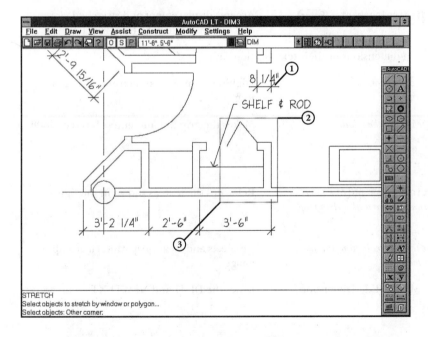

Figure 21.18

The drawing before editing.

21

Changing and Stretching Associative Dimensions

Continue from either of the two previous exercises.

Command: *Choose* **S**ettings, Di**m**ension Style *and click on* ARCH, *then choose* OK	Opens Dimension Styles and Settings dialog and sets the ARCH style current

continues

continued

Command: *Choose* **D**raw, **L**inear Dimensions,
Horizontal *and draw the dimension at* ①
(see fig. 21.18)

Command: **S** (Enter)   Issues the STRETCH command

STRETCH
Select objects to stretch by
window or polygon

Select objects: *Select a crossing window*
from ② *to* ③

Select objects: (Enter)

Base point or displacement: **12,0** (Enter)   Specifies the displacement

Second point of displacement: (Enter)   Accepts displacement and stretched closet
                                                    and dimension to 4'-6" (see fig. 21.19)

You can also stretch dimensions or their text location with grips.

Command: *Pick the dimension at* ①   Highlights the 8 ¼" dimension and shows
                                                    its grips

Command: *Pick the grip in the middle*   Makes the grip hot and enters Stretch mode
of the text

  ** STRETCH **

<Stretch to point>/Base point/Copy/   Relocates the text, as shown in the figure
Undo/eXit: *Turn on Ortho and pick* ④
(see fig. 21.19)

Command: *Choose the Cancel button and the*   Deselects and clears grips and cleans up the
Redraw button or tool   image

Command: *Choose* **M**odify, Ed**i**t Dimension,   Issues the DIM1 and NEWTEXT commands
Change Text

_dim1
Dim: _newtext

Enter new dimension text: **8"** (Enter)

Select objects: *Select the 8 ¼" dimension*   Updates the text to 8"
at ④ *and press Enter*

Command: *Choose* **M**odify, Ed**it** Dimension, **H**ome Position	Issues the DIM1 and HOMETEXT commands
Command: _dim1 Dim: _hometext	
Select objects: **P** (Enter)	Reselects the previously selected text
Select objects: (Enter)	Ends selection and moves the text back between the extension lines

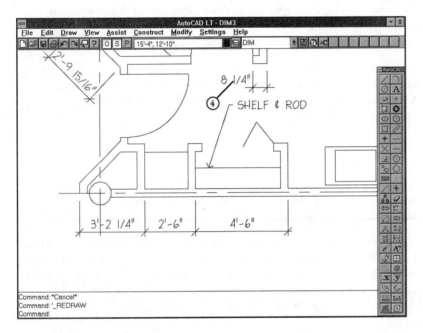

Figure 21.19

The dimensions after stretching, before NEWTEXT.

21

When you stretch an associative dimension or edit it with the NEWTEXT, HOMETEXT, or UPDATE command, the associative dimension is updated to the current dimension variable settings. Because of this updating, you must take care to ensure that all dimension variables are set appropriately for the dimension(s) being edited before you update them.

> Dim: **HOMETEXT.** The HOMETEXT dimensioning command restores associative dimension text to its original default position. You can use this command after you modify the text location. The **M**odify pull-down menu item for this command is **H**ome Position.

> Dim: **NEWTEXT.** The NEWTEXT dimensioning command changes selected existing associative dimension text; or, if you press Enter at the new text prompt, the NEWTEXT command restores selected existing associative dimension text to its default measured value. The **M**odify pull-down menu item for this command is **C**hange Text.

> Dim: **UPDATE.** The UPDATE dimensioning command changes selected existing associative dimension objects to the current unit, text style, dimension style, and dimension variable settings. The **M**odify pull-down menu item for this command is **U**pdate Dimension.

AutoCAD LT includes several other dimensioning commands for editing the appearance of associative dimensions. TEDIT changes the location and angle of dimension text, TROTATE (Text Rotate) rotates existing dimension text, and OBLIQUE changes the angle of extension lines.

TROTATE is another dimensioning command that enables you to edit dimension text. As its name implies, TROTATE rotates dimension text to the angle you specify.

The last dimensioning command, OBLIQUE, is useful for dimensioning isometric drawings or for angling the dimension lines when they do not fit in a tight spot. Oblique is useful for isometric dimensioning.

In the following exercise, you use a few dimension editing commands on some of the dimensions in the architectural DIM3 drawing. First you relocate the 4'-6" dimension to the right with TEDIT, and then you rotate the 8" dimension text 45 degrees. None of the drawing's features is really suitable for an oblique dimension, but try the OBLIQUE command anyway on the 8" dimension.

Editing Dimensions with the TEDIT, TROTATE, and OBLIQUE Commands

Continue from the previous exercise.

Command: *Choose* **M**odify, Ed**i**t Dimension,   Issues the TEDIT command
Move Text

_dim1
Dim: _tedit

Select dimension: *Select the 4'-6" dimension*

`Enter text location (Left/Right/` `Home/Angle):` *Move the cursor, noting* *how it drags the text, then enter* **R**	Moves the text to the right, as shown in figure 21.20
Command: *Choose* **M**odify, Ed**i**t Dimension, **R**otate Text	Issues the TROTATE command
`_dim1` `Dim: _trotate`	
`Enter text angle:` **45** (Enter)	Specifies a 45-degree angle
`Select objects:` *Select the 8" dimension*	
`Select objects:` (Enter)	Ends selection and rotates the text
Command: *Choose* **M**odify, Ed**i**t Dimension, **O**blique Dimension	Issues the OBLIQUE command
`_dim1` `Dim: _oblique`	
`Select object:` *Pick the 8" dimension*	
`Select object:` (Enter)	
`Enter obliquing angle` `(RETURN for none):` **-45** (Enter)	Obliques the dimension, as shown in the figure

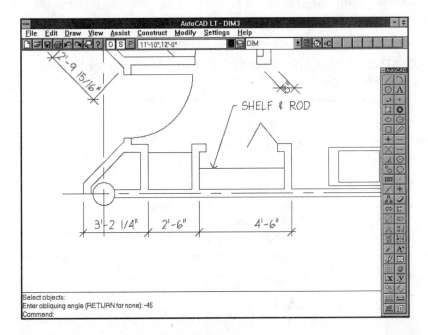

Figure 21.20

The modified dimensions.

21

You might want to experiment on this drawing by creating and editing more dimensions and dimension styles.

> `Dim:` **TEDIT.** The TEDIT (DIMension Text Edit) dimensioning command relocates existing dimension text. You can drag the dimension text into place with your pointing device; specify left, right, or home (original) justification; or specify a text angle.

The TEDIT command includes the following options:

◆ **Left.** The Left option relocates linear, radius, and diameter dimension text to the left side of the dimension line. The exact text location varies depending on the vertical placement of the dimension.

◆ **Right.** The Right option relocates linear, radius, and diameter dimension text to the right side of the dimension line. The exact text location varies depending on the vertical placement of the dimension.

◆ **Home.** The Home option restores dimension text to its original location (similar to the HOMETEXT dimensioning command).

◆ **Angle.** The Angle option rotates dimension text to the angle you specify (similar to the TROTATE dimensioning command).

◆ **Enter text location.** The Enter point option relocates dimension text to the point you specify (similar to using the STRETCH command).

> `Dim:` **TROTATE.** The TROTATE (Text Rotate) dimensioning command rotates existing dimension text to any angle.

 Note The TEDIT Angle option produces the same result as the TROTATE command, although TROTATE can change more than one dimension at a time.

> `Dim:` **OBLIQUE.** The OBLIQUE dimensioning command changes existing associative extension-line angles without changing the dimension text value. Press Enter at the angle prompt to restore the default angle.

Although the exercises in this chapter might not reflect your particular dimensioning standards, this and the previous chapters covered all the major aspects of AutoCAD LT dimensioning. By using a combination of dimension variables and dimension creation techniques, along with some dimension editing commands, you should be able to dimension a drawing to your specific standards.

This chapter made several references to the paper space environment. Understanding the paper space environment helps you to prepare your drawings for final plotting. This topic is covered next, in Chapter 22.

21

Structuring Your Drawing

In this chapter, you learn the proper techniques for laying out your finished drawing in preparation for plotting. Specifically, this chapter discusses the following topics:

◆ Applying your knowledge of views and viewports

◆ Laying out views and details to compose finished plots

◆ Using AutoCAD LT Release 2's Custom Setup feature to set up a new drawing in paper space

◆ Composing and scaling floating mview viewports in paper space

◆ Using multiple viewports in paper space

◆ Adding dimensions in floating mview viewports, and adjusting dimension scales automatically

◆ Inserting a border and a title block in paper space

Even though AutoCAD LT is supposed to be a "light" version of AutoCAD, the capability to create multiview plots at a variety of scale factors without modifying the original CAD model is a rather advanced CAD technique.

A simple CAD drawing with a plotting scale of 1:1 is ready to plot as soon as it is completed. If scaling factors will be used during plotting, you need to compensate by applying the appropriate text height, dimension feature scaling, and linetype and hatch scales. You will learn how to efficiently manage these scale factors through the use of paper space.

The exercises in this chapter use two common drawing applications: an architectural model and a mechanical model. The final architectural drawing contains a complete view of the building, along with several detailed views. This application demonstrates the power of paper space scaling. In addition, you prepare a three-dimensional mechanical model for plotting as several orthographic views and an isometric view, as shown in figure 22.1. In working with these two applications, you will discover the power and flexibility of AutoCAD LT.

Figure 22.1

A multiview drawing in paper space.

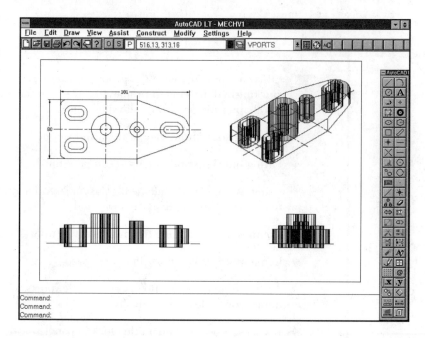

Applying Model Space Views and Viewports

What is model space? *Model space* is an AutoCAD LT command (MSPACE), but more important, model space is the CAD drafting environment to which you have become accustomed. You draw your model in model space in AutoCAD LT. This book has emphasized how important it is to draw objects (the model) full scale in a CAD environment. Whether you are designing microchips or skyscrapers, the model space environment in AutoCAD LT enables you to create your model at full scale.

In some CAD drafting applications, model space is the only environment you need to complete your work. The first drawing exercise in this chapter reviews the many viewing options available in model space. Because Chapter 5 explained these viewing commands, extensive coverage is not repeated here.

Using Views in Your Drawing

One of the most common initial objections to CAD is that people cannot imagine how they are going to work on large and complex drawings using a relatively small graphics window. As you become familiar with CAD, however, you learn to use the ZOOM and PAN options frequently to view the CAD model at various locations and scale factors.

The VIEW command enables you to name a given view so that it can quickly be recalled.

You begin the drawing exercises in this chapter by starting a new drawing named ARCHV1, which is based on the prototype ALT2201.DWG file. This file is the same as the plan at the end of the previous chapter, except the dimensions have been erased. You save several views of the ARCHV1 drawing for use in later exercises.

Saving Views in Your Drawing

Create a new drawing named ARCHV1, using the ALT2201.DWG file as a prototype, and using no setup method.

Command: *Choose* **V**iew, **V**iew, **S**ave	Issues the VIEW command with the Save option
`'_view ?/Delete/Restore/Save/Window:` `_save  View name to save:` **FULL** (Enter)	Saves the view under the name of FULL

continues

continued

Command: **V** (Enter)	Issues the VIEW command
VIEW ?/Delete/Restore/Save/ Window: **W** (Enter)	Specifies the Window option
View name to save: **BATH** (Enter)	Saves the view under the name of BATH
First corner: *Pick point* ① *(see fig. 22.2)*	
Other corner: *Pick point* ②	
Command: (Enter)	Repeats the VIEW command
VIEW ?/Delete/Restore/Save/ Window: **W** (Enter)	Specifies the Window option
View name to save: **ENT** (Enter)	Saves the entrance view under the name of ENT
First corner: *Pick point* ③	
Other corner: *Pick point* ④	

Save the drawing

Figure 22.2

Naming views in the drawing.

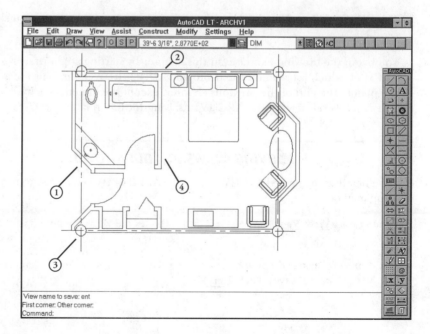

After you have named views, you can quickly access them by using the Restore option of the VIEW command. In the next exercise, you restore views.

Setting Up Model Space Tiled Viewports

If you find yourself frequently switching views during your drawing session, you might want to use multiple viewports to see several views of your drawing in the same graphics window. The VIEWPORTS (VPORTS) command enables you to partition the graphics window into a variety of different window arrangements.

The following exercise defines three viewports and specifies which view is to be displayed in each viewport. When you work in multiple viewports, remember to keep track of which viewport is *active*. The active viewport has a highlighted border, and you can activate any viewport by clicking in it. You also can name viewport configurations so that they can easily be retrieved.

Creating Model Space Viewports

Continue working with the ARCHV1 drawing.

Command: *Choose **V**iew, Viewp**o**rts, **3** Viewports*   Issues the VIEWPORTS command with the **3** Viewports option

```
_vports Save/Restore/Delete/Join/
SIngle/?/2/<3>/4: _3
Horizontal/Vertical/Above/Below/
Left/<Right>: (Enter)
```
Specifies a large view on the right

```
Regenerating drawing.
```

The right viewport should now be active.

Command: **V** (Enter)   Issues the VIEW command

```
VIEW ?/Delete/Restore/Save/
Window: R (Enter)
```
Specifies the Restore option

```
View name to restore: FULL (Enter)
```
Restores the FULL view in the right viewport

Command: *Click in the upper left viewport to make it active*

Command: **V** (Enter)   Begins the VIEW command

continues

22

continued

`VIEW ?/Delete/Restore/Save/` `Window:` **R** (Enter)	Specifies the Restore option
`View name to restore:` **BATH** (Enter)	Restores the BATH view in the upper left viewport
`Command:` *Click in the lower left viewport to make it active*	
`Command:` **V** (Enter)	Begins the VIEW command
`VIEW ?/Delete/Restore/Save/` `Window:` **R** (Enter)	Specifies the Restore option
`View name to restore:` **ENT** (Enter)	Restores the ENT view in the lower left viewport

Your drawing should now resemble figure 22.3.

`Command:` **VPORTS** (Enter)	Issues the VPORTS command
`Save/Restore/Delete/Join/SIngle/` `?/2/<3>/4:` **S** (Enter)	Specifies the Save option
`?/Name for new viewport` `configuration:` **MY3** (Enter)	
`Command:` (Enter)	Repeats the VPORTS command
`Save/Restore/Delete/Join/SIngle/` `?/2/<3>/4:` **SI** (Enter)	Specifies the SIngle option and creates a single viewport
`Regenerating drawing.`	
`Command:` **VIEW** (Enter)	Issues the VIEW command
`?/Delete/Restore/Save/Window:` **R** (Enter)	Specifies the Restore option
`View name to restore:` **FULL** (Enter)	Restores the FULL view

Save the drawing

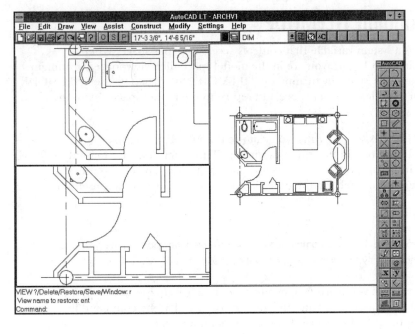

Figure 22.3

Three tiled viewports.

In the preceding exercise, you used the named views to set up your viewport configuration. You also can name the viewport configuration itself so that you can easily retrieve it at a later time.

Entering Paper Space

Have you ever been lost in paper space? You can easily become lost. When you leave the model space environment, you temporarily leave your model behind and enter a whole new drawing environment. You can create CAD objects in either model space or paper space. The rest of this chapter focuses on when to draw in model space and when to create objects in paper space. Paper space objects can never be viewed in model space; however, you can open windows in paper space to view the model space objects.

Simply stated, *paper space* is an environment that is used to compose a drawing sheet in order to prepare it for plotting. Plotting from paper space is done at a 1:1 ratio because the sheet border and the title block are created at full scale and all the model objects have been cut and pasted onto the sheet at the proper scale factors. This technique gives you much greater creativity in laying out CAD drawings for various plotting arrangements.

Understanding TILEMODE

TILEMODE is a system variable that controls access to paper space. When TILEMODE is set to 1 (on), you are in the model space tiled viewport environment. You can enter paper space by turning off TILEMODE (0). When you set TILEMODE back to 1 (on), you leave paper space and return to the model space environment with tiled viewports.

When TILEMODE is set to 1 (on), you can use the VPORTS command to create multiple tiled viewports in the graphics window. These viewports are helpful while you are drawing your model. Each viewport has its own display settings, but each is viewing the same model. On the other hand, tiled viewports are not useful for plotting.

 Note If you issue the PLOT command with multiple tiled viewports in the graphics window, only the active viewport will be plotted.

In the next exercise, you learn two ways to enter and leave paper space. You can use the View pull-down menu, or you can type the command at the command line. One of the most noticeable differences between model space and paper space is the different UCS icon that is used. To see the difference, turn on the UCS icon. Figure 22.4 shows your graphics window in paper space.

Figure 22.4

The paper space UCS icon.

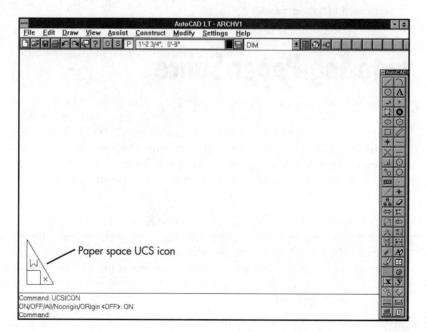

Paper space UCS icon

Entering and Leaving Paper Space

Continue working with your ARCHV1 drawing.

`Command:` *Choose* **A**ssist, U**CS** icon	Issues the UCSICON command
`_ucsicon ON/OFF/All/` `Noorigin/ORigin <OFF>:` **ON** (Enter)	Displays the UCS icon
`Command:` **TILEMODE** (Enter)	Accesses the TILEMODE variable
`New value for TILEMODE <1>:` **0** (Enter)	Turns TILEMODE off and enters paper space

`Entering Paper space.  Use MVIEW`
`to insert Model space viewports.`

`Regenerating drawing.`

`Command:` **UCSICON** (Enter)	Issues the UCSICON command
`ON/OFF/All/Noorigin/ORigin` `<OFF>:` **ON** (Enter)	Displays the paper space UCS icon
`Command:` **TILEMODE** (Enter)	Accesses the TILEMODE variable
`New value for TILEMODE <0>:` **1** (Enter)	Turns TILEMODE on and exits paper space

`Regenerating drawing.`

Now try entering paper space by using the **V**iew pull-down menu.

`Command:` *Choose* **V**iew, *then* **P**aper Space *(AutoCAD LT Release 1) or* **T**ile Mode *(AutoCAD LT Release 2)*	Turns TILEMODE off
`_tilemode New value` `for TILEMODE <1>: 0`	Enters paper space

`Regenerating drawing.`

`Command:` *Choose* **V**iew, Viewp**o**rts	Displays the Viewports submenu

Notice the Viewports options shown in figure 22.5.

`Command:` *Choose* **V**iew, *then* **P**aper Space *(AutoCAD LT Release 1) or* **T**ile Mode *(AutoCAD LT Release 2)*	Turns TILEMODE on

22

continues

continued

```
_tilemode New value                    Exits paper space
for TILEMODE <0>: 1

Regenerating drawing.
```

Command: *Choose* **V**iew, Viewp**o**rts   Displays the Viewports submenu

Notice the different set of Viewports options shown in figure 22.6.

Figure 22.5

*The AutoCAD LT
Releases 1 and 2
Viewports menus
with paper space
turned on and
TILEMODE off.*

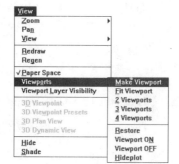

AutoCAD LT Release 1

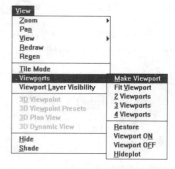

AutoCAD LT Release 2

Figure 22.6

*The AutoCAD
LT Releases 1
and 2 Viewports
menus with
paper space
turned off and
TILEMODE on.*

AutoCAD LT Release 1

AutoCAD LT Release 2

There is a minor difference in how the AutoCAD LT Release 1 and AutoCAD LT Release 2 menus indicate the status of TILEMODE. When paper space or a floating mview viewport in paper space is current (TILEMODE=0), the **P**aper Space item in the **V**iew pull-down menu has a check mark in AutoCAD LT Release 1, or the **T**ile Mode item is shown without a check mark in AutoCAD LT Release 2. When tile mode is current (TILEMODE=1), whether in a single full-window viewport or in multiple tiled viewports, the **P**aper Space item in the **V**iew pull-down menu is shown without a check mark in AutoCAD LT Release 1, or the **T**ile Mode item is shown with a check mark in AutoCAD LT Release 2. Choosing the **P**aper Space or **T**ile Mode item is the same as entering TILEMODE and turning it off if it was on, or on if it was off, at the command line.

Now that you understand how to enter and leave the paper space environment, continue to the next section, in which you learn to view your model in paper space.

Setting Up a Single Floating Mview Viewport in Paper Space

You can view objects that you have created in model space from paper space by opening one or more floating mview viewports. An *mview viewport* is a floating viewport, like a window you open in paper space through which you can view the model space objects. Floating mview viewports are much more flexible than tiled viewports. Unlike tiled viewports, floating mview viewports can be moved around and resized; they can even overlap each other. Before you open a floating mview viewport in paper space, it might be helpful to insert a B-size border and a title block so that you better understand the use of paper space.

Inserting a Border in Paper Space

Borders and title blocks used in paper space are always drawn for a 1:1 plotting scale. The B-size border drawing provided for this chapter is approximately 17 $1/2$ by 11 $1/2$ inches. In the following exercise, you insert this border in your existing drawing in paper space at the 0,0 point with a scale factor of 1. Most notes and symbols not directly tied to the model also should be added in the paper space environment. If you want text to appear at a height of $1/4$ inch, you must create this text at $1/4$ inch in paper space.

The following exercise demonstrates how to insert a border and a title block in the paper space environment.

Inserting a Border in Paper Space

Continue working with the ARCHV1 drawing. Create two new layers, BORDER and VPORT1, and make BORDER the current layer.

Command: *Choose* **V**iew, *then* **P**aper Space *(AutoCAD LT Release 1) or* **T**ile Mode *(AutoCAD LT Release 2)*	Turns off TILEMODE
`_tilemode`	
`New value for TILEMODE <1>: 0`	Enters paper space
`Regenerating drawing.`	
Command: *Choose* **D**raw, Insert Bloc**k**	Issues DDINSERT command and opens the Insert dialog box
`_ddinsert`	
In the **F**ile *text box, type* **ALTBORDR** *and turn off the* **S**pecify Parameters on Screen *parameter, then choose* OK	Inserts the ALTBORDR drawing at 0,0 with a scale of 1 and rotation of 0
Command: *Choose* **V**iew, **Z**oom, **A**ll	Shows the complete border (see fig. 22.7)

Save the drawing

Figure 22.7

Inserting the ALTBORDR border and title block.

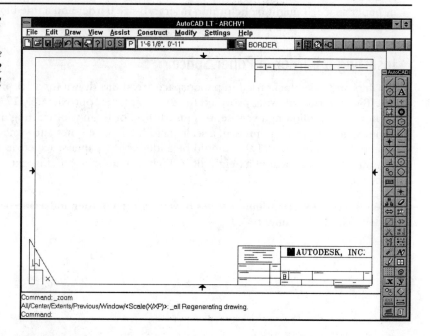

You now have a drawing with objects in model space (the architectural model) and in paper space (the border and title block). The next step is to create a floating mview viewport to view the model.

Using the MVIEW Command to Create a Viewport

When you choose the Viewports item from the **V**iew pull-down menu, the available options depend on whether TILEMODE is set to 0 or to 1. If TILEMODE is set to 1 (on), the VPORTS command is issued to create tiled viewports. If TILEMODE is set to 0 (off), the MVIEW command is issued.

> **MVIEW.** The MVIEW command creates viewports in paper space and controls the display of objects in those viewports. This command functions only when TILEMODE is set to 0.

The options of the MVIEW command are similar to those of the VPORTS command. The following list explains each of the MVIEW command options:

- ◆ **Make Viewport.** The **M**ake Viewport option enables you to specify a window that defines the floating mview viewport size and location by specifying two opposite corner points for the viewport.

- ◆ **Fit Viewport.** The **F**it Viewport option automatically creates a floating mview viewport to fill the size of the current drawing area.

- ◆ **2 Viewports.** The **2** Viewports option enables you to choose either a vertical or a horizontal partition between the two floating mview viewports; you then pick two opposite corner points or a window to define the size and location of both viewports. Figure 22.8 shows the results of both the vertical and horizontal choices.

- ◆ **3 Viewports.** The **3** Viewports option enables you to choose from several different view layouts—horizontal, vertical, large window on right, and so on. You then pick two points to define the size and location. Figure 22.8 shows two of the **3** Viewports options.

- ◆ **4 Viewports.** The **4** Viewports option enables you to create four equally sized floating mview viewports (see fig. 22.8).

- ◆ **Restore.** The **R**estore option restores a previously named and saved tiled viewport configuration, creating an equivalent floating viewport configuration in paper space.

22

◆ **Viewport O<u>N</u>/O<u>FF</u>.** The Viewport O<u>N</u> and Viewport O<u>FF</u> options control whether the contents of the viewport are displayed or hidden. The upper left floating mview viewport in figure 22.8 has been turned off by using this option.

◆ **<u>H</u>ideplot.** The <u>H</u>ideplot option causes hidden lines to be removed during plotting of specified floating mview viewports. This option is similar to the plotting option of removing hidden lines, but it applies only to selected floating mview viewports.

Note You can create as many floating mview viewports as you want, but AutoCAD LT displays the contents of only 15 viewports at a time.

Figure 22.8

Several floating mview viewport configurations.

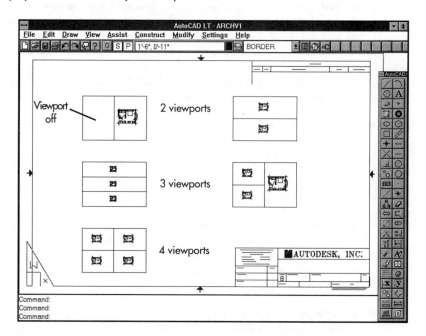

In the following exercise, try using the MVIEW command to create a floating mview viewport in paper space. You then use this floating mview viewport to view the architectural model. With this technique, you can lay out your final drawing sheet by creating and editing views of model space objects in paper space.

Creating a Floating Mview Viewport Using the MVIEW Command

Continue working with the ARCHV1 drawing. Make the VPORT1 layer current.

Command: *Choose* **V**iew, Viewp**o**rts, **M**ake Viewport	Issues the MVIEW command

`_mview`

```
ON/OFF/Hideplot/Fit/2/3/4/
Restore/<First Point>: Pick point
① (see fig. 22.9)
```

`Other corner:` *Pick point* ②	Specifies the size and location of the mview viewport

`Regenerating drawing.`

`Command:` *Click on the P button on the toolbar*	Issues the MSPACE command (see fig. 22.10)

`_MSPACE`

Try several ZOOM and PAN commands in this mview viewport.

`Command:` *Click on the P button on the toolbar* *again*	Issues the PSPACE command

`_PSPACE`

Try several more ZOOM and PAN commands to see how they affect the entire graphics window. Save the drawing for a later exercise.

In addition to using the MVIEW command, you used two other new commands in the preceding exercise, MSPACE and PSPACE.

Activating a Viewport in Paper Space

When TILEMODE is set to 0, you can switch between the paper space environment and a current mview viewport. To switch between the two environments, you use the MSPACE and PSPACE commands, or you click on the P button on the toolbar.

22

Figure 22.9

Creating a floating mview viewport with the MVIEW command.

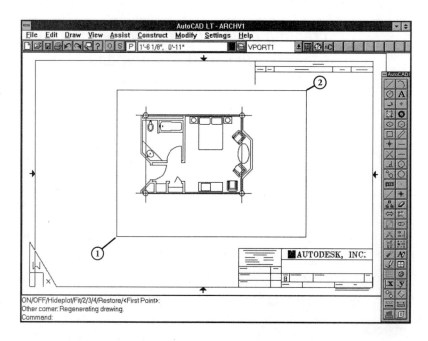

Figure 22.10

Using MSPACE to activate a floating mview viewport.

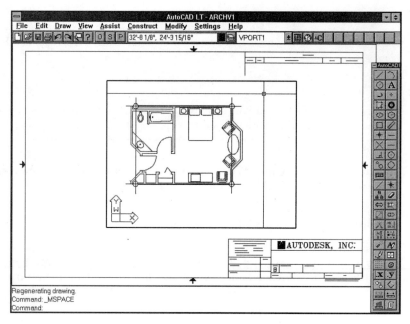

> **MSPACE.** The MSPACE command activates a floating mview viewport so that you can work in that viewport in the model space environment. This command functions only when TILEMODE is set to 0 and is effective only if there is a current mview viewport to activate.

> **PSPACE.** The PSPACE command switches from an active mview viewport to paper space. This command functions only when TILEMODE is set to 0.

You now have two choices for entering model space. Either you can turn TILEMODE on (1) to leave paper space, or you can use the MSPACE command to activate a floating mview viewport while TILEMODE is off (0).

If you are using AutoCAD LT Release 2, you have another option for inserting a title block and viewport in a new drawing. If you are using AutoCAD LT Release 1, skip to the "Composing a Multiview Drawing" section.

Using Custom Setup to Insert a Title Block and Viewport

If you are using AutoCAD LT Release 2, you can also use the Custom Setup feature in the Create New Drawing dialog box to insert a title block and viewport in a new drawing. As shown in figure 22.11, the Custom Drawing Setup dialog box offers control over units, size, all drawing aids, and the title block inserted. It also includes a time/date stamp feature, which inserts an attribute block.

ALT2

After you complete the desired settings in the Create New Drawing dialog box and choose OK, Custom Setup inserts the specified title block in paper space, inserts the date stamp block, creates a single floating mview viewport, and zooms model space in the viewport to the size you specified. It leaves model space current.

Try using Custom Setup to set up a new drawing similar to those in previous exercises.

Figure 22.11

The Custom Drawing Setup dialog box.

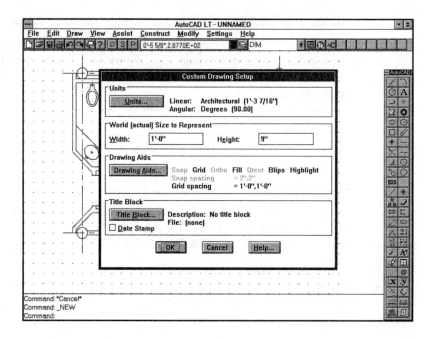

Figure 22.11

The Custom Drawing Setup dialog box.

Creating Floating Viewport with Custom Setup

Click on the New button (save the current drawing if prompted)

Opens the Create New Drawing dialog box

Enter **ALT2201** *in the* **P**rototype *edit box, choose the* **C**ustom Setup *radio button, then choose* OK

Opens the drawing in tilemode, then opens the Custom Drawing Setup dialog box

The Custom Drawing Setup dialog box inherits its default settings from the prototype drawing, except for the limits (World (actual) Size to Represent). Review them before proceeding (see fig. 22.11).

Enter **32'** *in the* **W**idth *box and* **24'** *in the* H**ei**ght *box*

Sets the limits***************

Choose Drawing **Ai**ds

Opens the Drawing Aids dialog box

Turn on Snap *and choose* OK

Sets snap and returns to the Custom Drawing Setup dialog box

Choose Title **B**lock

Opens the Title Block dialog box (see fig. 22.12)

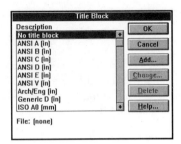

Figure 22.12

*The Title Block
dialog box.*

The Title Block dialog box displays descriptions for the title block drawings that have been placed on the Description list for easy access. Next you add the ALTBORDR drawing to the list.

Choose Add

Opens the Add New Title Block dialog box (see fig. 22.13)

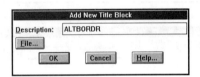

Figure 22.13

*The Add New
Title Block
dialog box.*

Enter **IA LT Border** *in the* **D**escription *box and
choose the* **F**ile *button*

Opens the Select Title Block File dialog box, a standard file dialog box

Select the **altbordr.dwg** *file from the* \DWGS\IALT
directory and choose OK

Selects the drawing to insert in paper space, and returns to the Add New Title Block dialog box, which now shows altbordr next to the **F**ile button

In the Add New Title Block *dialog box,
choose* OK

Closes the dialog box and shows IA LT Border selected in the Description list of the Title Block dialog box

In the Title Block *dialog box, choose* OK

Closes the dialog box and lists the IA LT Border description and altbordr.dwg file name next to the Title **B**lock button in the Custom Drawing Setup dialog box

In the Custom Drawing Setup *dialog
box, put a check in the* **D**ate Stamp *check box*

Activates the date stamp insertion feature

Choose OK

Inserts the title block in paper space and zooms to its limits, then prompts for the date stamp block insertion

continues

continued

```
REVDATE block insertion point
<0,0>: .5,.5 (Enter)
```

```
REVDATE block rotation (0 or 90      Inserts the date stamp block and creates
degrees) <0>: 90 (Enter)             a floating mview viewport in paper space
                                     (see fig. 22.14)
```

As the date stamp block indicates, the drawing is unnamed.

```
Command: Click on the Save button     Opens the Save Drawing As dialog box
```

Enter **CUSTOM** *and choose* OK   Names and saves the drawing

```
Command: Choose Modify, Date and Time   Updates the date stamp, changing the time
                                        and changing the drawing name to CUSTOM
```

Figure 22.14

An inserted title block, date stamp, and floating viewport in paper space.

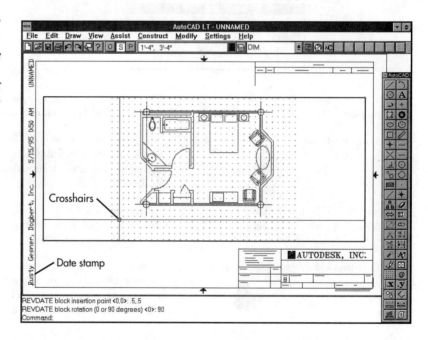

There are several limitations to Custom Setup:

◆ Snap and grid settings are the same in paper space and model space, requiring you to reset them to a more useful setting in one or the other.

◆ Size/scale-related settings are based on calculations controlled by the height entered in the Height box of the Custom Drawing Setup dialog box, instead of prompting you for intended plot scale and using it as a basis. This might yield silly settings such as 1 $^{43}/_{64}$ for text size or fillet radius.

◆ All size/scale-related dimension variables for the default *UNNAMED dimension style (unless DIMSCALE is set to 0) are based on calculations controlled by the height entered in the Height box, instead of considering intended plot scale. Named dimension styles are not affected. See the previous chapter for an important warning about the implications of this.

◆ The model space view is zoomed to fill the available viewport with the specified real world height, instead of being scaled relative to paper space (to an intended plot scale).

◆ The viewport is sized to fill the available space in the title block, instead of providing you control of its size or position.

◆ You cannot create multiple viewports with the Custom Drawing Setup dialog box.

You can either use your own setup methods, or reset size-related settings and edit or add to the floating viewports after setup to deal with these limitations.

The title block and date stamp settings remain the defaults for subsequent use of Custom Setup. Now that you have added the ALTBORDR title block to the list, you can easily select it if another title block has later been made the default.

Tip   You can change the user name in the date stamp by changing the user name in the Preferences dialog box, then updating it with the Date and Time menu item.

Composing a Multiview Drawing

In this chapter, the term *composing* refers to the final size and placement of views on the sheet to be plotted. Typically, the final drawing sheet is laid out in paper space at full scale. Most of the general notes, tables, and items not directly associated with the model are created or inserted in paper space.

Mview viewports are extremely flexible. In paper space, the mview viewports function like any other AutoCAD LT object. They can be moved, scaled, stretched, or erased.

Tip The mview viewport borders are convenient for manipulating the viewports, but you do not normally want to see them on the final plot. Create the mview viewport borders on a separate layer, and then turn off that layer to remove the borders.

Defining Multiple Mview Viewports

Without the paper space capabilities of AutoCAD LT, you would have to manually copy and scale different sections of your drawing to create multiple views. Another alternative would be to draw the other views separately. This method really creates problems, however, when engineering changes occur because you have to change every part of the drawing where that feature is shown. When you define multiple mview viewports, you are viewing the same model, but through many windows with different scale factors or viewing locations.

In the following exercise, you create several mview viewports. First you erase the single mview viewport and restore the MY3 viewport configuration created in the tiled viewports exercise at the beginning of the chapter. You can restore saved model space viewport configurations in paper space as a shortcut for creating similar mview viewport configurations. Then you create three new mview viewports and experiment with performing some of the common editing commands on these viewports.

Creating Multiple Mview Viewports

Reopen the ARCHV1 drawing that you saved in an earlier exercise.

Command: **E** (Enter)   Issues the ERASE command

ERASE Select objects: *Pick the border of the viewport*

1 found Select objects: (Enter)   Erases the single mview viewport

Command: *Choose* **V**iew, Viewp**o**rts, **R**estore   Issues the MVIEW command with the
                                                         Restore option

mview ON/OFF/Hideplot/Fit/2/3/4/   Specifies the MY3 tiled viewport
Restore/<First Point>:_restore   configuration to restore in paper space
?/Name of window configuration to
insert <*ACTIVE*>: **MY3** (Enter)

```
Fit/<First Point>: Pick point ①
(see fig. 22.15)
```

```
Second point: Pick point ②
```
Defines size and location and then creates the saved configuration

```
Regenerating drawing.
```

```
Command: U Enter
```
Undoes the last command

```
GROUP Regenerating drawing.
```

```
Command: Choose View, Viewports,
3 Viewports
```
Issues the MVIEW command with the 3 Viewports option

```
_mview ON/OFF/Hideplot/Fit/
2/3/4/Restore/<First Point>: 3
```

```
Horizontal/Vertical/Above/Below/Left
/<Right>: Enter
```

```
Fit/<First Point>: Pick point ①
(see fig. 22.15)
```

```
Second point: Pick point ②
```
Defines size and location

```
Regenerating drawing.
```
Creates three viewports

```
Command: Enter
```
Repeats the MOVE command

```
MOVE
```

```
Select objects: Pick the right
viewport border
```

```
1 found Select objects: Enter
```

```
Base point or displacement: 1,0 Enter
```
Specifies the displacement

```
Second point of displacement: Enter
```
Accepts the displacement and moves the viewport 1 inch to the right, as shown in figure 22.16

```
Command: Choose Modify, Move
```

```
_move
```

```
Select objects: Pick the lower left viewport
border
```

continues

22

continued

1 found Select objects: (Enter)

Base point or displacement: **0,-1** (Enter)

Second point of displacement:
(Enter)

Moves the viewport 1 inch down, as shown
in figure 22.16

Save the drawing

Figure 22.15

*Restoring the
MY3 viewport
configuration.*

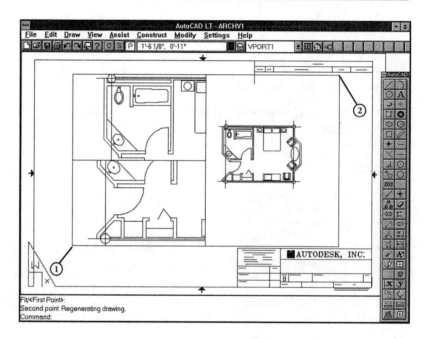

Notice how easy it is to edit the mview viewports by selecting the borders. The
STRETCH command is useful for changing the size and shape of the viewports.

The next step in composing a multiview drawing layout is to control the viewing scale
of the viewports.

Controlling the Display of Mview Viewports

When you model a design in AutoCAD LT, you draw it at full size. If the design is a
house or another large object, the model can be 100 or more feet in size. To show
such a large object to scale on a small sheet of paper, you scale the object's mview
viewport by using the XP option of the ZOOM command.

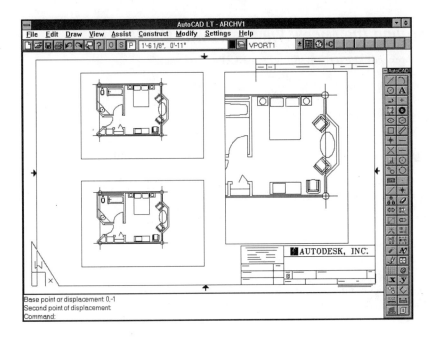

Figure 22.16

Mview viewports after moving.

◆ **ZOOM XP**. The XP option of the ZOOM command enables you to specify a scale factor as a proportion of the paper space scale factor.

The process of determining the scale factor for full-size models to fit standard-size drawing sheets has already been discussed in Chapter 8, "Preparing Your Workspace: CAD Concepts 1B." Chapter 23, "Producing Hard Copy," covers the topic of scale further with a discussion of plotting scale.

In this chapter, you use the architectural drawing to determine the scale factor of mview viewports. First, consider the paper size. To plot the 24-foot-long room at a scale of 1"=4'-0" (or a plot-scale factor of $1/48$: one plotted inch equals 48 drawing units) requires an area 6 feet long. A B-size (11"×17") page is sufficient for that view, along with several other views required to show better detail. The bathroom, measuring about 8 feet long, requires about 4 inches to show at a $1/2$"=1' or 1:24 scale.

In the following exercise, try using the ZOOM XP capability to give scale factors to the three mview viewports. To work inside the viewports in model space, you must first activate the mview viewports with the MSPACE command. Remember, before you issue the command you want to affect a viewport, you must click in that viewport to make it active.

Scaling the Mview Viewports with ZOOM XP

Continue from the preceding exercise, using the ARCHV1 drawing.

Command: *Click on the P button on the toolbar*	Issues the MSPACE command
Command: *If the right viewport is not active, click in it*	
Command: **Z** ⏎	Issues the ZOOM command
ZOOM All/Center/Extents/Previous/ Window/<Scale(X/XP)>: **1/48XP** ⏎	Zooms the right viewport to ¹⁄₄₈ of the paper space scale
Command: **P** ⏎	Issues the PAN command
PAN Displacement: *Pan to the view shown (see fig. 22.17)*	

Repeat this process by clicking in the upper left viewport, zooming it to 1/24XP, and panning to the proper view. Do the same on the lower left viewport.

Save the drawing

Figure 22.17

The mview viewports after zooming and panning.

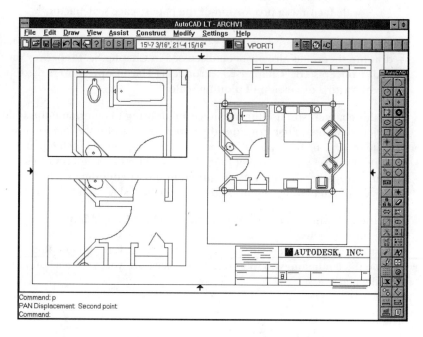

When you plot this drawing at a scale factor of 1=1, the model space objects will be properly scaled.

Sizing Text, Symbols, and Dimensions

When you add text, symbols, and dimensions to your drawing, remember to take advantage of paper space. Before adding text or symbols, you should ask this question: Is it necessary to add the text or symbol in model space? If your answer is no, you can alternatively enter the text in paper space at the actual size you want the text when you plot at full scale. If you want or need to enter the text in model space, you must consider the paper space viewport scale factor.

For text and unit-sized symbols drawn in model space, divide the desired plotted height by the ZOOM XP scale factor to determine the height in drawing units. As an example, to get $1/8$" plotted text with a $1/48$ plotting scale, you set the text size to 6 ($1/8$ divided by $1/48$ plot-scale factor = $48/8$ = 6). For symbols that are defined at their desired plot size, such as a $3/8$" bubble, you insert them at the inverse of the ZOOM XP scale. For paper space, just add the text of symbols at the desired plot height.

When you are dimensioning a drawing, you need to enter the dimensions in model space so you can take advantage of the associative nature of dimensions. When you add dimensions in model space, you have the same problems as you do with text and symbols added in model space. When you scale the viewport, the dimensions will not be the correct size for plotting. To get the correct text size, you must set the dimension height to the inverse of the ZOOM XP scale factor. You can use the DIMSCALE command to set the dimension scale. DIMSCALE is controlled by the **F**eature Scaling option in the Scale and Colors dialog box.

Tip You can add dimensions in model space or in paper space; however, paper space dimensions are generally not acceptable because they are not attached to the model and are not associative.

AutoCAD LT provides one other useful feature for dimensioning in mview viewports. A special function in the Scale and Colors dialog box enables you to specify that the paper space viewport scale factor be applied to all dimension features. You make this specification by checking the Use **P**aper Space Scaling box in the Scale and Colors dialog box (see fig. 22.18). This sets the DIMSCALE system variable to 0.

Tip If you set the Use **P**aper Space Scaling option to on and use ZOOM XP to scale your paper space viewports before you add dimensions, the dimensions are automatically scaled for you when you add them.

22

Figure 22.18

*The paper space
scaling option.*

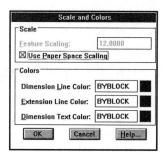

The following exercise shows how easy it is to keep your dimension feature scaling consistent when you dimension in mview viewports of different scale factors. You also use the VPLAYER command, which is explained after the exercise.

Dimensioning in Mview Viewports

Continue from the preceding exercise, using the ARCHV1 drawing. Set the current layer to DIM.

Command: *Choose* Settings, Di**m**ension Style, Scale and **C**olors	Opens the Scale and Colors dialog box
Turn on the Use **P**aper Space Scaling *option, then choose* OK *twice*	Sets dimensions to scale to the zoom XP factors to which you zoomed the viewports

Place the 20'-0" dimension at ① in the right viewport (see fig. 22.19).

Create a new layer called DIM1, make it the current layer, and add the 5'-0" dimension at ② in the upper left viewport (see fig. 22.19).

The dimensions appear rather small because they are scaled for plotting on a B-size sheet. Next, you zoom to the view shown in figure 22.20 for a closer look; you should zoom only in paper space to avoid altering the zoom XP scales you set earlier.

Command: *Turn on the P button*	Reenters paper space so you can zoom

Zoom to the view shown in figure 22.20.

Command: *Turn off the P button*	Reenters model space

The 5'-0" dimension also appears at ③ in the right viewport. You need to use the VPLAYER command to suppress the display of its layer in the right viewport, as follows.

Command: *Click in the right viewport
to make it active*

Command: *Choose* **V**iew, Viewport **L**ayer Visibility, **F**reeze	Issues the **VPLAYER** command with the Freeze option
```vplayer ?/Freeze/Thaw/Reset/Newfrz/ Vpvisdflt:_freeze Layer(s) to Freeze: DIM1 (Enter)```	
`All/Select/<Current>:` (Enter)	Accepts the current viewport
```?/Freeze/Thaw/Reset/Newfrz/ Vpvisdflt: (Enter)```	Completes the command and freezes the layer with the 5'-0" dimension from the viewport; it still appears at ④ but no longer appears at ⑤ in figure 22.20

Save the drawing

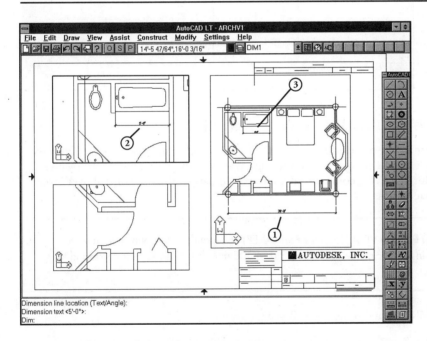

Figure 22.19

Dimensions in two mview viewports.

AutoCAD LT provides consistent feature scaling for your dimensions in all the mview viewports. Using this function is much easier than remembering to apply the inverse of the paper space scaling factor to all the dimensions.

One problem you might have noticed with figure 22.19 is that the 5' dimension shows in every viewport which displays that part of the model. In most cases, you want a dimension to appear only once on a multiview drawing. In the preceding exercise, you used the **VPLAYER** command to suppress the display of the 5-foot dimension in the right viewport (see fig. 22.20).

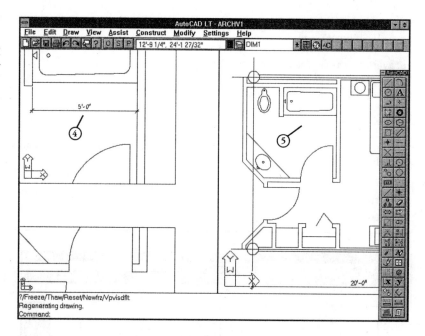

Controlling Viewport Layer Visibility

Because each mview viewport is viewing the same model, objects such as dimensions will appear in several viewports, even though you want them to appear in only one viewport. The VPLAYER command enables you to have complete control over layer visibility in viewports.

> **VPLAYER.** The VPLAYER (ViewPort LAYER) command controls which layers are visible in specific mview viewports. TILEMODE must be off (0) for this command to function.

The VPLAYER command has the following options:

◆ **Freeze.** The **F**reeze option freezes the specified layers in the selected viewports.

◆ **Thaw.** The **T**haw option thaws the specified layers in the selected viewports.

◆ **Reset.** The **R**eset option sets the visibility of layers to their current default settings.

◆ **New Freeze.** The **N**ew Freeze (Newfrz) option creates new layers that are to be frozen in all current viewports.

◆ **VP Default Visibility.** The <u>VP</u> Default Visibility (Vpvisdflt) option sets layers for a default visibility for each viewport.

◆ **List?.** The Lis<u>t</u>? option lists all the frozen layers for a specific viewport.

When the VPLAYER command prompts you for a layer name, you can use wild cards or several layer names separated by commas. At the `All/Select/<Current>:` prompt, you must specify the viewport with one of the options.

Stop
Be sure that layers are turned on and thawed before using them with the VPLAYER command.

The Layer Control dialog box (see fig. 22.21) also gives you some control over the layer visibility in mview viewports. From the Layer Control dialog box, you can specify that one or more layers be frozen or thawed in the current viewport or in new viewports.

Layer Control			
Current Layer: DIM1			
Layer Name	State	Color	Linetype
0	On	white	CONTINUOUS
BORDER	On	white	CONTINUOUS
CENTER	On	blue	CENTER2
DEFPOINTS	On	white	CONTINUOUS
DIM	On	white	CONTINUOUS
DIM1	On . . C .	white	CONTINUOUS
FIXTURE	On	magenta	CONTINUOUS
FURN	On	magenta	CONTINUOUS
VPORT1	On	white	CONTINUOUS
WALLS	On	red	CONTINUOUS

On Off
Thaw Freeze
Unlock Lock
Cur VP: Thw Frz
New VP: Thw Frz
Set Color...
Set Ltype...

Select <u>A</u>ll <u>N</u>ew Current Rename
Clear All
Filters
☐ O<u>n</u> S<u>e</u>t...
OK Cancel <u>H</u>elp...

Figure 22.21

The Layer Control dialog box.

22

Exploring Additional Paper Space Capabilities

Perhaps you work in a mechanical environment and your drawings do not resemble the architectural example presented so far in this chapter. The rest of the chapter uses a three-dimensional mechanical model to show you some additional capabilities of the paper space environment.

A three-dimensional model is often shown in several views so that the part features can be described completely. AutoCAD LT has many special viewing commands to enable you to view three-dimensional parts. Chapter 24, "Moving Beyond the Basics," explains these commands.

Setting Up Mview Viewports Using a 3D Model

A 3D model has been generated in AutoCAD LT from the mechanical part you dimensioned in Chapters 20, "Applying Dimensions in CAD," and 21, "Styling and Editing Dimensions." The units are in millimeters, and a metric B-size drawing sheet provides a good paper space working area for this drawing exercise.

In the following exercise, you begin by entering paper space and defining a B-size border. Because the model was created with four tiled viewports, that viewport configuration can easily be restored using the MVIEW command. Because the model space objects will be plotted full scale, you should zoom all the viewports to a scale factor of 1XP. The unwanted dimensions appearing in the isometric view can easily be removed by freezing the layer in the current viewport using the Layer Control dialog box. The Freeze option of this dialog box has an effect similar to that of the VPLAYER command.

Setting Up Orthographic Views from a 3D Model

Create a new drawing named MECHV1, using the ALT2202.DWG file as a prototype, and using no setup method.

Command: *Choose **V**iew, then **P**aper Space*   Turns TILEMODE off
*(AutoCAD LT Release 1) or **T**ile Mode*
(AutoCAD LT Release 2)

```
_tilemode
New value for TILEMODE <1>: 0

Entering Paper space.
Use MVIEW to insert Model space
viewports. Regenerating drawing.
```

Command: *Choose **D**raw, Rectangle*

```
_rectang

First corner: 0,0 (Enter)
```

Other corner: **450,300** (Enter)   Draws a B-size border

Change to the VPORTS layer.

Command: *Choose **V**iew, Viewp**o**rts,*   Issues the MVIEW command with the
Restore   Restore option

```
_mview
ON/OFF/Hideplot/Fit/2/3/4/Restore/
<First Point>: _restore
?/Name of window configuration to
insert <*ACTIVE>: 4VIEW (Enter)

Fit/<First Point>: F (Enter)
```

Regenerating drawing.   Displays four viewports

Command: **Z** (Enter)   Issues the ZOOM command

```
ZOOM All/Center/Extents/Previous/
Window/<Scale(X/XP)>: .9X (Enter)
```
Shows the borders of the drawing (see fig. 22.22)

Regenerating drawing.

Command: *Click on the P button on*   Issues the MSPACE command
the toolbar

```
_MSPACE
```

Command: **Z** (Enter)   Issues the ZOOM command

```
ZOOM All/Center/Extents/Previous/
Window/<Scale(X/XP)>: 1XP (Enter)
```

Continue by clicking in each of the mview viewports and zooming them to 1XP.

Command: *Click in the isometric*   Makes the isometric viewport active
viewport

Command: *Click on the Layers button on the*   Freezes the DIM layer in the current
toolbar and highlight the DIM *layer, then*   viewport (see fig. 22.23)
click on the Cur VP Fr *button and* choose OK

Save the drawing

Based on a single 3D model, you have quickly composed an orthographic view drawing that also contains an isometric view for better clarification. Before you prepare to plot this drawing, take a look at a few more techniques.

22

Figure 22.22

The orthographic view layout.

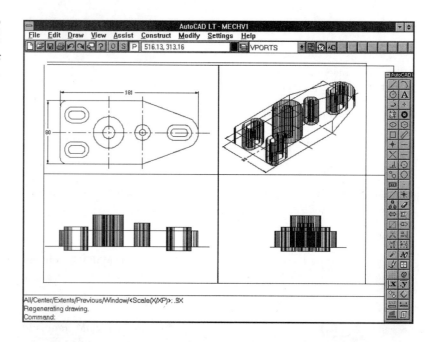

Figure 22.23

Removing dimensions from the isometric view.

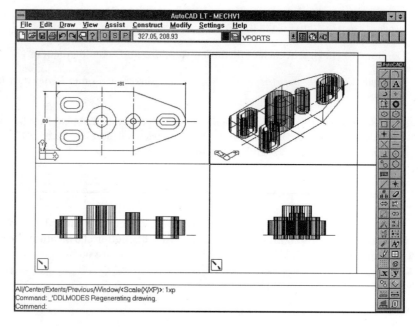

Controlling Hidden Line Visibility and Linetype Scale

AutoCAD LT employs a powerful command called HIDE to remove hidden lines that are behind surfaces in a three-dimensional drawing. Figure 22.24 shows the result of the HIDE command in the current drawing.

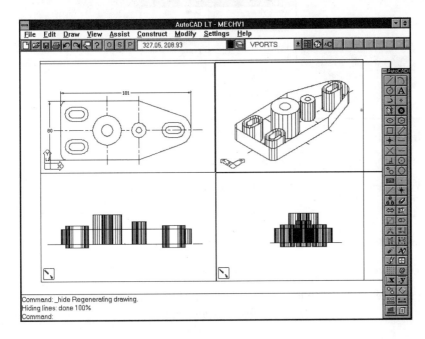

Figure 22.24

Using the HIDE command in the isometric view.

The hidden lines return with the next regeneration of the isometric view. The **H**ideplot option of the MVIEW command also enables you to select viewports that should have hidden lines removed in the finished plot.

AutoCAD LT also has the capability to apply a paper space linetype scale in each mview viewport so that the dash lengths are always based on paper space drawing units. The variable name is PSLTSCALE, and it can be turned on and off by a check mark in front of the **P**space LT Scale item in the **S**ettings pull-down menu (see fig. 22.25).

In the last portion of this drawing exercise, you use the hidden line and linetype scale techniques. When you have finished manipulating the mview viewports, you turn off the VPORTS layer in preparation for plotting.

Figure 22.25

*The menu
selection for paper
space linetype
scaling.*

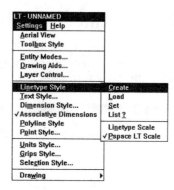

Controlling Hidden Lines and Linetype Scaling

Continue with the existing MECHV1 drawing. Be sure that the upper right viewport is active.

Command: *Choose* **V**iew, **H**ide   Issues the HIDE command

_hide Regenerating   Removes hidden lines
drawing. Hiding lines: done 0%
Hiding lines: done 100%

Command: *Choose* **V**iew, **Reg**en   Regenerates the view

Command: *Choose* **V**iew, Viewp**o**rts, **H**ideplot   Issues the MVIEW command with
                                             the Hideplot option

_mview
Switching to Paper space.
ON/OFF/Hideplot/Fit/2/3/4/
Restore/<First Point>: _hideplot
ON/OFF: **ON** (Enter)

Select objects: *Pick the edge of
the upper right viewport*

1 found Select objects: (Enter)   Causes upper right viewport to plot with
                                             hidden lines removed

Switching to Model space.

Click in the upper left viewport.

Command: **z** (Enter)   Issues the ZOOM command

ZOOM All/Center/Extents/Previous/
Window/<Scale(X/XP)>: **3XP** (Enter)

Notice the scale of the center lines.

Command: *Choose* **S**ettings,   Turns off the PSLTSCALE setting
Li**n**etype Style, **P**space LT Scale

New value for PSLTSCALE <1>: 0

Command: **REGEN** (Enter)

Notice the new center-line scaling, as shown in figure 22.26.

Zoom to the previous view, make layer 0 current, and turn off the VPORTS layer.

Command: **UCSICON** (Enter)   Issues the UCSICON command

ON/OFF/All/Noorigin/ORigin
<ON>: **ALL** (Enter)

ON/OFF/Noorigin/ORigin <ON>:   Turns off the UCS icon in each viewport
OFF (Enter)

Command: *Click on the P button
on the toolbar*

_PSPACE   Enters paper space

Save the drawing

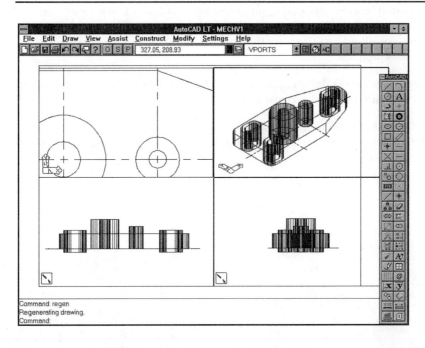

Figure 22.26

*The center-line
scaling with paper
space scaling
turned off.*

22

After some notes are added in paper space, this drawing (as it appears in fig. 22.27) will be ready to plot.

Figure 22.27

The completed drawing ready to plot.

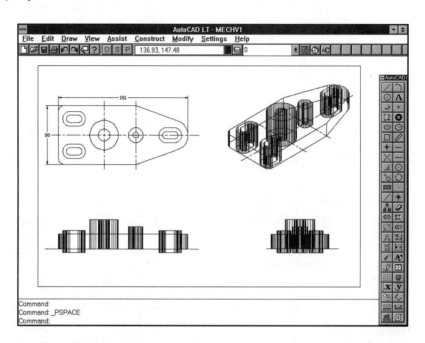

If you have created this type of drawing on a drawing board, you know the amount of planning you must do before any lines are drawn. Moreover, if you think paper space is a lot of work, you should try to create this type of drawing with the regular CAD copy and scale techniques.

The most important part of using paper space is determining which objects to draw in model space and which objects to create in paper space.

This chapter has mentioned plotting several times. You are now ready to proceed to Chapter 23, in which you learn to plot your drawings with AutoCAD LT.

Producing Hard Copy

The ultimate objective of spending hours in front of a computer screen using AutoCAD LT is to produce a hard-copy paper plot or printout of your work. After all, as of this writing, society has not yet progressed to the ideal of the paperless office predicted at the advent of computers. Paper is still the preferred medium of exchange for ideas. This chapter discusses the following procedures for producing hard-copy output:

◆ Making quick check plots

◆ Choosing a device for printing or plotting

◆ Saving and obtaining default settings for your plots

◆ Determining what part of your drawing to plot

◆ Setting pen weights and line styles

◆ Specifying paper size and units of measurement for your plot

◆ Setting the scale factor, rotation, and origin point of your plot

◆ Plotting to a file versus plotting directly to a plotter or printer

◆ Previewing your plot

◆ Managing your plotters and printers

◆ Managing your media and supplies

◆ Considering alternative forms of output

Because CAD drawings are typically used to share ideas and to provide instruction, this chapter focuses on the methods of output used to achieve these goals.

An understanding of the way in which AutoCAD LT prints or plots a drawing will eliminate some frustration and trial-and-error experimenting. To obtain the desired output, you must have a knowledge of scale factors, plot origins, rotation settings, pen assignments, and more. With this basic understanding, the plotting procedures should soon become habits, and you will be plotting your drawings with a minimum of trouble.

This chapter guides you through the basic principles of plotting and printing your drawings. In the past, the term "plotting" was reserved for output devices that used pens to plot the drawing. Printing usually meant a desktop printer in the form of a dot-matrix, inkjet, or laser type. For the purpose of this chapter, the terms "plotter," "plot," and "plotting" are used synonymously with the terms "printer," "printed hard copy," and "printing."

Printing and Plotting from AutoCAD LT

To make perfect final or presentation plots, AutoCAD LT provides a multitude of plotting selections, adjustments, settings, and parameters. Sometimes, however, you don't need a perfect plot; just a quick, not-to-scale plot will suffice for checking your drawing. Before getting involved in the complexities of plotting, try a quick check plot in the next section.

Making a Quick Check Plot

When your drawing is ready to plot, you can issue the PLOT command in one of three ways:

◆ Choose the Plot button on the toolbar (the printer icon)

◆ Choose the **P**rint/Plot item from the **F**ile pull-down menu

◆ Enter **PLOT** or the **PP** alias at the Command: prompt

> **PLOT.** The PLOT command is used to generate output from AutoCAD LT. This command outputs the current drawing in the form of hard-copy paper plots or in plot files. You can specify the drawing area to plot by current view, the drawing extents, the current limits, a named view, or a user-specified window. You can output the plot data to the default Windows printer or HPGL device or to a file on disk. The PLOT command uses the Plot Configuration dialog box, unless the CMDDIA system variable is set to 0 (off). If CMDDIA is off, or if the plot is initiated by a script file, then command-line plotting prompts are used.

After you issue the PLOT command, the Plot Configuration dialog box opens (see fig. 23.1). This dialog box controls the plotting options and settings with buttons, check boxes, and radio buttons. The default plotting device in AutoCAD LT is the current Windows default printer—the printing (and/or plotting) device that Windows is currently using. Most Windows printers can be used by AutoCAD LT, so try the following exercise to make a quick check plot. If it works, great. If not, don't worry; just read the following section about choosing a plotting device, and then try the check plot again.

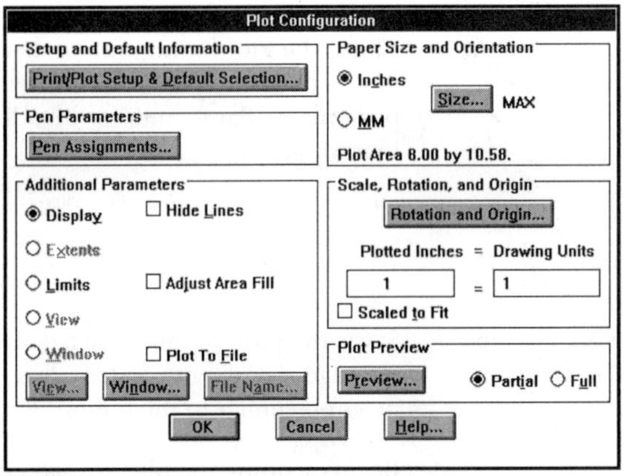

Figure 23.1

The Plot Configuration dialog box.

Before immersing yourself in the details of selecting plotting devices and setting options in the Plot Configuration dialog box, try to generate a quick plot in the following exercise. As a prototype drawing, you use the file ALT2301.DWG, which is similar to the SHELF drawing you completed in Chapters 16, "Increasing Your Drawing Power with Polylines and Double Lines," and 17, "Dressing Up Drawings with Hatching." The drawing contains a single mview viewport with 30×40 limits scaled 1:4 in a paper space view with 8.5×11 limits. You plot it to fit your current printing device, without worrying about scale or most of the settings. Even if you don't have any printer or plotter connected, you can still follow the exercise up to the "Choose OK" step.

Plotting a Drawing

Create a new drawing named SHELF, using the ALT2301.DWG file as a prototype and using no setup method. This drawing replaces the previous SHELF.DWG file.

Command: *Choose the Plot button*	Issues the PLOT command and opens the Plot Configuration dialog box (see fig. 23.1)
_PLOT	
Choose the Ex*tents radio button, then make sure that the* Plot To File *check box is clear and that there is a check in the* Scaled to Fit *check box*	Ensures that the full drawing extents will be plotted to fill the available area of the current device
Choose Full, *then* Preview *in the* Plot Preview *section*	Previews the plot in the drawing window (see fig. 23.2)

Your preview may be smaller and rotated from that shown, depending on your current device. You'll learn to change this later in the chapter.

Choose End Preview	Terminates the preview
If you have a device connected, make sure it is on and ready, then choose OK; *otherwise, choose* Cancel	Closes the Plot Configuration dialog box; depending on your device, you will see prompts similar to and/or including the following:
Effective plotting area: 7.90 wide by 10.53 high Position paper in plotter.	
Press RETURN to continue or S to Stop for hardware setup *Press Enter and answer other prompts, if any*	Starts the plot; you may see a dialog box message "Sending to System Printer" and prompts similar to the following:
Plotting viewport 2. Effective plotting area: 7.89 wide by 10.52 high Regeneration done 100% Vector sort done 100% Plot complete.	Begins sending the plot, displays progress, and completes sending the plot, which will take from several seconds to several minutes to print or plot, depending on your device

---

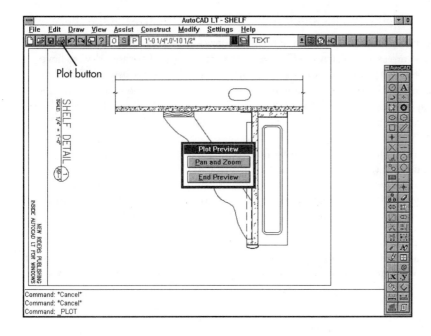

Figure 23.2

Previewing the check plot.

If the check plot worked, your current Windows printer (or plotter) will produce a plot similar to the preview after a few seconds or minutes. If the check plot didn't work, read the following section, select and/or reconfigure your printing or plotting device, and then try the check plot again.

Choosing a Device for Plotting

Plotting a drawing from AutoCAD LT uses either vector or raster output. *Vector output* consists of line segments (vectors) defined by their endpoints. Vector output translates and represents the objects that make up the drawing in the form of these vectors, which are accepted by vector devices such as pen plotters, most inkjet or bubblejet plotters, and PostScript printers. Thus a circle in your drawing is plotted as dozens of short line segments or vectors that simulate the circle's shape. At the resolution of most vector devices, the circle still looks round to the human eye.

Raster output consists of a multitude of dots defined by their positions, like the pixels that make up the on-screen drawing image. Raster output translates and represents the objects that make up the drawing in the form of these dots, which raster devices such as dot-matrix and some laser and inkjet printers accept. A line segment is simulated by a series of dots packed close together in a row. A circle is simulated by placing dots in a circular pattern.

Note All laser, dot-matrix, inkjet, and bubblejet devices are actually raster devices, but some are seen by AutoCAD LT as vector devices. Many other raster devices have built-in vector-to-raster conversion, so they can emulate vector devices. Built-in rasterizing hardware, software, or both convert the vector data into raster data for output to the print head. In fact, the PostScript language itself is a vector-based language, but it is usually output on raster devices.

You are probably thinking that this information might impress your friends but wondering what relevance it has for you as an AutoCAD LT user. The answer is that you should have a general knowledge of the type of output device for the purpose of setting up your plot. For example, the type of output device can affect how you configure your pens or even whether you can configure pen settings at all.

Printing and plotting from AutoCAD LT is handled through Microsoft Windows. In addition to hardware features and limitations, the available features and limitations of your printer or plotter depend on the device driver software installed in Windows.

Note See the Troubleshooting Guide appendix in the *AutoCAD LT Release 2 User's Guide* and the README.DOC files in AutoCAD LT Release 1 or 2 for more on plotter configuration, ports, cabling, and connections.

Selecting the Default Windows Printer

AutoCAD LT prints to the default Windows printer. You use the Windows Printers dialog box to install device drivers for printers, set the default printer, and see what printers you have installed. To open the Windows Printers dialog box, open the Main group in Program Manager, double-click on the Control Panel icon, then double-click on the Printers icon. You are presented with the Printers dialog box (see fig. 23.3), which contains a list of installed printers and various buttons for configuring and installing printers.

You set the default Windows printer from the Windows Printers dialog box by selecting a printer in the Installed **P**rinters list, and then choosing S**e**t As Default Printer. You choose Close after you have set the default printer. For other information on printer setup and configuration, see your Windows manual or the instructions supplied with your printer or plotter, or choose the **H**elp button for Windows Help.

Note If you are using a monochrome (black-and-white) device, such as a PostScript printer, you might need to set the device options to force all AutoCAD LT colors to black. Otherwise, the printer might use dot halftones to represent various colors.

This is called *dithering*, but is not supported by all Windows printer drivers. Dithering might cause some colors to print faintly or to disappear. If this happens, disable dithering. If dithering is disabled, a dithering disabled message appears in the Pen Assignments dialog box. The DITHER system variable (1=on, 0=off) controls dithering from AutoCAD LT. Some printers also have settings that affect dithering in their options or advanced options settings. You can, for example, set all colors to print black in a PostScript printer's dialog box by choosing **S**etup, **O**ptions, Ad**v**anced, then turning on the All **C**olors to Black check box. Printer settings made from within AutoCAD affect only the current session's printer settings, not the Windows defaults.

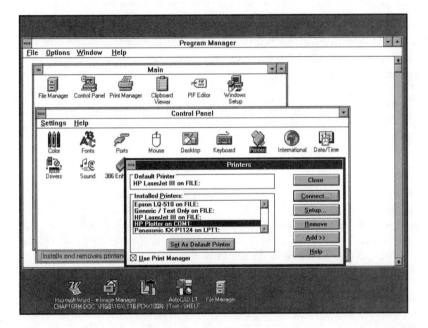

Figure 23.3

Accessing the Windows Printers (setup) dialog box.

If your plotting device is not supported by the standard Windows drivers, your printer or plotter manufacturer may be able to supply an appropriate driver. Autodesk has provided a driver that enables you to select from the available Windows devices from within AutoCAD LT (see the following note).

Note The original Microsoft Windows 3.1 HPGL printer/plotter driver does not properly support AutoCAD LT Release 1 (and other vector-based software products). Devices that do not properly plot with AutoCAD LT Release 1 include HP 7220, 7470, 7475, 7550, 7580, 7585, 7586, ColorPro, DraftPro, DraftPro DXL and EXL,

continues

Draftmaster I, and other vendors' plotters that use HPGL or emulate one of these. Until Microsoft and Hewlett-Packard correct and update the Windows driver, Autodesk has provided a substitute driver for AutoCAD LT Release 1 as an interim solution. This interim driver corrects many problems (including long plotting times) and is included on the IALT Disk supplied with this book. This interim driver also enables you to select any available Windows device from within AutoCAD LT AutoCAD LT Release 1, so you should install the driver if you have an HPGL-compatible device or more than one device of any type. See Appendix G for installation instructions. There is also available a PenSpeed utility that works with the AutoCAD LT Release 1 interim driver to provide greater control over pen speeds. You can obtain this from the AutoCAD Retail Products (GO ARETAIL) forum on CompuServe.

ALT2

AutoCAD LT Release 2 includes built-in support for HPGL devices and works similarly to the AutoCAD LT Release 1 interim solution, but does so without you having to worry about it.

Initially, AutoCAD LT Release 1 can use only the current Windows default device. If you install Autodesk's interim HPGL driver in AutoCAD LT Release 1 or are using AutoCAD LT Release 2, however, you can choose between the default Windows device and other devices, as explained in the next section called "Selecting a Printer in AutoCAD LT."

You can check your current device from the AutoCAD LT Plot Configuration dialog box (refer to previous fig. 23.1). To do so, choose the Print/Plot Setup & **D**efault Selection button to open the Print/Plot Setup & Default Selection dialog box (see fig. 23.4—the larger version is for AutoCAD LT Release 2). Then choose the S**h**ow Device Requirements button. A Show Device Requirements dialog box opens, with information about your current device.

Figures 23.5 and 23.6 show the Show Device Requirements dialog boxes for two different devices, an HP LaserJet III configured with the Windows driver and an HP DraftPro configured with the AutoCAD LT Release 1 interim Autodesk HPGL driver or with AutoCAD LT Release 2.

Figure 23.4

The Print/Plot Setup & Default Selection dialog boxes.

Figure 23.5

The Show Device Requirements dialog box for HP LaserJet III.

Figure 23.6

The Show Device Requirements dialog box for an HPGL device, the HP DraftPro.

23

Selecting a Printer in AutoCAD LT

Even if you do not have an HPGL printing or plotting device, using AutoCAD LT Release 2 or installing the AutoCAD LT Release 1 interim HPGL driver from Autodesk enables you to select from the available Windows devices from a Print Setup dialog box in AutoCAD LT.

In AutoCAD LT Release 1, if you have not installed the interim HPGL driver from Autodesk, the **P**rint/Plot Setup button in the Print/Plot Setup & Default Selection dialog box opens a Print Setup dialog box that merely tells you to use the Windows Printers dialog box to make changes to the default device.

If you use AutoCAD LT Release 2 or have installed the AutoCAD LT Release 1 interim HPGL driver from Autodesk, you can choose between the default Windows device and other devices during an AutoCAD LT session.

When you install the AutoCAD LT Release 1 interim HPGL driver, your AutoCAD LT **F**ile pull-down menu inherits two additional items: **H**PGL On and HPG**L** Off. These items enable you to choose whether your drawing will be plotted to the default Windows device or to an HPGL device. If you choose **H**PGL On, AutoCAD LT uses the interim HPGL driver, but other Windows programs still use the default Windows device. With HPGL on, the **P**rint/Plot Setup button in the Print/Plot Setup & Default Selection dialog box opens the HPGL Driver Setup dialog box shown in figure 23.7. You can select different HPGL plotting devices (Models) and ports (Output To) in this dialog box. The selection you make becomes the new AutoCAD LT default printer. This support is built-in in AutoCAD LT Release 2, so it does not have the **H**PGL On and HPG**L** Off menu items. The HPGL Driver Setup dialog box varies with the plotting device selected.

Figure 23.7

The HPGL Driver Setup dialog box.

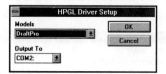

If you choose HPG**L** Off in AutoCAD LT Release 1, the **P**rint/Plot Setup button in the Print/Plot Setup & Default Selection dialog box opens an expanded Print Setup dialog box (see fig. 23.8). This expanded dialog box is the normal Print Setup dialog box in AutoCAD LT Release 2. It enables you to choose the Windows default (the **D**efault Printer radio button) or any installed Windows printer (the Specific **P**rinter radio button). The selection affects only the current AutoCAD LT session. Future AutoCAD LT sessions default to the Windows default (unless HPGL is on in AutoCAD LT Release 1).

Note With HPGL off in AutoCAD LT Release 1, the Print Setup dialog box may display choices for HPGL-compatible devices (such as HP Plotter on COM1 in figure 23.8), but you should not use these selections because they do not use Autodesk's interim HPGL driver. Autodesk's interim HPGL driver is not selectable from this dialog box. To use the interim HPGL driver, choose the **F**ile pull-down menu, and then choose **H**PGL On. In AutoCAD LT Release 2, you can use any available device.

In addition to device selection, the Plot Configuration dialog box offers many other choices, settings, and options.

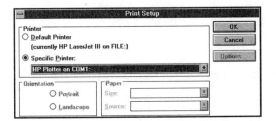

Figure 23.8

The expanded Print Setup dialog box.

Making Settings with the Plot Configuration Dialog Box

With the exceptions of selecting the default Windows printer, setting paper space or model space current, and predefining named views to plot, the Plot Configuration dialog box controls all aspects of plotting. The Plot Configuration dialog box is divided into groups of related items. The items in each of these groups are described in the following sections.

The Setup and Default Information group has a single button:

◆ **Print/Plot Setup & Default Selection.** The Print/Plot Setup & **D**efault Selection button opens the Print/Plot Setup & Default Selection dialog box (see previous fig. 23.4). This dialog box is used to set up the output device and to save and restore plot setup data in files. Your device manufacturer may have specific instructions for setting up your plotter for AutoCAD LT.

The Pen Parameters group also has a single button:

◆ **Pen Assignments.** The **P**en Assignments button opens the Pen Assignments dialog box (see fig. 23.9). This dialog box is used for assigning pen numbers, plotter linetypes, and pen widths to colors in AutoCAD LT. Depending on the

23

selected plotting device, various features of this dialog box may be grayed or unavailable.

Figure 23.9

The Pen Assignments dialog box.

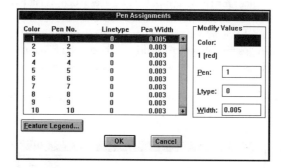

 Note Setting plotter linetypes is not recommended. Generally, it is better to use AutoCAD LT's linetype features.

The Paper Size and Orientation group has the following items:

◆ **Inches.** The Inches radio button selects inches as the unit of measurement for paper size and scaling factors.

◆ **MM.** The MM radio button selects millimeters as the unit of measurement for paper size and scaling factors.

◆ **Size.** The Size button opens the Paper Size dialog box (see the section called "Choosing the Proper Paper Size and Rotation" later in this chapter), in which you can select a predefined size or define and select custom user sizes.

The Additional Parameters group has the following items:

◆ **Display.** The Display radio button uses the current drawing display area to define the area of the drawing to be plotted.

◆ **Extents.** The Extents radio button uses the current drawing extents to define the area of the drawing to be plotted.

◆ **Limits.** The Limits radio button uses the current limits setting to define the area of the drawing to be plotted.

◆ **View.** The View radio button is turned on when you choose the View button (at the bottom of the Additional Parameters box) and specify a named view to plot. This radio button is grayed out unless a named view has been selected to plot.

◆ **Window.** The <u>W</u>indow radio button is turned on when you choose the Wi<u>n</u>dow button (also at the bottom of the Additional Parameters box) and specify a windowed area of the drawing to plot. This radio button is grayed out unless a windowed area has been specified to plot.

◆ **Hide <u>L</u>ines.** The Hide <u>L</u>ines check box determines whether hidden lines in a 3D drawing are removed in the plot.

◆ **Adjust Area Fill.** The Ad<u>j</u>ust Area Fill check box determines whether AutoCAD LT compensates for the pen width when filling in solid objects and wide polylines. If this box is checked, AutoCAD LT pulls in the boundaries of these objects by one-half the pen width for greater accuracy. This option is used for PC board artwork and on other plots that must be accurate to one-half the pen width.

◆ **Plot To <u>F</u>ile.** When you check the Plot To <u>F</u>ile check box, AutoCAD LT plots the drawing to a disk file rather than to the plotter output device. If you are on a network, you may have network spooling software that watches for plot files and sends them to the appropriate device. See the AutoCAD LT Release 2 README.DOC for shared plotters using Microsoft Windows for Workgroups. If you use a service bureau for plotting, you may use this option to have them plot the drawing for you.

◆ **Vi<u>e</u>w.** The Vi<u>e</u>w button opens the View Name dialog box (see fig. 23.10), from which you can select a named view defined in the drawing to plot.

◆ **Wi<u>n</u>dow.** The Wi<u>n</u>dow button opens the Window Selection dialog box (see fig. 23.11). This dialog box is used for specifying a window area of the drawing to plot.

◆ **File N<u>a</u>me.** When the Plot To <u>F</u>ile box is checked, the File N<u>a</u>me button is used to specify the path and file name of the plot file to be created. If none is specified, the default file name is the drawing name with an extension of PLT.

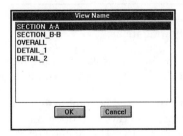

Figure 23.10

The View Name dialog box.

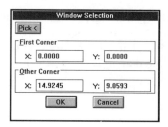

Figure 23.11

The Window Selection dialog box.

The Scale, Rotation, and Origin group has the following items:

- ◆ **Rotation and Origin.** The Rotation and Origin button opens the Plot Rotation and Origin dialog box (see fig. 23.12). This dialog box is used for adjusting the position and angle of the plot on the paper.

- ◆ **Plotted Inches = Drawing Units.** The Plotted Inches = Drawing Units input boxes specify the scale factor to be used when the drawing is plotted. The values determine the size to which AutoCAD LT scales the drawing when plotting. These settings are affected by the Scaled to Fit check box.

- ◆ **Scaled to Fit.** The Scaled to Fit check box, when checked, sets the Plotted Inches = Drawing Units input boxes to plot the specified area as large as possible, using the current Size and Rotation and Origin settings on the specified device. When cleared, it has no effect. You can use the Preview button to check whether you need to adjust the rotation to maximize the plot.

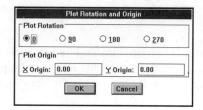

Figure 23.12

The Plot Rotation and Origin dialog box.

The Plot Preview group has the following items:

- ◆ **Preview button.** The Preview button displays how the plot will fit on the paper with the current paper size, rotation angle, and plot origin.

- ◆ **Partial.** The Partial radio button is used in conjunction with the Preview button. The Partial radio button sets Preview to open the Preview Effective Plotting Area dialog box (see fig. 23.13). This dialog box shows the drawing as a rectangular area in relationship to the paper size you have selected.

New Riders Publishing
INSIDE
SERIES

◆ **Full radio button.** The Full radio button is used in conjunction with the Preview button. The Full radio button sets Preview to simulate the plot in the drawing window (see fig. 23.14).

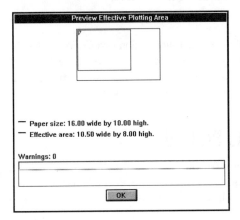

Figure 23.13

The Preview Effective Plotting Area dialog box.

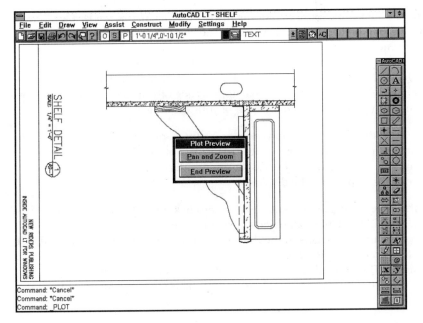

Figure 23.14

Full plot preview.

The Plot Configuration dialog box has three additional buttons:

◆ **OK.** The OK button closes the Plot Configuration dialog box and prompts Press RETURN to continue or S to Stop for hardware setup on the command line. Pressing Enter at this prompt plots the drawing. Canceling with Ctrl+C at this prompt cancels the plot.

◆ **Cancel.** The Cancel button aborts the PLOT command, closes the Plot Configuration dialog box, and returns to the `Command:` prompt.

◆ **Help.** The **H**elp button opens Windows Help.

 Tip   Cancelling with the Plot Configuration dialog box Cancel button discards dialog box settings. Cancelling with Ctrl+C or the toolbar Cancel button at the `Press RETURN to continue or S to Stop for hardware setup` prompt cancels the plot but saves any dialog box settings you have made.

Defining What Gets Plotted

After you have selected a device for output, you must decide what portion of your drawing to plot. In the Additional Parameters section of the Plot Configuration dialog box, AutoCAD LT gives you a choice of five ways to specify the area of your drawing to plot:

◆ **Display.** When you choose to plot the display by clicking on the Displa**y** radio button, AutoCAD LT plots literally what is shown in the current view of the drawing window—no more and no less. This option is useful for check plots, in which you may be zoomed in to a detailed portion on your drawing and need to have a hard-copy plot to check. This option also might be used to see how your pen weight settings will affect the final appearance of your plot. In this case, you would need to plot only a small portion of your drawing.

When calculating how to position the plot on the paper, AutoCAD LT takes into account everything in the current view, regardless of whether you are zoomed in or out. Any white space on the display is considered a part of the drawing when you specify plotting the display.

◆ **Extents.** When you choose to plot extents by clicking on the E**x**tents radio button, AutoCAD LT plots all objects (except those on frozen layers). The extents used are the extents of the drawing that were calculated by AutoCAD LT on the last screen regeneration. Before you plot extents, the safest way to see what AutoCAD LT will plot is to issue a ZOOM Extents command to make certain you don't have any "straggling" objects hanging out in space somewhere.

◆ **Limits.** When you choose to plot limits by clicking on the **L**imits radio button, AutoCAD LT plots only what is within the currently defined drawing limits. The value of the system variable LIMCHECK, which determines whether limits checking is on or off, has no effect on limits plotting.

◆ **View.** To plot a view, you first choose the View button (beneath the radio buttons in the Additional Parameters section of the Plot Configuration dialog box). You are presented with the View Name dialog box (refer to fig. 23.10), which lists the named views in your drawing. You then select the view you want to plot and choose OK, then choose the **V**iew radio button. Plotting a view is convenient on large drawings for which you have taken the time to establish named views, or if you define a view with a standard name such as PLOT in all drawings. Views are a powerful tool for plotting as well as for navigating around your drawing while editing. Refer to Chapter 5 for a discussion of named views.

◆ **Window.** To plot a window, you first choose the Wi**n**dow button (beneath the radio buttons in the Additional Parameters section of the Plot Configuration dialog box). You are then presented with the Window Selection dialog box (see fig. 23.15). In this dialog box, you can explicitly define the window area to plot by entering the coordinates of opposite corners of the window in the **F**irst Corner and **O**ther Corner input boxes. If you want to define the window on your drawing visually, you can choose the **P**ick button. You are then prompted to pick the two corners to window the area of the drawing you want to plot. The Window option of selecting an area of your drawing to plot is similar to the Display option. Whatever is within the user-specified window is plotted. After you specify the window, you choose the **W**indow radio button.

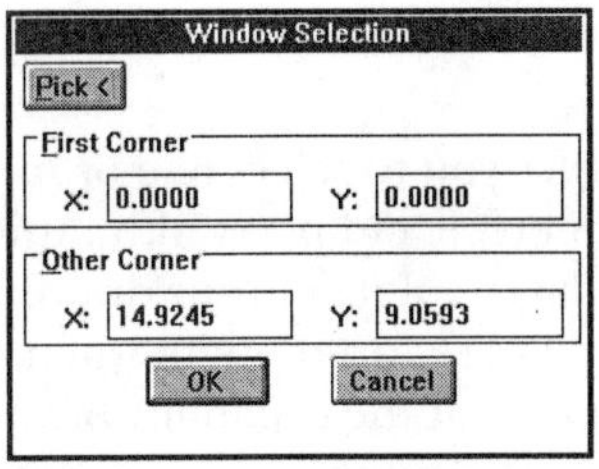

Figure 23.15

The Window Selection dialog box.

You can set limits by using the LIMITS command or by setting the system variables LIMMIN and LIMMAX. Some experienced CAD users prefer to use limits to define the area of their drawing that will be plotted, whereas others do not use limits at all but prefer to plot extents. Whether you use extents or limits is a matter of preference and depends on the way you like to construct your drawings.

Suppose that you work in an architectural design firm that is renovating some rest rooms in a public building. You have already entered the existing floor plan and the rest-room fixture layouts into AutoCAD LT. You might plot the area of one of the rest rooms for the other design disciplines to use as a background for the HVAC (Heating, Ventilation, and Air Conditioning), electrical, and plumbing details. While the other designers use this background drawing, you have time to finish the rest of the floor plan data on the rest of the building. You could use the Window option to pinpoint the areas of the drawing you want plotted.

Specifying Pen Weights and Line Styles

The **P**en Assignments button in the Plot Configuration dialog box opens the Pen Assignments dialog box shown in figure 23.16. Plotter pens, linetypes, and line weights (widths) are assigned by color. For example, if you assign pen 2 with linetype 0 (continuous) and width .005 to color 1 (red), then everything that is red in the drawing (whether by explicit object color or by layer color) will plot with these assignments.

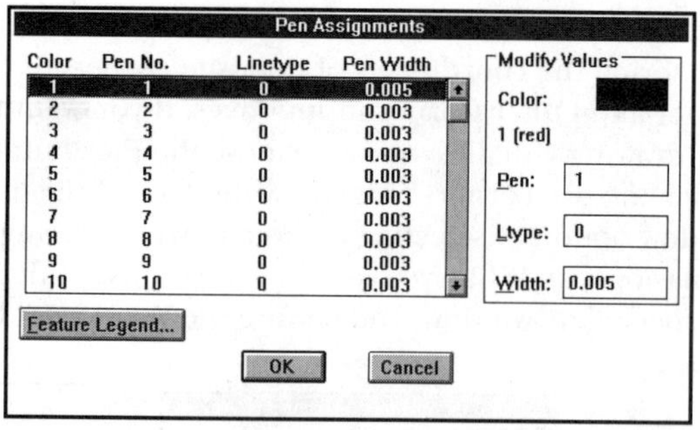

Figure 23.16

The Pen Assignments dialog box.

The Pen Assignments dialog box enables you to select one or more colors and assign them to a certain pen with a certain linetype and pen width. AutoCAD LT assigns pen numbers according to the object and layer colors in your drawing. For this plotting feature to work effectively, you must exercise forethought when constructing your drawing. You need to know beforehand what the capability of your output device is in terms of the number of pens it supports and their pen weights. You also need to determine what color you will use for a particular pen weight and to bear this in mind while editing your drawing.

If you work in an office with several other CAD users, you may have office standards established for pens, colors, and their corresponding line weights. If you do not have such standards, perhaps now is the time to establish some. A suggested method is to use the standard AutoCAD LT color numbers in order from the lightest pen weight to the heaviest. In other words, color 1 (red) could be 0.25 mm; color 2 (yellow), 0.35 mm; color 3 (green), 0.50 mm; and color 4 (cyan), 0.70 mm, and so on.

When you select one or more items in the Pen Assignments list box, you can specify a pen number, linetype, and width value in the **P**en, **L**type, and **W**idth input boxes, respectively (refer to fig. 23.16). The **P**en input box enables you to assign a pen number to the selected items. If you are using a pen plotter with a carousel for the

pens, the pen number corresponds directly with the number of the pen slot in the carousel. If you are using a raster device for output (such as a laser, inkjet, or electro-static plotter), your plotter driver may have *logical* (simulated) pens that you can assign. Each of these logical pens might have a different width or might be capable of generating custom patterns or screening.

Your plotting device may support built-in plotter linetypes. You specify the linetype assigned to each color in the **L**type input box. You can display the available plotter linetypes in the Feature Legend dialog box (see fig. 23.17) by choosing the **F**eature Legend button. The available linetypes depend on the selected plotting device. Generally, you should use plotter linetype 0 (continuous), which causes the plot to depend solely on AutoCAD LT's linetypes instead of plotter linetypes. This is prefer-able to using other plotter linetypes because AutoCAD LT handles linetype end alignments better than most plotters.

Figure 23.17

Plotter linetypes in the Feature Legend dialog box.

The **W**idth input box specifies what line width is drawn with a particular pen. The value entered in the **W**idth input box is in the units of measurement you specified in the Plot Configuration dialog box. On a pen plotter, the plotted width is, of course, the physical width of the pen assigned to the color. The **W**idth setting still has a meaning, however, because it tells the plotter how wide the pen is so that the plotter knows how closely to space strokes when filling solids and wide polylines. The **W**idth setting should be set to slightly less than the actual physical pen width.

On raster devices that support logical (simulated) pens, this **W**idth value specifies the width to be plotted by the logical pen assigned to the color. On laser and PostScript devices or PostScript plotting to file, a width of 0.003 works well.

Choosing the Proper Paper Size and Rotation

When you choose the **S**ize button in the Plot Configuration dialog box, the Paper Size dialog box opens (see fig. 23.18). The Paper Size dialog box lists the available plotting areas for the standard paper sizes from which you can choose; this list is dependent on your configured output device. You also can define custom paper sizes in the USER input boxes.

Note that the widths and heights listed in the Paper Size dialog box are the available plotting area of the specified size, not the actual sheet dimensions. For example, your plotter might require $1/2$-inch margins with $1\ 1/2$ inches on one end of the paper. To specify the plottable paper area in AutoCAD LT, you need to subtract these margins from the actual paper size.

Figure 23.18

The Paper Size dialog box.

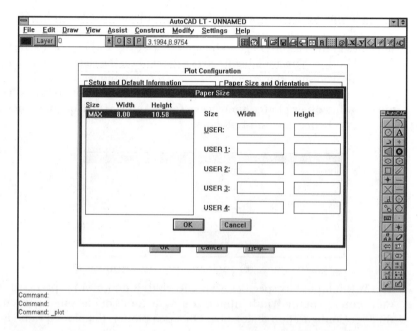

 Tip   With some plotting devices, AutoCAD LT does not offer a predefined B-size choice; however, you can define a user size with appropriate width and height.

When you choose the Rotation and Origin button in the Plot Configuration dialog box, the Plot Rotation and Origin dialog box opens (see fig. 23.19). The plot rotation options of 0, 90, 180, and 270 degrees enable you to rotate the plot on the paper. If your drawing is in *portrait* orientation (taller than it is wide), you may need to rotate the plot 90 degrees to position it correctly on the paper. Similarly, if your drawing is in *landscape* orientation (wider than it is tall) but your plotter normally outputs in portrait mode, you may need to rotate the plot on the paper.

The plot origin is where AutoCAD LT places the lower left corner of the drawing area that is being plotted (taking rotation into account). With some large-format plotters, the plot origin is assumed to be the lower right corner as you face the plotter with the paper loaded. With other plotters, the plot origin might be the upper left corner. In

any case, the default plot origin, 0,0, is at the corner of the plotter's currently specified extents, which is the plot area determined by the width and height of the current
size. In the following section called "Seeing a Preview," figure 23.20 shows the plot
origin in a preview.

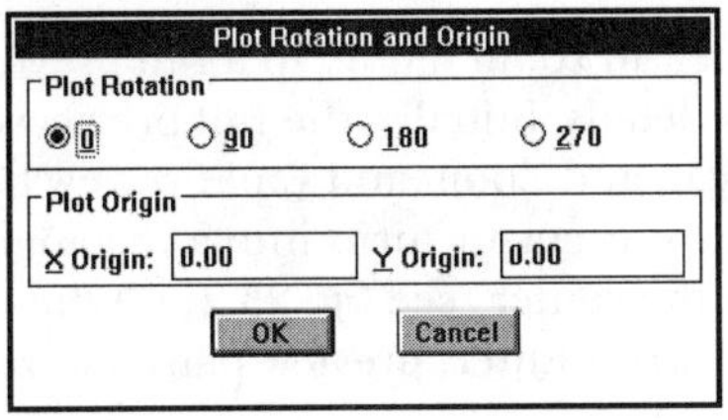

Figure 23.19

*The Plot Rotation
and Origin dialog
box.*

By adjusting the origin point in AutoCAD LT before plotting, you may be able to
compensate for the plotter not centering the plot properly or prevent AutoCAD LT
from chopping off a portion of your drawing at the margins. If you have several small
plots that can be plotted on one piece of paper, you can set the origin manually, leave
the paper in the plotter after the first plot, and define a new origin for the second
plot so that it is placed elsewhere on your paper. Using paper space to compose the
plot is easier, however, and enables you to preview the combined images (see Chapter
22, "Structuring Your Drawing").

The combination of plot rotation and plot origin controls the position and orientation of your plot on the sheet. You can use the plot preview feature to verify it.

Seeing a Preview

You used the preview feature in the quick check plot exercise. The Preview button in
the Plot Configuration dialog box enables you to preview the plot on screen before it
is actually plotted. You can see how your plot will be positioned and oriented (partial
preview; see fig. 23.20) or how the full plot will appear (see fig. 23.21). A partial
preview is always the default. You can control whether you see a partial preview or a
full preview by selecting the Partial or Full radio buttons in the Plot Preview section of
the Plot Configuration dialog box.

A partial preview shows you two rectangular areas on your screen. The red rectangle
represents the paper size you have selected for your plot, and the blue rectangle
represents the area that will be plotted. In a partial preview, you will sometimes see a
triangular shape in one corner. This triangular shape represents the origin of the plot
(see fig. 23.20).

A full preview provides more detail by actually plotting your drawing on screen. Full previews are useful to make sure that the plotting area you have defined will be sufficient and will fit on the paper appropriately. For very large drawings, however, full previews can be time-consuming because AutoCAD LT calculates and plots each vector. In most situations, a partial preview is sufficient.

Figure 23.21 illustrates a full preview in zoom mode. In a full preview, you can zoom and pan around the plot to check details. Initially, the full preview displays the Plot Preview dialog box, which offers **P**an and Zoom and **E**nd Preview buttons. When you choose the **P**an and Zoom button, your cursor turns into a rectangular zoom box, initially in pan mode with an X in the center (see fig. 23.21). When you place this box over the area you want to view and press Enter, preview pans and zooms the drawing to that area.

Figure 23.20

The plot origin in a partial preview.

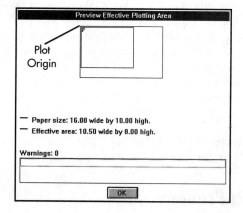

Each time you click the left mouse button, the zoom box switches between pan mode (panning the box) and zoom mode (resizing the box). In zoom mode, the box displays an arrow at the right side (see fig. 23.22). To change the size of the zoom box, you click to enter zoom mode and drag to make the box larger or smaller, then click again to return to pan mode and fix the box at the current size.

You press Enter to zoom to the area in the Plot Preview dialog box that offers **Z**oom Previous and **E**nd Preview buttons. You choose the **E**nd Preview button to end your full preview and return to the Plot Configuration dialog box.

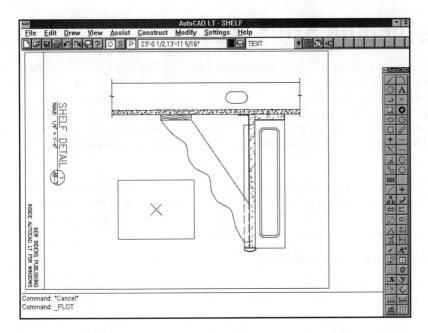

Figure 23.21

Panning the zoom box in a full plot preview.

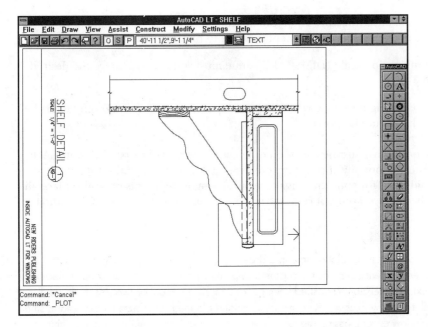

Figure 23.22

Sizing the zoom box in a full plot preview.

23

Understanding Scale Issues

One of the most confusing issues pertaining to plotting is the drawing size and scale factor of items in the drawing versus the plotting scale factor. You may sometimes have difficulty scaling a drawing properly so that it is large enough to fit on a sheet but also maintains readable text. Conversely, you may have difficulty scaling a drawing so that the entire drawing fits on the sheet properly and none of the plot is cropped or cut off. The scale factor and paper size determine whether your results are satisfactory.

A good CAD user almost never tackles a drawing without first considering the scale at which it will be plotted. You must put as much thought into your drawing as you would if you were to sit down with a large sheet of paper, a pencil, and a drawing scale. You should think about the following questions:

◆ How large should your final plot be?

◆ What plot scale will convey your ideas most effectively without being too small or too large ($^1/_4$"=1'-0" versus $^1/_8$"=1'-0" or 1:250 mm versus 1:50 mm)?

◆ What height must your text be drawn to plot at the desired height?

◆ What scale must linetypes and symbols (such as bubbles, boxed labels, flow diagram symbols, electrical receptacles) be to plot at the desired height?

◆ What dimension scale (DIMSCALE) value must you use to achieve the desired results?

◆ If you are using mview viewports in paper space, what must the zoom factors be for each of your viewports?

All of these questions must be considered before you draw your first line. AutoCAD LT is a wonderful tool, but it cannot make assumptions for you. You must still establish guidelines for your drawings to avoid having to redimension and replace all your notes because you did not remember to consider the scale factor of your final drawing.

Tip Before investing a lot of time in a drawing, create a few objects that fill out its overall extents, such as the outline of a plan or part. In one corner, add a piece of text, a dimension, a dashed linetype, and insert a symbol or two. Next, do a full plot preview to check your overall scale and planned sheet size. Finally, plot a small window encompassing the text, dimension, linetype, and symbol to check their legibility. It's a lot easier to adjust scale settings or planned sheet size before you've invested hundreds of hours in the drawing.

Although most drawing scale considerations are the same for paper space or model space plotting, the plot scale you use differs. First, look at scale in model space plotting.

Plotting from Model Space

You are in model space if TILEMODE is on (there is no check next to the **P**aper Space item in the **V**iew menu), or if you are in an mview viewport in paper space. You are in paper space if TILEMODE is off (there is a check next to the **P**aper Space item in the **V**iew menu) and you are not in an mview viewport. The P button on the toolbar is on when you are in paper space. Most drawing is done in model space, whether in tilemode or mview viewports. You must consider the final scale of your output before placing any text or dimensions in model space.

Suppose that you have a drawing you want plotted at a scale of $^1/_4$"=1'-0". This scale is equal to 1=48. When plotting at a scale of $^1/_4$"=1'-0", AutoCAD LT physically scales your plotted drawing 48 times smaller than it was drawn. Your plot scale factor is then 48. To end up with $^1/_8$-inch-high text on your plot, you must place the text on your drawing at a height of $^1/_8$ inch times 48 or 6 inches high. Similarly, you should set DIMSCALE to 48, insert symbols at a scale of 48, and set linetype scale proportionately to 48.

In the Plot Configuration dialog box, you can designate the plot scale factor by entering the values in the Plotted Inches = Drawing Units input boxes. For example, if you plan to plot your drawing at a scale of $^1/_4$"=1'-0", you could specify this scale factor in one of the following ways:

◆ $^1/_4$"=1'

◆ $^1/_4$=12

◆ $^1/_4$"=12"

◆ 1=48

◆ .25=12

Any combination will work, as long as the ratio of the Plotted Inches on your plot to the Drawing Units in your drawing remains the same.

Tip   To determine the maximum scale that will fit the sheet, you can put a check in the Scaled **t**o Fit check box, and then adjust the Plotted Inches = Drawing Units input boxes to the next smaller standard scale. For example, if Scaled **t**o Fit sets Plotted Inches = Drawing Units to 8 = 14.24, you would reset them to 8 = 16 or 1 = 2.

23

In the following exercise, you plot the SHELF drawing from model space. The drawing is initially in paper space, so you need to enter model space before plotting. Your plot should be at a scale factor of 1"=4".

Plotting from Model Space

Continue in the previous SHELF drawing, or begin a new drawing again named SHELF, using the ALT2301.DWG file as a prototype and using no setup method.

Make sure that you have a print or plot device set up in Windows or AutoCAD LT or both, as discussed in the earlier sections. (If not, just cancel the plot at the last step of this exercise.)

Command: *Click on the P button*   Enters model space in the mview viewport

_MSPACE

You could plot from here, or from tilemode after the following step; the result is exactly the same because you are in model space either way.

Command: *Choose* **V**iew, *then* **P**aper Space   Enters model space in tilemode
(AutoCAD LT Release 1) or **T**ile Mode
(AutoCAD LT Release 2)

tilemode   Changes the TILEMODE system
New value for TILEMODE <0>: 1   variable value to 1 (on)
Regenerating drawing.

Command: *Choose the Plot button*   Issues the PLOT command and opens the
                                                      Plot Configuration dialog box (see fig. 23.23)

Figure 23.23

*The Plot
Configuration
dialog box.*

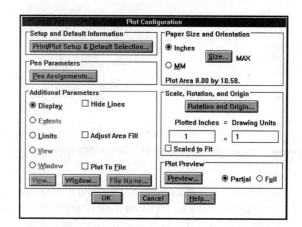

In the Paper Size and Orientation *area, make sure* Inc̲hes *is selected, then choose* **S̲ize**	Opens the Paper Size dialog box
Choose **S̲ize** A *or another size in the range of* 7.5"×10" *to* 8"×10.5"	Sets the plot size
In the Additional Parameters *area, choose the* Ex̲tents *radio button*	Defines the area of the drawing to plot
Enter **1** = **4** *in the* Plotted Inches = Drawing Units *input boxes*	Sets the plotting scale
Choose Fu̲ll, Pr̲eview	Previews the plot

The drawing image is too close to the corner of the sheet. Try again with limits, as follows.

Choose E̲nd Preview	Closes the Plot Preview dialog box
In the Additional Parameters *area, choose the* L̲imits *radio button*	Redefines the area of the drawing to plot
Choose Pr̲eview	Previews the plot

The corner-to-drawing image relationship is OK, but if it runs off the top of the sheet, adjust rotation as follows.

Choose OK	Closes the Plot Preview dialog box
If needed, choose Rotation and Orig̲in, *then the* 0 *or* 90 *radio button, (whichever is not already selected), then* OK	Opens the Plot Rotation and Origin dialog box, rotates the plot, then closes the dialog box

Preview it again; it should fit nicely on the sheet. End the preview.

Choose OK	Closes the Plot Configuration dialog box

Answer any further prompts to start the plot, or press Ctrl+C to cancel if you have no device available.

23

The preceding exercise plotted only the shelf detail, at $1/4$"=1'-0" scale. It plotted without the title block, however, because the title block was drawn in the paper space viewport. When plotting finished drawings from model space, you might want to insert a title block as an xref, scaled by the plot scale value, as shown in Chapter 18, "Leveraging Repetitive Design and Drafting." In the next exercise, you plot both the paper space title block and the model space drawing image at the same time, by plotting from paper space.

Plotting from Paper Space

If you are using paper space, your title block and border are typically drawn and plotted at a 1:1 scale factor. You insert the drawing image(s) in one or more mview viewports. Instead of scaling these images in the Plot Configuration dialog box, you scale them in the mviews. The same scaling considerations discussed in the previous "Plotting from Model Space" section apply to drawing and scaling the image in the mview viewport. You scale the images in mviews using the same plot scale factor that you would scale them when plotting from model space. You can scale each mview using the ZOOM XP option. The ZOOM XP factor is the reciprocal of the plot scale factor that you would use if plotting that viewport directly. For a 1:4 plot in the SHELF drawing, you could enter the ZOOM XP factor as **1/4XP** or **.25XP**.

Paper space enables you to compose the plotted sheet entirely in the paper space viewport. You insert and zoom mviews, and add titles and even annotation in the paper space viewport. Then you plot from the paper space viewport with a plot scale ratio of 1=1 in the Plotted Inches = Drawing Units input boxes. In paper space plotting, you should never draw or place anything in paper space that is not appropriate for plotting at a 1:1 ratio.

In the following exercise, you plot the SHELF drawing again. This time you plot it from paper space (TILEMODE=0). Because you are plotting from paper space, your plot scale should be 1=1.

Plotting from Paper Space

Create a new drawing again named SHELF, using the ALT2301.DWG file as a prototype and using no setup method. The P toolbar button indicates that you are in paper space.

Command: *Choose* **F**ile, **P**rint/Plot	Issues the PLOT command and opens the Plot Configuration dialog box
In the Paper Size and Orientation *area, make sure* In**c**hes *is selected, then choose* **S**ize	Opens the Paper Size dialog box
Choose **S**ize A *or another size in the range of* 7.5"×10" *to* 8"×10.5"	Sets the plot size
In the Additional Parameters *area, choose the* E**x**tents *radio button*	Defines the area of the drawing to plot
Enter **1** = **1** *in the* Plotted Inches = Drawing Units *input boxes*	Sets the plotting scale
Choose F**u**ll, **P**review	Previews the plot, similar to figure 23.24

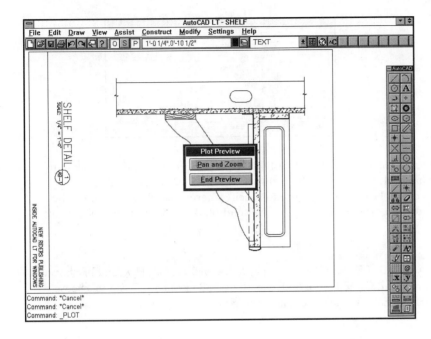

Figure 23.24

Full preview of paper space plot of SHELF drawing.

Choose **E**nd Preview	Closes the Plot Preview dialog box

If the preview ran off any edge of the sheet, adjust rotation, origin, or both with the Rotation and Ori**g**in button (see the preceding exercise), and then check the preview again.

Choose OK	Closes the Plot Configuration dialog box

Answer any further prompts to start the plot.

The resulting plot should include the title block at 1:1 scale as well as the shelf image at $\frac{1}{4}$"=1'-0" scale. The plot should look similar to the preview in figure 23.24.

Plotting to a File

You may need to plot to a file to enable network print/plot spooling software to handle sending plots to a shared network device, or you may need to create plot files for importation into other programs. Plotting to a file is just like plotting to a real device, except that you put a check in the Plot To **F**ile box in the Plot Configuration dialog box before choosing OK to plot. You can let it plot to the default file name (the current drawing name with a PLT extension), or you can choose the File N**a**me button in the Plot Configuration dialog box to specify a different name. The File N**a**me button opens a standard file dialog box, shown in figure 23.25.

Figure 23.25

The Create Plot File dialog box.

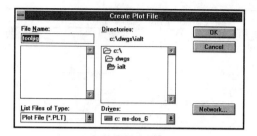

If you are on a network, the Create Plot File dialog box includes the Network button shown in figure 23.1. Clicking on the Network button opens a *<Network>* Drive Connections dialog box, which you use to specify where to send the plot file. The exact title and contents of this dialog box depend on the network to which you are attached.

ALT2 ◆ **Note**   In AutoCAD LT Release 2, you can plot to files in BMP, GIF, PCX, and TIFF bitmap formats, in 640×480, 800×600, and 1024×768 resolutions. To do so, choose Print/Plot Setup Default Selection and select the desired format.

Managing Plot Settings, Plotters, and Supplies

Most plots conform to some sort of standard, so you will find yourself repeatedly using several sets of settings in the Plot Configuration dialog box. After going to all the trouble of setting up the Plot Configuration dialog box, you probably want to be able to save the settings and restore them for later use. You can do so, as explained in the following section. Even if your drawing and plot dialog box settings are perfect, however, you won't get a good plot unless your plotting hardware is set up correctly and you are using appropriate supplies. This section discusses managing plot settings, plotter hardware, and plotting supplies.

Managing Standard Sets of Plot Settings

You can save and reload standard sets of plot settings. When you choose the Print/ Plot Setup & **D**efault Selection button in the Plot Configuration dialog box, you see the **S**ave Default To File and **G**et Default From File buttons for saving and restoring plot configurations to and from files. These buttons open the Save to File and Obtain from File dialog boxes, which are standard file dialog boxes. They save and restore plot configuration parameter (PCP) files that store plot parameters, such as pen

New Riders Publishing
INSIDE
SERIES

assignments, linetypes, paper size, and so on. By saving these defaults to a file, you have quick access to them the next time you need to generate a similar plot. You can have as many PCP files as needed. Perhaps you generate different types of plots for different clients. You could have a PCP file for each client to avoid having to remember pen settings and all the other details. In addition, if you have more than one plotting device, PCP files can be saved for each device.

PCP files are standard ASCII text files. The following is an excerpt from a PCP file:

```
;Created by AutoCAD LT on 03/04/1994 at 00:26
;From AutoCAD LT Drawing C:\DWGS\IALT\SHELF
;For the driver: System Printer ADI 4.2 - by Autodesk, Inc.
;For the device:

VERSION = 1.0
UNITS = _I
ORIGIN = 0.00,0.00
SIZE = MAX
ROTATE = 0
HIDE = _N
PEN_WIDTH = 0.010000
SCALE = _F
PLOT_FILE = _NONE
FILL_ADJUST = _N
OPTIMIZE_LEVEL = 4

BEGIN_COLOR = 1
  PEN_NUMBER = 1
  HW_LINETYPE = 0
  PEN_WEIGHT = 0.000984
END_COLOR

BEGIN_COLOR = 2
  PEN_NUMBER = 2
  HW_LINETYPE = 0
  PEN_WEIGHT = 0.000984
END_COLOR

.
.     (other color sets are stored here)
.
BEGIN_COLOR = 255
  PEN_NUMBER = 7
  HW_LINETYPE = 0
  PEN_WEIGHT = 0.000984
END_COLOR
```

23

Dealing with Equipment

Even with correct settings, you won't get a good plot unless your plotting hardware is set up correctly. If you can produce a correct plot preview and plot to a file but you are having difficulty plotting to your output device, some investigation is required. You should consider the following possibilities:

◆ Check the obvious. Is your plotter turned on?

◆ Does your plotter have paper loaded?

◆ Does your plotter have the correct pens loaded, and are they in the correct positions?

◆ If your pens are skipping, can you slow down the pen speed?

◆ If your plot starts but terminates before your entire drawing is plotted, check the communications parameters between the plotter and your computer. Check your plotter manual, or ask your AutoCAD dealer to assist you with this problem.

◆ Do you have the correct cable installed between your plotter and your computer system? If you are not getting any plots or if you are getting only partial plots, you may not have the correct cable to ensure that the computer system and plotter are communicating with one another.

◆ Are your plots truncated or chopped off at the margins? Check your paper size setting in AutoCAD LT. This setting should be no larger than the maximum plotting area your plotter can handle. In addition, check your plotting scale, and preview your plot to ensure that you are using the appropriate scale for your plot.

◆ Is your plot enormously out of scale? If you intended to plot from paper space, check to make sure that TILEMODE=0 and that you are not in model space inside a viewport. Every AutoCAD LT user will probably make this mistake sometime.

◆ Is your plot oriented correctly on the paper? Check to make sure that the rotation is set appropriately. The plot preview can be helpful in determining the correct orientation.

◆ Is your plot centered correctly on the page? Adjust the plot origin to compensate for the shift.

◆ Are the line weights incorrect? Check the line weight settings in the Pen Assignments dialog box. Make sure that you have designated the appropriate

units of measurement. A common mistake is to use millimeter values for pen weights when your plot dimension units are set to inches. Most pen manufacturers size their pens in millimeters. You must therefore convert this value to inches for correct line weights. In addition, make sure that the colors are mapped to the appropriate pen number and pen width.

◆ Are the linetypes not plotting, or are they plotting at the wrong scale? Check to see that the PSLTSCALE and LTSCALE system variables are set appropriately.

◆ Are the dimensions and plotted text too small to read? Check your plotting scale to determine if your text height is drawn accordingly.

Most plotters are fairly low maintenance; however, a little preventive maintenance every month is good insurance.

◆ Keep roller and pinch wheels clean. Pinch wheels press the paper against the roller, and rollers move the paper. Clean paper particles and residue from the pinch wheels with a stiff toothbrush.

◆ Check the paper sensors, if any. Plotters that use photodiodes to measure the paper have small holes in the back and front of the plate over which the paper moves. These holes have glass covers that can get dirty and cause problems loading the paper. Clean them with alcohol on a cotton-tipped swab.

◆ Keep printheads and other parts clean.

Sometimes plotting can be more of an art than a science. With experience, and some trial and error, you will soon be producing professional-looking plots most of the time.

Managing Media and Supplies

The acquisition of CAD software brings with it choices that must be made with respect to plotting media and supplies.

You must determine what type of output you generate most—8 $^1/_2$"×11" laser plots? 24"×36" D-size plots? This decision affects the type of media you buy. You must, of course, take into consideration the capabilities of your output device.

If you generate large-format plots, you need to decide which paper media will suit your needs. Bond paper is the least expensive and is used primarily for check plots or small plots that can be photocopied. Vellum is the second most expensive (next to polyester film) and is often used for generating low- to moderate-volume blue-line copies. *Polyester film* (such as Mylar) is used for high-volume copying and archival purposes only because it doesn't stretch, shrink, or fade. Translucent bond rides the middle ground in cost between bond and vellum; it provides a good mix for check plots and reproduces well.

Your choice of media also depends on the type of output device you have. Some manufacturers of electrostatic, laser, and inkjet plotters specify certain types and brands of media for the best results. Their recommendations may limit your choices of the type of media you use.

In addition to paper, you must decide on pens, toner, inkjet cartridges, and other supplies necessary to keep your plotter running. The type of pens you select depends on the type of paper you use. Pens made for use on vellum may not work as well on bond paper. Pens made for polyester film should be used only on polyester film.

Liquid roller-ball, ballpoint, and fiber-tip pens are OK for check plots. Ball pens work better on cheap paper than do fiber-tip pens, which bleed more. Ball and fiber-tip pens are disposable, but drafting-style ink pens are available in both disposable and refillable types. Speed, acceleration, force, and point quality affect the pen efficiency. Most plotters have adjustable speed and force (pen pressure). Many plotters sense the type of pen installed and use default settings that you can override to fine-tune your plot quality. Too high an acceleration can cause skips in the ends of lines. High acceleration speeds plotting of short line segments, text, and curves, where the pen has little room to get up to full speed. Ball pens accommodate rapid acceleration, making them ideal for check plots. Pressurized ballpoint pens plot as fast as 60 cps. Fiber-tip pens often work best around 40 to 50 cps. Fine-tuning the speed and acceleration can make a big difference in quality with ink pens, which range from 10 cps to 30 cps. Jewel tips handle higher speeds and outwear tungsten or ceramic. Stainless tips are suitable only for disposable pens. Tips wear much faster on polyester film than on vellum. Cross-grooved tips (don't use single grooved) can plot at higher speeds than plain tips can. Don't refill disposable pens; they aren't durable enough.

The most important part of ink pen maintenance is keeping them capped, even if in a pen carousel. Disposable ink pens usually have caps with rubber cushions inside to keep the tip from drying and clogging; however, for safety, keep them in a carousel or sealed container with a moist sponge (use a little bleach in the water to prevent mildew). A drop of pen cleaner in a cartridge full of ink also helps prevent clogging. A tap of the top of a well-maintained pen usually gets it running.

If you are new to CAD and plotting, it may take a while to determine what supplies you should have in stock. By establishing a usage trend, you can more accurately monitor your supplies. The last headache you want is to run out of ink or paper when a job deadline has you working at 2:00 a.m. and all your suppliers are closed.

Exploring Alternative Output

In addition to generating paper plots and plot files, AutoCAD LT has other forms of output. The sudden explosion in the desktop publishing (DTP) world has spilled over into the CAD area to some degree. Salespeople are looking for ways to incorporate their engineering department drawings into impressive sales reports and marketing brochures. Engineers are looking for ways to impress their superiors with their design ideas. The following three forms of alternative output are the most widely used.

◆ **PSOUT.** In the desktop publishing world, the PostScript language has become the actual standard for document publishing. The PostScript language is a vector-based language, which means that PostScript lettering fonts can be scaled without losing resolution. Fill patterns can be generated as well as lines of varying width and intensity. PostScript (EPS) files can be imported into many graphics, word processing, or desktop publishing packages. By importing, you can produce hybrid documents such as brochures and sales sheets that include AutoCAD LT drawings.

◆ **DXFOUT.** Another form of output in AutoCAD LT is the Drawing eXchange Format (DXF) file. The DXF file was created by Autodesk and is a standard in the industry. Most other CAD, word processing, and desktop publishing packages accept the DXF file as an import option, and many other CAD packages also can export DXF files. You can import DXF files into AutoCAD LT with the DXFIN command.

◆ **WMFOUT.** Windows Metafile Format (WMF) and bit-map (BMP) files are AutoCAD LT file formats that can be used in other software applications. A WMF file is a combination of vector and raster data that can be scaled and printed at any scale without losing resolution. The SAVEDIB command is used to generate a bit-map (BMP) or raster image file of everything that is on the AutoCAD LT screen, including menus, the toolbar, the toolbox, and any overlapping windows.

Now that you can plot whatever you can create in AutoCAD LT, you are ready to turn to the last chapter. Chapter 24, "Moving Beyond the Basics," explores several topics that can expand your horizons, both in AutoCAD LT and beyond AutoCAD LT, including sharing your CAD data with other programs.

23

Moving Beyond the Basics

I f you have worked through *Inside AutoCAD LT for Windows, Second Edition* to this point, you are becoming acclimated to drawing on a computer. There is much more to using CAD than just creating drawings, however, and many more sources are available for enhancing your drawings.

Although AutoCAD LT is marketed as a low-cost computer drafting package, it has many of the capabilities of its big brother, AutoCAD Release 12 for Windows. In this chapter, you look at many of the features that make AutoCAD LT more than a simple drafting package, as well as methods you can use to enhance your own use of the software. The items covered in this chapter include:

◆ Establishing layer-naming standards

◆ Guidelines for adding consistent style to your drawings

◆ Creating template drawings that contain the layers, text styles, and linetypes you use most

◆ Viewing and working with three-dimensional drawings

◆ Transferring data between different Windows and CAD programs

◆ What to look for when the capabilities of AutoCAD LT are no longer enough for you

A tutorial's primary purpose is to familiarize you with the software it is describing. *Inside AutoCAD LT for Windows, Second Edition* has been primarily concerned that you learn the tools you use on a regular basis. Drawing commands, object properties, viewing, layers, blocks—each of these you will use almost every time you work with AutoCAD LT.

Eventually, however, you will probably want to go beyond the basics and learn how to use more advanced features. AutoCAD LT is more than a simple drafting package. The next few sections of this chapter show you more of the advanced capabilities of the software, and how you can use those capabilities to make your drawings more accurate and professional.

Developing Standards

Standards, whether you define them or follow them, are meant to provide consistency in the way you work. Standards may be as simple as using a layer called NOTES for all text relating to the drawing you are working on, or as complex as using the ROMANS text style with a 15-degree obliquing angle on the layer EX-OWNERS for showing property owners on a survey plat. Standards set the tone for how you go about creating, organizing, and manipulating drawings.

Drafting on a computer is a simple but effective method for setting and maintaining standards. All the information you create is in an electronic format, which makes the job of maintaining standards from project to project as simple as reopening a file, saving the information to a new file name, and then deleting all the information that no longer pertains to the new project. What is left (layers, linetypes, text styles, and so on) becomes the basis for your new work.

Like the drawings you create, standards resemble the methods you use to create manual drawings. The same lessons you learned with manual drawing need to be applied to computer drawing, such as re-creating manual drafting styles in the computer, using templates for repeating parts or objects, and enforcing the use of standards. With the computer, you won't have to re-create all the standards you've developed for each new drawing, but you will need to learn a new way of applying those standards.

Each person's style of drawing differs. When you use CAD, your style carries over to the drawings you create. It may be in the letter styles you use for text and titles or in the way you use linetypes and line weights. Your style probably reflects the way you previously created manual drawings. If you don't have a manual drawing background, or if you simply want some tips for organizing and working with CAD, keep the information in this section in mind.

Using Standard Layer-Naming Schemes

Layers are one of the most controversial areas for applying standards. No matter what naming method you use, you should develop some sort of standard layer-naming scheme. Two schemes you can use as a reference are the American Institute of Architects CAD Layering Guidelines, and the Construction Standards Institute layer guidelines. Both of these documents provide examples for how to set up layer names for architectural-type projects. Both the AIA and CSI layering formats break down each portion of a building and assign it a layer name.

The AIA Format

The AIA format describes layers using a major group character, a minor group series of characters, and additional modifiers for differentiating between different groups. For example, the following layer names use the AIA format:

A-WALL

A-WALL-ELEV

A-WALL-MOVE

A-DOOR

A-DOOR-METL

A-DOOR-IDEN-METL

E-POWR

E-FIRE

E-LITE-SQUR

E-LITE-RECT

The first character is the Major Group type. Here the layers define "A" for architectural-related information, and "E" for electrical-related information. The AIA guidelines also use identifiers for Structural, Mechanical, Plumbing, Fire Protection, Civil Engineering, and Landscape Architecture. A single dash separates the major and minor groups, and then four characters describe the minor group information. In the previous layers, minor groups such as walls (WALL), doors (DOOR), power (POWR), fire alarms (FIRE), and lighting (LITE) are all identified.

Beyond the major and minor group information, a four-character group called a modifier and another four-character group for user-defined information are allowed. In the previous layer list, the layer A-DOOR-METL could be used to identify metal doors in a building, and the layer A-DOOR-IDEN-METL could be used for the metal door identification number. The AIA CAD Layer Guidelines document contains specific layer-naming suggestions that can be used to organize a complex project.

24

The CSI Format

The Construction Standards Institute (CSI) suggests that you follow the 16-division CSI format for identifying construction materials as the basis for your layer scheme. This format uses a five-number scheme to break down all building construction materials and services. The first two numbers of the scheme are direct from the CSI master divisions, which are defined as follows:

Division 01: General Data

Division 02: Sitework

Division 03: Concrete

Division 04: Masonry

Division 05: Metals

Division 06: Wood and Plastics

Division 07: Thermal and Moisture Protection

Division 08: Doors and Windows

Division 09: Finishes

Division 10: Specialties

Division 11: Equipment

Division 12: Furnishings

Division 13: Special Construction

Division 14: Conveying Systems

Division 15: Mechanical

Division 16: Electrical

Each of these categories is divided further based on the products that fall under the category. The three remaining numbers of the CSI layering format are used to define individual division types. For example, here are a few individual CSI elements:

02860 - Playground Equipment

05400 - Metal Studs

07555 - Ballast Roof

08833001 - Rolling Shutter Door

09700 - Abrasive Safety Floors

11700 - X-ray Machines

13046 - Prefabricated Offices and Booths

Most of the products that are defined by the CSI format easily fall into the five-number scheme, but a few subcategories like Rolling Shutter Doors are even more divided. The use of numbers for the layering scheme results in less typing to set up and manipulate layers. The problem with this format is that unless you know the division and subdivision numbers extremely well, you need to refer to some type of master index to determine which layer holds what type of data.

One advantage of following a layer-naming standard is easy manipulation of the layers. With both schemes, it's easy to turn off or on a group of layers. For example, if you are using the AIA standards and a drawing of a building and you want to work on the floor plan, you can turn off all the layers, then turn on all layers that begin with A. See Chapter 10, "Getting Organized: Drawing on Layers," for information on using wild cards with layers.

The AIA system of layer naming is much more conducive to working with the drawing as a whole; the CSI system works much better when you need to see all drawing elements of a certain type. As you can see, displaying layers that only contain certain types of information is a quick process, and not limited to only these types of layering systems.

Custom Layer Standards

You can create your own layer standards, which are a better reflection of the way you work. Because any layer name in AutoCAD LT can be up to 31 characters in length, you can be quite descriptive with your layer names. If you decide to make your own layer name scheme, try to be as descriptive as possible while using as few characters as possible. For example, you might use layer names such as the ones shown in table 24.1 in your drawings.

TABLE 24.1
Example Layer Names

Architectural	Mechanical
FLR1-WALLS	PART-HVY
FLR1-FIXTURES	PART-MED
FLR1-DOORS	PART-FINE
FLR1-STAIR	PART-XFINE
FLR1-STRUCT-COLS	PART-SECTION

continues

TABLE 24.1, CONTINUED
Example Layer Names

Architectural	Mechanical
FLR1-STRUCT-GRID	NOTE-FINE
FLR1-CLG-LIGHTS	NOTE-MED
FLR1-CLG-GRID	BORDER-FINE
FLR2-WALLS	BORDER-HVY
FLR2-FIXTURES	
FLR2-DOORS	

Table 24.1 shows a simple scheme to define the types of objects in a drawing. The architectural example breaks down objects by the floor number and the object type. By using the floor number as the prefix for the layer name, you can arbitrarily turn on only the layers that relate to the floor of a building you want to work on. In the mechanical example, the layer name corresponds to a pen weight that would be used to plot the drawing. HVY, for example, signifies a heavy line weight. You can assign layer colors to pen widths by using the **P**en Assignments option of the PLOT command. See Chapter 23, "Producing Hard Copy," for specific examples of corresponding layer colors to pen numbers.

When assigning layer names in your drawing, keep in mind the correlation you give between a layer color and plotter pen width. For example, the simple layer name scheme used for a mechanical drawing directly relates each layer to a single plotter pen weight or a linetype. The naming scheme can also be more complex, as in the case of the architectural layers, which break down the drawing objects into similar categories. Typically, all of your objects within a similar category will be plotted in the same manner. If you want some elements to plot differently, make up a new layer and assign different colors and linetypes to those elements.

Creating Custom Linetypes

The use of linetypes in your drawings largely depends on how you show information manually. For example, hidden lines are used to describe the edges of an object that is hidden by other objects, such as the edge-line in the underside of a part, or an underground foundation in a building elevation. Center lines are used to show structural grids or how screws join to a part in an assembly drawing, and a DASH2 linetype might be used to display a property line in a survey drawing.

If the linetypes you want to use in a drawing are not available from those found in the ACLT.LIN file, you have two options for creating a custom linetype. You can add the linetype to ACLT.LIN using an ASCII text editor, and then load it using the LINETYPE command Load option, or create it at the Command: prompt by using the LINETYPE command's Create option.

Creating Custom Linetypes

Create a new unnamed drawing, using the default prototype and no setup method.

Command: *Choose* **S**ettings, Li**n**etpe Style, **C**reate	Issues the LINETYPE command with the Create option
Name of linetype to create: **TEST-PATTERN** ⏎Enter	Specifies a name to be used for linetype
Type TEST *for the linetype file name*	Specifies a name for the file where the linetype will be stored
Descriptive text: **Test pattern for LINETYPE example** ⏎Enter	Specifies a short description for the linetype
Enter pattern (on next line): **A,1.0,-0.5,0,-0.5,1.0,-0.5** ⏎Enter	Specifies the actual linetype definition
>New definition written to file	Writes the linetype information to the TEST.LIN file
?/Create/Load/Set: **L** ⏎Enter	Loads the new linetype into the drawing
Linetype(s) to load: **TEST-PATTERN** ⏎Enter	Specifies the name of the linetype

Confirm that the highlighted file in the File **N**ame text box of the Select Linetype file dialog box is "TEST," and press Enter.

?/Create/Load/Set: **S** ⏎Enter	Uses the linetype for all new objects
New entity linetype (or ?) <BYLAYER>: **TEST-PATTERN** ⏎Enter	Specifies the name of the linetype you created
?/Create/Load/Set: ⏎Enter	Exits the LINETYPE command
Command: *Click on the Rectangle tool*	*Issues* the RECTANG command
First corner: *Pick* ① *(see fig. 24.1)*	Chooses the points for the rectangle corners
Other corner: *Pick* ②	

24

When you use this method for creating linetypes, you use the same format to describe the dashes and spaces that make up the linetype pattern as the format you used to define the linetype pattern in the ACLT.LIN file. Once the pattern is entered correctly, it can be used immediately, as shown in figure 24.1. The only drawback to this method of creating linetypes is that the linetype is not stored in a separate linetype file and cannot be loaded by another drawing. You have to recreate the linetype pattern in each drawing. If you want to access the linetype more easily, put the linetype definition into the ACLT.LIN file. You can then use the LINETYPE command Load option to add the linetype into other drawings.

Figure 24.1

A custom linetype.

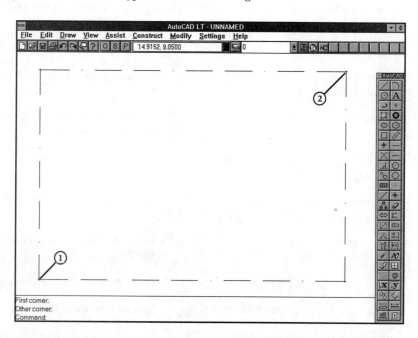

Linetypes are as easy to create and add as drawing names. Although the linetypes supplied with AutoCAD LT encompass a large number of possible uses, you may find that you need a linetype with a different pattern, or a smaller dash-space-dash sequence. You can view the existing linetype definitions in the file ACLT.LIN by using a program such as the Windows Notepad application. These definitions can give you ideas for specialized linetypes.

Using Hatch Patterns

The use of typical hatch patterns in a drawing is another method for establishing standards. Most drawing disciplines (architects, civil engineers, mechanical designers, surveyors) typically use hatch patterns to indicate a variety of different materials.

Architects use a line hatch pattern with a 45-degree slant between wall lines to indicate brick; a mechanical designer might use a net pattern to indicate a part that has been cut through; or a soils engineer might use a random pattern to describe a geological formation.

AutoCAD LT comes with a variety of hatch patterns in the ACLT.PAT file. This file is similar to the file used to define linetypes in that it allows patterns to be used across a group of drawings. Creating a hatch pattern is much more difficult, however, than creating a line pattern. In the linetype pattern, the only information required is how long the dash should be, and how long the space should be. With a hatch pattern, you must supply the angle of the line, the line's origin in the X and Y direction, the line's offset from the origin in the X and Y direction, and the dash/dot pattern for the hatch line. All of this information is needed just to create a single line in a repeating hatch pattern. For patterns such as concrete or brick pavers, you may have to write 30 or more lines of pattern code.

Regardless of their complexity, you can create your own hatch patterns. *Maximizing AutoCAD Release 12* by New Riders Publishing gives examples of creating simple and complex hatch patterns. The *AutoCAD Resource Guide* contains a list of all current application programs that enhance the AutoCAD software. In this list are several commercial hatch pattern packages that contain ready-to-use hatch patterns.

Using Text Styles

The use of text in a drawing is another area in which you can begin to establish standards. If you have previously created drawings by hand, you already have an idea of what the letters should look like in your computer drawings. If drafting is a completely new experience, you should use a simple text font that is readable at a variety of sizes, such as the ROMANS font. This font is composed of single-stroke characters that maintain smoothness, even among round letters, in sizes approaching two inches and larger. By using a finer pen with smaller-sized letters for general drawing text, and a wider pen with larger text for titles, you create a contrast that draws the viewer's eye to what you want him or her to see.

As you become more at ease with creating drawings on the computer, you'll probably want to make your drawings look more professional. AutoCAD LT comes with a wide range of fonts, from simple gothic and Cyrillic fonts to complex outline and filled PostScript fonts. In addition to the fonts that come with AutoCAD LT, a variety of third-party and shareware font packages work with AutoCAD. You also can create your own fonts, but this is very time-consuming. When custom designing a font, you must describe each stroke and arc of each character. To create a full character set, you will duplicate the design process almost a hundred times to create uppercase, lowercase, numeric, and punctuation characters.

24

By far the simplest and least expensive font option is to purchase a font package from a commercial developer. For prices ranging from $25 to $150, you can have a professionally crafted font that reflects a high-quality drawing. The New Riders Publishing book, *Killer AutoCAD Utilities*, comes with a variety of shareware fonts, and the *AutoCAD Resource Guide* contains lists and advertisements for developers who have font libraries for your use. If you are interested in creating your own font or special characters and symbols, the book *Maximizing AutoCAD Release 12* from NRP covers font creation in detail.

The final item to keep in mind about text and fonts is the type of font file used to generate the text characters. For many years AutoCAD has used the .SHX (shape) file format, which is designed for plotting on vector-based devices such as plotters and printers. AutoCAD LT also supports .PFB (PostScript) fonts, which can be plotted in an outline or filled format. Any plotter AutoCAD LT supports can plot PostScript outline fonts, but to plot the PostScript-filled fonts, the plotter must understand the PostScript language. For further information about plotting from AutoCAD LT, see Chapter 23, "Producing Hard Copy."

Working with Standard Template Drawings

In previous chapters, you learned how to use the DDLMODES, STYLE, and LINETYPE commands to create layers and text styles and to load linetypes into your drawing. For new drawings, though, AutoCAD LT has only the layer 0, the linetype CONTINUOUS, and the text style STANDARD available. In addition, settings such as the units, Snap mode, Ortho mode, and Grid mode all default to AutoCAD LT's original settings. If you want to create a single drawing that contains all the layers, linetypes, fonts, and settings that you use regularly, AutoCAD LT enables you to define this drawing as a template.

Template drawings, also known as *prototype drawings*, enable you to set up all your layers, linetypes, and text styles and use these settings when creating new drawings. These drawings can also contains settings for units, modes, and object creation. You can also predefine borders and viewports, and you can insert often-used blocks and xrefs. Even typical drawing details can form the basis of a template drawing. In general, a template drawing should contain all of the elements that would normally be a part of your drawing. Here are some specific recommendations for information that should be part of a template drawing:

- ◆ **Linetypes.** Make sure that any linetypes necessary for your layers are part of the prototype drawing. By doing this, you will save time and standardize available linetypes. Linetypes take up a relatively small amount of space, so you may want to load the full contents of your LIN file.

◆ **Layers.** If you have a standard layering scheme, or any layers you use consistently across drawings, set it up in your prototype. Be sure to include all the layer settings, such as color, linetype, and layer visibility.

◆ **Text Styles.** Any text styles that you use for typical notes, titles, logos, and so on should be placed in the drawing prototype.

◆ **Drawing Modes and Settings.** Many computer drafters have preferences about using Snap mode and Ortho mode, which can be turned on or off in the drawing prototype. The typical units for distance and angle can be preset by using DDUNITS. If you don't like to see the pick blips or solid fills, and if you like the grid turned on, you can use the DDRMODES command to set these preferences. You can also use the DDEMODES command to set the starting layer name and the current text style. Finally, the linetype scale settings can be preset in the prototype, which allows you to preset if linetypes are controlled with the paper space settings or only model space settings.

◆ **Dimension Settings.** Dimension styles are one of the best methods for managing the complexity of all the dimension settings. Set up and name any dimension styles you typically use, and then make sure that everyone is using the styles, rather than modifying the settings on an individual basis.

◆ **Borders and Viewports.** Every drawing you create will have some type of border. This may be as simple as a small company logo with the drafter's name and a scale, or it may be an outline of the sheet size you use, with north arrows and graphic scales, company and client logos, and project information. If you use paper space to arrange your drawings properly (the authors recommend this), you can also set up a typical viewport that takes up part of the sheet. You can even preset the display scale for the viewport with which you typically view model space elements.

◆ **Typical Drawing Elements.** Drawing objects should be the last items you place into a prototype drawing because they take up a lot of space. Also, it is sometimes easier to go to other drawings and use the WBLOCK and INSERT commands to move necessary elements into a drawing, rather than try to place every possible element into your prototype. Some of the objects you should consider placing in the prototype might be typical notes that do not change between drawings. Simple elements (such as lines and circles) that make up a structural grid can also be handy when they are part of the prototype.

Figure 24.2 shows a generic prototype drawing that was created for drawing floor plans. The border has been set up in paper space with all titles and scales already applied and a default viewpoint that has been created to show whatever model space elements the drafter creates.

24

Figure 24.2

*A generic
prototype
drawing.*

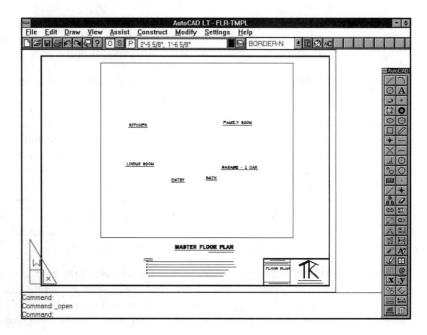

Creating a prototype drawing for any drawing you typically work with can save you quite a bit of time. With a single prototype drawing set up, you can quickly change such minor items as the linetype scale and dimension scale and have another proto-type drawing ready to use. This means that the time you spend setting up a single prototype can be recouped by not having to perform all those settings for each drawing you create thereafter.

Once you have a single prototype drawing, or a series of prototype drawings, you need only use the **P**rototype option of the Create New Drawing dialog box. Simply select the drawing that contains the appropriate settings for the new drawing you will create. After you press OK, all of the drawing settings are loaded in, and you are ready to draw. If you have a series of prototype drawings to choose from, place them in their own subdirectory for quicker access.

Using Libraries of Parts and Details

The AutoCAD program has been around for the majority of the life of the PC. Over that 10+ years, it has become the standard used by the majority of design profession-als. It is also the package of choice for manufacturers when creating libraries of their products for use in CAD.

A *library of parts* is a series of drawing files that contain standard details, drawing elements, or graphics you use when you create a drawing. For example, if you are an architect, your library of parts could contain toilet fixtures, furniture symbols, doors, windows, and structural columns. If you are a mechanical designer, your library could contain typical bolt plans and sections, dies, threads, and tapped sleeves. Your parts library does not have to be limited to small drawing elements. If you have a machine subassembly or a bathroom layout that you typically show on your drawings, this too can become a library element. A library enables you to take often-used objects and make them available for any drawing.

Arranging Your Own Library of Parts

If you would like to set up your own library of parts, you can organize it in one of two ways. The first method is to place all the library elements in a single subdirectory and assign descriptive file names. The file names should indicate the content of the library element by using similar prefix names. For example, you might use FURN as the first four characters of any furniture library element. The only drawback to this method is that if you have a lot of library elements, it may become difficult to decide on enough descriptive names when you are limited to eight characters for each file name. If you can manage it, you might have a subdirectory in the ACLT directory with library elements that look like figure 24.3.

```
ACLTWIN
  └─DETAILS
      └─BDR-PLAN.DWG      (Prototype plan sheet)
        BDR-SECT.DWG      (Prototype section sheet)
        BDR-ELEV.DWG      (Prototype elevation sheet)
        ARROW-1.DWG       (North arrow #1)
        ARROW-2.DWG       (North arrow #2)
        FURN-CHR.DWG      (Chair library part)
        FURN-TBL.DWG      (Table library part)
        FURN-SHL.DWG      (Shelf library part)
        FURN-CCH.DWG      (Couch library part)
        FIXT-WC.DWG       (Water closet fixture)
        FIXT-HWC.DWG      (Handicapped water closet fixture)
        FIXT-LAV.DWG      (Lavatory fixture)
        FIXT-HLV.DWG      (Handicapped lavatory fixture)
```

Figure 24.3

Library elements in a single directory.

Another method for arranging your library is to use different subdirectories to store different drawing elements. For example, one subdirectory holds prototype drawing borders, another holds furniture, and another subdirectory holds bathroom fixtures. You can separate library elements into logical groups and maintain descriptive names for each of the library elements. The only drawback to this method is that you must be extremely methodical about separating out the different types of library parts when you add them to your library. If you set up this type of library, your arrangement may look similar to figure 24.4.

24

Figure 24.4

Using multiple directories for library elements.

```
ACLTWIN
  └─DETAILS
      ├─BORDERS
      │    BDR-PLAN.DWG        (Prototype plan sheet)
      │    BDR-SECT.DWG        (Prototype section sheet)
      │    BDR-ELEV.DWG        (Prototype elevation sheet)
      │    ARROW-1.DWG         (North arrow #1)
      │    ARROW-2.DWG         (North arrow #2)
      ├─FURNITUR
      │    FURN-CHR.DWG        (Chair library part)
      │    FURN-TBL.DWG        (Table library part)
      │    FURN-SHL.DWG        (Shelf library part)
      │    FURN-CCH.DWG        (Couch library part)
      └─BATH-FIXT
           FIXT-WC.DWG         (Water closet fixture)
           FIXT-HWC.DWG        (Handicapped water closet fixture)
           FIXT-LAV.DWG        (Lavatory fixture)
           FIXT-HLV.DWG        (Handicapped lavatory fixture)
```

No matter how you arrange your part libraries, you want to have easy access to any element you need to add to a drawing. AutoCAD LT enables you to set support directories from the Preferences dialog box. *Support directories* are directories AutoCAD LT searches when inserting a file into the current drawing. By default, when you issue an INSERT command and the name you give is not currently a block within the drawing, AutoCAD LT will try to locate a matching file name in any support directories.

Tip The support directories that AutoCAD LT searches include more than just those listed in the Preferences dialog box **S**upport Dirs box. AutoCAD LT also searches the current directory and directories specified in the properties of the program item used to start AutoCAD LT. You can check the current search path by entering a nonsense name at the INSERT command's Block name (or ?): prompt. This displays all directories in the current search path in the error Message dialog box that appears.

You are not limited to a single support directory location for your library parts. If you choose the **B**rowse button in the Preferences dialog box, you open the Edit Path dialog box, which enables you to choose multiple locations as support directories. To add a path for AutoCAD LT to use when inserting library parts, choose it from the Directo**r**ies list box and select the Add button. The path name is added to the **S**earch Path list. You can also remove unneeded search paths from the list by highlighting the appropriate name and choosing **D**elete.

New Riders Publishing
INSIDE
SERIES

Tip Even though you may separate different types of library parts into various subdirectories, you should still be careful of the name you use for the library part. When you insert a part, AutoCAD LT searches the support directories in the order in which they appear in the **S**earch path list. The first matching file from the first support directory location is the part that will be inserted, even if you intended to insert a different part.

Using Third-Party Libraries

If you would like to use libraries of parts to store often-needed drawing elements, you can create the library elements yourself or purchase them from different manufacturers. Many manufacturers make their product libraries available in an AutoCAD-compatible format that often can be used with other Autodesk products, such as AutoCAD LT.

If you need the library of a manufacturer's product, make sure the product line does not require AutoLISP to access the library elements or to create them in the drawing. Many manufacturers use AutoLISP to create parts parametrically from dimensions you give in a drawing. AutoCAD LT does not support the AutoLISP language. For a list of manufacturers with parts libraries, refer to the *AutoCAD Resource Guide*, which is available from Autodesk or your local AutoCAD dealer.

If you have accumulated a variety of drawing elements that you want to turn into a library of parts, start by following the recommendations given earlier for creating and placing file names and directories. Add the appropriate support directories in the AutoCAD LT Preferences dialog box, and you are ready to go. If you are setting up a library of parts for coworkers to use, you might consider creating an icon menu for your library elements. This enables you to show each part in your library graphically and use whatever naming scheme you want for the part's file name. The person who is using the icon menu doesn't need to know the name of the file that contains the element he wants to use; he simply chooses it from the menu.

Tip Creating icon menus is beyond the scope of this book. You can read the New Riders Publishing book *Maximizing AutoCAD Release 12* for information on creating and using this type of menu.

Enforcing and Maintaining Standards

Before a company can establish a standard methodology for creating drawings, two steps must be taken in the standardization process. The first step is to create the standards, and the second step is to enforce those standards. Creating the standards

24

is usually the easier of the two steps. All that is required is taking items you may have used when you were drafting manually and translating them into a computer format. If you don't currently have a standard, you might look at what your competitors are doing. Borrow from what they appear to do right, and use your own ideas for what they do wrong.

Enforcing standards is often difficult, but it is necessary if you are to provide a consistent-looking product to your clients. Here are some tips for establishing and enforcing standards among coworkers:

◆ **Create and use prototype drawings.** This is one of the best methods for maintaining standards because it creates all the drawing properties first. The draftsman doesn't need to worry about creating a non-standard layer or using a non-standard font because all of these elements are already available.

◆ **Use dimension styles.** With over 50 different options for creating dimensions, dimensions can easily differ among users. By creating dimension styles and placing them in the prototype drawing, you can help eliminate some of the inconsistencies that occur when dimensioning drawings.

◆ **Maintain and use a library of parts.** Parts libraries make standard drawing symbols available to everyone. If drafters know that the drawing element has already been created, they will be more likely to use it rather than to create their own. The other thing to be aware of is that you must update libraries as drawing elements change. If the library contains only outdated parts, no one will want to use it.

◆ **Establish a standards committee.** The benefits of a committee are that the job of overseeing and maintaining standards can be shared, rather than being a burden to only one person. The committee can also make sure that as standards change, everyone is informed about the correct method to use in the future.

◆ **Review all drawings.** The final step is to review everything that leaves your office. This is probably something that is done to check the accuracy of the work, but you should also keep an eye out for consistency between drawings. Clients may not notice that one drawing uses a ROMAND font rather than a ROMANS, but if one set of dimensions is in architectural units and another in decimal, they are bound to wonder how well you checked for other problems. Remember that a consistent-looking set of drawings makes you look like a professional.

Working in Three Dimensions

One area in which AutoCAD Release 12 will always outshine AutoCAD LT is in the area of three-dimensional modeling. AutoCAD Release 12 contains many commands for the creation of primitive 3D shapes such as boxes, cones, tubes, and spheres. In addition, the Advanced Modeling Extension package enables you to create more complex 3D shapes through the use of Boolean operations such as addition and subtraction.

Although AutoCAD LT does not incorporate many of the advanced 3D features and object types found in AutoCAD Releases 12 or 13, it can take basic objects and give them height in 3D space. You can use AutoCAD LT commands to view 3D models from any point in space. Even the current drawing plane can be modified, allowing objects to occupy any location in 3D space.

A comprehensive tutorial for working with 3D elements is beyond the scope of this book. Although AutoCAD LT enables the user to edit complex 3D objects created in AutoCAD Release 12, it does not support the commands that create 3D objects. For true 3D modeling, the reader must use a more full-featured package, such as AutoCAD Release 12. The following sections are not designed to serve as an in-depth tutorial to creating 3D models, but as examples of the capabilities AutoCAD LT has when dealing with 3D elements.

Using the VPOINT Command to View 3D Drawings

Even though AutoCAD LT cannot create complex 3D drawings, the program has the same tools as AutoCAD Release 12 for viewing 3D drawings. The most useful of these tools is the VPOINT command. In the following exercise, you will be working with the file ALT2401, which is on the disk that accompanies this book. This drawing file is composed almost entirely of normal AutoCAD LT objects (lines, circles, polylines) that have been modified and manipulated to create a 3D model. The following exercises demonstrate AutoCAD LT's tools for viewing a 3D model, as well as how to use them when creating 3D drawings.

Viewing 3D Models with the VPOINT Command

Create a new drawing named 3D using ALT2401 as the prototype drawing, and using no setup method.

Command: *Choose* **V**iew, **3**D Viewpoint, **R**otate	Issues the VPOINT command with the Rotate option

continues

24

continued

Enter angle in XY plane from X axis <270d0'0">: **200** (Enter)	Sets the direction in the current drawing plane
`Enter angle from XY` `plane <90d0'0">:` **15** (Enter)	Sets the angle above the drawing plane from which the model will be viewed
Command: *Choose* **V**iew, **H**ide	Removes lines that are behind other objects

---

> **VPOINT.** The VPOINT command is used to view an object in the graphics area from any location in AutoCAD LT's 3D space. When you use this command, AutoCAD LT zooms to the drawing's extents as seen from the new viewing location.

The VPOINT command has three options for defining the point of view from which you look at a drawing.

◆ **Rotate.** With Rotate, you can precisely define a direction in the drawing plane and an angle above the drawing plane for viewing a drawing.

◆ **Globe and Axes.** This option enables you to choose your viewing location from a flattened globe that represents 3D space in the drawing. The globe is composed of two concentric circles with a crosshair drawn through the center. Your pointing device moves a small cross through the globe.

Moving the cross within the inner circle enables you to view the model from above; moving the cross in the outer circle enables you to view the model from below. As you move the cross through the circles, AutoCAD LT displays a 3D axis indicator that shows the directions for the X, Y, and Z planes. To use the Globe and Axes option, press Enter at the VPOINT prompt.

◆ **Point.** This option is used to specify an X,Y,Z coordinate that looks toward point 0,0,0. This becomes the direction from which you are viewing the 3D model. To use the Point option, specify any 3D point at the VPOINT prompt.

> **HIDE.** The HIDE command removes hidden lines of a 3D model from the current viewpoint. HIDE enables you to get a better understanding of where elements in a 3D model are located in relation to each other. The hidden lines are not actually removed from the drawing database, but simply not displayed in the drawing area. The REDRAW command or any command that redraws or regenerates the drawing will cause the hidden lines to be visible again.

In the preceding exercise, when you first opened the exercise drawing, the drawing was viewed in plan view, looking down on the drawing elements (see fig. 24.5). You then used the VPOINT command's Rotation option to see the 3D model from a different location in 3D space. To achieve the fastest possible speed, AutoCAD LT uses wireframes to represent 3D elements. To see how each of the 3D elements relates to the model, the HIDE command (see fig. 24.6) was used. This command removes any 3D objects that are hidden behind other objects in the model.

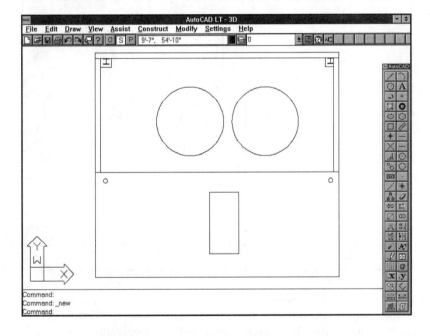

Figure 24.5

Viewing a 3D model in plan view—looking down on it.

AutoCAD LT also provides the SHADE command, which takes a 3D model and displays solid surfaces of color on any 3D elements. The HIDE command is much quicker, though, because it removes only elements that are hidden and shows only the edges of 3D elements. In addition, when you use the HIDE command, you can still use object snaps to select points on an object. The image generated with the SHADE command cannot be manipulated or referenced at all. For more information on the SHADE command, refer to the AutoCAD LT **H**elp menu and the *AutoCAD LT for Windows User's Guide.*

Using the VPORTS Command

24

Although the VPOINT command provides a quick method for viewing a 3D model, the process of actually working with and creating elements in 3D space can be difficult. Because AutoCAD LT displays 3D objects as wireframes, it is easy to become confused about the location of an element relative to the objects around it. To aid the designer when working in 3D space, AutoCAD LT provides the VPORTS command, which breaks the screen into rectangular windows. Each of these windows can be set to view the 3D model from a different location. The VPORTS command is similar to the MVIEW command, except that the viewports created cannot be moved or resized.

Figure 24.6

Viewing a 3D model from a point in 3D space.

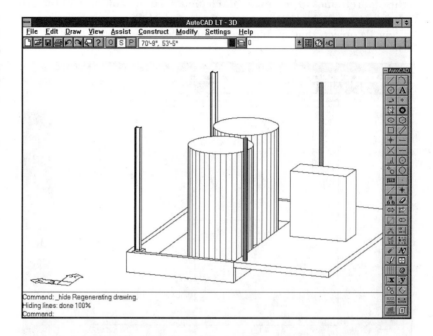

AutoCAD LT has several menu options that enable you to establish the viewing locations within the viewports created with the VPORTS command. In the following exercise, you continue to use the 3D drawing you created in the preceding exercise. This time, you use VPORTS to create and set the display in a series of viewports.

Creating Multiple Viewports

Continue from the preceding exercise.

Command: *Choose* **V**iew, 3D Vie**w**point Presets, **T**op	Issues the VPORTS command to restore the drawing to plan view
Command: *Choose* **V**iew, **Z**oom **E**xtents	Redisplays the drawing within the full extents of the window
Command: *Choose* **V**iew, Viewp**o**rts, **3** Viewports	Issues the VPORTS command to create three viewports

`Horizontal/Vertical/Above/Below/Left/` `<Right>:` (Enter)	Sets the location for the larger viewport
Pick in the lower left viewport	Selects the current, active viewport
`Command:` *Choose* **V**iew, 3D Vie**w**point Presets, Iso View N**E**	Sets the display direction from the upper left corner of the model
Pick in the right viewport	Selects the current, active viewport
Choose **V**iew, 3D Vie**w**point Presets, Iso View S**E**	Sets the display direction from the lower left corner of the model (see fig. 24.7)
`Command:` *Choose* **V**iew, Viewp**o**rts, **S**ave	Issues the VPORTS command to save the current viewport configuration
`?/Name for new viewpoint configuration:` **DEFAULT** (Enter)	Saves these viewport settings with a name for easy recall

Save the drawing

> **VPORTS.** The VPORTS command is used to create and arrange model space viewports. Each viewport serves as an independent viewing location into the drawing. This allows different viewports to contain different views of the model space elements. Any viewport can be made active by clicking in the viewport, or by pressing Ctrl+V.

The VPORTS command has the following options:

◆ **Save.** The Save option names and stores the current viewport configuration and includes the number of viewports and the viewpoint of each viewport. This option is useful for coming back to a certain arrangement of drawing views after you have modified the view with the ZOOM, PAN, and VPOINT commands. You can save multiple configurations and restore each as you need them.

◆ **Restore.** The Restore option restores a named viewport configuration stored previously with the Save option.

◆ **Delete.** The Delete option removes a named viewport configuration stored previously with the Save option. This is most useful when a saved viewport configuration is no longer useful in your work.

◆ **Join.** The Join option merges two viewports in the display screen into a single viewport.

24

◆ **SIngle.** The SIngle option enlarges the current active viewport to fill the display screen.

◆ **?.** This option lists any named viewport configurations. Information regarding each viewport and the viewing direction is displayed.

◆ **2/<3>/4.** These options are used to determine the number and arrangement of the viewports used to display the current drawing. The 2 option creates two viewports that split the drawing area or current viewport horizontally or vertically. The 3 option splits the drawing area or current viewport into half and then prompts you for the location of the third viewport. The 4 option breaks the drawing area or current viewport into four quarters.

To work effectively with 3D models, you usually need at least three viewports open. One viewport should show the model as seen from the top view or front view in the plan. The other two views should use whatever viewpoints are useful for constructing your model. One of the remaining two viewports is usually set to a side plan view, and the other is usually a 3D view of the model. Because AutoCAD LT allows you to use any viewport for selecting points, you can choose the viewport that gives you the best view of objects you want to select or points you want to pick (see fig. 24.7).

Figure 24.7

Multiple viewports used to display the 3D model.

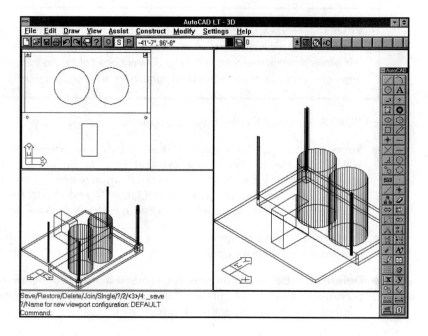

Using the DVIEW Command

Another method you can use to view 3D models is the DVIEW command. The DVIEW command also enables you to interactively specify the drawing view. It uses a camera metaphor to help you specify the view you want. This command also enables you to create perspective views from a 3D model, which is different from the axonometric display shown with the VPOINT command. In the following exercise, you use the DVIEW command to change the drawing view and create a perspective view of the drawing.

Creating a Perspective View from a Model

Continue from the preceding exercise.

Pick in the upper left viewport	Selects the current, active viewport
Command: *Choose* **V**iew, Viewp**o**rts, **S**ingle	Issues the VPORTS command and makes the current viewport fill the drawing window
Command: *Choose* **V**iew, 3D D**y**namic View	Issues the DVIEW command
Select objects: **ALL** (Enter)	Selects all the drawing objects for the perspective viewing
Select objects: (Enter)	
CAmera/TArget/Distance/POints/ PAn/Zoom/TWist/CLip/Hide/Off/ Undo/<eXit>: **CA** (Enter)	Specifies the CAmera option
Toggle angle in/Enter angle from XY plane <90.00>: **20** (Enter)	Sets the view angle in the drawing plane
Toggle angle from/Enter angle in XY plane from X axis <-90.00>: **-50** (Enter)	Sets the angle above the drawing plane
CAmera/TArget/Distance/POints/ PAn/Zoom/TWist/CLip/Hide/Off/ Undo/<eXit>: **D** (Enter)	Specifies the Distance option

continues

24

continued

```New camera/target distance <0'-1">: 75' (Enter)```	Sets the distance from the camera point to the target point in the 3D model and enters perspective mode
```CAmera/TArget/Distance/POints/ PAn/Zoom/TWist/CLip/Hide/Off/ Undo/<eXit>: (Enter)```	Exits the DVIEW command
Command: *Choose* <u>V</u>iew, <u>H</u>ide	Produces a hidden-line display of the perspective view

> **DVIEW.** The DVIEW command enables you to dynamically adjust the view of your drawing. After the DVIEW command is issued, you are prompted to select a representative sample of objects to help you set the view. Because the DVIEW command is interactive, you do not usually want to select all the objects in your drawing. The more objects you select, the slower the dynamic display updates. When you are finished setting the view, the entire drawing is displayed, using the parameters you specified in the DVIEW command. Pressing Enter at the Select objects: prompt uses AutoCAD's default DVIEW image (a house) to help you specify the view.

The DVIEW command has a number of options for controlling the view of your model:

◆ **CAmera.** The CAmera option is used to set the location of the viewer (the camera) in relation to the camera's target point. With this option, you specify an angle in the X,Y plane for the direction from which you are looking at the target, and an angle above the X,Y plane describing the elevation of the camera relative to the target point.

◆ **TArget.** The TArget option rotates the target point about the camera position. You specify an angle in the X,Y plane and an angle relative to the X axis.

◆ **Distance.** The Distance option enables you to determine the distance between the camera (you, the viewer) and the target point. Using this option turns on perspective viewing. You cannot pick points in a viewport that displays a perspective view. The UCS icon is replaced by the perspective icon (a box drawn in perspective) to indicate that the view is in perspective.

- **POints.** The Points option enables you to specify exact X,Y,Z coordinates for both the camera and target locations. This is handy for precisely locating a viewing height and direction.

- **PAn.** Because the normal PAN and ZOOM commands are not allowed in perspective mode, you must use the DVIEW command's equivalents to properly display the view. When you use this option, both the camera and target points move relative to the direction of the pan direction.

- **Zoom.** This option is similar to the zoom setting on a camera lens. When using this option, you are prompted for a scale factor that moves the camera closer or farther away from the model objects.

- **TWist.** The TWist option rotates the display along the camera/target line of sight. When you use this option, AutoCAD LT asks for the desired rotation angle.

- **CLip.** The CLip option enables you to define clipping planes in front of and behind the target point. These clipping planes enable you to screen out objects that obstruct your view of the model.

- **Hide.** This option is similar to the normal HIDE command, which removes lines behind other 3D objects. The advantage to this option is that you do not have to leave the DVIEW command to determine whether you are viewing the 3D elements of your drawing from the correct direction.

- **Off.** This option turns off perspective mode and returns you to AutoCAD LT's normal axonometric mode.

- **Undo.** The Undo option enables you to reverse any changes to the viewpoint you have made with the other options from within the DVIEW command.

- **eXit**. When you have completed the view changes, this option redraws all the drawing objects from the new viewpoint and returns you to the Command: prompt.

Using the Distance option of the DVIEW command puts AutoCAD LT into perspective view mode (see fig. 24.8). In this mode, you cannot use the PAN or ZOOM commands or choose points by picking with the mouse. In perspective view mode, AutoCAD LT only allows you to specify points by using exact coordinates (0,0,0) and relative locations (@120<225) from the keyboard. Visually locating points in a perspective view is much more difficult because all points converge in the distance. To work in AutoCAD LT's normal display mode, you must reissue the DVIEW command and use the Off option.

24

Figure 24.8

A hidden-line removal of a perspective view of the 3D model.

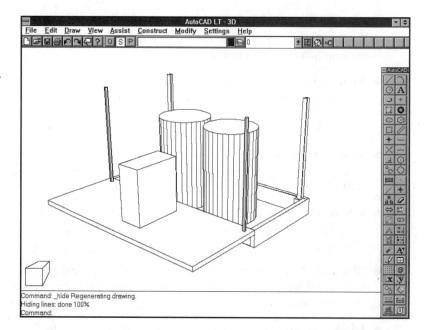

Modifying the Current Coordinate System

To work effectively in AutoCAD LT's 3D space, you must use the User Coordinates System (UCS). By default, the UCS is aligned with the World Coordinate System (WCS). The WCS is the global coordinate system AutoCAD LT uses to locate objects, and unless you are working in 3D, you don't really need to be concerned about the WCS. When creating 3D models, though, the WCS is usually the base on which you build your models.

You first learned about the UCS command in Chapter 2 for drawing in 2D. To draw in 3D space in AutoCAD LT, you use the UCS command to make working in 3D easier. This command, which stands for User Coordinate System, enables you to define any location in 3D space as the current drawing plane.

In the following exercise, you use the UCS command to easily place objects in 3D space without having to mentally calculate the 3D points.

Working in Other Coordinate Systems

Start a new drawing named 3D-UCS, using the default ACLT prototype drawing and no setup method. Then, set the snap increment to two inches, and turn on Snap.

Command: *Choose the Current Color button on the toolbar*   Opens the Entity Creation Modes dialog box

Enter **60** *in the* **T***hickness box, and choose* OK	Sets the current entity thickness—new objects will be drawn with a height of 60 in the Z axis
Command: *Choose* **A**ssist, U**C**S Icon	Issues the UCSICON command
`ON/OFF/All/Noorigin/` `ORigin <OFF>:` **ALL** (Enter)	Turns on the UCS icon in all viewports
`ON/OFF/Noorigin/` `ORigin <OFF>:` **ON** (Enter)	Turns on the UCS icon
Command: *Choose* **V**iew, Viewp**o**rts, **3** Viewports	Issues the VPORTS command to create three viewports
`Horizontal/Vertical/Above/` `Below/Left/<Right>:` (Enter)	Sets the location for the larger viewport
Command: *Choose* **V**iew, **Z**oom, **S**cale	Issues the ZOOM command
`All/Center/Extents/Previous/` `Window/<Scale(X/XP)>:` **.05** (Enter)	Sets the display scale factor for the right viewport

Click in each of the other two viewports and zoom them with a .05 scale.

Command: *Click on the Line tool*	Issues the LINE command
`From point:` **-50,0** (Enter)	Specifies the starting point
`To point:` **@100<0** (Enter)	Specifies the next two endpoint locations
`To point:` **@100<90** (Enter)	
`To point:` (Enter)	Ends the LINE command
Click in the lower left viewport	Makes the viewport active
Command: *Choose* **A**ssist, Set **U**CS **X** Axis Rotate	Issues the UCS command with the X option
`Rotation angle about X` `axis <0>:` **90** (Enter)	Rotates the Y and Z axes about the the X axis
Command: *Choose* **V**iew, 3D Vie**w**point Presets, Iso View **SE**	Changes the view orientation to look at the model from the southeast

Zoom to the view shown in figure 24.9.

Command: *Click on the Line tool*	Issues the LINE command
`From point:` *Use INT object snap to pick* ① *(see fig. 24.9)*	Starts the line at the displayed intersection

continues

24

continued

To point: **@100<90** (Enter)   Draws the line (see fig. 24.10)

Figure 24.9

A few simple lines created as 3D objects.

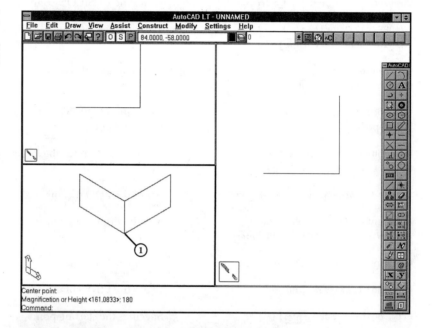

Figure 24.10

Creating more objects in different coordinate systems.

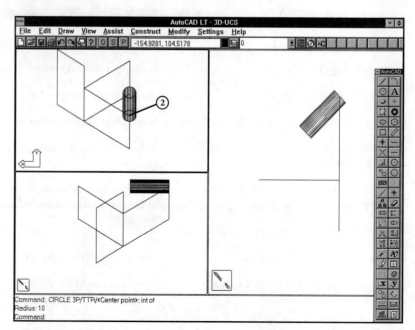

To point: **Enter**	Ends the LINE command
Click in the upper left viewport	
Command: *Choose* **A**ssist, Set **U**CS, **Y** Axis Rotate	Issues the UCS command with the Y option
Rotation angle about Y axis <0>: **-45** **Enter**	Rotates the X and Z axes about the Y axis
Command: *Choose* **V**iew, 3D Vie**w**point Presets, Iso View N**E**	Changes the view orientation
Zoom to the view shown in figure 24.10.	
Command: *Click on the Circle tool*	Issues the CIRCLE command
3P/TTR/<Center point>: *Use INT object snap to pick* ② *(see fig. 24.10)*	Locates the circle center point
Radius: **10** **Enter**	Specifies the circle radius and draws a 60 unit cylinder

> **UCS.** The UCS command enables you to change the location of the drawing plane in AutoCAD LT's 3D space. The UCS command is useful for taking simple objects and building somewhat complex 3D models.

The UCS command has several options for relocating the current drawing plane:

◆ **Origin.** The Origin option enables you to relocate the 0,0,0 point of the UCS to a new point of your choosing. This option is handy when you want to use X,Y coordinates that are relative to the current UCS's origin, and in the same X,Y plane orientation.

◆ **ZAxis.** The ZAxis option enables you to specify a new UCS by specifying a new origin point and a point on the new Z axis relative to the current UCS.

◆ **3point.** The 3point option enables you to specify three points to define a new UCS. The first point is the UCS origin, the second point specifies the direction along the X axis, and the third point is the direction of the Y axis. All specified points are relative to the current UCS.

◆ **Entity.** This option aligns the UCS with the coordinate system of a selected object. The Z axis is placed in the extrusion direction of the selected object.

24

◆ **View.** The View option rotates the UCS so that it is perpendicular to the current view.

◆ **X/Y/Z.** These three options enable you to choose the axis around which you rotate the UCS.

◆ **Prev.** This option, which stands for previous, will reset the UCS to the previous UCS.

◆ **Restore.** This option works in conjunction with the Save option. It enables you to restore the UCS to a previously named UCS setting.

◆ **Save.** This option names the origin location and direction of the X, Y, and Z axes of the current UCS. You can then modify your UCS and later return to the saved UCS settings by using the Restore option.

◆ **Del.** This option deletes a saved UCS.

◆ **?.** This option displays the names of and information about any saved user coordinate systems.

◆ **<World>.** This default option resets the UCS to the World Coordinate System.

When you first began the preceding exercise, you used the UCSICON command to turn on the coordinate system icon in all viewports so that you have a sense of the current direction observed by the coordinate system. If you do not pay attention to the orientation of the coordinate system icon, something as simple as moving @60<225 can throw objects into a position completely opposite of where you would like them. Also, as mentioned in the previous section, by creating several viewports, you can get a better feel for how elements are being created in 3D space. Although you drew only two lines initially, the lines form a pair of walls because you have set the entity (object) thickness property (refer to fig. 24.9).

You also used the UCS command to rotate the coordinate system about various axes and draw more objects (refer to fig. 24.10). You may have noticed that the UCS icon changed direction as the coordinate system was relocated. As you drew the final line and circle objects, their extrusion direction was perpendicular to the User Coordinate System, which is the way the thickness property is always handled. If you keep that in mind, it then becomes quite simple to create walls, sloped roofs, and multistory models using the simple tools of AutoCAD LT.

 Tip The UCS command, although quite powerful, is sometimes difficult to use if you are only making simple adjustments to the coordinate system you are working in. If you choose **A**ssist, and then **P**reset UCS, the UCS Orientation dialog box opens. This dialog box enables you to relocate the UCS plane either relative to the default

WCS, or relative to the current UCS. This can be extremely handy if you are drawing a wall and then want to change your UCS to add a roof. It also eliminates the need to remember whether the next UCS you are switching to is 90 degrees about the Y axis or the X axis.

Creating and Editing Objects in 3D Space

In the final example of this section, you continue to work with the 3D drawing file you created earlier and use the commands you have experimented with in the previous sections. In this example, you will add an enclosure around the tank area and modify the surface object that forms the slab of part of the model. This object is an AutoCAD Release 12 3Dface object, which can be modified in AutoCAD LT, but cannot be created.

Note AutoCAD LT for Windows can display, shade, and plot surface objects created in AutoCAD Release 12. AutoCAD LT for Windows can even edit surface objects with commands such as COPY, MOVE, STRETCH. However, AutoCAD LT for Windows cannot create surface objects.

Creating 3D Objects

Create a new drawing named 3D, overwriting the previous 3D drawing. Use ALT2402A as a prototype, and using no setup method. Turn on Ortho mode, and set Snap to 4" in each viewport.

Click in the upper left viewport	Makes the plan view viewport active
Command: *Choose* **V**iew, Viewp**o**rts, **Si**ngle	Issues the VPORTS command and makes the current viewport fill the drawing window
Command: *Choose the Current Color button on the toolbar*	Opens the Entity Creation Modes dialog box
Enter **15'** *in the* **T**hickness *box, and choose* OK	Sets the current entity thickness for new objects
Command: *Click on the Line tool*	
From point: *Pick* ① *(see fig. 24.11)*	
To point: *Pick* ②	Draws the first side of the enclosure, 15' high
To point: *Pick* ③	Draws the second side

continues

24

continued

`To point:` *Pick* ④	Draws the third side
`To point:` (Enter)	Ends the LINE command
`Command:` *Choose the Current Color button on the toolbar*	Opens the Entity Creation Modes dialog box
Enter **2'** *in the Thickness box, and choose* OK	Sets the object thickness
`Command:` *Click on the Line tool*	
`From point:` @ (Enter)	Starts at ④, the endpoint of the last line
`To point:` *Pick* ① *(see fig. 24.11)*	Draws back to the starting enclosure line
`To point:` (Enter)	Ends the LINE command

Until now, creating the enclosure has been boring—there's really not a lot to see when you are creating 3D elements in plan view (see fig. 24.11). Next, restore the viewport configuration that was saved as DEFAULT and then continue editing the drawing in 3D. The points you will choose to perform the editing of the next example are displayed in figure 24.13.

Figure 24.11

The enclosure walls as seen in plan view.

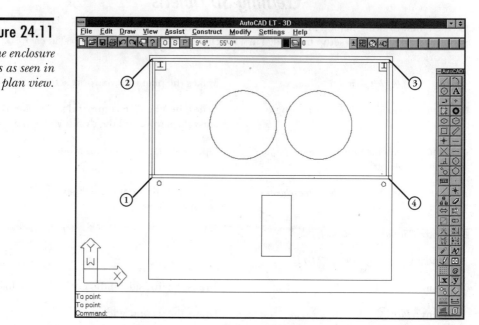

Modifying 3D Objects

Continue from the preceding exercise.

Command: *Choose* **V**iew, Viewp**o**rts, **R**estore	
Command: _vports	
Save/Restore/Delete/Join/SIngle/?/ 2/<3>/4: _restore	
?/Name of viewport configuration to restore: **DEFAULT** (Enter)	Specifies the DEFAULT viewport
Regenerating drawing	
Command: *Choose* **A**ssist, Set **UCS** **X** Axis Rotate	Execute the UCS command with the X option
Rotation angle about X axis <0d0'0">: **90** (Enter)	Rotates the Y and Z axes about the X axis (see the UCS icons in figure 24.12)
Command: *Click on the Move tool*	Issues the MOVE command, to move the last line up to form a fascia
Select objects: **L** (Enter)	Selects the 2' enclosure piece which was drawn last
Select objects: (Enter)	Ends object selection
Base point or displacement: **13'<90** (Enter)	Specifies the displacement
Second point of displacement: (Enter)	Accepts the displacement and moves the line up to the roof
Click in the lower left viewport	Makes it active
Command: *Turn off Ortho*	
Command: *Click on the Line tool*	Issues the LINE command, for drawing the roof
From point: *Use the ENDPoint object snap to pick* ① *(see fig. 24.12)*	Starts the line at the displayed intersection
To point: *Use the ENDPoint object snap to pick* ②	Draws the enclosure roof

continues

24

continued

Figure 24.12

The enclosure during modifications, before DDCHPROP.

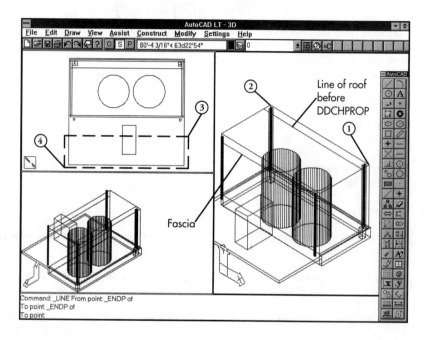

To point: (Enter)	Ends the line command

As you can see in figure 24.12, the roof is only 2' wide. Next you use DDCHPROP to widen it.

Command: *Click on the Change tool*	Issues the DDCHPROP command
Select objects: **L** (Enter)	Selects the last object drawn
Select objects: (Enter)	
In the Thickness box, change 2' to 15', press OK	Changes the thickness value for the roof, extending it over the fascia
Command: *Choose **A**ssist, Set **U**CS, **W**orld*	Changes the UCS back to the World Coordinate System
Click in the upper left viewport	Makes it active

Command: **ZOOM** (Enter)

All/Center/Extents/Previous/Windows/
<Scale[X/XP]>: **.9X** (Enter)

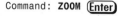

`Command:` *Click on the Stretch tool*	Issues the STRETCH command
`Select objects:` *Pick a crossing window from* ③ *to* ④*, then press Enter*	
`Base point or displacement:` **2'<90** (Enter)	Specifies the displacement
`Second point of displacement:` (Enter)	Accepts the displacement and shortens the platform and box
Pick in the right viewport	Selects the active viewport
`Command:` *Choose* **V**iew*, Viewp***o**r*ts,* **Si**ngle	Issues the VPORTS command and makes the current viewport fill the display
`Command:` *Choose* **V**iew*,* **H**ide	Produces a hidden-line-removed display of the enlarged viewport (see fig. 24.13)

The top edges of the fascia and columns are visible through the roof in the hidden-line-removed display because they are in the same plane. You can fix this by moving the roof up a fraction of an inch (use a displacement of 0,0,.1) and using HIDE again.

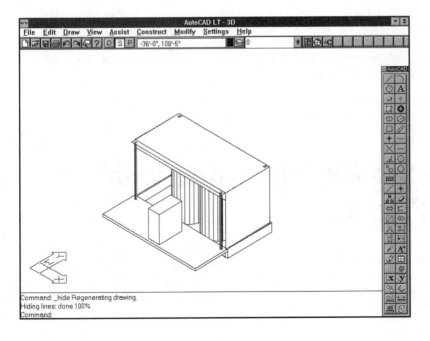

Figure 24.13

The enclosure in 3D with hidden lines removed.

24

In these few examples, you have not really used all the 3D commands with AutoCAD LT, but you have seen some of the capabilities of the commands. For more information on working in 3D space, see the New Riders Publishing book *Inside AutoCAD R12 for Windows*.

Sharing Data

One of the reasons for performing design work on the computer is the ease of modifying and sharing the electronic information you create. AutoCAD LT shares the capabilities of AutoCAD Release 12 for Windows for transferring information between other CAD software and other Microsoft Windows applications.

Because of AutoCAD's dominant position in the CAD industry most other CAD software provides output in a format that AutoCAD reads. However, different CAD software provide different features. Elements created in CAD package A do not always translate successfully to CAD package B, resulting in some loss of information. By and large, though, you should have no problem getting other types of electronic information into AutoCAD.

In addition to being able to transfer drawing information between different CAD software, AutoCAD LT is a true Microsoft Windows application. Unlike most CAD packages, AutoCAD LT can transfer information between other Windows applications across the Clipboard. These applications don't need to be able to understand AutoCAD LT's information because Windows translates it into a format that is easily understood by every application.

The following sections discuss the various methods for transferring information across a wide variety of CAD and Windows programs.

Exchanging File Information with Other Programs

AutoCAD LT for Windows supports a number of different file formats that can be used to transfer drawing information between different types of software. AutoCAD LT contains over ten different methods of exchanging information between different applications because it is the combination of a traditional CAD package and the Microsoft Windows environment.

Note In AutoCAD Release 2, you can use the plot-to-file feature to create bitmapped files in BMP, GIF, PCX, and TIFF formats, in 640×480, 800×600, and 1024×768 resolutions. To do so, choose Print/Plot Setup **D**efault Selection from the Plot Configuration dialog box (PLOT command), select the desired format, then choose the File N**a**me button from the Plot Configuration dialog box and specify a file name.

The next section discusses the file-based transfer methods available with AutoCAD LT. These transfer methods include the export of drawing objects into the Drawing Interchange Format (DXF), the Windows Metafile Format, and the PostScript page description language.

Using the Drawing Interchange Format (DXF)

AutoCAD LT for Windows and AutoCAD Release 12 for Windows are almost the same programs. AutoCAD LT lacks a few of the high-end features of its big brother, but all the basic functionality and most capabilities of AutoCAD Release 12 are built into AutoCAD LT. Because of this closeness between both software packages, AutoCAD LT also reads and write AutoCAD Release 12 DWG files. Any object created in AutoCAD Release 11 or 12 can be displayed in AutoCAD LT, and even though AutoCAD LT cannot create some of the objects that AutoCAD Release 12 creates, it can display, modify, and plot any object created with AutoCAD Release 11 or 12.

If you want to work with AutoCAD LT drawings with other software that does not read or write the DWG file format, you need to provide the data in another format. The most widely used format is the ASCII Drawing Interchange Format (DXF). This format, defined by Autodesk, describes all the elements that make up a drawing in a readable ASCII file. This file can contain descriptions of various AutoCAD LT elements, ranging from layers, linetypes, and blocks to lines, arcs, circles, and text.

Exchanging information using the DXF format is an extremely simple process. When exporting drawing information, you have the option of exporting selected objects or the whole drawing. To export DXF drawing data, you use the DXFOUT command; to import DXF data, you use the DXFIN command. In the following exercise, you export data to a DXF file.

Creating a DXF File

Create a new drawing named XPORT, using ALT2402 as a prototype, and using no setup method.

Command: *Choose* **F**ile, **I**mport/Export, **D**XF Out	Issues the DXFOUT command and displays the Create DXF File dialog box

continues

24

continued

Type **CH24-OUT** *in the* File **N**ame *edit box, click on* OK	Specifies the name to use for the DXF output file
Enter decimal places of accuracy (0 to 16)/Objects <6>: **Enter**	Accepts the default accuracy setting and creates the file

---

> **DXFOUT.** The DXFOUT command exports drawing objects using the Drawing Interchange Format defined by Autodesk. The file that is created has a DXF extension and is composed of ASCII information that can be modified with a variety of file-editing programs. This information includes object properties such as layer names, linetypes, and colors, as well as full coordinate information for each object within the drawing.

The DXFOUT command has two options, the first is to supply the accuracy used for object locations in the DXF file. AutoCAD stores all drawing objects with 16-place precision, but that much information can greatly increase the size of the DXF file that is created. The default value of six decimal places maintains high accuracy for the placement of objects.

The other option is Objects, which enables you to choose the objects that are exported to the DXF file. By default, the DXFOUT command exports all objects within the drawing.

Any kind of data stored in an AutoCAD LT drawing file can be transferred with the DXF file format. In the preceding exercise, you chose to output all the drawing objects with an accuracy of six decimal places. If you select the Objects option first, you choose the objects you want to export, and then a prompt asks you for the accuracy level you want.

On the other hand, importing information from a DXF file can be a little tricky. It's not that there are problems with importing objects in a DXF file—it's simply that AutoCAD LT must have the drawing set in a particular manner to import all the information correctly. If you have a file open that contains any objects or named items, and you use the DXFIN command to import DXF data, only objects are imported. If you are importing into a completely blank drawing, information such as layers, linetypes, blocks, and other drawing information is re-created.

Using the Windows Metafile Format (WMF)

The Microsoft Windows Metafile format (WMF) is another type of vector format that can be used to store AutoCAD LT object information. The DXF file format is composed of an ASCII description of each object and the objects properties; a Metafile is a series of binary records that convey to Microsoft Windows how the drawing data is to be re-created.

Because the information is already contained in a Windows-compatible format, WMF files can be displayed in a preview window. If you use the WMFIN command, a preview window displays the contents of a selected Metafile at the side of the Import WMF dialog box. This preview can save you a significant amount of time if you have a library of parts made up of WMF files.

The significant drawback to using metafiles as a method of data transfer is the loss of layers, linetypes, scale information, and 3D data. The WMF file only stores the graphic objects as they appear in the drawing area, rather than all the data that goes into creating the drawing properly in AutoCAD LT. For example, if you use the WMFOUT command to export a dashed line on a layer named HIDDEN, and then use the WMFIN command to import it back into the drawing, the object will be re-created as a series of short lines on layer 0.

The procedure for exporting drawing objects to a metafile (WMF) format is similar to the exporting of objects to a DXF file. In the following exercise, you export a WMF file.

Creating a WMF File

Continue from the preceding exercise or create a new drawing named XPORT, using ALT2402 as a prototype, and using no setup method.

Command: *Choose* **F**ile, **I**mport/Export, W**M**F Out	Issues the WMFOUT command and displays the Export WMF File dialog box
Type **CH24-W** *in the* File **N**ame *edit box and click on* OK	Defines the name to use for the WMF output file
Select objects: **ALL** (Enter)	Selects all the drawing objects
Select objects: (Enter)	Ends object selection and creates a WMF file

24

> **WMFOUT.** The WMFOUT command exports drawing objects using the Windows Metafile Format. This format stores objects as a series of records that correspond to Windows graphic drawing commands. The Metafile can then be read by other programs that support the WMF format.

The import of a Metafile is a simple process. The information in a WMF is scaled in the same manner as a block insert. Although the information stored with the Metafile loses much of its AutoCAD LT-specific data, all objects maintain the same accuracy that was used when the WMF file was created.

When importing data from a WMF, AutoCAD LT provides two options regarding the manner in which the data is re-created in the drawing. The WMFOPTS command enables you to determine if rectangles and circles will be filled or outlined, and whether wide lines are created with the width originally specified in the WMF.

In this next exercise, you import the Metafile you created in the previous example. You can start a new drawing and leave the current value of the WMFOPTS commands as they are, and then follow the example instructions.

Importing a WMF File

Start a new drawing.

Command: *Choose* File, Import/Export, **W**MF In	Issues the WMFIN command and opens the Import WMF File dialog box
Choose the CH24-W file, and click on OK	Specifies the name to use for the WMF file to import
Insertion point: **1,8** (Enter)	Specifies the insertion points
X scale factor <1> / Corner / XYZ: **1.5** (Enter)	Sets the scale factor for the imported objects
Y scale factor (default=X): (Enter)	Accepts the default scale
Rotation angle <0>: (Enter)	Accepts the default angle
Click on the Explode tool	Issues the EXPLODE command
Select objects: **L** (Enter)	Explodes the last object drawn (the WMF file)
Select objects: (Enter)	

Command: **ERASE** (Enter)

Select objects: *Pick* ① *(see fig. 24.14) and press Enter*	Selects and erases a portion of what was once a single line object with a center linetype, now made of many little lines

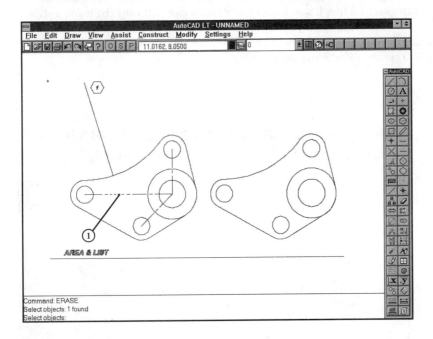

Figure 24.14

The objects imported using the WMFIN command.

WMFIN. The WMF command is used to import objects that have been saved to a file with a WMF extension. The data in the Metafile does not contain drawing data such as layer names and linetypes, and 3D information, so some modification of the final objects may be necessary.

Because the Metafile contains vector information, you can use the EXPLODE command to reduce the imported image to its component parts. As stated previously, the Metafile does not maintain any of the AutoCAD LT object property data.

Creating PostScript Output

PostScript is known as a *page description language*, used mainly by graphic illustrators and designers. PostScript is the language of choice on Macintosh computers. It is used for all types of output—from desktop publishing software to CAD. AutoCAD LT comes with several PostScript fonts that can be used in place of the default shape (SHX) fonts.

24

The use of PostScript for exporting drawing information makes the data more compatible with a wider range of output devices and applications that recognize PostScript objects. The standard file extension for PostScript is EPS (Encapsulated PostScript).

The PSOUT command, available from the **F**ile menu's **I**mport/Export, **P**ostScript Out item, creates an EPS file. If you have used a PostScript text font (by using a style defined with a font file that has a PFB extension), the fonts will be exported along with the rest of the image. The following exercise uses the file ALT2402, shown in figure 24.15, to create a PostScript output file.

Figure 24.15

A drawing containing objects and PostScript fonts for export using PSOUT.

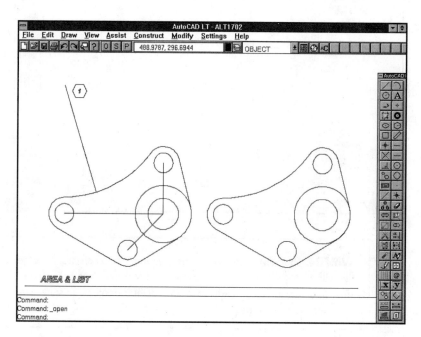

Exporting a PostScript File

Create a new drawing named XPORT using the ALT2402 drawing as a prototype, and using no setup method.

Command: *Choose* **F**ile, **I**mport/Export, **P**ostScript Out	Issues the PSOUT command, then displays the Create PostScript File dialog box
Type **CH24-P** *in the* File **N**ame *edit box*	Specifies the name to use for the EPS output file

```
What to plot—Display, Extents,          Accepts the default area of the drawing
Limits, View, or Window <D>: (Enter)     to be exported, the current display

Include a screen preview image in the
file? (None/EPSI/TIFF) <None>: (Enter)

Size units (Inches or Millimeters)       Specifies the type of units used to
<Inches>: (Enter)                        define the image

Output Inches=Drawing Units or Fit       Sets the scale for the image
or ? <Fit>: 1=1 (Enter)
```

PSOUT switches to the text screen and lists the sheet size choices.

```
Enter the Size or Width,Height           Specifies a C size sheet
(in Inches) <USER>: C (Enter)
```

PSOUT. The PSOUT command exports drawing data to an Encapsulated PostScript (EPS) file. This file can be used with a variety of PostScript-compatible software for page layout and printing at high resolutions. The use of this command is similar to using the PLOT command.

The options that the PSOUT command presents enable you to set scales, sheet sizes, and preview images. The prompts for the PSOUT options include:

◆ `What to plot—Display, Extents, Limits, View, or Window <D>:`. At this prompt, you define which portion of the current drawing will be placed in the PostScript output file.

◆ `Include a screen preview image in the file? (None/EPSI/TIFF) <None>:`. The EPS file format allows a preview image to be encapsulated with the other PostScript data. Not all programs can read or ignore this data, so it may be best to avoid using the preview feature if you are not sure of which program you will be using the file with.

◆ `Size units (Inches or Millimeters) <Inches>:`. This defines the units that will be used to encode the PostScript data.

◆ `Output Inches=Drawing Units or Fit or ? <Fit>:`. The selected portion of the drawing may be scaled to fit properly on a page. AutoCAD LT will apply any scale factor before encoding the data in the EPS file.

◆ `Enter the Size or Width,Height (in Inches) <USER>:`. You will be given a variety of sheet sizes in which the PostScript data can be drawn. If you are only going to a PostScript printer, use the A-size sheet option.

24

The file from which you created the PostScript output contains a variety of normal AutoCAD objects and PostScript fonts. When the EPS file you created in the exercise is sent to a PostScript printer, the linework will print with filled variations of the fonts. This occurs because AutoCAD will only display PostScript fonts in outline mode. For the proper fill to be applied to a filled PostScript font, it must be plotted on a PostScript printer.

Transferring Information through the Windows Clipboard

In addition to transferring information between AutoCAD LT and other CAD packages, the Microsoft Windows environment also is host to the exchange of information with other Windows applications. These other programs may have nothing in common with AutoCAD LT—they could be word processors, spreadsheets, or databases. As long as these programs can import certain generic Windows files formats, AutoCAD LT drawing information can be used.

Generally speaking, all Windows programs can transfer and import information through the Windows Clipboard. AutoCAD LT contains many options for placing drawing file information into the Clipboard in a variety of different ways. AutoCAD LT also has capabilities to import information from the Windows Clipboard. Over the next few sections, you learn about each of these capabilities.

You can view the current Clipboard contents by using the Clipboard Viewer that you should find in your Main group in Program Manager. If you are using Windows for Workgroups, you use the ClipBook Viewer to access the Clipboard. If the Clipboard is not visible when you open the ClipBook, choose **W**indow, then **1** Clipboard to display it.

Using the Copy Image Option

The Windows Clipboard can deal with information in a variety of formats. The first **E**dit menu option is Copy **I**mage, which copies a bitmap representation of a selected area of the drawing. A bitmap is an image that uses pixels to depict the position and color of objects. When you use the COPYIMAGE command, you select a portion of the drawing window that defines the size of the bitmap image. After the bitmap has been created, it can be imported into any other Windows application that can import bitmaps. In the following exercise, you use the Windows Write application to show how bitmaps can be imported into other programs by using the Windows Clipboard.

Transferring an Image through the Clipboard

Create a new drawing named XPORT using ALT2402 as a prototype, and using no setup method.

Command: *Choose* **E**dit, Copy **I**mage	Issues the COPYIMAGE command
Select an area of the screen *Pick a point at the upper left and another at the lower right of the drawing*	Defines the portion of the drawing to copy as a bitmap
In Program Manager, open Write from the Accessories group	Starts the Write application
In Write, choose **E**dit, **Pa**ste	Imports the image into the Microsoft Write word processor (see fig. 24.16)
Close the Write application and return to the AutoCAD LT graphics window	

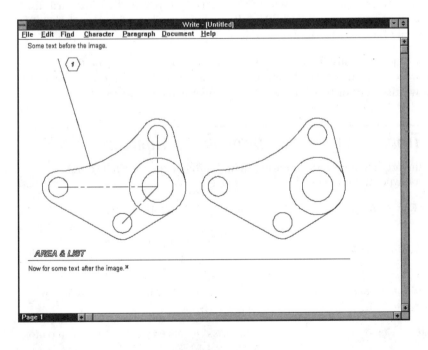

Figure 24.16

A portion of the drawing imported into the Write application.

> **COPYIMAGE.** The COPYIMAGE command is used to place a bitmap representation of a selected area of the drawing into the Windows Clipboard.

When the bitmap is pasted into another application—Windows Write in this example—its size in the receiving application will be the same as its size in AutoCAD LT (see fig. 24.16). Some applications may enable you to decrease or increase the size of the image, depending on how they handle imported bitmaps.

Using the Copy Vectors Option

In addition to pasting AutoCAD drawings as images to the Clipboard, AutoCAD LT drawings can be saved to the Clipboard as vector data (similar to the WMF format). Vector information can be pasted into a program, such as CorelDraw or PageMaker, and manipulated as individual objects.

The COPYCLIP command, which is issued when you choose the Copy **V**ectors item from the **E**dit menu, enables you to select the objects to copy into the Clipboard. In the following exercise, you use the COPYCLIP command to select a group of objects from the drawing file and then paste the objects into the Paintbrush application.

AutoCAD LT objects can also be pasted back into another drawing, using this method. Your work in AutoCAD LT may form the basis of an illustration that will be part of an advertisement or brochure when you copy the data as vectors.

Transferring Vectors through the Clipboard

Continue from the preceding exercise or create a new drawing named XPORT, using ALT2402 as a prototype, and using no setup method.

`Command:` *Choose* **E**dit, Copy **V**ectors	Issues the COPYCLIP command
`Select objects:` *Pick a few objects and press Enter*	
Go to the Program Manager and start the Paintbrush application	Starts the Paintbrush application to accept a paste operation
Choose **E**dit, P**a**ste	Imports the image into the Paintbrush editor (see fig. 24.17)

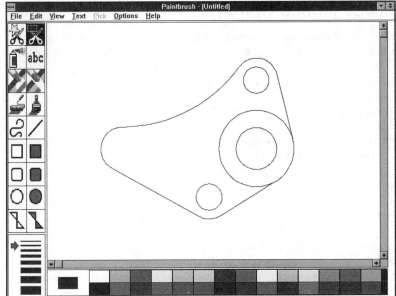

Figure 24.17

The drawing's bitmap image imported into the Paintbrush application.

COPYCLIP. The COPYCLIP command copies AutoCAD LT objects as vector information and places the data into the Windows Clipboard. If other Windows applications use the Paste option to import the data, Windows transfers it in the Metafile (WMF) format. If AutoCAD LT re-imports the data, the information is maintained as AutoCAD LT objects.

After importing the image into Paintbrush, the scale of the objects may be slightly reduced or enlarged (see fig. 24.18) because Paintbrush is essentially a bitmap editor, and must translate the WMF data passed to it in the clipboard into information it can work with.

The COPYCLIP command uses the Windows Metafile format to transfer vector information to other Windows applications through the Clipboard. As you learned in the section about using the WMF Out export option, the Metafile does not maintain all the object property information that AutoCAD LT stores. Transferring objects through the Clipboard in this manner will result in a loss of layer and linetype information.

24

Using the Copy Embed Option

The COPYEMBED command, issued by using the **E**dit menu's Copy **E**mbed item, establishes an OLE (Object Linking and Embedding) connection between AutoCAD LT and another Windows application. This connection places a linked copy of the selected objects into a Windows application. You can double-click on this copy of the objects, which causes Windows to execute the AutoCAD LT program and place the embedded objects in the drawing for modification.

The embedded data is actually a drawing file contained within the other Windows application. Even though this "drawing" file was created from objects in a normal drawing, changes you make to the original drawing will not be reflected in the embedded objects. Likewise, modifying the embedded objects will not affect the original drawing. If you want the link to be treated in a more dynamic fashion, you should use the COPYLINK command described in the next section.

 Stop Be careful when you give a coworker or client a document containing linked or embedded information. Windows expects the originating program to be available if called by the user to change an imported image. If the person to whom you are giving the file does not have the same software, he or she may not be able to work with your linked images.

Using the Copy Link Option

The COPYLINK command, issued by using the **E**dit menu's Copy **L**ink item, is used to establish an OLE (Object Linking and Embedding) connection between AutoCAD LT and another Windows application. This connection places an image of the selected objects into a Windows application, similar to an external reference in a drawing. The difference is that you can double-click on the linked image, and Windows will execute the AutoCAD LT program and open the drawing used for the link.

When data from an AutoCAD LT drawing is linked into another application, Microsoft Windows maintains a list of the creating program and the original image source. This information is used to execute the application and load the correct file when called upon by the user. If you start the linking document, the OLE server program that created the document will ask if you want to update the link. Answering Yes to this query will refresh the image based on the current contents of the drawing file; answering No will display the last image used for the link.

The COPYLINK command is more helpful than the COPYEMBED command because COPYLINK adds only an image of the file, not a copy of all the objects. For this reason, the file size of the linking document is much smaller.

Pasting Images into AutoCAD LT

One method for importing information into AutoCAD LT from the Clipboard is by using the Edit menu's Paste item. This process takes data from the Clipboard in a vector format (Metafile, or AutoCAD LT) and imports that data into the current drawing. The data will be inserted as a block that can be scaled, rotated, moved, and exploded.

In the following exercise, you paste the same objects used for the previous Copy Vectors example into a new drawing.

Pasting Information from the Clipboard

Create a new unnamed drawing, using the default prototype and no setup method.

Command: *Choose* Edit, Paste   Issues the PASTECLIP command

Insertion point: **0,0** (Enter)   Specifies the insertion point for the block
                                                 object that holds the clipboard contents

X scale factor <1> / Corner / XYZ: (Enter)   Accepts the default 1:1 scale factor

Y scale factor (default=X): (Enter)

Rotation angle <0>: (Enter)   Accepts the default rotation angle and pastes
                                                 the image

Command: *Choose* View, Zoom Extents   Redisplays the drawing within
                                                 the full extents of the window

---

> **PASTECLIP.** The PASTECLIP command takes any AutoCAD LT compatible information in the Windows Clipboard and places it into the drawing. The information is stored as a block object, which you can explode.

Although using the Clipboard works quite well for moving information between different drawings and applications, other programs also use the Clipboard to move information. If you are not careful, you can place data in the clipboard that deletes any drawing objects already in the clipboard.

24

Importing Text with the Paste Command

Another type of transfer of Windows information is pasting text data and single commands directly to the Text: prompt or command line. This is accomplished by using the Edit menu's Paste Command item. If you had the following text in the Windows Notepad, for example, you could use the Paste Command option to enter it in AutoCAD LT.

```
Masonry Opening 3'-4"W x 6'-8" H
Steel door frame to be shop primed
and painted before assembly in the
Field.
```

This information (which is in the ALT24CMD.TXT file from the IALT Disk) is exactly as you would enter it at the Text: prompt. In the following exercise, you paste this text to AutoCAD LT by using the Clipboard.

Pasting Commands from the Clipboard

Create a new unnamed drawing, using the default ACLT prototype and no setup method.

Start the Notepad application (from the Accessories group in Program Manager) and load the ALT24CMD.TXT file from the \DWGS\IALT directory.

In Notepad, choose Edit, Select All

Choose Edit, Copy

Switch to AutoCAD LT

In AutoCAD LT, click on the Text tool   *Issues the DTEXT command*

```
_DTEXT Justify/Style/<Start point>:
6,4 (Enter)
```

```
Height <0.2000>: (Enter)
```

```
Rotation angle <0>: (Enter)
```

Text: *Choose* Edit, Paste Command   Places the text in AutoCAD LT

```
Masonry opening 3'-4" W x 7'-4" H

Text: Steel door frame to be shop primed

Text: and painted before assembly in the

Text: field.

Text: (Enter)                                    Completes the DTEXT command
```

Note Paste **C**ommand does not work for issuing multiline command text to AutoCAD LT. It can be used at the Command: prompt, but only for pasting a single line of input at a time.

When pasting commands or text from the clipboard, you must make sure to format any text as if you were entering it at the keyboard. This means that for each AutoCAD LT prompt, you must supply some response, whether it is a coordinate point or simply a space, which is interpreted as pressing the Enter key.

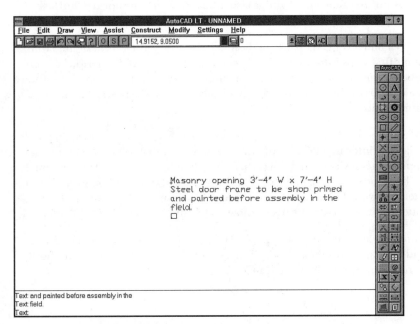

Figure 24.18

Text inserted from the clipboard.

Looking to Your Future with CAD

To expand the functionality of AutoCAD LT, look at add-in packages, parts libraries, and other options that may make your work easier. Autodesk is positioning itself to provide the core package; Autodesk wants all other elements (surface modeling, rendering, data exchange) to be plug-in modules. This arrangement gives you the advantage of having a single core, and a variety of packages that you can integrate tightly with that software.

AutoCAD LT can use a wide range of add-in symbols, menus, and DIESEL macros that are used in the more advanced AutoCAD Release 12. Sources for these add-ins are the AutoCAD forum on CompuServe and the majority of AutoCAD user groups. The New Riders book *Maximizing AutoCAD Release 12* describes the process of customizing AutoCAD in detail.

A good source for locating other products that enhance AutoCAD LT is the *AutoCAD Resource Guide.* This booklet contains extensive lists and advertisements of products that work with the range of Autodesk products such as AutoCAD Release 12, AutoCAD Release 12 for Windows, and 3D Studio. The *AutoCAD Resource Guide* is included with AutoCAD Release 12 and is also available from your local AutoDesk dealer. You can call 1-800-445-5415 to locate an Autodesk dealer near you.

AutoCAD LT is a mid-level CAD package designed for cost-conscious designers who are taking their first steps into the world of computer-aided drafting. Serious designers who are beginning to look for more automation and capabilities from the software they use on a daily basis should consider a more advanced package such as AutoCAD Release 12 for Windows.

Not only do software needs change, but hardware needs also change. If you move from an HP laser printer to a PostScript laser plotter, you need to be sure that your software supports the devices you work with. Soon you might not even be using mice or digitizers, but modifying a virtual reality that contains 3D models (many architects are experimenting with this right now). Are you ready to make that leap, or does basic computer drafting serve your needs, now and in the future?

As long as you keep an open mind toward CAD use, you can adapt to changes in hardware and software. This makes today's investment in a simple program a doorway to future increases in productivity for yourself and your clients.

Part IV

Appendices

A   *AutoCAD LT Installation and Setup* 959

B   *Troubleshooting Common Problems* 969

C   *Enhancing Performance* 981

D   *System Variables* 989

E   *Dimension Variables* 1019

F   *Command Reference* 1027

G   *The IALT Disk* 1049

New Riders Publishing
INSIDE
SERIES

A P P E N D I X

AutoCAD LT Installation and Setup

This appendix covers the installation and network setup of AutoCAD LT.

The following lists the hardware and software requirements for AutoCAD LT:

◆ MS-DOS 3.31 or later (6.1 or later recommended)

◆ Windows 3.1, running 386 Enhanced Mode, or Windows for Workgroups 3.11, or Windows NT (AutoCAD LT Release 2 reportedly runs under Windows 95, but has not been certified for it.)

◆ 386 DX (with a math coprocessor) or 486 or Pentium-based system, or a system with a compatible processor

◆ Mouse or other Windows-compatible pointer

◆ 4 MB of RAM minimum for AutoCAD LT Release 1 (8 MB or more recommended) or 8 MB of RAM minimum for AutoCAD LT Release 2 (more recommended)

◆ 10 MB for AutoCAD LT Release 1 or 16 MB for AutoCAD LT Release 2 of free
   hard disk space to install all the AutoCAD LT files

◆ Permanent swap file for Windows, recommended size two to four times the size
   of RAM (see Appendix C, "Enhancing Performance")

Preparing for Installation

You can install AutoCAD LT from disks, or if you have AutoCAD LT Release 2, from
CD-ROM. Before you install AutoCAD LT, make a backup copy of the installation
disks to protect yourself from disk accidents. It also is a good idea to prepare your
hard drive to get optimum Windows and AutoCAD LT performance.

Backing Up Your Original Software Disks

Before beginning any software installation, make a backup copy of your original
software disks. Always install the software from the backup set of disks, not the
originals. Before making backup copies, place a write-protect tab on each original
5 ¼-inch disk or slide the write-protect cover open on each original 3 ½-inch disk
to prevent accidental erasure or damage to it. You must have the same number and
type of backup disks as your distribution set.

The *source* disk is the disk you are copying (your original distribution disk), and the
destination disk is your duplicate (backup) disk. The destination disk does not need
to be formatted. File Manager automatically formats it if necessary.

Using File Manager to Back Up Your Disks

In Windows, double-click on the Main icon, then on the File Manager icon	Opens File Manager from the Main group in Program Manager

Place the source diskette to be copied from the drive and click on that drive's icon.

*Choose **D**isk, then **C**opy Disk, enter the drive letter in the **S**ource In and **D**estination In boxes, choose OK, and follow the prompts*	Copies the diskette

Repeat this process for each diskette to be copied.

Double-click on the control menu button (left side of the File Manager title bar)	Closes File Manager

---

Preparing Your Hard Drive before Installation

The speed with which files are accessed on your hard disk drive significantly affects AutoCAD's performance, because Windows must swap program and drawing data in and out to disk when the drawing becomes too big to fit entirely into available RAM. Disk-access time also is important when loading and storing drawing files, inserting blocks, and loading other files.

 Note   It helps to keep each application, such as AutoCAD LT, in its own subdirectory. It also helps to keep each application project's files in their own subdirectory. File access is faster, you are not as likely to get files mixed up, and future program upgrades are easier to install. In addition, it is much easier to back up your file system when programs are separated into individual directories.

When you create or install new files or programs, they fill any unused space, starting with the scattered or fragmented empty space left by deleted files. This fragments the new files or programs, slowing down their access time. Also, a fragmented disk can prevent the creation of a Windows permanent swap file, which requires a large contiguous file space. To prevent these problems, you should defragment your disk before installing new programs or creating a new Windows permanent swap file. See Appendix C, "Enhancing Performance," for more information.

Installing AutoCAD LT

Whether you install from disks or a CD-ROM, you start the setup program from Disk 1, in Windows, then insert the other disks or CD-ROM when requested. If you have any difficulty identifying which disk to begin with, just try each disk until Windows finds the setup program.

AutoCAD LT for Windows is installed from the Windows Program Manager. Auto-CAD LT Release 1 requires 9 MB of available hard disk space for a total installation and AutoCAD LT Release 2 requires 15 MB. If you want to install only the executable and support files, click in the Executable/Support files check box. You still need over 8 to 10 MB of available hard disk space for this option. Unless you do not want the symbol library for some reason, use the default Install ALL files option. In AutoCAD LT Release 1, if you do not install the symbol library files now, you can install them later by running the SETUP.EXE program again and clicking in the Symbol Library Files check box. You save only 1.1 MB of hard disk space by not installing the AutoCAD LT Release 1 symbol library files. In AutoCAD LT Release 2, if you can't install all files now, you can add files later by rerunning setup.

Note If you receive an error message similar to the following, you have insufficient disk space (the number of bytes shown as *xxxx* in the message) to install AutoCAD LT for Windows on the hard drive you have specified.

```
<drive>:\ALCTWIN has only xxxx bytes available.
10000000 bytes are required to install selected files.
```

You must cancel the installation, free up sufficient space, and restart the installation; or you can return to the directory path screen and specify a drive that has enough free space (refer to the discussion prior to the exercise). If you cancel the install-ation, you receive the message:

```
AutoCAD LT installation is not yet complete.
Are you sure you want to exit Setup?
```

Click on the appropriate **Y**es or **N**o response.

You now are ready to install AutoCAD LT for Windows by performing the steps described in the following exercise.

Installing AutoCAD LT for Windows

Click on **F**ile *in the Windows Program Manager menu bar*	Displays the **F**ile menu
Click on **R**un	Displays the Run dialog box
Type the letter of the disk drive where the Auto-CAD LT installation disk is located in the **C**ommand Line *edit box followed by* **:\SETUP** *(for example, A:\SETUP)*	Specifies that the SETUP program is to be run from that disk drive
Click on OK	Starts the SETUP program

While the program is loading, a window is displayed to let you know the program is working. After the program is fully loaded, if you are installing AutoCAD LT Release 1, you see the following:

```
Congratulations!
You have selected the world leader in design automation
software.
```

Click on OK

Next you see a dialog box with the `AutoCAD LT for Windows must be personalized before use.` message and boxes to enter your name and company.

Enter your name (4 characters min.) in the Name *box, use the Tab key to switch to the* Company *box, and enter your company name (4 characters min.)*	Requires a name and company name (you can use *None* if applicable)
Click on OK	Prompts you for confirmation:

```
AutoCAD LT for Windows will be personalized to:
Name: <Your Name>
Company: <Company Name>
```

Click on **O**K *if the names are correct, or click on* **C**hange *if they are not*	Accepts the names or returns to the previous screen

When you choose OK, it writes the personalization information to the installation disk.

If your AutoCAD LT for Windows has been previously installed, the user name and company name will be displayed, and you only need to click on OK to proceed.

You then are presented with setup options and their required file space:

```
AutoCAD LT for Windows - Setup options:
Install ALL files...
Executable/Support Files...
```

Unless you are short on disk space, you should use the default, `Install ALL files...`

Choose the desired option and press Enter or click on **O**K	Displays information on where to install files:

```
Installing AutoCAD LT for Windows:
Setup will install AutoCAD LT into the following directory,
which will be created on your hard disk.
If you want to install AutoCAD LT for Windows in a different
drive or directory, enter the new drive or directory path.
Click Continue to begin the installation.
Install AutoCAD LT to:
```

To change the default drive of C:\ACLTWIN, *press Home, then Delete, enter a different drive letter, and then press Enter*	

continues

continued

You also can similarly change the default installation path, but it is recommended that you use the default path name.

Press Enter or choose **C**ontinue   Starts the installation

Setup prompts you for the CD-ROM or each installation disk as it is required.

If using a CD-ROM, you might be prompted to `Please insert the CD or diskette labeled ACLT_2`, even if the CD-ROM is already in the CD-ROM drive. You need to enter the drive letter of the CD-ROM and choose OK before it is recognized.

Click on **O**K *after inserting each disk*   Reads the next disk

After all the disks and files have been installed, Setup displays its last screen, in which you specify the Program Group name and icon:

```
Setup will now create a Program Group. You can
enter a new or existing group name.
Program Group Name:
AutoCAD LT
```

AutoCAD LT is the default Program Group Name. If you want to use a different group name, type it in the Program Group Name text box.

Click on OK or press Enter after all the selections are the way you want them.

Then you are prompted to select the AutoCAD LT program icon you want to use, and specify the icon's caption:

```
Setup will place AutoCAD LT's icon into the Program
Group. You can select any of the ones below.
Select Icon:
```

Four icon options are offered; the default icon is on   Selects the icon used to run AutoCAD LT
the left. Click on the icon you want to use   from Program Manager

```
Setup will use the default below as the icon caption.
You can change it if desired.
Icon Caption:
```

The default Icon Caption is AutoCAD LT. If you want to have a different caption under the icon, type it in the Icon Caption text box.

| *After you have made all your choices, or to simply accept the defaults, press Enter or click on* OK | Completes the AutoCAD LT setup and displays the AutoCAD LT group in the Windows Program Manager, or issues the following prompt: |

```
AutoCAD LT has found AutoCAD or AutoCAD VQ .dwg files on your computer. You can
change the association of these files to AutoCAD LT so that when you click on
them, AutoCAD LT is launched, rather than AutoCAD or AutoCAD VQ.
```

| Would you like to do so? *Click on Yes* **only** *if you are* **sure** *you want to do so; if unsure, click on No and see your system manager* | Completes the AutoCAD LT setup and displays the AutoCAD LT group in the Windows Program Manager |

Next, test your installation.

| *In Program Manager, double-click on the AutoCAD LT program item icon (see fig. A.1)* | Starts AutoCAD LT, displaying its identification information and listing personalization and version data |

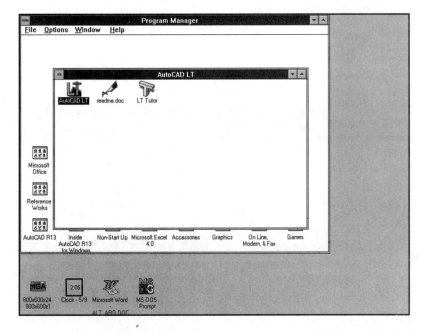

Figure A.1

AutoCAD LT group.

If you are using AutoCAD LT Release 2, the Create New Drawing dialog box is displayed (see fig. A.2). Click on Cancel to close it.

A blank, unnamed drawing is displayed (see fig. A.3).

continues

continued

Figure A.2

*AutoCAD LT
Release 2's Create
New Drawing
dialog box.*

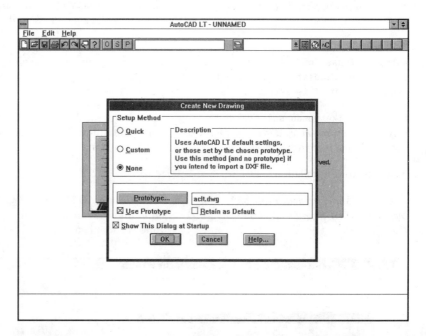

Figure A.3

*Blank, unnamed
AutoCAD LT
drawing.*

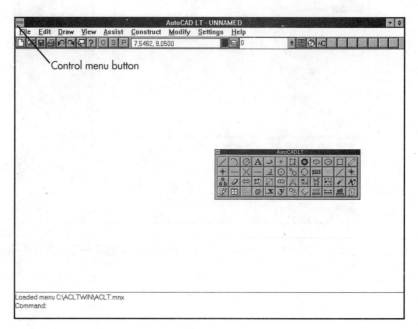

Choose **F**ile, *then* E**x**it, *or double-click on the control menu button (see fig. A.3)*	Closes AutoCAD LT

After you have run the Setup program, you might find your Program Manager window reduced in size when you return to it. Simply click on the Program Manager window's maximize icon (up arrow in the upper right corner) to restore it.

 Note One feature of Windows is the ability to select a data file and have Windows automatically start up the application that you use for that data file. You can automatically start AutoCAD LT and load a particular drawing by double-clicking on the file name of the drawing in File Manager.

If you used the default group name, you now have a new Program Group named AutoCAD LT with the icon you selected for launching AutoCAD LT. You also have an icon for launching the tutorial and one for viewing the README.DOC file, which contains explanations for any last-minute changes or corrections made to the program or manual.

During the transfer of files from the installation disks to the hard drive, you saw the following message:

```
This would be a great opportunity to register your AutoCAD LT for
Windows. By registering your AutoCAD LT, Autodesk can keep you
informed of new and exciting AutoCAD LTs and AutoCAD LT updates.
```

Registering your copy of AutoCAD LT for Windows as soon as possible is as important as installing the software. After your registration is received and filed by Autodesk, you become eligible for technical support as well as the notification of AutoCAD LT for Windows updates and bug fixes.

Making Settings

When you install AutoCAD LT, it creates a file named ACLT.INI in the program directory (default ACLTWIN). This file controls a number of settings that affect AutoCAD LT's appearance and behavior. These settings are changed in the Preferences dialog box (see Chapter 3, "Keeping Track of Your Work: Drawings as Files") and are documented in the "Customizing Initialization Files" chapter of the *AutoCAD LT Release 2 User's Guide.* When you first start AutoCAD LT, another file named ACLT.CFG is created, storing hardware configuration data.

If you are running AutoCAD LT Release 2 from a copy installed on a network drive, these files might need to be relocated to your local drive.

Network Configuration

If you are running AutoCAD LT Release 2 from a copy installed on a network drive, changes in settings made by other users can affect your settings unless you copy the ACLT.INI and ACLT.CFG files to your local drive. To do so:

1. Use File Manager to create a new directory on your local drive. You can name it ACLTWIN, or any name you like.

2. Use File Manager to locate the ACLT.INI and ACLT.CFG files on the network drive in the AutoCAD LT program directory (default ACLTWIN), and copy them to the new directory on your local drive.

3. In Program Manager, select the AutoCAD LT program item icon (refer to fig. A.1) by single-clicking on it. Then, while still in Program Manager, click on the **F**ile menu, then on the **P**roperties menu item. This opens the Program Item Properties dialog box.

4. To the end of the line in the Command Line box, add /c *d:\path* where *d:* is your local drive and *path* is the new directory on your local drive. If, for example, AutoCAD LT is installed in the F:\USER\ACLTWIN directory on the network and you created a new directory named MY_ACLT on your local drive C:, then the resulting Command Line box should contain F:\USER\ACLTWIN\aclt.exe /c C:\MY_ACLT.

You also should relocate the temporary files that AutoCAD LT creates and uses while it runs to your local drive. You do this with a setting in the Preferences dialog box (see Chapter 3, "Keeping Track of Your Work: Drawings as Files").

Troubleshooting Common Problems

The following sections list some common problems and solutions you can encounter in setting up and running AutoCAD LT.

Problems with Startup Files

When your system *boots*, or starts up, it runs through a self-test, reads hidden system files, then looks for two startup files in your root directory: CONFIG.SYS and AUTOEXEC.BAT. The settings, or lack thereof, in these files can cause problems, slow performance, or crashes with Windows. Because AutoCAD runs under Windows, its performance and behavior are dependent on that of Windows.

The CONFIG.SYS file contains entries that load system-level device drivers, such as memory managers, RAM drives, and disk caches. You also can load device drivers for peripherals (a mouse, for example) in CONFIG.SYS. In addition, this file contains entries that set the number of files that a program can have open at one time, and that specify the number of disk buffers to be created by the system.

The AUTOEXEC.BAT file contains entries to set your system prompt, set your path and other DOS environment variables, and call batch files or other programs to execute automatically during startup.

You can view and edit these files with Windows' text editor, Notepad. The icon to launch Notepad is located in the Windows Accessories group. Although Notepad cannot process extremely large files (it is limited to files of fewer than approximately 50,000 characters), it should be adequate for creating or editing most of the text files discussed in this book. For instructions on using Notepad, see your Windows reference manual, or launch Notepad and then press F1 or choose **H**elp.

 Tip   Keep your AUTOEXEC.BAT and CONFIG.SYS files as uncluttered as possible. Keep your path down to the absolute minimum to avoid possible conflicts, and install only device drivers that are necessary in CONFIG.SYS.

If you edit your CONFIG.SYS and AUTOEXEC.BAT files, your changes do not take effect until you reboot your computer. To perform a warm reboot of your system, exit Windows, then press Ctrl+Alt+Del.

Tailoring Your CONFIG.SYS File

The CONFIG.SYS file is read automatically by the system at boot, and it must be located in the root directory of the boot disk. To examine or edit your CONFIG.SYS file, open it in Notepad, as shown in the following exercise, or use the ASCII text editor of your choice.

Examining CONFIG.SYS

From the Windows Program Manager, double-click on the Accessories icon, then on the
Notepad icon.

Choose **F**ile, *then* **O**pen *and enter*
\CONFIG.SYS *in the* File name *box,*
and choose OK

Your CONFIG.SYS displays. A typical CONFIG.SYS file includes:

```
DEVICE=HIMEM.SYS
DEVICE=EMM386.SYS
BUFFERS=1
FILES=48
DEVICE=SMARTDRV.SYS
```

HIMEM.SYS and EMM386.SYS are memory managers used by Windows and DOS 5.0
and later. Your system might use other memory managers, such as QEMM386.SYS,
instead of HIMEM.SYS or EMM386.SYS. QEMM386.SYS (and associated utilities from
Quarterdeck Office Systems) can often provide better memory management and
more available memory than HIMEM.SYS and EMM386.SYS can.

If you are using DOS 6 (recommended), your CONFIG.SYS might also include
DOS=HIGH to increase memory available to Windows. Also, if you are using DOS 6
or QEMM (also recommended), the previous DEVICE= lines might instead begin
DEVICEHIGH or DEVICE=C:\BOOT\QEMM\LOADHI.SYS. DOS's DEVICEHIGH and QEMM's
LOADHI.SYS increase memory available to Windows.

BUFFERS allocate RAM to hold your recently used data. Use BUFFERS=20 or more
for AutoCAD LT. If a program frequently accesses recently used data, buffers reduce
disk accesses and increase speed. Each two-buffer increment uses 1 KB of base
(conventional) DOS memory. You might have to use a smaller number if AutoCAD
runs short of memory.

Note If you use a disk cache program, such as PC-CACHE, NCACHE, or SMARTDRIVE,
set BUFFERS to one. The cache program provides better performance than the use
of BUFFERS. One is the smallest value BUFFERS accepts.

FILES tells DOS the maximum number of files your applications expect to have open
at one time. Use FILES=40 or more for AutoCAD LT. FILES does not use much
memory; a large value helps with AutoCAD.

Note If you use QEMM, you can use a smaller value, such as 10, for FILES, and use QEMM's FILES command in your AUTOEXEC.BAT file to add more files in upper memory.

SMARTDRV.SYS is a disk-caching utility that speeds up hard-disk access. You can instead have another disk-caching utility installed, such as PC-CACHE from Central Point Software, Inc. Some disk-caching utilities get installed in your CONFIG.SYS, and others in your AUTOEXEC.BAT file, but you should only have one installed.

Tailoring Your AUTOEXEC.BAT File

The AUTOEXEC.BAT file is a batch file like any other, with one important exception: it is automatically executed every time the system is booted. Like CONFIG.SYS, it must be in the root directory.

The AUTOEXEC.BAT file is the place to install your TSR (Terminate-and-Stay-Resident) programs and to declare DOS environment settings that you need to complete an application environment (such as the ACAD support variable or the ACADCFG variable). Examine your AUTOEXEC.BAT file—it should include at least the lines shown in the following exercise.

To examine or edit your AUTOEXEC.BAT file, open it in Notepad, as shown in the following exercise, or use the ASCII text editor of your choice.

Examining the AUTOEXEC.BAT File

From the Windows Program Manager, double-click on the Accessories icon, then on the Notepad icon.

Choose **File**, *then* **O**pen *and enter*
\AUTOEXEC.BAT *in the* File name *box,*
and choose OK

Your AUTOEXEC.BAT displays. A typical AUTOEXEC.BAT file includes:

```
C:\BOOT\MOUSE
PROMPT=$P$G
PATH C:\;C:\DOS;C:\BAT;C:\WINDOWS
SET TEMP=C:\WINDOWS\TEMP
```

C:\BOOT\MOUSE loads a mouse driver. Mouse drivers are sometimes loaded in CONFIG.SYS instead of in AUTOEXEC.BAT.

PROMPT=PG tells DOS to display the current directory as part of the DOS command prompt, which helps you keep track of the current directory.

PATH C:\;C:\DOS;C:\BAT;C:\WINDOWS specifies the order of directories that DOS searches when you enter an executable program or batch file name. Your path may include other directories. In fact, when you install Windows, your Windows directory is automatically added to your path by the Windows installation program if you choose. You do not have to place your AutoCAD LT directory on your path; you specified the location of the AutoCAD LT executable file when you added the AutoCAD LT icon to the Windows Program Manager.

PATH is essential for automatic directory access to programs and DOS commands. The C:\ (root) and C:\DOS paths are essential to the recommended setup. If your DOS files are in a different directory, substitute the directory name for DOS in your path line.

 Tip Keep your path short; a long path takes DOS longer to search (the path line cannot exceed 144 characters). Many programs use an installation process that adds the program's directory to your path. In most cases, you can shorten the path by including a batch file directory, such as C:\BAT, on your path and by creating batch files in that directory to change directories and launch programs, instead of having each program's directory on the path. A batch file named WIN.BAT that contains the following lines, for example, starts Windows and enables you to delete C:\WINDOWS from your path:

```
C:
CD \WINDOWS
WIN
CD \
```

The SET line tells Windows where to place temporary files. Your batch file can include lines other than those listed here. Use whatever is relevant to your setup in your AUTOEXEC.BAT file.

Common Problems with CONFIG.SYS

If your CONFIG.SYS settings do not run smoothly, your only indication might be that some AutoCAD LT features do not work. If you receive the following error message, DOS cannot find the file as it is specified:

```
Bad or missing FILENAME
```

Check your spelling, and provide a full path. The following message means you made a syntax error, or that your version of DOS does not support the configuration command:

```
Unrecognized command in CONFIG.SYS
```

Check your spelling.

Watch closely when you boot (start) your system. These error messages flash by quickly. If you suspect an error, temporarily rename your AUTOEXEC.BAT file so that the system stops after loading CONFIG.SYS. You also can try to send the screen messages to the printer by pressing Ctrl+PrtSc as soon as DOS starts reading the CONFIG.SYS file. Press Ctrl+PrtSc again to turn the printer echo off.

If you are using DOS 6, you can single-step your CONFIG.SYS file to test it or temporarily bypass suspect lines. To do so, press the F8 key at the Starting MS-DOS prompt during bootup. Then enter **Y** or **N** when asked if you want to load each line.

Common Problems with AUTOEXEC.BAT

Errors in the AUTOEXEC.BAT file can have many causes and are harder to troubleshoot. Often, the system just does not behave as you think it should. The following lists some troubleshooting tips:

◆ Isolate errors by temporarily editing your AUTOEXEC.BAT file. You can disable a line with a leading colon, as in the following:

```
: NOW DOS WILL IGNORE THIS LINE!
```

◆ If you are using DOS 6, you can single-step the AUTOEXEC.BAT, as described in the previous paragraph for the CONFIG.SYS file.

◆ Many AUTOEXEC.BAT files have echo to the screen turned off by the command ECHO OFF or @ECHO OFF. Disable echo off to see what they are doing and put a leading colon on the line.

◆ To record or study what is happening more closely, echo to the printer by pressing Ctrl+PrtSc while booting.

◆ Make sure the prompt, path, and other environment settings precede any TSR (memory-resident) programs in the file.

◆ Check your path for completeness and syntax. Unsophisticated programs that require support or overlay files, in addition to their EXE or COM files, might not work, even if they are in the path. Directories do not need to be in the path unless you want to execute files in them from other directories.

◆ The APPEND command (DOS 3.3 or later) works like PATH to enable programs to find their support and overlay files in other directories. It uses about 5 KB of RAM. All files in an appended directory are recognized by programs as if they were in the current directory.

Stop If you use APPEND, use it *cautiously*. If you modify a file in an appended directory, the modified file is written to the current directory, *not* to the appended directory. When you load an AutoCAD MNU file from an appended directory, you create an MNX file in the current directory. AutoCAD searches an appended directory before completing its normal directory search pattern, so appended support files are loaded instead of those in the current directory.

◆ If your AUTOEXEC.BAT file does not seem to complete its execution, you might have tried to execute another BAT file from your AUTOEXEC.BAT file. This is called nesting the other BAT file's execution. If you nest execution of BAT files, the second one takes over and the first is not completed. To solve this problem with DOS 3.3 or later, use the following:

```
CALL NAME
```

◆ If you are fighting for memory, insert temporary lines in the AUTOEXEC.BAT file to check your available memory. After you determine the amount of memory allocated to each, you can decide what to sacrifice. Use the following at appropriate points to display the remaining memory:

```
CHKDSK
PAUSE
```

In DOS 5.0 or later, replace CHKDSK with **MEM**. Reboot to see the effect. Remove the lines after you are done.

◆ Run CHKDSK /F at the DOS prompt on a regular basis. It verifies your hard disk file structure and frees up any lost clusters found. Lost clusters are sometimes created when programs crash. Answer **N** when it asks if you want to convert the clusters to files. You cannot run CHKDSK /F from a Windows DOS prompt.

◆ If you have unusual occurrences or lockups, and you use TSRs, the TSRs might be the source of the problems, although cause and effect can be hard to pin down. Disable TSRs one at a time in your AUTOEXEC file, then reboot and test.

Memory Problems

Windows is highly dependent on memory and related resources. Even if you have considerably more than the minimum required amount of RAM, you still can suffer memory shortages. This is because portions of Windows depend on the limited 640 KB area of lower DOS memory. You should use DOS 6 or QEMM or a similar memory manager and load DOS and device drivers and TSR utilities in high memory to maximize the available lower DOS memory for Windows to use. (See Appendix C, "Enhancing Performance.")

Danger signs include strange behavior or system lockups. If you experience odd graphics behavior, such as icons or windows that flash or windows that are not fully restored, STOP! Then, close applications and save files before proceeding. If you continue to work, you might suffer a lockup, applications failing, or corrupted files.

The area of resources that most often limits Windows, particularly with graphics applications, is called GDI resources. If you experience the symptoms listed in the previous paragraph, you probably are low on GDI resources. You can check this in Program Manager by choosing **H**elp, then **A**bout Program Manager. The bottom two lines in the About Program Manager window that appears list memory and resources. If resources drops below 20 percent, you are in danger and should immediately close applications.

 Note   Microsoft Word and many graphics or paint programs are notorious consumers of memory and GDI resources, so use caution with such programs when AutoCAD LT is running.

If you exit AutoCAD LT Release 1, and then try to reopen it, you might see an `insufficient memory to run application` error message in an alert box. If so, choose OK and try again. It usually works the second time. If this does not work, you have to completely exit Windows, and then start Windows again.

Finding Support Files

When you ask AutoCAD LT to find a support file (such as a menu file), it searches in a particular order. AutoCAD LT typically searches the current directory, then the current drawing's directory, then the designated support directory(ies), and finally the program directory, home of ACLT.EXE. If you keep AutoCAD's search order in mind, you can prevent AutoCAD from finding the wrong support files. If AutoCAD loads the wrong support files, you might find that the designated support directory(ies) is set incorrectly.

In AutoCAD LT, you have three ways to specify configuration and support directories. You can set DOS environment variables before starting Windows, set parameters in the Preferences dialog box, and use command line parameters in the startup icon. The order of supersession is: command line parameter > environment dialog > DOS environment variable.

Tracing and Curing Errors

You are your own best source for error diagnosis. Log any problems as they occur so that you can begin to recognize any patterns. The following are some tips and techniques:

- ◆ Scroll back through the text window to see what happened.

- ◆ Write down what you did in as much detail as possible, as far back as you can remember.

- ◆ If you can repeat the problem, you might want to use a log file to track exactly what happened. You can create a log file showing all the commands you enter and all of AutoCAD LT's command responses. Just enter **LOGFILEON** at the Command: prompt to turn on the log feature; enter **LOGFILEOFF** when you are finished. The AutoCAD LT log file is named ACLT.LOG and is saved in the \ACLTWIN subdirectory. You can view or print the file using any ASCII text editor. Note that if a log file already exists, AutoCAD LT adds to the file. Be sure to delete the log file when you are done with it, or it could grow quite large. Do not save the log file in a word processor format, or AutoCAD LT will crash the next time you open it.

- ◆ Use the AutoCAD LT STATUS command to check settings.

- ◆ Check related system variable settings.

- ◆ Check the AutoCAD LT environment settings.

- ◆ Check AutoCAD LT startup command line parameters.

Clearing Up File Problems After a System Crash

When your system goes down unexpectedly in the middle of an AutoCAD LT session, you can end up with extraneous files on disk or with files locked and inaccessible.

Run SCANDISK (in DOS 6) or CHKDSK /F at the DOS prompt after exiting Windows to restore any disk space occupied by abandoned sessions. Do not run SCANDISK or CHKDSK /F from Windows.

Removing Extraneous Files After a Crash

When AutoCAD LT terminates abnormally, you might find files on your hard drive with the extension AC$. Normally, AutoCAD LT erases these files whenever you exit the program. If the system is turned off, crashes, or locks up for some reason, however, the files remain on your disk until you erase them. The $ is the convention for designating a temporary file. As long as no application programs are currently running, you can delete any file names that begin with a $ or that have a $ in their extension.

Look for these files in the drawing directory, the ACLTWIN directory, and in the root directory of the drive from which you started AutoCAD LT. Use the DOS DEL or ERASE commands, or choose **D**elete from the **F**ile pull-down menu in Windows' File Manager to erase these files. From DOS, you can erase all files having an extension of AC$ by entering the following in each directory where they are found:

```
DEL *.AC$
```

Unlocking Locked Files

If your AutoCAD LT session terminates abnormally and you have file locking turned on, the drawing file you were editing remains locked. If you try to edit it again, AutoCAD LT refuses access to the file. Locked files are designated by a small lock file with the same name as the file it locks, but with a K as the last letter of its extension. For example, the DRAWING.DWG file is locked if an DRAWING.DWK file exists in the same directory. The menu file and other support files might also be left locked, particularly in a networked system.

To unlock a locked file, first verify that the file is not actually in use by someone else, such as on a network. If it is not, choose **F**ile, then **U**nlock file. A standard AutoCAD LT file dialog box appears. Select all the files you want to unlock and click on OK. AutoCAD then unlocks the files.

Other Error Messages

Other specific error messages are documented at the end of the "Troubleshooting Guide" appendix in the *AutoCAD LT Release 2 User's Guide,* so they are not repeated here.

Bugs

The LT_BUG.TXT file, installed in the \DWGS\IALT directory by the IALT Disk installation, lists bugs that exist in some versions of AutoCAD LT Release 1. AutoCAD LT Release 2, at the time of this writing, is too new for such information to be available, but bugs in AutoCAD LT Release 2 might be added to this file when available.

AutoCAD LT and Other AutoCAD Releases

You can read and write AutoCAD Release 12, AutoCAD LT Release 1, and AutoCAD LT Release 2 drawings in any of these three versions of AutoCAD or AutoCAD LT. There are, however, limitations on what you can do to objects that are not supported in the version you are using. AutoCAD LT Release 2 associative hatches, for example, are not associative in AutoCAD LT Release 1 or Release 12.

AutoCAD Release 13 can read AutoCAD Release 12, AutoCAD LT Release 1, and AutoCAD LT Release 2 drawings (but AutoCAD LT Release 2 associative hatches are not associative in AutoCAD Release 13 or vice versa). AutoCAD Release 13 uses a different file format that is not readable by AutoCAD Release 12, AutoCAD LT Release 1, and AutoCAD LT Release 2. To read a drawing created in AutoCAD Release 13 in AutoCAD Release 12, AutoCAD LT Release 1, or AutoCAD LT Release 2, it must be saved in AutoCAD Release 13 by using the SAVEASR12 command.

Stop Saving a drawing in AutoCAD Release 13 by using the SAVEASR12 command translates or discards data not recognized by AutoCAD Release 12. Use a different name than the original drawing file if you need you keep the AutoCAD Release 13 data intact.

Enhancing Performance

AutoCAD LT shares your computer's resources with Windows, which, along with the overhead of the graphical user interface (GUI), affects its performance. Windows is highly dependent on memory and related resources, and AutoCAD LT requires far more resources than most programs. Because portions of Windows depend on the limited 640 KB area of lower DOS memory, you may experience resource shortages and impeded performance even if you have far more RAM than the minimum requirements.

The following recommendations can improve the performance of Windows and AutoCAD LT:

- ◆ Defragment your hard drive.

- ◆ Use a large permanent swap file.

- ◆ Use 32-bit file access.

- ◆ Use as fast a processor as you can afford.

- ◆ Install as much RAM as you can afford.

- ◆ Use a memory manager that puts DOS in high memory, and device drivers and TSRs in upper memory to maximize the available lower DOS memory for Windows.

◆ Use as fast a video card as you can afford, with as much resolution and as large a display as you can afford.

◆ Keep up-to-date.

◆ Use a disk cache program.

Disk Defragmenting

The DOS file system often causes files on your hard disk drive or floppy disk to be broken into segments scattered around, rather than stored in *contiguous* (side-by-side) sectors. This is called *fragmentation*. The more the disk is used, the more likely fragmentation will result. When you create or install new files or programs, they first fill the scattered empty space left by deleted files. This fragments the new files or programs, slowing down file access time. Fragmentation can also greatly impact performance by preventing the creation of a Windows permanent swap file, which requires a large contiguous file space.

If your drive has been in use for a long time, you should defragment or pack the disk. This process reorders the files, moving the data around so that your files are once again stored in contiguous sectors. Any small groups of unused sectors that were previously between files are reallocated in larger groups.

Stop Before you defragment or reformat any disk or drive, make sure you have a complete backup of all files on it, that you know how to restore them, and that you have a bootable diskette containing your CONFIG.SYS and AUTOEXEC.BAT files, as well as any files referenced by your CONFIG.SYS and AUTOEXEC.BAT files.

Use a disk optimizer or defragmentation program frequently to speed up file access on your hard disk. Some commercial disk-management programs not only pack the disk, but also repair errors and/or check and adjust performance and operating parameters of your hard drive, such as the disk's *interleave factor* (the ordering of the sectors on the disk). See any software dealer for recommendations.

Setting a Large Permanent Swap File and 32-Bit File Access

Windows must be configured with a permanent swap file to permit acceptable AutoCAD performance. The size of the swap file should be as large as Windows

allows. The optimum swap file size is 32 MB or even larger. The amount of RAM you have affects the size of the swap file Windows allows.

Windows swaps information to disk when it has used all the available RAM. Normally, Windows creates these files dynamically on your hard drive as it needs space. You can instruct Windows to create a permanent swap file on your hard drive. Performance is enhanced because the permanent swap file occupies contiguous, rather than scattered, disk space.

Swap file performance can be further enhanced by enabling 32-bit file access, which can decrease access time considerably.

 Note Do not confuse 32-bit file access with 32-bit disk access. Both improve performance, but 32-bit file access has considerably more effect than 32-bit disk access. 32-bit file access is compatible with almost all systems while 32-bit disk access is less compatible and might be unavailable on your system. Sometimes Windows lets you set 32-bit disk access, then later rejects it when restarting. If this happens, you have to redo your virtual memory settings, without 32-bit disk access.

The following exercise shows how to set up a permanent swap file and 32-bit file access.

Setting a Permanent Swap File and 32-Bit File Access

In Windows Program Manager, open the Main *group and double-click on the Control Panel icon*	Opens the Control Panel
Double-click on the 386 Enhanced *icon in the Control Panel*	Opens the 386 Enhanced dialog box
Choose **V**irtual Memory *in the* 386 Enhanced *dialog box*	Opens the Virtual Memory dialog box and displays the current swapfile settings
Choose **C**hange	

The dialog box expands to show New Settings, and displays the largest possible and the recommended swap file sizes. If the largest possible size is less than four times the actual RAM you have installed, yet you have plenty of disk space, you probably need to optimize the disk.

If you want to create a larger swap file on another drive, change the **D**rive setting to see if another drive has more space. If you still don't get a large enough size, see the Tip following the exercise. When a suitable maximum size displays that you are satisfied with, proceed.

continues

continued

*Change **T**ype to* Permanent

Enter the desired size in the New **S**ize *box*

If the Use 32-bit **F**ile Access check box is available (not grayed), put a check in it. If the **U**se 32-bit Disk Access check box is available (not grayed), you can also put a check in it. See your Windows reference manual for details on 32-bit file and disk access.

Choose OK

Restart Windows for your swap, file, and disk access changes to take effect.

 Tip

AutoCAD benefits from a huge Windows swap file, but normally limits the maximum size to four times the actual installed physical RAM memory. It lets you set the size larger, but does not use the extra space unless you make a special setting, called PageOverCommit. You can increase the usable size of the Windows swap file with the Windows Virtual Memory multiplier `PageOverCommit` switch in the [386Enh] section of the Windows SYSTEM.INI file. If not set, or set to the default value of four, Windows uses four times the physical memory. From 64 to 128 MB is recommended for the swap file, particularly for large, complex drawings and if running multiple applications in Windows.

With a 64 MB permanent swap file but only 8 MB of RAM, Windows will use only 32 MB (8 MB×4) unless you tell it to use more. To tell Windows to use 64 MB (8 MB×8), put the following line in the [386Enh] section of the SYSTEM.INI file:

```
PageOverCommit=8
```

Upgrading Your Processor

The faster the processor, the better. A Pentium is faster than a 486, which is faster than a 386. A 120 Mhz processor is faster than a 66 Mhz, which is faster than a 16 Mhz. You often can upgrade your processor without replacing your computer. Replacement processor chips are available for many computers, and cost much less than replacing the computer. The replacement chips plug into the original processor's socket or an additional socket on the system board. Replacement only takes a few minutes.

Installing Additional Memory

You can enhance your computer's performance by installing more RAM. When your drawings grow in size so that they no longer fit in RAM while you work on them in AutoCAD LT, Windows begins paging drawing and program data to disk. You begin to lose time as Windows reads to and from your disk. The more RAM you can install in your computer, the longer you can put off paging. To determine how much RAM you might need, use this rule of thumb:

$$3 \times \text{drawing size} + 6 \text{ MB AutoCAD LT} + 2 \text{ MB Windows}$$

A 1 MB drawing would require 11 MB RAM to forestall paging. If you typically create 1 MB drawings, you should have 11 MB RAM (or more) to accommodate AutoCAD LT and maximize performance. There are many types of memory. If you add more memory, make sure it is compatible with your system and that you have available memory slots before buying it. Then, shop around—prices vary widely.

Maximizing Available Memory

Free as much of the lower 640 KB of DOS RAM as you possibly can before running Windows, so that Windows and AutoCAD LT have as much RAM as possible for their use when you run them. To accomplish this, do the following:

◆ Load only memory-resident TSR programs you absolutely need. Windows reduces the need for TSRs. A TSR program like Sidekick, for example, provides a pop-up text editor in DOS. You don't need this in Windows because you can easily run a text editor in Windows while running AutoCAD LT.

◆ Use a smaller disk cache in Windows. Many disk cache programs have separate size settings for DOS and Windows. SMARTDRV and PC-CACHE from Central Point Software are such programs. SMARTDRV has a default size of 2048 KB on machines with 8 MB of RAM. A cache size of 512 KB is adequate for Windows.

◆ Try MultiMedia Cloaking from Helix Software—it puts the disk cache, CD-ROM, and mouse drivers in extended memory.

◆ Use EMS or XMS versions of network drivers and other device drivers, if applicable and available.

◆ Use a memory manager such as HIMEM.SYS (MS-DOS 5 or later), or QEMM386.SYS from Quarterdeck Office Systems, along with DOS=HIGH or DOS's LOADHIGH or QEMM's LOADHI, to maximize your available DOS memory. See an MS-DOS 5 (or later) or QEMM 386 manual for details.

C

Running Fewer Applications

You can improve performance by running only essential applications in Windows when using AutoCAD LT. Avoid running applications that process simultaneously when you are working in AutoCAD LT. The fewer applications you have running, the more system resources are available for AutoCAD LT's use. In particular, if you have a screen saver utility installed to blank the screen, you should be aware that it may slow down AutoCAD LT. (The built-in screen saver in Windows 3.1 does not slow AutoCAD LT; you can install it with the Desktop in the Control Panel group.)

Using Faster Video

Video boards vary widely in their hardware performance, as do their drivers also vary. A number of manufacturers offer video adapter boards optimized for Windows; they improve screen scrolling and redraw speed in AutoCAD LT. Some third-party video driver suppliers offer drivers that improve on the OEM (Original Equipment Manufacturers) drivers. Several of these manufacturers as well as other third-party ADI driver developers offer software video drivers that optimize AutoCAD LT video performance. See your AutoCAD dealer or computer dealer for details.

Using higher resolution video boards and displays indirectly improves performance by providing a larger and more usable drawing area and reducing pans, zooms, and redraws.

Keeping Up-to-Date

If you are not using them already, install Windows for WorkGroups 3.11, DOS 6.2, and the latest versions of other system utilities that you use. The latest versions often improve performance somewhat.

Using a Disk Cache

Disk caching programs buffer disk reads to minimize disk access time. SmartDrive, included with Windows and MS-DOS 5 or later, is adequate. The Norton Utilities NCACHE from Symantec, or PC-CACHE from Central Point Software, is better. A hardware caching hard-drive controller is best. MultiMedia Cloaking from Helix Software replaces Smartdrive with a version that uses extended memory.

Note Write-caching is not recommended with AutoCAD LT, nor do the authors recommend it in general.

Other Tips

For other performance tips, see the *AutoCAD LT for Windows User's Guide* and README.DOC file (use Windows Write to read the README.DOC file). You can also find more detailed information on Windows in *Inside Windows 3.11, Platinum Edition* (New Riders Publishing).

System Variables

This appendix contains two tables of AutoCAD LT system variables. Use these tables to find AutoCAD LT's environment settings and their values. Dimension variables, although they are technically system variables, are presented separately in Appendix E, "Dimension Variables."

Table D.1 presents all the system variables available through AutoCAD LT. The system variable name and the default AutoCAD LT prototype drawing (ACLT.DWG) settings are shown. A brief description is given for each variable, and the meaning is given for each code. Variable names shown italicized must be set by the SETVAR command. All others can be set directly by entering their name at the Command: prompt (or at the Dim: prompt in the case of dimension variables) or indirectly by using the command(s) shown. All values are saved with the drawing unless noted with (CFG) for ConFiGuration file, or (NS) for Not Saved.

Table D.2 presents variables that are present in AutoCAD LT only for drawing compatibility with AutoCAD.

Note Variables shown in bold and marked (RO) are read only, which means that you cannot change them directly. If you create a new drawing with other than the standard ACLT prototype drawing, your default values might differ from those shown in the tables. Default values that differ from AutoCAD LT Release 1 to AutoCAD LT Release 2 are indicated with the notations "in R1" or "in R2." AutoCAD LT Release 1 or 2 variables that are not present in both releases are indicated with the notations "R1 only" or "R2 only."

TABLE D.1
AutoCAD LT System Variables

Variable Name	Default Setting	Command Name	Variable Description
ACLTPREFIX	**C:\ACLTWIN**		**Directory search path set in the Support Dirs box in the Preferences dialog box (NS)(RO)**
ACLTVER	*Date or version*		**The release number of your copy of AutoCAD LT (RO)(NS)**
AFLAGS	0	DDATTDEF, ATTDEF	Current state of ATTDEF modes. The value is the sum of the following: 0 = Off 1 = Invisible 2 = Constant 4 = Verify 8 = Preset (NS)
ANGBASE	0	DDUNITS, UNITS	The direction of angle 0 in the current UCS
ANGDIR	0	DDUNITS, UNITS	The direction of angle measure: 1 = Clockwise 0 = Counterclockwise
APERTURE	10	DDOSNAP, APERTURE	Half the OSNAP target size in pixels (CFG)
AREA	**0.0000**	**AREA, LIST**	**The last computed area in square drawing units (RO)(NS)**

New Riders Publishing
INSIDE
SERIES

Variable Name	Default Setting	Command Name	Variable Description
ATTDIA	0		Controls the attribute-entry method: 1 = DDATTE dialog box 0 = Attribute prompts
ATTMODE	1	ATTDISP	Attribute display: 1 = Normal 2 = On 0 = Off
ATTREQ	1		Attribute values used by Insert: 1 = Prompts for values 0 = Uses defaults
AUNITS	0	DDUNITS, UNITS	The angular unit display code: 0 = Decimal deg. 1 = Degrees/min/sec 2 = Grads 3 = Radians 4 = Surveyors units
AUPREC	0	DDUNITS, UNITS	The number of angular units decimal places
BACKZ	**0.0000**	**DVIEW**	**The DVIEW back clipping plane offset in drawing units. See VIEWMODE. (RO)**
BLIPMODE	On	BLIPMODE	Controls blip display: On = Blips Off = No Blips

continues

D

TABLE D.1, CONTINUED
AutoCAD LT System Variables

Variable Name	Default Setting	Command Name	Variable Description
CDATE	*19931223.14464898*	**TIME**	**Current date and time in** *YYYYMMDD.HHMMSS(millisec)* **format (NS)(RO)**
CECOLOR	BYLAYER	DDEMODES, COLOR	The current entity color
CELTYPE	BYLAYER	DDEMODES, LINETYPE	The current entity linetype
CHAMFERA	0.0000 in R1 0.500 in R2	CHAMFER	The first chamfer distance
CHAMFERB	0.0000 in R1 0.500 in R2	CHAMFER	The second chamfer distance
CIRCLERAD	0.0000		The default radius value for new circle entities: 0 = None (NS)
CLAYER	0	DDLMODES, LAYER	The current layer
CMDACTIVE	1	CMDACTIVE	Indicates that an AutoCAD command is active (used by DIESEL): 0 = None 1 = Ordinary Command 2 = Ordinary and Transparent 4 = Script 8 = Dialog box (NS)(RO)

Variable Name	Default Setting	Command Name	Variable Description
CMDDIA	1		Controls whether the PLOT command issues dialog boxes or prompts; a nonzero setting issues dialog boxes, and 0 issues prompts (CFG)
CMDNAMES	""		**Names of any active commands (RO)(NS)** **(Used by DIESEL)**
COORDS	1	[^D] [F6]	Controls the updating of the coordinate display: 0 = Absolute upon picks 1 = Absolute continuously 2 = Relative only during prompts
CVPORT	2	VPORTS	The current viewport's number
DATE	*2448806.36807836*	TIME	**The current date and time in Julian format (NS)(RO)**
DBMOD	0	Most	**Describes modifications to the current drawing database (sum of the following):** **0 = None** **1 = Entities** **2 = Symbol table** **4 = Database variable** **8 = Window** **16 = View** **(Used by DIESEL) (RO)(NS)**

continues

D

TABLE D.1, CONTINUED
AutoCAD LT System Variables

Variable Name	Default Setting	Command Name	Variable Description
DIASTAT	1	DD????	**The last dialog box exit code:** **0 = Canceled** **1 = OK button** (Used by DIESEL) (RO)(NS)
DISTANCE	0.0000	DIST	**The last distance computed by the DISTANCE command (NS)(RO)**
DITHER	1		Use dithered output (for raster printers) 1 = On 0 = Off
DONUTID	0.5000		The default inner diameter for new DONUT entities; may be 0 (NS)
DONUTOD	1.0000		The default outer diameter for new DONUT entities; must be nonzero (NS)
DWGCODEPAGE	iso8859-1		A string indicating the code page used for the drawing (RO)
DWGNAME	UNNAMED		**The current drawing name supplied by the user when the drawing was begun (Used by DIESEL) (RO)**
DWGPREFIX	C:\ACLTWIN\		**The current drawing's drive and directory path (Used by DIESEL) (RO)(NS)**

Variable Name	Default Setting	Command Name	Variable Description
DWGTITLED	0	NEW	Indicates whether the current drawing has been named or not: 1 = Yes 0 = No (Used by DIESEL) (RO)(NS)
DWGWRITE	1	OPEN	Indicates that the current drawing is opened as read-only: 0 = Read-only 1 = Read/write (Used by DIESEL) (NS)
ELEVATION	0.0000	ELEV	The current elevation in the current UCS for the current space
EXEDIR	C:\ACLTWIN\ *R2 only*		The directory from which AutoCAD LT was executed
EXPERT	0		Suppresses successive levels of Are you sure? warnings: 0 = None 1 = REGEN/LAYER 2 = BLOCK/WBLOCK/SAVE 3 = LINETYPE 4 = UCS/VPORT 5 = DIM (NS)
EXTMAX	-1.0000E+20,-1.0000E+20		The X,Y coordinates of the drawing's upper right extents in the WCS (RO)

continues

D

TABLE D.1, CONTINUED
AutoCAD LT System Variables

Variable Name	Default Setting	Command Name	Variable Description
EXTMIN	**1.0000E+20,1.0000E+20**		**The X,Y coordinates of the drawing's lower left extents in the WCS (RO)**
FILEDIA	1		Controls the display of the dialog box for file name requests: 0 = Only when a tilde (~) is entered 1 = On (CFG)
FILLETRAD	0.0000 in R1 0.5000 in R2	FILLET	The current fillet radius
FILLMODE	1	FILL	Turns on the display of fill traces, solids, and wide polylines: 1 = On 0 = Off
FRONTZ	**0.0000**	**DVIEW**	**The DVIEW front clipping plane's offset, in drawing units. See VIEWMODE. (RO)**
GRIDMODE	0	DDRMODES, GRID	Controls grid display in the current viewport: 1 = On 0 = Off
GRIDUNIT	0.0000,0.0000	DDRMODES, GRID	The X,Y grid increment for the current viewport

Variable Name	Default Setting	Command Name	Variable Description
GRIPBLOCK	0	**DDGRIPS**	Controls the display of grips for entities in blocks: 1 = On 0 = Off (CFG)
GRIPCOLOR	5	**DDGRIPS**	The current color code of unselected (outlined) grips; can be a value of 0 to 255 (CFG)
GRIPHOT	1	**DDGRIPS**	The current color code of selected (filled) grips; can be a value of 0 to 255 (CFG)
GRIPS	1	**DDSELECT**	Controls the display of entity grips and grip editing: 1 = On 0 = Off (CFG)
GRIPSIZE	6	**DDGRIPS**	The size of grip box in pixels; equals 0 = PICKBOX (CFG)
HANDLES	0 *in R1* 1 *in R2*	**HANDLES**	Controls the creation of entity handles for the current drawing (not listed by SETVAR): 1 = On 0 = Off (RO)

continues

D

TABLE D.1, CONTINUED
AutoCAD LT System Variables

Variable Name	Default Setting	Command Name	Variable Description
HIGHLIGHT	1		Determines whether current object selection set is highlighted: 1 = On 0 = Off (NS)
HPANG	0	HATCH	The default angle for new hatch patterns (NS)
HPDOUBLE	0	HATCH	Controls user-defined hatch-pattern doubling: 1 = On 0 = Off (NS)
HPNAME	""	HATCH	The default name and style for new hatches (NS)
HPSCALE	1.0000	HATCH	The default scale factor for new hatches; must be nonzero (NS)
HPSPACE	1.0000	HATCH	The default spacing for user-defined hatch patterns; must be nonzero (NS)
INSBASE	0.0000,0.0000,0.0000	BASE	Insertion base point X,Y coordinate of current drawing in current space and current UCS

Variable Name	Default Setting	Command Name	Variable Description
INSNAME	""	DDINSERT, INSERT	The default block name for new insertions (NS)
LASTANGLE	0	ARC	**The end angle of the last arc in the current-space UCS (NS)(RO)**
LASTPOINT	0.0000,0.0000,0.0000		The current space and UCS coordinate of the last point entered (recall with "@") (NS)
LENSLENGTH	50.0000	DVIEW	**The current viewport perspective view lens length, in millimeters (RO)**
LIMCHECK	0	LIMITS	Controls limits checking for current space: 1 = On 0 = Off
LIMMAX	12.0000,9.0000	LIMITS	The upper right X,Y limit of current space, relative to the WCS
LIMMIN	0.0000,0.0000	LIMITS	The lower left X,Y limit of current space, relative to WCS
LTSCALE	1.0000	LTSCALE	The global scale factor applied to linetypes
LUNITS	2	DDUNITS, UNITS	The linear units format: 1 = Scientific 2 = Decimal 3 = Engineering 4 = Architectural 5 = Fractional

continues

D

TABLE D.1, CONTINUED
AutoCAD LT System Variables

Variable Name	Default Setting	Command Name	Variable Description
LUPREC	4	DDUNITS, UNITS	Units precision decimal places or fraction denominator
MACROTRACE	0		**Controls the DIESEL macro-debugging display:** **1 = On** **0 = Off** **(NS)**
MAXACTVP	16		**The maximum number of viewports to regenerate (NS)(RO)**
MAXSORT	200		The maximum number of symbols and file names sorted in lists, up to 200 (CFG)
MENUECHO	0		Controls the display of menu actions on the command line; the value is the sum of the following: 1 = Suppresses menu input 2 = Suppresses command prompts 4 = Suppresses disable ^P toggling 8 = Displays DIESEL input/output strings (NS)
MIRRTEXT	1		Controls reflection of text by the MIRROR command: 0 = Retain text direction 1 = Reflect text

Variable Name	Default Setting	Command Name	Variable Description
MODEMACRO	""		A DIESEL language expression to control status-line display (NS)
OFFSETDIST	-1.0000	**OFFSET**	The default distance for the OFFSET command; negative values enable the Through option
ORTHOMODE	0	[^O] [F8]	Sets the current Ortho mode state: 1 = On 0 = Off
OSMODE	0	DDOSNAP, OSNAP	The current object snap mode; the value is the sum of the following: 1 = Endp 2 = Mid 4 = Cen 8 = Node 16 = Quad 32 = Int 64 = Ins 128 = Perp 256 = Tan 512 = Near 1024 = Quick
PDMODE	0		Controls the graphic display of point entities
PDSIZE	0.0000		Controls the size of point graphic display: positive = absolute negative = relative to view

continues

D

Table D.1, Continued
AutoCAD LT System Variables

Variable Name	Default Setting	Command Name	Variable Description
PERIMETER	0.0000	**AREA, LIST**	The last computed perimeter (NS)(RO)
PICKADD	1	DDSELECT	Controls whether selected entities are added to, or replace (added with Shift+select), the current selection set: 1 = Added (Shift to remove only) 0 = Replace (Shift to add or remove) (CFG)
PICKAUTO	1	DDSELECT	Controls the implied (AUTO) windowing for object selection: 1 = On 0 = Off (CFG)
PICKBOX	3		Half the object-selection pick box size, in pixels (CFG)
PICKDRAG	0	**DDSELECT**	Determines whether the pick button must be depressed during window corner picking in set selection (MS Windows style): 1 = On 0 = Off (CFG)

Variable Name	Default Setting	Command Name	Variable Description
PICKFIRST	1	**DDSELECT**	**Enables entity selection before command selection (noun/verb paradigm):** **1 = On** **0 = Off** **(CFG)**
PLATFORM	**"Microsoft Windows"**		**Indicates the version of AutoCAD in use: a string such as "386 DOS Extender," "Sun 4/SPARCstation," "Apple Macintosh," etc. (RO)(NS)**
PLINEGEN	0		The control points for polyline generation of noncontinuous linetypes: 0 = Vertices 1 = End points
PLINEWID	0.0000	PLINE	The default width for new polyline entities
PLOTID	"System Printer"	PLOT	The current plotter configuration description (CFG)
PLOTTER	0	PLOT	The current plotter configuration number (CFG)
POLYSIDES	4	POLYGON	The default number of sides (3 to 1024) for new polygon entities (NS)
PSLTSCALE	1		Paper-space scaling of model space linetypes: 1 = On 0 = Off

continues

D

Table D.1, Continued
AutoCAD LT System Variables

Variable Name	Default Setting	Command Name	Variable Description
PSPROLOG	""		The name of the PostScript post-processing section of ACAD.PSF to be appended to the PSOUT command's output (CFG)
PSQUALITY	75	PSQUALITY	The default quality setting for rendering of images by the PSIN command (CFG)
QTEXTMODE	0	QTEXT	Sets the current state of Quick text mode: 1 = On 0 = Off
SAVEFILE	**AUTO.SV$ in R1** **auto.sv$ in R2**		**The default directory and file name for automatic file saves (CFG)(RO)**
SAVENAME	""	SAVEAS	The drawing name specified by the user to the last invocation of the SAVEAS command in the current session (RO)
SAVETIME	0		The default interval between automatic file saves, in minutes: 0 = Disable automatic saves (CFG) (RO)

Variable Name	Default Setting	Command Name	Variable Description
SCREENMODE	*3 in R1 only*	[F2]	**Indicates the active AutoCAD screen mode or window:** **0 = Text** **1 = Graphics** **2 = Dual screen** **3 = Windows** **(RO)(CFG)**
SCREENSIZE	574.0000,414.0000		**The size of current viewport, in pixels, X and Y (RO)**
SHADEDGE	3		Controls the display of edges and faces by the SHADE command: 0 = Faces shaded, edges unhighlighted 1 = Faces shaded, edges in background color 2 = Faces unfilled, edges in entity color 3 = Faces in entity color, edges in background
SHADEDIF	70		Specifies the ratio of diffuse-to-ambient light used by the SHADE command; expressed as a percentage of diffuse reflective light
SNAPANG	0	DDRMODES, SNAP	The angle of SNAP/GRID rotation in the current viewport, for the current UCS

continues

D

TABLE D.1, CONTINUED
AutoCAD LT System Variables

Variable Name	Default Setting	Command Name	Variable Description
SNAPBASE	0.0000,0.0000	DDRMODES, SNAP	The X,Y base point of SNAP/GRID rotation in the current viewport, for the current UCS.
SNAPISOPAIR	0	DDRMODES, SNAP [^E]	The current isoplane for the current viewport: 0 = Left 1 = Top 2 = Right
SNAPMODE	0	DDRMODES, SNAP [^B] [F9]	Indicates the state of Snap for the current viewport: 1 = On 0 = Off
SNAPSTYL	0	DDRMODES, SNAP	The snap style for the current viewport: 1 = Isometric 0 = Standard
SNAPUNIT	1.0000,1.0000 *in R1* 0.5000,0.5000 *in R2*	DDRMODES, SNAP	The snap X,Y increment for the current viewport

Variable Name	Default Setting	Command Name	Variable Description
SORTENTS	96	DDSELECT	A bit code corresponding to the type(s) of operations for which AutoCAD should not use spatial database organization and instead sort entities in the order created; the value is the sum of the following: 0 = Off 1 = Object selection 2 = OSNAP 4 = REDRAW 8 = MSLIDE 16 = REGEN 32 = PLOT 64 = PSOUT (CFG)
SPLFRAME	0		Controls the display of control polygons for spline-fit polylines, defining meshes of surface-fit polygon meshes, invisible 3D face edges: 1 = On 0 = Off
SPLINESEGS	8		The number of line segments in each spline curve

continues

D

TABLE D.1, CONTINUED
AutoCAD LT System Variables

Variable Name	Default Setting	Command Name	Variable Description
SPLINETYPE	6		Controls the spline type generated by the PEDIT command's Spline option: 5 = Quadratic B-Spline 6 = Cubic B-Spline
SYSCODEPAGE	iso8859-1		A string indicating the code page used by the system (RO)
TARGET	0.0000,0.0000,0.0000	DVIEW	The UCS coordinates of the current viewport's target point (RO)
TDCREATE	2448806.36779607	TIME	The date and time of the current drawing's creation, in Julian format (RO)
TDINDWG	0.00000000	TIME	The total amount of editing time elapsed in the current drawing, in Julian days (RO)
TDUPDATE	2448806.36779607	TIME	The date and time when the file was last saved, in Julian format (RO)
TDUSRTIMER	0.00000000	TIME	User-controlled elapsed time in Julian days (RO)
TEXTEVAL	0		Controls the checking of text input (except by DTEXT) for DIESEL expressions: 0 = Yes 1 = No (NS)

Variable Name	Default Setting	Command Name	Variable Description
TEXTSIZE	0.2000	DTEXT, TEXT	The height applied to new text entities created with nonfixed-height text styles
TEXTSTYLE	STANDARD	DTEXT, TEXT, STYLE	The current text style's name
THICKNESS	0.0000		The current 3D extrusion thickness
TILEMODE	1	TILEMODE	Release 10 VPORT compatibility setting; enables/disables paper space and viewport entities: 1 = On 0 = Off
TOOLTIPS	1 *R2 only*		Controls display of ToolTips: 0 = off 1 = on
TREEDEPTH	3020	DDSELECT	A code number (four digits) representing the maximum number of divisions for spatial database index for model space (first two digits) and paper space (last two digits)
TREEMAX	10000000	TREEMAX	The maximum number of nodes for spatial database organization for the current memory configuration (CFG)

continues

D

TABLE D.1, CONTINUED
AutoCAD LT System Variables

Variable Name	Default Setting	Command Name	Variable Description
UCSFOLLOW	0		Controls automatic display of the plan view in the current viewport when switching to a new UCS: 1 = On 0 = Off
UCSICON	0	UCSICON	Controls the UCS icon's display; the value is the sum of the following (not listed by SETVAR): 0 = Off 1 = On 2 = At origin
UCSNAME	""	DDUCS, UCS	The name of the current UCS for the current space: "" = Unnamed (RO)
UCSORG	0.0000,0.0000,0.0000	DDUCS, UCS	The WCS origin of the current UCS for the current space (RO)
UCSXDIR	1.0000,0.0000,0.0000	DDUCS, UCS	The X direction of the current UCS (RO)
UCSYDIR	0.0000,1.0000,0.0000	DDUCS, UCS	The Y direction of the current UCS (RO)

Variable Name	Default Setting	Command Name	Variable Description
UNDOCTL	5	**UNDO**	**The current state of UNDO; the value is the sum of the following:** **1 = Enabled** **2 = Single command** **4 = Auto mode** **8 = Group active** **(RO)(NS)**
UNDOMARKS	0	**UNDO**	**The current number of marks in the UNDO command's history (RO) (NS)**
UNITMODE	0		Controls the display of user input of fractions, feet and inches, and surveyor's angles: 0 = Per LUNITS 1 = As input
USERI1 - 5	0		User integer variables USERI1 to USERI5
USERR1 - 5	0.0000		User real-number variables USERR1 to USERR5
VIEWCTR	6.2433,4.5000	**ZOOM, PAN**	**The X,Y center point coordinate of the VIEW current view in the current viewport (RO)**
VIEWDIR	0.0000,0.0000,1.0000	**DVIEW**	**The camera point offset from target in the WCS (RO)**

continues

D

TABLE D.1, CONTINUED
AutoCAD LT System Variables

Variable Name	Default Setting	Command Name	Variable Description
VIEWMODE	0	DVIEW, UCS	The current viewport's viewing mode; the value is the sum of the following: 1 = Perspective 2 = Front clipping on 4 = Back clipping on 8 = UCSFOLLOW On 16 = FRONTZ offset in use (RO)
VIEWSIZE	9.0000	ZOOM, VIEW	The current view's height, in drawing units (RO)
VIEWTWIST	0	DVIEW	The current viewport's view-twist angle (RO)
VISRETAIN	0		Controls retention of Xref file layer settings in the current drawing: 0 = Off 1 = On
VSMAX	37.4600,27.0000,0.0000	ZOOM,PAN,VIEW	The upper right X,Y coordinate of the current viewport's virtual screen for the current UCS (NS)(RO)
VSMIN	-24.9734,-18.0000,0.0000	ZOOM,PAN,VIEW	The lower left X,Y coordinate of the current viewport's virtual screen for the current UCS (NS)(RO)

Variable Name	Default Setting	Command Name	Variable Description
WORLDUCS	1	UCS	**The current UCS, equivalent to WCS:** **1 = True** **0 = False** **(RO)(NS)**
WORLDVIEW	1	DVIEW,UCS	Controls the automatic changing of a UCS to the WCS during the DVIEW and VPOINT commands: 1 = On 0 = Off
XREFCTL	0		Controls the creation of an XLG log file that contains XREF results: 0 = No file 1 = XLG file (CFG)

D

TABLE D.2
AutoCAD Release 12 System Variables Present in AutoCAD LT

Variable Name	Default Setting	Command Name	Variable Description
AUDITCTL	**0** *R1 only*		**Controls the creation of an ADT log file containing AUDIT results:** **0 = No file** **1 = ADT file** **(CFG)**
CMDECHO	1		Controls AutoCAD Command: prompt echoing by AutoLISP: 1 = Echo 0 = No Echo (NS)
DRAGMODE	2		(Has no effect in AutoCAD LT) Controls object dragging on-screen: 0 = Off 1 = If requested 2 = Auto
DRAGP1	10		The regen-drag sampling rate (CFG)
DRAGP2	25		The fast-drag sampling rate (CFG)
ERRNO	0		An error number generated by AutoLISP and ADS applications.

Variable Name	Default Setting	Command Name	Variable Description
LOGINNAME	"AutoCAD LT User" *R1 only*		The name entered by the user or configuration file during login to AutoCAD (CFG)(RO)
MENUCTL	1		Command-line, input-sensitive, screen menu-page switching: 1 = On 0 = Off (CFG)
MENUNAME	ACAD	MENU	The current menu name, plus the drive/path if entered (RO)
PFACEVMAX	4		The maximum number of vertexes per face in a PFACE mesh (NS)(RO)
POPUPS	1		Determines whether the Advanced User Interface (dialog boxes, menu bar, pull-down menus, icon menus) is supported: 1 = Yes 0 = No (NS)(RO)
REGENMODE	1		Indicates the current state of Regenauto: 1 = On 0 = Off

continues

D

TABLE D.2, CONTINUED
AutoCAD Release 12 System Variables Present in AutoCAD LT

Variable Name	Default Setting	Command Name	Variable Description
RE-INIT	0		A code that specifies the type(s) of reinitializations to perform. The sum of: 0 = Off 1 = Digitizer port 2 = Plotter port 4 = Digitizer device 8 = Display device 16 = Reload ACAD.PGP (NS)
SCREENBOXES	**0**		**The number of available screen menu boxes in the current graphics screen area (RO)(CFG)**
SHPNAME	""		The default shape name (NS)
SKETCHINC	0.1000		The recording increment for SKETCH segments
SKPOLY	0		Controls the type of entities generated by SKETCH: 1 = Polylines 0 = Lines
SURFTAB1	6		The number of RULESURF and TABSURF tabulations, also the REVSURF and EDGESURF M-direction density

Variable Name	Default Setting	Command Name	Variable Description
SURFTAB2	6		The REVSURF and EDGESURF N-direction density
SURFTYPE	6		Controls type of surface generated by Pedit smooth option: Quadratic B-Spline=5 Cubic B-Spline=6 Bézier=8
SURFU	6		The M-direction surface density of 3D polygon meshes
SURFV	6		The N-direction surface density 3D polygon meshes
TABMODE	0		Controls tablet mode: 1 = On 0 = Off (NS)
TEMPPREFIX	**"" *R1 only***		**The directory configured for placement of AutoCAD's temporary files; defaults to the drawing directory (RO)(NS)**
TRACEWID	0.0500		The current width of traces

D

A P P E N D I X

E

Dimension Variables

This appendix contains a table of AutoCAD LT dimension variables. Use this table to find AutoCAD LT's dimensioning environment settings and values.

Table E.1 presents all the dimension variables available through AutoCAD LT. The variable name and the default AutoCAD LT prototype drawing (ACLT.DWG) settings are shown. A brief description is given for each variable, and the meaning is given for each code. These variables can be set directly by entering their name at the Command: prompt or at the Dim: prompt, or indirectly by using the command(s) shown. All values are saved with the drawing unless noted with (CFG) for ConFiGuration file, or (NS) for Not Saved.

Note Variables shown in bold and marked (RO) are read only, which means that you cannot change them directly. If you create a new drawing with other than the standard IALT prototype drawing, your default values might differ from those shown in the tables.

TABLE E.1
AutoCAD LT Dimension Variables

Variable Name	Default Setting	Command Name	Variable Description
DIMALT	0		Controls the drawing of additional dimension text in an alternative-units system: 1 = On 0 = Off
DIMALTD	2		The decimal precision of dimension text when alternative units are used
DIMALTF	25.4000		The scale factor for dimension text when alternate units are used
DIMAPOST	""		The user-defined suffix for alternative dimension text
DIMASO	1		Controls the creation of associative dimensions: 1 = On 0 = Off
DIMASZ	0.1800		Controls the size of dimension arrows and affects the fit of dimension text inside dimension lines when DIMTSZ is set to 0
DIMBLK	""		The name of the block to draw rather than an arrow or tick
DIMBLK1	""		The name of the block for the first end of dimension lines; see DIMSAH
DIMBLK2	""		The name of the block for the second end of dimension lines; see DIMSAH

Variable Name	Default Setting	Command Name	Variable Description
DIMCEN	0.0900		Controls center marks or center lines drawn by radial DIM commands: 0 = no center marks positive value = draw center marks (value = length) negative value = draw center lines (absolute value = mark portion)
DIMCLRD	0		The dimension line, arrow, and leader color number, any valid color number, or: 0 = BYBLOCK 256 = BYLAYER
DIMCLRE	0		The dimension extension line's color (see DIMCLRD)
DIMCLRT	0		The dimension text's color (see DIMCLRD)
DIMDLE	0.0000		The dimension line's extension distance beyond ticks when ticks are drawn (when DIMTSZ is nonzero)
DIMDLI	0.3800		The offset distance between successive continuing or baseline dimensions
DIMEXE	0.1800		The length of extension lines beyond dimension lines
DIMEXO	0.0625		The distance by which extension line origin is offset from dimensioned entity
DIMGAP	0.0900		The space between text and a dimension line; determines when text is placed outside a dimension (creates Basic dimension text boxes if negative)

continues

E

TABLE E.1, CONTINUED
AutoCAD LT Dimension Variables

Variable Name	Default Setting	Command Name	Variable Description
DIMLFAC	1.0000		The overall linear dimensioning scale factor; if negative, acts as the absolute value applied to paper space viewports
DIMLIM	0		Presents dimension limits as default text: 1 = On 0 = Off See DIMTP and DIMTM
DIMPOST	""		The user-defined suffix for dimension text, such as "mm"
DIMRND	0.0000		The rounding interval for linear dimension text
DIMSAH	0		Enables the use of DIMBLK1 and DIMBLK2 rather than DIMBLK or a default terminator: 1 = On 0 = Off
DIMSCALE	1.0000		The overall scale factor applied to other dimension variables except tolerances, angles, measured lengths, or coordinates 0 = Paper space scale
DIMSE1	0		Suppresses the first extension line: 1 = On 0 = Off
DIMSE2	0		Suppresses the second extension line: 1 = On 0 = Off

Variable Name	Default Setting	Command Name	Variable Description
DIMSHO	1		Determines whether associative dimension text is updated during dragging: 1 = On 0 = Off
DIMSOXD	0		Suppresses the placement of dimension lines outside extension lines: 1 = On 0 = Off
DIMSTYLE	**"*UNNAMED"**		**Holds the name of the current dimension style (RO)**
DIMTAD	0		Places dimension text above the dimension line rather than within: 1 = On 0 = Off
DIMTFAC	1.0000		Scale factor for dimension tolerance text height
DIMTIH	1		Forces dimension text inside the extension lines to be positioned horizontally rather than aligned: 1 = On 0 = Off
DIMTIX	0		Forces dimension text inside extension lines: 1 = On 0 = Off
DIMTM	0.0000		The negative tolerance value used when DIMTOL or DIMLIM is on

continues

E

TABLE E.1, CONTINUED
AutoCAD LT Dimension Variables

Variable Name	Default Setting	Command Name	Variable Description
DIMTOFL	0		Draws dimension lines between extension lines even if text is placed outside the extension lines: 1 = On 0 = Off
DIMTOH	1		Forces dimension text to be positioned horizontally rather than aligned when it falls outside the extension lines: 1 = On 0 = Off
DIMTOL	0		Appends tolerance values (DIMTP and DIMTM) to the default dimension text: 1 = On 0 = Off
DIMTP	0.0000		The positive tolerance value used when DIMTOL or DIMLIM is on
DIMTSZ	0.0000		When assigned a nonzero value, forces tick marks to be drawn (rather than arrowheads) at the size specified by the value; affects the placement of the dimension line and text between extension lines
DIMTVP	0.0000		Percentage of text height to offset dimension vertically
DIMTXT	0.1800		The dimension text height for nonfixed text styles

Variable Name	Default Setting	Command Name	Variable Description
DIMZIN	0		Suppresses the display of zero inches or zero feet in dimension text, and leading or trailing zeros in decimal dimension text: 0 = Feet & Inches=0 1 = Neither 2 = Inches Only 3 = Feet only 4 = Leading zeros 8 = Trailing zeros 12 = Both leading zeros and trailing zeros

E

Command Reference

This appendix contains definitions of the commands used in AutoCAD LT, followed by a table of the command shortcuts. The commands covered in more detail in previous chapters of this book are listed in **bold** type. The commands new to AutoCAD LT Release 2 are listed in *italic* (or ***bold italic***) type.

?. The ? (or HELP) command opens the AutoCAD LT Help window in Windows.

3DPOLY. The 3DPOLY command enables you to construct polylines in three dimensions (X,Y,Z). A 3D polyline can contain only line segments.

ABOUT. The ABOUT command displays information about your version of AutoCAD LT, such as the version number, serial number, and license information. ABOUT also displays any text in the ACAD.MSG message file, if found on the search path. You can modify the ACAD.MSG text file, using any text editor that can save an ASCII format file, to supply your own custom message. You can delete the file to prevent display of any message.

APERTURE. The APERTURE command specifies the object snap aperture size (APERTURE system variable) in pixels from the crosshairs to the edge of the aperture box. You normally use the Running Object Snap dialog box (DDOSNAP command) to set the aperture, but the APERTURE command provides a wider range (1–50 vs. 1–20).

ARC. The ARC command creates a circular arc. You can choose the arc's dimensions and location by specifying three pieces of information. This information can be any combination of the start point, a point on the circumference, endpoint, center, and included angle that defines an arc. The default is a three-point arc that uses a starting point, a point on the arc, and an endpoint.

AREA. The AREA command calculates and displays the total of one or more areas and perimeter distances defined by a series of three or more points that you pick (the default method), or defined by one or more selected circles or polylines (the Entity option).

ARRAY. The ARRAY command makes multiple copies of objects, creating a rectangular array (copies arranged parallel to the X,Y axis) or a polar array (copies arranged in a circular pattern). Objects in polar arrays can be rotated about the array's center point or copied with their original orientation.

ATTDEF. The ATTDEF command defines an attribute for inclusion and insertion in a block. An attribute consists of a tag name, an optional prompt (otherwise the tag is used), and an optional default value (otherwise blank) for insertion with the block. When an attribute is defined, its tag appears. When the attribute has been included in a block and inserted, its default value or the value you enter at the time of insertion appears. The attribute tag and value text can use any of the options available to normal text, such as style, height, or rotation. Attributes can be defined to insert as visible or invisible and constant or variable. They can be set to automatically insert default text.

ATTDISP. The ATTDISP command controls the visibility of block attributes. The setting is stored in the ATTMODE system variable.

ATTEDIT. The ATTEDIT command enables you to edit block attribute information, properties, and positions. See the DDATTE command, which provides the same function but in a dialog box.

ATTEXT. The ATTEXT command enables you to extract block attribute information to a file on disk. See the DDATTEXT command, which provides the same function but in a dialog box.

BASE. The BASE command resets the base point in the current UCS. The base point is used as the insert base point when the drawing is inserted in or attached to other drawings.

BHATCH. The BHATCH command (Boundary Hatch dialog box) is used to apply a predefined pattern (or *poché*) to one or more closed areas, automatically detecting islands within the area(s). A name, scale, and rotation angle must be specified for the pattern, or a user-specified pattern consisting of only evenly spaced lines also can be specified. A boundary selection set must be specified, either by selecting objects, by picking one or more points in the area(s) to hatch, or both. BHATCH finds the boundary of the specified area and does not require the defining objects to meet precisely, unlike the HATCH command. The HATCH command requires you to select every defining object and for their endpoints to meet in an end-to-end chain. Unlike hatch patterns created with the HATCH command, those created by BHATCH are associative and can be edited, automatically adjusting as their boundaries are modified.

BLOCK. The BLOCK command defines a block with the name and insertion (base) point you specify and the objects you select. The objects are erased upon completion.

BLIPMODE. The BLIPMODE command (stored in the BLIPMODE system variable) turns blips on and off. Blips are the tiny temporary crosses that display when you pick points.

BMAKE. The BMAKE command opens the Block Definition dialog box, which you can use to specify the parameters for a block definition. (It is generally easier to just use the BLOCK command.)

BREAK. The BREAK command erases portions of objects between two specified points. You can break lines, circles, arcs, and 2D polylines. The point you pick to select an object to break becomes the default first break point, but you can use the F option to respecify this first point.

BOUNDARY. The BOUNDARY command (Boundary Creation dialog box) creates polyline boundaries within one or more closed areas, automatically detecting islands within the area(s). A boundary selection set must be specified, either by selecting objects or by picking one or more points in the area(s). BOUNDARY finds the boundary of the specified area and does not require the defining objects to meet precisely.

CHAMFER. The CHAMFER command creates an angled line connecting two intersecting lines. You also can use CHAMFER to create an angled segment between two adjacent straight segments of a 2D polyline, or at all vertices of straight segments throughout a single 2D polyline. You can set the distance (default 0) measured from the real or projected intersection of the lines to the start of the chamfer on each line. CHAMFER extends or trims the lines to those distances from their intersection and then joins the endpoints with a new line or segment. The first line you select is modified by the first chamfer distance, and the second line is modified by the second distance. The default value for the second distance is always equal to the first.

F

CHANGE. The CHANGE command modifies the geometry and properties of existing objects. Its default is Change point, which specifies a new primary point for most objects. The effect varies with the object type.

CHPROP. The CHPROP command is used to change the object properties of existing objects in the drawing. These properties include color, layer, linetype, and thickness. The DDCHPROP command (Change Properties dialog box) provides the same function but in a dialog box.

CIRCLE. The CIRCLE command can draw circles by using nearly any geometric method. The most common method (the default) is to specify the center point and radius. You can drag and pick the size of the circle on-screen, or specify the radius with a keyboard entry.

COLOR. The COLOR command enables you to specify the current object color. The DDEMODES command provides the same function, but in the Select Color subdialog of the Entity Creation Modes dialog box.

COPY. The COPY command copies selected objects by the displacement you specify. The selected objects are not modified. You can indicate the displacement by two points, from which a relative distance and angle for the copy is derived. Or you can specify a coordinate value at the first displacement prompt and press Enter at the second displacement prompt, in which case the coordinate value is interpreted as the relative distance and angle, or displacement, for the copy. You can use the Multiple option to make multiple copies, specifying a single base point with multiple displacements (multiple second points).

COPYCLIP. The COPYCLIP command copies selected objects to the Windows Clipboard (or Clipbook). COPYCLIP is used to copy objects to other Windows applications. Objects are copied in all available formats (ASCII is the only available format for text objects).

COPYEMBED. The COPYEMBED command copies a specified area from the current viewport to the Windows Clipboard (or Clipbook). COPYEMBED is used for embedding drawings in other OLE applications.

COPYIMAGE. The COPYIMAGE command copies a specified area from the current viewport to the Windows Clipboard (or Clipbook). COPYIMAGE is used to copy an image to other Windows applications.

COPYLINK. The COPYLINK command copies the current view to the Windows Clipboard (or Clipbook). COPYLINK is used for linking to other OLE applications.

DDATTDEF. The DDATTDEF command brings up the Attribute Definition dialog box, in which you can create attribute definitions—text objects included in blocks that can be assigned different values with each insertion. An attribute definition

contains three parts: a tag that defines the type of information conveyed by the attribute, a prompt at which you supply a value when you insert the block, and a default value. Attributes appear on your screen as AutoCAD LT text. Part of the attribute definition process involves specifying height, justification, style, rotation, and position just as with AutoCAD LT's TEXT command. You also can assign one or more modes to your attribute definitions: Invisible, Constant, Verify, or Preset.

DDATTE. DDATTE (Dynamic Dialog ATTribute Edit) enables you to edit attribute string values by using the Attribute Extraction dialog box. You can either edit strings character by character or you can overwrite an entire line. If all of a block's attributes do not fit in a single dialog box screen, you can use the buttons in the dialog box to move through the various attributes.

DDATTEXT. The DDATTEXT command extracts attribute information from your drawing and stores it in a text file. You can analyze the extracted attribute data in a spreadsheet program, catalog it in a database program, or print it as a text report. DDATTEXT extracts information in one of three formats: Comma Delimited Format (CDF), Space Delimited Format (SDF), or Drawing Interchange Format (DXF). Use the format that is accepted by the program in which you want to use the extracted information.

DDCHPROP. The DDCHPROP command is used to change the object properties of existing objects in the drawing. These properties include color, layer, linetype, and thickness. After the DDCHPROP command is issued, the Change Properties dialog box is displayed. The current values of the selected objects' properties are displayed in the dialog box.

DDEDIT. The DDEDIT command (Dynamic Dialogue EDIT) prompts for a text or attribute string and opens the Edit Text dialog box with the selected string highlighted. DDEDIT can also be used to edit the tag, prompt, and default values of attribute definitions. Use DDATTE to edit attributes after they have been inserted as a block. DDEDIT repeats for additional text selections until you press Ctrl+C or Enter at its selection prompt.

DDEMODES. The DDEMODES command displays the Entity Creation Modes dialog box, which is used to control the properties of new objects. These properties include color, layer, linetype, and thickness. The property settings in the Entity Creation Modes dialog box affect the creation of all new objects. The Entity Creation Modes dialog box also enables you to set the elevation and the current text style.

DDGRIPS. Drawing objects in AutoCAD LT might display grips, small squares located at strategic points on the objects. You can enable grips by using the DDGRIPS command (which displays the Grips dialog box) or by setting the GRIPS system variable to 1. With grips enabled, the crosshairs snap automatically to a grip when the crosshairs pass over the grip. You can stretch, move, rotate, scale, or mirror the

F

gripped object by moving the grip. In addition to enabling or disabling grips, the DDGRIPS command also enables you to set the color and size of the grips.

DDIM. The Dimension Styles and Settings dialog box displayed by the DDIM command provides access to all of AutoCAD LT's dimensioning system variables. You also can create custom system variable settings and save them under unique dimension style names for later recall.

DDINSERT. The DDINSERT command displays the Insert dialog box for inserting blocks and drawing files into the current drawing.

DDLMODES. The DDLMODES (Dynamic Dialog Layer MODES) command uses the Layer Control dialog box to manage layer settings. DDLMODES also provides an easy way for you to check layer status. You can use the DDLMODES dialog box to turn layers on or off, lock or unlock layers, freeze or thaw layers, change color or linetype settings, and set a new current layer.

DDMODIFY. The DDMODIFY command opens the Modify *<Entity_type>* dialog box, which enables you to view and modify the properties and geometric data of the selected object.

DDOSNAP. The DDOSNAP command enables you to set AutoCAD LT's running object snap modes. The command displays the Running Object Snap dialog box. Object snaps enable you to manipulate objects and draw accurately by letting you specify points corresponding to the geometric features of a selected object. To enter a point with object snap, you need only specify an object snap mode and pick any point on an existing object. AutoCAD LT calculates the precise point coordinates according to the mode you specified and the object selected. You can set one or more modes to be applied to all point entry, or you can enter them on the fly at AutoCAD LT's command option prompts.

DDPTYPE. The DDPTYPE command opens the Point Style dialog box, which enables you to specify the display style and size of point objects. The settings are stored in the PDMODE and PDSIZE system variables.

DDRENAME. With the DDRENAME command, which displays the Rename dialog box, you can rename blocks, dimension styles, layers, linetypes, text styles, UCS configurations, views, and viewport configurations.

DDRMODES. DDRMODES (Dynamic Dialog dRawing MODES) controls drawing mode settings—snap, grid, blips, ortho, axis, and isoplane—by using the Drawing Aids dialog box. DDRMODES is also useful when you need to check the current status of the various drawing-mode settings.

DDSELECT. The DDSELECT command displays the Entity Selection Settings dialog box, in which you can tell AutoCAD LT which object selection modes to use when forming a selection set of objects that you want to edit.

DDUCS. DDUCS (Dynamic Dialog User Coordinate Systems) controls User Coordinate Systems (UCSs) through the UCS Control dialog box. You can change the current UCS, rename a previously defined UCS, list the specifications of a UCS, and delete a UCS through the DDUCS dialog box.

DDUCSP. DDUCSP opens the UCS Orientation dialog box, which enables you to choose predefined UCSs.

DDUNITS. AutoCAD LT allows for the display of coordinates, distances, and angles in several formats, so that, depending upon your profession, you can measure and notate in the most appropriate format. You set the format with the DDUNITS command. The main features of the Units Control dialog box are two sets of radio buttons. On the left, the Units buttons set the format used for distances and measurement.

DELAY. The DELAY command enables you to specify a time delay (in milliseconds) before the next command or line in a script file is processed.

DIM. The DIM command enters dimensioning mode, where AutoCAD LT displays the Dim: prompt in place of the Command: prompt and then accepts dimensioning commands and variables.

DIM1. The DIM1 command enters dimensioning mode and displays the Dim: prompt in place of the Command: prompt for one dimensioning command or variable only, then returns to the Command: prompt.

Dim: **ALIGNED.** The ALIGNED dimensioning command calculates the point-to-point dimension between the two extension-line origin points you specify and aligns the dimension line parallel to an imaginary line between the points. If you press Enter to select a line, a circle, an arc, or a 2D polyline to dimension, the dimension line aligns with the object.

Dim: **ANGULAR.** The ANGULAR dimensioning command dimensions an angle by picking one of the following object combinations: two nonparallel lines or polyline segments, an arc or polyline arc segment, a circle and another point, or three points. All object-selection methods require selection by picking points.

Dim: **BASELINE.** The BASELINE dimensioning command calculates and draws a dimension in a series from a single first extension-line origin. Create or select any linear dimension, and then use BASELINE to dimension successive distances. You enter only the second extension-line origin point for each successive dimension. Each dimension is offset from and parallel to the previous or the selected dimension and shares the same first extension-line origin.

Dim: **CENTER.** The CENTER dimensioning command draws a center mark (a cross) or a center mark and center lines in circles and arcs. The DIMCEN dimension variable controls the center-mark size and whether center lines also are drawn.

F

`Dim:` **CONTINUE.** The CONTINUE dimensioning command dimensions multiple distances, each measured from the previous or selected second extension-line origin. You create or select any linear dimension, and then you use CONTINUE to dimension successive distances. AutoCAD LT aligns each dimension with the previous or selected linear dimension and uses its second extension line as the new first extension line. You enter only the second extension-line origin point for each successive dimension.

`Dim:` **DIAMETER.** The DIAMETER dimensioning command dimensions arcs and circles. The dimension line is placed at the point where you pick the arc or circle. Whether the text is placed inside or outside the circle depends on the size of the text compared to the size of the circle. Several dimension variables, explained later in this chapter, also control the text placement.

`Dim:` **EXIT.** The EXIT dimensioning command leaves dimensioning mode and returns you to the `Command:` prompt.

`Dim:` **HOMETEXT.** The HOMETEXT dimensioning command restores associative dimension text to its original default position. You can use this command after you modify the text location. The **M**odify pull-down menu item for this command is **H**ome Position.

`Dim:` **HORIZONTAL.** The HORIZONTAL dimensioning command draws a horizontal dimension line. You can pick the first and second extension-line origins, or you can press Enter to select an object to dimension.

`Dim:` **LEADER.** The LEADER dimensioning command draws an arrowhead, one or more leader lines at any angle, and horizontal text.

`Dim:` **NEWTEXT.** The NEWTEXT dimensioning command changes selected existing associative dimension text; or, if you press Enter at the new text prompt, the NEWTEXT command restores selected existing associative dimension text to its default measured value. The **M**odify pull-down menu item for this command is **C**hange Text.

`Dim:` **OBLIQUE.** The OBLIQUE dimensioning command changes existing associative extension-line angles without changing the dimension text value. Press Enter at the angle prompt to restore the default angle.

`Dim:` **ORDINATE.** The ORDINATE dimensioning command draws a leader line and calculates dimension text for ordinate or datum dimensions. The text aligns with the leader line. You pick the feature to dimension (the leader's first point) and the leader endpoint. This command calculates the distance along the X or Y axis from 0,0 to the feature point, depending on the first (feature) and second leader points.

`Dim:` **RADIUS.** The RADIUS dimensioning command dimensions the radius of an arc or a circle. The point where you select the radius determines the leader placement for the radius dimension.

`Dim:` **ROTATED.** The ROTATED dimensioning command calculates the dimension and draws the dimension line at any specified angle. You can pick the first and second extension-line origins, or you can press Enter to select a line, a circle, an arc, or a polyline to dimension. ROTATED draws the extension lines perpendicular to the dimension line.

`Dim:` **TEDIT.** The TEDIT (DIMension Text Edit) dimensioning command relocates existing dimension text. You can drag the dimension text into place with your pointing device; specify left, right, or home (original) justification; or specify a text angle.

`Dim:` **TROTATE.** The TROTATE (Text Rotate) dimensioning command rotates existing dimension text to any angle.

`Dim:` **UNDO.** The UNDO dimensioning command cancels the latest dimensioning command, including any dimension variable settings made since the previous command. You can repeat UNDO to step back to the beginning of the current dimensioning session. After you exit dimensioning mode, however, AutoCAD LT treats the entire dimensioning session as a single step.

`Dim:` **UPDATE.** The UPDATE dimensioning command changes selected existing associative dimension objects to the current unit, text style, dimension style, and dimension variable settings. The **M**odify pull-down menu item for this command is **U**pdate Dimension.

`Dim:` **VERTICAL.** The VERTICAL dimensioning command draws a vertical dimension line. You can pick the first and second extension-line origins, or you can press Enter to select an object to dimension.

DIST. The DIST command calculates and displays the distance, angle, and X,Y,Z offsets between any two points that you specify.

DIVIDE. The DIVIDE command places point objects or blocks along the length or perimeter of existing objects, at intervals determined by the number of segments you specify. The point objects or blocks are placed in the Previous selection set for later selection.

DLINE. The DLINE command is used to construct parallel line and arc segments at a specified offset width.

DONUT. The DONUT command is used to create circular polylines that can vary in width. A donut is created by specifying an inside diameter and an outside diameter.

F

DSVIEWER. The DSVIEWER command opens the Aerial View, which enables you to interactively pan and zoom the drawing in the current viewport of the graphics window.

ELEV. The ELEV command enables you to specify the current object elevation and thickness (stored in the ELEVATION and THICKNESS system variables) for 3D work. It is generally better to use a UCS setting in lieu of setting an elevation. You can also use the DDEMODES command (Entity Creation Modes dialog box) to set elevation and thickness.

END. The END command saves the drawing and closes AutoCAD LT.

EXPLODE. The EXPLODE command replaces selected polylines with line and arc segments, or inserted blocks with the constituent objects of their block definitions. Mirrored or unequally scaled blocks cannot be exploded.

DTEXT. The DTEXT command places text objects in a drawing. It prompts for insertion point, text style, justification, height, and rotation, and places one or more lines of text, either directly below the first or at other locations selected. Preview text appears on-screen as it is entered.

DVIEW. The DVIEW command enables you to dynamically adjust the view of your drawing. After the DVIEW command is issued, you are prompted to select a representative sample of objects to help you set the view. Because the DVIEW command is interactive, you do not usually want to select all the objects in your drawing. The more objects you select, the slower the dynamic display updates. When you are finished setting the view, the entire drawing is displayed, using the parameters you specified in the DVIEW command. Pressing Enter at the Select objects: prompt uses AutoCAD's default DVIEW image (a house) to help you specify the view.

DXFOUT. The DXFOUT command exports drawing objects using the Drawing Interchange Format defined by Autodesk. The file that is created has a DXF extension and is composed of ASCII information that can be modified with a variety of file-editing programs. This information includes object properties such as layer names, linetypes, and colors, as well as full coordinate information for each object within the drawing.

ELLIPSE. The ELLIPSE command is used to create zero-width polylines simulating an elliptical shape. In AutoCAD LT, you can create an ellipse by specifying the major-and minor-axis endpoints, the endpoints of one axis, and a rotation angle (as if rotating a circle on a diameter axis) or by specifying the center point and the axis endpoints.

ERASE. The ERASE command deletes a selection set from the drawing database.

EXTEND. The EXTEND command projects selected lines, arcs, and open polylines to meet selected boundary edges. You can use lines, arcs, circles, and polylines as boundary edges. You can select an object as both a boundary edge and as an object to extend.

FILEOPEN. Opens an existing drawing file, prompting for the name at the command line. If the FILEDIA system variable is off (0), the OPEN command, which otherwise opens the Open Drawing dialog box, acts identically to FILEOPEN.

FILL. FILL turns the filling of solids and wide polylines on and off for display and plotting. The setting is stored in the FILLMODE system variable.

FILLET. The FILLET command creates an arc between any combination of two lines, circles, or arcs. You also can use FILLET to create an arc between two adjacent segments of a 2D polyline, or at all vertices of a single 2D polyline. If the selected objects do not intersect, or if they extend past their intersection, FILLET extends or trims them as needed. You also can use FILLET to set a default fillet radius (initially 0) that is used by subsequent FILLET commands.

GETENV. The GETENV command returns the value of a specified setting from the ACLT.INI file, for use in menu programming.

GRAPHSCR. GRAPHSCR displays the AutoCAD LT Release 2 graphics window, for display control by menus and scripts.

GRID. The GRID command controls the visibility and spacing of a visual reference grid of dots. The grid can also be set by using the Drawing Aids dialog box, without issuing the GRID command.

HATCH. The HATCH command is used to apply a predefined pattern (or poche) to an area. A boundary selection set must be specified in addition to the pattern name, scale, and rotation angle of the pattern. User-specified patterns consisting of only evenly spaced lines also can be used.

HATCHEDIT. The HATCHEDIT command opens the Hatchedit dialog box, which enables you to modify and update an associative hatch pattern created by BHATCH.

HELP. The HELP (or ?) command opens the AutoCAD LT Help window in Windows.

HIDE. The HIDE command removes hidden lines of a 3D model from the current viewpoint. HIDE enables you to get a better understanding of where elements in a 3D model are located in relation to each other. The hidden lines are not actually removed from the drawing database, but simply not displayed in the drawing area. The REDRAW command or any command that redraws or regenerates the drawing will cause the hidden lines to be visible again.

F

ID. The ID command prompts for a point and returns the X, Y, and Z coordinates of the point specified. The system variable LASTPOINT is set to the coordinates returned. Normally, the current elevation setting is used for the Z value. You can pick the point, and you can use snap, object snap, point filters, and absolute or relative coordinates.

INSERT. The INSERT and DDINSERT (Insert dialog box) commands insert an image of and reference to a previously defined block, or they insert a drawing file to create a block definition as well as an image of and reference to that new definition. The inserted block reference is a single object, regardless of the number of objects in the drawing file or previously defined block. If, however, the block name is prefaced with an asterisk (like ***NUT10**) with the INSERT command or the **E**xplode box in the Insert dialog box is checked, AutoCAD LT simply copies the objects in the block definition or drawing file and does not create a block reference or definition. The INSERT command and Insert dialog box have options for listing defined blocks, and for specifying the block's insertion point, scale, and rotation.

ISOPLANE. The ISOPLANE command sets the current isometric drawing plane in isometric snap/grid mode. You also can use the F5 or Ctrl+E keys or the DDRMODES command (Drawing Aids dialog box) to set the isoplane.

LAYER. The LAYER command offers the same control over layers as does the Layer Control dialog box (except for freezing of layers in specific mview viewports in paper space). LAYER's options—? (lists layers), Make (creates and sets current layer), Set (current), New, ON, OFF, Color, Ltype, Freeze, Thaw, LOck, and Unlock—provide the same functions as the features of the Layer Control dialog box. For an explanation of these features, see the previous option list for the Layer Control dialog box.

LIMITS. The LIMITS command defines the drawing area by the coordinates of its lower left and upper right corners. This command sets the extents of the grid in the World Coordinate System and defines the minimum area for the ZOOM All command.

LINE. The LINE command draws one or more straight 2D or 3D line segments. Press Enter at the From point: prompt to continue from the endpoint of the last line drawn or tangent to the last arc drawn. Enter **C** at the To point: prompt to close two or more line segments, creating a line from the last endpoint to the original start point. Press Enter or cancel at the To point: prompt to end the LINE command.

LINETYPE. The LINETYPE command enables you to load new linetypes into a drawing, list the currently loaded linetypes, and set the current new object linetype. This command is also used to create user-defined linetypes on the fly.

LIST. The LIST command prompts for a selection set, changes to the text window, and lists the object data for each selected object.

LTSCALE. The LTSCALE command enables you to set the linetype scale, the relative length of broken linetypes.

MEASURE. The MEASURE command places point objects or blocks along the length or perimeter of existing objects, at intervals determined by a distance you specify. The point objects or blocks are placed in the Previous selection set for later selection.

MINSERT. MINSERT is similar to a combination of the INSERT and ARRAY commands. MINSERT is limited to rectangular arrays. It inserts multiple images of, and a single reference to, a previously defined block (or a drawing file which it inserts to create a block definition). The inserted block array is a single object, regardless of the number of rows and columns or objects in the drawing file or previously defined block. You cannot preface the block name with an asterisk (like *NUT10) with the MINSERT command, and you cannot explode an array created with MINSERT. The MINSERT command has options for listing defined blocks, for specifying the block's insertion point, scale, and rotation, and for specifying the number and spacing of the rows and columns in the array it creates.

MIRROR. The MIRROR command creates a mirror image of selected objects. The selected entities can be retained (the default) or deleted.

MOVE. The MOVE command relocates selected objects by the 2D or 3D displacement you specify. You can indicate the displacement by two points, from which a relative distance and angle for the move is derived. Or you can specify a coordinate value at the first displacement prompt and press Enter at the second displacement prompt, in which case the coordinate value is interpreted as the relative distance and angle, or displacement, for the move.

MSLIDE. The MSLIDE command makes a slide image file of the contents of the current viewport.

MSPACE. The MSPACE command activates a floating mview viewport so that you can work in that viewport in the model space environment. This command functions only when TILEMODE is set to 0 and is effective only if there is a current floating mview viewport to activate.

MULTIPLE. The MULTIPLE command causes the next command to repeat until cancelled.

MVIEW. The MVIEW command creates viewports in paper space and controls the display of objects in those viewports. This command functions only when TILEMODE is set to 0.

NEW. The NEW command is used to create a new drawing in AutoCAD LT. A drawing name can be assigned, and a prototype drawing can be designated.

F

OFFSET. The OFFSET command creates a parallel copy of a selected line, circle, arc, or 2D polyline. The copy is created offset by a specified distance or drawn through a selected point (the initial default).

OOPS. The OOPS command restores the objects that were erased with the last ERASE command. (The BLOCK command, covered in Chapter 13, "Using Object Properties and Text Styles," also performs an erase operation, and OOPS will restore those objects as well.) OOPS restores the erased objects, even if other commands have been used after the ERASE command. OOPS only restores objects erased in the last erase operation; objects erased in earlier erase operations cannot be restored.

OPEN. The OPEN command closes the current drawing (prompting you to save any changes) and retrieves a specified drawing file from disk. You can specify the path as well as the file name.

ORTHO. The ORTHO command turns on and off the orthogonal cursor constraint. You also can use the F8 or Ctrl+O keys, the Ortho button on the toolbar, or the Drawing Aids dialog box to control ortho.

OSNAP. The OSNAP command enables you to set running object snap modes. You also can use the DDOSNAP command (Running Object Snap dialog box) to set running object snap modes.

PAN. The PAN command moves the view up, down, and sideways in the drawing without changing the current zoom magnification. You can pick points or enter a displacement (offset). PAN has no command options.

PASTECLIP. The PASTECLIP command takes any AutoCAD LT compatible information in the Windows Clipboard and places it into the drawing. The information is stored as a block object, which you can explode.

PEDIT. The PEDIT command enables you to alter a polyline. With PEDIT, you can add or move vertices, change overall and vertex width values, and break and straighten polylines. You also can apply three types of curves to a polyline.

PLAN. The PLAN command enables you to set the 3D viewpoint of the current viewport to the current UCS, a specific UCS, or the WCS.

PLINE. The PLINE command enables you to construct a single polyline object consisting of line and arc segments joined at their endpoints. A polyline can be opened or closed. A polyline contains width information for each vertex.

PLOT. The PLOT command is used to generate output from AutoCAD LT. This command outputs the current drawing in the form of hard-copy paper plots or in plot files. You can specify the drawing area to plot by current view, the drawing extents, the current limits, a named view, or a user-specified window. You can output the plot data to the default Windows printer or HPGL device or to a file on disk. The PLOT command uses the Plot Configuration dialog box, unless the CMDDIA system variable is set to 0 (off). If CMDDIA is off, or if the plot is initiated by a script file, then command line plotting prompts are used.

POINT. The POINT command draws a point object with X,Y,Z coordinates anywhere in space. Points are sometimes used for reference marks and as nodes to snap to with the NODe object snap mode.

POLYGON. The POLYGON command creates multisided polygons consisting of from 3 to 1,024 sides. The POLYGON command creates a polyline with no width value.

PREFERENCES. The PREFERENCES command opens the Preferences dialog box, which enables you to set your preferences for support and temporary file names and paths, interface colors and fonts, toolbar and toolbox availability, English/metric prototype default, automatic save, file locking, user name, default menu file, and beep-on-error warning.

PSOUT. The PSOUT command exports drawing data to an Encapsulated PostScript (EPS) file. This file can be used with a variety of PostScript-compatible software for page layout and printing at high resolutions. The use of this command is similar to using the PLOT command.

PSPACE. The PSPACE command switches from an active mview viewport to paper space. This command functions only when TILEMODE is set to 0.

PURGE. The PURGE command removes definitions of unused blocks, dimension and text styles, layers, linetypes, and shapes from a drawing. The PURGE command must be used on a newly opened drawing, before any drawing or editing commands are used. When you enter any option (type of named item), PURGE prompts for confirmation for purging each unreferenced definition of that type.

QSAVE. The QSAVE command saves your drawing to a file on disk. The current drawing's path and file name are used if a name has been assigned. If the file already exists, the SAVE command first renames it with a BAK extension. If the current drawing is unnamed, QSAVE opens the Save Drawing As dialog box.

RECTANG. The RECTANG command creates a rectangular polyline using the current polyline width. The rectangle is created by specifying its two opposite corners.

REDO. The REDO command restores everything undone by a U or UNDO command, if REDO is used immediately after the U or UNDO command. REDO reverses only a single previous U or UNDO command.

REDRAW. The REDRAW command cleans up the image in the current viewport, erasing blips and artifacts of edits.

F

REGEN. The REGEN command recalculates and regenerates the drawing and redraws all viewports, and updates the drawing database index to optimize display and selection operations.

RENAME. The RENAME command changes the names of blocks, dimension styles, layers, linetypes, text styles, UCSs, views, and viewports. All eight of its options work the same, prompting for the old name and then for the new name.

RESUME. The RESUME command restarts a paused script.

ROTATE. The ROTATE command rotates objects in the X,Y plane around a specified base point using a relative rotation angle that you enter or a reference angle that you indicate by picking points.

REVDATE. The REVDATE command inserts a revision date/time block consisting of three attributes: user name, current date and time, and drawing name.

RSCRIPT. The RSCRIPT command repeats a script.

SAVE. The SAVE command saves your drawing to a file on disk. The current drawing's path and file name are used if a name has been assigned. If the file already exists, the SAVE command first renames it with a BAK extension. If the current drawing is unnamed, SAVE opens the Save Drawing As dialog box.

SAVEAS. The SAVEAS command saves your drawing to a file on disk after renaming it. You can assign a new path as well as a new file name.

SAVEDIB. The SAVEDIB command (SAVE Device Independent Bitmap) saves the contents of the current AutoCAD LT graphics window (the drawing image(s), toolbar, toolbox, and the command lines) to a BMP file as a bit mapped image.

SCALE. The SCALE command changes the size of existing objects relative to a specified base point, by a specified scale factor, by referencing one specified distance to another, or by a combination of these two methods.

SCRIPT. The SCRIPT command runs the specified script file. A script file is an ASCII text file, a macro file of commands, options, and other imput just as you would type them at the AutoCAD command line.

SELECT. The SELECT command creates a selection set that you can later recall by using the Previous object selection option. Select can use all the selection options.

SETENV. The SETENV command sets the value of a specified setting in the ACLT.INI file for use in menu programming.

SETVAR. The SETVAR command lists and changes the values of system variables. You can enter a specific variable to change, or enter a question mark (?) to list one or more variables.

SHADE. The SHADE command renders a flat-shaded 3D image of the drawing in the current viewport. The shading method and ambient/diffuse light settings are controlled by the SHADEDGE and SHADEDIF system variables.

SNAP. The SNAP command turns the snap grid on and off, and sets its spacing. It also provides options for setting Aspect (different X and Y values) and switching to an isometric snap grid. The snap grid settings can also be made by using the Drawing Aids dialog box, without issuing the SNAP command.

SOLID. The SOLID command draws a 2D solid-filled object defined by three or four corner points.

STRETCH. The STRETCH command stretches objects that cross a crossing window. You can stretch lines, arcs, solids, traces, polylines (including all polyline and polyface meshes), and 3Dfaces. For stretchable objects, endpoints that lie inside the crossing window are moved while endpoints outside the window remain fixed. All objects entirely in the window move. Text, blocks, shapes, and circles move only if their insert or center points are in the window.

STYLE. The STYLE command enables you to create, name, and recall sets of text style parameters including font, text height, text width, and obliquing angle, as well as backwards, upside-down, and vertical orientation. The STYLE command sets a newly defined text style or a changed text style as the current style for the drawing.

TEXT. The TEXT command places text objects in a drawing. It prompts for insertion point, text style, justification, height, and rotation, and places one line of text. Unlike the DTEXT command, TEXT does not preview text on-screen as it is entered.

TEXTSCR. TEXTSCR displays the AutoCAD LT Release 2 text window, for display control by menus and scripts.

TIME. The TIME command displays the current time (and date) and, for the current drawing, the time created, time last updated, total editing time, elapsed timer reading (since last being reset), next automatic save time. With TIME's options, you can redisplay the time, turn the timer on and off, and reset the timer.

TOOLBOX. The TOOLBOX command cycles the toolbox to the next of each of its four positions.

TRIM. The TRIM command removes portions of lines, arcs, circles, and 2D polylines that cross a selected cutting edge. You can select lines, circles, arcs, and polylines as cutting edges. An object can act as a cutting edge *and* be an object that is trimmed within the same command.

U. The U command undoes or reverses the effects of the last previous command.

F

UCS. The UCS command is used to set up and manage User Coordinate Systems. It provides a range of options, including setting the origin, specifying rotation about any axis, aligning with objects, saving, listing, and restoring.

UCSICON. The UCSICON command controls the visibility and placement of the UCS Icon.

UNDO. The UNDO command reverses the effect(s) of one or more previous commands, and can step back through the drawing to its state at the beginning of the drawing session. The UNDO command includes options for controlling how many previous drawing steps are stored, controlling how far back to undo previous steps, grouping operations as if single steps, and for turning off the undo feature.

UNITS. The UNITS command enables you to set the current linear and angular drawing units and precision. The DDUNITS command provides the same functions, but in an easier-to-use dialog box.

UNLOCK. The UNLOCK command opens the File(s) to Unlock dialog box, which enables you to unlock locked files.

VIEW. The VIEW command saves the current viewport's view or a user-specified window as a named view (up to 31 characters). Saved views are then restored with the VIEW Restore option.

VPLAYER. The VPLAYER (ViewPort LAYER) command controls which layers are visible in specific mview viewports. TILEMODE must be off (0) for this command to function.

VPOINT. The VPOINT command is used to view an object in the graphics area from any location in AutoCAD LT's 3D space. When you use this command, AutoCAD LT zooms to the drawing's extents as seen from the new viewing location.

VPORTS or VIEWPORTS. With the TILEMODE system variable set to 1 (1 = on, which is the default), the VPORTS command divides your screen into tiled viewports. The current view (viewpoint or perspective) and the SNAP, GRID, ISOMETRIC, and UCSICON settings can differ in each viewport. Each viewport can be zoomed independently.

VPORTS. The VPORTS command is used to create and arrange model space viewports. Each viewport serves as an independent viewing location into the drawing. This allows different viewports to contain different views of the model space elements. Any viewport can be made active by clicking in the viewport, or by pressing Ctrl+V.

VSLIDE. The VSLIDE command displays a specified slide image file in the current viewport.

WBLOCK. The WBLOCK command creates a new drawing file or replaces an existing one with the data you select from the current drawing. As data to export, you can specify a block name defined in the current drawing, or press Enter and specify an insertion base point and select objects to export, or enter * to export the entire current drawing. Selected objects are erased upon completion. The WBLOCK command does *not* create a new block, either in the current drawing or in the drawing file it creates. The 0,0 base point of the new file is the insertion base point of the specified block, or the point specified at the `Insertion base point:` prompt for selected objects, or the 0,0 point of the current UCS if you enter * to export the entire drawing. Settings such as units, limits, snap, and grid are also exported.

WMFIN. The WMF command is used to import objects that have been saved to a file with a WMF extension. The data in the Metafile does not contain drawing data such as layer names and linetypes, and 3D information, so some modification of the final entities might be necessary.

WMFOUT. The WMFOUT command exports drawing objects using the Windows Metafile Format. This format stores objects as a series of records that correspond to Windows graphic drawing commands. The Metafile can then be read by other programs that support the WMF format.

WMFOPTS. The WMFOPTS command sets the options that control how objects such as rectangles, circles, and polygons are imported by WMFIN.

XBIND. The XBIND command enables you to convert specified dependent symbols (blocks, dimension or text styles, layers, linetypes, UCSs, views, and tiled viewports) that are defined in an externally referenced drawing into normal blocks, dimension or text styles, layers, linetypes, UCSs, views, and tiled viewports. You specify what type of symbol to bind at the initial `Block/Dimstyle/LAyer/LType/Style:` prompt, and XBIND prompts for a specific symbol name of that type. You can enter a single name, or several names separated by commas, or use wild cards. Each specified symbol is bound and becomes independently available in the current drawing. If a bound item references another dependent symbol in the xref, that other symbol is also bound. Binding a layer, for example, causes a linetype assigned to that layer to be bound as well.

XREF. The XREF command attaches references to external drawings, in a manner similar to inserting a block. The primary difference between an xref and a block is that a block is defined in the current drawing, while the xref's data resides entirely in the external drawing's database. Only a reference to the external file is placed in the current drawing's database. The XREF command options enable you to attach, detach, and list xrefs, to reload or respecify the path to an external drawing file to update the xref, and to bind (convert to a normal block) specified xrefs. Once bound, the named items defined in the external drawing, such as blocks, dimension or text styles, layers, linetypes, UCSs, views, and tiled viewports, can be used independently in the current drawing.

F

ZOOM. The ZOOM command controls the display in the current viewport, zooming in (magnifying the image) or zooming out (shrinking the image). Zoom in to view a small part of the drawing in greater detail, or zoom out to view a larger part in less detail.

Table F.1 shows the AutoCAD LT aliases, or convenient abbreviations for use at the keyboard, for most commands and selected settings. **Bold** type indicates aliases for AutoCAD LT Release 1 only, and *bold italic* type indicates aliases for AutoCAD LT Release 2 only.

TABLE F.1
Command Aliases

Command	Alias	Command	Alias	Command	Alias
ABOUT	AB	COLOR	CO	DDOSNAP	OS
APERTURE	AP	COPY	CP	DDRENAME	DR
ARC	A	COPYCLIP	CC	DDRMODES	DA
AREA	AA	COPYEMBED	CE	DDSELECT	SL
ARRAY	AR	COPYIMAGE	CI	DDUCS	UC
ATTDEF	AD	COPYLINK	CL	DDUCSP	UP
ATTDISP	AT	DDATTDEF	DAD	DDUNITS	DU
ATTEDIT	AE	DDATTE	DE	DIM	D
ATTEXT	AX	DDATTEXT	DAX	DIM1	D1
BASE	BA	DDCHPROP	DC	DIST	DI
BLIPMODE	BM	DDEDIT	ED	DLINE	DL
BLOCK	B	DDEDIT	TE	DONUT	DO
BREAK	BR	DDEMODES	EM	DSVIEWER	DS
CHAMFER	CF	DDGRIPS	GR	DTEXT	DT
CHANGE	CH	DDIM	DM	DTEXT	T
CHPROP	CR	DDINSERT	I	DVIEW	DV
CIRCLE	C	DDLMODES	LD	DXFIN	DN

Command	Alias	Command	Alias	Command	Alias
DXFOUT	DX	MINSERT	MN	PREFERENCES	PF
ELEV	EV	MIRROR	MI	PSLTSCALE	PC
ELLIPSE	EL	MOVE	M	PSOUT	PU
ERASE	ETH	MSLIDE	ML	PSPACE	PS
EXIT	**ET**	MSPACE	MS	PURGE	PR
EXIT	**Q**	MULTIPLE	MU	QTEXT	AT
EXIT	**QUIT**	MVIEW	MV	*QUIT*	*ET*
EXPLODE	EP	NEW	N	*QUIT*	*EXIT*
EXPLODE	X	OFFSET	OF	*QUIT*	*Q*
EXTEND	EX	OOPS	OO	RECTANG	RC
FILL	FL	OPEN	OP	REDO	RE
FILLET	F	ORTHO	OR	REDRAW	R
GRID	H	OSNAP	O	REGEN	RG
HATCH	H	PAN	P	RENAME	RN
HIDE	HI	PASTECLIP	PC	ROTATE	RO
INSERT	IN	PEDIT	PE	SAVE	SA
ISOPLANE	IS	PICKBOX	PB	SAVEAS	SS
LAYER	LA	PLAN	PV	SCALE	SC
LIMITS	LM	PLINE	PL	SCRIPT	SR
LINE	L	PLINEGEN	PN	SELECT	SE
LINETYPE	LT	PLOT	PP	SHADE	SH
LIST	LS	POINT	PT	SHADEDGE	SD
LTSCALE	LC	POLYGON	PG	SNAP	SN

continues

TABLE F.1, CONTINUED
Command Aliases

Command	Alias	Command	Alias	Command	Alias
SOLID	SO	UCSICON	UI	VSLIDE	VS
STRETCH	S	UNDO	UN	WBLOCK	W
STYLE	ST	UNITS	UT	WMFIN	WI
TEXT	TX	UNLOCK	FILES	WMFOUT	WO
THICKNESS	TH	UNLOCK	UL	XBIND	XB
TILEMODE	TM	VIEW	V	XPLODE	X
TIME	TI	VIEWPORTS	VW	EXREF	XR
TOOLBOX	TL	VPLAYER	VL	ZOOM	Z
TRIM	TR	VPOINT	VP		

The IALT Disk

A disk called the IALT Disk is included with *Inside AutoCAD LT for Windows, Second Edition.* The book and disk are designed for use on your AutoCAD LT workstation. The disk provides starting drawings and support files for many of the exercises, thus saving you time by bypassing initial drawing setup requirements. For example, if you want to learn about dimensioning, but you do not want to first create a drawing to dimension, you can move right to the dimensioning section by using a preset drawing from the disk.

The disk also includes the following useful extras:

◆ A bug list for AutoCAD LT Release 1 users

◆ Free architectural AutoCAD text fonts

◆ LTHook, a shareware program for assigning macros to keystrokes such as F3, Alt+J, or Ctrl+L

◆ An update patch from Autodesk for AutoCAD LT Release 1 c1 users

◆ An updated HPGL plotter driver from Autodesk for AutoCAD LT Release 1

◆ LT_BASIC, a BASIC Interpreter for programming AutoCAD LT

These items can be installed all at the same time, or some can be installed individually as needed.

Note   Your hard drive letter or directory names might differ from those shown in this appendix. If they do, substitute your hard drive letter and directory names wherever you encounter drive letters (such as the C in C:) or the directory names (such as \ACLTWIN) in this appendix. If your disk drive is not drive A, substitute your drive letter for A where A: is shown.

Installing the IALT Disk

The setup for *Inside AutoCAD LT for Windows, Second Edition* exercises requires you to set aside space on your hard disk for a directory called \DWGS\IALT. This setup ensures that any AutoCAD LT drawings used for the exercises in the book do not interfere with any other AutoCAD LT projects that you or your coworkers may be working on. Also, you can easily remove all practice files after you are through with the book's exercises. The installation program creates the \DWGS\IALT directory and then copies the files into it. The installation program also creates a program group for Inside AutoCAD LT for Windows and a startup icon you use when you want to use AutoCAD LT to perform the exercises in this book.

The following installation instructions assume that you are using the DOS operating system with Microsoft Windows 3.1, that AutoCAD LT is installed in the C:\ACLTWIN directory, and that AutoCAD LT runs and is configured properly.

Now you are ready to install the IALT Disk files.

Installing the IALT Disk

Put the IALT Disk in disk drive A: and open the Windows Program Manager.

Choose **F**ile, *then* **R**un   Displays the Run dialog box

In the **C**ommand Line *text box, type* **A:INSTALL**   Executes the installation program
then click on OK

The installation program prompts you and offers defaults for all necessary information. If you change the default parameters, be sure to follow the steps in the following section to make similar changes to the startup icon properties.

Choose Full Install to install everything, or choose Custom Install then Inside AutoCAD LT for Windows to install the minimum files.

G

| *In the Book Updates Readme dialog box, click on the* OK *button when you are finished reading the UPDATE.TXT file* | Closes the window and completes the IALT Disk installation |

The installation creates the Inside AutoCAD LT for Windows program group, shown in figure G.1. Even if you choose not to install all options, their "Readme" icons appear for more information. If you do choose to install all components, you will see additional icons.

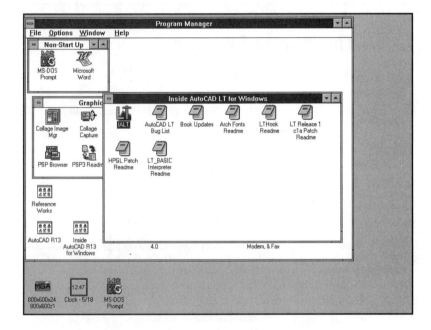

Figure G.1

The Inside AutoCAD LT for Windows program group.

Next, you need to test the installation and to ensure that you are using the default IALT prototype drawing.

Starting AutoCAD LT and Checking the Prototype Drawing

Now that the command line has been defined and the proper files copied to the IALT directory, you can start AutoCAD LT by double-clicking on the AutoCAD LT icon that the installation program created (or that you just modified).

Stop Always use this icon to start AutoCAD LT for use in this book. Otherwise, you might have trouble locating the book's files.

Also, if you or others have been using your AutoCAD LT installation for other work, you need to ensure that you are using the default ACLT prototype drawing so it matches this book's expectations. Use the version of the following two exercises that matches your version of AutoCAD LT—AutoCAD LT Release 1 or AutoCAD LT Release 2.

Checking Your AutoCAD LT Release 1 Installation and Checking the Prototype

Double-click on the IALT icon you installed	Starts AutoCAD LT Release 1
After the Command: *prompt appears,* *choose* File, New	Opens the Create New Drawing dialog box
_new	
Click on the New Drawing Name *button*	Opens the Create Drawing File dialog box

Under the **D**irectories label, the current path should display c:\dwgs\ialt, unless you specified a different directory when installing the IALT Disk.

Double-click in the File Name *edit box, then type* **ACLT** *and choose* OK	Closes the Create Drawing File dialog box and displays C:\DWGS\IALT\ACLT.DWG in the New **D**rawing Name edit box
Put a check in the **N**o Prototype *check box,* *then choose* OK	Ensures that the default settings are used and starts a new drawing
Command: *Choose* File, Save	Saves the new drawing in the IALT directory
_qsave	
Command: *Choose* File, New	Opens the Create New Drawing dialog box
If the Prototype *edit box does not display* ACLT *(with no path or the* \dwgs\ialt *path), double-click in it and enter* **ACLT**, *then put a check mark in the* **R**etain as Default *check box*	Sets the default prototype to the new file you just created

New Riders Publishing
INSIDE
SERIES

G

Choose OK	Starts a new, unnamed drawing with your new prototype
Choose **F**ile, E**x**it	Exits AutoCAD LT Release 1

Checking Your AutoCAD LT Release 2 Installation and Checking the Prototype

Double-click on the IALT icon you installed	Starts AutoCAD LT Release 2

After several moments, the Create New Drawing dialog box appears. If not, when the Command: prompt appears, choose **F**ile, then **N**ew to display the dialog box, and put a check in the **S**how This Dialog at Startup check box.

Make sure the **N**one *radio button is on in the* Setup Method *area, then clear the* **U**se Prototype *check box, then choose* OK	Ensures that the default settings are used and starts a new drawing
Command: *Choose* **F**ile, Save **A**s	Opens the Save Drawing As dialog box

`_saveas`

Under the **D**irectories label, the current path should display `c:\dwgs\ialt`, unless you specified a different directory when installing the IALT Disk.

In the File **N**ame *edit box, type* **ACLT**, *then choose* OK	Closes the Save Drawing As dialog box and saves the new drawing in the IALT directory

`Current drawing name set to C:\DWGS\IALT\ACLT.`

Command: *Choose* **F**ile, **N**ew	Opens the Create New Drawing dialog box
If the **P**rototype *edit box does not display* ACLT *or aclt.dwg (with no path or the \dwgs\ialt path), double-click* ? *in it and enter* **ACLT**, *then put a check mark in the* **R**etain as Default *check box*	Sets the default prototype to the new file you just created
Choose OK	Starts a new, unnamed drawing with your new prototype
Choose **F**ile, E**x**it	Exits AutoCAD LT Release 2

Tip   To open another software application without ending your AutoCAD LT for Windows session, you can click on the Minimize (down-arrow) button in the upper right corner of the AutoCAD LT window. This step reduces the AutoCAD LT window to an icon until you double-click on it to open the window again.

Installing the IALT Disk's Text Fonts

ARCHS is a proportional, single-stroke, hand-lettering font for general use. ARCHF is a TXT.SHX replacement to use for drawing creation and check plots. Both have identical character sets and lettering spacing, and are interchangeable. All of AutoCAD's standard font characters are supported, including those entered with control codes (%%nnn). Additional special and fractional characters are entered with control codes or <ALT> keys. ARCH-SS.SHX is a "bigfont" complement font, adding uppercase and numerical subscripts and superscripts to ARCHS and ARCHF.

Installing the IALT Disk's text fonts is a simple process. You can use them in the \DWGS\FONTS subdirectory that the disk installation program creates, but it is easier if you copy or move the SHX files from the \DWGS\FONTS subdirectory to the \ACLTWIN subdirectory. If AutoCAD LT is not installed in the \ACLTWIN subdirectory, copy the SHX font files to your alternate subdirectory (the subdirectory with ACLT.EXE).

If you did not install them in the first disk installation exercise, you do not yet have the files in the \DWGS\FONTS subdirectory. In that case, you must use the IALT Disk installation program to create this subdirectory and copy the font files from the IALT Disk. Perform the following exercise only if you do not have the files in the \DWGS\FONTS subdirectory.

Installing the Font Files

Put the IALT Disk in disk drive A: and switch to Program Manager.

Choose **F***ile, then* **R***un*	Displays the Run dialog box
In the **C***ommand Line text box, type* **A:INSTALL** *then click on* OK	Executes the installation program

The installation program prompts you and offers defaults for all necessary information.

Choose the **C***ustom Install button*	Enables you to choose installation components

Choose Arch Fonts *from the component list*	Specifies the font component to install
Choose the OK *button*	Installs the fonts
Click on the OK *button*	Closes the window

See Chapter 13, "Using Object Properties and Text Styles," for the use of text styles and fonts, and Chapter 21, "Styling and Editing Dimensions," for an example of using an architectural font in dimensioning text.

Note These fonts are currently free for your evaluation and feedback. If you find them useful or have suggestions, you can provide feedback to Chris Bryant via CompuServe at 72570,1012. It might become shareware in the future.

Neither New Riders Publishing nor the authors of this book are responsible in any way for these fonts. They are provided on the IALT Disk for your convenience and evaluation.

Installing LTHook

LTHook is a keyboard macro recorder/player for AutoCAD LT Releases 1 and 2. With LTHook, you can program your keyboard to play any AutoCAD LT command or sequence of commands just as if you had typed them in at the command prompt yourself.

The LTHook files are automatically installed if you performed a full installation of the IALT Disk. If you performed a custom installation of the IALT Disk and did not install the LTHook component, you must use the IALT Disk installation program to install LTHook.

The following exercise shows you how to install LTHook.

Installing LTHook

Put the IALT Disk in disk drive A: and switch to Program Manager.

Choose **F**ile, *then* **R**un	Displays the Run dialog box
In the **C**ommand Line *text box, type* **A:INSTALL** *then click on* OK	Executes the installation program

continues

continued

The installation program prompts you and offers defaults for all necessary information.

Choose the **C**ustom Install *button*	Enables you to choose installation components
Choose LTHook *from the component list*	Specifies the component to install
Choose the OK *button*	Installs LTHook
Click on the OK *button*	Closes the window
Double-click on the LTHook Readme icon in the Inside AutoCAD LT for Windows program group	Provides information on LTHook

The installation program automatically creates a startup icon for LTHook in the Inside AutoCAD LT for Windows program group. Double-click on the LTHook icon to start LTHook. It starts minimized, at the bottom of the Windows desktop. Double-click on it to open it. Use its **H**elp button for more information.

 Note LTHook is a shareware program, provided on the IALT Disk for your convenience and evaluation. If you find it useful and continue to use it, you must register it with Command Software & Consulting and pay $19. See the ORDER.TXT and LICENSE.TXT files in the \DWGS\LTHOOK directory for information. (The author of LTHook, William Blackmon, is also the technical editor and reviewer of this book.)

Neither New Riders Publishing nor the authors of this book are responsible in any way for LTHook. It is provided on the IALT Disk for your convenience and evaluation.

Installing the AutoCAD LT Release 1 c1a Patch

The AutoCAD LT Release 1 c1a Patch fixes a problem that caused linetypes with dots to not display correctly on all systems. This patch updates AutoCAD LT Release 1 c1 to c1a. This fix is not required for AutoCAD LT R1 c0 or AutoCAD LT Release 2, and should be used only to update AutoCAD LT Release 1 c1.

The AutoCAD LT Release 1 c1a Patch files are automatically copied to your disk if you performed a full installation of the IALT Disk. If you performed a custom installation of the IALT Disk and did not install the LT Rel. 1 c1a Patch component, you must use the IALT Disk installation program to copy the AutoCAD LT Release 1 c1a Patch files.

The following exercise shows you how to copy the AutoCAD LT Release 1 c1a Patch files.

Copying the AutoCAD LT Release 1 c1a Patch

Put the IALT Disk in disk drive A: and switch to Program Manager.

Choose **F**ile, *then* **R**un	Displays the Run dialog box
In the **C**ommand Line *text box, type* **A:INSTALL** *then click on* OK	Executes the installation program

The installation program prompts you and offers defaults for all necessary information.

Choose the **C**ustom Install *button*	Enables you to choose installation components
Choose LT Rel 1 c1a Patch *from the component list*	Specifies the component to copy
Choose the OK *button*	Copies the patch files
Click on the OK *button*	Closes the window

After you have copied the AutoCAD LT Release 1 c1a Patch files, you must execute the patch.

Executing the LT Release 1 c1a Patch

Double-click on the LT Release 1 c1a Patch Readme icon in the Inside AutoCAD LT for Windows program group and follow step 5 of the instructions that appear.

Updating AutoCAD LT Release 1's Plotter Driver

An updated plotter driver for AutoCAD LT Release 1 from Autodesk is also included on the IALT Disk. This driver provides plot device selection in AutoCAD LT, and should be used with Hewlett-Packard plotters and other plotters that are HPGL compatible. The file containing the updated HPGL driver is copied into the \DWGS\HPGL subdirectory when the full IALT Disk is installed.

 Stop If you use AutoCAD LT Release 2, do not install this driver. Its functionality is built-in in AutoCAD LT Release 2.

Even if you do not have an HPGL plotter, you should install the updated HPGL driver if you use AutoCAD LT Release 1. The updated driver enables you to have AutoCAD LT Release 1 configured for a different output device than the Windows system printer. See Chapter 23, "Producing Hard Copy," for information on using the updated driver to plot your drawings.

If you did not do a full installation of the IALT Disk, you must use the IALT Disk installation program to create the \DWGS\HPGL subdirectory and copy the driver files from the IALT Disk. Perform the following exercise only if you do not already have the files in the \DWGS\HPGL subdirectory; if you installed them in the first disk installation exercise, skip to the "Installing the Updated Plotter Driver" section.

Copying the HPGL Driver Files from the IALT Disk

Put the IALT Disk in disk drive A: and switch to Program Manager.

Choose **F**ile, *then* **R**un	Displays the Run dialog box
In the **C**ommand Line *text box, type* **A:INSTALL** *then click on* OK	Executes the installation program

The installation program prompts you and offers defaults for all necessary information.

Choose the **C**ustom Install *button*	Enables you to choose installation components

G

Choose HPGL Plotter Driver Update *from the component list*	Specifies the component to copy
Choose the OK *button*	Copies the files
Click on the OK *button*	Closes the window

Installing the Updated Plotter Driver

Follow the installation instructions that are in the README.TXT file in the \DWGS\HPGL subdirectory that was created when you installed the IALT Disk. You can double-click on the HPGL Patch Readme item in the Inside AutoCAD LT for Windows program group to read this file. In the installation instructions, specify the \DWGS\HPGL subdirectory when it asks you to copy files from the diskette or network.

 Note If you have a copy of the ACLT2.MNU file in any other directories other than ACLTWIN, copy the ACLT2.MNU file from the \DWGS\HPGL directory to those other directories. If the **F**ile menu in AutoCAD LT does not display HPGL On and HPGL Off items after you install the HPGL driver, then you need to locate and replace all copies of the ACLT2.MNU file. If you have customized your ACLT2.MNU, then see item 6 in the LTHPGL.TXT file instructions instead of copying the ACLT2.MNU file.

After you have installed the updated plotter driver, or if you use AutoCAD LT Release 2, you can delete the \DWGS\HPGL subdirectory from your hard disk. See Chapter 23, "Producing Hard Copy," for more about plotting and the updated HPGL driver.

Installing LT_BASIC

LT_BASIC is a minimal Basic Interpreter that works closely with AutoCAD LT. LT_BASIC is mainly a 2D user tool, not a tool for developing large applications. It enables AutoCAD LT users to write "more intelligent" scripts and macros. There are special commands for using it with LT. One major feature is the toolbox, where the user can add LT_BASIC commands to AutoCAD LT.

The LT_BASIC files are automatically copied to your hard disk if you performed a full installation of the IALT Disk. If you performed a custom installation of the IALT Disk and did not install the LT_BASIC component, you must use the IALT Disk installation program to copy the LT_BASIC files, as shown in the following exercise.

Copying the LT_BASIC Files

Put the IALT Disk in disk drive A: and switch to Program Manager.

Choose **F**ile, *then* **R**un	Displays the Run dialog box
In the **C**ommand Line *text box, type* **A:INSTALL** *then click on* OK	Executes the installation program

The installation program prompts you and offers defaults for all necessary information.

Choose the **C**ustom Install *button*	Enables you to choose components
Choose LT_BASIC *from the component list*	Specifies the component to copy
Choose the OK *button*	Copies the LT_BASIC files
Click on the OK *button*	Closes the window

After you have copied the AutoCAD LT_BASIC files, you must execute the LTB033.EXE file to complete the installation and to extract full documentation for LT_BASIC.

Completing the LT_BASIC Installation

Double-click on the LT_BASIC Interpreter Readme icon in the Inside AutoCAD LT for Windows program group and follow the instructions that appear.

Note LT_BASIC is a beta program and is currently free for your evaluation and feedback. If you find it useful or have suggestions, you can provide feedback to Stefan Dorsch via CompuServe at 100117,715. It might become a shareware program in the future.

Neither New Riders Publishing nor the authors of this book are responsible in any way for LT_BASIC. It is provided on the IALT Disk for your convenience and evaluation.

New Riders Publishing
INSIDE
SERIES

Index

Symbols

' (apostrophe), wild card, 396
(number sign), wild card, 396
(⌀), ANSI diameter symbol, 792
* (asterisk), wild card, 337, 370, 392, 395-396
+ option (Aerial View window), 180, 191
– (hyphen), wild card, 396
– option (Aerial View window), 180, 191
. (period), wild card, 396
< (left angle bracket), absolute polar coordinates, 87
>> (double angle brackets), transparent command prompt, 211
? (question mark), wild card, 337, 392- 393, 396
? (HELP) command, 1027
? option
  HATCH command, 652
  VIEW command, 205

  SETVAR command, 324
  UCS command, 98
@ (at sign)
  object displacement, 245
  relative coordinates, 87
  wild card, 396
[ ] (brackets), wild card, 396
[~] (bracketed tilde), wild card, 396
~ (tilde), wild card, 396
3 Point option (UCS command), 97
32-bit file access, setup, 983-984
3D models
  coordinate systems, 930-935
  lines, hiding, 922
  mview viewports, 862-863
  perspective views, 929
  shading, 923
  viewing, 921-923, 927-929
  viewports, 923-926

3D objects
creating, 935-940
editing, 935-940
isometric mode, 99
3DPOLY command, 605, 1027
3P option (CIRCLE command), 155
3point option (UCS command), 933

A

**About AutoCAD LT command (Help
pull-down menu), 59**
ABOUT command, 1027
absolute coordinates, 86-87
absolute polar coordinates, 87
ACLT.INI file, 967
ACLT.LIN file, 133
ACLT.MNU file, 133
ACLT.MNX file, 133
ACLT.PAT file, 133, 654
ACLTISO.LIN file, 133
ACLTISO.PAT file, 133
activating
layers, 376-377
paper space viewports, 845-847
active viewports, 215, 835
Add option (AREA command), 454, 461
adding
objects to selection sets, 226
tools to toolbox, 353-356
**Advanced options (Boundary Hatch
dialog box), 661-666**
Aerial View window, 54, 175-194, 246
closing, 189
dynamic zooming/panning, 189
menus, 190-194
nondynamic panning, 189
options, 180-184
PAN command, 199-201
panning, 189
Release 2 version, 184-190
scroll bars, 181

toolbar, 190-194
updating, 192
VIEW command, 201-206
ZOOM command, 194-199
zooming, 189
**AIA (American Institute of Architects)
format, layer names, 907**
aliases (commands), 44, 1046-1048
**ALIGNED dimensioning command,
782-785, 1033**
aligned dimensions, 782-785
alignment
block objects, 702-706
dimension text, 807
objects with coordinate systems, 83
point coordinates with
point filters, 430
ROTATE command, 571
text objects, 167-169
**All Control option (UNDO
command), 252**
ALL object selection method, 226
Alt+F4 key command, 128
Alt+minus key command, 247
Alt+P key command, 320
Alt+Tab key command, 209
Alt+Y key command, 365
**alternate measurement units (dimension
text), 810**
Angle option
ARC command, 150
Boundary Hatch dialog box, 660
angles
bisecting, 400
controlling with orthogonal drawing
aid, 83
included, 597
measuring, 451
ROTATE command, 569-575
**ANGULAR dimensioning command,
794-796, 1033**
angular dimensions, 794-796

anonymous block objects, **685**
ANSI diameter symbol, (⊘), **792**
aperture box (cursor), **402**
APERTURE command, **1028**
apostrophe ('), wild card, **396**
APPEND command, **975**
ARC command, **146-152, 1028**
architectural drawings
    dimension styles, 816-818
    plot sheets, 304-306
architectural measurement units, **320**
arcs
    clockwise, 151
    combining with lines, 151-152
    creating, 146-152
    dimensions, 149, 790-794, 803
    EXPLODE command, 619-621
    FILLET command, 536
    OFFSET command, 518
    orthogonal mode, 149
    polylines, 595-605
        center option, 599
        included angles, 597
        radius, 603
    radii, measuring, 448
    stretching, 266-271
    tangency to two circles, 414
area, measuring, **452-462**
AREA command, **452-462, 1028**
AREA system variable, **459**
ARRAY command, **279, 519, 699, 1028**
    multiple copies, 520
    Polar option, 523
    Rectangular option, 522
    unit cells, 522
arrays (block objects), inserting, **698-702**
Arrows dialog box, **806**
ASCII (American Standard Code for Information Interchange) characters, **123**
assigning commands to toolbox icons, **352, 356**

associative dimensions, **768**
    editing, 821-829
    object snaps, 419
    restoring, 825
    stretching, 823-825
    updating, 826
associative hatch patterns, **661**
    editing, 666-670
    updating, 670
Associative option (Boundary Hatch dialog box), **661**
asterisk (*), wild card, **337, 370, 392, 395-396**
at sign (@)
    object displacement, 245
    relative coordinates, 87
    wild card, 396
attaching xrefs, **722-725**
ATTDEF command, **708-710, 1028**
ATTDIA system variable, **715**
ATTDISP command, **719, 1028**
ATTEDIT command, **716-719, 1028**
ATTEXT command, **1028**
Attribute Definition dialog box, **708, 711**
attributes
    block objects, 467
    text
        defining, 708-712
        editing, 712, 716-719
        inserting definitions, 713-716
    xrefs, 725
AUto object selection method, **226**
Auto option (UNDO command), **251**
Auto Viewport option (Aerial View window), **180**
AutoCAD LT
    advantages, 27-28
    backups, 960
    bugs, 979
    c1a Patch, installation, 1056-1057
    compatibility with other releases, 979

data sharing capabilities, 940-948
enhancing performance, 981-987
hardware/software requirements, 959
installation, 961-967
launching, 31
network configurations, 968
plotter driver, updating, 1058
quitting, 128
system settings, 967-968
text references, 956
versus manual drafting, 26-27
AUTOEXEC.BAT files
editing, 972-973
errors, troubleshooting, 974-975
automated command sequences, 134
**Automatic Save Every: check box
(Preferences dialog box), 130**
automatic save feature, 132, 342
axes (coordinate systems), 66
displaying with UCS icon, 90
rotating, 90, 93

B

Back option (UNDO command), 251
backups (AutoCAD LT software), 960
backwards text, 504
BASE command, 757, 1028
**Base point option (stretch grip
editing), 266**
base points
block objects, 686, 690
drawings, setting, 756-759
objects, specifying for grip
editing, 279
**BASELINE dimensioning command,
778-779, 1033**
baseline dimensions, 778-779, 802
batch files, editing, 972-973
beep notification (errors), 342
**beveling corners with CHAMFER
command, 540**

**BHATCH command, 647-648, 655,
658, 1029**
Bind option (XREF command), 730
binding xrefs, 730-732
**Bird's Eye tool (Aerial View
window), 191**
bisecting angles, 400
**black-and-white screen illustrations,
optimizing, 347**
blip marks
commands, disabling, 40
object snaps, 429
BLIPMODE command, 1029
BLOCK command, 686, 742, 1029
Block Definition dialog box, 683, 742
block objects, 29, 674-675
alignment, 702-706
anonymous, 685
arrays, inserting, 698-702
attributes, 467
automated text, 707-719
base points, 686, 690
BYBLOCK properties, 747-749
BYLAYER properties, 745-746
colors, 745-751
components, restoring, 686
converting xrefs to, 724, 730-732
creating, 683-690
defining, 683-686
deleting, 763-764
editing, 738-742
explicit properties, 745
exploding, 681, 739-742
exporting, 753-756
grip editing, 759-761
grips, 259
inserting, 679-682, 690-702
*along divided/measured objects,
702-706*
drawings as, 676-682
layers, 745-751
libraries, 750-759
linetypes, 745-751

listing, 465-467
mirroring, 693-695
naming, 690
nesting in blocks/xrefs, 761-762
object manifestations, 686-690
object snaps, 419
presetting rotation/scale settings, 696-698
properties, 745-749
redefining, 742-745
rotating, 691-695, 759-760
scaling, 691-695
title, 707-719
unit scale parts, 688
block reference objects, 742
BMAKE command, 683, 1029
bond paper (plot sheet output), 901
bookmarks (drawings), 251
borders
    paper space, inserting, 841-843
    prototype drawings, 915
boundaries
    BHATCH command, 655, 658
    hatch patterns, 648-649, 662-666
BOUNDARY command, 462, 630-637, 1029
Boundary Creation dialog box, 634
Boundary Hatch dialog box, 647, 656, 663-666
Boundary option (Boundary Hatch dialog box), 660
BOX object selection method, 227
bracketed tilde ([~]), wild card, 396
brackets ([ ]), wild card, 396
BREAK command, 528-535, 1029
    erasing hidden objects, 534
    points, 534
Break option (PEDIT command), 613
bugs (software), 979
buttons (dialog boxes), 48
BYBLOCK properties, 479, 483, 747-749
BYLAYER properties, 479, 483, 745-746

C

c1a Patch (AutoCAD LT), installation, 1056-1057
caches (hard drives), 986
CAmera option (DVIEW command), 928
Cancel radio button (Open Drawing dialog box), 125
canceling commands, 39
Cartesian coordinate system, 66-72
CENTER dimensioning command, 790-794, 1033
CENter object snap, 402-408
Center option
    ARC command, 149
    arcs, 599
    ZOOM command, 197
Center point option (CIRCLE command), 155
center points (circles), 153
centering
    extension lines, 803
    text objects, 167
centerlines, 140-142
chained dimensions, 780-782
CHAMFER command, 535-542, 1029
    beveling corners, 540
    Distances option, 542
    Polyline option, 542
    polylines, 616-619
CHANGE command, 483, 553-559, 1030
    circles, 553
    lines, 557
    Ortho, 556
    points, 556
    text, 555
Change Properties dialog box, 490-492, 556, 740
character strings, 123
characters (ASCII code values), 123
check boxes, 48
CHKDSK /F command, 978

CHPROP command, 490-497, 556, 1030
CIRCLE command, 152-158, 1030
circles
    arc tangency, 414
    center points, 153
    CHANGE command, 553
    creating, 152-158
    dimensions, 790-794, 803
    OFFSET command, 518
    orthogonal mode, 154
    radii, 158, 448
    rubber-band, 153
    stretching, 266-271
    tangent-tangent-radius, 156-158
clearing
    drawings, 40
    files after system crashes, 977-978
    layer filters, 387
CLip option (DVIEW command), 929
Clipboard data transfers, 948-955
clockwise arcs, 151
Close option
    LINE command, 142-145
    PEDIT command, 606
closed polylines, 592
closing Aerial View window, 189
COLOR command, 1030
color filters (layers), 385
colors
    block objects, 745-751
    dimension lines, 814
    dimension text, 812-814
    extension lines, 814
    grips, 259-260
    layers, 366, 369-374
    naming, 374
    objects, 477-479, 492-493
    preferences, setting, 343-348
    xrefs, 752
Colors dialog box, 346
combining
    Aerial View window options, 184
    arcs with lines, 151-152

    object snaps, 424
    viewports, 215
command line, 33
command options, *see* **options**
command reference, accessing, 59
commands, 30
    ?, 1027
    3DPOLY, 605, 1027
    ABOUT, 1027
    aliases, 44, 1046-1048
    APERTURE, 1028
    APPEND, 975
    ARC, 146-152, 1028
    AREA, 452-462, 1028
    ARRAY, 279, 519-524, 699, 1028
    assigning to toolbox icons, 352
    ATTDEF, 708, 710, 1028
    ATTDISP, 719, 1028
    ATTEDIT, 716-719, 1028
    ATTEXT, 1028
    automated sequences, 134
    BASE, 757, 1028
    BHATCH, 647-648, 655, 658, 1029
    BLIPMODE, 1029
    blips, disabling, 40
    BLOCK, 686, 742, 1029
    BMAKE, 683, 1029
    BOUNDARY, 462, 630-637, 1029
    BREAK, 528-535, 1029
    canceling, 39
    CHAMFER, 535-542, 616-619, 1029
    CHANGE, 483, 553-559, 1030
    CHKDSK /F, 978
    CHPROP, 490-497, 556, 1030
    CIRCLE, 152-158, 1030
    COLOR, 1030
    context-sensitive help, 61
    COPY, 240-248, 1030
    COPYCLIP, 950-951, 1030
    COPYEMBED, 952, 1030
    COPYIMAGE, 950, 1030
    COPYLINK, 952, 1030

DDATTDEF, 708, 1030
DDATTE, 716, 1031
DDATTEXT, 1031
DDCHPROP, 490-497, 1031
DDEDIT, 579-581, 1031
DDEMODES, 477-489, 1031
DDGRIPS, 1031
DDIM, 801, 1032
DDINSERT, 353, 676, 1032, 1038
DDLMODES, 363, 367, 1032
DDMODIFY, 468-472, 494,
  505-507, 1032
DDOSNAP, 420, 1032
DDPTYPE, 1032
DDRENAME, 375, 503, 1032
DDRMODES, 1032
DDSELECT, 233, 1032
DDUCS, 99, 1033
DDUCSP, 1033
DDUNITS, 319, 1033, 1044
DELAY, 1033
DIM, 1033
DIM1, 1033
dimensioning, 770
    ALIGNED, 782-785, 1033
    ANGULAR, 794-796, 1033
    BASELINE, 778-779, 1033
    CENTER, 790-794, 1033
    CONTINUE, 780-782, 1034
    DIAMETER, 790, 1034
    EXIT, 773, 1034
    HOMETEXT, 825, 1034
    HORIZONTAL, 775, 1034
    issuing, 770
    LEADER, 789-790, 1034
    NEWTEXT, 826, 1034
    OBLIQUE, 826-828, 1034
    ORDINATE, 786-788, 1034
    prompts, 772-774
    RADIUS, 790-794, 1035
    ROTATED, 782-785, 1035
    STATUS, 820

    TEDIT, 826-828, 1035
    TROTATE, 826-828, 1035
    UNDO, 785, 1035
    UPDATE, 826, 1035
    VARIABLES, 820
    VERTICAL, 776-778, 1035
DIMSCALE, 857
DIMUPD, 810
DIST, 448-452, 1035
DIVIDE, 440-445, 702, 1035
DLINE, 637-644, 1035
DONUT, 623-628, 1035
drawing
    environments, 36
    files, 111-128
DSVIEWER, 185, 1036
DTEXT, 162-169, 501, 1036
DVIEW, 927-929, 1036
DXFOUT, 942, 1036
editing, 36
ELEV, 1036
ELLIPSE, 625-628, 1036
END, 1036
ERASE, 51-54, 237-240, 1036
EXIT, 128
EXPLODE, 619-621, 681,
  739-742, 1036
EXTEND, 543-550, 549, 1037
File menu
    Import/Export command, 134
    Print/Plot, 134
    Run Script, 134
    Save, 119
    Unlock Files, 134
FILEOPEN, 1037
FILL, 1037
FILLET, 535-542, 616-619, 1037
GETENV, 1037
GRAPHSCR, 1037
GRID, 80, 1037
HANDLES, 661
HATCH, 647-652, 1037

HATCHEDIT, 666-670, 1037
HELP, 57, 1037
help, 60
Help pull-down menu, 59
 Orientation, 63
 Tutorial, 62
 What's New, 61
HIDE, 922, 1037
ID, 426-430, 1038
importing to drawings from
 Clipboard, 954-955
INSERT, 676-682, 690-691,
 744-745, 1038
ISOPLANE, 1038
issuing, 34-46
 with keyboard, 43-45
 with mouse, 36-42
 with pull-down menus, 40
 with tools, 39
LAYER, 387-389, 483, 569, 1038
LIMITS, 299-303, 885, 1038
LINE, 139-146, 1038
LINETYPE, 370, 483, 1038
LIST, 462-468, 1038
LTSCALE, 1039
MEASURE, 440-445, 702, 1039
MINSERT, 699-702, 1039
MIRROR, 527, 1039
MOVE, 240-248, 1039
MSLIDE, 1039
MSPACE, 847, 1039
MULTIPLE, 1039
MVIEW, 843-845, 1039
NEW, 111-118, 1039
object snap overrides, 38
OFFSET, 513-519, 1040
offsets, 90
OOPS, 237-240, 1040
OPEN, 109, 125, 1040
ORTHO, 1040
OSNAP, 1040
PAN, 199-201, 1040

PASTECLIP, 953, 1040
PEDIT, 484, 605-619, 1040
PLAN, 1040
PLINE, 587-605, 1040
PLOT, 870-873, 1040
POINT, 158-162, 1041
POLYGON, 621-623, 1041
PREFERENCES, 341, 1041
prompts, 33
PSOUT, 947, 1041
PSPACE, 847, 1041
PURGE, 371, 389-391, 483, 756,
 763-764, 1041
QSAVE, 119, 1041
QUIT, 128
RECTANG, 628-630, 1041
REDO, 249-252, 1041
REDRAW, 39, 144, 922, 1037, 1041
REGEN, 159, 207, 1042
RENAME, 336, 375, 1042
repeating, 50
replicating
 ARRAY, 519-524
 MIRROR, 524-528
 OFFSET, 513-519
RESUME, 1042
REVDATE, 1042
reviewing with text window, 34
ROTATE, 569-575, 1042
RSCRIPT, 1042
SAVE, 111, 119-124, 1042
SAVEAS, 122, 1042
SAVEASR12, 979
SAVEDIB, 903, 1042
SCALE, 322, 575-578, 1042
SCANDISK, 978
screen regeneration, 206
SCRIPT, 1042
SELECT, 566-569, 1042
SETENV, 1042
SETVAR, 324, 459, 1042
SHADE, 923, 1043

SNAP, 80, 101, 1043
SOLID, 1043
STRETCH, 275, 559-569, 1043
STYLE, 497, 500, 816, 1043
TEXT, 165, 1043
TEXTSCR, 1043
TIME, 1043
TOOLBOX, 350, 1043
transparent, 207-212
   assigning to toolbox icons, 356
   display control, 211
TRIM, 543-550, 1043
troubleshooting errors, 50-54
U, 1043
UCS, 90, 97, 933, 1044
UCSICON, 93, 1044
UNDO, 50-51, 249-252, 1044
UNITS, 317, 1044
UNLOCK, 1044
VIEW, 201-206, 833, 836, 1044
VIEWPORTS, 835, 1044
VPLAYER, 389, 860-861, 1044
VPOINT, 921-923, 1044
VPORTS, 207, 212, 215, 835,
   923-926, 1044
VSLIDE, 1044
WBLOCK, 753-756, 1045
WMFIN, 945, 1045
WMFOPTS, 1045
WMFOUT, 944, 1045
XBIND, 732-735, 1045
XREF, 720-725, 1045
ZOOM, 194-199, 248, 287, 1046
see also function keys; key commands
computer processors, upgrading, 984
CONFIG.SYS files
   editing, 970-972
   errors, troubleshooting, 973-974
configurations
   networks, 968
   plot sheets, 879-890
   viewports, 216, 926

construction lines, 80
context-sensitive help, 61
CONTINUE dimensioning command,
   780-782, 1034
Continue option
   ARC command, 150
   LINE command, 145
Control option (UNDO command), 251
controlling hatch pattern boundaries,
   662-666
converting
   dependent symbols to
     block objects, 735
   drawing files
     to DXF, 941-942
     to PostScript format, 945-948
     to WMF, 943-945
   measurement units to/from other
     formats, 322
   xrefs to block objects, 724, 730-732
coordinate display, 45, 68-72
coordinate systems
   3D models, 930-935
   axes, 66, 93
   Cartesian, 66-72
   modifying, 930-935
   object alignment via orthogonal
     mode, 83
   UCS (User Coordinate System),
     90-99, 933
   WCS (World Coordinate System), 90
coordinated snap and grids, 76-83
coordinates, *see* **point coordinates**
COPY command, 240-248, 1030
Copy option (stretch grip editing), 266
COPYCLIP command, 950-951, 1030
COPYEMBED command, 952, 1030
COPYIMAGE command, 950, 1030
copying
   ARRAY command, 519-524
   MIRROR command, 524-528
   multiple copies, 520

objects, 240-248
  as vector data, 950-951
  to Clipboard, 948-950
  OFFSET command, 513-519
  selection sets, 240-248
COPYLINK command, 952, 1030
**corners, beveling with CHAMFER
  command, 540**
**CPolygon selection method (objects),
  226, 229, 232**
Create Drawing File dialog box, 115
**Create New Drawing dialog box, 31,
  112-113**
crosshairs (cursor), 36
**crossing selection method (objects),
  225, 228, 232**
**CSI (Construction Standards Institute)
  format, layer names, 908-909**
Ctrl+B key command, 45, 74
Ctrl+C key command, 39, 257
Ctrl+D key command, 45
Ctrl+E key command, 45, 101
Ctrl+G key command, 45, 80
Ctrl+O key command, 45, 83
current layers, 364, 365, 387, 487
**Current View tool (Aerial View
  window), 191**
cursor, 36
  aperture box, 402
  crosshairs, 36
  not-VP, 215
  pick boxes, 224
  pop-up menu, 399
  rubber-band, 451
**Custom Drawing Setup dialog box, 332,
  847-851**
**Custom Pattern option (Boundary
  Hatch dialog box), 660**
**Custom setup (prototype drawings),
  326, 330-331**
customizing
  layer naming standards, 909-910
  linetypes, 910-912

toolbar, 33
toolbox, 33, 350
**cutting objects with TRIM command,
  543-550**

D

data records (objects), 462-472
data transfers (Clipboard), 948-955
DDATTDEF command, 708, 1030
DDATTE command, 716, 1031
DDATTEXT command, 1031
DDCHPROP command, 490-497, 1031
DDEDIT command, 579-581, 1031
DDEMODES command, 477-489, 1031
DDGRIPS command, 1031
DDIM command, 801, 1032
**DDINSERT command, 353, 676,
  1032, 1038**
DDLMODES command, 363, 367, 1032
**DDMODIFY command, 468-472, 494,
  505-507, 1032**
DDOSNAP command, 420, 1032
DDPTYPE command, 1032
DDRENAME command, 375, 503, 1032
DDRMODES command, 1032
DDSELECT command, 233, 1032
DDUCS command, 99, 1033
DDUCSP command, 1033
DDUNITS command, 319, 1033, 1044
deactivating layers, 376-377
default line (polylines), 588-595
defaults
  fonts, 348
  object selection, 231
  printers, 874
  prototype drawings, 118
defining
  block objects, 683-686
  multiple mview viewports, 852-854
  plot sheets, 884-886
  text attributes, 708-712

defragmenting hard drives, 982
Del option (UCS command), 98
DELAY command, 1033
Delete option (VIEW command), 205
deleting
    block objects, 763-764
    layers, 389-391
    linetypes, 371, 483
    objects
        from selection sets, 226
        with ERASE command, 237-240
    text objects, 163
    viewports, 215, 925
dependent symbols (xrefs),
  728-730, 735
deselecting objects, 228
detaching xrefs, 722-725
dialog boxes
    Arrows, 806
    Attribute Definition, 708
    Block Definition, 683, 742
    Boundary Creation, 634
    Boundary Hatch, 647, 656, 663-666
    buttons, 48
    Change Properties, 490-492, 556, 740
    check boxes, 48
    Colors, 346
    Create Drawing File, 115
    Create New Drawing, 31, 112-113
    Custom Drawing Setup, 332, 847-851
    Dimension Line, 801-802
    Dimension Styles and Settings,
     800-814
    Drawing Aids, 76, 101, 142
    Edit Attribute Definition, 712
    edit boxes, 48
    Edit Path, 126
    Entity Creation Modes, 477
    Entity Selection Settings, 233-236
    Entity Sort Method, 235-237
    Extension Lines, 802-804
    Feature Legend, 887

Find File, 126-128
Fonts, 349
grayed items, 47
Grips, 254, 259-260
Grips Style, 759
Hatchedit, 666
HPGL Driver Setup, 878
Insert, 676, 681-682
Layer Control, 363-376, 487, 861
Modify <*Object_type*>, 469, 494
Modify Text, 506
navigating, 46-49
Open Drawing, 124
opening, 48
Opens Grips, 759
Pen Assignments, 879
Plot Configuration, 871-872, 879-890
Plot Rotation and Origin, 882, 888
Point Style, 159
Preferences, 129-133, 341
Preferences Fonts, 348
Print Setup, 878
Print/Plot Setup & Default
  Selection, 876
Printers, 874
Prototype Drawing File, 116
radio buttons, 49
Rename, 336
Running Object Snap, 420
Save Drawing As, 113-115, 120-122
Scale and Colors, 812-814, 857
Select Color, 371, 479
Select Hatch Pattern, 646, 650
Select Linetype, 372, 480
Select Text Font, 502
Select Text Style, 488, 497
Set Layer Filters, 384
Show Device Requirements, 876
slider bars, 49
Text Format, 808-811
Text Location, 807-808
Toolbox Customization, 352

UCS Control, 99
Units Control, 314
View Name, 881
Warning, 742
Window Selection, 881, 885
DIAMETER dimensioning command, 790, 1034
Diameter option (CIRCLE command), 155
DIM command, 1033
DIM1 command, 1033
DIMASO dimension variable, 822
DIMCEN dimension variable, 792, 803
Dimension Line dialog box, 801-802
dimension lines, 767
    colors, 814
    interior, 801
    settings, 801
    terminating, 806
Dimension Styles and Settings dialog box, 800-814
dimension variables, 768-769, 800, 1019-1025
    changing, 801
    DIMASO, 822
    DIMCEN, 792, 803
    DIMSCALE, 801, 812
    DIMTIX, 792
dimensioning commands, 770
    ALIGNED, 782-785, 1033
    ANGULAR, 794-796, 1033
    BASELINE, 778-779, 1033
    CENTER, 790-794, 1033
    CONTINUE, 780-782, 1034
    DIAMETER, 790, 1034
    EXIT, 773, 1034
    HOMETEXT, 825, 1034
    HORIZONTAL, 775, 1034
    issuing, 770
    LEADER, 789-790, 1034
    NEWTEXT, 826, 1034
    OBLIQUE, 826-828, 1034

ORDINATE, 786-788, 1034
prompts, 772-774
RADIUS, 790-794, 1035
ROTATED, 782-785, 1035
STATUS, 820
TEDIT, 826-828, 1035
TROTATE, 826-828, 1035
UNDO, 785, 1035
UPDATE, 826, 1035
VARIABLES, 820
VERTICAL, 776-778, 1035
dimensions
aligned, 782-785
angular, 794-796
architectural, styles, 816-818
arcs, 149, 790-794, 803
associativity, 768
    editing, 821-829
    object snaps, 419
    restoring, 825
    stretching, 823-825
    updating, 826
baseline, 778-779, 802
chained, 780-782
circles, 790-794, 803
erasing, 785-786
exploding, 822
extension lines, 767
    centering, 803
    colors, 814
    offsetting, 802
    settings, 802-804
    suppressing, 802
horizontal, 774-778
isometric drawings, 826
leaders
    inserting, 788-790
    styles, 819-820
linear, 774-786
mview viewports, 858
ordinate, 786-788
prototype drawings, 915

rotated, 782-785
rounding off, 808
scaling, 313, 808, 857-859
series, 778-782
settings, 798-821
stacks, 778-779
styles, 800
    creating, 814-821
    importing, 821
text, 767, 773
    alignment, 807
    alternate measurement units, 810
    colors, 812-814
    formats, 808-811
    gap settings, 802
    inserting, 788-790
    location settings, 807-808
    moving, 826
    prefixes/suffixes, 808
    rotating, 826
    scaling, 808, 812-814
    suppressing zeros, 809
    tolerance settings, 809
undoing, 785-786
vertical, 774-778
witness lines, 767, 802
DIMSCALE command, 857
DIMSCALE dimension variable, 801, 812
DIMSCALE system variable, 313, 857
DIMTIX dimension variable, 792
DIMUPD command, 810
directories (organizing drawings), 109-111
Directories box (Create New Drawing dialog box), 115
Directories drop-down list (Open Drawing dialog box), 125
disk caches, 986
displacement (objects), 244-248
displaying
layers with filters, 382-387
multiple mview viewports, 854-857

displays (plot sheets), 884
DIST command, 448-452, 1035
Distance option
CHAMFER command, 542
DVIEW command, 928
OFFSET command, 518
DITHER system variable, 875
dithering, 875
DIVIDE command, 440-445, 702, 1035
divided objects, inserting block objects, 702-706
dividing viewports, 216
DLINE command, 637-644, 1035
documents (online help), 61
DONUT command, 623-628, 1035
dots (grids), removing, 74
double lines, 637-644
Double option (Boundary Hatch dialog box), 660
drawing aids
coordinated snap and grids, 76-83
orthogonal mode, 83-85
reference grids, 72-73
snap grids, 73-74
Drawing Aids dialog box, 76, 101, 142
drawing commands, 36
drawing environment commands, 36
Drawing Extents tool (Aerial View window), 190
drawing modes (prototype drawings), 915
drawing windows, *see* **graphics windows**
drawings
3D models, 921-940
    coordinate systems, 930-935
    perspective views, 929
    shading, 923
    viewing, 921-923, 927-929
    viewports, 923-926
3D objects (isometric mode), 99
Aerial View window, 175-194

architectural
  creating dimension styles, 816-818
  plot sheets, 304-306
base points, setting, 756-759
bookmarks, 251
clearing, 40
Clipboard data, importing, 953
colors, setting preferences, 345-348
consistency, 333
construction lines, creating with snap
  and grid, 80
coordinate display modes, 45, 68-70
dimensions, 767-796
  scaling, 313
  settings, 798-821
environment preferences, 129-133
exporting, 754
extents, 207
file commands, 111-128
file name extensions, 110
file paths, 110
files
  automatic saving, 132
  finding, 126-128
  locking, 131, 342
  reopening, 135
  search paths, 132-133, 342
  temporary, 133
  unlocking, 134
fitting to plot sheets, 303-308
fonts, 348-350, 497-507
formats
  DXF, 941-942
  PostScript, 945-948
  WMF, 943-945
grid display, 45
importing
  Clipboard text, 954
  commands from Clipboard, 954-955
inserting as block objects, 676-682
isometric dimensions, 826
isometric mode, 99-105

isoplane modes, cycling, 45
layers, 29, 360-362
  activating/deactivating, 376-377
  changing, 142
  colors, 366, 369-374
  controlling object properties, 475
  creating, 363-368
  current, 364-365, 387
  customized naming standards,
    909-910
  deleting, 389-391
  deselecting, 365
  displaying with filters, 382-387
  filters, 366, 382-387
  freezing, 378-379
  frozen, 365
  grouping with wild cards, 392
  help, 366
  linetypes, 366, 369-374
  listing, 363-365
  locking, 366, 379-382
  multiple, 367-368
  naming, 367, 907-910
  naming conventions, 391-396
  properties, 368-374
  renaming, 365, 374-376
  selecting all, 365
  setting for objects, 487
  setting from toolbox, 362
  status, reading, 378
  thawed, 365
  thawing, 378-379
  unlocking, 366, 379-382
  xrefs, 730
limits, 299-303
linetypes
  customizing, 910-912
  deleting, 483
  loading, 483
  scaling, 313
measurement units, 313-322, 343-345
measuring, 448-462

model space, 833-837
multiple viewports, 212-218
naming, 114-115, 121-124
naming conventions, 335-338
object snaps, 158, 278-279, 398-426
    INSert, 165
    NODe, 161
objects, 53
    ALL selection method, 226
    arcs, 146-152
    AUto selection method, 226
    blocks, 29, 259, 674-675, 683-702
    BOX selection method, 227
    BYBLOCK properties, 479, 483
    BYLAYER properties, 479, 483
    circles, 152-158
    colors, 477-479
    copying, 240-248, 948-950
    CPolygon selection method, 226,
      229, 232
    crossing selection method, 225,
      228, 232
    data records, 462-472
    deselecting, 228
    displacement, 244-248
    elevation, 488-489
    enlarging, 289
    erasing, 51, 237-240
    exporting, 753-756
    fence selection method, 225, 232,
      240, 243
    grids, 29
    grip editing, 220, 254-258, 260-294
    grips, 220, 254, 259-260
    hatch patterns, 912-913
    highlighted, 51
    hot grips, 258
    last selection method, 226, 240
    libraries, 916-919
    lines, 139-146
    linetypes, 480-486
    listing, 462-468

    measuring, 448-462
    mirroring, 256, 292-294
    modifying, 468-472
    moving, 240-248, 256, 275-278
    multiple selection, 226, 230-231
    noun-verb editing, 224, 232-236
    parts, 686
    pick selection, 225
    placing point coordinates, 440-445
    point, 419
    point coordinates, 158-162
    polylines, 274
    previous selection method, 226,
      242-243
    properties, 474-497
    reducing, 289
    restoring with OOPS command,
      237-240
    rotating, 256, 279-286
    scaling, 256, 286-290, 308
    selecting, 221-237
    selection sets, 224, 227
    setting current layers for, 487
    SIngle selection method, 227
    snapping to grids, 278
    sorting selection, 237
    stretching, 255-257, 261-265
    symbols, 687
    tangency, 158
    templates, 687
    text, 162-169
    text styles, 488
    thickness, 475, 489
    unit parts, 687
    verb-noun editing, 224, 232-236
    verifying snap grid placement, 430
    viewing, 462-472
    window selection method, 225, 232
    WPolygon selection method, 226, 232
objects snaps, 227
OLE, 952
opening, 124-128

organizing, 29, 109-111
orthogonal mode, 45, 83-85
panning, 57, 178, 199-201
paper space, 837-847
planning, 332-338
plot scales, 307
plot sheets, 870-879
  alternative output, 903
  configurations, 879-890
  defining, 884-886
  hardware, 900-901
  output media, 901-902
  parameters, 880-881
  previewing, 889-890
  scaling, 892-898
  settings, 898-899
plotting, 870-873
  from model space, 894-895
  from paper space, 896-897
  to files, 897-898
printing, 870-879
prototypes, 111, 115-118, 325, 914-916
  protecting from overwriting, 126
  setup, 326-332
renaming, 335
safeguards, 29
saving, 119-124, 950-951
scale multipliers, 308
scaling, 298-325
screen regenerations, 206-207
snap mode, 45
standards, 333-335, 919-920
support directories, 918
support files, 132-133
symbols, importing, 134
templates, 914-916
temporary reference points, setting, 426
text, scaling, 309-312
text styles, 913-914
  creating, 497-502
  options, 503-504

tracking, 434-439
viewports, 212
  combining, 215
  configurations, 216
  deleting, 215
  dividing, 216
  inserting, 847-851
  multiple, 192
  restoring, 217
  saving, 216
views, 54-57, 201-206, 833-835
windows, 236
xrefs, 674-675, 719-735
  colors, 752
  layers, 752
  libraries, 750-759
  linetypes, 752
zooming, 54, 178, 194-199
drivers (printers), 875
Drives drop-down list box
  Create New Drawing dial box, 115
  Open Drawing dialog box, 125
DSVIEWER command, 185, 1036
DTEXT command, 162-169, 501, 1036
DVIEW command, 927-929, 1036
DWG file name extension, 114
DWK file name extension, 131
DXF (Drawing eXchange Format), 134, 941-942
DXFOUT command, 903, 942, 1036
dynamic Cartesian coordinates, 71
dynamic polar coordinates, 71
Dynamic Update option (Aerial View window), 181
dynamic zooming/panning (Aerial View window), 189

E

Edit Attribute Definition dialog box, 712
edit boxes, 48
Edit Path dialog box, 126

editing
3D objects, 935-940
associative dimensions, 821-829
associative hatch patterns, 666-670
AUTOEXEC.BAT files, 972-973
block objects, 738-742
CONFIG.SYS files, 970-972
inserted text attributes, 716-719
text, 579-581
text attributes, 712
xref source files, 725
see also grip editing; noun-verb
editing; verb-noun editing
editing commands, 36
ELEV command, 1036
elevation (objects), 488-489
ELLIPSE command, 625-628, 1036
ellipses, 586
END command, 1036
End option
ARC command, 149
UNDO command, 251
ENDPoint object snap, 402-408
**endpoints (CHANGE command),
553-559**
engineering measurement units, 318
enlarging
objects, 289
viewports, 926
entities, *see* **objects**
Entity Creation Modes dialog box, 477
Entity option
AREA command, 454, 459
UCS command, 98, 933
**Entity Selection Settings dialog box,
233-236**
Entity Sort Method dialog box, 235-237
**EPS (Encapsulated PostScript) format,
945-948**
ERASE command, 51-54, 237-240, 1036
erasing
dimensions, 785-786
hidden objects, 534
objects, 51, 237-240

error messages, 962
errors
AUTOEXEC.BAT files, 974-975
CONFIG.SYS files, 973-974
memory, 976
notification (beep), 342
tracing, 977
troubleshooting
with commands, 50-54
*with REDO/UNDO commands,
248-252*
EXIT command, 128
**EXIT dimensioning command,
773, 1034**
eXit option (stretch grip editing), 266
explicit properties (objects), 475, 745
**EXPLODE command, 619-621, 681,
739-742, 1036**
**Exploded option (Boundary Hatch
dialog box), 660**
exploding
block objects, 681, 739-742
dimensions, 822
hatch patterns, 655
nested block objects, 762
exporting
block objects, 753-756
drawings, 754
objects, 753-756
PostScript files, 946-947
EXTEND command, 543-550, 549, 1037
extension lines (dimensions), 767
centering, 803
colors, 814
offsetting, 802
settings, 802-804
suppressing, 802
Extension Lines dialog box, 802-804
extents
drawings, 207
plot sheets, 884
**Extents option (ZOOM command),
197, 248**
**extracting objects from
block objects, 739**

F

F1 function key, 57
F2 function key, 204, 348
F5 function key, 101
F7 function key, 80, 344
F8 function key, 83
F9 function key, 74, 320, 344
F10 function key, 179
Feature Legend dialog box, 887
fence selection method (objects), 225, 232, 240, 243
File Locking check box (Preferences dialog box), 130-131
File menu commands
   Import/Export, 134
   Print/Plot, 134
   Run Script, 134
   Save, 119
   Unlock Files, 134
File Name edit box
   Create New Drawing dialog box, 115
   Open Drawing dialog box, 125
file name extensions (drawings), 110
File Name list box (Create New Drawing dialog box), 115
FILEOPEN command, 1037
files
   32-bit access, 983-984
   ACLT.INI, 967
   AUTOEXEC.BAT
     editing, 972-973
     errors, 974-975
   CONFIG.SYS
     editing, 970-972
     errors, 973-974
   drawings
     automatic saving, 132
     converting to DXF, 941-942
     converting to PostScript format, 945-948
     converting to WMF, 943-945
     inserting as block objects, 676-682
     locking, 131
     naming, 122-124
     reopening, 135
     search paths, 132-133, 342
     support files, 132-133
     temporary, 133
     unlocking, 134
   hatch patterns, 654
   locking, 342
   plotting drawings to, 897-898
   PostScript, exporting, 946-947
   startup, troubleshooting, 970-975
   support, 976-977
   swap, 982-984
   system crash errors, 977-978
   unlocking, 978
   WMF, importing, 944-945
FILL command, 1037
FILLET command, 535-542, 1037
   arcs, 536
   Polyline option, 537
   Radius option, 537
filters
   layers, 366, 382-387
   point coordinates, 430-434
Find File dialog box, 126-128
Find File radio button (Open Drawing dialog box), 126
finding
   drawing files, 126-128
   point coordinates
     with coordinated snap and grids, 79
     with point filters, 431
     with reference grids, 72
     with snap grids, 73-74
   support files, 976-977
First point option (AREA command), 454
Fit option (PEDIT command), 610
floating mview viewports (paper space), 841

floating toolbox, 350
floating windows, 33
fonts, 497-507, 913-914
 IALT disk, installation, 1054-1055
 preferences, setting, 343, 348-350
Fonts dialog box, 349
formats
 AIA (layer names), 907
 CSI (layer names), 908-909
 dimension text, 808-811
 drawings
  DXF, 941-942
  PostScript, 945-948
  WMF, 943-945
**formatting hard drives for AutoCAD LT
 installation, 961**
freezing layers, 378-379
**From point option (LINE
 command), 144**
frozen layers, 365
function keys, 45
 F1, 57
 F2, 204, 348
 F5, 101
 F7, 80, 344
 F8, 83
 F9, 74, 320, 344
 F10, 179

G

GETENV command, 1037
Global View option (Aerial
 View window), 180
glossary, 60
graphics windows, 30, 45
GRAPHSCR command, 1037
GRID command, 80, 1037
grids
 activating/deactivating, 45
 coordinated snap and grids, 76-83
 dots, removing, 74

isometric snap/grids, 101
 objects, 29
 reference, 72
 snap, 73-74
grip editing, 220, 254-258
 block objects, 759-761
 multiple objects, 271-275
 operating modes, 258-294
 specifying object base points, 279
GRIPBLOCK system variable, 759
grips
 block objects, 259
 changing settings, 259-260
 colors, 259-260
 objects, 220, 254
 sizing, 259-260
 snapping to, 266
 stretching, 261-265
 vertices, 614
Grips dialog box, 254, 259-260
Grips Style dialog box, 759
GRIPS system variable, 221, 259
Group option (UNDO command), 251

H

HANDLES command, 661
hard copy, *see* plot sheets
hard drives
 caches, 986
 defragmenting, 982
 formatting for AutoCAD LT
  installation, 961
hardware
 AutoCAD LT requirements, 959
 plot sheets, 900-901
HATCH command, 647, 649, 1037
 ? option, 652
 name option, 652
 style option, 652
 U option, 652

hatch patterns, 646-649, 912-913
  ACLT.PAT file, 654
  applying, 649-656
  associative, 661
    editing, 666-670
    updating, 670
  BHATCH command, 655, 658
  boundaries, 648-649, 662-666
  exploding, 655
  island boundaries, 660
  point coordinates, specifying, 660
  previewing, 661
  scaling, 647-648
  selecting, 647-648
  stretching, 655
  user-defined, 653-654
HATCHEDIT command, 666-670, 1037
Hatchedit dialog box, 666
height (text), 503
Height option (DTEXT command), 166
help, 57-63
  accessing, 45
  commands, 60
  context-sensitive, 61
  layers, 366
  mouse, 38
  online documents, 61
  topics, searching, 60
HELP command, 57, 1037
Help Contents window, 60
Help pull-down menu commands, 59
  Orientation, 63
  Tutorial, 62
  What's New, 61
Help window, 58
hidden objects, 534
HIDE command, 922, 1037
Hide option (DVIEW command), 929
hiding
  lines
    in 3D models, 922
    in paper space viewports, 865
  toolbox, 351

highlighted objects, 51
HOMETEXT dimensioning command, 825, 1034
HORIZONTAL dimensioning command, 775, 1034
horizontal dimensions, 774-778
hot grips
  multiple, 271
  objects, 258
hot keys, 44
HPGL (Hewlett-Packard Graphics Language) driver
  installation, 878
  updating, 1058-1059
HPGL Driver Setup dialog box, 878
hyphen (-), wild card, 396

I

IALT (Inside AutoCAD LT) disk
  fonts, 1054-1055
  installation, 1050-1054
  starting, 1051-1054
  startup icon, changing, 1051-1052
icons
  toolbox, assigning commands to, 352
  UCS, 90
ID command, 426-430, 1038
implied windowing, 236
Import/Export command (File menu), 134
importing
  Clipboard data, 953-954
  commands, 954-955
  dimension styles, 821
  symbols, 134
  text, 581-584
  WMF files, 944-945
  xrefs, 732
included angles, 597
Inherit Properties option (Boundary Hatch dialog box), 661

INSERT command, 676-679, 681-682, 690-691, 744-745, 1038
Insert dialog box, 676, 681-682
INSert object snaps, 165, 402, 415-419
Insert option (PEDIT command), 613
inserting
  block objects, 679-682, 690-702
    along divided/measured objects, 702-706
    arrays, 698-702
  borders in paper space, 841-843
  drawings as block objects, 676-682
  exploded block objects, 681
  leaders in dimensions, 788-790
  objects into selection sets, 226
  text
    attribute definitions, 713-716
    in dimensions, 788-790
  title block objects, 847-851
  viewports, 847-851
insertion base points, *see* **base points**
installation
  AutoCAD LT, 961-967
  c1a Patch, 1056-1057
  fonts (IALT disk), 1054-1055
  HPGL driver, 878
  IALT disk, 1050-1054
  LT_BASIC interpreter program, 1059-1060
  LTHook macro program, 1055-1056
insufficient memory error message, 962
interface
  components, 29-34
  preferences, 340-350
interior dimension lines, 801
INTersection object snaps, 402, 408-415
islands (hatch patterns), 660
isometric drawing aid, 99-105
isometric drawings
  dimensions, 826
  snap/grids, 101
ISOPLANE command, 1038

isoplanes, 45, 100
issuing
  commands, 34-46
    with keyboard, 43-45
    with mouse, 36-42
    with pull-down menus, 40
    with tools, 39
  dimensioning commands, 770

J–K

Join option (PEDIT command), 606-607
Justify option (DTEXT command), 165, 167-169
justifying text objects, 167-169

key commands
  Alt+F4, 128
  Alt+minus, 247
  Alt+P, 320
  Alt+Tab, 209
  Alt+Y, 365
  Ctrl+B, 45, 74
  Ctrl+C, 39, 257
  Ctrl+D, 45
  Ctrl+E, 45, 101
  Ctrl+G, 45, 80
  Ctrl+O, 45, 83
  Shift, 236
  Shift+Tab, 49
keyboard
  accessing object snaps, 399
  characters (ASCII code values), 123
  entering transparent commands, 211
  function keys, 45
  functions, 46
  hot keys, 44
  issuing commands, 43-45
  placing point coordinates, 85-90
  selecting dialog box items, 49

L

landscape orientation, printing plot sheets, 888

last object selection method, 226, 240

LASTPOINT system variable, 426, 429

launching AutoCAD LT, 31

LAYER command, 387-389, 483, 569, 1038

Layer Control dialog box, 363-376, 487, 861

layers (drawings), 29, 360-362
activating/deactivating, 376-377
block objects, 745-751
changing, 142
colors, 366, 369-374
controlling object properties, 475
creating, 363-368
current, 364-365, 387, 487
deleting, 389-391
deselecting, 365
displaying with filters, 382-387
filters, 366, 382-387
freezing, 378-379
frozen, 365
grouping with wild cards, 392
help, 366
linetypes, 366, 369-374
listing, 363-365
locking, 366, 379-382
multiple, 367-368
mview viewport visibility, 860
naming, 367, 907-910
naming conventions, 386, 391-396
objects, 493
properties, 368-374
prototype drawings, 915
renaming, 365, 374-376
selecting all, 365
setting from toolbox, 362
status, reading, 378
thawed, 365

thawing, 378-379
unlocking, 366, 379-382
xrefs, 730, 752

LEADER dimensioning command, 789-790, 1034

leaders (dimensions)
inserting, 788-790
styles, 819-820

left angle bracket (<), absolute polar coordinates, 87

libraries
block objects, 750-759
objects, 916-919
xrefs, 750-759

limits
drawings, 299-303
plot sheets, 884

LIMITS command, 299-303, 885, 1038

LIMMAX system variable, 885

LIMMIN system variable, 885

LINE command, 139-146, 1038

linear dimensions, 774-786

linear distances, measuring, 452

lines
3D models, hiding, 922
centerlines, 140-142
CHAMFER command, 535-542
CHANGE command, 557
combining with arcs, 151-152
creating, 139-146
DLINE command, 637-644
double, 637-644
endpoints, 553-559
FILLET command, 535-542
measuring, 448
OFFSET command, 518
orthogonal mode, 146
paper space viewports, hiding, 865
polylines, 274, 586-621
3DPOLY command, 605
arcs, 595-605
CHAMFER command, 616-619

closed, 592

default line option, 588-595

ellipses, 586

EXPLODE command, 619-621

FILLET command, 616-619

grips, 614

included angles, 597

PEDIT command, 605-619

PLINE command, 587-605

vertices, 591

width, 594

rubber-band, 141

snap and grid spacing, 142

LINETYPE command, 370, 483, 1038

linetype filters (layers), 385

linetypes

block objects, 745-751

customizing, 910-912

deleting, 371, 483

layers, 366, 369-374

loading, 369-371, 483

logical, 369

objects, 480-486, 493

paper space viewports, scaling, 865

plot sheets, 886-887

polylines, 483-486

prototype drawings, 914

scaling, 313

xrefs, 752

list boxes, 48

LIST command, 462-468, 1038

List Files of Type drop-down list

Create New Draw dialog box, 115

Open Drawing dialog box, 125

listing

block reference object
properties, 742

layers, 363-365

objects, 462-468

viewport configurations, 926

xrefs, 724

loading linetypes, 369-371, 483

**Locate option (Aerial View window),
180, 183**

locking

drawing files, 131, 342

layers, 366, 379-382

logging errors, 977

logical linetypes, 369

**Lower left corner option (LIMITS
command), 303**

**LT_BASIC interpreter program,
installation, 1059-1060**

**LTHook macro program, installation,
1055-1056**

LTSCALE command, 1039

LTSCALE system variable, 313, 323, 373

**Ltype gen option (PEDIT
command), 612**

M

magnifying drawing zooms, 197

**Make option (LAYER command),
387-389**

Mark option (UNDO command), 251

maximizing memory, 985

**MEASURE command, 440-445,
702, 1039**

**measured objects, inserting block
objects, 702-706**

measurement units, 313-322

architectural, 320

converting to/from other
formats, 322

dimension text, 810

engineering, 318

metric, 344

plot sheets, 880

precision settings, 314-316

preferences, setting, 342-345

surveyor's, 321

measuring

area, 456-462

drawings, 448-462

objects, 448-462

media (plot sheets), 901-902
memory
   errors, troubleshooting, 976
   insufficient error message, 962
   maximizing, 985
   upgrading, 985
   virtual screen, 206
memory managers, 971, 985
Menu File edit box, 343
Menu menu (Aerial View window), 192
menus (Aerial View window), 190-194
merging viewports, 925
metric measurement units, 344
microprocessors, upgrading, 984
MIDpoint object snaps, 402-404
MINSERT command, 699-702, 1039
Minutes edit box (Preferences
  dialog box), 130
MIRROR command, 524-528, 1039
mirror operating mode (grip editing),
  292-294
mirroring
   block objects, 693-695
   objects, 256, 292-294
model space
   entering from paper space, 847
   plotting drawings from, 894-895
   viewports, 833-834
     active, 835
     creating, 835-836
     tiled, 835-837
modes (OFFSET command)
   Distance, 518
   Through, 518
Modify <*Object_type*> dialog boxes,
  469, 494
Modify Text dialog box, 506
modifying objects, 468-472
monochrome printers, 874
Monochrome Vectors check box
  (Colors dialog box), 347

mouse
   accessing cursor pop-up menu, 399
   functions, 46
   help, 38
   issuing commands, 36-42
   three-button, 36
   two-button, 36
MOVE command, 240-248, 1039
move operating mode (grip editing),
  275-278
Move option (PEDIT command), 614
moving
   dimension text, 826
   endpoints (lines), 559-569
   objects, 240-248, 256, 275-278
   origins (coordinate systems), 90, 93
   selection sets, 240-248
   toolbox, 350
MSLIDE command, 1039
MSPACE command, 847, 1039
MULTIPLE command, 1039
multiple copies, 520
multiple drawing viewports, 192
multiple layers, 367-368
multiple mview viewports (paper space)
   defining, 852-854
   display options, 854-857
   scaling, 854-857
multiple objects
   grip editing, 271-275
   selection, 226, 230-231
multiple viewports, 212-218, 843
MVIEW command, 843-845, 1039
mview viewports (paper space), 841-852
   3D models, 862-863
   dimensions, 858
   hiding lines, 865
   layer visibility, 860
   scaling, 857
   scaling linetypes, 865

N

name option (HATCH command), 652
named items (xrefs), 728-730
naming
    block objects, 690
    colors, 374
    drawings, 114-115, 121-124, 335-338
    layers, 365, 367, 391-396, 907-910
    plot sheets, 881
navigating
    dialog boxes, 46-49
    drawings via Aerial View window,
      175-194
NEArest object snap, 402, 415-419
nesting block objects in blocks/xrefs,
    761-762
networks (AutoCAD LT
    configurations), 968
NEW command, 111-118, 114, 1039
NEWTEXT dimensioning command,
    826, 1034
Next option (PEDIT command), 613
No Prototype check box (Create New
    Drawing dialog box), 117
NODe object snaps, 161, 402, 415-419
nondynamic panning (Aerial View
    window), 189
None Control option (UNDO com-
    mand), 252
NONe object snap, 402
not-VP cursor, 215
noun-verb editing, 220, 224, 232-236
number sign (#), wild card, 396

O

object snaps, 158, 398-426
    associative dimensions, 419
    blip marks, 429
    CENter, 402, 404-408
    combining, 424
    ENDPoint, 402, 404-408

    INSert, 165, 402, 415-419
    INTersection, 402, 408-415
    MIDpoint, 402, 404
    NEArest, 402, 415-419
    NODe, 161, 402, 415-419
    NONe, 402
    overrides, 38, 403-404
    PERpendicular, 403, 408-415
    QUAdrant, 403-404
    QUIck mode modifier, 425
    running, 420-426
    setting, 420-426
    TANgent, 403, 408-415
    using with snap grids, 227
    xrefs, 722
object types (STRETCH command), 565
objects, 53
    3D
      creating, 935-940
      editing, 935-940
      isometric mode, 99
    alignment with coordinate
      systems, 83
    ALL selection method, 226
    angles
      bisecting, 400
      controlling with orthogonal mode, 83
      dimensions, 794-796
      measuring, 451
    arcs
      combining with lines, 151
      creating, 146-152
      dimensions, 149, 790-794, 803
      orthogonal mode, 149
      stretching, 266-271
    area, measuring, 452-462
    AUto selection method, 226
    base points, specifying for grip
      editing, 279
    block references, 742
    blocks, 29, 674-675
      alignment, 702-706
      anonymous, 685

arrays, inserting, 698-702
attributes, 467
automated text, 707-719
base points, 686, 690
BYBLOCK properties, 747-749
BYLAYER properties, 745-746
colors, 745-751
converting xrefs to, 724, 730-732
creating, 683-690
defining, 683-686
deleting, 763-764
editing, 738, 740-742
explicit properties, 745
exploding, 681, 739 742
exporting, 753-756
grip editing, 759-761
grips, 259
inserting, 679-682, 690-702
inserting along divided/measured
   objects, 702-706
inserting drawings as, 676-682
layers, 745-749, 750-751
libraries, 750-759
linetypes, 745-751
listing, 465-467
mirroring, 693-695
naming, 690
nesting in blocks/xrefs, 761-762
object manifestations, 686-690
object snaps, 419
presetting rotation/scale settings,
   696-698
properties, 745-749
redefining, 742-745
rotating, 691-695
rotating with grips, 759-760
scaling, 691-695
title, 707-719
BOX selection method, 227
BYBLOCK color property, 479
BYBLOCK linetype property, 483
BYLAYER color property, 479

BYLAYER linetype property, 483
circles
   center points, 153
   creating, 152-158
   dimensions, 790-794, 803
   orthogonal mode, 154
   radii, 158
   rubber-band, 153
   stretching, 266-271
colors, 477-479, 492-493
copying, 240-248
   as vector data, 950-951
   to Clipboard, 948-950
CPolygon selection method, 226,
   229, 232
creating in orthogonal mode, 83-85
crossing selection method, 225,
   228, 232
current layers, setting, 487
data records, 462-472
deselecting, 228
displacement, 244-248
divided, inserting block objects,
   702-706
elevation, setting, 488-489
enlarging, 289
erasing, 51, 237-240
exporting, 753-756
extracting from block objects, 739
fence selection method, 225, 232,
   240, 243
grids, 29
grip editing, 220, 254-258, 260-294
grips, 220, 254
   changing settings, 259-260
   colors, 259-260
   sizing, 259-260
   snapping to, 266
   stretching, 261-265
hatch patterns, 912-913
highlighted, 51
hot grips, 258

last selection method, 226, 240
layers, changing, 493
libraries, 916-919
lines
    centerlines, 140-142
    combining with arcs, 151
    creating, 139-146
    measuring, 448
    orthogonal mode, 146
    snap and grid spacing, 142
linetypes, 480-486, 493
listing, 462-468
measured, inserting block objects, 702-706
measuring, 448-462
mirroring, 256, 292-294
modifying, 468-472
moving, 240-248, 256, 275-278
multiple, grip editing, 271-275
multiple selection, 226, 230-231
noun-verb editing, 224, 232-236
offsets, measuring, 452
parts, 686
perimeters, measuring, 452
pick selection method, 225
point, 419
point coordinates
    placing, 440-445
    tracking, 434-439
points
    creating, 158-162
    regenerating, 159
    sizing, 161
    styles, 161
polylines, 274, 586-621
    3DPOLY command, 605
    arcs, 595-605
    closed, 592
    default line option, 588-595
    ellipses, 586
    included angles, 597
    linetypes, 483-486

    listing, 465-467
    PEDIT command, 605-619
    PLINE command, 587-605
    vertices, 591
    width, 594
previous selection method, 226, 242-243
properties, 474-476
    changing, 489-497
    setting, 476-489
prototype drawings, 915
reducing, 289
restoring with OOPS command, 237-240
rotating, 256, 279-286
scaling, 256, 286-290, 308
selecting, 221-237
selection sets, 224, 227
    adding objects to, 226
    moving, 240-248
    removing objects from, 226
SIngle selection method, 227
snapping, 278
sorting selection, 237
stretching, 255, 257, 261-265
symbols, 687
tangency, 158
templates, 687
text
    centering, 167
    creating, 162-169
    deleting, 163
    justifying, 167-169
    object snaps, 419
text styles, setting, 488
thickness, 475, 489, 494
unit parts, 687
verb-noun editing, 224, 232-236
verifying snap grid placement, 430
viewing, 462-472, 841-852
window selection method, 225, 232
WPolygon selection method, 226, 232

**OBLIQUE dimensioning command,
826, 828, 1034**
obliquing angle (text styles), 504
OFF option (LIMITS command), 303
OFFSET commands, 513-519, 1040
offsets
    commands, 90
    extension lines, 802
    measuring, 452
    origins, 93
**OK radio button (Open Drawing
dialog box), 125**
**OLE (Object Linking and
Embedding), 952**
ON option (LIMITS command), 303
**One Control option (UNDO
command), 252**
online documents (help), 61
OOPS command, 237-240, 1040
OPEN command, 109, 125, 1040
Open Drawing dialog box, 124
opening
    dialog boxes, 48
    drawings, 124-128
    prototype drawings, 118
Opens Grips dialog box, 759
operating modes
    grip editing, 258, 260-294
    object snaps, 402
optimizing memory, 985
options
    Aerial View window, 180-184
    ANGULAR dimensioning command,
    795-796
    ARC command, 149-152
    AREA command, 454
    ATTDEF command, 710-711
    ATTEDIT command, 718-719
    Attribution Definition
    dialog box, 711
    Boundary Hatch dialog box, 659-666
    CIRCLE command, 155

DIST command, 451
DTEXT command, 165-166
DVIEW command, 928-929
HATCH command, 652
INSERT command, 690-691
    preliminary, 697
    preset, 697
LAYER command, 387-389
Layer Control dialog box, 365-366
LIMITS command, 303
LINE command, 144-146
MVIEW command, 843-844
ORDINATE dimensioning
    command, 788
PSOUT command, 947
rotate grip editing mode, 283-286
SETVAR command, 324
stretch operating mode (grip
    editing), 265-266
TEDIT dimensioning command, 828
text styles, 503-504
UCS command, 97, 933-934
UNDO command, 251-252
VIEW command, 205
VPLAYER command, 860-861
VPOINT command, 922
VPORTS command, 215, 925-929
XREF command, 724
ZOOM command, 197-199
**Options menu (Aerial View
window), 192**
**ORDINATE dimensioning command,
786-788, 1034**
ordinate dimensions, 786-788
**organizing drawings with directories,
109-111**
orientation (printing)
    landscape, 888
    plot sheets, 880, 882, 888
    portrait, 888
**Orientation command (Help pull-down
menu), 63**

Origin option (UCS command), 97, 933
origins (coordinate systems), 66, 90, 93
ORTHO command, 556, 1040
orthogonal mode, 83
    arcs, 149
    circles, 154
    drawings, activating/deactivating, 45
    lines, 146
OSNAP command, 1040
output media (plot sheets), 901-902
overrides (object snaps), 403-404

P

PAN command, 199-201, 1040
Pan option (Aerial View window),
  180, 929
panning
    Aerial View window, 189
    drawings, 57, 178, 199-201
paper size (plot sheets), 880, 887-889
paper space, 837-847
    borders, inserting, 841-843
    entering/leaving, 839-840
    plotting drawings from, 896-897
    viewports
        3D models, 862-863
        activating, 845-847
        creating, 843-845
        dimensions, 858
        hiding lines, 865
        layer visibility, 860
        multiple, 843
        multiple mview, 852-857
        mview, 841-852
        restoring, 843
        scale factors, 857
        scaling linetypes, 865
parameters (plot sheets), 880-881
parts (objects), 686
PASTECLIP command, 953, 1040
pasting Clipboard data into
  drawings, 953

paths
    drawing files, 110
    object library files, 918
    xref files, 724
Pattern option (Boundary Hatch dialog
  box), 660
Pattern Properties option (Boundary
  Hatch dialog box), 659
Pattern Type option (Boundary Hatch
  dialog box), 659
PDMODE system variable, 161
PDSIZE system variable, 161
PEDIT command, 484, 605-619, 1040
    Break option, 613
    Close option, 606
    Fit option, 610
    Insert option, 613
    Join option, 606, 607
    Ltype gen option, 612
    Move option, 614
    Next option, 613
    Previous option, 613
    Regen option, 614
    Spine option, 610
    Straighten option, 614
    system variables, 611
    Tangent option, 614
    vertices, 613
    Width option, 609, 614
Pen Assignments dialog box, 879
pens (plot sheet output), 902
PERIMETER system variable, 459
perimeters, measuring, 452
period (.), wild card, 396
PERpendicular object snap, 403,
  408-415
perspective views (3D models), 929
PFB file name extension, 133
pick boxes (cursor), 53, 224, 236
Pick Points option (Boundary Hatch
  dialog box), 660
pick selection method (objects), 225

PICKAUTO system variable, 225
PICKBOX system variable, 236
PLAN command, 1040
PLINE command, 587-605, 1040
PLINEGEN system variable, 484
PLOT command, 870-873, 1040
Plot Configuration dialog box, 871-872, 879-890, 883
Plot Rotation and Origin dialog box, 882, 888
plot scales, 307
plot sheets, 870-879
    alternative output, 903
    architectural drawings, 304-306
    configurations, 879-890
    defining, 884-886
    displays, 884
    DXFOUT (Drawing eXchange Format output), 903
    extents, 884
    hardware, 900-901
    limits, 884
    linetypes, 369, 886-887
    measurement units, 313-322, 880
    naming, 881
    output media, 901-902
    paper size, 880, 887-889
    parameters, 880-881
    pen assignments, 879, 886-887, 902
    previewing, 872, 882, 889-890
    printing
        orientation, 880, 882
        to disk, 881
    PSOUT (PostScript output), 903
    raster output, 873
    rotation (printing), 887-889
    scale factors, 880, 882
    scaling, 882, 892-898
    scaling drawings to, 303-308
    settings, 898-899
    standard sizes, 312
    vector output, 873

    views, 885
    windows, 885
    WMFOUT (Windows Metafile Format output), 903
plotter driver, updating, 1058
plotting drawings, 870-873
    from model space, 894-895
    from paper space, 896-897
    to files, 897-898
poché (hatch patterns), 646-649
POINT command, 158-162, 1041
point coordinates
    absolute, 86-87
    absolute polar, 87
    alignment with point filters, 430
    BREAK command, 534
    CHANGE command, 556
    coordinated snap and grids, 76-83
    dynamic Cartesian, 71
    dynamic polar, 71
    filters, 430-434
    finding
        with coordinated snap and grids, 79
        with reference grids, 72
    hatch patterns, specifying, 660
    object displacement, 244-248
    objects, placing, 440-445
    origins, 66, 93
    placing
        with keyboard, 85-90
        with snap grids, 73-74
    polar, 70, 86-87
    regenerating, 159
    relative, 87-88, 434-439
    relative polar, 88
    selecting, 69, 72-85
    specifying with object snaps, 407
    static, 71
    typing, 88-90
    verifying, 426
    X axis, 67
    Y axis, 67

point objects, 419
creating, 158-162
sizing, 161
styles, 161
Point Style dialog box, 159
pointing device, *see* mouse
POints option (DVIEW command), 929
polar coordinates, 70, 86-87
Polar option (ARRAY command), 523
polyester film (plot sheet output), 901
POLYGON command, 621-623, 1041
polygons, 562
Polyline option
CHAMFER command, 542
FILLET command, 537
polylines, 274, 586-621
3DPOLY command, 605
arcs, 595-605
center option, 599
included angles, 597
radius, 603
area, measuring, 457
BOUNDARY command, 630-637
CHAMFER command, 616-619
closed, 592
default line option, 588-595
DONUT command, 623-628
editing, 605-619
ELLIPSE command, 625-628
ellipses, 586
EXPLODE command, 619-621
FILLET command, 616-619
included angles, 597
linetypes, 483-486
listing, 465-467
OFFSET command, 519
PLINE command, 587-605
POLYGON command, 621-623
RECTANG command, 628-630
vertices, 591, 614
width, 594
pop-up menus, 399

portrait orientation (printing plot sheets), 888
PostScript
file format, 945-948
fonts, 505
precision settings (measurement units), 314-316
preferences, setting, 340-350
PREFERENCES command, 341, 1041
Preferences dialog box, 129-133, 341
Preferences Fonts dialog box, 348
prefixes (dimension text), 808
preliminary options (INSERT command), 697
preset options (INSERT command), 697
presetting block object rotation/scale settings, 696-698
Press Enter option (DTEXT command), 166
press-and-drag selection method (windows), 236
Prev option (UCS command), 98, 934
Preview Hatch option (Boundary Hatch dialog box), 661
previewing
hatch patterns, 661
plot sheets, 872, 882, 889-890
previous object selection method, 226, 242-243
Previous option
PEDIT command, 613
ZOOM command, 197
Print Setup dialog box, 878
Print/Plot command (File menu), 134
Print/Plot Setup & Default Selection dialog box, 876
printer drivers, 875
printers
default, 874
dithering, 875
monochrome, 874
plot sheet setup, 900-901

raster devices, 874
selecting, 873-879
vector devices, 874
Printers dialog box, 874
printing
drawings, 870-879
plot sheets to disk, 881
printouts, *see* **plot sheets**
processors, upgrading, 984
**Program Manager window,
restoring size, 967**
projecting objects, 549
prompts
commands, 33
dimensioning commands, 772-774
MIRROR command, 527
properties
block objects, 745-759
block reference objects, 742
layers, 368-374
objects, 474-476
changing, 489-497
setting, 476-489
xrefs
layers, 730
libraries, 750-759
**proportions (SCALE command),
575-578**
Prototype Drawing File dialog box, 116
**prototype drawings, 111, 115-118, 325,
914-916**
protecting from overwriting, 126
setup, 326-332
PSLTSCALE system variable, 865
PSOUT command, 903, 947, 1041
PSPACE command, 847, 1041
pull-down menu bar, 33, 45
pull-down menus
display options, 42
issuing commands from, 40
**PURGE command, 371, 389-391, 483,
756, 763-764, 1041**
purging block objects, 763-764

Q

QSAVE command, 119, 1041
QUAdrant object snap, 403, 404
**question mark (?), wild card, 337,
392-393, 396**
**QUIck mode modifier
(object snaps), 425**
**Quick setup (prototype drawings),
326-328**
**Quick Step, creating coordinated snap
and grids, 81-83**
**Quick Tour command (Help pull-down
menu), 59**
QUIT command, 128
quitting
Aerial View window, 189
AutoCAD LT, 128

R

radii
arcs, 603
circles, 158
measuring, 448
radio buttons, 49
**RADIUS dimensioning command,
790-794, 1035**
Radius option (CIRCLE command), 155
Radius option (FILLET command), 537
**RAM (random access memory),
adding, 985**
raster output (plot sheets), 873
**Read Only Mode check box (Open
Drawing dialog box), 126**
reading layer status, 378
**Real Time tool (Aerial View
window), 191**
records (objects), 462-472
RECTANG command, 628-630, 1041
rectangles, 628-630
**Rectangular option (ARRAY
command), 522**

redefining block objects, 742-745
redesigned Aerial View window (Release 2 version), 184-190
REDO command, 249-252, 1041
REDRAW command, 39, 144, 922, 1037, 1041
reducing objects, 289
Reference angle, rotating, 571
reference grids, 72
Reference option
    rotate grip editing mode, 283-286
    scale grip editing mode, 289
reference points (temporary), setting, 426
REGEN command, 159, 207, 1042
Regen option (PEDIT command), 614
regenerating point objects, 159
regens (screen regenerations), 206
relative coordinates, 71, 87-88
relative point coordinates, tracking, 434-439
relative polar coordinates, 88
reloading xrefs, 725-728
Remove Islands option (Boundary Hatch dialog box), 660
removing objects from selection sets, 226
RENAME command, 336, 375, 1042
Rename dialog box, 336
renaming
    drawings, 335
    layers, 365, 374-376
    xrefs, 723
reopening drawing files, 135
repeating commands, 50
replicating commands
    ARRAY, 519-524
    MIRROR, 524-528
    OFFSET, 513-519
resolved xrefs, 728
Restore option
    UCS command, 98
    VIEW command, 205

restoring
    associative dimensions, 825
    block object components, 686
    objects with OOPS command, 237-240
    paper space viewports, 843
    Program Manager window size, 967
    UCS settings, 934
    viewports, 217, 925
RESUME command, 1042
Retain as Default check box (Create New Drawing dialog box), 118
REVDATE command, 1042
ROTATE command, 569-575, 1042
rotate operating mode (grip editing), 279
ROTATED dimensioning command, 782-785, 1035
rotated dimensions, 782-785
rotating
    axes, 90, 93
    block objects, 691-695, 759-760
    dimension text, 826
    objects, 256, 279-286
    UCS, 93, 933
rotation (printing), plot sheets, 887-889
Rotation angle option (DTEXT command), 166
rounding off dimensions, 808
RSCRIPT command, 1042
rubber-band
    circles, 153
    cursor, 451
    lines, 141
Run Script command (File menu), 134
running object snaps, 420-426
Running Object Snap dialog box, 420

S

SAVE command, 111, 119-124, 1042
Save Drawing As dialog box, 113-115, 120-122

Save File Name edit box (Preferences dialog box), 130
Save option
   UCS command, 98
   VIEW command, 205
SAVEAS command, 122, 1042
SAVEASR12 command, 979
SAVEDIB command, 903, 1042
saving
   drawings, 119-124
      as vector data, 950-951
      automatically, 132
      views, 833-834
   UCS settings, 99, 934
   viewports, 216
Scale and Colors dialog box, 812-814, 857
SCALE command, 322, 575-578, 1042
scale factors
   block objects, 691
   paper space viewports, 857
   plot sheets, 880, 882
scale multipliers, 308
scale operating mode (grip editing), 286-290
Scale option (Boundary Hatch dialog box), 660
Scale(X/XP) option (ZOOM command), 197
scaling
   block objects, 691-695
   dimension text, 808, 812-814
   dimensions, 313, 808, 857-859
   drawings, 298-325
   hatch patterns, 647-648
   linetypes, 313, 865
   multiple mview viewports, 854
   mview viewports, 857
   objects, 256, 286-290, 308
   plot sheets, 882, 892-898
   text, 309-312
SCANDISK command, 978

screen regenerations, 206-207
SCRIPT command, 1042
script files, 134
scroll bars (Aerial View window), 181
Search for Help On... command (Help pull-down menu), 59-60
search paths (drawing files), 132-133, 342
searching help topics, 60
Second point option (ARC command), 149
Select Color dialog box, 371, 479
SELECT command, 566-569, 1042
Select Hatch Pattern dialog box, 646, 650
Select Initial View check box (Open Drawing dialog box), 126
Select Linetype dialog box, 372, 480
Select Objects (Boundary Hatch dialog box), 660
Select Text Font dialog box, 502
Select Text Style dialog box, 488, 497
selecting
   hatch patterns, 647-648
   objects for editing, 221-237
selection sets (objects), 224, 227
   adding objects to, 226
   copying, 240-248
   moving, 240-248
   removing objects from, 226
series dimensions, 778-782
Set Layer Filters dialog box, 384
SETENV command, 1042
setup
   32-bit file access, 983-984
   prototype drawings, 326-332
   swap files, 982-984
SETVAR command, 324, 459, 1042
SHADE command, 923, 1043
shading 3D models, 923
shape fonts, 505
Shift key command, 236

Shift+Tab key command, 49
Show Device Requirements
  dialog box, 876
SHX file name extension, 133
SIngle object selection method, 227
sizing
  grips, 259-260
  pick boxes, 236
  point objects, 161
  text in paper space, 857
SLD file name extension, 134
slider bars (dialog boxes), 49
snap and grid lines, 142
SNAP command, 80, 101, 1043
snap grids, 73-74
  coordinated snap and grids, 76-81
  creating with Quick Step, 81-83
  using with object snaps, 227
snap operating mode (grip editing),
  45, 266
snapping
  objects
    to angles, 278
    to distances, 278
    to grids, 278
  to grips, 266
software (AutoCAD LT
  requirements), 959
SOLID command, 1043
sorting (object selection methods), 237
spacebar, issuing commands from, 43
Spacing option (Boundary Hatch dialog
  box), 660
SPLFRAME (PEDIT command), 611
Spline option (PEDIT command), 610
SPLINESEGS (PEDIT command), 611
Spyglass tool (Aerial View window), 191
standards (drawings), 919-920
Start point option
  ARC command, 149
  DTEXT command, 165
starting IALT disk, 1051-1054

startup files, troubleshooting, 970-975
startup icon (IALT disk), changing,
  1051-1052
static coordinates, 71
Statistics option (Aerial View
  window), 180
STATUS dimensioning command, 820
Straighten option (PEDIT
  command), 614
STRETCH command, 275, 1043
  endpoints, 559-569
  object types, 565
  polygons, 562
  SELECT command, 566-569
  windows, 562
stretch operating mode (grip editing),
  261-265
Stretch to point option
  (grip editing), 265
stretching
  arcs, 266-271
  associative dimensions, 823-825
  circles, 266-271
  hatch patterns, 655
  objects, 255, 257, 261-265
STYLE command, 497, 500, 816, 1043
Style option
  DTEXT command, 165
  HATCH command, 652
styles
  dimensions, 800
    creating, 814-821
    importing, 821
  point objects, 161
  text, 913-914
    changing, 505-507
    creating, 497-502
    options, 503-504
    prototype drawings, 915
Subtract option (AREA command),
  454, 461
suffixes (dimension text), 808

support directories, 918
Support Dirs edit box (Preferences dialog box), 130
support files (drawings), 132-133, 976-977
suppressing
  extension lines, 802
  zeros in dimension text, 809
surveyor's measurement units, 321
swap files, setup, 982-984
symbol library, 134
symbols
  block objects, 688-690
  dependent (xrefs), 728
  importing, 134
  objects, 687
System Colors radio button (Colors dialog box), 346
system crashes, troubleshooting file errors, 977-978
system settings for AutoCAD LT, 967-968
system variables, 322-325, 989-1017
  AREA, 459
  ATTDIA, 715
  DIMSCALE, 313, 857
  DITHER, 875
  GRIPBLOCK, 759
  GRIPS, 221, 259
  LASTPOINT, 426, 429
  LIMMAX, 885
  LIMMIN, 885
  LTSCALE, 313, 323, 373
  PDMODE, 161
  PDSIZE, 161
  PEDIT, 611
  PERIMETER, 459
  PICKAUTO, 225
  PICKBOX, 236
  PLINEGEN, 484
  PSLTSCALE, 865
  TILEMODE, 215, 838-841
  VISRETAIN, 730

T

tags (text attributes), 707
tangency
  arcs (to two circles), 414
  objects, 158
TANgent object snap, 403, 408-415
Tangent option (PEDIT command), 614
tangent-tangent-radius circles, 156-158
TArget option (DVIEW command), 928
TEDIT dimensioning command, 826, 828, 1035
templates, 687, 914-916
temporary files (drawings), 133
Temporary Files radio button (Preferences dialog box), 131
temporary reference points, setting, 426
Terminate-and-Stay-Resident programs (TSRs), 972
terminating dimension lines, 806
text
  attributes, 707
    defining, 708-712
    editing, 712, 716-719
    inserting definitions, 713-716
  backwards, 504
  CHANGE command, 555
  Clipboard, importing into drawings, 954
  dimensions, 767, 773
    alignment, 807
    alternate measurement units, 810
    colors, 812-814
    formats, 808-811
    gap settings, 802
    inserting, 788-790
    location settings, 807-808
    moving, 826
    prefixes/suffixes, 808
    rotating, 826
    scaling, 808, 812-814
    suppressing zeros, 809
    tolerance settings, 809

editing, 579-581
font preferences, 348-350
height, 503
importing, 581-584
obliquing angle, 504
scaling, 309-312
sizing in paper space, 857
upside-down, 504
vertical, 504
width, 504
TEXT command, 165, 1043
Text Format dialog box, 808-811
Text Location dialog box, 807-808
text objects
centering, 167
creating, 162-169
deleting, 163
INSert object snaps, 165
justifying, 167-169
object snaps, 419
Text option (DTEXT command), 166
text styles, 913-915
changing, 505-507
creating, 497-502
setting, 488
text window, 34, 45
TEXTSCR command, 1043
thawed layers, 365
thawing layers, 378-379
thickness property (objects), 475, 489, 494
third-party object libraries, 919
three-button mouse, 36
Through mode (OFFSET command), 518
tilde (~), wild card, 396
tiled viewports (model space), 835-837
TILEMODE system variable, 215, 838-841
TIME command, 1043
title bar, 32
title block objects, 707-719, 847-851

To point option (LINE command), 145
tolerance settings (dimension text), 809
toolbar, 342
Aerial View window, 190-194
customizing, 33
issuing commands from, 39
toolbox, 342
customizing, 33, 350
floating, 350
hiding, 351
icons, assigning commands to, 352
issuing commands from, 39
moving, 350
tools, adding, 353-356
width, adjusting, 352
TOOLBOX command, 350, 1043
Toolbox Customization dialog box, 352
tools, 33, 353-356
ToolTips, 33
tracing errors, 977
tracking relative point coordinates, 434-439
translucent bond paper (plot sheet output), 902
transparent commands, 207-212
assigning to toolbox icons, 356
display control, 211
TRIM command, 543-550, 1043
TROTATE dimensioning command, 826, 828, 1035
troubleshooting
AUTOEXEC.BAT files, 974-975
CONFIG.SYS files, 973-974
errors
with commands, 50-54
with REDO/UNDO commands, 248-252
files after system crashes, 977-978
memory errors, 976
startup files, 970-975
TSR (Terminate-and-Stay-Resident) programs, 972

TTR (tangent-tangent-radius) option, CIRCLE command, 155-158
Tutorial command (Help pull-down menu), 62
TWist option (DVIEW command), 929
two-button mouse, 36
Type It radio button (Open Drawing dialog box), 125
typing point coordinates, 85-90

U

U (undo) command, 50-51, 1043
U option (HATCH command), 652
UCS (User Coordinate System), 90-99
   rotating, 93, 933
   settings
      restoring, 934
      saving, 99, 934
UCS command, 90, 97, 933, 1044
UCS Control dialog box, 99
UCSICON command, 93, 1044
UNDO command, 50, 249-252, 1044
UNDO dimensioning command, 785, 1035
Undo option
   LINE command, 142-145
   stretch grip editing, 266
unit cells (ARRAY command), 522
unit parts (objects), 687
unit scale part block objects, 688
UNITS command, 317, 1044
Units Control dialog box, 314
units, *see* measurement units
UNLOCK command, 1044
Unlock Files command (File menu), 134
unlocking
   drawing files, 134
   files, 978
   layers, 366, 379-382
UPDATE dimensioning command, 826, 1035

updating
   Aerial View window, 192
   associative dimensions, 826
   associative hatch patterns, 670
   HPGL driver, 1058-1059
   plotter driver, 1058
   xrefs, 724, 725-728
upgrading
   memory, 985
   microprocessors, 984
   video cards, 986
Upper right corner option (LIMITS command), 303
upside-down text, 504
Use Prototype check box (Create New Drawing dialog box), 117
User Coordinate System, *see* UCS
user interface
   components, 29-34
   preferences, 340-350
user name preferences, 343
user-defined hatch patterns, 653-654

V

variable name option (SETVAR command), 325
variables
   dimensions, 768-769
   system, 322-325, 989-1017
VARIABLES dimensioning command, 820
vector output (plot sheets), 873
vellum paper (plot sheet output), 901
verb-noun editing, 220, 224, 232-236
verifying point coordinates, 426
VERTICAL dimensioning command, 776-778, 1035
vertical dimensions, 774-778
vertical text, 504
vertices
   grips, 614
   polylines, 591, 613

video cards, upgrading, 986
VIEW command, 201-206, 833, 836, 1044
View Name dialog box, 881
View option (UCS command), 98, 934
View Selections option (Boundary Hatch dialog box), 661
viewing
    3D models, 921-923, 927-929
    objects, 462-472, 841-852
viewports, 212
    3D models, 923-926
    active, 215
    combining, 215
    configurations, 216, 926
    deleting, 215, 925
    dividing, 216
    enlarging, 926
    inserting into drawings, 847-851
    merging, 925
    model space, 833-834
        active, 835
        creating, 835-836
        tiled, 835-837
    multiple, 192, 212-218
    paper space
        activating, 845-847
        creating, 843-845
        multiple, 843
        multiple mview, 852-857
        mview, 841-852
        restoring, 843
        scale factors, 857
    prototype drawings, 915
    restoring, 217, 925
    saving, 216
VIEWPORTS command, 835, 1044
views
    drawings, 54-57, 201-206, 833-835
    plot sheets, 885
Virtual Drawing Area tool (Aerial View window), 191

virtual screen memory, 206
visibility filters (layers), 384
VISRETAIN system variable, 730
VPLAYER command, 389, 860-861, 1044
VPOINT command, 921-923, 1044
VPORTS command, 207, 212, 215, 835, 923-926, 1044
VSLIDE command, 1044

W

walls (double lines), 638
Warning dialog box, 742
WBLOCK command, 753-756, 1045
WCS (World Coordinate System), 90
What's New command (Help pull-down menu), 61
width
    plot sheet pen assignments, 887
    polylines, 594
    text, 504
    toolbox, adjusting, 352
Width option (PEDIT command), 609, 614
wild cards, 396
    filtering layers with, 386, 392-396
    naming drawings, 337
Window on Top option (Aerial View window), 181
Window option
    VIEW command, 205
    ZOOM command, 197
Window Selection dialog box, 881, 885
window selection method (objects), 225, 232
Windows (OLE with AutoCAD LT), 952
windows
    Aerial View, 54
    colors, 345-348
    floating, 33
    graphics, 30, 45

Help, 58
Help Contents, 60
implied windowing, 236
plot sheets, 885
press-and-drag selection method, 236
Program Manager, restoring size, 967
STRETCH command, 562
text, 34, 45
zoom, 54
witness lines (dimensions), 767, 802
WMF (Windows Metafile Format), 134, 943-945
WMFIN command, 945, 1045
WMFOPTS command, 1045
WMFOUT command, 903, 944, 1045
World Coordinate System (WCS), 90
World option (UCS command), 97
WPolygon selection method (objects), 226, 232

X

X axes, 66
X option (UCS command), 934
XBIND command, 732-735, 1045
XREF command, 720-725, 1045
xrefs (external references), 674-675, 719-735
attaching, 720-725
attributes, 725
colors, 752
converting to block objects, 724, 730-732
dependent symbols, 728-730
detaching, 722-725
file paths, 724
importing, 732
layers, 730, 752
libraries, 750-759
linetypes, 752
listing, 724
named items, 728-730
nesting block objects, 761-762
object manifestations, 686-690
object snaps, 722
properties, 730
renaming, 723
resolved, 728
source files, editing, 725
updating, 724, 725-728

Y–Z

Y axes, 66
Y option (UCS command), 934

Z axes, 66
Z option (UCS command), 98, 934
ZAxis option (UCS command), 933
zeros, suppressing in dimension text, 809
ZOOM command, 194-199, 248, 287, 1046
Zoom option (Aerial View window), 180, 929
zoom windows, 54
zooming
Aerial View window, 189
drawings, 54, 178, 194-199

FILE

File	
New...	
Open...	
Save	
Save As...	
Print/Plot...	
Import/Export	▶
Run Script...	
Unlock Files...	
Preferences...	
Exit	
1 C:\DWGS\IALT\ARCHV1	
2 C:\TEST	
3 C:\....\ALT2201	
4 C:\DWGS\IALT\TEST	

View Slide...
DXF In...
WMF In...
WMF In Options...
Make Slide...
DXF Out...
Block Out...
Attributes Out...
PostScript Out...
WMF Out...
BMP Out...

EDIT

Edit
Undo
Redo
Copy Image
Copy Vectors
Copy Embed
Copy Link
Paste
Paste Command
Text Window

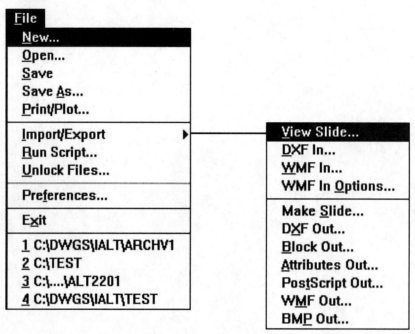

DRAW

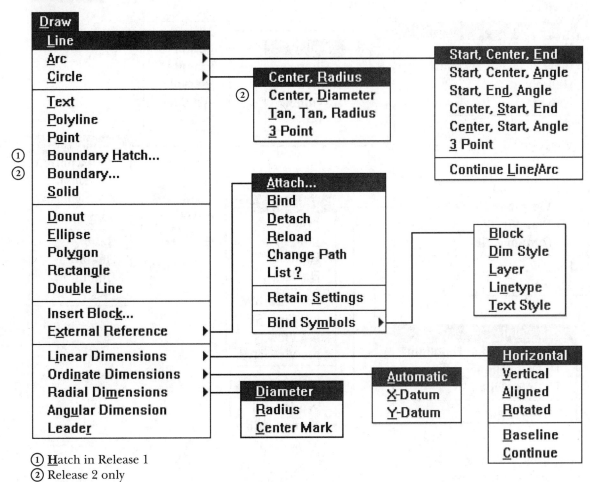

Draw
- **Line**
- **Arc** ▶
- **Circle** ▶
  - **Center, Radius**
  - ② **Center, Diameter**
  - **Tan, Tan, Radius**
  - **3 Point**
    - **Start, Center, End**
    - **Start, Center, Angle**
    - **Start, End, Angle**
    - **Center, Start, End**
    - **Center, Start, Angle**
    - **3 Point**
    - **Continue Line/Arc**
- **Text**
- **Polyline**
- **Point**
- ① **Boundary Hatch...**
- ② **Boundary...**
- **Solid**
- **Donut**
- **Ellipse**
- **Polygon**
- **Rectangle**
- **Double Line**
- **Insert Block...**
- **External Reference** ▶
  - **Attach...**
  - **Bind**
  - **Detach**
  - **Reload**
  - **Change Path**
  - **List ?**
  - **Retain Settings**
  - **Bind Symbols** ▶
    - **Block**
    - **Dim Style**
    - **Layer**
    - **Linetype**
    - **Text Style**
- **Linear Dimensions** ▶
  - **Horizontal**
  - **Vertical**
  - **Aligned**
  - **Rotated**
  - **Baseline**
  - **Continue**
- **Ordinate Dimensions** ▶
  - **Automatic**
  - **X-Datum**
  - **Y-Datum**
- **Radial Dimensions** ▶
  - **Diameter**
  - **Radius**
  - **Center Mark**
- **Angular Dimension**
- **Leader**

① Hatch in Release 1
② Release 2 only

VIEW

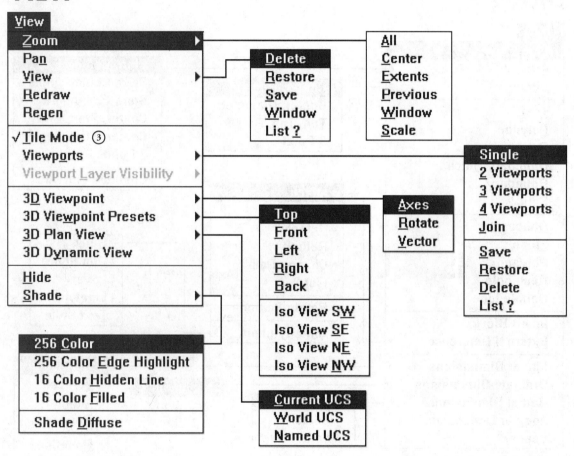

③ Paper Space in Release 1

ASSIST

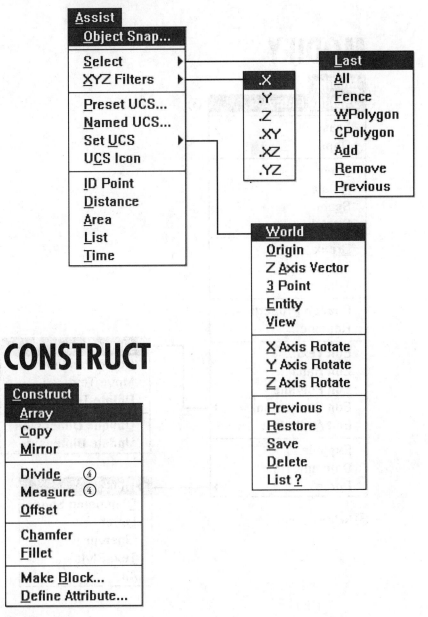

Assist
- Object Snap...
- Select ▶
- XYZ Filters ▶
- Preset UCS...
- Named UCS...
- Set UCS ▶
- UCS Icon
- ID Point
- Distance
- Area
- List
- Time

XYZ Filters
- .X
- .Y
- .Z
- .XY
- .XZ
- .YZ

Select
- Last
- All
- Fence
- WPolygon
- CPolygon
- Add
- Remove
- Previous

Set UCS / World
- World
- Origin
- Z Axis Vector
- 3 Point
- Entity
- View
- X Axis Rotate
- Y Axis Rotate
- Z Axis Rotate
- Previous
- Restore
- Save
- Delete
- List ?

CONSTRUCT

Construct
- Array
- Copy
- Mirror
- Divide ④
- Measure ④
- Offset
- Chamfer
- Fillet
- Make Block...
- Define Attribute...

④ Release 2 only

MODIFY

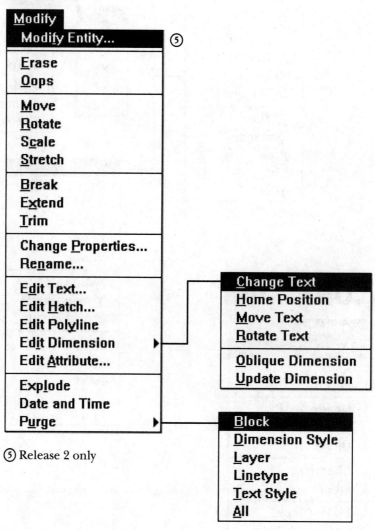

Modify
Modify Entity... ⑤
Erase
Oops
Move
Rotate
S**c**ale
Stretch
Break
E**x**tend
Trim
Change **P**roperties...
Re**n**ame...
E**d**it Text...
Edit **H**atch...
Edit Pol**y**line
Ed**i**t Dimension ▶
Edit **A**ttribute...
Exp**l**ode
Date and Time
P**u**rge ▶

Change Text
Home Position
Move Text
Rotate Text
Oblique Dimension
Update Dimension

Block
Dimension Style
Layer
Li**n**etype
Text Style
All

⑤ Release 2 only

SETTINGS

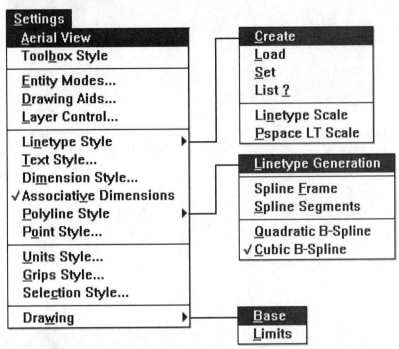

Settings
- Aerial View
- Toolbox Style
- Entity Modes...
- Drawing Aids...
- Layer Control...
- Linetype Style ▶
- Text Style...
- Dimension Style...
- √ Associative Dimensions
- Polyline Style ▶
- Point Style...
- Units Style...
- Grips Style...
- Selection Style...
- Drawing ▶

Linetype Style
- Create
- Load
- Set
- List ?
- Linetype Scale
- Pspace LT Scale

Linetype Generation
- Spline Frame
- Spline Segments
- Quadratic B-Spline
- √ Cubic B-Spline

Drawing
- Base
- Limits

HELP

Help
- Contents
- Search for Help on...
- How to Use Help
- Orientation ⑥
- What's New ⑥
- Tutorial ⑥
- About AutoCAD LT...

⑥ Release 2 only

PLUG YOURSELF INTO...

THE MACMILLAN INFORMATION SUPERLIBRARY™

Free information and vast computer resources from the world's leading computer book publisher—online!

FIND THE BOOKS THAT ARE RIGHT FOR YOU!

A complete online catalog, plus sample chapters and tables of contents give you an in-depth look at *all* of our books, including hard-to-find titles. It's the best way to find the books you need!

- ● STAY INFORMED with the latest computer industry news through our online newsletter, press releases, and customized Information SuperLibrary Reports.

- ● GET FAST ANSWERS to your questions about MCP books and software.

- ● VISIT our online bookstore for the latest information and editions!

- ● COMMUNICATE with our expert authors through e-mail and conferences.

- ● DOWNLOAD SOFTWARE from the immense MCP library:
  - Source code and files from MCP books
  - The best shareware, freeware, and demos

- ● DISCOVER HOT SPOTS on other parts of the Internet.

- ● WIN BOOKS in ongoing contests and giveaways!

| TO PLUG INTO MCP: → | WORLD WIDE WEB: http://www.mcp.com |

GOPHER: gopher.mcp.com

FTP: ftp.mcp.com

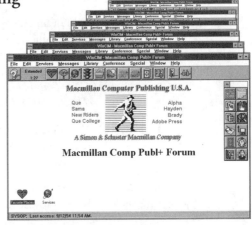

WANT MORE INFORMATION?

CHECK OUT THESE RELATED TOPICS OR SEE YOUR LOCAL BOOKSTORE

CAD and 3D Studio

As the number one CAD publisher in the world, and as a Registered Publisher of Autodesk, New Riders Publishing provides unequaled content on this complex topic. Industry-leading products include AutoCAD and 3D Studio.

Networking

As the leading Novell NetWare publisher, New Riders Publishing delivers cutting-edge products for network professionals. We publish books for all levels of users, from those wanting to gain NetWare Certification, to those administering or installing a network. Leading books in this category include *Inside NetWare 3.12*, *CNE Training Guide: Managing NetWare Systems*, *Inside TCP/IP*, and *NetWare: The Professional Reference*.

Graphics

New Riders provides readers with the most comprehensive product tutorials and references available for the graphics market. Best-sellers include *Inside CorelDRAW! 5*, *Inside Photoshop 3*, and *Adobe Photoshop NOW!*

Internet and Communications

As one of the fastest growing publishers in the communications market, New Riders provides unparalleled information and detail on this ever-changing topic area. We publish international best-sellers such as *New Riders' Official Internet Yellow Pages, 2nd Edition*, a directory of over 10,000 listings of Internet sites and resources from around the world, and *Riding the Internet Highway, Deluxe Edition*.

Operating Systems

Expanding off our expertise in technical markets, and driven by the needs of the computing and business professional, New Riders offers comprehensive references for experienced and advanced users of today's most popular operating systems, including *Understanding Windows 95*, *Inside Unix*, *Inside Windows 3.11 Platinum Edition*, *Inside OS/2 Warp Version 3*, and *Inside MS-DOS 6.22*.

Other Markets

Professionals looking to increase productivity and maximize the potential of their software and hardware should spend time discovering our line of products for Word, Excel, and Lotus 1-2-3. These titles include *Inside Word 6 for Windows*, *Inside Excel 5 for Windows*, *Inside 1-2-3 Release 5*, and *Inside WordPerfect for Windows*.

Orders/Customer Service **1-800-653-6156**   Source Code **NRP95**

New Riders Publishing 201 West 103rd Street ◆ Indianapolis, Indiana 46290 USA

REGISTRATION CARD

Inside AutoCAD LT for Windows, Second Edition

Name _____ Title _____

Company _____ Type of business _____

Address _____

City/State/ZIP _____

Have you used these types of books before? ☐ yes   ☐ no

If yes, which ones? _____

_____

How many computer books do you purchase each year? ☐ 1–5   ☐ 6 or more

How did you learn about this book? _____

Where did you purchase this book? _____

Which applications do you currently use? _____

_____

Which computer magazines do you subscribe to? _____

_____

What trade shows do you attend? _____

_____

Comments: _____

_____

_____

Would you like to be placed on our preferred mailing list? ☐ yes   ☐ no

☐ **I would like to see my name in print!** You may use my name and quote me in future New Riders products and promotions. My daytime phone number is: _____

New Riders Publishing 201 West 103rd Street ◆ Indianapolis, Indiana 46290 USA

Fax to **317-581-4670**   Orders/Customer Service **1-800-653-6156**   Source Code **NRP95**

Fold Here